Dreamweaver CS6

the missing manual®

The book that should have been in the box®

David Sawyer McFarland

O'REILLY®

Beijing | Cambridge | Farnham | Köln | Sebastopol | Tokyo

Dreamweaver CS6: The Missing Manual

by David Sawyer McFarland

Published by O'Reilly Media, Inc.,
1005 Gravenstein Highway North, Sebastopol, CA 95472.

O'Reilly books may be purchased for educational, business, or sales promotional
use. Online editions are also available for most titles (*http://my.safaribooksonline.com*).
For more information, contact our corporate/institutional sales department: (800)
998-9938 or *corporate@oreilly.com*.

July 2012:   First Edition.

Revision History for the 1st Edition:

   2012-07-02   First release

See *http://shop.oreilly.com/product/0636920022732.do* for release details.

ISBN-13: 978-1-449-31617-4
[M]

Contents

Part One: Building a Web Page

Part Two: Building a Better Web Page

The Missing Credits

ABOUT THE AUTHOR

 David Sawyer McFarland is president of Sawyer McFarland Media, Inc., a web development and training company in Portland, Oregon. He's been building websites since 1995, when he designed his first site, an online magazine for communication professionals. He's served as the Webmaster at the University of California at Berkeley and the Berkeley Multimedia Research Center, and he has helped build, design, and program numerous websites for clients including Macworld.com, among others.

In addition to building websites, David is a writer, trainer, and instructor. He's taught web design at the UC Berkeley Graduate School of Journalism, the Center for Electronic Art, the Academy of Art College, and the Art Institute of Portland. He currently teaches in the Multimedia Program at Portland State University. He's written articles about web design for *Practical Web Design*, *Macworld*, and CreativePro.com.

David is also the author of *CSS: The Missing Manual* and *JavaScript & jQuery: The Missing Manual*.

He welcomes feedback about this book by email at *missing@sawmac.com*. (If you need technical help, however, please refer to the sources listed in Appendix A.)

ABOUT THE CREATIVE TEAM

Peter McKie (editor) has a master's degree from Boston University's School of Journalism and lives in New York City, where he researches the history of old houses and, every once in a while, sneaks into abandoned buildings. Email: *pmckie@oreilly.com*.

Holly Bauer (production editor) lives in Ye Olde Cambridge, MA, where she is an avid home cook, prolific DIYer, and mid-century modern furniture design enthusiast. Email: *holly@oreilly.com*.

Nancy Wolfe Kotary (compositor) is a copyeditor, typesetter, and former O'Reilly production manager with more years of experience in publishing than she cares to count. She is from New Hampshire and lives in Massachusetts but does not worship squirrels or drive like a maniac.

Marcia Simmons (proofreader) is a writer and editor living in the San Francisco Bay Area. She's author of the book *DIY Cocktails*. Blog: *www.marciaisms.com*.

Julie Hawks (indexer) is an indexer for the Missing Manual series. She is currently pursuing a masters degree in Religious Studies while discovering the joys of warm winters in the Carolinas. Email: *juliehawks@gmail.com*.

Murray R. Summers (technical reviewer) is an Adobe Certified Dreamweaver Developer and Community Professional. He has co-authored and contributed chapters to several books on Dreamweaver, been the technical editor for the last seven editions of the Dreamweaver Missing Manual, and presented at multiple national conferences. His company, Great Web Sights, has been active in web development since 1998. Murray lives in southern Delaware with his wife Suzanne. One daughter attends Clemson University, and the other is a skilled web developer (*carolinawebcreations .biz*). His two sons live and work in Virginia Beach.

Danilo Celic, Jr. (technical reviewer) has been using Dreamweaver since version 1.2. In the years since, he has contributed to the Dreamweaver community in a variety of capacities. He has been a co-author, technical editor, and technical reviewer for a shelf full of Dreamweaver- and Web-related books. He loves sharing what he has learned over the years of the inner workings of Dreamweaver and various web technologies. Danilo lives in the suburbs of Chicago with his wife, Melissa, who patiently forgives the late hours he puts in in front of a glowing screen. Email: *danilo@ shimmerphase.com*.

ACKNOWLEDGMENTS

Thanks to all those who have helped with this book (and all of my books over the years): my students, colleagues, and the wonderful people at O'Reilly. Thanks to Murray Summers and Danilo Celic for their careful scrutiny and erudite corrections to my writing; thanks also to Peter McKie, for making my writing more energetic and clearer.

— *Dave McFarland*

THE MISSING MANUAL SERIES

Missing Manuals are witty, superbly written guides to computer products that don't come with printed manuals (which is just about all of them). Each book features a handcrafted index.

Recent and upcoming titles include:

- *Access 2010: The Missing Manual* by Matthew MacDonald
- *Abobe Edge Preview 5: The Missing Manual* by Chris Grover
- *Buying a Home: The Missing Manual* by Nancy Conner
- *CSS: The Missing Manual, Second Edition* by David Sawyer McFarland
- *Creating a Website: The Missing Manual, Third Edition* by Matthew MacDonald
- *David Pogue's Digital Photography: The Missing Manual* by David Pogue
- *Dreamweaver CS5.5: The Missing Manual* by David Sawyer McFarland
- *Droid 2: The Missing Manual* by Preston Gralla
- *Droid X2: The Missing Manual* by Preston Gralla

- *Excel 2010: The Missing Manual* by Matthew MacDonald
- *Facebook: The Missing Manual, Third Edition* by E.A. Vander Veer
- *FileMaker Pro 11: The Missing Manual* by Susan Prosser and Stuart Gripman
- *Flash CS6: The Missing Manual* by Chris Grover
- *Galaxy S II: The Missing Manual* by Preston Gralla
- *Galaxy Tab: The Missing Manual* by Preston Gralla
- *Google+: The Missing Manual* by Kevin Purdy
- *Google Apps: The Missing Manual* by Nancy Conner
- *Google SketchUp: The Missing Manual* by Chris Grover
- *HTML5: The Missing Manual* by Matthew MacDonald
- *iMovie '11 & iDVD: The Missing Manual* by David Pogue and Aaron Miller
- *iPad: The Missing Manual, Fourth Edition* by J.D. Biersdorfer
- *iPhone: The Missing Manual, Fifth Edition* by David Pogue
- *iPhone App Development: The Missing Manual* by Craig Hockenberry
- *iPhoto '11: The Missing Manual* by David Pogue and Lesa Snider
- *iPod: The Missing Manual, Tenth Edition* by J.D. Biersdorfer and David Pogue
- *JavaScript & jQuery: The Missing Manual, Second Edition* by David Sawyer McFarland
- *Kindle Fire: The Missing Manual* by Peter Meyers
- *Living Green: The Missing Manual* by Nancy Conner
- *Mac OS X Lion: The Missing Manual* by David Pogue
- *Mac OS X Snow Leopard: The Missing Manual* by David Pogue
- *Microsoft Project 2010: The Missing Manual* by Bonnie Biafore
- *Motorola Xoom: The Missing Manual* by Preston Gralla
- *Netbooks: The Missing Manual* by J.D. Biersdorfer
- *NOOK Tablet: The Missing Manual* by Preston Gralla
- *Office 2010: The Missing Manual* by Nancy Conner, Chris Grover, and Matthew MacDonald
- *Office 2011 for Macintosh: The Missing Manual* by Chris Grover
- *Palm Pre: The Missing Manual* by Ed Baig
- *Personal Investing: The Missing Manual* by Bonnie Biafore

- *Photoshop CS6: The Missing Manual* by Lesa Snider
- *Photoshop Elements 10: The Missing Manual* by Barbara Brundage
- *PHP & MySQL: The Missing Manual* by Brett McLaughlin
- *PowerPoint 2007: The Missing Manual* by E.A. Vander Veer
- *Premiere Elements 8: The Missing Manual* by Chris Grover
- *QuickBase: The Missing Manual* by Nancy Conner
- *QuickBooks 2012: The Missing Manual* by Bonnie Biafore
- *Quicken 2009: The Missing Manual* by Bonnie Biafore
- *Switching to the Mac: The Missing Manual, Lion Edition* by David Pogue
- *Wikipedia: The Missing Manual* by John Broughton
- *Windows Vista: The Missing Manual* by David Pogue
- *Windows 7: The Missing Manual* by David Pogue
- *Word 2007: The Missing Manual* by Chris Grover
- *Your Body: The Missing Manual* by Matthew MacDonald
- *Your Brain: The Missing Manual* by Matthew MacDonald
- *Your Money: The Missing Manual* by J.D. Roth

For a full list of all Missing Manuals in print, go to *www.missingmanuals.com/library .html.*

Preface

Websites evolve every year, growing in scope and complexity, with new features popping up to make sites look and work ever better. Even people building personal sites use various programming languages and server technologies to dish up content.

Throughout its history, Dreamweaver has managed to keep pace with the changing web-development landscape, and Dreamweaver CS6 is no exception; it's capable of doing more than any previous version of the program. Whether you want to use Cascading Style Sheets (CSS) for cutting-edge design, dip into the world of JavaScript-powered dynamic pages, explore HTML5 and CSS3, build websites for mobile devices, use content management systems like WordPress or Drupal, or simply stick to straightforward HTML, Dreamweaver has just about all the tools you need.

Any enterprising designer can create web pages, Cascading Style Sheets, and even JavaScript programs with a simple text editor. In fact, Dreamweaver CS6's powerful text editor lets you handcraft text files to create basic or complex database-driven pages. However, hand-typing HTML, CSS, and JavaScript is not only a recipe for carpal tunnel syndrome, it's also a slow and typo-prone way to build web pages. Dreamweaver provides buttons, dialog boxes, and panels that let you add HTML, CSS, and JavaScript quickly, with fewer keystrokes. A simple button lets you insert the complex HTML required to build an HTML table in a matter of seconds, for example. And Dreamweaver is flexible enough to let you both hand-code and use its time-saving HTML shortcuts. The choice is yours.

■ What Dreamweaver Is All About

Dreamweaver is a complete website development and site management program. It works with web technologies like HTML, XHTML, CSS, JavaScript, and PHP.

Its CSS support lets you create fast-loading, easily modified pages, while its unique "Spry" technology provides one-click access to complex, interactive layout options like drop-down menus.

Dreamweaver also includes plenty of tools for managing websites once you build them. You can check for broken links, use templates to streamline site-wide page changes, and reorganize your site in a flash with the program's site management tools.

NOTE If you're not already familiar with the acronym CSS, it stands for Cascading Style Sheets—a set of rules you write that dictate the look of your pages. Dreamweaver includes advanced tools to create, test, and edit CSS in your pages.

If you've built one or more sites without Dreamweaver, you don't have to start over again. The program happily opens web pages and websites created in other programs without destroying any of your carefully handcrafted code.

■ Why Dreamweaver?

You can find other web design programs on the market—dozens of them, in fact. But Dreamweaver is one of the leaders, thanks to key benefits like these:

- **Visual page-building**. If you've spent any time using a text editor to punch out HTML for your web pages, you know the tedium involved in adding even a simple photograph. When your boss asks you to add her photo to the company home page, you launch your trusty text editor and type in something like *<img src="images/staff/bigcheese.jpg" width="100" height="150" alt="The Boss">*. Not only is this approach prone to typos, it also separates you from what you want the page to *look* like.

  Dreamweaver, on the other hand, gives you a several ways to stay in touch with your page's visual design. If your interest is in design and not HTML, you can work in the program's Design view. Drag an image to your budding web page there, and Dreamweaver displays the picture on the page. Just as a word processor displays documents as they'll look when you print them out, so Dreamweaver gives you a close approximation of what your page will look like in a web browser.

  Another development approach web designers commonly use is keeping a page's code and its browser-rendered look side-by-side. Dreamweaver's Split view handles that, giving you direct access to the HTML of a page on one half of the screen and to its visual look in the other half.

Finally, because Dreamweaver's Design view is only an approximation of what a page looks like in a browser, the program offers "Live view"—a real-time look at your page in a web browser built right into Dreamweaver. That way, you can see what a page looks like and how it behaves without leaving Dreamweaver!

- **Complex interactivity, simply**. You've probably seen web pages where an image (on a navigation bar, for example) lights up or changes appearance when you mouse over it. Dynamic effects like this—mouse rollovers, alert boxes, and drop-down menus—usually require JavaScript programming, a language browsers understand. While JavaScript can do amazing things, it requires time and practice to learn.

  Dreamweaver includes an easy-to-use JavaScript-based technology called the *Spry Framework*. With Spry, you can easily create interactive, drop-down menus (Chapter 4), add advanced layout elements like tabbed panels (Chapter 13), and include sophisticated validation to prevent site visitors from submitting incomplete forms (Chapter 12).

- **Solid code**. Every now and then, even in Dreamweaver, you may want to put aside the visual view and look at a page's underlying HTML. You may want to tweak the code that Dreamweaver produces, for example, or you may wonder how Dreamweaver codes.

  Adobe realizes that many professional web developers do a lot of work "in the trenches," typing HTML, CSS, and JavaScript code by hand. In Dreamweaver, you can edit a page's raw HTML to your heart's content. Switching back and forth between Design view and Code view is seamless and, best of all, non-destructive. Unlike many visual web page programs, where making a change in the visual mode stomps all over the underlying HTML, Dreamweaver respects hand-typed code and doesn't try to rewrite it (unless you ask it to). You can even use Dreamweaver's Split view to see your HTML side-by-side with a representation of your final page, or you can switch between Code and Design view.

  In addition, Dreamweaver can open many other types of files commonly used on websites, such as external JavaScript files (.js files), so you don't have to switch to another program to work on them. Dreamweaver's Related Files toolbar lists all JavaScript, CSS, or server-side files the current document uses. For hand-coders, this feature means that editing a page's CSS or JavaScript is just a click away (instead of a time-draining File→Open hunt for that danged file). Chapter 7 has the full scoop on how Dreamweaver handles writing and editing code.

- **Site management tools**. Rarely will you build just a single web page. More often, you'll create and edit pages that work together to form part of a website. Or you may be building an entire website from scratch.

Either way, Dreamweaver's site management tools make your job easier. They automate many of the routine tasks every webmaster faces, from managing links, images, pages, and other media to working with a team of people and moving your site to a web server. Part Four of this book looks at how Dreamweaver helps you build and maintain websites.

Hand Coding vs. Visual Editors

At one time, creating web pages in a text editor was considered the best way to build websites. The precise control that hand-written code gave you over HTML was (and often still is) seen as the only way to assure quality web pages.

Professional site developers championed hand-coding because many early visual page-building programs added unnecessary code—code that affects how a page appears and how quickly it downloads over the Internet. But hand-coding is time-consuming and error-prone. One typo can render a web page useless.

Fortunately, Dreamweaver creates solid code even in a visual environment. Since its earliest incarnation, Dreamweaver has prided itself on its ability to produce clean HTML and its tolerance for code created by other programs—including text editors. In fact, Dreamweaver includes a powerful built-in text-editing mode that lets you freely manipulate the HTML of a page—or any other code, including JavaScript, Visual Basic, XML, PHP, and ColdFusion Markup Language.

But the real story is that the code Dreamweaver produces when you work in Design mode is as solid and well-written as hand-hewn code. Knowing this, feel free to take advantage of the increased productivity that Dreamweaver's visual-editing mode brings to your day-to-day work with its one-click objects, instant JavaScript, and simplified layout tools. Doing so won't compromise your code and will certainly let you finish your website in record time.

Honestly, no web design program is really WYSIWYG ("what you see is what you get"). Because every browser interprets the HTML language slightly differently, web design is more like WYSIRWYGOAGD: "what you see is roughly what you'll get, on a good day." That's why Dreamweaver's Live View and integrated Adobe BrowserLab (a browser-testing service) can help you make sure your pages look the way you *really* want them to.

Finally, if you have experience hand-coding HTML and CSS, you'll be pleasantly surprised by Dreamweaver's powerful text-editing capabilities. In fact, even though Dreamweaver has a reputation as a *visual* web page editor, it's also one of the best text-editing programs on the market.

- **Have it your way**. As if Dreamweaver didn't have enough going for it, the program's engineers have created a completely customizable product, or, as they call it, an *extensible* program. Anyone can add to or change Dreamweaver's menus, commands, objects, and windows.

  Suppose, for example, that you hardly ever use any of the commands in the Edit menu. By editing one text file in the Dreamweaver Configuration folder, you can get rid of unwanted menu items—or even add commands of your own creation. This incredible flexibility lets you customize Dreamweaver to fit the way you work, and even add features that Adobe's programmers never imagined. Best of all, the Adobe Exchange website includes hundreds of free and commercial extensions for Dreamweaver. See Chapter 20 for details.

■ What's New in Dreamweaver CS6

If you've never used Dreamweaver before, see Chapter 1 for the grand tour. If you're upgrading from Dreamweaver CS3 or some other version of the program, you'll find that Dreamweaver CS6 offers a host of new features:

- **HTML5** is touted by everyone from AT&T to Google to *Newsweek* as the next big thing (described in more detail on page 10). It's the first major change to HTML in years and promises to make building powerful website easier than ever. Dreamweaver CS6 provides basic support for HTML5. That means that it understands the new HTML5 tags and provides code hints as you type those tags in Code view (code-hinting lets you type a few letters of a tag and then select the tag you're after from a pop-up menu—in other words, less typing, fewer typos, faster web page building). Unfortunately, code-hinting is only helpful if you type HTML by hand. If you prefer using Design view and clicking buttons on a user-friendly palette of HTML options, you'll have to wait for the next version of Dreamweaver for Dreamweaver-produced HTML5 code.

- **CSS3** is, like HTML5, a new (and evolving) standard for web designers. It promises many new formatting controls to make web pages look beautiful, including drop shadows for text, rounded corners on boxes, background gradients, borders made of graphics, and even animated transitions from one set of CSS properties to another. Dreamweaver CS6 includes code-hinting for CSS3 and adds many CSS3 properties to the CSS Styles panel.

  Dreamweaver CS6 also adds helpful tools for some of CSS3's most exciting offerings: the new web fonts manager (page 146) frees you from the boredom of the same limited set of fonts (Arial, Helvetica, and Times New Roman, for example) that web designers have been using for years. Now, Dreamweaver provides an easy way to use any of hundreds of freely available fonts to enliven the typography on your pages. And the new CSS transitions panel (page 405) lets you easily add animations to mouse rollovers, so you can turn a navigation bar into an animated visual delight.

- **Mobile Web Design**. iPhones, iPads, Android gadgets, tablets, and other mobile devices are popping up like weeds. Web developers need to know not only what their site looks like in the many browsers on the market, but they also need to customize their sites for mobile browsers. Dreamweaver CS6 builds on the mobile tools added in CS5.5 (multiscreen preview to see designs at different screen sizes and media query support to craft your CSS to respond to different screen widths). CS6 introduces a new "fluid grid layout" tool that lets you build designs that re-flow content to match different devices: For example, using the same HTML, you can create designs that fit in a single column for a phone, two columns for a tablet, and three or more columns for a spacious desktop monitor.

- **Mobile Application Development**. Dreamweaver CS6 includes built-in support for jQuery Mobile and PhoneGap—two programming technologies that let you build mobile phone applications using just HTML, CSS, and JavaScript. The new PhoneGap Build service simplifies the headache-inducing hurdles usually involved in creating native applications for iOS, Android, and Blackberry devices. With it, you can write an application using HTML, CSS, and JavaScript and turn it into standalone phone app you can sell in iTunes' App Store or one of the many other smartphone marketplaces.

- **Under the hood improvements**. Of course, any new version of software includes numerous bug fixes and performance improvements. Most notably, the Dreamweaver engineers have streamlined file transfers from your computer to your web server. In previous versions of the program, you had to transfer files one at a time; now you can move multiple files simultaneously.

■ What's Old in Dreamweaver CS6

Unfortunately, not everything in Dreamweaver CS6 is shiny and new. Dreamweaver's "Server Behaviors," which let you save form information, retrieve information from databases, and password-protect web pages, have gotten old from neglect. This once-innovative feature was a boon to designers who needed complex features but didn't know how to program. However, Adobe has basically ignored this feature for several versions of the program. The programming behind these behaviors is now old and unprofessional. While Adobe hasn't yet removed the tools, this book no longer includes a section dedicated to teaching them. It's not in your interest to learn how to use them, nor in our interest to lead you toward a tool that's no good. (Having said that, there are some excellent Dreamweaver extensions from WebAssist [*www .webassist.com*] that let you tap into the power of database programming, bypassing the old Dreamweaver tools.)

■ HTML, XHTML, CSS, and JavaScript 101

Underneath the hood of any web page—whether it's your uncle's "Check out this summer's fishin'" page or the front door of a billion-dollar online retailer—is nothing more than line after line of ordinary text. You embed simple commands, called tags, within this text. Web browsers know how to interpret the tags to properly display your pages.

When you create a page with tags in it, the document becomes known as an HTML page (for Hypertext Markup Language). HTML is still at the heart of most of the Web.

The HTML code that creates a web page can be as simple as this:

```
<!DOCTYPE HTML PUBLIC "-//W3C//DTD HTML 4.01 Transitional//EN" "http://www.
w3.org/TR/html4/loose.dtd">
<html>
<head>
<title>Hey, I am the title of this Web page.</title>
</head>
<body>
<p>Hey, I am some body text on this Web page.</p>
</body>
</html>
```

While it may not be exciting, this short bit of HTML is all you need to create an actual web page.

■ Document Types

The first line of the code above:

```
<!DOCTYPE HTML PUBLIC "-//W3C//DTD HTML 4.01 Transitional//EN" "http://www.
w3.org/TR/html4/loose.dtd">
```

is called a "doctype," and it simply identifies what flavor of HTML you used to write the page. Developers have used two doctypes for years—HTML 4.01 and XHTML 1.0—and each has two styles: *strict* and *transitional*. Dreamweaver can create any of these types of HTML documents—you simply tell it which one you want when you create a new web page (see page 44) and Dreamweaver handles the rest.

Dreamweaver even lets you use the latest, greatest, and simplest doctype, HTML5. It replaces the extraneous code of earlier doctypes with much simpler and straight-forward code:

```
<!DOCTYPE HTML>
```

Yep, that's it. HTML5 is intended to be much easier to use in many ways, and Dreamweaver CS6 provides limited support for this new version of HTML. This book uses the HTML5 doctype—it's short, simple, and supported by every major browser (even back to Internet Explorer 6). And because HTML5 is the future of the Web, there's no reason to use older doctypes any longer.

But no matter which doctype you're interested in, it's important that you always use one, because without it, different browsers display CSS differently, and your pages will look different depending on your visitor's browser.

Different doctypes do require that you write your HTML in a particular way. For example, the line break tag looks like this in HTML 4.01:

```
<br>
```

But in XHTML, it's written this way:

```
<br />
```

HTML5 lets you write it either way. Fortunately, you won't have to worry about these subtle differences when you use Dreamweaver to insert your HTML—it automatically adjusts to the doctype and inserts the appropriate HTML.

■ Of Tags and Properties

In the preceding example—and, indeed, in the HTML of any web page you examine—you'll notice that most commands appear in *pairs* surrounding a block of text or other commands.

These bracketed commands, like the <p> command that denotes the beginning of a paragraph, constitute the "markup" part of HTML (hypertext *markup* language) and are called *tags*. Sandwiched between brackets, tags are simply instructions that tell a web browser how to display a page.

The starting tag of each pair tells the browser where the instruction begins, and the closing tag tells it where the instruction ends. A closing tag always includes a forward slash (/) after the first bracket symbol (<), so the closing tag for the paragraph command above is </p>.

Fortunately, Dreamweaver can generate all these tags *automatically*. You don't have to memorize or even type them in (although many programmers still enjoy doing so for greater control). Behind the scenes, Dreamweaver's all-consuming mission is to convert your visual design into underlying code, like this:

- The <html> tag appears once at the beginning of a web page and again (with an added closing slash) at the end. This tells a browser that the information between these two tags is written in HTML, as opposed to some other language. All the contents of the page, including any other tags, appear between these opening and closing <html> tags.

  If you were to think of a web page as a tree, the <html> tag would be its trunk. Springing from the trunk are two branches that represent the two main parts of any web page: the head of the page and the body.

- The *head* of a web page contains the title of the page ("Izzie's Mail-Order Pencils"). It may also include other, invisible information, such as a page description, that browsers and search engines use. You surround the head section with opening and closing <head> tags.

In addition, the head section can include information that browsers use to format the page's HTML and to add interactivity. You can store CSS styles and Java-Script code in the head, for example, or you can embed links to external CSS and JavaScript files there. In fact, the interactivity you'll see in Dreamweaver's Spry widgets (Chapter 13) work with the help of JavaScript code stored in separate files on a server; the link to these files resides in the page's head section.

The *body* of a web page, identified by its beginning and ending <body> tags, contains all the information that appears inside a browser window—headlines, text, pictures, and so on. When you work in Dreamweaver's Design view, the blank white portion of the document window represents the body area. It resembles the blank page of a word-processing program.

Most of your work with Dreamweaver involves inserting and formatting text, pictures, and other objects in the body portion of a document. Many tags commonly used in web pages appear within the <body> tag. Here are a few:

- You can tell a web browser where a paragraph of text begins with a <p> (opening paragraph) tag, and where it ends with a </p> (closing paragraph) tag.

- The <strong> tag emphasizes text. The text between an opening and closing <strong> tag shows up as boldfaced type. The HTML snippet <strong>Warning!</strong> tells a web browser to display the word "Warning!" in bold type on the screen.

- The <a> tag, or anchor tag, creates a link (hyperlink) on a web page. A link, of course, can lead anywhere on the Web. How do you tell a browser where the link should point? Simply give address instructions inside the <a> tags. For instance, you might type *<a href="http://www.missingmanuals.com">Click here!</a>*.

The browser knows that when your visitor clicks the words "Click here!", it should go to the Missing Manuals website. The *href* part of the tag is called, in Dreamweaver, a *property* (you may also hear the term *attribute*), and the URL (the Uniform Resource Locator, or web address) is the *value* of that property. In this example, *http://www.missingmanuals.com* is the value of the *href* property.

Fortunately, Dreamweaver exempts you from having to type any of this code, letting you add properties to tags (and other page elements) through an easy-to-use window called the *Property Inspector*. To create links the Dreamweaver way (read: the easy way), turn to Chapter 4.

NOTE For a full-fledged introduction to HTML, check out *Creating a Website: The Missing Manual*, 3rd Edition. For a primer that's geared to readers who want to master CSS, pick up a copy of *CSS: The Missing Manual*. And if you want to add interactivity to your web pages (beyond the cool, ready-to-use features that Dreamweaver offers), you might be interested in *JavaScript & jQuery: The Missing Manual*. End of advertisements: Now back to your regularly scheduled book.

■ XHTML

Like any technology, HTML has evolved over time. Although standard HTML has served its purpose well, it's always been a somewhat sloppy language. Among other things, it allows uppercase, lowercase, and mixed-case letters in tags (<body> and <BODY> are both correct, for example) and permits unclosed tags (so that you can use an opening <p> tag without a closing </p> tag to create a paragraph). While this flexibility may make page-writing easier, it also makes life more difficult for web browsers, smartphones, and other technologies that must interact with data on the Web. Additionally, HTML doesn't work with one of the hottest Internet languages, XML, or Extensible Markup Language.

To keep pace with the times, an improved version of HTML, called XHTML, was introduced back in 2000, and you'll find it used frequently on many sites (in fact, XHTML is just an "XML-ified" version of HTML). Dreamweaver CS6 can create and work with XHTML files as well as plain old HTML pages.

XHTML was seen as the future back in 2000, but HTML5 has since supplanted it. While web browsers still understand XHTML (and probably will for a long time), you won't be using it in this book.

■ HTML5

HTML5 isn't some radically new technology. In fact, unlike XHTML, which was in-tended to foster a new way to build web pages, HTML5 is about making sure the web continues to work as it always has. Most of the basics of HTML are still in place. HTML5 adds a few new elements, meant to support the way web designers currently build websites. In HTML5, for example, the <header> tag can contain the content you'd usually find at the top of a page, such as a logo and site-wide navigation links; the new <nav> tag encloses the set of links used to navigate a site; and the <footer> tag houses the stuff you usually put at the bottom of a page, like legal notices, email contacts, and so on.

In addition, HTML5 adds new tags that let you insert video and audio into a page, and new form tags that add sophisticated form elements, like sliders and drop-down date pickers, as well as built-in browser support for form validation to make sure visitors correctly fill out your forms. Unfortunately, browser support for these new features isn't consistent and it's therefore difficult to use the new tags without some pretty elaborate workarounds to ensure cross-browser support.

In addition, Dreamweaver CS6 doesn't provide quick tools for inserting HTML5 tags. While Dreamweaver offers click-to-insert buttons that make it easy to insert HTML4 tags like the <img>, <table>, or <p> tags, it doesn't provide similar buttons for HTML5 tags like <header>, <footer>, <article>, or <section>. You can, of course, type HTML5 tags directly into the code of any page in Dreamweaver—the program even provides "code hints" for the tags.

But new tags are just one small part of the HTML5 story. HTML5 started life as a product of the Web Hypertext Application Technology Group (WHATG), which wanted to create a version of HTML that provided the tools needed to build powerful, browser-based applications like Gmail. So, much of HTML5 is devoted to powerful (and complicated) technologies like Canvas (for drawing pictures and diagrams on a web page), data storage (for storing information like game scores, preferences, and notes on a visitor's computer), drag and drop functionality, "web workers" for making JavaScript programs run faster and more efficiently, and "web sockets" for streaming data from a web server. All these technologies are promising, but browser support for them varies. In addition, Dreamweaver doesn't provide any easy-to-use tools to tap into these complicated technologies, so you're a few years off from being able to easily include most HTML5 functionality on your sites.

■ Add Style with Cascading Style Sheets

HTML used to be the only language you needed to create web pages. You could build them with colorful text and graphics, and make words jump out using different fonts, font sizes, and font colors. But today, you can't add much visual stimulation to a site without CSS. CSS is a formatting language that lets you design pages with sophisticated layouts and enhanced text. For example, it provides site-wide design consistency for headings and subheads, creates unique-looking sidebars, and adds special graphics treatment for quotations.

From now on, think of HTML as merely the scaffolding you use to organize a page. It helps identify and structure page elements. Tags like <h1> and <h2> denote headlines and reflect their relative importance: A *Heading 1* is more important than a *Heading 2*, for example (and can affect how a search engine like Google adds a page to its search listings). The <p> tag indicates a basic paragraph of information. Other tags provide further structural clues: For example, a <ul> tag identifies a bulleted list (to, say, make a list of recipe ingredients more intelligible).

Cascading Style Sheets, on the other hand, add design flair to that highly structured content, making it more beautiful and easier to read. Take a look at the CSS Zen Garden site (*www.csszengarden.com*). Each of the striking, very different websites profiled there use the same underlying HTML. The only difference among them—and the sole reason they look so different—is that each uses a different style sheet. Essentially, a CSS style is just a rule that tells a browser how to display a particular element on a page—to make an <h1> tag appear orange, 36 pixels tall, and in the Verdana font, for example.

But CSS is more powerful than that. You use it to add borders, change margins, and even control the exact placement of an element on a page.

To be a successful web designer, you need to get to know Cascading Style Sheets. You'll learn more about this exciting technology throughout this book.

■ Add Interactivity with JavaScript

A normal web page—just regular HTML and CSS—isn't very responsive. About the only interaction visitors have with the page is clicking a link to load a new page. JavaScript is a programming language that lets you supercharge your HTML with animation, interactivity, and dynamic visual effects. It can also make a web page more responsive to visitors by supplying immediate feedback. For example, a JavaScript-powered shopping cart can instantly display the total cost of your purchase, with tax and shipping, the moment a visitor selects a product to buy; or JavaScript can produce an error message immediately after someone attempts to submit a web form that's missing information.

JavaScript's main selling point is immediacy. It lets web pages respond instantly to your visitors' actions: clicking a link, filling out a form, or merely moving the mouse around the screen. JavaScript doesn't suffer from the frustrating delay associated with "server-side" interactive programming languages like PHP, which require that a web browser communicate with a remote web server—in other words, JavaScript doesn't rely on constantly loading and reloading pages. It lets you create pages that look like and respond with the immediacy of a desktop program.

If you've visited Google Maps (*http://maps.google.com*), you've seen JavaScript in action. Google Maps lets you zoom in on a map to get a detailed view of streets and zoom out to get a birds-eye view of how to get across town, the state, or the nation, all from the same web page. While there have been lots of map sites before Google, they always required loading a new web page every time you changed a view (a usually slow process).

The JavaScript programs you create can range from the really simple (such as pop-ping up a new browser window with a web page in it) to full-blown "web applications," such as Google Docs (*http://docs.google.com*), which let you edit documents, build spreadsheets, and create presentations using your web browser—all as though the program were running on your computer.

JavaScript programming can be difficult, but Dreamweaver has plenty of tools that let you add sophisticated interactivity to your sites—from animations to drop-down navigation menus—with just a few clicks of your mouse.

■ Mobile Web Design

There's no doubt that mobile phones are changing how we live our lives. They're also changing how we build websites. The small screens of iPhones and Android phones don't treat wide, three-column web pages kindly. Many sites shrink down to postage-stamp size when you look at them on phones, requiring you to pinch and zoom and swipe and scroll to find what you're looking for. Fortunately, there are ways to make websites redraw themselves to fit the smaller sizes of mobile phone screens. Dreamweaver CS6 includes several solutions: the new fluid grid layout tool (page 521) lets you design three different layouts (for phones, tablets, and desktop screens) using the same HTML. In other words, you only have a single web page, but using CSS, you can alter the design depending on the width of the viewing screen. You can also craft your own "media queries" (a CSS3 feature discussed on page 510) to create CSS styles that apply only to screens at particular widths or within a particular range of widths.

Dreamweaver CS6 also provides tools for creating mobile-only websites using jQuery Mobile (page 537), a JavaScript tool that makes traditional websites look and function more like mobile applications (and less like web pages).

■ The Very Basics of Reading This Book

You'll find very little jargon or nerd terminology in this book. You will, however, encounter a few terms and concepts you'll come across frequently in your computing life:

- **Clicking**. This book gives you three kinds of instructions that require you to use your computer's mouse or trackpad. To *click* means to point the arrow cursor at something on the screen and then—without moving the cursor—press and release the clicker button on the mouse (or laptop trackpad). To *double-click*, of course, means to click twice in rapid succession, again without moving the cursor. And to *drag* means to move the cursor while holding down the button.

- **Keyboard shortcuts**. Every time you take your hand off the keyboard to move the mouse, you lose time and potentially disrupt your creative flow. That's why many experienced computer fans use keystroke combinations instead of menu commands wherever possible. Ctrl+B (⌘-B for Mac folks), for example, gives you boldface type in Dreamweaver documents (and most other programs).

  When you see a shortcut like Ctrl+S (⌘-S), it's telling you to hold down the Ctrl or ⌘ key and type the letter S, then release both keys. (This command, by the way, saves changes to the current document.)

- **Choice is good**. Dreamweaver frequently gives you several ways to trigger a particular command—by selecting a menu command *or* by clicking a toolbar button *or* by pressing a key combination, for example. Some people prefer the speed of keyboard shortcuts; others like the satisfaction of a visual command available in menus or toolbars. This book lists all the alternatives; use whichever you find most convenient.

About This Book

Despite the many improvements in software over the years, one feature has grown consistently worse: documentation. Until version 4, Dreamweaver came with a printed manual. In MX 2004, all you got was a *Getting Started* booklet. Now, you're lucky just to get a cardboard box with a DVD in it. To get any real information, you need to delve into the program's online help screens.

But even if you have no problem reading a help screen in one window as you work in another, something's still missing. At times, the terse electronic help screens assume you already understand the discussion at hand and hurriedly skip over important topics that require an in-depth explanation. In addition, you don't always get an objective evaluation of the program's features. Engineers often add technically sophisticated capabilities to a program because they *can*, not because you need them. You shouldn't have to waste your time learning tools that don't help you get your work done.

The purpose of this book, then, is to serve as the Dreamweaver manual that should have been in the box. You'll find step-by-step instructions for every Dreamweaver feature, including those you may not otherwise have understood, let alone mastered, such as Libraries, Design view, behaviors, and Dreamweaver's Spry tools. In addition, you'll find honest evaluations of each tool to help you determine which ones are useful to you, as well as how and when to use them.

> **NOTE** This book periodically recommends *other* books, covering topics that are too specialized or tangential for a manual on Dreamweaver. Careful readers may notice that not every one of these titles is published by *Missing Manual* parent O'Reilly Media. While we're happy to mention other Missing Manuals and books in the O'Reilly family, if there's a great book out there that doesn't happen to be published by O'Reilly, we'll let you know about it.

Dreamweaver CS6: The Missing Manual is designed to accommodate readers at every technical level. The primary discussions are written for advanced-beginner or intermediate computer users. But if you're new to building web pages, special sidebar articles called Up To Speed provide the introductory information you need to understand the topic at hand. If you're a web veteran, on the other hand, keep your eye out for similar boxes called Power Users' Clinic. They offer more technical tips, tricks, and shortcuts for the experienced computer fan.

About→These→Arrows

Throughout this book, and throughout the Missing Manual series, you'll find sentences like this one: "Open the System→Library→Fonts folder." That's shorthand for a much longer instruction that directs you to open three nested folders in sequence, like this: "On your hard drive, you'll find a folder called System. Click to open it. Inside the System folder is a folder called Library; double-click it to open it. Inside *that* folder is yet another folder called Fonts. Double-click to open it, too."

Similarly, this kind of arrow shorthand helps to simplify the business of choosing commands in menus, as shown in Figure I-1.

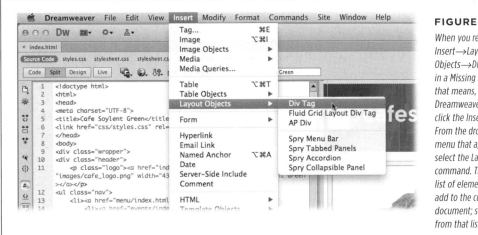

FIGURE I-1

When you read "Choose Insert→Layout Objects→Div Tag" in a Missing Manual, that means, "From Dreamweaver's menu bar, click the Insert command. From the drop-down menu that appears, select the Layout Objects command. That opens a list of elements you can add to the currently open document; select Div Tag from that list."

▮ Macintosh and Windows

Dreamweaver CS6 works almost precisely the same way on the Macintosh as it does in Windows. Every button in every dialog box is exactly the same; the software response to every command is identical. In this book, the illustrations have been given even-handed treatment, alternating between the various operating systems where Dreamweaver feels at home (Windows 7, Windows Vista, Windows XP, and Mac OS X).

One of the biggest differences between Windows and Mac software is the keystrokes, because the Ctrl key in Windows is equivalent to the Macintosh's ⌘ key. And the key labeled Alt on a Windows PC (and on non-U.S. Macs) is the equivalent of the Option key on American Mac keyboards.

Whenever this book refers to a key combination, therefore, you'll see the Windows keystrokes listed first (using the + symbol for compound commands, as is customary in Windows documentation); the Macintosh keystrokes follow in parentheses (with - symbols, in time-honored Mac fashion). In other words, you might read, "The keyboard shortcut for saving a file is Ctrl+S (⌘-S)."

■ About the Outline

Dreamweaver CS6: The Missing Manual is divided into six parts, each with several chapters:

- Part One explores Dreamweaver's main screens and takes you through the basic steps of page-building. It explains how to add and format text, how to link from one page to another, how to spice up your designs with graphics, and introduces you to Cascading Style Sheets.

- Part Two takes you deeper into Dreamweaver and provides in-depth CSS coverage. In addition, you'll get step-by-step instructions for creating advanced page layouts, as well as advice on how to view and work with the underlying HTML of a page.

NOTE Previous versions of this book contained a chapter on HTML frames—a method of displaying several web pages in a single browser window. This technique is going the way of the dodo bird. Since Dreamweaver CS6 is full of so many useful and exciting features and this book's already bursting at its seams (any more pages, and it would have to come with a medical warning to those with bad backs), the frames chapter has been removed.

- Part Three helps you add interactivity to your site. From forms that collect information from visitors to interactive page widgets like tabbed interfaces using the Spry Framework, this section guides you through adding animation, multimedia, and other interactive effects with ease.

- Part Four covers the big picture: managing the pages and files on your site, testing links and pages, and moving your site onto a web server connected to the Internet. And since you're not always working solo, this section covers features that let you work with a team of web developers.

- Part Five shows you how to take full advantage of such timesaving features as Libraries, Templates, and History panel automation. It also covers Dreamweaver's Extension Manager, a program that can add hundreds of free and commercial features to the program.

■ Living Examples

This book is designed to get your work onto the Web fast and professionally; it's only natural, then, that part of the value of this book also lies on the Web.

As you read the book's chapters, you'll encounter a number of *living examples*—step-by-step tutorials you can build yourself, using raw materials (like graphics and half-completed web pages) you can download from either *www.sawmac.com/dwcs6* or this book's Missing CD page at *http://missingmanuals.com/cds/dweaver6tmm*.

You might not gain very much from simply reading these step-by-step lessons while relaxing in your hammock. But if you take the time to work through the tutorials, you'll discover that they give you unprecedented insight into the way professional designers build Web pages.

You'll also find the URLs of the finished pages, so you can compare your Dreamweaver work with the final result. In other words, you won't just see pictures of Dreamweaver's output in the pages of the book; you'll find the actual, working pages on the Internet.

■ Online Resources

As the owner of a Missing Manual, you've got more than just a book to read. Online, you'll find example files, and you can also communicate with the Missing Manual team to tell us what you love (or hate) about the book. Head over to *www.missingmanuals.com*, or go directly to one of the following sections.

The Missing CD

This book doesn't have a CD pasted inside the back cover, but you're not missing out on anything. Go to *http://missingmanuals.com/cds/dreamweavercs6mm/* to download the tutorials and sample pages mentioned in this book. And so you don't wear down your fingers typing long web addresses, the Missing CD page offers a list of clickable links to the websites mentioned in the book, too.

Registration

If you register this book at *oreilly.com*, you'll be eligible for special offers—like discounts on future editions of this book. If you buy the ebook from oreilly.com and register your purchase, you get free lifetime updates for this edition of the ebook; we'll notify you by email when updates become available. Registering takes only a few clicks. Type *www.oreilly.com/register* into your browser to hop directly to the Registration page.

Feedback

Got questions? Need more information? Fancy yourself a book reviewer? On our Feedback page, you can get expert answers to questions that come to you while reading, share your thoughts on this Missing Manual, and find groups for folks who share your interest in Dreamweaver. To have your say, go to *www.missingmanuals.com/feedback*.

Errata

To keep this book as up to date and accurate as possible, each time we print more copies, we'll make any confirmed corrections you suggest. We also note such changes on the book's website, so you can mark important corrections into your own copy of the book, if you like. And if you bought the ebook from us and registered your purchase, you'll get an email notifying you when you can download a free updated version of this edition of the ebook. Go to *http://tinyurl.com/c9cz8kv* to report an error and view existing corrections.

■ Using Code Examples

This book is here to help you get your job done. In general, you may use the code in this book in your programs and documentation. You don't need to contact us for permission unless you're reproducing a significant portion of the code. For example, writing a program that uses several chunks of code from this book does not require permission. Selling or distributing a CD of examples from O'Reilly books does require permission. Answering a question by citing this book and quoting example code does not require permission. Incorporating a significant amount of example code from this book into your product's documentation does require permission.

We appreciate, but do not require, attribution. An attribution usually includes the source book's title, author, publisher, and ISBN. For example: "*Dreamweaver CS6: The Missing Manual* by David Sawyer McFarland (O'Reilly). Copyright 2012 Sawyer McFarland Media, Inc., 978-1-449-31617-4."

If you feel your use of code examples falls outside fair use or the permission given above, feel free to contact us at *permissions@oreilly.com*.

■ Safari® Books Online

 Safari® Books Online is an on-demand digital library that lets you search over 7,500 technology books and videos.

With a subscription, you can read any page and watch any video from our library. Access new titles before they're available in print. Copy and paste code samples, organize your favorites, download chapters, bookmark key sections, create notes, print out pages, and benefit from tons of other time-saving features.

O'Reilly Media has uploaded this book to the Safari Books Online service. To have full digital access to this book and others on similar topics from O'Reilly and other publishers, sign up for free at *http://my.safaribooksonline.com*.

Building a Web Page

Dreamweaver CS6 Guided Tour

D reamweaver CS6 is a powerful program for designing and building websites. If you're brand-new to Dreamweaver, turn to page 2 for a quick look at what this program can do; if you're a longtime Dreamweaver fan, page 5 tells you what's new in this, its latest incarnation.

This chapter gives you an overview of Dreamweaver—a guide to the windows, tool-bars, and menus you'll use every time you build a web page. It also shows you how to set up the program so you can begin building pages. And, because *doing* is often a better way to learn than just *reading*, you'll get a step-by-step tour of web page design—the Dreamweaver way—in the tutorial at the end of this chapter.

■ The Dreamweaver CS6 Interface

When you open Dreamweaver, you'll be greeted by the program's Welcome screen (Figure 1-1). This simple starting point lets you open any one of the nine most re-cently opened files, create a new web page, view instructional videos, and access online help.

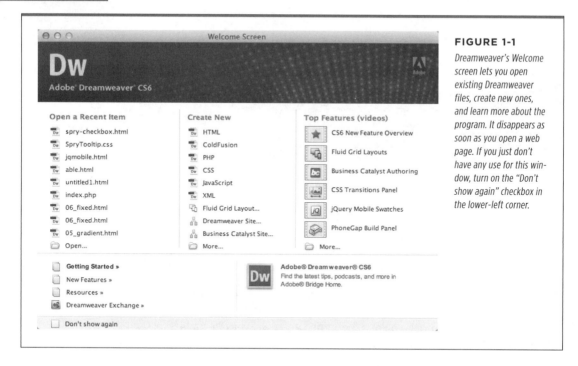

FIGURE 1-1
*Dreamweaver's Welcome
screen lets you open
existing Dreamweaver
files, create new ones,
and learn more about the
program. It disappears as
soon as you open a web
page. If you just don't
have any use for this window, turn on the "Don't
show again" checkbox in
the lower-left corner.*

Dreamweaver CS6's interface shares the look and feel of other programs, like Photoshop, Illustrator, and Flash, in Adobe's "Creative Suite." Out of the box, Dreamweaver's
various windows are a unified whole (see Figure 1-2). That is, the edges of all the
windows touch each other, and resizing one window affects the others around it.
This type of interface is common on Windows computers, but Mac fans accustomed
to independent floating panels might find it strange. Give it a chance. As you'll soon
see, this layout has its benefits. (If you just can't stand this locked-in-place style,
you can detach the various panels and place them wherever you like; see page 34
for instructions.)

Document tabs　Document toolbar　　　　　　　　Application bar

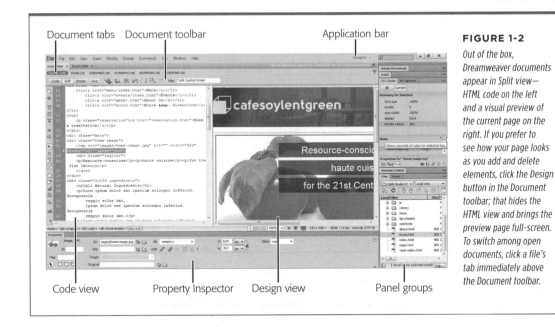

FIGURE 1-2

*Out of the box,
Dreamweaver documents
appear in Split view—
HTML code on the left
and a visual preview of
the current page on the
right. If you prefer to
see how your page looks
as you add and delete
elements, click the Design
button in the Document
toolbar; that hides the
HTML view and brings the
preview page full-screen.
To switch among open
documents, click a file's
tab immediately above
the Document toolbar.*

Code view　　　　　Property Inspector　　Design view　　　　　Panel groups

Many of the program's individual windows help you handle specific tasks, like build-ing CSS styles. You'll read about each panel in relevant chapters later in the book, but you'll frequently interact with three main groups of windows: the document window, a set of "panels," and the Property Inspector.

NOTE　The look of Dreamweaver's windows depends on what kind of computer you use (Windows or Mac-intosh) and what changes you make in the program's Preferences settings. Even so, the features and functions generally work the same way. In this book, where the program's operation differs dramatically in one operating system or the other, special boxes and illustrations (labeled "For Windows Only" or "For Macs Only") will let you know.

The Document Window

What you see on a web page is the end result of the interaction between your browser and the page's HTML, CSS, and (sometimes) JavaScript. Because of this interrela-tionship, Dreamweaver's *document window* lets you view pages-in-progress four ways: as straight code (in Code view), in an editable, visual view (called Design view, pictured in Figure 1-3), with both views side-by-side (known as Split view, pictured in

Figure 1-2), and as it will appear in a web browser (Live view, which turns the document window into a real web browser). If your monitor is wide enough, Split view is a great way to work: click into the Design view half of the document window to add HTML visually, and, when it's easier just to type HTML, click into the Code view part of the document window and type away. Split view even lets you see the code in one half, and turn on Live view in the other half so you can work on the HTML code and see the page as it will appear in a real web browser (you can't, however, edit any page content in Live view). In addition, if you're new to HTML, Split view is a great way to learn the language: add elements like paragraphs, headlines, and tables in Design view and see the relevant HTML in Code view. (You work in the document window's Design view much as you do in a word processor: To add text to a page, for example, you simply click inside the window and start typing.)

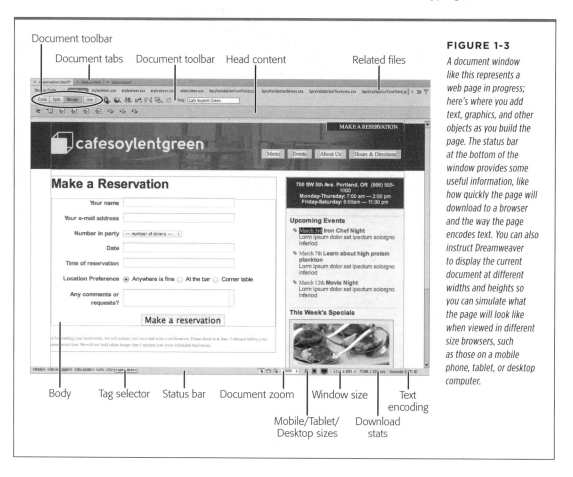

Document toolbar
Document tabs   Document toolbar   Head content   Related files

Body   Tag selector   Status bar   Document zoom   Window size   Text encoding
Mobile/Tablet/Desktop sizes   Download stats

FIGURE 1-3

A document window like this represents a web page in progress; here's where you add text, graphics, and other objects as you build the page. The status bar at the bottom of the window provides some useful information, like how quickly the page will download to a browser and the way the page encodes text. You can also instruct Dreamweaver to display the current document at different widths and heights so you can simulate what the page will look like when viewed in different size browsers, such as those on a mobile phone, tablet, or desktop computer.

When you build a page, you work in the document window, and, as you add pages to your site or edit existing ones, you open new document windows.

Several other screen components provide useful information about your document. They may appear in different locations on Windows and Mac computers (see Figure 1-2 and Figure 1-3, respectively), but they work the same way.

For example:

- **Document tabs**. When you have more than one web document open at a time, small tabs appear at the top of the document window—one for each open file. The name of the file appears in the tab; to switch to it, just click its tab.

TIP If you mouse over a document tab and pause, the location of the file appears in a small pop-up window called a *tooltip*.

- **Related Files bar**. The Related Files bar lists all CSS (Cascading Style Sheets), JavaScript, and server-side programming pages (like PHP) the current web page uses. You'll learn more about these external files later in this book, but as a quick summary, it's common in current web design to have other files supply design and interactivity to a page of HTML. Web designers frequently work on these files in addition to the basic HTML file, so the Related Files bar lets you quickly jump to and work on these "helper" files.

- **Document toolbar**. The Document toolbar lets you change the title of a page, switch between Design and Code views, jump to Live view (to see how the page looks and works in a web browser), preview the page in different browsers, make sure your page is free of HTML errors, and change the look of the document window. (If you don't see the Document toolbar, choose View→Toolbars→Document.) You'll read about its various buttons and menus in the relevant chapters of this book, but you'll want to be aware of the Code, Split, and Design buttons (circled in Figure 1-3). They let you see the page you're working on in the four views described above.

NOTE You may find two other toolbars, the Standard toolbar and Style Rendering toolbar, useful. The Standard toolbar is common on many Windows programs and includes buttons for frequent file and editing tasks, like creating a new page, opening a page, saving one or all open documents, canceling and repeating commands, and cutting, copying, and pasting page elements. (Dreamweaver hides this toolbar until you summon it by choosing View→Toolbars→Standard.) The Style Rendering toolbar comes in handy when you work with CSS. You'll learn how to use it on page 401.

- **Head content**. Most of what you put on a web page winds up in the body of the page, but some elements are specific to a region of the page called the *head*. This is where you put things like the page's title, the *meta tags* that provide information for some search engines and browsers (for example, a description of the page or keywords used in the page), JavaScript programs, and links to CSS files (Chapter 3).

None of this information actually appears on your page when it's "live" on the Internet, but you can have a look at it in Dreamweaver by choosing View→Head Content. You'll see a row of icons representing the different bits of information in the head.

- **Tag Selector**. The Tag Selector is extremely useful. It provides a sneak peek at the HTML that composes your web page, behind the scenes. It indicates how Dreamweaver nests HTML tags in your document to create what you see on the page. In addition, it lets you isolate, with a single mouse click, an HTML tag and all the information inside it. That means you can cleanly remove a page element or set its properties (see page 31), and precisely control the application of styles to it (Chapter 4).

You'll make good use of the Tag Selector in the tutorials to come. For experienced Dreamweaver fans, it's one of the program's most useful tools.

NOTE In Design view, clicking the <body> tag in the Tag Selector is usually the same as pressing Ctrl+A (⌘-A) or choosing Edit→Select All. It selects everything in the document window. However, if you click inside a table (Chapter 6) or a <div> tag (see page 438), choosing Edit→Select All selects only the contents of the table cell or the <div> tag. In such a case, you need to press Ctrl+A (⌘-A) several times to select everything on the page. After you do, you can press the delete key to instantly get rid of everything in your document.

Careful, though: Pressing Ctrl+A (⌘-A) or choosing Edit→Select All in Code view selects *all* the code, including the information in the head section of the page. Deleting all the code gives you an empty file—and an invalid web page.

The Insert Panel

Dreamweaver provides many windows for working with the various technologies required to build and maintain a website. It calls most of its windows *panels*, and they sit in tidy groups on the right edge of your screen. The various panels and their uses will come up in relevant sections of this book, and you'll learn how to organize the panels on page 34. But two are worth mentioning up front: the Insert panel and the Files panel.

If the document window is your canvas, the Insert panel holds your brushes and paints, as you can see in Figure 1-4. You can create a page simply by typing HTML in Code view, but it's often easier to work in Design view, where the Insert panel can simplify the process of adding page elements like images, horizontal rules, forms, and multimedia content. Want to put a picture on your web page? Just click the Images icon in the Insert panel.

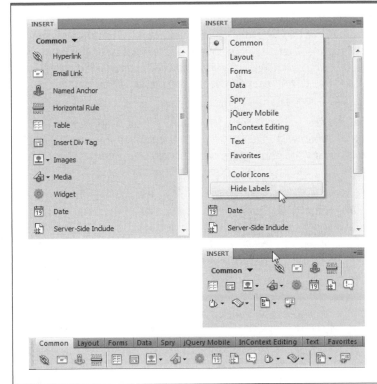

FIGURE 1-4

The Insert panel has many faces; choose the one that works best for you. Normally, the panel displays page elements under each of its drop-down menus in a single list with an icon and a name—for example, the picture of an envelope and the label "Email Link" (top left). Unfortunately, this tall list takes up a lot of screen real estate. You can display the Insert panel's buttons in a more compact way by hiding the labels. When you choose Hide Labels from the panel's category drop-down menu (top-right image), Dreamweaver displays the icons side by side in rows, taking up a lot less space (middle-right image). Finally, you can turn the Insert panel into an Insert bar that appears above the document window instead of grouped with the right-hand panels; this space-saving option is a favorite among many web developers. To get the Insert toolbar, either drag the Insert panel under the Application bar or choose Window→Workspace Layout→Classic (see Figure 1-7).

NOTE Adding elements to your web page using the Insert panel may feel like magic, but it's really just a quick way to add HTML to a page. Clicking the Images icon, for instance, simply inserts the <img> tag into the underlying HTML of your page. Of course, Dreamweaver's visual approach hides that code and cheerfully displays a picture on the page.

When you first start Dreamweaver, the Insert panel is open. If you ever close it by mistake, you can open it again by choosing Window→Insert or by pressing Ctrl+F2 (⌘-F2). On the other hand, if screen space is at a premium, you can close the Insert panel and use the Insert *menu* instead. The menu offers all the objects available from the Insert panel or toolbar, though not grouped by sets, as the panel and toolbar are. (You can turn the Insert panel into a toolbar above the document window, as described in Figure 1-4.)

The Insert panel offers nine sets of objects, each available from the drop-down menu at the top of the panel (see Figure 1-4, top right) or by clicking one of the tabs on the Insert toolbar (bottom image in Figure 1-4):

- **Common objects**. In addition to images, tables, and email links—which you'll use frequently in everyday web design—this category of the Insert panel offers access to Dreamweaver's *template* features. Templates let you build basic web-page designs that you can use over and over again, speeding up page development and facilitating easy updates. See Chapter 19 for details.

- **Layout objects**. The objects in this category help you control the layout of a web page by organizing its contents using CSS or HTML tables. In addition, this panel includes some of Dreamweaver's Spry widgets, which let you add interactive elements like drop-down menus and animated, collapsible panels to a page so you can fit more information in less space (see Chapter 13).

- **Form objects**. Want to get some input from visitors to your website? Use forms to let them make comments, order products, or answer questions. The Forms category lets you add form elements like radio buttons, pull-down menus, and text boxes (see Chapter 12). Dreamweaver includes sophisticated form validation so you can make sure visitors input the correct information *before* they submit a form.

> **NOTE** In Web parlance, a *form* is a web page that lets visitors type in information that your web server processes. For example, you might ask a guest to type in his email address when he signs up for a newsletter.

- **Data**. The Data category provides tools that help you build dynamic pages: controls that add records to your database, for example, or that update information already in a database. Unfortunately, these tools haven't been updated for years, and it appears that Adobe will phase these out in the future. You will, however, find several data tools here that aren't related to dynamic pages. Dreamweaver's Spry dataset feature lets you display interactive data in a table, so visitors can sort the data by column and even change the information displayed on the page by interacting with the data—all without having to reload an additional web page; you'll find Spry datasets discussed on page 661.

> **NOTE** If you're a longtime Dreamweaver user, you know that versions of the program before Dreamweaver CS4 displayed tool buttons in color; now it displays them in the Insert panel in black-and-white. If you liked it better the old way, right-click the Insert panel and then choose Color Icons. Better yet, you can move the Insert panel back to its old location above the document window by selecting Classic from the Workspace Switcher menu (jump ahead to Figure 1-7). This action not only brings back the old Insert bar, it also adds color to all the buttons.

- **Spry**. Spry is a technology from Adobe that lets you easily add interactive features to your site, from drop-down navigation menus to animated effects to complex displays of data. Basically, Spry is a simple way for web designers to insert complex JavaScript programming into websites. The Spry category of the Insert panel gathers together all of Dreamweaver's Spry tools. You'll find the same buttons spread throughout the Insert panel; for example, the Spry tools related to form validation also appear in the Forms category, while the Spry dataset buttons are also available from the Data category.

- **jQuery Mobile**. jQuery Mobile is a JavaScript-powered toolset for building websites that work well on mobile devices, like iPhones and Android phones. The objects listed here simplify the creation of page elements like lists, form fields, and text areas for mobile-enhanced websites. You'll learn about these tools in Chapter 11.

- **InContext Editing**. If you build websites that non-web-savvy folk will update, Adobe offers a commercial service called InContext Editing, which lets nontechnical people edit web pages using a simple web-based interface. Unfortunately, while Adobe used to offer this as a standalone tool that you could use with any website, InContext Editing is now available only when you use Adobe's Business Catalyst (*www.businesscatalyst.com*). Business Catalyst is a web-hosting service for web designers whose clients require sophisticated e-commerce capability, mail-list management, advanced web statistics, and automated tools to manage and update their sites. The service offers hosting packages ranging from a $9-a-month "starter" package to a $79-per-month "pro" package. Dreamweaver includes a Business Catalyst panel that lets you manage hosted sites. Of course, if you already have a web hosting company or don't want to use Business Catalyst, you should steer clear of this category.

- **Text objects**. This category of objects lets you format type—make it bold or italic, for instance. Unfortunately, clicking some of the buttons in this category can introduce HTML errors if you don't know what you're doing. If you're not too comfortable with HTML, the Property Inspector (introduced on page 31, and discussed in depth in Chapter 2) is a much more effective tool for creating headlines, bulleted lists, and bold and italic text. The one useful button in this category is Characters, which lets you insert text that's not easy to type on a keyboard, like the trademark and copyright symbols (see page 92 for more).

- **Favorites**. Perhaps the most useful category, Favorites can be anything you want it to be. After you discover which objects you use the most (like the Image command, if you work with a lot of graphics), you can add those objects to this set of personal tools. You may find that once you populate this category, you'll never again need the other categories in the Insert panel. For instructions on adding objects to the Favorites category, see the box on page 31.

The Files Panel

The Files panel is another Dreamweaver element you'll turn to frequently (see Figure 1-5). It lists all the files—web pages, graphics, CSS, and JavaScript—that make up your website. It gives you a quick way to open the files you want to work on (just double-click the file name in the panel). It also lets you switch among different sites you're building or maintaining, and provides some valuable tools for organizing your files. If the Files panel isn't open, summon it by choosing Window→Files or by pressing F8 (Shift-⌘-F on Macs).

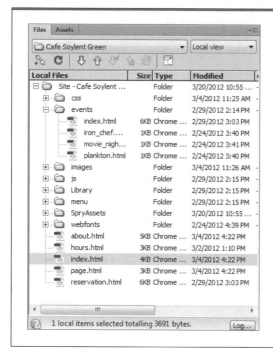

FIGURE 1-5

The Files panel provides a bird's-eye view of your site's files. But it's more than just a simple list—it also lets you quickly open files, rename and rearrange them in the site, and switch among sites. Later in this chapter, you'll learn how to organize your files using this panel.

To use the Files panel effectively, you need to create a local site for each website you work on—setting up a site is a specific Dreamweaver task and one of the most important steps in using Dreamweaver correctly. You'll learn how to set up a site later in this chapter, starting on page 40.

Adding Favorite Objects to the Insert Panel

Help! I'm tired of wading through so many pull-down menus to find all my favorite Dreamweaver objects. How can I see my most-used objects in one place?

Dreamweaver includes a marvelous productivity tool: the Favorites category of the Insert panel. It lets you collect your most-used objects in a single place, without any interference from the buttons for HTML tags and objects you never use. Maybe you use the Common category's Email Link object all the time but never touch the Named Anchor object, for example. This is the timesaving feature for you.

To add objects to the Favorites category, right-click (Control-click) anywhere in the Insert panel (or the Insert toolbar, if you're using Dreamweaver's Classic view as described on page 38). From the contextual menu, choose Customize Favorites to open the Customize Favorite Objects window. All the objects available in all the Insert categories appear in the left-hand list. Select an object and then click the >> button to add that object to your Favorites list. (You can view the objects for just one category by selecting the category from the "Available objects" menu.) Repeat with other objects, if you like.

To rearrange the order of the toolbar buttons, click one and then click the up or down arrow. Depending on whether you display the panel buttons with or without labels, buttons you put higher in the list appear either toward the top of the panel or toward the beginning of the rows of buttons. You can even use the Add Separator button to insert a thin gray line between buttons—to separate one group of similar objects (graphics-related objects, say) from another (such as form objects). Unfortunately, you can't group Favorite objects into submenus. Each item you add becomes a single button on the Insert bar.

To delete a button or separator from the list, select it and then click the trash icon. Click OK to close the window and create your new list of Favorite objects, which are now available under the Favorites category of the Insert panel.

After you create your Favorites tab, you can always add more objects (or delete ones you no longer need) by right-clicking (Control-clicking) the Insert bar and then, from the shortcut menu, choosing Customize Favorites.

The Property Inspector

After dropping in an image, table, or anything else from the Insert panel, you can use Dreamweaver's Property Inspector to fine-tune the element's appearance and attributes (see Figure 1-6). Suppose, for example, that your boss has decided she wants her picture to link to her personal blog. After highlighting her picture in the document window, you can use the Property Inspector to add the link.

FIGURE 1-6

If you don't see the Property Inspector, open it by choosing Window→Properties or pressing Ctrl+F3 (⌘-F3).

The Property Inspector is a chameleon. It's aware of what you're working on in the document window—a table, an image, some text—and displays the appropriate set of properties (that is, options). It works whether you're in Design view or Code view. You'll use the Property Inspector extensively in Dreamweaver.

For now, though, here are two essential tips to get you started:

- In the Property Inspector, double-click any blank gray area to hide or show the bottom half of the Inspector, where Dreamweaver displays a set of advanced options. (It's a good idea to leave the Inspector fully expanded, since you may otherwise miss some useful options.)

- At its heart, the Property Inspector simply displays the attributes of HTML tags. The *src* (source) attribute of the image tag (<img>), for instance, tells a web browser where to find an image file.

  You can most easily make sure you're setting the properties of the correct object by clicking its tag in the Tag Selector (see page 26).

NOTE When you work with text, the Property Inspector has two buttons—labeled HTML and CSS—that let you either work with the page's HTML properties related to text or create CSS styles. You'll read more about this in Chapter 3, but here's a quick pointer: When you want to create paragraphs, headlines, bulleted lists, and bold or italic text, click the HTML button. When you want to change the appearance of text (its font, color, and size), use the CSS button—or, better yet, use the CSS Styles panel, described on page 126, to choose from a much wider range of formatting options.

The Application Bar

The Application bar's main purpose is to let you switch between document views (for example, between Code and Design view), to configure the program's windows, and to give you a shortcut for defining sites, downloading extensions, and searching Adobe's online help. You can find all the options listed here in the program's main menus, too. Figure 1-7 shows its location on Windows PCs (top) and Macs (bottom).

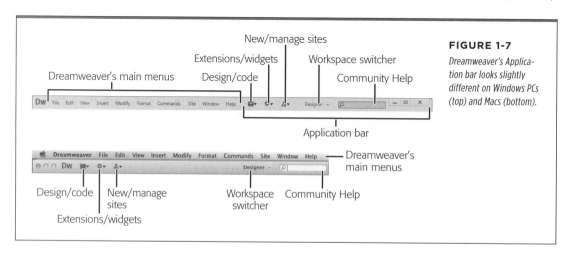

FIGURE 1-7

Dreamweaver's Application bar looks slightly different on Windows PCs (top) and Macs (bottom).

Here's what it offers:

- The **Layout** menu lets you switch between the raw HTML view and the visual Design view (a rough approximation of what a page will look like in a web browser). You can also see both the code and design at the same time by selecting Split view. You can access all the same options from Dreamweaver's View menu.

TIP The Application bar's Code/Design view options are mostly duplicated on the Document toolbar using easier-to-access buttons. However, the Split Code option (which you won't find on the toolbar) is useful if you love to hand-code. Selecting this option lets you view the code for a page in two windows, side-by-side. This way, you can work on both the HTML at the top of a web page and the HTML at the bottom of the page without scrolling. Or better yet, you can work on the CSS of a page on one half of the document window and the HTML for that page on the other half.

- The **Extend Dreamweaver** menu gives you quick access to Dreamweaver's Extension Manager and the Adobe Exchange website. Extensions are add-on features (some are free and some cost money) that let you do more with Dreamweaver. You'll find extensions discussed on page 900. You can also use the menu to open a Widget Browser to locate and install prepackaged programs that add JavaScript-driven interactivity to a page. You'll learn about the Widget Browser on page 699.

- The **Site** menu lets you define a new website or manage the sites you already have. You'll learn a lot more about Dreamweaver sites later in this chapter (in "Setting Up a Site" on page 40), but basically a site is defined as the folder where you keep all the files that make up one particular website. If you're designing more than one website, you can define multiple sites within Dreamweaver. Both the new site and manage site options listed here are available from the Sites menu.

- On the far right of the toolbar, the **Workspace Switcher** lets you reorganize Dreamweaver's layout. You can choose one of the workspaces Dreamweaver supplies or, as discussed in "Workspace Layouts" on page 37, you can design your own layout to create the ultimate workspace. You can access these same options from the Window→Workspace Layout menu.

- The **Community Help** field is a search function. But unlike the help feature you find in most programs, this search field lets you search the entire Internet for useful information related to Dreamweaver. Type a search term in the field and then hit Enter (Return)—the Adobe Help program launches, loading a web page related to your search and offering a list of links to other, related web pages. This help function is a bit better than just using Google—you never know what that'll turn up—because Adobe hand-picks the sites that turn up in the search. So you won't be getting "helpful" advice from the blogger down the street who just bought Dreamweaver and decided to post his thoughts. You can also tap this option by selecting Help and typing your search terms into the Search field that appears.

Hiding the Application Bar

On Windows PCs, the Application bar is unobtrusive – it just sits to the right of Dreamweaver's main menu items. However, if you have a particularly small monitor, the Application bar will drop down below the menu, taking up a good chunk of vertical space on the screen. Fortunately, you can hide the Application bar if you like. Choose Window→Application Bar. Since the options available in the Application bar are also available from the main menus, it's no big loss to hide it.

On Macs, the Application bar always sits on its own. With just a few menu items and a search field, the Application bar is mostly a waste of space. You can hide it on Macs as well, but at a cost: You'll lose the Application Frame, which binds all the panels, toolbars, and windows into a cohesive whole. With the Application Frame turned on, if you change the width of the panel groups on the right side on the screen, the document window and Property Inspector will also resize. If you turn off the Application bar, however, the document window, Property Inspector, and panel group act as separate windows you can resize independently of each other.

So, if you're a Mac user willing to give up the unified workspace of the Application Frame, here's how to hide the Application bar: Turn off the Application Frame by choosing Window→Application Frame, and then choose Window→Application Bar to hide the Application bar. You can always turn the Application Frame back on, but doing so automatically brings the Application bar back.

Organizing Your Workspace

Dreamweaver's basic user interface includes the Document window, Application bar, Property Inspector, and panel groups. All these windows act like a unified whole; that is, if you resize one window, the other windows resize to fit the space. For example, you can drag the left edge of the panel groups (circled in Figure 1-8) to the left to make the panels wider or to the right to make them thinner. The windows that touch the panels (the document window and the Property Inspector) change their widths accordingly. This kind of joined-at-the-hip interface is common in Windows applications, but may feel a bit weird for Mac enthusiasts. (If you prefer the "floating palette" look and feel common to a lot of Mac programs, you can set up Dreamweaver that way—see page 36.)

NOTE On Macs, if you turn off the Application Frame, Dreamweaver's windows act independently of each other. See "Hiding the Application Bar" above for more.

You can control the panel group in many ways to customize your workspace:

- You can open a particular panel from the Window menu. For example, to open the Files panel, choose Window→Files.

- If the panel is closed but its tab is visible (for example, the Insert tab in Figure 1-7), click the tab once to open it. Double-click the tab again, and the panel (and any other panels grouped with it) closes.

- Drag the horizontal line between an open panel and another panel to resize the panel. For example, to make the CSS Styles panel taller, grab the thick border between that panel and the Business Catalyst panel and then drag down. The CSS Styles panel gets taller and the open panel below it gets shorter.

- To completely close a panel so that even its tab no longer appears, right-click (Control-click) the tab and then choose Close. (Choose Close Tab Group to hide all the tabs in a group.) To get the panel back, you need to use the Window menu or use the panel's keyboard shortcut—for example, the F8 key (Shift-⌘-F on Macs) opens and closes the Files panel.

- If you want to hide all windows *except* for documents, choose Window→Hide Panels or press F4—a useful trick when you want to maximize the amount of screen space for the web page you're working on. To bring back all the panels, press F4 again or choose Window→Show Panels. (On a MacBook, you have to press the "fn" key in combination with F4 for this to work.)

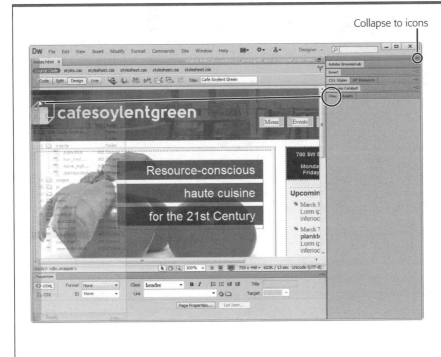

Collapse to icons

FIGURE 1-8

You're not limited to keeping all of Dreamweaver's panels on the right side—you can move individual panels to other parts of the screen. In this figure, grabbing the Files panel's tab lets you drag the panel to the left edge of the screen. A ghosted version of the panel appears as you do. When you see a thick blue line on the screen's edge, drop the tab to create a panel that takes up the entire edge of the screen. In other words, in this figure, dropping the Files panel tab creates a full-height column on the left edge of the screen composed entirely of Files panel objects—the document window and Property Inspector move to the right to make room.

◼ FLOATING PANELS

As mentioned earlier, you can drag a panel by its tab to another part of the screen. Dragging it to the edge of the screen docks the panel to that edge. However, if you drag a panel and drop it when it's not near a screen's edge, it becomes a floating panel (see Figure 1-9). Floating panels are often nuisances, since they hide whatever is beneath them, so you often end up having to move them out of the way just to see what you're doing. However, they come in handy when you have two monitors. If that's the case, you can dedicate your main monitor to the document window and Property Inspector (and maybe your most important panels), and then drag a bunch of floating panels onto your second screen.

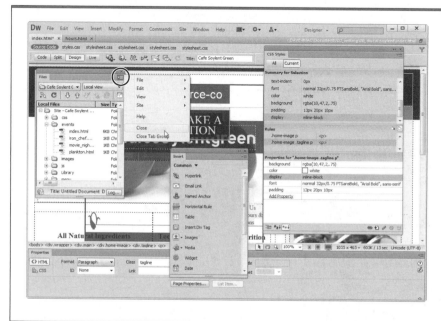

FIGURE 1-9

Here, the Files, Insert, and CSS Styles panels float. Each panel has its own Context menu icon (circled on the right side of the Files panel). Clicking the button reveals a shortcut menu that lets you work with features specific to that panel. This menu also offers generic panel actions, such as closing the panel. If you find you've made a mess of your workspace and want to return Dreamweaver to the way it normally lays out panels, use the Workspace Switcher, discussed next.

To "unfloat" a floating panel, simply drag it to the edge of your screen (if you have more than one monitor, drag the panel to one of the edges of your *main* monitor). If you already have panels at that edge, drag the panel to either the bottom of the panels (to dock it at the bottom of the column of panels), between the bottom edge of one panel group and the top edge of another (to insert the panel in its own group between the other panels), or next to another panel's tab to group the panels together.

TIP Drag a panel to either side of a docked column of panels to create a second column. In other words, you can create two side-by-side columns of panels.

■ ICONIC PANES

As if you didn't already have enough ways to organize your panels, Dreamweaver includes yet another way to display them. By clicking the "Collapse to Icons" button at the top right of a column of panels, you can shrink the panels to a group of much smaller icons. To reopen the controls for a panel you shrunk, just click the panel name. For example, in Figure 1-10, clicking CSS Styles opens the CSS Styles panel to the left. Once you finish working with the panel, click the panel name again or click elsewhere on the screen and the pop-up panel disappears. This so-called iconic view is particularly good if you have a small monitor and need to preserve as much screen real estate as possible.

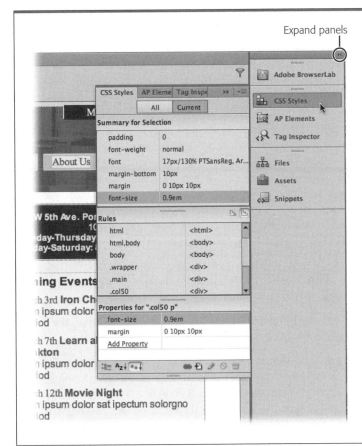

Expand panels

FIGURE 1-10

Iconic panes let you preserve screen real estate. To return to normal-width panels, click the Expand Panels button.

■ WORKSPACE LAYOUTS

Sometimes too much choice is a bad thing, and even though Dreamweaver's interface means you can pretty much organize its windows and panels any way you like, it also means you can easily accidentally click or drag the wrong thing and suddenly find panels strewn across the screen or completely gone.

Fortunately, Dreamweaver includes a wonderful, timesaving productivity enhancer that ensures you always have your windows organized the way you want, and you can quickly return to that setup if you accidentally move anything. The Workspace Layouts feature lets you save the position and size of Dreamweaver's panels and windows as a custom "layout" that you can return to by simply selecting the layout's name from the Workspace Switcher menu in the Application bar or by choosing Window→Workspace Layout.

For example, when you work on a database-driven website, you may like to have the Application panel group and the Snippets panel open, and the CSS panel tucked away. When you work on design-heavy sites, on the other hand, you probably want the CSS panel open but couldn't care less about the Tag Inspector. You can create a different layout for each situation and then simply switch between them.

> **NOTE** The Classic layout is a great way to free up space in the already crowded grouping of panels on the right edge of the screen. It moves the Insert panel to the top of the screen, converting it into an Insert "bar"—one long row of icons with tabs for the categories of HTML objects.

In addition, Dreamweaver comes preprogrammed with eight workspace layouts designed to configure the interface to match the needs of designers, coders, application developers, and those who like to spread their windows and panels across two monitors. You should try each one (use the Workspace Switcher menu in the Application bar) to see which you like best. You can then tweak that layout by closing or opening other panels, rearranging panels, and so on, until you find the perfect layout for you. Then just save it as a custom layout (as described below) so you can call it up any time. Here are a few other tips when you're ready to lay down a custom layout:

- Open the panels you work with most frequently. For example, choose Window→Files to open the Files panel.

- Increase or decrease the height of a panel by dragging up or down the empty space to the right of a panel or panel-group name (see Figure 1-11).

- You can move a panel to another area of your screen by dragging its tabs as described earlier. This trick is especially useful if you have a large monitor, since you can place one group of panels on the right edge of the monitor and another group either next to the first one or on the left side of the monitor. As described in "Floating Panels" on page 36, you can also create untethered panels. If you've got two monitors, you can spread the panels across both screens.

To save your layout, select New Workspace from the Workspace Switcher menu in the Application bar, or choose Window→Workspace Layout→New Workspace. The Save Workspace dialog box appears; type in a name for the layout and then click OK. (If you type in a name that's the same as one you already used, Dreamweaver lets you know and gives you the option to replace the old layout with the new one. That's the only way to update a workspace layout you previously created.) Dreamweaver saves your new layout.

FIGURE 1-11

Resizing a panel vertically is as easy as dragging its bottom border up or down (circled at bottom of Insert panel). If you're lucky enough to have a large monitor, it's often helpful to put the Files panel by itself on either the left or right side of the screen.

TIP The Workspace Layout feature is also handy if you share your computer with other people. You can create your own workspace layout ("Bob's Workspace," for example) with the panels and windows exactly where you like them. Then, when you go to use the computer and the bozo before you has rearranged the entire workspace, just select your layout from the Application bar or the Window→Workspace Layouts menu.

To switch to a layout you already saved, simply select your workspace from the Application bar or choose Window→Workspace Layout→*Name of Your Layout*. After a brief pause, Dreamweaver switches to the selected layout.

■ Setting Up a Site

Whenever you build a new website or want to edit a site you created outside of Dreamweaver, you have to introduce the program to the site—a process Dreamweaver calls *setting up a site*. This is *the* most important first step when you start using Dreamweaver, whether you plan to whip up a 5-page site, build a 1,000-page online store, or edit the site your sister built for you. At its most basic, defining a site lets Dreamweaver know where you store your web pages on your computer. It also helps Dreamweaver correctly insert images and add links from one page to another in your site. In addition, if you want to take advantage of Dreamweaver's many timesaving site-management tools, such as the link checker (see page 765), Library items (Chapter 18), templates (Chapter 19), and FTP feature for moving your files to a web server (Chapter 17), you *have* to set up a site.

There are a lot of ways to configure a site, depending on your needs. For example, if you're ready to move pages to the Web, you need to tell Dreamweaver how to connect to your web server. But to get started with a new site, you only need to provide a couple of pieces of information:

1. **Choose Site→New Site to open the Site Setup window (see Figure 1-12).**

   You'll supply the basics of your site here.

2. **In the "Site name" field, type a name for your site.**

   The name you type here is solely for your own reference, to help you identify the site when it appears in the Files panel; the name won't show up on the Web.

> **NOTE** In Web argot, a *field* is simply a box where you type in information.

3. **Click the folder icon to the right of the "Local site folder" field.**

   The Choose Root Folder window opens, where you select a folder on your hard drive to serve as your *local site, or more specifically, your local site's main, or root, folder.* You'll store all your site's files—HTML documents and graphics, CSS files, and all the other files that make up your site—in this local root folder or in the root's subfolders (such as an Images subfolder).

> **NOTE** Another way to think of the local site folder: It's the folder on your computer in which you'll put your site's home page.

4. **Browse to and select a folder for your site's files.**

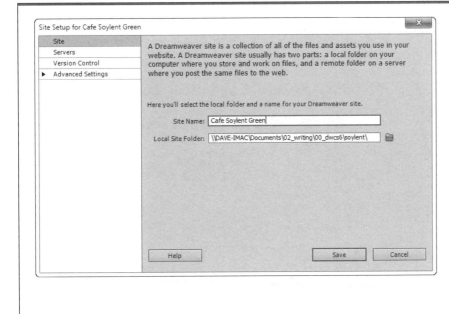

FIGURE 1-12

The Site Setup window lets you tell Dreamweaver about your site—where you store your files, how to connect to your web server so you can upload pages to the Internet, and so on. But to get started, you only need to fill in these two fields. You'll find the other Site Setup categories, listed on the left above, discussed later: The Servers category lets you point Dreamweaver to your online web server so you can upload files to your live site (Chapter 17) and to a "testing server" so you can put complex, database-driven websites through their paces before going live (Chapter 21); the Version Control category is for those using the (very complex) Subversion system (most people—the author of this book included—never use this option, but if you're curious, see the box on page 810 for more information). You'll find the Advanced settings discussed in step 5 below and elsewhere in this book.

Figure 1-13 demonstrates the process. If you're editing an existing site, select the folder that contains the site's files. If you're creating a new site, create a folder for that site using the New Folder button in this window.

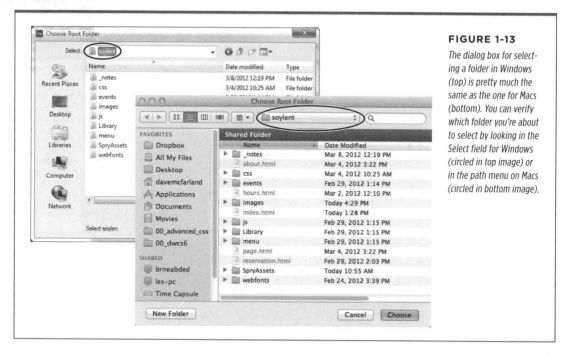

FIGURE 1-13

The dialog box for selecting a folder in Windows (top) is pretty much the same as the one for Macs (bottom). You can verify which folder you're about to select by looking in the Select field for Windows (circled in top image) or in the path menu on Macs (circled in bottom image).

5. **For a few additional options, select Advanced Settings from the left-hand list of setup categories (see Figure 1-14).**

   This step is optional and you can happily skip it to begin building web pages. You'll find most of the categories listed here discussed elsewhere in the book, but you may want to visit the options in the Local Info category:

   - The "Default Images folder" field lets you select (or create) a folder inside your local site folder to hold the images you'll use on your web pages. Choosing a default images folder is useful only if you tend to add images to your pages-in-progress from outside your local site folder—if, for example, you add images that are sitting on your desktop or in another folder on your hard drive. In that case, Dreamweaver automatically copies those files to the Images folder on your local site; that way, when you upload your local site to your online web server, all your images go along for the ride. (Dreamweaver will still copy "outside" image files you use on your pages to your local site without setting this option, but each time you add an image, you have to tell Dreamweaver where to save the file. If you'll primarily use images you already saved in your local site, skip this setting.)

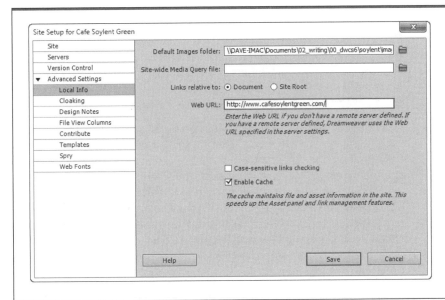

FIGURE 1-14

You can happily use Dreamweaver without ever visiting the Advanced Settings options in the left-hand column of the Site Setup window. The Local Info options are discussed above, and the other options are discussed elsewhere in this book: Cloaking on page 804, Design Notes on page 817, File View Columns on page 830, Templates in Chapter 19, Spry on page 215, and Web Fonts on page 146.

- The "Site-wide Media Query file" field is useful when you design a site for visitors who use tablets and mobile phones as well as desktop web browsers. Media queries are a CSS-based tool that let you trigger different page-formatting rules based on (among other things) the screen width of the device used to visit your site. In other words, you can design a site that displays differently on the small screen of a mobile device (for example, it may show just a single column of content) than it does on the much larger screen of a desktop browser (where you can fit, for example, a three-column design). You'll learn about media queries in Chapter 11.

- The "Links relative to" setting determines how Dreamweaver writes links to other pages in your site, links to images in your site, and links to external files, like Cascading Style Sheets, Flash movies, and so on. Unless you're an experienced web designer, stick with the normal "Document" setting here—you can read about the difference between (and uses for) document- and site root-relative links on page 185.

- Type the web address for your site in the Web URL field: for example http://www.cafesoylentgreen.com/. If you don't yet have a web address, you can leave this blank. In some cases, you may need to add some more information after the domain name. For example, if you're a teacher and you have a site on your college's web server, its address might look something like this: www.somecollege.edu/~bob. Or you might be responsible for maintaining just part of a larger site—sometimes called a "sub-site"—so you might need to append, for example, */marketing* to the end of the URL. Regardless, just type the address you normally type into a web browser to visit your site. For example, www.mybigcompany.com/marketing.

- Leave the "Case-sensitive links checking" checkbox turned off. This is useful only when you have web pages and files on a Unix server that allows files with the same name but different letter cases: for example, *HOME.html*, *home.html*, and *HoMe.html*. Since Windows PCs and Macs don't let you do this, you'll probably never have a site with file names like these.

- Keep the Enable Cache checkbox turned on. Dreamweaver creates a site cache for each site you set up. That's a small database that tracks pages, links, images, and other site components. The cache helps Dreamweaver's site-management tools avoid breaking links, lets Dreamweaver warn you when you're about to delete important files, and lets you reorganize your site quickly. The only reason to turn off this checkbox is if you have a really large website (tens of thousands of pages and images) and you notice that Dreamweaver is really slow whenever you begin to work on the site, move a file, change a file's name, delete a file, or perform one of Dreamweaver's other site-management tasks. In that case, you may see a box saying "updating the site cache" or "checking links" that stays open and prevents you from using Dreamweaver for a minute or more—basically your site is so big that Dreamweaver has to spend a lot of time keeping track of your files and links.

6. **Click the Save button to finish the site setup.**

   Your site's files (if there are any yet) appear in the Files panel. Now you're ready to create and edit web pages and take advantage of Dreamweaver's powerful site-building tools.

> **NOTE** Dreamweaver lets you set up *multiple* websites, a handy feature if you're a web designer with several clients, or if your company builds and manages more than one site. To define an additional site, choose Site→New Site and then repeat the steps starting on page 40. You can then switch from one site to another using the Sites menu at the top-left of the Files panel.

■ Creating a Web Page

After you define a site, you'll want to start building pages. Just choose File→New or press Ctrl+N (⌘-N on Macs) to open Dreamweaver's New Document window (see Figure 1-15). It's a little overwhelming at first. You have so many options it's hard to know where to start. Fortunately, when you just want to create a new HTML file, you can skip most of these options.

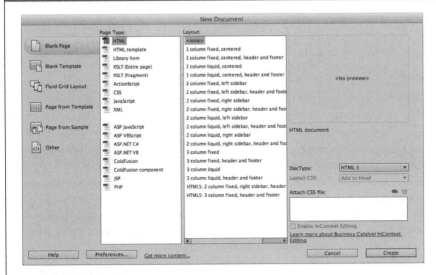

FIGURE 1-15

*The New Document
window lets you create
nearly every type of web
document under the
sun. Dreamweaver CS6
includes a set of prepackaged CSS layouts that use
the latest web design
techniques, including
HTML5. You'll learn more
about these layouts in
Chapter 10.*

To create a basic HTML file for a web page:

1. **From the left-hand list of document categories, choose Blank Page.**

    The Blank Page category lets you create a new empty document—maybe a web page or something a bit more esoteric, like an XML file, an external JavaScript file, or one of the several types of server-driven pages (such as a PHP file, discussed in Chapter 21).

    The Fluid Grid Layout option is new in Dreamweaver CS6. It lets you create a web page that adapts to three browser widths: one for a phone, a tablet, and a desktop browser. You'll learn how to use this feature on page 521.

    Both the Blank Template and "Page from Template" categories relate to Dreamweaver's Template feature discussed in Chapter 19. The "Page from Sample" category lets you choose from several files with already-created designs. Most of the designs are old and left over from earlier versions of Dreamweaver, aren't very attractive, and don't use the best techniques for building a web page. However, Dreamweaver CS6 includes some starter pages for creating mobile-only websites. You can learn more about these on page 537. The last category, Other, lets you create documents for different programming languages like ActionScript or Java. Unless you're a Flash or Java programmer, you probably won't ever need these.

2. **From the Page Type list, choose HTML.**

   You can create other types of documents, too, some of which you'll learn more about later in this book, such as templates (Chapter 19), Library items (Chapter 18), and CSS files (Chapter 4).

Terms Worth Knowing

During the tutorial in these pages—and, indeed, everywhere in Dreamweaver—you'll encounter a few terms frequently heard at web designer luncheons:

Root folder. The first rule of managing a website is that every piece of the site you're working on—web page (HTML) documents, images, sound files, and so on—must sit in a single master folder on your hard drive. This is the *root* folder for your website, and because it's on your computer, it's called the *local* root folder, though Dreamweaver calls it your local site folder. The *root* (a.k.a site) folder is the master, outer, main folder. Think of it as the edge of the known universe for that site; nothing exists outside the root. Of course, to help organize your site's files, you can include any number of subfolders *within* that main folder.

When you finish creating a site on your computer, you'll move the files in your local root folder onto a web server for the world to see. You call the folder where you place your site files on the server the *remote root folder*.

Local site. The usual routine for creating web pages goes like this: You create the page on your own computer—using a program like Dreamweaver—and then you upload it to a computer on the Internet called a web server, where your handiwork becomes available to the masses. So, it's very common for a website to exist in two places at once, one copy on your computer and the other on the server.

The copy on your computer is called the *local site*, or the development site. Think of the local site as a sort of staging ground, where you build your site, test it, and modify it. Because the local site isn't on a web server, the public can't see it and you can freely edit and add to it without affecting the pages your visitors see (they're on the remote site, after all).

Remote site. When you add or update a file, you move it from your local site to the remote site. The *remote*, or live, site is a mirror image of your local site. Because you create the remote site by uploading your local site, the folder on your web server has the same structure as the folder on your local site, and it contains the same files. Only polished, fully functional pages go online to the remote site; save the half-finished, typo-ridden drafts for your local site. Chapter 17 explains how to use Dreamweaver's FTP features to define and work with a remote site.

3. **From the Layout list, choose "<none>."**

   This choice creates a blank document. The other choices ("1 column elastic, centered," "1 column elastic, centered, header and footer," and so on) are predesigned page layouts. These designs (not to be confused with the designs under the "Page from Sample" category) use CSS, which you'll learn much more about starting in Chapter 3. You'll learn more about this feature in Chapter 10.

4. **Select a document type from the DocType menu.**

   Selecting a *doctype*, or document type, identifies the type of HTML you'll use to create your page. It affects how Dreamweaver writes HTML code and how a web browser understands it. Fortunately, since Dreamweaver writes all the code for you, you don't need to worry about the subtle differences between the different document types.

HTML5 is the normal setting in Dreamweaver. HTML5 is the new HTML stan-dard—it's what all the cool kids on the block are using, and you should too. However, XHTML 1.0 Transitional, as well as HTML 4.01 Transitional, HTML 4.01 Strict, and XHTML 1.0 Strict also work just fine; so if you're working on a site whose pages use one of these older doctypes, you might want to stick with it.

If you don't really understand or care about doctypes, just select HTML5. But make sure you avoid None (which can force browsers to display pages in what's called "quirks mode" and makes perfecting designs difficult), XHTML Mobile, and XHTML 1.1 (which is not only obsolete, it also requires a special setting on your web server to work properly).

TIP If you don't want to deal with the New Document window every time you create a page using Dream-weaver's New Document keyboard shortcut (Ctrl+N in Windows, ⌘+N on Macs), choose Edit→Preferences in Windows (Dreamweaver→Preferences on Macs). In the Preferences dialog box, click the New Document category and then turn off the "Show New Document Dialog on Ctrl+N (⌘+N)" checkbox.

While you're at it, you can specify the type of file Dreamweaver creates whenever you press Ctrl+N (⌘-N). For example, if you usually create plain HTML files, choose HTML. But if you usually create dynamic pages, choose a different type of file—PHP, for example. You can also select the default doctype—choose HTML5—for all new pages.

Once you set these options, pressing Ctrl+N (⌘-N) instantly creates a new blank document using the doctype you chose above. (Choosing File→New, however, still opens the New Document window.)

5. **Click Create.**

   Dreamweaver opens a new, blank web page ready for you to save and title (see Figure 1-16).

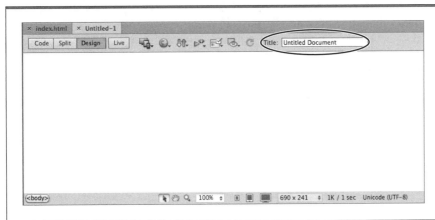

FIGURE 1-16

Here's a new blank web page. Always remember to title the page by click-ing inside the Title field at the top of the document window (circled) and then entering a descriptive name.

6. Choose File→Save.

The Save As dialog box appears. You need to save the file somewhere inside your local site folder. You can save it inside any subfolder within the root folder as well.

TIP If you've set up a site, Dreamweaver provides a quick shortcut to the local root folder. When you save a web page, click the Site Root button in the Save As dialog box—this jumps directly to the local root folder. The Site Root button appears at the bottom-right of the Save As dialog box in Windows, and at the bottom-left of that window on Macs.

---

7. Type a name for the file and then click Save.

Make sure the name doesn't contain spaces or any characters except letters, numbers, hyphens, and underscores, and that it ends in either .html or .htm.

Although most operating systems let you save files with long names, spaces, and characters like #, $, and &, some browsers and servers have trouble interpreting anything other than letters and numbers.

Furthermore, web servers rely on file extensions like .htm, .html, .gif, and .jpg to know whether a file is a web page, graphic, or some other type of file. Dreamweaver for Windows automatically adds the extension to your saved document names. But on Macs—which let you save files without extensions—make sure the file ends in the suffix .html when you save it.

8. At the top of the document window, click inside the Title field and then type a name for the page.

Every new document Dreamweaver creates has the unflattering name "Untitled Document." If you do a quick search on Google for "Untitled Document," you'll find (at the time of this writing) 52,800,000 pages (that's 25,300,000 more untitled documents than there were when the last edition of this book came out—obviously some people still need to pick up a copy). Dreamweaver probably created most of those pages. You should change this to a descriptive title indicating the main topic of the page, like "Directions to Cafe Soylent Green," "About Cafe Soylent Green," or "Technical Specifications for the Anodyne 3000 Indoor Lawn Mower." Not only is replacing "Untitled Document" more professional, but providing a descriptive title can improve a web page's ranking among search engines.

Naming Your Files and Folders

The rules for naming files and folders in Windows and on Macs are fairly flexible. You can use letters, numbers, spaces, and even symbols like $, #, and !.

Web servers, on the other hand, are far less accommodating. Because many symbols—such as &, ⌘, and ?—have special significance on the Web, using them in file names can confuse web servers and cause errors.

The precise list of no-no's varies from web server to web server, but you'll be safe if you stick to letters, numbers, hyphens (-), and underscore characters (_) when you name files and

folders. Stay away from spaces. File names like *company logo .gif* or *This company's president.html* may or may not work on a web server. Replace spaces with underscores or inner caps—*company_logo.gif* or *companyLogo.gif*—and remove all punctuation marks.

Sure, some operating systems and web servers permit strange naming conventions, but why take the chance? Someday you may need to move your site to another, less forgiving server. Play it safe: Keep your file names simple.

Managing Files and Folders with the Files Panel

Dreamweaver's Files panel provides a fast way to add blank web pages to your site. With one click, you can create a new page in any folder, saving you several steps compared to using the File menu. In addition, you can use the Files panel to add folders, rename files and folders, and move files into and out of folders on your site.

Adding Files

To create a new, blank web page, open the Files panel using one of the methods described on page 30 (for example, choose Window→Files), and then right-click (Control-click) on a file or folder in the Files panel. In the shortcut menu that appears, choose New File. Dreamweaver creates a new, empty page in the folder where the selected page resides or, if you selected a folder, Dreamweaver adds a new page there.

The type of file Dreamweaver creates depends on the type of site you're creating. For a plain HTML site, Dreamweaver creates a blank HTML page. If you're building a dynamic, database-driven site, however (like those described in Chapter 21 of this book), Dreamweaver creates a blank page based on the type of server model you select. For example, if you build a site using PHP and MySQL, Dreamweaver creates a blank PHP page (named *untitled.php*).

NOTE The doctype (page 7) of a new web page created with the Files panel depends on your Dreamweaver Preferences settings: Choose Edit→Preferences (Dreamweaver→Preferences on Macs), select the New Document category, and choose HTML5 (or whichever doctype you prefer) from the Default Document Type menu. You can set other options for new documents in this window as well, such as the file extension you prefer (.html or .html, for instance).

The new file appears in the Files panel with a highlighted naming rectangle next to it; type a name for the page here. Don't forget to add the appropriate HTML extension (.htm or .html) to the end of the name—if you do forget, Dreamweaver creates a completely empty file, no starter HTML included (and changing the name by adding the .html extension won't fix the problem). If this happens, delete the file and create a new one. (If you're creating a PHP file, make sure the file name ends in .php.)

NOTE If, immediately after creating a new file in the Files panel, you rename that file and add a new extension, the contents of the file update to reflect the new file type. For example, changing *untitled.html* to *global.css* erases all the HTML code in the file and turns it into an empty CSS file.

Adding Folders

You can add folders to your site directly in Dreamweaver using the Files panel. Just right-click (Control-click) on any file or folder. From the shortcut menu, choose New Folder. If you click a file, Dreamweaver creates the new folder in the same folder as that file; if you click a folder, you get a new folder inside the existing one.

If you crave variety, you can add a folder another way. Select a file or folder in the Files panel and then click the contextual menu button (at the top-right of the Files panel) and select File→New Folder. Finally, in the naming rectangle that appears in the Files panel, type a name for the new folder.

Moving Files and Folders

Because the Dreamweaver Files panel looks and acts so much like Windows Explorer and the Macintosh Finder, you may think it does nothing more than let you move and rename files and folders. You may even be tempted to work with your site files directly on the your Windows or Mac desktop, thinking that you're saving time. Think again. When it comes to moving files and folders in your site, Dreamweaver does more than your computer's desktop ever could.

In your Web travels, you've probably encountered the dreaded "404: File Not Found" error. This "broken link" message doesn't necessarily mean that the page doesn't exist; it just means that your web browser didn't find the page at the location (URL) specified by the link you just clicked. In short, someone working on the website probably moved or renamed a file without updating the link. Because website files are interrelated in such complex ways—pages link to other pages, which include paths to graphics, which in turn appear on other pages—an action as simple as moving one file can wreak havoc on an entire site. That's why you shouldn't drag website files around on your desktop or rename them in Windows Explorer or the Macintosh Finder.

In fact, moving and reorganizing website files is so headache-ridden and error-prone that some web designers avoid it altogether, leaving their sites straining under the weight of thousands of poorly organized files. But you can avoid that: Dreamweaver makes reorganizing a site easy and error-free. When you use the Files panel to move files, Dreamweaver looks for actions that could break your site's links and automatically rewrites the paths of links, images, and other media (see the cautionary note below).

TIP Note to JavaScript coders: If your custom JavaScript programs include paths to web pages, images, or other files on your site, Dreamweaver can't help you. When you reorganize your site with the Files panel, the program updates *links* it created, but not *paths* in your JavaScript programs.

Just be sure to do your file- and folder-moving from within Dreamweaver, like this: In the Files panel, drag the file or folder into its new folder (see Figure 1-17). To move multiple files, Ctrl-click (⌘-click) each and then drag them as a group; to deselect a file, Ctrl-click or ⌘-click it again. You can also select one file or folder and Shift-click another to select all files and folders in between the two.

NOTE Close *all* your web documents *before* you reorganize your files this way. Dreamweaver has been known to not always correctly update links in open files. But if you do end up with malfunctioning links, you can always use Dreamweaver's Find Broken Links tool (see "Finding Broken Links" on page 765) to ferret out and fix them.

When you release the mouse button, the Update Files dialog box appears (Figure 1-17); just click Update. Dreamweaver updates all the links for you.

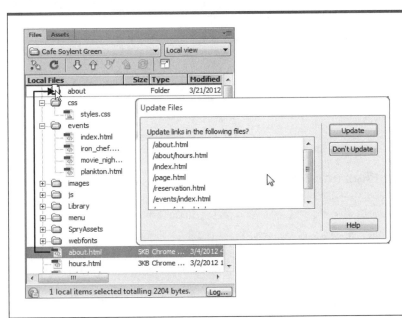

FIGURE 1-17

You can move files and folders within the Files panel just as you would in Windows Explorer or the Macintosh Finder. Simply drag the file into (or out of) a folder. But unlike your computer's file system, Dreamweaver monitors the links between web pages, graphics, and other files. If you move a file using Windows Explorer or the Finder, you'll most likely end up breaking links to that file or, if it's a web page, breaking links within that file. By contrast, Dreamweaver is smart enough to know when moving files will cause problems. The Update Files dialog box lets you update links to and from the files you move so your site keeps working properly.

NOTE If you accidentally drag a file or folder to the wrong location, click Don't Update. Then drag the file or folder back to its original location and, if Dreamweaver asks, click Don't Update once again.

Renaming Files and Folders

Renaming files and folders poses the same problems as moving them. Because links include file and folder names, altering a name can break a link just as easily as moving or deleting a file or folder.

For example, say you create a new site with a home page named *home.html*. You cheerfully continue building the other pages of your site, linking them to *home.html* as you go along. But after reading this chapter and checking the default file name your web server requires (see "Setting Up a Site" on page 40), you find you need to rename your home page *index.html*. If you were to rename the file *index.html* using Windows Explorer or the Macintosh Finder, every link to *home.html* would result in a "File not found" error!

Dreamweaver handles this potential disaster effortlessly, as long as you rename the file in the Files panel. To do so, click the file or folder name in the panel. Pause a moment, and click the *name* of the file or folder. (The pause ensures that Dreamweaver won't think you just double-clicked the name to edit the file.)

A renaming field appears; type the new name. Be sure to include the proper extension for the type of file you're renaming. For example, GIFs end with .gif and Cascading Style Sheets end with .css. Although Dreamweaver lets you name files without using an extension, extension-less files won't work when you move them to a web server, and Dreamweaver itself may not open the file correctly without an extension.

Finally, in the Update Files dialog box, click Update. Dreamweaver updates all the links to the file or folder to reflect the new name.

WARNING It bears repeating: Never rename or move files and folders *outside* of Dreamweaver. If you use Windows Explorer or the Macintosh Finder to reorganize your site's files, links will break, images will disappear, and the earth will open underneath your feet. (Well, that last thing won't happen, but it can *feel* that way when your boss comes in and says, "What happened to our website? Nothing works!")

If you move files outside of Dreamweaver by accident, see "Finding Broken Links" on page 765 to fix the links.

Deleting Files and Folders

It's a good idea to clean up your site from time to time by deleting old and unused files. Just as with moving and renaming files, you delete them from the Files panel.

To delete a file or folder, click to select it in the Files panel and press Backspace or Delete. (To select multiple files or folders, Ctrl-click [⌘-click] them.) If no other page references the doomed file or folder, a simple "Are you sure you want to delete this file?" warning appears; click Yes.

However, if other files link to the file or to files within the folder you want to delete, Dreamweaver displays a warning dialog box (Figure 1-18) informing you that you're about to break links on one or more pages.

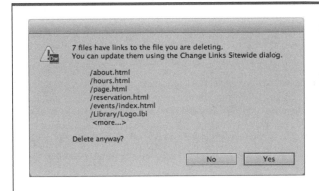

FIGURE 1-18

When you delete files in the Files panel, Dreamweaver tells you if other pages link to the file. If they do, you need to repair the links. Dreamweaver makes that easy via the Change Links Sitewide command (see "Changing a Link Throughout a Site" on page 771)—and it reminds you of the feature in this dialog box.

The message even lists the first few pages that use the file. If you made a mistake, click No to leave your site untouched.

If you're sure you want to delete the file or folder, click Yes. And yes, this move does *break links* in all the pages listed. Repairing those links, which usually means linking them to a new page, requires a separate step: using the Site→Change Links Sitewide command, as described on page 771.

NOTE If you move files into your site folder using Windows Explorer or the Mac Finder, Dreamweaver might not be aware of those files or links between those files and others in your site. If that's the case, when you move or delete files, Dreamweaver may not correctly update links or warn you of broken links caused by deleting a necessary file. To make Dreamweaver aware of any new files you add, choose Site→Advanced→Recreate Site Cache. Dreamweaver will scan all the files in the local site folder and update the cache (its database of files and links in the site).

■ The Dreamweaver Test Drive

Although reading a book is a good way to learn the ins and outs of a program, nothing beats sitting in front of a computer and putting that program through its paces. Many of this book's chapters, therefore, conclude with hands-on training: step-by-step tutorials that show you how to create a real, working, professionally designed website for a fictional café, Cafe Soylent Green.

The rest of this chapter introduces Dreamweaver by taking you step by step through the process of building a web page. It shouldn't take more than an hour. When it's over, you'll have learned the basic steps for building any web page: creating and saving a new document, adding and formatting text, inserting graphics, adding links, and tapping the program's site-management features.

If you already use Dreamweaver and want to jump right into the details of the program, feel free to skip this tutorial. (And if you're the type who likes to read first and try second, read Chapters 2 through 5 and then return to this point to practice what you just learned.)

NOTE The tutorial in this chapter requires the example files from this book's website, *http://www.sawmac .com/dwcs6/*. Click the Download Tutorials link to save the files to your local drive. The tutorial files are in Zip format, a technology that compresses a lot of files into one, smaller archive file.

Windows folks should download the Zip file and then double-click it to open the archive. Click the Extract All Files option and then follow the instructions the Extraction Wizard gives you to store the files on your computer. Mac users can just double-click the file to decompress it.

After you download and decompress the Zip file, you should have an MM_DWCS6 folder on your computer, containing all the tutorial files for this book.

FREQUENTLY ASKED QUESTION

Beware "Site-Less" Web Design

Why doesn't Dreamweaver update links when I move a file or warn me when I delete a file that other pages link to?

Dreamweaver's site-management tools always have your back—unless you're not working within a site. That can happen if you make the wrong choice in the Files panel.

The Files panel lets you browse all the files on your local drive, just like Windows Explorer or the Mac Finder does. If you click the Sites menu in the Files panel (where you'd normally switch between sites) and scroll to the top of the list, you'll see a list of all the hard drives and other storage devices on your home or office network.

Sometimes people accidentally select their hard drive (C: or Macintosh HD, for example) instead of the site they want to work on in the Sites menu, and *then* they navigate to the folder holding their site's files. They begin working, blissfully unaware

that they're doing so without Dreamweaver's safety net. When you work on your files this way, Dreamweaver doesn't monitor the changes you make to your site files—like moving, deleting, or renaming them. In other words, Dreamweaver normally rewrites page links when you move a file that other pages link to, and it warns you when you delete a file that other pages use. But when you're working in "site-less" mode, with your hard drive selected in the Sites menu, Dreamweaver can't help you. Similarly, all of Dreamweaver's other site-management features, like Libraries (Chapter 18), templates (Chapter 19), and file transfers (Chapter 17), don't work when you're off in Unmonitored-Site Land. In other words, it's best to always set up a local site, and always make sure you select the site's name in the Files panel to work on pages in that site.

Phase 1: Getting Dreamweaver in Shape

Before you start working in Dreamweaver, make sure the program's set up to work for you. In the following steps, you'll double-check some key Dreamweaver settings and organize your workspace using Dreamweaver's Workspace Layout feature.

First, make sure your preferences are all set:

1. **If it isn't already open, start Dreamweaver.**

   Hey, you've got to start with the basics, right?

2. **Choose Edit→Preferences (Windows) or Dreamweaver→Preferences (Macs).**

The Preferences dialog box opens, listing a dizzying array of categories and options (see Figure 1-19).

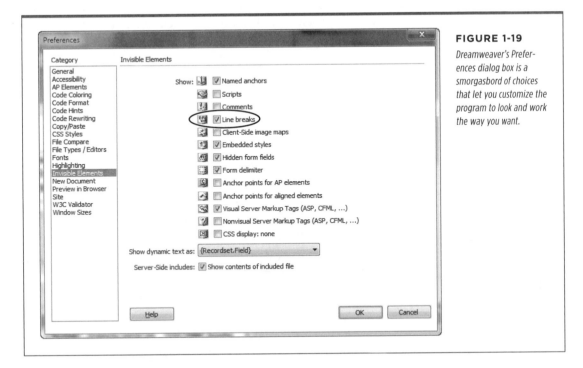

FIGURE 1-19

Dreamweaver's Preferences dialog box is a smorgasbord of choices that let you customize the program to look and work the way you want.

3. **In the Preferences dialog box, select the Invisible Elements category and then turn on the fourth checkbox from the top, "Line Breaks" (circled in Figure 1-19).**

Sometimes, when you paste text from other programs, like Microsoft Word or an email program, Dreamweaver displays what were once separate paragraphs as one long, single paragraph broken up with invisible characters called *line breaks* (for you HTML-savvy readers, this is the <br> tag). Normally, you can't see the line break character in Dreamweaver's Design view. This setting makes sure you can—it represents breaks in the document window using a little gold shield. The shield gives you an easy way to select a line break and remove it to create a single paragraph by combing the text before and after the line break, or to create two paragraphs.

4. **Click OK.**

The Preferences dialog box closes. You're ready to get your workspace in order. As noted at the beginning of this chapter, Dreamweaver offers many windows to help you build web pages. For this tutorial, though, you need only three: the Insert panel, the document window, and the Property Inspector. But, for good measure (and to give you a bit of practice), you'll open another panel and rearrange the workspace a little. To get started, have Dreamweaver display the space-saving Classic workspace.

5. **From the Workspace Switcher on the Application bar, select Classic (see Figure 1-20), or go to Window→Workspace Layout from the main menu and then select Classic from the drop-down list.**

   If you see Classic already selected, choose Reset 'Classic,' which moves any panels that were resized, closed, or repositioned back to their original locations. The Classic workspace puts the Property Inspector at the bottom of the screen, turns the Insert panel into an Insert toolbar that appears directly below the Application bar, opens the CSS Styles and Files panels on the right edge, and displays other closed tabs (for Adobe BrowserLab and a group of tabs for working with server-side programming and databases).

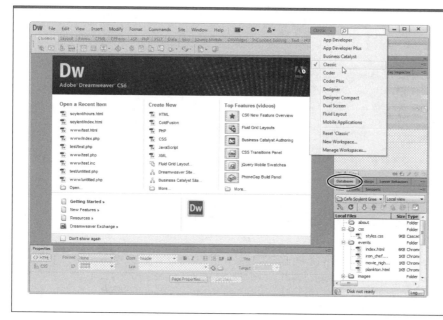

FIGURE 1-20

The Dreamweaver Welcome screen pictured in the middle of this figure lists recently opened files in the left column. Clicking one of the file names opens that file for editing. The middle column provides a quick way to create a new web page or define a new site. In addition, you can access introductory videos and other getting-started material from the screen's right-hand panel. You see the Welcome screen only when you have no other web files open.

Adobe BrowserLab, discussed on page 760, provides a quick way to see what your web page will look like in different browsers on both Windows and Mac PCs. You won't be needing the server-side tabs (Databases, Bindings, and Server Behaviors); Dreamweaver uses them with its outdated server-side tools, so you're best off avoiding them. Fortunately, you can close a group of tabs to get them out of the way.

6. **Right-click (Control-click) the Databases tab (circled in Figure 1-20), and choose Close Tab Group from the drop-down menu.**

The Databases panel and its two other tabs disappear (you can always get them back by selecting Window→Databases).

The CSS Styles panel is very useful; it also comprises three panes stacked one on top of the next, so giving it plenty of vertical room is a good idea.

7. **Drag the thick line that appears between the top of the Files panel and the bottom of the CSS Styles panel (circled in Figure 1-21) down until the Files panel is about half the size of the CSS Styles panel.**

Now the workspace looks great. It displays most of the panels you need for this tutorial (and for much of your web page building). Since this arrangement is so useful, you'll want to save it as a custom layout (OK, maybe you don't, but play along).

FIGURE 1-21

Make a panel taller or shorter by dragging the thick line separating two panels (circled). The options in some panels, like the CSS Styles panel here, are dimmed if you don't have a web page open. You can also minimize a panel group by double-clicking its tab. For example, double-clicking the Files tab in this figure hides the Files panel (the list of files) and expands the CSS Styles panel—a good technique if you need more space for a particular panel. To re-open a closed panel, just click its tab once.

8. **From the Application bar's Workspace Switcher, choose New Workspace.**

   The Save Workspace window appears, waiting for you to name your new layout.

9. **Type *Missing Manual* (or any name you like), and then click OK.**

   You just created a new workspace layout. To see if it works, switch to another one of Dreamweaver's layouts, see how the screen changes, and then switch back to your new setup.

10. **From the Workspace Switcher, choose App Developer Plus.**

    This moves the panels around quite a bit, and even displays some panels in Dreamweaver's iconic mode (described on page 37). This layout is a bit too complicated for your needs, so you'll switch back.

11. **From the Workspace Switcher, choose Missing Manual (or whatever you named your custom space in step 9).**

    Voilà! Dreamweaver resets everything the way you had it before. You can create multiple workspaces for different websites or different types of sites.

Phase 2: Creating a Website

As discussed on page 40, whenever you use Dreamweaver to create or edit a website, your first step should always be to show Dreamweaver the location of your *local site folder* (also called the local root folder)—the master folder for all your website's files. You do this by *setting up a site*, like so:

1. **Choose Site→New Site.**

   The Site Setup window appears. You only need to provide two pieces of information to get started.

2. **Type *Test Drive* in the Site Name field.**

   The name you type here is solely for your own reference; it lets you identify the site in Dreamweaver's Site menu. Dreamweaver also asks where you want to store the website's files. In this example, you'll use one of the folders you downloaded from this book's website (at other times, you'll choose or create a folder of your own).

3. **Click the folder icon next to the label "Local site folder."**

   The Choose Root Folder window opens so you can navigate to a folder on your hard drive to serve as your local folder. (This is the folder on your computer where you'll store the HTML documents and graphics, CSS, and other web files that make up your site.)

4. **Browse to and select the Chapter01 folder located inside the MM_DWCS6 folder you downloaded earlier.** Click the Select (Choose) button to set this folder as the local root folder.

At this point, you've given Dreamweaver all the information it needs to successfully work with the tutorial files.

NOTE You'll find finished versions of all the tutorials in this book in the MM_DWCS6 folder; the completed files have "_complete" appended to the chapter name. The finished version of *this* tutorial is in the Chapter01_finished folder.

---

5. **Click Save to close the Site Setup window.**

   After you set up a site, Dreamweaver creates a *site cache* for it (see page 44). Since there are hardly any files in the Chapter01 folder, you may not even notice this happening—it goes by in the blink of an eye.

Phase 3: Creating and Saving a Web Page

"Enough already! I want to build a web page," you're probably saying. You'll do just that now:

1. **Choose File→New.**

   The New Document window opens. Creating a blank web page involves a few clicks.

2. **From the left-hand list of document categories, select Blank Page; in the Page Type list, highlight HTML; and from the Layout list, choose <none>.** From the DocType menu in the bottom-right, select HTML 5.

   As discussed on page 7, HTML comes in a variety of flavors, called doctypes. HTML5 is the latest and greatest version, so use it.

3. **Click Create.**

   Dreamweaver opens a new, blank HTML page. Even though the underlying code for an HTML page differs in slight ways depending on which document type you chose (HTML 4.01 Transitional, XHTML 1.0 Strict, HTML5, and so on), you have nothing to worry about: When you add HTML in Design view, Dreamweaver writes the correct code for your doctype.

   If you see a bunch of strange text in the document window, you're looking at the underlying HTML, and you're in either Code or Split view. If your monitor is wide enough to view both the Code and Design views side-by-side, select the Split button at the top of the document window; if your monitor is on the small side, click Design. (If you don't see these buttons, choose View→Toolbars→Document.) You'll work mainly in the visual Design view for this tutorial.

4. **Choose File→Save.**

   The Save As dialog box opens.

   Always save a newly created page right away. This good habit prevents serious headaches if the power goes out as you finish that beautiful—but unsaved—creation.

5. **Save the page in the Chapter01 folder as *index.html*.**

You could also save the page as *index.htm*; both .html and .htm are valid extensions for HTML files. On most web servers, you'll name the home page *index.html* (see the box on page 735 for an explanation).

Make sure you save this page in the correct folder. In Phase 2 (page 58), you told Dreamweaver to use the Chapter01 as the site's root folder—the folder that holds all the pages and files for the site. If you save the page in a folder outside of Chapter01, Dreamweaver gets confused and its site-management features won't work correctly.

TIP When you save a file, you can quickly jump to the current site's root folder. In the Save As dialog box, click the Site Root button—that takes you right to the root folder. This little trick also works when you link to or open a file.

6. **If the document window toolbar isn't already open, choose View→Toolbars→ Document to display it.**

The toolbar at the top of the document window provides easy access to a variety of tasks you'll perform frequently, such as titling a page, previewing it in a web browser, and looking at the HTML.

7. **In the toolbar's Title field, select the text "Untitled Document," and then type in "Welcome to Cafe Soylent Green."**

The Title field lets you set a page's title—the information that appears in the title bar of a web browser. The title also shows up as the name of your page when someone searches the web using a search engine like Google or Bing. In addition, a clear and descriptive title that identifies the main point of the page can also help increase a page's rank among the major search engines.

If you have Split view turned on, you'll notice that in Code view, Dreamweaver updated the <title> tag in the HTML to read "<title>Welcome to Cafe Soylent Green</title>."

8. **In the Property Inspector, click the Page Properties button, or choose Modify→Page Properties.**

The Page Properties dialog box opens (see Figure 1-22), letting you define the basic look of each web page you create. Six categories of settings control attributes like text color, background color, link colors, and page margins.

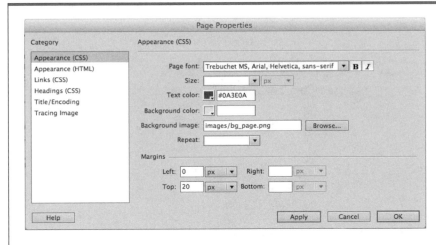

FIGURE 1-22

Dreamweaver clearly indicates which property settings use CSS and which rely on HTML. You should avoid the category labeled "Appearance (HTML)." The options in that category add old, out-of-date code to your pages.

9. **From the "Page font" menu, select "Trebuchet MS, Arial, Helvetica, sans-serif."**

   This sets a basic font (and three backup fonts, in case your visitor's machine lacks Trebuchet MS) that Dreamweaver automatically uses for all the text on the page. However, as you'll see later in this tutorial, you can always specify a different font for selected text.

   Next, you'll set a basic text color for the page.

10. **Next to "Text color," click the small gray box.** From the pop-up color palette, choose a color (a dark green color works well with this site).

    Unless you intervene, all web page text starts out black; the text on this page reflects the color you select here. In the next step, you'll add an image as a background to liven up the page.

NOTE Alternatively, you could type a color value, like *#333333*, into the field beside the palette icon. That's *hexadecimal* notation, which is familiar to HTML coding gurus. Both the pop-up color palette and the hexadecimal color-specifying field appear fairly often in Dreamweaver. Dreamweaver CS6 even lets you specify a color using other values, such as RGB (red-green-blue) and HSL (hue-saturation-lightness) values. See page 160 for more on setting colors in Dreamweaver.

---

11. **To the right of the "Background image" field, click the Browse button.**

    The Select Image Source window appears (see Figure 1-23). Use it to navigate to and select a graphic.

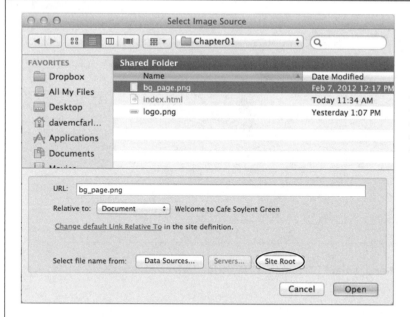

FIGURE 1-23

Use the Select Image Source window to insert graphics on a web page. The Site Root button (circled) is a shortcut to your local site's main, or root, folder—a nifty way to quickly get to your root folder when you search for a file. On Windows, the Site Root button appears at the top of the window.

12. **Click the Site Root button at the top of the window (bottom of the window on Macs).** Select the file *bg_page.png*, and then click OK (Open).

   In Dreamweaver, you can select a file *and* close the selection window just by double-clicking the file name.

> **NOTE** Windows Users: Normally, Windows doesn't display a file's extension. So when you navigate to the images folder in step 13 above, you might see *bg_page* instead of *bg_page.png*. Since file extensions are an important way people (and web servers) identify the types of files a website uses, you probably want Windows to display extensions. Here's how you do that: In Windows Explorer, navigate to and select the MM_DWCS6 folder. If you use Windows 7 or Vista, choose Organize→"Folder and search options." If you use Windows XP, choose Tools→Folder Options. In the Folder Options window, select the View tab, and then turn off the "Hide extensions for known file types" checkbox. To apply this setting to the tutorial files, click OK; to apply it to all the files on your computer, click the "Apply to Folders" button, and then click OK.

13. **In the Left margin field, type 0; in the Top margin field type *20*.**

   The *0* setting for the left margin removes the little bit of space web browsers insert between the contents of your web page and the left side of the browser window. The *20* adds 20 pixels between the top of the browser window and the page contents.

If you like, you can change this setting to make the browser add more space to the top and left side of the page, or set both values to *0* to remove any space between the page's content and the browser window edges. In fact, you can even add a little extra empty space on the *right* side of a page. (The right margin control is especially useful for languages that read from right to left, like Hebrew or Arabic.)

14. **Back in the Category menu (far left of the Page Properties window), click Links, and then add the following properties: In the "Link color" field, type *#336633*; in the "Visited links" field, type *#999999*; in the "Rollover links" field, type *#CC9900*; and in the "Active links" field, type *#FF0000* (see Figure 1-24).**

   These hexadecimal codes specify web page colors (see "Picking a Font Color" on page 157 for more on choosing colors for web pages).

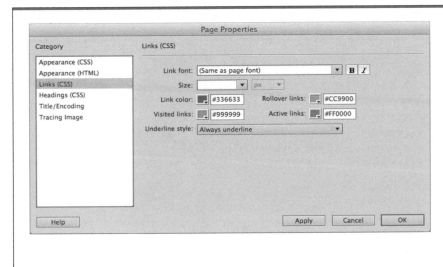

FIGURE 1-24

You can set several hyperlink properties using the Links category of the Page Properties dialog box. You can choose a different font and size for links, as well as specify colors for four different link states. Finally, you can choose whether (or when) a browser underlines links. Most browsers automatically do, but you can override that behavior with the help of this dialog box and the Cascading Style Sheet Dreamweaver creates.

Links come in four varieties: regular, visited, active, and rollover. A *regular* link is a plain old link, unvisited, untouched. A *visited* link is one you've already clicked, as noted in your browser's History list. An *active* link is one you're currently clicking (you're pressing the mouse button down as you hover over the link). And finally, a *rollover* link indicates what the link looks like when you mouse over it without clicking. You can choose different colors for each of these link states.

While it may seem like overkill to have four different colors for links, the regular and visited link colors provide useful feedback to web visitors by telling them which links they've already followed and which remain to be checked out. For its part, the rollover link gives you instant feedback, changing color as soon as you move your cursor over it. The active link color isn't that useful for navigating a site since its color changes so briefly you probably won't even notice it.

NOTE Although Dreamweaver uses the term *rollover* link, in the world of Cascading Style Sheets, this is called a *hover* link.

---

15. **Click OK to close the window and apply the changes to the page.**

    If you look at the top of the document window, you'll see an asterisk next to the file name—that's Dreamweaver's way of telling you that you haven't saved a page you edited, a nice reminder to save your file frequently and prevent heartache if the program suddenly shuts down (see circled image in Figure 1-25).

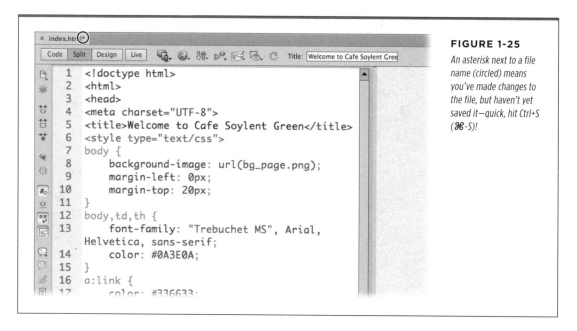

FIGURE 1-25

An asterisk next to a file name (circled) means you've made changes to the file, but haven't yet saved it—quick, hit Ctrl+S (⌘-S)!

If you've been working in Split view, you'll also notice that Dreamweaver added the HTML <style> tag with some other code inside it—this is called a CSS style sheet and the code includes formatting information that dictates how a browser displays various tags (you'll learn all about this in Chapter 3.)

16. **Choose File→Save (or press Ctrl+S [⌘-S]).**

    Save your work frequently. (This isn't a web technique so much as a computer-always-crashes-when-you-least-expect-it technique.)

Phase 4: Adding Images and Text

Now you'll add the real meat of your web page, words and pictures.

1. **On the Insert bar's Common tab, from the Image menu, select Image (see Figure 1-26).**

   Alternatively, choose Insert→Image. Either way, the Select Image Source dialog box opens. (If you didn't choose the Classic view from the Workspace Switcher—step 5 on page 56—then the Insert bar is really the Insert panel and it appears in the right-hand group of panels.)

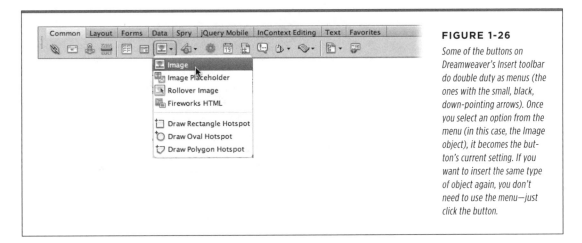

FIGURE 1-26

Some of the buttons on Dreamweaver's Insert toolbar do double duty as menus (the ones with the small, black, down-pointing arrows). Once you select an option from the menu (in this case, the Image object), it becomes the button's current setting. If you want to insert the same type of object again, you don't need to use the menu—just click the button.

2. **Make sure you're in the local root folder and double-click the *logo.png* graphics file.**

   The Image Tag Accessibility window opens. Fresh out of the box and onto your computer, Dreamweaver automatically turns on several accessibility preferences. They're designed to make your pages more accessible to people who use alternative devices for viewing websites—for example, people with viewing disabilities who require special web browser software, such as a screen reader, which reads the contents of a web page out loud. Of course, images aren't words, so they can't be spoken. But you can describe an image by adding what's called an *alt* property. This is a text description of the graphic (an *alt*ernative to seeing the image) that's useful not only for screen-reading software, but for people who deliberately *turn off* pictures in their web browser so pages load faster. (Search engines also look at *alt* properties when they index a page, so an accurate description can help your site's search-engine rankings.)

NOTE If you don't see the Image Tag Accessibility window, press Ctrl+U (⌘-U) to open the Preferences panel, select the Accessibility category, turn on the Images checkbox, and then click OK.

3. **In the "Alternate text" field, type *Cafe Soylent Green.*** Click OK to add the image to the page.

The café's banner appears at the top of the page, as shown in Figure 1-27. A thin border appears around the image, indicating that you have it selected. Note that the Property Inspector changes to reflect the properties of the selected item, the image in this case.

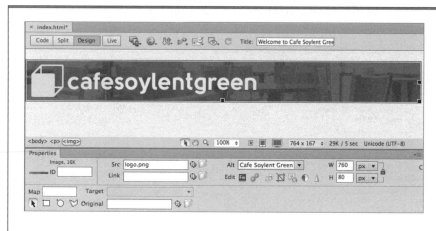

FIGURE 1-27

When you select an image in the document window, the Property Inspector reveals the image's dimensions. In the top-left corner of the Inspector, a thumbnail of the image appears, as does the word "Image" (to identify the type of element you selected), and the image's file size (in this case, 16 KB). You'll learn about other image properties in Chapter 5.

NOTE You can also add or edit *alt* text in the Property Inspector.

4. **Deselect the image by clicking anywhere else in the document window or by pressing the right arrow key.**

Keep your keyboard's arrow keys in mind—they're a great way to deselect a page element *and* move your cursor into place to add text or more images.

5. **Press Enter (Return) to create a new paragraph.** Type *Welcome to Cafe Soylent Green.*

Make sure you're in Design view here—pressing Enter (Return) in Code view simply inserts a carriage return and no paragraph tags. Notice that the text is a dark color and uses the Trebuchet (or, if you don't have Trebuchet MS installed, the Arial) font; you set these options earlier, in the Page Properties dialog box. The Property Inspector now displays text-formatting options.

NOTE The key called Enter on a Windows keyboard is named Return on most Macintosh keyboards and Enter on others. So on Macs, you press either Return or Enter.

6. **In the Property Inspector, click the HTML button and then, from the Format menu, choose Heading 1 (see Figure 1-28).**

   The text you just typed becomes big and bold—the default style for Heading 1. The Format menu offers a number of paragraph types. Right now, the text doesn't stand out enough, so you'll change its color.

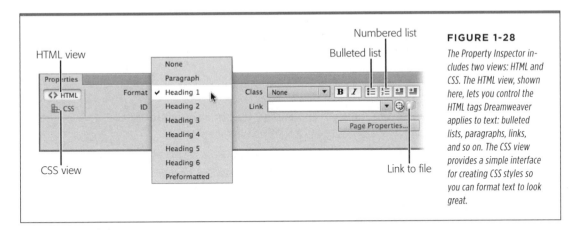

FIGURE 1-28

The Property Inspector includes two views: HTML and CSS. The HTML view, shown here, lets you control the HTML tags Dreamweaver applies to text: bulleted lists, paragraphs, links, and so on. The CSS view provides a simple interface for creating CSS styles so you can format text to look great.

7. **Select the text you just typed.**

   You can do so either by dragging carefully across the entire line or by triple-clicking anywhere inside the line. (Unlike the Format menu, which affects an entire *paragraph* at a time, many options in the Property Inspector—like the one you'll use next—apply only to text you've *selected*.)

8. **In the Property Inspector, click the CSS button to switch to CSS properties.**
   From the "Targeted rule" menu, choose New CSS Rule. In the Color field of the Property Inspector, replace the value that's listed with *#CC9900* (or select a color using the color box, if you prefer), and then hit Enter (Return).

   The New CSS Rule window opens. This window (which you'll learn a lot more about in Chapter 3) lets you create new CSS styles. In this case, you'll create a type of style, called a tag style, that Dreamweaver applies to any Heading 1 (<h1> tag) on a page.

9. **From the top menu, select "Tag (redefines an HTML element)."**

   Notice that the field below that menu changes to display "h1." This is called a selector—and once you define its characteristics, it tells web browsers how to display any level-1 heading (in other words, any text that has an <h1> tag applied to it).

   Don't worry about any of the other settings in this window; you'll learn the details soon.

10. **Click OK.**

    Dreamweaver has just created a new CSS style. Now, wasn't that easy? Next, you'll change the font for this text.

11. **Make sure you still have the headline selected.** In the Property Inspector, choose "Palatino Linotype, Book Antiqua, Palatino, serif" from the Font menu.

    This time, Dreamweaver doesn't open the New CSS Rule window; that's because you're simply adding more styling information to the style you created in step 9. Now the heading will have the color you specified in step 8 and the font you chose in this step.

    Time to add more text.

12. **Click to the right of the heading text to deselect it.** Press Enter (Return) to create a new paragraph below the headline.

    Although you may type a headline now and again, you'll probably get most of your text from word processing documents or emails from your clients, boss, or coworkers. To get that text into Dreamweaver, you simply copy it from the document and paste it into your web page.

13. **In the Files panel, double-click the file *home-page.txt* to open it.**

    This file is just plain text—no formatting, just words. To get it into your document, you'll copy and paste it.

14. **Click anywhere inside the text, and then choose Edit→Select All, followed by Edit→Copy.** Click the *index.html* tab to return to your web page and, finally, choose Edit→Paste.

    You should see a few gold shields sprinkled among the text (circled in Figure 1-29). If you don't, make sure you completed step 3 on page 55. These shields represent line breaks—spots where text drops to the next line without creating a new paragraph. You'll often see these in pasted text. In this case, you need to remove them, and then create separate paragraphs.

15. **Click one of the gold shields and then press Enter (Return).** Repeat this for all the other gold shields in the document window.

    This deletes the line break in the document (it actually deletes the HTML tag <br>) and creates two paragraphs out of one. Repeat this step for the gold shields beside the words Location, Hours, and Specialties.

    At this point, the pasted text is just a series of paragraphs. To give it some structure, you'll add headings and a bulleted list.

16. **Click in the paragraph with the text "About the Cafe."** In the Property Inspector, click the HTML button, and then choose Heading 2 from the Format menu.

   That changes the paragraph to a headline, making it bigger and bolder.

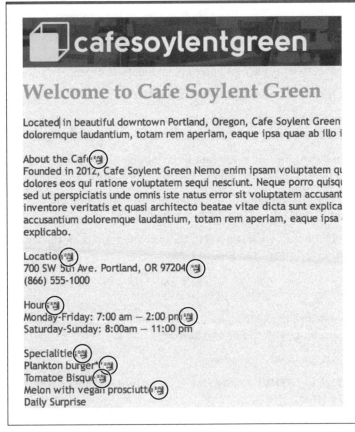

FIGURE 1-29

Line breaks (circled) often crop up when you copy and paste text from other programs into Dreamweaver. Follow the steps on page 55 to make sure you can see the line breaks in Design view.

17. **Repeat the last step for the lines of text "Location," "Hours," and "Specialties" (near the end of the page).**

   You now have one Heading 1 and four Heading 2 headlines. The Heading 2 headlines could use a little style also.

18. **Triple-click the headline "About the Cafe" to select it.** In the Property Inspector, click the CSS button. In the Size field, delete "none", and type 20.

   The New CSS Rule window appears again. Now you'll create a style for <h2> tags.

19. **From the top menu, select "Tag (redefines an HTML element)."**

   You should see h2 in the middle field.

20. **Click OK.**

Notice that the text gets a little smaller—the style you just created applies to all <h2> tags, and they now share the same font size, 20 pixels. Next, you'll change the text's color.

21. **Make sure you still have the headline selected and, in the Property Inspector, click in the field next to the color box, and replace the color currently there with #339966.**

You've changed the color to a lighter and brighter shade of green.

22. **In the Property Inspector, click the I (for italics) button.**

This italicizes the text and updates the h2 style you created earlier—that's why the other Heading 2 headlines are now italicized, too.

23. **Select the four paragraphs under the headline "Specialties"; drag from the start of the first paragraph to the end of the fourth paragraph.**

You can also drag up starting from the end of the last paragraph. Either way, you select all four paragraphs listing the café's specialties.

24. **In the Property Inspector, click the HTML button, and then click the Unordered (bulleted) List button (see Figure 1-28).**

The paragraphs turn into a bulleted list of items, called an "unordered list" in HTML-speak. Finally, you'll highlight location and hours.

25. **Select the two paragraphs below the Location headline (beginning with 700 SW 5th and ending with the phone number).**

You'll make the address bold.

26. **Make sure you have the HTML button pressed in the Property Inspector, and then click the B button.**

The text changes appearance but the New CSS Rule window doesn't appear. Even though you find the B (for bold) button on both the HTML and CSS views of the Property Inspector, they do different things. When you select it in HTML mode, Dreamweaver inserts the HTML <strong> tag—used to "strongly" emphasize text. But when you press the B button in CSS mode, Dreamweaver adds CSS code to the page to make the text look bold. It's a subtle but important difference—in HTML mode, you change the formatting of just the selected text, but in CSS mode, you'd create a style, and that style would change the formatting of all the text that shared the same tag, the paragraph tag (<p>) in this example. (You'll read more about this on page 130.) In this case, you want to use the HTML <strong> tag to emphasize the selected text.

27. **Repeat step 26 for the two paragraphs below the Hours headline, and then save the page.**

You'll add a few more design touches to the page, but first you should see how the page looks in a real web browser.

The Mysterious Haunted Steering Wheel

When I select a paragraph, an image...heck, anything at all, in Design view, a weird icon appears. It looks like a ship's steering wheel. What is it and how do I get rid of it?

You click this steering-wheel icon to open the Code Navigator window. That window (described on page 397) lists the CSS styles related to whatever page element you selected. It's useful for people who like to skip Dreamweaver's user-friendly CSS Styles panel and create and edit CSS by hand. If you're new

to CSS, this isn't a useful tool and that goofy icon, which looks like something Ahab's ghost misplaced, gets in the way. To hide it, click the icon to open the Code Navigator and turn on the "Disable indicator" checkbox in the bottom-right. If you ever want to turn the Navigator back on, choose View→Code Navigator to open the Code Navigator window, and then turn off the Disable checkbox.

Phase 5: Preview Your Work

Dreamweaver's Design view gives you a visual way to add and edit HTML. However, its display is frequently a long way off from that of a real web browser. Dreamweaver may display *more* information than you'd see on the Web (including "invisible" objects, like table borders and those line breaks you removed earlier), or it may display *less* (it sometimes has trouble rendering complex designs).

Furthermore, much to the eternal woe of web designers, different browsers display pages differently. Pages you view in Internet Explorer don't always look the same in other browsers, like Firefox or Safari. In some cases, the differences may be subtle (for example, text may be slightly larger or smaller). In other cases, the changes can be dramatic: Earlier versions of Internet Explorer, for example, can't display the text or box drop shadows discussed on page 421.

NOTE If you don't happen to have a Windows computer, a Mac, and every browser ever made, you can take advantage of Adobe's BrowserLab service, which takes screenshots of your page in a variety of browsers running on a variety of operating systems. You'll learn about BrowserLab on page 760.

If you're designing web pages for a company intranet and only have to worry about the one web browser your IT department puts on everyone's computer, you're lucky. Most people have to deal with the fact that their sites must withstand scrutiny from a wide range of browsers, so it's a good idea to preview your pages using whatever browsers you expect your visitors to use. Fortunately, Dreamweaver lets you preview a web page using any browser you have installed on your computer.

NOTE With the increasing popularity of tablets and mobile phones, you can no longer just worry about how your web pages look in desktop browsers; you also have to think about how they look on the small screens of an iPhone, Android phone, or Windows phone. Chapter 11 has information on how Dreamweaver CS6 can help you make your websites mobile-ready.

One quick way to check a page in a web browser is to use Dreamweaver's built-in Live view, which lets you preview a page using a browser that's built into Dreamweaver.

1. **In the Document toolbar, click the Live button (circled in Figure 1-30).**

   The Live button highlights. The page doesn't look that different—for a simple page like this it won't, but Live view is great for previewing more complex CSS and for testing JavaScript interactivity, like the kind Dreamweaver's Spry tools, such as the Spry Menu Bar provide (page 210).

FIGURE 1-30

Dreamweaver's Live view lets you preview a page in a real web browser, one built into Dreamweaver.

There is one problem with Live view: It uses WebKit, the engine behind Apple's Safari browser and Google's Chrome browser. This isn't the only browser out there, so it's not how all visitors will view your site. You want to test your page designs in other browsers, too. Fortunately, Dreamweaver makes it easy to jump straight to any web browser installed on your computer.

2. **Click the Live button again to exit Live view.**

   This is an important and easily overlooked step. When you're in Live view, you can't edit a page in Design view. Since a page in Live view can look very much like it does in Design view, it's easy to try to work on the page while you're in Live view and say "Hey, what's going on? Dreamweaver isn't working any more!" So always remember to exit Live view when it's time to work on your pages.

   To preview your page in a web browser, you need to make sure Dreamweaver knows which browsers you have installed and where they are.

TIP While you can't edit a page in Design view while Live view is on, you can edit the HTML code in Code view. One common technique among HTML jockeys is to display Split view, and then turn on Live view. This opens the HTML code on the left and a live browser display on the right. They then merrily edit the HTML and view the changes in Live view. However, to see the effect of any changes you make in Code view, you need to click into the Live view area or press F5.

3. **Choose File→"Preview in Browser"→Edit Browser List.**

   The "Preview in Browser" preferences window opens (see Figure 1-31). When you install Dreamweaver, it detects the browsers on your computer; a list of them appears in this window. If you installed a browser *after* you installed Dreamweaver, it doesn't appear here, and you need to follow steps 4 and 5 next; otherwise, skip to step 6.

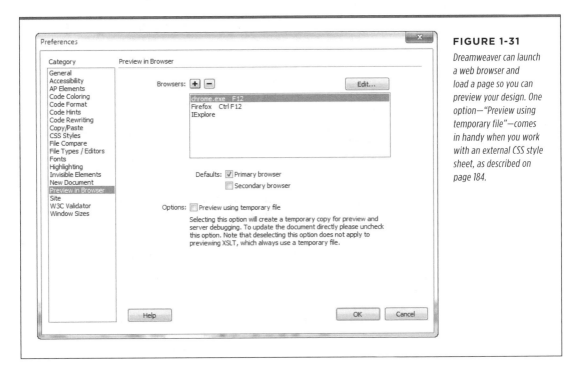

FIGURE 1-31

Dreamweaver can launch a web browser and load a page so you can preview your design. One option—"Preview using temporary file"—comes in handy when you work with an external CSS style sheet, as described on page 184.

4. **Click the + button.**

   The Add Browser or Select Browser window opens.

5. **Click the Browse button.** Search your hard drive to find the browser you want to add to the list.

   Dreamweaver inserts the browser's default name in the Name field. If you wish to change it for display purposes within Dreamweaver, select it, and then type in a new name. (But don't do this *before* you select the browser, since Dreamweaver erases anything you typed as soon as you select a browser.)

6. **In the window's Browser list, select the browser you most commonly use.** Turn on the Primary Browser checkbox. Click OK.

   You just designated this browser as the *primary* one when you work in Dreamweaver. You can now preview your pages in this browser with a simple keyboard shortcut: F12 (Option-F12 on a Mac). (Macintosh fans: Unfortunately, Apple has assigned the F12 key to the Dashboard program, so it takes two keys to preview the page—Option and F12 together; you can change this by creating your own keyboard shortcut, as described on page 911. If you're using a Macintosh laptop, you may have to press Option-F12 and the function [fn] key in the lower-left corner of the keyboard.)

   If you like, you can choose a secondary browser, which you launch by pressing Ctrl+F12 (⌘-F12) key combination.

   Now you're ready to preview your document in your favorite browser. Fortunately, Dreamweaver makes it easy.

   NOTE Windows PCs don't list Google Chrome in the Program Files directory, as they do most other programs. Depending on your version of Windows, you'll find Chrome in one of these locations:

   - Windows 7: C:\Users\Username\AppData\Local\Google

   - Vista: C:\Users\UserName\AppDataLocal\Google\Chrome

   - XP: C:\Documents and Settings\UserName\Local Settings\Application Data\Google\Chrome

7. **Press the F12 key (Option-F12), or choose File→"Preview in Browser" and then, from the menu, select a browser.**

   The F12 key (Option-F12) is the most important keyboard shortcut you'll learn; it opens the web page in your primary browser so you can preview your work.

   You can also use the "Preview in Browser" menu (the globe icon) in the document window to preview a page (see Figure 1-32).

   NOTE If you use the "Preview in Browser" menu to select a browser, you'll notice one other option: "Preview in Adobe BrowserLab." BrowserLab is an online service that takes screenshots of your web page using different browsers on both Windows and Mac machines—it's a great way to make sure your design works in as many browsers as possible. You'll learn about BrowserLab in depth on page 760.

8. **When you finish previewing the page, go back to Dreamweaver.**

   Do so using your favorite way to switch programs on your computer—by using the Windows taskbar or the Dock in Mac OS X.

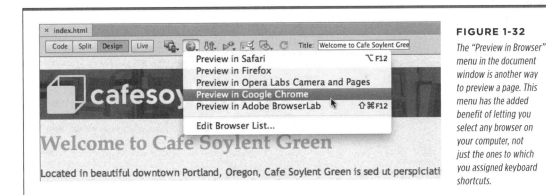

FIGURE 1-32

The "Preview in Browser" menu in the document window is another way to preview a page. This menu has the added benefit of letting you select any browser on your computer, not just the ones to which you assigned keyboard shortcuts.

Phase 6: Finishing the Page

You've covered most of the steps you need to finish this web page. Now you just need to add a graphic, format the copyright notice, and provide a little more structure to the page.

1. **Scroll to the bottom of the page and select all the text in the copyright paragraph.**

   You can either triple-click inside the paragraph or drag from beginning to end.

2. **Click the CSS button in the Property Inspector and then, from the Size menu, choose 12.**

   The New CSS Rule window opens again. This time you want to create a style that applies only to this paragraph of text—not every paragraph—so you need to use what's called a class style.

3. **Leave the default setting— "Class (can apply to any HTML element)"—for the Selector Type field, type *.copyright* in the Selector Name field (Figure 1-33), and then click OK.**

   Class names begin with a period—that's how browsers identify the CSS style as a class. You can see that the copyright text gets smaller when you apply the *.copyright* class, which specifies a type size of 12 pixels.

   Another way to separate the copyright notice from the page's main content is to add a simple line above it. CSS lets you do that with a property called Border; however, you can't set that property using the Property Inspector; you need to use the CSS Styles panel.

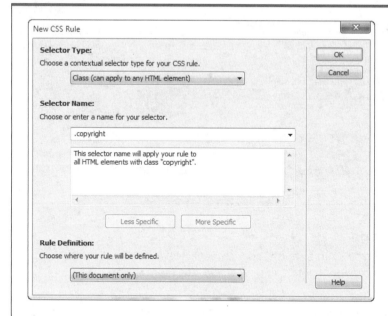

FIGURE 1-33

The New CSS Rule window lets you create CSS styles. You can choose among many types of styles. In this case, you're creating a class style named .copyright. Class styles work a lot like styles in word processors—to use them, you select the text you want to format, and then apply the style.

4. **If it isn't already open, open the CSS Styles panel by choosing Window→CSS Styles.**

   The CSS styles panel is the command center for working with style sheets (see Figure 1-34). It lists all the styles available to the current web page and lets you edit them and add new styles. You'll learn all about it in Chapter 3, but for now you'll get a taste of using it to edit a style.

5. **Click the + (flippy triangle on Macs) button to the left <style> to display the list of styles on this page.** Double-click the style *.copyright* at the bottom of the list of styles.

   The CSS Rule Definition window opens (see Figure 1-35). This window lets you set dozens of CSS properties, including controls for formatting text, adding borders, and positioning elements on a page. You'll learn about these properties throughout this book, but for now you'll look at a couple of properties categories.

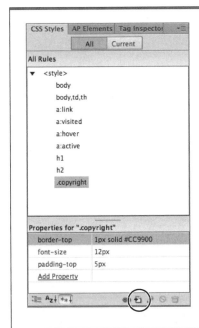

FIGURE 1-34

The CSS Styles panel has two views: All and Current. The All view, pictured here, lists all the styles available to the current page. You can edit a style by double-clicking its name, or add a new style by clicking the New Rule button (circled). You'll learn about the Current view on page 393.

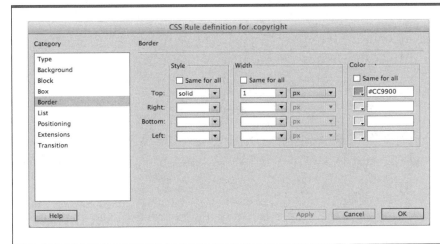

FIGURE 1-35

The CSS Border settings let you add a border line around any (or all) of the four edges of any page element. In this case, you're adding a line just above the copyright notice, but when formatting a "What's new" box, you might add a border around all four edges to make it stand out.

6. **Click Border in the left-hand list of categories.** Turn off the three "Same for all" checkboxes along the top and choose "solid" for the Top style, type *1* for the top width, and *#CC9900* for the top color.

The window should now look like Figure 1-35. Borderlines touch the content of the element they surround—in other words, this top line sits very close to the copyright text. It'll look better if there's a bit of space between it and the copyright notice.

7. **In the CSS Rule Definition window, click the Box category.** Under the Padding settings, turn off the "Same for all" checkbox, type 5 in the Top field, and then click OK.

Padding is the space that appears between an element's content (like the text in a paragraph or the graphic in the image tag). Adding padding increases the space between the border and the content. The window should now look like Figure 1-36.

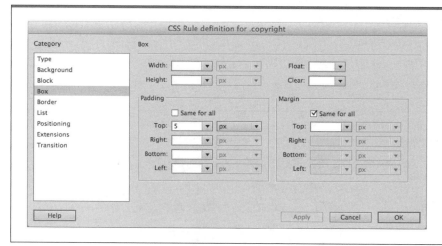

FIGURE 1-36

The CSS Box category lets you create page elements like sidebars. You'll learn a lot more about these Box properties on page 447.

8. **Click OK to finish editing the style.**

You'll now see a brownish line above the copyright notice, nicely setting it off from the rest of the page. Next, you'll link to a map that shows the location of the restaurant.

9. **In the middle of the page, select the parenthetical text "click to see map."**

To create a link, you just need to tell Dreamweaver which page you want to link to. You can do this several ways. Using the Property Inspector is the easiest.

10. **In the Property Inspector, click the HTML button, and then click the folder icon that appears to the right of the Link field.**

The Select File dialog box appears.

11. **Click the Site Root button (at the top of the dialog box in Windows, the bottom of the dialog box on Macs), and double-click the file *map.html*.**

The Site Root button jumps you right to the folder containing your site. It's a convenient way to move quickly to your root folder. Double-clicking the file name tells Dreamweaver to insert the HTML needed to create a link along with the link's address.

If you save the page and then preview it in a web browser, click the link you just added. The browser jumps to another page (one already created for you). You'll notice that there's text near the bottom of the map that reads "back to home page." Since you just learned the powerful link-adding skill, open *map .html* and add a link to that page. Select the text "back to home page" and link to the *index.html* file by following steps 10 and 11, and then save the *map.html* file. We'll wait for you....

You may have noticed that the map page's content is contained in a box that's nicely centered in the middle of the screen. That would look great on the home page you've created as well. You'll create a new layout element to achieve this effect.

12. **Return to the *index.html* file; click anywhere inside the page, and then choose Edit→Select All or press Ctrl+A (⌘-A).**

You selected the entire contents of the page. You'll wrap all the text and images in a <div> tag to create a kind of container for the page contents.

13. **Choose Insert→Layout Objects→Div Tag.**

The Insert Div Tag window opens (see Figure 1-37). A <div> tag simply provides a way to organize content on a page by grouping HTML—think of it as a box containing other HTML tags. For example, to create a sidebar that includes navigation links, news headlines, and Google ads, you'd wrap them all in a <div> tag. It's a very important tag for CSS-based layouts. You'll read more about it on page 438.

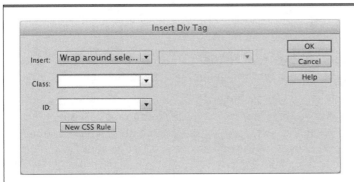

FIGURE 1-37

The Insert Div Tag window provides an easy way to divide sections of a web page into groups of related HTML—like the elements (graphic, navigation bar, and so on) that make up a page banner, for example. You'll learn about all the different functions of this window on page 440.

Next, you need to create a style that provides the instructions that format this new <div> tag. You've already used the Property Inspector to create a style, but that works only for text. To format other tags, you need to create a style in another way.

14. **Click the New CSS Rule button at the bottom of the Insert Div Tag window.**

    The New CSS Rule window appears (a CSS style is technically called a "rule"). This window lets you specify the type of style you create, the style's name, and where Dreamweaver should store the style information. You'll learn all the ins and outs of this window in Chapter 3.

15. **From the top menu, choose "Class (can apply to any HTML element)," and then type *.container* in the "Choose or enter a name" field.** Make sure you have "This document only" selected in the bottom menu. Click OK.

    The "CSS Rule definition" window appears. (There's a lot going on in this box, but don't worry about the details at this point. You'll learn everything there is to know about creating styles later in this book. This part of the tutorial is intended to give you a taste for some of a web designer's daily page-building duties. So relax and follow along.) First, you'll add a border around the edges.

16. **From the left-hand list of categories, select Border.** Leave the three "Same for all" checkboxes turned on, and choose "solid" for the style, type 1 for the width, and then type #336633 for the color.

    This action adds a green border around the edges. Next, you'll give the div tag a set width and center it on the page.

17. **Click the Box category, and then, in the width field, type *760*.**

    This makes the box 760 pixels wide—the same width as the banner. To make sure the text doesn't butt right up against the edge of the box, you'll add a little padding around the inside of this style.

18. **Make sure the "Same for all" checkbox is turned on, and then type *10* in the Top field under Padding.**

    This adds 10 pixels of space inside the box, essentially pushing the text and the graphics away from the edges of it.

19. **Under the Margin settings, turn off the "Same for all" checkbox, and then, for both the right and left margin menus, select "auto."**

    The window should now look like Figure 1-38. Selecting "auto" for the left and right margins is your way of telling a web browser to automatically supply values for those margins—in this case, as you'll see in a moment, it has the effect of centering the <div> element in the middle of a browser window.

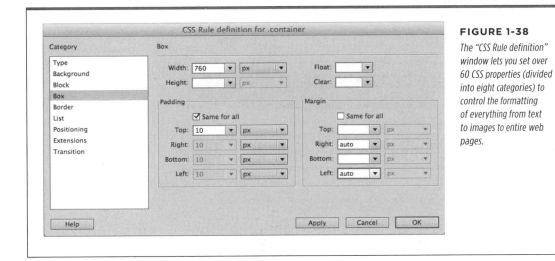

FIGURE 1-38

The "CSS Rule definition" window lets you set over 60 CSS properties (divided into eight categories) to control the formatting of everything from text to images to entire web pages.

20. **Click OK to complete the style.**

    The Insert Div Tag window reappears, and the name of the style you just created—"container"—appears in a field labeled Class.

21. **In the Insert Div Tag window, click OK.**

    This inserts the new <div> tag and at the same time applies the style you just created. Now it's time to take a look at your handiwork.

22. **Choose File→Save.** Press the F12 key (Option-F12) to preview your work in your browser (Figure 1-39).

    Test the link to make sure it works. Resize your browser and watch how the page content centers itself in the middle of the window.

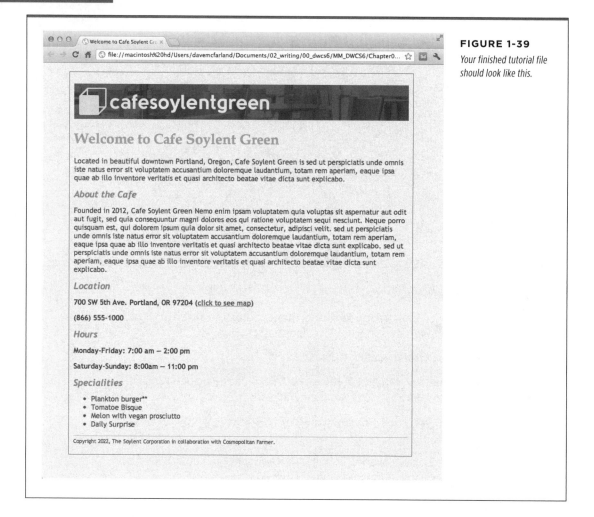

FIGURE 1-39

Your finished tutorial file should look like this.

Phase 7: Organizing Your Files

There's one last housekeeping chore to attend to. If you look at the Files panel, you'll notice that there are two web pages, three graphics (.png files), and a text file. Most web designers like to organize graphics files into folders to keep them in one place. You could create a folder in Windows Explorer or the Mac Finder, but why bother when you can do it directly in Dreamweaver?

1. **In the Files panel, right-click (Control-click) the Site folder listed under "Local view" (circled in Figure 1-40).** From the drop-down menu, choose New Folder.

Dreamweaver adds a new "untitled" folder to the files list and highlights the name, ready for editing.

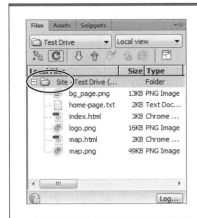

FIGURE 1-40

Dreamweaver's Files panel is more than just a way to see all the files in your site. You can use it to open a file (double-click the file name), rename a file (click the file name, pause, and then click the file name again), add folders (right-click on a file or folder and choose New Folder), and move files around (drag a file into a folder, for example).

2. **Type *images* to name the folder, and then press Enter (Return).**

   The folder might still read "untitled" if you click elsewhere in the program before you edit the name; doing so deselects the folder. If that happens, simply click "untitled" to select the folder, pause a moment, and then click "untitled" again to highlight the name so you can change it.

   Now you just need to get your images into this new folder.

3. **Ctrl-click (⌘-click) the three image files (*bg_page.png*, *logo.png*, and *map.png*) to select them, and then drag them into the images folder.**

   The Update Files window appears, letting you know that by moving these files, you'll affect the *index.html* and *map.html* files. That's because those pages use these images. Normally, moving a web file that another page uses breaks the link between the files. Fortunately, Dreamweaver's smart enough to update the links so they still work.

4. **Click Update.**

   Dreamweaver quickly updates the web pages so that they now reference the new location for the three images.

5. **Choose File→Save All to save all the changes you just made.**

   The Save All command is an invaluable tool. It saves any changes you've made to all opened files.

Congratulations! You just built your first web page in Dreamweaver, complete with graphics, formatted text, and links. You've even used one of Dreamweaver's site-management features to create a new folder and organize your site's files without breaking them! If you want to compare your work with the finished product, go to Chapter01_complete in the Tutorials folder and load the file *index.html*.

Much of the work of building websites involves the procedures covered in this tutorial—defining a site, adding links, formatting text, placing graphics, creating styles, and inserting <div> tags. The next few chapters cover these basics in greater depth and introduce other important tools, tips, and techniques for using Dreamweaver to build great web pages.

TIP To get a full description of every Dreamweaver menu, see Appendix B, "Dreamweaver CS6, Menu by Menu."

Adding and Formatting Text

Nowadays, streaming video, audio, and high-quality graphics are what draw most people to websites. After all, it's exciting to hear the latest song from your favorite band, see a preview of a yet-to-be released blockbuster, or tune in to YouTube to see the kid down the street embarrass himself in front of a billion Web viewers.

But the fact is, the Web is woven primarily with *words*. iPad reviews, Justin Bieber and Lady Gaga gossip, and countless personal blogs about cats still drive people to the Internet. As you build web pages and websites, you'll spend a lot of time adding and formatting *text*. To get your message across effectively, you need to understand how Dreamweaver works with text.

That's what this chapter is all about—it covers the not-always-simple act of getting text *into* your Dreamweaver documents. In Chapter 3, you'll learn how to format that text so it looks professionally designed.

■ Adding Text in Dreamweaver

In Design view, Dreamweaver works much like a word-processing program. When you create a new document, the blinking cursor appears at the top of the page, ready for you to begin typing. When you finish typing a paragraph, you press Enter (Return) to start a new one. Text, as well as anything else you add to a web page, starts at the top of the page and works its way to the bottom.

If you build websites for clients or as part of a team, your writers likely send you their text as a word-processing document. You can copy text from that document (or from another source, like an email message) and paste it into Dreamweaver's Design view; you have a couple of options for doing that.

> **TIP** If the text you want to paste comes from a Microsoft Word or Excel file, you're lucky. Dreamweaver includes special commands for pasting text from these two programs (see "Paste Special" below). If you use Windows, you can *import* Word and Excel files directly into a web page using Dreamweaver's File→Import→[Word/Excel] Document command (see page 91).

Simple Copy and Paste

For non-Microsoft-spawned documents, you can, of course, simply copy and paste text, like generations of web designers before you.

Open the document in whatever program created it—WordPad, TextEdit, your email program, whatever. Select the text you want (by dragging through it, for example), or choose Edit→Select All (Ctrl+A [⌘-A]) to highlight all the text. Then choose Edit→Copy, or press Ctrl+C (⌘-C), to copy it. Switch to Dreamweaver, and, in the Design view of the document window, click where you want the text to go, and then choose Edit→Paste (Ctrl+V [⌘-V]).

This drops the text into place. Unfortunately, you lose any formatting the text had (font type, size, color, bold, italics, and so on), as shown in Figure 2-1.

Furthermore, you may find the pasted paragraphs in the resulting HTML separated by line-break characters instead of true paragraph tags, <p>. In HTML, the line-break character—the <br> tag—adds a "soft" carriage return, simply dropping the text that follows onto the next line. This means that when you paste in a series of paragraphs, Dreamweaver treats them as though they were one gargantuan paragraph, which can pose problems when you try to format what you *think* is a single paragraph. To get true paragraphs, you first have to make the line breaks visible. Choose Edit→Preferences (Dreamweaver→Preferences) or press Ctrl+U (⌘-U). Click the Invisible Elements category. Make sure you have the Line Breaks checkbox turned on. Now you see each line break as a small gold shield. (If you still don't see the line break character, choose View→Visual Aids, and make sure you have the Invisible Elements checkbox turned on.) Select the shield and then hit Enter (Return) to eliminate the break *and* create a true paragraph.

> **TIP** If you *have* to copy and paste text from non-Microsoft programs, you do have one way to get paragraphs (and not just lines separated by the line-break character) when you paste text into Dreamweaver. Just make sure whoever's typing up the original document inserts an empty paragraph between each paragraph of text. Pressing Enter (Return) twice at the end of a paragraph does that. When you copy and paste, Dreamweaver removes the empty paragraphs *and* pastes the text as regular paragraphs.

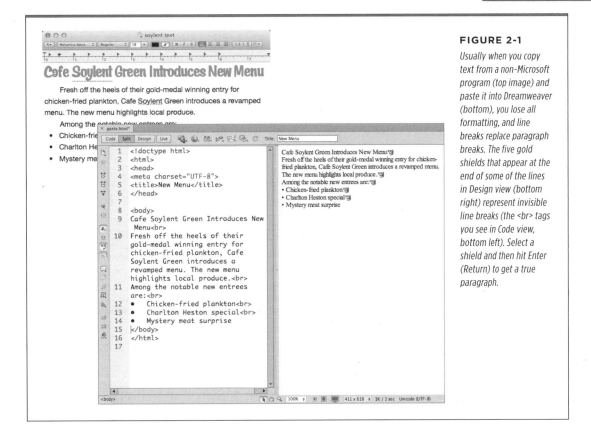

FIGURE 2-1

Usually when you copy text from a non-Microsoft program (top image) and paste it into Dreamweaver (bottom), you lose all formatting, and line breaks replace paragraph breaks. The five gold shields that appear at the end of some of the lines in Design view (bottom right) represent invisible line breaks (the <br> tags you see in Code view, bottom left). Select a shield and then hit Enter (Return) to get a true paragraph.

Paste Special

Dreamweaver's Paste Special command supports four document formats, ranging from plain text to highly designed HTML (see below). In actual use, however, Dreamweaver supports only the first two formats listed below for *all* pasting operations; the other two work only with Microsoft Word or Excel documents.

Note that these options work only when you paste text in Design view—if you paste a document in Code view, Dreamweaver just dumps in the plain text, without paragraphs, line breaks, or any other formatting.

- **Text only**. This is the most basic option of all. It pastes text without any formatting whatsoever, ignoring even paragraphs and line breaks (this is also how text appears when you paste it in Code view). You end up with one long, uninterrupted series of sentences. Though you won't want this effect often, it can come in handy when you copy a long paragraph of text from an email program that adds unnecessary line breaks at the end of each line of text.

- **Text with structure**. Here, Dreamweaver tries to preserve the structure of the text, including paragraphs, headers, bulleted lists, and so on. This option doesn't retain any formatting applied to the text, such as boldface or italics. You'll use this option with most non-Microsoft Office-copied text. In most cases, however, Dreamweaver ends up preserving only paragraphs and misses bulleted lists and headers.

- **Basic formatting**. When you paste text using this option, Dreamweaver formats the same elements as the "Text with structure" option but also preserves text formatting, such as boldface, italics, and underlines. This is the method Dreamweaver uses when pasting Microsoft Word or Excel text and numbers, as described in the next section.

- **Full formatting**. This option includes everything you get with basic formatting but also converts Word formatting into CSS styles, placing them in an internal style sheet in the <head> section of the web page. These styles control text font size and color, paragraph margins, and so on. Full formatting is available only when you copy and paste from Word or Excel (see the next section).

> **NOTE** You can copy an entire page of HTML from Firefox or Internet Explorer, and then paste it into Dreamweaver. Click inside a web page, press Ctrl+A to select the entire page, and then press Ctrl+C to copy the HTML. Then switch to Dreamweaver, click inside an empty page, and press Ctrl+V to paste. Dreamweaver copies all the HTML and, sometimes, even graphics. The text comes in with "full formatting," but note that no style sheets come along for the ride, so you'll lose any CSS-driven styles.

■ CHANGING PASTE SPECIAL'S DEFAULT BEHAVIOR

If you always work with the same type of documents, you can set Dreamweaver's default behavior for the Paste Special command. Choose Edit→Paste Special to open the Paste Special window (see Figure 2-2). Here, you can choose which of the four techniques you wish to use as the default. Well, sort of. You're limited to what Dreamweaver can actually paste. For non-Microsoft Office products, that means only the first two options—the others are grayed out—whereas you can choose from any of the four options with text copied from Word or Excel.

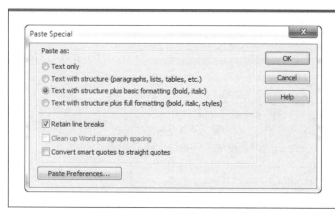

FIGURE 2-2

The Paste Special command lets you paste text copied from other programs. If you want Dreamweaver to use the same option each time you use the Paste Special command, click the Paste Preferences button. This opens the Preferences window. Select whatever settings—Basic formatting, for example—you want Dreamweaver to apply any time you click Paste Special.

For text copied from most programs, it's best to use "Text with structure" and keep the "Retain line breaks" checkbox turned on. You still have to manually replace line breaks with paragraphs, as described in the Note on nonbreaking spaces (page 94), but without "Retain line breaks" turned on, Dreamweaver removes single hard returns, resulting in one long paragraph of text.

In addition, when you paste text that includes traditional quotation marks (also called "curly" quotes), you can tell Dreamweaver to insert "straight" quotes by turning on the "Convert smart quotes to straight quotes" checkbox. This option forces Dreamweaver to replace opening and closing double quotes (" and ") with the " character, and single quotes (' and ') with straight single quotes ('). Only turn on this option if you really like the "Hey, I wrote this on a dumb computer that has no understanding of real typography" look, or if you're pasting HTML code from a Word document that accidentally placed all HTML properties inside curly quotes (like that happens a lot). For Word or Excel files, there are a few options worth considering, as described next.

Pasting Text from Microsoft Word: The Basic Method

While text pasted from non-Word applications doesn't retain much formatting beyond paragraphs, Dreamweaver includes both basic and advanced ways to copy and paste Word text.

Frequently, you'll just want to preserve basic formatting, like bold or italic text, headlines, and bulleted lists. You won't need (and in most cases, won't want) more extravagant formatting, like different fonts, colors, or margin settings. After all, you're the web designer, and you'll use your own design sense and CSS formatting rules to add beauty to basic text.

Pasting Word text works like any copy/paste action described in the previous section. Select the desired text in Word, copy it, switch to Dreamweaver, and then choose Edit→Paste to drop the text into a web page. You don't have to spend a lot of time reformatting the pasted text since Dreamweaver preserves many basic formatting options:

- Paragraphs formatted with Word's built-in heading styles (Heading 1, Heading 2, and so on) get HTML heading tags: <h1> (for Heading 1), <h2>, <title>, and so on.

- Paragraphs remain paragraphs...most of the time. Actually, the way Dreamweaver pastes paragraphs depends on both how Word formatted the paragraphs to begin with and whether you turned on the Paste Special window's "Clean up Word paragraph spacing" setting (see Figure 2-2). If you did, paragraphs you paste from Word can sometimes appear as one large paragraph, with line break characters at the end of each one—not the best way to get an HTML paragraph. To get Dreamweaver to paste each paragraph *as* a paragraph, choose Edit→Paste Special, turn off the "Clean up Word paragraph spacing" checkbox, and then click OK.

NOTE If the source Word document has an empty line between each paragraph (in other words, an empty paragraph generated by pressing the Enter key twice after each real paragraph), make sure you *do* have the "Clean up Word paragraph spacing" checkbox turned on. That eliminates the empty paragraphs.

- Bold and italic text maintain their look in Dreamweaver (Dreamweaver uses the HTML <strong> tag for bolded text and the <em> tag for italicized text, as described on page 116).

- Basic text-alignment options (left, right, and center) remain intact. Justified text, on the other hand, gets pasted as left-aligned text. (You can compensate for this using the Justify option in the Property Inspector, as described on page 161.)

- Numbered lists come through as numbered lists in Dreamweaver (see page 106) *if* you used Word's Automatic Numbered-List feature to create them.

NOTE Suppose you copy some HTML, maybe out of the Source view of an actual web page or from a "How to Write HTML" website. You'll notice that when you paste it into Dreamweaver's Design view, all the HTML tags appear in that view, complete with brackets (< >) and other assorted messiness. To get HTML into a page (and make it work like HTML), you have to go into Code view and paste the code directly into the page's HTML. To see the HTML for a page, click the Code view or Split view buttons at the top of the document window.

- If you paste text created using Word's built-in list-bulleting feature, you end up with a proper HTML bulleted list (see page 106). If you create your own bulleted list style in Word, make sure you select the "list" type when you create the style; otherwise, copying and pasting the custom list might just paste plain paragraphs of text.

- Graphics from Word documents get pasted as graphics. In fact, even if the original graphics aren't in a web-ready format (if they're BMP, TIFF, or PICT files, for example), Dreamweaver converts them to either the GIF or JPEG format, which web browsers understand. Dreamweaver even copies the files to your local site folder *and* links them correctly to the page. (Chapter 5 covers images in depth.)

NOTE Keep in mind a couple of caveats when you paste from Word. First, you can't copy and paste more than a couple hundred KB worth of text, so you have to transfer really long documents in pieces (or better yet, spread them out among multiple web pages). Second, the ability to keep basic HTML formatting in place when you paste works only with versions of Word later than Office 97 (for Windows) or Office 98 (for Macs).

Pasting Text with Word Formatting

If you simply *must* keep that three-inch-tall, crazy, cartoon-like orange font you used in a Word document, you can turn to the "Text with structure plus full formatting" option of the Paste Special command. After copying text from Word and returning to Dreamweaver, choose Edit→Paste Special or press Ctrl+Shift+V (⌘-Shift-V). When the Paste Special window appears, choose the "full formatting" option, and then click OK.

Dreamweaver pastes the text with as much formatting as possible, including margins, fonts, and text colors and sizes. Behind the scenes, Dreamweaver pastes the text *and* adds CSS formatting that attempts to approximate the look of the text as it appeared in Word.

NOTE Sometimes when you paste from Word (even using the standard Paste command), you end up with empty <a> tags in your HTML. They appear as gold shields in Dreamweaver's Design view (circled in Figure 2-3). The links might look something like this: <a name="OLE_LINK1" id="OLE_LINK1"></a>. Feel free to delete them—they're unnecessary crud that Word adds.

Unfortunately, all this extra code increases the document's file size and download time, and can interfere with future formatting changes. What's worse, most of your visitors won't even be able to *see* some of this formatting—if you use an uncommon font, for example. For these reasons, it's best to skip this feature, paste Word text using the regular Paste command, and then create your own styles to make the text look great (you'll learn how to do that in the next chapter).

Pasting Excel Spreadsheet Information

Dreamweaver also lets you paste text and numbers from Microsoft Excel. Options include a basic method—using the standard Edit→Paste command (Ctrl+V [⌘-V])—and a format-rich method, using the "full formatting" option of the Paste Special window: choose Edit→Paste Special (or press Ctrl+Shift+V [⌘-Shift-V]), choose "Text with structure plus full formatting" from the Paste Special window, and then click OK.

Both methods paste spreadsheet information as an HTML table composed of cells, rows, and columns. (See Chapter 6 for more on tables.) But unlike pasting from Word, using the basic Paste command with Excel files preserves *no* formatting—it doesn't even hang on to bold and italic text. The "full formatting" option, however, preserves advanced formatting like fonts, font sizes, text colors, and cell background colors.

Importing Word and Excel Documents (Windows)

Windows fans can import documents directly from a Word or Excel file. In Design view, position your cursor where you want to insert the text or spreadsheet on your web page, and then choose File→Import→Word Document (or Excel Document). An Open File dialog box appears; find and double-click the Word or Excel file you want.

Dreamweaver captures the information just as if you'd used Edit→Paste. That is, for Word documents, Dreamweaver carries over basic formatting like bold, italics, headlines, and paragraphs, and imports and converts images. The importing process doesn't create style sheets or apply advanced formatting. For Excel documents, you get just an organized table of data—no formatting.

Adding Special Characters

Many useful special characters—such as copyright or trademark symbols—don't appear on your keyboard, making them difficult or impossible to type. Dreamweaver's Insert toolbar's Text tab lets you use a variety of symbols and international characters simply by clicking an icon.

To open the Text tab:

1. **On the Insert panel, choose the Text category.**

   If you can't see the Insert panel, choose Window→Insert to open it, or use the keyboard shortcut Ctrl+F2 (⌘-F2). The panel shown in Figure 2-3 appears. (If you're using the "Classic" workspace layout discussed in the box on page 38, the Text category is a tab on the Insert toolbar [Figure 2-3, bottom].)

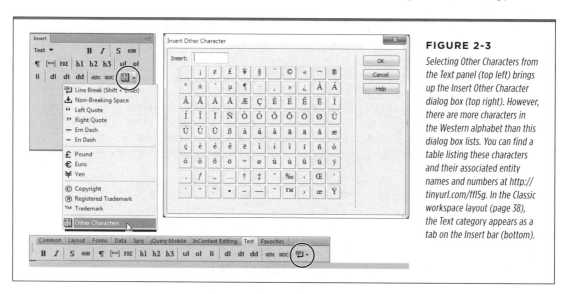

FIGURE 2-3

Selecting Other Characters from the Text panel (top left) brings up the Insert Other Character dialog box (top right). However, there are more characters in the Western alphabet than this dialog box lists. You can find a table listing these characters and their associated entity names and numbers at http://tinyurl.com/ffl5g. In the Classic workspace layout (page 38), the Text category appears as a tab on the Insert bar (bottom).

Many of the options let you add common HTML tags, like the bold (<b>) and strong (<strong>) tags, most of which you can apply more easily using the Property Inspector or keyboard shortcuts, as discussed in the next chapter. This panel also features less frequently used tags, like those for abbreviations (<abbr>) and a definition list (<dl>). You can satisfy your curiosity about these tags by using Dreamweaver's HTML reference (see page 370), but their names alone give you an idea of when you might want to use them.

The last option on the panel, Other Characters (highlighted in Figure 2-3) is actually a menu that offers a range of symbols and international characters. Unlike regular Western characters, such as *a* or *z*, Dreamweaver represents these characters in HTML by a code name or number. For instance, it adds the trademark symbol (™) to a page's HTML as *™* (another way to write this symbol in HTML is *™*).

NOTE If you like card games or just want to add a heart to a web page without using a graphic, choose the Other Characters option from the Insert panel and type *♥*. Type *♦* for a diamond, *♠* for a spade, or *♣* for a club. (Don't forget the semicolon at the end of each—that's part of the code.)

2. **From the menu at the end of the Insert panel, select the symbol you want to insert.**

   Dreamweaver inserts the appropriate HTML into your web page. (Alternatively, you can select the Other Characters option to bring up the wider-ranging Insert Other Character dialog box.)

NOTE If you set the encoding of your page to anything other than Western European or Unicode (UTF-8) in the Page Properties window (by choosing Modify→Page Properties, and then clicking the Title/Encoding category), you can reliably insert only line breaks and nonbreaking spaces. The other special characters available from the Character category of the Objects panel may not work (see the box on page 100 for more about how encoding works).

Line Breaks

Pressing Enter (Return) in Dreamweaver's Design view creates a new paragraph, just as it does in a word processor. Unfortunately, web browsers add extra space above and below paragraphs—which is a real nuisance if you want to create several single-spaced lines of text, like this:

> 702 A Street
> Boring, OR
> 97009 USA

Here, each part of the address is on its own line, but the entire address still represents just a single paragraph (and each of the lines share that paragraph's formatting, as you'll learn in the next chapter).

NOTE If you want to *entirely* dispense with the space that browsers insert between paragraphs, don't use line breaks each time. Instead, use CSS to eliminate the top and bottom margins of the <p> tag, as described in the Tip on page 163.

To create this single-spaced effect in HTML, you need to insert a *line break* at the insertion point, using one of these techniques:

- Press Shift+Enter.
- Select Line Break from the Characters menu in the Insert panel's Text category.
- Choose Insert→HTML→Special Characters→Line Break.

Keyboard Shortcuts for Special Characters

Dreamweaver uses UTF-8 (also called Unicode) encoding when you create a new page (unless you specify otherwise). Without getting into the messy details, UTF-8 lets you include almost any type of character available to the languages of the world—it lets a Chinese speaker embed actual Chinese characters in a page, for example. When you use the Other Characters window, Dreamweaver inserts what's called an HTML *entity*—a code that replaces the real character. For example, the HTML entity for the © symbol is *©*. But UTF-8 lets you add the actual symbol to a page—the trick is knowing how to do that through your keyboard.

On the Mac, you have a handful of keyboard shortcuts for directly typing a special character like a curly quote mark in a page. Here are a few of the most common:

- Ellipsis (three periods in a row): Option+;
- Em dash (—): Option+Shift+-
- Opening single quote ('): Option+] for opening
- Closing single quote ('): Option+Shift+]
- Opening double-quote ("): Option+[
- Closing double-quote ("): Option+Shift+[
- Copyright symbol (©): Option+G

You can also use the Mac Character Palette to insert unusual symbols using Unicode (for information on the Mac character palette visit *http://tinyurl.com/7c8aqrw*).

In Windows, you must press the Alt key, type the Unicode value using your keyboard's numeric keypad, and then release the Alt key. Note that you can't use the regular number keys for this—you must use the numeric keypad. For example, to add an ellipsis, hold down the Alt key, type *0133*, and then release the Alt key. Here are a few others:

- Open single quote: Alt+0145
- Closing single quote: Alt+0146
- Opening double-quote: Alt+0147
- Closing double-quote: Alt+0148

In Windows, it's easier to use the character map to insert special symbols and characters. Visit *http://tinyurl.com/5blqek* to learn how.

NOTE When you insert a line break in Dreamweaver, the Design view may give you no visual hint that the break is even there; after all, a regular paragraph break and a line break both create a new line of text. This is especially likely if you copy text from programs other than Microsoft Word or Excel. You might find text from those other programs—especially email programs—loaded with an infuriating number of line breaks. To add to the confusion, a line break may go unnoticed if it occurs at the end of a long line.

Your only hope is to make line breaks visible. To do that, choose Edit→Preferences (Dreamweaver→Preferences), or press Ctrl+U (⌘-U). Click the Invisible Elements category. Make sure the Line Breaks checkbox is turned on. Now you see each line break as a small gold shield. (If, after doing this, you still don't see the line break character, choose View→Visual Aids, and make sure you have the Invisible Elements checkbox turned on.)

You can select a line break by clicking the shield, and then delete it just as you would any other page element. Better yet, select the shield, and then hit Enter (Return) to eliminate the line break *and* create a new paragraph.

Nonbreaking Spaces

Sometimes the way a sentence breaks over two lines in your text can distort what you're trying to say, as shown in Figure 2-4. If that's the case, a *nonbreaking space* can save the day. It looks just like a regular space, but it acts as a glue that prevents the words on either side of it from being split apart at the end of a line. For example, adding a nonbreaking space between the words "farmer" and "says" in Figure 2-4 ensures that those words won't get split across a line break and helps clarify the presentation and meaning of this headline.

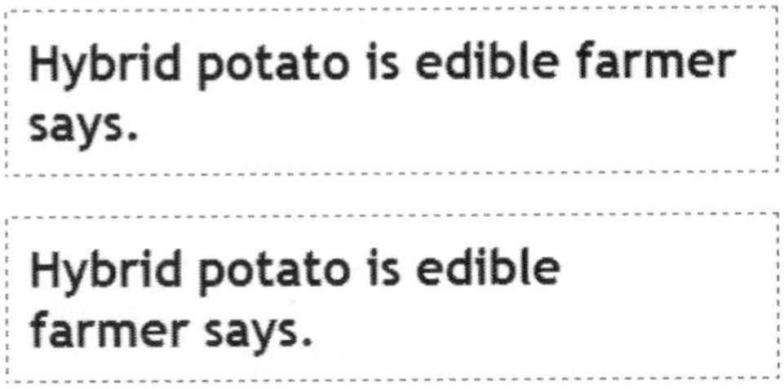

Hybrid potato is edible farmer says.

Hybrid potato is edible farmer says.

FIGURE 2-4

Headlines sometimes break between lines, leaving a single word alone on a line (top)—in typography this is known as a "widow." Adding a nonbreaking space (bottom) can prevent widows and clarify a headline's meaning.

To insert a nonbreaking space between two words, delete the regular space already there (for example, by clicking after the space and pressing the backspace key), and then do one of the following:

- Press Ctrl+Shift+space bar (⌘-Shift-space bar).
- On the Insert panel's Text category, from the Characters menu, select Non-Breaking Space.
- Choose Insert→HTML→Special Characters→Non-Breaking Space.

Multiple Spaces

You may have noticed that if you type more than one space in a row, Dreamweaver ignores all but the first one. This isn't a glitch in the program, it's standard HTML. Web browsers ignore any spaces following the first one.

Therefore, a line like "Beware   of   llama," with several spaces between each word, appears on a web page like this: "Beware of llama." Not only do web browsers ignore multiple spaces, they also ignore any spaces that aren't *between* words. So if you hit the space bar a couple of times to indent the first line of a paragraph, you're wasting your time. A browser won't display any of those spaces (and Dreamweaver doesn't display them, either).

This feature makes good sense, because it prevents web pages from being littered with extraneous spaces that many people insert when writing HTML. (Extra spaces in a page of HTML often makes the code easier to read.)

There may be times, however, when you *want* to add more space between words. For example, consider the text navigation bar at the bottom of a web page, a common element that lists the sections of a website. Visitors can click one of the section titles to jump directly to that area of the site. For clarity, many designers like to add multiple spaces between the links, like this:

News   Classifieds   Jobs

One simple way to add space is to insert multiple nonbreaking spaces as described in the previous section. A browser *does* display every nonbreaking space it encounters, so you can add multiple nonbreaking spaces between words, letters, or even at the beginning of paragraphs. This technique has a few downsides, though: You have to type the code for a bunch of nonbreaking spaces, which takes work, and it adds code to your web page, making it download a bit slower.

Alternatively, you can enlist Cascading Style Sheets (CSS) to add spaces. While you won't get in-depth detail on CSS until the next chapter, here are a few CSS *properties* (formatting rules) to tuck in the back of your mind when you need to add space to your text:

- To indent the first line of a paragraph, use the *text indent* property (page 165).

- To add space between words in a paragraph, use the *word spacing* property (page 164).

- To increase or decrease the space between letters, use *letter spacing* (page 164).

- And, if you want to increase the space between text links as in the example above, you can add either left and right *margins* or *padding* to each link (page 449).

NOTE If you often add multiple spaces, Dreamweaver offers a shortcut. Choose Edit→Preferences (Dreamweaver→Preferences) to open Dreamweaver's Preferences window. Click the General category. Then, under "Editing options," turn on "Allow multiple consecutive spaces." Now, whenever you press the space bar more than once, Dreamweaver inserts *nonbreaking* spaces.

In fact, Dreamweaver is even smarter than that. It inserts a regular space if you press the space bar just once, a nonbreaking space followed by a regular space if you hit the space bar twice, and multiple nonbreaking spaces followed by a regular space if you hit the space bar repeatedly. Why does Dreamweaver automatically add the regular spaces? Since nonbreaking spaces act like glue that keeps words stuck together, the regular spaces let the lines break normally, if necessary.

Adding a Date to Your Page

The Insert panel's Common category offers an icon called Date (it looks like the page of a calendar). Clicking this icon or choosing Insert→Date opens the Insert Date dialog box (Figure 2-5), which lets you insert today's date, as your computer understands it, into your web page-in-progress. You can also specify whether to include the day of the week and the current time.

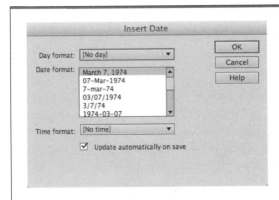

FIGURE 2-5

When you insert a Date object (a placeholder for the actual date) onto a web page, you have several additional options: If you want to add the day of the week, choose the format you want from the "Day format" drop-down menu. You may also add the current time in hours and minutes—in either military time (22:18) or regular time (10:18 PM)—from the "Time format" drop-down menu.

Select the format you wish from the Date Format list. You have 13 configurations to choose from, such as March 7, 1974 or 3/7/74.

You may wonder why Dreamweaver includes an insert-date function anyway. How hard is it to type *Thursday, July 12*?

Actually, the real value of the Insert Date feature lies in the "Update automatically on save" checkbox. Choosing this option forces Dreamweaver to *update* the date each time you save the document.

You can use this feature to stamp a web page with a date that indicates when the contents were last updated. For example, you might type *This page was revised on:* and then choose Insert→Date and turn on the "Update automatically on save" checkbox. Now, each time you make a change to the page, Dreamweaver changes the date to reflect the last time you saved the document. You never have to worry about dating pages again.

■ Selecting Text

After you get text into your Dreamweaver document, you'll undoubtedly need to edit it. You'll delete words and paragraphs, move sentences around, add words, and fix typos.

The first step in any of these procedures is learning how to select text, which works much as it does in a word processor. You drag your cursor across text to highlight it, or click at the beginning of the selection, and then hold down the Shift key as you click at the end of the selection; you'll automatically select everything in between. You can also use shortcuts like these:

- To select a word, double-click it.

- To select a paragraph, triple-click anywhere in it.

- To select a line of text, move your cursor to the left of the line until the cursor changes from an I-beam to an arrow, signaling that you've reached the left-margin selection strip. Click once to highlight one line of text; click once, and then drag vertically in this selection strip to select multiple lines.

- While pressing Shift, use the left and right arrow keys to select one letter at a time. Use Ctrl+Shift (⌘-Shift) and the left and right arrow keys to select one *word* at a time.

- Ctrl+A (⌘-A) selects everything in the body of a page—text, graphics, and all. (Well, this isn't 100 percent true: If you use tables or <div> tags [page 438] to organize a page, Ctrl+A may select just the text within a table cell or <div> tag; clicking the <body> tag in the Tag Selector [page 26] is the sure-fire way to select everything on a page.)

Once you select text, you can cut, copy, or delete it. To move it to another part of the web page, or even to another Dreamweaver document, use the Cut, Copy, and Paste commands in the Edit menu. You can also move text around by dragging and dropping it, as shown in Figure 2-6.

Once copied, the text remains in your clipboard and you can place it again and again (until you copy something else to the clipboard, of course). When you cut (or copy) and paste *within* Dreamweaver, all the code affecting that text comes along for the ride. If you copy a paragraph that includes bold text, for example, then you copy the HTML tags for both creating the paragraph and for producing bold text.

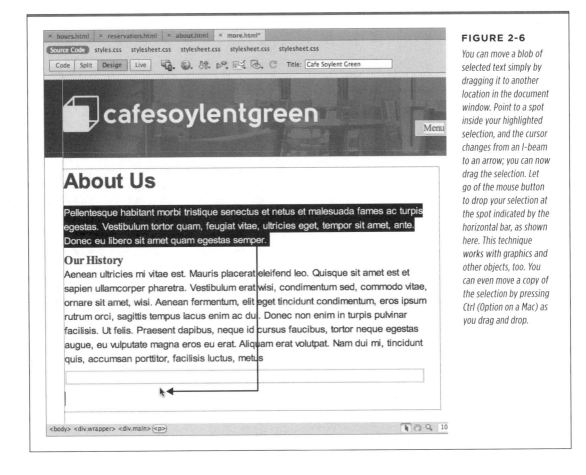

FIGURE 2-6

You can move a blob of selected text simply by dragging it to another location in the document window. Point to a spot inside your highlighted selection, and the cursor changes from an I-beam to an arrow; you can now drag the selection. Let go of the mouse button to drop your selection at the spot indicated by the horizontal bar, as shown here. This technique works with graphics and other objects, too. You can even move a copy of the selection by pressing Ctrl (Option on a Mac) as you drag and drop.

Decoding Encoding

In some cases, when you copy a symbol like © from Microsoft Word and then paste it into Dreamweaver, you see *©* in the HTML. Other times, you see the actual symbol (©). Which you get depends on the type of *encoding* Dreamweaver uses on your web page. Unless you work with languages other than English, encoding isn't much of an issue; you can work happily without ever worrying about how Dreamweaver encodes your HTML. But if you commonly need to type characters that don't appear on the standard English keyboard, such as Chinese, Kanji, or simply the accented letters of French or Spanish, Dreamweaver's encoding method is helpful.

Computers don't think in terms of letters or any of the other symbols we humans normally use to communicate with each other. Computers think in terms of bits and bytes. They represent every letter or symbol on a web page by a numeric code. The process of converting those letters and symbols to computer-friendly code is called *encoding*. But since the world is filled with symbols from many different languages—Latin, Chinese, Arabic, Cyrillic, Hebrew, and so on—there are many *encoding schemes* used to accommodate the different alphabets of the world. Versions of Dreamweaver prior to CS3 used Western Latin encoding, which handles most of the characters in English and Western European languages. But it doesn't handle all the symbols. That's why, when you copy a © symbol from Word and paste it into a web page with Western Latin encoding, you end up with *©* in your HTML instead of the copyright symbol. *©* is called an *entity*, and browsers know that when they see that particular entity, they should display a true copyright symbol.

Dreamweaver uses a newer type of encoding when it creates a web page—Unicode. Unicode, which Dreamweaver refers to as *Unicode (UTF-8)*, accommodates many of the alphabets of the world, so you can mix Kanji with Cyrillic with English on a single page, and all the characters display as they should. A page encoded with Unicode also produces slightly different HTML when you paste symbols from other programs. Instead of using entities in the page, like *”* for a curly right quotation mark, you see the actual character (") in the HTML. This quality generally makes HTML much easier to read. However, if you've previously built a site using a different encoding scheme, like *Japanese (Shift JIS)*—yes, that's the actual format name—you may want to stick to that method.

You probably won't ever need to change Dreamweaver's encoding scheme, but if you update a site and want to upgrade to the new Unicode encoding (maybe so you can type © instead of *©* in your HTML), choose Modify→Page Properties, click the Title/Encoding category, and then select a method from the encoding menu. If you want to change the default encoding for all new documents (for example, if you absolutely must stick with the *Shift JIS* to match the encoding method of other pages on your site), choose Edit→Preferences (Dreamweaver→Preferences), click the New Document category, and then select an option from the Default Encoding menu.

Note that if, later on, you switch back to Unicode (UTF-8), make sure you select "C (Canonical Decomposition)" from the Normalization field, and leave the Include Unicode Signature checkbox *turned off* (otherwise the page may not display correctly in current browsers).

Finally, if you use the Insert Special Character menu (page 92), Dreamweaver always inserts an HTML entity (*®*, for example) instead of the actual symbol (™), even in a UTF-8 page. You can, however, type many of these symbols on your keyboard, as described in the Power Users' Clinic on page 94.

NOTE Not *all* formatting necessarily comes along for the ride. For example, if you format text using an external style sheet (see page 123) and you cut and paste that text into a web page that's not linked to the CSS file, the formatting does *not* show up in the new page. So on some occasions, you may copy text from one document, paste it into another, and find that the formatting disappears.

To delete any selection, press Delete or choose Edit→Clear.

HTML Formatting

Getting text onto a web page is a good start, but effective communication requires effective design. Large, bold headlines help readers scan a page's important topics. Colorful text focuses attention. Bulleted sentences crystallize and summarize ideas. Just as a monotonous, low-key voice puts a crowd to sleep, a vast desert of plain HTML text is sure to turn visitors away from the important message of your site. In fact, text formatting could be the key to making your *Widgets Online 2012 Sale-a-Thon* a resounding success instead of an unnoticed disaster.

Text formatting is actually a two-step process. First you apply the appropriate HTML tag to each chunk of text, and then you create styles using a formatting language called CSS (Cascading Style Sheets) to make that text look great. You add HTML tags not so much to format text (though they *can* do that, with the undesired side effect that different browsers can interpret the tags differently); rather, you use them to *structure* the text into logical blocks. Once you set up those blocks, you can use CSS to format them to your liking—and not just in the current page, but across your site. That's one of the big benefits of CSS.

For example, you'd use the <h1> (Heading 1) tag to indicate the most important heading on a page, and the <ol> (ordered list) tag to list a series of numbered steps. Structuring your text with HTML like this not only adds some rudimentary formatting (the resulting page has a large, boldfaced headline and a numbered list), but it also structures your text so that search engines and alternative browsing devices, like screen readers for the vision-impaired, can weight the relative importance of each block of text. However, HTML's limited formatting options aren't very appealing. That's where CSS comes in. You use CSS to fine-tune the visual appeal of text by changing fonts, applying color, adjusting font size, and a lot more.

The fundamental difference between HTML and CSS is so important that Dreamweaver treats these two technologies separately by splitting the Property Inspector into two tabbed areas, one for HTML and the other for CSS. That way, you always know when you're applying which type of formatting code (see Figure 2-7). In this chapter, you'll learn to use HTML tags to structure text on a web page; in the next chapter, you'll create beautiful typography with CSS.

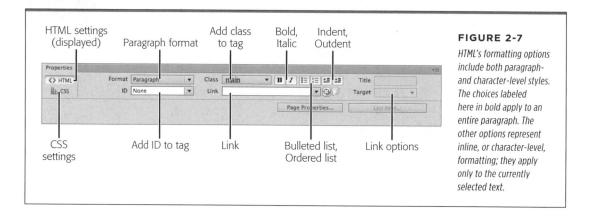

FIGURE 2-7

HTML's formatting options include both paragraph- and character-level styles. The choices labeled here in bold apply to an entire paragraph. The other options represent inline, or character-level, formatting; they apply only to the currently selected text.

■ Paragraph Formatting

Just as you use paragraphs to help organize your thoughts into clear, well-structured units when you write a paper or letter, you also organize content on web pages into blocks of information using HTML tags (see page 8 for more about tags). The most basic block of information is the simple paragraph, which you identify in HTML with a paragraph tag, like this:

```
<p>Hello. This is a paragraph on a web page.</p>
```

A web browser considers everything between the opening <p> tag and the closing </p> tag as part of the same paragraph. You can apply many Dreamweaver format-ting options—headlines, lists, indentations, and alignment, for example—only to full paragraphs rather than individual words. In a word processor, you call this kind of formatting *paragraph* formatting; in web design, it's called *block-level* formatting. Either way, the idea is the same: The formatting you apply affects an entire paragraph (that is, a *block* of text, whether that block consists of just a single sentence or of several sentences). On the other hand, you can apply *character-level* formatting to individual words or even letters. Character-level formatting includes bold and italic attributes. In the world of HTML, *inline elements*, like the <strong> and the <em> tags, provide character-level formatting.

Paragraphs

If you create a new document in Dreamweaver and start typing right away, the text you type has no paragraph formatting at all, as indicated by the word "None" in the Format menu at the left side of the Property Inspector (see Figure 2-7). (*None* isn't an HTML tag; it just means that you aren't using *any* of the text tags this menu offers—<p>, <h1>, and so on.)

However, when you press Enter (Return), Dreamweaver transforms that text into a new paragraph, complete with opening and closing <p> tags. Still, your newly born paragraph has no *design* applied to it. When a visitor looks at the paragraph, he doesn't see text in *a* font and size of your choosing; rather, he sees it formatted according to his browser's Preferences settings. For example, if a visitor sets his browser to display unformatted text as Vladimir Script, your page will look as though John Hancock wrote it. However, since most people don't bother to do this, browsers usually use some version of Times New Roman for paragraphs (you'll be able to specify your own fonts using CSS, as described on page 145).

UP TO SPEED

Separating Structure from Presentation

HTML isn't about good looks or fancy design, it's about page architecture. HTML tags apply *structure* to your page, providing search engines with valuable insight into how you organize your content. In fact, most visitors to your site won't ever see, and probably don't care, which HTML tags you use. But Google, Bing, and other search engines do. They use your tags to determine which text is the most important and to understand what your page is really about.

Google, for example, puts a lot of stock in <h1> tags, seeing the text inside as defining the page's subject. That's why search engine experts recommend using only one <h1> tag per page, and suggest that you make the text very descriptive: <h1>My page</h1> isn't good, but <h1>The Ultimate Chia Pet Resource</h1> is.

In general, use HTML to structure your page just as you'd structure a report or term paper. For example, the Heading 1 (<h1>) tag indicates a headline of the highest level and, therefore, of greatest importance; the smaller Heading 2 (<h2>) tag represents a headline of slightly less importance: a subhead. You

can see this kind of structure in this book. Each section begins with a headline and includes subheads that further divide the content into logical blocks of information.

Structure is more about organizing content than it is about making a page look pretty. Even if this book used different colors and fonts for every headline, its fundamental organization—chapter title, main headlines, subheads, bulleted lists, numbered instructions, and paragraphs of information—remains the same.

HTML is also important for devices that don't read or can't display CSS. For example, people with vision impairment often rely on screen readers (programs that literally read the text on a page out loud) to surf the Web. For screen readers, good HTML structure is the only way they can understand a page—clear use of headline, paragraph, and other tags help screen readers convey the structure of a page.

You can add the paragraph tag to any block of text. Since that attribute affects all the text within the block, you don't need to select any text as a first step. Simply click anywhere inside the block of text, and then do one of the following:

- In the Property Inspector, choose Paragraph from the Format drop-down menu.

- Choose Format→Paragraph Format→Paragraph.

- Press Ctrl+Shift+P (⌘-Shift-P).

NOTE Much to the chagrin of web designers, web browsers display a line's worth of blank space before and after many block-level elements, like headings and paragraphs. If you find this visual gap distracting, you can't, unfortunately, get rid of it with regular HTML. However, many of the formatting limitations of HTML, including this one, go away when you use CSS. See page 163 to fix this problem.

Headlines

Headlines announce information ("The Vote Is In!") and help organize content. Just as this book uses different levels of headings—from chapter titles all the way down to subsections— to introduce its topics, HTML headings come in a variety of sizes to reflect a piece of content's importance. Headlines range in size from 1 (most important) to 6 (least important), as shown in Figure 2-8.

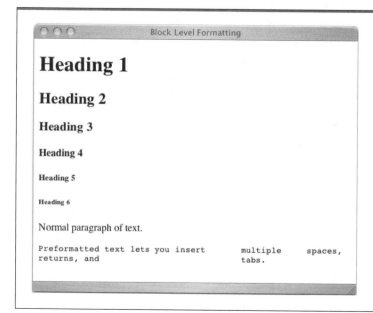

FIGURE 2-8

You can apply any of eight basic paragraph formats to a block of plain old text: Headings 1 through 6, Paragraph, and Preformatted. Normally, browsers vary the size, font, and weight (boldness) of these tags (unless you add some of the CSS magic discussed in the next chapter).

To turn a paragraph into a headline, click anywhere inside the line, or block, of text and then do one of the following:

- From the Format menu in the Property Inspector, select one of the heading levels (Heading 1 through Heading 6).

- Choose Format→Paragraph Format→Heading 1 (or Heading 2, Heading 3, and so on).

- Press Ctrl+1 (⌘-1) for the Heading 1 style, Ctrl+2 (⌘-2) for Heading 2, and so on.

Preformatted Text

Web browsers normally ignore extra spaces, tabs, and other blank-space characters in the underlying HTML when they display web pages. However, the Preformatted paragraph format overrides this behavior. Preformatted paragraphs display *every* text character in a paragraph, including tabs, multiple spaces, and line breaks, so you don't have to resort to multiple nonbreaking space characters (see page 95) to insert more than one space at a time.

The original idea behind the Preformatted format was to display tabular data—like that in a spreadsheet—without the use of tables. That's why preformatted paragraphs use a *monospaced* font like Courier. In a monospaced font, each letter of the alphabet, including *i* and *w*, have the same width, making it easy to align letters in columns. That's also why, when you use the Preformatted paragraph style, you can use tabs to align text in columns. (When you use any other paragraph format, web browsers ignore tabs.) However, using an HTML table is a much better way to display data in columns; see Chapter 6.

Nonetheless, the Preformatted format can still be useful—when you want to display sample HTML or programming code, for example. You can add the Preformatted format to any block of text. Simply click inside the block, and take one of these two steps:

- In the Property Inspector, choose Format→Preformatted.
- Choose Format→Paragraph Format→Preformatted Text.

Keep in mind that preformatted text appears exactly as you type it in. Unlike normal paragraph text, lines of preformatted text don't automatically wrap if they're wider than your visitor's display. That means that if you present your visitor with a really long line of preformatted text, she has to scroll horizontally to see all of it. To end a line of preformatted text and create another, you must press the Enter (Return) key, thus creating a manual line break.

Indented Paragraphs

Dreamweaver's Property Inspector includes a button that looks like the indent buttons in word processors. However, the button doesn't really create an indent; it actually inserts the HTML blockquote tag (though the Indent button has a different function when you apply it to working with lists, as described on page 111).

The blockquote tag was designed to set apart quoted material, such as an excerpt from a book or part of a famous speech. However, since HTML indents blockquotes from the left edge of the page, some novice web designers use it to indent text. That's not a good idea for a couple of reasons. First, the tag indents text from *both* sides of a page, so it doesn't make sense as a way to indent a paragraph. In addition, you don't have any control over how *much* space a visitor's browser adds to the margins of a blockquote. Most insert about 40 pixels of blank space on the left and right sides.

As you'll see on page 449, CSS gives you precise control over indented elements using the *margin* or *padding* properties. However, if you *do* want to quote passages of text, you should use the blockquote tag. To do so, just click inside a paragraph or any block-level element (like a paragraph), and do one of the following:

- In the Property Inspector, click the Blockquote button (see Figure 2-7, where it's labeled "Indent").

- Choose Format→Indent.

- Press Ctrl+Alt+] (⌘-Option-]).

If you ever want to remove the block quote, you can use Dreamweaver to *outdent* it (yes, *outdent* is a real word—ever since Microsoft made it up).

To remove a <blockquote> tag, click inside the paragraph, and then do one of the following:

- In the Property Inspector, click the Outdent button.

- Choose Format→Outdent.

- Press Ctrl+Alt+[(⌘-Option-[).

◼ Creating and Formatting Lists

Lists organize the everyday information of our lives: to-do lists, grocery lists, least favorite celebrity lists, and so on. On web pages, lists are indispensable for presenting groups of items, such as links, company services, or sets of instructions.

HTML offers formatting options for three basic types of lists (see Figure 2-9). The two most common are *bulleted* lists (called *unordered* lists in HTML) and *numbered* lists (called *ordered* lists in HTML). The third and lesser-known list type, the *definition* list, comes in handy when you want to create glossaries or dictionary entries.

Bulleted and Numbered Lists

Bulleted and numbered lists share similar formatting. Dreamweaver automatically indents list items in both cases, and automatically precedes each item with a character—a bullet, number, or letter, for example:

- Unordered, or bulleted, lists, like this one, are good for groups of items that don't necessarily follow a sequence. Browsers precede each list item with a bullet.

- Ordered lists are useful when you want to present items that follow a sequence, such as the numbered instructions in the section below. Instead of a bullet, a number or letter precedes each item in an ordered list. Dreamweaver suggests a number (1, 2, 3, and so on), but you can substitute Roman numerals, letters, and other variations.

You can create a list from scratch within Dreamweaver, or apply list formatting to text that's already on a page.

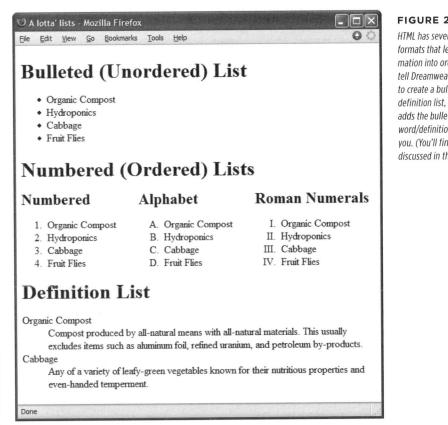

FIGURE 2-9

HTML has several predefined list formats that let you organize information into orderly units. Once you tell Dreamweaver that you intend to create a bulleted, numbered, or definition list, it automatically adds the bullets, numbers, or word/definition formatting for you. (You'll find definition lists discussed in the next section.)

■ **CREATING A NEW BULLETED OR NUMBERED LIST**

When you make a new list in Dreamweaver, first choose a list format, and then type in the list items:

1. **In Design view in the document window, click the point on a page where you want to start the list.**

2. **In the Property Inspector, click the Ordered List or Unordered List button to apply the list format (see Figure 2-7).** (The Unordered option is also known as a bulleted list.)

   Alternatively, you can choose Format→List→Unordered List or Ordered List. Either way, the first bullet or number appears automatically in your document.

3. **Type in the first list item, and then press Enter (Return).** Repeat this step until you add all the items in the list.

The text you type appears after the bullet or number (*Organic Compost*, for example, in the bulleted list in Figure 2-9). When you press Enter (Return), a new bullet or number appears, ready for your next item. (If you just want to move to the next line *without* creating a new bullet, then insert a line break by pressing Shift+Enter [Shift-Return].)

> **NOTE** You can use the Property Inspector to create a numbered or bulleted list in Code view, but Dreamweaver won't automatically add a new list item each time you hit return. To insert a new list item, you must click outside the current list item (either before an opening <li> or after a closing </li>) and either choose Insert→HTML→Text Object→List Item, or just type the HTML yourself (for example: <li>New item</li>). As you can see, using Design view to add lists is a lot easier. The only benefit of the Code view is that you can insert paragraphs, headlines and other elements inside the <li> tags, which is perfectly valid HTML, but which Dreamweaver doesn't let you do in Design view.

4. **When you finish the list, press Enter (Return) twice.**

The double hard return ends the list and creates a new empty paragraph.

■ FORMATTING EXISTING TEXT AS A LIST

You may have several paragraphs of text you already typed up or pasted in from another program. You can easily change any such group of paragraphs into a list:

1. **Select the text you wish to turn into a list.**

The easiest way to do this is to drag from the first list item straight down to the last one. Lists are block-level elements; each paragraph, whether it's a headline or a regular block of text, becomes one bulleted or numbered item in the list.

> **NOTE** You can use the Property Inspector to change existing text into a list in Code view as well.

2. **Apply the list format.**

Just as you created a list from scratch as described above, click either the Un-ordered List or Ordered List button in the Property Inspector, or choose from the Format→List submenu. The selected paragraphs instantly take on the list formatting, complete with bullets or automatic numbering.

> **NOTE** You may sometimes run into this problem: You select what looks like a handful of paragraphs and apply the list format, but only one bullet (or number) appears. This glitch arises when you use the line break <br> tag to move text down a line in a paragraph. While it's true that using the <br> tag visually separates lines in a paragraph into separate blocks, the text is still part of a single paragraph, and it appears as only *one* bulleted or numbered item. The presence of multiple <br> tags can be a real problem when you paste text from other programs. See page 93 for more on the <br> tag and how to get rid of these pesky critters.

Whichever way you create your list—either by typing it in from scratch or formatting existing text—you're not stuck with the results of your early decisions. You can add onto lists, add extra spaces, and even renumber them, as described in the following section.

Reformatting Bulleted and Numbered Lists

HTML tags define lists, just as they define other web page elements. Making changes to an existing list is a matter of changing those tags, using Dreamweaver's menu commands and Property Inspector.

> **TIP** Web browsers generally display list items stacked directly one on top of the other. If you want to add a little breathing room between each item, use the CSS *margin* property to add space above or below <li> tags, as described on page 449.

ADDING NEW ITEMS TO A LIST

Once you create a list, you can easily add items. To add an item at the beginning of a list, click in front of the first character of the first list item (not its bullet or number), type the item you wish to add, and then press Enter (Return). Your first item now sits beside the first bullet or number, and pressing the Enter (Return) key automatically generates the next bullet or number (and renumbers the other list items, if necessary).

> **NOTE** Adding items this way works only in Design view, not Code view.

To add an item to the middle or end of a list, click at the end of the *previous* list item, and then press Enter (Return). The insertion point appears after Dreamweaver adds a new bullet or number; type your list item on this new line.

FORMATTING BULLETS AND NUMBERS

Bulleted and numbered lists aren't limited to just the standard round black bullet or the numbers 1, 2, and 3. You can choose from two bullet types and a handful of numbering schemes. Here's how to change these settings:

1. **Click once inside any list item.**

   Strangely enough, you can't change the properties of a list if you first select the entire list, a single list item, or several list items.

> **NOTE** Most of the settings in the List Properties dialog box produce invalid HTML for HTML5, as well as the strict versions of HTML 4.01 and XHTML 1.0. If you use this dialog box, stick to XHTML transitional or HTML transitional document types (see page 7 for more on picking a document type).

2. **Open the List Properties dialog box (Figure 2-10).**

Either click the List Item button in the bottom half of the Property Inspector or choose Format→List→Properties. (If the list is inside a table cell, your only choice is to use the Format menu. In this situation, the List Item button doesn't appear in the Property Inspector.)

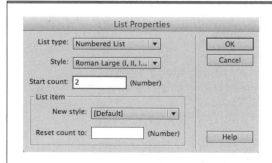

FIGURE 2-10

The List Properties dialog box lets you set the type and style of a list. For example, if you select a numbered list, you can choose from five number styles: Number (1, 2, 3); Roman Small (i, ii, iii); Roman Large (I, II, III); Alphabet Small (a, b, c); and Alphabet Large (A, B, C). While the options in the top half of this window apply to an entire list (every item with the <ol> or <ul> tag), the options below the label "List Item" apply to just the single list item you clicked before opening the List Properties dialog box.

3. **Skip the "List type" drop-down menu.**

It lets you turn a numbered list into a bulleted one, and vice versa. But why bother? You can achieve the same thing by simply selecting a bulleted list and clicking the numbered list button in the Property Inspector and vice versa. In addition, this menu has two other options—Directory List and Menu List—which insert obsolete HTML, so avoid it.

4. **Choose a bullet or numbering style.**

Bulleted lists can have three styles: *default, bullet,* or *square.* In most browsers, the default style is the same as the bullet style (a simple, solid, black circle). As you might guess, the square style uses a solid black square for the bullet character.

Numbered lists, on the other hand, offer a greater variety of style options. Dreamweaver starts you off with a simple numbering scheme (1, 2, 3, and so on), but you can choose from any of five styles for ordered lists, as explained in Figure 2-10.

TIP You can achieve the same effect as step 4 above using CSS. Not only does CSS give you more options—you can use a graphic you created as a bullet, for example—but you avoid inserting obsolete HTML. See page 166 for CSS list options.

---

5. **Set the starting number for the list.**

   You don't have to begin a numbered list at 1, A, or the Roman numeral I. You can start it with any number you wish—a trick that can come in handy if, for example, you create a web page that explains how to rebuild a car's engine. As part of each step, say you want to include a photograph. You create a numbered list, type in the directions for step 1, hit Return, and then insert an image (as described in Chapter 5). You hit Return again, and then type in the text for step 2. Unfortunately, the photo, because it's technically an item in an ordered list, now has the number 2 next to it, and your real step 2 is listed as step 3!

   If you remove the list formatting from the photo to get rid of the 2, then you create one list above it and another below it. Step 2, *below* the photo, now thinks it's the beginning of a new list—and starts over with the number 1! The solution is to make the list below the photo think it's a *new* list that begins with 2.

   To start a list at something other than 1, type the starting number in the "Start count" field (Figure 2-10). You must enter a number, even if you want the list to use letters. So, to begin a list at D instead of A, type *4* in the "Start count" field.

   You can even change the style of a *single* list item. For instance, you could change the third item in a numeric list from a 3 to the letter C. (Of course, just because you *can* doesn't mean you should. Dreamweaver is very thorough in supporting the almost overwhelming combination of options available in HTML, but, unless you're building a Dadaist revival site, how often do you want a list that's numbered 1, 2, C, iv, 1?)

6. **Click OK to apply the changes.**

■ NESTED LISTS

Some complex outlines require multiple *levels* of lists. Legal documents, for instance, may list major clauses with capital letters (A, B, C, and so on) and use Roman numerals (i, ii, iii, and so on) for subclauses.

You can easily create such nested lists in Dreamweaver using the Property Inspector's indent button; Figure 2-11 shows you the steps.

You can change the style of a nested list—for example, change the nested list in Figure 3-6, bottom, into a bulleted list—by clicking the appropriate list type in the Property Inspector. Changing the nested list's type doesn't affect the parent list type (that is, the outer list); for example, changing the nested list in Figure 2-11 from a numbered list to a bulleted list doesn't change the outer list to a bulleted list.

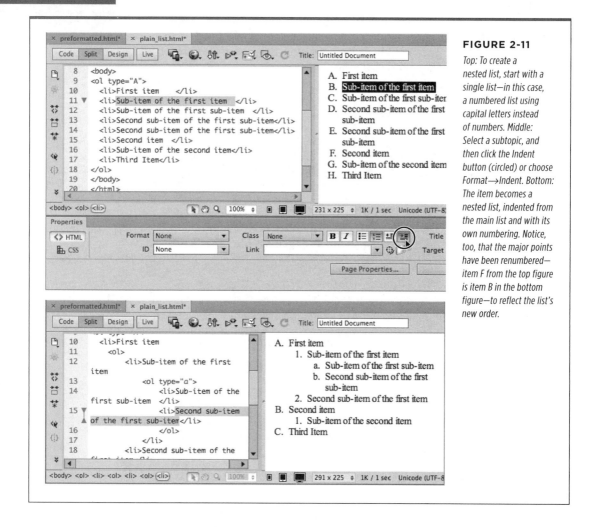

FIGURE 2-11

Top: To create a nested list, start with a single list—in this case, a numbered list using capital letters instead of numbers. Middle: Select a subtopic, and then click the Indent button (circled) or choose Format→Indent. Bottom: The item becomes a nested list, indented from the main list and with its own numbering. Notice, too, that the major points have been renumbered— item F from the top figure is item B in the bottom figure—to reflect the list's new order.

TIP You can also create a nested list by hitting the tab key to indent a list item to another level. Shift-Tab outdents the list item.

Definition Lists

You can use *definition lists* to create dictionary or glossary entries, or whenever you need to present a term and its definition. Each item in a definition list is composed of two parts: a word or term and its definition.

NOTE Behind the scenes, Dreamweaver creates an entire definition list using the <dl> tag. Then it applies two tags to each item in the list: <dt> for the word or term you want to define, and <dd> for the definition itself.

As you can see in Figure 2-9, definition lists aren't as fancy as they sound. HTML presents the first item in the list—the word or term—on its own line with no indent, and the second item—the definition—appears directly underneath, indented.

You can't create a definition list using the Property Inspector. Instead, start by creating a list of definitions and terms: Each term and definition should be in its own paragraph, and the definition should immediately follow the term. Next, highlight the paragraphs that contain the terms and definitions, and then choose Format→List→Definition List.

To turn a definition list *back* to regular paragraphs, select the list, and then choose Format→List→None, or, in the Property Inspector, click the Outdent button.

FREQUENTLY ASKED QUESTION

When Not to Approach the Insert Panel

I like the convenience of the Insert panel. Should I use its Text category to format text?

In a word, no. Unlike the way web designers use most of the other categories in the Insert panel, they use the Text category mainly when working in Code view or to insert special characters, like the copyright symbol as described on page 92. It contains many of the same formatting options as the Property Inspector; the Insert panel's *h1, h2,* and *h3,* for instance, are the same as Headings 1, 2, and 3 in the Property Inspector's Format drop-down menu.

However, using some of the panel's text options, such as *li,* can generate invalid HTML if you don't use it correctly. Furthermore, despite its usual tidiness, Dreamweaver doesn't clean up the code produced this way.

In fact, some of these options, when used in Design view, actually split the document window in two, showing the HTML code on one side and Design view on the other. This arrangement is confusing if you're not accustomed to seeing—or if you're not interested in—the raw HTML. All major text-formatting options are available from the Property Inspector and Format menu. If you stick to these two tools, you can safely avoid the Text category.

Removing and Deleting List Items

Dreamweaver lets you take items out of a list two ways: either by removing the list *formatting* from items (and changing them back to normal paragraphs) or by deleting their text outright.

■ REMOVING LIST FORMATTING

To remove list formatting from one or more list items (or an entire list), highlight the lines in question, and then choose Format→List→None (or, in the Property Inspector, just click the Outdent button). You've just removed all list formatting; the text remains on the screen, now formatted as standard paragraphs. For nested lists, you need to click the Outdent button once for each level of indent.

If you reformat an item in the middle of a list using this technique, it becomes a regular paragraph, and Dreamweaver turns the items above and below it into separate lists.

■ DELETING LIST ITEMS

You can easily delete a list or list item with the Tag Selector in the document window's status bar (see Figure 2-12). To delete an entire list, click anywhere inside it, click its tag in the Tag Selector—<ul> for a bulleted list, <ol> for a numbered list—and then press Delete. You can also, of course, drag through all the text in the list, and then press Delete.

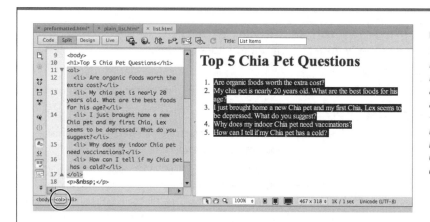

FIGURE 2-12

The Tag Selector (at the bottom left of the document window) is a great way to quickly and accurately select an HTML tag and its contents. Clicking the <ol> (ordered list) tag, for instance, selects the entire numbered list, as shown here. Clicking the <li> tag selects just one list item.

To delete a single list item, click that item in the document window, click the <li> tag in the Tag Selector, and then press Delete.

> **TIP** You can rearrange a list in Design view by dragging a list item to another position within the list. If it's an ordered list (1, 2, 3, and so on), Dreamweaver automatically renumbers it.

However, selecting a list item can be tricky. If you simply drag to select the text, you don't actually select the list item itself, with all its formatting and numbering. To be sure that you select a list item *and* its formatting, click the <li> tag in the Tag Selector in the document window's status bar (see Figure 2-12). Now, when you drag the selection to a new position in the list, the number (or bullet) goes along for the ride. You can also copy or cut the selected list item, and then paste it into another position in the list.

■ Text Styles

The formatting you can apply through HTML tags isn't much to write home about, much less to advertise on a résumé. It's pretty basic; browsers generally display a Heading 1, for instance, in black and bold using a large Times New Roman font. As mentioned in the "Headlines" section on page 104, HTML paragraph formatting is intended to provide *structure*, not good looks. To create standout web pages, you need to use Cascading Style Sheets; CSS lets you apply different fonts, colors, and sizes to your text, and you'll learn how to do that in the next chapter.

Still, HTML offers a handful of tags you can apply to text. Dreamweaver refers to these tags as *styles*, but they really just format text for specific, often obscure, purposes (see Figure 2-13). For example, the Code and Variable styles are intended to format programming code, while the Sample style represents the output from a computer program—not exactly styles you need often in promoting, say, your *Cheeses of the World* mail-order company.

FIGURE 2-13

Top: While the Property Inspector lets you apply bold and italic formats to text, the Format→Style menu offers a larger selection of styles. Don't be confused by the term "styles," which, in this case, merely refers to different HTML tags. They're unrelated to CSS styles and are intended to identify very specific types of text, like citations from a book or magazine, or programming code.
Bottom: As you can see, the many style options usually include bold, italic, the browser's monospaced font (usually Courier), or some combination of the three. But don't worry about how they look "out of the box"—as you'll learn in the next chapter, you can make any of these tags appear any way you want by applying CSS.

To use an HTML style, select the text, and then select a format from the Format→Style menu. (You can also use the Property Inspector to apply the <strong> or <em> tags to emphasize text by making it bold or italic.)

NOTE Use italics with care. While printed material uses it frequently to add *emphasis* or to reference a book title, it can be difficult to read on a computer screen, especially at small type sizes.

UP TO SPEED

When Bold and Italics Are Neither

You may be confused by the HTML Dreamweaver produces when you tell it to make text bold or italic. Instead of using the <b> tag—the original HTML code for bold—Dreamweaver uses the <strong> tag. And instead of using <i> for italic, clicking the Property Inspector's I button gets you <em> tag, the one for emphasis. That's because Adobe decided to follow industry practices rather than stick to an old tradition.

For most purposes, <strong> and <em> behave identically to <b> and <i>. The results look the same—bolded or italicized text—in most browsers. However, when screen readers (programs or equipment that reads web pages aloud for the benefit of the visually impaired) encounter these tags, the <strong> tag triggers a loud, strong voice. The <em> tag also brings an emphasis to the voice of screen readers, though with less strength than the <strong> tag.

Since most browsers simply treat the <strong> tag like the <b> tag and the <em> tag like the <i> tag, you'll probably never notice the difference. However, if you prefer the simple <b>

and <i> tags, choose Edit→Preferences. Select the General category, and then turn off the checkbox labeled "Use <strong> and <em> in place of <b> and <i>."

HTML5 slightly redefines all these tags. It rewrote the <i> tag for text in an "alternate voice," such as a foreign word, a technical term, or typographically italicized text such as a book title, like *Dreamweaver CS6: The Missing Manual.* You use the <b> tag just to make text look bold so that it stands out visually. Basically, imagine you're reading text out loud. If you encounter a word that you would emphasize with your voice ("That's so Raven," for example), use the <em> tag; if you'd shout the word ("Help!!!"), use the <strong> tag. If you simply want text to look a certain way, you can use the <i> or <b> tags, or, better yet, the CSS *font-weight* and *font-style* properties described in "CSS Type Properties in the Rule Definition Window" on page 161. You can read more about HTML5 and the <b>, <strong>, <i>, and <em> tags at *http://tinyurl.com/yau4mze.*

Unless you intend to use HTML tags that properly format your content, like using the Code style to display computer code, you're better off avoiding such styles. But if you think one of them might come in handy, you can find more about these styles in Dreamweaver's built-in HTML reference; see page 370.

NOTE The teletype (<tt>) tag is obsolete and has been removed from HTML5, so avoid it.

■ Spell Checking

You spend a lot of time perfecting your web pages, making sure that the images look great, the text is properly formatted, and everything aligns to make a beautiful visual presentation. But one step is often forgotten, especially given the hyper-speed development process of the Web—making sure your web content is free of typos.

Spelling mistakes look unprofessional and imply a lack of attention to detail. Who wants to hire an "illustraightor" or "Web dezyner?" Dreamweaver's spell checking feature can help.

About Dictionaries

Before you start spell checking, make sure you have the right *dictionary* selected. Dreamweaver comes with 36 of them, ranging from Bulgarian to Turkish (including three variants of English, and four of German). When it checks your spelling, the program compares the text in your document against the list of words in one of these dictionaries.

To specify a dictionary, choose Edit→Preferences (Dreamweaver→Preferences) or press Ctrl+U (⌘-U) to open the Preferences dialog box. Select the General category and then, from the Spelling Dictionary drop-down menu at the bottom of the window, choose a language.

Performing a Spell Check

Once you select a dictionary, open the web page whose spelling you want to check. You can check as much or as little of the text as you like, as follows:

1. **Highlight the text you want to check (which can even be a single word).**

   If you want to check the *entire* document, make sure you have nothing selected in the document window (one good way to do this is to click in the middle of a paragraph of text).

NOTE Unfortunately, Dreamweaver doesn't offer a site-wide spell-checking feature. You must check each page individually.

GEM IN THE ROUGH

Clean Up Word

From Word, you can save any document as a web page, essentially turning it into an HTML page—except that Word produces hideous HTML. One look at it, and you'd think that your cat fell asleep on the keyboard.

Here's what happens: To let you reopen the document as a Word file when the time comes, Word injects reams of information that adds to the file size of the page. This is a particular problem with the latest versions of Word, which add loads of XML and Cascading Style Sheet information.

Fortunately, Dreamweaver's Clean Up Word HTML command strips out most of that unnecessary code and produces leaner web pages. To use it, open the Word HTML file just as you would any other web page, by choosing File→Open. Then choose Commands→Clean Up Word HTML.

The Clean Up Word HTML dialog box opens; Dreamweaver automatically detects whether the HTML was produced by Word 97/98 or a later version, and then applies the appropriate rules for cleaning up the HTML.

Unfortunately, Dreamweaver doesn't always catch all the junk Word throws in, so if you have the original Word document, you're better off just opening it, copying the contents, and pasting it into Dreamweaver. Then you can use Dreamweaver's tools for formatting the text so that it looks just the way you want it to, without any unnecessary code.

2. **Choose Commands→Check Spelling (or press Shift+F7).**

   The Check Spelling dialog box opens (see Figure 2-14). If a word isn't in Dreamweaver's dictionary, it appears in the top box, along with a list of suggested spellings.

   The first suggestion is listed in the "Change to" field.

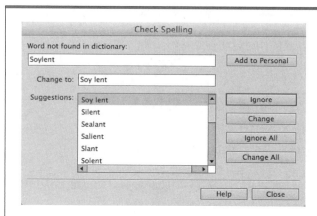

FIGURE 2-14

Dreamweaver's spell-checking feature checks only words in the document window. It can't check the spelling of comments, <alt> tags, or any text that appears in the head of the document, with the exception of the page's title. Nor can you spell check an entire website's worth of pages with a single command; you need to check each page individually.

3. **If the "Change to" field is correct, click Change.**

   If Dreamweaver correctly flags a word as misspelled but the correct spelling isn't in the "Change to" field, double-click the correct spelling in the list Suggestions list below it. If the correct spelling isn't *there*, type it into the "Change to" box yourself. Then click the Change button to correct this one instance, or click Change All to replace this misspelled word everywhere in the document.

   Dreamweaver makes the change and moves on to the next questionable spelling.

4. **If the word is actually correctly spelled but not in Dreamweaver's dictionary, click Ignore, Ignore All, or "Add to Personal."**

   If you want Dreamweaver to ignore this word *every* time it appears in the document, rather than just this instance of it, click Ignore All.

   On the other hand, you'll probably use some words that Dreamweaver doesn't have in its dictionaries. You may, for instance, use a client's name throughout your pages. If that name isn't in Dreamweaver's dictionary, it consistently flags the name as a spelling error.

To teach Dreamweaver the client's name so that the Check Spelling dialog box doesn't pop up at every instance, click "Add to Personal." Dreamweaver adds the word to your personal dictionary, which is a special file that Dreamweaver also consults when checking your spelling.

After you click Ignore or Change, Dreamweaver moves on to the next word it doesn't recognize. Begin again from step 3. If you didn't start the spell check from the beginning of the document, once Dreamweaver reaches the end, it asks if you want to continue spell checking from the beginning.

5. **To finish the spell check, click Close.**

Introducing Cascading Style Sheets

What you see on a web page when you use garden-variety HTML tags like <h1>, <p>, and <ul> pales in comparison to the text and styling on display in, say, a print magazine. If web designers had only HTML to make their sites look great, the Web would forever be the ugly duckling of the media world. HTML doesn't hold a candle to the typographic and layout control you get when you create a document in even the most basic word processing program.

Fortunately for web designers, you can change the ho-hum appearance of HTML using a technology called Cascading Style Sheets (CSS). CSS gives you the tools you need to make HTML look beautiful. If you think of HTML as the basic structure of a house (the foundation, walls, and rooms), then CSS is the house's interior decoration (the paint, carpeting, and the color, style, and placement of furniture). CSS gives you much greater control over the layout and design of your pages. Using it, you can add margins to paragraphs (just as in a word processor), colorful and stylish borders to images, and even dynamic rollover effects to text links. Dreamweaver's streamlined approach to CSS makes it fast and easy to create styles and store them in a central style sheet that controls the look of all the pages in a site.

CSS is a big topic. It's also the heart of today's cutting-edge web design. So instead of dedicating just a single chapter to it, this book provides instruction in the fine art of using CSS in nearly every chapter. In this chapter, you'll learn the basics of CSS and how to use Dreamweaver's powerful CSS tools. In the next few chapters, you'll learn how CSS can improve the look of common web page elements like links, images, and tables. Once you're comfortable with the basics, you'll find in-depth information on CSS in Chapter 8. In Chapter 9, you'll learn how to harness the power of CSS to fully control the layout of a web page. And in Chapter 10, you'll learn how to troubleshoot CSS problems with Dreamweaver.

■ Cascading Style Sheet Basics

If you've used styles in programs like Microsoft Word or Adobe InDesign, CSS will feel familiar. A *style* is simply a rule describing how a browser should format a particular HTML tag. A *style sheet* is a collection of these styles.

You can create a single style that formats text with the font Arial, colored red, and with a left margin of 50 pixels, for example. You can also create styles specifically for images; for instance, you can create a style that aligns an image along the right edge of a web page, surrounds the image with a colorful border, and adds a 50-pixel margin between the image and the surrounding text.

Once you create a style, you can apply it to text, images, or other elements on a page. For example, you could select a paragraph of text and apply a style to it to instantly change the text's size, color, and font. You can also create styles for specific *tags*, so that, for example, a browser displays all <h1> elements in the same style, no matter where they appear on your site.

Why Use CSS?

In the past, HTML alone provided basic formatting options for text, images, tables, and other web page elements. But today, professional web designers use CSS to style their pages. In fact, the older HTML tags used to format text and other page elements have been phased out by the World Wide Web Consortium (W3C), the organization that defines Web standards, in favor of CSS. Following industry practice, Dreamweaver CS6 has made it impossible to add obsolete HTML tags, such as the <font> tag (unless you write the code yourself).

CSS has many benefits over HTML. With it, you can format paragraphs to resemble those that appear in a book or newspaper (with the first line indented and no space between paragraphs, for example), and control the leading (the space between lines of type in a paragraph). When you use CSS to add a background image to a page, you get to decide how (and whether) it tiles (repeats). HTML can't even begin to do any of these things.

Style sheets also make it easier to update your site. You can collect all your styles into a single file linked to every site page. When it's time to change every <h2> tag to lime green, you edit a style in the style sheet file, and that change immediately ripples throughout your site, *wherever* you used that style. You can thus completely change the appearance of a site simply by editing a single style sheet.

Getting to Know (and Love) CSS

Cascading Style Sheets are an exciting—and complex—addition to your web-building toolkit, worthy of entire books and websites. For example:

- For an excellent tutorial on CSS, visit W3 Schools' CSS tutorials at *http://tinyurl.com/rqrw*.

- If you like video tutorials, Sitepoint's CSS Video Crash Course (*www.sitepoint.com/videos/videocss1/*) will teach you a lot about CSS in under 3 hours.

- If you want to get help *and* learn more about CSS, the Sitepoint CSS Forums (*http://tinyurl.com/cmeaubn*) are always busy with advice from a great community of CSS enthusiasts.

- Sitepoint also provides a great online CSS reference at *http://reference.sitepoint.com/css*. This site is a dictionary-like resource of all CSS properties, including information on which browsers support which properties.

- For the ultimate authority, turn to the World Wide Web Consortium's website: *www.w3.org/Style/CSS*. The W3C is the body responsible for many of the standards that drive the Web—including HTML and CSS. (Beware: This site reads like a college physics textbook.)

- For a great list of CSS-related sites, visit the Information and Technology Systems and Services website at the University of Minnesota, Duluth (*http://tinyurl.com/jg2fe*).

- If you just love to curl up by the fireplace with a good tech book, try *CSS: The Missing Manual* by David McFarland (hey, that name rings a bell!). It's written in the same style as this book, with in-depth coverage of CSS and step-by-step tutorials that guide you through every facet of this complicated technology.

CSS may sound like a cure-all for HTML's anemic formatting powers, but truth be told, it's a bit tricky to use. For example, CSS support varies from browser to browser, so you need to test your pages thoroughly on a variety of browsers. Fortunately, Dreamweaver has built-in support for Adobe's BrowserLab service, which generates screenshots of your page taken from a wide range of browsers on both Windows and Mac computers. You'll learn how to use this service on page 760.

Internal vs. External Style Sheets

As you create new formatting styles, you'll add them to a style sheet you store either in the web page itself (in which case it's an *internal style sheet*), or in a separate file called an *external style sheet*.

Internal style sheets appear in the <head> portion of a web page and contain styles that apply only to that page. An internal style sheet is a good choice when you have a very specific formatting task for a single page. For example, if the marketing department wants a one-page online "flyer" with a unique format and its own distinctive look.

TIP When you create a new page design, it's often easier to add styles to an internal style sheet. Once you're satisfied with the design, you can export the styles to an external style sheet—for use by all your site's pages—as described on page 385.

An external style sheet, on the other hand, contains only styles—no HTML—and you can link numerous pages to it. In fact, you can link every page on your site to it, giving your site a uniform, site-wide set of styles. For instance, you can put a headline style in an external style sheet and link every page on the site to that sheet. Every headline on every page then shares the same look—instant design consistency! Even better, when the boss (or the interior decorator in you) calls up and asks you to change the color of the headlines, you need to edit only a single file—the external style sheet—to update hundreds or even thousands of web pages.

You can create both types of style sheet easily in Dreamweaver, and you aren't limited to choosing one or the other. A single web page can have both an external style sheet (for styles that apply to the whole site) and an internal style sheet (to format just that page). You can even attach multiple external style sheets to a single page.

Types of Styles

Styles come in several flavors. The most common are *class, ID*, and *tag* styles.

A *class style* is one you create, name, and attach manually to an HTML tag or to selected text (in other words, text you select with your cursor). Class styles work much like styles in word processing and page layout programs. If you want to display the name of your company in bold and red wherever it appears in a web page, you can create a class style named *company* that formats text in boldface and red letters. You would then select your company's name on the page and apply this style to it.

An *ID* style lets you format a *unique* item on a page. Use ID styles to identify an object (or an area of a page) that appears only once—like a website's logo, copyright notice, main navigation bar, banner, or a particular field in a form. An ID style is similar to a class style in that you name the style and apply it manually. But you can apply a class to many different elements on a page, and you can apply an ID to only one tag or object per page. (It's okay to use multiple IDs on a single page, so long as each ID name is different.) ID styles aren't as popular as they once were—partly because you can only use the ID (and thus the style) once per page, but mostly because ID styles pose problems when your site's styles grow more complex and your style sheets longer. You'll learn why IDs are often avoided in greater depth on page 393; for now, just keep in mind that class styles can do anything an ID style can do, an you'll use those and the tag styles (discussed next) instead of ID styles in this book.

The other major type of CSS style is called a *tag style*, and it applies to an individual HTML tag globally, as opposed to individual pages or selections. Suppose you want to display every Heading 1 paragraph in the Arial font. Instead of creating a class style and applying it to every Heading 1 on the page, you could create a tag style for the <h1> tag. In effect, you redefine the tag so that a browser displays it in Arial.

The main benefit to redefining an HTML tag this way is that you don't have to apply the style by hand. Since the new style says that *all* <h1> tags must use Arial, a browser displays <h1> tags in Arial wherever it encounters them.

Transforming HTML tag styles is the easiest way to format a page. For one thing, there's no need to select the tag manually and apply the style; wherever the tag appears, a browser automatically applies the style.

Nevertheless, sometimes only a class style will do, such as when you want to format just a few words in a paragraph. Simply redefining the <p> tag won't do the trick, since that would affect the entire paragraph (and every other paragraph on your site). Instead, you have to create a class style and apply it to just the words you wish to style. In addition, class styles are handy when you want to format just one instance of a tag differently from others. If you want to format the introductory paragraph on a page one way and all the other paragraphs a different way, you create a class style and apply it to that first paragraph. (Another solution is a slightly more complicated, but more flexible, type of style called a *descendent selector*—you'll read about those later, on page 377.)

NOTE In addition to class and tag styles, other types of styles provide added control for particular situations. You can read about these more advanced styles starting on page 375.

■ Creating Styles

Dreamweaver gives you several ways to create CSS styles. For text, you can use the Property Inspector's CSS mode to apply a font, font size, font color, font weight, and alignment to selected text. To create styles for elements other than text (like images or tables), or to tap into the dozens of other CSS properties not listed in the Property Inspector, you use the CSS Styles panel (see Figure 3-1). To get a complete overview of the style creation process, you'll look at both methods—starting with the more versatile CSS Styles panel, then moving on to the Property Inspector.

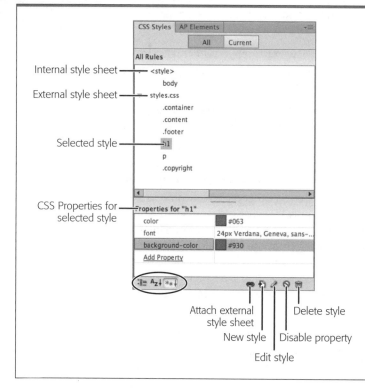

Internal style sheet
External style sheet
Selected style
CSS Properties for
selected style

Attach external
style sheet
New style
Edit style
Disable property
Delete style

FIGURE 3-1

With the "All" button selected, the CSS Styles panel lists the names of all the styles the current page uses, including those in both external and internal style sheets. Here, one external style sheet—styles.css—contains six styles. The first three are class styles (notice that the names begin with a period), while the next two are tag styles (note that their names match HTML tags), and the last one is another class style. You also see one tag style defined in an internal style sheet—the one listed below "<style>." Click the minus-sign (-) icon (flippy triangle on Macs) to the left of the style sheet to collapse the list of styles, hiding them from view. The "Properties" list in the bottom half of the panel lets you edit a style (see page 382); the three buttons at the bottom left of the panel (circled) control how Dreamweaver displays the Properties list.

Phase 1: Set Up the Style

Dreamweaver gives you many ways to create a new style: On the CSS Styles panel, click the new style button (which Dreamweaver calls the New CSS Rule button). Or right-click (Control-click) anywhere in the CSS Styles panel, and then, from the menu that appears, select New. Alternatively, choose Format→CSS Styles→New. The New CSS Rule dialog box appears (Figure 3-2), where you begin creating your style. (In the technical language of CSS, a style is actually called a *rule*, but for simplicity's sake, this book uses the term *style*. After all, *Cascading Rule Sheets* doesn't have much of a ring to it.)

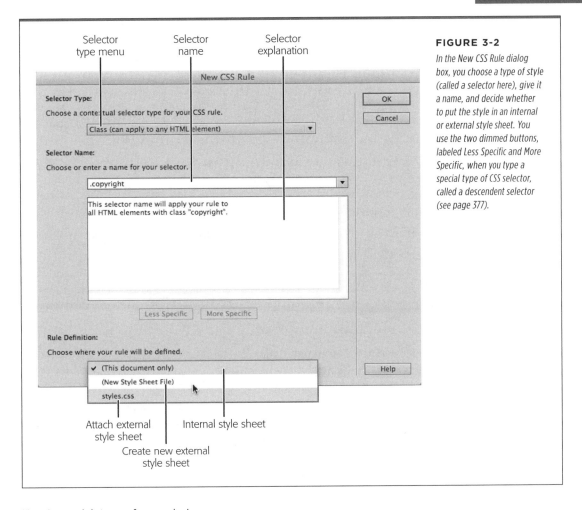

FIGURE 3-2

In the New CSS Rule dialog box, you choose a type of style (called a selector here), give it a name, and decide whether to put the style in an internal or external style sheet. You use the two dimmed buttons, labeled Less Specific and More Specific, when you type a special type of CSS selector, called a descendent selector (see page 377).

Here's a quick tour of your choices:

- **Selector Type**. From the Selector Type menu, choose the kind of style you want to create. *Class* creates a style that you manually apply to page elements, *ID* creates a style that you can use only once on the page, and *Tag* creates an HTML style that Dreamweaver applies to each occurrence of the tag.

  You'll want to use a fourth type of CSS style, *Compound*, to create more advanced style types, such as pseudo-classes, attribute selectors, and descendent selectors. You'll learn about these styles in various parts of the book; you can find a detailed discussion starting on page 375.

NOTE If you've highlighted an element on a page (say a bulleted list item) that's inside another element (like the body tag) that itself has a class or ID style applied to it and then you create a new style, Dreamweaver highlights the Compound option in the CSS Rule dialog box. In addition, in the Selector Name field, Dreamweaver suggests a name—for example, .container li. That's called a descendent selector and you'll learn about them on page 377.

- **Selector Name**. If you selected Class or ID from the Selector Type menu, enter a name for the new style. According to the rules of CSS, you have to start class style names with a period—*.copyright*, for example—and ID style names with the # symbol—*#banner*, for example. Dreamweaver automatically adds the proper symbol if you forget.

  Another class or ID style name rule: A letter must follow the period or # symbol. After that, you can use any combination of letters and numbers, but avoid unusual characters and spaces. For example, *.logo, .main_content, and #email* all work fine. Dreamweaver lets you know if you use any invalid characters.

  If you chose the Tag style instead, choose the HTML tag you want to redefine from the Selector Type drop-down menu.

NOTE If you're an HTML guru, you may find it faster to skip the Selector Name drop-down menu and just type the tag (minus the brackets) in the text box. For example, if you want to create a style for all unordered (bulleted) lists, type *ul*.

If you select the Compound option, Dreamweaver lets you type any valid CSS selector type in the Selector field. You use this feature for some advanced CSS tricks, but you can also use it just to create a class, ID, or tag style.

Note that when you add a class, ID, tag, or other selector to the Selector Name field, Dreamweaver briefly explains to which HTML elements it will apply the selector. For example, Figure 3-2 displays the New CSS Rule dialog box in the process of creating a new class style named *.copyright*. The dialog box explains that Dreamweaver will apply this rule to all the HTML elements to which you assigned the *class* property *.copyright* (in other words, to all the text and tags to which you applied the class "copyright"). You'll learn how to apply a class on page 132. For simple styles like class and tag styles, this explanation is pretty much like "Uh, yeah. Tell me something I don't know, Dreamweaver." But for complex selectors such as the descendent selectors you'll learn about on page 377, this explanatory box helps clarify which page element Dreamweaver will apply an otherwise confusing selector name to.

- **Rule Definition**. The Rule Definition menu at the bottom of the dialog box lets you specify where you want to put the CSS code for the style you're about to create. Choose "This document only" if you want to use the style only on the current web page, thus creating an *internal* style sheet as described on page 123. To create a new *external* style sheet, choose New Style Sheet File from the

Rule Definition drop-down menu. This option not only creates a new external CSS file (which you can save anywhere in your site folder), but also adds the necessary code in the current document to link to that file.

If you previously linked an external style sheet to this document, then that style sheet's name appears in the drop-down menu (*styles.css*, for example in Figure 3-2), indicating that Dreamweaver will add the new style to this style sheet file.

NOTE If you create a bunch of internal styles on a particular page and later realize you'd like to turn them into an external style sheet that you can use in other pages, you're in luck. Dreamweaver includes many tools for managing your style sheets. You'll learn them starting on page 385.

If you indicate that you want to create a new, external style sheet, clicking OK brings up a Save Style Sheet As dialog box. Navigate to your site's folder, and then type in a name for the new external CSS file. Just as HTML files end in .html, so CSS files end in .css.

NOTE If you'll use this style sheet for all your site's pages, you may want to save it in your site's root folder, or in a folder specifically dedicated to style sheets, and give it a general name like *site_styles.css*, *main.css*, styles.css, or *global.css*. (You don't have to type the .css file name extension, by the way. In this case, Dreamweaver adds it.)

No matter what Selector Type you select (Class, ID, Tag, or Compound), clicking OK brings you to the CSS Rule Definition window, discussed next.

Phase 2: Defining a Style

The CSS Rule Definition window lists all the available properties for styling text, graphics, tables, and other HTML tags (see Figure 3-3). You'll learn about each of the properties throughout this book.

When you finish defining a style, click OK at the bottom of the window. Dreamweaver adds the style to the specified style sheet and displays it in the CSS Styles panel.

The real trick to defining a style is mastering all the properties available, such as borders, margins, and background colors, and *then* learning how to apply them so they work reliably in different browsers.

NOTE The CSS properties listed in the Rule Definition window don't include all the CSS properties available. In fact, most of the newer properties introduced in CSS3 (the third version of CSS), aren't available in the Rule Definition window. You'll learn how to use these newer properties on page 418.

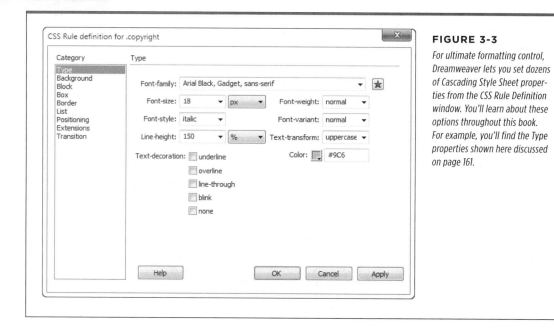

FIGURE 3-3

For ultimate formatting control, Dreamweaver lets you set dozens of Cascading Style Sheet properties from the CSS Rule Definition window. You'll learn about these options throughout this book. For example, you'll find the Type properties shown here discussed on page 161.

Creating a Style with the Property Inspector

The Property Inspector's CSS mode lets you quickly create (or modify) styles, such as choosing a font or a font size (see Figure 3-4) for text you select. In CSS mode, the Property Inspector looks a lot like the formatting bar in a word processing program: dedicated buttons let you make text bold or italic, control alignment, and set font type, size, and color. All these options rely on CSS properties.

To use the Property Inspector's CSS mode, select some text on the page (drag your cursor to select a swath of copy, double-click to select a word, and triple-click to select a paragraph or headline). Then, from the Property Inspector, select an option—for example, choose a font set from the Font drop-down menu. If you don't have a style currently applied to the selection, you see <New CSS Rule> in the Targeted Rule menu (see Figure 3-4, top), and when you apply a format, Dreamweaver opens the New CSS Rule dialog box.

Now it's up to you to pick the type of style (class, ID, tag, or compound), name it, and decide where to store it; just follow the same steps you used to create a new style using the CSS Styles panel, as described on page 125. After you create the new style, you return to the Property Inspector, skipping the Rule Definition window. The Inspector then lists the new style name in the Targeted Rule menu and displays the format settings you selected (for example, the font you chose appears in the Font menu).

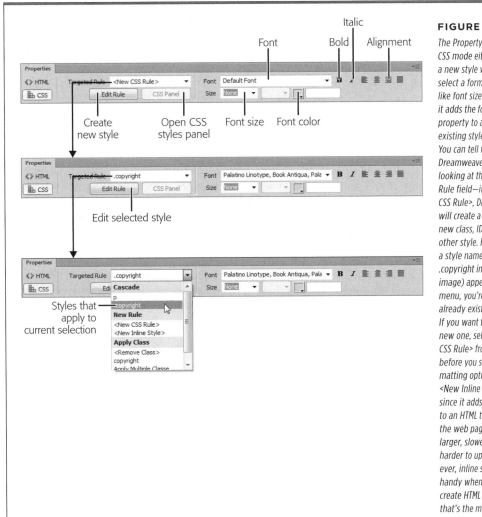

FIGURE 3-4

The Property Inspector's CSS mode either creates a new style when you select a formatting option like font size (top) or it adds the formatting property to an already existing style (middle). You can tell which action Dreamweaver will take by looking at the Targeted Rule field—if it says <New CSS Rule>, Dreamweaver will create a brand-new class, ID, tag, or other style. However, if a style name (like "p" or .copyright in the middle image) appears in that menu, you're editing an already existing style. If you want to create a new one, select <New CSS Rule> from the menu before you select a for-matting option. Avoid the <New Inline Style> style, since it adds CSS directly to an HTML tag, making the web page's file size larger, slower to load, and harder to update. How-ever, inline styles come in handy when you need to create HTML emails, since that's the most reliable way to add CSS to an email message.

Look at a basic example: Suppose you want to format a copyright notice at the bottom of a page in a way that's different from other text on the page. You would first triple-click the copyright paragraph to select the text, and then choose whatever formatting options you want from the CSS mode of the Property Inspector—for example, select 12 from the Size menu to create small, 12-pixel type.

At this point, Dreamweaver opens the New CSS Rule dialog box and, from the Selector Type menu, you select Class, and then, in the Selector Name field, type *.copyright*. You could then store the style's attributes in either an external or internal style sheet, as described on page 123. When you close the New CSS Rule window, Dreamweaver applies the new class style named *copyright* to the paragraph and displays "12" in the Size box in the Property Inspector to denote the text's pixel size.

The Property Inspector's CSS mode behaves differently, however, if you already have a style applied to the selected text. In that case, the style appears in the Targeted Rule menu. For example, in Figure 3-4 (middle), you already applied the class style *copyright* to the selected text, so you see ".copyright" listed in that menu (Figure 3-4, bottom). At this point, choosing another formatting option from the Property Inspector—for instance, clicking the bold button or selecting a font from the font menu—doesn't create a new style, it simply adds this new format to the existing style.

Say you create a *.copyright* class style with a font size of 12 pixels. If you select that copyright text again and then select a font color, Dreamweaver updates the *.copyright* class style—it adds the CSS color property to the style. Making additional formatting choices also updates the style.

Using Styles

After you create a tag style, your work is done. The browser automatically applies the style to the appropriate tag on the page. For example, if you create a "p" tag style, any paragraph (anything with the HTML <p> tag applied to it) on the page reflects the formatting dictated by that style. However, when you create class or ID styles, you need to take an extra step: You must assign the class or ID to the tag you wish to format.

Applying a Class Style

You can apply class styles to any selection in the document window, whether it's a word, an image, or an entire paragraph. In fact, you can apply a class style to *any* individual HTML tag, such as a <p> (paragraph), <td> (table cell), or <body> tag. You can even select just a single word within a paragraph and apply a style to *it*.

APPLYING A CLASS STYLE TO TEXT

Start out by selecting some words. Then, from the Property Inspector, select the style name—you can do this either in HTML mode, in which case you select the name from the Class drop-down menu (Figure 3-5, top) or in CSS mode, where you use the Targeted Rule menu (Figure 3-5, bottom).

To style an entire paragraph, triple-click within the paragraph to select it, and then use the Property Inspector to select a style. When you style an entire paragraph, you're actually telling Dreamweaver to apply the style to the <p> tag. In that case, Dreamweaver adds a special *class* property to the page's code, like this: <p class="company"> (for a class style named .*company*).

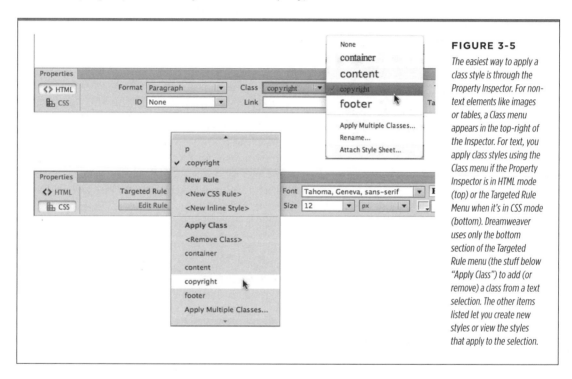

FIGURE 3-5

The easiest way to apply a class style is through the Property Inspector. For non-text elements like images or tables, a Class menu appears in the top-right of the Inspector. For text, you apply class styles using the Class menu if the Property Inspector is in HTML mode (top) or the Targeted Rule Menu when it's in CSS mode (bottom). Dreamweaver uses only the bottom section of the Targeted Rule menu (the stuff below "Apply Class") to add (or remove) a class from a text selection. The other items listed let you create new styles or view the styles that apply to the selection.

TIP You can also add a class style to an entire paragraph or heading simply by clicking anywhere inside the paragraph or heading, and then, from the Property Inspector, choosing the class name—just make sure you don't select a piece of text, or Dreamweaver applies the style just to the selected text, not the entire paragraph.

Anatomy of a Style

When you style a page, Dreamweaver can automatically handle the details of adding the proper CSS code to it, but if you're looking for a way to impress your neighbors, here's the behind-the-scenes scoop on how it works.

When you create an internal style sheet, Dreamweaver adds a pair of <style> tags to the head of the page. The opening <style> tag tells a web browser that the following information isn't HTML—it's CSS code. When the browser encounters the closing </style> tag, it knows that it's at the end of the style definition.

Within the <style> tag, you see one or more styles (reminder: in CSS-speak, styles are also called rules). An HTML tag style for the Heading 1 tag (<h1>), for example, might look like this:

```
h1 {
    font-size: 24px;
    color: #003399;
}
```

The first part—h1—is called a *selector*, and it identifies the style's target. In this case, a browser applies this style wherever an <h1> (Heading 1) tag appears in a web page's code.

The information between the braces—{}—defines the formatting the browser should apply. The preceding code contains two formatting instructions for the <h1> tag. Each is called a *declaration* and is composed of a *property* and a *value*. For instance, *font-size: 24px* is one declaration, which has a property of *font-size* and a value of *24px*. In other words, this rule

tells a browser that it should make the text inside an <h1> tag 24 pixels tall. The second declaration makes a browser display the text of all <h1> tags in the color #003399.

A class style looks just like a tag style, except that instead of the selector being a tag, it's a name *you* supply, preceded by a dot, like this:

```
.company {
    font-size: 24px;
    color: #003399;
}
```

Styles in an external style sheet look exactly the same; the only difference is that external style sheets are separate files whose names end in .css, they don't include the <style> tags and must not include any HTML. You link an external style sheet to a web page using the <link> tag. For example, to link a style sheet named *styles.css* to a web page, you could add this HTML code to the page:

```
<link href="styles.css" rel="stylesheet"
type="text/css">
```

In Dreamweaver, you can easily get a look at the style definitions in an external style sheet:

Near the top of the document window, in the list of related files, just click the CSS file's name (see Figure 1-2).

On the other hand, if you apply a class style to a selection that isn't a tag—like a single word that you double-click—Dreamweaver wraps that selection within a <span> tag, like this: <span class="company">Cafe Soylent Green</span>. This tag, in other words, applies a class to a *span* of text that doesn't have its own tag.

■ APPLYING A CLASS STYLE TO OBJECTS

To apply a class style to an object (like an image or a table), start by selecting the object. As always, the Tag Selector at the bottom of the document window is a great way to select a tag. Then, at the top right of the Property Inspector, use the Class drop-down menu to select the style name.

> **NOTE** You can apply any class style to any element, although doing so doesn't always make sense. If you format a graphic with a style that specifies bold, red Courier type, it doesn't look any different.

■ OTHER CLASS STYLING OPTIONS

You can also apply a class style by selecting whatever element you want to style, choosing Format→CSS Styles, and then, from the submenu, selecting the style. Or you can right-click (Control-click) the style's name in the CSS Styles panel, and then, from the pop-up menu, choose Apply. Finally, you can also apply a class from the document window's Tag Selector, as shown in Figure 3-6.

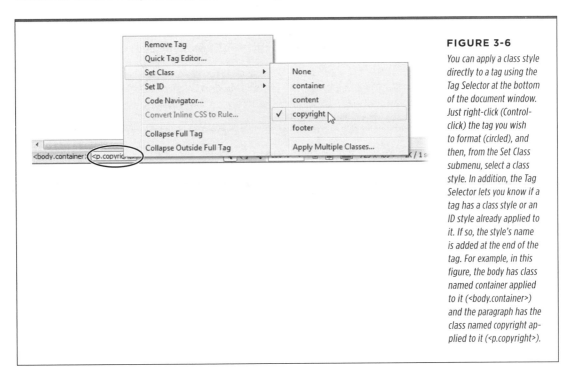

FIGURE 3-6

You can apply a class style directly to a tag using the Tag Selector at the bottom of the document window. Just right-click (Control-click) the tag you wish to format (circled), and then, from the Set Class submenu, select a class style. In addition, the Tag Selector lets you know if a tag has a class style or an ID style already applied to it. If so, the style's name is added at the end of the tag. For example, in this figure, the body has class named container applied to it (<body.container>) and the paragraph has the class named copyright applied to it (<p.copyright>).

Applying Multiple Classes

The rules of HTML and CSS let you apply more than one class to a single tag. This technique is handy when you have page elements that share similar formatting but have their own style requirements as well. For example, say you want to add a border and colorful background to a set of images in a portfolio (you'll learn how to add borders and backgrounds on page 260 and 262). You could then create a class style (for example .portfolioImage) with those properties.

However, some of the photos will appear on the right side of the page and others on the left (you'll learn how to do this on page 257). In other words, you'll format the images similarly, but position them differently. In this case, you can create two new class styles (.imageLeft and .imageRight, for instance). You could then apply both the .portfolioImage and the .imageLeft classes to images you want to have a border and align to the left, and add the .portfolioImage and .imageRight classes to the other images.

Using multiple classes is increasingly common in web design, but until CS6, the only way you could do this in Dreamweaver was to type the multiple classes in code view. Fortunately, Dreamweaver CS6 provides a simple way to use the Property Inspector to add more than one class to a tag:

1. **Select the element you want to add more than one class to.**

   This could be a headline, a paragraph, an image, a <div> tag (page 438), and so on.

2. **From the Property Inspector, click the Class menu and select Apply Multiple Classes.**

   This option is available both in the HTML and CSS modes of the Property Inspector. In either case, the Multiclass Selection window appears (see Figure 3-7).

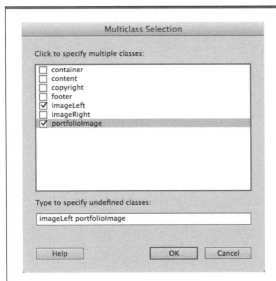

FIGURE 3-7

Dreamweaver CS6's new Multiclass Selection window lets you apply more than one class to an element. You can choose from a list of classes that already exist in a style sheet by turning on the appropriate checkbox, or simply type the class names (separated by spaces) in the text field at the bottom.

NOTE You can also apply multiple classes to a tag using the Tag Selector at the bottom of the document window. Right-click (option-click) on the tag and choose Set Class→Apply Multiple Classes (see Figure 3-6).

3. **In the Multiclass Selection window, select the classes you wish to apply to the selected tag.**

   Only CSS classes you already added to a page's internal or external style sheet appear in this window, so it's best to create the CSS styles before applying the class names to the HTML tag. However, you can still apply the names of classes even if they don't appear in a page's style sheet. Type each class name into the text field at the bottom of the window, just add a space between each class name and don't include the period that precedes a class in a style sheet. For example, portfolioImage imageLeft is correct, but .portfolio.imageLeft is not.

4. **Click OK to close the Multiclass Selection window and apply the multiple classes to the tag.**

    Under the hood, Dreamweaver simply adds the class names to the HTML tag: for example, <img class="portfolioImage imageLeft" src="photo.jpg">.

You can always remove or add additional classes by selecting the tag again and choosing Apply Multiple Classes from the Property Inspector's Class menu. If you deselect all the class names, Dreamweaver removes the class attribute from the tag. Alternatively, you can use the technique described next to remove all the classes from a tag.

Removing a Class Style

To remove a class style from text, select the text and then, from the Property Inspector, choose None from the Class menu (HTML mode) or <Remove Class> from the Targeted Rule menu (CSS mode). To remove a class style from another object (like an image), select the object, and then, from the Property Inspector's Class menu, choose None. You can also choose Format→CSS Styles→None to remove a style from any selection (even non-text elements like images or tables).

TIP If you applied a class style to a selection of text, you don't have to select *all* the text to remove the style. Just click anywhere inside it, and then select None from the Property Inspector's Class menu or <Remove Class> from the Targeted Rule menu. Dreamweaver is smart enough to realize that you want to remove the style applied to the text. (If you applied the style to a tag, then Dreamweaver removes the Class property. If you applied the style using the <span> tag, Dreamweaver removes the <span> tag.)

You can't, however, remove *tag* styles from HTML tags. For example, suppose you redefined the <h2> tag using the steps outlined on page 125. If your page has three Heading 2 (<h2>) paragraphs, and you want the third heading to have a different style from the other two, you can't simply "remove" the <h2> style from the third heading. You need to create a new class style with all the formatting options you want for that heading, and then apply it directly to this particular <h2> tag. (By the magic of CSS, the class formatting options override any existing tag style options— see page 391 for more on this sleight of hand.)

Applying IDs to a Tag

As discussed on page 124, ID styles aren't used as much as they used to be. However, if you're working on an older site with previously created ID styles, you can still apply them in Dreamweaver. To apply an ID to text, just select the text and use the ID menu in the HTML mode of the Property Inspector (see Figure 3-5, top). Since you can apply each ID name only once per page, the menu lists only unassigned IDs—IDs that exist in your style sheet but that you haven't applied to a tag on the current page.

For non-text elements, select the element, and then, in the Property Inspector, type the iD name into the ID field. (For some elements, the ID field is unlabeled, but you can always find it on the far left of the Property Inspector.)

You can also use the Tag Selector as outlined in Figure 3-6. Just use the Set ID menu in the contextual menu that appears when you right-click (Control-click) the tag.

NOTE The Tag Selector tells you whether you applied an ID to a tag by including the # symbol with the ID name. For example, *body#catalog* indicates that the <body> tag has an ID named *catalog* applied to it.

Whenever you apply an ID to a tag, Dreamweaver adds a bit of HTML to your page. For instance, an ID style named *#copyright* applied to a paragraph looks like this in the HTML: <p id="copyright"> (this is just like the "class" property that's added when you use class styles, as described on page 133).

To remove an ID from a text element, select the text, and then, from the Property Inspector's ID menu, select None. For non-text elements, select the element, and then, in the Property Inspector's ID field, delete the ID name.

Linking to an External Style Sheet

Whenever you create an external style sheet while adding a style to a web page, Dreamweaver automatically links it to the current document. To use its styles in a different web page, you must *attach* it to the page.

To do so, open the web page to which you want to add the style sheet. Then, in the CSS Styles panel, click the Attach External Style Sheet button (see Figure 3-1). (If the CSS Styles panel isn't open, choose Window→CSS Styles or press Shift-F11.)

TIP You can also use the Property Inspector to attach a style sheet. Just select "Attach Style Sheet" from the Class menu in HTML mode (see Figure 3-5, top).

The Attach External Style Sheet window appears (see Figure 3-8). Click Browse. In the Select Style Sheet File dialog box that appears, navigate to and double-click the CSS (.css) file you want to attach to the document. If the style sheet you select is outside the current site—for example, it's in another of your websites—Dreamweaver offers to copy the style sheet file into your site's root folder; click Yes.

The Attach External Style Sheet window provides two other options: how to attach the style sheet and what type of "media" you want the styles to apply to. The "media" setting is optional and dictates when Dreamweaver applies the styles. For example, you can use one set of styles when you print a page and another set when a browser displays the page. You'll find in-depth information on media types and how to use them on page 399. If you simply want to attach a style sheet to a page so that the styles always apply (when viewed on a screen *or* printed out), leave the Media option blank.

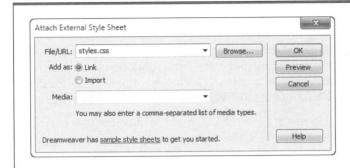

FIGURE 3-8

*Adding styles from an external style sheet is as
simple as browsing for the file and then clicking OK.
Choosing a media type is optional.*

When you attach an external style sheet, you can either "link" it or "import" it. These two choices are nearly identical; they're simply two different ways to attach an external style sheet to a web page. The method preferred by the pros, linking to the style sheet, is also Dreamweaver's suggested choice. Save yourself an extra click and go with the link option.

TIP You can preview the effect of the style sheet on your page by clicking the Preview button in the Attach External Style Sheet window.

After choosing your options, click OK, and Dreamweaver adds the necessary HTML to the head of the web page and automatically formats any tags in the document according to the style sheet's tag styles. In Design view, you see the formatting changes take place immediately after you attach the style sheet.

If the style sheet contains *class* styles, on the other hand, you don't see their formatting effects until you apply the class to an element on the page, as described on page 132.

■ Manipulating Styles

As with anything in Dreamweaver, styles are easy enough to edit, delete, or duplicate; all you need is a map of the terrain.

Editing Styles

While building a website, you almost always continually refine your designs. That chartreuse color you assigned to the background of your pages may have looked great at 2 a.m., but it loses something in the light of day.

Fortunately, one of CSS's greatest selling points is how easy it is to update a website's formatting.

NOTE Although this section focuses mainly on how to style your text, you also use CSS styles to add background colors, background images, borders, and to accurately position elements on a page. The next few chapters show you how to style links, images, tables, forms, and other page elements with CSS.

Dreamweaver provides many ways to edit styles:

- In the CSS Styles panel, select a style and then click the Edit Style button to open the Rule Definition window (this is the same window you used to create the style). Make your changes, and then click OK to return to the document window. Dreamweaver reformats the page to reflect your changes.

- Double-click the name of a style in the CSS panel to open the Rule Definition window. Actually, depending on a preference setting—or a setting someone else may have tweaked while using your computer—double-clicking a style in the CSS panel may display the—eek!—raw CSS code in Code view. To change this behavior, open the Preferences window (Ctrl+U [⌘-U]), click the CSS Styles category, and then select the "Edit using CSS dialog" button.

- In the CSS Styles panel, right-click (Control-click) the name of a style, and then, from the shortcut menu, choose Edit, which also opens the Rule Definition window. Make your changes to the style and then click OK to return to the document window.

FREQUENTLY ASKED QUESTION

When Formatting Disappears

Sometimes when I copy text from one web page and paste it into another, all the formatting disappears. What's going on?

When you use Cascading Style Sheets, keep in mind that the actual style information is stored either in the <head> of a web page (for internal style sheets) or in a separate CSS file (an external style sheet). If a page includes an internal style sheet, when you copy text, graphics, or other page elements, Dreamweaver copies those elements and any class or ID style definitions that content uses. When you paste the HTML into another page, Dreamweaver writes the styles into the <head> of that page. This feature can save you some time, but it doesn't solve all your woes. It doesn't, for example, copy any *tag styles* you created, nor does it carry over most advanced styles (see page 375 for more on advanced styles). So if you copy and paste some text—say, an <h1> tag styled with an h1 tag style—the <h1> tag and its contents end up in the other page, but the style information doesn't.

In addition, if you copy and paste text from a page that uses an external style sheet, the styles themselves don't go along for the ride. So if you copy a paragraph that has a class style applied to it and paste it into another document, the code in the paragraph gets pasted (<p class="company"> for instance), but the actual *.company* style, with all its formatting properties, doesn't.

The best solution is to use a common external style sheet that you attach to all the pages on your site. That way, when you copy and paste HTML, all the pages share the same styles and formatting. So in the preceding example, if you copy a paragraph that includes a class style—class="company"—into another page that shares the same style sheet, the paragraphs look the same on both pages. See page 128 for more on how to create an uber site-wide external style sheet.

NOTE   The properties pane in the CSS Styles panel offers yet another, faster way to edit a style. This advanced technique requires a bit of CSS savvy and is discussed on page 382.

Deleting a Style

At some point, you may find you created a style that you don't need after all. Maybe you redefined the HTML <code> tag and realized that you never use it. You don't need to keep it around, taking up precious space in the style sheet.

To delete a style, make sure you have the CSS Styles panel open (Window→CSS Styles) and the All button highlighted. Click the name of the style you wish to delete, and then press your keyboard's Delete key (you can also click the Trash can icon at the bottom of the panel). You can remove all the styles in an internal style sheet (as well as the style sheet itself) by selecting the style sheet—indicated by "<style>" in the CSS Styles panel—and pressing Delete (or clicking the Trash can icon). If you trash an *external* style sheet, however, you merely unlink it from the current document without actually deleting the .css file.

Unfortunately, deleting a class style *doesn't* delete any references to the style in your site's pages. For example, if you created a style called *.company* and applied it throughout your site, and you then delete that style from the style sheet, Dreamweaver doesn't remove the <span> tags or class properties that refer to the style. Your pages are still littered with orphaned code like this—<span class="company">Cafe Soylent Green</span>—even though the text loses its styling. (See how to solve this problem using Dreamweaver's powerful "Find and Replace" tool in Chapter 20.)

Renaming a Class Style

You can rename any style by selecting it in the CSS Styles panel, pausing a second, and then clicking the name again. This makes the name editable, at which point you can type a new name in its place. Of course, if you change a style named *p* to a style named *h1*, you've essentially removed the style for the <p> tag and added an <h1> style to the style sheet—in other words, all the paragraphs in your pages would lose their formatting, and all <h1> tags would suddenly change appearance. Alternatively, you could open the .css file in Code view and then edit the name. However, when it comes to class styles, just changing the name doesn't do much good if you already applied the style throughout your site. The *old* class name still appears in the HTML everywhere you used it.

When Undo Won't Do

Sometimes when I edit a style—say, to change a font color—I can undo that change. But sometimes, I'm unable to undo changes I make to a style. What gives?

You can undo only changes made to a document that's currently open in the document window. If you're working on an HTML file in either Design, Code, or Split view, you can undo any changes you make to that file. For example, say you add an internal style sheet to a document. If you edit one of those styles, Dreamweaver lets you undo those changes. Because the styles in an internal style sheet are a part of the web page you're working on, choosing Edit→Undo undoes the last change you made.

However, if you're working on a web page with an external style sheet, you're actually working on two *different* files at the same time—the web page you're building and the style sheet file in which you add, delete, or edit styles. So if you're designing a web page and edit a style in the external style sheet, you're actually making a change to the style sheet file. In this case,

choosing Edit→Undo undoes only the last change made to the *web page.* If you want to undo the change you made to the external style sheet, you need to use Dreamweaver's related files feature. The name of the external style sheet appears on the Related Files toolbar, which appears below the title of the web page file; click the file's name to move to its code, and then choose Edit→Undo. Click the Source Code button to return to your web page (you'll learn more about the Related Files toolbar on page 353).

If you're in Split view with the HTML code displayed on the left, and the Design view on the right, you can click the .css file in the Related Files toolbar and see the CSS code for that .css file in the left. At this point, the undo command works on whichever document the cursor is inside—in other words, click in the CSS code on the left-hand .css file and Edit→Undo undoes the last change to the CSS; click in the Design view on the right hand side and Edit→Undo undoes the last change to the HTML of the web page.

What you really need to do is rename the class style, and *then* perform a find-and-replace operation to change the name wherever it appears in your site. Dreamweaver includes a handy tool to simplify this process.

To rename a class style:

1. **In the Property Inspector, choose Rename from the Class menu (on the HTML tab of the Property Inspector).**

   The Rename Style window appears (Figure 3-9).

FIGURE 3-9

The Rename Style tool is a fast and easy way to change the name of a class style even if you used the style hundreds of times throughout your site.

TIP You can also right-click (Control-click) a style name in the CSS styles panel and choose Rename Class to open the Rename Class window.

2. **From the top drop-down menu, choose the name of the style you want to rename.**

   This menu lists all the class styles in the page's style sheets, both internal and external.

3. **In the "New name" box, type the new style name.**

   You must follow the same rules for naming class styles as described on page 128. But, just as when creating a new class in Dreamweaver's New CSS Rule window, you don't need to precede the name with a period.

4. **Click OK.**

   If the style whose name you're changing is an internal style, Dreamweaver makes the change. Your job is done.

   If the style belongs to an external style sheet, however, Dreamweaver warns you that other pages on the site may also use this style. To successfully rename the style, you have to use Dreamweaver's "Find and Replace" tool to search the site and update all the pages that use the old style name. In that case, continue to step 5.

5. **If you get cold feet, click Cancel to call off the name change, or click Yes to open the "Find and Replace" window, where you should click Replace All.**

   One last warning appears, reminding you that you can't undo the find-and-replace.

NOTE If you click No in the warning box that appears after step 5, Dreamweaver still renames the style in the external style sheet, but it doesn't update your pages.

6. **Click Yes.**

   Dreamweaver goes through each page of your site, dutifully updating the name of the style everywhere it appears.

NOTE Dreamweaver doesn't supply a similar tool for renaming ID styles. While you can change the name of an ID style in the CSS styles panel—select the style, pause, then click it's name for editing—Dreamweaver doesn't automatically update the HTML that references that style. You can use Dreamweaver's find-and-replace feature (Chapter 22) to do that.

Duplicating a Style

Dreamweaver makes it easy to duplicate a CSS style, which is handy when you want to use the formatting options from one style as a starting-off point for a new style.

You can duplicate a style two ways. The easiest is to open the CSS Styles panel (Window→CSS Styles), right-click (Control-click) the name of the style you want to duplicate, and then, from the shortcut menu, choose Duplicate.

The Duplicate CSS Rule window appears (Figure 3-10), where you can give the duplicated style a new name, reassign its Type setting, use the "Define in" menu to move it from an internal to an external style sheet, and so on.

When you click OK, Dreamweaver adds the duplicate style to the page or external style sheet. You can then edit the new style just as you would any other, as described above.

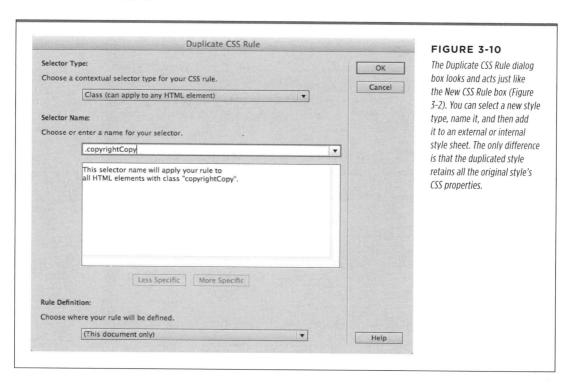

FIGURE 3-10

The Duplicate CSS Rule dialog box looks and acts just like the New CSS Rule box (Figure 3-2). You can select a new style type, name it, and then add it to an external or internal style sheet. The only difference is that the duplicated style retains all the original style's CSS properties.

■ Text Formatting with CSS

One of the best uses of Cascading Style Sheets is to convert the drab appearance of HTML text into lavishly designed prose. Or, if you like a somber, corporate style, CSS can help with that, too. Whatever your design inclination, you can improve the look of your web text using CSS.

You can define six text-related CSS properties using the CSS mode of the Property Inspector, or use the full-blown CSS Rule Definition window to deploy more than 64 CSS properties. The most commonly used properties for text are stored in the Type and Block categories, while the List category offers several options for formatting bulleted and numbered lists.

NOTE You can apply nearly every CSS property to text. For example, you can use the border property to underline text and the margin property to remove space between paragraphs. You'll find those properties and others not listed in the Type or Block categories introduced later in this book (you don't want to blow your circuits too quickly). For now, you'll learn the most type-centric properties.

Choosing a Font

There are two ways to include fonts on a web page: The traditional method uses fonts installed on a visitor's computer, while a newer technique lets you use specially prepared fonts—called *web fonts*. Dreamweaver CS6 provides a new tool for working with web fonts, which you'll learn about on page 146.

The traditional method relies on fonts already installed on a visitor's computer. This mimics the way you use fonts in a word processor. For example, as you craft a document in Microsoft Word, you can select any font on your computer, even that fancy font you just bought from a small font company in Nome, Alaska. Unfortunately, when you email that document to your boss, she won't see the same design when she opens the document on her computer. That's because she doesn't own the same fonts. She'll see some default font—Times, perhaps. Fonts show up in a distributed document only if each recipient has the same fonts installed.

Unless you use web fonts, you're in the same predicament when crafting web pages. You're free, as a web designer, to specify any font you want in a web page, but it doesn't show up on a viewer's computer unless she's installed the same font on her system. If she hasn't, her browser displays your text in a default font, which is usually some version of Times, Arial, or Courier.

You can deal with this dilemma several ways. One is to convert your text into graphic images—unfortunately that process takes time and forces your web visitors to download byte-hogging images just to read your web page. Another is to specify the font you'd *like* to use; if your visitor's computer has the specified font, that's what she'll see. You can specify secondary or tertiary fonts, too, in case the preferred font isn't available. In fact, Dreamweaver offers prepackaged lists of such "first choice, second choice, third choice" fonts, as you'll find out in the following section.

■ APPLYING FONT FORMATTING

To use a font, you select it from either the Font menu in the Property Inspector's CSS mode or from the CSS Rule Definition window's Font-family menu. In either case, you're actually either creating a new style (as described on page 125) or updating an existing one.

You'll soon discover that Dreamweaver's font menus aren't quite what you're used to. When you apply a font to text, you choose from one of the prepackaged lists just described; a typical choice is something like "Arial, Helvetica, sans-serif." In other words, you don't just choose a single font, such as Helvetica.

If the first font isn't installed on your visitor's computer, the browser looks down the list until it finds a font that is. Different operating systems use different fonts, so these lists include one font that's common on Windows PCs and another, similar-looking font that's common on Macs. Arial, for instance, is found on all Windows machines, while Macs offer the similar Helvetica font.

That's it. You've just selected one of Dreamweaver's predefined font lists, and any text the CSS style formats will use the font you selected. If you'd like a greater degree of control over the fonts your page displays, read on.

> **NOTE** Technically, you can specify any number of fallback fonts in one of these lists, not just first, second, and third choices. Your list can range anywhere from just a single font to a long list arranged in order of preference.

UP TO SPEED

Knowing Your Font Types

You can choose from literally tens of thousands of fonts to express your every thought, from bookish, staid, and classical typefaces to rounded, cartoonish squiggles.

Most fonts are divided into two categories: serif and sans-serif. Graphic designers often use serif fonts for long passages of text, as it's widely believed that serifs—small decorative strokes ("hands" and "feet") at the extremities of a letter's main outline—gently lead the eye from letter to letter, making the text easier to read. Examples of serif fonts include Times, Times New Roman, Georgia, and Minion.

Designers often use sans-serif ("without serifs") fonts for headlines, thanks to their clean and simple appearance. Arial, Helvetica, Verdana, and Formata are all sans-serif fonts (you're reading Gotham right now). Some people believe that you should use only sans-serif fonts on web pages because they think the delicate decorative strokes of serif fonts don't display well on the coarse resolution of a computer screen. This is an aesthetic judgment, so you should feel free to pick the fonts you think look (and read) the best.

There are other classes of fonts as well, such as monospace fonts like Courier, in which all letters are the same width (useful for aligning text into columns.) This type of font resembles type from a typewriter (remember those mechanical beasts?). Script fonts resemble handwriting, and they're usually bold, fun, and difficult to read at small font sizes. However, the different operating systems have few of these types of fonts in common, so if you do want to use a fancy-looking font, you'll have to use a web font (described below).

Using Web Fonts

A newer technique for using fonts on the web lets visitors download the fonts they need, either from your site or from another site (Google is one example) that has those fonts available. This approach, using what are known as "web fonts," lets you use any font you want, but a visitor has to download it first.

This technique may sound like the answer to a designer's dreams, but there are a few drawbacks. First, you need different types of fonts for different browsers (for example, Internet Explorer 8 and earlier require a special font format called .eot, while Safari on many iPhones requires an SVG font). Creating these font types isn't easy. Second, font files can be large, forcing visitors to wait for lengthy downloads.

However, web fonts are an exciting addition to a web designer's toolbag, since using distinctive fonts can help set off your site from the pack. Best of all, Dreamweaver CS6 now includes a tool that makes using web fonts easy.

■ MANAGING WEB FONTS

Using web fonts is a two-step process in Dreamweaver. First, you have to add your web fonts to Dreamweaver using the Web Fonts manager window. This step simply registers the fonts with Dreamweaver, so that you can use them on any site you create. Second, once you add a web font to Dreamweaver, you can then add it to any CSS style you create; the process is pretty much the same as when you pick one of the font sets ("Arial, Helvetica, sans-serif," for example) that Dreamweaver already displays in the font menu. However, there are some subtle differences, as described on page 150. When you add a web font to a style sheet, Dreamweaver actually makes a *copy* of the font files and makes them available to the site you're working on (see page 152).

To begin using web fonts, you first need to get some fonts and then add them to Dreamweaver, like this:

1. **Get a font.**

   Unfortunately, you can't just use any old font on your computer. First, there's a legal reason: The companies that create fonts don't always want you to use them on the web. Because web fonts are literally just sitting on your web server, someone could download the font and start using it free of charge. Basically, these companies are worried about software piracy and losing sales.

   Second, fonts come in different formats for different browsers. For example, Internet Explorer 8 and earlier only support a special format called EOT (Embedded OpenType). EOT was developed by Microsoft as a way to protect fonts from piracy. Unfortunately, no other browser can read an EOT font. Firefox, on the other hand supports both WOFF (Web Open Font Format) and TTF (TrueType Font) fonts. And iOS devices (iPhones, iPads, and iPod Touches) running version 4.1 or earlier of the iOS operating system require an SVG (Scalable Vector Graphic) format. EOT, WOFF, TTF, SVG, oh my!

   The easiest way to get fonts that are both free to use and come in these different formats is from a website named, strangely enough, FontSquirrel.com. In fact, this site offers hundreds of free "@font-face kits" (@font-face is the CSS command you use to add a font from your server to a style sheet). These kits include fonts in EOT, TTF, SVG, and WOFF formats. Just visit *www.fontsquirrel .com/fontface*, browse through the collection, and then click "Get Kit" next to any font you like. Doing this downloads a folder containing the necessary font files. You can save these anywhere on your computer.

> **TIP** If you don't find a font you like among FontSquirrel's collection, you can use the site's @font-face Generator to create the required font formats. Just visit *www.fontsquirrel.com/fontface/generator*, click the Add Fonts button, and select a TrueType font (.ttf file) from your computer. Turn on the "Yes, the fonts I'm uploading are legally eligible for web embedding" checkbox and click the Download Your Kit button. In a few moments, you'll have a folder with your font in the four web font formats.

2. **In Dreamweaver, choose Modify→Web Fonts.**

   The Web Fonts manager window appears (see Figure 3-11). You use this window to add your downloaded web fonts.

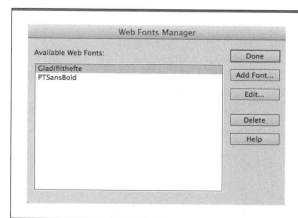

FIGURE 3-11

The Web Fonts Manager window lets you select web fonts from your computer to use on your web sites. At first, this window will be empty, but as you add web fonts, the window displays their names. In this example, the fonts PTSansBold and Gladifilthefte (yes, that's really the font's name) have already been added.

3. **Click the Add Font button.**

   The Add Web Font window appears (Figure 3-12).

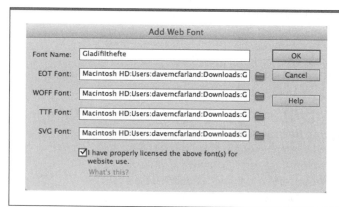

FIGURE 3-12

You must turn on the "I have properly licensed the above font(s)" checkbox to add web fonts to Dreamweaver. Since you can't legally put just any font you own on the Web, turning on this box absolves Adobe of any legal responsibility ("I'm Adobe's Legal Counsel, and I approve this message.") Fortunately, fonts you download from FontSquirrel.com site are free for web use.

4. **Type a name for the font in the Font Name box.**

This step is optional; if you leave it blank, Dreamweaver names the font using the name from the font file you select (as described in the next step). However, when you download web fonts from FontSquirrel.com, you'll notice that some fonts have strange, long, or difficult-to-translate names; in these cases, it's often a good idea to provide a name of your choosing. In addition, if the font is bold or italic, or bold and italic, you should add that as part of the name. For example, the font PT Sans (available from *www.fontsquirrel.com/fonts/PT-Sans*) comes in a variety of formats—bold, italic, narrow, and so on—with hard-to-decipher names like PT75F. It's better to supply a recognizable name, like PTSansBold for the bold version of the font, PTSansItalic for the italic version, and so on.

5. **Click the folder icon to the right of the EOT Font text field.**

The Open dialog box appears—this is just a basic file-selection dialog box. You simply need to select the EOT font.

6. **Navigate to the folder containing the EOT font you wish to use; select the file and click the Open button.**

Dreamweaver adds the path to the EOT file in the EOT Font text field. In addition, if the folder containing the selected EOT file also contains WOFF, TrueType, and SVG versions of the font, Dreamweaver automatically fills in the those paths as well. If, for some reason, you store the WOFF, TrueType, or SVG versions in another folder, you'll have to repeat this step to select each of them (in other words, just keep the different versions of a font together in the same folder on your computer).

> **NOTE** You don't need to store the web font files in your site when you add them to the Web Fonts manager. In fact, the Web Fonts manager window handles web fonts for all your sites. Once you add a web font, Dreamweaver makes it available to any page in any site you work on. When you add the font to a style as described below, Dreamweaver copies those font files to your site.

7. **Turn on the "I have properly licensed the above fonts" checkbox and click the OK button.**

The Add Web Font window closes, returning you to the Web Fonts Manager window. You can add additional web fonts by clicking the Add Font button and repeating the above steps.

8. **In the Web Fonts Manager window, click Done.**

You've added the font to Dreamweaver, and it's now available to any CSS style as described next.

NOTE When you add web fonts, Dreamweaver makes copies of the font files and places them in your Dreamweaver configuration folder. This means that if you move or even delete the original font files from your computer Dreamweaver still has access to them. To remove *these* files, use the Manage Web Fonts window to delete them, and Dreamweaver removes the fonts from its configuration folder. (If you're curious about where the configuration folder lives, see the box on page 907.)

9. **If you later decide that you wish to delete or edit (to change the font's name, for example) a web font from Dreamweaver, just choose Modify→Web Fonts to open the Manage Web Fonts window again.** Select the font and click Edit, which returns you to the Edit Web Font window (which looks just like the Add Web Font window in Figure 3-12). You can then change the font's name or choose different font files. Note that this has no effect on any site that already uses the web font; for example, it won't change the font name in any style sheet that specifies that font.

10. **To remove the web fonts from Dreamweaver, select the font name from the Manage Web Fonts window and click Delete.** Note that this doesn't delete the font files from your computer, nor does it remove the font from any site that uses this font.

TIP If you don't like the fonts available at FontSquirrel.com, you'll find over 500 free fonts at Google's Web Fonts website, *http://www.google.com/webfonts*. Google provides another way to use web fonts, which involves adding a link to a CSS file on Google's computers. You can find instructions at *http://tinyurl.com/7dd6oed*. Alternatively, you can download the font from Google in TrueType format and use FontSquirrel's @font-face Generator (*www.fontsquirrel.com/fontface/generator*) to create EOT, WOFF, and SVG versions; you can then use those fonts using Dreamweaver's web fonts manager.

■ USING A WEB FONT

Once you add a web font to Dreamweaver, you can use it in CSS styles.

1. **Create a new style as described on page 125.**

   For example, on the CSS Styles panel click the New Style button (see Figure 3-1). Then choose the selector type, name the style, and choose where you wish to store the CSS.

2. **Select the Type category of the "CSS Rule definition" window, and choose the web font from the Font-family menu (Figure 3-13).**

   All the web fonts you added to Dreamweaver appear below the main Dreamweaver font list. Dreamweaver only lists one font there, the web font you selected. As mentioned on page 145, it's a good idea to include a few back-up fonts in case your visitor can't access the first font listed. In the case of web fonts, that could happen if your guest's browser doesn't support web fonts or if it couldn't download the font for some reason.

NOTE Web fonts you add to Dreamweaver also appear in the font menu in the Property Inspector, discussed on page 130.

3. **Choose "normal" from the font-weight menu and "normal" from the font-style menu.**

   This step can help make your text look better. Some browsers will attempt to make a font look "bold" or "italic" artificially—that is, make the font look thicker if it's a headline or the font-weight property is set to bold, or slant the text to make it look italicized. For example, if you pick a bold web font and apply it to a headline, Firefox tries to make the font even bolder (because headline tags are normally bold) by thickening its outline. The result looks awful.

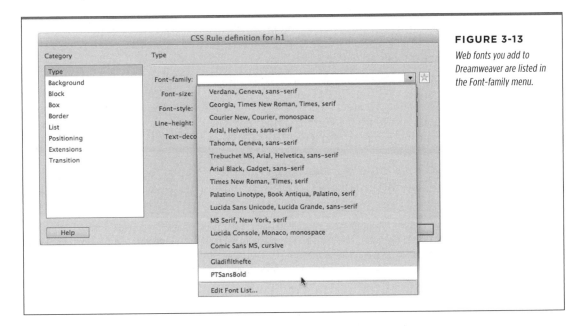

FIGURE 3-13

Web fonts you add to Dreamweaver are listed in the Font-family menu.

NOTE One downside to web fonts is that web browsers won't automatically pick an italic or bold version of the font if you italicize or bold the text. For example, say you add two web fonts, one the regular version of the font, the other a bolded version. If you apply the regular version to a paragraph, then select a word in that paragraph and click the B button in the Property Inspector to make that text bold, the web browser won't use the bold version of the font—it still uses the regular version (the results vary from browser to browser, as some browsers, like Internet Explorer, will make the text artificially bold, and others, like Chrome, will leave the text in its regular unbolded state). One solution is to create a tag style for the <strong> tag and assign the bold version of the web font to it.

4. When you finish setting all the properties for the new style, click OK.

If this is the first time you've used the web font on the current site, Dreamweaver does a couple of things. First, it creates a folder named webfonts in your site's local root folder (page 46). Inside that folder, Dreamweaver puts another folder named after the font name—PTSansBold, for example. Dreamweaver puts all the web font files (the .eot, woff, .ttf, and .svg fonts) in that folder, along with an external style sheet named *stylesheet.css*. That style sheet contains the CSS required to correctly include the web fonts on a page.

Finally, Dreamweaver attaches that external style sheet to the current page (if that page uses an internal style sheet) or to another external style sheet (if the page uses an external style sheet). This last part is a little confusing. For some reason, the Dreamweaver engineers decided to put the CSS for each web font you use into its own folder and then attach that style sheet to your main style sheet using what's called an @import directive. The code in the page's style sheet looks something like this:

```
@import url("../webfonts/PTSansBold/stylesheet.css");
```

The @import directive is simply a way of importing the contents of an external style sheet into the current style sheet. The important thing to keep in mind is that the contents of the webfonts folder in your site are critical—don't delete the folder or you'll erase the fonts from your site. And, when it's time to upload your site to the web (described in Chapter 17), don't forget to place this folder on your web server.

> **TIP** Normally, when you use a web font, Dreamweaver copies the font files to a folder named webfonts in your site's local root folder. If you want Dreamweaver to put those fonts in another folder on your site, choose Site→Manage Sites. In the Manage Sites window, select your site, and click the Edit button (the pencil icon) to open the Site Setup window. Expand the Advanced Settings list, click the Web Fonts category, and click the folder icon to navigate to and select your site's web fonts.

Creating Custom Font Lists

Dreamweaver CS6 comes with 13 preset font lists, which incorporate fonts common to both Windows and Mac PCs. However, you might want to customize this list by adding additional fonts or creating font lists that mix web fonts and the fonts common to all operating systems.

Here's how you create a new "first choice, second choice, third choice" font list.

1. Open the Edit Font List dialog box.

From the Property Inspector's Font menu (visible only in CSS mode), choose Edit Font List, or choose Format→Font→Edit Font List. Either way, the Edit Font List dialog box appears (Figure 3-14).

2. **Select a first-choice font from the "Available fonts" list, or type in the font name.**

Dreamweaver lists all the fonts installed on your computer in the "Available fonts" menu. Simply click to select the font you wish to add.

Alternatively, type a font's name into the box that appears directly below the list of available fonts—a handy trick if you want to include a font that isn't installed on your computer (a Windows font when you're working on a Mac, for example).

TIP You can add a web font when you create a custom font list—the web fonts you add to Dreamweaver appear at the bottom of the "Available fonts" menu in the Edit Font List window.

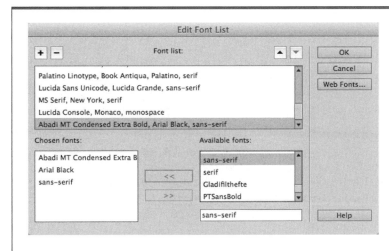

FIGURE 3-14

In the Edit Font List dialog box, not only can you create your own font lists, but you can also edit, remove, or reorder the predefined lists. When you click a list in the "Font list" menu, the "first choice, second choice, third choice" fonts appear in the lower-left corner. To remove a font from that list, click the font name, and then click the >> button. To add a font to the list, select a font in the "Available fonts" menu, and then click the << button. Finally, to reorder the font lists that appear in the Property Inspector, click the CSS Rule Definition window's Font menu, or Format→Font menu, and then click the arrow keys near the upper-right corner of the dialog box.

3. **Add the font you just highlighted to your new, custom font list by clicking the << button (or just double-clicking the font name).**

Your first-choice font appears in the "Chosen fonts" list.

4. **Repeat steps 2 and 3 for each font you want to include in your custom list.**

The order in which you add the fonts is the order in which they appear on the list. These become the "first choice, second choice, third choice" fonts.

Unfortunately, there's no way to change the order of the fonts once you add them. So if you accidentally put the fonts in the wrong order, you must delete the list by clicking the minus-sign (-) button in the upper-left corner of the dialog box and start over.

5. **Add a generic font family.**

This last step isn't strictly necessary, but it's a good idea. If your visitor is some kind of anti-font radical whose computer doesn't have *any* of the fonts you chose, his browser will substitute the generic font family you specify here.

Generic fonts are listed at the bottom of the list of "Available fonts" and include "cursive," "fantasy," "monospace," "sans-serif," and "serif." On most systems, the monospaced font is Courier, the serif font is Times, and the sans-serif font is Arial or Helvetica. Select a generic font that's similar in appearance to the fonts in your list. For instance, choose "sans-serif" if your list consists of sans-serif fonts like Helvetica or Arial; choose "serif" if you specified fonts like Times or Georgia; or choose "monospace" for a font like Courier.

6. **Click OK.**

Your new font package appears in the Property Inspector's Font menu, ready to apply.

Changing the Font Size

Varying the sizes of fonts on a web page is one way to direct a viewer's attention. Large type screams "Read Me!"—excellent for attention-grabbing headlines—while small type fades into the background, perfect for necessary but unexciting legal mumbo-jumbo like copyright notices.

Unless you specifically define its size, text in a regular paragraph appears at the default size specified by your visitor's browser, usually 16 pixels. However, not only can people change that default size (much to the eternal frustration of web designers), but different operating systems have been known to display text at different sizes. Bottom line: You can't really assume that text will appear at the same size on all your guests' monitors.

To set a font size, you can use either the Size menu in the Property Inspector's CSS mode (Figure 3-15) or the CSS Rule Definition window's Font-size menu (Figure 3-16). Whichever you choose, you're either creating a new style as described on page 125 or updating an existing style (page 139).

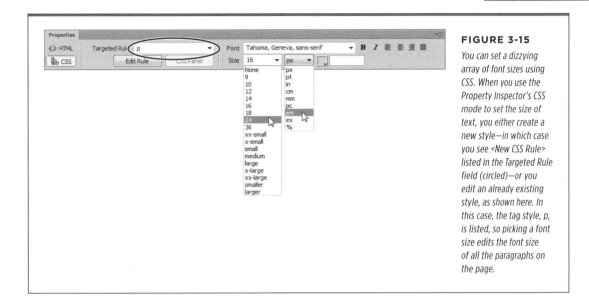

FIGURE 3-15

You can set a dizzying array of font sizes using CSS. When you use the Property Inspector's CSS mode to set the size of text, you either create a new style—in which case you see <New CSS Rule> listed in the Targeted Rule field (circled)—or you edit an already existing style, as shown here. In this case, the tag style, p, is listed, so picking a font size edits the font size of all the paragraphs on the page.

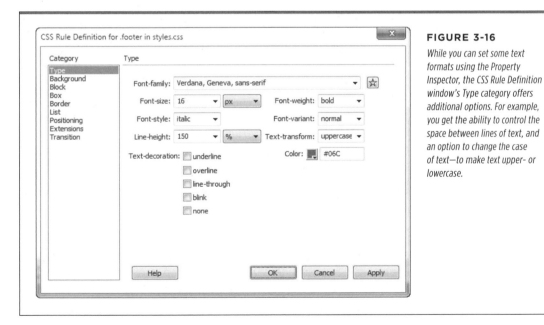

FIGURE 3-16

While you can set some text formats using the Property Inspector, the CSS Rule Definition window's Type category offers additional options. For example, you get the ability to control the space between lines of text, and an option to change the case of text—to make text upper- or lowercase.

The choices available from the Size menu break down into four groups:

- The *None* option removes any size information applied to the text. The text returns to its default size.

- The numeric choices—9 through 36—indicate how tall you wish to make the text, measured in pixels. Nine-pixel-tall text is nearly unreadable, while 36-pixel copy makes a bold statement. One benefit of specifying pixel sizes is that the resulting text appears nearly the same across different browsers and operating systems, obviating the problems mentioned above.

- The options *xx-small* through *xx-large* indicate fixed sizes, replacing the sizes 1 through 7 used with the old HTML <font> tag. The *medium* size is usually the same as the standard browser font size of 16 pixels.

- The last two choices—*smaller* and *larger*—are relative sizes, meaning that they shrink or enlarge the selected text based on the default size in your page. These choices come in handy when you define a base font size for the entire page using the Page Properties window (see Figure 1-22).

   Suppose you set the default text size for a web page at 12 pixels. If you apply a "larger" size to a selection of text, then it gets bigger (the exact amount varies by web browser). If, later, you change the base size to 14 pixels (in Page Properties), all of that "larger" text will increase proportionally.

To change the size of text, simply select it, and then, from the Property Inspector, choose a new size or edit the appropriate CSS style as described on page 139. If you applied a pixel value, you have an additional option: You can type in any number you wish if you don't like any of the sizes listed. In fact, unlike HTML, browsers can handle humongous text—hundreds of pixels tall, if that's what you're into.

You're not limited to pixels, either. The Units drop-down menu (Figure 3-15, to the right of the Size menu) lets you use as the unit of measure pixels, points, inches, centimeters, millimeters, picas, ems, percentages, or exes (an *ex* is the width of the letter X in the current font). Most of these measurement systems aren't intended for on-screen display. The most useful options are:

- *Pixels* are great for ensuring that text looks the same size across different browsers and operating systems.

- *Ems* are a relative measurement, meaning that the actual font size varies.

   One em is equal to the default font size. So suppose a web browser's default font size is 16 pixels. In that case, 1 em would mean 16 pixels tall, 2 ems would be twice that (32 pixels), and 1.5 ems would be 24 pixels.

   The advantage of ems is that they let web visitors control the browser's base font size to fit their vision. For example, if text is normally too small, they can increase the base font size. Any text measured in ems then changes according to the web browser's new setting. (For a good set of instructions on how to change the starting font size in all major browsers visit: *http://tinyurl.com/7b9ndbg*.)

NOTE You don't need to use ems to allow browsers to resize text. All current browsers have a Zoom command that enlarges not only text, but also all other page elements (pictures, navigation links, and so on), too.

You can use pixels and ems together. You could, for instance, set the base font size of your page to 16 pixels, and then use ems for other parts of the page. For example, you could set headlines to 2 ems, making them 32 pixels tall. If you later thought the overall text size of the page was too small or too large, you could simply change the base font size for the page, and the headlines and other text would resize proportionally.

NOTE As you get more advanced with CSS, you'll probably run into some weird problems with em or percentage text sizes due to an advanced concept known as the *cascade.* The gruesome details begin on page 391.

- *Percentages* (%) are another relative size measurement. When applied to text size, they're functionally equivalent to ems—100% is the same as 1 em, 200% is 2 ems, and 75% is .75 ems. If you're more comfortable with the notion of percentages than the typography-inspired ems, use percentage values.

The other measurement options, like inches and millimeters, don't make as much sense as pixels, ems, and percentages because you can't consistently measure them on monitors. Thanks to the wide array of monitors and displays and their different pixel densities, there's no reliable way to measure "pixels-to-the-inch" on computer screens. The upshot is that you're safe using pixel values—they're easier to understand, more consistent across browsers, and compatible (to keep parallel structure of list) with the zoom feature of all currently shipping browsers.

Picking a Font Color

To set the color of text, use the CSS *color* property. You can do so in the Property Inspector's CSS mode or by assigning text color in the Text category of the CSS Rule Definition window.

Most color formatting in Dreamweaver, whether for text or the background of a web page, makes use of Dreamweaver's *color box.* You can pick a color by clicking the color box and, from the pop-up color palette, selecting a hue (see Figure 3-17). Or click the System Color Picker button to launch the Windows or Mac color-picker dialog box, which lets you choose from a much wider selection of colors.

In addition, you can use the eyedropper cursor that appears when you click the color box. This cursor is "loaded," meaning you can click any spot on your screen—even outside the dialog box—to select a color, a trick that comes in handy when you want to use a color from an image elsewhere in your document (to have headline text match the color in an image, for example). You can even sample a color from another application (from any visible window, Dreamweaver or not): Just move the eyedropper over the color, and then click. (This click may take you out of Dreamweaver. Just return to Dreamweaver, and the color you sampled is listed in the color property box.)

Normally, Dreamweaver uses what's called "hexadecimal notation" to specify the color you select (see the box below). However, Dreamweaver CS6 offers a wide range of color notations, including hexadecimal (or "hex"), RGB, HSL, RGBa, and HSLa (see the box on page 160). To use one, click the contextual menu button in the color selector (circled in Figure 3-17), click Color Format, and then select an option from the Color Format menu. You can then sample a color from the page, from the color palette or even from the System color picker, and Dreamweaver writes the correct code for that color.

WARNING Internet Explorer 8 and earlier support only the RGB and two hex color formats. Until Internet Explorer users upgrade to IE 9 or switch to Firefox, Chrome, Safari, or Opera, you're better off sticking with RGB or hex color values for your pages.

If you decide you don't want to add color, or you want to remove a color you already applied, click the Default Color button. Without a color specified, web browsers use default colors for the element in question. For instance, text on a web page is usually black unless you specify otherwise.

Next to the color box in any Dreamweaver dialog box is a blank text field. If you know your web colors, you can type its value into this box, which is sometimes faster and more precise than clicking the rainbow palette.

Adding Bold and Italic

You can use the Property Inspector to make text bold or italic. Depending on which mode the inspector is in—HTML or CSS—clicking the B or I button does different things. In HTML mode, the B button wraps selected text with the <strong> tag, while the I button wraps it with the <em> (for emphasis) tag. In CSS mode, the B button sets the CSS *font-weight* property to bold, while the I button sets the CSS *font-style* property to italic. In other words, these two buttons either insert HTML tags or add CSS properties to a style.

If you just want to change the appearance of text, use CSS mode. But if you actually want to emphasize some text because it's important for the sentence's meaning (and therefore important to the way search engines perceive the sentence), use HTML mode. For example, if you want the word "Monday" to stand out on a page, use CSS. But, for a sentence like "He *never* makes mistakes," the emphasis on "never" is important to understanding the sentence; in that case, use HTML mode. The people viewing your site might not notice the difference, but Google, other search engines, and screen readers will.

NOTE If you use the Property Inspector's CSS mode, the B button only makes type bold or removes bold formatting that you previously applied. In the case of headlines, which browsers automatically display as bold, clicking the B button has no effect. To remove the bold formatting from headlines, you have to use the CSS Style Definition window, and, from the font-weight menu, select *normal*.

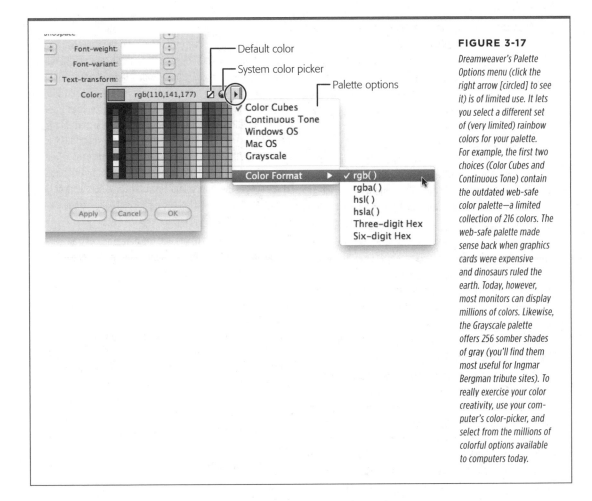

FIGURE 3-17

Dreamweaver's Palette Options menu (click the right arrow [circled] to see it) is of limited use. It lets you select a different set of (very limited) rainbow colors for your palette. For example, the first two choices (Color Cubes and Continuous Tone) contain the outdated web-safe color palette—a limited collection of 216 colors. The web-safe palette made sense back when graphics cards were expensive and dinosaurs ruled the earth. Today, however, most monitors can display millions of colors. Likewise, the Grayscale palette offers 256 somber shades of gray (you'll find them most useful for Ingmar Bergman tribute sites). To really exercise your color creativity, use your computer's color-picker, and select from the millions of colorful options available to computers today.

Web Colors

CSS supports several color notations: hexadecimal, RGB, HSL, RGBa, and HSLa. These formats are just different ways to specify a color, and you can get the same color using any of them.

Traditionally, you specify colors in CSS using hexadecimal notation. "Hex" represents colors using a six-digit code, like this: #fe3400. (Hexadecimal notation is a system computers use for counting. In this system, you count like this: 0, 1, 2, 3, 4, 5, 6, 7, 8, 9, a, b, c, d, e, f. The # symbol tells a computer that the following sequence is a series of hexadecimal numbers.) The best way to find a color's hex value is to choose the color you want by clicking on it in the palette and then looking at the code that Dreamweaver writes in the text box next to it.

Hex colors comprise three pairs of numbers. For example, the number above, #fe3400, is really fe, 34, and 00. Each pair represents a number for red, green, and blue color values, which, when combined, make up a color. You sometimes see only three numbers, like this: #f00—that's shorthand used when both numbers in a pair are the same. For example, you can shorten #ff0011 to just #f01. In the color box's "Color format" menu (see Figure 3-17), Dreamweaver refers to these formats as "six-digit hex" and "three-digit hex."

However, CSS supports other formats for specifying color. RGB stands for "Red Green Blue" and is the format most commonly associated with computer graphics. Most graphics programs let you pick colors using RGB, and, in fact, hex colors are really just RGB values specified using hex numbers. For example, the hex color #ff0033, looks like this as an RGB value in CSS: rgb(255,0,51). Each value represents a color and uses a number from 0 to 255, so rgb(255,0,51) means 255 red, 0 green, and 51 blue. RGB color values work in all web browsers (even Internet Explorer 6), so if you're more comfortable with RGB, feel free to use this option.

HSL stands for "Hue, Saturation, Lightness" and is yet another way to specify colors based on its color (hue), intensity (saturation), and lightness (how close a color is to white or black). You specify the hue using a number from 0 to 360 (representing the degrees around a color wheel with red being 0 and 360, green 120, and blue 240), the saturation is a percentage from 0 (gray) to 100 (full intensity), and lightness is a percentage from 0 (black) to 100 (white). That hex color above, #ff0033, is written like this in HSL: hsl(348,100%,50%). Some people find HSL colors easier to understand than RGB or hex, but all three let you specify the same colors. However, HSL colors work only in Internet Explorer 9 and later. Since IE 8 and 7 still are popular, you're better off skipping HSL for now.

Finally, RGBa and HSLa colors add the dimension of transparency to color: The "a" stands for alpha transparency and refers to how transparent the color is. In other words, you can create "see-through" colors. For example, you could make the color of a headline partially transparent so that a background image on the page shows through the headline. There are many fun and creative effects possible with alpha transparency (for example, the article at *http://tinyurl.com/ydj8658* uses RGBa color). Unfortunately, Internet Explorer 8 and earlier don't understand RGBa or HSLa, so use these formats with caution. If you do want to explore them, they work just like their non-transparent counterparts, with the addition of one extra value from 0 (completely invisible) to 1 (completely opaque). So if you wanted a vivid red color that was 50 percent transparent, you'd specify an RGBa value using this notation: rgba(255,0,0,.5). In HSLa notation, that color is hsla(0,100%,50%,.5). If you use Dreamweaver's Color Format menu to select an RGBa or HSLa color, Dreamweaver always sets the transparency to 1; you can change it in the color field to anything from 0 to 1 (such as .25 to get 25 percent transparency).

Aligning Text

The alignment buttons in the Property Inspector's CSS mode set the CSS text-align property to either *left, right, center*, or *justify*. These same options are available under the Block category of the CSS Rule Definition window (to see them, jump ahead to Figure 3-20).

CSS Type Properties in the Rule Definition Window

As its name implies, the Rule Definition window's Type category lets you format text. Several of the settings are the same as those available from the Property Inspector's CSS mode, and you learned about them in depth starting on page 144. To summarize, this category of CSS properties includes:

- **Font**. You choose a font for the new CSS style rule from the Font menu. As discussed on page 145, you choose from Dreamweaver's pre-programmed *groups* of fonts or web fonts you added to Dreamweaver (page 146).

- **Size**. As described on page 154, you can choose from many different measurement standards to size text, but the most common are pixels, ems, and percentages.

- **Weight**. Weight refers to the thickness of a font. The Weight menu offers 13 choices. Normal and Bold are the most common, and they work in all browsers that understand CSS. See Figure 3-18 for details.

- **Style**. In this peculiar instance, "Style" means italic, oblique, or normal text. Technically, italic is a custom-designed, emphatic version of a typeface, *like this*. Oblique, on the other hand, is just a computerized adaptation of a normal font, in which each letter is inclined a certain number of degrees to the right. In practical application, there's no visible difference between italic and oblique in web browsers.

- **Variant**. This drop-down menu simply lets you specify small-caps type, if you like—a slightly formal, fancy-looking type style much favored by attorneys' offices.

- **Line height**. Line height, otherwise known as *leading* (pronounced "led, lc"), refers to the space between lines of text in a paragraph (see Figure 3-19). To create more space between lines, set the line height greater than the font size. (If you type a number without a % sign, Dreamweaver assumes you're specifying a line height in pixels. You can change the units of measure using the drop-down menu to the right of the Line-height field.)

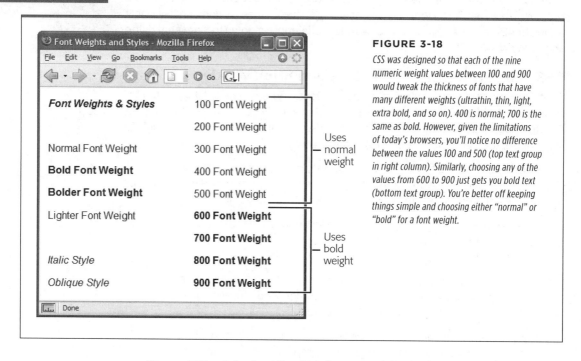

FIGURE 3-18

CSS was designed so that each of the nine numeric weight values between 100 and 900 would tweak the thickness of fonts that have many different weights (ultrathin, thin, light, extra bold, and so on). 400 is normal; 700 is the same as bold. However, given the limitations of today's browsers, you'll notice no difference between the values 100 and 500 (top text group in right column). Similarly, choosing any of the values from 600 to 900 just gets you bold text (bottom text group). You're better off keeping things simple and choosing either "normal" or "bold" for a font weight.

"Normal," the default setting (third paragraph in Figure 3-19), uses a line height that's slightly larger than the height of the text. You don't get access to the drop-down menu of measurement units (pixels, points, %, and so on) unless you type a number in this box.

> **TIP** A good approach for line height is to type in a percentage measurement, such as *120%*, which is relative to the size of the text; so if your text were 10 pixels tall, the space from the base of one line of text to the next would be 12 pixels (120% of 10). Now, if you change the size of the text, the *relative* space between lines remains the same.

- **Text-transform**. From this menu, you can automatically capitalize text. To capitalize the first letter of each word, choose "capitalize." The "uppercase" option gives you all capital letters, while "lowercase" makes all the letters lowercase. The factory setting is "none," which has no effect on the text.

- **Decoration**. This strange assortment of five checkboxes lets you dress up your text, mostly in unattractive ways. "Underline," "overline," and "line-through" add horizontal lines below, above, or directly through the affected text, respectively. Turning on "blink" makes text blink on and off (but only in a few browsers); unless you want to appear on one of those "worst website of the week" lists, avoid it. You can apply any number of decorative types per style, except with "none," which, obviously, you can't choose along with any of the other options. The "none" setting is useful for hiding the underlines that normally appear below links.

- **Color**. Set the color of the style's text using Dreamweaver's color box, described on page 157.

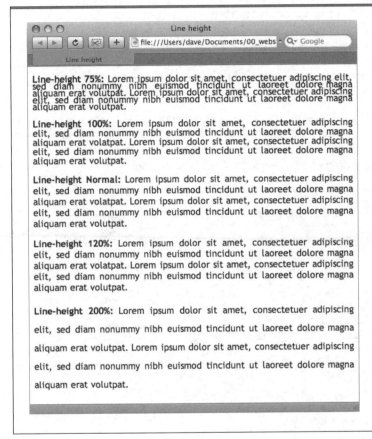

FIGURE 3-19

Control the space between lines with the Line-height property in the CSS Rule Definition dialog box. In this example, each paragraph's text is set in 16-pixel Trebuchet MS. With CSS, you can make lines bump into each other by setting a low line-height value (top paragraph), or spread them far apart by using a larger value (bottom paragraph).

Block Properties

The Block Properties panel is a hodgepodge of CSS settings that affect how browsers display letters and words (see Figure 3-20).

TIP To completely remove the space between paragraphs, set the Top and Bottom margin for paragraphs to 0 in the CSS Rule Definition window's Box category. Headlines also have space before and after them, so if you want to remove space between a headline and paragraph, you need to remove the bottom margin of the headline and the top margin of the paragraph. To indent paragraphs, set the Left and Right margin properties.

Despite this category's name, these properties don't just apply to block-level elements (paragraphs, headlines, and so on). You can apply a style you define here to even a single word or two. (The one exception is the Text-align property, which applies only to paragraphs and other block-level elements.) Here are your choices:

- **Word-spacing**. This property helps you clean up text by adding or removing space *between* words. The default value, "normal," leaves a normal, single space between words. If you want words in a sentence to be spaced   apart   like   this, then type a value of about 10 pixels (choose Value from the first drop-down menu and then the units you want from the second one). The bigger the number, the larger the gap between words. You can also *remove* space between words by using a negative number—a great choice when you want to make your pages difficult to read.

- **Letter-spacing**. This property works just like word spacing, but governs the space between *letters*. To add space l i k e t h i s, type a value of about 5 pixels. The result can make long passages hard to read, but a little space between letters can add a dramatic flair to short headlines and movie titles.

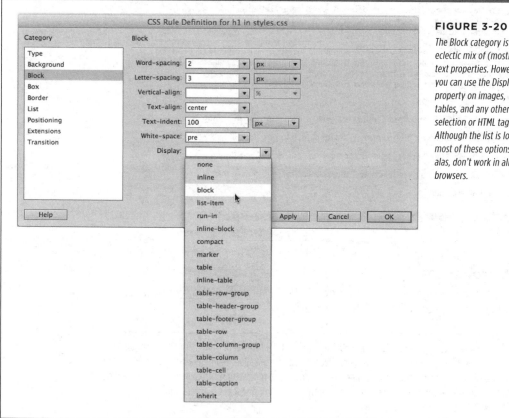

FIGURE 3-20

The Block category is an eclectic mix of (mostly) text properties. However, you can use the Display property on images, tables, and any other selection or HTML tag. Although the list is long, most of these options, alas, don't work in all browsers.

- **Vertical-align**. With this property, you can change the vertical placement of an object—such as text or an image—relative to the items around it. For example, you could move text above or below the surrounding text to format a trademark character, copyright symbol, or footnote reference using the options "super" and "sub." If you wanted to add the trademark symbol to, say, *Chia Pet*™, then you'd select the letters TM and set the vertical alignment to "super." In addition, for more accurate control, you can type a value (like 10%) to raise an object above its normal baseline or a negative value (like -10% or -5 pixels) to move an object down.

  Vertical alignment also works with graphics, and designers often use the options Top, Bottom, and Middle with HTML table cells to position content within a cell.

NOTE The "sub" and "super" alignment options don't change the size of the selected text. If you want to create true subscript or superscript characters (for chemical symbols, trademark or copyright symbols, and so on), you should also use a smaller font size in the style; 75% works great.

- **Text-align**. This property controls the alignment of a block-level element, like a paragraph or table. You can choose from among the usual suspects—"left," "center," "right," or even "justify." (Like the text in this paragraph, justified text aligns copy on both the left and right edges.)

  Use the "justify" option with care, however. Because web browsers don't have the advanced controls that page-layout software does, they usually do an awful job of justifying text on a computer screen. The results can be difficult to read—and ugly.

- **Text-indent**. This useful option lets you indent the first line of a paragraph. If you enter 15 pixels, each paragraph gets an attractive first-line indent, exactly as in a real word processor.

  You can also use a *negative* number, which makes the first line extend past the *left* margin of a paragraph, creating a hanging indent (or *outdent*)—a nice effect for a sentence that introduces a bulleted list or for glossary pages. If you use a negative number, it's a good idea to set the left margin for the paragraph equal to the value of the negative text indent (see page 449). Otherwise the first line might extend too far to the left, off the screen!

- **White-space**. This property controls how a browser displays extra white space (spaces, tabs, returns, and so on). Browsers normally ignore extra spaces in the HTML of a page, reducing them to a single-space character between words and other elements, as described on page 95. The "pre" option functions just like the HTML <pre> tag: Extra white space (like tabs, multiple spaces, and hard returns) that you put *in the HTML code* appear in the document window. The "nowrap" option prevents lines from breaking (and wrapping to the next line) when they reach the end of the browser window.

- **Display**. This property defines how a browser displays a particular element, like a paragraph or link. The range of choices here may overwhelm you—but you may be underwhelmed when you find out that browsers don't support all these options.

  The only four that work reliably across browsers are "none," "inline," "block," and "inline-block." The "block" option treats any item styled with this property as a block—separated from other content by space above and below it. Paragraphs and headings normally appear this way. But you can apply this value to a link (which normally appears inside a block-level element like a paragraph) to turn it into its own block. Usually, you have to click directly on the text or image inside a link to jump to the linked page. But when you set a link's display to "block," guests can click anywhere in the entire width of the block—even areas where no text appears.

  The "inline" option treats the item as though it's part of the current block or paragraph, so that any item styled with this property (like a picture) flows together with other items around it, as if it were part of the same paragraph. People frequently use this property to take a bulleted list of links and turn it into a horizontal navigation bar. For a good tutorial on this topic, visit *http://tinyurl.com/as4rk*.

  "Inline-block" is like inline, in that the element sits on the same line as other content. However, adding top and bottom margins when you use the "inline" option has no effect (the space for the margin is never added). With inline-bock, you can add top and bottom margins for greater control of spacing around the element.

  The "none" option is the most fun: It turns off the display of an item. In other words, any text or item styled with this option doesn't appear on the page. You can use JavaScript programming to switch this property on and off, making items seem to appear and disappear.

List Properties

To exercise greater control over bulleted and numbered lists, use the options in the CSS Rule Definition window's List category (see Figure 3-21):

- **List-style-type**. Select the type of bullet you want in front of a list item. Options include: "disc," "circle," "square," "decimal" (1, 2, 3), "lower-roman" (i, ii, iii), "upper-roman" (I, II, III), "lower-alpha" (a, b, c), "upper-alpha" (A, B, C), and "none" (no bullet at all).

- **List-style-image**. For the ultimate control of your bullet icon, skip the boring options preprogrammed into a web browser (like disc, circle, square, or decimal) and supply your own. Click the Browse button, and then, from your site folder, select a graphics file. Make sure the graphic is appropriate bullet material—in other words, small.

TIP The Background Image property, which you'll learn about on page 262, is a more versatile solution to adding bullet images to a list. The List-style-image property does let you specify a graphic to use as a bullet, but there are no controls for positioning that image. On the other hand, you can accurately position a background image, so it's much easier to tweak the placement of your bullet using the Background Image property. Here's how: Create a style for the <li> tag (or a class style that you apply to each <li> tag); make sure you set the List-style-type property type to "none" (this hides the bullet); set the background image to your graphical bullet; and play with the background position values (page 264). Playing with the padding values (page 449) helps position the text relative to the image.

- **List-style-Position**. This property controls where the bullet appears relative to the list item's text. The "outside" option places the bullet outside the margin of the text, exactly the way bulleted lists normally look. "Inside," on the other hand, displays the bullet within the text margin, so that the left edge of the *bullet* aligns with the left margin of the text; Figure 3-21 makes the effect clear.

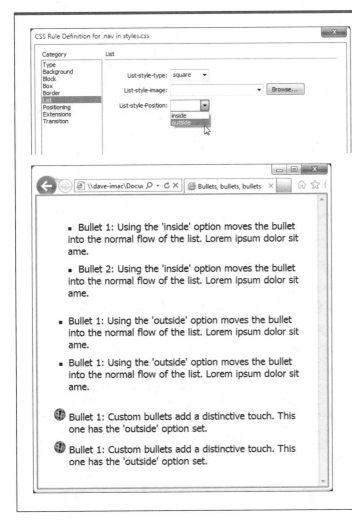

FIGURE 3-21

Top: Take control of your bulleted and numbered lists using the CSS Rule Definition window's List category. With Cascading Style Sheets, you can even supply your own graphic bullets. Bottom: A bullet-crazed web page, for illustration purposes. Parading down the screen, you can see "inside" bullets, "outside" bullets, and bullets made from graphics.

NOTE If you want to adjust the amount of space web browsers normally use to indent lists, set the left padding property (see page 449) to 0, and set the left margin (see page 449) to the amount of indent you'd like. Sometimes you want no indent at all—for example, if you're creating a list of links that should look like buttons, not bulleted items—set both the left padding and left margin to 0 (and while you're at it, set the bullet type to "none," as described above).

■ Cascading Style Sheets Tutorial

In this tutorial, you'll practice the basic techniques required to create and edit styles. Make sure you grasp the fundamentals covered in the following pages; you'll be building lots of style sheets in the other tutorials in this book using these same methods.

In this tutorial, you'll create an external style sheet that formats pages on the Cafe Soylent Green website.

NOTE Before getting started, download the tutorial files from *www.sawmac.com/dwcs6*. See the Note on page 54 for more details.

Setting Up

Once you download the tutorial files and open Dreamweaver, you need to set up a site for this tutorial. You learned how to do this in the first chapter, but here's a quick recap—practice makes perfect!

1. **Choose Site→New Site.**

   The Site Setup window appears.

2. **For the Site Name, type *CSS Tutorial*.**

   The only other step required to set up a site is to tell Dreamweaver where to find the site's files.

3. **To the right of the "Local site folder" box, click the folder icon.**

   The Choose Root Folder window appears. This is just a window onto your computer's file system; navigate to the proper folder just as you would when working with other programs.

4. **Navigate to and select the Chapter03 folder located in the MM_DWCS6 folder.** Click the Select button (Choose on Macs) to select this folder, and then, in the Site Setup window, click Save to complete the process of defining a site.

   You should see two files—*about.html* and *events.html*—in the Files panel. (If you don't see the Files panel, choose Window→Files to open it.)

Adding Web Fonts

In this tutorial, you'll use Dreamweaver CS6's new web fonts feature. The first step is adding web fonts to Dreamweaver's web fonts manager.

1. **Choose Modify→Web Fonts.**

   The Web Fonts Manager window opens. You'll add your first font.

2. **Click the Add Font button.**

   The Add Web Font window appears (see Figure 3-22).

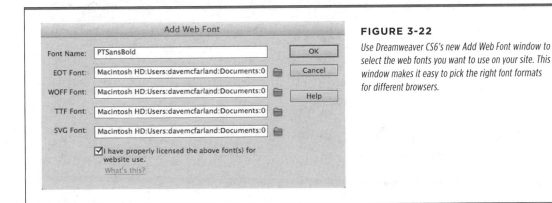

FIGURE 3-22

Use Dreamweaver CS6's new Add Web Font window to select the web fonts you want to use on your site. This window makes it easy to pick the right font formats for different browsers.

3. **Type PTSansBold in the Font Name field.**

   If you leave this field blank, Dreamweaver will fill it in with a name taken from the font file's name. However, since font names aren't always easy to understand, it's best to type a name that indicates the font and any special features, like bold, italic, or bold and italic.

4. **Click the folder icon to the right of the EOT Font field.**

   The Open dialog appears.

5. **Navigate to the Fonts folder inside the MM_DWCS6 folder (the main tutorials folder).** Select the PTSansBold.eot file inside the Bold folder, and click Open.

   The window closes and Dreamweaver adds the path to the PTSansBold.eot file to the text field. In fact, since the other versions of that font (.ttf, .svg, and .woff) are also in that folder, Dreamweaver fills out the other three fields as well.

6. **Turn on the "I have properly licensed the above fonts" checkbox, and click OK.**

   Since PTSans is a free font, licensed for web use, it's OK to use it on this site. You've added one font to Dreamweaver. You can now use this font on any page in any site you build. But before you start using it, you'll add three more fonts to Dreamweaver.

7. **Repeat steps 2-6 to add three more fonts.** Name the fonts PTSansBoldItalic, PTSansItalic, and PTSansRegular.

The fonts you need are in the Fonts folder in the MM_DWCS6 folder. Look inside the Bold Italic, Italic, and Regular folders, respectively. Once you're done, the Web Fonts Manager window should look like Figure 3-23.

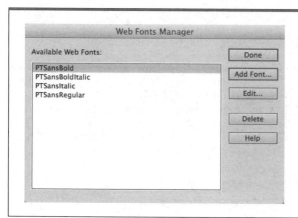

FIGURE 3-23

You use the Web Fonts Manager window to add or remove web fonts from Dreamweaver. When you select a font and press Delete, Dreamweaver removes the font from its font list but doesn't remove the font from any site or style sheet that uses it.

8. **Click Done.**

The Web Fonts Manager window closes and, behind the scenes, Dreamweaver adds those fonts to its font list, makes copies of the font files, and places them inside the program's Configuration folder. You can now use those fonts on any page and any site you create with Dreamweaver.

Creating an External Style Sheet

Now that you've got Dreamweaver ready to use web fonts, you'll create a new external style sheet and start adding styles.

1. **In the files panel, double-click the file named *about.html*.**

The web page contains headlines, paragraphs, and a copyright notice. The page's text is plain, boring-looking HTML, so you'll use CSS to spiff it up. To start, you'll create a style for the first headline.

NOTE You can, of course, also open a file by choosing File→Open and navigating to the folder where the file resides.

2. **Triple-click the headline "About Us."**

This selects the entire headline. You'll now use the Property Inspector to select a font.

3. **Click the CSS button in the Property Inspector and then, from the Font menu, choose PTSansBold.**

   Because the headline had no style applied to it, Dreamweaver opens the New CSS Rule window (see Figure 3-24). You'll pick the type of style you want to create.

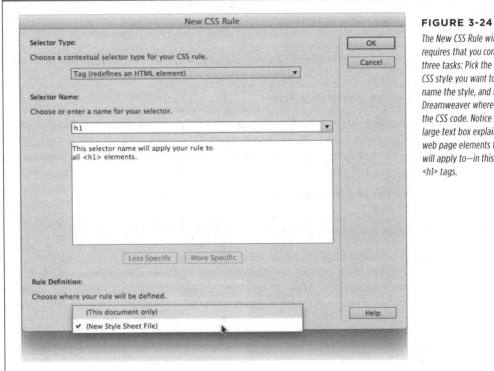

FIGURE 3-24

The New CSS Rule window requires that you complete three tasks: Pick the type of CSS style you want to create, name the style, and tell Dreamweaver where to store the CSS code. Notice how the large text box explains what web page elements the style will apply to—in this case all <h1> tags.

4. **From the Selector Type menu at the top of the window, select Tag.**

   This step lets you create a style for a particular HTML tag, in this case, the <h1> tag. In other words, you're going to create a formatting rule that automatically applies to every heading 1 paragraph.

5. **The Selector Name field should have "h1" listed, but if it doesn't, use the middle drop-down menu to select "h1."**

   Next you'll choose where to store the CSS code for this new style—in this case, in an external style sheet.

6. **From the bottom menu, choose New Style Sheet File, as pictured in Figure 3-24.** Click OK.

   The Save Style Sheet File As dialog box appears. You're about to create the file—an external style sheet—that stores the styles for this page.

7. **Click the Site Root button (top of the dialog box on Windows, bottom right on Macs).**

   The Site Root button is a handy shortcut. It automatically takes you to the local site folder for the site you're currently working on, saving you the effort of manually navigating there. (OK, in this example, you're already in the local site folder, but you should know about this button and what it does—it really does come in handy for getting you to the top-level folder of the current site after you open files elsewhere on your hard drive or folders deeply nested inside the current site.)

8. **In the Save Style Sheet File As" box, type *styles.css*, and then click Save.**

   Cascading Style Sheet files always end in .css; that's how web servers and browsers can tell what kind of files they are.

   Notice that the headline looks exactly the same. Unfortunately, Dreamweaver can't display web fonts in Design view. The only way to see the effect of the new style is to click the Live button in the Document toolbar or to preview the page in a web browser.

9. **Click the Live button in the Document toolbar.**

   The headline now uses the bold version of the PTSans font. Unfortunately, you can't edit text in Live view, so you need to return to Design view to keep working.

   NOTE Because Live view often looks just like Design view, it's easy to get caught in the frustrating situation where Dreamweaver won't let you select text or edit the web page. If this happens, take a breath, look to see if the Live button is dark grey (meaning it's selected), then click it to turn off Live view. Dreamweaver switches to Design view, where you can edit. If you're in split view, you can always edit the HTML code and leave the Live view turned on. HTML pros often work this way, typing HTML tags into the code half of Split view and checking the updated display in Live view.

10. **Click the Live button once again to return to the editable Design view.**

    You created a style and added an external style sheet to your site in just a couple steps. Now, you'll add some color.

11. **Make sure you still have the headline selected, and then, in the Property Inspector's Color field (beside the palette box icon), type *#145207* (see Figure 3-25).**

    You can use the color box to select another color if you prefer.

    The New CSS Rule window doesn't appear this time, because now you're editing the h1 tag style you created previously. Time to change the size of the font.

FIGURE 3-25

*Choosing properties for
an element that already
has a style applied to
it—like the h1 tag style
here—updates that style.*

NOTE   If the New CSS Rule window appears again at either step 11 or 12, something went wrong. Click the
Cancel button. You must have accidentally selected some other text—maybe just part of the headline—before
using the Property Inspector. To get back on track, triple-click the "About Us" headline again, and then repeat
step 11 or 12.

12. **In the Property Inspector's Size box, type *36*.**

    The Property Inspector should now look like Figure 3-25. You just set the font
    size to 36 pixels tall. You've pretty much reached the limit of what the Property
    Inspector is capable of, but you've barely scratched the surface of Cascading
    Styles Sheets. In the next part of this tutorial, you'll learn how to edit a style
    and access the wide range of formatting options that CSS offers.

Editing a Style

You won't always create styles perfectly—you may make a mistake, or simply wish
to change the font, font size, or color. Fortunately, Dreamweaver makes it as easy
to edit a style as it does to create a style.

1. **Make sure you have the CSS Styles panel open (Window→CSS Styles) and
   the All button selected at the top of the panel.**

   This displays all the style sheets attached to this page (in this case, just
   styles.css).

2. **If it isn't already, expand the list of styles in the *styles.css* style sheet by
   clicking the + icon (flippy triangle on Macs) to the left of "styles.css."**

   You'll notice another external style sheet, *stylesheet.css.* This style sheet contains
   the CSS code necessary to load the web font you selected earlier. In addition,
   you'll see one tag style, the h1 style you created previously.

3. **In the list, double-click "h1."**

This opens the CSS Rule Definition window, where you can access a range of CSS properties (see Figure 3-26). If you preview the page in Internet Explorer, Firefox, and Opera, there's a big problem. The headline looks really thick and chunky. That's because headlines are bolded by default, and those browsers take the current font (in this case PTSansBold) and try to make it bold. But the font you're using is already a bolded version, so trying to make a bold font look "bold" only makes it look ugly. To overcome this, you need to set the font-weight to normal.

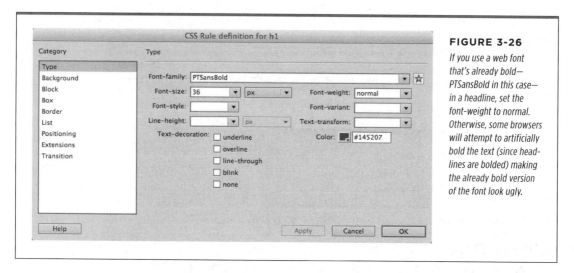

FIGURE 3-26

If you use a web font that's already bold—PTSansBold in this case—in a headline, set the font-weight to normal. Otherwise, some browsers will attempt to artificially bold the text (since head-lines are bolded) making the already bold version of the font look ugly.

4. **In the Type category of the Rule Definition window, select "normal" from the Font-weight menu.**

When formatting text, you can use many other non-text-related CSS properties. For example, you can add border lines to any element on a page.

5. **In the category list, click Border.**

The CSS Rule Definition window now displays all the properties that add a border around a style (see Figure 3-27). You can control each border individually, or use the same line style for all four edges. In this case, you'll add lines to just the top and bottom of the headline.

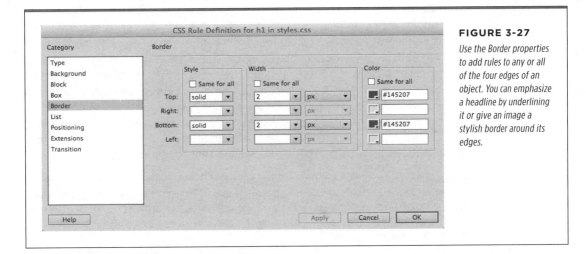

FIGURE 3-27

Use the Border properties to add rules to any or all of the four edges of an object. You can emphasize a headline by underlining it or give an image a stylish border around its edges.

6. **Turn off all three "Same for all" checkboxes.** For the Top border, choose "solid" from the top Style menu, type *2* in the top Width box, and type *#145207* in the top Color box. For the Bottom border, choose "solid" from the Style menu, type *2* in the Width box, and *#145207* in the Color box.

   If you click the Apply button now, you may notice that the top border is a little too close to the top of the headline. You can add a little breathing room using the CSS Padding property.

7. **In the Rule Definition window, click the Box category.** Turn off the "Same for all" checkbox underneath Padding, and then, in the "Top padding" box, type *2*.

   Padding is the space between the edge of an element (where the border appears) and the stuff inside the element (like text). In this case, adding 2 pixels of top padding adds 2 pixels of space between the top border line and the headline's text. You'll learn more about padding on page 449.

8. **Click OK to close the window and complete editing the style.**

   Now you have a distinctive-looking headline. But you've just started building styles for this page.

9. **Choose File→Save All Related Files.**

The Save All Related Files command can be a real lifesaver when you work with external style sheets. Even though you're looking at and working on a web page (*about.html* here), each time you add a style, Dreamweaver updates the external style sheet file (*styles.css*). So most of the work you've done so far has gone into updating the *styles.css* file. Unfortunately, the regular keyboard shortcut to save a file, Ctrl+S (⌘-S), saves only changes to the file you can see—in this case, the web page. Make sure you use the Save All Related Files command frequently, otherwise you could lose all the changes you make to an external style sheet if Dreamweaver or your computer crashes. (To make things easier, you can create your own keyboard shortcut for the Save All Related Files command. See page 911 for details on creating keyboard shortcuts.)

> **NOTE** The File→Save All command is also useful. It saves every file you have open that has unsaved changes. Feel free to use this command frequently even if you might want to undo some of those changes—Dreamweaver's smart enough to let you undo changes you made to a file even after you save those changes (but only if don't close the file in the meantime).

Adding Another Style

The Property Inspector isn't the only way to create a style—in fact, since it offers a limited number of formatting options, it isn't even the best way. The CSS Styles panel provides a faster way with more choices.

1. **At the bottom of the CSS Styles panel, click the New CSS Rule button (the + button pictured in Figure 3-1).**

   The New CSS Rule window appears. You'll create another tag style for the Heading 2 tag.

2. **From the top menu, choose Tag; in the Selector Name field, type *h2* (or select "h2" from the drop-down menu); in the bottom menu, make sure you have "styles.css" selected.** Click OK.

   This action adds a new tag style to the *styles.css* style sheet. You'll set a few text properties next.

3. **From the Font-family menu, choose "PTSansBold."**

   You'll use the same font as in Heading 1, but you'll change its size and color.

4. **In the Font-size box, type *24*, and, in the Color box, type *#033E00*.**

   This creates medium-sized, dark-green text. To make the headline stand out a bit, you'll make all the text uppercase. Fortunately, you don't have to hold down the caps-lock button and retype each headline to do so—there's a CSS property that does it for you.

5. **From the Text-transform menu, choose "uppercase."**

One problem with this page is the large gap between the subheads and the paragraphs following them. The Heading 2 headlines ("Our History," for example) introduce the paragraphs that follow. Removing the gap that appears between the heading and the following paragraph would visually tie the two together better. To make this change, you must first remove the margin below each headline.

6. **In the left-hand list of CSS categories, select Box.** In the Margin area, turn off the "Same for all" checkbox; in the Bottom box, type *0*.

   This should remove any space that appears below the Heading 2 tags.

7. **Click OK to close the Rule Definition window and finish editing the style.**

   The space between the headlines and the paragraphs hasn't changed a bit! What gives? Paragraphs and headlines have space both above *and* below. The space you're seeing is actually the *top* margin of the paragraph tag.

   Top and bottom margins have a peculiar feature: They don't add up like 1+1=2. In other words, a web browser doesn't add the bottom margin of Heading 2 to the top margin of the paragraph to calculate the total space between the two blocks of text. Instead, a web browser uses the margin with the *largest* value to determine the space between paragraphs (a lot of text layout programs, including word processors, share this behavior).

   For example, say the <h2> tag has a bottom margin of 12 pixels, while the paragraph following it has a top margin of 10 pixels. The total space between the two isn't 22 pixels (10+12)—it's 12 pixels (the value of the larger margin). So, if you remove the bottom margin of the headline, the gap between the two blocks of text isn't gone—it's now 10 pixels, the top margin value for the paragraph. That's the situation here: You need to modify the paragraphs' top margin as well. You can do that by creating another style.

8. **In the CSS Styles panel, click the New CSS Rule button.**

   The New CSS Rule window appears. You'll create a tag style to control how browsers format paragraphs.

9. **From the top menu, choose Tag; in the Selector Name box, type *p*, and then, in the bottom menu, make sure you have "styles.css" selected.** Click OK to create the style.

   Before getting to that pesky margin, first set some basic type options.

10. **From the Font-family menu, choose PTSansRegular.**

    This is one of the web fonts you added earlier.

11. **In the Font-size box, type *14*, and from the Font-weight menu select normal.**

    CSS provides a lot of control over type, including the ability to adjust the leading, or space between, lines in a paragraph.

12. **In the Line-height box, type *150*, and then, from the drop-down menu to the right, choose *%*.**

The line-height property controls the space between lines of text. In this case, you've set that space to 150%, which means that each line will be 150 percent (or 1.5 times) the size of the font. A setting of 150% adds more space than usual between each line of text in a paragraph—the result is more white space and a more luxurious feel.

Now back to that margin problem.

13. **Click the Box category; in the Margin section, turn off the "Same for all" checkbox.** Type *5* in the Top box and *75* in the Left box.

The window should now look like Figure 3-28. The 5-pixel top margin adds just a small amount of space between the paragraph and the <h2> tag above it—completely removing all space between the two would make them seem crowded together. The 75-pixel left margin is just for fun. This margin indents the paragraphs from the left edge of the page by 75 pixels, creating a distinctive look that makes the Heading 2 paragraphs stand out even more.

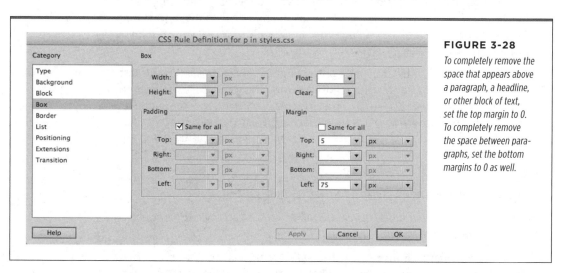

FIGURE 3-28

To completely remove the space that appears above a paragraph, a headline, or other block of text, set the top margin to 0. To completely remove the space between paragraphs, set the bottom margins to 0 as well.

14. **Click OK; choose File→Save All Related Files.**

The page is nearly complete, but you may notice something strange when you preview the page in a browser. In Chrome and Safari, the paragraph text that should be bolded (in the first paragraph following the "Our History" headline and the last paragraph) and the text in the paragraph following the "Our Founders headline" that should be italicized are neither bold nor italic. In addition, that text might look less than spectacular in Internet Explorer, Firefox, and Opera. That's because those browsers aren't using the bold or italic version of the web font; they're merely adding more weight or slanting the text artificially. This is one drawback of web fonts; the web browser doesn't know how to automatically swap in the bold version of the font. You'll need to tell it which fonts to use in those cases.

15. **In the CSS Styles panel, click the New CSS Rule button.**

   The New CSS Rule window appears. You'll create a tag style to control how browsers format paragraphs.

16. **From the top menu, choose Tag; in the Selector Name box, type _strong_, and then, in the bottom menu, make sure you have "styles.css" selected.** Click OK to create the style.

   You only need to pick a font, and set the font-weight to normal.

17. **From the Font-family menu, choose PTSansBold.** Choose "normal" from the Font-weight menu. Click OK to complete the style.

   If you set the font weight to normal, browsers won't try to make the font bold. The same is true for italics,

18. **Repeat steps 15-16 to create a new style for the em tag.** Choose PTSansItalic from the Font-family menu and then set its Font-style property to normal. Click OK to complete the style.

   The HTML <em> tag normally italicizes text. In this case, you'll simply swap in the italic version of the PTSans font.

Creating a Class Style

Now you'll create a style to format the copyright notice at the bottom of the page. It's inside a regular paragraph (<p> tag), so it's getting all its formatting from the p tag style. Here's an instance where you'd like to style a single paragraph without affecting the other paragraphs on the page. A class style is perfect for this kind of task.

1. **On the CSS Styles panel, click the New CSS Rule button.**

   The New CSS Rule window opens. This time, you'll create a class style rather than an HTML tag style.

2. **From the top menu, select Class.** In the Selector Name box, type _.copyright_ (with a period before it).

   Class styles always begin with a period—however, if you leave it out, Dreamweaver puts it in.

> **NOTE** Some beginners think that whenever you create a new style, you also need to create a new external style sheet. On the contrary, you can—and should—store more than one style in a single external style sheet. In fact, if you're creating a set of styles for an entire site, put them all in the same external style sheet.

3. **Make sure you have "styles.css" selected in the bottom menu, and then click OK.**

You're adding yet another style to the external style sheet you created at the beginning of this tutorial. The CSS Rule Definition window appears. You'll add a few new properties to make this style look different from the rest of the text on the page.

4. **From the Font-family menu, choose PTSansBold.** In the Font-size box, type *12*; from the Font-weight menu, choose "normal"; and for the Color, type *#FFFFFF* or use the color box to select a white.

Because the text is now white (the same color as the page), you'll change the background color to make the copyright stand out.

5. **In the category list, click Background.**

The CSS Rule Definition window now displays all the properties used to add a background color or background image to an element. You'll add a background color now (background images are discussed on page 262).

6. **In the Background-color box type *#145207*.**

To allow a little breathing room around the copyright text, you'll add some padding.

7. **In the left-hand list of CSS categories, click the Box category.** Type *5* in the Padding's Top box.

While margins control the space between elements (like the gap between paragraphs), *padding* controls the space between the content and the content's border, which also includes the area where a browser paints the background. In other words, adding padding extends the background around the text (or other content) you're styling.

You'll change the copyright notice's margin settings as well.

8. **In the Margin area, turn off the "Same for all" checkbox, and then type *25* in the Top box and *0* in the Left box.**

The window should look like Figure 3-29 The 25 pixels of top margin pushes the copyright notice away from the bottom of the paragraph of text above it. In addition, since Dreamweaver indents all the paragraphs 75 pixels from the left edge, you need to set the left margin here, in the copyright notice, to 0. This overrides the 75-pixel margin from the <p> tag style and lets the copyright notice hug the left edge of the page.

9. **Click OK.**

The Rule Definition window closes, but this time nothing's changed in the document window. Unlike HTML tag styles, class styles don't show up anywhere until you apply them by hand.

10. **Scroll to the bottom of the page and select the last paragraph, the one with the copyright notice.**

This action sets you up for applying the style. You can also just click anywhere inside the paragraph (without selecting any text) to apply a class style to it.

11. **In the Property Inspector, click the HTML button, and then, from the Class menu, choose "copyright" (see Figure 3-30).**

Boom—the copyright notice suddenly changes size and color, and grows a line above it. Magic.

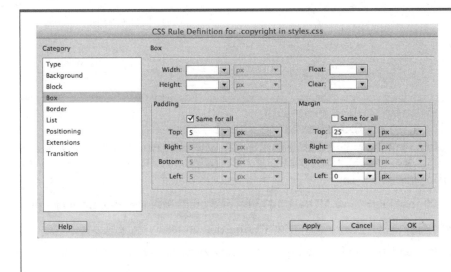

FIGURE 3-29

The difference between padding and margin settings is subtle but important. Both properties add space around content you're styling. And if you don't have a background color, image, or border, both properties pretty much act the same. However, when you do have a background color, image, or border, padding adds space between the content and the edge of the backgrounds and borders. Margins add space outside the border and background.

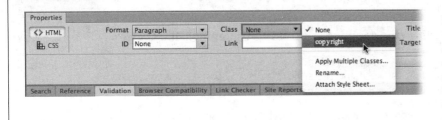

FIGURE 3-30

The Class menu in the HTML mode of the Property Inspector lists all class styles. It also displays the style name using the style's text formatting—in this case, bold, white text, with a dark green background. Notice that the menu lists only class styles; tag styles don't appear in this menu, since you don't apply them manually. You can also apply a class using the Property Inspector's CSS Mode, as described on page 133.

Attaching an External Style Sheet

Now that you've created these styles, you may wonder how you can use them on other pages—after all, that's the beauty of external style sheets. Once created, it's a simple process to link other pages in the site to that style sheet.

1. **Choose File→Save All Related Files, and then close the *about.html* page.**

   You'll open a new web page to attach the external style sheet to it.

2. **In the Files panel, double-click the file *events.html* to open it.**

   This file is another page for the café's website. It has no formatting yet, so you'll attach the external style sheet you just created.

3. **On the CSS Styles panel, click the Attach Style Sheet button (the chain link button at the bottom of the CSS Styles panel).**

   The Attach External Style Sheet window appears.

4. **Click the Browse button.**

   The Select Style Sheet dialog box appears.

5. **Navigate to the Chapter03 folder (or click the Site Root button), and then double-click the *styles.css* file.**

Don't forget the Site Root button. It appears on every window in which you need to save, open, or select a file. It's a great shortcut to make sure you're working in the correct folder for your site.

You can ignore the other settings in the Attach External Style Sheet window for now (they're described on page 138).

6. **Click OK to attach the style sheet to the page.**

Dreamweaver instantly formats the headlines and main text of the story. Pretty cool—and very efficient. You need to apply the .*copyright* class style only to the last paragraph on the page.

7. **Scroll to the bottom of the page, and then click anywhere inside the paragraph with the copyright notice.**

Next you'll add a style to the paragraph.

8. **From the Class menu on the Property Inspector, select "copyright."**

This page is almost done. Preview it in a web browser to see what you need to do next.

9. **Press F12 (Option-F12) to preview the page.**

Dreamweaver probably prompts you to save your files; go ahead and do that. The page opens in a browser; notice that the bulleted list doesn't use the same font as the paragraph text. You'll change that now.

10. **Return to Dreamweaver and add a style for the <ul> tag.**

In other words, click the New CSS Rule button in the CSS Styles panel, choose "tag" for the selector, type *ul* for the selector name, and then click OK to create the style (refer to steps 1 and 2 on page 176 if you need more details on creating a new tag style).

11. **Choose PTSansRegular from the Font-family menu; type *14* in the Font-size box.** Click the Box category, turn off the Margin "Same for all" checkbox, and then type *50* in the Left margin box.

This matches the settings for the paragraph text. Lastly, change the bullet to a square shape.

12. **Click the List category in the CSS Rule Definition window; choose "square" from the List-style-type menu and then click OK.**

You finished the style for the bulleted list items.

13. **Press F12 (Option-F12) to preview the page.**

Dreamweaver probably prompts you to save your files; go ahead and do that. The finished page should look something like Figure 3-31. If you'd like to compare your finished product to the completed version, you'll find those pages in the Chapter03_complete folder in the tutorials folder.

NOTE   You may need to hit your browser's Refresh button to see the most recent changes you made to the style sheet. This is one problem you'll encounter when you design pages with external style sheets—web browsers often *cache* them (see page 44). Normally that's a good thing—it means repeat visitors to your site have to wait only once for the CSS file to download—the first time they visit your site. But when you're in the midst of a design, frantically switching back and forth between Dreamweaver and a web browser preview, the browser might retrieve the obsolete version of the external style sheet saved in its cache rather than the newly updated file on your computer. (The Safari browser is particularly aggressive at holding onto cached files, so if you preview in that browser, make sure to reload the page when you do.)

You can work around this problem: Open the Preferences window (Edit→Preferences [Dreamweaver→Preferences]), select "Preview in Browser," and then turn on the "Preview using temporary file" checkbox. Now when you preview the page, Dreamweaver makes a temporary file on your computer that incorporates both the CSS and HTML of the page. This defeats a browser's cache so that now you're seeing the very latest changes. This setting has the added benefit of stopping Dreamweaver's annoying "You must save your file before previewing" dialog box each time you preview an unsaved page.

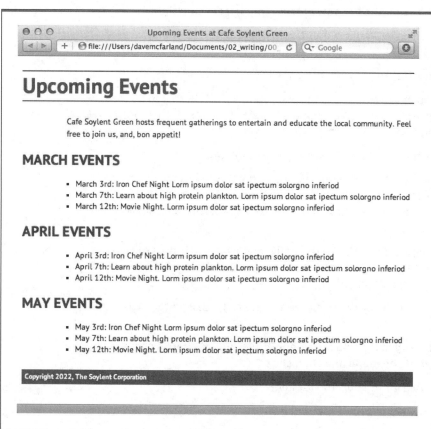

FIGURE 3-31

CSS offers a lot of design tools to produce beautiful typography for your web pages. In addition, an external style sheet lets you quickly, easily, and consistently style hundreds of pages without much work.

Links

The humble hyperlink may not raise eyebrows anymore, but the notion that you can navigate a whole sea of information, jumping from one island of content to another with a simple click, is a powerful phenomenon. Interested in a particular band? Go to Google, type in the band's name, *click* to go to its website, *click* to go to the page that lists its upcoming gigs, *click* to go to the venue's website, and then *click* to buy tickets.

Although embedding links is a basic task in building web pages, and even though Dreamweaver—for the most part—shields you from the complexities of doing so, links can be tricky to understand. The first section of this chapter gives you an overview of links, including some of the technical distinctions between the different types of links. The rest of the chapter, with sections on formatting the appearance of your links and creating navigation menus, will help turn you into a link-crafting maestro.

> **NOTE** If you already understand links or you're eager to start using Dreamweaver, jump to the tutorial on page 223.

■ Understanding Links

Links are snippets of code that give web browsers directions to get from one page to another on the Web. What makes links powerful is that the distance covered by those directions doesn't matter. A link can lead to another page on the same site just as easily as it can lead to a page on a web server halfway around the globe.

Behind the scenes, a simple HTML tag called the anchor tag (<a>) makes each and every link work. Links come in three flavors: *absolute, document-relative*, and *root-relative*. Page 190 shows you examples of each in practice.

Absolute Links

When people want to mail you a letter, they ask for your address. Suppose it's 123 Main St., Smithville, NY 12001, USA. No matter where in the country your friends are, if they write *123 Main St., Smithville, NY 12001, USA* on an envelope and mail it, their letters will get to you. That's because your address is unique.

Similarly, every web page has a unique address, called a *URL* (most people pronounce it "you-are-el"), or Uniform Resource Locator. If you open a web browser and type http://www.cafesoylentgreen.com/events/index.html into the address bar, the events page for Cafe Soylent Green opens.

This URL is an *absolute link*—it's the complete, unique address for a single page. Absolute links always begin with *http://*, and an absolute link leads to the same destination page, no matter what website page you put that link on—an absolute link in a web page can call up another page within the same site or a page on another site entirely. You'll use absolute links any time you link to a web page *outside of your own site*—that's the *only* way a web browser can go from a page on your site to a page outside of your site. However, when you want to call up a page *within* your site, there's another way to write the link (described next), one that lets you view your pages without an Internet connection, right on your desktop—a feat that's impossible with absolute links.

The bottom line: Use absolute links when you want to link to a page on another website.

Document-Relative Links

Suppose you, the resident of 123 Main Street, drop in on a couple who just moved into a house directly across the street from you. After letting them know about all the great restaurants nearby, you tell them about a party you're having at your place.

When they ask you where you live, you could say, "I live at 123 Main St., Smithville, NY 12001, USA," but your neighbors would probably think you needed psychiatric help. Instead, you'd say something like, "Just walk across the street, and there you are." Of course, you can't use these instructions as your mailing address, and they wouldn't make sense, either, for a neighbor who lived seven houses down. Those directions only help the neighbors directly across the street get from their house to yours.

When you want to create a link from one web page to another within the same website, you use a similar shorthand, called a *document-relative link*. In essence, a document-relative link—like the directions you gave your neighbor—tells a browser where to find a page *relative* to your current location, in this case relative to the current web page you're on. If two pages are in the same folder, for instance, the path is as simple as "Go to that page over there." In this case, the link is simply the name of the file you wish to link to: *index.html*, for example. You can leave off all that http://www.your_site.com/ business, because you're already on that site and within that directory.

Document-relative links can be finicky, however, because they're completely dependent on the location of the page containing the link. If you move that page to another part of your site—filing it in a different folder, for example—the link won't work (it's as though your neighbors moved across town—they couldn't walk across the street to get to your house any longer). That's why working with document-relative links has traditionally been one of the most troublesome chores for web designers, even though this kind of link is ideal for linking from one page to another in the same site.

Fortunately, Dreamweaver makes working with document-relative links so easy you may forget what all the fuss is about. In Dreamweaver, whenever you save a page that has a document-relative link to a folder different from the page's original folder—a maneuver that would normally shatter all the links on the page—Dreamweaver quietly *rewrites* the links so they still work. Even better, using the program's site management tools, you can cavalierly reorganize your site without fear, moving files and folders without harming the delicate connections between your site's files. (You'll learn about Dreamweaver's site management features in depth in Part 4 of this book.)

Root-Relative Links

Root-relative links, also called *site root-relative links*, describe how to get from one page to another within the same site, just like document-relative links. However, in this case, the link describes the path relative to the site's *root folder*—the folder that contains the home page and all the other pages, folders, and files that make up your site. (For a detailed description of the root folder and structuring a website, see Chapter 15.)

Imagine you work in a big office building. Say you need to get to a co-worker's office in the same building, so you call her for directions. She may not know the precise directions from your office to hers, but she can tell you how to get from the building's entrance to her office. Since you both know where the building's front door is, these directions work well. In fact, she can give the same directions to anyone else in the building, and since they all know where the entrance is, they'll be able to find her office, too. Think of the office building as your site, and its front door as the *root* of your site. Root-relative links always begin with a slash (/). This slash is a stand-in character for the root folder—the front door—of your site. The same root-relative link always leads to the same page, no matter where it is on your website.

If you use Dreamweaver for all your web page development, you probably won't need root-relative links, but they can come in handy. For example, suppose you're asked to create a new page for an existing website. Your client gives you text, some graphics, and a list of the other pages on the site that this page needs to link to. The problem is, your client doesn't know where on the site the new page needs to go, and his webmaster won't return your calls.

Fortunately, you can use root-relative links to solve this dilemma. Since these links work no matter where the page is on your site, you could complete the page and let the client put it where it belongs—and the links will still work.

There's one major drawback to root-relative links: They don't work when you test them on your own computer. If you view a web page sitting on your computer's hard drive, clicking a root-relative link in your browser either doesn't work or produces only a "File not found" error. Root-relative links work only when the pages that have them reside on a web server. That's because the technology behind web servers understands root-relative links, but your personal computer doesn't.

One solution to the root-relative links problem is to install a web server on your computer and put your site files inside it. This is the approach you take when building the dynamic sites discussed in Chapter 21.

UP TO SPEED

Parts of a URL

Each chunk of a URL helps a web browser locate the proper web page. Take the following URL, for instance: http://www.cafesoylentgreen.com/events/index.html.

- **http://**. This portion of the address specifies the *protocol*, the communications technology a browser uses to interact with the web server. *HTTP* stands for *hypertext transfer protocol*; you use it to go to a web page. You use other protocols for other Web tasks, such as *ftp* when you want to transfer files to and from a server and *mailto* when you want to send email messages to mail servers. *HTTPS* stands for hypertext transfer protocol secure, and you write it as https:// in the address bar of a browser. HTTPS requires a special server setup, and it encrypts the communications between a browser and a web server so snoops can't see the information you send and receive. Bank websites, e-commerce sites, and other sites that deal with sensitive information use HTTPS web servers.

- **www.cafesoylentgreen.com.** This is the Web address of the computer dishing out the pages for Café Soylent Green's website—that is, it's the address of the web *server* where all the café's pages reside. The *www* part identifies a website within the *domain "cafesoylentgreen.com."* You can have multiple websites in a single domain, such as http://news.cafesoylentgreen.com, http://secret.cafesoylentgreen.com, and so on. Many websites these days even leave off the www, and you can find them simply by their domain name, like this: http://cafesoylentgreen.com.

- **/events/**. This is the name of a folder (also called a directory) on the web server.

- **index.html**. This is the name of the file the web browser will open—it's the file name of the web page itself, the HTML document you created in Dreamweaver.

NOTE There's one exception to the "root relative links don't preview correctly" dilemma. Dreamweaver provides two ways to preview a web page: *with* a temporary file or *without* one. The temporary-file option has a couple of advantages: You can preview a page without having to save it first, and you can preview—on your local computer—any root-relative links you create.

To turn this feature on, go to Edit→Preferences (Dreamweaver→Preferences), click the "Preview in Browser" category, and turn on the Preview Using Temporary File checkbox. Behind the scenes, Dreamweaver secretly rewrites root-relative links as *document-relative* links whenever it creates a temporary file. If you see files in your site with weird names like TMP2zlc3mvs10.htm, those are the temporary files Dreamweaver creates. Feel free to delete them.

Unless you have a specific reason to use root-relative links (like your IT department says you have to), it's best to stick to document-relative links for your pages. But keep this discussion in mind. Later in the book, you'll see that Dreamweaver's site management features use root-relative paths behind the scenes to track your site's files.

NOTE You can run into trouble with root-relative links if the site you're working on is located in a folder inside a web server's root folder. For example, say your buddy gives you space on his web server. He says you can put your site in a folder called *my_friend*, so your URL is http://www.my_buddy.com/my_friend/. In this case, your web pages don't sit at the root of the site—they're in a folder *inside* the root. So a root-relative link to your home page would be /my_friend/index.html. Dreamweaver can handle a situation like this, but only if you provide the correct URL for your site—http://www.my_buddy.com/my_friend/—when you set it up (see Figure 4-1).

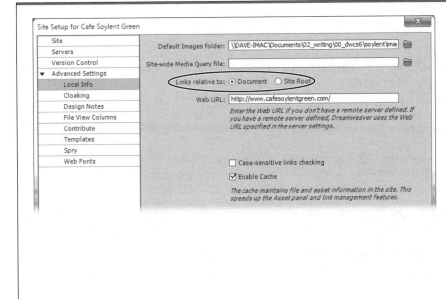

FIGURE 4-1

When you set up a site in Dreamweaver, you can identify the URL of the site even if it's in a subfolder within the root folder—it's the site's actual address on the Internet. Expand the list of Advanced Settings options on the left of the Site Setup window, click the Local Info category, and then type the full web address of your site in the Web URL box. You can also tell Dreamweaver which type of link— document-relative or site root-relative—it should use when it creates a link to another page on your site (circled). You can always return to this window to change this option: Choose Site→Manage Sites, select your site, and then click Edit.

Link Types in Action

Figure 4-2 shows a website as it appears on a hard drive: folders filled with HTML documents and graphics. Here's a closer look at some links you might find on those pages and how they might work.

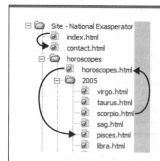

FIGURE 4-2

Here are a few examples of links for a fictitious website located at http://www.nationalexasperator.com. The three arrows show the connections between the original page (where each arrow starts) and the page it links to (where each arrow ends).

■ LINK FROM THE HOME PAGE (INDEX.HTML) TO THE CONTACT US PAGE (CONTACT.HTML)

Most websites call the home page *index.html* or *index.htm*. You can link from this page to the *contact.html* page—identified by the number 1 in Figure 4-2—using any of the three link types:

- **Absolute link address:** http://www.nationalexasperator.com/contact.html. What it means: Go to the website at http://www.nationalexasperator.com and download the page *contact.html*.

- **Document-relative link address:** *contact.html*. What it means: Look in the same folder as the current page is in and download the page *contact.html*.

- **Root-relative link address:** */contact.html*. What it means: Go to the top-level folder of this site and download *contact.html*.

> **TIP** If you can write an absolute URL, you can easily write a root-relative URL. Simply strip off the *http://* and the web server name. In the example above, erasing the http://www.nationalexasperator.com in the absolute address leaves */contact.html*—the root-relative path.

■ LINK FROM THE HOROSCOPES PAGE TO THE PISCES PAGE

Now imagine you built a web page that you want to link to a page in a subfolder of your site. Here's how you'd use each of the three link types to open a document nested in a subfolder (In this example, a subfolder called "2005"), as identified by the number 2 in Figure 4-2:

- **Absolute link address:** http://www.nationalexasperator.com/horoscopes /2005/pisces.html. What it means: Go to the website at http://www.national exasperator.com, look in the folder *horoscopes*, then look in the folder *2005*, and then download the page *pisces.html*.

- **Document-relative link address:** *2005/pisces.html*. What it means: From the current page, look in the folder *2005* and download the page *pisces.html*.

- **Root-relative link address:** */horoscopes/2005/pisces.html*. What it means: Go to the top-level folder of this site, look in the folder *horoscopes*, then look in the folder *2005*, and then download the page *pisces.html*.

■ LINK FROM THE SCORPIO PAGE TO THE HOROSCOPES PAGE

Now suppose you're building a web page that's in a deeply nested folder, and you want it to link to a document outside of that folder, like the link labeled 3 in Figure 4-2:

- **Absolute link address:** http://www.nationalexasperator.com/horoscopes/horoscopes.html. What it means: Go to the website at http://www.national exasperator.com, look in the folder *horoscopes*, and download the page *horoscopes.html*.

- **Document-relative link address:** *../horoscopes.html*. What it means: Go up one level—outside of the current folder—and download the page *horoscopes.html*. In website addresses, a slash / represents a folder or directory. The two dots (..) mean, "Go up one level," into the folder that *contains* the current folder. So to link to a page that's up two levels—for example, to link from *scorpio.html* to the home page (*index.html*)—you would use *../* twice, like this: *../../index.html*.

- **Root-relative link address:** */horoscopes/horoscopes.html*. What it means: Go to the top-level folder of this site, look in the folder *horoscopes*, and download the page *horoscopes.html*.

Executive Summary

In short: Use absolute URLs to link to pages *outside* your site folder, use document-relative links to link to pages *within your site*, and, unless you know what you're doing (or your IT department tells you that you have to), avoid using root-relative links altogether.

■ Adding a Link

If all that talk of links gets you confused, don't worry. Links *are* confusing, and that's one of the best reasons to use Dreamweaver. If you can navigate to a document on your own computer or anywhere on the Web, you can create a link to it in Dreamweaver, even if you don't know the first thing about URLs and don't intend to learn the details of writing them.

Browsing for a File

To create a link from one page to another on your local website, use the Property Inspector's "Browse for File" button (see Figure 4-3) or its keyboard shortcut, as described in the following steps.

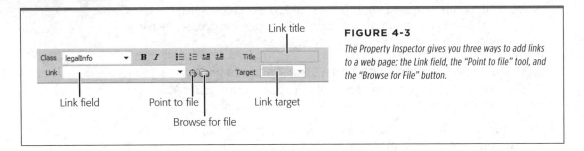

FIGURE 4-3

The Property Inspector gives you three ways to add links to a web page: the Link field, the "Point to file" tool, and the "Browse for File" button.

To browse for a file in Dreamweaver, you use the same type of dialog box that you use to open or save a file, making "Browse for File" the easiest way to add a link. (To link to a page on *another* website, you need to type the web address into the Property Inspector. Turn to page 196 for instructions.)

1. **In the document window, select the text or image you want to link from.**

    You can select a single word, a sentence, or an entire paragraph. When you add a link to text, the selected words appear in blue and underlined (depending on your visitors' web browser settings), like billions of links before them.

    In addition, you can turn a picture into a link—a great way to add attractive graphics-based navigation buttons.

> **NOTE** When you add a link to an image, Internet Explorer 8 and earlier draws a blue border around the image, just like linked text has a blue underline. Fortunately, with some simple CSS, you can get rid of that blue outline—see the Tip on page 195.

2. **In the Property Inspector, click the folder icon—that's the "Browse for File" button.**

    Or, choose Modify→Make Link, or press Ctrl+L (⌘-L). In any case, the Select File dialog box opens (see Figure 4-4 for Windows, Figure 4-5 for Macs).

3. **Navigate to and select the file you want the link to open.**

    The file should be a web page that's part of your site. In other words, it should be in the local root folder (see the box on page 46) or in a folder therein.

    Remember: To a website, the root folder is like the edges of the known universe—nothing exists outside of it. If you try to link to a file *outside* the root folder—like to a file on your desktop—Dreamweaver tells you it's a problem and offers to copy the file to the root folder. Accept the offer.

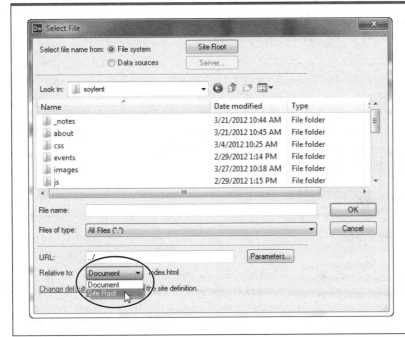

FIGURE 4-4

In Windows, use the Select File dialog box to browse your computer to select the target file for a link. When you set up your site, you can tell Dreamweaver whether to use document- or site root-relative links. However, if you ever find the need to temporarily switch to a different type of link (to a root-relative link, for example, if you set up your site to use document-relative links), use the "Relative to" drop-down menu (circled). You probably won't ever need to do this, but Dreamweaver gives you the option.

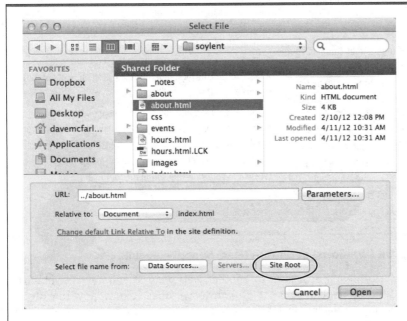

FIGURE 4-5

Every file in a website needs to be somewhere inside a local root folder (see the box on page 46). This master folder holds all the files for your site, including other folders with other files. Because it's so central to your web files, Dreamweaver includes a Site Root button (circled) in every window that requires selecting or saving a file. (This example shows what you see on a Mac; on Windows PCs, the button's at the top of the window, as shown in Figure 4-4.) Click this button and you jump straight to your site's root (so you know exactly where you are on your hard drive), making it easy to navigate to the file you need.

NOTE You can double-click the name of a file in the Select File dialog box and Dreamweaver selects the file *and* closes the Select File dialog box in one step.

4. **Make sure you select the correct type of link—document- or site root-relative—from the "Relative to" menu.**

   As noted earlier in this chapter, document-relative links are usually the best choice. Root-relative links (a.k.a. *site root-relative links*) don't work when you preview your site on your own computer. (They do, however, work once you move them to your web server.)

NOTE You can skip step 4; just set the type of link you want in the Site Setup window, and then forget about it. Dreamweaver always uses the link type you specified there. See Figure 4-1 for details.

FREQUENTLY ASKED QUESTION

The Mysterious Triple Slashes

Why do my links start with file:///?

Links that begin with *file:///* (file:///C:/missingmanual/book_site/cafe/events.html, for example) aren't valid links on the Web. Rather, they're temporary addresses that Dreamweaver creates as placeholders for links it will rewrite later. (A *file:/// path* tells Dreamweaver to look for the file on your computer.) You'll spot these addresses when you add document-relative links to a page you haven't saved, or when you work with files outside of your site's local root folder.

Suppose you're working on a web page that contains your company's legal mumbo-jumbo, but you haven't yet saved it. After adding a document-relative link to your home page, you notice that the Property Inspector's Link field begins with *file:///*. Since you haven't saved your legal page, Dreamweaver doesn't know its folder location and can't create a relative link telling a browser where to go to get the page. So it creates a temporary link, which helps it keep track of which page to link to. Once you save the page somewhere in your site, Dreamweaver rewrites the link in proper document-relative format, and the temporary *file:///* link disappears.

Likewise, Dreamweaver can't write a "legitimate" link (a link that really *will* work in a web browser) to a file outside the local root folder. Since it considers anything beyond the root folder outside the bounds of the site, Dreamweaver can't write a link to "nowhere." So, if you save a page *outside* the local root folder, Dreamweaver writes all document-relative links on that page as file paths beginning with *file:///*. (This problem can also crop up if you use Dreamweaver without first setting up a site—that's why that simple site setup process, described on page 40, is so important.) To avoid this invalid link problem, always save your web pages inside the local root folder or in a folder *inside* the local root folder. To learn more about root folders and websites, see Chapter 15.

If you set up a site and you *link to* a page—or add an image (Chapter 5)—stored outside the local root folder, Dreamweaver has the same problem. However, in this instance, Dreamweaver gives you the option of copying the out-of-bounds file to a location of your choosing within the root folder.

---

5. **Click OK (Windows) or Choose (Mac) to apply the link.**

   The text or image now links to another web page. If you haven't yet saved the other web page in your site, Dreamweaver doesn't know how to write the document-relative link. Instead, it displays a dialog box saying that it will assign a temporary path for the link until you save the page—see the box above.

After you apply a link, in Design view, the link text appears underlined and colored (using the color defined by the Page Properties window, shown in Figure 1-22). Press F12 (Option-F12 on Macs) to preview the page in your browser, where you can click the link.

You can use the browse-to-file method when you work in Code view, too: select text in Code view and follow the steps above.

TIP Internet Explorer displays a colored border around linked images. To get rid of that border, create a CSS style for the <img> tag (see page 125 if you're unsure about creating styles). Under the Border category of the CSS Rule Definition window, set the border style to "none" (see page 260 for more information on CSS borders).

Using the Point-to-File Tool

You can also create links by dragging an icon from the Property Inspector to the Files panel (see Figure 4-6). If your site involves a lot of links, learning to use the Point-to-File tool will save you time and energy.

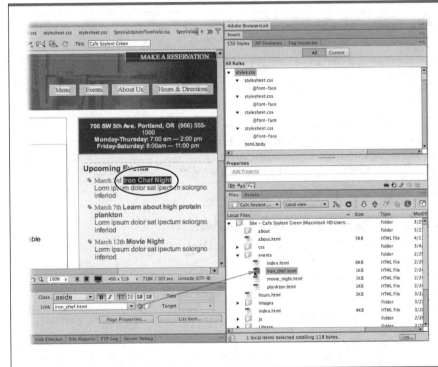

FIGURE 4-6

In the document window, select the text (circled) you want to turn into a link. To link to another page, drag the Point-to-File icon (the bull's-eye icon in the Property Inspector) to a web page in the Files panel (right). In this example, Dreamweaver creates a link to the web page called directions.html. You could also Shift-drag from the selected text to the directions.html page in the Files panel to create the same link.

To use this trick effectively, position your document window and Files panel side by side.

1. **In the document window, select the text or image you want to turn into a link.**

   Make sure you have both the Property Inspector and Files panel open. To open the Property Inspector, choose Window→Properties. To open the Files window, choose Window→Files. (Before using the Files window, you need to create a local site, as described on page 40.)

   > **NOTE** The point-to-file tool works in Code view as well.

2. **Drag the Point-to-File icon from the Property Inspector onto a web page in the Files window.**

   Or you can Shift-drag the selected text or image in the document window to any web page in the Files panel, bypassing the Property Inspector altogether (this method only works in Design view, however).

   > **TIP** You can also drag a file from the Files panel into the Link box in the Property Inspector to link to it.

3. **After dragging over the correct web page, release the mouse button.**

   The selected text or image in your web page now links to the file you just pointed to.

   > **NOTE** **Bizarre Bug Alert**: If you use two monitors as you build web pages, the Point-to-File icon might not work. If your main monitor (the one with the Start menu for Windows, or the one where a program's menu bar appears on Macs) is on the right, and the second monitor is on the left, the Point-to-File icon *may not* work. Then again, it might! Strange, but truly infuriating.

Typing (or Pasting) the URL or Path

If you need to link to another website, or you feel comfortable working with document-relative links, you can also simply type the URL or path to the page into the Property Inspector. Note that this technique and the hyperlink object tool discussed next are the *only* ways to add links to pages *outside* the current website.

1. **In the document window, select the text or image you want to make into a link.**

2. **In the Property Inspector's Link field (Figure 4-3), type the URL (the path) to the file.**

   If the link leads to another website, type an absolute URL—that is, a complete web address, starting with *http://*.

TIP An easier approach is to copy a complete URL—including the *http://* part—from the address bar in your browser window and paste it into the Link field.

To link to a page on your own site, type a document-relative link (see page 190 for some examples). Letting Dreamweaver write the correct path using the point-to-file or browsing technique described above is a good way to avoid typos. But typing the path can come in handy when, say, you want to create a link to a page you haven't yet created, but know where it'll go.

3. **Press Enter (Return) to apply the link.**

   While you don't necessarily have to hit Enter (Return)—sometimes you can just click elsewhere on the page and keep working—Dreamweaver has been known to forget the link and not apply it. This is true for most fields in the Property Inspector—so if you type information directly into the Property Inspector (to create a link, add a title, and so on) get into the habit of hitting the Enter (Return) key to make sure your change sticks.

NOTE If you add an absolute link to a website without specifying a web page, add a final forward slash (/) to the end of the address. For example, to link to Yahoo, type *http://www.yahoo.com/*. The final slash tells the web server that you're requesting the default page (the home page) at Yahoo.com.

Although leaving out the slash works, too (*http://www.yahoo.com*), the server has to do a little extra work to figure out which page to send back, resulting in a slight and unnecessary delay.

Also include the final slash when you provide a link to the default page inside a folder on a site, like this: *http://www.sawmac.com/dwcs6/*. That saves the browser from first requesting a file named *dwcs6*, and then requesting the default page inside the folder dwcs6.

Using the Hyperlink Object

Dreamweaver gives you yet another way to add a link. The Hyperlink object in the Common category of the Insert panel (Figure 4-7) lets you insert a link with many optional properties. Its only real benefit is that it lets you add text and a link in one step (instead of adding text to a page, selecting it, and *then* specifying a link address). Unfortunately, this tool only works with text (not graphics), and some of the optional properties don't work in all browsers.

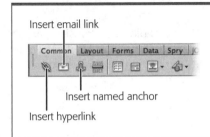

FIGURE 4-7

The Insert panel's Common category includes three link-related objects: the Hyperlink (to add links), the Email link (to link to an email address), and the Named anchor (to link to a specific spot [a bookmark] in the current page or another page in the same site). As discussed in Figure 1-3, the Insert options can appear in a toolbar (as pictured here) or as a panel grouped with other site panels on the right side of the screen.

If you're still interested, here's how it works. Start by clicking on the page where you want to insert a link. Then:

1. **Choose Insert→Hyperlink or click the chain icon on the Insert toolbar.**

   The Hyperlink dialog box opens (see Figure 4-8). To apply a link to text already on the page, select the text first, and then choose Insert→Hyperlink.

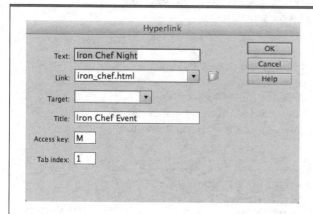

FIGURE 4-8

As an alternative to using this dialog box, you can specify all the options you see here, except the "Access key" and "Tab index" properties (see steps 6 and 7 below), to existing text or images from the Property Inspector. Also, keep in mind one somewhat special case. If you want to add an access key and tab index to an already existing link, you have a couple of options: Go into Code view (as described in Chapter 7) and hand-edit the HTML, or use the Tag Inspector to see all the properties available to a particular link. (For details, see page 362.)

2. **In the Text box, type the text you want to appear on the page.**

   Whatever you type here is what you'll see on the page, and what your audience will click to follow the link. If you previously selected some text on the page, it shows up in the Text box automatically.

3. **Click the folder icon and search for the page you want to link to.**

   Alternatively, you can type a URL in the Link box.

4. **Set the target window for the link.**

   If you want the linked page to open in the same window—as most linked pages do—don't select anything. To make the page open in a new window, select the _blank option (see the box on page 199 for more on targeting a link).

   The last three options are more interesting.

5. **Type a title for the destination page.**

   This property is optional. As described in the preceding box, most browsers display the title in a small tooltip window when a visitor moves his mouse over the link.

Targeting and Titling Links

What are the Title box and Target menu in the Property Inspector for?

A link's *Title* property supplies additional information about a link, usually to clearly indicate where the link leads. For example, if you linked the words "Click here for more" to an article describing different types of termites, the link text alone doesn't clearly explain where the link leads—"Click for more *of what?*" you might ask. In this case, you could add the title "A complete list of termite species" in the Property Inspector (see Figure 4-3). The Title property is optional, and if the link text already clearly explains where the link leads, don't bother setting it. In fact, you can avoid the Title property altogether if you write text that explains where the link leads: "Click here for a complete list of termite species," for example.

However, in the case of linked images (such as a logo that also acts as a link back to a site's home page), adding a title is a very good idea. Search engines like the Title property in this case, because it lets them know the purpose of the link; people who use screen readers (programs that help those with vision problems surf the Web) also benefit, since the Title property can be read out loud and the visitor will know where the link goes. The Title property has one other unique feature: Web browsers display a drop-down tooltip with the title's text in it when a guest moves her mouse over the link.

The *Target* menu has nothing to do with the accuracy of your links, nor with shooting ranges. It deals with how a browser displays the destination page when you click a link.

You can have the new page (a) replace the current page in the browser window (the way most links work); (b) open in a new browser window (choose the *_blank* option); or (c) appear in a different *frame* on the same page (an obsolete HTML feature).

_blank is pretty much the only option used these days, but be careful if your pages use the "Strict" forms of HTML 4.01 and XHTML 1.0; the Target attribute isn't valid code for these doctypes. However, HTML5, recognizing the usefulness of being able to open links in a new tab or window, allows the *_blank* target...and so does every browser on the planet).

6. **Type a key in the "Access key" box.**

   An *access key* lets you trigger a link from your keyboard. Internet Explorer and Safari for Windows understand this property in conjunction with the Alt key; Alt + Shift + the access key works on Firefox and Google Chrome for Windows; Control + the access key for Firefox and Safari 3 on Macs; Control + option + the access key for Chrome and Safari 4 and later on Macs; and Shift + Esc + the access key for Opera. For example, if you type *h* in the "Access key" box, then a visitor using Internet Explorer can press Alt+H to mouselessly open that link. Of course, unless people who visit your site are psychic, it's a good idea to provide the access key next to the link itself, as in "Home Page (Alt+H)."

7. **In the "Tab index" box, type a number for the tab order.**

   In most browsers, you can press the Tab key to step through the links on a page (and boxes on a form). This feature not only gives you a handy way to go from link to link from your keyboard, but it also lets people who can't use a mouse due to disabilities cycle through the links.

Normally when you press Tab, web browsers highlight links in the order they appear in the page's HTML. The Tab index, by contrast, lets *you* control the order in which links light up as visitors tab through them. For example, you can give your navigation buttons priority when someone presses Tab, even if they aren't the first links on the page.

For the first link in the order, type *1* here. Number other links in the order you want the Tab key to follow. If you aren't concerned about the order of a particular link, leave this option blank or type in *0*. The web browser will highlight that link after the visitor has tabbed through all links that *do* have a Tab index.

EXTENSION ALERT

QuickLink Is Quick Work

Dreamweaver makes it easy to add innovative commands and tools—including those written by independent, non-Adobe programmers—to your copy of the program. You can read a lot more about these add-on programs, called *extensions*, in Chapter 20.

When you work with links, one extension that really comes in handy is QuickLink. Created by Dreamweaver guru Tom Muck, this extension instantly turns text into either a *mailto* or an *absolute* URL. You can find QuickLink at *http://tinyurl .com/3cquzkl*. Amazingly, even though this extension hasn't been updated since Dreamweaver MX 2004, it still works in CS6.

Once you install the extension, here's how it works: Suppose you insert your cursor somewhere on a web page in Dreamweaver and type the text, "You can download the free PDF viewer at *http://www.adobe.com*." To turn *http://www .adobe.com* into a real link, you can either select the text, go

to the Property Inspector, and then type *http://www.adobe .com*, or—with QuickLink—simply select the text and choose Commands→QuickLink. QuickLink writes the proper code in the Property Inspector, including the initial (and mandatory) *http://*, even if those characters were missing from the original text. (Note that this extension has one small bug: After you install it, the QuickLink command will appear *twice* in the Commands menu. Either one works.)

QuickLink also converts email addresses to proper *mailto* links: Just select the email address (*missing@sawmac.com*, say), apply the QuickLink command, and watch as the extension automatically inserts the correct code (mailto: *missing@ sawmac.com*) into your page.

For even faster action, create a keyboard shortcut for this command; Shift+Ctrl+L is a good one. (See page 911 for more on keyboard shortcuts.)

■ Adding an Email Link

If you want to invite your site visitors to email you, an *email link* is the perfect solution. When someone clicks an email link, his email program launches automatically, and a new message opens with your email address already in the "To:" field. Your guest can then just type his message and send it off.

An email link looks like this: *mailto:chef@cafesoylentgreen.com*. The first part (*mailto*) indicates the type of link, while the second part (*chef@cafesoylentgreen.com*) specifies the email address.

NOTE Email links work only if the person who clicks the link has an email program set up and running on his computer. If someone visits your site from a computer at the public library, for example, he might not be able to send email. Likewise, if he's using a web-based email client, like Gmail, clicking an email link won't open his Gmail page in a web browser.

You can create an email link much the way you create any other Dreamweaver link: by selecting text or an image and typing the *mailto* address, as shown above, into the Property Inspector's Link field. To simplify this process, Dreamweaver offers a quick way to insert an email link:

1. **Under the Insert panel's Common category, click the "Email link" icon, which looks like an envelope (see Figure 4-7).**

   Alternatively, choose Insert→Email Link. Either way, if you already typed the text (*Email me!*) on your web page, select it first. The Email Link dialog box opens (see Figure 4-9).

FIGURE 4-9

The Email Link dialog box lets you specify the text for the email link and the email address. You can also select text in your document and click the Email Link icon on the Objects panel. The text you select appears in the Text field in this dialog box.

2. **In the Text field, type the text that you want to appear on the web page.**

   This text can indicate the link's purpose, like *Email the webmaster.* (If you select text in the document first, it automatically appears in the Text field.)

3. **Type an email address into the Email field.**

   This is the address that appears in your visitors' email program when they click the link. (You don't have to type *mailto:*—Dreamweaver adds it automatically.)

4. **Click OK.**

   Dreamweaver adds the text to the page, complete with a *mailto* link.

NOTE Some people don't add email links to their websites because they're afraid of spammers' automated programs that search the web and collect email addresses. There are some tricks to fool these "spambots," but spammers have figured most of them out. The fact is, spammers can attack even "Contact Us" web forms.

If you're absolutely obsessed with never being spammed, leave your email address off your site. However, many businesses rely on people contacting them for more information, and the harder you make it for a legitimate visitor to contact you, the fewer legitimate contacts you'll receive—after all, you wouldn't have much of a freelance design business if you never provided a way for someone to contact you. Your best bet is to let the spam come, but add a spam filter to your email program to separate the wheat from the chaff.

■ Linking Within a Web Page

Clicking a link usually loads a web page into the browser window. However, what if you want to link not only to a web page but to a specific *spot* on that page? You'll see this frequently on long web pages, where links at the top of the page let visitors jump down to specific content lower on the page; see Figure 4-10 for an example. You can create in-page links two ways: by using a *named-anchor* or by adding an ID to the target section. The named-anchor method has been around since the earliest days of the Web; it uses a special type of link. With the ID technique, you give the destination spot a unique ID and then link to that ID. Although this method is newer, it works with all current web browsers. You'll learn about both methods below.

Method 1: Creating a Named Anchor

Creating a Named Anchor link is a two-step process: First you add an anchor to a spot on a page and name it, thus identifying the destination for the link; then you add a link that goes to that named anchor. For instance, in the Table of Contents example shown in Figure 4-10, you'd add a Named Anchor at the beginning of each chapter section.

To create a named anchor:

1. **In the document window, click the spot where you want your visitors to end up.**

    You want to add a Named Anchor here.

2. **Insert a Named Anchor.**

    You can do so using any of three methods: Choose Insert→Named Anchor, press Ctrl+Alt+A (⌘-Option-A), or, from the Insert toolbar, select the Common category and click the Named Anchor icon (see Figure 4-7).

3. **Type the name of the anchor in the Insert Named Anchor dialog box.**

    Give each anchor a unique name (something short and easy to remember). HTML doesn't allow spaces or punctuation marks, and if you include any, Dreamweaver displays an error message and strips out the offending characters.

4. **Click OK to insert the anchor.**

    Dreamweaver displays a gold shield with an anchor icon in it. Click this icon to see the name of the anchor in the Property Inspector. (If you don't see it, see page 204 for details on hiding and showing anchors.)

The Named Anchor icon (the gold shield) is the key to removing or editing the anchor later: Just click the icon and press Delete to get rid of it, or click it and change its name in the Property Inspector. (Deleting the name in the Property Inspector deletes the anchor from the page.)

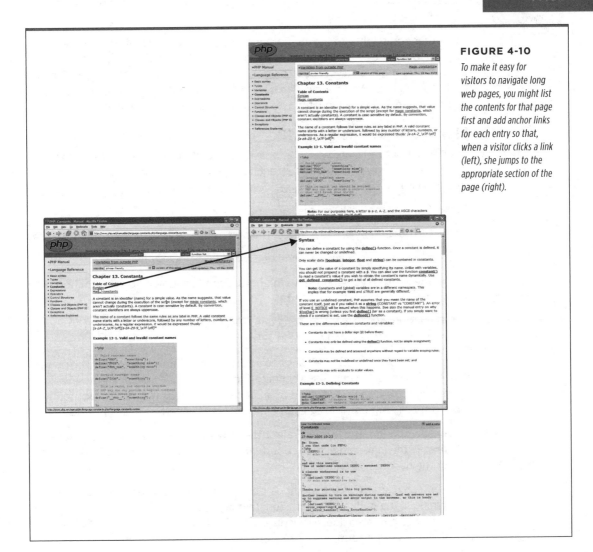

FIGURE 4-10

To make it easy for visitors to navigate long web pages, you might list the contents for that page first and add anchor links for each entry so that, when a visitor clicks a link (left), she jumps to the appropriate section of the page (right).

Method 2: Adding an ID

Instead of adding a Named Anchor, you can assign an ID to the destination spot on a page. For example, if you want to link to a subhead way down on a page (a Heading 2, or <h2> tag, for example), you can assign an ID to that heading. For text, you add an ID by clicking anywhere inside a paragraph and, in the Property Inspector's ID box, type the name you want to use. As with Named Anchors, you can't use spaces or punctuation marks.

For non-text elements, like images or tables, select the tag (the Tag Selector discussed on page 26 is the best way), and type a name in the ID box on the left side of the Property Inspector.

One other You might use IDs in another context, to identify and style discrete sections of your page by adding an ID to a tag and then styling the page using CSS (see page 124 for more on ID styles). The good news is you can use that same ID name for both purposes. You can add an ID to a tag whether you style the tag or not; if you decide to style the tag later, you can use the same ID name in the style sheet.

Linking to an Anchor or ID

Creating a link to a Named Anchor or ID isn't all that different from linking to a web page. Once you create and name an anchor or add an ID name to a tag, you can link to it from within the same web page or from a different page.

To link to an anchor or ID on the same page:

1. **In the document window, select the text or image you want to turn into a link.**

   For example, drag across some text, or highlight a graphic.

2. **In the Property Inspector's Link field, type #, followed by the anchor or ID name.**

   The # sign indicates that the link goes to an anchor or ID. So, to link to an anchor named *directions*, you'd type in *#directions*.

You can also link from one web page to a particular location on another web page in your site. You need to first add a Named Anchor or ID to the destination page. Then the process is the same as linking to an anchor on the same page, except that you have to specify not only the anchor name, but also the path to the web page as well.

3. **In the document window, select the text or image you want to turn into a link.** In the Link field of the Property Inspector, type or choose the URL or path of the destination page.

   You can use any of the methods described above: browsing, point-to-file, or typing in the path name. Unfortunately, if you browse to select the destination file, Dreamweaver doesn't display any of the anchors or IDs on that page, so you need to perform one extra step.

4. **Click at the end of the URL or path.** Type # followed by the anchor or ID's name.

   In the end, the Link field should look something like this: *contact.html#directions*.

Viewing and Hiding Anchors

A Named Anchor isn't visible in a web browser; it appears in Dreamweaver as an anchor-on-a-gold-shield icon. (If anchors don't appear, visit the Preferences window and, in the Invisible Elements category, make sure you have the Anchor checkbox turned on.)

If Dreamweaver displays Named Anchors and you'd prefer to hide them, turn off the Anchor box in the Invisible Elements category. To hide *all* invisible elements, choose View→Visual Aids→Invisible Elements, or choose Visual Aids→Invisible Elements from the Visual Aids menu in the toolbar (see Figure 9-12).

However, if you link within a page using an ID, Dreamweaver doesn't display any gold shield at all. That's because Dreamweaver never displays ID names in Design view, and there's no way to change that.

FREQUENTLY ASKED QUESTION

Anchors Away

When I click a link to an anchor or ID, the web browser is supposed to go to the page and display the anchor or the tag with the specified ID at the top of the browser window. But sometimes the linked-to spot appears in the middle of the browser. What's that about?

Web browsers can't scroll beyond the bottom of a web page, so if you have an anchor or ID near the bottom of a page, the browser can't pull the page all the way up to the anchor point.

If one of your own web pages exhibits this problem and it really bothers you, the fix is simple: create a style for the <body> tag and add *bottom padding* (page 449). This adds space after the last bit of content on the page, so browsers can scroll the page all the way to the anchor.

■ Modifying a Link

At some point, you may need to change or edit a link. Perhaps the URL you were linking to has changed, or you simply no longer need that link.

Changing a Link's Destination

As you'll read in Part 4, Dreamweaver provides some amazing tools for automatically updating links in your pages to keep your site in working order, even if you move files around. But even Dreamweaver isn't smart enough to know when a page on someone *else's* website has been moved or deleted. And you may decide you simply need to change a link so that it points to a different page on your own site. In both cases, you need to change the links by hand:

1. **Select the text or picture link.**

   The existing link path appears in the Property Inspector's Link field.

2. **Use any of the techniques described on page 191 to specify the link's new target.**

   For example, click the "Browse for File" button in the Property Inspector and locate a different web page in your site, or type a complete URL to point to a page outside your site. The destination of the link changes to the new URL, path, or anchor.

Removing a Link

Sometimes, you want to stop a link from linking—when the web page you were pointing to no longer exists, for example. You want to keep the originating text or image, but remove the outdated link. In that case, select the link text or image and then use one of these tactics:

- Choose Modify→Remove Link, or press Ctrl+Shift+L (⌘-Shift-L).

- Delete the text in the Link field of the Property Inspector and then press Enter (Return).

The text or image remains on your web page, but it no longer links to anything. If it's a text link, the color changes from your site's link color to the normal text color for the page.

Of course, if you're feeling particularly destructive, you can delete the link's text or image itself, which simultaneously deletes the link.

■ Styling Links

You can control the basic look of links from the Links category of the Page Properties window (Figure 4-11). To open it, choose Modify→Page Properties→Links (CSS), press Ctrl+J (⌘-J)→Links (CSS), or click the Page Properties button in the Property Inspector (the button appears only when you have either nothing on the page selected or you have text selected; it doesn't appear if you have an image selected, for example). In the Category list, click "Links (CSS)."

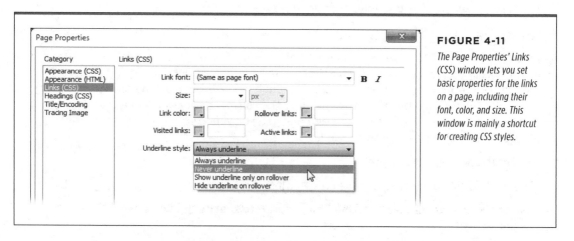

FIGURE 4-11

The Page Properties' Links (CSS) window lets you set basic properties for the links on a page, including their font, color, and size. This window is mainly a shortcut for creating CSS styles.

The top set of options—font, size, bold, italic—sets the basic formatting for every link on the page. The next group of options sets the color of the links under specific conditions. Web browsers keep track of how a visitor interacts with the links on a page: when he moves his mouse over a link, for example. Each link has four modes (called *states*): a plain, unvisited link is simply called a *link*; a link that a visitor has already clicked (determined by your guest's browser history) is called a *visited* link; a link that a guest's mouse is currently pointing to is technically called a *hover* state, though Dreamweaver refers to it as a *rollover* link; and a link in the process of being clicked (where a visitor has pressed but not released his mouse button) is known as an *active* link.

Each of these states provides useful feedback for your visitors, and you can style each one individually. In most web browsers, a plain link appears blue until you visit the linked page—then the link turns purple. This helpful color-coding lets a visitor know whether to follow a link: "Hey, there's a page I haven't seen," or, "Been there, done that."

The rollover (or hover) link is particularly useful in telling visitors they can click the link, and it lends itself to a lot of creative potential. For example, you can completely change the look of a link when a visitor mouses over it; you can change its color, add a background image, or change its background color. (To get neat effects like this, you need to go beyond the Page Properties window and set styles for your links, as described in the next section.)

Finally, an *active* link is for that fleeting moment when a visitor clicks a link but has yet to release the mouse button. It happens so fast that it's usually not worth spending too much time formatting the state.

NOTE Internet Explorer applies the active link style to any link a visitor *tabs* to (some web surfers can't, or don't want to, use a mouse and rely on the keyboard to navigate websites). Firefox, Safari, Opera, and Chrome use yet another link state, called *focus*, to style links that someone reaches via the Tab key. See the note on page 209 for more on a link's focus state.

The Page Properties window lets you change the color for each link state. In addition, the "Underline style" menu lets you control whether a browser underlines a link (the default), displays nothing beneath the link, displays an underline when a guest mouses over the link, or underlines the link by default but removes it once a visitor mouses over it. Since web surfers are accustomed to thinking of underlined text as a big "CLICK ME" sign, think twice before removing underlines from links. Without some clear indication that the text is a link, visitors may never see (or click) the links on your page.

One problem with using the Page Properties window to style links is that the settings apply only to the current page. That's because the Page Properties window saves the CSS styles to an internal style sheet in the current page. Fortunately, you don't need to set the Page Properties on every page of your site; you can move the styles you create in Page Properties to an external style sheet (see page 123 for a refresher on external style sheets). If you use the Page Properties window for one page, you can export those styles or even drag them into an external style sheet. (To learn how, see page 385.) Alternatively, you can bypass the Page Properties window altogether and create CSS link styles from scratch—which you'll learn about in the next section.

CSS and Links

Using the CSS Styles panel to create styles for your links gives you access to many more formatting options besides the font, color, and size options offered in the Page Properties window. In fact, you can apply nearly every CSS property to links. For example, you can use all the text options discussed on page 161—font size, weight, variant, letter spacing, and so on—to format a link. In addition, you can add a border (page 260) and a background color to a link to make it look like a button.

To format the look of all your links, create a tag style (page 124) for the <a> tag (the tag that creates links) using the instructions on page 125. To create a different look for a particular link (if you want that "Buy Now!" link to be bigger and bolder than other links on a page, for example), create a class style (page 124) and apply it directly to that link.

To control how a link looks for different states (link, visited, hover, and active), you need to dip a little deeper into the CSS pool and use what's called a *pseudo-class*. As you've read, a selector is merely the part of a style that instructs a browser where to apply the style—*h1* is the selector for formatting every Heading 1, for example. When you select Compound from the Selector Type menu at the top of New CSS Rule window, Dreamweaver lets you select one of four *pseudo-classes*, each of which refer to a different type of link, as shown in Figure 4-12. These four options (*a:link, a:visited, a:hover*, and *a:active*) correspond to the link states you saw in the Page Properties window.

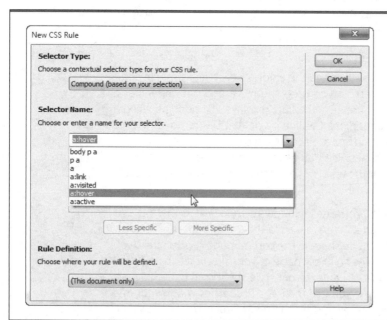

FIGURE 4-12

The drop-down menu that appears when you select "Compound" as the selector type from the top menu lists the four link pseudo-classes. You may see one or more other names at the top of the list, too—for example, the "body p a," "p a," and "a" selector names you see in this menu. The Selector Name menu lists the style names you can apply to what you have selected on the page. In this case, you put the cursor inside a link, which was inside a paragraph. As a result, Dreamweaver suggests creating a "body p a" style or a "p a" style. These styles are called descendent selectors—you'll learn about them on page 377.

To use a pseudo-class, open the New CSS Rule window (click the + icon in the CSS Styles panel or go to Format→CSS Styles→New), select Compound from the Selector Type menu, and then choose the appropriate selector from the Selector Name drop-down menu. For example, to format the way a link looks when a guest mouses over it, choose *a:hover*. You don't have to set all four pseudo-classes; if you're not interested in how your links look during the nanosecond that a visitor clicks it, skip the *a:active* option. If you want to set more than one pseudo-class, you must create them in the order that they appear in the menu, or the styles may not display as you intend them. (A helpful mnemonic for remembering this rule is LoVe HAte—that is, *:link* comes before *:visited*, which comes before *:hover*, which comes before *:active*.)

NOTE Safari, Firefox, and Chrome browsers understand an additional pseudo-class related to links: *a:focus*. This selector applies when a visitor uses the Tab key to move from one link to another on a page. Each time she jumps to a new link, the browser highlights it and gives the link "focus." All versions of IE treat *a:active* as if it were *a:focus*.

To create a style that formats a link when a visitor tabs to it (instead of mouses over it), create what's called a group style. Here's how: When you create the "highlighted" style, choose Compound for the selector type. For the selector name, type in *a:focus, a:active*. This applies the "tabbed to" highlight style for all current browsers.

Using these styles, you can make your link text appear red and underscored before a visitor clicks the link, twice as large when he mouses over it, purple and boldfaced when he clicks it, and pale pink after he visits the linked site. (Granted, if you try this design, Martha Stewart may never hire you to design her site, but you get the point.)

NOTE For security reasons, current browsers limit the styling you apply to a visited link to just a different color. In other words, say you create the pseudo-class style a:visited and change the font, font-size, background-color, underline, and set its text color to red; the only visual change the browser will make to a visited link is to change its text color to red—the font, background-color, and other settings are simply ignored.

Note that these link pseudo-classes have one drawback: setting them affects *all* the links on a page. In that respect, adding pseudo-classes to the a tag (a:active, a:hover, and so on) is like creating tag styles.

TIP Dreamweaver lets you quickly preview link states in Design view. Choose View→Toolbars→Style Rendering to open the Style Rendering toolbar sandwiched between the Related Files toolbar (page 353) and the Document toolbar (page 25). Buttons labeled *:l* (for the link state), *:v* (for visited), *:h* (for hover), *:a* (for active) and *:f* (for focus) appear at the right side of the toolbar. Click any of them to see the CSS design for the selected state: for example, click the *:h* button to see all the links on a page as they'll appear when a mouse hovers over them. You'll learn more about the Style Rendering toolbar on page 402.

If you want to apply a style to only certain links on a page, here's what to do: create a new style (click the + button in the CSS Styles panel, for example), choose Compound from the Selector Type menu in the New CSS Rule window, and then, in the Selector Name box, type a class name followed by a colon and the appropriate link state. For example, to change the look of a "Buy Now!" link only, you could create a style called *.buyNow:link*; to make that link look different when someone mouses over it, you'd name the link *.buyNow:hover*.

After naming the style (and saving it to an external style sheet), follow the steps on page 129 to create the look for that style (choose a font, select a color, and so on). After you create the style, simply apply the style class to the link (or links) you want to style using any of the techniques described on page 132. (In the example above, the class name is *buyNow*, and that's what you'll see listed in the Property Inspector's Class menu.)

> **NOTE** Descendent selectors provide a more efficient—but more complex—way to format specific links differently from all the others on a page. You'll find this CSS concept discussed on page 377.

Creating a Navigation Menu

Every website should have navigation links that let visitors quickly jump to the site's main areas. On a shopping site, those links might point to the categories of products for sale—books, DVDs, CDs, electronics, and so on. For a corporate intranet, links to human resources, office policies, company events, and each department might be important. Whatever the site, a web designer should strive to get visitors where they want to go via the shortest route possible.

Dreamweaver CS6 includes a powerful and easy navigation-building tool—the Spry menu bar. With it, you can put all your site's most important links into a compact horizontal or vertical menu (see Figure 4-13). Each button supports two levels of drop-down submenus, so a visitor can quickly jump to a page buried deep within your site.

The Spry Menu Bar is just one of the many "Spry" tools in Dreamweaver CS6. You'll learn a lot more about what Adobe calls the Spry Framework in Chapter 13, but in a nutshell, Spry is a collection of advanced JavaScript programs that let you add lots of dynamic effects to your web pages. (If you're familiar with the old Dreamweaver Behaviors, Spry is like those—on steroids.)

Adding a Menu

The first step in inserting a Spry menu is deciding where on the page to put it. A horizontal menu bar, with buttons sitting side by side, works well near the top of a page, either at the very top or below the area dedicated to a logo (often called a "banner"). A vertical menu bar, whose buttons are stacked one on top of the other, usually sits at the left edge of a page, below the banner area.

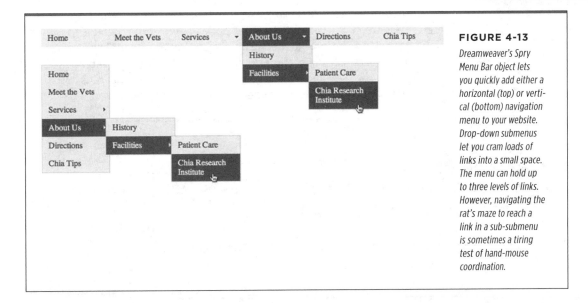

FIGURE 4-13

Dreamweaver's Spry Menu Bar object lets you quickly add either a horizontal (top) or vertical (bottom) navigation menu to your website. Drop-down submenus let you cram loads of links into a small space. The menu can hold up to three levels of links. However, navigating the rat's maze to reach a link in a sub-submenu is sometimes a tiring test of hand-mouse coordination.

To add a Spry menu:

1. **In the document window, click the spot where you want to insert the menu.**

   You can add a Spry menu bar in either Design view or Code view. When you learn more about web page layout in Chapter 9, you'll discover that most elements on a page—like graphics, paragraphs, and menus—go inside <div> tags, which you use to define the beginning and end of that element.

2. **Click the Spry Menu Bar button in the Layout category of the Insert panel (Figure 4-14).**

   You'll also find this button on the Spry tab of the Insert toolbar, or you can choose Insert→Spry→Spry Menu Bar. In any case, the Spry Menu Bar window appears, asking whether you want a horizontal or vertical bar.

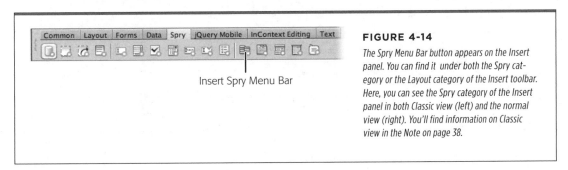

Insert Spry Menu Bar

FIGURE 4-14

The Spry Menu Bar button appears on the Insert panel. You can find it under both the Spry category or the Layout category of the Insert toolbar. Here, you can see the Spry category of the Insert panel in both Classic view (left) and the normal view (right). You'll find information on Classic view in the Note on page 38.

3. **Depending on the type of menu you want, choose either the Horizontal or Vertical radio button and then click OK.**

Dreamweaver inserts a "starter" menu containing a few links and drop-down menus (Figure 4-15). The blue tab that appears above the menu is the selection tab: click it to select the menu so you can change and add links using the Property Inspector (discussed next). If you can't see the blue tab, make sure the "show invisible element" setting is on: Choose View→Visual Aids and make sure you have Invisible Elements checked and Hide All unchecked.

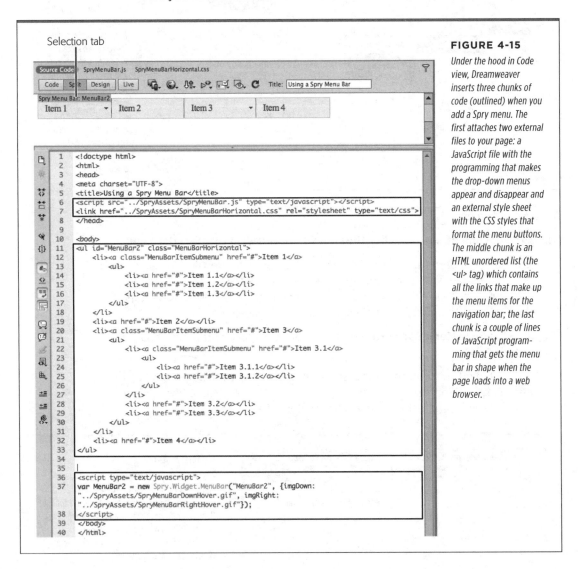

FIGURE 4-15

Under the hood in Code view, Dreamweaver inserts three chunks of code (outlined) when you add a Spry menu. The first attaches two external files to your page: a JavaScript file with the programming that makes the drop-down menus appear and disappear and an external style sheet with the CSS styles that format the menu buttons. The middle chunk is an HTML unordered list (the <ul> tag) which contains all the links that make up the menu items for the navigation bar; the last chunk is a couple of lines of JavaScript programming that gets the menu bar in shape when the page loads into a web browser.

Adding, Editing, and Removing Spry Menu Links

The starter Spry menu that Dreamweaver inserts into your page isn't very useful (unless you coincidentally have four sections on your site named Item 1, Item 2, Item 3, and Item 4). To make the menu your own, you need to re-label the buttons and link them to pages on your site; you can also add more buttons and assign links to each of them.

To edit the Spry menu, select it by clicking the blue Spry selection tab. Once selected, the menu's labels and links appear in the Property Inspector (Figure 4-16).

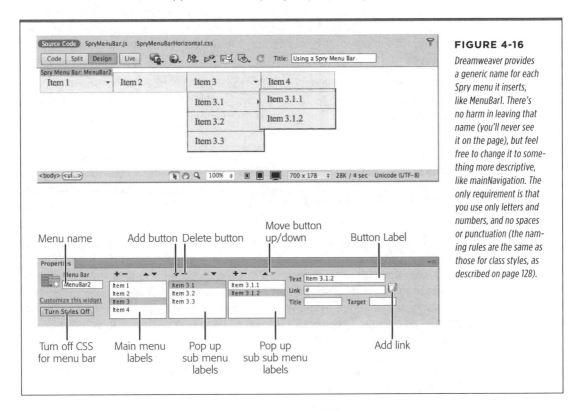

FIGURE 4-16

Dreamweaver provides a generic name for each Spry menu it inserts, like MenuBar1. There's no harm in leaving that name (you'll never see it on the page), but feel free to change it to something more descriptive, like mainNavigation. The only requirement is that you use only letters and numbers, and no spaces or punctuation (the naming rules are the same as those for class styles, as described on page 128).

A Spry menu supports up to three levels of menus. Dreamweaver always displays the main navigation buttons; each can have its own drop-down menu, which only appears when a visitor mouses over the button. And each button on the *second* level of menus (the first drop-down menu) can have its own drop-down menu (making it the third level of menus). The Property Inspector gives each level its own column (see Figure 4-16), and each column has its own set of controls so you can add, delete, and move menu buttons.

To edit one of the main navigation buttons on a Spry menu, select the button's label (for example, Item 1) in the left-hand column of the Property Inspector; in the Text box, type the label you want to appear on the navigation button ("Home" or "About Us," for example). Then create the link using the "Browse for File" button or by typing the URL into the Link box (see page 191 for more on setting links). You can leave the Title and Target boxes empty (see the box on page 199 for descriptions of these properties).

To add a button to the main menu, click the + button above the left-hand column. Dreamweaver inserts a new "Untitled Item" in the list of links. Change the button's label in the text box, and then set a link using either method discussed in the previous paragraph.

To delete a button from the main nav bar, click its name in the left-hand column, and then click the minus-sign button (-) at the top of the column. You can also rearrange the order of the buttons by selecting a name from the list and clicking the up or down arrow (on a horizontal menu bar the up arrow moves the button to the left, while the down arrow moves the button to the right).

You add, edit, and arrange submenus the same way. Select the Spry menu (click the blue menu tab) and then, in the Property Inspector, select the menu item to which you want to add a submenu. For example, in Figure 4-16, to add another button to the drop-down menu that appears when a visitor mouses over the "Item 3" button, select Item 3 from the left-hand column, and then click the + button in the *middle* column. Dreamweaver highlights the new button, and you can delete and rearrange buttons in the submenu using the minus and up and down arrow buttons at the top of that menu's column. To work with a sub-submenu (the third level of menus), first select an item from the left-hand column, and then click an item in the middle column.

NOTE You can also edit a Spry menu's text and links in the document window. The main nav buttons are always visible, so you can click inside one to edit the text or change the link. To see a drop-down menu in the document window, select the Spry menu (click the blue tab); in the first column of the Property Inspector, select a menu item that has a drop-down menu, and then select any button in the drop-down submenu list. That drop-down menu appears in the document window (as pictured in Figure 4-16). In fact, the menu won't *disappear* (potentially covering other content on your page) until you select one of the other main nav buttons from the left-hand column in the Property Inspector.

When Dreamweaver inserts a Spry menu, it adds a bunch of files to your site. Dreamweaver places those files in a folder named SpryAssets in your site's local root folder (a message listing the names of the files appears as soon as you save a page after inserting a menu). These files control the look and functionality of the menu:

Dreamweaver adds one CSS file, one JavaScript file, and some image files (for the arrows used to identify buttons with submenus). When you eventually move your pages to a web server, make sure you upload these ancillary files as well.

NOTE If you don't like the folder name SpryAssets, or if you'd like to store these supporting files in a different folder, choose Site→Manage Sites to open the Manage Sites window, select your site from the list, and then click the Edit button. Doing so opens the Site Setup window (the one you used when you first defined the site).

Click Advanced Settings on the left side of the window. Click the Spry category, and then click the Folder icon to locate another folder on the site. If you select a new folder after you inserted a Spry object into a page, just drag the files from the SpryAssets folder to the new folder in the Files panel (the one you just told Dreamweaver to use for all Spry files). (See page 50 for more information on moving files using the Files panel.) You can then safely delete the empty SpryAssets folder.

Changing the Look of the Navigation Menu

The "direct from the manufacturer" look of Spry menus leaves something to be desired. The battleship gray buttons and vibrant, "Hey, look at me, I'm purple!" rollovers aren't the most pleasing combination. Because Dreamweaver formats the menu with a collection of CSS styles, the power to improve the look of Spry menus is within your reach. Unfortunately, decoding Dreamweaver's tangle of CSS requires a guidebook. Basically, the process involves identifying the name of the CSS style responsible for the format you want to change, and then editing that style using the basic techniques you learned on page 139, or using one of the advanced methods discussed on page 382.

TIP You can preview the Spry menu bar—complete with interactive drop-down menus—by using Dreamweaver's Live view. Click the Live button at the top of the document window or choose View→Live View. Now you can mouse over the menu and see its buttons highlight and submenus drop down. In other words, it's just like viewing the page in a web browser. To leave Live view, click the Live button a second time, or choose View→Live View again.

For example, if you want to change the font that a menu uses, open the CSS Styles panel (Window→CSS Styles) and then click the All button to see all the styles available for a page. Dreamweaver stores the styles for menu bars in their own style sheets (*SpryMenuBarVertical.css* for vertical menu bars and *SpryMenuBarHorizontal.css* for horizontal bars). Expand the list of styles (click the + symbol to the left of the style sheet name in the CSS Styles panel), and then double-click *ul.MenuBarVertical a* (if you're working on a vertical menu) or *ul.MenuBarHorizontal a* (for horizontal menus). This opens the Style Definition window for that style. You can then change the menu's font (see page 145).

NOTE The Spry menu bars are formatted using an external style sheet (page 123). If you edit the CSS of a Spry menu bar on one page, that change will apply to the Spry menu bar on every other page of your site.

Spry Menus Behind the Scenes

A Spry menu might look like a fancy navigation bar made up of colorful buttons and interactive menus, but under the hood it's just a simple bulleted list of links. Some pretty clever CSS creates the cool-looking buttons, and well-crafted JavaScript provides the dynamic behavior that makes the menus work.

Since the HTML behind a menu is so simple, it can be easier to edit Spry menus if you remove the fancy CSS. To do this, select the Spry menu by clicking its blue tab and then, in the Property Inspector, click the Turn Styles Off button. Bam! You have an ugly bulleted list, just like the ones you learned about in Chapter 2. In fact, you can use the same techniques described on page 106 to add, edit, and delete bulleted items. The text you add to each bulleted item will appear on the navigation button: Select this text and add a link as described on page 191.

The primary set of bullets (the ones furthest to the left) represent the main navigation buttons. The drop-down menus are just nested lists, as described on page 111. Take this simple list:

```
* Home
* Our Services
    * Consultation
    * Garden Planning
        * Basic Apartment Plan
        * Deluxe Apartment Plan
* Contact Us
```

This would produce a navigation bar with three buttons, labeled "Home," "Our Services," and "Contact Us." Moving the mouse over the "Our Services" button would open a drop-down menu with two other buttons, labeled "Consultation" and "Garden Planning." In other words, the bullets labeled "Consultation" and "Garden Planning" are a nested list inside the bulleted item named "Our Services," while the two bullet items "Basic Apartment Plan" and "Deluxe Apartment Plan" are a nested list inside the "Garden Planning" bulleted item.

If you decide to take this quick-and-dirty approach to editing Spry menus, keep one thing in mind: Dreamweaver expects any bulleted item containing a nested list (a drop-down menu) to have a special CSS class applied to it: *MenuBarItemSubmenu*. In the example above, you need to apply this style to both the "Our Services" and "Garden Planning" list items. To do so, click inside the bulleted item (the one containing the nested list), and use the Class menu in the Property Inspector's HTML mode to apply the *MenuBarItemSubmenu* style (turn to page 132 for a refresher on applying class styles).

NOTE The strange style names Dreamweaver uses for Spry menus (*ul.MenuBarVertical a*, for example) are called *descendent selectors*. They're an advanced type of CSS selector used to pinpoint very specific elements in a page. You can read about them on page 377, but for now, here's the ultra-quick cheat sheet for descendent selectors: Read them from right to left. The element on the far right is the element that Dreamweaver will ultimately style. In this example, it's a link—the "a" represents the <a> tag used for the links in the navigation bar. The "ul.MenuBarVertical" part specifies an unordered list (<ul>) that has a class *MenuBarVertical* applied to it. So running that selector through the universal translator produces this instruction: "Format every <a> tag that appears inside a bulleted list with the class MenuBarVertical like this...." In other words, only the links inside the Spry menu bar are affected by this style.

Spry menus offer two types of button: one for a regular menu item, and one for a submenu item (see Figure 4-17). A regular menu item is a button without a drop-down menu attached; a guest clicks the button and goes to a new page. A submenu button is any button that produces a drop-down menu when a visitor mouses over it. In addition, these two button types each have two looks: the button as it sits on the page, and the button as your guest mouses over it (its rollover look).

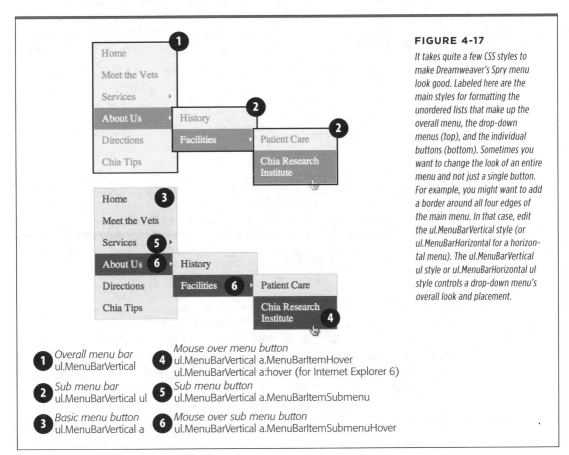

FIGURE 4-17

It takes quite a few CSS styles to make Dreamweaver's Spry menu look good. Labeled here are the main styles for formatting the unordered lists that make up the overall menu, the drop-down menus (top), and the individual buttons (bottom). Sometimes you want to change the look of an entire menu and not just a single button. For example, you might want to add a border around all four edges of the main menu. In that case, edit the ul.MenuBarVertical style (or ul.MenuBarHorizontal for a horizontal menu). The ul.MenuBarVertical ul style or ul.MenuBarHorizontal ul style controls a drop-down menu's overall look and placement.

1 Overall menu bar
ul.MenuBarVertical

2 Sub menu bar
ul.MenuBarVertical ul

3 Basic menu button
ul.MenuBarVertical a

4 Mouse over menu button
ul.MenuBarVertical a.MenuBarItemHover
ul.MenuBarVertical a:hover (for Internet Explorer 6)

5 Sub menu button
ul.MenuBarVertical a.MenuBarItemSubmenu

6 Mouse over sub menu button
ul.MenuBarVertical a.MenuBarItemSubmenuHover

NOTE A submenu button can also be a link. For example, say you had a button labeled Animals; rolling over that button makes another menu appear with three other buttons—Dogs, Cats, Camels. The Animals button can be both a link—leading to a page about animals—and the "trigger" that makes the drop-down menu appear.

■ FORMATTING REGULAR MENU BUTTONS

You can define the look of a regular menu button, and simultaneously set the basic look for all the menu bar buttons, by editing the *ul.MenuBarHorizontal a* style (for a horizontal menu) or *ul.MenuBarVertical a* style (for a vertical menu). Just double-click the style's name in the CSS Styles panel to edit it.

You can set any of the CSS text properties discussed on page 161, such as font, font size, and font color. All the buttons will share these settings (except font color, because it always changes when a visitor rolls her mouse over any button—if you want to use the same font color in that instance, you need to specify that color in the styles discussed in the next section).

In addition, this style controls the background color of both regular buttons and submenu buttons. To change the background color, edit the appropriate style (for example, *ul.MenuBarVertical a* for a vertical menu) and change the background color option found under the Background category of the Rule Definition window.

You can also add border lines to the buttons—for example, a line separating each button—by setting the border properties for the style (see page 260 for more on CSS borders). Set the *padding* (page 449) to control the space between the text on a button and the edge of the button. To make the text appear close to the edges of the button, decrease the padding; to place empty space around the text, increase the padding.

> **NOTE** If you add a horizontal menu bar, you may run into one particularly frustrating problem: That's when a column of your page, which should appear right below the menu bar, actually appears much further down the page, usually beneath another column, such as a sidebar. This problem only appears under unusual circumstances—when you use CSS-based layouts with the Float property and when one of the menu buttons is taller than the others (and even then you won't always see the problem). The dreaded "float drop" (no joke) causes this problem, and you'll find a solution on "Avoiding 'Float Drops'" on page 502.

◼ FORMATTING ROLLOVER MENU BUTTONS

Visitors get instant feedback when they interact with a Spry menu. Moving the mouse over a menu button changes the color of the button and its text, letting visitors know "Hey, I'm a link, click me!" The rollover buttons Dreamweaver creates have a purple background and white text, but you can change those settings by editing either the *ul.MenuBarVertical a.MenuBarItemHover* or the *ul.MenuBarHorizontal a.MenuBarItemHover* style (depending on whether you inserted a vertical or horizontal menu).

> **NOTE** If you're worried about Internet Explorer 6, you must edit a separate style—ul.MenuBarVertical a:hover or ul.MenuBarHorizontal a:hover—to achieve a hover effect for menu button. Since IE 6 is quickly disappearing, you might not bother.

Locate a style in the CSS Styles panel, and double-click it to edit it. Dreamweaver-created styles only set text color and background color properties, but you're free to change any CSS property. For example, if you added border lines between buttons in the menu bar, you could alter the color of those lines for the rollover button. Or you could make text appear bold when a guest hovers over a button.

NOTE The name of the style used for rollover menu buttons is actually a combination of three different selectors and is so long that its full name doesn't even fit in the CSS Styles panel: "*ul.MenuBarHorizontal a.MenuBarItemHover, ul.MenuBarHorizontal a.MenuBarItemSubmenuHover, ul.MenuBarHorizontal a.MenuBarSubmenuVisible*" (the name will be slightly different for a vertical menu). This peculiar style is called a *group selector*. It's an efficient way to apply similar formatting rules to multiple elements on a page (see page 381 for an explanation of group selectors).

FREQUENTLY ASKED QUESTION

Stopping Content From Wrapping Around a Menu

When I add a horizontal Spry menu bar, then add a paragraph after the menu bar, that paragraph appears to the right of the menu bar. How do I make that paragraph go below the menu?

What you're encountering here is a problem common to the CSS float property. The float property is used to make an element move to the left or right, and allow content to wrap around it. For example, say you have a photo and you want it to appear on the right side of a page. However, you also want the text that follows the photo to wrap around the photo's left side, the way photos often appear in magazines. You could float the image to the right using the CSS float property (in fact, you'll learn just how to do this on page 257). In addition, site developers use floats extensively in page layout and you'll learn how to use them to create side-by-side columns in Chapter 9.

In the case of a horizontal Spry menu bar, Dreamweaver uses the CSS float property to make the buttons in the main menu bar appear side-by-side. Of course, the downside of this is that text following the menu will appear to the right of the menu instead of below it. To get around this problem you need to edit the ul.MenuBarHorizontal style: in the CSS Styles panel, locate and double-click the ul.MenuBarHorizontal style to open it for editing in the CSS Rule Definition window. Select Block from the left-hand list of categories. From the Display menu, choose inline-block. Click OK to finish editing the style. Unfortunately, Dreamweaver's Design view doesn't understand this little trick and will continue to display the paragraph next to the menu bar instead of below it. However, if you click the Live button to enter Live view (page 72) or preview the page in a web browser (page 73), you'll see that it works.

■ FORMATTING SUBMENU BUTTONS

Submenu buttons (the buttons that produce a drop-down menu when a guest mouses over them) look nearly identical to other menu buttons. In fact, the two styles mentioned above, which control a menu in its normal and rollover states, define the basic formatting for submenu buttons as well. The only visible difference is the small arrow that appears on the right edge of a submenu button (see Figure 4-17). It visually indicates the presence of a drop-down menu; it's a kind of "there's more this way" icon.

You can replace the graphics Dreamweaver uses for submenus: they're named *SpryMenuBarDown.gif, SpryMenuBarDownHover.gif, SpryMenuBarRight.gif*, and *SpryMenuBarRightHover.gif*. (You'll find the two "down" arrow graphics only in horizontal menus.) Create your own arrow graphics (in GIF format) with the same names and replace the original graphics files, which are located in the SpryAssets folder (unless you changed the name and location as described in the Tip on page 215). The graphics should be small enough to be visible in the menu buttons—the ones that Dreamweaver supplies are 4 x 7 pixels (right arrow) and 7 x 4 pixels (down arrow)—and you should include versions for both the normal and roll-over states of the submenu button.

TIP You can *permanently* replace the arrow graphics Dreamweaver uses with your own. First, go into the Dreamweaver configuration folder. In Windows, you'll find them at C:\Program Files\Adobe\Adobe Dreamweaver CS6\configuration\Shared\Spry\Widgets\MenuBar; on Macs you'll find them in Applications→Adobe Dreamweaver CS6→Configuration→Shared→Spry→Widgets→MenuBar. Make sure your graphic files have the exact same names as those Dreamweaver uses. (The CSS files that provide the basic styles for the Spry menu bar are also in this folder, so you could even edit these if you wanted a different set of "starter styles" for your menus—just make sure to back up the original CSS files!)

If you want to further customize the submenu buttons' appearance (for example, to change the font just for submenu buttons), edit either the *ul.MenuBarVertical a.MenuBarItemSubmenu* or *ul.MenuBarHorizontal a.MenuBarItemSubmenu* style. The *ul.MenuBarVertical a.MenuBarItemSubmenuHover* style controls the rollover state for submenu buttons in vertical menus; for horizontal menus, it's *ul.MenuBarHorizontal a.MenuBarItemSubmenuHover*.

■ CHANGING THE WIDTH OF MENUS AND BUTTONS

Spry menu buttons have preset widths. The main navigation buttons are each 8 ems wide, while the buttons on drop-down menus are 8.2 ems wide (see page 156 for information on ems). If your navigation buttons have a lot of text on them, 8 ems may be too narrow to fit everything in. Or, 8 ems may be too much space if the menu text is small and made up of short words like "Home," "About," and "Contact." You can adjust the width of buttons and menus by opening the appropriate CSS Style (discussed next) and adjusting the style's *width* property. For example, double-click the style name in the CSS Styles panel, and then change the *width* property in either the Box or Positioning categories of the CSS Rule Definition window. (The CSS Properties pane provides an even quicker method, as discussed in Figure 4-18.)

Here are the settings you can edit:

- **Main menu width**. The *ul.MenuBarVertical* style sets the overall width of a menu. (Setting the width of a horizontal menu has no effect, since the width of a horizontal menu is determined by the number of buttons on the menu.) For a vertical menu bar, use the same width for the menu as you do for the button (discussed next).

- **Main menu button width**. The width of the buttons that appear on the main Spry menu are determined by the *ul.MenuBarVertical li* style or *ul.MenuBarHorizontal li* style. You may want the button to be just as wide as the text inside it—in other words, have buttons of different widths based on the amount of text in the button's label. For this effect, set the width of this style to *auto*. Variable-width buttons look good for horizontal menus, but not for vertical menus, where the staggered right edges of the column of buttons looks uneven and distracting.

- **Drop-down menu width**. Control the overall width of drop-down menus with the *ul.MenuBarVertical ul* or *ul.MenuBarHorizontal ul* style. The width you set for this style should match the width of the drop-down menu buttons, covered next.

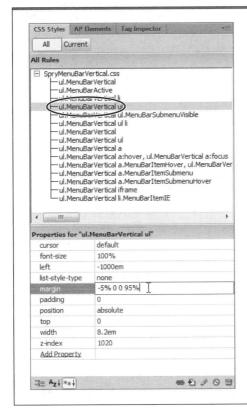

FIGURE 4-18

Dreamweaver's CSS style sheet for Spry menus lists the drop-down menu style—ul.MenuBarVertical ul, in this case, ulMenuBarHorizontal ul for horizontal menus—twice. The first one listed (circled) controls the positioning of the drop-down menu. The second one controls the border around it (why two? Great question, for which nobody except Adobe has an answer—and they're not telling.) Double-click the style to edit its properties using the Rule Definition window. For a really quick edit, like changing the position of a drop-down menu by adjusting its margin property, you can use the Properties pane of the CSS Styles panel (pictured in the bottom half of this image). Just select the current value for the property and type in a new value. For example, in this image, clicking the "-5% 0 0 95%" value (which represent the top, right, bottom, and left margin values, respectively) to the right of the word "margin" lets you type in a new value: 0 0 0 100%, say. You'll learn to edit using the Properties pane on page 382.

- **Drop-down menu button width**. The *ul.MenuBarVertical ul li* and *ul.MenuBarHorizontal ul li* styles control the width of the drop-down menu buttons on the vertical and horizontal menu, respectively. Dreamweaver's normal setting is 8.2 ems, but you can adjust this to create wider or narrower buttons.

NOTE If you want to add space between buttons in a horizontal menu bar, add some left or right margin to the *ul.MenuBarHorizontal li* style. You then have to set that same margin (left or right) for the *ul.MenuBarHorizontal ul li* style to 0, so that the margins on the drop-down submenus aren't affected.

■ POSITIONING DROP-DOWN MENUS

The drop-down menus on vertical menu bars overlap the button that opens them (see Figure 4-17). This stacking appearance gives the menu a 3-D look, as if the drop-down menu really were popping out of the page. However, you may want the drop-down menu to appear directly next to the menu button, or to overlap it even more dramatically.

To change the position of the menu, edit the *ul.MenuBarVertical ul* (or *ul.MenuBarHorizontal ul*) style. The CSS *margin* property controls the placement of the menu. For a vertical menu, the drop-down menu has a -5% top margin; this places the top of the drop-down menu a little *above* the submenu button that triggers it. The left margin is set to 95%, which moves the drop-down menu to the far right of the submenu button. To make the drop-down menu appear directly to the right and aligned with the top of the submenu button, change the top margin to 0 and the left margin to 100%. To make the drop-down menu overlap even more, you could change -5% to -10% for the top margin, and 95% to 85% for the left margin.

A horizontal menu's drop-down menu appears directly below the submenu button that triggers it. Its margin setting is 0. If you wish to make that menu overlap the submenu button, change the top margin to -5% and the left margin to 5%.

NOTE The look of sub-submenus for the horizontal menu bar is controlled by a style named *ul.MenuBarHorizontal ul ul*. There is no sub-submenu style for vertical menus, but you could create one named *ul.MenuBarVertical ul ul*.

■ REMOVING A SPRY MENU

To get rid of a Spry menu, select it (for example, click the blue tab shown in Figure 4-15), and then press the Delete key. In addition to removing the HTML for the menu, Dreamweaver also—as long as there are no other Spry menus on the page—removes the menu's linked external style sheet and JavaScript file.

■ REUSING A SPRY MENU

Of course you're not just going to create a Spry menu for a single page. Spry menus are intended to act as global navigation for an entire site (or least a significant subsection of a site), and so should appear on most if not all of your site's pages. There are a couple ways you can reuse a Spry menu once you create it:

- **Copy and paste.** If you click the blue tab of a Spry menu, you'll select its HTML in Code view; however, Dreamweaver's smart enough to know that there's more than just HTML needed to make a Spry menu. When you copy the menu (Edit→Copy), open another page, click in that page, and choose Edit→Paste, Dreamweaver not only pastes the HTML for that menu, it also adds the necessary code to link to the external style sheet and JavaScript files, as well as the JavaScript code that makes the menu work.

  One downside to this method is that Dreamweaver doesn't make sure the links will work when you paste the menu into another page. In other words, if you paste the menu into a page that exists in a directory other than the one housing the page you copied the menu from, the menu links probably won't work. Remember that document-relative links (page 186) describe the path from the current page to the linked-to page, so the path from page A to page B may not be the same as the path from page C to page B if pages A and B are in different directories. To get around this, you could start with a "flat" file setup—that is, don't create any subfolders for your site and place all your web pages in the root directory. That way, a document-relative path to a page in the site will be the same for all pages in the site. After you finish building the site, you could create subfolders and move your files around, letting Dreamweaver update all of the links so they continue to work (see page 49 for instructions on using the Files panel to organize site files).

> **TIP** If your Spry menu bars have broken links, use Dreamweaver's Check Links Sitewide tool to fix them (see page 765). For example, if you copy a Spry menu and paste it in another page, inadvertently placing it in a page in a subfolder (essentially breaking the links for that menu), you can have Dreamweaver identify and help fix them with this handy site-management tool.

- **Use Save As.** Another approach is to build a page for your site, complete the Spry menu, and then choose File→Save As to save a copy of that file. You can continue to use the Save As command to populate the rest of your site. The downside of this approach is that you need to build your menu before you build your pages, and that means you can't create links using the Browse for File technique you learned in this chapter (that tool assumes the linked-to pages already exist in your site). Instead, you'll need to figure out ahead of time how many pages you want and what you'll name their files, and you need to manually type the links as you build the menu bar. This is a labor-intensive approach that's prone to typos.

- **Use Dreamweaver templates.** Dreamweaver's Template feature, described in Chapter 19, is a great aid in building multi-page websites that use consistent design elements. Templates let you build pages that share common elements, like a layout, footer, banner, and, yes, navigation bars. With a template, you can manage your Spry menu bar from a single file—the template file. When you change a template file, like adding a button to a Spry menu bar or changing a link in a menu bar), Dreamweaver automatically passes those changes on to the other pages in the site.

> **NOTE** Dreamweaver has another site management feature called Library items (Chapter 18), which seem like they'd work great for managing Spry menu bars. They're intended to hold chunks of HTML that you want to reuse throughout a site. But Spry menu bars are more than just a chunk of HTML—they also require JavaScript and links to CSS and JavaScript files to work, so you can't make a Spry menu a Library item.

■ Link Tutorial

In this tutorial, you'll put what you learned in this chapter to use. You'll see how to link to other pages on your own site, link to another site on the Web, and use Dreamweaver's Spry menu bar to create a great-looking navigation bar—complete with fancy JavaScript-driven drop-down menus. (To see the completed page, skip ahead to Figure 4-28.)

TIP You'll need to download files from *www.sawmac.com/dwcs6* to complete this tutorial. See the Note on page 54 for details.

Linking to Other Pages and Websites

Once you downloaded the tutorial files and open Dreamweaver, set up a new site as described on page 40. In a nutshell, Choose Site→New Site. In the Site Setup window, type *Links Tutorial* into the Site Name field, click the folder icon next to the Local Site Folder field, navigate to and select the Chapter04 folder inside the MM_DWCS6 folder, and then click Choose or Select. Finally, click OK.

Once again, you'll be working on a page from Cafe Soylent Green.

1. **In the files panel, double-click the file named *index.html*.**

   You can also open the file by choosing File→Open, selecting its name, and then clicking OK (Select on Macs). You're looking at a basic web page, with a banner, some text, and a footer. It's all contained inside a <div> tag that's 800 pixels wide and centered in the screen (you learned how to do this trick in the tutorial from Chapter 1 on page 79).

   If your screen is wide enough to show both the code and design view side-by-side, click the Split button in the top-left of the document window. If you can't fit both comfortably, then click the Design button to display Design view.

   At the end of the last paragraph, in the section that begins with the headline "All Natural Ingredients," you'll see the text "Read more about our natural ingredients." This should link to another page.

2. **Select the text "Read more about our natural ingredients."** In the Property Inspector, to the right of the Link box, click the "Browse for File" button.

   The Select File window opens.

3. **Click the Site Root button (at the top of the dialog box in Windows, the bottom-right on Macs) to go to the site's main, or root, folder.** Double-click the file named *ingredients.html*.

   The Select File window closes. That's it? Yup. You just created a link. Now, you'll learn an even faster way to do that.

4. **In the last paragraph before the footer of the page, select the text "Read more about our nutritional principles."**

   Make sure the Files panel is open (Window→Files).

5. **In the Property Inspector, drag the small Point-to-File icon (see Figure 4-6) beside the Link box into the Files panel; move your mouse over the file *nutrition.html*, and then release the mouse button.**

Dreamweaver adds the link to your page. (If you have the double-monitors configuration discussed in the Note on page 196, this point-to-file technique won't work. In that case, use the method in steps 3 and 4 to link to *nutrition.html*.)

Note that if you wanted to link the text in the examples above to a page on another website, you couldn't use either of the methods outlined here. Instead, you'd need to type an absolute URL into the Link box, as you'll see in the next two steps.

6. **Scroll to the bottom of the page.** In the footer, you see small gray type that reads "in collaboration with Cosmopolitan Farmer." Select the text *"Cosmopolitan Farmer."*

You want this text to link to this site's parent company.

7. **In the Property Inspector's Link box, type *http://www.cosmofarmer.com/*, and then press Enter (Return).**

Now the text links to the CosmoFarmer website. Unfortunately, the blue links don't fit in with the cafe's color palette. You'll remedy that next.

Formatting Links

You can change the look of links using a little CSS.

1. **Make sure the CSS Styles panel is open (Window→CSS Styles); at the bottom of the panel, click the + button.**

The New CSS Rule window opens. (For a refresher on creating CSS styles, see page 125.)

2. **From the top menu, select Tag; in the Selector Name box, type *a* (or choose it from the drop-down menu); and, at the bottom of the window, select *styles.css* from the Rule Definition menu.** Click OK to create the style.

Now you'll pick a font and font color for links.

3. **In the Type category's Font-family drop-down menu, choose PTSansBold.**

You just selected one of the web fonts you added in the last tutorial (if you don't see PTSansBold at the bottom of the Font-family menu, repeat the steps on page 169 to add the PTSansBold web font to Dreamweaver).

4. **In the color box, type #417F2C , and then click OK.**

The links on the page change to green. You won't see the font change because Dreamweaver's Design view doesn't display web fonts. However, you can click the Live button in the Document toolbar to see what the font looks like. Make sure to click Live again to exit Live view so you can go back to editing the page.

You'll now change what the links look like when a guest hovers over them.

5. **In the CSS Styles panel, click the + button; in the New CSS Rule window's Selector Type drop-down menu, select Compound, and then, from the Selector Name pull-down menu, select *a:hover*.** Click OK.

   Again, the CSS Rule Definition window appears.

6. **From the CSS Rule Definition window's Type category, type *#0A2F02 in the Color field*, and then, in the Text-decoration list, turn on the "none" checkbox (see Figure 4-19).** Click OK to finish the style and return to the document window.

   To see how this rollover style works, you'll use Dreamweaver's Live view.

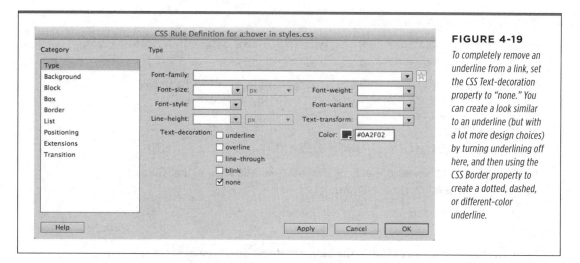

FIGURE 4-19

To completely remove an underline from a link, set the CSS Text-decoration property to "none." You can create a look similar to an underline (but with a lot more design choices) by turning underlining off here, and then using the CSS Border property to create a dotted, dashed, or different-color underline.

7. **At the top of the Document window, click the Live button (or choose View→Live View).**

   Live view lets you preview the look (and functionality) of a web page directly in Dreamweaver. Dreamweaver includes an embedded version of the WebKit browser (which is pretty much the Chrome and Safari browser). With Live view, you can interact with JavaScript as well as view CSS hover effects. Move your mouse over the various links on the page, and you see the link change to dark green and the underline disappear. (Of course, Safari and Chrome aren't Internet Explorer or Firefox, so you need to preview the page in those browsers, too, to make sure it looks good.)

8. **Click the Live button (or choose View→Live View) a second time to leave Live view.**

   You can't edit a page in Live view, so you always need to click out of it when you're ready to work on your page again. Now you'll add a Spry menu bar.

Adding an Email Link

You'll find an email address—*info@cafesoylentgreen.com*—at the bottom of the page. Clicking it, however, doesn't do anything. Here's how you turn that address into an email link that opens an email program when a visitor clicks the link:

1. **Select the text "info@cafesoylentgreen.com."**

   The text you select doesn't have to be an email address. It could simply say "Email us." Likewise, if you haven't yet added any text, just click where you'd like to insert the email link and move on to step 2.

2. **Choose Insert→Email Link (or click the Email link button under the common category of the Insert panel shown in Figure 4-7).**

   The Email Link window appears (Figure 4-20). Dreamweaver's already filled out the text and email boxes.

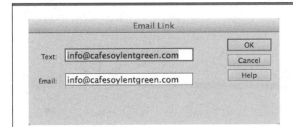

FIGURE 4-20

When you insert an email link, Dreamweaver copies any text you selected on the page into the Text field. If the text also matches the format of an email address, the program helpfully copies that into the Email field.

3. **Click OK.**

   Dreamweaver adds the email link (pretty easy, huh?).

Adding a Navigation Bar

One of Dreamweaver's most exciting tools is the Spry Menu Bar. This sophisticated combination of HTML, CSS, and JavaScript lets you easily create slick-looking navigation bars with rollover effects and drop-down menus. Since the Dreamweaver engineers have done all the complex programming for you, you just have to insert, modify, and format the menu to make it fit perfectly into your website design.

1. **Return to Dreamweaver and make sure you have the file *index.html* open; at the top of the page click just to the right of the word "Green" in the banner.**

   You'll insert a horizontal menu bar that spans most of the page's width. Placing it near the top of the page, as part of the banner, lets site visitors easily find and use it.

2. **Choose Insert→Spry→Spry Menu Bar.**

   Alternatively, you could click the Spry Menu Bar button on the Layout tab of the Insert toolbar (Figure 4-14). Either way, the Spry Menu Bar window appears.

3. **Choose the Horizontal option, and then click OK.**

   A gray menu appears at the top of the page with four buttons: Item 1, Item 2, Item 3, and Item 4 (see Figure 4-21).

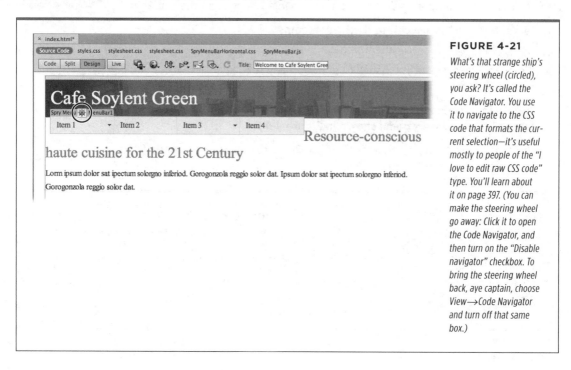

FIGURE 4-21
What's that strange ship's steering wheel (circled), you ask? It's called the Code Navigator. You use it to navigate to the CSS code that formats the current selection—it's useful mostly to people of the "I love to edit raw CSS code" type. You'll learn about it on page 397. (You can make the steering wheel go away: Click it to open the Code Navigator, and then turn on the "Disable navigator" checkbox. To bring the steering wheel back, aye captain, choose View→Code Navigator and turn off that same box.)

4. **Choose File→Save.**

   A window appears letting you know that Dreamweaver just added six new files to your site. Click OK to dismiss this window. Dreamweaver places these files inside a new folder named SpryAssets. You can see the folder listed in the Files panel, although you may need to press the "Refresh" button (the circle with an arrow tip) first.

   You've probably noticed the menu bar pops out of the bottom of the green banner box; what's worse is part of the second headline on the page, beginning with "Resource-conscious haute cuisine," has moved to the right of the navigation bar. The CSS that positions the menu bar buttons side-by-side causes this effect (described in the box on page 219). If you preview the page in a web browser (or click the Live button) you'll see that, indeed, this is how the browser displays the page. What a mess. Fortunately there's an easy solution.

5. **In the CSS Styles panel, click the All button and locate *SpryMenuBarHorizontal.css*.** Click the + button (flippy triangle on Macs) to display all the styles in the style sheet.

This is the external style sheet that Dreamweaver attached to the page, and that formats the Spry menu bar. While you're at it, you should temporarily hide the styles in the *styles.css*—there's no need to look at those styles now, since you'll only be working on the menu bar for the rest of this tutorial. Click the minus icon (flippy triangle on Macs) next to the *styles.css* to collapse the list.

6. **Double-click the first style in the *SpryMenuBarHorizontal.css* style sheet, ul.MenuBarHorizontal.**

   The CSS Rule Definition window appears. You need to set the display property for this element.

7. **Select Block from the list of categories on the left.** From the Display menu, choose "inline-block" (see Figure 4-22). Click OK to finish editing the style and close the CSS Rule Definition window.

   Huh? Nothing's changed. Unfortunately, Dreamweaver's Design view doesn't always display a page the same way that a web browser does. This is especially true when you use some CSS tricks of the trade, like this one. Click the Live button to see what a browser does with this new instruction—the banner expands to contain the menu, and the headline drops down. Click Live again to exit Live view.

   The next step is to change the menu bar buttons' labels, add new buttons, and create links.

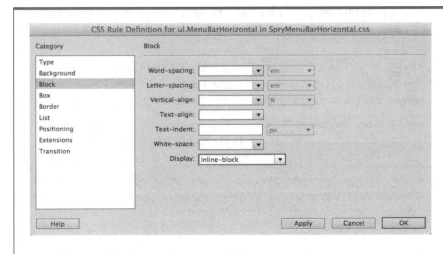

FIGURE 4-22

The CSS Display property's inline-block value is strange but useful. It takes any element and treats it like a block—that is, you can give it a height, set margins around it, and add padding to it, but inline-block doesn't place the element on its own line. You can use inline-block in many creative ways; visit www.impressivewebs.com/inline-block/ and http://tinyurl.com/ycxwyq5 to see some examples.

8. **In the document window, click the blue Spry Menu Bar tab, which appears just above the new menu.**

   If you don't see that tab, move your mouse over the menu until it appears. (If you still can't see it, see Figure 4-14 for a solution.) The Property Inspector displays the menu bar's properties.

9. **In the Property Inspector, select Item 1 from the left column of button labels; in the Text box, type Home (see Figure 4-23), and then press Enter (Return).**

   Notice that the first button now says "Home." Now you'll add a link.

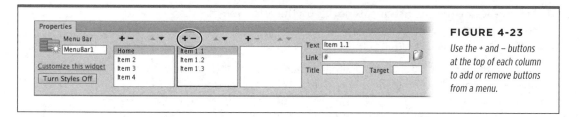

FIGURE 4-23

Use the + and – buttons at the top of each column to add or remove buttons from a menu.

10. **To the right of the Link box, click the "Browse for File" button (the folder icon).**

   This is the same process you followed earlier to add a link to one of the sidebar paragraphs.

11. **In the Select File window, click the Site Root button (top of the window in Windows, bottom right on Macs); double-click the *index.html* file.**

   You've labeled your first button and created the first link on this menu bar. Unfortunately, Dreamweaver has added a drop-down menu to this button with three additional buttons. Since the Home button isn't really a "section" of the site with additional pages, you don't need the submenu.

12. **In the middle column in the Property Inspector, select item 1.1 and press the - (minus) button at the top of that column (circled in Figure 4-23).**

   Dreamweaver removes the top button from the list. If you look in the document window, you'll see the drop-down menu. When you select an item in one of the submenu columns in the Property Inspector, Dreamweaver temporarily displays the drop-down menu. This is a great way to preview what the drop-down menu will look like.

   If the Property Inspector no longer shows the properties for the Spry Menu Bar, just click the bar's blue tab in the document window.

13. **Repeat step 12 for Item 1.2 and Item 1.3.**

   After removing Item 1.3, notice that the down-pointing arrow on the Home button disappears. Because there's no longer a drop-down menu associated with this link, Dreamweaver removes the arrow graphic. Now you'll add another button.

14. **Repeat steps 9–11 for Item 2: Change its label to Menu, and then link to the** *menu.html* **file located in the root folder.**

    The button's text on the page changes. Next you'll add a drop-down menu to this button.

15. **Make sure you still have the Spry Menu bar selected (if not, click its blue tab) and that Menu is selected in the left column in the Property Inspector.** Click the + button in the middle column to add a new button for the drop-down menu.

    This adds a new menu item label, too, labeled "Untitled Item." You just need to re-label and link it.

16. **In the Text field, type** *Breakfast*, **and add a link to the file** *breakfast.html.*

    Now you'll add one more button to this drop-down menu.

17. **Click the + button in the middle column to add another button to the Menu drop-down menu.** Label it *Lunch*, and then link it to *lunch.html.*

    You'll now add one last button for this menu.

18. **Click the + button in the middle column to add another button.** Label it *Dinner*, and then link it to *dinner.html.*

    Now you'll return to the main menu and change Item 3.

19. **Repeat steps 9–11 for Item 3: Change its label to** *About Us*, **and then link it to** *about.html.*

    This button also has a drop-down menu, but instead of deleting it, you'll just change the button labels to match the site.

20. **In the middle column in the Property Inspector, select Item 3.1; change its label to** *Directions*, **and then link it to** *directions.html.*

    This button has its own drop-down menu (a sub-submenu), but you don't need it here.

21. **From the far right column in the Property Inspector, select and delete Item 3.1.1 and Item 3.1.2.**

    Use the same technique described in Step 12 (select the item, and then click the - button at the top of its column).

22. **Repeat step 20 for Item 3.2.** Label it *Hours*, and then link it to *hours.html.*

    This drop-down menu has one extra button, but there's no page on the site for this, so you'll delete it.

23. **Select Item 3.3 in the middle column and click the - button to delete it.**

    This site's pretty simple, so that third button in the menu bar isn't needed.

24. **In the Property Inspector, select Item 4 from the left column and click the - button.**

    The fourth button disappears. You're done! Thankfully, once you craft a navigation bar, you can reuse it throughout your site, so you don't have to go through this laborious procedure for each page of your site. (Dreamweaver's Template feature can make the process even easier, as described in Chapter 19.)

    You can press the Live button to test the menu bar without leaving Dreamweaver. Make sure to click the Live button again when you're done.

25. **Choose File→Save All.** Choose File→"Preview in Browser" and select your favorite browser from the list.

    The browser opens with the *index.html* page displayed. Mouse over the buttons in the Spry menu bar and try the links. Unfortunately, only *index.html* actually has a menu.

Adding the Menu to Other Pages

You've built a menu that links to other pages in the site. The problem is that those pages don't have the same navigation bar. Fortunately, Dreamweaver lets you copy and paste a Spry menu bar to another page.

1. **Back on the *index.html* page, click the blue tab for the Spry menu bar, and choose Edit→Copy.**

   When you click the blue tab, Dreamweaver selects the HTML for the menu—a basic HTML unordered list.

2. **Open the file *about.html*.**

   You can do this either by double-clicking the file name in Dreamweaver's Files panel, or by choosing File→Open and navigating to *about.html* in the site's root folder.

3. **Click to the right of "Cafe Soylent Green" in the green banner and choose Edit→Paste.**

   Dreamweaver not only pastes the HTML for the menu bar, but also links to the external style sheet and JavaScript file that Spry requires, and adds some JavaScript code near the bottom of the page.

   As discussed on page 222, pasting a menu bar like this won't always work. If the page you're pasting into is in another directory of the site, any document-relative links (page 186) you used in the menu probably won't work.

4. **Paste the menu bar into the other pages in the Files panel.**

There are quite a few files, but make sure you paste the menu into enough files that you're comfortable with the process.

TIP What do you do if you need to change one of the links in the menu bar? Now that you've added the same HTML to many different pages, any changes you need to make, like adding or removing links, need to be reflected in every page. You have a couple of options: you could use Dreamweaver's Templates feature discussed in Chapter 19. That lets you maintain one copy of the menu, and when you change it, Dreamweaver automatically updates all the pages on your site.

Second, you could use Dreamweaver's powerful Find and Replace command (Chapter 20) to find the HTML for the old menu and replace it with the HTML for the new menu across your site; that lets you update all your pages in a matter of moments. Lastly, you could use the more technical "server-side includes" approach discussed on page 921.

If you simply want to change the *appearance* of the menu bar, no problem. Since a single external style sheet controls the menu's look, any changes you make to it will automatically apply to all your pages.

Styling the Menu Bar

The basic look of a Spry menu probably doesn't fit the design of your site, so learning to edit the CSS that Dreamweaver supplies is an important skill. In this part of the tutorial, you'll edit the look of the buttons and drop-down menus, and replace the pre-made arrow graphics with custom images.

1. **Start with the basic look of the buttons.**

   Make sure you have the CSS Styles panel open (Window→CSS Styles) with the All button at the top of that panel highlighted.

   When you inserted the menu bar, Dreamweaver attached an external style sheet named *SpryMenuBarHorizontal.css* to the page. This style sheet contains all the styles you need to modify the look of the menu.

2. **In the CSS Styles panel, double-click the style *ul.MenuBarHorizontal a* (it's about halfway down the list of styles).**

   The CSS Rule Definition window opens, displaying the current settings for this style. This particular style is a descendent selector. You'll learn about descendent selectors on page 377, but in a nutshell, you read the style from right to left, with the rightmost element being the object of this style. In this case, the style applies to an <a> tag (a link), but only when the link is inside an unordered list (*ul*) that has the class *MenuBarHorizontal* applied to it. In other words, this style applies to every link inside the Spry menu bar. You'll make some type changes first.

3. **From the Font-family menu, select PTSansBold; in the Font-size menu, type *13*; from the Text-transform menu, choose "uppercase;" and change the color to *#F2E5C2*.**

   The window should look like Figure 4-24. Next, you'll change the background color of the buttons to green.

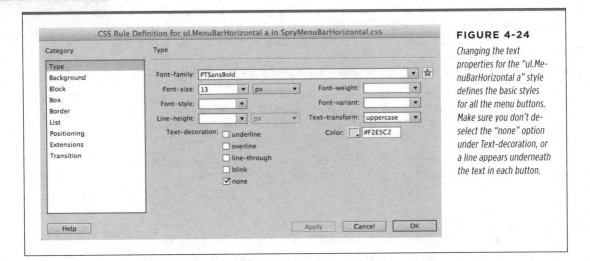

FIGURE 4-24

Changing the text properties for the "ul.MenuBarHorizontal a" style defines the basic styles for all the menu buttons. Make sure you don't deselect the "none" option under Text-decoration, or a line appears underneath the text in each button.

4. **Click the Background category, and type** *#468531* **for the background color.**

   The buttons will look better with thick, distinctive borderlines around them.

5. **Click the Border category; for the top border, select "solid" from the Style menu, type** *1* **in the Width menu, and set the color to** *#F2E5C2*.

   Next, you'll give the text inside a little breathing room.

6. **Click the Box category; change the Padding settings so that the top and bottom padding are 5px and the left and right padding are 20px each.**

   The window should now look like Figure 4-25. You can quickly set these values by typing in *5px* (*20px* for the left and right padding), instead of typing *5* (or *20*) in the first box, and then choosing *px* from the menu to the right.

7. **Click OK to finish editing the style.**

   The text on the buttons looks pretty good, but the labels inside the main menu are short, so the buttons look too wide. They'd also look better if the buttons were spread out a bit.

8. **In the CSS Styles panel,** *select* **the** *ul.MenuBarHorizontal li* **style (circled in Figure 4-26).**

Don't double-click the style name or that'll open the Style Definition window—you'll use a quicker method to edit this style. Here's another descendent selector style; it applies to every <li> tag (list item) inside the menu bar. For a quick edit to an already defined property, in the CSS Styles panel, you can use the Properties pane (it's at the bottom of the CSS Styles window; you may have to extend it by hovering over it until your cursor changes to a double line, and then drag the border up). Notice that the style currently has a fixed width of "8em." You'll change that.

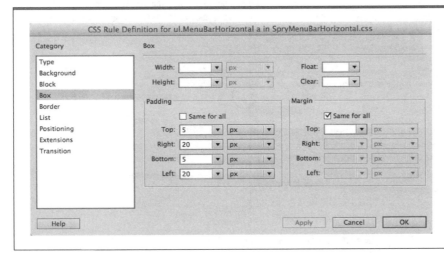

FIGURE 4-25

Adding padding to the navigation buttons adds space inside the button, separating the text from the button's edges. This makes for a larger clickable target and more prominent buttons.

9. **Click "8em" to the right of "width" in the Properties pane, and delete it.**

   This removes a set width for the buttons, and makes each button vary in width, just wide enough to hold its label and the left and right padding you set in step 6. You can also *add* a CSS property using the Properties pane.

10. **At the bottom of the Properties pane, click the Add Property link; either type *margin-right* in the box or click the menu button and select "margin-right" from the list of CSS properties; press the Tab key, and then type *20px.* ** Hit Enter (Return) to make your edits take effect.

    The CSS Properties pane should look like Figure 4-26. You just added 20 pixels of space to the right side of each list item. This effectively spreads out the buttons, adding a bit of space between each. If you save and preview the page now (or press the Live button at the top of the document window), you see that the drop-down menus look a bit weird—there's a strange border that doesn't fit the buttons.

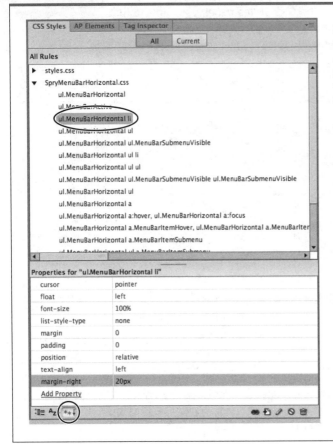

FIGURE 4-26

When you select a style name in the CSS Styles panel, all its properties appear in the Properties pane in the bottom half of the panel. To see only the properties currently set for the style, make sure you have the "set properties" button (bottom circle) pressed. Click any value (for example, "20px," in the margin-right field here) to edit the CSS property.

NOTE When setting a measurement (like width or height) in the Properties pane, you don't have to type a value in the first field, and *then* use the measurements menu to select a value like px, em, or %. It's faster to type the measurement value *along with* the number—for example, type *125px*—and then hit Enter (or Return) to make the change stick.

11. **In the CSS Styles panel, select the second *ul.MenuBarHorizontal ul* (about half way down the list of styles), and click the trashcan icon in the lower-right of the CSS Styles panel to delete it.**

You can also delete this style by selecting it and pressing Delete. Make sure you select the *second* instance of the ul.MenuBarHorizontal ul style (yes, it appears twice in the style sheet). You can verify that this is the correct style by looking in the Properties pane of the CSS Styles pane: if you see just a single property, the Border property, you've selected the correct style.

If you preview the page now, you'll see that the drop down menu's top border appears below the bottom border of the main menu buttons. This double border doesn't look great, so you'll move the drop-down menu up 1 pixel.

12. **Double click the remaining *ul.MenuBarHorizontal ul* style to (the fourth style in the SprymenuBarHorizontal.css stylesheet) open it in the CSS Rule Definition window.** Click the Box category and change its width from 8.2em to 125px. Turn off the "same for all" box under the Margin settings and type -1px for the top margin. Click OK to finish editing the style.

   Margins are the spaces between one element (or tag) and another. CSS allows negative margin values, so you can actually have one element move over another. In this case, the negative 1-pixel margin moves the drop-down menus up 1 pixel, so that their top border overlaps the bottom border of the main menu buttons. Lastly, you'll adjust the width of the drop-down menu buttons themselves.

13. **In the CSS Styles panel, select the style *ul.MenuBarHorizontal ul li*.** Using the Properties pane, set the width to 125px. Set the top margin to -1px as you did in the previous step for the drop down menu.

   This style, another descendent selector, applies to list items (the <li> tag), but only to list items that appear inside a <ul> tag that is itself inside a <ul> tag with the class *MenuBarHorizontal* applied to it. In other words, this style affects the buttons inside a drop-down menu.

Rollover Buttons

Overall, the menu bar looks good and works well. There are just a few tweaks left. The rollover buttons don't look so great—electric purple just doesn't fit the look of the cafe.

1. **In the CSS Styles panel, select the style that begins with *ul.MenuBarHorizontal a.MenuBarItemHover* (a little over half of the way down the list of styles).**

   You may need to expand the width of the Styles panel to see the full name of the styles: Drag the gray bar separating the document window and panel groups to the left. Actually, it's a much longer group of selectors named "*ul.MenuBarHorizontal a.MenuBarItemHover, ul.MenuBarHorizontal a.MenuBarItemSubmenuHover, ul.MenuBarHorizontal a.MenuBarSubmenuVisible*," but you'll probably only be able to see the first part. Notice that, in the Properties pane, a background color and text color are set; you'll change these.

2. **In the Properties pane, select the #33C in the field to the right of "back-ground-color," and then type #F2E5C2; click the #FFF value next to "color," and then type #333.**

Alternatively, you could click the color box to the right of the Background-color property in the Properties pane: that opens Dreamweaver's color picker and changes the cursor to an eyedropper. Mouse over the tan footer at the bottom of the page and click to select that color for the background. For the Color property, click the color box and select a dark gray color from the color picker. Now you'll replace Dreamweaver's default arrow graphics with arrows custom-made to match the Café Soylent Green site.

NOTE Internet Explorer 6 is nearly extinct in much of the world, but, if you still need to support it, you'll need to edit another style, *ul.MenuBarHorizontal a:hover, ul.MenuBarHorizontal a:focus*, to control the rollover state for the menu buttons.

3. **Open the Files panel (Window→Files) and expand the folder named NEW_NAV_IMAGES so you can see the two files inside it.**

To expand the folder, click the + button (flippy triangle on Macs). The two image files in this folder have the same names as the ones Dreamweaver supplies. You can just drag these files into the SpryAssets folder to replace the old ones.

4. **In the NEW_NAV_IMAGES folder, click one of the image files to select it, hold down the control key (⌘ key), and then click the other file.** Once selected, drag them into the SpryAssets folder (see Figure 4-27).

Dreamweaver lets you know that you're about to replace some existing files; that's what you want to do, so click the "Yes to All" button.

5. **Choose File→Save All Related Files; Press the F12 (Option-F12) key to pre-view the finished product.**

Move your mouse over the buttons. The result should look like Figure 4-28 (you may need to press your browser's Reload button to make it load the new graphics and revised external style sheet). (You can find a completed version of this tutorial in the Chapter04_complete folder that accompanied the downloaded tutorial files.)

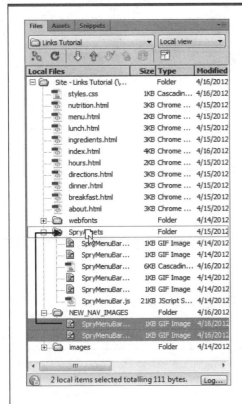

NOTE When you preview an unsaved page or a page that uses an external style sheet that's opened and unsaved, Dreamweaver pops up an annoying "save these files" window. You must click Yes to see the newest version of the page. If you're getting tired of this window, you can use the "Preview using temporary file" feature described on page 14.

FIGURE 4-27

The Files panel offers more than just a list of files in a website. It also lets your rearrange, rename, and create web page files. You learned how to use the Files panel to manage your site's files on page 49.

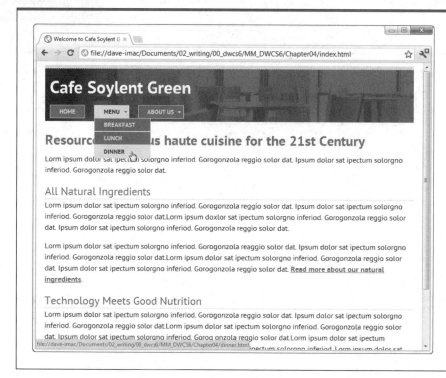

FIGURE 4-28

Adding a Spry menu may take quite a few steps, but it delivers a high-quality dynamic navigation bar and saves you countless hours of JavaScript programming and browser testing.

TIP To get a full description of every Dreamweaver menu, see Appendix B, "Dreamweaver CS6, Menu by Menu."

Images

Nobody believes that a picture is worth a thousand words more than today's web designers, as evidenced by the highly visual nature of the Internet. In fact, it's not difficult to stumble onto a home page composed almost entirely of graphics, as you can see in Figure 5-1.

FIGURE 5-1

Some websites rely almost exclusively on graphics for both looks and function. The home page for the Curious George website at http://pbskids .org, for instance, uses graphics not just for pictures of the main character, but also for the page's background and navigation buttons.

Even if you don't want to go that far, understanding how to effectively use graphics on a web page is invaluable. Whether you want to plop a simple photo onto your page, cover it with clickable "hotspots," or design an interactive set of buttons that light up when a cursor passes over them, Dreamweaver makes the job easy.

■ Adding Images

If you were writing out the HTML instructions for your web page by hand, you'd insert an image using the image tag: <img>. For example, the HTML snippet <img src="images/george.jpg"> tells a browser to display a graphic file named *george.jpg*, which it can find in the *images* folder. (An image tag's primary property is called the *source* [src] property; it indicates the URL or path to the graphics file.)

Dreamweaver automatically does all the necessary coding for you when you insert a picture into your fledgling page. Here are the steps:

1. **Save the web page that will include the image.**

   To insert an image, Dreamweaver has to know where to find it, which could be anywhere on your hard drive. As with links, saving the page before you proceed lets Dreamweaver correctly determine the path from the page you just saved to the image.

2. **In the document window, put your cursor where you want to insert the image.**

   You can choose anywhere within a paragraph, a cell in a table (see Chapter 6), or a <div> tag (see page 438). To set your graphic apart from the text on the page, press Enter (Return) to create a blank line to give the image its own paragraph.

3. **Choose Insert→Image.**

   Alternatively, from the Insert panel's Common category, you can click the Image button (see Figure 5-2). Or, if you're a keyboard shortcut fan, press Ctrl+Alt+I (⌘-Option-I).

   In any case, the Select Image Source dialog box opens. This box is nearly identical to the Select File window that appears when you add a link to a page (see *Figure 4-4*).

4. **Browse to and then select the graphics file you want to add to the page.**

   The file must be in one of the formats that work on the Web: GIF, JPEG, or PNG.

   Store the file somewhere in your local site folder (see page 46) or in one of its subfolders. If you don't, Dreamweaver can't add the correct path to your web page.

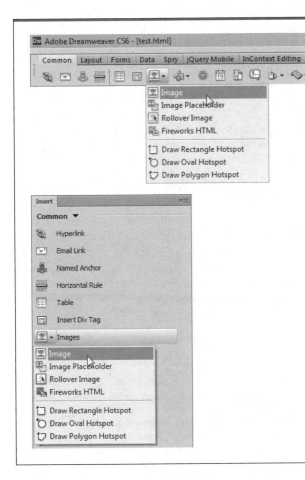

FIGURE 5-2

The Image menu on the Insert panel's Common category provides tools that let you add graphics to your pages. If you're using Dreamweaver's "Classic" workspace or have dragged the insert panel to the top of the screen between the Document toolbar and the Application bar (top), the Insert panel is actually a toolbar near the top of your screen. The "Designer" workspace layout (bottom) displays the Insert panel grouped with other panels on the right edge of the screen. See page 37 for more on Dreamweaver workspaces.

NOTE The primary file format for Fireworks, Adobe's web-friendly image-editing program, is PNG (just as Photoshop's format is PSD). However, a native Fireworks file contains additional data the program uses to keep track of fonts, layers, and other information. That extra data significantly increases the file size. So always make sure you use the Fireworks' Export command to properly compress the image into a GIF, JPEG, or PNG file without all the extra info. Fortunately, Fireworks CS6 now adds .fw to the filename—logo.fw.png, for example—so you won't mistakenly add one of the much larger Fireworks PNG files to a page.

That's why, if you try to insert a graphic that's not in your site folder, Dream-weaver offers to add a *copy* of it to that folder. If you choose Yes, a Copy File As dialog box opens so you can save the file in your local root folder, renaming it if you wish. If you choose No, Dreamweaver uses a file-relative path (beginning with *file:///*) for the image's location. But clicking No is a bad idea: While you can see the graphic as you work in Dreamweaver on your computer, the graphic doesn't appear once you move the document to the Web (see the box on page 194).

NOTE Dreamweaver lets you choose a Photoshop (PSD) file from the Select Image dialog box when you insert an image, but it doesn't actually insert the PSD file. It opens a second window where you can save the image as a GIF, JPEG, or PNG file with web-appropriate optimization settings. Page 247 has the full story.

5. **Click OK (Windows) or Choose (Macs).**

   You should see an Image Tag Accessibility Attributes window (Figure 5-3), which lets you add an "alternate" (text) description of the image (for the benefit of those who can't see your images—those using screen-reading software, for instance). If you don't see this window, somewhere along the line, you or someone else turned off this option—you can turn it back on by going to Edit→Preferences→Accessibility (Dreamweaver→Preferences→Accessibility) and turning on the checkbox for Images; see page 256.

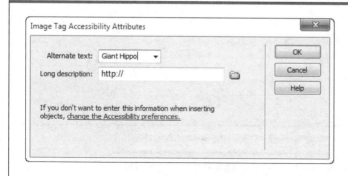

FIGURE 5-3

For complex images, you can use the Accessibility Attributes window's second option—Long Description—to link to another page with detailed information about an information-heavy graphic, such as a chart or map. However, for most images, a short alternate text description is all you need. For details on how the Long Description works, see the box on page 256.

6. **Type a short text description of the image, and then press OK.**

   Dreamweaver inserts the image. The options in the Image Tag Accessibility Attributes window are described in greater detail on page 254 and in the box on page 256, but in a nutshell, you should add a brief description for any image that adds meaning to a page. For example, if you insert a graphic of your company's logo, the alternative text should be your company's name. You can skip the Long Description box—Dreamweaver uses it to link to a separate web page that describes the image in greater depth: Sure, a picture is worth a thousand words, but that doesn't mean you need to add a thousand-word-long web page for each image in your site!

TIP Dreamweaver offers several drag-and-drop techniques so you can quickly add images to your pages.

Make sure you set up a site as described on page 40. Then open the Files window (press F8). You can drag any graphics file from that window right into an open Dreamweaver document. You can also drag graphics from the Assets panel, as described on page 751.

Dreamweaver even lets you drag a graphic from your desktop (including Photoshop images) onto a web page. If you do this, Dreamweaver dutifully informs you that you must copy the file into your site folder (and provides a dialog box that lets you specify *which* folder), so that the image shows up when you transfer your site files to the Web. (You can even define a default Images folder for a site, so that when you drag an image onto a page, Dreamweaver automatically copies it into the correct folder [see page 737].)

Adding an Image Placeholder

You may find yourself working on a website without all the pieces of the puzzle; for example, you may start building a page even before your client gives you all the necessary text. Or you may find that a photograph hasn't been shot, but you want to get the page ready for it. Other times, you may be responsible for building web pages while another designer creates banners and navigation buttons.

To help you out in these situations, Dreamweaver includes the Image Placeholder button. It lets you insert a placeholder—called an *FPO* (For Placement Only) image in publishing lingo—so you can stake out space on a page for a graphic that isn't ready yet. This way, you can lay out the structure of a page without waiting for all its graphics.

To insert a placeholder, do one of the following:

- Choose Insert→Image Placeholder.

- In the Insert bar's Common category, select the Image Placeholder icon from the Image menu (see Figure 5-2).

In the window that appears (see Figure 5-4), type a width and height for the image, which determines how much space the placeholder reserves on the page. This should match the dimensions of the final image. The Name and "Alternate text" fields are optional. (If you fill them out, they appear in the Name and Alt boxes of the image's Property Inspector, as discussed next.)

The Color box lets you specify a color for the placeholder—presumably to make the placeholder more colorful than the default gray. Avoid this option: It inserts inline CSS that Dreamweaver doesn't remove when you substitute the real graphic, adding unnecessary code to the page. Worse, if the image you eventually use has any transparent areas, the color defined here shows through the graphic!

FIGURE 5-4

*The values you type for Name, Width, Height, and "Alternate text"
appear in the Property Inspector after you insert the placeholder.
The Color option lets you choose a color for the placeholder,
but avoid it or you'll add unnecessary code to your page, which
Dreamweaver doesn't remove once you add the real graphic.*

WARNING Dreamweaver takes the name you give a placeholder and uses it as an ID attribute to the <img>
tag. Both JavaScript and CSS use IDs. If the name you provide for the placeholder is the same as an ID name for
a CSS style you created, you can run into some weird display problems. Bottom line: Unless you plan on using a
CSS ID style to format the image or JavaScript to control the image, leave the Name field empty when you insert
the placeholder.

Of course, using a placeholder doesn't do you any good if you don't eventually
replace it with a real image. Once you've got the actual image, double-click the
placeholder. The Select Image Source window appears. Follow steps 4–5 on pages
242 and 244 to insert the new image.

If you also own Fireworks, Adobe's web graphics companion program, the image
placeholder gives you an added benefit. When you select an image placeholder in
the document window, the Property Inspector includes a button called Create. Click
this button to launch Fireworks and open a new, blank graphics document set to the
exact dimensions you specified earlier. You can then create your graphic in Fireworks.
After you save the file, Fireworks exports it to whatever folder you specify, and
then automatically inserts it into your document, replacing the placeholder image.

Finally, PNG32 offers one more feature that no other format does: 256 levels of
transparency (also called *alpha* transparency), which means you can actually see
the background of a web page through a drop shadow on a graphic, or even create a graphic with 50 percent opacity (meaning you can see through it) to create a
ghostly translucent effect on a page. This feature is very useful when you want to
place an image with a drop shadow onto a colored background—drop shadows are
generally see-through, so that opacity means you can place an image with a drop
shadow on any colored background and the background color will mix naturally
with the drop shadow.

GIFs, JPEGs, and PNGs: The Graphics of the Web

Computer graphics come in hundreds of file formats. The assorted acronyms can be mind-numbing: GIF, JPEG, PNG, TIFF, PICT, BMP, EPS, SVG, and so on.

Fortunately, the limited graphics formats the Web uses makes things simpler. All of today's web browsers support three common graphics formats, each of which provides good *compression*; through clever computer manipulation, compression reduces a graphic's file size so it can travel more rapidly across the Internet. The graphics format you choose depends on the image you wish to add to your page.

GIF (Graphics Interchange Format) files provide good compression for images with big areas of solid color: logos, text, simple banners, and so on. GIFs also offer single-color transparency, meaning you can make one color in the graphic disappear, permitting the background of a web page to show through part of the image. In addition, you can create limited animations with GIF files (like a flashing "Buy Me" button).

GIF images support a maximum of only 256 shades of color, generally making photos look posterized (in other words, not completely realistic). That radiant sunset photo you took with your digital camera won't look so good as a GIF file.

JPEG (Joint Photographic Experts Group) graphics, on the other hand, pick up where GIFs leave off. JPEGs support millions of colors, making them ideal for photos. Not only that, but they compress multicolored images much better than GIFs, because the JPEG compression formula considers how the human eye perceives adjacent color values; when your graphics software saves a JPEG file, it runs a complex color analysis to lower the amount of data required to accurately represent the image. On the downside, JPEG compression makes any text you have in an image and large areas of solid color look blotchy, so it's not a good choice for logos or simple drawings.

Finally, the PNG (Portable Network Graphics) format includes the best features of GIFs and JPEGs, but you need to know which version of PNG to use for which situation. PNG8 is basically a replacement for GIFs. Like a GIF, it supports 256 colors and basic one-color transparency. And while PNG8 usually compresses images to a slightly smaller file size than GIF, Dreamweaver's image optimization tool does the opposite, making PNG8 files slightly larger than GIF versions of the same graphic.

PNG24 and PNG32 offer the expanded color palette of JPEG images, without any loss of quality. This means that photos saved as PNG24 or PNG32 tend to be of higher quality than JPEGs. But before you jump on the PNG bandwagon, JPEG images offer very good quality and a *much* smaller file size than either PNG24 or PNG32. In general, JPEG is a better choice for photos and other images that include lots of colors.

Inserting an Image from Photoshop

Since Adobe makes the world's most popular image-editing program, Photoshop, it only makes sense that Dreamweaver's engineers provide a streamlined process for moving images back and forth between Photoshop and Dreamweaver. You can add a Photoshop document to a web page two ways: Insert a PSD file (Photoshop's native format), or copy an image from Photoshop, and then paste it into a Dreamweaver document.

The first method—inserting a PSD file—supports what Adobe calls *Smart Objects*, which lets Dreamweaver keep track of whether you update the original Photoshop file, and, if so, gives you the option to update the compressed, web-ready version of the image, too. Nice. That's great news if you're the type who constantly tweaks your artwork in Photoshop. The second method—copying and pasting from Photoshop—doesn't keep track of any changes to the original file. Both methods are explained in the following pages.

Method 1: Using the Insert Photoshop Images

You can insert a regular Photoshop file using the same steps described on page 242 for inserting GIF, JPEG, or PNG files. For example, use the Image button on the Insert panel, or choose Insert→Image. The Select Image Source window appears, just as it does when you insert a standard web-ready file. You can then choose a Photoshop document (a .psd file), and click OK (Choose on Macs).

> **NOTE** You can also insert a PSD file by dragging it directly from the desktop (or any folder) and dropping it into a Dreamweaver document. If you stored the PSD file somewhere inside your local root folder, you can drag it from the Files panel and drop it onto the page.

1. **Choose Insert→Image.**

   You can insert a regular Photoshop file using the same steps described on page 242 for inserting GIF, JPEG, or PNG files. Alternatively, you can use the Image button on the Insert panel. Either way, the Select Image Source window appears, just as it does when you insert a standard web-ready file.

2. **Choose a Photoshop document (a .psd file), and click OK (Choose).**

   Dreamweaver places the image on the page and opens an Image Optimization window (see Figure 5-5).

3. **Choose your optimization settings.**

   You have two options:

   - **Select one of Dreamweaver's 6 image presets.** The Preset menu lists six pre-programmed options. They include different settings for the three basic image formats described in the box on page 247: GIF, JPEG, and PNG. You can select one and then further refine it by changing the settings for that particular file type as described on pages 250–253.

   - **Select an image format from the Format menu and tweak the available settings for the image.** The format menu lets you select either GIF, JPEG, or one of the three versions of the PNG format (PNG8, PNG24, and PNG32). Once you select a format, Dreamweaver displays options for that form. For example, Figure 5-5 displays the options for the PNG8 format, including color palette, number of colors, and matte setting. You'll see the options for each file type discussed below.

When you select an option from this menu, Dreamweaver updates the image on the page so you can preview the optimization setting you select.

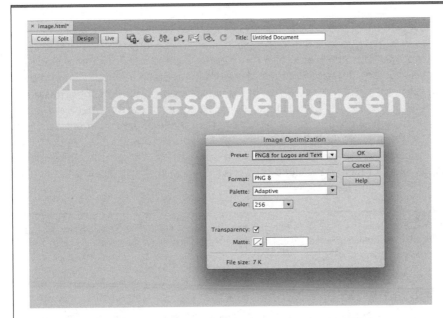

FIGURE 5-5

Dreamweaver CS6 lets you insert a Photoshop (.psd) file directly into Dreamweaver, and in the process choose how you want to convert that file into a web-ready GIF, JPG, or PNG file. You can choose a graphic file type such as PNG8 and set various options that help compress the image to a smaller file size.

4. **Click OK in the Image Optimization window.**

   The Save Web Image window appears.

5. **Navigate to a location in the site where you wish to save the web-ready image (for example, an images folder in the site's root folder).**

   Click Save.

   Dreamweaver optimizes the image (converting it to a GIF, JPEG, or PNG format) and saves it to the site.

6. **The Image Tag Accessibility window appears; follow the instructions in step 6 on page 244 to fill out this window.**

   When you finish, you'll see a small icon in the upper-left corner of the image. It indicates that the image is a *Smart Object*, meaning that it retains a link to the original PSD file. What makes it "smart" is that Dreamweaver tracks any changes you make to the PSD file—if you decide to open Photoshop and add some cool effect to the image, Dreamweaver knows you changed the original. At this point, you can update the image on your web page directly in Dreamweaver. Page 270 shows you how.

NOTE You can't import animated GIFs using the Image Preview window; instead, you need to first export the animated GIF from the program in which you created it (like Fireworks or Photoshop), and then import it into Dreamweaver.

When you insert a Photoshop image this way, Dreamweaver, unfortunately, ignores images you made using Photoshop's "slice" tool. This handy tool lets web designers export just bits and pieces of a complete web page design in Photoshop—for example, you could design the look of a site's home page in Photoshop and then show it to your client for feedback. Then you can export just parts of the design as separate image files, like a logo in the upper-left corner of the document, individual navigation icons along the top, or a photo in the middle of the document. So if you want to use an exported slice as a graphic on your web page, the import-from-Photoshop technique isn't the best; Dreamweaver tries to insert the entire image, not just slices of it. To get around this, you'll need to stick with Photoshop and its "Save for Web and Devices" command.

NOTE Dreamweaver CS6 has completely revamped the process of inserting Photoshop files. When you inserted a Photoshop file in CS5 and 5.5, Dreamweaver presented you with a large, confusing Image Preview window with dozens of controls.

■ JPEG OPTIMIZATION OPTIONS

Dreamweaver doesn't give you many choices for optimizing JPEG images. There are two presets:JPEG for photos and "JPEG for Maximum Compatibility." These presets don't really do anything besides choose the JPEG format and set the Quality level to 100 or 80. You're better off just selecting JPEG from the Format menu and then choosing a quality setting from 1 to 100 (see Figure 5-6).

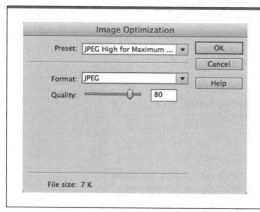

FIGURE 5-6

Move the quality slider down (for smaller files, but worse-looking images) or up (for larger files and better-looking images). Keep an eye on the file size listed at the bottom of the window. It indicates the size of the web-ready JPEG file Dreamweaver will create.

The quality level affects both how good the image looks and its file size. The higher the quality, the larger the file; the worse the quality, the smaller the file. Dream-weaver's Quality setting runs from 1 (low quality/small file) to 100 (high quality/large file). Eighty is a good choice for very good quality and manageable file size; 60

works when you want to keep file size on the slim side. The exact setting depends on what the image looks like, so move the Quality slider back and forth until the image preview looks good.

■ GIF AND PNG8 OPTIMIZATION OPTIONS

GIF and PNG8 files have nearly identical optimization settings. The number of colors an image has—the size of its *palette*, in other words—contributes most to its file size. Fewer colors mean a smaller file size. Most of the settings available for GIF and PNG8 images control the number and type of colors you can use (see Figure 5-7).

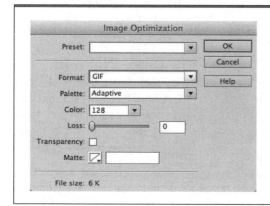

FIGURE 5-7

GIF and PNG optimization settings are nearly identical when you insert a Photoshop image in Dreamweaver. The only difference is the "loss" option—it's only available for GIFs, and it trades image quality for smaller file size.

For optimal compression settings with a GIF or PNG8 image, follow these steps:

1. **From the Palette menu, select Adaptive.**

   Since both image types are limited to just 256 colors, this menu determines which colors your image will use. You have a lot of options here, but you can ignore all of them but Adaptive, which means that Dreamweaver picks the best 256 colors from the image itself. The only other option, Grayscale, converts the graphic to a black-and-white image.

2. **In the "Number of Colors" menu, select a value.**

   You can tell Dreamweaver to use 2 to the maximum of 256 colors in the image. If the original Photoshop image started out with only 64 colors, choosing 256 doesn't add colors or quality to the image. However, you can often choose a *lower* number, eliminating colors from the graphic and reducing the file size significantly without overly harming the image's final quality. Again, each image is different, so trial and error is the best way to balance the minimum number of colors you need with the quality you want.

3. **Choose a value for "Loss" (available only for GIF images).**

   The Loss option decreases file size at the cost of image quality. In general, increasing the "loss" setting makes an image look spotted and windswept, so unless you're going for a special effect, use a low setting or none at all.

4. **If the Photoshop image has a transparent background, turn on the Transparency checkbox.**

In the case of GIFs, you should also click the Matte color box and select a color that matches the background color of the page or the background color of the element you've placed the image in. You can do this by clicking the color box and using the eyedropper to sample the color. This mixes the semi-transparent areas of the image (like a see-through drop shadow or the edges around the visible part of the graphic) with the background color, creating a more natural-looking image. If the matte color doesn't match the background, you can end up with unattractive "halos" around the visible part of the graphic.

In the case of PNG8 images, you don't need to select a matte color as long as the Photoshop image has a completely transparent background. Dreamweaver is smart enough to apply an "alpha transparency" to this kind of image.

If the graphic doesn't have any transparency in it, and you choose the GIF format, the Matte setting performs a different function: It removes a selected color from the image, making that part of the image transparent. Click the Matte color box and use the eye dropper to pick the soon-to-be-transparent color on the graphic. Generally, the results don't look very good, however. You're better off creating the transparent effect in Photoshop.

> **TIP** If you're inserting an image that has a transparent background and is a good candidate for a GIF or PNG8 (that is, large areas of solid color as described in the box on page 247), choose PNG8 and turn on the Transparency checkbox. Dreamweaver saves PNG8 images with full alpha transparency, which looks a lot better than the color transparency GIF images offer.

■ PNG OPTIMIZATION OPTIONS

If you save a file in the PNG8 format, you have the same options as GIF images (see the previous section). If you choose PNG24 your choice is simple...well, actually, you don't have a choice. In the Image Preview window, just click OK, and then save the file. As mentioned in the box on page 247, PNG24 images aren't a good choice for web pages. While they provide better quality than JPEG images, they produce significantly larger file sizes.

As with PNG8 images, you can turn on the Transparency checkbox for PNG32 pics (see Figure 5-8). In fact, you'd only want to use PNG32 if an image contains an alpha transparency channel (256 levels of transparency) and the image has lots of colors: for example a gradient that transitions from a solid color to a transparent background or a photograph whose edges fade off to a transparent background. In other words, use PNG8 with transparency if the image has 256 colors or less (like a logo), and choose PNG32 with transparency if the image has more than 256 colors and has transparent areas. (See the box on page 247 for more on choosing a graphic file format.)

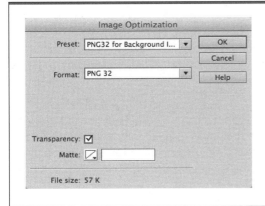

FIGURE 5-8

Saving a Photoshop file as a PNG32 image doesn't provide a lot of choices. In fact, the only advantage using PNG32 is the transparency option. Skip selecting a matte color for PNG32 images—you only need to turn on the Transparency checkbox to use the alpha transparency already provided by PNG32.

Modifying an Image

After you insert a graphic, you can manipulate it several ways: You can attach a link to it, apply a CSS class style to it, and even create an "image map" so that different areas on the image link to different web pages. You can also use some of Dreamweaver's basic editing tools to crop, resize, optimize, sharpen, and adjust the image's contrast and brightness.

As with most objects on a web page, you set image properties using the Property Inspector (see Figure 5-9).

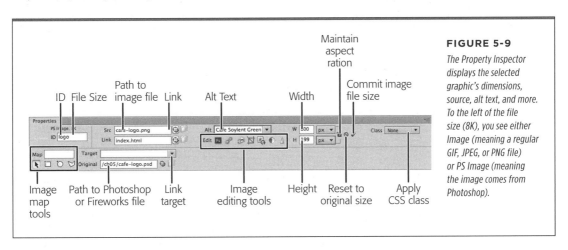

FIGURE 5-9

The Property Inspector displays the selected graphic's dimensions, source, alt text, and more. To the left of the file size (8K), you see either Image (meaning a regular GIF, JPEG, or PNG file) or PS Image (meaning the image comes from Photoshop).

Adding an ID to an Image

In the Property Inspector, just to the right of an image's thumbnail, you'll see a small field where you can type in an ID. Most of the time, you'll leave this field blank. But if you plan to add interactive effects to the image, like the rollover effect discussed on page 276 using Dreamweaver behaviors (see Chapter 13) or your own Java-Script programming, you'll need to add an ID. Use only letters and numbers in the name—no spaces or other punctuation. Furthermore, since this adds an ID to the image, the name must be unique to the page. Following this rule lets JavaScript "talk" to a specific image.

When you add an ID, Dreamweaver adds both a Name property and an ID property to the image tag. The ID is JavaScript's standard way to identify an object on a page. (Cascading Style Sheets also use IDs, as described on page 124, so you could also use the CSS ID you give an image to create a unique format for just that image—for example, to add a border.)

Unfortunately, Dreamweaver also adds a name attribute to the image tag when you add an ID in the Property Inspector, creating code like this:

```
<img src="logo.png" name="logo" width="544" height="142" id="logo">
```

The name attribute isn't valid HTML5, so whenever you set the ID for an image with the Property Inspector, you're also creating invalid HTML (see page 773 for more on validating web pages). If you need to add an ID to an image on an HTML5 page, you're better off going into Code view (page 335) or using the Tag Selector (page 26).

Adding a Text Description to an Image

Not everyone who visits your website gets to see those stunning photos of your summer vacation. Some people deliberately turn off graphics when they surf, enjoying the web without the wait, since graphics-free pages appear almost instantly. Other people have vision impairments that prevent them from seeing the web's visual aspects. They rely on special software that reads web page text aloud, including any labels you give your graphics.

To assist web surfers in both situations, make a habit of setting an image's *Alt* property. Short for *alternative text*, the Alt property is text that describes images.

> **NOTE** Dreamweaver normally reminds you to add an Alt property when you add an image to a page, but you can turn off this setting. See the box on page 256 to make sure it's on.

To add a description to an image, type it in the Property Inspector's Alt field (see Figure 5-9). If you're naming navigation buttons, for example, you could use the text that appears on the button, such as *Home* or *Products*. For images that carry greater meaning—such as a photo of the product itself—you might use a more detailed description: "Photo of Sasquatch relaxing at his lodge in the Adirondacks."

NOTE In some cases, a description is more of a distraction than a help. For example, you might insert an image of an intricate swirling line to act as a visual divider between two paragraphs. The image doesn't actually convey any meaningful information; it's just for decoration. In an instance like this, click the drop-down menu to the right of the Alt field in the Property Inspector. It lets you choose one option: <empty>. Use it for images that don't add meaning to a page, like decorative elements. This trick helps your pages meet accessibility requirements without adding distracting and unnecessary descriptions.

Changing an Image's Size

A graphic's Width and Height properties do more than determine its size on-screen; they also help web browsers load the graphic quickly and efficiently. Since the HTML of a web page downloads before any graphics do, browsers display the text on a page first and add images as they arrive. If you don't include width and height attributes with an image, the browser doesn't know how much space on the page to reserve, so it has to redraw the page after it downloads each image. As a result, the pages appear to "stutter" with each redraw. This disconcerting behavior does little for your reputation as a cool, competent web designer.

Fortunately, you don't have to worry about specifying a picture's dimensions yourself. Whenever Dreamweaver inserts an image into a page, it automatically calculates its width and height, and enters those values into the Property Inspector's W and H fields (see Figure 5-7).

You can, if you like, *shrink* a graphic by typing smaller values into the W and H fields, but doing so doesn't do anything to speed up the page's download time. You make the picture *appear* smaller, but a browser still has to download the entire file. To make your graphic smaller in both appearance and file size, you have to shrink it in an image-editing program like Fireworks or Photoshop, or use Dreamweaver's Resample Image tool, described on page 266. Not only do you get an image that's exactly the size you want, but the image usually looks better and you trim a few bytes off its file size (and maybe even save a second or two of download time).

On the other hand, setting width and height values that are *larger* than the dimensions of a graphic merely distorts the image by stretching it, creating an undesirable pixellated effect. If you want a larger image without distortion or pixellation, start with a larger original image. To do so, return to your digital camera or stock photo file or recreate the graphic at a larger size in Photoshop or Fireworks.

Dreamweaver provides some helpful tools when you resize an image. The lock icon to the right of the Width and Height boxes (see Figure 5-9) maintains the aspect ratio of the image when locked: For example, say you insert an image that is 200 pixels wide and 100 pixels tall. You click in the W (width) box in the Property Inspector and type *100* because you want the image to be smaller: If the lock icon is closed, the H box will change to 50 pixels. In other words, Dreamweaver maintains the proportions of the image when you type a value in either the W or H boxes. On the other hand, if you click the icon to unlock it, you can then type values in the W and H boxes that stretch the image beyond its normal proportions. (You'll probably also stretch your client's patience when she sees what a mess you made of her company's logo.)

In addition, if you're not happy with the new dimension you typed (or you accidentally resized the image by typing in the W or H boxes or grabbing the image resize handles discussed in the box on page 257), click the "Reset to original size" button (see Figure 5-9). That returns the image to its original dimensions. Finally, if you do change the image's size and you're happy with the new look, click the "Commit image size" button, which permanently alters the file (basically, it does the same thing as the Resample Image tool described on page 266).

Making Accessible Websites

Some people using the Web have disabilities that make reading, seeing, hearing, or using a mouse difficult. Visually impaired people, for example, may not benefit from images on the screen, even if they have software that reads a web page's text aloud.

Dreamweaver includes a number of features that make your websites more accessible. That's good news if you're building a site for the federal government or one of the many states that support Section 508 of the Workforce Investment Act, the law that requires websites built for or funded by the government to offer equal or equivalent access to everyone. Throughout this book, you'll find tips for using Dreamweaver's accessibility features.

The Alt property described on page 254 is an important first step in assisting visually impaired web surfers. For complex images, such as a graph that plots changes in utility rates over time, you can supply a more detailed description on a separate web page. The *Longdesc* (long description) property of an image lets you specify a link to a page containing a text description of the image. Some web browsers understand this property, letting visually impaired visitors jump to that description page.

While you can't find the *Longdesc* property in the Property Inspector, Dreamweaver displays a field for it in the Accessibility Options window every time you insert a graphic. If you don't see the window, turn it on by choosing Edit→Preferences (Dreamweaver→Preferences) to open the Preferences window. Select the Accessibility category, and then turn on the Images checkbox.

Now, whenever you insert a graphic, you can quickly set its Alt text and specify an HTML page for the long description. (You can also use the Tag Selector described on page 26 to add a *Longdesc* property to a graphic already on a page.)

Note that you're *not required* by Section 508 to use the long description property for images. It's merely recommended if the image is particularly complex or includes information that you can't explain in the limited space of an Alt property—for example, graphs or images that include a lot of text. You'll probably rarely, if ever, find yourself adding a long description for an image.

For an overview of web accessibility and helpful tips on making accessible sites, visit *www.w3.org/WAI/gettingstarted/*.

NOTE Earlier versions of Dreamweaver also included an alignment menu and a border and margin settings box in the Property Inspector. The Dreamweaver engineers removed those from CS6 because they're better handled with CSS as described next.

Watch Those Resize Handles!

After you insert an image in the document window, a thin black border appears around it, indicating that it's selected. Three small black squares—resize handles—appear on the right edge, bottom edge, and lower-right corner.

Dragging these handles changes the graphic's width and height—or, rather, it changes the Width and Height properties in the Property Inspector. Pressing Shift while dragging the corner handle keeps the proportions of the image the same. The graphic file itself remains unchanged.

However, dragging one of these handles to make the picture appear bigger is almost always unsuccessful, resulting in distortion and ugly pixellation.

You can far too easily accidentally grab and drag those pesky resize handles. In fact, sometimes you may resize a graphic and not even know it. Perhaps you accidentally dragged the left resize handle a few pixels, making the graphic wider, but not enough to notice.

Fortunately, the Property Inspector lets you know when a graphic differs from its original size: If you see the "Reset to original size" button (the little circle with a slash icon pictured in Figure 5-9), you know you've resized the image. Click this button to resize the pic back to its original dimensions.

◼ Controlling Images with CSS

Cascading Style Sheets aren't just for stylizing text. You can also use its design power to add borders to an image, force text to wrap around an image, and even add images to the background of other elements. For example, the CSS *background-image* property lets you place an image in the background of a web page, or add a graphical background to a link, headline, or any HTML tag.

In general, you probably don't want to create a tag style (see page 124) for the <img> tag. That type of style affects *every* image on a page (or on an entire site if you use a site-wide external style sheet). And while you may want a bright-red, 10-pixel border around each thumbnail in a photo gallery, you probably don't want that border around the site's logo or the navigation buttons on the same page. You're more likely to create class styles that you manually apply to certain graphics. In the thumbnail example, you'd create a class style with the proper border setting, and then apply that class to each gallery image (you can be even more efficient and use a *descendent selector* as described on page 377).

Wrapping Text Around an Image

When you add an image to a page, you might initially find yourself staring at a bunch of empty white space around the image (see Figure 5-10, top). Not only does this waste precious screen real estate, it's usually unattractive. Fortunately, you can wrap text around images using the CSS *float* property (see Figure 5-10, bottom).

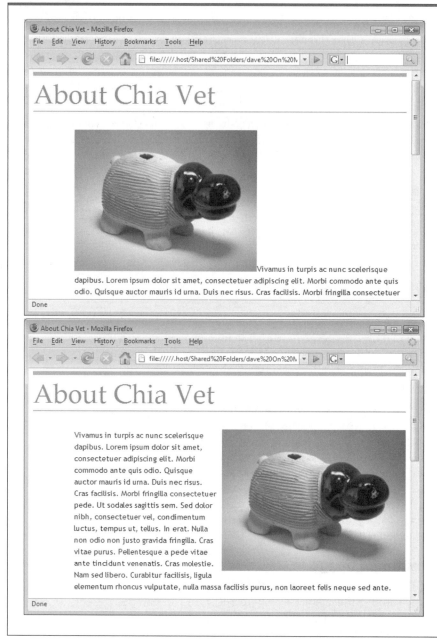

FIGURE 5-10

Placing an image on the same line as text (top) creates unsightly open space, which you can put to better use. By floating an image to the right (bottom) or left, you force content that would otherwise sit beneath the image to wrap around it.

To do so, in the CSS Rule Definition window's Box category, set the *float* property (see Figure 5-11). You can float an element *left* or *right*. If you want an image to appear on the right side of a page and have text flow around its left and bottom edges, choose "right" from the Float menu. The Float property behaves just like the right and left alignment options for images (see the following note).

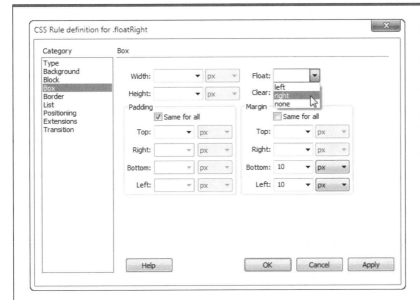

FIGURE 5-11

The Box category contains some of the most-used CSS properties: the Float property to align images and other page elements to the left or right; the Margin property to add or remove space between elements (like adding space between the edge of a right-floated image and the text that wraps around it); and the Padding property to add space between the content within an element and the edges of the element.

NOTE The Float property has many uses, from positioning images on the right or left side of a page to creating thumbnail photo galleries to laying out entire web pages. You'll learn about using it for layout in Chapter 9. For an excellent introduction and set of tutorials on the float property in general, visit *http://css.maxdesign.com.au/floatutorial*. Book lovers should pick up *CSS: The Missing Manual* for an in-depth discussion, tutorials, and practical tips on using floats.

One thing to keep in mind with floats: The floated element must appear *before* anything you want to wrap around it. Say you have a paragraph of text you'd like to wrap around a right-floated image. You need to insert the image before the text (a good spot is before the first letter in the wraparound paragraph). If you float an image to the right but place the image after the text, the image moves to the right, but the paragraph remains above the image.

You'll frequently use the Margin property with floats (see Figure 5-11). A margin is the outermost space surrounding an element. It lets you add space between one element and another. So, for a right-floated image, it's usually a good idea to add a little *left, bottom*, and *top* margin. This creates a bit of breathing room between the image and anything that wraps around it; omitting a left margin on a right-floated image can cause text to butt right up against the image.

You can specify a margin using any of the measurement values—pixels, percentages, and so on—that CSS supports.

Adding Borders

As you saw in the tutorial for Chapter 3, you can add a border to any element on a page—a paragraph or even a single word. But borders can really add impact to a photo on a page, because they give the image a polished "frame-like" appearance; in addition, borders can help unify a page full of thumbnail images.

You control the border, logically enough, from the CSS Rule Definition window's Border category (see Figure 5-12).

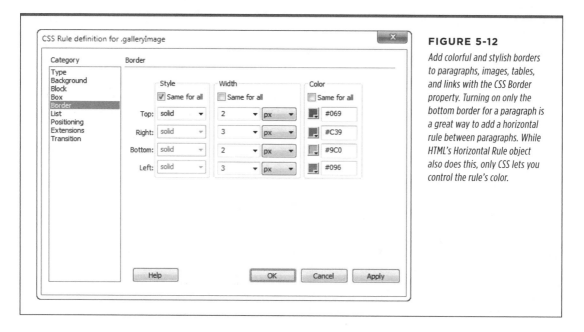

FIGURE 5-12

Add colorful and stylish borders to paragraphs, images, tables, and links with the CSS Border property. Turning on only the bottom border for a paragraph is a great way to add a horizontal rule between paragraphs. While HTML's Horizontal Rule object also does this, only CSS lets you control the rule's color.

You can control each *side* of the border independently, with its own width and color settings by specifying the three main border properties:

- **Style**. This menu lets you specify the type of line a web browser draws for the border. It gives you more options than a frame shop: none (the default), dotted, dashed, solid, double, groove, ridge, inset, and outset (see Figure 5-13). You can use a different style for each edge, or, from the top menu, select a style, and then turn on the "Same for all" checkbox to apply a style to all four borders.

NOTE You have to select a style from the drop-down menu to see the borders. If you leave this option blank or select "none," you don't see the borders even if you set its width and color properties.

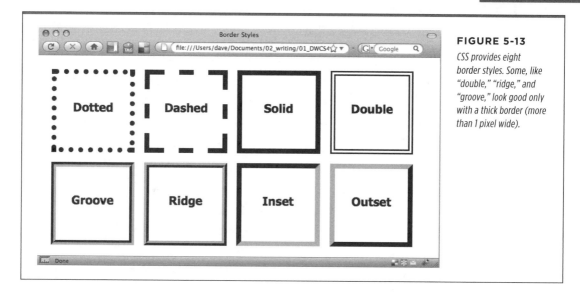

FIGURE 5-13

CSS provides eight border styles. Some, like "double," "ridge," and "groove," look good only with a thick border (more than 1 pixel wide).

- **Border Widths**. You can set border widths for each side of a styled object. Choose one of the preset widths—"thin," "medium," "thick," or "auto"—or choose "(value)" from the pop-up menu, type a value into the Width box, and then, from the drop-down menu to the right, select a unit of measure. Again, you can choose from a range of units: pixels, percentage, inches, and so on (see page 156 for more on CSS units of measure). If you want to eliminate the border on one side, type *0* into the appropriate box (or, from the Style menu, choose "none").

- **Border Colors**. You can color each of the four borders individually using the ubiquitous Dreamweaver color box. If you don't assign any colors but do assign border *widths*, the borders match the color of the surrounding text.

If you use borders to "frame" an image, you can use the *padding* property to add space between the image and the border—this simulates the appearance of the cardboard mat used in professionally framed photographs. Padding is the gap that separates content—such as a paragraph of text or an image—and its border.

You set the padding from the CSS Style Definition window's Box category (see Figure 5-11). If you put a 1-pixel border around an image and want to add 10 pixels of space between the image and the border, type *10* into the Top padding box, and then, from the drop-down menu, choose "pixels." Turn off the "Same for all" checkbox to set the padding around each edge separately; then, type values into each of the other three boxes.

Background Images

Adding an image to a page as described on page 242 isn't the only way to add graphical beauty. CSS also lets you add an image to the *background* of any tag. You can put a graphic in the background of a page, enhance a headline with an icon, or add your own custom graphics to links (in fact, the arrow icons used for the Spry Menu Bar discussed on page 210 are images applied to a link's background).

You control background images by setting the following properties in the CSS Rule Definition window's Background category (see Figure 5-14).

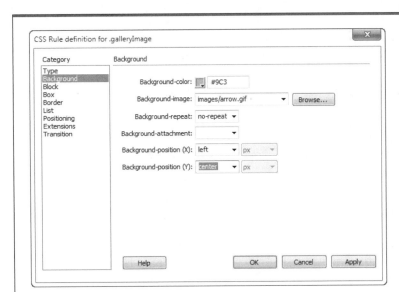

FIGURE 5-14

The CSS Background property lets you specify a background color and image for a style. While you won't frequently apply a background color to an image (after all, the image would usually cover up anything behind it), it can come in handy when you use it with the Padding property (see page 449) to create a customized "matte" to surround the image.

■ BACKGROUND IMAGE

Add a background image to a tag by clicking the Browse button, and then selecting an image from your site. You can also type in an absolute URL, starting with *http://*, to use an image off the Web.

To fill the background of your entire web page with a repeating graphic, you could either redefine the <body> tag using this property, or create a class or ID style with a Background Image property, and then apply the class or ID to the <body> tag as described on page 132 (the tutorial from Chapter 1 uses this technique to add a background pattern to the page).

You can even control how an image tiles (repeats) and where Dreamweaver puts it on a page (see below). Furthermore, you can add background images to any *individual* element on your page: paragraphs, tables, divs, and so on.

Background images appear above any background color, so you can (and often will) combine the two. For example, you may want to position an interesting graphic on top of a colorful background image.

NOTE One common byte-saving technique when you use navigation buttons on a site is to create an image that has all the characteristics of a button—burnished edges and so on—except for a label. You use this generic button as the background image for navigation links on a page. The links themselves include regular text—"Home," "About Us," and so on—but the background of each link makes them look like graphical buttons. This main benefit to this technique is that you don't need to create separate graphics for each button.

■ BACKGROUND REPEAT

When displaying the background for a web page, a browser usually *tiles* the background image. That is, it repeats the image over and over again, across and down. A small image of a carrot added to the background of a page appears as a field of carrots—one next to another, row after row. (Not all web designers use a background images for their pages; some leave the background white or set a color property, such as black for sites that use white text.)

But with CSS, you can control *how* the background image repeats. You can select from the following options:

- *repeat* tiles the image horizontally and vertically. This is how browsers normally display a background image.

- *repeat-x* and *repeat-y* display a horizontal and vertical band of images, respectively. If you want a single row of images at the top of a page, use the *repeat-x* option; it's a good way to add a graphical background to a banner. *repeat-y*, on the other hand, is great for a graphical sidebar that appears down the edge of a page.

- *no-repeat* displays the image only once (see the examples in Figure 5-15).

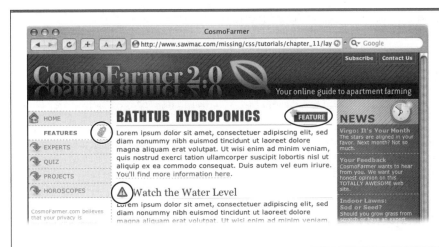

FIGURE 5-15

Background images aren't just for the body of a web page. You can apply styles that include background images to any page element, including links, headlines, and paragraphs of text. The circled graphics in this image are just a few examples of background images with the "no-repeat" setting.

■ BACKGROUND ATTACHMENT

By default, the background image on a page scrolls with the rest of the page, so that as you scroll down to read a long web page, the image scrolls "off the screen" along with the text.

But using CSS, you can lock the image in place by choosing *fixed* from the Attachment menu. Say you add your company's logo to the background of a page and set the Repeat property (described above) to "no-repeat." The logo now appears only once in the upper-left corner of the page. If you use the "fixed" option for this property, when a visitor scrolls the page, the logo remains fixed in the upper-left corner. (Choosing "scroll" from the Attachment menu means, of course, that the background image scrolls with the page—this is a default behavior, so you don't need to choose this option.) Note that "fixed" really works out only when you apply an image to the body of a page—the image stays fixed when the rest of the content scrolls.

■ HORIZONTAL AND VERTICAL POSITION

Using these controls, you can specify a position for the affected text or other web page element. The Horizontal Position options are: "left," "center," and "right." You can also choose "(value)," type an exact number in the box, and then, from the menu to the right, select a unit of measure. Similarly, the Vertical Position options include "top," "center," and "bottom," or you can enter a specific value.

These positioning options refer to the position of the styled object. Suppose you create a class style that includes a background image with both the horizontal and vertical positions set to *center*. Then, say you apply that class style to a paragraph. The background image would appear in the center of that *paragraph*, not in the center of the web page.

Likewise, if you set the horizontal position of an image to 10 pixels and the vertical position to 20 pixels, the image would start 10 pixels from the left edge of the paragraph and 20 pixels from the top edge.

And if you wanted to place an image in the exact center of a page, you'd choose "center" from both the Horizontal and Vertical Position menus, set the Repeat property to "no-repeat," and then apply the style to the page's <body> tag.

NOTE You can even use percentage values to position a background image. For information on how that works, visit *http://tinyurl.com/6ogmd36*.

■ Editing Graphics

Nothing's ever perfect, especially when you're building a website. Corrections are par for the course—not just to a web page, but to the pictures on it as well. Perhaps a picture is a tad too dark, or you'd like to crop out the rowdy coworker being escorted out by security from your company's holiday party.

In the hands of less capable software, you'd face a tedious set of steps each time you wanted to edit a graphic. You'd have to open Photoshop, Fireworks, or whatever graphics program you prefer; choose File→Open; navigate to your website folder; find the graphic that needs touching up (if you can even remember its name); and then open it to make your changes.

Dreamweaver includes tools that handle many basic graphics-editing tasks. For more complex work, like changing the text on a button from "Now Firing" to "Now Hiring," you do need to switch to a different program. But even here, Dreamweaver is considerate of your time; it lets you access your favorite graphics program with just a couple of clicks.

Dreamweaver's Built-In Editing Tools

Dreamweaver includes four tools that crop, resize, sharpen, and adjust the brightness and contrast of an image (see Figure 5-16). Suppose your boss emails you his portrait with instructions to put it on his "Meet the boss" page. Unfortunately, the picture's too big and too dark. Rather than launch a separate image-editing program, you can simply add the photo to the page, and then make the corrections within Dreamweaver.

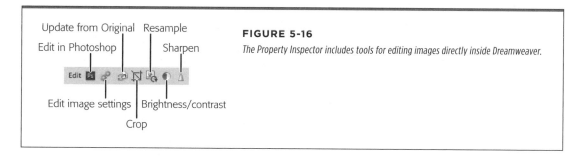

FIGURE 5-16

The Property Inspector includes tools for editing images directly inside Dreamweaver.

But first, a warning: All of Dreamweaver's tools change the *original* GIF, JPEG, or PNG image in your site folder. If you shrink a graphic and later change your mind, you may be out of luck. It's a good idea, therefore, to back up your images before you use these tools. In addition, if you add a Photoshop document and create a Smart Object (page 247), the tools discussed next break the link with the Photoshop file. That means that, for Smart Objects, you're better off editing the original Photoshop document as discussed on page 270. The reason? That retains the relationship between the image on your web page and Photoshop; if you edit the graphic in Photoshop at some point, Dreamweaver notifies you, and you can update the image on your site.

Furthermore, remember that if you use that same file on other pages, your modifications appear on those pages, too. For instance, if you decide to shrink your company logo on one page, you may find the smaller logo on *every* page on your site! What's worse, the image's width and height settings don't change on the other pages, so the logo looks unnaturally pixellated there. If you want to change a graphic on only one page, make a copy of it first, insert the *copy* in the page you wish to change, and then modify just that image file. That way, the rest of your site keeps the original graphic.

Of course, if you discover right away that you made a change you don't want, you can choose Edit→Undo or press Ctrl+Z (⌘-Z). Until you close the page, you can undo multiple image changes.

Meet the Geeks Behind Dreamweaver

Want to see pictures of the engineers behind Dreamweaver? OK, maybe you don't, but you *can*. Go to the Property Inspector and select an image in the document window. On the left side of the Inspector, Ctrl+double-click (⌘-double-click) the thumbnail of the graphic. A picture of one of Dreamweaver's programmers appears, along with his or her name. Ctrl+double-click (⌘-double-click) the thumbnail repeatedly to cycle through the names and pictures of other members of the Dreamweaver team.

■ CROPPING AN IMAGE

Dreamweaver's Crop tool can remove extraneous or distracting parts of an image. You can use it to focus on a single person, or to get rid of those teenagers making faces in the corner.

To do so, select the graphic you want to crop, and then, in the Property Inspector, click the Crop tool (see Figure 5-16). Alternatively, choose Modify→Image→Crop.

You'll see a rectangular box with eight handles appear inside the image; anything outside the box is cropped out. Move this box (by dragging it) and resize it (by dragging the handles) until you've got just what you want inside the box.

When you're done, double-click inside the box, or click the Property Inspector's Crop tool again. Dreamweaver crops the image, discarding the graphic's unwanted areas.

To undo a crop you don't like, simply press Ctrl+Z (⌘-Z). In fact, you can back out before you've used the Crop tool at all; click anywhere on the page outside the image to make the cropping box go away.

■ RESAMPLING AN IMAGE

If a photo is just too big to fit on a web page, you could select the image and use one of the resize handles to alter its dimensions. Unfortunately, graphics you shrink this way give you the worst of both worlds: They look muddier than they were before, and they download slowly because you're still grabbing the larger image.

You can, however, use this resizing technique with Dreamweaver's Image Resample tool to resize the actual graphic. You'll end up with a trimmed-down file with its appearance intact.

To use the Resample tool, select an image and then resize it using the resize handles. (Shift-drag to prevent distortion.) When you're done, click the Resample button in the Property Inspector (Figure 5-16), and Dreamweaver resizes the image file.

You can even make an image *larger* than the original using this technique. The end result isn't perfect—even Dreamweaver can't create image information that was never there—but the program does its best to prevent the image from looking pixellated. You don't want to enlarge images this way often, but in a pinch, it's a quick way to make a photo just a little bit larger.

TIP When working with a Photoshop Smart Object, you can make the image on the page in Dreamweaver smaller, and then click the Update from Original button to create a smaller version without resizing the Photoshop file (see page 270).

Dreamweaver changes the actual graphic file, altering its width and height. If you change your mind about resampling the image, your only option is the old Undo command, Ctrl+Z (⌘-Z).

■ BRIGHTNESS AND CONTRAST

If an image on a page is too light, dark, or washed-out, you can use Dreamweaver's Brightness/Contrast dialog box to fix it.

First, select the picture, and then click the Brightness/Contrast icon in the Property Inspector. In the Brightness/Contrast dialog box (Figure 5-17), move the Brightness slider to the right to lighten the image (great for underexposed interior shots), or to the left to darken the image. The Contrast control works the same way: right to increase contrast (making dark colors darker and light colors lighter), left to decrease contrast (moving all colors toward gray).

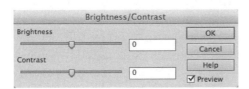

FIGURE 5-17

If you've ever used image-editing software like Fireworks or Photoshop, this dialog box should look familiar. Make sure you have the Preview checkbox turned on so you can see your changes right in the document window before you click OK.

You'll often use the Brightness and Contrast sliders together. Brightening (lightening) an image also has a fading effect. By increasing the contrast at the same time, you restore some punch to a brightened image.

As with the other image-editing controls, if you're unhappy with the changes you make, choose Edit→Undo or press Ctrl+Z (⌘-Z) to return the image to its previous glory.

■ SHARPENING IMAGES

Sometimes graphics, even those from scanners and digital cameras, can look a little fuzzy, especially if you resample the image (see previous page). Dreamweaver's Sharpen tool helps restore clarity and make such images "pop." It works like similar tools in graphics-editing programs: It increases the contrast between an image's pixels to create the illusion of sharper, more focused graphics (insert your own Sharper Image joke here).

To use the tool, select a graphic, and then, in the Property Inspector, click the Sharpen icon (Figure 5-16). The Sharpen window appears, with a single slider. Move the slider to the right to increase the amount of sharpening, or type a number in the box (*10* is maximum sharpening; *0* is no change). You probably won't use the maximum setting unless you're going for a special effect, since it tends to highlight "noise" in the image, creating an unappealing halo effect around the pixels. Once you select a level of sharpening you like, click OK.

If you're unhappy with the results, just press Ctrl+Z (⌘-Z), or choose Edit→Undo.

Setting Up an External Editor

When you double-click an image file in the Files panel, your favorite image-editing program launches and opens the file, ready for you to edit. When you first install Dreamweaver, it tries to figure out which program to use by looking through the software installed on your computer. But if you want to use a program other than the one Dreamweaver assigns, you need to tell Dreamweaver.

1. **Choose Edit→Preferences (Dreamweaver→Preferences).**

    The Preferences dialog box opens, as shown in Figure 5-18.

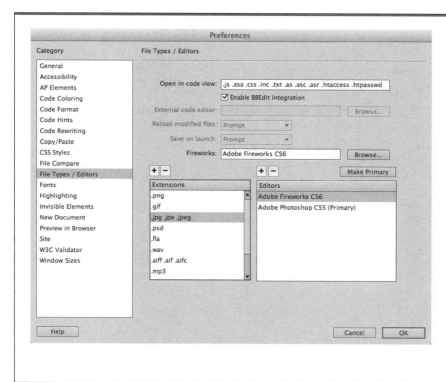

FIGURE 5-18

You can tell Dreamweaver to use certain programs for editing different types of files, such as GIF, JPEG, or PNG files. If you have .fla (Flash files), .mp3 (music files), or other types of non-HTML files on your site, you can assign programs to those file types as well— double-clicking the file in the Files panel launches the associated editing program. The BBEdit integration box is just for Mac users, who might as well turn off this checkbox— you won't need this code editor since Dreamweaver has its own powerful text editor (see Chapter 7 for more on Dreamweaver's code-editing features).

2. **In the left pane, click File Types/Editors.**

The Preferences box displays your preferred editing programs for different types of files. In the bottom half of the box, two columns appear: Extensions and Editors.

3. **From the Extensions list, select a graphics-file extension.**

The box lists three types of files: GIFs, JPEGs, and PNGs. You can choose a different editing program for each type if you like. You can add filename extensions for file types not shown by clicking the + button above the Extensions list.

4. **Click the + button above the Editors list.**

The Select External Editor dialog box opens.

5. **On your hard drive, find the program you want to use to edit the selected type of graphics file.**

It can be Photoshop, Photoshop Elements, Fireworks, or whatever.

6. **If you wish to make this program your primary image-editing tool, click Make Primary.**

This *primary* editor is the one Dreamweaver opens when you choose to edit a graphic. (You can define other, less frequently used editors, as well. See the tip at the end of this list.)

7. **Repeat steps 3–6 for each type of graphics file you work with.**

Dreamweaver treats GIFs, JPEGs, and PNGs as separate file types, so you need to assign an editor to each. Of course, most people choose the same program for all three types.

8. **Click OK to close the Preferences dialog box.**

From now on, whenever you need to touch up a graphic on your web page, just select it, and then click Edit in the Property Inspector. Alternatively, in the Files panel, you can simply double-click the file, or Ctrl-double-click (⌘-double-click) the image on the page. In any case, your graphic now opens in the program you set as your primary editor.

NOTE If you insert a Photoshop image, clicking the Property Inspector's Edit button launches Photoshop and opens the original PSD file—no matter what the image's file type in Photoshop.

Now you can edit the graphic and save changes to it. When you return to Dreamweaver, the modified image appears on the page. (If you're a Photoshop or Fireworks fan, you're in even better shape; read on.)

NOTE You aren't limited to just one external editor for each file type. For instance, if there's a Fireworks feature you need, even though Photoshop is your primary editor, you can still jump to Fireworks directly from Dreamweaver.

The trick is to right-click (Control-click) the image you want to edit, whether it's in the document window or the Files panel. Choose the Open With menu. If you added the image editor to your preferences (Figure 5-18), the submenu lists that editor. Otherwise, from the contextual menu, select Browse, and then, in the resulting dialog box, choose the editing program you want to use. That program opens, with the graphic you clicked open and ready for your edits.

Editing Smart Objects

Since Adobe makes the ubiquitous Photoshop as well as Dreamweaver, it makes sense that the two programs work together. As you read on page 247, you can get a Photoshop image by simply inserting the PSD file, just as you would insert a regular web-ready graphic. Doing this creates a *smart object*.

Smart Objects really are a, well, smart idea. They let you preserve an original high-resolution Photoshop file as the main source of one or more web-ready graphics. Since producing web graphics often entails reducing a file's size, any edits you make to the image are best made to the highest-quality version you have. For example, if you want to change the font in your company's logo, don't edit the GIF or PNG file you used on a web page. Instead, edit the higher-quality PSD version in Photoshop. Smart Objects make that easy.

You can launch Photoshop and then open the PSD file to work on it, or, better yet, you can launch Photoshop directly from Dreamweaver—on your web page, select the Smart Object, and then click the Property Inspector's "Edit in Photoshop" button (see Figure 5-19). This opens the PSD file in Photoshop, where you can make the desired edits—modify the company logo, crop the image, use creative filters, and so on. When you're done, save and close the file.

TIP You can also launch Photoshop to edit a Smart Object's original Photoshop document directly from the Files panel. Right-click (Control-click) the Smart Object—which is a GIF, JPEG, or PNG file in the Files panel—and then, from the contextual menu that appears, choose "Edit Original with Photoshop."

Smart objects are "smart" because they keep track of any changes to the original PSD file. You can recognize a Smart Object by the recycling logo that appears in the upper-left corner of the image in Dreamweaver's Design view (see Figure 5-20). Immediately after you insert a Photoshop image, the two arrows in the icon are green, meaning that the image on the page is based on the latest version of the file (Figure 5-20, top). If you update the Photoshop document in Photoshop, the bottom arrow turns red (Figure 5-20, middle). This means someone modified the original Photoshop document. To sync the web page file with the original, select the image, and then click the Update From Original button in the Property Inspector. You can also right-click (Control-click) the image and select Update From Original from the contextual menu.

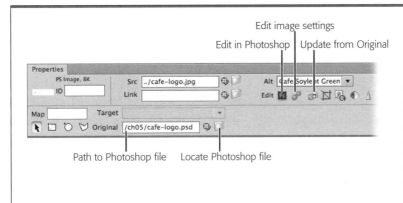

Edit image settings

Edit in Photoshop | Update from Original

Path to Photoshop file   Locate Photoshop file

FIGURE 5-19

When you use Smart Objects on a page, the Property Inspector includes an "Update from original" button, which lets you update the image on a page whenever you change the image's original Photoshop file. You can also revisit the original image settings—for example if you decide you want a PNG8 image instead of a GIF or if you want to change the compression settings—by clicking the Edit Image Settings button.

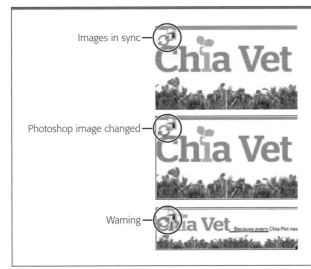

Images in sync

Photoshop image changed

Warning

FIGURE 5-20

A Smart Object is a GIF, JPEG, or PNG file you imported from Photoshop. In Design view, Dreamweaver displays an icon in the top-left corner of the image indicating that it's a Smart Object. If one of the arrows in the icon is red, the image on the page doesn't match the Photoshop file. If the bottom arrow is red (middle), someone has changed the Photoshop file since you inserted it. Dreamweaver also displays a warning symbol (a yellow triangle with an exclamation mark) in certain situations, described below.

When you update an image this way, Dreamweaver retains all the previous optimization settings—including the file format (GIF, JPEG, or PNG), cropping, resizing, and file name.

■ SMART OBJECT WARNINGS

Sometimes you see a warning symbol (a yellow triangle with an exclamation mark) as part of the Smart Object icon (see Figure 5-20, bottom). That means one of two things: Either Dreamweaver can't locate the original PSD file, or you resized the inserted image in Dreamweaver—probably by dragging the resize handles, as discussed on page 257.

If Dreamweaver loses track of a PSD file, simply select the Smart Object (you need to be in Design view), and then click the folder icon in the Property Inspector (to the right of the Original box). This opens the Select Original File window—just a basic "pick a file on your computer" dialog box. Navigate to the PSD file, and then select it. Unfortunately, once Dreamweaver loses track of the PSD file, it also loses all the optimization information, such as the file format and the name of the web-ready file. You have to set all these options again, as described on pages 250–252.

The second instance in which you can see the yellow warning symbol is when you resize an image in Dreamweaver. If you make the image on the page *smaller* than the original PSD file (for example, by dragging the resize handles or entering smaller width and height values in the Property Inspector), click the Property Inspector's "Update from Original" button (see Figure 5-19). Doing so re-exports the original image (using all your optimization settings) so that it matches the new size you set on the page. (This has no affect on the original PSD image; it always remains the same.)

However, if you resize the image on the page so that it's *larger* than the original PSD file, the yellow warning icon remains, no matter what. In this case, it indicates that the PSD file doesn't have enough pixels to make the image the size you want it without affecting the image's quality. In other words, you can't make the images on your page larger than the Photoshop file they come from without getting a worse-quality image.

NOTE If you resize a Smart Object on a page, you can return it to its original size (that is, the size of the image in the original Photoshop file). In Design view, right-click (Control-click) the Smart Object, and then, from the menu that appears, choose "Reset size to original."

Optimizing an Image

You can optimize an image—compress it so it downloads faster—by clicking the "Edit image settings" button (the one with the two green gears) in the Property Inspector (see Figure 5-19). After clicking the button, the Image Optimization window appears. This is the same one that appears when you import a Photoshop file. Although the Optimize feature does leave you with a smaller image file, you should only use it if you're applying it to a Photoshop Smart Object. If you try to optimize a regular GIF, JPEG, or PNG, you're compressing an already compressed file. Applying additional optimization degrades the image's quality. However, clicking the "Optimize image" button after selecting a Photoshop file lets you create a new web-ready file—GIF, JPEG, or PNG—from the original Photoshop file without any loss of quality.

If you have do have a JPEG file that you think should be a GIF (see the box on page 247 for some guidelines), or you simply want to see if you can shave a few more bytes from a file by optimizing it again, it's best to return to the original file (Fireworks, Illustrator, or whatever program you used to create the graphic), if available, and use that program's export or "Save for Web" feature to generate a new GIF, JPEG, or PNG.

If you decide to ignore this warning (or you don't have the original image and really need to optimize the image further), follow the directions on pages 250–252. Once you make your changes, click OK in the Preview Image window. Dreamweaver optimizes the image again. You can choose Edit→Undo to back out of the change.

■ Image Maps

As Chapter 4 makes clear, you can easily turn a graphic into a clickable link. You can also add *multiple* links to a single image.

Suppose your company has offices all over the country and you want to provide an easy way for visitors to locate the nearest one. One approach is to list all the state names and link them to separate pages for each state. But that's boring! Instead, you could use a map of the United States—a single image—and turn each state's outline into a hotspot linked to the appropriate page, listing all the offices in that state.

The array of invisible link buttons (called *hotspots*) responsible for this magic is called an *image map*. Image maps contain one or more hotspots, each leading somewhere else.

Here's how to create an image map:

1. **Select the graphic you want to make into an image map.**

   The Property Inspector displays that image's properties and, in the lower-left corner, the image map tools (see Figure 5-21, bottom). (You see these tools only with the Property Inspector fully expanded—double-click the empty grey area to show the full Property Inspector.)

2. **In the Property Inspector's Map field, type a name for the map.**

   The name should contain only letters and numbers, and can't begin with a number. If you don't give the map a name, Dreamweaver automatically assigns it the ingenious name *Map*. You don't really need to change the name; your visitors never see it, and a browser uses it just to find the file. If you create additional image maps, Dreamweaver calls them *Map2*, *Map3*, and so on.

3. **Select one of the image map tools.**

   Choose the rectangle, circle, or polygon tool, depending on the shape you have in mind for your hotspot. For instance, in the image in Figure 5-21, the polygon tool was used to draw each of the oddly shaped hotspots.

NOTE   If you have Dreamweaver's Image Accessibility preference setting turned on (page 256), you get a window reminding you to add an Alt property to the hotspot you're about to draw. Each hotspot can have its own Alt description.

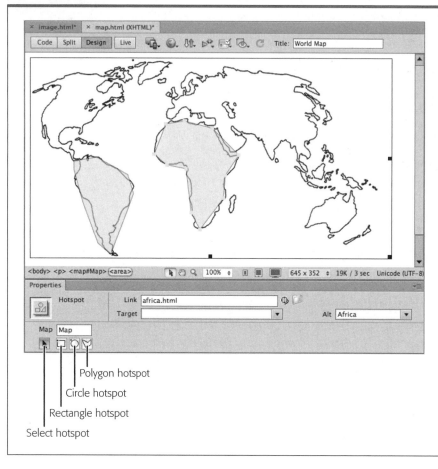

FIGURE 5-21

Each link on an image map is called a hotspot. Shown here are hotspots around South America and Africa. When you select a hotspot, the Property Inspector displays its Link, Target, and Alt properties. The lower half of the inspector displays the name of the map, as well as tools for selecting and drawing additional hotspots.

4. **Draw the hotspot.**

   To use the rectangle and circle tools, click directly on your picture, and then drag diagonally to form a rectangle or circle. To make a perfect square, press Shift while you drag the rectangle tool. (The circle tool always creates a perfect circle.)

   To draw an irregularly shaped hotspot using the polygon tool, click once to define one corner of the hotspot. Continue clicking until you define each corner of the hotspot. Dreamweaver automatically joins the corners to close the shape.

   Dreamweaver fills the inside of the hotspot with a light blue tint to make it easy to see (your visitors won't see the blue highlighting).

If you need to adjust the hotspot you just drew, click the Arrow button in the Property Inspector. You can drag the light blue square handles to reshape or resize the hotspot, or drag inside it to move the hotspot as a whole. If you change your mind about the hotspot, press Delete to get rid of it.

NOTE After you draw a hotspot, the drawing tool remains active so you can draw additional hotspots. To disengage it, click the Arrow button.

5. **Add a link to the hotspot.**

   After you draw a hotspot, that hotspot is selected; its properties appear in the Property Inspector. Use any of the techniques discussed on "Adding a Link" on page 191 to link this hotspot to another web page or anchor.

6. **If necessary, set the Target property.**

   Most of the options in the Target drop-down menu are useful only when you work with frames, as discussed on page 199. The "_blank" option, however, is useful any time: It forces your visitor's browser to load the linked page into a *new* browser window. The original page remains open, underneath the new window.

7. **Set the hotspot's Alt property.**

   By typing a label into the Property Inspector's Alt box, you provide a written name for this portion of the graphic. As noted on page 254, *alt* tags are extremely important to people who surf the web with graphics turned off or use text-to-speech reading software.

8. **Repeat steps 2–7 for each hotspot you wish to add to an image.**

   As you work, you can see the light blue hotspots filling in your image map.

Editing a Hotspot's Properties

As noted in step 4, you can change a hotspot's shape by dragging its tiny square handles. But you can also change its other properties—like which web page it links to.

To do so, click to select the image map. Click the black Arrow button—the hotspot selection tool—on the Property Inspector's far left side (see Figure 5-21), then click the hotspot you want to edit. Then use the Property Inspector controls to edit the Link, Target, and Alt properties.

If you're having a fit of frustration, you can also press Delete or Backspace to delete the hotspot altogether.

Rollover Images

Rollover images are common interactive elements on the Web. Webmasters frequently use them as navigation buttons (see Figure 5-22), but you can use them anytime you wish to dramatically swap one image for another. Say you put a photo of a product you're selling on a web page. The photo links to a page that describes the product and lets your visitor buy it. To add emphasis to the image, you could add a rollover image so that when a visitor moves his mouse over the photo, *another* image—for example, the same image but with "Buy Now!" or "Learn more" banner printed across it—appears. You've almost certainly seen rollovers in action, where your mouse moves over a button on a web page and the image lights up, or glows, or turns into a frog.

FIGURE 5-22

Rollover graphics appear frequently in navigation bars. Before your cursor touches a rollover button, like the Horoscopes link here (top), it just sits there. But when your cursor arrives, the button changes appearance (bottom) to indicate that the graphic has a functional purpose—in this case, it now reads "I'm a link. Click me."

This simple change in appearance is a powerful way to inform visitors that the graphic is more than just a pretty picture—it's a button that actually does something. Rollovers usually announce that the image is a link, though you can use them for other creative effects, as described on page 695.

Behind the scenes, you create a rollover by preparing *two different* graphics—a "before" version and an "after" version. One graphic appears when the web page first loads, and the other appears when your visitor mouses over the first. If your guest moves her cursor away without clicking, the original image pops back into place.

You achieve this dynamic effect by using *JavaScript*, a programming language that lets you add interactivity to web pages. You saw JavaScript in action with the Spry menu bar (page 210). Aside from Spry objects, Dreamweaver includes many prewritten JavaScript programs, called *behaviors*, that let you add rollover images and other interactivity to your pages. (You'll find more about behaviors in Chapter 13.)

To insert a rollover image, start by using a graphics program to prepare the "before" and "after" images. Unless you're going for a bizarre distortion effect, both images should be exactly the same size. Store them somewhere in your website folder.

Then, in the document window, click the spot where you want to insert the image. If you're building a navigation bar, you might place several images (the buttons) side by side.

Choose Insert→Image Objects→Rollover Image (or, on the Insert panel's Common category, click the Rollover Image button). Either way, the Insert Rollover Image dialog box appears (see Figure 5-23).

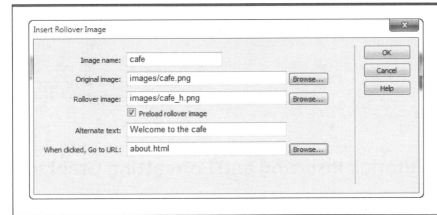

FIGURE 5-23

This box lets you specify the name, link, and image files browsers use to create a rollover effect. "Preload rollover image" forces the browser to download the rollover image along with the rest of the page to avoid a delay when a guest mouses over the image for the first time.

Fill in the blanks like this:

- **Image name**. Type a name for the graphic. JavaScript requires *some* name for the rollover effect. If you leave this blank, Dreamweaver gives the image an unimaginative name—like Image2—when you insert a rollover. However, if you plan to later add additional interactive effects (Chapter 13), you may want to change the name to something more descriptive, to make it easier to identify the graphic later.

- **Original image**. When you click the top Browse button, a dialog box appears, prompting you to choose the graphic you want to use as the "before" button—the one that appears when the web page loads.

- **Rollover image**. When you click the second Browse button, Dreamweaver prompts you to choose the "after" graphic—the image that appears when your visitor mouses over the original button.

- **Alternate text**. You can add a text description for a rollover button just as you can for any other graphic, as described on page 254.

- **When clicked, go to URL**. Most web pages use rollover images as navigation elements that, when clicked, take a web surfer to another page. In this box, you specify the destination page. Click the Browse button to select a page from your site, or, if you wish to link to another site, type an absolute URL (see page 186) beginning with *http://.*

When you click OK, you return to your document window, where only the "before" button appears. You can select and modify it just as you would any other image. In fact, it's just a regular image with a link and a Dreamweaver behavior attached.

You can see the rollover in action right from Dreamweaver. Click the Live button near the top of the Document window—this turns on the embedded WebKit browser so you can actually see the JavaScript work just as it will in a "live" browser (or as it will in Google's Chrome and Apple's Safari browsers, which both use WebKit). When you're done, click the Live button again to return to editing the page. To see how the rollover works in other browsers, press the F12 key (Option-F12) or use the File→"Preview in Browser" command.

You can achieve the same effect as the rollover behavior with a little more effort using Dreamweaver's Swap Image behavior, discussed on page 695. In fact, this versatile behavior lets you create multiple, simultaneous image swaps where several images change at the same time.

■ Tutorial: Inserting and Formatting Graphics

In this tutorial, you'll learn how to insert a photo, add a rollover image, and apply CSS to improve the look of a web page. You'll also learn how to use background images to enhance the look of headlines.

> **TIP** You'll need to download the tutorial files from *http://www.sawmac.com/dwcs6* to complete this tutorial. See the note on for more details.

Setting Up

Once you download the tutorial files and open Dreamweaver, set up a new site as described on page 40. You should be pretty good at this routine by now, but here's a quick recap, as well as an introduction to another setting that's helpful when you work with images.

1. **Choose Site→New Site.**

   The Site Setup window appears.

2. **For the Site Name, type *Images Tutorial*.** To the right of the Local Site Folder box, click the folder icon.

   The Choose Local Root Folder window appears. This is just a window into your computer's file system; navigate to the proper folder just as you do when you work with other programs.

3. **Navigate to MM_DWCS6 folder, and then select Chapter05.** Click Select (Choose) to identify this folder as the local root folder.

   These steps are the only ones required to define a new site; however, you'll find one other setting useful when working with images.

4. **Click the Advanced Settings option in the left-hand side of the window to reveal seven additional categories.**

Most of the options are related to Dreamweaver's site-management tools, its Spry widgets, and the Contribute web-editing program, but the options in the Local Info category are useful for links and inserting images.

5. **Select the Local Info category.** To the right of the "Default Images folder" box, click the folder icon. Inside the Chapter05 folder, double-click the Images folder to select it. Click" to begin a new sentence, click Save to complete the process of setting up the site.

By defining a default destination for image files, certain operations, like dragging an image from the desktop or inserting a Photoshop image, go faster— Dreamweaver already knows where you want those images to go.

Adding an Image

Once again, you'll work on a page from the Cafe Soylent Green site.

1. **In the Files panel, double-click the file named *index.html*.**

If you need a refresher on the Files panel, see page 30 and *Figure 1-5*.

2. **Click at the beginning of the paragraph immediately following the headline "All Natural Ingredients" (before the "L" in "Lorem ipsum").**

You'll add an image here.

3. **Choose Insert→Image (or click the Image button on the Common tab of the Insert panel).** Navigate to the images folder, and then double-click the file *special1.jpg*.

The Image Tag Accessibility Attributes window appears. (If it doesn't, that's OK, just fill out the Property Inspector's Alt box with the text *Plankton Carpaccio* and skip the next step.)

4. **In the "Alternate text" box, type Plankton Carpaccio, and then click OK.**

A photo of one of the cafe's dishes appears. A black outline and three black boxes (resize handles) indicate that you have the image selected—if you don't see the boxes, click the image to select it.

Next you'll link this image to another page.

5. **In the Property Inspector, to the right of the Link box, click the folder icon.** Click the Site Root button to make sure you have the Chapter05 folder (the local site folder) selected and then double-click the *menu.html* page.

If you need a recap on linking, check out page 191.

The image is a bit too close to the headline, and the large empty white space to the right of the graphic is distracting. Fortunately, CSS can help with both those problems.

6. **Make sure the CSS Styles panel is open (Window→CSS Styles); in the panel's bottom-right, click the Create New Rule button (the + icon).**

   The New CSS Rule window appears. You'll create a class style to apply to the image, and store the CSS information in an already attached external style sheet.

7. **From the top menu, select Class; in the Selector Name box, type .*imageRight*; in the bottom menu, select *styles.css*, and then click OK.**

   The CSS Rule Definition window appears.

8. **From the Rule Definition window, select the Box category, and choose right from the Float menu; turn off the "Same for all" checkbox under Margin, and type *10* in the Top box, *10* in the Bottom box and *15* in the Left box; leave the Right box blank.**

   The CSS Rule Definition window should look like Figure 5-24. The "right" setting for the CSS Float property will move the image to the right of the page, forcing the text that follows it to wrap around the left side of the image. The margin settings add space on top (to move the image down from the headline border) and to the left and bottom (to add some space between the text and the graphic.) Next you'll add a decorative border.

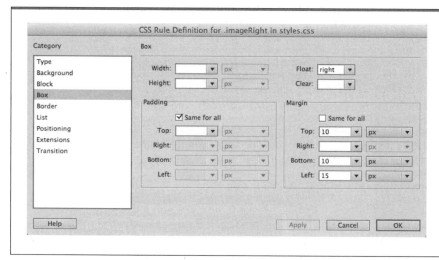

FIGURE 5-24

Float is one of the most commonly used CSS properties. It lets you align an element, like an image, to the left or right. Content adjacent to the floated element wraps around it; when you use the Float property on <div> tags, it helps you create multi-column page designs (which you'll learn about in Chapter 9).

9. **Select the Border category.** Choose "solid" from the Top style menu; type *4* in the Width box; and type *#F2E5C2* in the Color box. Click OK to complete the style.

   Nothing happens, yet. You have to apply the class style.

10. **Click the image to select it.** In the Property Inspector, from the Class menu, choose *imageRight*.

A tan border appears around the image, it moves to the right of the content, and scoots down from the headline 10 pixels.

11. **Click at the beginning in the paragraph immediately following the second headline.** Repeat steps 3–5 to insert the image *special2.jpg*. Select the graphics file *special2.jpg*, and type *Grilled Mozzarella* for the Alt text; link it to the *menu.html* file.

    You've inserted a second graphic and link; now you'll apply the class you created earlier.

12. **Click the *special2.jpg* image to select it.** In the Property Inspector, from the Class menu, choose *imageRight*.

    The café name at the top of the page looks a bit drab; let's replace it with the café's logo.

Inserting a Photoshop File

Dreamweaver makes it easy to insert and optimize files from Photoshop.

1. **Select the text "Cafe Soylent Green" at the top of the page and press Delete to remove it.** Choose Insert→Image.

   The Select Image Source window appears. Now you'll select a Photoshop (.psd) file. You can also drag the PSD file from the Files panel and drop it into the empty space where the text used to be.

2. **Click the Site Root button, and then double-click the *cafe-logo.psd* file.**

   The Image Optimization window appears.

3. **Choose PNG8 from the Format menu and turn on the transparency checkbox.**

   The Photoshop file has a transparent background—that's not so important right now since the logo is sitting on a white page, but if you add an image behind the logo (which you soon will) it's important to make sure that the transparent areas of the graphic are see-through.

4. **Click the OK button, and in the "Save Web Image" box, save the file as *cafe-logo.png*.**

   Notice that when the Save Web Image window appears, Dreamweaver has the Images folder already selected—that's because of step 5 on page 279, where you specified the default images folder.

5. **In the Image Tag Accessibility Attributes window's Alternate Text box, type Cafe Soylent Green, and then click OK.**

   A big photo appears on the page (see Figure 5-25). You'll notice the Smart Object logo in the top-left corner (circled in Figure 5-25), and three resize handles (black squares that appear on the bottom right corner, bottom edge, and right edge of the photo). The logo is a bit large, but you can resize it in Dreamweaver.

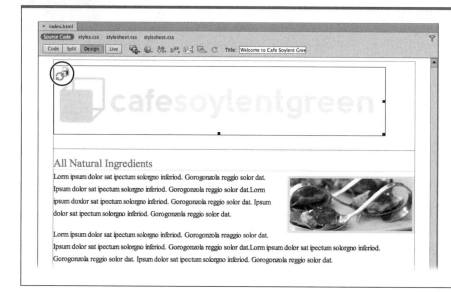

FIGURE 5-25

Photoshop Smart Objects look just like regular images; the only difference is the small icon in the top-left (circled).

6. **Hold down the Shift key and drag the image's bottom-right resize handle up and to the left until the image is about 110 pixels tall (look in the Property Inspector's H box to see the image's height).**

   If you don't see the resize handles, click the image to select it. The Shift key makes sure the image scales proportionally, which, in turn, ensures that you don't accidentally distort the image.

   Now you see a yellow warning sign in the image's upper-left corner (see Figure 5-26). This means that the dimensions of the image no longer match the width and height specified in the HTML—by resizing the image, you change the HTML but not the actual image file. As mentioned in the box on page 257, this isn't a good idea—the image doesn't look as good and the file is larger than it needs to be (meaning it will download more slowly). Fortunately, because this is a Smart Object, you can easily recreate a PNG file that matches the smaller dimensions you just specified while maintaining the image's original quality.

FIGURE 5-26

When you see a warning icon (the yellow triangle) on a Smart Object, it usually means you resized the image on the page. The "Update from Original" button lets you recreate the image from the original to match the dimensions you're after.

7. **In the Property Inspector, click the "Update from Original" button (the one with the recycle icon, circled in Figure 5-26).**

    Dreamweaver re-optimizes the image based on the Photoshop file. This means that, behind the scenes, Dreamweaver creates a new PNG file—complete with all your original optimization settings (PNG8 with transparency). Modifying an image using Smart Objects, aside from being very fast, is the best way to assure a high-quality web image.

    If you own Photoshop CS5 or CS6, launch it now (if you don't have Photoshop, just skip to the next paragraph); then, in the Chapter05 folder, open the *cafe-log.psd* file, and edit it—apply a filter, add some text, or whatever. Save the file, and then return to Dreamweaver. You'll see a red "out-of-sync" arrow on the image. Select it, press the "Update from Original" button again, and Dreamweaver creates a new image from the edited PSD file. You'll now see the new, filter-enhanced version of the image without having to make a stop at the Image Preview window. Very cool.

Using Background Images

The HTML <img> tag isn't the only way to add an image to a web page. You can also use the CSS *background-image* property to give any HTML tag a graphical backdrop. You added a background image to the body of a web page in the first tutorial. In fact, a little-known trick is adding a background image to the <html> tag and another to the <body> tag: This basically lets you overlap two different images that cover the canvas of your web page.

1. **Make sure the CSS Styles panel is open (Window→CSS Styles); in the panel's bottom-right corner, click the Create New Style button (the + icon).**

   The New CSS Rule window appears. You'll create a style for the <html> tag.

2. **From the top menu, select Tag; in the Selector Name box, type *html*; in the bottom menu, select *styles.css*, and then click OK.**

   The CSS Rule Definition window appears.

3. **In the Rule Definition window, select the Background category; click the Browse button, navigate to the Images folder, and then double-click the file *bg_page.png*.**

   The image is a simple textured sand-color background.

4. **Click OK to finish the style.**

   What gives? There's no background image! Again, Dreamweaver's Design view fails us—many common CSS tricks, like adding a background image to the <html> tag, just won't appear in Design view. Only when you view the page in a browser, or in Dreamweaver's Live view, will you see the background effect.

5. **Click the Live button in the Document toolbar.**

   The background texture looks great! Unfortunately, the color matches the word "Soylent" in the logo. To get the logo back, you can add another background image.

6. **Click the Live button again to exit Live view.**

   You'll next add a background image to the <body> tag. There's already an existing style, so you just need to edit it.

7. **In the CSS styles panel, locate the body style near the bottom of the list *styles.css* stylesheet. Double-click the body style to open it for editing.**

   The CSS Rule Definition window appears.

8. **In the Rule Definition window, select the Background category; click the Browse button, navigate to the Images folder, and then double-click the file *bg_banner.png*.**

   The image is a dark-green bar that will run along the top of the page. Normally, background images tile from left to right and top to bottom, which would fill the body element here. If you press the Apply button you'll see this effect in Design view...not pretty. Fortunately, you can control how a background image tiles.

9. **From the Background-repeat menu select "repeat-x."**

   The CSS Rule Definition window should now look like Figure 5-27. "Repeat-x" repeats the image horizontally, along the x-axis.

10. **Click OK to complete the style.**

    Time to create a style for the list items.

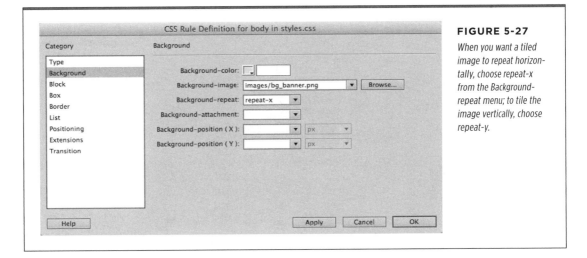

FIGURE 5-27

When you want a tiled image to repeat horizontally, choose repeat-x from the Background-repeat menu; to tile the image vertically, choose repeat-y.

11. **In the CSS Styles panel, click the Create New Style button (the + icon).**

    The New CSS Rule window appears again. You'll create a style for the <li> element this time.

12. **From the top menu, select Tag; in the Selector Name box, type *li*; in the bottom menu, select *styles.css*, and then click OK.**

    The CSS Rule Definition window appears.

13. **In the Rule Definition window, select the Background category; click the Browse button, navigate to the Images folder, and then double-click the file *list_dignbat.png*.**

    The image is a small icon with a green box. You encounter the same problem here as you did in step 8 above; the entire unordered list (<ul>) area is filled with little green boxes.

14. **From the Background-repeat menu, select "no-repeat"; type 1 in the Background-position (X) box, and 4 in the Background-position (Y) box.**

    The CSS Rule Definition window should look like Figure 5-28. The no-repeat setting means that the background image will appear only a single time; you can control where the image appears in the background of the element with the two position settings specified above. In this case, the 1 and 4 mean place the image 1 pixel from the left edge of a list item and 4 pixels down from the top of the element. Why those values? Trial and error! Each image and element will probably require different position values to look good.

Because you're using an image for the list item's bullet, you need to make sure web browsers don't also display the normal bullet icon.

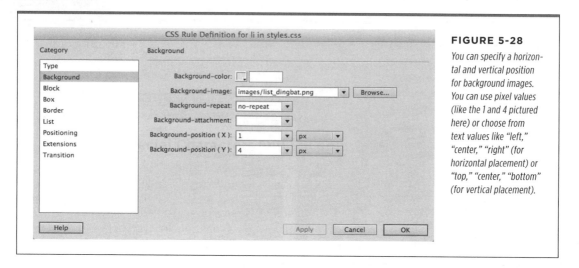

FIGURE 5-28

You can specify a horizontal and vertical position for background images. You can use pixel values (like the 1 and 4 pictured here) or choose from text values like "left," "center," "right" (for horizontal placement) or "top," "center," "bottom" (for vertical placement).

15. **Select the List category in the CSS Rule Definition window; select "none" from the List-style-type menu.** Click OK to complete the style.

    The image is in place but doesn't look right. The text is covering it up! Whenever you use a background image as an icon like this, you also need to add padding to scoot the tag's content out of the way. You'll need to go back and edit the style.

16. **Make sure you have the All button selected in the CSS Styles panel: double-click the "li" style (it should be listed at the bottom of the list of styles.)**

    If you don't see any styles listed, make sure the "styles.css stylesheet" is expanded (click the + button [flippy triangle on Macs] to the left of "styles.css"). This opens the CSS Rule Definition window again, with the "li" style opened for editing.

17. **Select the Box category: Type *0* in the Margin box; turn off the "Same for all" checkbox under Padding, and type 20 in the Left padding box.**

    The CSS Rule Definition window should look like Figure 5-29. You're done!

18. **Click OK to complete the style.** Choose File→Save All and preview the page in a web browser (File→Preview in Browser).

    The finished page should look like Figure 5-30. As you can see, you can use graphics in numerous ways to enhance the look of a web page. For an added exercise, you'll find two other graphic files—*tech-icon.png* and *ingredient-icon.png*—in the Images directory. Create styles for the first two headlines on the page so that those graphics appear as icons to the left of the text. (Hint: You'll need to use class styles [page 124] to achieve this.)

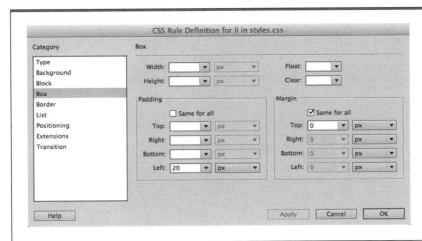

FIGURE 5-29

When inserting a background image, you'll frequently add padding to scoot text or other content away from the image. In this case, an icon appears on the left edge of a list item, so adding left padding adds space to the left of the text, making room for the icon.

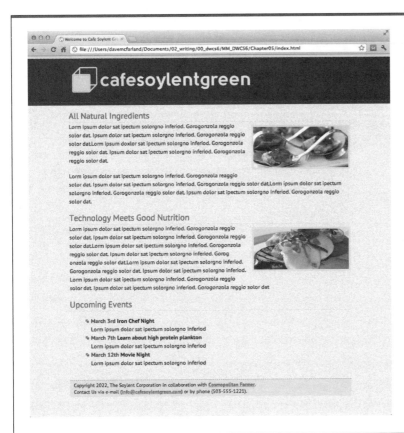

FIGURE 5-30

Photos, icons, and other graphic elements add visual interest to any web page.

Tables

The HTML <table> tag has had a somewhat infamous existence in the world of web design. It was originally intended to present scientific data in a spreadsheet-like manner. But as the web grew, graphic designers got into the web design game. They wanted to recreate the types of layouts they saw in magazines, books, and newspapers (in other words, they wanted to make good-looking websites). The most reliable tool at the time was the <table> tag, which designers morphed into a way to create columns, sidebars, and, in general, to precisely position elements on a page.

Today, with nearly everyone on the planet using advanced browsers like Internet Explorer, Firefox, Safari, and Opera, web designers use a more facile page-styling technique—CSS-based layout. Table-based layout is an aging dinosaur that produces pages heavy with code (which means they download slower), harder to update, and hostile to alternative browsers, like screen readers, mobile phones, and text-only browsers.

This chapter shows you how to use tables for their intended purpose: displaying data and other information best presented in rows and columns (Figure 6-1). If you're a long-time web designer who still uses tables for page layout, you can use Dreamweaver and the instructions in this chapter to continue that technique. However, you're better off making the switch to CSS-based layout. Dreamweaver's advanced CSS tools make building well-designed pages much simpler. You'll learn all about CSS layout in Chapter 9.

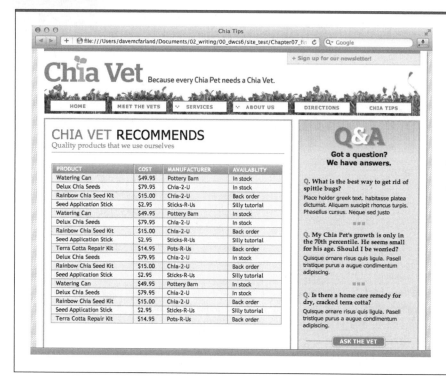

FIGURE 6-1

You can do all your page layout and design with CSS, and use tables for their intended purpose—displaying rows and columns of information. The list of products on this page is nestled inside a basic <table> tag, while the rest of the page is laid out using CSS.

■ Table Basics

A table is a grid of rows and columns that intersect to form *cells*, as shown in Figure 6-2. If you've used a spreadsheet before, an HTML table should feel familiar.

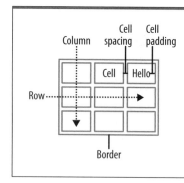

FIGURE 6-2

Rows, columns, and cells make up a table. Cell spacing specifies how many pixels of space appear between cells. Cell padding, on the other hand, adds space between the four sides of a cell and the cell's content.

A table row usually represents a collection of data for a single item. In Figure 6-1, for example, each row holds data for one product. A table *column* represents data of a particular type. The first column in Figure 6-1 contains the name of each product, while the second column displays its cost. A table cell, then, holds one piece of data for a particular row, like the exact price of the Rainbow Chia Seeds.

At a minimum, you use three HTML tags to create a table (there are actually quite a few tags related to table design, as you'll read about soon). You set the boundaries of the table with the <table> tag. Then, within this structure, you add table rows using the <tr> tag. Finally, you divide a table row into individual cells, each of which holds one piece of data.

You create a cell that holds data—$49.95, for instance—with the <td> or *table data* tag. Browsers align the text inside a <td> to the left edge of the cell.

A fourth tag, the <th>, or table head tag, also creates cells within a row, but instead of holding data, a table header tells you the *kind* of information you'll find in a row or column. Text inside a <th> tag appears centered and in boldface.

Figure 6-1, for example, contains one table (it uses one <table> tag), and 18 rows (18 <tr> tags). The top row contains four table headers (<th>) that identify the type of data in the cells below: Product, Cost, and so on. The other 17 rows contain data, and you create them with simple <td> tags.

Inserting a Table

One of the main problems with HTML tables is that they require a lot of code. Not only is this one reason why CSS is a better page layout method than HTML, it's also a good reason to use Dreamweaver to create a table. If you've ever hand-coded an HTML table, you know what a tangled mess of code it requires; one typo can sink your whole page. Fortunately, Dreamweaver makes the process simple.

1. **In the document window, position your cursor where you want to insert a table.**

   You can add a table anywhere you can add a paragraph of text. You can even add a table inside *another* table, by clicking inside a table cell.

2. **Choose Insert→Table.**

   You can also click the Table button on the Insert panel (it's under both the Common category and the Layout category). You can also press Ctrl+Alt+T (⌘-Option-T). Either way, the Table dialog box opens (see Figure 6-3).

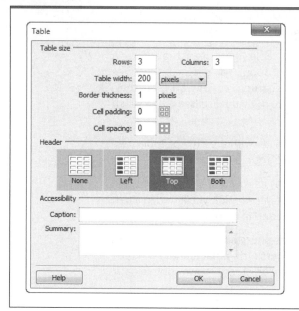

FIGURE 6-3

The Table dialog box lets you control a table's appearance. Leaving the Cell Padding and Cell Spacing fields empty isn't the same as setting them to 0. If these properties are empty, most browsers insert 1 pixel of cell padding and 2 pixels of cell spacing into tables. If you notice unwanted gaps between cells in a table, or between content in a table and the cell's edges, empty settings here are the likeliest culprit. To truly leave zero space, set Cell Padding and Cell Spacing to 0. (Dreamweaver remembers the settings you use. When you use the Insert Table dialog box again, it starts with the same settings you entered previously.)

3. **Using the Rows and Columns fields, specify how many rows and columns you want in your table.**

Don't fret too much over your estimate, since you can always add or remove rows and columns later.

4. **Type the amount of cell padding, in pixels, you want for the table.**

Cell padding is the buffer around the content within a cell—the space from the edge of the cell to the contents inside (see Figure 6-2). Unfortunately, this property applies to *every* cell in a table (it also applies equally to all four sides of the cell). You can't specify cell padding for individual cells, nor can you use different cell padding for each edge of the content (you can't for example, specify 10 pixels of padding on the left side of the cell, but only 5 pixels at the top) unless you use the CSS *padding* property as described on page 449. Designers often type either 0 or leave this box empty, and then use CSS to control the spacing in individual cells (via the <td> and <th> tags).

5. **Type the amount of cell spacing, in pixels, you want for the table.**

Cell spacing specifies how many pixels of empty space separate one cell from another. Like cell *padding*, this property applies to every cell in a table. CSS provides an equivalent property, *border-spacing*, but Dreamweaver's CSS Rule Definition window doesn't list that property—you'll need to use the CSS Properties pane to add this property to the table (see page 382). In addition, Internet

Explorer 7 and earlier ignore border spacing. So if you want space between each cell, it's easiest to add a value here (you can change it later). Type *0* to remove any space between cells. (Note that leaving these fields empty isn't the same as setting them to 0; see the caption in Figure 6-3.)

6. **Using the "Table width" field, specify how wide you want the table (in units you specify using the field's drop-down menu).**

   Tables can have either a specified, fixed minimum width, or they can take up a specified percentage of the space available on the page. To set a fixed width, choose Pixels as the unit of measure, and then, in the "Table width" field, type a pixel amount. Fixed-width tables remain the same size regardless of the browser window's size.

   Percentage-width tables grow or shrink relative to the space available. If you place a 100% wide table on a blank web page, the table stretches all the way across your visitor's browser window, no matter how wide or narrow he has it set. But the percentage isn't always based on the overall browser window width. If you place a table *inside* another object—for example, within a <div> tag—and that <div> has a set width, Dreamweaver calculates the percentage based on that object. Say you have a sidebar on a page, and the sidebar is 300 pixels wide; if you insert an 80% wide table inside the sidebar, then the table takes up 80 percent of 300 pixels, or 240 pixels.

7. **In the "Border thickness" box, type a number, in pixels, for the border.**

   If you don't want a border, type *0*. Dreamweaver uses dotted lines in Design view to help you identify rows, columns, and cells whose border is 0. (The dotted lines won't appear on your finished page.) Again, CSS offers a much better way to add borders, so it's best to set this to 0 and use CSS to control the borders (see page 260).

8. **Using the buttons in the middle of the dialog box, select a Header option.**

   The Header property inserts the table header <th> tag that creates the specialized cells in the top row or left-hand column. The <th> tag indicates that a cell is a *headline* for a column or row of data, and it identifies the kind of information in the cells below or to the right of the headline. A table that displays a company's yearly sales figures, broken down by region, might have a top row of headers for each year ("2010," "2011," "2012"), while the left column would have table headers identifying each region ("Northwest," "West," "South," and so on).

   The only visible change you get with a <th> tag is that web browsers display the text center-aligned and in bold type. However, this option also makes the table more accessible by telling screen readers (used by the visually impaired) that the cell serves as a header for the information in the column or row. (You can always change the look of these cells using CSS; just create a style for the <th> tag.)

9. **In the bottom section of the Table dialog box, add any Accessibility settings you wish to use.**

In the Caption box, type information identifying the table; it appears, centered, above the table. Use the Summary box when you want to explain a particularly complex table. This information doesn't show up in a browser window; it's intended to clarify the contents of a table to search engines and screen readers. Basic data tables (simple rows and columns) don't need a summary; search engines and screen readers can understand them just fine. It's only when you create a complex table with merged cells (see page 308) and multiple levels of headers that you might want to fill out the Summary box.

For more information on these options, and to get a complete rundown on table accessibility, visit *http://tinyurl.com/5vgvv2e*.

10. **Click OK to insert the table.**

Once you add a table to a page, you can begin filling its cells. A cell works like a small document window; you can click inside it and add text, images, and links using the techniques you've already learned. You can even insert a table inside a cell (a common technique in the bad old days of table-based layout).

To move your cursor from one cell to the next, press Tab. When you reach the last cell in a row, the Tab key moves the insertion point to the first cell in the row below. And if the insertion point is in the last *cell* of the last row, pressing Tab creates a new row at the bottom of the table.

Shift+Tab moves the cursor in the *opposite* direction—from the current cell to the previous cell.

■ Selecting Parts of a Table

Tables and their cells have independent properties. For example, a table and a cell can have different alignment properties. But before you can change any of these properties, you must first *select* the tables, rows, columns, and cells you want to affect.

Selecting a Table

You can select a table in the document window a number of ways:

• Click the upper-left corner of the table, or anywhere on the bottom or right edges. (Be careful using the latter technique, however. It's easy to accidentally *drag* the border, adding a height or width property to cells in the table.)

• Click anywhere inside the table, and then select the <table> tag in the document window's status bar (see page 26 to learn about the Tag Selector).

- Click anywhere inside the table, and then choose Modify→Table→Select Table.

- Right-click (Control-click) inside a table, and then, from the shortcut menu, choose Table→Select Table.

- If the insertion point is in any cell inside the table, pressing Ctrl+A (⌘-A) twice selects the table.

Once selected, a table appears with a thick black border and three tiny, square resize handles—at the right edge, bottom edge, and lower-right corner.

Selecting Rows or Columns

You can also select an entire row or column of cells by doing one of the following:

- Move your cursor to the left edge of a row or the top edge of a column. When it changes to a right- or down-pointing arrow, click, as explained in Figure 6-4.

- Click a cell at either end of a row, or the first or last cell of a column, and then drag across the cells in the row or column to select them.

- Click any cell in the row you want to select, and then click the <tr> tag in the Tag Selector (the <tr> tag is how HTML indicates a table row). This method doesn't work for columns.

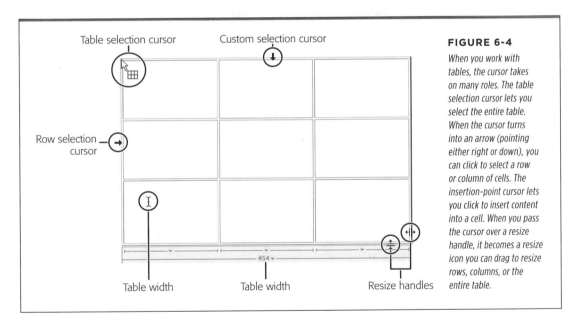

Table selection cursor   Custom selection cursor

Row selection cursor

Table width   Table width   Resize handles

FIGURE 6-4

When you work with tables, the cursor takes on many roles. The table selection cursor lets you select the entire table. When the cursor turns into an arrow (pointing either right or down), you can click to select a row or column of cells. The insertion-point cursor lets you click to insert content into a cell. When you pass the cursor over a resize handle, it becomes a resize icon you can drag to resize rows, columns, or the entire table.

When you select a cell, its border turns dark. When you select multiple cells, each has a dark border.

Selecting Cells

To select one or more cells:

- Drag across adjoining cells. A solid black border appears around a cell or cells when you select them.

- To select several cells that aren't necessarily adjacent, Ctrl-click (⌘-click) them one at a time. (You can also Ctrl-click [⌘-click] an already selected cell to deselect it.)

- Click a cell, and then Shift-click another cell. Your two clicks form diagonally opposite corners of an imaginary rectangle; Dreamweaver highlights all cells within it.

- Use the Tag Selector (see page 26) to select a cell. Click inside the cell you wish to select, and then click the <td> (or <th> for table headers) tag in the Selector. HTML identifies table cells with the <td> tag for table data, and the <th> tag for table headers.

- If the insertion point is inside the cell you want to select, press Ctrl+A (⌘-A).

■ Expanded Table Mode

If you remove all padding, cell spacing, and borders from a table, you may find it hard to select tables and individual cells. This is especially true if you nest tables within table cells (a common table-layout technique). To help you out, Dreamweaver offers an Expanded Table mode. Clicking the Expanded button on the Layout category of the Insert panel adds visible borders to every table and cell, and increases onscreen cell padding. (Choosing View→Table Mode→Expanded Tables does the same thing.) Expanded Table mode never changes the actual page code; it merely affects how the page looks in Design view. The guideline borders and extra spacing don't appear in web browsers.

If you simply use tables to display data, you'll probably never need Expanded Table mode, but if you have to edit old web pages built with complicated table layouts, Expanded mode is a big help.

To return to Standard view, click the Standard button on the Layout category of the Insert panel, or choose View→Table Mode→Standard Mode. You can also click the Exit link that appears in the blue toolbar above the document window (this toolbar appears only when you're in Expanded Table mode).

■ Formatting Tables

When you first insert a table, you set the number of rows and columns, as well as the table's cell padding, cell spacing, width, and borders. You're not stuck, however, with the properties you first give a table; you can change any or all of them, and set a few additional ones, using the Property Inspector.

When you select a table, the Property Inspector changes to reflect that table's settings (see Figure 6-5). You can adjust the table by entering different values for width, rows, columns, and so on in the appropriate fields.

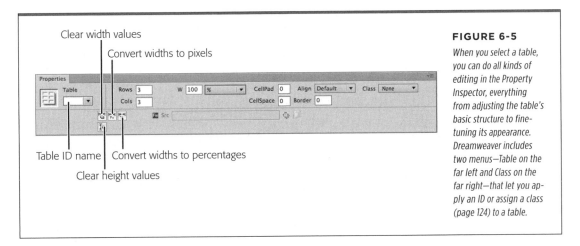

Clear width values
Convert widths to pixels
Table ID name
Convert widths to percentages
Clear height values

FIGURE 6-5

When you select a table, you can do all kinds of editing in the Property Inspector, everything from adjusting the table's basic structure to fine-tuning its appearance. Dreamweaver includes two menus—Table on the far left and Class on the far right—that let you apply an ID or assign a class (page 124) to a table.

In addition, the Property Inspector lets you set alignment options and add colors or a background image, as described next.

Aligning Tables

In the normal flow of a web page, a table acts like a paragraph, header, or any other HTML block-level element. Browsers align it to the left of the page, with other elements placed either above or below it.

But you can make several useful changes to the way a table interacts with the text and other elements on a page. After selecting the table, use one of the three alignment options in the drop-down menu on the right of the Property Inspector:

- The Left and Right options align the table with the left or right page margins. Anything you then add to the page—including paragraphs, images, or other tables—wraps around the right or left side of the table. You can apply the CSS Float property to a table (just as with images) to achieve the same effect (see page 257).

- The Center option makes the table sit in the center of a page, interrupting the flow of the elements around it. Nothing wraps around the table.

NOTE   Some of the properties Dreamweaver lets you adjust to make tables look better aren't technically valid for some of the different HTML document types that Dreamweaver creates. Dreamweaver can create HTML 4.01 Transitional, XHTML 1.0 Transitional, and several other types of HTML documents. In general, HTML 4.01 Transitional and XHTML 1.0 Transitional are commonly used document types—XHTML 1.0 Transitional is the "out of box" setting in Dreamweaver. However, the more "strict" types, like HTML 4.01 Strict and XHTML 1.0 Strict, don't support some table properties, and the *align* property, discussed above, is one of them.

HTML5 is even more strict. Not only is the align property considered obsolete, but so are the table width, cell padding, and cell spacing options.

This discrepancy is more a technicality than a design nuisance; most web browsers still display the alignment you select, even when you create HTML5, HTML Strict, and XHTML Strict documents. The newer and recommended method is to use CSS properties to accomplish the same display goals; for example, using CSS to set the left and right margins of a table to *auto* centers the table on the page, while applying a CSS Left Float or Right Float property is the same as the Left and Right alignment options. The CSS Width (page 448) and Padding properties (page 449) for tables are fine replacements for their HTML equivalents.

Clearing Height and Width Values

When creating complex table designs, it's easy to get yourself into a situation where width and height measurements conflict and produce unreliable results. For example, it's possible to set one cell to 300 pixels wide, and later set another cell *in the same column* to 400 pixels wide. Since a browser can't do both (how can one column be both 300 *and* 400 pixels wide?), you might not get the results you want.

In tables with many cells, these kinds of problems are tough to ferret out. That's when you'll find the following timesaving tools—located behind the obscure-looking buttons in the Property Inspector's bottom half (see Figure 6-5)—handy. They let you delete the width and height measurements and start from scratch (see page 299).

- Clicking the Clear Height Values button removes the height properties of the table and each cell. Doing so doesn't set the heights to zero; it simply deletes the property altogether.

- Clicking the Clear Width Values button does the same thing with the width properties of a table and its cells.

Two additional buttons let you convert pixel-based table widths to percentage measurements and vice versa. In other words, if a table is 600 pixels wide and you click the "Convert Widths to Percentages" button, Dreamweaver assigns percentages to the table and each cell whose width you specified using pixels.

These percentages depend on how much of the document window your table takes up when you click the button. If the document window is 1200 pixels wide, that 600-pixel-wide table changes to a 50% wide table. Because you'll rarely do this, don't waste your brain cells memorizing such tools.

WARNING Dreamweaver CS6 doesn't provide access to outdated table properties like *border color, background color,* and *background image* from the Property Inspector. Instead, you should use the CSS equivalents: *border* (page 260), *background-image* (page 262), and *background-color.* You'll find examples of how to use CSS to add background images, colors, and borders to a table in the tutorial at the end of this chapter. In addition, you'll learn how to use the very valuable *border-collapse* property on page 326.

Resizing a Table

While you define the width of a table when you first insert it, you can always change it later. To do so, select the table, and then take either of these steps:

- Type a value into the W (width) box in the Property Inspector, and then choose a unit of measure, either pixels or percentages, from the drop-down menu.

- Drag one of the resize handles on the right edge. Avoid the handle in the right corner of the table—this adds a *height* property to the first cell in the bottom row. If you do add a *height* property this way, you can easily remove it using the "Clear Height Values" button in the Property Inspector.

In theory, you can also convert a table from a fixed unit of measure, such as pixels, to the stretchy, percentage-style width setting—or vice versa—using the two "Convert Table Width" buttons at the bottom of the Property Inspector (see Figure 6-5). What these buttons do depends on the size of the current document window in Dreamweaver. For example, suppose the document window is 700 pixels wide, and you inserted a table that's 100 percent wide. Clicking the "Convert Table Widths to Pixels" button sets the table's width to around 700 pixels (the exact value depends on the margins of the page). However, if your document window were 500 pixels wide, clicking the same button would produce a fixed-width table of around 500 pixels wide.

NOTE The HTML <table> tag doesn't officially have a Height property. Dreamweaver, however, adds Height properties to table cells when you drag their top or bottom borders, but it won't add a Height property to the table tag, which is a good thing, since it's invalid HTML. You could add it manually—<table height="500">—since most browsers understand the Height property and would obey your wishes. But since it's not standard code, there's no guarantee that newer browsers will support it.

You have a couple of alternatives: First, you could decide not to worry about height. After all, it's difficult to control the height of a table precisely, especially if there's text in it. Since text sizes appear differently on different operating systems and browsers, the table may grow taller if your guest's text is larger, no matter what height you set.

Your second option is to use the CSS *height* property (page 448) to set the table's stature.

The "Convert Table Width to Percentages" buttons take the opposite tack. They set the width of a table and its cells to percentages based on the amount of the document window's width and height they cover at the moment. The bigger the current document window, the smaller the percentage.

Because the effects of these buttons depend on the document window's size, you'll find yourself rarely, if ever, using them.

Modifying Cell and Row Properties

Cells have their own properties, separate from the properties of the table itself. So do table *rows*—but not columns (see the box on page 302).

When you click inside a cell, the top half of the Property Inspector displays the cell's text formatting properties; the bottom half shows the properties of the cell itself (see Figure 6-6).

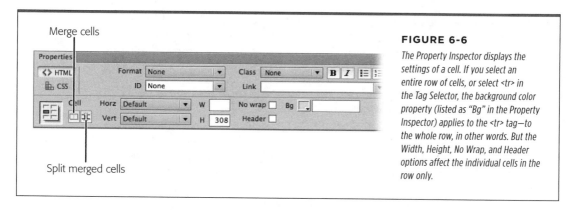

FIGURE 6-6

The Property Inspector displays the settings of a cell. If you select an entire row of cells, or select <tr> in the Tag Selector, the background color property (listed as "Bg" in the Property Inspector) applies to the <tr> tag—to the whole row, in other words. But the Width, Height, No Wrap, and Header options affect the individual cells in the row only.

Alignment Properties

At the outset, a cell's contents hug the left wall and float halfway between the top and bottom of the cell. After selecting a row, a cell, or several cells, you can change these alignments in the Property Inspector. For example, the "Horz" (horizontal) menu offers Left, Center, Right, and Default alignment. ("Default" gives you the same effect as "Left" without adding any extra HTML code.)

Note that these options are distinct from the *paragraph* alignment options discussed in Chapter 3. In fact, you can mix and match the two. Suppose you have a table cell containing four paragraphs, and you want to center-align all but the last paragraph, which you want right-aligned. To do so, you could set the alignment of the *cell* to Center, and then select just the last paragraph and set its alignment to Right. The paragraph's alignment overrides the alignment applied by the cell.

You can set the vertical alignment property in the same manner. Select the relevant cells, and then use one of the five options available in the Property Inspector's "Vert" (vertical) menu: Default (the same as Middle), Top, Middle, Bottom, or Baseline. The Baseline option aligns the bottom of the first line of text in the cell to the baseline of text in all the other cells in the row—really only useful if the type in the different cells is different sizes and you're an extremely picky designer (which you might be, and that's OK).

NOTE The CSS *text-align* property (in the Block category of the CSS Rule Definition window) provides the same effect as horizontal cell alignment; the *vertical-align* property (in the Block category of the CSS Rule Definition window) is the CSS replacement for a cell's vertical alignment.

Table Header

The Table Header option lets you convert a <td> tag to a <th> tag, which is useful when you want to turn, say, the row at the top of a table into a header. It works just like the column or row header options available in the Table dialog box, described on page 293.

NOTE You can also turn off the Table Header box to turn a table header into a regular table cell. This is handy when you insert a table that shouldn't have headers, but you forgot to unselect the header option in the Table dialog box.

You usually use this option for tables that include actual tabular data, like a spreadsheet, to identify the type of data that appears in the other cells in a row or column. For example, you may have a table containing data from different years; each cell in the top row could identify the year the data in the cells below it was compiled.

While Dreamweaver lets you change a single cell into a header, you'll most likely apply this to the top row or left column of cells.

A Property to Forget

The No Wrap option is of such little value that you'll probably go your entire web career without using it.

But for the sake of thoroughness—and in case you actually find a use for it—here's a description. The No Wrap property prevents a web browser from wrapping a line of text within a cell onto multiple lines. The browser widens the cell instead, so that it accommodates the line without breaks. The result is almost never useful or attractive. Furthermore, in some browsers, if you specify a width for the cell, the browsers ignore the No Wrap option!

Cell Decoration

Cells needn't be drab. As with tables, you can give individual cells background colors, or even background graphics. However, just as with tables, you should avoid the decorative table cell options available in the Property Inspector. Instead, use CSS's *background-color* property to add color to a cell, the *background-image* property (see "Background Images" on page 262) to add a graphic to the background of a cell, and the *border* property (see "Adding Borders" on page 260) to add color borders around cells.

POWER USERS' CLINIC

The Dawn of Columns

As far as the standard HTML language is concerned, there really isn't any such entity as a column. You create tables with the <table> tag, rows with the <tr> tag, and cells with the <td> tag—but there's no column tag. Dreamweaver calculates the columns based on the number of cells in a row. If there are seven rows in a table, each with four cells, the table has four columns. In other words, the number of cells you add to a row determines the number of columns in a table.

Two tags introduced in HTML 4—the <colgroup> and <col> tags—let you control various attributes of columns in a table. Unfortunately, Dreamweaver provides no easy way to add the tags. You can find out more about them, however, from *http://tinyurl.com/3whpctc*.

FREQUENTLY ASKED QUESTION

Suddenly Jumbo Cells

When I added some text to a cell, it suddenly got much wider than the other cells in the row. What gives?

It isn't Dreamweaver's fault, it's how HTML works.

Web browsers (and Dreamweaver) display cells to match the content inside. For example, say you add a three-column table to a page. In the first cell of the first row, you type in two words, leave the second cell empty, and add a 125-pixel-wide image in the third cell of that row. Since the image is the biggest item, its

cell is wider than the other two. The middle cell, with nothing in it, is given the least amount of space.

Usually, you don't want a web browser making these kinds of decisions. By specifying a width for a cell (below), you can force a browser to display a cell with the dimension you want. But keep in mind that there are exceptions to this rule; see "The contents take priority" on page 303.

Setting Cell Dimensions

Specifying the width or height of a particular cell is simple: Select one or more cells, and then type a value in the Property Inspector's W (width) or H (height) field. You can specify the value in either pixels or percentages. For instance, if you want a 50-pixel-wide cell, type in *50*. For a cell that you want to take up 50 percent of the total table width, type in *50%*. Read the next section for details on the tricky business of controlling cell and table dimensions.

You can also resize a column or row of cells by dragging a cell border. As your cursor approaches the cell's edge, it changes shape to indicate that you can begin dragging. Dreamweaver also provides an interactive display of cell widths (circled in Figure 6-7) when you use this method. This helpful feature lets you know the exact width of your cells at all times, so you can drag a cell to a precise width. When you resize table cells this way, Dreamweaver sets the width of the cell using the type of measure you specified for the overall table width—percentages or pixels. In other words, if you insert a table and set its width to 100%, when you drag the side wall of a cell to resize that cell, Dreamweaver sets the cell width using a percentage value (30%, for example); however, if you initially set the table to 500 pixels wide, Dreamweaver displays the cell widths as pixel values when you resize them.

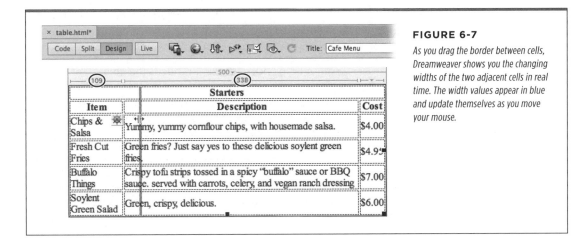

FIGURE 6-7

As you drag the border between cells, Dreamweaver shows you the changing widths of the two adjacent cells in real time. The width values appear in blue and update themselves as you move your mouse.

Tips for Surviving Table-Making

Nothing is more confounding than trying to get your tables laid out exactly as you want them. Many beginning web designers throw their hands up in despair when working with tables, which often seem to have minds of their own. Here are a few problems that often confuse designers—and some ways that make working with them more straightforward.

■ THE CONTENTS TAKE PRIORITY

Say you create a 300-pixel-wide table and set each cell in the first row to 100 pixels wide. You insert a larger graphic into the first cell, and suddenly—kablooie! Even though you set each cell to 100 pixels wide, as shown in Figure 6-8, the column with the graphic is much wider than the other two.

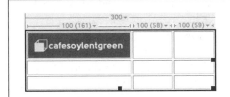

FIGURE 6-8

Because a web browser can't shrink an image or hide part of it, the top-left cell above has to grow to fit it. That first column of cells now measures 161 pixels wide; the other two columns must shrink in order to keep the table 300 pixels wide. The numbers at the top of each cell indicate its width as set in the HTML—100—and, in parentheses, the actual width as displayed in Dreamweaver (161, 58, and 59).

That's because an individual cell can't be smaller than the largest piece of content inside it. In this case, although you told the cell to be 100 pixels wide, the image is 161 pixels wide, which forces the first column to grow (and the other columns to shrink) accordingly.

■ THERE'S NO SUCH THING AS COLUMN WIDTH—ONLY CELL WIDTH

To set the width of a column of cells, you have to set the width of only *one* cell in that column. Say you have a table with three rows and three columns. You need to set only the width for the top row of cells; you can (and should) leave the cell widths for the remaining cells in the two bottom rows empty. In fact, that's what Dreamweaver does automatically—when you drag a vertical border between cells, Dreamweaver only modifies the Width property of the top cells.

This principle can save a lot of time and, because it reduces the amount of code on a web page, it makes your pages load (and therefore appear) faster. The same holds true for the height of a row. You need only to set the height of a single cell to define the height for its entire row. When you drag a horizontal border, Dreamweaver adds a Height property to the first cell in the row above the border.

> **TIP** You can actually set the width of a column if you use the <colgroup> and <col> tags when creating a table. Unfortunately, Dreamweaver doesn't provide any way, aside from hand coding, to add those tags. But if you're interested, you can learn more about using those tags and CSS to define the width of individual table columns at *http://tinyurl.com/5qt25f*.

■ DO THE MATH

Calculators are really useful when you build tables. Although you *could* create a 400-pixel-wide table with three 700-pixel-wide columns, the results you'd get on the screen could be unpredictable (after all, 700 plus 700 plus 700 does not equal 400).

As it turns out, web browsers' loyalty is to *table* width first, and then to column width. If the combined widths of your columns add up to the width of your table, you'll save yourself a lot of headaches.

Don't forget that you need to account for borders, cell padding, and cell spacing. For example, say you create a 500-pixel-wide table with two columns and 10 pixels of padding. If you want the first column 100 pixels wide, you'd set the width value to 80 pixels: 10 pixels of left padding plus 80 pixels of cell space plus 10 pixels of right padding equals 100 pixels total width.

The same is true when you use percentage values for tables and cell widths. Just make sure the value of the widths of the cells in a row totals 100%. That is, if you have three columns and you want the first column to be twice as wide as the other two, you could set it's width to 50% and the other two cells' widths to 25% each. This is true even if you set the initial width of the entire table to something smaller than 100%, say, 80%. That 80% table width simply means that the table will be 80% of the width of its container—the page for example, or a <div> tag. Even though the table takes up only 80% of the browser window, for instance, all the cells together still make up 100% of the table width.

Beware the Resize Handles

Dreamweaver provides several techniques for resizing tables and cells in Design view. Unfortunately, the easiest way to resize a table—dragging a cell or table border—is also the easiest way to make a mistake. Because moving the cursor over any border turns it into the Resize tool, almost every Dreamweaver practitioner drags a border accidentally at least once, overwriting carefully calculated table and cell widths and heights.

In addition, if you grab either of the two bottom resize handles (they look like black squares) when you have a table selected,

you'll set the table's Height property. As mentioned in the note on page 299, it's actually invalid HTML to add a height attribute to the table tag.

On occasions like these, don't forget Dreamweaver's undo feature, Ctrl+Z (⌘-Z). And if all is lost, you can always clear the widths and heights of every cell in a table (using the Property Inspector's buttons) and start over by typing in new cell dimensions (see Figure 6-5).

Adding and Removing Cells

Even after you insert a table into a web page, you can add and subtract rows and columns. The text or images in the columns move right or down to accommodate their new next-door neighbors.

Adding One Row or Column

To add a single row to a table, use any of these approaches:

- Click inside a cell. On the Insert panel's Layout category, click the Insert Row Above button (see Figure 6-9) to add a row above the current row. Click the Insert Row Below button to add a row below the current row.

- Click inside a cell. Choose Modify→Table→Insert Row, or press Ctrl+M (⌘-M) to insert a new row of cells above the current row. Alternatively, you can right-click (Control-click) a cell, and then, from the shortcut menu, choose Table→Insert Row.

- To add a new row at the end of a table, click inside the last cell in the table, and then press Tab.

FIGURE 6-9

Four buttons in the Layout category of the Insert panel make it easy to add columns and rows. They also make it easy to control where a new row or column goes—a feat not possible with a simple keyboard shortcut.

The new rows inherit all the properties (except width) of the row you originally clicked.

To add a single *column* of cells:

- Click inside a cell. On the Insert bar's Layout tab, click the "Insert Column to the Left" button to add a column to the left of the selected one. Click the "Insert Column to the Right" button to add a column to the right of the current column.

- Click inside a cell, and then choose Modify→Table→Insert Column.

- Click inside a cell, and then press Ctrl+Shift+A (⌘-Shift-A).

- Right-click (Control-click) a cell, and then, from the shortcut menu that appears, choose Table→Insert Column.

In each case (except for the "Insert Column to the Right" button), a new column appears to the left of the current one.

Adding Multiple Rows or Columns

If you need to add a lot of rows or columns to a table, you use a special dialog box.

1. **Click inside a cell.** Choose Modify→Table→Insert Rows or Columns.

   The "Insert Rows or Columns" dialog box appears (see Figure 6-10).

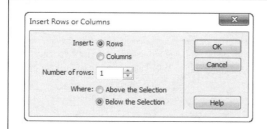

FIGURE 6-10

The "Insert Rows or Columns" dialog box lets you add multiple rows or columns to a table. The wording of the options changes depending on which you want to do.

2. **Click either Rows or Columns.** Type the number of rows or columns you wish to add.

   Windows users can also click the tiny up- and down-arrow buttons next to "Number of rows" (or columns).

3. **Tell Dreamweaver where you want the new rows or columns to appear, relative to the cell you selected, by clicking Above or Below (for rows), or Before or After (for columns).** Click OK to insert them.

Using the dialog box gives you an advantage over the single row/single column expansion described above. There, new rows always go above the current cell, and new columns always go to the left. This dialog box lets you choose whether the new row or column comes *before* or *after* the selected cell.

Deleting Rows and Columns

To delete a row from your table, use one of the following techniques:

> **NOTE** When you remove a row or column, Dreamweaver eliminates everything inside the cells. So before you start hacking away, it's a good idea to save a copy of the page.

- Select the row (see "Selecting Rows or Columns" on page 295) and then press Delete to remove all the row's cells—and everything in them.

- Click a cell. Choose Modify→Table→Delete Row, or use the keyboard shortcut Ctrl+Shift+M (⌘-Shift-M).

- Right-click (Control-click) inside a cell, and then, from the shortcut menu, choose Table→Delete Row.

Deleting a column is equally straightforward:

- Select the column, and then press Delete. You just eliminated all the selected cells and everything in them.

- Click a cell, and then choose Modify→Table→Delete Column, or use the keyboard shortcut Ctrl+Shift+Hyphen (⌘-Shift-Hyphen).

- Right-click (Control-click) inside a cell, and then choose Table→Delete Column from the shortcut menu.

WARNING Dreamweaver doesn't let you delete a row if you *merged* one of its cells with a cell in another row. Nor can you delete a column if it contains a cell merged with an adjacent cell. (You'll learn about merged cells in the next section.)

Deleting a column like this is actually quite a feat. Since there's no column tag in HTML, Dreamweaver, behind the scenes, has to select individual cells in multiple rows—a task you wouldn't wish on your worst enemy if you had to do it by editing the raw HTML.

Merging and Splitting Cells

Cells are very basic creatures with some severe limitations. For example, all the cells in a row share the same height. One cell can't be taller than the cell next to it, which can pose some serious design problems. In the old days of table-based design, designers solved this problem by combining multiple cells to form, for example, one tall banner area that spanned three table columns.

But even when your tables contain just data, there are times when you need to combine cells. The table in Figure 6-11, for example, breaks down data for a single year—like 2006—into two demographic groups—men and women. Since the data in the "men" and "women" columns pertain to particular years, you can merge two table cells to identify the first year, 2006, and combine two additional cells for the year 2007. Dreamweaver provides several ways to persuade cells to work well together. The trick is to *merge* cells—combine their area—to create a larger cell that spans two or more rows or columns.

CosmoFarmer Subscriber Information by Year

Year	2006		2007	
Gender	Men	Women	Men	Women
Number	10,000	15,000	25,000	27,000
Average Age	39	34	33	30
Avg Yearly Income	$65K	$66K	$100K	$100K

FIGURE 6-11

You can create cells that span multiple rows and columns by merging adjacent cells. This is one way to represent multiple related rows or columns of information using a single table header.

To merge cells, start by selecting the cells you want to merge, using any of the methods described in "Selecting Parts of a Table" on page 294. You can only merge cells that form a rectangle or square. You can't, for instance, select three cells in a column, and only one in the adjacent row, to create an L shape. Nor can you merge cells that aren't adjacent; in other words, you can't merge a cell in one corner of a table with a cell in the opposite corner.

Then, in the Property Inspector, click the Merge Cells button (Figure 6-12) or choose Modify→Table→Merge Cells. Dreamweaver joins the selected cells, forming a single new super cell.

FIGURE 6-12

The Merge Cells button is active only when you select multiple cells. The Split Cells button appears only when you select a single cell or when you click inside a cell (see below for more on splitting cells).

TIP Better yet, use this undocumented keyboard shortcut: the M key. Just select two or more cells, and then press M. It's much easier than the keyboard shortcut listed in the online help: Ctrl+Alt+M (⌘-Option-M).

You may also find yourself in the opposite situation: You have one cell that you want to *divide* into multiple cells. To split a cell, click or select a single cell. In the Property Inspector, click the Split Cells button. (Once again, you can trigger this command several ways. You can choose Modify→Table→Split Cell, or if you prefer keyboard shortcuts, you can press Ctrl+Alt+S [⌘-Option-S]. You can even right-click [Control-click] the selected cell, and then, from the shortcut menu, choose Table→Split Cell.)

When the Split Cell dialog box opens (Figure 6-13), click one of the buttons to indicate whether you want to split the cell into rows or columns. Then type the number of rows or columns you want to create, and click OK.

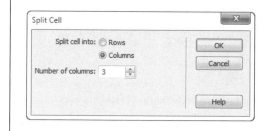

FIGURE 6-13

The Split Cell dialog box lets you divide a single cell into multiple cells. You can choose whether to divide the cell into rows (multiple cells on top of one another) or columns (multiple cells side by side).

If you split a cell into columns, everything in the cell winds up in the left column, with the new, empty column or columns to the left. When you split a cell into rows, the current contents end up in the top row.

◼ Tabular Data

Since tables are meant to display data, Dreamweaver provides useful tools so you can import and work with data.

Importing Data into a Table

Say your boss emails you your company's yearly sales information, which includes data on sales, profits, and expenses organized by quarter. She asks you to get this up on the Web for a board meeting she's having in half an hour.

This assignment could require a fair amount of work: building a table and then copying and pasting the correct information into each cell of the table, one at a time. Dreamweaver makes your task much easier, because you can create a table and import data into its rows and columns in one pass.

For this to work, the table data you want to import must begin life in a *delimited* format. Most spreadsheet programs, including Excel, and database programs, such as Access or FileMaker Pro, export delimited data easily. In most programs, you do this by choosing File→Export or File→Save As, and then choose a tab-delimited or comma-separated text file format.

> **NOTE** Dreamweaver for Windows users don't need to create a delimited-format file for Microsoft Excel data. It directly imports the data and converts it into a well-organized table. See page 91 for details.

In a delimited file, each line of text represents one table row. You keep the individual pieces of information in that line of text discrete using a special character called a delimiter—most often a tab, but possibly a comma or colon. Each discrete piece of data will go into a single cell in the row. In a colon-delimited file, for example, Dreamweaver would convert the line *Sales:$1,000,000:$2,000,000:$567,000:$12,500* into a row of five cells, with the first cell containing the word *Sales*.

Once you save your boss's spreadsheet as a delimited file, you're ready to import it into a Dreamweaver table:

1. **Choose File→Import→Tabular Data.**

   The Import Tabular Data dialog box appears (see Figure 6-14).

2. **Click Browse.** In the Insert Tabular Data dialog box, find and select the delimited text file you want to import.

The delimited file is not a spreadsheet, but a plain text file. Navigate to and double-click the file name in the dialog box.

3. **From the drop-down menu, select the delimiter you used to separate the data in the file.**

You choose from Tab, Comma, Colon, Semicolon, or Other. If you select Other, an additional field appears, where you type in the character used as the delimiter.

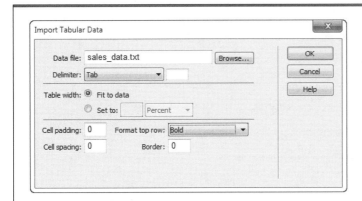

FIGURE 6-14

The Import Tabular Data dialog box lets you select a data file to import and choose formatting options for the resulting table.

4. **Select a table width.**

Choose "Fit to data" if you want the table to fit itself to the information you're importing—an excellent idea when you aren't completely sure how much information the file contains. (You can always modify the table after you import the data.)

On the other hand, if your web page needs a table of a certain size, you can specify it by selecting the Set button, and then typing a value in the field next to it. Select "pixel" or "percentage value" (see page 293).

5. **Set values for "Cell padding," "Cell spacing," and Border, if you like.**

See page 292 for details.

6. **Select a formatting option for the top row of data.**

If the first line in the text file has column headings—Quarter 1 Sales, Quarter 2 Sales, and so on—Dreamweaver lets you choose Bold, Italic, or Bold Italic to set this row apart from the rest of the table. Unfortunately, this option doesn't turn the cells in the first row into table header (<th>) tags, which is what they should be. It's best to choose no formatting, manually select the cells, and then turn them into table header (<th>) tags as described on page 301.

7. **Click OK to import the data and create the table.**

Dreamweaver adds the table to your web page. It's a regular HTML table at this point, and you can edit the contents as you normally would or modify the table (add rows and columns, for example) using any of the techniques discussed in this chapter.

Sorting Data in a Table

If you have a table that lists employee names, you probably want to present that list in alphabetical order—or alphabetically *and* by department. Dreamweaver's Sort Table command takes a lot of the drudgery out of this task.

1. **Select the table you want to sort.**

See page 294 for some table-selection techniques.

2. **Choose Commands→Sort Table.**

The Sort Table dialog box appears (Figure 6-15).

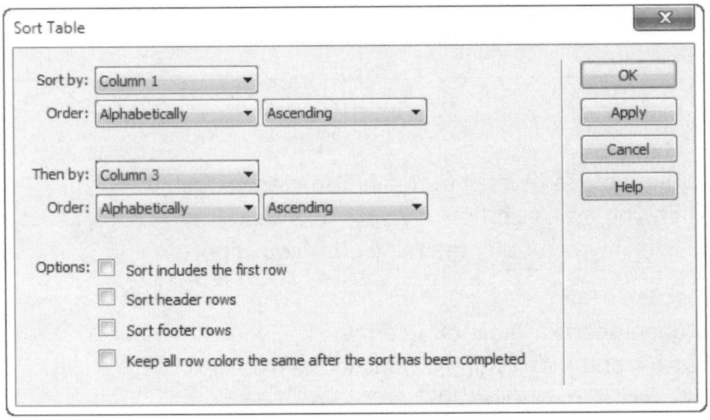

FIGURE 6-15

The Sort Table command works well with Dreamweaver's Import Tabular Data feature. Imagine you get a text file listing all your company's employees, import the data into a table, and then realize that the names aren't in any particular order.

3. **Using the "Sort by" drop-down menu, choose the column by which you want to sort.**

You can choose any column in the table. Suppose you have a table listing a bunch of products. Each row has the product name, number, and price. To see the products listed from least to most expensive, sort by the column with the product prices.

> **TIP** The Spry Data Set tools let you create a table that your website guests can sort *interactively*. Read about this cool tool on page 661.

4. **Use the next two drop-down menus to specify how you want Dreamweaver to sort the data.**

   You can sort it alphabetically or numerically. To order the product list in the example above by price, choose Numerically from the Order drop-down menu. If you're sorting a Name column, choose Alphabetically.

   Use the second drop-down menu to specify whether you want an Ascending (A–Z, 1–100) or Descending (Z–A, 100–1) sort.

5. **If you like, choose an additional column to sort by, using the "Then by" drop-down menu.**

   This secondary sort can come in handy when several cells in the *first* sorting column have the same value. If several items in your product list cost $100, a sort by price would place them consecutively in the table; you could then specify a secondary sort that would place the products in alphabetical order within each price group. Doing so lists all the products from least to most expensive, *and* lists all same-priced products alphabetically within their group.

6. **If the first row of the table contains data you want to sort, turn on "Sort includes the first row."**

   If, however, the first row contains *headings* for each column, leave this box turned off.

7. **Choose whether you want to sort header rows and footer rows as well.**

   The Sort Header Row option isn't referring to cells that have the "header" property set (see page 301). This option, and the next one, refer to the <thead> (table header) and <tfoot> (table footer) tags, which let you turn one or more rows into repeating headers and footers for long tables. Since Dreamweaver doesn't insert these tags for you, you'll most likely never use these options.

8. **Choose whether to keep row colors with the sorted row.**

   One way to visually organize a table is to add color to alternate rows. This every-other-row pattern helps readers focus on one row at a time. However, if you sort a table formatted this way, you'd wind up with some crazy pattern of colored and uncolored rows. The bottom line: If you applied colors to your rows and you want to keep those colors in the same order, leave this checkbox turned off.

   Dreamweaver is even in step with current web design practices, which don't assign a background color to table rows by using the outmoded *bgcolor* HTML property but instead use CSS. A common approach to coloring table rows is to apply a CSS class style to every *other* row in a table. That class style might have the *background-color* property set so that alternating rows are colored. When you use the Sort Table command, Dreamweaver keeps the class names in the proper order. That is, it keeps the classes applied to every other row, even when you reorganize the data with the Sort Table command. This only works if you *don't* turn on the "Keep all row colors the same" checkbox—so don't turn it on!

9. **Click Apply to see the effect of the sort without closing the dialog box.**

If the table meets with your satisfaction, click OK to sort the table and return to the document window. (Clicking Cancel, however, doesn't undo the sort. If you want to return the table to its previous sort order, choose Edit→Undo Sort Table after closing the sort window.)

Exporting Table Data

Getting data out of a table in Dreamweaver is simple. Just select the table, and then choose File→Export→Table. In the Export Table dialog box that appears, select the type of delimiter (Tab, Comma, Space, Colon, Semicolon, or Other) and the destination computer's operating system (Windows, Mac, or Unix), and then click OK. Give the file a name and save it on your computer. You can then import this delimited file into your spreadsheet or database program.

■ Tables Tutorial

In this tutorial, you'll create a menu for the café site you've been working on. In addition, you'll use some Cascading Style Sheet magic to make the table look great (skip ahead to Figure 6-27 to see the finished page).

> **TIP** You need to download files from *www.sawmac.com/dwcs6* to complete this tutorial. See the Note on page 54 for more details.

Once you download the tutorial files and open Dreamweaver, set up a new site as described on page 40: Name the site *Tables Tutorial*, and select the Chapter06 folder (inside the MM_DWCS6 folder). (In a nutshell: choose Site→New Site. In the Site Setup window, type *Tables Tutorial* into the Site Name field, click the folder icon next to the Local Site Folder field, navigate to and select the Chapter06 folder, and then click Choose or Select. Finally, click OK.)

Adding a Table

Once again, you'll be working on a page for the good people who run *Cafe Soylent Green*.

1. **Choose File→Open.**

You'll work on a page similar to the ones you've built so far.

2. **Navigate to the Chapter06 folder and double-click the file named *menu. html*.** Click in the empty space beneath the headline "Cafe Soylent Green Menu."

You'll insert a table into this space.

3. Choose Insert→Table.

You can also click the Table button in the Insert panel's Common category. Either way, the Table window appears (see Figure 6-16). You need to define the table's basic characteristics.

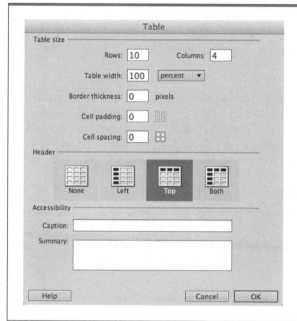

FIGURE 6-16

Inserting a table into a web page is a matter of making a few choices in the Table dialog box. Any text you type into the Summary box doesn't appear in a browser window, so you probably won't use this option much. It's intended to explain a particularly complicated table to non-visual web browsers (like search engines such as Google and Bing, or screen readers used by the visually impaired).

4. Type *10* in the Rows box and *4* in the Columns box.

Time to set the width, spacing, and padding properties.

5. Set "Table width" to 100 percent. Type *0* in the "Border thickness," "Cell padding," and "Cell spacing" boxes.

Setting a table's width to 100 percent makes it fit the available space given to it—in this case, you're about to insert this table into a <div> tag that has a set width of 800 pixels. The browser will make this table fill that space and, in effect, display an 800-pixel-wide table. Using a percentage value is a good idea, because if you decide to change the width of the main content area of the page (make it 1,000 pixels wide instead of 800 pixels, for example), the table grows to fit the new dimensions. If you use pixels for the width, you'd have to go back to the table and change its width every time you decided to change the width of the main content region.

Setting the other three properties here to 0 is common. You have greater control of borders and cell attributes using CSS.

6. **In the window's Header section, select Top.**

The header setting indicates which cells Dreamweaver will mark as "table headers"—these cells contain labels that describe the kind of information in the cells below (when you select Top), or the in the cells of a row (when you select Left). Now that you've picked Top, the top row of cells will hold labels like Product, Cost, and Manufacturer.

You can skip the caption. It's not a requirement, and the page's title makes clear what the table is all about. The window should now look like Figure 6-16.

7. **Click OK.**

A new table appears on the page, filling the space provided by the main content <div> tag. At this point, you could begin adding content by clicking into a cell and typing. However, this book isn't about improving your typing skills, so you'll forego typing in all the menu items the café offers and, instead, use Dreamweaver's very useful Import Tabular Data command.

Importing Tabular Data

While it's not difficult to type data into a table, it does take time. And, if you already have the data you want to insert in spreadsheet format, there's a better way to fill up that table. In this section of the tutorial, you'll use the Insert Tabular Data command to create and fill a table in several easy steps—but first, you need to remove the table you just added.

1. **Select the table and press Delete (or select Edit→Cut).**

As described on page 294, there are several ways to select a table. One is to click the top-left corner. But when a table has no borders, padding, or cell spacing, that can be tricky. Clicking the Expanded button in the Insert panel's Layout category temporarily adds borders, padding, and spacing, so you can more easily select the table. (Choosing View→Table Mode→Expanded Tables Mode does the same thing.)

An easier way is to just click inside any cell in the table and then, in the Tag Selector (page 26) in the bottom left of the document window, simply click the <table> tag to select the table and all its contents. Then click Delete to remove it.

Now you'll import a text file.

2. **Make sure the cursor is still in the empty space below the café's headline and choose File→Import→Tabular Data.**

Dreamweaver opens the Import Tabular Data window (Figure 6-17).

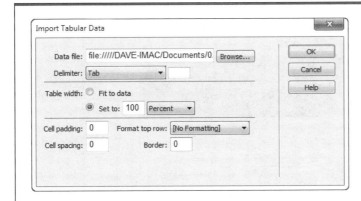

Import Tabular Data

FIGURE 6-17

Dreamweaver makes it easy to import a text file's worth of data into a brand-new HTML table. Leave the "Format top row" menu on "No Formatting." You're better off controlling the formatting, including the border, padding, and spacing attributes you earlier set to 0, with CSS.

3. **Click the Browse button to open a file selection window and double-click the file *menu.txt* in the Chapter06 folder.**

   This file contains what's called "tab-delimited" data. That is, each line in the file represents one row in a table, and each cell is separated by a tab character. This format is a common way to export information from a spreadsheet program like Microsoft Excel or Apple Numbers or even from a database.

4. **Make sure Tab is selected in the Delimiter menu.**

   The option you select from the Delimiter drop-down menu depends on the file you're importing. The file you just selected has each piece of information separated by a tab character. Dreamweaver can use that tab to identify the data for individual cells and figure how many columns the table will need. When you export a spreadsheet, you can use other delimiting characters, including commas, semicolons, and colons to demarcate each cell.

5. **In the "Table width" section, select "Set to," type *100*, and then choose Percent.** Set the "Cell padding," "Cell spacing," and Border boxes to *0*.

   The window should now look like Figure 6-17.

6. **Click OK to import the data and create a new table.**

   Dreamweaver creates the new table, 3 columns wide by 16 rows high, and inserts all the information for the café's menu (see Figure 6-18).

   The café divides its menu into three categories, Starters, Main, and Dessert. In the first row, you'll see the word "Starters" sitting in a single cell on the left. This really should span the entire table, since it's introducing this section of the menu. Fortunately, that's easy to do.

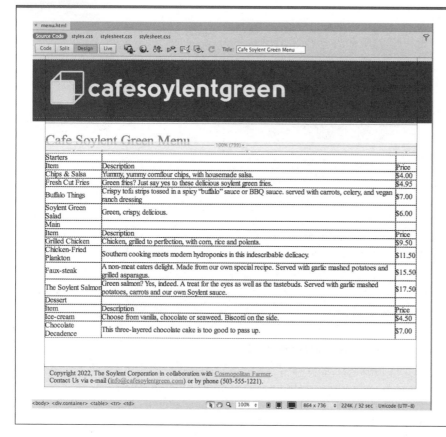

FIGURE 6-18

Dreamweaver's import tabular data command makes it easy to convert a comma- (or tab-) separated value file into a complex HTML table. It's certainly a lot easier than filling out each table cell individually. When you need to create a HTML table filled with data, try to get your table data in a CSV (comma separated value) file.

7. **Ctrl-click (⌘-click) the three cells in the top row.** Press the M key to merge those cells.

   The three cells turn into one big cell that spans the width of the table. You could also have selected the row using any of the methods described on page 295— for example, in Expanded Table Mode (choose View→Table Mode→Expanded Tables Mode), you could click on the left edge of the first cell to select the row, or you could click in the left cell and drag to the right until you select all the cells.

   You can also merge those cells by clicking the Merge Selected Cells icon in the Property Inspector (circled in Figure 6-19).

   Because this row introduces the content that follows, it's a good candidate for the table head (<th>) tag described on page 301.

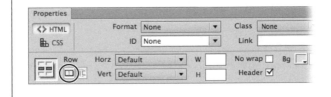

FIGURE 6-19

The Header checkbox turns the selected table cell into a table head using the <th> tag. You see the Header box only if you click inside a table and the Property Inspector is completely expanded, as described on page 32. The Merge Selected Cells button (circled) combines table cells.

8. **In the Property Inspector, turn on the Header checkbox.**

   This converts a regular table cell (<td> tag) into a table header (<th> tag).

9. **Repeat steps 7–8 for the two rows with the text "Main" and "Dessert" in them.**

   Below those rows is another set of cells which make good candidates for table headers: the "Item," "Description," and "Price" cells all indicate what type of information will appear in that column.

10. **Click inside each of the three "Item," "Description," and "Price" cells (that's nine cells altogether), and then turn on the Header checkbox in the Property Inspector.**

    A quick way to do this is to Ctrl+click (⌘-click) all nine cells, and then turn on the Header checkbox. Just as in step 8, this turns each <td> tag into a <th> tag.

    You've discovered that a couple of items are missing from the menu, so it's time to add them.

11. **Click in the very last cell of the table, the one with $7.00 price and press the Tab key.**

    Dreamweaver adds a new row to the table.

12. **Type *Hot Fudge Sundae*, and press Tab to jump to the next cell.** Type The ultimate dessert experience. Press tab again, type $5.00, and press Tab one last time.

    You added a row's worth of information, and then added another blank row to the end of the table. Unfortunately, that was a mistake. You don't need that last row. What an excellent time to learn how to delete a row.

13. **Click in the last cell in the bottom-right.** Drag to the left until you select all three empty cells. Press Delete.

Dreamweaver removes the row easily. Now you need to add another row in the middle of the table. The tab-to-add row technique only works if you're in the last table cell. To add a row in the middle of a table, you need to try something else.

14. **Click in the cell with the text "The Soylent Salmon."** Select Insert→Table Objects→Insert Row Below.

    Dreamweaver inserts a new, blank row. You can also use the Insert panel's Layout category to add a row above or below the current row (see Figure 6-9). The last step is to add another entrée to the menu.

15. **Click in the first cell of the newly inserted row.** Type *Shiitake Burger*, and press Tab to jump to the next cell. Type The best hamburger mushroom's can buy. Press Tab one last time and type $12.00.

    The menu's complete. Now it's time to make it look good.

Formatting the Table

Tables, like everything HTML, are drab by themselves. To make data really stand out, you need to turn to the power of Cascading Style Sheets. In this section, you'll format the table's basic font attributes, make the headers stand out, and add lines around the cells.

1. **Make sure the CSS Styles panel is open (Window→CSS Styles); in the bottom-right of the panel, click the Create New Style button (the + icon).**

    The New CSS Rule window appears. You'll create a class style for the table tag headers and store the CSS information in an already attached external style sheet. (For a recap on creating style sheets, turn to page 125.)

2. **Choose Class from the top menu, type *.menu* in the Selector Name box, select *styles.css* in the bottom menu, and then click OK.**

    The CSS Rule Definition window appears. Instead of creating a style for the <table> tag, you're creating a class style. That's because, if you created a *tag* style, it would apply to every instance of that HTML tag. So if this site had other tables in it, that single <table> tag style would format *all* of the site's tables, and that might not be what you want. By using a class style, you have the flexibility to create different designs for different tables.

3. **From the Font-family menu, select PTSansRegular.** In the Font-size box, type *14*.

    You'll only see PTSansRegular if you completed the tutorial in Chapter 3, which added the PTSans web fonts to Dreamweaver (see page 169).

    The table is a bit close to the bottom of the headline above it; adding a little margin to the top of the table will help.

4. **Select the Box category; turn off the Margin's "Same for all" box, and type *20* in the Top box.** Click OK to complete the style.

This class style doesn't take effect until you apply it.

5. **Click the bottom border of the table to select it (or use any of the techniques described on page 294).** From the Property Inspector's Class menu, choose menu.

The menu scoots down the page a bit, and the font gets smaller. You won't see the effect of the PTSansRegular font, since Dreamweaver can't display web fonts in Design view; however, if you preview this in a browser or click the Live button, you'll see the new font in action.

The table headers don't really command enough attention. You'll make them stand out by using a background graphic and increasing the space inside each cell.

6. **Click the Create New Style button.** In the CSS Rule Definition window, choose Compound from the top menu (see Figure 6-20).

A "compound" style is usually what CSS veterans know as a descendent selector—a style name composed of two or more CSS selectors. You'll learn more about this setting in the next chapter, but for now, keep in mind that you want to create a style that affects only the table headers that appear inside the table on this page—<th> tags that appear inside a table that's styled with the *menu* class.

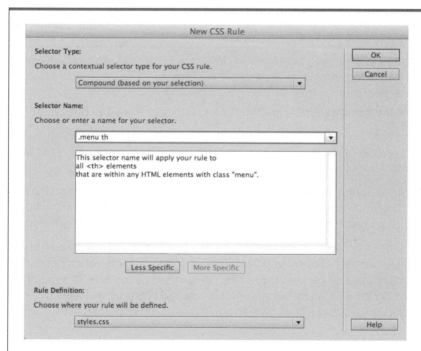

FIGURE 6-20

What Dreamweaver calls a compound style is really just a catch-all term for any type of style including class, tag, or ID styles. More significantly, Dreamweaver uses compound styles to create one of the most important types of CSS styles: descendent selectors, like the .menu th selector pictured here. This selector homes in on a very specific group of tags: <th> tags inside any other tag that has the class .menu applied to it.

7. **Replace whatever's currently listed in the Selector Name box with *.menu th* and make sure you have *styles.css* selected in the bottom menu.** Click OK to create the style.

    Here's a descendent selector, this time defining the look of every <th> tag inside another tag with the class *.menu* applied to it. You'll make the text green on a tan background.

8. **In the Type category, select PTSansBold from the Font-family menu; type 16 in the Font-size box; and type *#468531* in Color box.**

    This makes the text green and 16 pixels tall. Now you'll add a color for the background.

9. **Click the Background category.** Set the background color to #F2E5C2 (a tan).

    Currently, Dreamweaver has centered the column headers in their cells. To have them match the appearance of the other cells, you'll align them to the left.

10. **Click the Block category, and then, from the Text-align menu, choose "left."**

    You could also use the Property Inspector to set the horizontal alignment of each table header to Left, but not only is that more work, it also adds extra HTML to your page. The CSS method is easier and makes for faster-loading web pages.

    If you click the Apply button now, you see how this style is shaping up. The text is a bit cramped inside each cell. To add some breathing room between the edges of each cell and the text inside it, you'll use the CSS *padding* property.

NOTE If you accidentally press the OK button before completing the style, just double-click the style's name (*.menu th*) in the CSS Styles panel to re-open the Style Definition window.

---

11. **Click the Box category.** Type *5* in the Padding property's Top box.

    Since the "Same for all" checkbox is turned on, the 5-pixel setting applies to all four sides of the table header. One last touch: a border separating the table headers from the rows below it.

12. **Click the Border category.** Turn off the three "Same for all" boxes. From the Bottom drop-down menu in the Style category, choose "solid;" type *1* in the Width box, and make the color *#EC6206*. Click the OK button to complete the style.

    This adds a border below each table header (see Figure 6-21). In this particular table, you have two rows of different types of headers: the category headers (Starters, for example) and the headers that announce the dish, its description, and its price. Sharing the same style, the stacked header rows look a bit...well, boring. You'll create a class style to apply to each category of dishes.

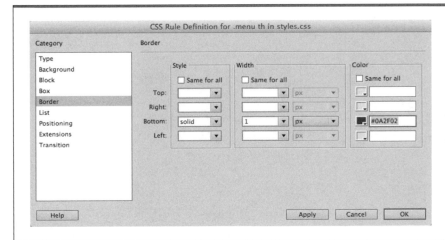

FIGURE 6-21

Borders can apply to any or all sides of an element. When you apply a border to a table, you're assigning lines around the outside of the entire table. But table cell borders apply to the four edges of each cell. In this case, each <th> tag will have a border underneath it.

13. **Click the Create New Style icon.** In the CSS Rule Definition window, choose Compound from the top menu, type *.menu .course* in the Selector Name box, make sure you have *styles.css* selected in the bottom menu, and then click OK.

This is another descendent selector. This one is composed of two class names and can be translated to mean, "Apply this style to an element with a class of .course, but only when it's inside another element with a class of *.menu*." In other words, you're about to create another style that includes a new class name, *.course*, which you'll apply to the first table header in each section of the menu.

14. **In the Type category's Font-size box, type 18, choose "uppercase" from the Text-transform menu, and then select white (#FFFFFF) for the color.**

Because you left the "Same for all" box turned on, 5 pixels of padding will appear around all four sides of each table cell. Time to add a background image.

15. **Click the Background category.** Type *#0A2F02* in the Background-color box. Click the Browse button, and then, in the site's images folder, select the file *bg-th.jpg*. Choose "center" from the "Background-position (X)" menu and "top" from the "Background-position (Y)" menu.

The window should look like Figure 6-22. Just a few last touches and you'll be done.

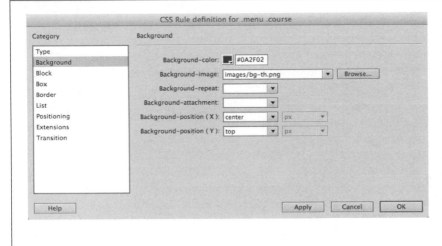

FIGURE 6-22

Why add a background color when you're also using a background image? Remember that, in the last step, you made the text white. To make sure visitors can read your text, you need a dark background (white on white isn't so easy to read). If, for some reason, the graphic doesn't appear (the visitor has turned off graphics, for example, or the image doesn't download properly), the table headers would appear as white text on a white background. By setting a dark background color too, you're covered—if the image doesn't download, the text is still readable—white text on a dark green background.

16. **Click the Block category, and choose "center" from the Text-align menu.**

    This centers the text in the row. To scoot these table headers down a little, you'll add a bit of padding.

17. **Click the Box category.** Turn off the Padding "Same for all" box and type *13* in the Top box. Click OK to complete the style.

    Nothing happens...you need to apply the class to the table header.

18. **Click inside the table head with the text "Starters."** From the Property Inspector's Class menu, select "course."

    The text centers, turns white and a green gradient background image appears. You need to do the same for the other two rows.

19. **Repeat step 18 for the table headers "Main" and "Dessert."**

    Now it's time to tackle the look of the main table cells.

20. **Click the Create New Style button.** In the CSS Rule Definition window, choose Compound from the top menu, type *.menu td* in the Selector Name box, make sure you have *styles.css* selected in the bottom menu, and then click OK.

    You should be getting the hang of these descendent selectors by now: This style will apply to every <td> tag (that's an individual table cell) within another tag that has the class named *.menu* applied to it. You'll add padding and border lines to clearly indicate each cell.

21. **Click the Box category.** Under the Padding category, type *5* in the Top box.

    Because the "Same for all" box is turned on, 5 pixels of padding will appear around all four sides of each table cell. Time to add some borders.

22. **Click the Border category and leave the "Same for all" checkboxes turned on.** Choose "solid" from, the Style category's Top menu, type *1* in the Width box, and make the color white—#FFFFFF. Click OK to complete the style.

    If you preview the page in a browser (F12 [Option-F12]) or click the Live button at the top of the document window, you'll notice that, where two cells touch, the borders are a bit thick (see Figure 6-23). Because you added a border around all four sides of each cell, the border is twice as thick and looks a little chunky where two cells meet (circled in Figure 6-23). You could edit the style and add a border to only some sides of the cell (like the left and bottom sides) so that the borders don't double up, but CSS gives you an easier way.

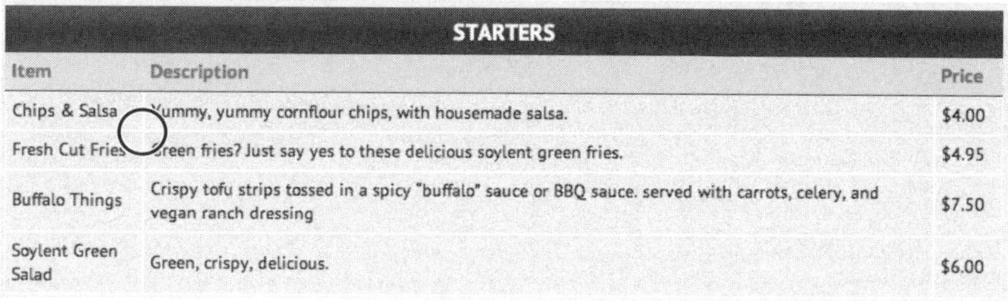

STARTERS		
Item	Description	Price
Chips & Salsa	Yummy, yummy cornflour chips, with housemade salsa.	$4.00
Fresh Cut Fries	Green fries? Just say yes to these delicious soylent green fries.	$4.95
Buffalo Things	Crispy tofu strips tossed in a spicy "buffalo" sauce or BBQ sauce. served with carrots, celery, and vegan ranch dressing	$7.50
Soylent Green Salad	Green, crispy, delicious.	$6.00

FIGURE 6-23

Adding a border to table cells creates slightly chunky double borders where cells touch each other. Fortunately, with a little-known CSS property, you can overcome that aesthetic nuisance.

NOTE Make sure to exit Live view when you finish viewing your page—just click the Live button a second time. If you don't leave Live view, you can't edit your page.

Final Improvements

To finish this tutorial, you'll get rid of the double-border problem, and make the table rows easier to read by coloring every other row.

1. **Make sure the CSS Styles panel is open (Window→CSS Styles) and that you have the All button at the top of the panel selected.**

The All button lets you view all the styles attached to a page. In this case, there's just one external style sheet, styles.css, attached to the page. It has two style sheets inside it (those two style sheets, both named stylesheet.css, are for the web fonts you used for the table (see page 146 for more on web fonts.]) You're going to edit an already existing style in the *styles.css* file.

2. **If you can't see any styles listed under "*styles.css*" in the Styles panel, click the + button (flippy triangle on Macs) to the left of "*styles.css*" to expand the list.** Locate the style named *.menu*, and then select it.

   Don't double-click the style name—that opens the CSS Rule Definition window. You're about to add a CSS property that Dreamweaver doesn't make available in that window. Instead, you need to use another technique for adding properties to a style—the Properties pane.

   The Properties pane is at the bottom of the CSS styles panel. It should look like Figure 6-24.

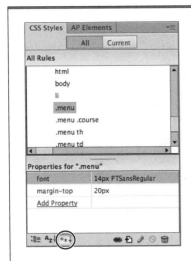

FIGURE 6-24

When you select a style in the "All" view of the CSS Styles panel, the properties for that style appear in the Properties pane below. In this case, you selected the style .menu and Dreamweaver displays its three properties (font-family, font-size, and margin-top). You can add more properties by clicking the Add Property link. There are actually three views to the Properties pane, but it's most useful to see just the currently set properties. Click the "Show only set properties" button (circled) for the view above. (You'll learn about the Properties pane in depth on page 382.)

3. **Click the Add Property link, and then, in the box, type *border-collapse*.**

   Border-collapse is a special CSS property that forces adjoining cells to "collapse" onto each other. Essentially, it removes space between cells and prevents this double-border problem.

4. **From the menu to the right of the Border-collapse property you just added, select "collapse" (see Figure 6-25).**

   That removes the double-border between adjacent cells (you don't see this effect in Dreamweaver's Design view, but if you click the Live button or preview the page in a browser, you will). Now you'll highlight alternating table rows.

This technique makes tables easier to scan, since your eye can easily identify the cells that make up a row. To do this, you'll create an advanced CSS style.

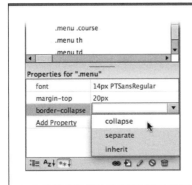

FIGURE 6-25

The Border-collapse property is an official CSS property, even though it doesn't appear in Dreamweaver's CSS Rule Definition window. You can, however, add it by hand from the Properties pane.

5. **Click the Create New Style button.** In the CSS Rule Definition window, choose Compound from the top menu, and then type .menu *tr:nth-child(odd)* in the Selector Name box. Make sure you have *styles.css* selected in the bottom menu, and then click OK.

   This style is an advanced CSS selector. In a nutshell, it selects every odd table row inside the table with the class *.menu* applied to it. There's a similar style you could use for every even table row: *tr:nth-of-type(even)*. All you need to do now is define a background color.

6. **In the CSS Rule Definition window, select the Background category; click the color box to open the color palette, and then click the arrow in the top-right (circled in Figure 6-26).** Select "rgba" from the Color Format menu.

   As mentioned on page 160, CSS supports several color formats; "rgba" stands for "red, green, blue, alpha," and it lets you pick a color that is partially transparent. This is provides a neat effect since this lets colors or images below the element show through.

7. **Choose white from the color picker.**

8. **You'll see "rgba(255,255,255,1)" in the Background-color box.** The *255,255,255* specifies the color white, while the *1* means 100% opaque—in other words, you can't see through it.

9. **Change the *1* to *.5* so that the color value now reads "rgba(255,255,255,.5)."** Click OK to complete the style.

   You won't see any effect in Design view, but if you preview the page in a web browser or use Live view you'll see every other table row with a slightly lighter background. One last design change and you're done. The menu items don't really stand out. Simply making them bold will help guide visitors' eyes to the tasty food the café offers.

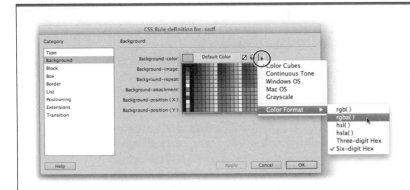

FIGURE 6-26

Hidden in Dreamweaver's color palette is the Color Format menu. It lets you choose different ways to express a color value, including "rgba," which lets you modify the color's visibility (page 159 has more details).

WARNING Neither the nth-of-type selector nor RGBA colors work in Internet Explorer 8 or earlier. While all other browsers, including IE 9 and 10, display this style correctly, if you want to add striped rows to your tables and you want it to work in Internet Explorer 8, you need to instead create a class style—.odd, for example—with a background color of your choosing (but using only Hexadecimal [#FFFFFF] or RGB [for example, "rgb(255,255,255)"] colors). You then need to manually apply the style to every other table row by selecting the row and then using the Property Inspector to apply the class to that row (which is a lot of work!).

10. **Click the Create New Style button.** In the CSS Rule Definition window, choose Compound from the top menu, and then type .menu *td:first-child* in the Selector Name box. Make sure you have *styles.css* selected in the bottom menu, and then click OK.

    Here's another new type of style: *:first-child* is called a *pseudo-element*, and it selects an element that's the first child nested inside another tag. In this case, *td:first-child* means "Select the first table cell (the first <td> tag) that's nested inside its parent." To understand how it works, it helps to examine the HTML for one row from the table:

    ```
    <tr>

        <td>Chips & Salsa</td>

        <td>Yummy, yummy cornflour chips, with housemade salsa.</td>

        <td>$4.00</td>

    </tr>
    ```

    The element that wraps around the <td> tags here is the <tr> tag. In CSS-speak, the <tr> tag is called a parent, while the <td> tags that appear immediately inside it are called children. In this example, there are three <td> tags, thus three children. The first child is the <td> with the name of the menu item Chips

& Salsa in it. So the new selector *.menu td:first-child* will select that <td> and every other first table cell inside a row that's also inside a table with the class *.menu* applied to it. Wow, that seems like a pretty complex selector, but you'll see in a moment how it will make formatting this table easy.

NOTE Unlike the *:nth-of-type selector*, the *:first-child* selector works in Internet Explorer 7 and later. Only the nearly extinct IE 6 doesn't understand it, so you should feel free to use it.

11. **From the Font-family menu select PTSansBold.** Click OK to complete the style. Press the F12 (Option-F12) key to preview your hard work in a browser.

    The complete page should look like Figure 6-27. Notice that the name of each food item is bold, but none of the other cells in each row are. Without that *:first-child* selector, the only way to achieve this effect would be to manually select each food item and make it bold or apply a class style to it.

    You'll find a completed version of this tutorial in the Chapter06_complete folder that accompanies the downloaded tutorial files.

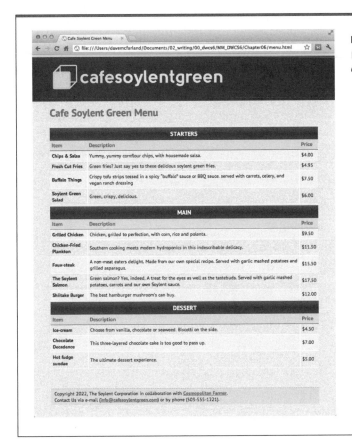

FIGURE 6-27

With Dreamweaver and a little CSS, you can make elegant HTML tables.

HTML: Under the Hood

Dreamweaver started life primarily as a visual web page editor, but over the years, its code-editing tools have evolved to rival the best text editors, including those that hard-core handcoders use. Some people bypass Dreamweaver's Design view entirely and use only its Code view, where they edit their HTML, CSS, and JavaScript directly. In fact, you can use Dreamweaver to edit any text-based file, including XML, Java, ActionScript, and just plain text itself.

Dreamweaver's code editor includes professional features like customizable syntax highlighting, auto indenting, line numbering, and code hints; code collapse, so you can concentrate on just the code you want; and the Code view toolbar, which provides one-click access to frequently used hand-coding commands. Dreamweaver may be the only web-page creation program that hardcore code junkies ever need. In fact, Adobe aimed many of Dreamweaver CS6's improvements at those who use Code view to edit pages in HTML, CSS, JavaScript, and the server-side programming language PHP.

■ Controlling How Dreamweaver Handles HTML

Unlike many other visual HTML editors, Dreamweaver has always graciously accepted HTML written by hand (and even by other programs). This openness lets you write code the way you want, without worrying that Dreamweaver will change it. For example, suppose you have a particular way of formatting your handwritten code. Maybe you insert an extra hard return after every <td> (table cell) tag, or you like to use multiple tabs to indent nested tags. In cases like these, Dreamweaver doesn't rewrite your code to fit its own style—unless you ask it to.

Auto-Fixing Your Code

That's not to say that Dreamweaver doesn't ever change your code. In fact, the program can automatically fix errors when you open a page created in another program, including:

- **Overlapping tags**. Take a look at this example:

```
<p><strong>Fix your tags!</p></strong>
```

  This HTML is invalid, because both the opening and closing <strong> tags should appear *inside* the <p> tag. Dreamweaver rewrites this snippet correctly:

```
<p><strong>Fix your tags!</strong></p>
```

- **Unclosed tags**. Tags usually come in pairs, like this:

```
<em>This text is in italic</em>
```

  But if a page is missing the ending tag (<em>*This text is in italic*), Dreamweaver adds it.

- **Extra closing tags**. If a page has an *extra* closing tag (<strong>bold text </strong> </strong>), Dreamweaver helpfully removes it.

> **NOTE** If you only use Dreamweaver's Design view to create the HTML for your web pages, you don't have to worry about these code-rewriting options. Dreamweaver adds the HTML correctly.

This auto-fix feature comes turned *off* in Dreamweaver. If you work on a site that was hand-coded or created by a less capable web-editing program, it's wise to turn this feature on, since all those errors are improper HTML that can cause problems for browsers. (Once upon a time, for example, some web developers deliberately omitted closing tags to save a few kilobytes in file size. Although most browsers can still interpret this kind of sloppy code, it's poor practice.)

You can turn on auto-fixing in the Code Rewriting category of Dreamweaver's Preferences window (see Figure 7-1); turn on the checkboxes next to "Fix invalidly nested and unclosed tags" and "Remove extra closing tags." If you leave these options turned off, Dreamweaver doesn't fix the HTML, and there's no command you can run to correct the tags. Instead, Dreamweaver highlights the mistakes in Design and Code views (skip ahead to Figure 7-5 to get a glimpse of what that looks like).

> **NOTE** The "Warn when fixing or removing tags" option doesn't really warn you so much as report code that Dreamweaver has already gone ahead and fixed. You can't undo these changes, but you can close the file without saving it to retain the old (improperly written) HTML.

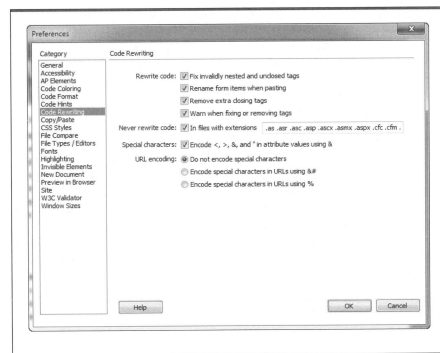

FIGURE 7-1

You don't want Dreamweaver trying to "fix" some types of code. For example, many server-side programming languages mix HTML and server-side code in a way that confuses Dream-weaver's code-rewriting tool. For that reason, turn on the checkbox next to "Never rewrite code." The box to the right of that checkbox lists the most common server-side file extensions, such as .php, .asp, and so on. If you write pages that end in an extension not listed— for example, Ruby on Rails files end in .rb—add the extension to this box.

Dreamweaver can also change the capitalization (case) of HTML tags and properties if you want. For example, you might prefer lowercase letters for tags and proper-ties, like this:

```
<a href="nextpage.html">Click here</a>
```

Dreamweaver can convert uppercase tags (<A HREF="next.html">) to lowercase (and vice versa) when it finds them in pages created by other programs. You can turn on this feature in the Code Format section of the Preferences menu (Edit→Preferences [Dreamweaver→Preferences]), as described in "Line breaks" on page 93.

Server-Side Web Pages

Dreamweaver can leave pages with certain file name extensions untouched—pages created with a server-side programming language like PHP, Cold Fusion, C#, or Ruby. (Server-side programming lets web pages talk to databases, process HTML forms, and send email.) Server-side programming relies on code within the HTML of a page—code that Dreamweaver might "fix," mistakenly interpreting it as errors in the HTML.

Unless you change its settings, Dreamweaver doesn't rewrite the code in files whose names end in .asp (Active Server Pages that run on Microsoft's IIS Web Server), .aspx (Microsoft's .NET technology), .cfm and .cfml (ColdFusion Markup Language pages that run on Adobe's ColdFusion Server), .jsp (JavaServer pages that run on any Java Server), or .php (PHP pages), among others. Nor does it rewrite code inside an external JavaScript file (a .js file), since it's common practice to write JavaScript that creates HTML on the fly—many times this means JavaScript coders add HTML fragments (incomplete tags and code) to their files. If you edit other types of files with Dreamweaver and don't want it interfering with them, add their file extensions to the "Never rewrite code" list in the Preferences window, as shown in Figure 7-1.

Special Characters and Encoding

The Code Rewriting preferences window also lets you control how Dreamweaver handles special characters, like <, >, &, and " whenever you enter them into the Property Inspector or a dialog box. (This doesn't apply, however, when you type these characters in Code view or in the document window in Design view. Dreamweaver always encodes special characters you type directly into a page in Design view; conversely, it never encodes special characters in Code view.) Some characters have special meaning. For example, the "less than" symbol (<) indicates the beginning of an HTML tag, so you can't just link to a page named *bob<zero.html*. If you typed this in, a browser would read it as the start of a new HTML tag (called *zero*).

You can avoid this problem several ways. First, whenever possible, avoid strange characters when you name pages, graphics, CSS styles, or any other object in your site. Stick to letters, numbers, hyphens, and underscores (_) to make your life easier.

You can also let Dreamweaver *encode* special characters. Encoding a character simply means using a code to represent it, since the character itself, like the < sign, may have a special meaning in HTML (the beginning of a tag in this example). For example, you can produce a space on your web page using the code *%20*, or a < symbol using *<*. Thus, the infamous *bob<zero.html* file becomes *bob<zero .html*, and your link works just fine. Other characters, like ™ or ©, get encoded as *™* and *©*, respectively. To set up encoding, choose Edit→Preferences (Dreamweaver→Preferences on Macs) and select Code Rewriting from the category list. Your options are as follows:

- **Special characters**. Turn on this checkbox to have Dreamweaver convert the <, >, &, and * characters to the specially encoded format mentioned above. (This feature has no effect on code you type in Code view, nor on text you type into the document window in Design view.)

- **Do not encode special characters**. Select this option, the first of three under "URL encoding," to tell Dreamweaver not to touch any web addresses you enter (in the Property Inspector's Link box, say). (Again, selecting this option has no effect on links you add in Code view.)

- **"Encode special characters in URLs using &#" is the safest choice**. It's especially helpful if you use a language that has a non-Latin alphabet. If you name your files using Japanese characters, for example, choosing this option translates them into code that successfully transmits over the Internet.

- **"Encode special characters in URLs using %" is intended for use with older browsers** (and we're talking *old*, as in pre-Internet Explorer 4), so unless you've got a time machine and plan on going back to 1998 to build websites, skip this option.

■ Code View

Dreamweaver provides several ways to view a page's HTML:

- **Code view**. In Code view, Dreamweaver displays your page's raw code, just as any text editor would.

- **Split view**. This view displays both the HTML code and the visual design of the web page (Design view) side-by-side: code on the left, design on the right. You can reverse this order or stack one view on top of the other from the Code/Design view menu on the Application bar (Figure 7-2). In addition, if the page has an external style sheet, you can use Dreamweaver's Related Files feature (page 353) to display the CSS code in one half of the document window and the visual Design view in the other half.

- **Split Code view**. This option is for serious coding junkies. It lets you view the code *twice*, so you can work on two sections of a page at once. That's useful for pages with lots of HTML and can come in handy when you want to edit the CSS in the <head> region of a page while crafting HTML in the <body> section. It also works with Dreamweaver's Related Files feature (page 353); in Split Code view, you can check the HTML for a web page in one half of the document window and the CSS for an external style sheet in the other half (or the JavaScript from an external JavaScript file for that matter).

- **Code Inspector**. The Code Inspector displays your HTML in a floating window so you see your working pages in their full glory in the document window, rather than have them cut in half in Split view. To open the Code Inspector, choose Window→Code Inspector, or press F10 (Option-F10). If you have multiple monitors, the Code Inspector is especially handy, because you can display your HTML code on one monitor and the document window on the other. Multitasking code warriors can also use the Code Inspector to look at one area of code while using the main document window to work on another area of code (though the Split Code view works well for this, too).

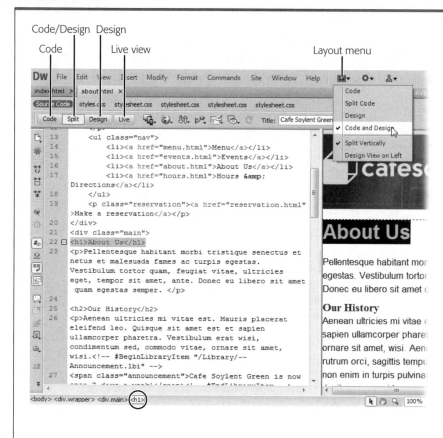

FIGURE 7-2

In Split view (called Code and Design view in the drop-down View menu), you can display raw code right beside the visual Design view. Normally, Dreamweaver displays the code on the left and the design on the right. However, from the View menu, you can select "Design view on Left" to switch them. Leave the Split Vertically option selected; otherwise Dreamweaver displays the code on top and Design view on the bottom, which doesn't leave much space to work on either the code or the design. In Split view, when you select an object in the visual half (the selected "About Us" headline, for example), Dreamweaver selects the corresponding HTML in the code half (the highlighted <h1> tag in Code view in this figure)—a great way to identify an object in your HTML. As you work in one half of the Split view, Dreamweaver updates the other half. Use the buttons (labeled) in the document window's toolbar to jump between the different views. (Notice that the Tag Selector at the bottom of the document window [circled] also identifies the selected tag.)

The rest of this chapter assumes that you're using Code view to edit your HTML.

Dreamweaver gives you three ways to select a view. From the View menu, choose Code, Split Code, Design, or "Code and Design" (a.k.a. Split view); you can also click one of the buttons in the document window's toolbar or use the menu in the Application bar at the top of Dreamweaver.

TIP You can quickly jump between Code and Design views by pressing Control+ ` (on both Windows and Macs). In Split view, this shortcut jumps between the two views, so you can insert an image in the design half of Split view, and then press Control+ ` to jump right into the HTML for that image in the code half of the window. (If you have the Code Inspector open, this keyboard shortcut jumps between the Code Inspector and the document window.)

Code view functions much like a text editor (only better, as you'll soon see). You can click anywhere inside the window and start typing in HTML, JavaScript, CSS, or any other programming code you want (such as PHP or ColdFusion).

You don't have to type out *everything* by hand; the Insert panel, Insert menu, and Property Inspector also function in Code view. Use these sources of canned HTML to combine hands-on HTML coding with convenient, easy-to-use Dreamweaver objects. This trick can be a real timesaver when you need to add a table, which would otherwise be a multiline exercise in typing accuracy.

You can also select a tag (like an image's <img> tag) in Code view and use the Property Inspector to modify it.

NOTE When you add HTML in Code view, Dreamweaver doesn't automatically update Design view, which can be disconcerting when you work in Split view. (After all, how would Dreamweaver display a half-finished tag like this: *<img src="?*) In the Property Inspector, click the Refresh button (see Figure 7-3) or press F5 to update the visual display.

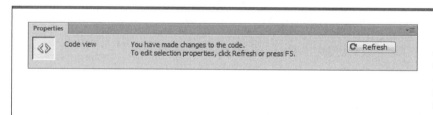

FIGURE 7-3

After you change code on the code side of Split view, click the Refresh button in the Property Inspector to update the Design view.

To help navigate your code, Code view provides several visual cues. They include:

- **Syntax coloring**. Dreamweaver displays different elements in different colors. Comments, for example, are gray; text is black; most HTML tags appear in blue, though form tags are orange; image tags are purple; and links are green. You can change any of these colors, and even specify unique colors for different types of tags, using the Preferences window (see Figure 7-4).

To really make a tag stand out, you can underline, boldface, or italicize it, and even give it a background color. Dreamweaver offers separate color schemes for 25 types of documents, such as CSS, ASP, and XML files. (But do you really need different colors for HTML forms in JavaScript files, HTML pages, and PHP pages? You be the judge.)

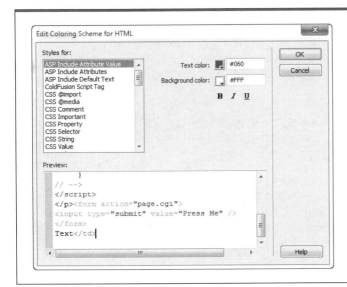

FIGURE 7-4

From the Preferences window (Edit→Preferences in Windows, Dreamweaver→Preferences on Macs), you can control the color Dreamweaver uses to display HTML, CSS, and script in Code view. To do so, select the Code Coloring category, select the type of document you're working on—HTML, CSS, PHP, or whatever—and then click Edit Coloring Scheme. In the Edit Coloring Scheme window (shown here), select an item whose color you want to change—like Library Item or HTML Form Tags, for example—and set a text and/or background color using the color boxes. You can also make the code bold, italic, or underlined using the appropriate formatting buttons.

- **Bad code highlighting**. When you type incorrect code (say an opening tag without a closing tag, or improperly nested tags), Dreamweaver highlights it in yellow (circled in Figure 7-5), but only if you turn on the Highlight Invalid Code option (View→Code View Options→Highlight Invalid Code) or click the Highlight Invalid Code button in the Coding toolbar (see Figure 7-6).

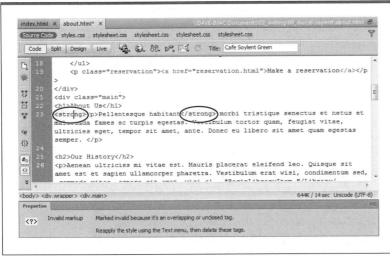

FIGURE 7-5

Dreamweaver highlights incorrect HTML in bright yellow in Code view (like the <strong> tags circled here). If you click the yellow area, the Property Inspector reveals the mistake. In this case, a tag is improperly nested—part of it lies outside the <p> tag. (In Design view, on the other hand, Dreamweaver indicates mistakes by showing the HTML tag—</strong> for example—in front of a bright yellow background.)

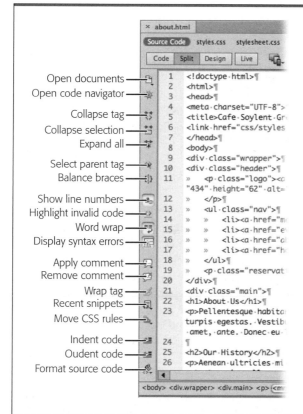

Open documents
Open code navigator
Collapse tag
Collapse selection
Expand all
Select parent tag
Balance braces
Show line numbers
Highlight invalid code
Word wrap
Display syntax errors
Apply comment
Remove comment
Wrap tag
Recent snippets
Move CSS rules
Indent code
Oudent code
Format source code

FIGURE 7-6

Code view provides easy access to common code-writing commands in the Coding toolbar (left edge). Using the toolbar, it's easy to wrap a selection of HTML in an HTML comment, hide code you don't want to see or edit, or turn on and off Code view options like line numbering and highlighting invalid code.

- **Templates**. Regions you can't edit in the pages that Dreamweaver templates create (Chapter 18) appear in light gray. This coloring scheme is a little confusing since Dreamweaver also displays HTML comments in gray, and you *can* edit those. You can change either color, however, as shown in Figure 7-4.

- **Browser compatibility highlighting**. Much to the anguish of web designers, browsers sometimes react differently to CSS formatting. What looks great in Firefox may crumble in Internet Explorer 6. Dreamweaver's Browser Compatibility Checker alerts you to possible cross-browser CSS problems. When you see a squiggly line underneath code, Dreamweaver is telling you there's a potential problem. You only see the squiggly lines if you first run the Check Browser Compatibility command (see the Note on page 491). Unfortunately, this tool is so woefully out of date, you should avoid it.

- **Library Items**. Code from Library items (Chapter 18) has a light yellow background.

You can also control the following Code view display features from the View→Code View Options submenu:

- **Word Wrap**. This option makes long lines of code wrap (at the window's edge) to the next line, so you don't have to scroll horizontally to see it all. This option affects only how Dreamweaver *displays* the line; it doesn't actually change your code by introducing line breaks. Dreamweaver turns this option on by default.

- **Line Numbers**. Automatic line-numbering can come in handy when you encounter an error in a page containing JavaScript (the code Dreamweaver's Spry widgets use, for example) or server-side code (such as PHP, described in Chapter 21). In Code view, you can click a line number to select the entire line, which is a great way to delete or cut a line of code. Normally, Dreamweaver displays line numbers, but if you don't see them in Code view, click the "Show line numbers" button in the Coding toolbar (Figure 7-6) or choose View→Code View Options→Line Numbers to turn them on.

- **Hidden Characters**. Some characters you type on a keyboard don't show up on-screen: the end of a line, created by hitting the Enter or Return key, for example. Occasionally, these hidden characters can cause big trouble. When you work with dynamic, server-side web pages, for example, you might find some cool code on the Web and copy it to your own page. Sometimes copying and pasting code from a web page introduces hidden characters that prevent the code from working. Turning on the Hidden Characters option helps ferret out problem characters so you can eliminate them. Spaces appear as dots, paragraph breaks as paragraph symbols, and tabs as a set of double arrows (see the code in Figure 7-6).

- **Highlight Invalid Code**. This option is the on/off switch for highlighting bad HTML in Code view (see Figure 7-5). Dreamweaver normally turns this option off, but it's a good idea to turn it on: go to View→Code View Options→Highlight Invalid Code.

- **Syntax Coloring**. This option turns tags, comments, and text into colorful (and informative) text (see Figure 7-4). Dreamweaver turns this option on by default.

- **Auto Indent**. When you work with nested HTML tags, it's often helpful to press Tab to indent each level of nested tags, making it easier to identify large blocks of HTML (such as a table and all its contents). The Auto Indent option carries the same size indent onto the next line when you hit Enter (Return).

  Suppose you hit the Tab key twice, type a line of code, and then hit Enter (Return). Dreamweaver puts the insertion point on the next line, indenting it two tabs. To outdent, press the Backspace key. Dreamweaver normally turns this option on.

- **Syntax Error Alerts in Info Bar**. This feature benefits JavaScript and PHP programmers. When you turn it on, Dreamweaver highlights potential syntax errors in both languages (meaning it signals typos or improper code) and displays a yellow info bar at the top of the document window. You can also turn this feature off and on from the Coding toolbar (Figure 7-6).

Coding Toolbar

Dreamweaver includes a handy toolbar on the left edge of the document window in Code view that makes many basic hand-coding tasks go much more quickly. If you don't see it, turn it on by choosing View→Toolbars→Coding or by right-clicking (Control-clicking) on another toolbar, such as the Insert or Document toolbar, and then, in the drop-down menu, selecting the Coding option. Use the same technique to close the toolbar if you don't use it.

The toolbar's buttons duplicate tasks and preference settings from other parts of Dreamweaver. Here's a quick rundown, with brief explanations of what the buttons in Figure 7-6 do and, when applicable, a cross-reference to a more detailed description of the tool or action:

- **Open Documents**. This pull-down menu displays all your open documents so you can switch among them. Since it's actually easier to click a document's tab at the top of the document window, you probably won't use this button much.

- **Open code navigator**. The code navigator lets you see which CSS styles affect the currently selected HTML. If you have no HTML selected, the navigator displays the HTML tag in effect at the cursor location. It also lets you jump quickly to the code in a style sheet so you can edit the CSS. Read more about this feature in "Using the Code Navigator" on page 397.

- **Collapse Full Tag/Collapse Selection/Expand All**. These three buttons work with Dreamweaver's Code Collapse feature described in "Code Collapse" page 348. They let you collapse (and expand) multiple lines of code, essentially hiding those lines on-screen so you can concentrate on another piece of code.

- **Select Parent Tag**. This handy feature lets you quickly select the tag that surrounds your current selection. Say you select the text inside a link tag (<a>), or just click inside that tag, and your cursor is blinking happily. Click this button, and Dreamweaver selects the entire <a> tag and all its contents. Click it again, and you select that link's parent tag. If you really want to be productive, the keyboard shortcut Ctrl+[⌘-]) is quicker.

- **Balance Braces**. If you do a lot of programming in JavaScript or a server language like PHP, .NET, ColdFusion, or Java Server Pages, this button helps you find the matching brace ({ or }) in a chunk of program code—actually this tool selects *all* the code between an opening and closing brace, but doing so lets you identify where the braces begin and end. Just click to the right of an opening brace ({), and then click this button to find the closing brace. To find a closing brace's mate, click to the left of the brace, and then click this button. You can also find matching parentheses this way. The keyboard shortcut Ctrl+' (⌘-') is even faster.

- **Apply/Remove Comments**. Comments let you include helpful notes in your code, which don't appear when a browser displays the page. For example, you may want to leave explanatory notes to help future generations of web developers. Or you might put a comment before a <div> tag that explains what should go inside it—"Put corporate logo and navigation bar here." People frequently use comments to mark the end of a page section—"End of navigation bar." These buttons let you add or remove comments in HTML, CSS, JavaScript, PHP, and VBScript code, as demonstrated in Figure 7-7.

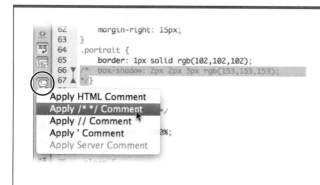

FIGURE 7-7

The Coding toolbar lets you wrap HTML, CSS, JavaScript, and other program code within comment characters. Just select the code you wish to turn into a comment, click the Apply Comment button (circled), and then select the type of comment you want to add: Use the HTML comment option to hide HTML code; the / */ option to hide multiple lines of CSS, JavaScript, or PHP code; the // option to hide each line of JavaScript or PHP code; and the ' option to hide VBScript code. The last option, Apply Server Comment, hides server-side code; use it to comment both HTML and server-side programming code in one step. To remove a comment, select all the code (including the comment markers), and then click the Remove Comment button (hidden in this figure; it's just below the Apply Comment button).*

TIP You can easily turn style properties on and off in Cascading Style Sheets by taking advantage of "comment" behavior. Open a CSS file, select a property inside a style, and stick a pair of comment tags around it (/* at the beginning and */ at the end). When you preview a page that uses the style, you see the style minus the property you "commented out," as programmers call it. This maneuver lets you add a new style and preview it, temporarily hiding the effect of one or more other style properties without permanently deleting them. It's also a great help in debugging problematic styles. In fact, it's so useful the CSS Styles panel provides a button that makes it easy to turn style properties on and off (see Figure 8-5).

- **Wrap Tag**. Works the same way as the Quick Tag editor described on page 361.

- **Recent Snippets**. This drop-down menu lists all the snippets (see page 829) you recently used. Select an item and Dreamweaver inserts it into your web page.

- **Move or Convert CSS**. This drop-down menu lets you move an inline CSS style to either an internal or external style sheet, or lets you move a rule from an internal to an external style sheet. You'll find more details on page 385.

- **Indent/Outdent**. These buttons indent or outdent lines of selected code, using the settings you defined in the Indent box of the Code Format preferences window (see page 350).

- **Format Source Code**. This button lets you enforce a consistent style for your code by applying specific formatting to an entire web page or to just a section of code. It uses the code-formatting options you set up in the Code Format preferences window (see page 350) and the rules defined in the type-A-uber-geek-what-a-lot-of-work Tag Library described in the box on page 355. In other words, if you want to make your HTML easier to read (by making Dreamweaver write every opening <tr> tag and closing </tr> tag separately on their own lines, for example), you can.

Code Hints

Typing code can be a chore, which is why even longtime hand-coders take advantage of anything that speeds up the process. A perfect example is Dreamweaver's Code Hints feature (shown in Figure 7-8). It lets you select tags, attributes, and even Cascading Style Sheet styles from a drop-down menu as you type.

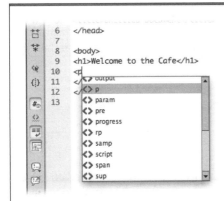

FIGURE 7-8

The Code Hints feature saves your tired fingers from typing tags and tag properties. As soon as you type <, Dreamweaver displays a drop-down list of tags. Select the one you want, and Dreamweaver types it in for you. Dreamweaver's even thoughtful enough to show you all available CSS styles when you insert a class attribute in a tag.

NOTE Code Hints work with other tags as well as scripting languages like JavaScript, PHP, ASP.NET, and ColdFusion. In addition, Dreamweaver includes CSS code hints, so if you write your style sheets by hand, you can take advantage of the auto-completion features of Code Hints to quickly type out CSS style properties.

Here's how it works. When you begin a new tag by typing an opening bracket (<), a menu pops up, listing all the available HTML tags. Use your mouse or arrow keys to select a tag, or type in the first few letters of it, and Dreamweaver finds the closest match. When you press Enter (Return), Dreamweaver automatically fills in the tag name. Even better, a second menu pops up, listing all the properties of that tag.

TIP You can also open the Code Hints menu by pressing Ctrl+Space bar (in both Windows and on Macs). This shortcut's really useful when you're editing code and want to add a property or edit the property of a tag you already created. For example, you could click inside the name of a class style applied to a tag, for instance—inside the word "copyright" in the code *class="copyright"*—and then press Ctrl+Space bar. This action not only selects the name so you can change it, but it also opens a menu listing all the classes available to the page. Then you can use the up and down arrow keys (or even your mouse) to select a different CSS style.

If Code Hints annoy you, you can turn off the feature completely, rein it in by setting a delay (so that lists don't appear immediately), or turn it off for selected types of elements (such as tag properties). To make any of these adjustments, open Dreamweaver's Preferences window (Ctrl+U [⌘-U]), and then select Code Hints. Make your desired changes, and then click OK.

Dreamweaver also simplifies writing closing tags: As soon as you type </ (the first two characters for any closing tag), Dreamweaver automatically finishes your thought by closing the tag for you. For example, after you type an opening <p> tag and add the paragraph's content, Dreamweaver finishes the closing tag—</p>—the moment you type </. For a longer tag, like the </address> tag, this feature saves your fingers a lot of work. You can change this behavior to make Dreamweaver automatically insert the closing tag immediately after you finish typing the opening tag, or, if you just can't stand the feature, turn off "Enable code hints" in the Code Hints preferences window.

NOTE If you like Code Hints, you'll love the Snippets panel, which makes reusing code a snap. See Chapter 18 for details.

HTML5 CODE HINTS

While Dreamweaver CS6 doesn't provide any visual tools for working with HTML5 (for example, you won't find any objects for inserting HTML5 tags listed in the Insert panel), you'll find HTML5 code hints in Dreamweaver, which work just like code hints for regular HTML. In other words, if you type <he in Code view, the code hint window pops up listing not only HTML4 tags like <head> or <thead>, but also the HTML5 tag <header>.

JAVASCRIPT CODE HINTS

JavaScript programmers also have access to a wide array of code-hint features that make programming go faster. In general, JavaScript code hints work just like HTML hints. As you type in JavaScript, Dreamweaver pops up a box of suggestions that match what you're typing. But JavaScript code hints go much further than simple lists of JavaScript keywords. Dreamweaver provides hints for basic JavaScript objects like arrays, dates, numbers, and strings. For example, say you create an array (gentle reader, if you have no idea what a JavaScript array is, feel free to skip this section). If you then write the array's name in your code, a hint box pops up listing all the methods and properties of JavaScript array objects.

In addition, Dreamweaver keeps track of JavaScript functions *you* create and provides code hints using your own function names, as well as custom-created classes. Even better, Dreamweaver is aware of document object model (DOM) properties and provides hints for all the properties and methods of DOM objects. Finally, if you use either the Spry or Prototype JavaScript library, Dreamweaver has built-in code-hints for those as well.

JQUERY CODE HINTS

jQuery is a popular JavaScript library used on millions of websites, from one-person blogs to ESPN, NBC, and even Microsoft. jQuery lets web designers jump into Java-Script programming by simplifying many common JavaScript programming tasks. It's so popular that Dreamweaver CS6 adds detailed code hints for jQuery. If you've no idea what jQuery is, skip this section, or better yet, pick up a copy of *JavaScript & jQuery: The Missing Manual*, which covers JavaScript and jQuery programming in detail.

Dreamweaver's jQuery code-hinting feature is very sophisticated. Not only does Dreamweaver provide hints for all of jQuery's built-in functions, but it also provides hints for all class and ID selectors on a page, along with tooltips for functions with multiple properties (see Figure 7-9.)

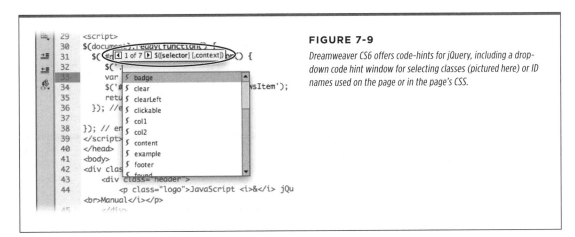

FIGURE 7-9

Dreamweaver CS6 offers code-hints for jQuery, including a drop-down code hint window for selecting classes (pictured here) or ID names used on the page or in the page's CSS.

Dreamweaver CS6 adds a kind of built-in jQuery cheat sheet as well. When you type in a jQuery function, a yellow box appears above the code (circled in Figure 7-9). It displays the function's name as well as which "arguments" it accepts (in program-ming, an argument is a piece of information that you can hand off to a command, and it affects how that command works). In some cases, a built-in jQuery function might work in several ways, each requiring a different kind of argument. In the example in Figure 7-9, a programmer has begun typing jQuery's $( ) function. The yellow pop-up box indicates that there are seven ways to use that function. Clicking the left or right arrow keys steps you through examples of the methods, indicating the number and type of arguments you would provide in each case.

PHP CODE HINTS

Dreamweaver includes advanced code-hinting for the server-side programming language PHP, too (but not for other server-side technologies, like .NET, ColdFusion, Ruby on Rails, or Java Server Pages). Not only does Dreamweaver support code-hinting for built-in PHP functions, but it also makes note of variables, functions, and classes you create (see Figure 7-10).

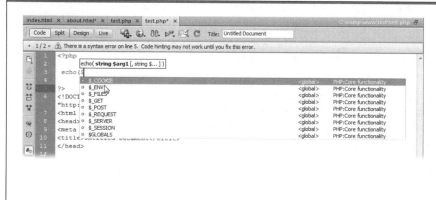

FIGURE 7-10

Dreamweaver is pretty unforgiving of syntax errors (typos or missing punctuation) in PHP code. Most of the time, you start typing PHP code and Dreamweaver displays a yellow "there is a syntax error" bar along with a red mark at the point it thinks you made an error. Don't worry, this happens a lot as you program. The important thing is that, once you finish, there's no syntax error message. If there is, you probably left off a closing), }, ', or ".

Since it's common for programmers to create multiple PHP files and add them all to (or include them all in) a master file, Dreamweaver CS6 searches through all the files the current working file references and analyzes (or *parses*) them. Then, as you type more PHP code, Dreamweaver displays code hints based on the names of variables, functions, and classes you defined in these files. In other words, Dreamweaver personalizes its code hints for your site and for the PHP programming you added to it.

In addition, since many PHP frameworks, like CakePHP and Zend, and many PHP-based content management systems (CMSes), like Drupal, Joomla and WordPress, rely on many separate PHP files, Dreamweaver includes something called site-specific code hints. This is only available for PHP-based websites (you can read how to set up a site for PHP in Part 6 of this book), and it's intended to let you identify which folders Dreamweaver scans to create its code hints for your site.

Dreamweaver's site-specific code hints have a few benefits. First, if you often include PHP files outside the root folder (for example, the Zend framework keeps its Include files outside the web-accessible root folder), you can tell Dreamweaver to scan the folder above the current local root folder. Second, many CMS systems and PHP frameworks use tons of files with tons of variables, functions, and class names. Sites like these use the files internally, in the programming that drives the systems. You, as a programmer, don't ever need to see most of them, and you certainly don't want their elements cluttering up your code-hint window.

You can turn site-specific code hints on by choosing Site→Site-Specific Code Hints. This opens a new window (see Figure 7-11). If you're using either WordPress, Drupal, or Joomla, you can select your environment from the top Structure menu, and Dreamweaver automatically identifies the proper folders, files, and paths. Click OK, and you're done.

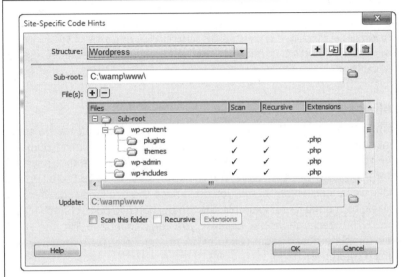

FIGURE 7-11

To add the function names, class names, and variable names you use in your site's PHP code to Dreamweaver's Code Hint feature, you need to choose Site→Site-Specific Code Hints and tell Dreamweaver which files and folders to scan.

If, however, you're using a PHP framework or some other PHP CMS, you need to tell Dreamweaver which folders to analyze by following these steps:

1. **Pick the folder containing your site and all the PHP files you want Dreamweaver to scan by clicking the folder icon and selecting the folder.**

   If you don't have any PHP files outside your local root folder, you can skip this step because Dreamweaver automatically selects the local root folder. However, you may have PHP files one level up from the local root folder. In this case, click the folder icon and select the folder one level up that contains both the PHP files and your local site root.

2. **Click the + button.**

   The Add File/Folder window opens. You can click another icon to select either one particular PHP file or a folder's worth of PHP files. If you pick a folder, turn on the checkbox labeled Recursive if you want Dreamweaver to scan the files in subfolders within this main folder. You can ensure that Dreamweaver searches only .php files by clicking the + button to the right of the Extensions label, and then typing in *.php*. Dreamweaver won't look through any other files and, as a result, it displays code hints faster. But if you do use other extensions for your PHP files, such as .inc, make sure to add them as well.

You can prevent Dreamweaver from scanning a folder you added from the main Site-Specific Code Hints window, too. Select the folder from the Files list, and turn off the "Scan this folder" checkbox. You can also turn off recursive scanning and change the file extensions from this window.

3. **Click OK to finish.**

   Dreamweaver scans the selected files and creates a list of code hints for your site.

NOTE You may find that Dreamweaver doesn't always automatically pop up a box for site-specific code hints as it does for regular PHP functions. You may need to coax Dreamweaver into displaying them by using the keyboard shortcut Ctrl-space bar.

Code Collapse

One problem with raw HTML, CSS, JavaScript, and PHP is that, well, it's raw—a bunch of letters, numbers, and symbols that tend to blend together in a mind-numbing sea of code. This can make locating a particular bit of code needle-in-a-haystack tough. On large pages with lots of code, you can easily get lost as you scroll up and down to make a change. In many cases, you don't need to see all the code, because you're not likely to change it—for example, the top portion of a page containing the doctype and *HTML* declarations—or because you can't change it—like the HTML embedded in template-based pages (Chapter 19), or pages that have Dreamweaver Library items (Chapter 18).

Fortunately, Dreamweaver lets you get that in-your-way code out of your face. The Code Collapse feature condenses multiple lines of code into a single highlighted box of 10 characters. The basic process is simple: Select the code you want to collapse—like all the code above the <body> tag—and then click one of the icons that appears just to the left of both the first and last line you wish to collapse (Figure 7-12). In Windows, this icon is a small box with a minus sign (-) in it; on Macs, it's a down-pointing arrow at the beginning of the selection and an up-pointing arrow at the end. The code collapses into a gray outlined box. To expand the code, select the condensed code and then click the "expand" icon (a plus sign [+] in Windows, a flippy triangle on Macs).

TIP To quickly select multiple lines of HTML (or any code, for that matter), click in the line-number area to the left of the code at the beginning of your selection, and then drag to the line where you want to end the selection. (If you don't see any line numbers, turn them on using the Coding toolbar or by clicking View→Code View Options→Line Numbers.)

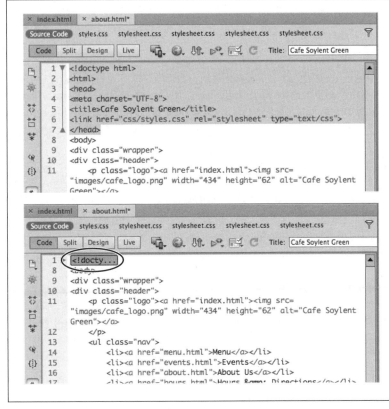

FIGURE 7-12

Now you see it, now you don't. You can collapse a multiline section of code (top) into a compact little gray box (circled in the bottom image). The collapsed code is still there in your page—you haven't deleted it—but now it's conveniently tucked out of sight. If you need a reminder of what the code is, move your mouse over the gray box and a tooltip displays the hidden code.

Dreamweaver includes a few more nuanced ways to collapse code. You can:

- **Collapse an individual tag**. Say you want to hide a long paragraph of text. Instead of selecting it, click anywhere inside the paragraph tag (<p>), and then either click the Coding toolbar's Collapse Tag button, choose Edit→Code Collapse→Collapse Full Tag, or press Ctrl+Shift+J (⌘-Shift-J).

  This feature works on the tag nearest the cursor. Say you have a paragraph of text and, inside it, a link. If you click inside the <a> tag and use this feature, the <a> tag collapses. But if you click anywhere else inside the paragraph (but not inside any other tag), the paragraph itself collapses. This behavior is a little confusing, but it can be really useful. Say you want to hide everything inside a page's <head> tags. Instead of having to select all the lines inside the <head> tag, click anywhere between the beginning and ending <head> tags (but make sure you're not inside *another* tag, like the <title> tag), and use any of the commands mentioned in the previous paragraph.

- **Collapse the code outside an individual tag**. This lets you hide everything *except* the code you want to work on. Suppose you want to see only the code inside the body tag. Click immediately after the opening <body> tag (in other words, inside the <body> tag, but not inside any other tags within the <body> tag), press the Alt (Option) key and then, on the Coding toolbar, click the Collapse Tag button. Choosing Edit→Code Collapse→Collapse Outside Full Tag or pressing Ctrl+Alt+J (⌘-Option-J) also works.

- **Collapse the code outside the current selection**. This is another way to view only the code you want to work on. Select the code, and then either press the Alt (Option) key and click the Coding toolbar's Collapse Selection button, choose Edit→Code Collapse→Collapse Outside Selection, or press Ctrl+Alt+C (⌘-Option-C).

- **Expand All**. If you miss all that hidden code, you can quickly restore it to its full glory by clicking the Coding toolbar's Expand All button, choosing Edit→Code Collapse→Expand All, or pressing Ctrl+Alt+E (⌘-Option-E).

> **NOTE** You can only invoke Collapse Full Tag and Collapse Outside Full Tag features when you work with HTML. These commands have no affect on CSS, JavaScript, or PHP pages.

You can hide any number of code regions in a page—for example, the top portion of a page, a navigation sidebar that never gets edited, or the copyright notice at the bottom of a page—so you can easily identify the code you really want to work on. Dreamweaver even remembers the state of these sections, so if you collapse a section and then close the document, the collapsed section remains hidden when you reopen the file.

Setting Code Formats

Whenever you use the Insert panel, Dreamweaver adds a chunk of HTML preformatted for easier reading. Dreamweaver indents the code for table rows, for instance, using two spaces; it indents the code for table *cells*, meanwhile, by four spaces. If you're particular about how your HTML is written, Dreamweaver gives you plenty of control over these settings.

> **NOTE** If you don't work in Code view frequently, you may not care a whit how Dreamweaver formats your HTML—and that's fine. As long as the underlying HTML is valid (and Dreamweaver writes valid HTML), web browsers can display HTML that's been formatted in many different ways. In fact, browsers simply ignore multiple spaces, empty lines, and other "white space" characters you might use to make HTML code more readable.

You can change basic code settings in the Preferences window; to change advanced settings, see "Advanced formatting options" below. For obsessive code jockeys who want to control how Dreamweaver formats individual tags, see the box on page 355.

For basic formatting settings, open the Preferences window (Edit→Preferences [Dreamweaver→Preferences] or Ctrl+U [⌘-U]), and then click the Code Format category (see Figure 7-13). While Dreamweaver's standard settings work fine, you can still configure a number of options.

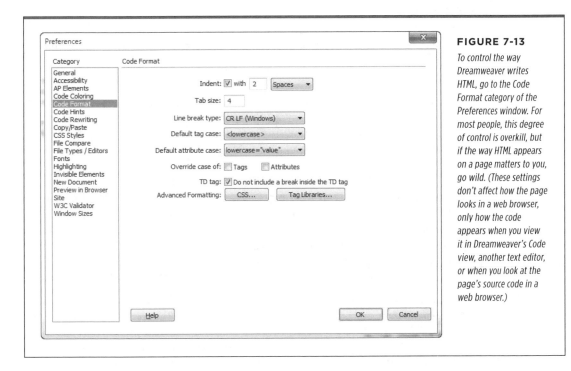

FIGURE 7-13

To control the way Dreamweaver writes HTML, go to the Code Format category of the Preferences window. For most people, this degree of control is overkill, but if the way HTML appears on a page matters to you, go wild. (These settings don't affect how the page looks in a web browser, only how the code appears when you view it in Dreamweaver's Code view, another text editor, or when you look at the page's source code in a web browser.)

■ INDENTS

To make your code easier to read, it helps to indent nested tags and other block-level elements. But if you prefer that Dreamweaver quit auto-indenting such elements, turn off the Indent checkbox. This is also your opportunity to tell Dreamweaver whether you want to indent code using spaces or tabs and to set the amount of indentation:

- If you select **Spaces** in the Indent menu, type in the number of spaces you want Dreamweaver to move the code over in the Indent field. The default setting is 2, meaning that Dreamweaver will indent your code two spaces in from the edge of the preceding code.

- If you select **Tabs** in the Indent menu, the number in the "Tab size" field indicates the size of each tab, measured in spaces. (The size you specify here affects only the display in Code view. In the code itself, Dreamweaver simply inserts a plain tab character.)

> **NOTE** If you choose to indent using tabs, you can save yourself a few bits of file size. Since Dreamweaver defaults to two-space characters for each tab, switching to tabs saves you one character (that is, there will be just one tab instead of two spaces for each indent).

■ LINE BREAKS

The Windows, Mac, and Unix operating systems each look for a different invisible character at the end of each line of code. This can cause problems if you create a page under one operating system and the remote server uses another. Fortunately, Dreamweaver fixes the problem when it transfers files to a web server.

If you plan to use another text editor to edit Dreamweaver-built pages you copy from a server, select that server's operating system from the "Line break type" drop-down menu. Doing so assures that the program on the receiving end will properly read the line breaks in your Dreamweaver-produced pages.

■ CHARACTER CASE FOR TAGS AND ATTRIBUTES

In standard HTML, you can write tag and property names using either uppercase letters (<B>bold</B>) or lowercase (bold); browsers don't care. However, *you* may care how they appear in Code view. Choose your preference from the two "case" drop-down menus, "Default tag case" and "Default attribute case." Most web developers today write tags in lowercase, so if you share your pages with colleagues, you're best off selecting lowercase (see the Note below).

> **NOTE** HTML may treat upper- and lowercase tags identically, but XML does not. Both it and the hybrid language *XHTML* require all-lowercase tag and property names. That's why many web developers now strictly use lowercase characters, even in their HTML. And that's why, if you select the XHTML option when you create a new page, Dreamweaver ignores any uppercase preferences you set—even if you turn on the "Override case of" checkboxes.

If you turn on the "Override case of" checkboxes, Dreamweaver scans tags and properties when it opens a page someone else (or some other program) created. If the case doesn't match your preference, Dreamweaver rewrites the code.

■ THE <TD> TAG

Adding a line break after an opening <td> (table cell) tag may look good in Code view, but in some browsers it adds an unwanted extra space character in the table cell. The extra space can wreak havoc on your design, so make sure you always turn this box on.

■ **ADVANCED FORMATTING OPTIONS**

For real format sticklers, two Advanced formatting buttons (Figure 7-13) let you control the way every aspect of your HTML and CSS code looks. The CSS button opens the CSS Source Format Options window, which lets you dictate how Dreamweaver writes your CSS—whether it indents properties, whether it uses separate lines for each property, where it puts the opening brace in CSS rules, and whether it inserts a blank line between rules to make your CSS more readable. All these options are matters of personal preference and don't affect the performance of your web pages or CSS.

The Tag Libraries button opens the same-named dialog window, discussed in the box on page 355.

If you find yourself wading through lots of HTML and CSS, you might want to experiment with these settings to make the code Dreamweaver produces more readable. Both the Tag and CSS format windows give you a preview of your customized HTML and CSS.

Keep in mind that these settings don't affect how *you* write code. But if you do find that your own HTML or CSS hand-coding doesn't look as elegant as Dreamweaver's, you can turn to the Apply Source Formatting command (Commands→Apply Source Formatting) to make Dreamweaver clean up your code. That command changes a page's code—adds indents, line breaks, and so on—based on the instructions defined in these two options.

NOTE Another set of preference settings affects how Dreamweaver creates its CSS code. The Preferences window's CSS Styles category tells Dreamweaver whether or not to use CSS shorthand properties. See "Fast Style Editing with the Properties Pane" for more on CSS shorthand properties.

Related Files

With external style sheets, JavaScript libraries like the Spry Framework (Chapter 13), and server-side programming becoming more and more a part of the average web designer's toolbox, Dreamweaver includes a feature that makes it easier for code jockeys to jump around the vast collection of files required to make a single web page work. The Related Files toolbar (see Figure 7-14) lists all the files a current web page uses. (Can't find the toolbar? See the Note below.) This includes external style sheets, external JavaScript files (like those that create the Spry navigation bar), and server-side files such as server-side includes.

Web page   Related files

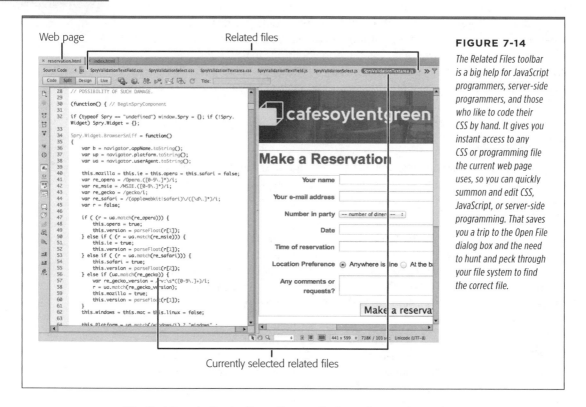

Currently selected related files

FIGURE 7-14

The Related Files toolbar is a big help for JavaScript programmers, server-side programmers, and those who like to code their CSS by hand. It gives you instant access to any CSS or programming file the current web page uses, so you can quickly summon and edit CSS, JavaScript, or server-side programming. That saves you a trip to the Open File dialog box and the need to hunt and peck through your file system to find the correct file.

The first item in the toolbar—Source Code—refers to the web page you're currently editing. The other items represent linked files. For example, the page in Figure 7-14 has six related files—four external style sheets and two JavaScript files.

> **NOTE** If you don't see the Related Files toolbar, it may have gotten turned off. To turn it back on, choose Edit→Preferences (Dreamweaver→Preferences), click the General category, and then make sure you turn on the Enable Related Files checkbox.

When you click the name of a related file in the toolbar, Dreamweaver displays that file's code. If you're in Design view, Dreamweaver switches to Split view and displays the web page in the Design window and the code for the related file in the other pane. If you're in Code view, Dreamweaver simply switches from the HTML of the web page to the CSS, JavaScript, or server-side code of the related file.

Take Control of Code Formatting

For ultimate control over tag formatting, Dreamweaver includes the Tag Library Editor. Not only does it let you control *exactly* how Dreamweaver formats every HTML tag it inserts into a page, it lets you dictate the formatting for nine other Tag Libraries, such as PHP, ASP, JSP, and ColdFusion tags.

Even if you're using some new bleeding-edge tag language unfamiliar to Dreamweaver, you're not out of luck. You can create additional Tag Libraries and even import custom ASP, NET and JSP tags, as well as DTD Schemas for XML. You can also add additional tags to any library; so if the HTML standard suddenly changes, you can add new or remove obsolete tags.

To control the way Dreamweaver formats tags in a library, choose Edit→Tag Libraries, which opens the Tag Library Editor window. Dreamweaver displays a list of all the tag libraries. Click the + symbol (flippy triangle on Macs) to the left of a tag library name to see a list of tags for that library. Select a tag, and then, from the Tag Format area in the bottom half of the window, select formatting options. Here's a shortcut for quickly reformatting a particular tag already present on a page: Select the tag in the Tag Selector first, and then choose Edit→Tag Libraries; Dreamweaver preselects that tag for you.

You can control where a line breaks in relation to the tag. You have four choices:

- **No line breaks at all**. So if you apply this option to the <a> tag, you end up with code like this:

  ```
  <p>Here is a <a href="home.html">link</a></p>
  ```

- **Line breaks before and after the tag**:

  ```
  <p>Here is a
  <a href="home.html">link
  </a>
  </p>
  ```

- **Line breaks before, inside, and after the tag**:

  ```
  <p>Here is a
  <a href="home.html">
  link
  </a>
  </p>
  ```

- **After the tag only**:

  ```
  <p>Here is a <a href="home.html">link</a>
  </p>
  ```

In addition, you can choose whether Dreamweaver applies formatting rules to the contents of a tag and choose the case—upper, lower, or mixed—that Dreamweaver uses when it adds tags to your code.

When you work on the related file, all the normal file operations apply only to that file. For example, if you select a CSS file from the Related Files toolbar and edit and save it, Dreamweaver saves only that file when you choose File→Save; it doesn't record any changes you made to the web page's code or to any other related files (see the Tip on page 356). Likewise, if you choose Site→Put to move a file to your web server (as described on page 798), that CSS file gets whisked off to the server, but the web page itself stays put. This sequence gets a little confusing when you work on related files in Split view, because the web page appears on one half of the screen while the code for a different file appears in the other half.

Note, however, that when you work on the web page in the Design view half of Split view, Dreamweaver applies all your file operations to that web page document.

TIP When working with the Related Files feature, you may be editing multiple files (for instance, the web page, the CSS, and the JavaScript) at the same time. To make sure you save the changes to *all* the files, use the File→Save All Related Files command, which saves the current web page and all its helper files. Better yet, create a keyboard shortcut (see page 911) for this useful command.

The Related Files feature works hand in hand with the Code Navigator. As described on page 397, the Code Navigator (the small ship steering wheel icon floating above page elements) displays a drop-down list of all the CSS styles applied to the page element under your cursor. If you click one of the styles and it happens to be in an external style sheet, Dreamweaver switches to Split view, opens the CSS file, and positions your cursor on the appropriate style so you can edit it. (That said, you might find the other methods of editing CSS, described on pages 139 and 382, easier and more error-free.)

■ FINDING NESTED PHP FILES

When programmers write code in the server-side language PHP, it's common to include several levels of programming files. For example, the popular blogging system WordPress uses a single file, *index.php*, to control an entire blog—this one file manages every one of the blog's pages, from the home page, to a category page, to a single blog post. To do this, the *index.php* file includes tons (really, we mean a *lot*) of other PHP files. With other text editors, the only way to edit WordPress files is to open each file manually. With Dreamweaver, however, you simply open the *index.html* file and then let Dreamweaver "discover" all related PHP files. To do this, you need to follow a few steps:

1. **Set up a staging server.**

   A staging server (also called a "testing server") is basically a server you set up (frequently on your own computer or a networked computer in your office) so you can test your PHP files before moving them to the Internet for all the world to see.

   It's not too difficult to set one up on your own computer. Windows users can learn how at *http://uptospeedguides.com/wamp* and Mac fans can learn how at *http://uptospeedguides.com/mamp*.

   After you set up a testing server, you need to edit the Site Definition settings (Site→Manage Sites) to let Dreamweaver know about it. You can review that process on page 931.

2. **Open a PHP file.**

   There are a couple of ways to "include" a PHP file in another PHP file. Dreamweaver has a command that lets you add basic Includes—Insert→Server-Side Include (see page 937). It automatically sees PHP files you include this way and displays them in the Related Files toolbar with no further effort on your part. But you might also include PHP files within *other* Include files. In cases like these, you need to tell Dreamweaver to "discover" them.

3. **Click the "Discover" link in the Document toolbar above the document window (see top image in Figure 7-15).**

   Dreamweaver displays a warning dialog box saying that it will execute the scripts on this page. That's not a problem, so turn on the "Don't warn me again" checkbox. Dreamweaver finds all the PHP files the currently open dynamic page uses. This may be just a few files, or, in the case of a complex PHP application like WordPress, quite a few. For example, in the bottom image of Figure 7-15, you can see that the Related Files toolbar is chock-full of file names.

4. **Select a related file to work on.**

   Once Dreamweaver discovers all related PHP files, you can use the Related Files toolbar as you normally would to open a file. If there are a lot of files, as in the case of a WordPress site, navigate through the list by clicking the left- and right-arrow buttons, or click the Show More button to see a drop-down menu of all the related files. Select a name from that list to open the file in Code view.

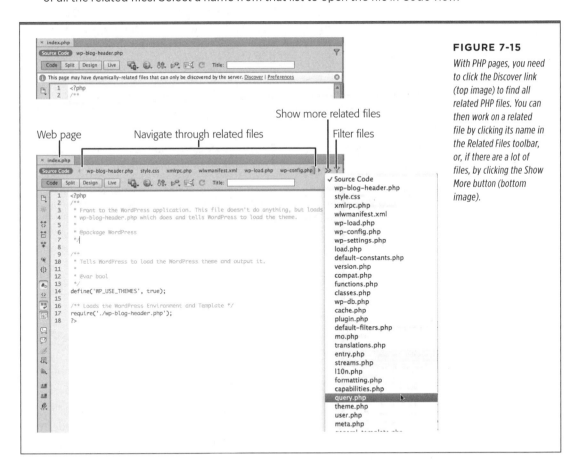

FIGURE 7-15

With PHP pages, you need to click the Discover link (top image) to find all related PHP files. You can then work on a related file by clicking its name in the Related Files toolbar, or, if there are a lot of files, by clicking the Show More button (bottom image).

5. **Filter the list if necessary.**

You may not want to see or work on some of the files in the Related Files toolbar. For example, in the case of WordPress, you'll see many PHP files listed, most of which you never want to touch since they're part of the core WordPress program and editing them might break your blog.

Fortunately, you can filter the list of related files so you see just the ones you want. The Filter button in the top-right corner of the Related Files toolbar lets you do two things. First, clicking it pops up a menu that lets you filter by file type—meaning you can show or hide CSS, PHP, and JavaScript files, and any other file type that your web page references. By default, Dreamweaver selects all the file types, so to hide one, click the Filter button and then click the extension (.css, .php, .js, and so on) for the file type you want to hide. To show those file types later, select them again from the Filter menu.

You can also create a custom filter. Click the Filter button, choose Custom Filter, and a dialog box pops up. Type in the file names and/or file types you want to see. For example, with WordPress, you're interested in editing the PHP theme files—the ones WordPress uses to create your blog's look. To show the relevant files, enter their names separated by a semicolon, like this: *index.php; footer .php; header.php*, and so on. You can also filter by file type. To show all Java-Script files plus *index.php, footer.php*, and *header.php*, type this in the Related Files toolbar: *index.php; footer.php; header.php;.js* (temporarily disable your pop-up blocker).

When you're done, click OK to close the Custom Filter. Dreamweaver displays only those files in the Related Files toolbar.

NOTE Custom Filters are useful but, unfortunately, Dreamweaver doesn't save them, so once you close a file, that filter is lost and you have to recreate it the next time you open the file. In addition, you can't filter by folder—all PHP files within a particular folder only, for example—although that would be really helpful when you work with certain CMS systems, like WordPress, which keep files related to the design of the site in one particular folder. Maybe next time.

■ Live Code

Live Code works in conjunction with the Live view option discussed on page 72. (The short version: Live view lets you see what an in-progress web page actually looks like in a browser...right within Dreamweaver.)

The Live Code button (circled in Figure 7-16) makes Dreamweaver jump to Split view, with the page's Live view in one half of the document window and the underlying HTML in the other half. In Live Code view, HTML appears with a yellow background, and, as with Live view in general, you can't edit it. So what is Live Code for? Or, more accurately, *who* is it for?

Hear ye! Hear ye! Calling all programmers. Live Code provides valuable insight into web pages that are either manipulated with JavaScript programming or constructed with server-side code, like the pages discussed in Part 6 of this book.

JavaScript programming usually involves manipulating the HTML of a page to make elements appear or disappear. For example, programmers often make forms more usable by adjusting the options the site displays based on selections the visitor makes. If someone checks the "married" button on a form under a question about marital status, for example, JavaScript can make the page display a *new* set of questions, ones that apply just to a married person. In other words, JavaScript actually changes the page's HTML.

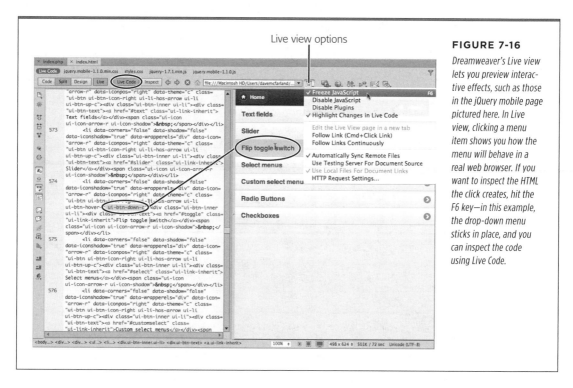

Live view options

FIGURE 7-16

Dreamweaver's Live view lets you preview interactive effects, such as those in the jQuery mobile page pictured here. In Live view, clicking a menu item shows you how the menu will behave in a real web browser. If you want to inspect the HTML the click creates, hit the F6 key—in this example, the drop-down menu sticks in place, and you can inspect the code using Live Code.

Live Code gives JavaScript programmers a glimpse into those changes. It lets you see if a JavaScript program correctly changes how a page looks. If you're a Java-Script programming type, you probably know about the DOM, or Document Object Model. Live Code gives you a direct view into the DOM—into how a browser sees the underlying HTML. This view is useful when a JavaScript program doesn't change the page the way you think it should.

Activating Live Code is pretty straightforward. First, get yourself into Live View by going to the Document toolbar and then clicking the Live button. Next, turn on its neighboring Live Code button (circled in Figure 7-16). Now you're ready to see how a page's HTML changes based on your interaction with the page. Dreamweaver even highlights *what's* changed with a pink background, so you can see the code JavaScript adds.

And if you're not a JavaScript programmer? You still might have an interest in Live Code. It's useful if you're using someone else's JavaScript, such as Dreamweaver's built-in Spry tools or a program you found online, like one of the many marvelous jQuery plug-ins (*http://plugins.jquery.com*). Using Live Code, you can see the HTML and the class and ID names it generates. Looking at JavaScript-generated HTML, it's pretty easy to figure out some of the CSS that formats the page, such as a class style (page 124) if the JavaScript adds class names to tags, an ID style (page 124) if it adds ID names to tags, or descendent selectors (page 377) that match the HTML.

For example, in Figure 7-16, you see a page with Live Code turned on. It captures the exact moment when a mouse clicked on a jQuery mobile list item (thanks to the Freeze JavaScript command described in the Tip below). It also shows you the HTML that the JavaScript inserted. In this case, it adds a class to a list item—*ui-bnt-down-c*—whenever you click it. That class isn't in the regular HTML; JavaScript adds it in response to the mouse click on one of the links in the menu bar. With this knowledge in hand, you now know you can edit the *MenuBarItemHover* class in the Spry Menu Bar style sheet to change the appearance of this button when a visitor mouses over it.

> **TIP** The F6 key freezes any currently running JavaScript, so you can make a drop-down menu "stick" in place when you mouse over it. It's like freezing the entire page, and it's great for working with Live Code, since you can freeze a dynamic rollover effect and see how the JavaScript programming affects the HTML of the page.

> **NOTE** You can also use the Live view Options menu to freeze a JavaScript program, as pictured in Figure 7-16 (but you can't freeze JavaScript you trigger by moving your mouse over an element, like a drop-down menu. That's because, when you move your mouse to the Live view options menu to freeze the JavaScript, the menu disappears).

Code view is also useful for server-side programmers who use multiple files (called "includes") to build a page. For example, the popular WordPress blogging software loads dozens of separate files just to display a single page; each of those files performs a different task and creates a different part of the page. If you open the main *index.php* file (in WordPress, this single file controls every page displayed), you'll see just a few lines of HTML and PHP programming. But if you go into Live view and then press the Live Code button, you'll see the HTML that the *index.php* file actually produces. This is one way to make sure that your server-side programming is putting together the finished HTML the way you want it.

Quick Tag Editor

Code view is great when you really need (or want) to jump into the trenches and fine-tune your HTML. But if you're aesthetically oriented, you probably spend most of your time in Design view, enjoying the pleasures of its visual authoring environment.

Occasionally, however, you want to dip into the HTML pond, especially when you need to use some HTML that's unavailable from the Insert panel. You might wish you could type out a quick HTML tag on the spot, right there in Design view, for example, without having to make the mental and visual shift to Code view.

That's what Dreamweaver's Quick Tag Editor is all about. To access it, in Design view press Ctrl+T (⌘-T)—or, if you're feeling especially mouse-driven, in the Property Inspector, click the Quick Tag Editor button (circled in Figure 7-17).

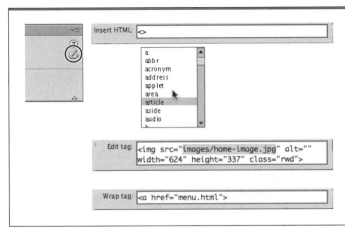

FIGURE 7-17

Left: You can quickly work with tags by clicking the Quick Tag Editor button in the Property Inspector's upper-right corner (circled). (You only see the button in Design view.) The Quick Tag Editor lets you insert new tags, edit old ones, or wrap a new tag around a selection. If the Editor window blocks the area of the page you're modifying, drag it out of the way by its handle (the edit mode name).

Depending on what you selected in the document window, the Quick Tag Editor opens in one of the following three modes:

- **Insert HTML**. Inserts a new tag in the page. You get this mode if you haven't selected anything in your document window.

- **Edit tag**. Lets you edit the tag for whatever element you selected in the document window (a graphic, for example). You can also edit all of that element's properties.

- **Wrap tag**. If you select a swath of text or other objects (like two images), the editor opens in this mode, which lets you easily wrap a new tag around that selection.

> **TIP** You can cycle through modes by repeatedly pressing Ctrl+T (⌘-T).

Using the Quick Tag Editor

You can type tag names, properties, and property values directly into the Quick Tag Editor. If you're editing a selected tag, you can change any of the properties listed, and even add new ones. When you're done, press Enter (Return). The Quick Tag Editor closes, and the changes take effect.

To make all this even easier, the Quick Tag Editor sports a helpful list—called *Tag Hints*—of HTML tags and properties for your selection pleasure. It's much like Code view's Code Hints (in fact, in the Preferences window, the Code Hints category also controls tag hints). When you're in Insert HTML mode, for example, a menu of available tags appears (top-right in Figure 7-17). Use the up and down arrow keys or the scroll bar to move through the list, or type in the first few letters of a tag or property, and Dreamweaver jumps to the nearest match.

To choose the highlighted name, press Enter (Return). Dreamweaver adds that tag or property name to the Quick Tag Editor. If you select a tag property, Dreamweaver adds the proper punctuation (href=" ", for example), and the cursor appears between the quotation marks, waiting for you to type in the property's value.

> **TIP** When editing an existing tag in the Quick Tag Editor, press Tab to select the next property or property value. You can then type a new property or value. Shift+Tab selects the *previous* property or value.

■ The Tag Inspector

The Property Inspector is a handy tool. It lets you adjust properties for all sorts of HTML tags, like a table's width or a paragraph's font. But even the Property Inspector doesn't tell the whole story. Some HTML tags have additional properties that don't appear there, such as the <a> tag's *tabindex* property, which lets you control the order in which Dreamweaver highlights links as a visitor presses the Tab key.

For these hard-to-reach properties, turn to the *Tag Inspector* (see Figure 7-18). Think of it as an uber-Property Inspector. For hard-core HTML fanatics, it's the best way to set properties for every HTML tag. To display it, press the F9 key (Option-F9 on Macs), or choose Window→Tag Inspector (the same procedure also hides this panel).

When you select a tag on the page (in either Code or Design view), Dreamweaver displays *all* its properties in the panel. To edit any of them, click in the space to the right of the property name. You can type in a new value or, for certain properties, choose from a list of values from a drop-down menu. For color properties, use Dreamweaver's ubiquitous color box to select the shade you want.

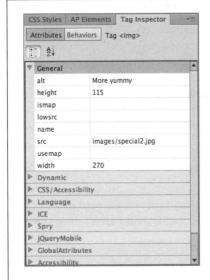 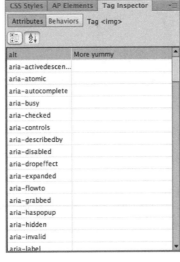

FIGURE 7-18

Dreamweaver's Tag inspector lets you edit every property of every tag on a page. What it lacks in user-friendliness—you need to know a lot about HTML to use it—it makes up for in comprehensiveness. It has two faces: Category view (left) and List view (right). The List view is just that: a list of all the properties for the selected tag. The Category view imposes a bit of order on this mess by organizing the different properties into related categories.

NOTE If you don't see a list of HTML properties, you may be in the Behaviors area of this panel. Just click the Attributes button at the top of the panel to use the Tag Selector. Oddly, the Behaviors button adds Dreamweaver behaviors (see Chapter 13) and isn't really used to inspect tags at all.

Unfortunately, you need to understand HTML fairly well to set values correctly—Dreamweaver doesn't make the process foolproof, so you could enter an invalid property. (To learn more about HTML tags and their properties, turn to Dreamweaver's built-in HTML reference, described on page 370.)

Comparing Versions of a Web Page

Sometimes you make a change to a page, save it, preview it, close it, and move along to the next assignment for the day. Only later, when you take a second look at your day's changes before moving pages to your web server, do you see that one of them has a problem you didn't notice at first. Perhaps the left sidebar is suddenly wider than it was before. Since you already closed the file, you can't use the Undo command to reverse whatever pesky mistake you made. You could, of course, retrieve the current version of the page from the server, thus overwriting your changes. But what if you did a lot of good work on the page—added text, graphics, and links—that you don't want to lose? Ideally, you'd like to see all the changes you made to the page, and selectively undo the mistake you accidentally introduced.

Enter the Compare File command. With it, you can compare two files and identify lines of code that differ between them. This tool is a perfect solution for problems like the unintentionally botched sidebar above. Compare the local file (the one with the messed-up sidebar) with the remote file (the live version of the website page that works, but is missing your most recent edits). You can then identify any changes you made and smoke out your mistake.

Dreamweaver doesn't actually have this tool built into it. Instead, it just passes the files to a separate file-comparison utility (often called a "diff" tool, since it identifies *differences* between files). Before you use Dreamweaver to compare files, you need to download one of these utilities, and you have a lot to choose from. Fortunately, several of them are free utilities for both Windows PCs and Macs (see the following boxes).

After you download and install the file-comparison utility, you need to tell Dreamweaver where to find it:

1. **Open the Preferences panel, by choosing Edit→Preferences (Dreamweaver→Preferences) or pressing Ctrl+U (⌘-U), and then click the File Compare category.**

   There's not much to this Preferences category, just a single box and a Browse button.

2. **Click the Browse button, and then navigate to and select the file-comparison utility.**

   For example, on Windows you might find your utility at *C:\Program Files\ WinMerge\WinMergeU.exe*.

WINDOWS ONLY

Getting Your Hands on the Goodies

You can find lots of file-comparison tools for Windows. Beyond Compare from Scooter Software (*www.scootersoftware.com*) is a $30 commercial product that offers a wide range of comparison options. For a free alternative, check out WinMerge (*http://winmerge.org*). This open-source software provides all the basic options you need. Here's how you get it: Go to *http://winmerge.org*. Click the "Download Now" button. At this point you're asked to save the file to your computer—of course, if you're using Internet Explorer, one of those yellow "Warning, warning, enemy attack" banners appears at the top of the page—you need to click that, and then choose "Download File" to actually download the file to your computer.

Once you download the program, the process of installing it is like most other Windows programs. Double-click the file to launch an installer, and follow the step-by-step instructions. You have several options along the way; accept the suggested settings and you'll be fine. Once you install it, you're ready to proceed as described below.

On Macs, the process is slightly different. Instead of selecting the text-editing program Text Wrangler or BBEdit, you need to specify the proper "diff" tool, which is stored in a special location on your computer. Navigate to the */usr/bin* folder (fortunately Dreamweaver drops you there automatically when you browse for the file-comparison tool)—something like this: *Macintosh HD:usr:bin*—and select the correct file. For Text Wrangler, it's *twdiff*; for BBEdit, it's *bbdiff*; and for FileMerge, it's *opendiff*.

3. **Click OK to close the Preferences window.**

Dreamweaver's been notified of the utility's location, so you're ready to compare files.

MACS ONLY

What Difference Does It Make?

The Mac version of Dreamweaver supports only three file comparison tools: File Merge (which is a Mac developer program that comes with the XCode tools on your Mac OS X installation disc), BBEdit (the powerful, $125 commercial text editor), and Text Wrangler (the free little brother of BBEdit). Bare Bones Software (*www.barebones.com*) produces both BBEdit and Text Wrangler, but since Text Wrangler is free, it's the best place to begin.

Point your Web browser to *http://tinyurl.com/ctwmby* and click any of the download links to save the program to your computer. As with many Mac applications, this download opens a disk image—just like a folder—with the program inside it. Just drag it to your Applications folder to install it.

The Compare File command works with either two local files that you select in the Files panel (see the Tip on page 367 for an explanation) or, more commonly, for a local file and a remote file, so you need to have a site defined with both local and remote root folders (see Chapter 17 for details on how to configure this). In addition, since you're comparing two files, you need to make sure you've got a version of the same file on both your local computer and remote site—for example, a copy of your home page both locally and on your server. To compare the files, follow these steps:

1. **In the Files panel, select the location of the first file you want to compare.**

Use the drop-down menu in the top-right of the panel to choose either "Local view" or "Remote server.".

2. **In the Files panel, right-click (Control-click) the file, and then, from the pop-up menu that appears, select "Compare with Remote Server" (if you're in the Remote Server view, this menu says "Compare with Local").**

Dreamweaver does a little behind-the-scenes trickery before passing the files off to the file comparison program. It first creates a folder (if it's not already created) named *_compareTemp* in the local root folder of your site. It then creates a temporary copy of the remote file and stores that in the new folder. So, you don't actually compare the live file on the server with the local file on your computer; you compare a *copy* of the remote file with the local file. This distinction is important if you want to incorporate changes to the live file, as described in step 3.

Then your selected file-comparison program—for example, WinMerge or Text Wrangler—starts up and compares the two files. If it finds no differences—if they're *exactly* the same—you'll most likely get a message saying something like "The Selected Files are Identical." Your work is done. If there *is* a difference, the file-comparison program displays the two files and identifies the code that differs between them (see Figure 7-19 and Figure 7-20).

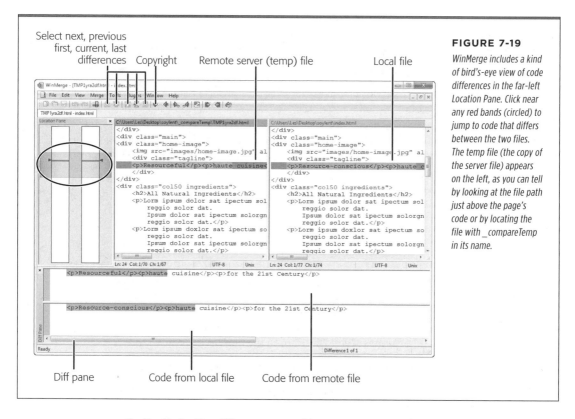

Select next, previous first, current, last differences Copyright Remote server (temp) file Local file

Diff pane Code from local file Code from remote file

FIGURE 7-19

WinMerge includes a kind of bird's-eye view of code differences in the far-left Location Pane. Click near any red bands (circled) to jump to code that differs between the two files. The temp file (the copy of the server file) appears on the left, as you can tell by looking at the file path just above the page's code or by locating the file with _compareTemp in its name.

3. **Evaluate the differences, and incorporate any changes into your local file.**

   All file-comparison programs work the same way. When they compare two files, you see the code for each side by side. In addition, they highlight the differences in some way. You can then review the differences and merge the changes into one file or the other. For example, say you accidentally delete a table from your local file; a comparison of this file with the remote file shows the table intact in the remote file, but missing in the local file. You can copy the table code from the remote file into the local file. If, however, you deleted the table purposefully, then do nothing, and move on to evaluate the next difference.

Here's where Dreamweaver's little bait-and-switch mentioned in step 2 becomes important. You're not actually comparing the remote file with the local file; you're comparing a *copy* of the remote file saved locally in the _compare Temp folder. As a result, you want to move changes in only one direction—from the temporary server file to your local file. That's because any changes you make to the temporary file have no effect on the live file on your web server.

So how do you update the remote file? Make changes to your local file, save it, return to Dreamweaver, and upload the local file to your remote site folder. Then pour yourself a cup of tea and be thankful you don't have to do *that* very often.

Remote temporary file   Local file

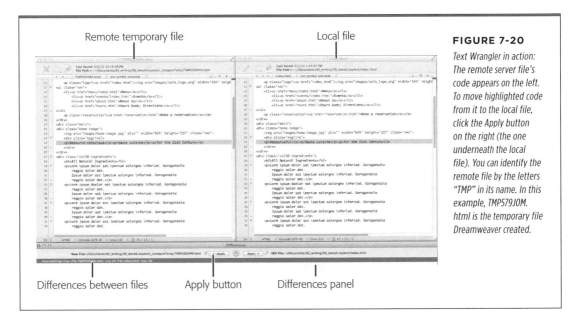

FIGURE 7-20

Text Wrangler in action: The remote server file's code appears on the left. To move highlighted code from it to the local file, click the Apply button on the right (the one underneath the local file). You can identify the remote file by the letters "TMP" in its name. In this example, TMP579J0M. html is the temporary file Dreamweaver created.

Differences between files   Apply button   Differences panel

4. **Save any changes, return to Dreamweaver, and then move your newly up-dated local file to your web server.**

   The exact process varies from program to program, but see the next two sections for examples using WinMerge and Text Wrangler.

TIP You can also compare two files on your local hard drive (the home page of the site you're working on against a backup of that page you made last week, for example). If the two files are in the same site (perhaps you have a backup folder in your local root folder), select them in the Files panel. If the files aren't in the same local root folder, go to the Files panel and then, from the site list, select your hard drive (instead of a defined site). In this mode, the Files panel acts just like Windows Explorer or the Mac Finder.

Using WinMerge to Compare Files

If you've got a Windows PC and want to take Dreamweaver's Compare Files command for a test drive, see the box on page 364 for instructions on downloading WinMerge, and then follow these steps:

1. **Once you download and install WinMerge, follow the steps on page 364 to set up Dreamweaver to work with WinMerge.**

   You need to make sure Dreamweaver knows that you want to use WinMerge for file comparisons.

2. **Follow steps 1 and 2 on page 365 to select a file and tell Dreamweaver to compare it with its sibling on the remote web server.**

   WinMerge launches, and if there are any differences between the files, the program shows the code for the two files side by side, with the differences highlighted.

   WinMerge highlights differences using one or more yellow bars in the Location Pane (circled in Figure 7-19), and the *code* is highlighted either in yellow or gray indicating areas where the files differ.

3. **Click anywhere in either file's code, and then click any of the "diff" navigation buttons—"next diff," "previous diff," "first diff," or "last diff"—to move from one code difference to another.**

   "Diff" stands for difference. WinMerge identifies the mismatched code by highlighting it in red. It pinpoints the exact differences in the Diff Pane below the files. You can now figure out which code you wish to keep.

4. **If the code in the remote server file looks correct, click the Copy Right button.**

   The live server file (a temporary file with a name like *TMP4wr997.html*) appears on the left and the local file appears on the right. Remember you only want to make changes to your local file. Hitting the Copy Right button copies the code from the live server file to the local file.

   You don't need to do anything if the code in the local file looks OK.

5. **Continue with steps 3 and 4 until you evaluate all the code differences in the two pages.**

At this point, the "perfect" copy is your local file. It has all the correct code from the server file and all the correct code from the local file. Now you just need to move it to your web server.

6. **Move your local file to your server using one of the techniques described on page 798.**

Using Text Wrangler to Compare Files

Mac owners can download the free Text Wrangler program to compare files (see the box on page 365). And since BBEdit is a more powerful version of Text Wrangler, these steps work for that program as well:

1. **Once you install Text Wrangler, follow the steps on page 364 to set up Dreamweaver's preferences.**

   You need to tell Dreamweaver you want to compare files using Text Wrangler.

2. **Follow steps 1 and 2 on page 365 to select a file and tell Dreamweaver to compare it with its sibling on the remote web server.**

   Text Wrangler launches and displays any code differences between the two files (see Figure 7-20). It also breaks out the problematic code in the Differences panel below the two pages.

   Text Wrangler tells you how the lines differ: For example, "Nonmatching lines" means the lines are similar (some of the code is the same) but not identical, while "Extra lines before line 678" means that one file uses a line of code that's completely different from the other file.

   If the files are identical, Dreamweaver pops up a "No difference found between these files" message (although sometimes, if there's no difference, you don't see any message at all).

3. **In the Differences panel, double-click the difference you want to inspect.**

   It's a good strategy to just start at the top of the list and work your way down.

4. **If the code in the live server file looks correct, click the Apply button to transfer the code from the remote file to your local file.**

   Remember, you only want to make changes to your local file, since the "live server" file is actually a temporary file that Dreamweaver downloaded from your server. The live server file appears on the left, and the local file on the right, so make sure to hit the Apply button that points to the *right*.

   You don't need to do anything if the code in the local file looks OK.

5. **Continue with steps 3 and 4 until you evaluate all the differences in the two pages.**

   At this point, the "perfect" copy is your local file. It has all the correct code from the remote file, and all the correct code from the local file. You just need to move it to your server.

6. **Move your local file to your Web server, using one of the techniques described on page 798.**

You can also use the file-compare feature to compare two local files or two remote files (see the Tip on page 367). In the case of two remote files, download them first, and then compare them.

■ Reference Panel

When it comes to building websites, there's a lot to know. After all, HTML, Cascading Style Sheets, and JavaScript are filled with cryptic terms and subtle nuances. Dreamweaver provides a Reference panel to make your search for knowledge a little bit easier. Unfortunately, the references supplied are so out of date that none but the HTML Reference has any relevance (as long as you're working with just XHTML 1.0 or HTML 4.01; if you're working with HTML5, then "Hello, Google").

To open the Reference panel, choose Help→Reference or press Shift+F1. The Reference panel appears at the bottom of the screen, docked with the Results panel group. The first menu at the top of the panel (Book) lets you choose the reference "book" you want to use. Again, only the HTML reference is any good, and only if you're sticking with standard HTML 4 tags. Once you select your reference, choose an HTML tag from the Tag menu to the right of the Book menu. A description of the tag appears in the main window. A secondary menu to the right, the Attribute menu, lets you access additional information about a property or tag. For example, if you want to see information about the <a> tag's *tabindex* property, choose "a" from the Tag menu and then, from the Attribute menu, click "tabindex."

For information on other topics, you're better off turning to the Web and Google. Here are a few good resources:

- For CSS help, SitePoint.com's free, online reference to CSS is great: *http://reference.sitepoint.com/css*.

- For JavaScript, W3Schools.com provides an in-depth reference: *www.w3schools.com/jsref/default.asp*.

- For PHP, you can't beat the Source. The official PHP site has excellent documentation on every aspect of PHP: *www.php.net/manual/en*.

■ Inserting JavaScript

Dreamweaver includes many fun and useful interactive effects—Spry menus, Spry form validation, Spry effects, Dreamweaver behaviors, and so on. JavaScript is the "engine" behind all of them. Of course, you can do a lot of other cool things with JavaScript that Dreamweaver hasn't programmed. In these cases, you need to wade into the depths of JavaScript programming yourself.

The most straightforward approach, especially if you're familiar with JavaScript, is to simply switch into Code view (Ctrl+` [Option-`]), and then code away. If you prefer, you can use Dreamweaver's Script window to add JavaScript code (see Figure 7-21).

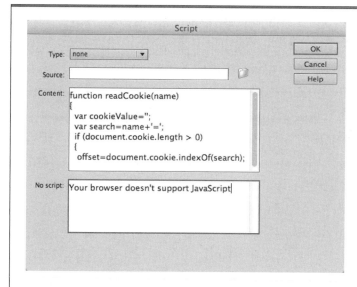

FIGURE 7-21
Unlike Code view, the Script window doesn't respond to the Tab key; if you're accustomed to indenting your code, you need to use spaces. You can also insert a message in the "No script" box, which appears if the web browser doesn't understand JavaScript.

To add JavaScript code, click in either the head or body section of a page and then choose Insert→HTML→Script Objects→Script. In the Script window that appears, from the Type menu, choose "none" if you're working on an HTML5 page or "text/javascript" for XHTML or HTML 4 pages.

> **TIP** You can use the Insert Script command in Design view also, but to add a script to the <head> of a page, first choose View→Head Content, which opens a small bar below the Document toolbar that lists all the different tags, like <title>, <script>, and <meta>, that appear in the head of a page. Click here, and follow the preceding recipe for inserting a script.

In the Content section, type in your script (no need to include <script> tags, as Dreamweaver handles that for you), and then click OK. If you insert the script in the body of the document, a small gold icon (indicating an invisible element on the page) marks its location.

You can edit your script in Code view, of course. In Design view, select the gold icon, and then, in the Property Inspector, click Edit.

> **NOTE** Dreamweaver includes an "Externalize JavaScript" command under the Commands menu. It's intended to make your pages leaner by taking JavaScript out of a page and putting it into a separate file. But it just ends up making any of the Spry widgets (like the Spry menu bar discussed on page 210) or Dreamweaver behaviors (Chapter 13) uneditable, except in Code view.

If you use external JavaScript files, you can link to them directly in the Script window. Instead of typing in any code, click the familiar "Browse for File" icon (to the right of the Source box), locate the external JavaScript file, and then click OK. Dreamweaver adds the appropriate code to link the script file to the web page (see Figure 7-21).

Dreamweaver also lets you open and work on external JavaScript files (.js files) right in Code view and, with the Related Files toolbar discussed on page 353, you can easily jump to the JavaScript code in the external file. Then you can use Code views' built-in text-editing capabilities to write your JavaScript program.

NOTE JavaScript programming is no walk in the park. Although it's certainly easier to learn than full-featured languages like Java or C++, it can still be challenging. If you want to get your feet wet, here's a great resource for basic tutorials and information on JavaScript: *http://www.w3schools.com/js*. For more in-depth coverage, check out *JavaScript & jQuery: The Missing Manual.*

Building a Better Web Page

Advanced CSS

Chapter 3 introduced the basics of Cascading Style Sheets. In other chapters, you learned how to use CSS to style links, navigation bars, text, and tables. You can go a long way in web design with just those techniques (and many people do). However, to really become a web design expert, you should become familiar with a handful of advanced CSS concepts. Fortunately, Dreamweaver includes tools to help you with these concepts so you can work more efficiently and avoid those head-scratching "Why the heck does my design look like that?!" moments. In addition, Dreamweaver CS6 includes a few approaches for adding the shiny, new CSS3 properties and a fun tool for adding basic CSS animations. (Even if you're not ready for some of the advanced CSS concepts discussed in this chapter, don't skip the section on CSS Transitions [page 405] because they're fun and easy to create.)

NOTE This chapter will help you on your journey from CSS novice to master. But keep in mind that it's the rare mortal who understands everything about CSS from reading a single chapter. If you really want to know the ins and outs of CSS, check out *CSS: The Missing Manual*.

■ Compound Selectors

It's pretty easy to learn how to use tag, class, and ID styles. To be technically accurate, all these styles aren't really styles. In CSS lingo, they're *selectors*, instructions that tell a browser *what* it should look for so it can apply CSS formatting rules. For example, a tag selector (not to be mistaken with Dreamweaver's time-saving selection tool, the Tag Selector) tells a browser to apply formatting to *any* instance of a particular tag on the page. Thus, browsers apply *h1* tag styles to *all* <h1> tags on a page. They apply class selector styles, on the other hand, only when they encounter the class name attached to an element on a page. Similarly, browsers apply ID selector styles to a tag with a matching ID name, for example <body id="home">. (Flip back to page 124 for a review of key differences between class and ID selectors.)

NOTE For a detailed discussion of selectors, visit *http://tinyurl.com/29dnb4.*

But tag, class, and ID selectors are just the tip of the selector iceberg. CSS offers many other selector types that let you format even the smallest page element; Dreamweaver lumps these laser-focused selectors under the term *compound selectors.* "Compound selector" is a Dreamweaver term, not a CSS term, so don't go using it at your weekly web designer get-togethers. Dreamweaver uses the term to describe advanced selectors, such as the "pseudo-class" styles you use to format different link states (*a:link, a:visited, a:hover,* and *a:active,* as described on page 206) or the descendent selectors the Spry menu bar uses (page 210).

The CSS arsenal includes a variety of advanced selectors (you'll find a few of the most common and useful ones mentioned below), but in Dreamweaver, you write all of them the same way. You start by creating a CSS style, following the instructions on page 125. But when you get to the New CSS Rule window (Figure 8-1), instead of selecting the Class, ID, or Tag Selector type, choose the Compound option.

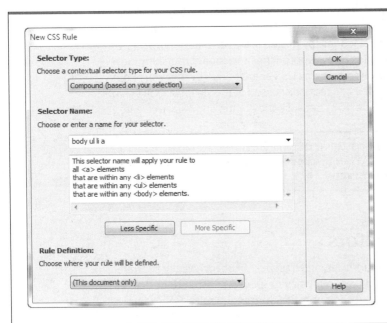

FIGURE 8-1

The Compound selector option lets you type any valid CSS selector in the Selector Name box. You can even create class, tag, and ID styles after choosing the Compound selector option. For a new class, type the name of the class preceded by a period, like this: .copyright. To create a tag style, type the tag name without brackets: p for the <p>, or paragraph, tag, for instance. And, to create a new ID style, type the # symbol followed by the ID name: #firstName, for example.

Unless you're styling one of the four link-state options listed in the Selector Name's drop-down menu, you have to type the name of any advanced selector you want to use. As described in the following sections, you use a different syntax (naming convention) for each type of selector. (The rest of the process for creating an advanced style works just like creating a tag or class style, and the process of editing or deleting the styles is also identical.)

Descendent Selectors

Tag styles have their drawbacks. While a tag style for the <p> tag makes simple work of formatting every paragraph on a page, it's also indiscriminate. You may not *want* every paragraph to look the same.

Suppose you want to divide a web page into different sections—a sidebar and a main content area—using smaller size text for the sidebar's paragraphs and headings. You *could* create two class styles—such as *.sidebarText* and *.mainText*—and then apply them to the appropriate paragraphs (<p class="sidebarText"> for sidebar paragraphs and <p class="mainText"> for body text). But who has that kind of time?

What you really need is a "smart" tag style, one that can adapt to its surroundings like a chameleon and apply the appropriate format depending on where it finds the element on a page. Enter *descendent selectors*.

Essentially, you use descendent selectors to format every instance of a particular tag (just like tag selectors do)—but only when those tags appear in a particular part of a web page. In effect, it's like saying, "Hey, you <a> tags in the navigation bar, listen up. I've got some formatting for you. All you other <a> tags, move along, there's nothing to see here." In other words, a descendent selector lets you format a tag based on its *relationship* to other tags. To understand how it works, you need to delve a little more deeply into HTML.

Think of the HTML that forms any web page as a kind of "family tree," like the one shown in Figure 8-2. The first HTML tag you use on a page—the <html> tag—is the grandpappy of all the other tags. In essence, when a tag is *inside* another tag, it's a *descendent* of that tag. In Figure 8-2, the text "wide range of topics" is bolded in the long paragraph. You get that format by applying a <strong> tag to that phrase. Because that bolded text sits inside a paragraph (inside a <p> tag, in other words), the <strong> tag is a descendent of that paragraph.

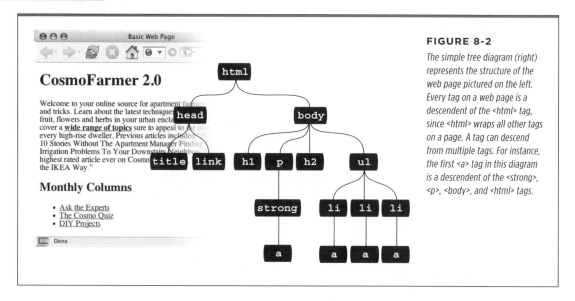

FIGURE 8-2

The simple tree diagram (right) represents the structure of the web page pictured on the left. Every tag on a web page is a descendent of the <html> tag, since <html> wraps all other tags on a page. A tag can descend from multiple tags. For instance, the first <a> tag in this diagram is a descendent of the <strong>, <p>, <body>, and <html> tags.

Descendent selectors let you take advantage of the HTML family tree by formatting tags differently when they appear inside certain other tags. For example, say you have an <h1> tag on your web page, and you want to emphasize a word within that heading. One option is to select the word and press the B button on the Property Inspector—that applies the <strong> tag to that word. The trouble is, most browsers boldface the words in both heading tags and <strong> tags, so your visitors won't see any difference between the emphasized word and the other words in the headline. Creating a tag selector to change the <strong> tag's color and make it stand out from the headline isn't much of a solution: you end up changing the color of *every* <strong> tag on the page, even ones inside paragraphs or bulleted lists, whether you like it or not. A descendent selector lets you do what you really want to do: change the color of the <strong> tag *only when* it appears inside of an <h1> tag.

Creating descendent selectors isn't much more difficult than creating any other type of style. You follow the same process—click the New Rule button at the bottom the CSS Styles panel—but in the New CSS Rule window, select Compound from the Selector Type menu. You then type the descendent selector's name in the Selector Name box. Figuring out how to name the selector is the tricky part.

You name a descendent selector by tacking together a series of selectors (separated by spaces) that identify the location in the family tree of the element you want to style. The most distant ancestor is on the far left and the element you wish to style is on the far right. Consider the example of the bolded word inside the headline discussed above. To style that bolded text (but leave any other bold text as it is), the descendent selector is *h1 strong*. You read this from right to left, so <strong> is the actual tag you're formatting, but only when it's inside an <h1> tag.

Figure 8-2 shows another example of descendent selectors. There are four links (<a> tags) on the page. Three of them appear inside bulleted list items (that's the <li> tag). If you want to create a style that applied only to those three links and leave the fourth link untouched, you'd create a descendent selector like this: *li a*. Again, the actual tag you want to format—the <a> link—appears on the far right, while the tag that wraps around the link—the <li> tag—appears to the left.

A descendent selector can contain more than just two elements. The following are all valid selectors for the <a> tags inside the bulleted lists in Figure 8-2:

- li a
- ul li a
- body li a
- html li a
- html body ul li a

These five selectors—all of which do the same thing—demonstrate that you don't have to describe the entire lineage of the tag you want to format. For instance, in the third example—*body li a*—you don't need the ul. This selector works as long as there's an <a> tag that's a descendent (somewhere down the line) of an <li> tag (which itself is a descendent of the <body> tag). This selector can just as easily apply to an <a> tag inside an <em> tag, inside a <strong> tag, that's inside a <li> tag, and so on.

> **NOTE** One reason you might make a descendent selector longer by tacking on additional selectors is if you've written several different rules that simultaneously format a tag. The more selectors that appear in a style name, the more powerful that style is and the more likely it is to override any conflicts with other styles. (More on this concept on page 391.) However, it's best to keep your selectors as short as possible to get the job done. In the above example, all five selectors work, but li a is the shortest, and therefore the best one to use.

When you choose Compound from the Selector Type menu in the New CSS Rule window, Dreamweaver suggests a descendent selector based on what you currently have selected on the page (or, if you have nothing selected, where the cursor is). For example, say you had the page pictured in Figure 8-2 open in Dreamweaver. If you selected the link with the text "Ask the Experts," created a new style (for example, by clicking the New CSS Rule button on the CSS Styles panel), and then selected Compound from the Selector Type menu, you'd see something like Figure 8-1. Having Dreamweaver compose the selector for you is, as you can imagine, a brain-cell saver. In this case, Dreamweaver suggests "body ul li a"—a descendent selector style that formats every link (<a>) inside a list item (<li>) that's part of an unordered list (<ul>) that is itself inside the body of the page (<body>).

> **NOTE** When you write your own descendent selectors, Dreamweaver's selector explanation box (the text box that appears below the Selector Name field) is a big help. It explains, in plain English, what elements that descendent selector will apply to (see the box below the *body ul li a* selector name in Figure 8-1, for example).

That's a pretty long-winded style name and, as mentioned above, you don't have to have all that information to accurately target the elements on a page for a style. For example, a simpler name, *li a*, would also get the job done. Dreamweaver generally suggests the most complete descendent selector, meaning the tag you want to format and every ancestor tag (every tag wrapped around the selected element). In most cases, you won't need such complicated descendent selector names. You can replace Dreamweaver's suggestion with a simpler one; just delete what Dreamweaver provides and type in another selector name. You can also click the Less Specific button on the New CSS Rule window. Each click removes the ancestor on the far left of the list. For example, in Figure 8-1, clicking Less Specific once changes the descendent selector to *ul li a*; clicking it a second time makes it *li a*.

■ DESCENDENT SELECTORS WITH CLASS AND ID STYLES

You're not limited to using tag selectors in your descendent selector names, either. You can build complex descendent selectors by combining different types of selectors. Suppose you want links to appear in yellow in introductory paragraphs (which you designate with a class style named *intro*). The following selector does the trick: *.intro a*. This descendent selector formats any link (<a>) inside any other tag that has the *intro* class applied to it.

Web designers frequently format the same tag differently, depending on where the tag appears in a layout. For instance, you'll often want paragraphs in the main content area of a page to look different from paragraphs in sidebars (you might use a different font and a smaller font size, for example). You'll usually wrap each section of a page inside a <div> tag that has a class applied to it. For example, you might wrap the main content area in a <div> tag and apply the class name *.content* to it. To format just the paragraphs inside the <div> tag, you'd use the descendent selector *.content p* (don't leave out the period). You'll use this technique frequently when you work with CSS layouts like those discussed in the next chapter.

You can apply either class names or ID names to div tags to create sections within a web page. While web designers used to use IDs with divs to identify unique page-layout elements, such as banners (for example, <div id="banner">), classes work just as well (<div class="banner", for example). In either case, you might want to target specific tags inside those divs. The process is the same whether you use IDs or class names, so if you want to define the look of bulleted lists wherever they appear inside a tag with an ID named *#banner*, you'd type *#banner ul* in the Selector Name box; if the tag had the class *.banner*, then the selector for a bulleted list inside that div would be .banner ul.

TIP When you work with descendent selectors, it helps to read the selector name *backwards, from right to left*. Take, for example, the selector *#content .nav li*. The *li* means "This style applies to the <li> tag;" the *.nav* means "But only when it's inside a tag with a class of nav applied to it;" and *#content* means "And only when that tag is inside another tag that has the ID *#content* applied to it."

After you name the descendent selector, save it to either an internal or external style sheet as described on page 123. Then click OK in the New CSS Rule window. You're ready to start adding the CSS properties that define the formatting your descendent selector will apply. Proceed as you normally would when you create *any* type of style (see page 125 for a refresher).

Styling Groups of Tags

Sometimes you want to apply the same formatting to several different elements. Say you'd like all headers on a page to share the same color and font. Creating a separate style for each header—*h1, h2, h3, h4, h5, h6*—is way too much work. In addition, if you later want to change the color of all the headers, you'd have to update six styles. A more streamlined approach is to use a *group* selector, which lets you apply a style to multiple selectors at the same time.

To write a style that applies to several different elements at once, create a new style by clicking the New Rule button at the bottom of the CSS Styles panel, and then choose Compound from the top menu in the New CSS Rule window (see Figure 8-3). In the Selector Name box, type a list of selectors separated by commas. To style all heading tags with the same formatting options, for example, you'd create the following selector: *h1, h2, h3, h4, h5, h6*.

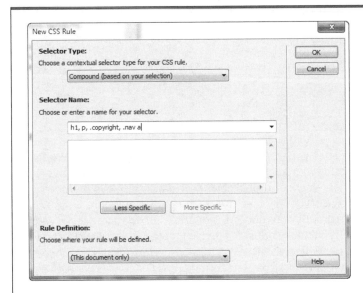

FIGURE 8-3

You can apply group selectors to more than just a single tag. You can use any valid selector (or combination of selector types) in a group selector. For example, the selector listed here applies to the <h1> tag, the <p> tag, any tag styled with the .copyright class, and any links inside another tag with the class .nav.

TIP At times, you may want a bunch of page elements to share *some*—but not all—formatting properties. Suppose you want to use the same font for several tags, but apply different font colors to each of those tags. You can create a single style using a group selector with the shared formatting options, and separate styles with unique formatting for each individual tag. That's a perfectly valid (and common) approach: web browsers just "tally up" all the different CSS properties applied to a tag to create a kind of uber style, as described on page 391.

Fast Style Editing with the Properties Pane

The CSS Rule Definition window can be a rather tedious way to edit CSS properties. It's easy to use, but opening the window and jumping around the categories and menus may slow down experienced CSS jockeys. Fortunately, Dreamweaver offers the Properties pane (Figure 8-4) for fast CSS editing. It displays a selected style's currently defined properties.

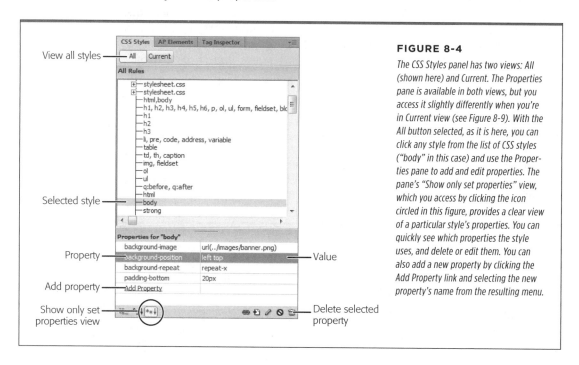

View all styles

Selected style

Property ———— Value

Add property

Show only set
properties view ———— Delete selected
property

FIGURE 8-4

The CSS Styles panel has two views: All (shown here) and Current. The Properties pane is available in both views, but you access it slightly differently when you're in Current view (see Figure 8-9). With the All button selected, as it is here, you can click any style from the list of CSS styles ("body" in this case) and use the Properties pane to add and edit properties. The pane's "Show only set properties" view, which you access by clicking the icon circled in this figure, provides a clear view of a particular style's properties. You can quickly see which properties the style uses, and delete or edit them. You can also add a new property by clicking the Add Property link and selecting the new property's name from the resulting menu.

Start by selecting the style you want to edit in the CSS Styles panel. The Properties pane (found in the bottom third of the Styles panel) displays CSS properties in one of three views: a "Show only set properties" view, which displays the properties defined for the selected style only (see the circled button in Figure 8-4); a Show category" view, which groups different CSS properties into the same seven categories used in the Rule Definition window (circled in Figure 8-5, left); and a List view, which provides an alphabetical listing of *all* CSS properties (circled in Figure 8-5, right). Click the buttons at the bottom-left corner of the CSS Styles panel to switch among these views.

The CSS Styles panel lists property names on the left, and their values on the right. Figure 8-4 shows an example of a style for the <body> tag, which lists four properties (*background-image* and *padding-bottom*, for example) and their corresponding settings ("url(../images/banner.png)," 20px, and so on).

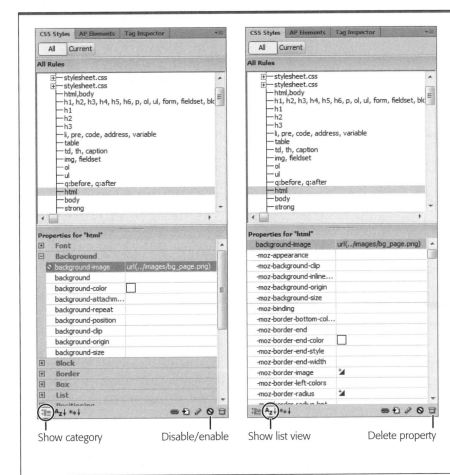

FIGURE 8-5

The Properties pane's two other views aren't as streamlined or as easy to use as the "Show only set properties" view pictured in Figure 8-4. You add new properties in these views by simply typing a value in the empty box to the right of the property name. In the panel on the left, for example, you'd type a value in any of the empty background boxes (for example the box to the right of background-repeat). However, since these views aren't the fastest way to edit CSS, you're better off not using them. On a side note, you can click the Delete button to remove a property from a style, and the Disable/Enable button to turn a property off or on—a useful tool to quickly preview, in Design or Live view, how one property affects the appearance of an element.

Show category   Disable/enable

Show list view   Delete property

To add a new property (in the "Show only set properties" mode pictured in Figure 8-4), click the Add Property link below the list of properties in the Properties pane, and then select the property name from the drop-down menu. You set (and can edit) the value of a particular property in the space to the right of the property name. Frequently, you don't have to type in the value. Dreamweaver provides the tools you're likely to need for each property: the ubiquitous color box (see page 159) for any property that requires a color, like a font; a drop-down menu for properties that have a limited list of values, like "Repeat-y" for the *background-repeat* property; and the familiar "Browse for File" folder icon for properties that require a path to a file, such as the *background-image* property.

NOTE The CSS Properties menu that appears when you click inside the Add Property box on the Properties pane provides a comprehensive list of CSS properties. Unlike the CSS Rule Definition window, which only lists well-supported CSS properties from the CSS 2.1 standard, the Properties menu lists not-yet-supported properties from the CSS3 standard, as well as some properties (like "zoom") that apply to only a single browser. In other words, be careful selecting any property that isn't also available from the CSS Rule Definition window...it may not work in all (or even any) browsers. See the section on CSS3 beginning on page 418.

Some other properties, however, require that you know enough CSS to enter the value manually and in the correct format. That's what makes the Properties pane a good advanced option for experienced CSS gurus.

But even those not so experienced with CSS should find the Properties pane helpful. First, it's the best way to get a bird's-eye view of a style's properties. Second, for really basic editing, such as changing the colors used in a style or assigning a style a different font, the Properties pane is as fast as it gets.

To remove a property from a style, delete its value in the right-hand column. Dreamweaver not only removes the value from the style sheet, it deletes the property name as well. In addition, you can right-click (Control-click) a property name and then select Delete from the pop-up menu, or simply click a property name and either press Delete or click the trashcan icon to banish it from your style sheet.

FREQUENTLY ASKED QUESTION

CSS Shorthand

In the CSS Properties pane, sometimes I'll see all the font properties grouped into a single property named font; *other times, font properties are listed individually, like* font-family, font-size, *and so on. Why is that?*

Some CSS properties seem to go together: font properties, background properties (like *background-color, background-image, background-repeat*, and so on), margin, border, padding, and *list-style* properties. CSS supports a shorthand that combines related properties into a single property name. For example, it can combine the *font-family, font-size, font-weight, font-style*, and *line-height* properties into a single property it calls *font*. This shorthand makes writing CSS by hand faster. Instead of typing all the above font properties—one line of CSS code per property—you can combine them into a single line like this:

```
font: italic  bold 16px/150% Tahoma, Ver-
dana, Arial, Helvetica, sans-serif;
```

Dreamweaver uses either the shorthand or longhand method depending on your Preferences settings. Choose Edit→Preferences (Dreamweaver→Preferences) or use the keyboard shortcut Ctrl+U [⌘-U]); click the CSS Styles category to view the settings Dreamweaver uses when it writes CSS code. The top group of checkboxes lets you turn on and off shorthand mode.

If you hand-edit your CSS, you might want to leave the shorthand boxes turned on. If Dreamweaver writes all your CSS code, turn off these boxes, for two reasons. First, unless you know your CSS well, shorthand versions of CSS properties are harder to edit in the Properties pane—it's very easy to mistype something, and many of the friendly drop-down menus (like a list of fonts you can apply to text) that Dreamweaver displays for "longhand" versions of properties don't appear for shorthand versions. Second, with the *background* shorthand property, you can sometimes find yourself in a weird mess, where background colors and images disappear from elements on a page.

■ Moving and Managing Styles

In the old days, when CSS support in web browsers was new, site designers would create just a handful of styles to format headlines and text. Keeping track of a site's styles back then wasn't too hard. Today, with great CSS support in browsers and CSS-based layout the norm, it's not uncommon to create a style sheet with hundreds of styles.

You might want to take a really long, complicated style sheet and split it up into several smaller, easier-to-read external style sheets. One common design practice is to store styles that serve related functions in separate style sheets—for example, all the styles related to formatting web forms would be in one style sheet, styles for text in another, and styles for page layout in yet another. You can then link each of the external style sheets to your site's pages as described on page 138.

Or you might find yourself in the opposite situation: You have too many style sheets and want to combine the styles into a single sheet to cut down on the number of files a web browser needs to download from your web server.

NOTE For really busy websites, the conventional wisdom is to use only a single external style sheet. That's because each request for a new file takes time and server power, so the more requests a browser makes for files, the slower the server performs. But unless your site is as busy as Yahoo, Google, or Amazon, your visitors won't notice if you use one or five external style sheets.

Even if you're not worried about creating new external style sheets (or cutting down on the number you have), it's still useful to organize the styles *within* a style sheet. Web designers frequently use this strategy; for example, they keep all the styles for basic layout in one section of a style sheet, basic tag selectors in another section, and styles for text, images, and other content grouped according to where they use them (sidebar, banner, and so on). By grouping related styles, it's a lot easier to find a particular style when it comes time to edit it.

Fortunately, you don't need to venture into Code view to move styles around in your style sheets. Dreamweaver provides a simple and logical way to do so (and to move styles from one style sheet to another, too).

- To move a style from one place to another in the same style sheet, drag the style in the CSS Styles panel (see Figure 8-6, left). Dreamweaver lists the styles in the order in which they appear in the actual CSS code—so dragging one style below another repositions the CSS code in the style sheet. (Order can be important in CSS for reasons you'll learn starting on page 391, but in a nutshell, CSS gives styles listed lower in a style sheet greater priority if that style conflicts with other styles.) You can select and move more than one style at a time by Ctrl-clicking (⌘-clicking) each style you wish to move and then dragging the highlighted group (Ctrl-click [⌘-click] a selected style to deselect it). Select a range of styles by clicking one style and then Shift-clicking another style: That highlights every style between the two mouse clicks.

 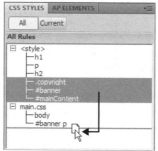

FIGURE 8-6

In the CSS Styles panel, you can drag styles to different locations within a style sheet (left). In this case, dragging the styles below the h1 style groups all the basic tag selectors (body, h1, p, and h2) together. You can also drag styles from one style sheet to another. In the Styles panel on the right, you're moving three styles from an internal style sheet to a CSS file named main.css.

NOTE You'll see the full list of styles in a style sheet (and be able to rearrange those styles) only when you select the All button (circled in Figure 8-6, left) in the CSS Styles panel.

- To move one or more styles *between* two style sheets, drag the style from one sheet to another in the CSS Styles panel. This works both for moving a style from an internal style sheet to an external one and for moving a style from one external style sheet to another. Say you create an internal style sheet for a page and attached an external style sheet to the same page. Dragging a style from the internal style sheet (represented by <style> in the CSS Styles panel) to the external style sheet (represented by its file name—*main.css*, for example) moves the style *out* of the internal style sheet and *into* the external style sheet (Figure 8-6, right). Dreamweaver then deletes the CSS code for the style from the first sheet. You can use the same method to move a style between two attached external style sheets.

  You need to give Dreamweaver a little help if you drag a style into another style sheet and the destination sheet contains a style with the same name. For example, say you define a style for the <body> tag in an internal style sheet, and you've got an external style sheet attached to the same page that also has a body tag style (perhaps with different properties). If you drag the body tag style from one style sheet into another, you're trying to add the same-named style a second time. When this happens, Dreamweaver informs you of the potential problem (see Figure 8-7).

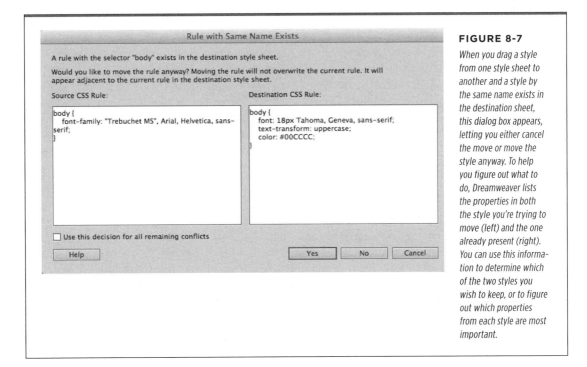

FIGURE 8-7

When you drag a style from one style sheet to another and a style by the same name exists in the destination sheet, this dialog box appears, letting you either cancel the move or move the style anyway. To help you figure out what to do, Dreamweaver lists the properties in both the style you're trying to move (left) and the one already present (right). You can use this information to determine which of the two styles you wish to keep, or to figure out which properties from each style are most important.

NOTE Unfortunately, Dreamweaver doesn't give you a way to reorder the sequence of internal and external style sheets on a page. They're attached to the page in the order in which you added them. For example, if you attach an external style sheet to a web page and then create an internal style sheet, the internal style sheet's code appears *after* the link to the external style sheet. The order of style sheets dictates the order in which a browser downloads those style sheets and can affect how a browser applies styles with conflicting properties (thanks to the CSS Cascade described on page 391). To change the order of the style sheets in the HTML, you have to go into Code view (View→Code) and reorder the <link> tags in the <head> of the HTML document.

You have two choices at that point. You can decide not to move the style and click the No button (the Cancel button has the same effect), and Dreamweaver will close the window without moving the style. Or you can click the Yes button and Dreamweaver will move the style to the style sheet. It doesn't replace the old style, nor does it merge the properties of the two styles. It simply adds the new style to the destination style sheet—in other words, you end up with a style sheet that has two separate styles, each with the same name. Even though this is perfectly valid CSS, it's confusing. Delete one of the styles, and, if necessary, edit the remaining one to add any properties you wanted from the deleted style.

NOTE Dreamweaver says that it will place a style "adjacent" to the style with the same name when it moves like-named styles, but it doesn't. It positions the style wherever you drop it in the list of styles in the destination style sheet.

- You can also move one or more styles to an external style sheet that's not attached to the current page. As discussed on page 123, external style sheets are the most efficient way to style a website's collection of pages. But it's often easier to use an internal style sheet when you first start a design. That's because, as you tweak your CSS, you only have to edit one file (the web page with the internal style sheet in it) instead of two (the web page *and* the external CSS file). But once you finish your design, it's best to move the styles from an internal sheet to an external one. This process is as easy as a right-click (Control-click).

  In the CSS Styles panel, select the styles you want to move to an external style sheet (Ctrl-click [⌘-click] each style name to select it). Right-click (Control-click) the selected styles and choose "Move CSS Rules" (see Figure 8-8, top). The "Move to External Style Sheet" window opens (Figure 8-8, bottom). You can then either add the rules to an existing external style sheet by clicking the browse button and selecting the CSS file or turn on the "A new style sheet" radio button to create a new CSS file and move the styles there. When you click OK, Dreamweaver either moves the styles to an existing CSS file, or it displays a dialog box letting you name and save the new CSS file. Either way, Dreamweaver removes the styles from the internal style sheet and places them into an external sheet; even better, if the external CSS file isn't already attached to the current page, Dreamweaver attaches it for you, which lets you skip the process of manually attaching the sheet.

NOTE If you move all the styles from an internal style sheet to an external one, Dreamweaver still leaves some useless <style> tags in your web page. To remove those, select *style* from the list of styles in the CSS Styles panel and then press the Delete key or click the trashcan icon in the lower-right corner of the Styles panel.

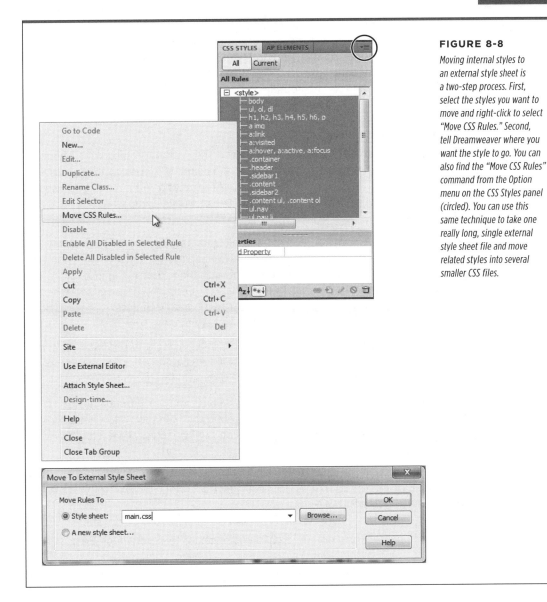

FIGURE 8-8

*Moving internal styles to
an external style sheet is
a two-step process. First,
select the styles you want to
move and right-click to select
"Move CSS Rules." Second,
tell Dreamweaver where you
want the style to go. You can
also find the "Move CSS Rules"
command from the Option
menu on the CSS Styles panel
(circled). You can use this
same technique to take one
really long, single external
style sheet file and move
related styles into several
smaller CSS files.*

More About CSS

As you begin to pile more and more styles into your pages, you may notice that a page might not look exactly as you expect. A paragraph of text might be green even though you didn't create a style for a green paragraph. Or you may have styled a particular paragraph to appear with green text, but it refuses to change color. Most of the time, peculiar behaviors like these occur when styles collide. The rules governing these interactions can be complex, but they boil down to two main concepts: *inheritance* and *the cascade*.

Inheritance

Imagine you create a new style by redefining the paragraph tag (<p>). The style specifies red text displayed in the Arial font at a height of 24 pixels. Then you select a single word in a paragraph and apply bold formatting to it. When you use the Property Inspector's bold button to do this, Dreamweaver wraps that word in a pair of <strong> tags.

When a browser loads the page, it formats all the paragraphs in red Arial text with a font size of 24 pixels, because that's how you defined the <p> tag. But what happens when the browser encounters the paragraph with the <strong> tag in it? Since you didn't redefine the <strong> tag in red, Arial, 24 pixels, the browser scratches its little silicon head: Should the browser resort to its *default* font, text size, and color when it gets to the <strong> tag, ignoring your style rules?

Of course not. The bolded word should look just like the rest of the paragraph: red, Arial, 24 pixels high—and now boldfaced, *too*. And indeed, that's how CSS works: The <strong> tag *inherits* the formatting of the surrounding <p> tag.

Just as human babies inherit traits like eye color from their parents, nested HTML tags inherit the properties of tags that surround them. In fact, a tag nested inside another tag—such as that <strong> tag inside the <p> tag—is called a *child*, while the enclosing tag is called the *parent*.

> **NOTE** As you read on page 377, a tag inside another tag is also called a *descendent* tag, while a tag that surrounds another tag is called its *ancestor*.

Inheritance passes from parent to child and ancestor to descendent. So in this example, the <p> tag (the parent) passes on the red color, Arial font, and 24-pixel size to the <strong> tag (the child). But just as children have their own unique qualities, the <strong> tag adds its own quality—boldness—to the properties it inherits from its parent.

> **NOTE** Inheritance applies to all styles, not just tag styles. For example, if you apply a class style to the <body> tag, then all the tags inside the <body> tag—paragraphs, images, and so on—inherit the properties of the class style.

Inheritance comes in quite handy at times. Say you want to display *all* the text on a page (paragraphs, headings, unordered lists, and links) in the Verdana font. You could dedicate yourself to a lengthy tagging extravaganza and redefine *every* HTML tag used to format text—<h1>, <h2>, <p>, <a>, <ul>, and so on—or create a class style and then manually apply it to all the text on the page.

However, a better and faster technique is to take advantage of inheritance. Every web page contains a <body> tag, which contains *all* the elements of your page. The <body> tag, therefore, is an ancestor to *all* the HTML you see on a page—images, paragraphs, headings, and so on. To quickly format all the text, you can create a style for the <body> tag and set the font to Verdana, or create a class style using that font and apply it to the <body> tag. Every bit of text inside the body—all children—will inherit the Verdana font property.

NOTE Actually, tags don't inherit all CSS properties. For the most part, the exclusions are logical. For example, say you create a border around an unordered list to visually set it off in its own box. If the border property were inherited, all the elements *inside* the unordered list—like list items, links, or bolded words—would each have their own box around them as well. Padding and margin are two other common properties that tags don't inherit.

The Cascade

At times, styles can conflict. Let's say you redefine the <h1> tag in an external style sheet, so that all <h1> headings show up in red Arial font. Then you attach this external style sheet to a web page that has an *internal* style sheet where you set the <h1> tag style to the Times font at 24 pixels high.

When a browser displays an <h1> heading, it runs into a little dilemma. The page specifies two styles—two sets of formatting rules—for the *same tag*. To make matters even more confusing, suppose one <h1> tag has a class named *.highlight* applied to it. The *.highlight* class style sets the font family to Trebuchet MS and makes all the text uppercase. So which style does the browser choose: the style from the internal style sheet, the style from the external style sheet, or the class style?

The answer is "All of them." The browser adopts elements of the three styles according to these hierarchical rules (hence the term "cascade" in "Cascading Style Sheets"):

- Properties that don't conflict are applied as usual. In the previous example, the red color property exists only in the external style sheet, while the internal style specifies only a font *size*. And the class is the only style to specify uppercase text. So far, the browser knows that, for this page, text inside <h1> tags should be red, 24 pixels tall, and uppercase.

- When properties *do* conflict, the browser uses the property from the style with the greatest specificity. Specificity is just CSS jargon that means "the style with the most authority." The type of selector you use on a page is one way to affect specificity: ID selectors are considered more specific than class styles, which are more specific than tag styles. In general, this means that properties from an ID style override properties from a class style, and properties from a class style override conflicts with a tag style. For an amusing—but accurate—description of specificity, read this article: *http://tinyurl.com/7ogaq*. Make sure you print out the accompanying *Star Wars*-themed chart, which visually explains specificity by equating class selectors with Darth Vader and IDs with the Dark Emperor himself: *http://tinyurl.com/dz9cf*. May the force be with you. (If you're more an aquatic-type there's also a CSS "Specifishity" chart at *http://tinyurl.com/89bafl2*.)

- If two styles with the same specificity conflict—like the *h1* style in the external style sheet and the *h1* style in the internal style sheet in this example—the browser chooses the properties from the styles that were added to the page last. Say you first create an internal style sheet (at which point Dreamweaver inserted the appropriate HTML and CSS code into the web page) and *then* attach an external style sheet. That means the link to the external style sheet appears *after* the internal style sheet in the web page. In this case, a style from the external style sheet with the same name as a style from the internal style sheet wins out. Similarly, if you attach the external style sheet first and then create the internal style sheet, the internal style sheet wins.

To summarize this example, then: Once the browser sorts things out, it determines that the text inside an <h1> tag on this web page should be Trebuchet MS and uppercase (from the class style), red (from the *h1* style in the external style sheet), and 24 pixels high (from the *h1* style in the internal style sheet).

NOTE Descendent selectors, which include combinations of tag, class, and ID names, such as *#banner h1*, *.main p*, or *h1 strong*, have even more authority than a tag or class style by themselves, since Dreamweaver calculates specificity by combining all the selectors listed. Say you create a <p> tag style that produces bright-red text, and a descendent selector, *.sidebar p*, with purple text. Any paragraphs inside another element (like a <div> tag) that use the *.sidebar* style are purple—*not* red. Fortunately, Dreamweaver provides several ways to decipher this confusing jumble of conflicting styles (described in the next section).

Inherited properties, however, have no specificity, so when child elements inherit properties from parent elements (as described on page 390), any style applied directly to the child element overrules properties from the parent element—no matter the specificity of the parent tag's style. Suppose you create an ID style named *#homepage* with the following properties: purple text and the Arial font. If you apply the *#homepage* ID to the <body> tag, the child elements (anything within the <body> tag) inherit those properties. If you then redefine the paragraph tag so that it displays text as green, the paragraph text inherits the Arial font from the body, but ignores the purple color in favor of the green. Even though an ID style like *#homepage* has greater authority than a simple *p* tag selector, the properties applied to the paragraph through the <p> tag style overrule the properties inherited from the ID selector.

Because ID selectors are so powerful (they have greater specificity than either class or tag selectors) many web designers steer clear of them. For example, when you create a descendent selector like *#main p*, you can override that style unless you create an even more powerful selector like *#main .special*. This can lead to some really long descendent selectors. If you stick with class and tag selectors, you won't need to work so hard to overcome conflicts caused by the cascade.

To learn more than you probably ever wanted to know about the cascade, visit *www.w3.org/TR/css3-cascade/*.

In *CSS: The Missing Manual*, you'll find chapters dedicated to both inheritance and the cascade.

The Other Side of the CSS Styles Panel

If you haven't yet put this book down in hopes that the swelling in your brain will subside, you've probably absorbed the notion that using multiple style properties can get complex. With all this inheritance and cascading going on, it's easy for styles to collide in hard-to-predict ways. To help you discern how styles interact and to ferret out possible conflicts, Dreamweaver includes a helpful view in the CSS Styles panel (see Figure 8-9); when you click the Current button, the panel switches to Current Selection mode, which tells you how a web browser formats a selected item—such as an image, paragraph, table, or <div> tag—once it takes into account inheritance and the cascade.

Current Selection mode is an invaluable tool in diagnosing weird CSS behavior associated with inheritance and cascading. But like any incredible tool, it requires a good user's manual to learn how it works. The panel crams in a lot of information, but here's a quick overview of what it provides:

* The "Summary for Selection" pane gives you a summary of the style properties for the currently selected item. Remember that whole thing about how parent tags pass on attributes to child tags, and how, as styles cascade through a page, they accumulate (which means, for example, that it's possible to have an <h1> tag formatted by multiple styles from multiple style sheets)? The "Summary for Selection" pane is like the grand total at the bottom of a spreadsheet. It tells you what a selected element—a paragraph, a picture, and so on—will look like when a web browser tallies up all the styles and displays the page. For serious CSS fans, this pane is almost worth the entire price of Dreamweaver.

* The About pane displays the origin of a particular property (Figure 8-9, top). If a headline is orange but you never created an <h1> tag that specified orange text, you can find out which style sheet passed the hideous orange on to the heading. This pane isn't very useful, however, since you can get the same information by mousing over any property in the Summary section. In addition, when you have the About pane visible, you can't see the much more useful Rules pane, discussed next. So you're better off skipping this pane.

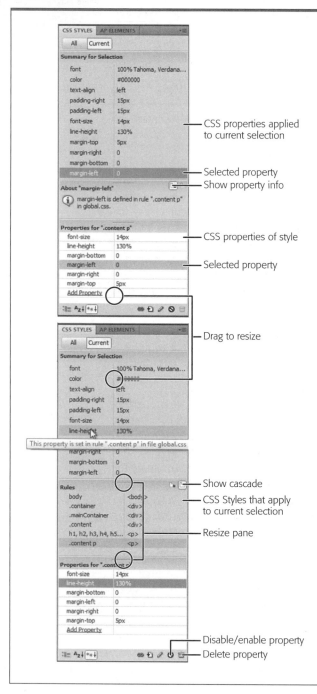

FIGURE 8-9

When you're in Current Selection mode, the views for the middle pane—Property Information (top) and Cascade (bottom)—are mostly the same. Property Information tells you where the selected item gets its properties—that is, the style and style sheets Dreamweaver uses to define the property. Cascade view, however, is far more useful. You can get the same information as in the Property Information view simply by mousing over a CSS property in the Summary pane. For example, in the bottom image, pointing your mouse at the line-height property opens a pop-up tooltip that explains that the property exists in a descendent selector named .content p, defined in an external style sheet named global.css. In addition, Cascade view lists all the styles applied to the currently selected tag. In this case, six styles help format the text currently selected. Unfortunately, out of the box, Dreamweaver thinks you should be looking at the Property Information pane, so one of the first things you should do when you start working with CSS is click the Current button at the top of the CSS Styles panel, and then click the Show Cascade button. Thankfully, Dreamweaver remembers which view you select, so the Cascade view remains selected when you quit and restart Dreamweaver.

- The Rules pane (also called Cascade view) lists the styles that apply to the current selection (Figure 8-9, bottom). Since any element can be on the receiving end of countless CSS properties handed down by parent tags, it's helpful to see a list of all the styles contributing to the current appearance of the selected object.

- The Rules pane shows the order of the cascade. Not only are the styles applied to the current selection listed here, they're listed in a particular order, with the most general at the top and the most specific at the bottom. When the same property exists in two (or more) styles, the style listed last (farthest down the list) wins.

A few examples help demonstrate how to read the CSS Style panel in Current Selection mode. The images in Figure 8-9 show the CSS properties affecting a selection of text (in this case, a paragraph within the main content area of a web page). The "Summary for Selection" pane lets you know that if you viewed this page in a browser, it would display text in the Tahoma typeface in black (#000000), left-aligned, with 15 pixels (px) of left and right padding, at a font size of 14 pixels, with a 130% line height (the space between each line of text), and with 5 pixels of space for the top margin. When you select a property from the "Summary for Selection" pane and then click the Show Property Information button (Figure 8-9, top), the About pane displays where the property comes from—in this case, the margin property settings belong to a descendent selector—*.content p*—which is defined in an external style sheet named *global.css*.

You've seen the bottom part of this pane before. It's the Properties pane, and you use it to delete, add, and edit a style's properties. Simply click in the area to the right of the property's name to change its value, or click the Add Property link to select a new property for the style. Notice that in this example, the Properties pane contains fewer properties than the Summary view. That's because it displays only the properties of a single style (the *.content p* descendent selector), while the Summary view shows all the properties the current selection inherits.

TIP Sometimes, it's hard to see all the information in one or more of the three panes. You can use the gray bars containing the panes' names as handles and drag them up or down to reveal more or less of each pane (see Figure 8-9), or double-click the tab of another open panel (like the Files panel) to close it and provide more room for the CSS Styles panel.

Clicking the Show Cascade button (Figure 8-9, bottom) reveals a list of all the styles that affect the current selection. In this case, you can see that six styles—the body tag style, three class styles (*.container, .mainContainer*, and *.content*), a group selector (*h1, h2, h3, h4, h5, h6, p*), and, finally, the descendent selector *.content p*—contribute to the way the selected paragraph looks. In addition, as mentioned above, the order of the styles is important. The lower the name appears in the list, the more "specific" that style is—in other words, when several styles contain the same property, the property belonging to the style *lower* on the list wins out. (See "The Cascade" on page 391 for more on conflicts caused by cascading styles.)

Clicking a style name in the Rules pane reveals that style's properties in the Properties pane below. This pane not only lists the style's properties, but also crosses out any properties that don't apply to the selected tag. A property doesn't apply to a selection for one of two reasons: either a more specific style overrides the property, or the selected tag doesn't inherit that property.

For example, Figure 8-10 (bottom left), shows that four styles affect the formatting of a single headline: two tag styles (<body> and <h2>) and one class style (.highlight). In the left-hand image, the *color* and *font-size* properties for the *h2* style are crossed out—those properties don't apply to the current selection. The *font-family* property, on the other hand, isn't crossed out, indicating that Dreamweaver displays the current selection using the font Verdana. Because that *h2* appears near the middle of the list of styles in the Rules pane, you can determine that that style is less "specific" (less powerful) than styles listed later. The style that appears last on the list—.highlight in this example—is most "specific" and its properties override conflicts from any other style. Selecting .highlight in the Rules pane (Figure 8-10, bottom right) demonstrates that, yes indeed, its font size and color properties "win" in the battle of cascading style properties.

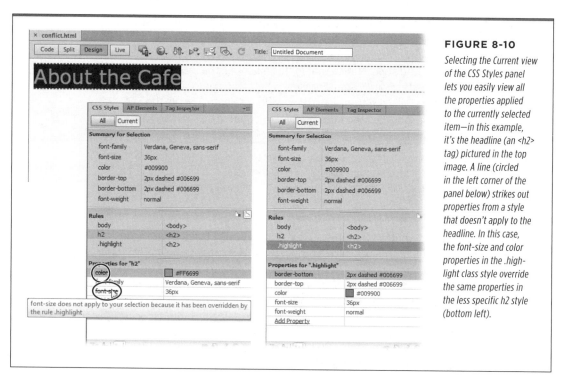

FIGURE 8-10

Selecting the Current view of the CSS Styles panel lets you easily view all the properties applied to the currently selected item—in this example, it's the headline (an <h2> tag) pictured in the top image. A line (circled in the left corner of the panel below) strikes out properties from a style that doesn't apply to the headline. In this case, the font-size and color properties in the .highlight class style override the same properties in the less specific h2 style (bottom left).

TIP If you mouse over a property that's crossed out in the Properties pane, Dreamweaver pops up a tooltip explaining why a browser won't apply that property. If the property is crossed out because a more specific style overrules it, Dreamweaver also tells you which style won out. For example, in Figure 8-10 (bottom left), mousing over the *font-size* property of the *h2* style opens a tooltip explaining that a more specific class style overrides this property.

If your web pages are elegantly simple and use only a couple of styles, you may not find much need for this aspect of the CSS Styles panel. But as you become more proficient (and adventurous) with CSS, you'll find this panel a great way to untangle masses of colliding and conflicting styles.

TIP One way to make a style more "powerful"—so that its properties override properties from conflicting styles—is to use a descendent selector. For example a *body p* descendent selector has more authority than just a plain *p* tag style, even though both styles target the exact same tags. Likewise, a *.content p* style is more powerful than a *body p* style since it applies a class selector (which is more powerful than a tag selector) and one tag selector. You can quickly rename a style or create a more long-winded and powerful descendent selector using the CSS Styles panel; select the name of the style in the CSS Styles panel (you must use the All view), and then click the style name a second time to edit it.

Using the Code Navigator

Dreamweaver includes yet another valuable CSS tool, this one aimed at CSS pros who like to use Code view when they write and edit CSS. The Code Navigator gives you a quick way to see all the CSS styles applied to any element you click on. It's kind of like the Rules pane of the CSS Styles panel, but the CSS styles appear in a pop-up window directly in the document window (see Figure 8-11).

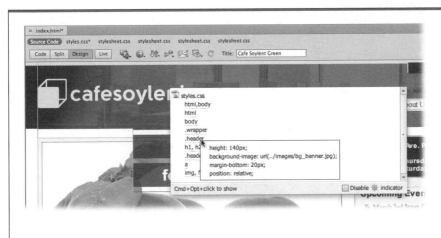

FIGURE 8-11

The Code Navigator displays a list of CSS styles applied to any element on a page. In fact, it can show more than just CSS; if you're working with templates (see Chapter 19) or dynamic, server-side web pages (see Chapter 21), the Code Navigator lists other files that impact the current document, such as a template file or a file with server-side programming.

To launch the Code Navigator, hold down the Alt key and click an element on the page (Mac owners need to press ⌘-Option and click). You can click any element whose CSS you wish to examine: an image, a heading, a paragraph, a table, and so on. For example, in Figure 8-11, Alt-clicking (⌘-Option) the café's logo opened the Code Navigator, which lists the styles that apply to that headline.

You can launch the Code Navigator several other ways:

- Click the Code Navigator icon (the ship steering-wheel icon, circled in Figure 8-12). This icon appears next to an element you select on a page (or above an element when you put your cursor on it). It usually takes a second or so to appear, so you may want to stick with the keyboard shortcut (Alt-click or ⌘-Option-click).

- Right-click any item on the page, and choose Code Navigator from the pop-up menu.

- Select an item on a page and choose View→Code Navigator, or press Ctrl-Alt-N (Windows) or ⌘-Option-N (Macs).

FIGURE 8-12

If the Code Navigator's ever-present steering wheel icon bothers you, get rid of it by turning on the Disable checkbox in the Code Navigator window (see Figure 8-11). From that point on, you open the Code Navigator using the keyboard shortcut or one of the other methods discussed above.

Once the Code Navigator window opens, you see all the CSS styles that affect the current item. In Figure 8-11, for example, the Code Navigator lists nine styles that impact the formatting for the logo image. If you move your mouse over one of the styles, you'll see a list of that style's CSS properties. In Figure 8-11, hovering over the *.header* style lists that style's properties: normal *height* (140px), a *background-image*, and so on. Although this is a quick way to view styles and their properties, it isn't as useful as the Current view of the CSS Styles panel, which shows you exactly which *properties* (not just which styles) apply to the current selection. In addition, the Code Navigator window doesn't always accurately display the CSS cascade (page 391)—it does list the styles in order of specificity, but it splits up the list of styles by style sheet, so if a page has more than one style sheet, you may not get a clear picture of the cascade. The CSS Rules pane (page 393), on the other hand, shows a complete list of styles from least to most specific, regardless of how many style sheets you use.

If you're a code jockey who prefers to type CSS code instead of relying on Dreamweaver's windows and panels, the Code Navigator lets you jump immediately to a style sheet. Open the Code Navigator and click any style listed; Dreamweaver jumps into Split mode (with a view of both the raw code and the page's design) and displays the CSS for the selected style (you'll find more on Split mode on page 335). Of course, you need to know how to write CSS for this to be useful. If you're not comfortable with that, you should stick with the CSS Styles panel and the methods for editing styles, discussed on pages 139 and 382.

◼ Styling for Print

You may be surprised to see a section on print design in a book dedicated to creating beautiful on-screen presentations. However, it's common to see people print out web pages—directions to a concert, a list of product names and ratings, or a long-winded treatise that's easier to read on paper while reclining in a favorite chair.

Unfortunately, some web pages just don't print well. Sometimes the banner's too big to fit on one sheet of paper, so it spans two printed pages; or the heavy use of ads wastes toner. And some CSS-based layouts simply print as jumbled messes. Fortunately, CSS has an answer: *printer style sheets*. The creators of CSS realized that people might use web pages in different ways, such as printing them out. In fact, they went so far as to define a large group of potential "media types" so web designers could customize pages for different output devices, including Teletype machines, Braille readers, and more.

Basically, by specifying a media type, you can attach an external style sheet Dreamweaver applies *only* when someone sends the page to a particular device. For instance, you could have a style sheet that works only when someone looks at a web page on a monitor and another that applies only when they print the page. You can tweak a page's styles so it looks good when you print it out without affecting its appearance on-screen. Figure 8-13 shows the concept in action.

The basic process involves creating an external style sheet that contains styles for the particular media type, and then attaching the style sheet to a web page and assigning the appropriate media type.

You learned how to attach an external style sheet on page 138, but in a nutshell, you simply click the Attach External Style Sheet button on the CSS Styles panel (see Figure 3-1). That opens the Attach External Style Sheet window (see Figure 8-14). Click the browse button and locate the CSS file, select the media type from the drop-down Media menu, and then click OK.

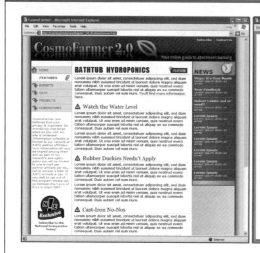

FIGURE 8-13

*When you print a web
page (left), you really
don't need its navigation
links or information unrelated to the topic at hand.
Create a print style sheet
to eliminate unneccessary
content and format the
page so it looks nice
when printed (right).*

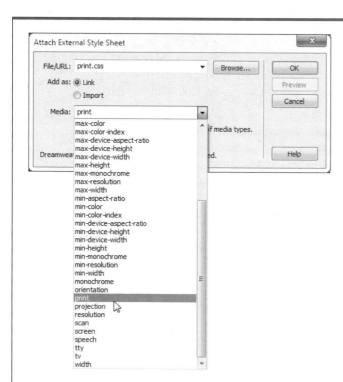

FIGURE 8-14

*When you attach an external style sheet, you can
assign it to a specific output device, such as a printer
("print") or monitor ("screen"). Or, you can use a
single style sheet no matter what the output device
("all"). Leaving the Media option blank is the same as
selecting "all." Dreamweaver CS6 includes lots of options in the menu, like max-width or min-color. You
use them to specify styles used only when a browser
encounters certain conditions (like a screen that's no
wider than 480 pixels). Most of these options aren't
that useful, but some are great for creating different
designs for mobile phones. You'll learn about these
other "media queries" on page 510.*

Although Dreamweaver lists many media types, it includes only three related to crafting printer style sheets: *print, screen*, and *all*. "Print" specifies that the styles apply only when someone prints the page; "screen" indicates a style sheet that takes effect only when the page appears on a display; and "all" is the same as not selecting anything—the style sheet applies when you print the page, view it on a monitor, feel it on a Braille reader, and so on. The "all" option comes in handy when you want to create a style sheet that defines the basic look of your website—such as its font, line height, and text alignment—no matter whether someone prints it or views it on-screen. You can create two additional style sheets from this basic one, one specifically designed for print, the other for monitors.

Previewing Media Styles in Dreamweaver

Web designers use Dreamweaver mainly to create pages that people view on-screen. Because of that, the program displays formatted pages only when you either haven't selected a media type at all or when you specify the "all" or "screen" type. So how can you see what a printed version of the page will look like when you design a print style sheet? Dreamweaver sports a fancy toolbar just for this purpose: the Style Rendering toolbar (Figure 8-15). To turn it on, choose View→Toolbars→Style Rendering, or right-click (Control-click) the Document toolbar, and then choose Style Rendering.

Each button in the toolbar lets you view the page as it will look onscreen, in print, or with one of the other media types. Click the Screen button to see how Dreamweaver (and a web browser) normally display the page. Click the Print button, and any styles attached using the "print" and "all" media types appear; in other words, when you design a page for print, click the Print button.

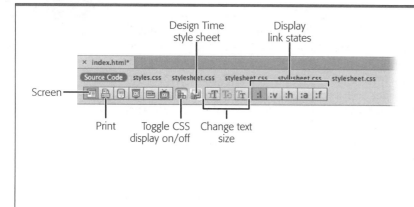

FIGURE 8-15

The Style Rendering toolbar lets you see styles that match the media type you selected when you attached the style sheet to the page. It also includes buttons to attach a Design Time style sheet (see the box on page 405) and to hide all the styles. This last option is particularly useful when you create complex CSS-based designs, which can sometimes make selecting and editing HTML difficult. Click the Toggle CSS Display button to temporarily hide the styles and display just the simple, unadorned HTML.

NOTE If your CSS styles don't seem to have any effect on a page, you either have the wrong media type selected in the Style Rendering toolbar, or you might have turned off the effect of CSS by clicking the Toggle CSS Display button. Click the button again to display the CSS-styled page.

FREQUENTLY ASKED QUESTION

Other Options in the Style Rendering Toolbar

There are other buttons besides the media buttons on the Style Rendering toolbar. What do they do?

The Style Rendering toolbar provides a few other options for previewing HTML elements in Design view. Three buttons control the size of text and five others let you preview links in different "states" (see Figure 8-15). From left to right, the three text buttons let you increase, reset, and decrease the size of text; that lets you see what happens to your design when someone increases or decreases the default text size in a browser. While this might have been a cool tool a few years back (when all browsers had an "increase text size" command), times have changed. Browsers now rely on a "zoom" feature, which not only increases the size of text, but of everything else on the page, too. In other words, these buttons aren't really useful, so skip them.

The link buttons, however, *are* useful—they let you preview your links in various states. As mentioned on page 206, you can style links to look different depending on whether a visitor has yet to click a link, is currently clicking it, has already clicked it, moves her mouse over it, or tabs to it. Normally, Dreamweaver displays just the plain-vanilla link style—the way a link looks when a guest has never visited it. Click any link button: *:l* for the unclicked state, *:a* for the active (being clicked) state, *:v* for the *:visited* state, *:h* for the *:hover* (mouseover) state, and *:f* for the *:focus* (tabbed-to) state. In other words, if you create different styles for different link states, these buttons let you see what they look like.

Tips for Printer Style Sheets

A printer style sheet can redefine the look of any element on a page when you print that page. You can change fonts, adjust type size, increase leading (the space) between lines of text, and so on. You can use any CSS property you want, and modify any style to your liking, but there are a few common tasks that most printer style sheets perform.

- **Override properties from another style sheet**. If you attach an external style sheet with the "all" media type or you didn't specify any media type at all, the printed page uses styles from that style sheet. When you create the print style sheet, you may need to override some of the settings in the web page's style sheet. The best way to do this is to simply create styles with names that match the styles you wish to override. For example, if a style sheet attached to a page has a *p* tag style that specifies a font size of 12 pixels, you can create another *p* tag style in the print style sheet that changes the font size to 12 points. (Due to the rules of the cascade [page 391], the printer style sheet needs to be attached *last* to the web page for its styles to overrule similarly named styles in another sheet.)

  Another solution is to simply create two style sheets—one for print and one for monitors—and attach each with its respective media type. This way, there won't be any overlap between styles in the two sheets.

- **Text size and color**. You size text that appears on-screen using pixels, ems, or percentages (see page 154). Unfortunately, these units of measure don't make a lot of sense to an inkjet printer. If you've used Microsoft Word, you probably know the measurement of choice for printed text is points. If you don't like the size of type when you print a page, redefine font sizes using a printer-friendly size. In addition, while bright yellow type on a black background may look cool on-screen, black type on white paper is the easiest to read. If you colored your text, it may print out as a shade of gray on a black-and-white printer. Setting text to black in a print style sheet can help your visitors' weary eyes.

- **Hide unnecessary page elements**. Guests don't really need to (and often times don't want to) print some parts of a web page (a navigation menu or a sidebar of links, for example). After all, you can't click them! Fortunately, CSS provides a property that lets you hide unwanted page elements on printed pages. Just create a style that applies to the part of the page you want to hide—for instance, with CSS-based layouts, you typically divide a page into sections using <div> tags, each with its own unique ID. Say you have the site's navigation bar inside a tag that has a class named *.navbar* attached to it. To hide the nav bar when someone prints the page, create another class style named *.navbar* in your print style sheet. In the CSS Rule Definition window, click the Block category and then choose "None" from the Display property menu. (In Figure 8-13, right, for example, the banner and both sidebars don't appear in the printed version of the page.)

- **Adjust margins and widths**. To make a website look more elegant, you might increase the margins around the edges of a page. But this extra space only wastes paper when printed. In the print style sheet, remove any margins you applied to the body tag. In addition, if you hide parts of a page when it's printed, it's possible that the remaining page elements won't fill the printed page. In this case, add a style to the print style sheet that changes the widths of the printed elements. For example, if you have a two-column design—a sidebar with links and other site-specific info and a main column filled with all the useful info that should appear on a printed page—and you hide one column (the sidebar), you'd then set the width of the remaining column to 100% and remove any margins on its left and right sides. That way, the printed information fills the width of the page.

- **Take advantage of !important**. As mentioned earlier, sometimes the print style sheet needs to override certain CSS properties from another style sheet. Thanks to the cascade (page 391), a style must have greater "specificity" to overrule another style. If you're trying to override, say, the font color used for a descendent selector named *body #wrapper #maincontent p*, you have to add the same long-winded style name to your print style sheet. Fortunately, CSS provides a simpler method: the *!important* directive. Adding *!important* to a property in a CSS style lets that property overrule any conflicting property values from other styles, even if those other styles are more specific.

Unfortunately, Dreamweaver doesn't give you a way to easily add this option. You have to manually edit the style sheet in Code view. Say you want the text of all paragraph tags to print black. Create a *p* tag style in the print style sheet and set the *color* property to "black." Then open the print style sheet in Code view and add *!important* after the color value and before the semicolon. Here's what that would look like in Code view:

```
p {
    color: #000000 !important;
}
```

When you print the page, this style overrides any color settings for any paragraph tags in a competing style sheet—even a much more specific style.

A Time to Design

A Dreamweaver feature called *Design Time style sheets* lets you quickly try different CSS style sheets as you develop web pages. With it, you can hide (external) style sheets you've attached to a web page and substitute new ones.

Design Time style sheets come in handy when you work on HTML that, later on, you intend to make part of a complete web page. Dreamweaver Library items are a good example; this feature (discussed in Chapter 18) lets you create a chunk of HTML that any number of pages on your site can use. When you update the Library item, Dreamweaver updates every page that uses it. A timesaving feature, for sure, but since a Library item is only *part* of a page, it doesn't include the <head> portion needed to either store styles or attach an external style sheet. So when designing a Library item, you're working in the dark (or at least without any style). By using Design Time style sheets, you can access all the styles in an external style sheet and even preview the effects directly in Design view.

You can apply a Design Time style sheet by clicking the Design Time style sheet button in the Style Rendering toolbar (see Figure 8-15) or by choosing Format→CSS Styles→Design-Time.

The Design-Time Style Sheets window appears. Click the top + button to select an external style sheet. Note that clicking this button doesn't attach the style sheet to the page; it merely lets you access the properties of a .css file as you work on a page.

To properly view your page with this new style sheet, you may need to get an attached external style sheet out of the way. To do that, use the bottom + button to add it to the Hide list.

You can only use Design Time style sheets when you work in Dreamweaver. They have no effect on how a page looks in a web browser. That's both the good news and the bad news. Although Dreamweaver lets you apply class styles from a Design Time style sheet to your web page, it doesn't actually attach the sheet to the page. For example, if you use a Design Time style sheet to design a Library item, Dreamweaver doesn't guarantee that the web page using the Library item has the style sheet you're using attached to it. You have to attach it yourself, or else your visitors will never see your intended result.

CSS Transitions

In Chapter 4 you learned about the *:hover* pseudo-class, which lets you change the style of a link as a visitor mouses over it. For example, the background color of a link in a navigation bar might be deep blue, but when a visitor mouses over that link, the background changes to bright orange. That change, from blue to orange, is instantaneous, but it might feel a bit abrupt to some. What if you could animate the change so that the link starts out blue and then morphs, moving through a range of colors on the way to turning solid orange. When you mouse off the link, the color would animate back from orange to blue. Now *that* would be cool...and, thanks to CSS3's new CSS Transitions property, it's easy to achieve.

In a nutshell, a CSS transition is an animation between one or more CSS properties to another set of CSS properties. Web browsers handle the animation: You only need to supply the starting point (the blue background of a link, for instance) and the ending point (the orange background). You also need to add the CSS Transition property, which, unfortunately, requires a fair amount of code. However, Dreamweaver CS6 provides a simple, straightforward tool for creating that code: the new CSS Transitions panel. Here's how you use it:

NOTE CSS transitions are fun and look great, but they're relatively new, so not all browsers support them. While Safari, Firefox, and Chrome understand CSS transitions, only version 10 of Internet Explorer (which isn't even shipping at the time of this writing) does. That means that over half of the web-surfing world won't be able to enjoy your finely crafted CSS transitions...yet. But since CSS transitions are really just eye candy anyway, visitors coming to your site with IE 7, 8, or 9 won't know what they're missing.

1. **Create a style for an element on your page.**

   That element can be a class, tag, ID, or any CSS selector style. The element's style represents the beginning of the animation, and you can use a wide range of CSS properties, including *background-color, background-position* (page 264); *border-color* and *border-width* (page 260); *color* (page 157); *font-size* (page 154); *font-weight* (page 161); *margins* (page 449); *padding* (page 449); *width* and *height* (page 448); the left, top, bottom and right position settings (page 470); *word-spacing* (page 164); and more. (You can find a complete list of valid, animate-able properties at *http://tinyurl.com/dxjbdhd*, though not all browsers support all the properties.)

   If you're creating a style for a nav button, for example, you could start with a simple class (*.nav*) that you apply to each link you want to animate. Or, if all the nav buttons are together inside a single div tag or unordered list, you could add a class name to the div or list tag (<ul class="nav", for example) then use a descendent selector (discussed on page 377) like .nav a to style all the links.

2. **Choose Window→CSS Transitions to open the CSS Transitions panel (see Figure 8-16).**

   The CSS Transitions panel lists any CSS transitions already applied to the page. You can use the panel to add new transitions or edit or delete existing ones.

TIP When you first open the CSS Transitions panel, it appears as a floating window; you can dock it with any other group of panels simply by dragging the panel over the tab in any panel group; when a blue outline appears around the panel group, let go; the CSS Transitions panels then pops into place. A good spot to dock it is next to the CSS Styles panel.

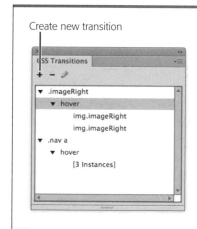

Create new transition

FIGURE 8-16

The CSS Transitions panel lets you add, edit, and delete animations between CSS properties. It lists all the CSS transitions defined in the style sheet (or style sheets) for the currently open web page.

3. **Click the New Transition button (the + sign).**

The New Transition window appears (see Figure 8-17).

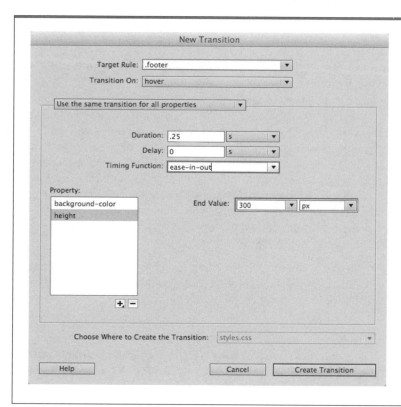

FIGURE 8-17

The New Transition window looks a bit overwhelming at first, but it's really an easy way to create a CSS transition: identify a page element you want to animate using the Target Rule menu, specify a trigger for the animation (the "Transition on" option), choose a CSS property you want to animate, and then set some timing options.

4. **From the Target Rule menu, select the style you created in step 1.**

This menu lists all the styles in the page's style sheet, including tag styles, class styles, IDs, and so on. It also lists any IDs applied to page elements, even if you never created an accompanying ID style, which comes in handy if you simply want to animate an element without first creating an ID style for it.

5. **From the Transition On menu, select the trigger for the animation.**

Unfortunately, you can't just animate an element whenever you like—you're limited to a handful of events related to CSS selectors. The :*hover* pseudo-class is the most well-known, but there are others you can tap into:

- *active* refers to the moment you click on a link. It's the same as the :*active* pseudo-class discussed on page 206. Browsers also apply an active state to any time you click on an element and hold the mouse button down. In other words, you could create a CSS animation so that when a visitor clicks on a particular <div> element and holds the mouse button down, that div's background color changes, its width increases, and its font size grows.

- *checked* applies to checkboxes (page 576) and radio buttons. However, there aren't a lot of CSS properties that apply to checkboxes and radio buttons that are worth animating.

- *disabled* and enabled apply to form elements visitors can't select or change. Since you can't disable or enable a form element without JavaScript, you probably won't ever need to use either of these settings.

- *focus* refers to text fields in web forms. When a visitor either clicks into or tabs to a text field, that field receives what's called "focus." You can apply a separate set of styles to a field when it's focused and animate the change between the look of the field as it normally appears and as it appears when a guest clicks into it to type. For example, you could set the height of a multi-line text field (also called a *textarea*, as described on page 575) to 100 pixels, and then create a CSS transition that changes the field's height to 500 pixels. When a visitor clicks into that text box, it grows to 500 pixels high, and when the visitor tabs or clicks out of the box, it shrinks back to 100 pixels. Likewise, you could set the background color of a text field to white, but when a visitor clicks into it, the background slowly changes to bright yellow.

- *hover* is the most commonly used option. It applies when a visitor mouses over an element. While you'll commonly use the hover transition with links, you can apply it to any page element: paragraphs, div tags, headlines, and so on.

- You probably won't ever use the *indeterminate* setting. It applies only to checkboxes and radio buttons, and refers to a checkbox or radio button that is neither turned on or off. Sounds very Zen, but it's also very useless. You can only specify the *indeterminate* setting using JavaScript, and since you probably won't ever need to use the state, there's no need to create an animation for it, either.

- *target* applies to named anchors, described on page 202, and it applies when a visitor clicks a link that jumps to that anchor. For example, say you add a link at the top of a page that jumps down the page to a named anchor. You could add a background color and a CSS transition to that named anchor so that when a visitor clicks the link and jumps to that spot on the page, the color fades into view.

> **NOTE** For some ideas on what you can do with the CSS *:target* pseudo-class check out *http://tinyurl .com/6mxqbz7* and *http://css-tricks.com/on-target/*.

6. **Choose either "Use the same transition for all properties" or "Use a different transition for each property."**

   As you'll see in steps 7-9, you can set a duration for the animation (how long it takes), a delay (how long before it begins), and a "timing function" (the rate of change during the animation). You can apply the same settings to all CSS properties or set different timings for each property. For example, if, when a visitor mouses over a navigation button, you want that button to change from blue to orange, have its text grow from 16 to 25 pixels, and enlarge its border from 1 pixel to 10 pixels in width, you have a choice. You can have all three animations occur at the same rate, or set different rates for each. For example, you could have the background color change quickly, make the border change more slowly, and wait for a second before the text increases in size; to do this, you'd choose the "Use a different transition for each property" option.

   Depending on which selection you make, the next steps will vary. If you selected the "Use the same transition" option, continue to the next step. If you selected "Use a different transition," skip to steps 10 and 11 to add a CSS property to animate, and then jump back to steps 7– 9 to set the duration, delay, and timing function for that property.

7. **Type a number in the Duration box and select either "s" (for seconds) or "ms" (for milliseconds) from the menu to the right.**

   The duration specifies how long the animation takes. While it may seem cool to slowly change the background color over the course of 10 seconds, most web surfers are impatient and don't want to wait to savor your carefully choreographed animation. A good value is .25 seconds (250 milliseconds)—that speed is fast enough for anxious visitors, but slow enough so they can see it. However, you may want to try .5 seconds (500 milliseconds) or longer to see how the effect looks.

   As mentioned in step 6, you can set different timings for each property, so you might want one animation to happen really quickly (like a change in the text size), but another (like a change in background color) to happen more slowly.

NOTE Don't leave the Duration box blank. Otherwise, the transition takes place immediately, with no animation.

8. **Type a number in the Delay box and select either "s" (for seconds) or "ms" (for milliseconds) from the menu to the right.**

The delay value indicates how long the browser should wait before starting the animation. In general, it's best to type 0, since waiting for any significant amount of time before starting the animation might confuse visitors. In addition, an animated transition reverses itself the moment the "trigger" stops: In other words, if a visitor mouses over a link, the animation begins, but when he moves the mouse off the link, the animation stops (even if the animation hasn't ended) and goes back to the original CSS property. If you add a long delay, then, your visitors may never see the animation.

9. **Choose an animation speed from the Timing Function drop-down menu.**

While the duration setting indicates how long the animation takes from start to finish, the timing function (also known as an "easing" function) controls the rate of change in an animation. Normally, a CSS transition doesn't progress at the same speed for the entire animation. That is, if you're changing the background of a link from blue to orange, the background color will start moving toward orange slowly at first; more quickly in the middle, reaching a more orangish color rapidly; and then slowly turning solid orange at the end. Different timing functions specify different rates of change. You can get some interesting and more "natural"-looking animations with different options:

- The cubic Bezier setting is the most complex. It requires four numbers that plot four "control points" along a line. Each point is a number from 0 to 1. In reality, all the timing functions follow what's called a Bezier curve that plots the amount of visual change over time (if you've worked with a drawing program, you've probably used Bezier "handles" to add curves to lines). The math isn't worth explaining (that's just our way of saying it's too confusing even for us), so you're better off using an online tool to create and test different settings. The "CSS cubic-bezier Builder" tool at *http:// tinyurl.com/bljzsxl* is particularly good. It lets you drag the control handles around and test how the animation changes over time. Once you find a curve you like, just note the four numbers and type them into the Timing Function box: for example, cubic-bezier(.17, 1, .78, .42).

- The ease option is the normal way a transition animates: slowly at first, rapidly in the middle, and then slowly at the end.

- The ease-in setting begins slowly at first, then picks up speed to finish the animation rapidly.

- The ease-in-out option begins very slowly, proceeds very rapidly in the middle and ends very slowly.

- The ease-out option begins very quickly, and then ends slowly.

- The linear option provides a smooth animation, where every step in the show represents the same amount of progress. There's a reason that this setting isn't the default for animations...it's just boring.

TIP The best way to pick a timing function is simply by experimenting. Try different settings and see which you like best. You can always go back and edit the setting, as described in Figure 8-18.

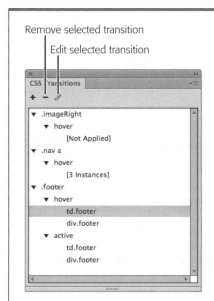

Remove selected transition

Edit selected transition

FIGURE 8-18

To edit a transition, simply select the triggering event (hover, active, and so on) in the CSS Transitions panel, and then click the edit button. Deleting a transition is a bit more complicated, as explained next.

10. **From the Property menu (Figure 8-17) pick the CSS Property you want to animate.**

While the list is very long, there are a few properties that work particularly well. Any property that uses color, like the *background-color, border-color,* and *color* properties, are good candidates; positioning properties like left, right, top, and bottom (used with absolutely positioned elements, described in Chapter 9) also look great when animated, as do the width and height properties. Some animated properties don't look very good or don't work at all in most browsers. For example, while Chrome can animate a change in *background-image*, no other browsers can, and animating *font-weight* (from normal to bold, for example) doesn't work in any browser.

You should select a CSS property that you specified in the original selector you chose for step 4. For example, if you want to animate the background color of an element, make sure you first give the element a background color before you add a CSS transition to it. While it's possible to animate a property without first adding that property to the beginning style (the Target selector), it sometimes produces weird results.

11. **Set the value for the property in the End Value box.**

What you add to this box depends on what property you selected. If you pick the *background-color* property, for example, Dreamweaver displays a color picker box; either select a color from it or type a color value into the box (see page 160 for more on CSS colors). If you pick a property that requires a numeric value, like *width*, *height*, *margin-left*, and so on, Dreamweaver displays two options: a box to enter a value and a menu for selecting a measurement unit, like px (pixels), em, or % (see page 154 for more on CSS measurement units).

If, in step 6, you chose to set a different transition for each property, go back to steps 7– 9 to set the timing options for this particular property.

12. **Continue to add additional properties following steps 10 and 11.**

You don't need to animate every CSS property applied to an element. Trying to add too many visual changes at once not only slows down the browser, it also probably distracts your audience. One or two animated changes is often enough to capture people's attention.

13. **From the "Choose Where to Create the Transition" menu, select which style sheet you want to add the transition information to.**

CSS transitions are really just CSS styles, so you store them in either an internal or external style sheet. This is the same choice you make when creating any CSS style, as described on page 128. In general, it's best to store the style in the same external style sheet you use for all the styles in your site.

14. **Click Create Transition.**

Dreamweaver closes the New Transition window, adds the required CSS to the page's style sheet, and lists the animation in the CSS Transitions panel (see Figure 8-18).

NOTE If you choose to create a CSS transition using a class style as the target (step 4 on page 408), Dreamweaver adds the class name to the HTML element currently selected (or where your cursor is currently positioned). This can be a bit disorienting since, if you aren't paying attention and simply create a CSS transition, Dreamweaver will apply that class to the current element, possibly significantly altering the look of that tag. Simply remove the unwanted class from the tag (see page 137); this won't remove the CSS transition, so it will still work for the elements you intended.

Understanding the CSS Transitions Panel

Dreamweaver's CSS Transitions panel isn't completely straightforward. There are three parts to each transition listed in the panel: the target selector, the triggering event, and a list of matched elements. On the far left are the CSS selectors—they represent the selectors the transition targets, and they're the same as the targets you selected in step 4 on page 408, when you created the transition. For example, in Figure 8-18 you can see *.imageRight*, *.nav a*, and *.footer*. Those are three selectors: two class selectors and a descendent selector (*.nav a*), which targets links inside another element that has the class *.nav* applied to it.

Next, the action that triggers the transition appears indented underneath each selector. For example, the *.imageRight* class has a hover transition, as do all the links inside another page element with the class .nav.

You can have more than one trigger listed for a target. For example, you could create a transition that appears when a visitor mouses over an element and a different transition when a visitor clicks the link (or makes it active): That's the case for the *.footer* element in Figure 8-18.

Indented below the trigger event is a list of the elements that match the target selector. While the list of target selectors and triggers are defined in the style sheet the page uses, the elements list is specific to each page. For example, in Figure 8-18, Dreamweaver lists the hover transition for the *.imageRight* class selector as "[Not applied]." That means that Dreamweaver won't apply the transition to any element on the page because no HTML tag has the *.imageRight* class applied to it; there may be a tag with that class applied to it on another page that uses the same style sheet, but not on this page.

The same transition may also apply to more than one element on the page. This is common when you apply a CSS transition to each button in a navigation bar. In Figure 8-18, for example, the panel states that there are "[3 instances]" of the button transition on the page, meaning three links on this page use the same transition. Likewise, you see *td.footer* and *div.footer* listed under both the active and hover triggers of the *.footer* selector. This means that there is one <td> tag and one <div> tag with the *.footer* class applied to them, and both of those elements have a CSS transition for hover and active states. If you apply the *.footer* class to additional elements on the page, Dreamweaver lists those as well.

Deleting a CSS Transition

Deleting a CSS transition is more complicated than you might think. As discussed in the box on page 416, Dreamweaver acts on two styles each time you add a transition: the initial target selector (the style before the animation begins) and the finished state (a pseudo-class like *:hover* or *:active* [see page 206]). So when you delete a CSS transition, Dreamweaver can immediately tell which styles you wish to edit.

To remove a CSS transition:

1. **Select the target selector (for example, *.imageRight*, *.nav a*, or *.footer*) and click the minus-sign icon (a.k.a. the Remove Transition button).**

   Dreamweaver opens the Remove Transition window (Figure 8-19).

   If you have more than one trigger event (like hover and active) on the same element, you can select the trigger to remove just that transition (active, for instance), and leave the other one alone (the hover transition, for example). If there are two trigger events and you choose the target selector, you can delete all the transitions for that selector.

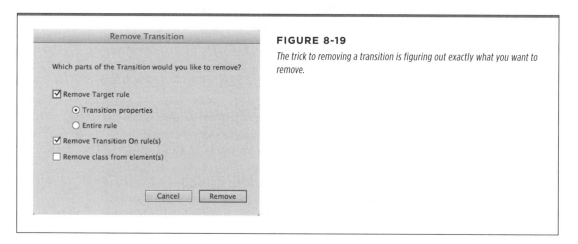

FIGURE 8-19

The trick to removing a transition is figuring out exactly what you want to remove.

2. **In the Remove Transition window, turn on the checkboxes that tell Dreamweaver what you'd like to remove.**

   Here's the confusing part about deleting a transition. Dreamweaver gives you several options, which have different effects.

   • The Remove Target rule option relates to the style that controls the appearance of the target element—that is, the style that defines the look of the element before the transition begins. As mentioned in the box on page 416, that initial style also contains the CSS transition property—the CSS property that tells a web browser that you want to animate a change in the CSS.

   Choose the "Transition properties" radio button if you simply want to remove the CSS transition property but leave the rest of the style untouched. You'll usually select this option, since the style will also contain properties you'd like to preserve, like the *font*, *font-size*, *background-color*, *margin*, *padding*, and so on. However, if you really want to completely remove a style, formatting and all, turn on the "Entire rule" radio button. Just keep in mind that this removes all the formatting applied by that style to the target element.

- Turn on the Remove Transition On rule(s) checkbox to delete the pseudo-class style (*:hover*, *:active*, and so on) that Dreamweaver added to your style sheet. This removes the end result of the animation—the style that formats the element when a visitor interacts with it (by hovering over the element, for example). Leave this checkbox turned off if you simply want to remove the animation. For example, you may find that you like the abrupt change in background when a visitor mouses over a link and you prefer to not have a smooth animated change. If that's the case, turn on the "Remove Target rule" checkbox, and select the "Transition properties" button, but leave the "Remove Transition On rule(s)" and the "Remove class from element(s)" checkboxes turned off.

- The Remove class from element(s) checkbox appears only if you apply a transition to a class selector (*.imageRight*, for example). Turning on this checkbox simply removes that class from any HTML tag on the page, so use this checkbox when you want to completely remove all traces of a transition, including the styles and classes used in it. However, if you're keeping the initial class style and its formatting (but not its transition properties), don't turn on this checkbox—that way, you'll leave the class on the HTML tag, and the remaining styling information will still apply to that element.

So, in a nutshell, if all you want to do is remove an animation, turn on the "Remove Target rule" checkbox, turn on the "Transition properties" radio button, and leave all the other checkboxes turned off. If you want to erase everything Dreamweaver added, turn on the "Remove Target rule" checkbox, select the "Transition properties" button, and turn on the "Remove Transition On rule(s)" checkbox.

3. **Click Remove.**

The Remove Transition window closes and Dreamweaver makes the requested changes, altering styles and the HTML where needed. Because Dreamweaver might make several changes at this point, you can't simply choose Edit→Undo to reverse the Remove Transition action, so be careful when you delete a transition.

Behind the Scenes of CSS Transitions

Dreamweaver CS6's CSS Transitions panel makes it easy to create complex animated transitions. Behind the scenes, however, Dreamweaver generates quite a bit of CSS. As you've read, a CSS transition is an animation between changes in CSS properties. You define those properties in two separate styles, the first defines the beginning of the animation, and the second specifies the final set of properties at the end of the animation. For example, creating an a tag style for the <a> tag sets the style for links on a page, while an a:hover style sets the appearance of links when a visitor mouses over them.

When you create a CSS transition and set the Transition On property to "hover" (see step 5 on page 408), Dreamweaver creates a new style with the *:hover* pseudo-class for whatever selector you chose in step 4 on page 408. For example, say you had an image on the page with the class .imgBorder applied to it. You want to add a cool animation that changes the border color around that image when a visitor mouses over it. By following the steps starting on page 406, you add a new CSS transition. Dreamweaver creates a new style named .imgBorder:hover with the new border color you specified. The CSS for that would look something like this:

```
.imgBorder:hover {
    border-color: #457348;
}
```

By itself, this new rule doesn't have any special CSS transition magic at all. It simply changes the border color when someone mouses over that image. To get the animation effect, Dreamweaver has to add another CSS property to the original style—in this example, to the *.imgBorder* class style. That's how CSS transitions work: You add the transition property to the starting point for the animation, the style that formats the element when the page first loads. That way, a web browser knows that it needs to animate the changes from this style to the *:hover* style.

Unfortunately, because the transition property hasn't yet been finalized by the W3C (the group that determines how CSS works), each browser requires its own special version of the transition property, which is preceded with a special prefix, -ms for Internet Explorer, -webkit (Safari and Chrome), -moz (Firefox), and -o (Opera). That means that to add a CSS transition, Dreamweaver actually has to write 5 lines of CSS, not just one:

```
.imgBorder {
    border: 10px solid #758837;
    -webkit-transition: border-color .5s
ease-out;
    -moz-transition: border-color .5s ease-
out;
    -ms-transition: border-color .5s ease-
out;
    -o-transition: border-color .5s ease-
out;
    transition: border-color .5s ease-out;
}
```

Thankfully, Dreamweaver takes care of all this coding for you.

Another Way to Create CSS Transitions

Dreamweaver CS6 adds yet another way to create CSS transitions, though this method requires that you know how CSS transitions really work (to find out, read the box above). To animate CSS transitions, you use the CSS3 Transition property. Dreamweaver CS6 lets you add that property when you create a style using the CSS Rule Definition window (see Figure 8-20).

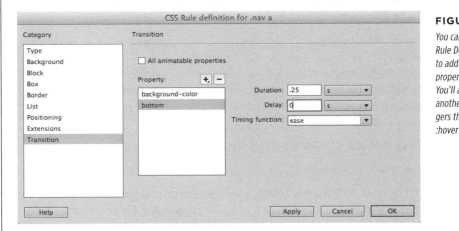

FIGURE 8-20

You can use the CSS Rule Definition window to add a CSS transition property to any element. You'll also need to create another style that triggers the transition, like a :hover pseudo-class style.

To create a transition using the Transition property:

1. **Create a style to format the element whose transition you want to animate.**

   For example, a link in a navigation bar, a form field, and so on. This style represents the beginning of the animation. (See page 125 for a recap on how to create a style.)

2. **Make sure the Rule Definition window is open for that style and select the Transition category.**

   You can add a transition after you create a style—just edit the existing style by double-clicking its name in the CSS Styles panel.

3. **Choose which property you wish to animate by turning off the "All animatable properties" checkbox, clicking the + button, and then selecting a CSS property (like background color or height).**

   Of course, instead of picking which property to animate, you can leave the "All animatable properties" checkbox turned on. This tells a browser to animate any changes in style properties. This may be what you're after, but in many cases you'll only want one property to change. For example, say you have a link with a background color, a font color, and a 1-pixel border. You then create a *:hover* pseudo-class style that sets different background and font colors and a different size border. If you want the browser to animate both color and border changes, then you'd leave the "All animatable properties" box turned on. But if you want only the background color animated, you'd turn off the checkbox, click the + button, and then select *background-color* from the menu.

4. **Type a Duration and Delay amount, and pick a timing function.**

   These settings are described in steps 7–9 on page 409–410.

5. **Repeat steps 3–4 to add more CSS properties, and then click OK to complete the style.**

   Dreamweaver writes the necessary CSS code to add a transition to the style—but you're not done yet. There won't be any animation until you also add a style that defines the formatting for the end of the transition. Dreamweaver's New Transition window (Figure 8-17) handles this part automatically, but when you create a transition using the Rule Definition window, you need to define this style yourself.

6. **Click the New CSS Rule button on the CSS Styles panel.**

   The New CSS Rule window appears, and you're ready to create a second style.

7. **In the New CSS Rule window, choose Compound from the Selector Type menu, and type a name with a pseudo-class in the Selector Name box.**

   Since CSS transitions only animate a change in styling, you must use one of the handful of CSS pseudo-classes that dynamically change an element. These include the same options mentioned on step 5 on page 408, hover, active, focus, target, checked, disabled, enabled, and indeterminate. Hover is the most common.

   The name of the selector should match the one for the style you created in step 1 above. Say, for example, the original style is for a descendent selector for all the links inside an element that has the class *.nav* applied to it. That style would be named .nav a. To create a style to format those links when the mouse hovers over them then you'd create a style named .nav a:hover. (Note that there's no space between the "a" and the ":hover.") To create a style for the active state of those same links, you'd name it .nav a:active.

8. **Add the properties you want using the Rule Definition window and then click OK to complete the style.**

   Now you have two styles—the starting style that has the CSS transition property, and the hover (or active or focus, and so on) style. You're done!

■ Using CSS3

The web continually evolves—not only do new websites appear (Facebook, YouTube, Twitter), but the fundamental technologies used to build websites change and grow. Web designers used to use HTML tables to lay out pages; now we use CSS. The web design world today is abuzz with the next incarnation of the CSS standard: CSS3. CSS3 adds amazing new design effects to websites, such as drop shadows for text or page elements, animated effects, rounded corners on images, gradient backgrounds, and more (see a list of the most popular CSS3 properties on page 421).

But there are drawbacks to CSS3. First, it's a work in progress; the W3C is still hammering out the list of CSS3 properties and how they work. As a result, browser support for CSS3 varies significantly. Internet Explorer 6 was created long before CSS3, and even Internet Explorer 9 doesn't understand many aspects of the standard. Some browsers don't support any of the properties proposed in CSS3. In addition, to get some CSS3 properties to work in the browsers that *do* support them, you have to use special "browser vendor prefixes." For example, the *box-shadow* property adds a drop shadow to page elements (like a sidebar, div, or headline). You'd use this CSS3 code to add a box shadow:

```
box-shadow: 2px 3px 4px #000;
```

But to get a box shadow in Safari and Chrome browsers, you have to write that same code like this:

```
-webkit-box-shadow: 2px 3px 4px #000;
```

And for Firefox, you'd write this:

```
-moz-box-shadow: 2px 3px 4px #000;
```

In other words, to add a drop shadow to an element, you have to write three lines of code, and even then it won't work in Internet Explorer 8 or earlier!

Because the CSS3 standard isn't complete and doesn't work universally across browsers, Dreamweaver doesn't support it in the same way that it supports the W3C-sanctioned CSS 2.1 standard. CSS 2.1 has wide support among web browsers—even Internet Explorer 6 understands most of its properties—and Dreamweaver's CSS Rule Definition window reflects this. You can find most of the CSS 2.1 properties in that window, but you won't find any of the new CSS3 properties there.

That's not to say that Dreamweaver CS6 doesn't support some of those properties. You already used two of them, web fonts and CSS transitions. Other CSS3 properties are available in the Properties pane; see the next section for details.

> **TIP** If you want to know which browsers support which CSS properties, visit the "When can I use…" website at *http://caniuse.com/*. It's an invaluable resource for web designers.

The Properties Pane

As you read on page 382, you can add CSS properties to a style using the Properties pane: Click the Add Property link and select a property from the drop-down list. Dreamweaver CS6 includes CSS3 properties in this list. As with CSS 2.1 properties, you simply select a CSS3 property from the list, and then type a proper value in the box to the right. Unfortunately, you need to know what the proper value is, and for many CSS3 properties, Dreamweaver doesn't help you out (see the end of this section for links to resources on CSS3). However, for some of the most commonly used CSS3 properties, Dreamweaver provides a bit more help in the form of pop-up dialog boxes. For example, if you add the *text-shadow* property, a small icon (circled in Figure 8-21) appears in the Value column; click it and a dialog box appears. Fill out the three boxes to define the placement and appearance of the drop shadow, and to pick a color for it. Dreamweaver provides similar functionality for the *box-shadow*, *border-image*, and *border-radius* properties.

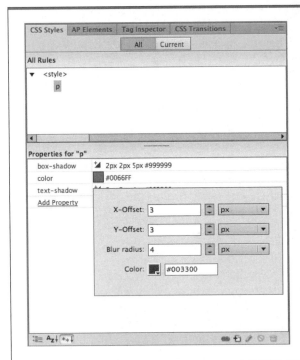

FIGURE 8-21

While Dreamweaver doesn't provide much assistance in using most CSS3 properties, it does give you an easy-to-use and -understand dialog box for a handful of CSS3 properties, like text-shadow, pictured here.

Code Hinting

Dreamweaver also includes CSS3 code hints. You read about code-hinting in the last chapter, but in a nutshell, it's a helpful aid for designers who like to type their HTML, CSS, and JavaScript by hand. As you type a CSS property into a style sheet, Dreamweaver lists properties that match as you type away. For example, type *co* and Dreamweaver lists *color, column-count,* and other CSS properties that begin with *co*. In Figure 8-22, for instance, after typing -webkit-, Dreamweaver lists all WebKit-specific CSS3 properties. You can click on the property with your mouse or, even better, use the up and down arrows on your keyboard to select the desired property; hitting Return makes Dreamweaver type the rest of the property for you. That's a great way to cut down on typing and increase your productivity. Unfortunately, code-hinting is really a power user's tool: You need to know how the CSS3 property works to correctly fill out the required value.

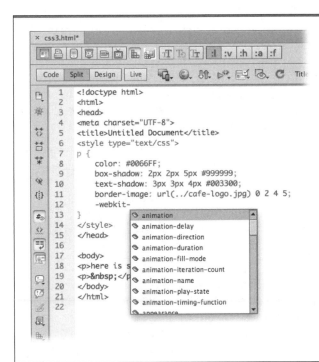

FIGURE 8-22

Dreamweaver's code-hinting feature is a time- and finger-saver. As you type a few letters of a CSS property, Dreamweaver opens a window that lists matching properties. You can select a property from the list and let Dreamweaver type the rest. This feature works with HTML tags and JavaScript programming as well.

Common CSS3 Properties

Although CSS3 is still in development, a range of browsers support a limited set of its properties. Many web designers have begun testing the CSS3 waters and include judicious amounts of CSS3 in their pages. Some of the most exciting (and supported) properties are:

- **Text-shadow**. Adds a drop shadow to headlines or any other text. Unfortunately, no version of Internet Explorer (even IE 9) supports this property, but it works in Safari, Firefox, Chrome, and Opera without a special vendor-specific prefix (like -webkit or -moz). You can use Dreamweaver's Properties pane to add *text-shadow* to a style (see Figure 8-21). For more on the *text-shadow* property and a useful tool for previewing its effect, visit *http://tinyurl.com/cxxhavg*.

- **Box-shadow**. Adds a drop shadow to any HTML element, like a sidebar, banner, or any box on a page. You can even add a rectangular shadow around headlines and paragraphs of text. All major browsers (except IE 8 and earlier) support this property. Unfortunately, like many CSS3 properties, you'll need to use special prefixes to make this work in some browsers (for example, you need to specify

-webkit-box-shadow instead of *box-shadow* for version 5 of Safari and early versions of Safari for iOS). Visit this useful tool for previewing box-shadow effects: *http://tinyurl.com/c2h2rrv*.

- **Border-radius**. If you've ever struggled trying to create rounded corners using multiple background images, this CSS3 property is for you. The *border-radius* property lets you round the corners of any HTML element—you can even round just one, two, or three corners, or provide different radii for each. Again, IE 8 and earlier can't take advantage of this fun property, and you need to provide additional properties for this to work in Safari, Firefox, and Chrome. Visit the Hands-On CSS Border Radius Generator at *http://tinyurl.com/bpkamka*.

- **Gradient**. CSS3 lets you add a gradient to the background of any element, so you could, for example, create a background that fades from white to dark gray without using graphics. You can create either linear (top to bottom or left to right) or radial gradients (circular from the center outward). Internet Explorer doesn't support this property, and the other major browsers require different property names for it. For a great tool to help you preview and write the required CSS, visit *http://www.colorzilla.com/gradient-editor/*.

- **Transforms**. Have you ever wanted to rotate an element on a page—perhaps make a <div> tag look like a piece of paper that's been set down askew on a table top? Well, even if you haven't, you can! Thanks to CSS3 you can rotate, skew, and scale an element with the Transform property. You'll need vendor-specific prefixes for Internet Explorer 9 (-ms-transform), Safari and Chrome (-webkit-transform), Firefox (-moz-transform), and Opera (-o-tranform). Of course, IE 8 and earlier are left out of the party. To learn how to use this property and test it out, visit *http://tinyurl.com/d8dle98*.

■ Advanced CSS Tutorial

In this tutorial, you'll create a descendent selector, and use Dreamweaver CS6's new CSS Transitions tool.

> **TIP** You need to download files from *www.sawmac.com/dwcs6* to complete this tutorial. See the Note on page 54 for details.

Once you download the tutorial files and open Dreamweaver, set up a new site as described on page 40. In a nutshell, choose Site→New Site. In the Site Setup window that appears, type *Adv CSS Tutorial* into the Site Name field. Click the folder icon next to the Local Site Folder field, navigate to and select the Chapter08 folder inside the MM_DWCS6 folder, and then click Choose (Select). Finally, click OK.

Creating a Descendent Selector

Once again, you'll be working on a page for the good people who run *Cafe Soylent Green*.

1. **Choose File→Open.**

   You'll work on a page similar to the ones you built in Chapter 5.

2. **Navigate to the Chapter08 folder and double-click the file _index.html_.**

   You can also double-click the _index.html_ file in the Files panel to open it. You'll notice a simple navigation bar in the upper-right corner of the page. These links would look a lot better as buttons, so you'll add a style to make that happen.

3. **Make sure you have the CSS Styles panel open (Window→CSS Styles), and then click the New Rule button in the bottom-right of the panel.**

   The New CSS Rule window opens (see Figure 8-23).

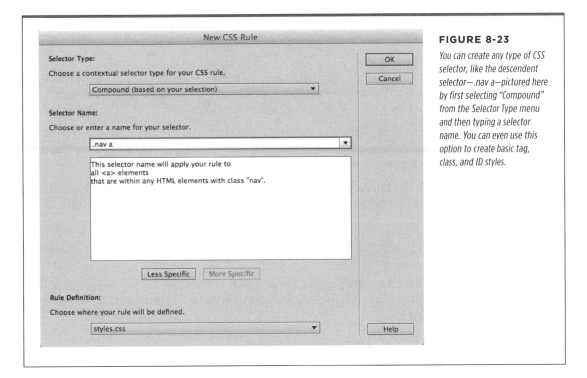

FIGURE 8-23

You can create any type of CSS selector, like the descendent selector—.nav a—pictured here by first selecting "Compound" from the Selector Type menu and then typing a selector name. You can even use this option to create basic tag, class, and ID styles.

You follow the same process you do to create any style (see page 125 if you need a recap). You want to style these links (navigation links in this example), but creating an <a> tag style would affect every link on the page (in this case, the links at the bottom of the page, and those associated with the two images). A better option is a descendent selector that targets just the navigation links (About Us, Menu, and Home). In this case, the links are actually bulleted list items that have a bit of styling already. The outer <ul> tag has a class applied to it: <ul class="nav">. This class name is all you need to create a style that affects just the links inside the bulleted list.

4. **Choose Compound from the Selector Type menu, type .nav a in the Selector Name box, and than choose "styles.css" from the bottom menu.** The New CSS Rule window should look like Figure 8-23.

The selector you just typed—*.nav a*—is a descendent selector. The element on the far right of the selector, "a", is the target. The selector to the left, *.nav*, is an element that wraps around the <a> tag. Time to create the style.

5. **Click OK to add the style.**

The CSS Rule Definition Window appears.

6. **In the Type category, choose PTSansBold from bottom of the Font-family menu, and turn on the "none" checkbox under Text-decoration.**

If you don't see PTSansBold, you may not have installed it yet. This is a web font introduced in the Chapter 3 tutorial. You can either go back to page 169 and follow the instructions to install PTSansBold, or select another font from the Font-family list.

7. **Click the Background category, and then type #0A2F02 in the Background-color box.** Select the Block category and select "inline-block" from the Display drop-down menu.

As described on page 166, the inline-block setting is useful if you want to add margins and padding to an inline element.

8. **Click the Border category, choose "solid" from the Top style menu, type 1 in the Top Width box, and then type #1C6300 in the Top Color box.**

This adds a green border around all four sides of each link, creating a button-like box effect. Because the border lines will come very close to the link text, you'll add some padding to push the border away from the text.

9. **Click the Box category, and then turn off the "Same for all" checkbox under Padding.** Type *3* in the Top box, *10* in the Right box, *3* in the Bottom box, and *10* in the Left box.

The window should look like Figure 8-24. You're all done with this style.

10. **Click OK to complete the style and close the window.**

Because the unordered list already had a *.nav* class applied to it, the styling you just created immediately appears on the links at the top of the page. Now it's time to add a CSS transition.

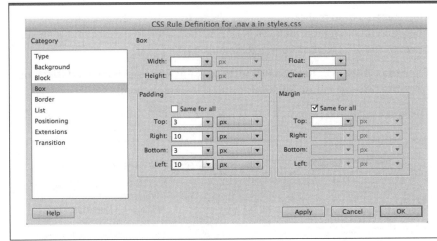

FIGURE 8-24

Whenever you add a border around an element that has text, it's usually a good idea to add some padding as well. Padding pushes the border away from the text so the text doesn't look cramped.

Adding a CSS Transition

CSS transitions are simple animations between two sets of CSS rules. Dreamweaver CS6 makes it easy to add these fun CSS3 effects.

1. **Choose Window→CSS Transitions**

   Dreamweaver opens the CSS Transitions window. This window begins life as a floating panel. If you want, drag it over the tab in the CSS Styles panel to dock it at the side of the screen with the styles panel.

2. **Click the + icon (the Create New Transition button).**

   The New Transition window launches. You'll specify what element you wish to animate.

3. **From the Target Rule menu, select .nav a.**

   This menu lists all the CSS styles available to the page, as well as any IDs used in the page's HTML. In this case, you chose the descendent selector you just created since you want to add a transition to the navigation links.

4. **From the Transition On menu, select "hover."**

   While Dreamweaver gives you other options, many aren't useful. The hover option is by far the most common, as it animates an element's appearance when a visitor mouses over it.

5. **Make sure you have "Use the same transition for all properties" selected from the drop-down menu.** Type *.25* in the Duration box, 0 in the Delay box, and choose "ease-in-out" from the Timing Function menu.

This creates an animation that takes .25 seconds from start to finish, with no delay and an animation that starts slowly, then change rapidly, and then slow down as the .25 seconds comes to an end.

6. **Click the + button below the Property box, and choose "background-color" from the pop-up menu.** Type #E1EBEB in the End Value box.

The window should now look like Figure 8-25. You're done.

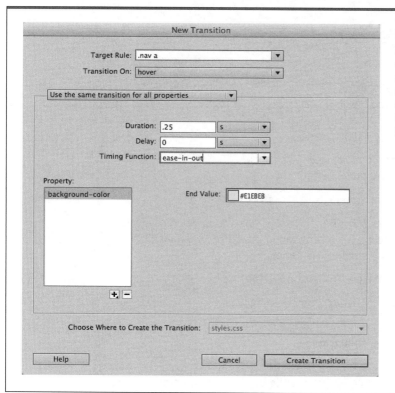

FIGURE 8-25

It's possible to animate each CSS property differently (choose "Use a different transitions for each property"). However, animating each property at a different rate, with a different delay and a different timing function, can result in a confusing animation.

7. **Click Create Transition to close the window and complete the transition.**

Behind the scenes, Dreamweaver adds a new style, *.nav a:hover*, and the proper CSS transition code to the *.nav a* style. Time to check out your work.

8. **Click the Live button in the Document toolbar to preview the transition.** Mouse over the various links.

The background color gently fades into view when you mouse over the links, and fades out when your mouse moves out. If you don't see this effect, you may have accidentally selected a different transition trigger (like "active" or "focus" instead of "hover"). If that's the case, select the transition in the CSS Transitions panel and click the minus-sign button to delete it.

9. **Click the Live button again to exit Live view.**

Now you'll add a CSS3 property to the links.

Adding CSS3 Properties

While you can't add most CSS3 properties to your styles using Dreamweaver's Rule Definition window, you can use the Properties pane on the CSS Styles panel.

1. **Open the CSS Styles panel (Window→CSS Styles).** Make sure you have the All button selected, and then locate and select the *.nav a* style.

   To add a CSS3 property to a style, you first select it and then use the Properties pane to add it.

2. **Click the Add Property link at the bottom of the Properties list and, in the menu that appears, select "border-radius."**

   You'll see *border-radius* appear in the list of properties and, to the right, a square icon with a + sign and a black triangle in it (circled in Figure 8-26).

3. **Click the icon to open a settings window and type 3 in the Top Left box.** Click outside the window to make the change take effect.

   You won't see the rounded corners in Dreamweaver's Design view, but if you preview the page in a browser or click Dreamweaver's Live button, you'll see the effect (make sure you exit Live view before continuing). Next, you'll add some CSS3 magic to the two photos on the page.

4. **In Design view, select the first photo (the one below "All Natural Ingredients") and, from the Property Inspector, choose *imageRight* from the class menu.**

   This is the same style you created in Chapter 5's tutorial. It floats the image to the right and adds a border around it.

5. **Repeat the previous step for the next photo (below the headline "Technology Meets Good Nutrition").**

   Now you'll add another CSS3 property.

6. **In the CSS Styles panel, select the *.imageRight* style (it's near the bottom of the list).** In the Properties pane, click the Add Property link, choose "opacity" from the list of properties, and then type *.75 in the box to the right*.

   The opacity property controls the transparency of an element. You can use a value of between 0 and 1. Zero makes the element completely invisible, while 1 makes it completely opaque. A value in between, like .75 here, lets a little bit of the background show through while still displaying the element. Why would you want to do this? So you could animate it with a CSS transition, of course!

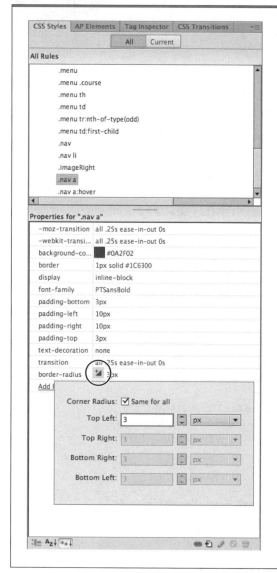

FIGURE 8-26

The CSS border-radius property adds rounded corners to elements. You can give all four corners the same radius (as in this case) or turn off the "Same for all" checkbox and type different radii for each corner. If you want to create a completely rounded "box" then use 50% for all four corners.

NOTE As with the *border-radius* property, you can't see the effect of the opacity property in Dreamweaver's Design view.

Adding One Last Transition

1. **Click to select one of the two images.**

   When you create a CSS transition from a class selector (the *.imageRight* style you applied in the previous step), Dreamweaver has the unfortunate habit of adding that class to whatever element is currently selected on the page. If you don't select one of the images, Dreamweaver ends up adding the *.imageRight* class to another element on the page, causing unwanted animation when someone mouses over that element.

2. **Open the CSS Transitions window (Window→CSS Transitions), and then click the New Transition button (the + icon).**

   The New Transition window appears. You'll specify what element you want to animate.

3. **From the Target Rule menu, select .imageRight.**

   This is the class style where you just added the opacity property.

4. **From the Transition On menu, select "hover."**

   This time, you'll set different timings for two different CSS properties.

5. **Choose "Use a different transition for each property."**

   The window changes

6. **Click the + button below the Property box, and choose "border-color" from the pop-up menu.** Type *1* in the Duration box and *0* in the Delay box. Choose "ease-in-out" from the Timing function menu, and then type #0A2F02 in the End Value box.

   This creates an animation that lasts 1 second (pretty long), gradually changing the border color around the image to dark green.

   Now, you'll add the opacity property.

7. **Click the + button below the Property box and choose "opacity" from the pop-up menu.** Type *.5* in the Duration box and *0* in the Delay box. Choose "ease-out" from the Timing function menu, and then type 1 in the End Value box.

   The window should look like Figure 8-27. This animation makes the images appear vibrant and colorful when a mouse moves over them. Since it only takes half a second to complete, it will happen more quickly than the changing border color.

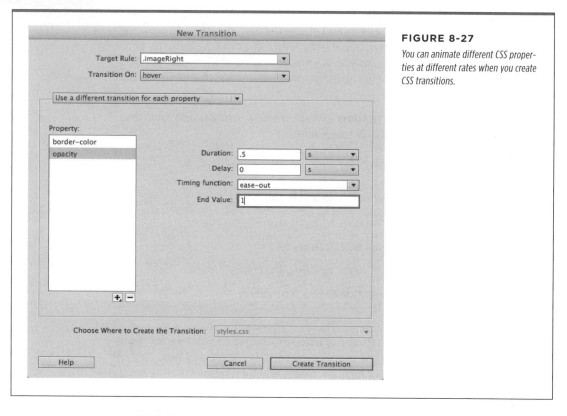

FIGURE 8-27

You can animate different CSS proper-
ties at different rates when you create
CSS transitions.

8. **Click Create Transition to close the window and complete the transition.**

   Behind the scenes, Dreamweaver adds a new style, *.imageRight:hover* and the proper CSS transition code to the *.imageRight* style. Time to check out your work.

9. **Click the Live button in the Document toolbar to preview the transition.** Mouse over the two photos.

   The photos should pop vibrantly from the page, while the border will more slowly change to dark green (see Figure 8-28). You can find a completed version of this tutorial in the Chapter08_complete folder that accompanies the downloaded tutorial files.

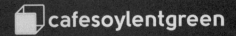

All Natural Ingredients

Lorm ipsum dolor sat ipectum solorgno inferiod. Gor(ogonzola reggio solor dat. Ipsum dolor sat ipectum solorgno inferiod. Gorogonzola reggio solor dat.Lorm ipsum doxlor sat ipectum solorgno inferiod. Gorogonzola reggio solor dat. Ipsum dolor sat ipectum solorgno inferiod. Gorogonzola reggio solor dat.

Lorm ipsum dolor sat ipectum solorgno inferiod. Gorogonzola reaggio solor dat. Ipsum dolor sat ipectum solorgno inferiod. Gorogonzola reggio solor dat.Lorm ipsum dolor sat ipectum solorgno inferiod. Gorogonzola reggio solor dat. Ipsum dolor sat ipectum solorgno inferiod. Gorogonzola reggio solor dat.

Technology Meets Good Nutrition

Lorm ipsum dolor sat ipectum solorgno inferiod. Gorogonzola reggio solor dat. Ipsum dolor sat ipectum solorgno inferiod. Gorogonzola reggio solor dat.Lorm ipsum dolor sat ipectum solorgno inferiod. Gorogonzola reggio solor dat. Ipsum dolor sat ipectum solorgno inferiod. Gorog onzola reggio solor dat.Lorm ipsum dolor sat ipectum solorgno inferiod. Gorogonzola reggio solor dat. Ipsum dolor sat ipectum solorgno inferiod. Lorm ipsum dr sat ipectum solorgno inferiod. Gorogonzola reggio solor dat. Ipsum dolorolo sat ipectum solorgno inferiod. Gorogonzola reggio solor dat

FIGURE 8-28

You can enliven any web page by adding CSS transitions to links, navigation bars, and even images. In this example, a "soft" image becomes vibrant and its border slowly turns dark green when a visitor mouses over the picture. There's no need for JavaScript— just a little CSS3 magic. (Unfortunately, you'll find that these effects won't work in Internet Explorer 9 or earlier.)

Page Layout

Web design, unfortunately, isn't like most other forms of graphic composition. For magazine and book projects, software like InDesign lets you place text and images anywhere you want—and even rotate and overlap them. But web designers are stuck with the basic technology of HTML, which wants to flow from the top of a browser window to the bottom, in one long column. To place elements around the page and create multiple columns of content, you need to resort to some fancy footwork.

For much of the Web's short life, designers have used the HTML <table> tag to control the position of elements on a page—to create columns, sidebars, banners, and so on. But the <table> tag was intended to display information in a spreadsheet-like format, and bending it to a web designer's vision often resulted in complex HTML that downloaded slowly, displayed sluggishly, and challenged coders.

Now that CSS-friendly web browsers like Internet Explorer, Safari, Firefox, Chrome, and Opera rule the Web, designers can safely rely on a much better (though often frustrating) method: Cascading Style Sheets. That's right; not only is CSS great for formatting text, navigation bars, images, and other bits of a web page, it also has all the tools you need to create sophisticated designs, like the ones shown in Figure 9-1.

FIGURE 9-1

CSS Zen Garden (www.csszengarden.com) is the original show-case for CSS layout. Although the designs haven't been updated in a while, in its day it caused many a web designer to bow down and proclaim, "I'm not worthy, I'm not worthy." The site not only demonstrates great design, it shows you the power of CSS-based layout. Each page includes the same content and the same HTML. The only difference is their external style sheets and graphics. CSS lets you redesign sites without rewriting any HTML.

CSS provides a couple of ways to control the placement of elements on a page. The most common is to create multiple-column layouts using the CSS Float property (the same property you used in Chapter 5 to position an image to the left or right of a page).

Dreamweaver includes a starter set of 18 CSS layouts that use this float-based approach. These stock pages cover the most commonly used page layouts—designs with one, two, or three columns of content, a header for a logo and banner, and a footer for a copyright notice, for example. These layout files aren't complete page designs so much as basic building blocks you can modify to match your sensibility.

CSS also includes a Position property, which lets you place elements "absolutely"—that is, at a pixel-specific position on the page. While this might sound like the answer to page layout, absolute positioning has its own set of problems, and web designers don't often use it for full page layout. Instead, they usually use it to accurately place small elements in an exact position on a page, or they use it in conjunction with Java-Script to make elements pop onto the page above other elements—Dreamweaver's Spry menu bar (page 210), for example, uses absolute positioning to place the bar's drop-down menus on top of the page.

NOTE CSS layout is one of those complex topics that is sometimes better learned by doing instead of by reading. To get a taste of how CSS layout works, try the tutorial on page 479, then flip back to the beginning of this chapter for all the messy details.

This chapter introduces the basic concepts behind float-based layouts—what they are, how they work, and how to create one; it also provides instructions for modifying Dreamweaver's CSS designs. In addition, you'll learn about absolute positioning, and how to use it to place select elements where you want them.

■ Types of Web Page Layouts

Being a web designer means dealing with the unknown. What kind of browsers do your visitors use, will your design work in all browsers, and so on. But perhaps the biggest challenge designers face is creating attractive designs that work across different size screens. Monitors vary in size and resolution, from petite 15-inch 640 x 480 pixel displays to 30-inch monstrosities displaying, oh, about 5 million x 4.3 million pixels. (In addition, designers now have to cope with the very small displays found on millions of cell phones and other mobile devices. Chapter 11 has information on how you can use CSS to create sites for those devices.)

NOTE A new approach to web layout, called Responsive Web Design, uses a liquid layout and some fancy CSS to completely change a page's design at different screen resolutions. That is, you can create one design for a phone, a different design for a tablet, and a third layout for desktop browsers. You'll learn about this technique, as well as a new tool in Dreamweaver CS6 to build these kinds of layouts, in Chapter 11.

Float-based layouts offer two approaches to this problem: *fixed-width* or *liquid layouts* (the latter also called *fluid layouts*). A fixed-width layout gives you the most control over your design but can inconvenience some of your visitors. Folks with really small monitors have to scroll to the right to see everything, and those with large monitors see wasted space that could display more of your excellent content. Liquid layouts make designing pages more challenging for you but make the most effective use of your guests' screen sizes.

- **Fixed-width layout**. Many designers prefer the consistency of a set width, like the page shown in Figure 9-2, top. Regardless of how wide a browser window is, the page content's width remains the same. In some cases, the design clings to the left edge of the browser window. More often, the content is centered. With the fixed-width approach, you don't have to worry about what happens to your design on a very wide (or very small) monitor.

  Fixed-width designs can range anywhere from 760 pixels in width to 1,000 pixels or more wide. To fit a fully maximized browser window on an 800 x 600 pixel screen, you'd use 760 pixels. These days, however, the screens on even tiny 10-inch netbooks or Apple iPads are at least 1,024 pixels wide, and all desktop computers support at least 1024 x 768 pixels, so most new sites use much bigger dimensions—960 pixels wide is now common for fixed-width designs, but you'll also see 1,000 pixels and even a bit more on some sites.

- **Liquid layout**. Sometimes, it's easier to roll with the tide instead of fighting it. A liquid design adjusts a page's dimensions to fit a browser's width—whatever that may be. Your page gets wider or narrower as your visitor resizes his browser window (Figure 9-2, bottom). While liquid design makes the best use of browser real estate, you have to do more work to make sure your design looks good at different window sizes. On very large monitors, these types of designs can look ridiculously wide.

  Fixed-width designs are probably the most common type of layout on the Web, since they provide a consistent display and make it much easier for designers to work with.

FIGURE 9-2

CSS gives you several ways to deal with the uncertain widths of browser windows and browser font sizes. You could simply ignore the fact that your site's visitors have different-resolution monitors and force a single, unchanging width on them, as the Target.com website does. As you can see in the top two images, resizing the browser window doesn't change the page—it remains the same width (but centered in the browser window) when you make the browser window wider. Many websites take this approach. Alternatively, you could create a liquid design whose content flows to fill whatever width window your visitor uses. That's how Amazon's site works (bottom two images).

Float Layout Basics

Float-based layouts take advantage of the CSS *float* property to position elements side by side and create columns on a page. As you read on page 257, you can float an image to make text wrap around a photograph. But it's also a powerful layout tool that lets you move a bunch of related page elements (like a list of links you want to appear in a left-hand column) to one side of the page or the other. In essence, the *float* property moves a page element to the left or the right. Any HTML that appears *after* the floated element moves up on the page and hugs the side of the float.

Float is a CSS property, available when you create a CSS style (see page 125 for instructions on creating styles). It's listed in the CSS Rule Definition window's Box category (see Figure 9-3). Choose the "left" option, and the styled element floats to the left; choose the "right" option and the element moves to the right.

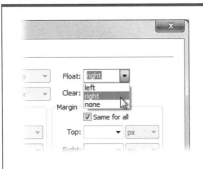

FIGURE 9-3

You have just three options when you want to float an element: left, right, and none. You might never need "none"—it simply positions an element as though it were a normal, unfloated element. Since this is the regular behavior of any element, you need this option only if you want to turn off a float applied by another style (see page 391 for more on how multiple styles can affect the same element).

The Mighty <div> Tag

Whatever layout method you use, web page design involves putting chunks of content into different regions of a page. With CSS, the most common way to organize content is with the <div> tag. The <div> tag is an HTML element that has no inherent formatting properties (besides the fact that browsers treat it as a block element, with a line break before and after it); you use the div to define a logical grouping of elements (a *division*) on a page, a chunk of HTML that belongs together.

For example, the elements comprising the logo and navigation bar in Figure 9-4 occupy the top of the page, so it makes sense to wrap a <div> tag around them (labeled "banner div" in the figure). At the very least, you would include <div> tags for all the major regions of your page, such as the banner, main content area, sidebar, footer, and so on. But it's also possible to wrap a <div> tag around one or more *other* divs. People often wrap all the HTML inside the <body> tag in a <div> tag. This tag, therefore, wraps around all the other divs on the page, and you can set some basic page properties by applying CSS to this *wrapper* div. For example, you can style a div to set the overall width for the page, set left and right margins, or center all the page's content in the middle of the screen.

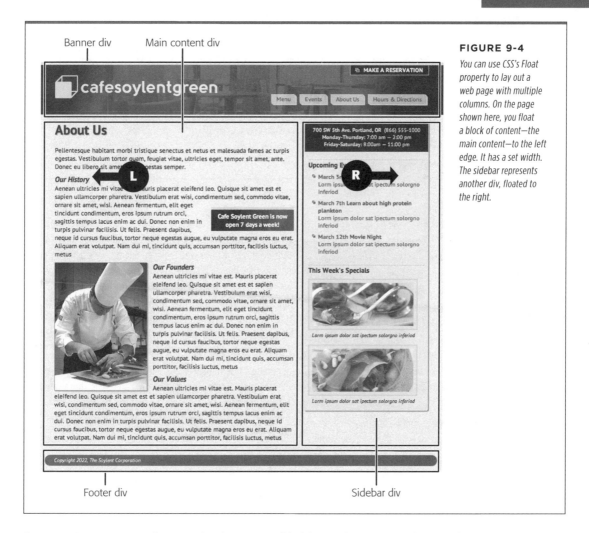

Banner div   Main content div

FIGURE 9-4

You can use CSS's Float property to lay out a web page with multiple columns. On the page shown here, you float a block of content—the main content—to the left edge. It has a set width. The sidebar represents another div, floated to the right.

Footer div   Sidebar div

Once you've got your <div> tags in place, you add either a class or ID style to each one so you can style each div separately. For parts of a page that form the basic building blocks of the page, designers usually apply either an ID or a class (page 124) to the div. For example, the <div> tag for a page's banner area might look like this: *<div id="banner">* or *<div class="banner">*.

There are only a few differences between using a class and an ID to identify a region of a page. Recall that you can use an ID only once per page, so if you have an element that appears multiple times, use a class instead. For example, if you have several divs that position photos and their captions, you'd add a class to each div rather than an ID, like this: *<div class="photoBox">*. Another difference: ID selectors in CSS take precedence over class selectors in the case of a style conflict. For example, if you apply both an ID and a class to the same <div> tag and then you create ID and class styles, any properties in the ID style that conflicted with those in the class would win out. This is one of the basic rules of the CSS cascade, described on page 391. Because ID selectors are so powerful when it comes to conflicts in CSS, many web designers now always use classes—even for elements that appear a single time on a page—because they can help you write shorter CSS selector names.

NOTE If you select a <div> tag in the document window, the Property Inspector provides two menus: one to apply an ID to the div and another to apply a class style to it.

FREQUENTLY ASKED QUESTION

HTML5 Elements

I hear that HTML5 has lots of new elements that replace the <div> tag. Is the <div> tag still relevant?

It's true that HTML5 introduces many new tags to help organize web page content. These "sectioning elements" are intended to let you group specific types of content. For example, you'd use the <header> tag for grouping content that appears at the top of the page (like a banner). The <section> tag is intended to set off—wait for it—a "section" of your page. The <article> tag is for grouping all the tags that make up an individual article. The <aside> tag is for content that's related to other content and can be used to create sidebars. There are many other tags as well.

Basically, you use these tags to group common sections of a page, and they're meant to take the place of the humble <div> tag you use for all the content listed above (headers, articles, and so on).

However, the <div> tag works just as well as all those tags. In fact, there's nothing inherently different in how the new tags display or act in a web browser, and from a site visitor's perspective, there's no difference whatsoever. You can style divs with CSS the same way you'd style the new HTML5 tags. Then why the new tags? The HTML5 sectioning elements are intended to help *computers* understand a page's structure better. For example, Google might look for an <article> tag in a page to better identify key content.

In addition, Internet Explorer 8 and earlier don't understand the new HTML5 tags. This means you can't style those tags without the help of some JavaScript. At this point, it's fine to continue using <div> tags for structuring your page content, and it will be for years ahead.

The Insert Div Tag Tool

Because grouping parts of a page using <div> tags is such an important part of CSS layout, Dreamweaver includes a tool to simplify the process. The Insert Div Tag tool lets you wrap a <div> tag around a selection of page content, or simply drop an empty div onto a page that you can fill with images, links, paragraphs of text, or whatever.

To use this tool, either select the content you want to wrap (for example, click at the beginning of the selection and drag to the end of it) or click on the page where you wish to insert an empty <div> tag. Then click the Insert Div Tag button in the Layout category of the Insert panel (see Figure 9-5). You can find that button listed in the Common category, too, or you can choose Insert→Layout Objects→Div Tag.

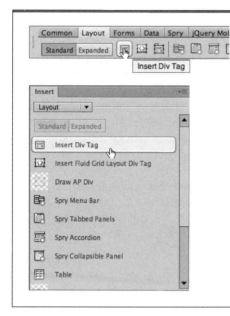

FIGURE 9-5

The Layout category of the Insert panel includes buttons for adding both <div> tags and absolutely positioned divs (see page 465). In this figure, the top image is the Insert bar in Classic view (as described on page 38), and the bottom is the Insert panel as Dreamweaver displays it by default.

In any case, the Insert Div Tag window appears (Figure 9-6).

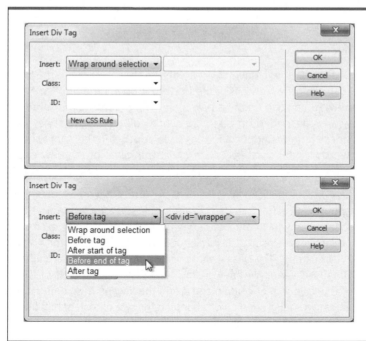

FIGURE 9-6

The Insert Div Tag tool tells Dreamweaver where to place a div in relation to other tags on the page (bottom image, drop-down menu on left). The Insert drop-down menu to the right of that lets you choose the precise tag for the div insertion point. That menu lists tags that have an ID applied to them, or, if you chose "After start of tag" or "Before end of tag" from the left-hand menu, it lists the <body> tag. Suppose, for example, you want to insert a <div> tag to display a footer at the bottom of a page. Because you know the footer will go last on the page, you click the Insert Div Tag button, select "Before end of tag" from the left menu, and <body> from the right menu. Dreamweaver puts the <div> tag at the very end of the page's content, just before the closing </body> tag.

If you click OK, Dreamweaver wraps any selected content in a <div> tag, or, if you didn't select anything on the page, it drops a new <div> tag onto the page with the text "Content for New Div Tag Goes Here" (of course, you'll replace that with your own content). But, usually, you'll take an additional step: applying either an ID or class to the div. You do this a couple of ways:

- **Choose a class from the Class menu or choose an ID from the ID menu**. The Class menu on the Insert Div Tag window lists all the class styles available to the current page. A class is the way to go if you want to format several divs the same way. For example, you might use a <div> tag to position an image and a caption on a page or create a pull-quote in the middle of an article; if you had multiple instances of photos with captions, you could create a class style (like .*figure*) to format each photo-caption pair. You could then select a photo and caption on the page, use the Insert Div Tag tool, and then select the class name (figure in this example) from the class menu. You could repeat this procedure multiple times on a single page. But you can also apply a class to a div even if you use it for a unique set of elements—such as the banner at the top of the page (Dreamweaver's CSS Layouts, discussed on page 452, use class names and styles only).

  The ID menu on the Insert Div Tag window behaves a bit differently. Since you can only use an ID once per page (see page 124 for the reason), the ID menu lists IDs that exist in your style sheet, but only those you haven't yet applied to any tags. Say you create an ID style named *#banner* that you plan to apply to a <div> tag to define the banner area of your page. You select the banner content (like the site logo and navigation bar), and then click the Insert Div Tag button. At this point, you'd select *banner* from the ID menu. If you then insert a second div on the page using the Insert Div Tag tool, *banner* no longer appears in the ID menu.

- **Create a new class or ID**. If you haven't yet created a style to apply to the new <div> tag, you can click the New CSS Rule button. It opens the familiar New Style Rule window, so you can create a new style. The process is the same as creating any style, as described on page 125. Once you define the style, you return to the Insert Div Tag window, and that style appears in the appropriate box. (In other words, if you created a class style, the name of the new class would appear in the Class box; similarly, a new ID name appears in the ID box.)

After you apply a class or ID and click OK, Dreamweaver inserts the new <div> tag, complete with the appropriate HTML needed to apply the style: for example, *<div id="banner">*. (Note that when you create an ID style, you add a # sign—for example, *#banner*—but when Dreamweaver inserts the HTML for the ID name, it omits the # sign. The same applies to class names: <div class="photo"> is correct, <div class=".photo"> is not.) In addition, Dreamweaver applies any styling you create for the class or ID to the div. In the case of CSS layout, that could mean sizing the div and positioning it on the page, as well as adding a background color, changing the size of text, or any other CSS formatting. You can add new content inside the div, edit what's there, or delete the div completely.

NOTE CSS-based layout is a big topic, worthy of a book or two by itself. For more in-depth coverage, including solutions to common float problems, pick up a copy of *CSS: The Missing Manual.*

A Simple Example

To get a better idea of how divs help with page layout, look at the layout in Figure 9-4. This design has a banner (a logo and navigation bar), a left-hand sidebar (a list of story titles and links), and the main story. Figure 9-7, left, shows the order in which the HTML appears on the page: The banner elements come first, the sidebar second, and the main story (headlines, paragraphs, photo, and so on) last. (Remember, what you're seeing demonstrates the power and beauty of the HTML/CSS tango: Your HTML file contains your structured chunks of content, while your CSS controls how a browser displays that content.) Viewed in a web browser, without any CSS styling, these different HTML sections would all appear stacked one on top of the other.

NOTE You don't have to create and name divs to get started with CSS layout. Dreamweaver ships with 18 premade designs called CSS Layouts. You can read about then on page 452.

To create a two-column design, follow these steps:

1. **Select the contents of the banner.** Then, on the Layout category of the Insert panel, click the Insert Div Tag button.

   For example, click before the logo image and drag to select the navigation bar. With this HTML selected, you can wrap it in a <div> tag.

2. **In the class box, add a class name (or use an ID if you prefer).**

   You can name the style several ways, depending on whether you want to create the style immediately, whether you've have already created the style, or whether want to create the style later on.

   • To create a class or ID style, click the New CSS Rule button. The process at this point is the same as that for creating any new style, as described on page 125. In this case, you might name the class style .banner (or the ID style *#banner*). You can set any CSS properties you want for the banner: add a border around all four sides, color the background, or even specify a width.

   • Select a class name from the Class menu, or an ID name from the ID menu. The web page may already have an external style sheet attached, which contains all the necessary styles for the layout. Just select the class name for the div you're inserting (for example, *.banner*).

   • Type a name in the Class (or ID) box. If you don't want to create a style, you could just type *banner* in the Class or ID box, and create the style later.

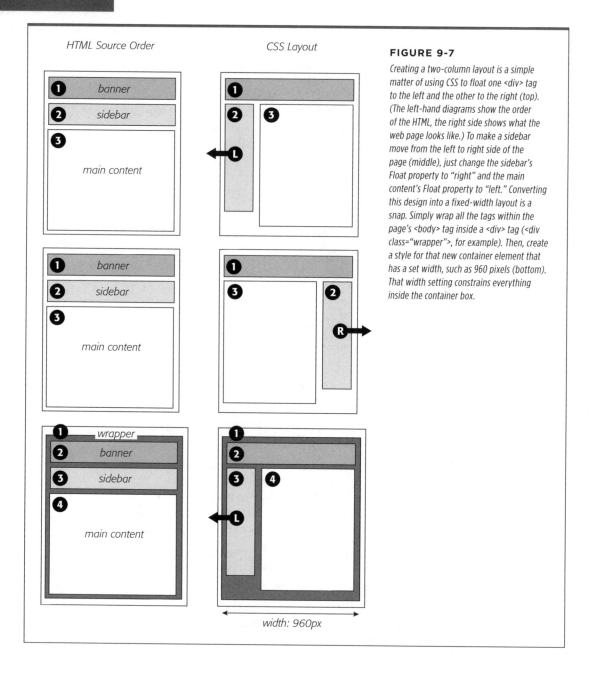

HTML Source Order

CSS Layout

FIGURE 9-7

Creating a two-column layout is a simple matter of using CSS to float one <div> tag to the left and the other to the right (top). (The left-hand diagrams show the order of the HTML, the right side shows what the web page looks like.) To make a sidebar move from the left to right side of the page (middle), just change the sidebar's Float property to "right" and the main content's Float property to "left." Converting this design into a fixed-width layout is a snap. Simply wrap all the tags within the page's <body> tag inside a <div> tag (<div class="wrapper">, for example). Then, create a style for that new container element that has a set width, such as 960 pixels (bottom). That width setting constrains everything inside the container box.

NOTE When you create a class style using the New CSS Rule box, you have to start the class name with a period, like this: *.banner*. However, when you add the class in the Insert Div Tag window, you omit the period; you just type *banner (or select banner from the Class menu)*. The same applies to ID styles—use a # when you create a style in the New CSS Rule box (*#banner*, for example), but omit it in the Insert Div dialog box.

3. **Click OK to close the Insert Div Tag window.**

   Dreamweaver wraps the selected HTML with a <div> tag, and (if you created a new style) formats the banner.

4. **Select the contents of the sidebar, and then, on the Insert bar, click the Insert Div Tag button.** Click the New CSS Style button and create a another class (or ID) style. Name it whatever you like, such as *.sidebar* or *.sectionNav*, and then click OK.

   This style formats and positions the left sidebar. You're finally getting to the "float" part of this design.

5. **In the CSS Rule Definition window, click the Box category, and then, from the Float menu, select "left" (see Figure 9-8).**

   When you work with floats, the source order (the order in which you add HTML to a file) is important. The HTML for the floated element must appear *before* the HTML for the element that wraps around it.

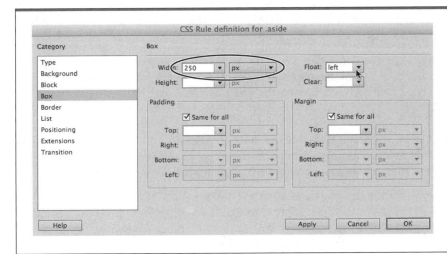

FIGURE 9-8

Whenever you float an element (other than an image), always set a width. It constrains the floated element so that a browser can wrap other content around it.

Figure 9-7 shows three two-column layouts. The diagrams on the left show the page's HTML source order: a <div> for the banner, followed by a <div> for the sidebar and, lastly, a <div> for the main content. On the right, you see the actual page layout. The sidebar comes *before* the main content in the HTML, so it can float either left (top, bottom) or right (middle). The main text area then moves up the page and wraps around the floated element.

6. **Type a value in the Width box (circled in Figure 9-8).**

Unless you're floating an image with a predefined width, you should always give your floats a width. That way, you create a set size for the floated element, allowing the browser to wrap other content around it.

You can use a fixed width, say *250px*, or you can specify a percentage for a flexible design based on the width of the browser window (see page 436 for more about the pros and cons of set versus variable dimensions). If you set the sidebar to 20% of the width of the browser window and the window is 700 pixels wide, the sidebar will be 140 pixels wide. But if your visitor stretches her window to 1,000 pixels wide, the sidebar grows to 200 pixels. Fixed-width sidebars make page design easier, since you don't have to fret over differently sized browser windows.

NOTE If you set a fixed width for your overall design (by wrapping all the page contents in a <div> tag with its width property set), percentage width values for the sidebar are based on the fixed width-containing element—it isn't based on the window size and doesn't change when the browser window size changes. This is true of any element whose width you specify by using percentage values: The percentage is based on the width of the tag that surrounds the element.

7. **Complete the style, and then insert the div.**

At this point you can continue to style the sidebar. You could add a background color, set a font family, that, thanks to inheritance (see page 390), will apply to all the text inside the div, and so on.

When you're done, click OK in the Style Definition window; you return to the Insert Div Tag window with the class box filled out with your freshly created style's name. Click OK to insert the div, and then watch the sidebar float.

Now it's time to style the main column.

8. **Follow the same steps for the main content div: select the page elements that form that main content on the page, click the Insert Div Tag button, and then create a new class (or ID) style for the page's main content region.**

In this instance, you don't need to float anything. You merely have to add a left margin to the main content so that it won't try to wrap *below* the end of the sidebar. If the sidebar is shorter than the other content on the page, the text from the main column wraps underneath the sidebar. It's much like how the main text interacts with the right-floated photo in Figure 9-4. If the main content wrapped underneath the sidebar, the appearance of two side-by-side columns would be ruined. Adding a left margin that's equal to or greater than the width of the sidebar indents the main content of the page, creating the illusion of a second column.

By the way, it's usually a good idea to make the left margin a little bigger than the width of the sidebar: That creates some empty space—a gutter—between the two elements. So if the sidebar is 170 pixels wide, adding a left margin of 185 pixels for the main content div adds an extra 15 pixels of space. If you use percentages to set the width of the sidebar, use a slightly larger percentage value for the left margin.

In addition, avoid setting a width for the main content div. It's not necessary, since browsers simply expand it to fit the available space. Even if you want a fixed-width design, you don't need to set a width for the main content div, as described in Figure 9-7.

Expanding the two-column design into a three-column design isn't difficult either (see Figure 9-9). First, add another <div> *between* the two columns and float it to the right. Then add a right margin to the middle column, so that if the text in the middle column runs longer than the new right sidebar, it won't wrap underneath the sidebar.

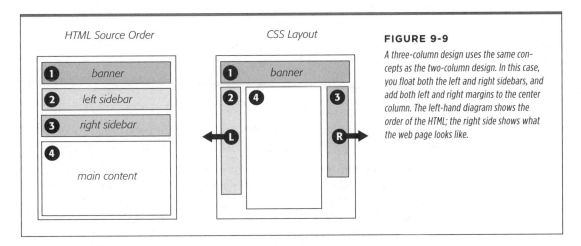

FIGURE 9-9

A three-column design uses the same concepts as the two-column design. In this case, you float both the left and right sidebars, and add both left and right margins to the center column. The left-hand diagram shows the order of the HTML; the right side shows what the web page looks like.

TIP If you're concerned about displaying your HTML in a specific order—for example, you'd like the main content region to appear before the sidebar—you can do that simply by floating the main content and the sidebar boxes. You'll see an example of this in the tutorial at the end of this chapter.

Understanding the Box Model

It's no coincidence that you find the Float property in the Box category of the CSS Rule Definition window (Figure 9-10).

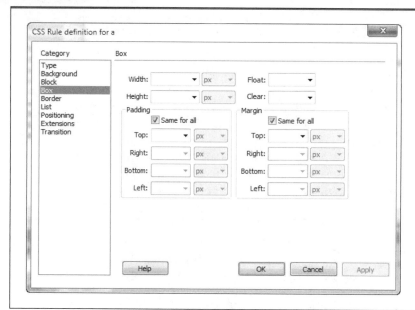

FIGURE 9-10

Use the Box category to define the dimensions of a style, to position an object on the page, and to add space between the styled object and the objects around it.

To fully understand CSS layouts and make the most of floats, you need to understand the other CSS properties in this category: width, height, padding, margin, and clear.

- **Width and height**. You can specify the width and height for any styled object using these properties. If you want a paragraph that's 100 pixels wide, create a class style with the Width property set to 100 pixels, and then apply it to the paragraph. You'll often use the Width property in conjunction with the Float property (see the following paragraph) to do things like create a box with a set width that floats to either the left or right side of the page—a common format for pull-quotes, message boxes, and sidebars.

  Be careful with the Height property. Many designers use it for precise control over page elements. Unfortunately, height is tricky to control. If you set a height for a sidebar that contains text, and you later add more text, you can end up with text spilling outside the sidebar—the same thing can happen if a visitor increases the text size in his browser. In other words, set the height of an object only if you're *sure* the content inside will never get taller—for example, if the content is an image.

- **Float**. To force an object to the left or right side of a page and have other content wrap around it, use the Float property. Of course, that's been most of the point of this chapter, so you probably understand this property by now. However, there's one important point to keep in mind: Floating an object doesn't necessarily move it to the side of a page or browser window. A floated object merely goes to the left or right edge of what's called its "containing block." If you float a div to the left of a page to create a sidebar, and then insert an image into the sidebar and float that image right, the image goes to the right edge of the sidebar, *not* to the right edge of the page. In addition, if you float multiple elements, they can often end up sitting beside each other—you use this technique to create four-column layouts, where each column floats next to the other.

- **Clear**. Clear *prevents* an element from wrapping around any object with a right or left Float property. This property comes in handy when you want to force an element to appear *below* a floated object instead of wrapping around it. The classic example is a page's footer (the area at the bottom of the page that usually contains contact information and a copyright notice). If a page has a left-floated sidebar that's longer than the main content, the footer can move up the page and wrap around the sidebar. In this case, the bottom of the sidebar is at the bottom of the page, and the footer is somewhere in the middle. To fix this problem, set the footer's Clear property to *both*. That forces the footer to drop below both left- and right-floated elements. (If you merely want something to drop below a left-floated element, but still wrap around anything floated right, choose the *left* option; to clear a right-floated element, choose *right*.) In other words, if you ever see page content next to a floated element instead of underneath it, use the *clear* property to properly position that content.

- **Padding**. Padding is the gap that separates the content of a page element—like a paragraph of text or an image—and its border. If you put a 1-pixel border around an image and want to add 10 pixels of space between the image itself and that border, type *10* into the Top padding box, and then choose "pixels" from the drop-down menu. To set the padding around each edge separately, turn off the "Same for all" box and then type values into each of the four boxes.

- **Margin**. The margin is the amount of space *surrounding* an element. It surrounds the border and padding properties of the style, and lets you add space between elements. Use any of the values—pixels, percentages, and so on—that CSS supports.

Padding, margins, borders, and the content inside the styled tag make up what web designers call the CSS Box Model, seen in Figure 9-11. Margins and padding are invisible. They also have similar effects: 5 pixels of left padding adds 5 pixels of space to the left edge of a style; the same happens when you add a 5-pixel left margin. Most people use margins to put space between elements (for example, between the right edge of one column and left edge of an adjacent one) and padding to add space between an element's border and its content (like moving text within a column away from a surrounding borderline). Because you can't see padding or margins (just the empty space they make), it's often difficult to know if the gap between, say, the banner at the top of your page and the main area of content results from the banner's style or the main area's style.

FIGURE 9-11

In what web designers call the CSS Box Model, every style is composed of multiple boxes, one inside the other. Each box controls certain display properties of the style. The outermost box is called the margin. It controls the space between the border of the styled object and any other objects around that object, such as images, paragraphs, or tables; padding is the space between the border and the content itself (the innermost box). The area within the border, which includes the content and the padding, may also have a background color. Actually, the background color is drawn underneath the border, so if you assign a dashed or dotted border, the background color appears in the gaps between the dots or dashes.

NOTE Dreamweaver includes a tool to help you visualize the margins and padding of elements. To learn how to use Inspect mode, see page 494.

You also can't always tell if the extra space comes from the padding or the margin setting. Dreamweaver includes a helpful diagnostic tool (see Figure 9-12) that lets you see these invisible properties.

When you select a <div> tag with margin or padding properties set, Dreamweaver draws a box around the div and adds slanting lines to indicate the space the margins and padding occupy (Figure 9-12 shows the box and lines in action).

Margins appear outside padding, and Dreamweaver represents them by lines that slant *downward* from left to right; padding appears inside the margin, and Dreamweaver indicates them with lines that go *upward* from left to right. When you select a <div> tag (the Tag Selector discussed on page 26 is a great way to do this), Dreamweaver highlights the margins and padding values defined in that ID style.

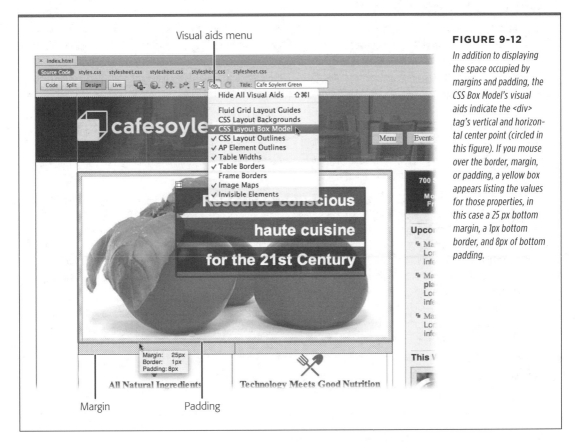

Visual aids menu

Margin   Padding

FIGURE 9-12

In addition to displaying the space occupied by margins and padding, the CSS Box Model's visual aids indicate the <div> tag's vertical and horizontal center point (circled in this figure). If you mouse over the border, margin, or padding, a yellow box appears listing the values for those properties, in this case a 25 px bottom margin, a 1px bottom border, and 8px of bottom padding.

As you can see, there's a considerable amount of margin on the bottom and a small amount of padding (8 pixels' worth) applied to the top, left, bottom and right edges.

If you find these visual aids confusing, you can turn them off via the Visual Aids menu in the document window (see Figure 9-12) or by choosing View→Visual Aids→Layout Box Model. These same steps turn the margin and padding visual aids back on.

FREQUENTLY ASKED QUESTION

When Width Doesn't Equal Width

In my style sheet, the CSS Width property of one of my styles is 150 pixels. But when I preview the page in a web browser, the <div> tag I applied the style to is much wider than 150 pixels. Is there a bug in my browser?

No, you're browser is fine. The problem lies with the difference between the CSS *width* property and the final calculated width of an element onscreen. The width you see onscreen is the sum total of several separate CSS properties, not just the Width property. The Width property merely defines the width of the content area of the style—the place where the text, images, or other nested tags sit.

The actual width—that is, the amount of screen real estate assigned by the web browser—is the *total* of the widths of the left and right margins, left and right padding, left and right borders, *and* the Width property. So say you create a style with a width of 100 pixels, 10 pixels of padding on all four sides, a 2 pixel border, and 20 pixels of space in the left margin. While the space dedicated to the content inside the style is 100 pixels wide, any tag with this style will have an onscreen width of 144 pixels: 100 (width) + 10 (left padding) + 10 (right padding) + 2 (left border) + 2 (right border) + 20 (left margin).

This can cause problems if you're not careful. For example, in a fixed-width layout, you might create a div that wraps around all other page elements. Its width is 960 pixels, so everything inside that div must fit in that 960-pixel space. If you wanted to create a four-column layout, you might insert four divs and create styles that set the width of each to 240 pixels (960 divided by 4).

However, if you added even a 1-pixel border to one of the divs, they'd suddenly take up more than 960 pixels, and you'd find that the last column wouldn't fit—in fact, it would drop down *below* the other three columns, creating a very weird-looking layout.

So if you find yourself floating lots of elements, and one of them drops below another when it should sit beside it, odds are pretty good that the elements are just too wide to sit side by side. So decrease the width, margins, padding, or borders until the elements fit (breaking out a calculator and adding up the margins, padding, borders, and widths can also help).

The CSS Height property and the final height of a style behave the same way. The onscreen height of an element is a combination of the height, top and bottom margins, padding, and borders.

■ Dreamweaver's CSS Layouts

You'll contend with many details when you build CSS-based layouts. For example, you need to understand the intricacies of the CSS Box Model, as well as the sometimes-bizarre behavior of floats. In addition, different browsers handle some CSS properties differently, which sometimes means a design that looks great in Firefox but completely falls apart in Internet Explorer 6. (Remember, even though much of the Windows-loving world has upgraded to IE 8 and IE 9, there are still plenty of folks cruising around the Web in IE 6 jalopies.) Fortunately, Dreamweaver is ready to give you a helping hand with 18 predesigned CSS Layouts.

Dreamweaver's CSS Layouts aren't finished web page designs. They don't have graphics, fancy text, drop-down menus, or any whiz-bang features. They're basic designs intended to lay the foundation for *your* design talents. Each layout is a simple HTML file and style sheet, each works with all current browsers, and each design's handcrafted CSS code irons out the many wrinkles in troublesome browsers (most notably Internet Explorer 6). In other words, instead of spending a day stretching and sizing your own canvas, a Dreamweaver CSS Layout is like going to the art store and buying a ready-made and primed canvas so you can get busy painting.

Creating a new CSS layout page takes just a few steps:

1. **Choose File→New.**

   This is the same first step you take when creating any new web page. The New Document window appears (Figure 9-13). You can also use the Ctrl+N (⌘-N) keyboard shortcut to open this window (however, it's possible to disable this keyboard shortcut, as described on page 47; you might want to do that if you'd rather skip this clunky window whenever you just want a new, blank web page).

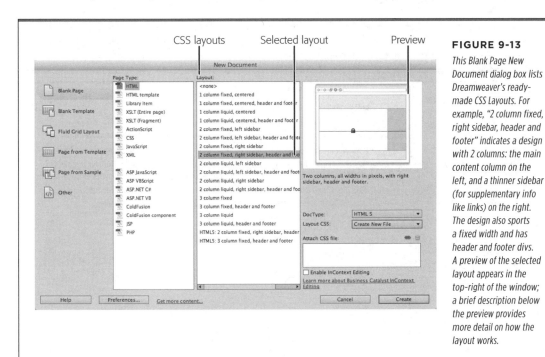

FIGURE 9-13

This Blank Page New Document dialog box lists Dreamweaver's ready-made CSS Layouts. For example, "2 column fixed, right sidebar, header and footer" indicates a design with 2 columns: the main content column on the left, and a thinner sidebar (for supplementary info like links) on the right. The design also sports a fixed width and has header and footer divs. A preview of the selected layout appears in the top-right of the window; a brief description below the preview provides more detail on how the layout works.

2. **Choose Blank Page from the left column, and the type of page you wish to create in the Page Type column.**

   Usually, you'll select HTML from the Page Type category, since most of the time you'll create regular web pages. However, if you're creating a page that uses a server-side language like PHP, you'd select it from the list.

TIP The Page From Sample category in the left column of the New Document window (see Figure 9-13) is mostly useless. It includes sample pages with some rudimentary design, but you can write better style sheets on your own. However, Dreamweaver CS6 includes a "Mobile starters" category for creating mobile sites (see on page 537 for a discussion of this feature).

3. **From the Layout column, select a page layout.**

   This is where the fun begins. As you've read before, choose *<none>* here to create an empty web page. The other options, however, let you choose one of 18 prefab CSS-based layouts. Basically, you decide how many columns you want (one, two, or three), whether you want a header and footer (like a banner at the top or a copyright notice at the bottom), and the type of web page layout (fixed-width or liquid).

   A fixed-width design maintains a constant page width no matter the width of a visitor's browser window. A liquid design lets the overall width of the page change with the size of a browser window. See page 435 for more on these types of layout.

   Dreamweaver previews each design in the top-right of the New Document window. See Figure 9-14 to decipher the visual codes that help you understand how the layouts behave.

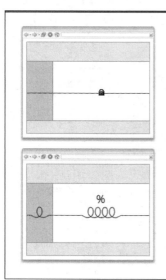

FIGURE 9-14

The layout previewed in the Blank Page New Document window visually identifies the type of CSS layout you select. A small lock icon indicates a fixed-width design (top); the layout sets the width of each column using pixel values, and the widths don't change when a guest resizes her browser window. The % symbol indicates a liquid design (bottom). It defines column widths using percentage values that change based on the width of the browser window; a wider browser window means wider columns. Liquid designs fill the entire width of a browser (well almost—the liquid designs provided with Dreamweaver are actually 80% of the width of the browser window).

4. **Choose a doctype from the DocType menu.**

   Here's where you decide which type of HTML/XHTML you want to use for the page. It's the same option you face when you create a new, blank web page, as described on page 46. You're safe going with the default option of HTML5.

5. **From the Layout CSS menu, select where you want to store the layout's CSS code.**

Each Dreamweaver CSS Layout requires its own style sheet of all the styles that make the layout work. When you create a new page from a CSS Layout, you can store that style sheet several places. The "Add to Head" option creates an internal style sheet in the HTML file Dreamweaver creates. Most of the time, you don't want this option, since external style sheets are more efficient (see page 123 for an explanation).

You can also store the CSS Layout styles in a new, external style sheet. Choose Create New File to let Dreamweaver store the necessary CSS rules there. You choose this option when you first use one of Dreamweaver's CSS layouts to create a new page. This creates a separate file with all the CSS necessary to control the page's layout. To add another page to your site using a layout you've already used (for example, a two-column fixed design with a header and footer), read on.

The "Link to Existing File" option sidesteps the entire process of creating new CSS styles. It assumes you have the appropriate styles defined in another external style sheet. If you previously created a web page using the same type of CSS layout, choose this option. Say you created a two-column fixed layout using a Dreamweaver CSS Layout. At that time, you saved the necessary styles for that layout in an external style sheet and saved the sheet to your site. Now, you can create a *new* two-column fixed-layout page using this external style sheet. Choose "Link to Existing File," and then proceed to step 6 to link the external style sheet on your site.

Keep in mind, however, that each CSS Layout has its *own* style sheet. So if you create a two-column fixed-layout page and then want to create a three-column liquid layout page, you can't link to the style sheet Dreamweaver created for the two-column layout. In other words, whenever you create a new *type* of CSS layout (two-column fixed, three-column liquid, and so on), choose the Create New File option so Dreamweaver creates the appropriate CSS in a new external style sheet.

TIP You don't need to go through these steps each time you want to create a new page using a CSS layout you've used before. Suppose you want to build a 40-page site with two-column, fixed-layout pages. Instead of going through the New Document dialog box (and the steps listed here) 40 times, use the New Document dialog box to create the initial page, and then choose File→Save As to save a copy of that design for the next two-column page you want to create. Better yet, use Dreamweaver's Template tool described in Chapter 19 to manage pages that have the same layout.

---

6. **Click the Attach Style Sheet button to attach any external style sheets to the page (see Figure 9-15).**

This is an optional step, but if you already have an external style sheet you want to use to format your site, now's the time to link to it. In addition, if you chose "Link to Existing File" in the previous step, you have to link to an external style sheet to create a particular layout type. The process of linking to external style sheets is the same as with any other web page, as described on page 138.

NOTE If, when you create a new web page, you link to an external style sheet as described in step 6, Dreamweaver may pop up a warning message that says something about needing to save your web page in order to correctly attach the style sheet. You can safely ignore this message. In fact, turn on the "Don't show me this message again" checkbox so you don't see this annoying message in the future.

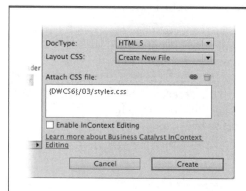

FIGURE 9-15

You can attach more than one external style sheet when you create a CSS-based layout. One might define the basic look of headlines, text, images, and other elements, for example, while another controls column layout, and a third "printer" style sheet might dictate how the page will look when printed (see page 399).

7. **Click the Create button to bring your new web page to life.**

If you selected the Create New File option in step 5, Dreamweaver asks you to name the new style sheet and select where you want to save it (just like when you create a new external style sheet, as described on page 128). Dreamweaver suggests names for the CSS files for each of its layouts—such as *twoColFixRtHdr.css* for a two column, fixed design with a right sidebar and a header and footer. You can change the name if you like, but the name Dreamweaver suggests is descriptive.

After all of that, you end up with a page that has a basic structure and some instructional text telling you to fill in the different areas of the page (see Figure 9-16). Don't forget to save and title the page.

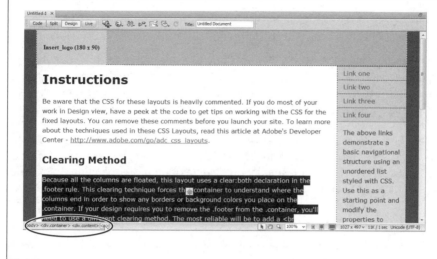

FIGURE 9-16

It doesn't look like much, but a CSS Layout page has the basic scaffolding of a bona fide web page in place: <div> tags to organize the page and CSS styles to position those divs. Click inside any area of the page, and the Tag Selector (circled) shows you the structure of the HTML at that point. In this case, if you click inside a paragraph in the middle column, the Tag Selector shows you which tags wrap around that paragraph. You read this info from right (the selected <p> tag) to left (the <body> tag that contains everything you see inside the document window). For this two-column design, the <p> tag is inside a div with a class of .content (that's what the <div.content> means), which is itself inside a div with a class of .container. Finally, the <body> tag encloses all the other tags.

The Structure of Dreamweaver's CSS Layouts

Dreamweaver's CSS Layouts are made up of a handful of page elements: Some pages have a header and footer, others have one or two sidebars, and all have a section of main content. The layout circumscribes each section with a <div> tag, and each div has its own class. The layout's accompanying style sheet defines the class styles and controls where a browser positions the different divs on the page.

To keep the CSS Layouts consistent, Dreamweaver uses the same class names for every layout (see Figure 9-17). It calls the class for the <div> tag containing the main content; if the layout has a sidebar, Dreamweaver applies the sidebar class *sidebar1* to it; if there's a second sidebar, Dreamweaver calls it *sidebar2*. Likewise, the header div has a class of *header*, while the div at the bottom of the page is *footer*. Dreamweaver uses one other <div>, and it surrounds all the other divs: Its class is *container*.

You may wonder: If all the CSS Layouts share the same names for their divs, how do you end up with different types of designs, like fixed and liquid? Each page has its own style sheet. When you create a new CSS Layout page and save those styles in an external style sheet (as described in step 5 on page 455), Dreamweaver suggests a name such as *thrColFixHdr.css* (for a three-column, fixed design with a header and footer), or *twoColLiqRt.css* (for a two-column, liquid design with a right sidebar). Each style sheet has different rules for its container, content, sidebar, and header, and footer styles. This means that if you plan on using more than one CSS Layout page, you need to keep separate style sheets for each type—in other words, if you attach the *twoColLiqRt.css* file to a three-column, fixed design, you end up with some weird results.

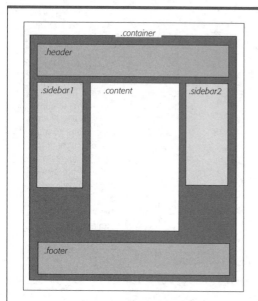

FIGURE 9-17

Each Dreamweaver CSS Layout's basic structure is the same. Several <div> tags identify the various regions of a page. Each div has its own class name, which a class style in the design's style sheet controls.

So what do you do if you want to, say, have the same design for all the paragraphs inside the main content div (<div class="content">) when you're using two different CSS Layouts? Create a third style sheet, named something like *global.css* or *site .css*, attach it to both types of pages, and create a descendent selector (page 377) like this: *.content p*. This formats just paragraphs inside another tag with the class *content*, and since it's in a style sheet shared by both pages, it works in both designs.

■ Modifying Dreamweaver's CSS Layouts

The basic look of a freshly minted Dreamweaver CSS Layout doesn't have much to recommend it: Fixed-width layouts have a green and tan color scheme, while liquid layouts are grayish-blue. One of the first things you want to do with a CSS Layout is remove some of Dreamweaver's formatting. In addition, you might want to tweak some of the basic layout properties, like the width of a fixed-width design or the width of sidebars and main columns.

Making General Changes to a CSS Layout

One of your first tasks should be to remove (or change) the background colors for the sidebar and other page elements of a CSS Layout page (unless you really like them, in which case your job is a lot easier). This generally means editing the styles in the Dreamweaver-supplied style sheet. You already know several ways to edit styles—like double-clicking the style's name in the CSS Styles panel (page 139) or using the Properties pane (page 382). The real trick is locating the correct style to edit. Here's the fast method:

1. **On the CSS Styles panel, click the Current button (see Figure 9-18, right).**

   If you don't have the Styles panel open, choose Window→CSS Styles. The Current view in this panel shows the styles and properties that Dreamweaver applied to whatever you select in the document window.

2. **Make sure that, in the Rules pane, you have the Show Cascade button selected.**

   The Show Cascade option lists all the styles that affect the current selection in the order of the "cascade"—least specific style at the top of the list, most specific at the bottom (see page 391 for a refresher on the cascade and specificity).

3. **Highlight the div you want to format.**

   For example, if you want to reformat the header, select the *header* div. You can select a div a couple of ways:

   - Click inside the div, and then click the corresponding <div> in the Tag Selector at the bottom left of the document window (see Figure 9-18, left). For example, click inside the header and then click *<div.header>* in the Tag selector.

   - Click inside the div, and then press Ctrl+A (⌘-A), or choose Edit→Select All. This selects the contents of the div and highlights the associated style for that div in the CSS Styles panel. (Pressing Ctrl+A twice selects the <div> tag itself.) To highlight a <div> tag that wraps around the div you clicked into, press Ctrl+A (⌘-A) twice more. For example, to select the *container* div that surrounds the header, sidebars, main content, and footer, you can click the header region, press Ctrl+A once to highlight the header style in the CSS Styles panel, and then press Ctrl+A twice more to highlight the *container* div.

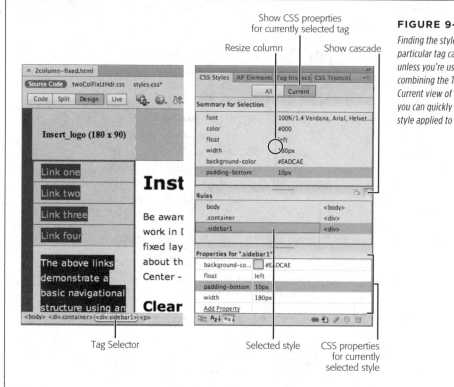

Show CSS proeprties
for currently selected tag

Resize column

Show cascade

Tag Selector

Selected style

CSS properties
for currently
selected style

FIGURE 9-18

*Finding the style that formats a
particular tag can be tricky—
unless you're using Dreamweaver. By
combining the Tag Selector and the
Current view of the CSS Styles panel,
you can quickly identify and edit a
style applied to any tag on a page.*

After you highlight the div, its style appears in the CSS Styles panel's Rules pane. In Figure 9-18, selecting the sidebar div—*<div.sidebar1>*—from the Tag Selector (left) selects that div's style (right). At this point, you can use the Properties pane (directly below the Rules pane) to edit the style as described on page 382, or simply double-click the style name to open the user-friendly Style Definition window.

> **NOTE** The styles for Dreamweaver CSS Layouts use what's called CSS "shorthand properties." These combine several CSS properties under a single property name. For example, you can combine the values for *background-color* and *background-image* into a single property named *background*, while you can specify all four margins (top, right, bottom, and left) with just one property: *margin*. This makes for more compact styles, but it also means that, to edit a shorthand property in the Properties pane, you need to know how to write the values yourself.

Dreamweaver doesn't provide a color box, link button, or any other of the helpful tools it provides when you set the values of a "longhand" property like *background-color*. In other words, unless you know CSS well, if you want to really make changes to one of the layout's styles, you're better off double-clicking the style's name in the Rules pane to access the much more user-friendly Rule Definition window.

Once you select a layout region on the page (header, sidebar, and so on), you probably want to make a few common changes:

- **Background colors**. To completely remove a div's background color, delete the value next to the *background-color* property in the Properties pane. You can also double-click the style's name in the CSS Styles panel to open the Rule Definition window, and then select the Background category to edit the color.

- **Text formatting**. You can modify the text and other content of a page to your heart's content. This book's earlier chapters show you how to format headlines, paragraphs, images, and links. However, when you create styles for these elements, use an external style sheet other than the one Dreamweaver supplies for the layout styles. You can store these types of styles in a generic style sheet like *styles.css*, instead of the layout-specific style sheet, such as *twoColFixLtHdr .css*. See step 5 on page 455 for the reason.

FREQUENTLY ASKED QUESTION

Paying Attention to Conditionals

I've noticed that when I create a page using any of Dreamweaver's two- or three-column liquid CSS layouts, the page has some weird-looking code just above the ending </head> tag. What's that about?

If you go into the Code view of any of the two- or three-column liquid layouts, you'll notice some grayed-out HTML that begins with *<!—[if lte IE 7]>* and ends with *<![endif]—>*. It's grayed out because Dreamweaver treats this code as an HTML comment. People who hand-code their pages use HTML comments to leave notes about their page—like why they added a chunk of HTML, (add comma after "HTML") or to identify which div a particular closing </div> tag belongs to. Dreamweaver and browsers ignore HTML comments.

However, this particular HTML comment, while ignored by every other browser, has special significance for Internet Explorer. HTML comments that begin like this *<!—[if IE]>* are actually secret messages, called *conditional comments*, intended just for Internet Explorer. Conditional comments let you send HTML, CSS, and JavaScript to Internet Explorer only; you can even send special HTML to particular versions of Internet Explorer. For example, *<!—[if lte IE 7]>* sends HTML to versions 7 and earlier of Internet Explorer (the "lte" part stands for "less than or equal to," so it addresses Internet Explorer 7 and those "less" than 7—IE 5 and IE 6, in other words).

You'll only encounter conditional comments in the two- or three-column liquid layouts. There, you find two styles squirreled away in conditional comments in the <head> of the page:

```
.content    {   margin-right:   -1px;
}
ul.nav a { zoom: 1; }
```

You might not need either of these to display your page correctly. The first helps IE determine the exact width for a percentage-based layout and only affects IE 6 and 7 (not 8 or 9). Try removing this style and testing your page in IE 6 and 7—if the column widths look and fit the same way they do in other browsers, you don't need this style. If they don't, test again with the style in place.

The second style—*ul.nav a*—applies only to the navigation buttons in the sidebar of some of these designs. If you remove the navigation bar (for example, if you have no navigation in the sidebar or use the Spry Menu [page 210] instead), remove this style.

In addition, IE 6 is nearly gone (see the box on page 504), and IE 7 is following close behind it. Odds are that soon you won't need to worry about either of these browsers and, depending on how tech-savvy your audience is, you might be able to stop supporting IE 7 now.

For a brief tutorial on conditional comments, visit: *www .javascriptkit.com/howto/cc2.shtml*.

Modifying Fixed Layouts

The width of any Dreamweaver fixed layout is 960 pixels. That's a common page width. It fits 1,024-pixel-wide screens (most netbooks, laptops, tablets, and desktop computers are at least that wide). However, that width may be too wide or too narrow for your tastes. If you're designing for the cinema-screen audience, you might want a page that takes advantage of a wider screen, so you might bump the width to 1,100 pixels or more. In addition, you may want to change the widths of columns on a page. Here's how you make a few key layout changes:

- **Page width**. Dreamweaver fixes the area of the page that includes the header, sidebars, and main content at 960 pixels. This setting is defined in Dreamweaver's *container* div. Select the div and change 960 to whatever width you want.

> **NOTE** Nine hundred and sixty pixels is way too wide for mobile phones. Fortunately, Dreamweaver CS6 includes support for a CSS technique called "media queries" which lets you adjust a page's layout based on the screen dimensions of the device viewing the page. In other words, you can design both a 960-pixel-wide layout for desktop computers and a 320-pixel-wide layout for phones. See Chapter 11 to learn how to use media queries.

- **Column width**. Dreamweaver makes the sidebar columns 180 pixels wide, and the main content region 780 pixels wide for two-column designs, or 600 pixels wide for three-column designs. Select the sidebar you wish to make wider or narrower, and then adjust its *width* property.

  Unfortunately, you often have to do a little math if you want the three columns to sit side by side. Since the container has a set width (960 pixels by default), the width of the three columns should also add up to 960 pixels. If their total is bigger, the content area actually drops below the two sidebars. So if you increase the size of one sidebar, you need to decrease the width of the main content area (the *.content* style) by the same amount. For example, in a two-column fixed design, if you increase the sidebar to 200 pixels wide (20 pixels more than it starts out with), you need to subtract 20 pixels from the width of the *content div:* In other words edit the *.content* style and change its width to 760 pixels.

  Things get even trickier if you add margins, padding, or a border to the left or right of any column. As discussed in the box on page 452, the actual horizontal space of any element is the sum of its width, left and right margins, left and right padding, and left and right border. If you add a 1-pixel right border to a sidebar, you increase the total width of all the columns to 961 pixels (1 pixel more than the container's 960-pixel width). The result? The main content area drops below the sidebar. Aye carumba! In other words, if you make a change to a sidebar, or the main content area, and the *content div* suddenly drops down on the page, check your math!

TIP If you use Dreamweaver CSS Layouts often, you may frequently make the same adjustments over and over again. For example, you might always remove the padding and background color, and adjust the column widths. Instead of repeatedly doing that, edit the default HTML and CSS files Dreamweaver uses when it creates a new blank CSS Layout page. In Windows, you find them in the C:\Program Files\Adobe\Adobe Dreamweaver CS6\Configuration\BuiltIn\Layouts folder, and on the Mac, they're in the Applications→Adobe Dreamweaver CS 6→Configuration→BuiltIn→Layouts folder.

NOTE You can also clean up this folder by deleting designs you don't use. Just make sure you back up the folder before you do anything to the files inside. And then, back up your new designs so that if you ever have to reinstall Dreamweaver, you have a backup of your modified templates.

Modifying Liquid Layouts

Liquid layouts adjust to the width of a browser window. Columns grow wider as visitors widen the window and shrink when the browser window shrinks. However, you can still control the relative widths of the page:

- **Page width**. Although a page adjusts its width with a liquid layout, Dreamweaver's default styles make the 80% of the window width. In other words, Dreamweaver always leaves some empty space on either side of the container div (10%, to be precise). To remove this space to make the page fill the entire width of the browser window, edit the *.container* style: Just delete the width entirely—don't set its width to 100 percent. (Doing so can make the page appear a little *wider* than the browser window, forcing visitors to scroll right to see all of a page's content. See the box on page 452 for an explanation.)

NOTE The liquid layouts that come with Dreamweaver have built-in limits for the width of the container div. Dreamweaver sets two additional *.container* style properties—*max-width* and *min-width*. Max-width defines the maximum width of the div (1,260 pixels) and keeps it from becoming unreadably wide on extremely large screens. The *min-width* property, by contrast, keeps the div from shrinking past 780 pixels. To change these values or delete them entirely, use the Properties pane (see page 382).

- **Column width**. As with fixed layouts, Dreamweaver sets the sidebar and main content widths using the Width property. The only difference is that it does so using percentages, with the combined width of the sidebars and the content div at 100%. Just as with fixed layouts, if you change the width of one div, you need to adjust the width of another. So in a three-column liquid design, to make the left sidebar, say, 25% instead of the usual 20%, you need to remove 5% from the *content* div, the right sidebar, or split that between the two: for example, change the *.content* style to a width of 57% (from its normal 60%) and the *.sidebar2* style to 18%.

Other Styles to Change

Dreamweaver's CSS Layouts include a few other styles you might want to modify or delete.

- **Text spacing**. It's common for web designers to add some empty space between the edge of a column and the content inside it. This "white space" makes the text feel less cramped and more readable. You can add padding to the div that creates the column—for example, the <div class="content"> element the CSS Layouts use to create the main content region. However, as mentioned above, adding padding to that div increases its overall width, potentially making the column too wide to fit next to the other columns. So, instead of adding padding to the sidebars or main content styles, Dreamweaver uses a group style ("h1, h2, h3, h4, h5, h6, p") that includes left and right padding. Because it applies the padding to tags inside the column and not the column itself, the overall width of each column remains the same. You get the same visual result—added white space on either side of each column—without having to futz with width settings.

  The only downside to this approach is that it will apply to every header and paragraph on the page. What if you want a little less white space inside the left sidebar and a little more inside the main content area? The answer is descendent selectors (see page 377). For example, to create a style that affects the padding of just the headings and paragraphs in the first sidebar, you'd create this (long-winded) group style:

  .sidebar1 h1, .sidebar1 h2, .sidebar1 h3, .sidebar1 h4, .sidebar1 h5, .sidebar1 h6, .sidebar1 p

  Then, any left and right padding you add to the *.sidebar* style applies only to the headings and paragraphs *inside* the sidebar (see page 381 for instructions on creating a group style).

  You'll also find styles named *.content ui and .content ol*, which Dreamweaver uses to add white space around bulleted and numbered lists inside the main content area. You may want to adjust or delete these styles as well.

- **Links**. The CSS Layouts also include styles for the link states discussed on page 206 (*a:link, a:visited*, and so on). You may not like these, so feel free to change or delete them. And if the pages in your site use different CSS Layouts (two-column fixed and three-column fixed pages, for example) you're better off creating a shared, external style sheet (*site.css* or *styles.css*, for instance), putting your link styles there, and then linking the external style sheet to all your pages (see page 138 to learn how to link to an external style sheet, and page 385 for how to move styles between style sheets). That way, all your pages, even ones with different layouts, will have consistent link styles.

- **Navigation bar**. Some of Dreamweaver's layouts include a simple navigation bar in a sidebar. If you like this, you can change its appearance by editing the various styles that begin with *ul.nav* in the layout's style sheet. They control the appearance of the list and the links inside. If you don't plan on using the navigation bars, feel free to delete the styles entirely.

NOTE The style sheets Dreamweaver supplies with CSS Layouts are chock-full of CSS comments. This is a good thing when you're getting started, because they're like a mini-lesson in CSS layout. Read through the comments in at least one of the style sheets and you're sure to learn a few things. However, when it's time to put your site on the Web, all those comments are unnecessary bloat that slow page downloads. You can delete them by hand (CSS comments are grey in Code view and begin with /* and end with */) or you can use Dreamweaver's Find and Replace tool to quickly remove them all.

For a little help, download Dreamweaver expert David Power's "Dreamweaver query" (basically a saved find-and-replace command) from *http://tinyurl.com/4ywjk42*. You can read about Dreamweaver's powerful Find and Replace tool in Chapter 20.

Absolute Positioning

Beyond float-based layouts, CSS's other main technique for placing elements on a page, absolute positioning, lets you specify the exact position on a page for any element. But before you start thinking you've found page-layout heaven, keep in mind that the Web is a fluid environment that's difficult to control with pixel-level precision. If a visitor increases the font size in her browser, the enlarged text may spill out of your carefully crafted layout. In addition, it's nearly impossible to force a footer to the bottom of a page laid out using absolute positioning (a trivial task with float-based layouts). That's why most CSS Layouts use floats and the techniques discussed at the beginning of this chapter.

That's not to say you shouldn't use absolute positioning. It's great for moving small elements, like a logo, image, or short set of links, to a specific position on a page. And it's the only way to have one element overlap another (see Figure 9-19). As long as you don't try to dictate the exact width, height, and position of every page element, you'll find absolute positioning powerful and helpful.

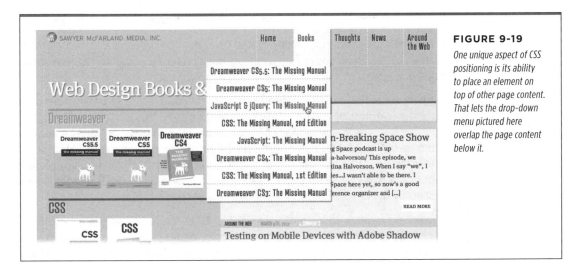

FIGURE 9-19

One unique aspect of CSS positioning is its ability to place an element on top of other page content. That lets the drop-down menu pictured here overlap the page content below it.

The CSS Positioning Properties

Several CSS properties position elements onscreen. You'll find them under the Positioning category of the CSS Rule Definition window (Figure 9-20).

■ POSITIONING TYPE

Normally, browsers position elements on the screen in the order they appear in the HTML; the first element tagged in the HTML appears at the top of the browser window. Similarly, HTML at the end of web-page files appears at the bottom of the browser window. In Figure 9-21, the top-left image shows a headline, followed by a paragraph of text, followed by a headline, an image, and another paragraph. This is the order in which the elements appear in the HTML, top to bottom.

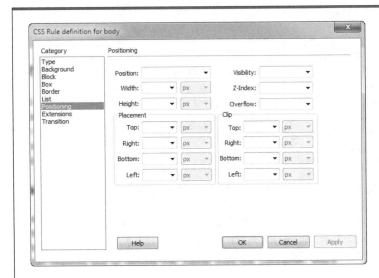

FIGURE 9-20

Dreamweaver gives you easy access to its many CSS Positioning properties. You'll never need to set all of them, and web designers rarely use a few of them, like those found in the Clip section of this dialog box (see page 472 for details on the Clip property).

The CSS *position* property, however, lets you alter the order of a styled element on-screen by assigning one of four available position types: *absolute, relative, static,* and *fixed.*

- **Absolute** is the most common option. It lets you place a tag anywhere on a page, regardless of the tag's position in the page's HTML. The top-right image in Figure 9-21 displays a graphic of a sticky note. Even though the image falls after the text "Malorum Gipsum" inside the headline in the page's HTML, it appears at the top of the page (and even a little bit off the top) because it's absolutely positioned (AP). The space the graphic used to occupy (top-left image) is now filled by the paragraph of text beneath the second headline.

  In other words, with absolute positioning, HTML code can go *anywhere* inside a <body> tag and still appear *anywhere* on a page—its location in the code has nothing to do with its location on-screen. In addition, absolutely positioned elements are removed from the normal flow of a page—other tags on the page aren't even "aware" that the AP (absolutely positioned) element exists.

After you select the Absolute option, use the Placement properties (see page 470) to specify a position.

Browsers, however, don't always put absolutely positioned elements in relation to the page itself. If you create a style to position an element inside another element that's either positioned relatively (see the next bullet point) or absolutely, the browser positions the first element *in relation to the latter element*, not in relation to the page itself. The next bullet point clarifies this confusing concept.

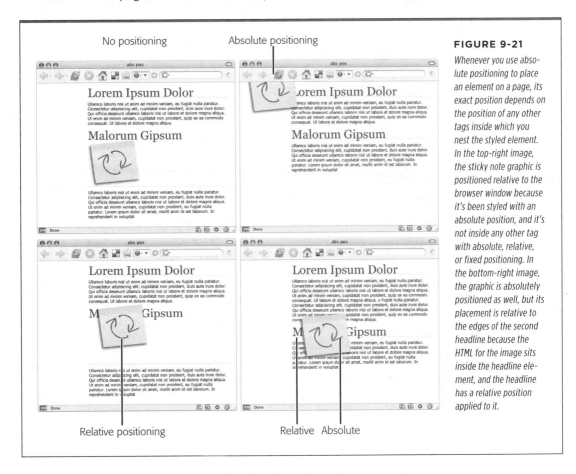

No positioning

Absolute positioning

Relative positioning

Relative   Absolute

FIGURE 9-21

Whenever you use absolute positioning to place an element on a page, its exact position depends on the position of any other tags inside which you nest the styled element. In the top-right image, the sticky note graphic is positioned relative to the browser window because it's been styled with an absolute position, and it's not inside any other tag with absolute, relative, or fixed positioning. In the bottom-right image, the graphic is absolutely positioned as well, but its placement is relative to the edges of the second headline because the HTML for the image sits inside the headline element, and the headline has a relative position applied to it.

• The **Relative** option lets you position a tag relative to its position in the HTML. When you choose this option, the positioned element appears relative to where it appears in the HTML. The bottom-left image in Figure 9-21 shows the same sticky note positioned using the Relative property. Although it has the same top and left placement values (page 470) as the top-right image, the browser now positions the sticky note relative to where its tag sits in the HTML—just below the "Malorum Gipsum" line. Even so, the note sits in the top-left position of that line, reflecting the values in the Relative property. Another side effect of relative positioning is that the space formerly taken up by the image (top-left in Figure 9-21) remains. Notice that the last paragraph doesn't try to fill up the space where the graphic was—there's still a big empty area.

At first glance, the Relative option might seem less than useful. After all, what's the point of positioning something on a page, just to leave a big empty ("I *was* here") space? In many cases, you don't actually apply relative positioning to an *element* you want to position. You apply it to a *tag* that wraps *around* the element you want to position, in order to create a new set of coordinates for an absolutely positioned element to use.

Say you put an image inside a headline, and you want the image to appear on the left edge of that headline. If you simply position the image in an exact spot in the browser window on the left edge of the headline tag, you're taking your chances. If the headline moves (say you add some new body text above it), the absolutely positioned image stays glued to its assigned spot. Instead, what you want to do is position the image *relative* to the headline tag, so that when the headline moves, so does the image. Look at the bottom-right image of Figure 9-21. The headline ("Malorum Gipsum") is relatively positioned, and the sticky note is absolutely positioned, but it's absolutely positioned *inside the headline tag.* Even when, later on, you add a little more text to the top of the page (thereby forcing the headline to move down), the sticky note travels along for the ride.

- **Static** positioning is the normal behavior of HTML. Static simply means the content follows the normal top-down flow of HTML. Why would you want to assign an element static positioning? The short answer: You probably never will.

- **Fixed** positioning is similar to the "fixed" value of the CSS attachment property used to lock a background image in place (see page 262). This option "fixes" the element in place in the browser window. When you scroll down the page, the AP element doesn't move, it remains in a precise spot in the browser window. It's a cool option with exciting possibilities. For example, you could create a navigation bar that sticks to the top of the browser window. When visitors scroll down the page, the navigation bar stays in place. Internet Explorer 6 ignores the fixed option, but since that browser is nearly extinct, it's worth experimenting with this property.

■ WIDTH AND HEIGHT

These properties, logically enough, set the width and height of the element. You can use any of the available CSS units of measure, like pixels, ems, and percentages. In most cases, when you want precise control over the dimensions of your tags—that is, a page element that's *exactly* 200 pixels wide and won't change even if a visitor changes the size of his browser window—use pixels. However, if you want the element to resize as the visitor resizes his browser, use percentages. That way, you can specify a style that's 50% the width of the browser window, no matter the size of the window.

NOTE The Width and Height properties available under the Positioning category of the CSS Rule Definition window are identical to the options of the same name under the Box category (see Figure 9-10). Also note that CSS calculates the total width of a style as the width value *plus* any borders, margins, or padding (see the box on page 452 for more). The same is true for the height of an element.

■ VISIBILITY

Left to its own devices, a web browser makes the contents of all tags visible on the page, so you'll usually leave this property blank. After all, if you put something on your page, it's usually because you want people to see it. But there are situations in which you may want to make a certain tag (and its contents) invisible to your visitors.

For example, you might want a page element to appear when a visitor clicks a button or mouses over another element (this is how the Spry tooltips, discussed on page 656, work). However, most web designers use the Display property (page 166) and not the Visibility property for this. To make an element disappear, set the display property to none; to make it visible, set the display property back to block (for block-level elements like headlines, paragraphs, and divs) or inline (for inline-elements like images, links, and <span> tags).

In other words, skip the Visibility property.

■ Z-INDEX

Welcome to the third dimension. Absolutely positioned tags are unique in the world of web elements because they "float" above (or even behind) a web page and can overlap each other, completely or partially.

If you were awake in high school geometry, you may remember the graphing system in which the x-axis specified where a point was in space from left to right and the y-axis specified where the point was from top to bottom. And if you were awake *and* paying attention, you may remember that the z-axis denotes a point's position in *front-to-back* space. When you draw a three-dimensional object on this type of graph, you need to use all three axes: x, y, and z.

The Z-Index of an absolutely positioned element doesn't make your web page *appear* three-dimensional; it simply specifies the "front-to-backness" of overlapping AP elements. In other words, the Z-Index, represented by a number in the Z-Index field, controls the stacking order of AP elements on a page.

The page itself lies behind all AP elements, and the AP elements stack up from there. In other words, the higher the Z-Index number, the higher the AP element in the "stack," so an AP element with a Z-Index of 4 appears *behind* an overlapping AP element with a Z-Index of, say, 7.

Z-Index numbers have no relation to the actual number of absolutely positioned items on a page. You can have three AP elements with Z-Indexes of, say, 2, 499, and 2000 if you choose. You'd still just have three AP elements, one on top of the other in ascending order. Spacing your Z-Index numbers in this somewhat arbitrary manner is helpful, since it lets you insert divs between already positioned divs as you develop your page, without having to renumber the Z-Indexes of all your AP elements.

■ OVERFLOW

Suppose you create a square div that's 100 x 100 pixels. Then you fill it with a graphic that's 150 x 162 pixels—that is, larger than the div itself.

You've already seen how a table cell reacts to this situation: It simply grows to fit the content inside it. Divs (and other elements), however, are more (or less) flexible, depending on your choice of Overflow option in the Property Inspector. The following options let you decide how browsers handle the excess part of the image:

- **Visible** will display any content that doesn't fit inside the element. It doesn't actually expand the size of the element itself, however, something you'll notice if you apply a background or borders to the element. In the example above, if you add a border to an element, a browser would draw the border only around the 100- x 100- (100- by 100-pixel) pixel square defined by the style. The graphic would simply "pop out" of the box.

- **Hidden** chops off the excess content. In the example above, you'd only see the top left 100 x 100 pixels of the image.

- **Scroll** adds scroll bars to the element, so that a visitor can scroll to see all of the element's contents. It's like having a miniature browser window embedded in the page. This feature offers an interesting way to add a small, scrollable window within a web page: Imagine a small "Latest Company News" box that visitors can scroll through to read the text inside without disturbing anything else on the page.

- **Auto** adds scroll bars to an element *only* if necessary to accommodate oversize contents.

In Design view, if you select any option besides "Visible," you see the div's set dimensions—for example, 100 pixels by 100 pixels. Dreamweaver doesn't display any content outside that area—the overflow, in other words.

You may have content you'd like to edit that's part of the overflow—like the "Latest Company News" box mentioned above. Dreamweaver gives you an easy way to edit any of that hidden content—just double-click the element. Doing so expands the div (just as if you'd selected the Visible option) so you can edit it. To reset the element back to its original dimensions, right-click (Control-click) the element and, from the shortcut menu that appears, select Element View→Hidden.

NOTE You can use the Overflow property on any element, not just on absolutely positioned divs. For example, if you want to create a 100-pixel-tall div with scrollbars and lots of content inside that visitors can scroll through, just create a style with a 100-pixel height and the Overflow property set to *Scroll*, and apply that style to the div. No positioning required.

■ PLACEMENT

These properties let you specify an absolutely positioned element's position, which is, after all, the whole point of AP elements. The four Placement properties control where each of the four edges of the AP element begin. Setting the Top box to 200 pixels positions the top of the AP element 200 pixels down the screen, whereas the Bottom option identifies where the bottom of the AP element starts. Similarly, the Left and Right properties set the beginning of the left edge and right edge of the AP element.

You'll frequently use a combination of the Width property (page 448) and the Top and Left or Right properties. To place a 150-pixel-wide sidebar 200 pixels from the top of the page and 15 pixels in from the left, you'd set the Width property to 150 pixels, the Top property to 200, and the Left property to 15 pixels.

You'll also find the Right property handy. Say you want to put a 200-pixel-wide sidebar on the right side of a page. Since you don't know the exact width of a visitor's browser—580 pixels, 1,200 pixels?—you can't know ahead of time how far the AP element needs to be from the left edge of the window. So you can set the Right property to 0—if you want the sidebar to touch the right edge of the page. If you want to indent the AP element 20 pixels from the right edge of the window, type *20*.

In addition, you can skip setting a width by assigning both Left and Right positioning simultaneously—say, placing an AP element 50 pixels from the left edge and 20 from the right. You can do the same with Top and Bottom settings as well—don't set the height of an element, just set its Top and Bottom values.

TIP Here's a cool trick: absolutely position a div and set its top, left, bottom, and right positions to 0. You'll have a div that fills the browser window—even when someone resizes the window.

Positioning isn't quite as straightforward as it may seem. The exact location of a positioned div is a combination of not only these position values, but also of what type of placement you choose for the AP element—absolute or relative. As noted earlier, with relative positioning, the numbers you type for Top or Left, for instance, are calculated based on where the AP element already appears in the HTML code and on the screen. So setting the Top property to 100 pixels doesn't place the AP element 100 pixels from the top of the browser window; it places it 100 pixels from where it would appear on the screen based on the HTML code.

Absolute positioning, however, lets you place an AP element at an exact spot on a page. So setting the Top and Left properties for an absolutely positioned AP element to 100 and 150 pixels *will* place that AP element 100 pixels from the top of the browser window and 150 pixels from the left edge.

NOTE There's one additional wrinkle to absolute positioning. For a div nested inside another div that has either a Relative or an Absolute position setting, the browser calculates position values based on the position of the *parent* div. If you have one AP element 300 pixels from the top of a page, an absolutely positioned AP element nested inside *that* AP element with a Top position of 20, it doesn't appear 20 pixels from the top of the page. It appears 20 pixels from the top of the parent AP element, in this case 320 pixels from the top of the page.

■ CLIP

The Clip property can hide all but a rectangular piece of an AP element. In most cases, you should avoid this property, since it's rarely useful, and it's also a waste of precious bandwidth.

Suppose you put a large graphic into an AP element, but you want to display only one small area. You *could* use the Clip property, but a browser still has to download the *entire* graphic, not just the clipped area. You're much better off preparing the smaller graphic at the right size to begin with. The kilobytes you save may be your own.

You can use JavaScript to *move* the clipping area, creating an effect like a spotlight traveling across the AP element. Although that may be a more useful purpose for the Clip property, Dreamweaver doesn't support it, unfortunately.

The four clipping settings—top, right, bottom, and left—specify the positions of the clipping box's four edges. In other words, these indicate the borders of the visible area of the AP element.

■ Adding an AP Element to Your Page

In most cases, the <div> tags you'll position will have a variety of HTML elements—images, paragraphs, headlines, and so on. For example, to place a series of links at the top of a page, you could wrap those links in a <div> tag and position that div. In this case, you can use the Insert Div Tag tool discussed on page 440. Start out by selecting existing content, or just click where you want to add a new absolutely positioned div. Either way, you either need to create a class or ID style first (with the positioning properties discussed above), and then select that style from the Class or ID menu of the Insert Div Tag window; alternatively, you can create the class or ID style by clicking the New CSS Style button in the Insert Div Tag window (see Figure 9-6).

But absolute positioning isn't just for <div> tags; any HTML tag—forms, paragraphs, headlines and images—can be positioned absolutely. You just need to create a style and set the Position property to Absolute (page 466), and, voila, you have an absolutely positioned element.

> **NOTE** Dreamweaver includes some other tools for working with what the program calls "AP Divs." But you should avoid both the Draw AP Div tool and the Insert AP Div command (Insert→Layout Objects→AP Div). These tools create internal CSS style sheets, along with less-than-obvious ID names. In addition, you can't control where in the page these tools dump the HTML they create. Another tool to skip: the AP Elements panel (Window→AP Elements). You can use the Property Inspector (discussed below) to make the same changes (and more) the panel offers.

Unless you add a background color or border to your AP element, it's difficult to identify its boundaries. To make working with AP elements easier, Dreamweaver provides visual cues in Design view, as shown in Figure 9-22, and explained in the following list:

- **AP element marker**. The gold shield with the letter C (huh?) represents the position in the underlying HTML where the code for the AP element actually appears. (Actually, the shield appears for any tag with either absolute or relative positioning.)

Dreamweaver doesn't display these markers by default. To see them, you have to turn them on in the Preferences window: Press Ctrl+U (⌘-U) to open the window, click the Invisible Elements category, and turn on "Anchor points for AP elements."

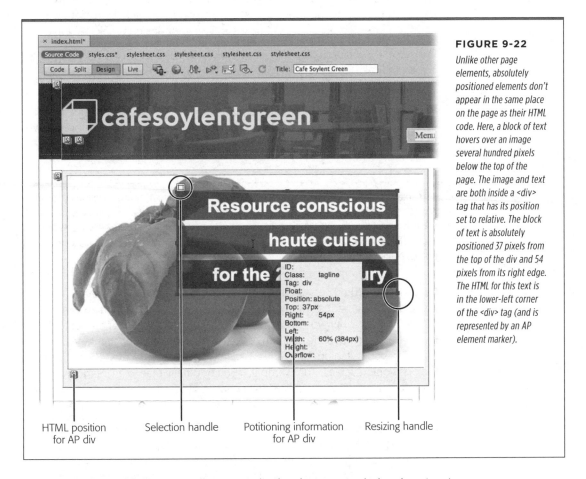

HTML position
for AP div

Selection handle

Potitioning information
for AP div

Resizing handle

FIGURE 9-22

Unlike other page elements, absolutely positioned elements don't appear in the same place on the page as their HTML code. Here, a block of text hovers over an image several hundred pixels below the top of the page. The image and text are both inside a <div> tag that has its position set to relative. The block of text is absolutely positioned 37 pixels from the top of the div and 54 pixels from its right edge. The HTML for this text is in the lower-left corner of the <div> tag (and is represented by an AP element marker).

While HTML objects generally appear in the document window in a top-to-bottom sequence that mirrors their order in the HTML, the position of AP elements *doesn't* depend on where the AP element-creating code appears in the page's HTML. In other words, you can have an AP element in the first line in the body of the HTML page while the element appears near the bottom of the final line on the page.

To move the HTML of the AP element, drag the shield icon. You can place this at the beginning, end, or anywhere else in your HTML, but you need to be careful. As discussed on page 466, when you position an element absolutely, its exact location depends on whether its parent element has either a relative or absolute position. If the parent element is itself positioned and you drag the element outside its parent, its top, left, bottom, and right coordinates will change—a browser may now position that element in relation to the browser window. Likewise, if you drag the shield inside another element that's positioned, the browser will display that element in relation to the new parent element. In other words, it can get pretty confusing when you start dragging the shield icon around, so be careful and remember to press Ctrl+Z (⌘-Z) if your design breaks as you do so.

Conversely, if you drag the selection handle of the element, it moves the element but leaves the HTML in the same location (described next).

That distinction often confuses Dreamweaver users. For instance, if you want to reposition an AP element on the page, don't drag the AP element's marker (the gold shield that represents the HTML code) into a table. This simply moves the HTML to another spot inside the code but doesn't reposition the div on the screen.

NOTE The AP element marker (the gold shield) takes up room on the screen and can push text, graphics, and other items out of the way. In fact, even the thin borders that Dreamweaver adds to indicate divs take up space in the document window, and the space they occupy may make it difficult to place AP elements precisely. The keyboard shortcut Ctrl+Shift+I (⌘-Shift-I) hides or shows invisible items like AP element markers. The Hide All Visual Aids option from the Document toolbar does the same thing (see Figure 9-23).

- **Selection handle**. The selection handle provides a convenient way to grab and move an AP element around a page. The handle appears when you select the AP element, or when you click inside the AP element to add material to it. The handle lets you move the position of the AP element without changing the position of its code. Behind the scenes, Dreamweaver updates the CSS by updating the positioning values. For example, if you originally placed an image by setting the left and top values, Dreamweaver changes those to match the new location; if you used right and bottom settings, Dreamweaver updates those...pretty nifty.

- **AP element outline**. Unselected absolutely positioned elements have a thin, gray, 3-D border. Like the AP element marker and selection handle, it's only there to help you see the boundaries of the AP element, and doesn't show up in web browsers. You can turn it on and off, but to turn it off, you need to make sure you turn off two options in the View→Visual Aids menu: AP Element Outlines and Layout Outlines. You can also use the Visual Aids menu in the document window.

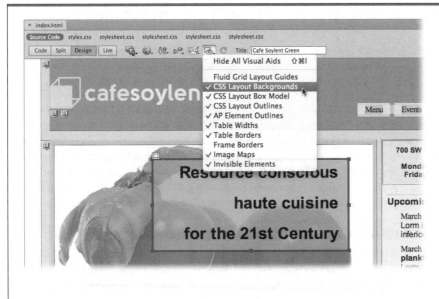

FIGURE 9-23

Choices 3 to 6 in the Visual Aids menu provide visual cues to help you with CSS Layouts in Design view. The CSS Layout Backgrounds option— selected here—lights up each <div> tag on a page with a hideous, randomly selected background color. It also highlights any element whose display property you set to "block" (page 166), or that uses either absolute or relative position- ing. You'll find the CSS Layout Box model option discussed in Figure 9-12.

NOTE If one AP element overlaps another, the top AP element—the one with the higher Z-Index, as described on page 469—has a solid outline; the lower element's outline appears as a dashed line where the top AP element overlaps it.

- **AP element positioning summary**. If you select an AP element and hover your mouse over that div, Dreamweaver pops up a box with information about that AP element (see Figure 9-22), including the name of the ID or class, what type of positioning you used, the AP element's dimensions, and so on. This gives you a bird's-eye view of the CSS properties defining the AP element's place- ment on the page.

Modifying AP Element Properties

Once you add an AP element, you don't need to go back to the CSS Rule Definition window to edit many of its positioning properties. Using the Property Inspector, you can rename, resize, move, and align the div with other AP elements, and set many other properties.

But first, you have to select the AP element using one of these methods:

- Click the AP element's selection handle (see Figure 9-22).

- Click the AP element's border. The border turns red when you move your mouse into the proper position.

- Click the AP element marker that indicates the HTML code for the absolutely positioned item. (Out of the box, Dreamweaver hides these markers, since they can get in the way of your design work; to show them, see the note on page 474.)

And if those aren't enough ways to select an AP element—Adobe's programmers never sleep—you can also Shift-click one. This Shift-click technique offers another advantage: you can select multiple AP elements simultaneously and set the properties of (or align) many AP elements at once. If you're working in an AP element or have an AP element selected, Shift-clicking another AP element selects them both. You can continue to Shift-click to select additional AP elements. (Shift-click a second time to deselect a selected element.)

Resizing Absolutely Positioned Elements

When you select an AP element, eight handles appear around its edges element (see Figure 9-22). You can drag any of them to change the element's dimensions. The corner handles resize both the width and height simultaneously.

You can also use the keyboard to resize an absolutely positioned element. First, select the AP element, and then do one of the following:

- Press the Ctrl (⌘) key, and then press the arrow keys to change the AP element's size by one pixel. The up and down arrow keys adjust the AP element's height; the left and right arrows affect its width.

- To change the size *10* pixels at a time, press Ctrl+Shift (⌘-Shift), and then press the arrow keys.

For better precision, use the Property Inspector to set an exact width and height for the element (see Figure 9-24). Type values in the W and H boxes to change the width and height, respectively. You can specify any unit of measure that CSS understands: px (pixels), pc (picas), pt (points), in (inches), mm (millimeters), cm (centimeters), em (height of the current font), ex (height of the current font's x character), or % (percentage)—see page 156. To pick your measurement unit, type its abbreviation *immediately* after you type in the size value. For example, type *100px* into the W box to make the AP element 100 pixels wide. Don't leave out the measurement unit—px, em, or %, for example—or browsers won't display the correct dimensions of the AP element.

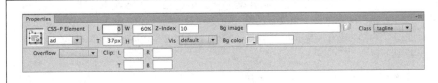

FIGURE 9-24

The Property Inspector controls many AP element properties (although some require you to edit CSS styles).

Another benefit to using the Property Inspector is that Dreamweaver lets you resize multiple AP elements at once. Shift-click two or more elements to select them, and then type new widths and heights. Dreamweaver sets all the selected AP elements to these dimensions.

Moving AP Elements

Moving an absolutely positioned element is just as simple as resizing it. Drag any border of the element, or the AP element's selection handle. Avoid the eight resize handles, however, because they'll change the size of the AP element when you drag them.

For less speed but greater precision, you can use the keyboard. First, select the element and then do one of the following:

- To move an AP element one pixel at a time, press the corresponding keyboard arrow key.

- Press Shift while using an arrow key to move the element 10 pixels at a time.

As you'd guess, you can also control an AP element's placement by using the Property Inspector. Dreamweaver measures an AP element's position relative to the left and top edges of the page (or, for nested AP elements, from the left and top edges of a parent div when you set the Position property to either absolute or relative). The Property Inspector provides two boxes for these values: L specifies the distance from the left edge of the page to the left edge of the selected AP element; T specifies the distance from the top of the page to the top of the selected AP element.

NOTE You can't edit an AP element's Right or Bottom positioning properties from the Property Inspector. For these properties, edit the AP element's style by either double-clicking the style in the CSS Styles panel, or selecting the style and using the Properties pane (page 382).

To position an AP element using the Property Inspector, select the div (for example, by clicking the div's border or by selecting its name in the AP Elements panel), and then type distances in the L and T boxes. You can use any of the units of measure mentioned previously. You can even use negative values to move part or all of an AP element off the page entirely (offstage, you might say), which you might want to do if you intended a subsequent animation to bring it *onstage*, into the document window using JavaScript.

If you draw a 100-pixel-tall and 50-pixel-wide AP element, you can move it to the very top-left corner of the page by selecting it, and then typing *0* in both the L and T boxes. To position that same AP element so that it's just off the left edge of the page, type *-50px* in the L box.

Aligning AP Elements

At times, you may want to align several AP elements so that their left, top, bottom, or right edges line up with each other. Dreamweaver's Align command does just that; it can even make the width and height of selected AP elements the same.

To use this feature, select two or more AP elements (by Shift-clicking them), choose Modify→Arrange, and then select one of the following options from the submenu:

- Align Left aligns the left edges of all selected AP elements. In other words, it gives each AP element the same L property.

- Align Right aligns the right edges.

- Align Top aligns the top edges, so that all the T properties are the same.

- Align Bottom aligns the bottom edges of the AP elements.

- Make Same Width sets the same width for all the selected AP elements (in the W box in the Property Inspector). Make Same Height does the same for the height of the AP elements.

The AP element you select *last* dictates how Dreamweaver aligns the AP elements. Say you have three AP elements—A, B, and C—and you select them in order from A to C. You then set their align property to *Left*. Dreamweaver uses the left edge of AP element C (the last one you selected) as the value for the other AP elements.

Background Image and Color

To add a background image to an AP element, click the folder icon next to the "Bg Image" field, and then select an image from your site folder. As usual, Dreamweaver tiles the image, if necessary, to fill the entire AP element's area with repeating copies of the graphic. (To adjust how or whether the image tiles, you need to edit the AP element's style using the normal CSS style-editing techniques; see page 139.)

Setting a background color is even easier. Just use the Bg Color box to select a color or to sample one from your screen.

CSS Layout Tutorial

In this tutorial, you'll create a two-column web page using CSS floats. You'll also use absolute positioning to control the placement of navigation elements (skip ahead to Figure 9-33 to see the end result). You can achieve a design like this many ways. You could, for example, use Dreamweaver's CSS Layouts (page 452), start with a blank web page, add divs, position them using CSS, and then add content. In this exercise, you'll start with an already created web page: It contains basic HTML, but no divs to organize that content or style sheets to format the page.

> **NOTE** You need to download the tutorial files from *www.sawmac.com/dwcs6* to complete this tutorial. See the note on page 54 for more details.

Once you download the tutorial files and open Dreamweaver, set up a new site as described on page 40. Name the site *CSS Layout*, and select the Chapter09 folder (inside the MM_DWCS6 folder). (In a nutshell: choose Site→New Site. In the Site Setup window, type *CSS Layout* in the Site Name field, click the folder icon next to the Local Site Folder field, navigate to and select the Chapter09 folder, and then click Choose or Select. Finally, click Save.)

1. **In the Files panel, double-click the file *about.html*.**

   Alternatively, choose File→Open and double-click the file *about.html*. Dreamweaver opens a web page with content and basic HTML formatting. You'll start by grouping the banner content—the logo, nav bar, and "Make a reservation" link.

2. **Click to the right of "Make a reservation" and drag up until you select the link, navigation bar, and logo image at the top of the page.**

   You'll wrap all this in a <div> tag.

3. **Choose Insert→Layout Objects→Div Tag.**

   Or, click the Insert Div Tag button under the Layout tab of the Insert panel. Either way, Dreamweaver opens the Insert Div Tag window. You want to create a CSS style to format this div.

4. **Click the New CSS Rule button, and in the New CSS Rule Window, choose Class from the selector type menu, type *.header* in the Selector Name field, and choose New Style Sheet file in the Rule Definition menu.**

   The window should look like Figure 9-25.

5. **Click OK and save this style sheet file as *styles.css* in the CSS folder of the site.**

   The CSS Rule Definition window appears. You're creating a style for the page's banner, and, as you can see in Figure 9-4, it's just a box that stretches across the page. You don't need to float or absolutely position it, but you'll add a background image and a few other properties.

6. **Select the Background category.**

   Click the Browse button to the right of the Background-image property and select the file *bg_banner.jpg* from the Images folder.

   This box holds only a bit of content—the logo and navigation elements—so you'll set a height for it to match the final design.

7. **Select the Box category and type *140* in the Height box.**

   Turn off the margin setting's "Same for all" checkbox and type *20* in the Bottom margin box. Click OK.

   Dreamweaver returns to the Insert Div Tag window. Notice that header (the style you just created) appears in the Class box (see Figure 9-26).

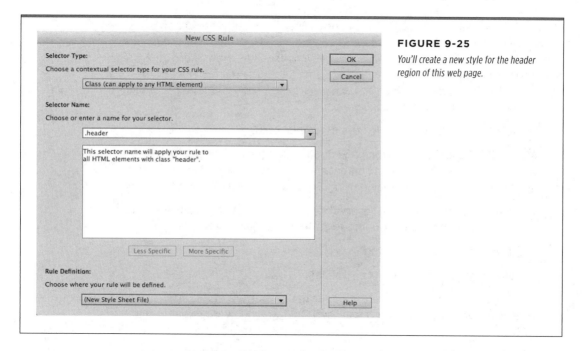

FIGURE 9-25

You'll create a new style for the header region of this web page.

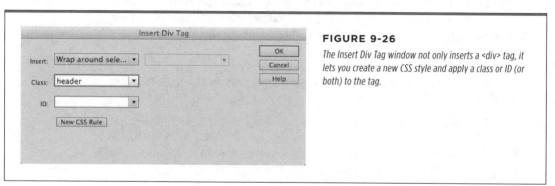

FIGURE 9-26

The Insert Div Tag window not only inserts a <div> tag, it lets you create a new CSS style and apply a class or ID (or both) to the tag.

8. **Click OK.**

   Dreamweaver adds the div tag to the page. There's something a bit wrong with it—the navigation bar and the link to the "Make a reservation" page don't fit. That's OK for now. Later in this tutorial, you'll use absolute positioning to relocate these elements in the upper right of the banner.

9. **Click to the left of the "About Us" headline and drag down until you select the headlines, paragraphs, and images up to the Cafe's address and phone number (don't select those).**

   This area is the main content of the page and should be in its own div.

10. **Choose Insert→Layout Objects→Div Tag.**

    Dreamweaver opens the Insert Div Tag window. You want to create a CSS style to format this div, too.

11. **Click the New CSS Rule button, and in the New CSS Rule Window, choose Class from the selector type menu; type *.main* in the Selector Name field.** Select styles.css from the bottom Rule Definition menu and click OK.

    These are the same steps you followed for the previous div.

12. **Select the Box category; type *64* in the Width box and then select *%* from the drop-down menu to the right.** Choose "left" from the Float menu, turn off the margin setting's "Same for all" checkbox, and type *25* in the Bottom margin box.

    The CSS Rule Definition window should look like Figure 9-27. Here, you're using a percentage width, so the main column will change its width as a guest changes the width of his browser window. The "left" float places this column on the left of the browser window.

13. **Click OK to return to the Insert Div Tag window, and click OK again to close the window and insert the new <div> tag.**

    The main text floats to the left of the page, and the content that was previously below it wraps around the right side, creating two columns (see Figure 9-28). You'll also float the sidebar column.

14. **Click to the left of the address (700 SW 5th Ave), and drag down to select everything up to the copyright notice (the black-highlighted area in Figure 9-28).**

    This area is the sidebar and you'll add a div to it as well.

15. **Choose Insert→Layout Objects→Div Tag to open the Insert Div Tag window.**

    Click the New CSS Rule button, and in the New CSS Rule Window, choose Class from the selector type menu; type *.aside* in the Selector Name field, and then click OK.

    These are the same steps you followed for the previous div.

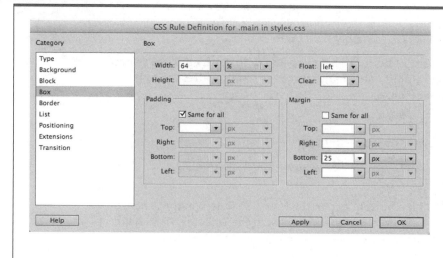

FIGURE 9-27

Percentage-width values make an element change size based on the width of its parent element. For example, a 64% wide box placed inside the body of a web page makes that box 64% of the browser window's width. As a visitor resizes the window, the box changes width. However, if you place that box inside another div with a pixel-value width—say 1,000 pixels wide—that box will now be a fixed width (64% of the 1,000-pixel-wide container, or 640 pixels).

16. **Select the Background category and, in the Background-color box, type #E7EBE0.**

    This adds a greenish background to the sidebar. You'll add a border next.

17. **Select the Border category.**

    Select "solid" from the Style menu, type *1* in the Width box, and type *#E5E5E5* in the color box.

    You added a grey border to the box. Time to position it.

18. **Select the Box category, type *33%* in the Width box, choose "right" from the Float menu, turn off the margin setting's "Same for all" checkbox, and then type *25* in the Bottom margin box.**

    In this case, you'll float the div to the right of the window. Notice that the width of this column (33%) and the main column (64%) don't add up to an even 100%. There's a couple of reasons for that. First, since the two columns are floated in opposite directions, the remaining space (3%) will appear as a bit of white space (a "gutter") between the two columns. Second, when using percentage widths, you need to be careful when you add padding, margins, or borders: As you read in the box on page 452, the actual width of an element is a combination of the border, padding, and width values.

Because you added a border to the sidebar, its screen width will be slightly wider than the 33% you specified. If you set the two columns' width values to equal 100%, they wouldn't fit side by side, since 100% width plus 2 pixels of left and right borders would total great than 100%; the sidebar would end up dropping below the main column

19. **Click OK to return to the Insert Div Tag window, and then click OK again to close the window and insert the new <div> tag.**

Dreamweaver adds the tag to the page. The sidebar column appears with a green background. You'll add a couple of CSS3 properties next.

FIGURE 9-28

A simple left float and a set width is the easiest way to get multiple columns to sit side by side.

Adding CSS3 Properties

Dreamweaver doesn't make it easy to add most CSS3 properties. Aside from the new web fonts feature (page 146) and CSS Transitions panel (page 405), you have to either hand-type CSS3 properties in your style sheets or use the CSS Properties pane.

1. **In the CSS Styles panel, click the All button, and select the *.aside* style.**

   You might need to click the + icon (flippy triangle on Macs) to the left of "styles.css" to expand the list and display the styles.

2. **In the Properties pane, click the Add Property link and select "border-radius" from the drop-down menu.**

   Click the icon to the right of "border-radius" (circled in the left image in Figure 9-29), and type *5* in the Top Left box, as pictured in Figure 9-29, right.

   This adds rounded corners to the sidebar. The *border-radius* property works only in modern browsers (that excludes IE 8 and earlier). Next, you'll add a drop shadow.

3. **In the Properties pane, click the Add Property link and select Box-shadow from the drop-down menu.**

   Click the icon to the right of box-shadow.

   Dreamweaver opens a window for setting CSS3 box-shadow properties.

4. **Type *2* in the X-Offset box, *2* in the Y-Offset box, *2* in the Blur-radius box and type *#999999* in the Color box (see Figure 9-30).**

   Press Enter (Return) to close the settings box.

   This adds a drop shadow to the sidebar, but you won't see anything in Dreamweaver's Design view. You need to preview the page in a browser (even Dreamweaver's Live view won't display the drop shadow).

   You're almost done with the layout. If you look at the page, you'll notice that the copyright notice appears below the sidebar and to the right of the main content column. It should drop below both columns.

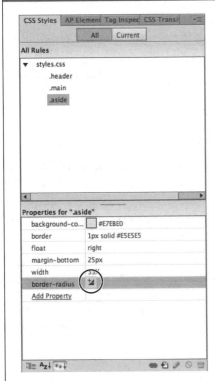

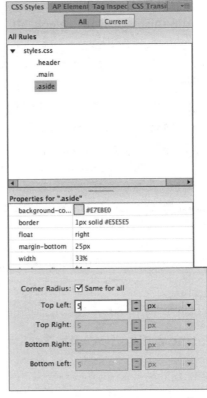

FIGURE 9-29

The CSS3 Border-radius property lets you add rounded corners to one, two, three, or all four corners of an element. Make sure you add either a background color or border to the element; otherwise you won't be able to see the rounded corners!

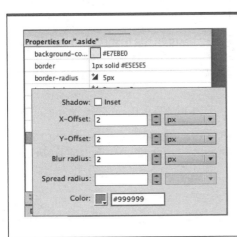

FIGURE 9-30

The CSS3 Border-radius property lets you add drop shadows to any element. You can learn more about this property at http://css-tricks.com/snippets/css/css-box-shadow/.

5. **Select the paragraph with the copyright notice ("Copyright 2022, The Soylent Corporation").**

You're going to wrap this in a new div. You should be having a sense of déjà vu at this point.

6. **Choose Insert→Layout Objects→Div Tag to open the Insert Div Tag window.**

Click the New CSS Rule button, and in the New CSS Rule Window choose Class from the selector type menu; type *.footer* in the Selector Name field, and then click OK.

These are the same steps you followed for the previous div.

7. **Select the Box category and, from the Clear menu, select "both."**

The Clear property prevents an element from wrapping around a floated element. The "both" setting prevents the footer from wrapping around either left- or right-floated elements.

8. **Click OK to return to the Insert Div Tag window, and then click OK again to close the window and insert the new div tag.**

The basic structure is in place. You have a two-column layout with a header and footer. If you preview the page in a web browser, you'll see that the design uses a "liquid" layout—that is, it grows wider or becomes narrower as the browser window's width changes. That's because you used percentage widths for the columns. However, you can easily turn this design into a fixed-width layout.

Creating a Fixed-Width Design

To turn the current liquid layout into a fixed-width layout, you simply wrap the contents of the page in a <div> tag with a set pixel width.

1. **In the Tag Selector at the bottom left of the document window, click <body>.**

You just selected the entire body of the web page. (The Tag Selector, discussed on page 26, is the best way to select a tag).

2. **Choose Insert→Layout Objects→Div Tag to open the Insert Div Tag window.**
Click the New CSS Rule button and, in the New CSS Rule Window, choose Class from the selector type menu, type *.container* in the Selector Name field, and then click OK.

Now you'll set the width for this tag, and position it in the middle of the screen.

3. **Select the Box category; type *1000* in the Width box, turn off the "Same for all" checkbox in the Margin settings, and then choose "auto" from both the Left and Right margin boxes.**

The window should look like Figure 9-31.

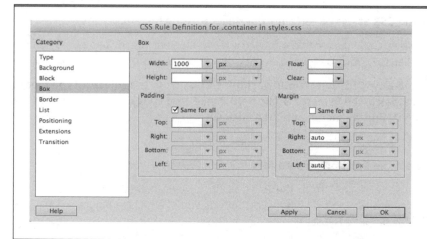

FIGURE 9-31

To center a div on a page, give it a fixed width and set its left and right margins to "auto."

4. **Click OK to return to the Insert Div Tag window, and then click OK again to close the window and insert the new <div> tag.**

   The new div wraps around all the other content on the page. By giving this container div a set width, browsers constrain all the contents inside to this width.

Adding Styles and Using Absolute Positioning

At this point, you could create new styles to format this page using the techniques you read about earlier in this book—change the fonts and font sizes, add underlines to headlines, change the look of links, and so on. For the sake of keeping this book shorter than *War and Peace* (actually, this edition is just about 50 pages shy of that), we assume you've already got those skills under your belt, so you'll attach a style sheet with some already created styles.

1. **In the CSS Styles panel, click the Attach Style Sheet button (the icon that looks like a chain link in the bottom-right of the CSS Styles panel).**

   The Attach External Style Sheet window opens.

2. **Click the Browse button, and then navigate to the "css" folder; double-click the file *final.css*.**

   In the Attach External Style Sheet window, click OK.

   Dreamweaver links the style sheet to the page, and styles the page's content. The new styles really change the look of the page, but there's nothing about them that you haven't already learned. For example, the picture of the chef is simply aligned to the left using the *float* property. The text is set to different sizes and colors with CSS, and so on.

One thing that does need some changing is the banner. The navigation bar and the reservation link are crowded together, and there's too much empty space on the right. You'll use absolute positioning to move them into place.

3. **In the CSS Styles panel, click the New CSS Rule button.**

   The New CSS Rule window opens. The navigation bar already has a class—.nav—applied to it. You just need to create a new .nav class style to position the nav bar.

4. **In the New CSS Rule Window, choose Class from the selector type menu; type .nav in the Selector Name field, make sure styles.css is selected in the Rule Definition menu, and then click OK.**

   Dreamweaver opens the CSS Rule Definition window.

5. **Select the Positioning category.**

   Choose "absolute" from the Position drop-down menu; type *0* in the Right Placement box and *32* in the Bottom Placement box (see Figure 9-32). Click OK to complete the style.

   Where did the navigation bar go? If you preview the page in a browser (or click the Live button), you'll find it at the bottom and right edge of the document window. Normally if you absolutely position an element on a page, the coordinates you use (top, left, right, and bottom) are set in relation to the browser window. But that's not what you want here. You want to position the navigation bar in relation to the bottom and right edges of the header div. To do that you just need to give the header div a position of "relative."

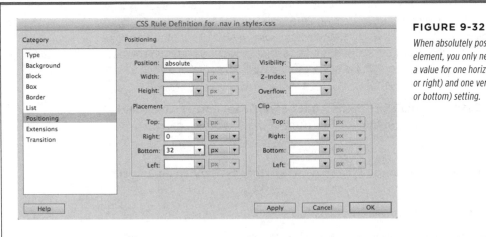

FIGURE 9-32

When absolutely positioning an element, you only need to type a value for one horizontal (left or right) and one vertical (top or bottom) setting.

6. **In the CSS Styles panel, locate the .header style in the styles.css stylesheet.**

   Double-click it to open the CSS Rule Definition window. Select the Positioning category and choose "relative" from the Position menu. Click OK.

The navigation bar pops into placed inside the header (you may need to click in the document window for Dreamweaver to display the change). Now you'll position the reservation link.

7. **Repeat steps 3–5.**

Create a new class style named *.reservation*; set its Position property to "absolute;" set its top position to *8* and its right position to *0*. Click OK to complete the style.

The navigation bar pops into placed inside the header (you may need to click in the document window, for Dreamweaver to display this change). Now, you'll position the reservation link.

8. **Press F12 (Option-F12) to preview your hard work in a browser.**

The complete page should look like Figure 9-33.

You'll find a completed version of this tutorial in the Chapter09_complete folder that accompanies the downloaded tutorial files.

NOTE To get a full description of every Dreamweaver menu, see Appendix B, Dreamweaver CS6, Menu by Menu, on page 933.

FIGURE 9-33

It doesn't take much CSS to create a multi-column layout, or to accurately place elements like a navigation bar.

Troubleshooting CSS

C ascading Style Sheets are the most important technology in a web designer's toolkit. Unfortunately, they're also the source of many frustrations. As you pile style upon style in your site to transform drab HTML into beautiful web pages, you increasingly run the risk that those styles may interact in ways you don't expect. As discussed in Chapter 8, the CSS concepts of "inheritance" and the "cascade" dictate how styles interact on a page, and those concepts have their own complicated rules. Adding to the confusion, different browsers can display CSS differently—this is especially true with older versions of Internet Explorer. Even newer browsers exhibit some frustrating inconsistencies in how they display CSS.

In this chapter, you'll look at Dreamweaver's tools for diagnosing CSS problems, as well as common problems you'll encounter as you build the kinds of CSS layouts discussed in the previous chapter.

NOTE Dreamweaver includes a Check Browser Compatibility tool. It's intended to warn you when the CSS in your web page won't work in a particular browser. Sounds good, right? It would be if it worked, but it doesn't. The information it provides is outdated (mostly covering Internet Explorer 6), and the "community" part of the tool (which allows people to add browser compatibility information to the Adobe website) is littered with off-topic posts.

■ Analyzing CSS with Dreamweaver

Dreamweaver's CSS tools are as good as they come—you can use them to build complex designs without ever dipping your toe into code. You can manage complex style sheets easily, and quickly add external style sheets to your pages. But building and managing styles is only one part of the CSS puzzle. You also need to analyze what the CSS is doing to the tags on your page—to see why text, for example, is purple instead of the green you specified. Dreamweaver provides help for this as well.

As described on page 393, the CSS Styles panel has two views: All and Current (see Figure 10-1). The All button is the best way to see all the styles you can draw on for the current document. When you select this button, you see not only the styles in the page itself (in an internal style sheet), but also the styles in all the external style sheets linked to the page.

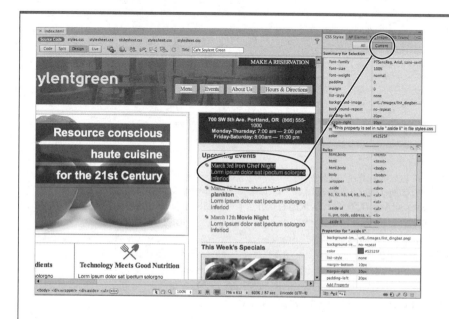

FIGURE 10-1

The Current view of the CSS Styles panel is one of Dreamweaver's best design tools. After you select a tag on a page, the Summary pane (top) lists all the properties that format your selection. Just below that, the Cascade pane (middle) lists all the styles affecting the selection. However, you only get the Cascade view if you select the Cascade button (the stair-step icon in the top-right of the middle pane). Make sure you do, since the other button ("Show information about se-lected property"), which is Dreamweaver's normal choice, isn't very useful.

The Current view, however, is where you can start analyzing how styles affect a particular tag on a page. As you read on page 390, tags can inherit properties (like color and font) from tags that wrap around them. For example, if you create a body tag style with a color property of *#F00*, a browser displays the text inside the body (and even text inside other tags, such as <p>, <h1>, and <li>) as red. In other words, the styling of any one tag may be a combination of properties from multiple styles. The ultimate set of properties that format a tag is the result of the complex interaction of styles governed by the rules of CSS inheritance (page 390) and the cascade (page 391).

You can view this combined, "calculated" style by selecting the tag you want to analyze (a <p> tag, a div tag, an image, and so on). Then click the Current view in the

CSS Styles panel and look at the list of properties in the Summary pane. In Figure 10-1, for example, the Summary pane lists properties such as *font-family, font-size, font-weight and padding* for a list item on the page. If you hover your mouse over one of the properties (*margin-right* in Figure 10-1), Dreamweaver displays a pop-up box listing the name of the style that property belongs to and which style sheet contains the CSS for it.

NOTE While the Summary pane of the CSS Styles panel is a fantastic tool, it does make mistakes. In particular, it gets confused when one style uses a "shorthand" property (see the box on page 384) that combines several CSS properties and another style uses individual property names.

For example, you can use a form of shorthand to set top, right, bottom, and left margins all at once, like this: *margin: 5px 0 0 0.* Or, you can set one margin with its individual property name: *margin-top: 0.* Unfortunately, Dreamweaver sees these as two separate properties and doesn't correctly determine which properties should apply.

You can see this mistake in Figure 10-1. Notice that both *margin-right* and *padding-left* properties are listed, but so is the shorthand for margin and padding properties. They can't both be right, so, to determine which is correct, click each property—the style that property belongs to will then appear in the Cascade view (middle pane). The style that appears lower in that list is the "more specific" style, and therefore its properties take precedence. In other words, that's the style you want to edit to change the padding property. (For a more detailed explanation of the cascade, see page 391.) One way to avoid this problem is to tell Dreamweaver to use long-hand properties when it writes CSS, as described on page 384.

Editing CSS Properties

There are lots of ways to change CSS properties and styles in Dreamweaver. For example, when you have the All button selected, a complete list of styles appears in the CSS Styles panel. Double-click the style you wish to edit and use the Rule Definition window to tweak its properties. If you understand CSS, you can select the style and then use the CSS Properties pane at the bottom of the Styles panel to quickly change and add properties.

These techniques are all well and good if you know which style you need to edit, but if you have a really long list of styles or you're working on a site for the first time in a while, you may not know which style you're after. In that case, use the Current view to home in on just the properties you want to change. Here's a quick step-by-step guide to that process:

1. **In the document window, select the element whose style you want to change.**

    For example, if a paragraph has green text and you want to make it blue, select that paragraph using one of the many techniques Dreamweaver offers: triple-click to select the paragraph, click once in the paragraph and then click the tag's name in the Tag Selector at the bottom of the document window, or just drag to highlight the whole paragraph.

TIP These steps work in Code view just as well as they do in Design view.

2. **Click the Current button on the CSS Styles panel.**

This divides the panel into three panes. The top one, the Summary pane, lists all the properties a browser will apply to the selection, even when the properties come from different styles. The middle pane lists the names of all the styles that affect the selection, with the least powerful (least "specific") at the top and the most powerful ("most specific") at the bottom—in other words, if more than one style assigns a value to the same property (for example, if two styles specify different text colors), the style listed last wins (but you need to click the Cascade button—top-right of the pane—to see the cascade). Finally, the bottom pane lists all the CSS properties for the style selected in the Cascade pane. This functions just like the Properties pane in the All view; in it, you can edit the individual properties of the selected style.

3. **In the Summary pane, double-click the property you want to change.**

This opens the Rule Definition window (the same window you used to create the style), where you can edit that property's (or any other property's) style. In the example above (the green paragraph you want to turn blue), you'd double-click the *color* property in the Summary pane to open the style that specifies the color, change the color property from green to blue, and then close the style. The paragraph now sports the new color.

Alternatively, you can click the property in the Summary pane to select it. The Cascade pane highlights the style that property belongs to, and the Properties pane lists all the properties (not just the one you selected) for that style. You can then edit the property.

As you can see, you can go a long way in tweaking a site's styles simply by selecting elements in the document window and using the Current view of the CSS Styles panel to quickly locate and edit properties you want to change.

TIP Even if you're not as interested in editing an existing property as you are in *adding* one, the CSS Styles panel can still be a big help. Select the element you wish to embellish with a new property—the font for the copyright notice, for example. You can look at the Cascade view to see all the styles that apply to that paragraph. If you see a style that specifically targets the paragraph (like a class selector named *.copyright* or a descendent selector like *.footer p*), you can double-click the style to add a *font-family* property. Or, if there isn't a style that formats the copyright notice's font, you can create one.

Analyzing CSS in JavaScript and Server-Side Pages

The CSS Styles panel is great at locating and editing styles that affect the elements on a page, but what about the HTML you don't normally see in the document window? These days, lots of sites use fancy JavaScript effects to display content; for example, the Spry tooltips (page 656), Spry form validation (page 588), and Spry menu bar (page 210) display certain page elements only when someone interacts with the page. Likewise, when you create server-side-driven pages, like PHP pages that retrieve information from a database, you see the completed page and all its elements only *after* a web server has processed the server-side programming and sent a completed web page back to your browser.

> **NOTE** You can't change a page in Live view—that is, you can't click into a paragraph and add new text, for example. However, you can edit the HTML, CSS, and JavaScript in Split view (page 335), and Live view will reflect those changes. You can also edit the CSS of a page in Live view using the CSS Styles panel. To exit Live view, click the Live button in the Document toolbar or choose View→Live View. You can also use the keyboard shortcut Alt-F11 (Option-F11) to turn Live view off (or on).

So how do you make sure pages that require real-time interaction with a web browser look and act the way you want? Easy; Dreamweaver includes a Live view feature called Inspect mode. Live view lets you see your page as it appears in a web browser (specifically, in browsers based on WebKit, the visual engine behind Apple's Safari and Google's Chrome browsers). Once in Live view, you can click the Inspect button (circled in Figure 10-2) to mouse around a page and analyze its CSS. You can even interact with JavaScript-driven page effects, such as a drop-down menu in a Spry menu bar (page 210), and analyze the CSS of page elements that aren't normally visible in Design view.

A few things happen when you're in Inspect mode:

- **Dreamweaver highlights a tag's box, padding, and margins**. As you mouse around the page, Dreamweaver highlights the "box model" of each tag you mouse over. As you can read on page 447, every block-level tag (like a headline, div or paragraph) in HTML is basically a box with a width, height, margins, padding, and borders. When you mouse over a tag in Inspect mode, the box turns blue to reveal its dimensions; padding appears in light purple, and margins show up in light yellow. Not every element has all these properties, so you may see some but not others. In fact, since you can set padding and margin values individually for each side of a tag, you might only see padding or a margin on one side of the element. For example, in Figure 10-2, hovering over a <div> in a sidebar reveals that the designer set only the top padding and a right margin for the div.

- **The Tag Selector displays the HTML structure**. When you mouse over page elements, such as images, paragraphs, <div> tags, and so on, the Tag Selector at the bottom of the document window identifies the tag you're over, as well as the tags that wrap around the current one. For example, in Figure 10-2, the Tag Selector highlights *<article>*, meaning your mouse is over an <article> tag that has the class *.sayfalist1* applied to it (<article> is a new HTML5 tag). The page's HTML encloses that tag in several other tags—a bunch of <div> tags.

Element (blue)　　Padding (purple)　　Margin (yellow)

FIGURE 10-2

Dreamweaver's Inspect mode is a great way to see which CSS styles affect which elements on a page. It's especially useful for pages with a lot of JavaScript-created elements, like drop-down menus and tooltips, or pages that include server-side programming, like PHP files. This figure shows a blog post made with the popular WordPress blogging system. In WordPress and other "content management systems," like Joomla and Drupal, web "pages" aren't individual files like the ones you've been building in this book, they're dynamically created screens that pull information from a database and construct the HTML for the page on the spot. Live view lets you see what a page created with server-side programming looks like in a browser; Inspect mode lets you analyze the CSS that formats the different parts of the page, like the sidebar pictured here.

- **The CSS Styles panel updates**. If you select the Current view in the Styles panel, you'll see the Summary list change as you mouse over the page in the document window, with Dreamweaver displaying the properties for each tag you hover over. The Cascade and Properties panes update as well. In other words, you're getting a birds-eye view of the page's CSS by mousing over page elements. In Figure 10-2, for example, the mouse sits over an <article> tag with the class *.hentry*—a class style with that same name appears in the middle Rules pane, and a list of all of the properties for the style appears in the bottom Properties pane.

If you decide to edit the styles for a particular element, click the element while you're in Inspect mode; this selects the element and displays its CSS rules and properties in the CSS Styles panel. You can then edit the styles either in the Properties pane as described on page 382, or double-click the style name in the Rules pane to edit the style in the Rule Definition window, as described on page 139.

Once you click an element, Dreamweaver exits Inspect mode (although it stays in Live view). You need to press the Inspect mode again (or use the keyboard shortcut Shift-Alt-F11 [Shift-Option-F11]) to re-enter Inspect mode.

TIP In Inspect mode, it's sometimes hard to select the exact tag you want to analyze in the Styles panel. For example, when you mouse over a div nested inside another div, Dreamweaver highlights the innermost div, and selecting the outer, parent div may not be easy. The solution? While you mouse over an element in Inspect mode, press the left arrow key to highlight the next-nearest parent element (the tag wrapped around the currently highlighted tag). You can keep pressing the left arrow to move up the nest of HTML tags. (Press the right arrow key to move back down to the original element.) Finally, when the tag you're interested in gets highlighted, click the mouse button to select that tag. Dreamweaver displays all its CSS properties and styles in the Styles panel.

■ FOLLOWING LINKS IN SERVER-SIDE PAGES

Dreamweaver CS6 includes a Browse function in Live view. That is, you can actually click links in Live view to jump to different pages within your site: The linked page then appears in the document window. This is kind of cool, but not that useful for links that call up other pages on the Web—you can't edit those live pages. It's not even that useful for regular web pages within your own site—after all, you can just open those pages from the Files panel to edit them.

NOTE The information in this section applies to server-side-driven pages, such as pages written in the PHP programming language. You need to have a web server set up on your own computer (a.k.a. a "testing" server; see page 913 for instructions) or access to your server on the Internet to correctly view these pages in Live view and analyze them with the Inspect mode. Chapter 21 discusses server-side programming with Dreamweaver.

However, the Browse function is a great feature for server-side-driven pages, which often use information passed in links to operate correctly. In other words, clicking a link sends additional information to the server, which then displays the page in a way you couldn't if you just opened the page in Dreamweaver. For example, the Web's most popular blogging system, WordPress, uses a complex set of PHP files to provide all of the system's amazing features. But you can only see those features in action if you can launch the pages from your local or Internet-based server.

One peculiar feature of WordPress (well, not that peculiar if you're a programmer) is that just one file, *index.php*, is responsible for displaying most of the pages on the site—from the home page to an archive listing of blog posts to an individual blog post. In other words, if you want to see your most recent blog post, you'd have to open the *index.php* page and follow a link from the home page to the post—and, strangely, that link still points to the *index.php* page. Here's the catch: The link includes information that instructs the *index.php* page to display a particular blog post. This makes editing the CSS of server-side pages the regular way—by opening the page in Design view—impossible. Instead, you need to go into Live view, click the links until you get to the page you're interested in, and then use Inspect mode (and the CSS Styles panel) to analyze and edit the styles that format the page.

To follow links on a page you need to:

1. **Enter Live view.**

   Click the Live button in the Document toolbar, choose View→Live View, or press Alt+F11 (Option-F11).

2. **Ctrl-click (⌘-click) a link.**

   This loads the new page into Dreamweaver's Live view. In the case of some dynamic pages, like WordPress, Dreamweaver doesn't actually load a new page, it just provides a specific request to the web server and the *index.php* file, which does a bunch of behind-the-scenes magic to generate a new chunk of HTML.

   When you're in Live view, you have to Ctrl+Click (⌘-Click) links to follow them. To make the links respond without resorting to keystroke combinations, click the Live view options menu in the Browser Navigation toolbar (circled in Figure 10-3) and select Follow Links Continuously.

FIGURE 10-3

The Browser Navigation toolbar acts like the toolbar you see in web browsers. You can refresh a page, go backward or forward through the links you've visited, and even type a URL in the address bar. The toolbar only appears when you're in Live view, and it's most useful if you work with server-side pages.

■ Overcoming Common CSS Problems

As you get more adventurous with CSS, you'll probably encounter—as many web designers have before you—some of the weird intricacies of working with floated elements ("floats"). This section describes a few common problems and their solutions. (And if you ever stumble on a problem not listed here, you can always take it to one of the online forums listed in Appendix A on page 929.)

Clearing and Containing Floats

As you learned in the last chapter, the CSS *float* property is a powerful design tool. It's the only way to get content to wrap around other content: Floating a photo lets text below it move up and wrap around the image. When you create float-based column designs, though, sometimes you *don't* want content to move up and next to a floated element. For example, you probably want to keep copyright notices, contact information, and other housekeeping details at the bottom of your web page, below all the other content.

In the CSS layouts discussed in the last chapter, you saw that if the main column of content is shorter than either of the floated sidebar columns, the footer moved up and around the left-floated column (Figure 10-4, left, circled). To make the footer stay below the sidebars, you use the *clear* property (page 449). It prevents an element from wrapping around floats (Figure 10-4, right, circled).

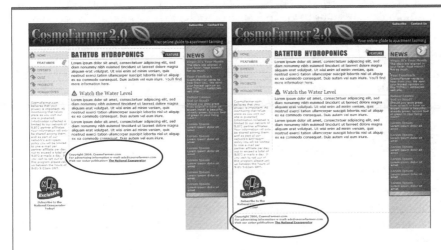

FIGURE 10-4

You don't always want an item to wrap around a floated element (left). Copyright notices and other housekeeping info that belong at the bottom of a page usually need to clear any floats they encounter. The clear property forces the copyright notice to the bottom of the page, below any floated elements (right).

Add the *clear* property to the style for any tag you want to prevent from wrapping around a floated element (you find the property in the Box category of the CSS Rule Definition window). You can make an element drop below a left-floated object by selecting the "left" value in the Clear drop-down menu, or below a right-floated object by selecting "right." For footers and other items that need to appear at the bottom of the page, select "both" to drop below left- and right-floated elements.

Another problem occurs when you float one or more elements inside a non-floated containing tag, like a <div>. When the floated element is taller than the other content inside the div, it sticks out of the bottom of the enclosing element. This snafu is especially noticeable if that tag has a background or border. The top image in Figure 10-5 shows a <div> tag that has an <h1> tag and two columns created by floating two divs. The enclosing div's style applies background and border properties to the entire box, but they appear only around the <h1> tag. That's because the floated columns are bigger than their container. So, instead of expanding the borders of the box, the columns pop out of the bottom of it. What you really want is something like the bottom image in Figure 10-5.

NOTE For a good explanation of why floated elements can pop out of their enclosing tags, read *http://css-tricks.com/snippets/css/css-boxshadow/*.

You see a similar problem with the three boxes that contain photos in the top image in Figure 10-5. In this case, the style floats each image left inside a containing <div> that has a border. Because the images are taller than their boxes, they pop out of the bottom. Unfortunately, this problem is even worse than the previous one, because each image causes the image below it to wrap to the right, creating an ugly staggered effect.

You can tackle the problem of renegade floats many ways. You'll learn several of the most common techniques below, because it's good to have more than one solution under your belt.

- **Add a clearing element at the bottom of the containing div**. This solution's the most straightforward. Simply add a tag—like a line break or horizontal rule—as the last item in the <div> containing the floated element (that is, right before the closing </div> tag). Then use the *clear* property to force that extra tag below the float. This trick makes the enclosing div expand, revealing its background and border. You can add a line break—
 (HTML) or
 (XHTML)—*before* the closing </div> tag and add a class to it: *<br class="clearfloat">*. You'll most likely need to manually type this in Code view.

  You then need to create a CSS class style (page 124) and set the Clear property to *both* (see below). (If you're using Dreamweaver's CSS Layouts, the style sheets already include a class style named *.clearfloat* with all the proper CSS for this trick.)

- **Float the containing element**. An easier solution is to float the div that contains the floated elements. A floated container <div> expands to fully include the floated elements inside it. In Figure 10-5, top, for example, the *float* property's been added to the div containing the heading and the two floated columns. In the process, the div's entire box—right down to its background and borders—expands to fit everything inside it, including the floated elements. Strange, but true.

  If you go this route, make sure you add a *clear* property to whatever element follows the floated container so the following element drops below the container.

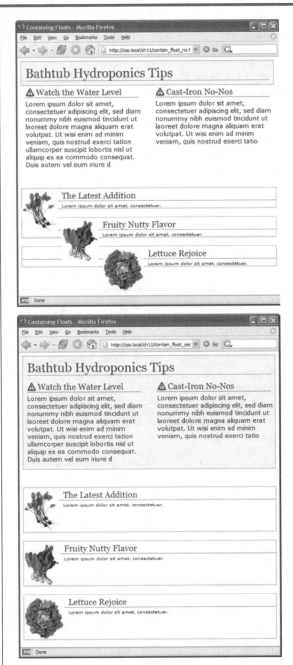

FIGURE 10-5

A floated element can escape its containing <div> if it's taller than the container. If the containing tag includes a background or border, the escaping elements can look like they're not even part of the container, as you can see in the top image—the bathtub tips should have the same tinted background as the headline does (bottom image). In addition, a floated element can bump into other elements—including other floats, thereby creating a "stair-step" effect, like the one you see in the three boxed elements in the top image. You really want the nicely stacked boxes you see in the bottom image.

- **Use overflow:hidden**. Another common technique is to add the *overflow* property (page 470) to the tag that wraps around the floated elements. Choose the "hidden" value from the Overflow menu listed in the Positioning category of the CSS Rule Definition window (see Figure 9-20).

  The *overflow:hidden* property is just another one of those weird CSS things: It forces the containing block to expand and contain the floated elements.

  In general, this technique works very well. However, if you have any absolutely positioned elements (see page 465) inside the container, they may not show up. Because the CSS hides the "overflow," it hides the stuff that appears outside the container, such as an element absolutely positioned outside it. You'll experience this if you have a drop-down menu inside another tag and the drop-downs, when they appear, should be outside the container element. If that's the case, use one of the float-taming methods described above.

Avoiding "Float Drops"

Suddenly, one of your columns simply drops down below the others (see Figure 10-6). It looks like there's plenty of room for all the columns to coexist side by side, but they don't. You've got the dreaded "float drop." This can happen when you work with Dreamweaver's CSS layouts. A floated column drops down because there's not enough room to fit it.

Be careful setting widths for *each* column. If the available space in the browser window (or in a <div> tag that contains the columns in a fixed-width design) is less than the *total* widths of the columns, you're asking for a float drop. So you need to make sure the math works. If you're using one of Dreamweaver's fixed-width layouts, a <div> tag with the ID *.container* wraps around the other tags on the page. Dreamweaver's stock style sheet sets the div to a width of 960 pixels. In a two-column design, you'll find two other divs, one for the main content and the other for a sidebar. If the combined widths of these two divs is greater than 960 pixels, the main content div drops below the sidebar.

Also, keep the CSS box model in mind: As discussed in the box on page 452, the width of an element displayed in a browser window isn't the same as its *width property*. The displayed width of any element combines the element's width, left and right border sizes, left and right padding, and left and right margins. For columns to fit side by side, the browser window (or containing div) must accommodate the total of all those widths.

While miscalculated column widths are the most common cause of dropped floats, they can also result from rounding errors if you use percentage widths. Browsers sometimes make mistakes when calculating the actual number of pixels needed to display something on the screen. That is, they can round numbers up, making elements slightly too large for the available space. So be careful when you set widths in percentages—err on the side of caution and make your percentage widths total slightly less than 100 percent.

Bottom line: The only reason you'll see a float drop is because there's not enough room to hold all of a page's columns side by side. Rather than strive to use every last pixel of screen space, give your elements a little wiggle room. Get in the habit of making the overall column widths a bit smaller than the max, and you'll spend less time troubleshooting float drops.

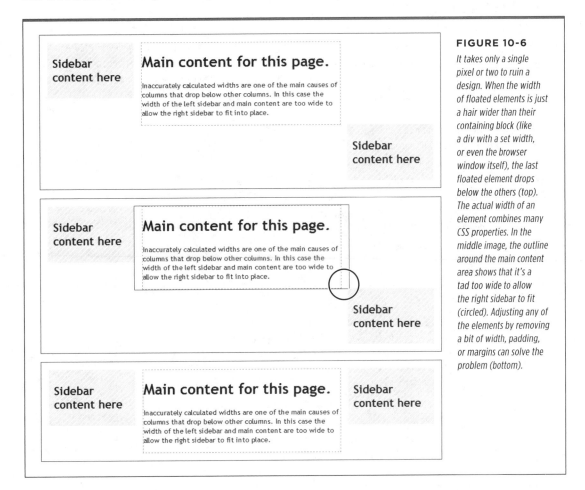

FIGURE 10-6

It takes only a single pixel or two to ruin a design. When the width of floated elements is just a hair wider than their containing block (like a div with a set width, or even the browser window itself), the last floated element drops below the others (top). The actual width of an element combines many CSS properties. In the middle image, the outline around the main content area shows that it's a tad too wide to allow the right sidebar to fit (circled). Adjusting any of the elements by removing a bit of width, padding, or margins can solve the problem (bottom).

Should I Care About IE 6?

I keep hearing that Internet Explorer is dead and we don't need to worry about it anymore. Is this true?

If you're a web designer, you've probably got the latest version of Internet Explorer, Safari, Firefox, Chrome, or Opera on your computer. Previous versions of this book talked quite a bit about Internet Explorer 6 and even provided a section on how to deal with IE 6 bugs. You won't find that section in this edition because IE 6 is rapidly disappearing.

If you're building sites with a US audience in mind, less than 0.2 percent of web surfers use that outdated browser; in the UK, it's 1.4 percent. The exact figure varies depending on whom you ask (for example, *http://css-tricks.com/snippets/css/css-boxshadow/* has worldwide IE 6 usage at 1.17 percent and *http://www.IE6countdown.com* says it's at 7.1 percent). In China, IE 6 is still widely used.

However, even statistics that include the geographic region of your site's audience don't truly reflect what visitors to your site use. If you build a site aimed at tech-savvy web designers, odds are that IE 6 hasn't tapped your site in a long time. However, if your site is aimed at people in China, you may need to contend with IE 6. The best way to find out how much of your traffic comes via IE 6 is to look at your web server's log files or sign up for Google Analytics (*http://www.google.com/analytics*) so you can track your visitor's browsers (among many other things).

For the great majority of web design projects, IE 6 is effectively gone. Hooray!

Designing Websites for Mobile Devices

Web designers used to build web pages for the 800 x 600 pixel resolution of 15-inch monitors. Then, as large LCD screens became popular, most web wizards designed pages for monitors that measured 1024 pixels wide and larger. Today, the explosive growth of smartphones, like the iPhone and Android models, make it clear that designers need to craft sites for much smaller screens, too. A majestic, panoramic web page that looks beautiful on a 27-inch monitor may turn into a tiny, unreadable postage stamp on an iPhone.

You can accommodate the multitude of mobile browsing devices several ways. Some designers build separate, mobile versions of their sites (see Figure 11-1). Using server-side programming, these sites detect the type of device your visitor has and deliver a web page customized for that device. An iPhone web surfer, for example, will see the mobile version of a site, which provides a greatly simplified experience: a single-column design with most of the navigation elements removed, but with a prominent search box added. Of course, not all of us have the time to create two versions of a website, or the technical skills to program a server to detect a visitor's browser.

Fortunately, Dreamweaver CS6 includes several tools that tackle the problem of mobile site design. The most straightforward of them uses CSS; CSS3 offers a feature called *media queries* that lets you check the resolution of a device (how many pixels wide a screen is) and supply styles for just that resolution. For example, if a screen is 320 pixels wide (typical for phones held vertically, in "portrait" mode), you can apply styles that format the page for that dimension. In other words, instead of sending out different versions of the site to different-size devices, you distribute the same site, but use different style sheets to format the HTML.

FIGURE 11-1

Many large companies, like Amazon.com and Target.com (pictured), create mobile versions of their sites, optimized for display on handheld devices like the iPhone.

In addition, Dreamweaver CS6 introduces a new feature called *fluid grid layouts*. It combines the results of a media query with a fancy grid-based layout tool to create pages designed for the destination device (that's called "Responsive Web Design" in Web argot). Based on media query results, the site changes to a layout based on one of three basic browser widths—mobile, tablet, and desktop—and then uses percentage widths to scale the layout for a specific device—after all, not all mobile phones have screens that are 320 pixels wide, and not all tablet screens are 760 pixels wide. Using this flexible layout, you can create designs that scale to a range of widths and adapt for the myriad screen sizes on mobile and tablet devices.

On top of that, Dreamweaver CS6 provides tools for building pages using jQuery Mobile, a JavaScript library that helps you build websites specifically tailored to mobile devices. With some simple HTML, some fancy CSS, and some complex JavaScript programming, jQuery Mobile lets you create the common navigation elements found on smartphone applications. You can create a website that really feels like a phone application, or you can use HTML, CSS, and jQuery Mobile to actually *create* a phone application that you can install on Android devices or upload to Apple's App Store for use on an iPad, iPhone, or iPod Touch. Dreamweaver CS5.5 introduced this jQuery tool, and CS6 adds more features to it, including a "swatches" panel that lets you quickly apply different designs to a jQuery mobile-powered web page.

■ Previewing Pages at Different Resolutions

Testing web pages in different browsers has always been a chore for webmasters, and that's especially true for mobile design. To preview a web page on a phone, you have to store the page on your server and use your mobile phone to connect to the website to see how it looks. Fortunately, Dreamweaver CS6 simulates different mobile devices' screen sizes so you can avoid this time-consuming step.

TIP If you own an iPhone, iPad, or Android phone or tablet, Adobe offers free software that lets you preview a mobile web page that's sitting on your desktop computer directly on your phone or tablet. Adobe Shadow (*http://labs.adobe.com/technologies/shadow/*) uses a combination of a desktop program, an app for your phone or tablet, and a Google Chrome browser plug-in to literally beam web pages that you view in Chrome on your desktop straight to your phone or tablet. In fact, you can beam a page to all your iOS or Android phones and tablets simultaneously.

Multiscreen Preview

Once you finish designing your site, select Multiscreen Preview from the Multiscreen menu in the Document toolbar (circled in Figure 11-2). You can also choose File→Multiscreen Preview to open a window with three views of your page, one each for a smartphone, a tablet, and a desktop browser (see Figure 11-3). Each version has a different width and height, and, because Dreamweaver displays the pages using its WebKit browser, each represents a "live" view of the page. That means that rollover effects, JavaScript, and links actually work.

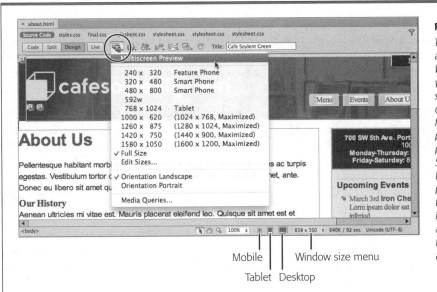

FIGURE 11-2

The Edit Sizes option at the bottom of the Window Size menu lets you customize the list of screen sizes Dreamweaver offers. For example, if Microsoft introduces a phone with a 120 x 120 pixel screen, select Edit Sizes from this menu, and then, in the Window Sizes preferences window, click the + button and type in a new width, height, and description. After that, the new resolution appears in this menu.

Mobile

Tablet Desktop

Window size menu

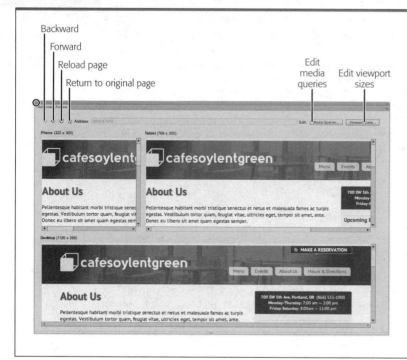

Backward
Forward
Reload page
Return to original page

Edit media queries
Edit viewport sizes

FIGURE 11-3

The Multiscreen Preview window lets you view a web page at three sizes, representing three different devices. In addition, Dreamweaver displays the pages in Live view (page 72)— that is, using its embedded WebKit browser. As a result, links are active and if you click one, the linked-to page will appear in each view, just as in a real browser. In fact, the preview window includes navigation buttons (Back, Next, Refresh, and Home) just like a real browser. The Home button simply returns you to the original document you were working on—the one currently open in the document window.

Since the page is live, you can't edit any HTML in this preview window. However, if you have a big enough monitor (or better yet, two monitors), you can move the preview window out of the way and then edit the HTML and CSS in Dreamweaver's document window. After making changes to the page, hit the Refresh button in the preview window to see those changes.

Unfortunately, the size of the three preview windows (Dreamweaver calls them "viewports") don't really match the actual size of most devices. For example, the smartphone viewport measures 320 x 300 pixels—too small for most phones. The iPhone and many Android phones' screens, for example, measure 320 x 480 pixels. That means that while the width is correct, the height Dreamweaver displays doesn't really match any phone. The same is true for the tablet setting—Dreamweaver displays a 768 x 300 pixel screen, but the iPad, for example, is 768 pixels x 1024 pixels.

Fortunately, you can change Dreamweaver's default viewport sizes: click the Viewport Sizes button in the Multiscreen Preview window and, in the window that appears, type new width and height values for the three devices. Just be careful of setting the height too tall, or there won't be enough screen space to display all three views. For example, if you set the tablet view to a height of 1024 pixels to match an iPad, there won't be enough room (on most monitors, even large ones) to display the desktop browser view.

When you're done with the Multiscreen Preview, click the "close" icon in the top-left corner of the window (circled in Figure 11-3).

Previewing Other Resolutions

While Multiscreen Preview is the only way to see side-by-side comparisons of a page at different resolutions, it has its limitations. You don't see the real size of a particular device, for example, just a cropped version. In addition, you can't edit the page, and the preview window is so big that unless you have a really big monitor (or two monitors), you can't simultaneously edit the page and preview your changes. And, finally, Dreamweaver limits the Multiscreen Preview to just three resolutions, and in the ever-changing mobile phone and tablet landscape, you'll no doubt have to design for many additional resolutions.

Fortunately, Dreamweaver offers an alternative to the multiscreen preview. You can work on your mobile page-in-progress one device at a time in the document window. Here's how you make that happen. After you design a page in the document window, choose a resolution from the Multiscreen menu (circled in Figure 11-2) or from the Window Size menu (bottom-right of the document window—see Figure 11-2). For example, if you select "320 x 480 Smart Phone," you'll see your page inside a small, 320 x 480 pixel frame within the document window (see Figure 11-4).

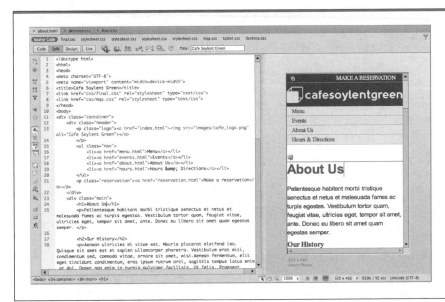

FIGURE 11-4

The "320 x 480 Smart Phone" preview is almost as good as seeing your page on an actual phone. It's the size screen you find on many smartphones, including the iPhone. Most desktop browsers won't let you resize their windows that small, so checking your site using a browser outside of Dreamweaver might not work. That makes Dreamweaver's preview a great way to see how a page will look on the small screen.

When you view your page at one of these preset resolutions, you can edit the HTML by selecting either Design or Split view. In addition, you can click the Live view button and even use Live Code (page 358) and Inspect Mode (page 494).

To exit a preset-resolution window, choose Full Size from the Multiscreen menu, or choose View→Window Size→Full Size.

Dreamweaver also provides three pre-programmed buttons at the bottom of the document window for changing the screen size in Design and Live view (see Figure 11-2). The Mobile button creates a 480 x 800 pixel frame; the Tablet button creates a 768 x 1024 pixel frame, and the Desktop button sets the frame to 1000 pixels wide and as tall as the Document window allows. Unfortunately, you can't assign different dimensions to these buttons—they're intended to work with Dreamweaver CS6's new Fluid Grid Layout feature described on page 521.

Media Queries

As mentioned at the beginning of this chapter, CSS3 includes a concept called *media queries*, which lets you assign styles to a page based on the width and height of the destination browser. So you can create custom styles for mobile phones, tablets, and desktop browsers, and, in turn, customize your site's presentation so that it looks its best on each type of device. Because media queries are part of the yet-to-be-finished CSS3 standard, not all browsers support them. Fortunately, the browsers you're most interested in—those for mobile phones and tablets—do, so even though Internet Explorer 8 doesn't know what a media query is, your good old iPhone or Android device does.

> **TIP** You can make IE 8 and earlier understand your media queries by adding a bit of JavaScript to the <head> of your document. You'll need to download the *respond.js* file from *http://tinyurl.com/7w49a6z*. Put the file in your site, and then link it to your page using the <script> tag. For example:
>
> ```
> <script src="respond.min.js"></script>
> ```
>
> This little maneuver forces IE 8, 7, and 6 to understand media queries. In fact, Dreamweaver CS6's new Fluid Grid Layout automatically adds this JavaScript to your pages (see page 521).

A "query" is just a question asked of a web browser: "Is your screen 320 pixels wide?" If the answer is Yes, the browser launches a style sheet for just that size device (a style sheet that you supply, as explained on page 513). The code that makes this happen looks pretty much the same as that for any external style sheet:

```
<link href="css/phone.css" rel="stylesheet" type="text/css" media="only

screen and (width:320px)">
```

The one addition to this standard style sheet link is the *media* attribute, which sets up the conditions under which Dreamweaver uses a particular sheet. You encountered the media attribute in Chapter 8 to tell a browser to apply different styles depending on whether you print out a page or view it on-screen (see page 399). Media queries are just an addition to the media attribute. In the example above, a browser loads the *phone.css* external style sheet when someone views your site with a browser whose width measures 320 pixels.

Because 320 pixels is very precise—what if there's a phone with a slightly smaller screen, say one that's just 300 pixels wide—it's best to use a range of values in your media query. For example, you might want to apply a particular style for screens that are less than or equal to 480 pixels wide. You do that like this:

```
<link href="css/phone.css" rel="stylesheet" type="text/css" media="only

screen and (max-width:480px)">
```

The notation "max-width:480px" is the same as saying "for screens that are at most 480 pixels wide." So the body tag style would apply to screens that are 480px wide, 320 pixels wide, and 200 pixels wide, for example.

Likewise, there's a Min Width option that determines whether a browser is at least a certain width. This is useful when you target a device that's bigger than a mobile phone or tablet. For example, you could write this link to apply styles to screens wider than the 768 pixels of many tablets:

```
<link href="css/desktop.css" rel="stylesheet" type="text/css" media="only

screen and (min-width:769px)">
```

To use this style sheet, a browser window must be at least 769 pixels wide—that's 1 pixel wider than a tablet.

And finally, you can set both Max Widths and Min Widths to target devices that fall between phones and desktop browsers. For example, to create a set of styles for a tablet that's 768 pixels wide, you could use this CSS code:

```
<link href="css/tablet.css" rel="stylesheet" type="text/css" media="only

screen and (min-width:481px) and (max-width:768px)
```

In other words, the browser's screen must be at least 481 pixels wide, but not more than 768 pixels wide. The stylesheet listed above wouldn't apply to a 320-pixel-wide smartphone, nor would it apply to a desktop browser with a screen width of 1024 pixels.

NOTE CSS3 media queries can do more than just check the width of a browser. The current Media Queries standard states that you can check for height, orientation (whether a visitor holds a mobile phone upright in "portrait" mode, or sideways in "landscape" mode), and even whether a device uses a color or monochrome screen. There are a few other browser characteristics you can check with media queries, but not all browsers support the queries, and Dreamweaver doesn't provide any direct support for them, either. You can learn more about media queries at the W3C website: *www.w3.org/TR/css3-mediaqueries*.

Fortunately, Dreamweaver doesn't require you to know all this code or add it yourself. It includes a Media Queries tool that adds the required programming and lets you use the CSS tools you already know. Used in conjunction with the window size previews discussed in the previous section, you can build media queries and preview their effects directly in Dreamweaver.

Dreamweaver CS6's Approach to Media Queries

Dreamweaver uses a separate external style sheet for each screen size you target: a phone style sheet, a tablet style sheet, a desktop style sheet, and so on. You can have as many style sheets as you want, each for a different resolution screen.

Dreamweaver can either attach those style sheets directly to a web page (see Figure 11-5, top) or to an intermediary style sheet—called a site-wide media queries file—that is, in turn, attached to the web page (Figure 11-5, bottom). The benefit of the site-wide file is that you need only one line of code to attach a style sheet to the page, instead of one line of code for each style sheet you create (for example, three lines of code that load phone, tablet, and desktop style sheets).

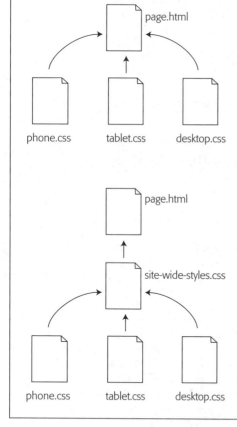

FIGURE 11-5

Dreamweaver's Media Queries tool lets you attach multiple style sheets—each for a custom screen width—to a page (top). This requires a line of code for each style sheet you create—for example, three style sheets need three links on the web page. Alternatively, you can attach a site-wide media queries file to each page on the site. That file contains links to the other style sheets (bottom). To target another device with another style sheet, you simply add one more line of code to the site-wide file, instead of editing every page on your site.

In addition, by using the site-wide media queries file, it's easier to add or remove style sheets for different devices. For example, say you start off with three style sheets, one for smartphones, one for tablets, and a third for desktop browsers, and you attached those sheets to each page on your site. If you later decide you only need style sheets for phone and desktop browsers, you need to edit every page on your site to remove the link to the tablet style sheet. If, however, you use a site-wide media queries file, you only need to edit the site-wide file to remove the tablet style sheet. Since each page on your site links to the site-wide file, any change you make to that file automatically applies to every page.

NOTE If you use a site-wide file, Dreamweaver adds a link to that file using the regular <link> tag—the same way it attaches any external style sheet (see page 138). However, the site-wide media queries file itself doesn't have the CSS styles; instead, it uses a rule called *@import* in conjunction with a media query to attach device-specific style sheets:

```
@import url("phone.css") only screen and (max-width:320px);
```

Using Dreamweaver's Media Queries Tool

To get started with media queries in Dreamweaver, open a web page and then launch the Media Queries window using one of these techniques:

- Choose Insert→Media Queries.

- Choose Modify→Media Queries.

- Choose Media Queries from the Multiscreen menu (see Figure 11-2).

Whichever method you choose, the Media Queries window opens (see Figure 11-6). You need to follow a few steps to get started, but the most important decision is determining where you should write the media queries: in a site-wide file or in the current page.

■ USING A SITE-WIDE MEDIA QUERIES FILE

A site-wide media queries file is a single, external style sheet with media queries that point to different style sheets—one for each target device. Each page in the site links to the site-wide file, which in turn loads the style sheet appropriate for the target device. As mentioned above, this approach means you add just one line of HTML to your page (for the site-wide file), and it's easier to add or remove a media query from your site because you edit only one site-wide file. In addition, as you'll see on page 517, it's faster to add the site-wide file to a web page using Dreamweaver. Because of these advantages, it's generally a good idea to use the side-wide media queries file.

NOTE The one downside to a site-wide media queries file is that it requires one additional request of the web server—the receiving browser has to download the site-wide file *and* the style sheet for your visitor's device. Downloading that additional file results in a slight performance hit, but unless you get huge amounts of traffic, no one will notice.

To use a site-wide media queries file:

1. **On the Media Queries window, turn on the "Site-wide media queries file" radio button (see Figure 11-6).**

   Next, specify the file name, or create a new site-wide media queries file.

2. **Click the "Specify..." button to the right of the radio button in step 1.**

The "Specify Site-wide Media Query File" window appears. Here, you either select an existing file or create a new one.

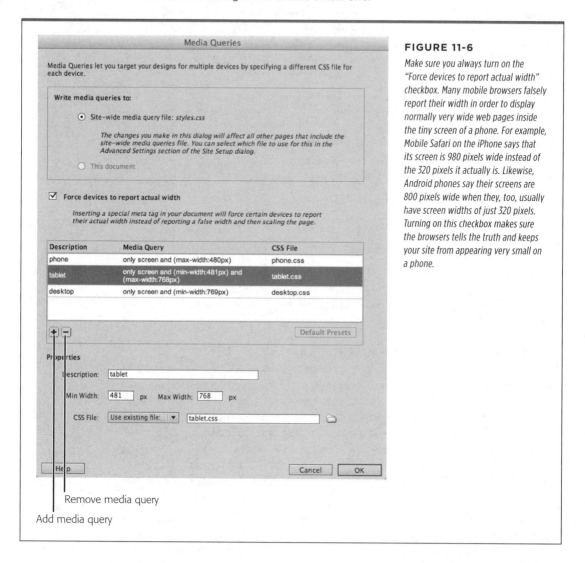

FIGURE 11-6

Make sure you always turn on the "Force devices to report actual width" checkbox. Many mobile browsers falsely report their width in order to display normally very wide web pages inside the tiny screen of a phone. For example, Mobile Safari on the iPhone says that its screen is 980 pixels wide instead of the 320 pixels it actually is. Likewise, Android phones say their screens are 800 pixels wide when they, too, usually have screen widths of just 320 pixels. Turning on this checkbox makes sure the browsers tells the truth and keeps your site from appearing very small on a phone.

NOTE If you don't see the "Specify..." button in the Media Queries window but you do see an external style sheet listed, you already set up a site-wide media queries file. If you press the OK button at the bottom-right of the window, you apply that file to the web page, and you're done with the page.

3. **Choose "Use existing file" or "Create new file" from the drop-down menu.**

Web designers who use media queries often start with a general CSS file that contains all the styling that applies to the site no matter what the browser window width. For example, you'll probably have the same page background color and same fonts and font colors no matter whether the page appears on a phone, tablet, or desktop browser. You can put these general styles in an external style sheet (*styles.css*) for example, and then select that style sheet in this step. Dreamweaver inserts the media queries, which link to the style sheets for different devices. However, every browser (mobile, tablet, or desktop) still loads and uses the styles from the main style sheet.

If you do select "Use existing file," click the folder icon, and then navigate to and select the external style sheet (a file ending in .css).

If you don't yet have an existing style sheet, select "Create new file."

4. **If you select "Create new file," click the folder icon, navigate to the destination folder, and then type a file name for the style sheet (*styles.css*, for example).**

Once you create (or link to) the site-wide file, you add media queries to it to determine the width of the destination device and then load a style sheet specific to it.

5. **Click the + button to add a new query (circled in Figure 11-6).**

You can also remove an existing query by selecting it in the list and then clicking the minus-sign (-) button.

6. **Type a name for the media query file in the Description box.**

Dreamweaver displays the name in the Media Queries window and adds a comment to the CSS file. You don't need to make the description anything complex—something as simple as "Phone," "Tablet," or "Desktop" is good enough.

7. **Type a minimum width (in pixels) in the Min Width box.**

The Min Width setting is the same as saying "the browser window must be at least this wide" for the style sheet to apply. For example, if you type *769* in this box, only browsers at least 769 pixels wide will load the style sheet (which you'll specify in step 9). It also applies to wider browser windows (1024 pixels, 2000 pixels, and so on), but not to narrower browser windows—768 pixels, 480 pixels, 320 pixels, and so on.

NOTE Media queries let you check not only the width, but also the height, of a browser window. However, Dreamweaver's Media Queries window won't let you specify a height. In general, that's all right. The biggest problem with viewing most websites on a phone is that their pages are just too wide, forcing you to either zoom in and scroll left and right to read the page, or squint and try to make out the tiny-tiny type of a three-column web page displayed at 320 pixels. Most web pages are already too tall to fit inside a browser window without scrolling anyway, so worrying about a browser's height doesn't make much sense.

You could use Min Width to open a desktop browser style sheet, too. However, since the still-popular IE 8 browser doesn't understand media queries, it will fail to load the desktop sheet. If you're worried about IE 8, either skip setting up a media query for desktop browsers and just put all the desktop styles inside the main style sheet or use JavaScript to force IE 8 to understand the desktop media query (see the Tip on page 510).

You *should* use Min Width, however, when you target a device in between the smallest and the largest browsers (a tablet, for instance). In this case, you use Min Width in conjunction with Max Width, as described in step 8.

You can leave the Min Width box empty: in fact, you will when you create a media query to target a mobile phone, as discussed in the next step.

8. **Type a maximum width in the Max Width box.**

The Max Width setting is the same as saying "the browser window must be no more than this wide" for a web browser to apply the style sheet. For example, if you type *480* in this box, Dreamweaver applies the style sheet you specify in step 9 only if the browser window is 480 pixels wide or less (400 pixels, 320 pixels, and so on). Dreamweaver won't apply the sheet for wider windows—481 pixels, 768 pixels, 1024 pixels, and so on. (If you target a desktop browser, you can leave the Max Width box empty, though you have to supply a value in the Min Width box.)

Your Max Width value should reflect the smallest device you target. For example, to target a phone, type in the width of the phone's screen. For many phones, the screen is 320 pixels wide in portrait mode, and 480 pixels wide in landscape mode. So if you type *480* in the Max Width box, a browser loads the style sheet for phones held in either orientation.

Use the Max Width setting in conjunction with Min Width to target devices that fall in between two resolutions. For example, a tablet's screen is wider than a phone's screen, but thinner than most desktop monitors' displays. If you wish to create a style sheet for tablets, you need to specify a Min Width that's wider than a phone browser's width (for example, 481 pixels) and a Max Width that's thinner than a desktop browser's width (for example, 768).

Tablets come in a variety of dimensions. The Kindle Fire measures 600 pixels by 1024 pixels, for example, as does the Samsung Galaxy Tab 2. The iPad is 768 pixels by 1024 pixels wide. Of course, if you hold any of these tablets in landscape mode, they'll measure 1024 pixels wide. Since 1024 pixels is wide enough to fit most web pages, there's really no reason to create a separate style sheet for these tablets when held in landscape mode, but you might want to tighten up the design for tablets held in portrait mode—for example, you might take a three-column design for the desktop and convert it to a two-column design for tablets. In that case, type *481* in the Min Width box and *768* in the Max Width box. The style sheet you'll specify in the next step loads only when a browser window measures at least 481 pixels wide (which excludes phones) but no more than 768 pixels wide (which excludes desktop browsers and a tablet held in landscape mode).

9. **Choose either "Use existing file" or "Create new file" from the CSS File menu, click the folder icon, and then either select an already existing site-wide style sheet or name and save a new one.**

Unless you already use media queries and have an appropriate style sheet, select the "Create a new file" option. After clicking the folder icon, navigate to a destination folder and supply a name that describes the style sheet—for example, *phone.css, tablet.css, desktop.css*, and so on.

10. **Repeat steps 5–9 until you create as many media queries and style sheets as you want.**

While you can create as many media queries as you like, life's always better when you keep it simple. At a minimum, you want style sheets for phones and desktop browsers, but if you're ambitious and have time on your hands, you might create a third style sheet for tablets. See page 518 for tips on building device-specific style sheets.

11. **Click OK to close the Media Queries window.**

Dreamweaver adds the code to your page, creates the site-wide media queries file, and includes all the style sheets you specified. At this point, you start adding styles to the sheets, as you normally would (see page 125 if you need a refresher course in creating styles).

Once you create a site-wide media queries file, applying that file to other pages is a snap:

1. **Open a web page to which you want to attach a site-wide media query file.**

2. **Use any of the methods described on page 513 to open the Media Queries window.**

For example, choose Insert→Media Queries.

3. **Turn on the "Site-wide media queries file" radio button, and then click OK.**

Dreamweaver links the already created site-wide media queries file to the page, and you're done.

When you attach a site-wide media queries file to a page, it appears in the CSS Styles panel, just as every other external style sheet does. Select it in the panel and click the trash can icon if you want to remove it from the page (see page 141 for more on removing an external style sheet).

■ **APPLYING MEDIA QUERIES TO THE CURRENT DOCUMENT**

The Media Queries window also lets you attach media queries directly to the current web page. This approach bypasses the site-wide media queries file: Dreamweaver simply links to the different style sheets using the appropriate query. For example, this <link> tag adds loads a style sheet only when a browser is 320 or fewer pixels wide:

```
<link href="phone.css" rel="style sheet" type="text/css" media="only screen

and (max-width:320px)">
```

The downside to this technique is that you have to add the media queries on a page-by-page basis. To do so, you must:

1. **Open the page to which you want to add the media query.**

2. **Choose Insert→Media Queries.**

   Or use any of the other methods discussed on page 513. The Media Queries window opens.

3. **Turn on the "This document" radio button.**

   At this point, the process is the same as when you first created a site-wide media query file: add a media query and select a style sheet.

4. **Follow steps 5–9 on pages 515 to 517 for each media query you wish to apply.**

   In other words, if you have a *phone.css* style sheet for mobile phones, a *tablet .css* style sheet for tablets, and a *desktop.css* style sheet for desktop browsers, you have to repeat steps 5–9 on pages 515 to 517 three times.

5. **Repeat the above steps for each page in your site.**

   This can be a pain. Even with just a single media query, attaching a single style sheet involves several more steps than using a site-wide file does. However, you can use Dreamweaver's Template tool (Chapter 19) to greatly simplify the process of building multiple web pages with queries in them.

■ Strategies for Using Media Queries

Now that you know how to add media queries to a page, what's the best way to use them to make your site mobile-friendly? Most site pages are just too wide to look good on a mobile phone. Phone browsers typically zoom out to give you a bird's-eye view of the page. If the page has multiple columns and was designed at a width of 960 pixels, it's impossible to read on a phone without zooming in and dragging the page around.

Web designers use a few techniques for mobile design:

• **Remove columns**. Multiple side-by-side columns look great on a big monitor (and even on a tablet in landscape mode), but not so much on a phone. Remove the floats (see page 448) to stack a page's content divs one on top of the other.

- **Remove widths**. If you use a fixed-width design, your pages won't look good on a phone. A 960-pixel-wide page is just too much for the 320 or 480 pixels of a phone. For a phone, a good approach is setting the widths of your content divs to *Auto* or *100%*. This converts your page from a fixed-width design to a liquid, or flexible, design. In other words, no matter how wide a phone's screen, the divs will fit 100 percent of it. If a person holding an iPhone in portrait mode (so that the screen width is 320 pixels) suddenly turns the phone horizontally (changing the screen width to 480 pixels), divs set to Auto or 100% simply resize to fit the new space.

- **Tighten up white space**. Ample space between headlines, graphics, and other page elements adds breathing room to a design on a 23-inch monitor, but creates a scattered design and wastes space on a phone's small screen. Shrinking *margin* (page 449) and *padding* (page 449) values lets you fit more onto those small screens.

- **Shrink fonts**. Large fonts look good on large screens, but take up too much room on handheld devices. Change the fonts on your page so they're smaller but still readable.

- **Hide content**. Many designers strip away content from mobile versions of sites. While it's easy to scan several columns and hundreds of lines of text on a desktop monitor, too much information on a phone can be overwhelming. You can use CSS to simply hide content that you think is superfluous for mobile users by setting the CSS display property to none (page 166).

- **Use background images**. If you put a 960-pixel banner on a page, no phone will display it without zooming out. One approach is to make sure your images are small enough to fit inside a phone's screen or use CSS background images instead (see page 262). For example, you could create a div and add a class to it like this: <div class="logo">. Then, in the style sheet for the desktop browser, set the div's width and height to match the size of the large logo, using the Background-image property to insert the image into the background. For example:

```
.logo {
    width: 960px;
    height: 120px;
    background-image: url(images/large_logo.png)
}
```

You could then put another style inside the style sheet used for mobile phones that resizes that div and uses a different background image:

```
.logo {

    width: 320px;

    height: 60px;

    background-image: url(images/small_logo.png)

}
```

TIP Web designer Ethan Marcotte suggests another way to deal with images in mobile design. His "fluid images" technique is described at *http://tinyurl.com/ch9e43*. Fluid images are part of the "Responsive Design Approach" used in the new Fluid Grid Layouts tool described on page 521.

Organizing Your Style Sheets for Media Queries

So how do you actually resize your site based on screen resolution? There are several approaches:

- **Create separate style sheets for each device**. In other words, create a phone style sheet, a tablet style sheet (if you're concerned about those), and a desktop style sheet, and then use Dreamweaver's media queries tool to attach each sheet to its respective page. However, since Internet Explorer 8 and earlier browsers don't understand media queries, attaching a desktop style sheet using a media query in IE 8 and earlier won't work. One way around this is to use JavaScript (see the tip on page 510) to make IE 8 understand media queries. Another approach is to use an IE conditional comment (see the box on page 461) to attach the desktop style sheet. To do this, add the following code after the media queries on your page:

```
<!--[if lt IE 9]>

<link href="desktop.css" media="screen" rel="stylesheet">

<![endif]-→
```

You need to change the *href* value above to specify the path to your desktop CSS file. Dreamweaver can't insert this code for you, and its link management tools don't know how to locate and track it, so if you move the CSS file, you need to change the *href* value to point to the new location.

The other downside to this approach is that you need to specify all the styles in *each* style sheet. If you want to use the same font for an <h1> tag, for instance, and you use three style sheets (one for phones, one for tablets, and one for desktop browsers), you need to add the h1 style to each sheet.

- **Use a master style sheet and then individual style sheets for each device**. This method is similar to the one described for print style sheets on page 399. Basically, you start by creating a style sheet for the desktop version of the site, just as you'd normally do. Then you use the Media Queries tool to attach style sheets for other devices: one for phones, for example. In this second style sheet, you add styles that override the styles in the master sheet.

For example, say the main style sheet (the one attached without a media query) has a style for a div with the class *content*. You name the style *.content*, and float it to the right, with a fixed width of 564 pixels. In the phone style sheet, add another style named *.content*, but set its *float* property to *none* and its *width* to *auto*. Because of the rules of the Cascade (see page 391), and because the phone style sheet appears second in the HTML, its *.content* style overrules the style with the same name in the master style sheet. You can continue adding styles to the phone style sheet that override those in the master sheet.

The phone style sheet doesn't have to override *all* the styles from the master sheet—that's one of the benefits of this approach. So if you don't create a style with the same name as one in the master sheet, the style from the master sheet prevails. Because of this, you only need to create a single style (in the master style sheet) for any site-wide formatting you want to see in phone, tablet, and desktop browsers (like fonts, page colors, and so on). Having the desktop styles in the main style sheet also avoids the need to use the IE conditional comment mentioned above.

Adding Styles to Media Query Style Sheets

Dreamweaver's Media Queries tool simply adds the media query needed to load a specific style sheet for a specific device. In other words, media queries merely control when a browser uses a specific style sheet—the actual style sheet (*phone .css, tablet.css, desktop.css*) is otherwise the same as any other external style sheet. You use the same Dreamweaver tools described elsewhere in this book to add, edit, delete, and manage the styles in those sheets. For example, follow the steps on page 125 to add a style, page 139 or 382 to edit a style, and page 141 to delete a style.

■ Fluid Grid Layouts

Dreamweaver CS6 adds another tool for building web pages that adapt to different browser widths. Its new Fluid Grid Layout lets you create a single HTML file whose layout morphs to fit phones, tablets, and desktop browsers. It's based on a technique called "responsive Web design," which includes CSS media queries, flexible column layout (that is, the columns adjust their width to match the browser width), and fluid images (see Figure 11-7).

FIGURE 11-7

The web design site Smashing Magazine (http://smashing magazine.com), uses responsive Web design to customize the site's layout for phones (top left), tablets (top right), and desktop browsers (bottom). Each device receives the same HTML file, but CSS media queries direct different CSS to each device, creating unique layouts appropriate to the devices' browser window widths.

NOTE Responsive Web design (RWD) is a term coined by the web designer Ethan Marcotte. You can learn more about it from the article that kicked off the RWD movement: *www.alistapart.com/articles/responsive-web-design/*.

Understanding Fluid Grid Layouts

Dreamweaver's Fluid Grid Layouts combine lots of concepts, and to use them correctly you need to understand a few key ideas:

- **Grid layout.** Graphic designers have been using grids for centuries to design books, brochures, and other printed materials. A grid is an invisible pattern that underlies the design of a page (see Figure 11-8). In web design, a grid is a pattern of columns used to define the width of divs placed on a page. The page's designer dictates the number of columns that comprise the grid. That layout then determines the width of the <div> tags used to place content on the page.

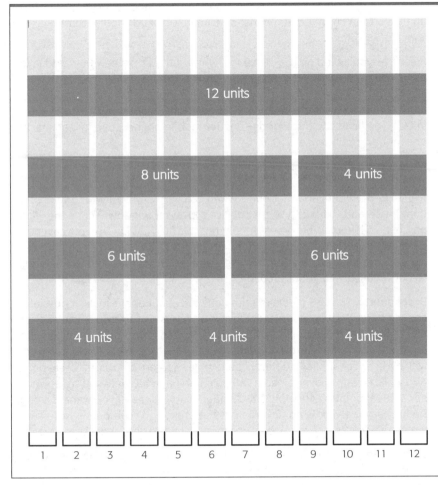

FIGURE 11-8

A layout is simply a grid of columns that provides the organizational structure for a page. In this example, the layout grid is composed of 12 columns. Those 12 columns provide 12 units that the page's designer can distribute among any number of actual layout elements. For example, a <div> tag for housing the page's header would fill the entire page, taking up all 12 columns (or units).

For example, the grid in Figure 11-8 comprises 12 columns. Think of each column as a single unit; the width of the page is the equivalent of all 12 columns, so the page is 12 units wide. A header div that spans the entire page, then, would also be 12 units wide. To add side-by-side columns, you simply divide those 12 units among the number of columns you want. For example, say you want to place the page's main content in a wide column and include some sidebar information in a narrower column to the right. You might divide that page into two columns and specify a main content column of 8 units, while the sidebar would be 4. Likewise, you could create two equal-width columns of 6 units each, or three side-by-side columns of 4 units apiece.

Another thing to keep in mind is that you have to define your columns in whole units—you can't have a column that's 2.5 units wide and another that's 9.5 units wide, for example.

Finally, as you'll read on the next page, when you set up a new fluid grid layout page, you get to define the underlying grid yourself. For example, you may not like 12 columns as an organizing principle; maybe you like more or fewer columns. Dreamweaver lets you pick your grid—anywhere from 2 to 24 columns. In fact, you'll specify three grids—one for mobile phones, one for tablets, and one for desktop browsers.

- **Fluid layout.** The width of each unit of the grid system can vary. That is, there is no fixed width, say 100 pixels, for a unit. Each unit represents a part of the overall grid's width, and that unit's width can vary depending on the destination device and the width of that device's browser window. That's the "fluid" part of fluid layout. When you add columns to a fluid layout, Dreamweaver uses percentage values to size the columns you insert. That means the columns resize to fit the available space in the browser window (this is the same as the "liquid" layouts you learned about on page 436).

- **Breakpoints.** The CSS media queries you read about above make it possible to apply different styles for different browser widths. For example, you can send one style sheet to a mobile browser whose screen is 480 or fewer pixels wide, and another sheet to a browser that's at least 789 pixels wide. The dimension at which a browser applies a different style sheet is referred to as its "breakpoint." And while Dreamweaver's Media Queries tool (page 510) lets you set any number of breakpoints (and apply any number of style sheets) you want in a page, Dreamweaver's Fluid Grid Layouts put the brakes on that idea—it offers only three breakpoints, one for mobile, one for tablets, and one for desktop browsers.

Dreamweaver adds styles for mobile devices whose width is 480 pixels or less. Tablet layouts kick in when pages are between 481 and 768 pixels wide, and desktop layouts take over for pages between 769 and 1232 pixels wide. These numbers are hard-wired into Dreamweaver's fluid grid system, and you can't change them without breaking the fluid grid tools.

- **Flexible Media.** Another key feature of Responsive Web Design is "flexible media," or images that resize based on the width of their containers. In Responsive Web Design, if a column containing an image gets thinner, the image gets narrower, too. So an image that's, say, 600 pixels wide when viewed on a desktop browser, will automatically scale down to fit the limited space of a mobile phone. This happens thanks to some clever CSS (in fact, you don't need to do anything to get this feature, just insert images as your normally would, as explained on page 242).

Creating a Fluid Grid Layout Page

Dreamweaver CS6's Fluid Grid Layout pages are a special breed: They use some special CSS, media queries, a bit of JavaScript, and a dedicated visual tool to get the job done. Because of this, you can't "turn" a regular web page into a Fluid Grid Layout page with the push of a button. In fact, the CSS and HTML for the grid layout is so complex you have to start by creating a new page, and then adding content. If you want to convert an older website into a fancy responsive design, you've got your work cut out for you. You'll need to create the Fluid Grid page first, and then move content into the new design: in other words, copy from the old pages and paste into the new.

1. **Choose File→New Fluid Grid Layout.**

   Dreamweaver opens the New Document window with the Fluid Grid Layout category selected (see Figure 11-9).

2. **Type the number of columns to form the grid you'd like to use for each device (mobile, tablet, and desktop) in the boxes inside the device outlines (the area with the pink columns).**

   Here, you're not saying how many columns you will actually insert in the web page. Rather, you're letting Dreamweaver know how many columns to draw on the screen to form the page grid. You use these screen columns as units of measure when you specify the number of columns you want on the page. What you type here really depends on the design you're after. Here are a few guidelines:

   - For mobile design, web designers often use just a single column for content (see the top-left image in Figure 11-7). Because of the narrow screen (480 or fewer pixels wide), placing more than one column in a row makes designs look squished. However, Dreamweaver won't let you type *1* in the Mobile Column box, so you need to type *2* or a larger number. If you're going to simply stack the content blocks one on top of the next (as many web designers do), it doesn't matter what you type here. If you *do* plan to place columns side by side (and you should probably stick with two columns as the maximum for mobile design), the number you type here determines the ratio of one column to the next. Type *2* if you want two equally sized columns sitting side by side. If you want columns of different proportions, type a larger number here to set up the ratio you want. For example, if you type *3*, you can make one column 2 units wide and the second column 1 unit wide.

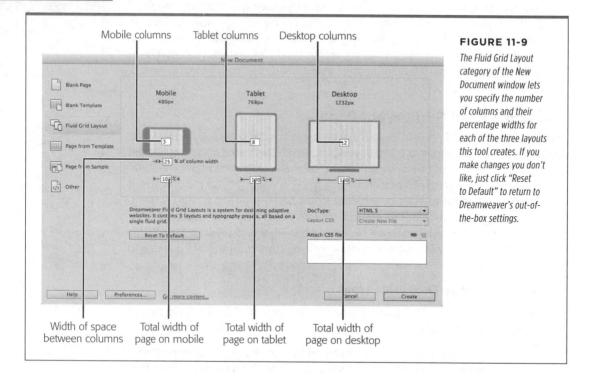

Mobile columns   Tablet columns   Desktop columns

Width of space between columns
Total width of page on mobile
Total width of page on tablet
Total width of page on desktop

FIGURE 11-9

The Fluid Grid Layout category of the New Document window lets you specify the number of columns and their percentage widths for each of the three layouts this tool creates. If you make changes you don't like, just click "Reset to Default" to return to Dreamweaver's out-of-the-box settings.

- For tablet design, type a number large enough to accommodate the different combinations of columns you envision for this design. If you think that you might want two equally sized columns, make sure the number is even; if you want three equally sized columns, you need a number divisible by 3. Twelve is a good number to use since it's divisible by 2, so you can create two columns that are each 6 units wide. If you want three columns in a 12-unit grid, you can make each one 4 units wide. In short, 12 units gives you lots of combinations of column number and browser widths. Keep in mind that this number only applies to devices whose width is between Mobile (greater than 480 pixels) and 768 pixels. In other words, this would apply to an iPad in portrait orientation (768 pixels wide), but not one that you hold in landscape mode (1024 pixels wide). Nor would this apply to a Kindle Fire or a Samsung Galaxy Tab 2, no matter which way you hold it, since the screens on those tablets measure 1024 by 800 pixels. In those cases, the tablet's browser would use the desktop design.

- For desktop design, use the same logic that you applied to tablets: how many columns do you want, and what proportion do you want to set for them? Twelve is a good value here, too, since it gives you many unit combinations for a wide number of columns, but Dreamweaver will accept a value up to 24.

3. **In the "% of column width" box, type a value for the space between columns.**

The space that separates columns (called the "gutter" in graphic design) is defined as a percentage of an individual column width. You can't set a different value for each type of layout: The mobile, tablet, and desktop layouts all share the same percentage. However, since you can set different numbers of grid columns for each layout, the actual width of the gutter will vary. Unfortunately, once you pick a gutter value, there's no way to return to this screen and change it. In fact, since Dreamweaver uses this value to make some complex calculations concerning the columns you insert, there's no easy way to change this value once you create the layout. A good value is between 20% and 30%, though you might want to create a couple of pages with different values and test them out before you commit to one value and build an entire site.

4. **Type a percentage width for each layout.**

The content for a flexible grid layout page sits inside a container div. You can set a width for that div to control how much of the browser window your design will fill. The normal values are 91%, 93%, and 90%. Why? We don't know. It seems weird that you'd choose not to use the entire width of a mobile phone's already thin screen. In fact, it seems weird that you wouldn't use all of the horizontal space allowed. So set the value to 100% for each layout.

5. **Click Create.**

Dreamweaver opens the Save Style Sheet File As dialog. You're about to save an external style sheet that contains all the styles necessary to control the layout of the page.

6. **Type a style sheet name—like *layout.css*—and then click Save.**

Dreamweaver saves the style sheet file to your site and displays the page in Mobile view (see Figure 11-10).

7. **Choose File→Save and save the HTML page to your site.**

Dreamweaver saves the web page and opens a "Copy Dependent Files" window informing you that it needs to save two files, *boilerplate.css* and *respond.min .js*, to your site. The *boilerplate.css* file is an external style sheet based on the HTML5 boilerplate template (*http://html5boilerplate.com/*); it sets up many basic CSS properties and provides a baseline for displaying various HTML tags. The *respond.min.js* file targets just Internet Explorer 8 and earlier and forces that browser to understand the media queries that the flexible grid layout uses.

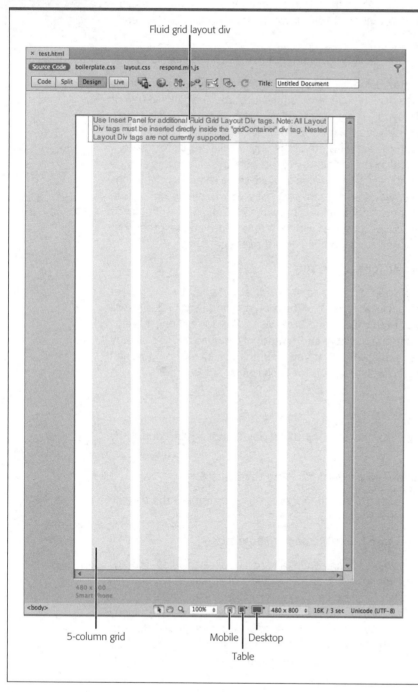

Fluid grid layout div

5-column grid

Mobile

Table

Desktop

FIGURE 11-10

A newly minted Flexible Grid Layout page starts with a single <div> tag spanning the top of the page. Dreamweaver gives this div a green background. You build the page by adding more divs, filling them with content, and moving them into columns. The pink columns form the grid itself, and two things determine the number of columns you see: the view you're in (Mobile, Tablet, or Desktop), and the column number and percentage values you specified in step 2 above. To turn off the pink grid and the green div background , uncheck Fluid Grid Layout Guides from the Document toolbar's Visual Aids menu (circled), or choose View→Visual Aids→Fluid Grid Layout Guides.

When you first create a flexible grid layout page, Dreamweaver inserts a single div at the top of the page (see Figure 11-11). It slaps a generic ID on the div, *LayoutDiv1*. The first thing you should do is change this name to something more descriptive, like banner or header.

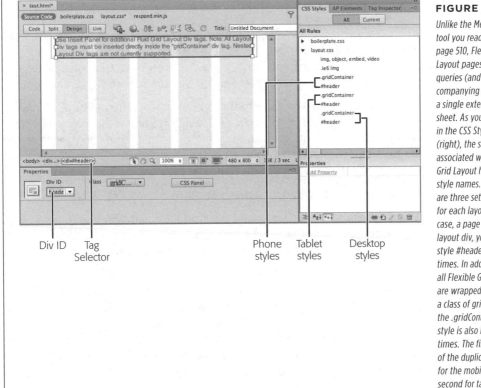

Div ID Tag Selector

Phone styles Tablet styles Desktop styles

FIGURE 11-11

Unlike the Media Query tool you read about on page 510, Flexible Grid Layout pages put media queries (and their accompanying styles) into a single external style sheet. As you can see in the CSS Styles panel (right), the style sheet associated with a Flexible Grid Layout has triplicate style names. In fact, there are three sets of styles for each layout div. In this case, a page with a single layout div, you see the ID style #header listed three times. In addition, since all Flexible Grid Layouts are wrapped in a div with a class of gridContainer, the .gridContainer class style is also listed three times. The first instance of the duplicate styles is for the mobile layout, the second for tablet layout, and the third for desktop layout. See page 535 for more on Fluid Grid Layout style sheets.

1. **Click inside the div, or click the `<div>` tag in the Tag Selector at the bottom of the document window.**

   This selects the div and displays its properties in the Property Inspector.

2. **In the ID field, select *LayoutDiv1* and type a more descriptive name.**

   Use a name that matches the content you expect to put in this div—banner, header, logo, or nav, for example. When you rename the div, Dreamweaver also updates the name of the ID style that formats this div in the external style sheet you created in steps 5 and 6 on page 527.

Inserting Fluid Grid Layout Divs

Once you create a Fluid Grid Layout page, it's time to insert the basic building blocks of the design. As with any CSS design (see Chapter 9), the fundamental unit of page layout in a fluid grid page is the humble <div> tag (page 438), the box that holds your content. Creating a page layout using Dreamweaver's fluid grid tool is largely a process of inserting divs, sizing them to create columns, and then filling them with content.

Like a regular web page, when you insert what Dreamweaver calls a "Fluid Grid Layout div," Dreamweaver adds an HTML <div> tag to the page. You place your content (images, headlines, paragraphs, and so on) in the div. Every device—phone, tablet, and desktop browser—downloads the same HTML with the same div tags and content.

However, unlike a regular web page, these divs can appear differently in each device, thanks to the power of CSS media queries. That is, on a phone, the divs might stack one on top of the other to form a single column; on a tablet, some divs might sit side by side to form a two-column layout; while the wide screen of a desktop browser lets you organize the same divs into a four-column design.

Before you start inserting divs, however, keep in mind a couple of rules:

- You must place a Fluid Grid Layout Div inside the container div. This is a <div> tag with the class gridContainer applied to it. You can tell if your cursor is inside the container by looking at the Tag Selector at the bottom-left of the document window (see Figure 11-11).

- You place new divs either before or after existing divs. You can't, for example, put a Fluid Grid Layout div inside another Fluid Grid Layout div—your design won't work if you do. For the most accurate placement of a new div, first click inside an already existing div before (or after) which you want to place the new div. Then use the Tag Selector to highlight the div, and click the left arrow key to place your cursor before the div, or the right arrow key to place the cursor after the div.

- When you insert a div in one view— Desktop view, for example—Dreamweaver adds that same div to the phone and tablet versions as well. The HTML is always the same for the three devices, though the page's appearance might differ because the browser applies different CSS styles based on the browser window width.

Once you place the cursor where you wish to insert the new div, you're ready to add a Fluid Grid Layout div:

1. **Click the Fluid Grid Layout div button on the Layout category of the Insert Panel (see Figure 11-12), or choose Insert→Layout Objects→Fluid Grid Layout Div Tag.**

    Either way, the Insert Fluid Grid Layout Div Tag window appears (Figure 11-13).

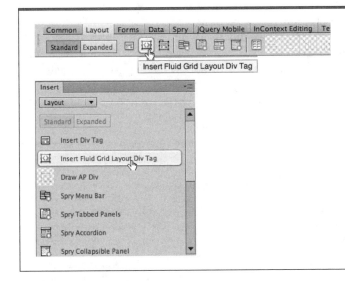

FIGURE 11-12

The insert Fluid Grid Layout Div Tag button is available from the Layout category of the Insert panel. The panel's Classic view (page 38) is displayed above, top, and the panel view appears below that.

FIGURE 11-13

The Insert Fluid Grid Layout Div Tag window adds a new div to a fluid grid page.

2. **Type a descriptive name for the new ID (for example, sidebar, footer, content).**

   Dreamweaver uses this name as the ID for the div—<div id="sidebar">, for example—and also creates an ID style—#sidebar, for example. In fact, Dreamweaver adds three copies of the ID style to the page's style sheet. They dictate the width and placement of the div for mobile, tablet, or desktop browsers.

3. **Leave the "Start new row" checkbox turned on, and click OK to insert the new div tag.**

   The "Start new row" checkbox dictates whether the div should sit on a row by itself (turned on) or should be inserted as a column next to another row (turned off). It's easiest to leave this checkbox turned on when you insert the div, and then adjust the divs after you insert them (as described next).

Formatting Fluid Grid Layout Divs

Once you insert divs into a Fluid Grid Layout page, you can begin to organize them into columns. Dreamweaver CS6's new tools make this easy. But first, you need to understand that each device—mobile, tablet, and desktop—has its own view, which you control by clicking the appropriate window size button in the bottom-right of the document window (see Figure 11-14). When you change the width of a div, or turn it into a column that sits next to one or more other divs, Dreamweaver updates the CSS for just that one view. In other words, you create separate layouts for mobile, tablet, and desktop browsers by clicking the appropriate window size button, and then resizing the divs for that view.

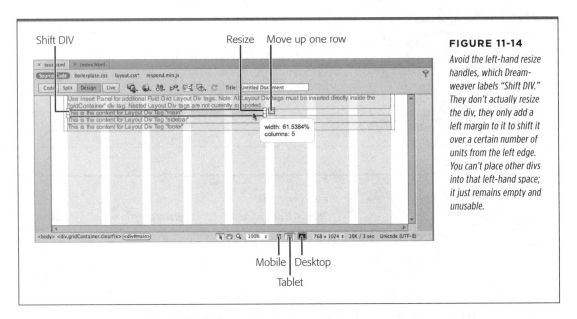

FIGURE 11-14

Avoid the left-hand resize handles, which Dream-weaver labels "Shift DIV." They don't actually resize the div, they only add a left margin to it to shift it over a certain number of units from the left edge. You can't place other divs into that left-hand space; it just remains empty and unusable.

To resize a div, simply click inside it and use the resize handle (to the right of the div) to change its width. Although the div displays three resize handles (boxes) on the right side, you can change only the width of the div; you can't, for example, grab the bottom handle and pull it down to make the div taller. The sole purpose of these handles is to make a div a certain number of grid units wide so you can place it next to one or more other divs in the same row.

To place columns side by side in a row, follow these steps:

1. **For the first div in a row, grab its right resize handle and drag to the left to set its width (No.1 in Figure 11-15).**

   As described on page 523, the underlying grid you selected in step 2 on page 525 dictates the possible widths for the div. Dreamweaver will snap the div to the nearest grid column. For example, in the page pictured in Figure 11-15, the underlying grid is 8 columns wide. Dragging the second div's resize handle to match up with Column 5 (top image) sets that column's width to 5 grid units.

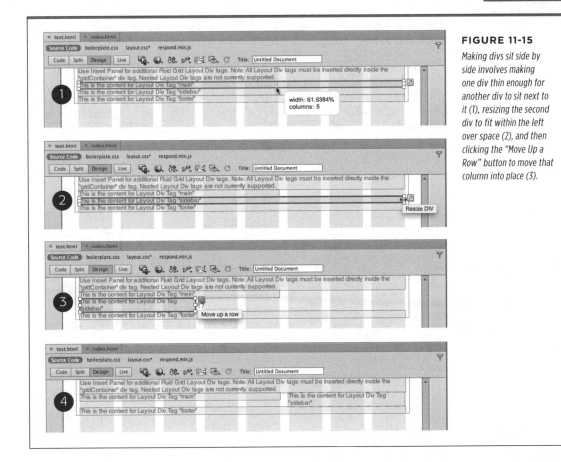

FIGURE 11-15

Making divs sit side by side involves making one div thin enough for another div to sit next to it (1), resizing the second div to fit within the left over space (2), and then clicking the "Move Up a Row" button to move that column into place (3).

NOTE Dreamweaver snaps the div's width to the nearest grid column, so you don't need to be super-accurate when you resize the width of a Fluid Grid Layout div.

---

2. **Grab the right resize handle for the div directly below the one you modified in step 1 and drag it to set its width (No. 2 in Figure 11-15).**

   For this div to sit next to the one you just set up, its width must be equal to or less than the remaining column units for the row. For example, in Figure 11-15, the second div on the page is five columns wide, and the overall grid width is 8 units. So if you want to create a two-column layout, set the width of this div to the space remaining after you resize the first div in the column. In the example in Figure 11-15, that would be 3 columns.

NOTE When you resize a div you want to move up and to the right of another div, it's tempting to grab the handles on the left side of the div. Don't!!! See Figure 11-14 for an explanation.

3. **Move the lower div up by clicking the "Move up a row" button (No. 3 in Figure 11-15).**

   As pictured in No. 4 in Figure 11-15, Dreamweaver moves the div up to the row above it (as long as the div is thin enough to fit in the available space). You can continue to resize the divs—for example, to make one column thinner and another wider—but Dreamweaver will only let those divs sit side by side if the total widths of the divs is equal to or less than the total number of grid units. If you resize one div to 6 columns in an 8-column grid, and set the second div to 3 columns, the two columns can't fit next to each other, so the second one drops below the first.

If you decide you want a div to move to its own row, click the "Starts new row" icon at the right edge of the div (circled in Figure 11-16, top).

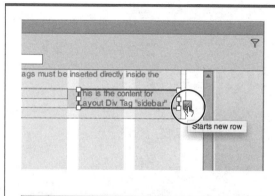

FIGURE 11-16

If, when you insert a Fluid Grid Layout div onto a page, you turn off the "Start new row" checkbox (see step 3 on page 531), you'll end up with a div that's slightly indented (bottom image). To remove this indent and move the div to its own row, click the "align div with grid" icon (circled).

Remember that each view—mobile, tablet, and desktop—has its own formatting for these divs. You need to click the appropriate view button (Figure 11-14), to switch to a different view, and *then* adjust the divs' widths to match your design.

NOTE For a mobile design, it's not uncommon to leave all the divs on their own row. For the thin display of a phone, it's difficult to insert multiple side-by-side columns without making the design feel cramped.

Adding Content to Fluid Grid Layout Pages

Adding content to a Fluid Grid Layout page is no different from adding content to any other web page. You insert images and text inside the layout divs, just as you normally insert HTML content into a web page. For example, you'd copy and paste text, and use the Property Inspector to create headlines, paragraphs, lists, and bold and italic characters. To insert an image, for instance, use the Insert→Image command).

NOTE When you insert an image into Fluid Grid Layout page, Dreamweaver doesn't assign a width or height to the image as it does in other types of web pages (see page 525). Instead, it leaves those values blank and uses some tricky CSS to makes the image "fluid"—that is, to make the image itself shrink in size as the div gets smaller. (To learn how this works, read the original article on this technique by Ethan Marcotte: *www.alistapart.com/articles/fluid-images/*.)

Styling Fluid Grid Layout Pages

Dreamweaver CS6's Fluid Grid Layout tools are merely intended to control the layout of divs in browsers on mobile, tablet, and desktop devices. They don't do anything to help style the look of the content you place *inside* those divs. You can use the regular CSS tools you learned about in this book to style headlines, add background colors to divs, and so on. However, before you jump into styling, you need to understand how Dreamweaver organizes the styles in the external style sheet for Fluid Grid Layout pages.

That style sheet contains styles for mobile, tablet, and desktop browsers; however, it includes only two media queries. The first part of the style sheet contains the styles for the mobile layout. Dreamweaver doesn't include those styles in a media query, so they actually apply to all browsers at any width.

So how do you get a different design for tablets? The first media query in the style sheet specifies a min-width of 481 pixels. That is, the styles in this part of the sheet apply to any device over 480 pixels wide. Dreamweaver inserts styles inside this media query with the same ID selector names that appeared earlier in the style sheet. Thanks to the CSS Cascade discussed on page 391, these styles override the same-named selectors used for mobile devices. It's kind of like the style sheet saying "Hey browser, here's some styles to use...oh, wait a minute, I see that you're wider than 480 pixels, so why don't you use these styles instead."

For example, if you look at the style sheet Dreamweaver creates when you build a Fluid Grid Layout page (see step 6 on page 527), you first see a class style named *.gridContainer*. This sets up the overall width of the page; that same style—*.gridContainer*—appears a second time in the style sheet, within the "min-width: 481px" media query. If the web browser is wider than 480 pixels, it applies this style, and any properties that conflict with the *.gridContainer* style listed earlier win.

The same happens for the desktop version, but it's even more confusing. That is, all the styles that appear in the beginning of the style sheet apply to mobile, tablet, and desktop devices. All the styles inside the first media query ("min-width: 481px") apply to both tablet and desktop machines (since tablet and desktop browser are wider than 480 pixels). A second media query with a *min-width* of 769 pixels applies another round of styles to just the desktop.

Here are some tips for styling HTML for different devices:

- **Styles that apply to all devices.** Say you want all <h1> tags to be bright red regardless of whether the visitor has an Android Phone, iPad, or Chrome desktop browser. Put the style anywhere before the second *.gridContainer style*.

- **Styles that apply only to mobile browsers.** This one is a bit tricky. You need to insert the style before the second *.gridContainer* style (as in the previous bullet point) but, because this style applies to all browsers, you need to create another style with the same name after the second *.gridContainer* (but before the third *.gridContainer*). This style needs to reset the CSS properties from the first style to match what you want for tablets and desktop browsers.

  For example, say you want the <h1> tag to be smaller on mobile devices, say 18 pixels. You'd create an <h1> tag style with Font-size set to 18px and put it near the beginning of the external style sheet. Then you'd create another <h1> tag style, setting its font size larger (say 36px) for tablets and desktop browsers, and place the style after the second *.gridContainer* style.

- **Styles that apply to tablets and desktop browsers.** Create a new style and place it between the second and third *.gridContainer* style.

- **Styles that apply only to tablets.** As with mobile-only styles, you need to create two styles with the same name. One goes between the second and third *.gridContainer* styles (this is the tablet-only style) and another after the third *.gridContainer* style, which resets the CSS properties to match the mobile design.

- **Styles that apply only to desktop browser.** This one, fortunately, is easy. Just place the new desktop-only style after the third *.gridContainer* style; it will fall inside the "min-width: 769px" media query and apply only to browsers with a width greater than 768 pixels.

TIP If you select a style in the CSS styles panel and then click the New CSS Rule button, Dreamweaver inserts the new style you create directly after the selected style in the style sheet. For example, if you want to place a style directly after the first *.gridContainer* style, just select *.gridContainer* (circled in Figure 11-17), and then click the New CSS Rule button. Create a style as you normally would (page 125), and when you're done, Dreamweaver inserts the CSS inside the style sheet directly after the *.gridContainer* style.

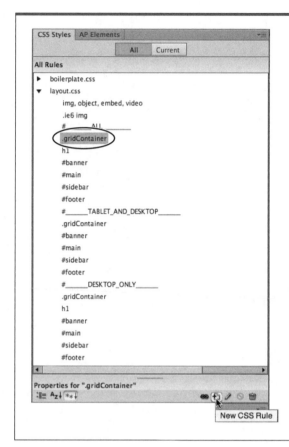

FIGURE 11-17

The CSS for Dreamweaver's Fluid Grid Layout pages can get pretty confusing. Because the styles for mobile, tablet, and desktop browsers all live inside the same style sheet, you'll need some help to figure out where to place styles to change the formatting for each device. Here's a tip: Create three "fake" styles in the CSS styles panel and place one before each .gridContainer style. In this example, the style sheet has a #_____ALL_____ style before the first .gridContainer. It acts as a note indicating that any style you place after this will apply to all devices. A second style, #_____TABLET_AND_DESKTOP_____, (placed directly before the second .gridContainer style), marks the beginning of the first media query. Any styles that go here apply to both tablet and desktop browsers. Finally, the style #_____DESKTOP_ONLY_____, placed before the third .gridContainer style, indicates the second media query, and these styles apply only to desktop browsers. (See page 385 to learn how to move styles within the CSS styles panel.)

jQuery Mobile

Media queries and the Fluid Grid layouts let you take one website and give it different designs for different devices. But what if you just want to create a mobile site from the get-go? Perhaps you want to design a "mobile-only" version of your site, one optimized to look and perform like a native phone application (see Figure 11-18). Dreamweaver lets you do just that with its support for jQuery Mobile.

FIGURE 11-18

Unlike a regular website, a jQuery Mobile site, like this one for the educational site Khan Academy (www.khanacademy.com), replicates the screen elements found in phone applications.

jQuery Mobile is a "mobile development framework," which means that it provides the tools you need to build web pages that act more like mobile applications than traditional web pages. A page built with jQuery Mobile includes screen transitions (one web page slides into view as the old one slides out), a more phone-like interface (large, rounded-corner buttons and smooth color gradients), and support for non-mouse-like interactions (like screen taps and swipes).

jQuery Mobile (*http://jquerymobile.com*) is a project of the enormously popular JavaScript framework jQuery (*http://jquery.com*), which simplifies the process of writing JavaScript. jQuery solves cross-browser problems and makes normally complicated JavaScript programming a lot easier. It provides JavaScript programming specific to phones, as well as the CSS that formats the HTML so your site mimics the screens you see in iPhone and Android apps.

So how do you use jQuery Mobile? In a nutshell, you construct a page using the basic building blocks of HTML—divs, images, paragraphs, and headers—and jQuery Mobile transforms them, through the power of JavaScript and some fancy CSS, into something that looks and feels a lot different from a regular web page. For example, the Khan Academy website, pictured in Figure 11-18, uses basic HTML, transformed into a phone-like presentation by jQuery Mobile.

If you have a smartphone, now's a good time to whip it out and visit a few sites that use jQuery Mobile—it's more informative to experience it rather than just read about it. (Here are a few mobile sites worth trying: True Value Paint [*http://truevaluepaint .com/*], Macworld [*www.macworld.com*], and Moulin Rouge [*http://m.moulinrouge .fr*].)

You can build a basic, mobile-only web page with just HTML and Dreamweaver CS6, as you'll see next.

NOTE To get the most out of jQuery Mobile, you need to be a pretty proficient JavaScript programmer. In fact, with some programming chops (and some patience), you can build true, native phone applications that work in iPhones, Android devices, Blackberries, Symbian phones, and more (see the box on page 560).

Creating a Basic jQuery Mobile Page

Fortunately, while there's a lot of complex programming behind a jQuery Mobile web page, actually adding content and building a page uses techniques you already learned in this book: inserting divs (page 440), typing in text, and adding images.

1. **Choose File→New.**

   The familiar New Document window opens—the same one you use to create a blank, new HTML file (Figure 11-19).

2. **Select the Page From Sample category from the left-hand list of options (circled in Figure 11-19), and then click the Mobile Starters folder from the Sample Folder column.**

   You'll see three options listed in the Sample Page category. The three options specify three different ways to include the required jQuery mobile files.

3. **Select either *jQuery Mobile (CDN)*, *jQuery Mobile (Local)*, or *jQuery Mobile with theme (Local)*.**

   The first option, CDN, refers to a "content delivery network," which simply means you don't keep the required external files on your computer. Instead, jQuery's web server stores the files for you. When someone visits your site, her browser downloads your page from your server, but downloads the JavaScript, CSS, and graphic files from jQuery.com. This has some benefits: jQuery.com manages those files, so you save your web server the effort and expense. However, the CDN option won't work without an Internet connection, and you're dependent on the jQuery.com servers—if they break down, your site won't work. (Also, if you're not connected to the Internet when you use Dreamweaver to build your jQuery Mobile site, the CDN option won't work properly—you won't be able to preview your page to see if it works.) In addition, since the CSS file sits on jQuery's server, you can't edit it, so customizing the look of the site is difficult.

The second option, *jQuery Mobile (Local)*, puts all the required files in your site folder. This gives you everything you need to work with jQuery Mobile, as well as a style sheet you can modify to make the site look the way you wish.

The most flexible option, however, is the last: *jQuery Mobile with theme (Local)*. Like the second option, Dreamweaver deposits all necessary files in your local site folder. However, Dreamweaver breaks the CSS file into two external files. The first style sheet, *jquery.mobile.structure-1.0.min.css* provides all the CSS required for the basic functions and layout of a jQuery Mobile site. In other words, the CSS in that file is crucial to the working of jQuery Mobile, and you shouldn't edit it. The second CSS file—*jquery.mobile.theme-1.0.min.css*—contains styles that affect the basic look of a jQuery Mobile site, including the fonts, colors, drop-shadows, and so on. This option is particularly useful because it works with jQuery Mobile's ThemeRoller website, which lets you visually customize the look of jQuery Mobile elements and then download a new mobile theme CSS file. In other words, when creating a new jQuery Mobile page, choose this option because it provides the easiest way to customize the look of your mobile site (see page 558 for more on styling a jQuery Mobile site).

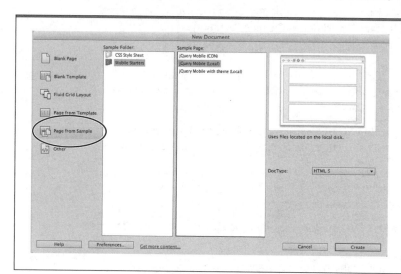

FIGURE 11-19

When you create a sample jQuery Mobile page, make sure you leave the HTML5 doctype selected. If you select another doctype, like HTML 4.01 Transitional, some of jQuery Mobile's features won't work.

4. **Click Create.**

   Dreamweaver creates a new, simple-looking web page with some sample content (see Figure 11-20). If you chose either of the Local options in the previous step and then saved the page, Dreamweaver saves the additional files mentioned in the previous step to your computer and places them in a *jquery-mobile* folder on your site.

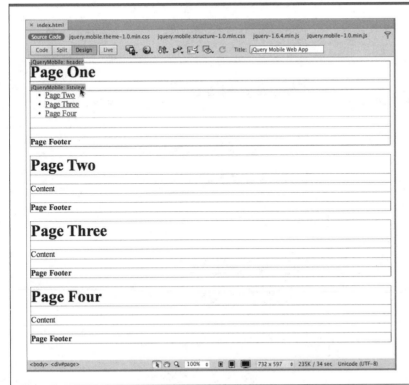

FIGURE 11-20

A jQuery Mobile page is made up of a bunch of nested divs. Dreamweaver applies a special attribute to each div that tells jQuery Mobile what to do with the div. For example, a screen's worth of information is one div, and its code looks like this: <div data-role="page">. Within that div are other divs: one for the header (<div data-role="header">), one for the content (<div data-role="content">), and one for the footer (<div data-role="footer">). When you mouse over one of the divs, Dreamweaver displays a blue tab indicating that div's role.

NOTE At the time of this writing, jQuery Mobile is currently at version 1.1.0. Dreamweaver CS6 ships with jQuery Mobile version 1.0. To upgrade, go to the jQuery Mobile site (*http://jquerymobile.com*) and download the latest version. Replaces the files in the *jquery-mobile* folder that Dreamweaver created. You also need to remove the links to the old files from the <head> of the page and attach the new style sheet (see page 138 for a refresher on attaching external style sheets) and the two JavaScript files (see page 370 for information on attaching a JavaScript file to a web page).

Anatomy of a jQuery Mobile Page

One peculiar feature of a jQuery Mobile site is that it's just a single file. When a guest visits the site, his browser downloads a single HTML file, but only display a *portion* of the HTML at a time. For example, the left image in Figure 11-21 represents Dreamweaver's stock jQuery Mobile page: one page with multiple div tags. However, when you look at the page in a browser, the browser converts that HTML into separate "pages." The top-right image in Figure 11-21 represents the "home page." It lists three links: Page Two, Page Three, and Page Four. Clicking the Page Four link loads that page's <div> and its contents (bottom, right).

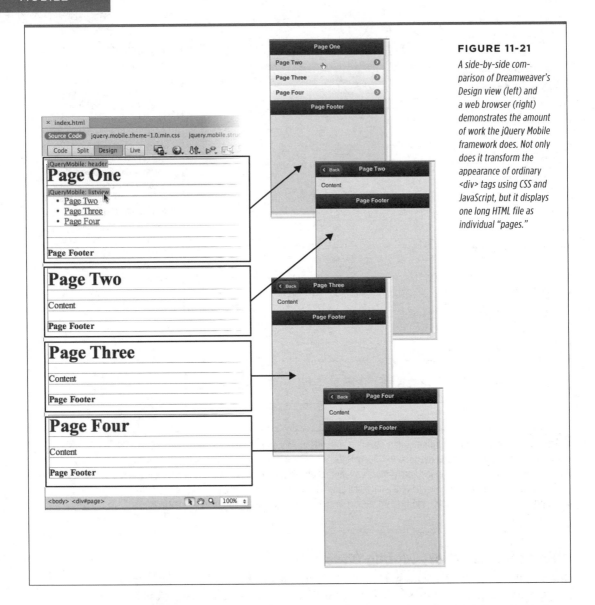

FIGURE 11-21

A side-by-side com-parison of Dreamweaver's Design view (left) and a web browser (right) demonstrates the amount of work the jQuery Mobile framework does. Not only does it transform the appearance of ordinary <div> tags using CSS and JavaScript, but it displays one long HTML file as individual "pages."

TIP Dreamweaver's Live View (page 72) and Window Size menu (Figure 11-3) provide a great combination for previewing a jQuery Mobile site. Choose the "320 x 480 Smart Phone" option and then click the Live View button on the Document toolbar. It's like having a smartphone built right into Dreamweaver (minus the roaming charges).

jQuery Mobile's programming converts those divs into separate screens, and applies the CSS that formats the page elements. But how does jQuery Mobile know which div is a page, and how does it make the other elements, such as a link, look like a button? The secret is a creative use of HTML attributes applied to HTML tags. The jQuery Mobile programming reads the attributes you apply to a tag and then formats that tag based on those attributes. For example, the basic structure of Dreamweaver's stock mobile page looks like this:

```
<div data-role="page" id="page2">
    <div data-role="header">
        <h1>Page Two</h1>
    </div>
    <div data-role="content">
        Content
    </div>
    <div data-role="footer">
        <h4>Page Footer</h4>
    </div>
</div>
```

As you can see, the "page" is a div tag with data-role="page" added to it. When the page loads in a browser, the jQuery Mobile programming kicks in and transforms the div into a "page." Dreamweaver usually includes three other divs within that "page," one for a header, one for the content, and the third for a footer. Thanks to their respective "data-role" values, each div looks different. jQuery Mobile formats the header and footer as dark stripes with light text, while it gives the content area a light background with dark text.

jQuery Mobile also applies special attributes to other HTML tags. For example, it creates the list of links in the top right image in Figure 11-10 (called a "list-view" in jQuery Mobile) using a simple unordered list:

```
<ul data-role="listview" data-inset="true">

    <li><a href="#page2">Page Two</a></li>

    <li><a href="#page3">Page Three</a>

    <li><a href="#page4">Page Four</a></li>

</ul>
```

By adding data-role="listview" to a <ul> tag, you can change the list from a basic bulleted set to a special, mobile-enhanced list. jQuery Mobile provides other, similar mobile elements, as described in the next section.

NOTE Although Dreamweaver CS6's starter file puts all the site's "pages" into a single file, you can create a mobile site with true multiple pages, just as you can in a regular site.

Adding Content to a jQuery Mobile Page

As you can see in Figure 11-20, a jQuery Mobile page is just some very basic HTML: divs, unordered lists, and links. To add content, select the dummy text Dreamweaver provides and change it. For example, to change the "Page One" headline that appears on the first page, highlight the text and type in your own headline: "My Great Web App," for example. Likewise, you can change the footer text—"Page Footer"—by selecting it inside the footer div and changing it.

> **NOTE** If you type a long sentence in either the header or footer and then preview the page in a phone, you'll notice that jQuery Mobile keeps the text to a single line and simply cuts off anything that doesn't fit. Because of that, keep the text in a header or footer short.

The central div in each page is where you add the main content. Dreamweaver places the word "content" inside that div, but you can delete it and add HTML as you normally would: headlines, paragraphs, bulleted lists, and images. In addition, you can insert special jQuery Mobile items—list views, layout grids, collapsible blocks, and link buttons—as well as additional "pages" using the Insert panel (see Figure 11-22).

■ ADDING LISTS

jQuery Mobile includes its own "widgets"—elements for links, layout, and content display. The page, header, and footer divs are widgets, for example. You can also insert a list of links that lets guests navigate from page to page of your mobile site. Dreamweaver's stock mobile "home page" includes a list of links to Page Two, Page Three, and Page Four for example (Figure 11-21, top right). Dreamweaver calls a list like this the "list view," and jQuery Mobile supplies several variations (see Figure 11-23).

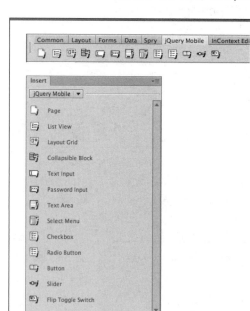

FIGURE 11-22

If you chose the Classic view for your workspace (page 38), the Insert panel appears as a bar at the top of your screen (top). Otherwise, the Insert panel hangs out on the right-hand side of your monitor. The jQuery Mobile category provides one-click access to common screen elements.

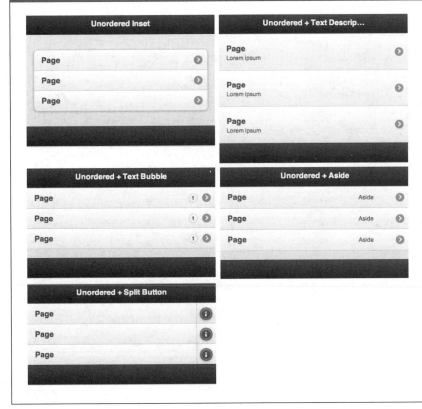

FIGURE 11-23

jQuery Mobile List views are either ordered (numbered) or unordered lists, created using the <ol> and <ul> tags. You can display these two types of list five ways: inset (with the list enclosed in its own box with rounded corners, as pictured at top left), with a text description (top right), with a text bubble (middle left), with an "aside" or small bit of text on the right (middle right), or with a "split button" that includes both text and a graphic (bottom left).

To add a list:

1. **Click inside the content div of a "page" div and click the List View button on the Insert panel (Figure 11-22).**

   Alternatively, choose Insert→jQuery Mobile→List View. Either way, the jQuery Mobile List View window opens (Figure 11-24).

2. **Choose Ordered or Unordered from the List Type menu.**

   Ordered lists include numbers on the left side of each item (Figure 11-25, bottom right). Use ordered lists for "top 10" items, or to indicate the specific order of steps in a process, like baking a soufflé. If the order isn't important, use an unordered list.

3. **Choose the number of list items from the Items menu.**

   You can choose from 1 to 10 items; however, since a List View is simply an HTML list, you can use the technique described on page 106 to add as many items as you want.

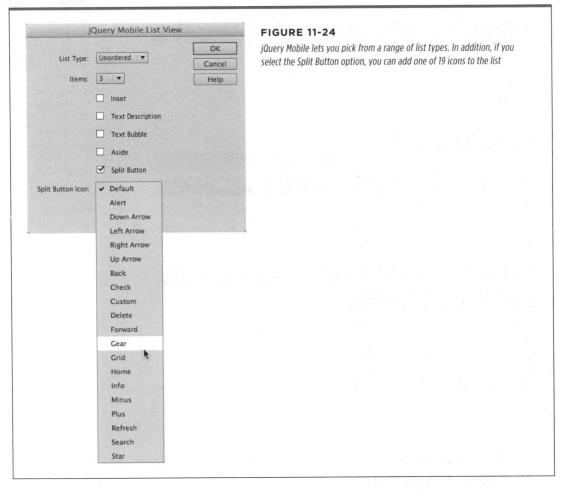

FIGURE 11-24

jQuery Mobile lets you pick from a range of list types. In addition, if you select the Split Button option, you can add one of 19 icons to the list

4. **Turn on one or more checkboxes to pick the type of list you want.**

   jQuery Mobile provides five basic lists, but you can combine list types to vary your options. For example, you can create an inset list (Figure 11-23, top left) that also includes a split button (Figure 11-23, bottom left). Try different combinations of checkboxes to produce different types of lists.

5. **If you select the Split Button option, choose an icon from the Split Button Icon menu.**

NOTE A Split Button list type inserts both text and an icon in a button, and each provides a link that can point to separate pages. For example, the text portion might lead to a page of detailed information, but the icon might link to a short page of supplementary information.

6. **Click OK to insert the new list view.**

    Depending on the list type you select, Dreamweaver inserts either an HTML unordered list (<ul> tag) or a numbered (ordered) list (<ol> tag). You can edit these list items as you would any other list (see page 106).

TIP If you add data-rel="dialog" to a link (an <a> tag) on a jQuery Mobile page, the linked page pops into view like a dialog box, complete with a close button.

7. **Change the text and link for each list item.**

    Each list item includes the text "Page" with an empty link (# appears in the Property Inspector's link box). You can select the text and type in whatever you wish. Then link that text to another page. If you link to another website, just type a complete, absolute URL beginning with http://. If you link to another HTML file on your site, you can use any of the techniques described on page 191.

    If you use Dreamweaver's suggested approach to mobile site development—one HTML file with multiple "page" divs inside it—you link to another "page" just as you would to a named anchor, as described on page 202. For example, if you want to link to a "page" div with an ID of "page8," you type #page8 in the Property Inspector's link box.

    Some of the list view types include additional text you can edit. For example, the "Text Description" option (Figure 11-25, top right) includes text ("Lorem ipsum") you can change. This is a good list type to pick when you need a bit of explanatory text ("See a complete list of our products"). In some cases, like the Text Bubble list type, the extra text isn't visible in Design view—you have to look in the HTML code to see and change it.

Unfortunately, as with all of Dreamweaver's jQuery Mobile objects, once you insert a list view into a page, there's no way to return to the List View window and change its settings. For example, you can't change an insert list into a "split button" list. You can, however, go into Code view and edit the HTML. The jQuery Mobile website provides helpful information on creating lists, including some even fancier ones, at *http://tinyurl.com/d8sjfhz.*

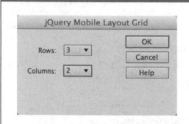

FIGURE 11-25

The layout grid in Dreamweaver's Design view (middle image) looks decidedly less glamorous than what it looks like in a web browser (bottom image).

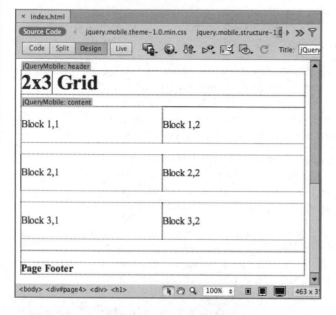

ADDING A LAYOUT GRID

Although phone screens are small, that doesn't mean that all your content has to sit inside one long column. You might want to present some small content in rows and columns. For example, if you have a bunch of 30-pixel by 30-pixel thumbnail images, you can arrange them in several side-by-side columns. jQuery Mobile provides "layout grids" for just that purpose.

A layout grid is basically a series of div tags that jQuery floats to create columns, the same technique you used to create the multi-column layouts described in Chapter 9. To insert a layout grid:

1. **Click inside the content div of a "page" div and then click the Layout Grid button on the Insert panel (Figure 11-22).**

   Alternatively, choose Insert→jQuery Mobile→Layout Grid. Either way, the jQuery Mobile Layout Grid window opens (top image in Figure 11-25).

2. **Choose the number of rows and columns you want.**

   There's not too much to this step, but keep in mind the limitations of a phone's screen. Choosing five columns and trying to put a lot of text into each column in one row will probably make the page wider than a phone's screen can handle.

3. **Click OK.**

   Dreamweaver inserts a number of <div> tags into the page. They don't look like much in Design view, but you can add any content you like (just make sure it isn't too big for a phone's screen).

You can't revisit the Layout Grid window, so if you want to change a three-column grid to two columns, you have to dip into the HTML. Fortunately, it's not so difficult. Here's the HTML for a one-row, two-column grid:

```
<div class="ui-grid-a">

    <div class="ui-block-a">Block 1,1</div>

    <div class="ui-block-b">Block 1,2</div>

</div>
```

jQuery Mobile uses a <div> tag to define layout grids. In the above example, that's <div class="ui-grid-a">. The letter in the class name determines the grid's number of columns: For example, *ui-grid-a* is a two-column grid, *ui-grid-b* gives you a three-column grid, *ui-grid-c* results in a four-column grid, and *ui-grid-d* is a five-column grid.

jQuery Mobile includes additional divs within this tag that define each block of content. So the above example includes two div tags. The class on those tags determines into which column jQuery Mobile inserts the content. For example, ui-block-a is the first column in a row. Say you want to turn the above two-column, one-row grid into a three-column, one-row design. You simply change the class name on the grid's div and then add a div for the new block, like this:

```
<div class="ui-grid-b">

    <div class="ui-block-a">Block 1,1</div>

    <div class="ui-block-b">Block 1,2</div>

    <div class="ui-block-c">Block 1,3</div>

</div>
```

In other words, you change <div class="ui-grid-a"> to <div class="ui-grid-b"> and add another block: <div class="ui-block-c">. You just have to be sure you keep the block's class names in order—a, b, c, and so on—and that you have the proper number of blocks for the type of grid you specify. For example, since the ui-grid-b class defines a three-column layout, you need three div tags per row. To add an additional row, duplicate the div tags from the previous row, like this:

```
<div class="ui-grid-b">

    <div class="ui-block-a">Block 1,1</div>

    <div class="ui-block-b">Block 1,2</div>

    <div class="ui-block-c">Block 1,3</div>

    <div class="ui-block-a">Block 2,1</div>

    <div class="ui-block-b">Block 2,2</div>

    <div class="ui-block-c">Block 2,3</div>

</div>
```

You can read more about jQuery Mobile grids at *http://tinyurl.com/cdwdlk7*.

■ ADDING A COLLAPSIBLE BLOCK

A collapsible block is a combination of a header and a hidden chunk of content. Click the header and the content reveals itself (bottom image in Figure 11-26). It's a good way to keep your page simple and short for phone-viewing—content only appears when a guest clicks a headline, and it disappears when he clicks the headline a second time.

To insert a collapsible block in Dreamweaver:

1. **Click inside the content div of a "page" div and click the Collapsible Block button in the Insert panel (Figure 11-22).**

   Alternatively, choose Insert→jQuery Mobile→Collapsible Block. Unlike other jQuery Mobile objects, there's no dialog box for this: Dreamweaver just drops a series of div tags into the page (Figure 11-26, top).

2. **Edit the headline and the content.**

Select the dummy "Header" text and type in your own headline. Remember to keep it short, however, since jQuery Mobile limits the header to a single line. You can change the dummy content Dreamweaver inserts—a simple <p> tag with the text "Content" inside it—to anything you want. You can even insert multiple paragraphs, lists, and images.

Dreamweaver inserts four div tags when you add a collapsible block to a page. The HTML looks like this:

```
<div data-role="collapsible-set">

    <div data-role="collapsible">

        <h3>Header</h3>

        <p>Content</p>

    </div>

    <div data-role="collapsible" data-collapsed="true">

        <h3>Header</h3>

        <p>Content</p>

    </div>

    <div data-role="collapsible" data-collapsed="true">

        <h3>Header</h3>

        <p>Content</p>

    </div>

</div>
```

The outer div—<div data-role="collapsible-set">—indicates that the div tags inside are part of a group (a "block") of collapsible elements. Each collapsible element—a header/content pair—sits inside another div, <div data-role="collapsible">. If you wish to have only two collapsible elements, delete one of the divs Dreamweaver inserts. If you want more, copy the div (including the header and content) and paste it before that last closing </div> for the set.

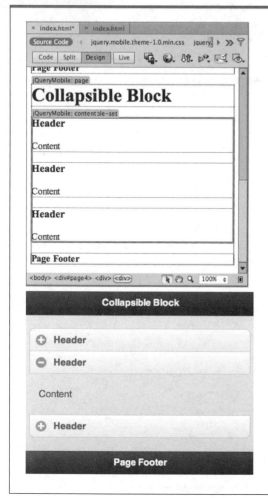

FIGURE 11-26

Collapsible blocks are a good way to keep a page's appearance simple, because the blocks hide content until a visitor wants to read it.

By default, all collapsible blocks start life closed. You can make sure that a collapsible block's content is visible by adding data-collapsed="false" to the <div> tag for a header/content pair. The first header/content pair in a collapsible block starts off hidden:

```
<div data-role="collapsible">

    <h3>Header</h3>

    <p>Content</p>

</div>
```

But you can show the content when the page first loads by adding an attribute to the div for that block:

```
<div data-role="collapsible" data-collapsed="false">

        <h3>Header</h3>

        <p>Content</p>

    </div>
```

You can read more about collapsible blocks at *http://tinyurl.com/cd63jv2*.

■ ADDING FORM ELEMENTS

The jQuery Mobile category of the Insert panel includes many form elements—text fields, password fields, checkboxes, radio buttons, and so on. However, these fields don't work like traditional form fields (which you'll learn about in the next chapter). In fact, they don't work at all unless you add JavaScript programming. And, unfortunately, Dreamweaver CS6 doesn't provide any tools to do so. In other words, to use any of these form elements effectively, you need to learn JavaScript and jQuery programming.

However, the button element isn't restricted to forms page; you can use it anywhere to insert links that *look* like buttons, too.

To insert button links:

1. **Click inside a div in one of the "pages" in the jQuery Mobile file.**

   For example, in the "content," "header," or "footer" divs described on "Anatomy of a jQuery Mobile Page".

2. **Click the Button button on the Insert panel (Figure 11-22).**

   Alternatively you can choose Insert→jQuery Mobile→Button. Either way, the jQuery Mobile Button window appears (Figure 11-27).

3. **Select the number of buttons you want on the page.**

   You can choose between 1 and 10 buttons, but remember you're designing for a small phone screen, so 10 buttons won't sit side-by-side.

4. **Choose Link from the Button Type menu.**

   The two other options (Button and Input) insert buttons in a form (like a "Submit" button); they require custom programming to work.

5. **Choose either Inline or Group from the Position menu.**

   The Inline option creates separate lozenge-shaped boxes for each button, while the Group option treats the buttons as a homogenous group (see the two bottom examples in Figure 11-28).

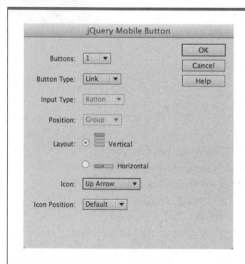

FIGURE 11-27

Unless you know how to write JavaScript, select only "Link" from the Button Type menu. This lets you insert regular page links that look like attractive buttons. The Input Type menu is only available when you select "Input" from the Button Type menu, and it lets you select one of the HTML form buttons discussed on page 585—but again, this is only an option if you're comfortable programming the buttons yourself to make them do something.

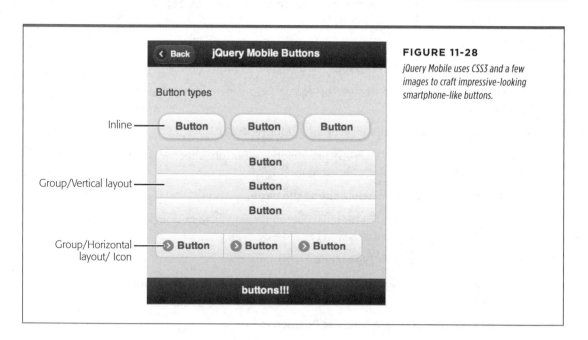

FIGURE 11-28

jQuery Mobile uses CSS3 and a few images to craft impressive-looking smartphone-like buttons.

6. **Choose a Vertical or Horizontal layout.**

These options are only available when you select "Group" in the previous step, and they affect how the grouped buttons appear on a page, either stacked one on top of the other ("Vertical") or side-by-side ("Horizontal"), as pictured in Figure 11-28. Keep in mind that if you place too many buttons side-by-side, some will drop down to the next space on the page and turn into stacked rows of buttons.

7. **Choose an option from the Icon menu.**

This step is optional, but it adds a neat graphical touch to each button. jQuery gives you 18 graphics to choose from (Right Arrow, Gear, Star, and so on), and if you don't want any of them, choose None. (In Figure 11-28, the bottom row of buttons have a right arrow icon applied to them.) You can see all 18 icons in action at *http://tinyurl.com/c2z6hyu.*

8. **If you selected an icon in the previous step, place it using the Icon Position menu.**

You can choose Left or Right to put the icon at either the left or right edge of the button, and Top or Bottom to place the icon either above or below the button's text. Choose No Text to display only the icon.

9. **Click OK to insert the button(s).**

Dreamweaver inserts as many buttons as you selected in step 3. In Design view, they don't look like much—just the word "button" repeated once for each one you added. Select that text to change it to something better. In addition, the text has a regular HTML link attached to it, just like the ones you learned about in Chapter 4. You can change the link using the Property Inspector, just as you would for a regular link.

If you plan to link to another "page" within the jQuery file, use the # symbol followed by the ID you apply to the <div> tag for that "page." For example, to link to "page2" in the sample jQuery Mobile file Dreamweaver supplies, you type #page2 in the Property Inspector's Link field. This is the same as linking to a named anchor within a page, as described on page 202.

Unfortunately, once you insert one or more buttons, you can't revisit the jQuery Mobile Button window (Figure 11-27) to edit them—in other words, you can't change the buttons' icons, grouping, or positioning once you insert them. Well, you can, but you have to go into Code view and change the attributes applied to the buttons. For example, to change a button's icon, go into Code view, locate the <a> tag for that button, and change the *data-icon* attribute to the proper value. For instance, changing data-icon="arrow-r" to data-icon="gear" changes a button's icon from a right-pointing arrow to a gear. The web page for jQuery Mobile buttons is an invaluable aid in this process: *http://tinyurl.com/d78s8pt.*

▪ ADDING NEW "PAGES"

As you read above, you can put multiple "pages" into a single HTML file. jQuery Mobile then hides all but one "page" when a browser loads the file. As you click links, the browser displays different portions of the page as if they were separate web pages (thanks to jQuery Mobile's JavaScript programming). A "page" is really just a div tag with an ID and a special HTML attribute—for example, <div data-role="page" id="page4">.

The stock mobile page Dreamweaver supplies has four "pages" but you can add more. It's important to make sure, however, that you don't insert a page inside another page's div. The best way to ensure this is to use the Tag Selector (page 26). For example, say you want to insert another page after the last page in a mobile file:

1. **Click inside the div for the last "page."**

   For example, inside the header, footer, or content div.

2. **In the Tag Selector, click the div for that page (see Figure 11-29).**

   You'll see something like <div#page4> in the Tag Selector.

3. **Press the right arrow key to move the cursor outside of the div.**

   The right arrow key moves the cursor below the div, so you can insert a new page after the currently selected one. To insert a page *before* the currently selected one, press the left arrow key.

4. **Click the Page button from the jQuery Mobile category of the Insert panel.**

   Alternatively, choose Insert→jQuery Mobile→Page. Either way, the jQuery Mobile Page window opens (Figure 11-30).

5. **Type an ID for the page, and then select whether you want a header and footer.**

   The ID can be anything you like. For example, if the page contains information about your company, you might name it "about." The ID you provide is important for links—you use that ID when you create a link that points to this new page, as described on "Adding lists". Normally, pages include a header and footer; if you don't want them, turn off their checkboxes.

6. **Click OK.**

   Dreamweaver inserts the <div> tags needed to add a page to the file, as described on page 541. You can add content to this new page following the instructions on page 544.

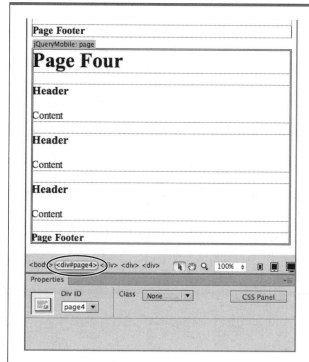

FIGURE 11-29

The Tag Selector is the most accurate way to select and navigate among HTML tags.

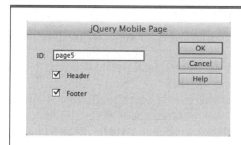

FIGURE 11-30

jQuery Mobile "pages" are just a series of divs—one for the header, one for content, and one for a footer. You can choose to leave out either the header or footer (or both).

Formatting a jQuery Mobile Page

When viewed in Dreamweaver's Design view, a jQuery Mobile Page is pretty unimpressive (Figure 11-21, left). However, the browser view of the same HTML is astonishingly different (Figure 11-21, right). The formerly ho-hum HTML turns into a slick, mobile page with subtle gradients, rounded corners, shadows, and sophisticated icons. Where does this design come from? jQuery Mobile is more than JavaScript—it's also complex CSS that makes the HTML for mobile devices look like an application for a smartphone.

You can use the CSS skills you picked up in this book to change the appearance of your jQuery Mobile site, but you're in for a lot of work if you do. The CSS is complex, and there are literally hundreds of styles required to make jQuery Mobile work. If you want to give it a try, Dreamweaver's Inspect mode (described in "Analyzing CSS in JavaScript and Server-Side Pages") is your best bet at deciphering the CSS.

Another approach is to use one of jQuery Mobile's five themes. That's right, jQuery Mobile has five built-in designs that you can switch among simply by adding attributes to the HTML tags. By default, jQuery Mobile uses its "a" theme for pages, but you can choose its b, c, d, and e themes. To change a theme, specify a data-theme for a jQuery Mobile-specific tag. For example, to change one page to the "b" theme add data-theme="b" to that page's <div> tag like this:

```
<div data-role="page" id="page" data-theme="b">
```

To change a List View to the "e" theme, add *data-theme="e"* to the list view div:

```
<ul data-role="listview" data-theme="e">
```

Fortunately, you don't need to add that theme data by hand. Dreamweaver CS6 includes a handy, context-sensitive jQuery Mobile Swatches panel (see Figure 11-31). You open it by choosing Window→jQuery Mobile Swatches.

You apply a swatch simply by clicking into a jQuery mobile element. The Swatches panel displays the formatting options for the current element. For example, in Figure 11-31, Dreamweaver displays the options for the selected link (circled) inside a jQuery mobile list view (page 544). In this instance, you could apply one of five swatches (labeled a to e) to the list itself, as well as other swatches for the different types of available lists. Clicking into another element, like a page header, updates the Swatches panel to list just the swatches available for page headers. Click a swatch to apply it to the selected page element.

If you want to create your own look for a jQuery Mobile site, visit the jQuery Mobile ThemeRoller website (*http://jquerymobile.com/themeroller/*). There, you can try different fonts, colors, borders, and shadows, and see a live, interactive rendering of your design choices. Once you're satisfied, click the Download button. You'll end up with a CSS file containing your design, as well as an Images folder containing the icons for the design. Simply move those files into the *jquery-mobile* folder in your site (replacing the original files). Change the link from the CSS file Dreamweaver supplies (*jquery.mobile.theme-1.0.min.css*) to your new theme file, and you're done. In fact,

Dreamweaver is smart enough to realize you're using a new theme, and displays it in the jQuery Mobile Swatches panel.

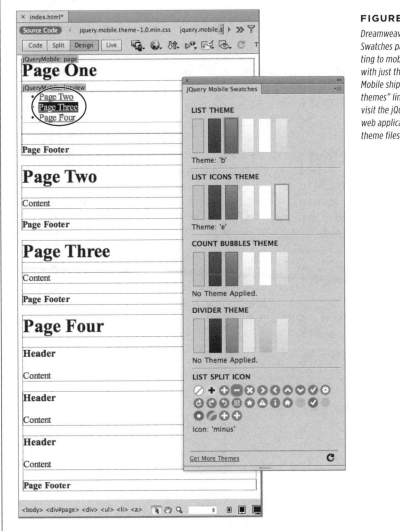

FIGURE 11-31

Dreamweaver CS6's new jQuery Mobile Swatches panel makes it easy to apply formatting to mobile page elements. You're not stuck with just the five basic swatches that jQuery Mobile ships with, either. Click the "Get more themes" link to launch a web browser and visit the jQuery Mobile ThemeRoller—an online web application for visually creating mobile theme files.

Launching Your jQuery Mobile Site

When you finish building your mobile website, put it on the web just as you would any other site. You can use the tools discussed in Chapter 17 to connect to your web server and transfer your files. Once on the web, any phone with a web browser can visit the page and see its awesome mobile-enabled beauty.

If the mobile site is a supplement to a regular site, you may want to add "See the mobile version of this site" somewhere on your main site, with a link to the mobile version.

Mobile Application Development

Using jQuery Mobile, you can build a website that looks great on mobile phones, but it's still a website: A visitor uses the browser in her phone to go to the site and clicks through pages just as she would on any other site.

However, you can also use jQuery Mobile to build an application for the iPhone, Android phones, and other devices. Although you use HTML, CSS, and JavaScript to build the application, you can turn it—or "compile" it—into a native phone application that guests can download from that phone's "app store." So instead of viewing the jQuery Mobile site in a browser, you actually download it from the phone's app store, install it on your phone, and launch it just as you would any other application.

The real trick lies in converting the HTML to a native application. Usually this involves downloading an "SDK," or Software Development Kit, for each phone you want to target—iPhones, Android phones, Windows Phone, WebOS, and so on. This step is fraught with peril for all but diehard software developers.

Dreamweaver CS6, however, provides a direct line to something called the "PhoneGap Build Service" (*http://build.phonegap .com/*). This site can ingest your HTML, JavaScript, and CSS and,

through some magic on their end, turn out native applications you can install on a phone.

Unfortunately, Dreamweaver doesn't provide the tools for actually creating the application; you need to be a very competent JavaScript programmer to get your app to actually do anything. Mobile application development is a world unto itself, and this book can't even begin to scratch the surface of the intricacies involved. However, there are a couple of books devoted to the subject, both by Jonathan Stark: *Building iPhone Apps with HTML, CSS, and JavaScript*, and *Building Android Apps with HTML, CSS, and JavaScript.*

However, once you build your app, you can go straight to the PhoneGap build service by selecting Site→PhoneGap Build Service→PhoneGap Build Service. For more information on how this works, check out the videos at *http://tinyurl.com/ d34aw4k* and *http://tinyurl.com/cunv958.*

Bringing Your Pages to Life

Forms

A website is a great way to brand your company, announce a new product, post late-breaking news, or just rant about the state of the world. But all that's *one-way* communication, and you may want to interact with your audience more—to get some feedback, for example. Or you may want to build your business by selling your product online, and you need a way to gather vital stats from customers.

If you want to *receive* information as well as deliver it, it's time to add *forms* to your web design repertoire (see Figure 12-1 for a simple example). Whatever type of information you need to collect on your site, Dreamweaver's *form objects* make the task easy.

◼ Form Basics

A form begins and ends with the HTML <form> tag. The opening tag (<form>) indicates the beginning of a form and sets its properties; the closing tag (</form>), of course, marks the form's end.

You add different objects between these tags to deck out your pages with the form elements your visitors interact with—radio buttons, text fields, and pull-down menus are just a few you can choose from to gather input. It's perfectly OK to include other HTML elements inside a form, too. In fact, your visitors would be lost if you didn't add (and format) text that explains each element's purpose. And if you don't use a table or Cascading Style Sheets to lay out your form in an organized way, it can quickly become an unreadable mess (see the box on page 583).

FIGURE 12-1

A form can be as simple as a single empty text box (called a field) and a button, or as complex as a 100-question survey composed of fill-in-the-blank and multiple-choice questions.

Every form element, whether it's a text field or a checkbox, has a *name* and a *value*. You supply the name, which should reflect the information you're trying to collect. For example, if you want a visitor to type his email address into a text field, you might name that field *email*. The value, on the other hand, is what your *visitor* types in—the text he enters into a text field, for example, or the selections he makes from a pull-down menu.

After a visitor fills out a form and clicks the Submit button, his browser sends each form element as a name/value pair, like this: *email=bob@bobville.com*. Submitting both pieces of information helps the program that processes the form figure out what the input means. After all, without a name, a value of "39" doesn't mean much (39 what? Potatoes, steps, days until Christmas?). The name/value pair (*age=39*) provides context for your visitor's input.

The Code Backstage

Creating a form is just the first step in collecting information. You also need to *transmit* that information to a program that actually *does* something with it. The program may then simply take the data from the form and email it to you. But it could also do something as complex as contacting a bank, processing a credit card payment, creating an invoice, or notifying the shipping department to deliver a poster of Justin Bieber to someone in Nova Scotia.

A form is pretty useless if you don't have a form-processing program on the other end of things—running on your web server. These information-crunching programs come in a variety of languages—Perl, C, C#, Visual Basic, VBScript, Java, ColdFusion Markup Language, PHP, Ruby—and may be part of a dedicated application server, like Adobe's ColdFusion Server or Microsoft's .NET technology.

While writing the necessary behind-the-scenes processing software can be complex, the concepts behind the forms themselves are straightforward:

1. **First, someone fills out a form on your website and clicks the Submit button (or Search, Buy, or whatever you actually label the button that transmits information).**

2. **Next, the browser transmits the form data over the Internet to a processing program on your web server.**

3. **The form-processing program collects the data and does something with it— whatever you and the programmer decide it should do.** It could, for example, send the data off as an email to you, search a vast database of information, or store the information in a database.

4. **Finally, the server returns a page to the browser, which your visitor sees.** It may be a standard web page with a message like "Thanks for the info," or a page the program generates on the fly that includes information like a detailed invoice or the results of a search.

So how do you create the processing half of the forms equation if you're not a programmer? Your web hosting company may offer free form-processing programs as part of their services. Contact them and ask; most companies provide basic instructions on how to use these programs. If you're part of a company's web development team, you may already have programmers on staff who can create the processing program. You can also find Dreamweaver Extensions that can help with a variety of form-processing tasks (see the boxes on pages 585 and 589).

If you feel adventurous, many form-processing programs are available free on the Web. For a thorough sampling, see the CGI Resource Index at *http://cgi.resource index.com*. Using these free programs can be tricky, however, because you need to download the appropriate program and install it on your web server—something not every web host allows.

Lastly, you can use a form-processing service like Wufoo (*http://wufoo.com*), which handles all the complicated parts of collecting and storing information from forms and provides tools for retrieving that information in a variety of formats.

Creating a Form

In Dreamweaver, you can build forms with one-click ease using the Insert panel's Forms category (see Figure 12-2).

To begin, you need to insert a <form> tag in your web page to indicate the boundaries of the form:

1. **In Design view, click the location in the document window where you want to insert the form.**

   You might decide to place it after a paragraph of introductory text, for example, or into a <div> tag that holds the page's main content.

NOTE If you plan to use an HTML table to organize a form's fields (see page 291), insert the form first, and then insert the table inside the <form> tag.

---

2. **On the Insert panel, select the Forms category.**

   The tab reveals 22 form-building tools.

3. **Click the Form icon (the very first icon in the list).**

   If you're a menu-driven person, choose Insert→Form→Form.

NOTE What you see when you insert an object using the Insert panel depends on whether you position your cursor in Design view or Code view. These instructions assume you're inserting form elements in Design view. If you're in Code view, you'll get Dreamweaver's Tag Editor instead. Basically, the Tag Editor provides more options up front, but nothing you can't set later with the Property Inspector. In addition, unless you know HTML well, the Tag Editor can easily insert improper HTML.

   Either way, a red, dashed-line rectangle appears in the document window, indicating the form's boundaries. (If you don't see it, choose View→Visual Aids→Invisible Elements.) The top line represents the opening <form> tag; the bottom represents the closing tag. Make sure you always insert form objects, like buttons and menus, *inside* these lines. Otherwise, Dreamweaver thinks you're trying to create a second form on the page. (It's perfectly valid to include more than one form per page [as long as you don't try to insert a form inside *another* form], but your visitor can submit only one form—and its data—at a time.)

TIP An even faster way to insert a <form> tag is to bypass step 3 and insert just a form element—like a text field or radio button; Dreamweaver asks if you want to add the <form> tag at the same time.

   Since you can place so many other HTML elements inside a form, you'll often find it easier to insert the form first, and then add tables, graphics, text, and form objects later.

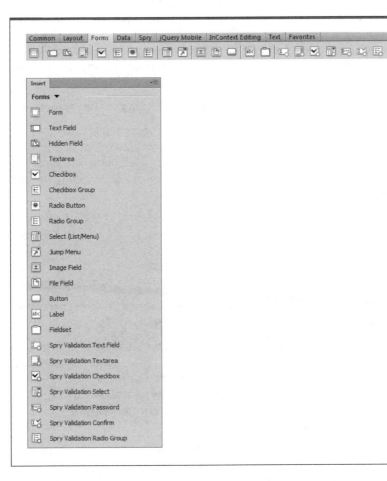

FIGURE 12-2

*Choosing the "Classic" view from the
Workspace Switcher, as described in
the Note on page 38, turns the Insert
panel into a toolbar that runs along
the top of Dreamweaver's workspace
(you can also just drag the Insert
panel up to the top of the screen to
turn it into a toolbar). If you prefer
the Insert panel where it normally
appears (bottom), select the Forms
category to get one-click access to
all the form elements—buttons, text
fields, checkboxes, and so on. Since
the Forms category has so many
buttons, you might want to turn off
the labels that appear next to each
icon, as described on page 27. That
way, you can see all the form buttons
without using your monitor's entire
height.*

4. **If it isn't already selected, click the dotted red line to select the form.**

   This step not only selects the form, it highlights everything inside the red lines,
   too. The Property Inspector displays the Form ID ("reservation" here) in the
   upper-left corner, as shown in Figure 12-3.

FIGURE 12-3

*Unless you're creating a
search form, you'll generally want to use the POST
method of sending data
to your server. Step 7 has
the details.*

5. **If you like, type a name for your form into the Form ID field.**

   This step is optional. Dreamweaver supplies a generic ID—*form1*—but you don't need to name a form for it to work. A name is useful if you use the JavaScript or the Spry form validation tools discussed later in this chapter (page 588) because they both interact with the form or its fields, and the tools need a way to uniquely identify each form. But the name doesn't appear anywhere on the page, so you can leave the default name if you wish.

6. **In the Action field, type a URL, or select a file by clicking the tiny folder icon.**

   Your mission here is to specify the location of the program that processes the form. If someone else is responsible for the programming, ask that person what to enter here. It's a standard web address—either an absolute URL (one that begins with *http://*) or the path to the server's form-processing program (see page 185 for more on these different kinds of links).

   Either way, the file name you add to the Action field *doesn't* end in *.html*. The path might be, for example, ../scripts/mail-form.php. In this case, the .php extension indicates a program written in the PHP programming language. Other common file extensions for web programs include .cfm (for ColdFusion Markup Language), .aspx (.NET pages), .jsp (Java Server Pages), or .cgi (CGI programs).

7. **Using the Method pop-up menu, specify how you want a browser to transmit the form data to the processing program (see Figure 12-3).**

   Basically, browsers can transmit form data to a web server in either of two ways. You'll use the more common method, called POST, most often. It sends form data in two steps. First, the browser contacts the form-processing program at the URL you specified in the previous step; then it sends that data to the server. This method gives your data a bit more security, and it can easily handle forms with lots of information.

   The GET method, on the other hand, adds the form data to the destination URL, like this: *http://search.yahoo.com/ search?p=dogs*. (Even though the GET method *sends* data, it's named GET because its purpose in life is to *receive* information—such as the results of a search.) The characters following the *?* in the address represent the form data. This code submits a single form field named *p*, with the value *dogs*, to the server. If a form has lots of fields and accepts lots of user input, a GET URL can become extremely long. Some servers can't handle very long URLs, so don't use the GET method if your forms collect a lot of data.

NOTE The GET method has one big benefit: You can *bookmark* it, which is great if you want to save and reuse a common search request for Google, for example, or you want to send someone Google Maps driving directions, or a list of Dreamweaver books you searched for on Amazon. That's why search engines use the GET method for form submissions.

---

8. **If you're using frames, select a Target option.**

You'll most likely skip this menu. Frames are *so* 1998 web design, and they pose serious problems for web designers and search engines. But even if you're not using frames, you can choose the "_blank" option to open a new browser window to display the results. (See page 199 for more on the Target property.)

9. **Select an encoding type, if you like.**

You usually don't have to select anything from the Enctype menu. Leaving this box empty is almost always correct, and is the same as selecting the much more long-winded "application/x-www-form-urlencoded" option.

But if you use the File Field button (see page 583) to let visitors upload files to your site, you should use the "multipart/form-data" option. In fact, Dreamweaver automatically selects this option when you add a File Field to a form. See the box below for more info on potential problems with File Field forms.

You've laid the foundation for your form. Now you're ready to add the input controls—menus, checkboxes, and so on—as described in the next section.

FREQUENTLY ASKED QUESTION

Using a Form to Upload Files

I want to let visitors upload photos to my site, but when I include a File Field button in one of my forms, I get an error message from the server when I try to submit the form. Why?

To upload files from a web page, you need to do two things: Change the encoding method (see step 9 above) to "multipart/form-data" and set up your server to receive files. Dreamweaver automatically takes care of the first part: Whenever you insert a form field, it changes the form's encoding method to "multipart/form-data."

The second part is up to you (or your web hosting company). Many web servers have this option turned off for security reasons. Check to see if your web host lets you use forms to upload files to your server. If it doesn't, find a hosting company that does.

In addition, you have to program the form-processing script to accept data in the "multipart/form-data" format. Since this task is challenging, you might want to enlist some help. The box on page 585 provides several resources for commercial Dreamweaver extensions that can help.

If you decide that's too much trouble and you delete the File Field button, you're still in trouble. Dreamweaver doesn't reset the encoding method to the original "application/x-www-form-urlencoded" setting, so when visitors try to submit the form (even without the File Field), they'll get a nasty error message from the server. You must remedy the situation manually, by selecting the form, and then using the Property Inspector to change the encoding method back to "application/x-www-form-urlencoded."

■ Adding Form Elements

Unless you've never used a computer before, the user interface elements available for HTML forms should look familiar (Figure 12-4): text fields where people can type in information (names, addresses, phone numbers, and so on); checkboxes for making multiple-choice selections; and menus for picking items from a list. The Insert panel's Forms category lets you create all these elements and more.

Dreamweaver includes some special form elements, called Spry validation widgets. They're like the form elements discussed below, but they can *verify* the contents of a form field, which prevents visitors from submitting a form they haven't filled out correctly. The Spry validation widgets are discussed on page 588.

What All Form Elements Have in Common

Adding form elements to your document always involves the same steps:

1. **In the document window, insert a form (see page 566).**

   If the page already has a form, click inside its red border (we're talking about the visual Design view here; while you can use the Insert panel while working in Code view, you'll have to fill out the Tag Editor window).

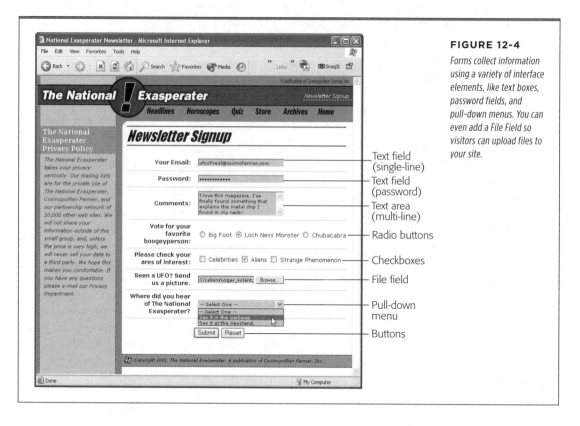

FIGURE 12-4

Forms collect information using a variety of interface elements, like text boxes, password fields, and pull-down menus. You can even add a File Field so visitors can upload files to your site.

Text field (single-line)
Text field (password)
Text area (multi-line)
Radio buttons
Checkboxes
File field
Pull-down menu
Buttons

TIP You can skip step 1 and have Dreamweaver add a form element when you first add the form field to a page. When you insert a field (step 2) and there's no form yet, Dreamweaver asks if you'd like to add the proper <form> tag. Click Yes and Dreamweaver automatically creates the red dotted-line form boundaries (and, behind the scenes, inserts the corresponding <form> tags). You should *always* click the Yes button. A form field that isn't surrounded by the proper form tag doesn't work in all browsers.

2. **In the Insert panel's Forms category, click the appropriate button (see Figure 12-2).**

   Alternatively, use the Insert→Form submenu. Dreamweaver represents every form object on the Insert panel with a command on the Insert menu, too (for example, Insert→Form→Text Field).

3. **In the Input Tag Accessibility Attributes window, type an ID (see Figure 12-5).**

   This window serves a couple of functions: It lets you assign an ID (this step) and set a few accessibility options for a form element. These options add information and tools for the benefit of those who surf using *assistive technologies* like screen readers, or those who use their keyboard (rather than their mouse) to jump from one field to another.

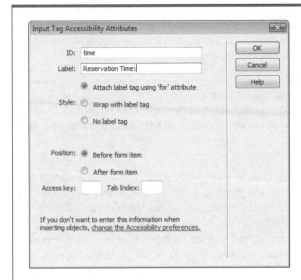

FIGURE 12-5

This window appears when you insert a form element. If you don't see it, you or someone else has turned off Dreamweaver's factory setting to automatically launch this window. To summon the window, choose Edit→Preferences (Dreamweaver→Preferences), click the Accessibility category, and then turn on the Form Objects checkbox.

The ID you type in this field also *names* the field. Remember, each field has a name so that the form-processing program can identify the information it receives (see page 565). Say you add a text field to a page to collect a visitor's town name. In the ID box, if you type *town*, then, when Dreamweaver inserts the text field onto the page, the underlying HTML that Dreamweaver writes looks like this: <input type="text" name="town" id="town">.

Be sure to follow the same naming conventions you use for CSS ID names: Begin with a letter; use only numbers, letters, hyphens, or underscores; and skip spaces, punctuation, and other characters. (Keep in mind that adding an ID to an HTML tag doesn't create a CSS ID style—but if you want to create a special look for just that one field, you *can* create a CSS ID style using the name you supply for the form element.)

NOTE The ID value you type in step 3 has a slightly different effect when you add radio buttons. What you type becomes the radio button's ID value, but Dreamweaver sets its name to "radio." That's because you can only use an ID once per tag on a page, but radio buttons that form part of a group (like answers to a multiple-choice question) must share the same name. Using the same name for more than one button tells a web browser that a visitor can select one and only one radio button from the group (see page 579). Therefore, make sure you rename your radio button using the Property Inspector, as described on page 579.

4. **Type a label, and then select label options.**

The label option lets you add text that identifies the form element's purpose. In fact, Dreamweaver wraps whatever text you type in an HTML tag, named, logically enough, the <label> tag. This tag identifies the form field's purpose, and your visitors see the text you enter here as they fill out the form. The label usually appears either to the left or right of the form field. For example, if you add a text field to collect someone's name, you might use the label *Name:*. Someone filling out the form then sees the word "Name:" followed by a box where they can type in their name. It's always a good idea to add a label. (You can read more about the <label> tag on page 587.)

NOTE Sometimes you don't need or want a label. For example, HTML's buttons—like Submit or Reset—already have a label, so you don't need to add another. In cases like this, either click the Cancel button, which adds the form field without an ID, label, or any other *accessibility* property, or leave the label box empty, and select the "No label tag" radio button.

After you type in a label, you choose from a couple of options in the Style part of the window. You can attach the label to a form element two ways. The first method, "Attach label tag using 'for' attribute," wraps the text you type inside a <label> tag. The form field itself isn't inside the label tag, but the two elements (the label and the field) are connected by a *for* property that Dreamweaver adds to the <label> tag, which tells browsers which form element the label is "for." This is a good option when a label and its form field don't appear directly next to each other in the HTML code. For example, web designers often use a table to visually organize forms (see the box on page 583). By placing text labels in one column of the table and form fields in an adjacent column, you can neatly align the labels and their corresponding fields, but the label and their associated fields appear in far different places in the HTML.

Here's an example that might make this all a bit clearer: Say you add a text field that lets someone enter her email address to subscribe to your site's newsletter. If, when you insert the field, you use the ID *email*, the label "Your email address:", and the "Attach label tag using the 'for' attribute" option, you end up with this HTML code:

```
<label for="email">Your email address:</label>

<input type="text" name="email" id="email" />
```

At this point, you can move the <label> tag (or the text field) to any other location on your web page, and the label remains related to the field. Of course, if you place the label at the top of the page and the field at the bottom, your visitors don't know they're related, so it makes sense to keep them in close proximity. People often put the <label> tag in one table cell of a row, and the field in a table cell to the right. (The label tag has one added benefit: click it and you select the associated form field, ready for the visitor to type in a response.)

The second option for attaching a label, "Wrap with label tag," wraps the <label> tag around both the text you type and the form element itself. This keeps the two elements together and easily identifies which label goes with each form field. And while wrapping a field with the <label> tag produces valid HTML, screen readers can't decipher it, so the "Attach label tag using 'for' attribute" is generally considered the best way to go.

NOTE You can skip the <label> tag entirely simply by choosing "No label tag." Any text you type in the label field is just dumped onto the page as regular text positioned next to the form field.

5. **Optionally, type an "Access key" and a Tab Index number, and then press OK.**

These steps let visitors hop to form fields using keyboard shortcuts instead of a mouse. If you specify *M* as a form element's access key, for example, visitors can jump to that element by typing *M* plus one or more other keys, depending on their browser:

- For Internet Explorer and Safari for Windows, the key combination is Alt + the access key (in this example, Alt+M).

- For Firefox for Windows and Google Chrome for Windows, visitors would type Alt + Shift + the access key (Alt+Shift+M).

- For Firefox on Macs and Safari 3 on Macs, guests would use Control + the access key (Control-M).

- For Google Chrome on Macs and Safari 4 and later on Macs, the combination is Ctrl + Option + the access key (for example Control-Option-M).

- For the Opera browser, guests would type Shift + Esc + the access key (Shift+Esc+M).

The biggest problem with this feature is that it's not at all obvious to your visitors what keyboard shortcuts work where. To make access keys useful, you need to list the shortcuts next to the form elements or create a "user's manual" of sorts that explains the shortcuts. You're probably best off leaving "Access key" blank.

The Tab Index lets you number each field in your form and, in the process, set the focus order for the fields as a visitor presses the Tab key. Number 1 indicates the first field selected when a visitor presses Tab, and each number after that—2, 3, 4, and so on—dictates the rest of the selection order on each click of the Tab key. You don't usually need to go to this extreme, since most browsers automatically jump to the next form field when you press the Tab key anyway, but it sometimes comes in handy when you have a particularly complex form and you use either tables or CSS to lay it out. In some cases, the default focus order doesn't match the visual presentation of the form. If that's the case, set the Tab Index so you can specify the correct order.

6. **In the Property Inspector, set the form element's properties (Figure 12-6).**

   Some elements let you specify things like width, height, and other variables, for instance. The following descriptions indicate the options available for each form element.

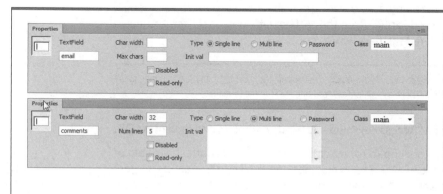

FIGURE 12-6

The Property Inspector looks slightly different depending on the type of form element you choose. For example, the properties for a regular text field (top) differ from those for a multiline text field—actually called a "textarea" in HTML-speak (bottom).

Text Fields

When you need to collect a specific piece of information, like a person's name, phone number, or address, use a text field (shown in Figure 12-4). Text fields accept typed responses, and they're great for open-ended questions. They come in three flavors: *single-line* fields for short responses, *password* fields that hide what people type from snooping eyes, and *multiline* fields for longer replies.

Once you insert a text field, you can adjust the following settings in the Property Inspector:

- **Char Width**. The width of a text field is measured in characters, so if you type *20* for the Char Width (character width) setting, Dreamweaver creates a text field that holds 20 typed letters. Be aware, however, that the *physical* width of the field (how many inches or pixels wide it is) can vary from browser to browser. (You can use Cascading Style Sheets to set an exact width using the *width* property described on page 448.)

- **Type**. You can choose from three types of text field:

  - A *single-line* text field, of course, holds just one line of text. This is the most common text field; use it for collecting small pieces of information, like a last name, Social Security number, or credit card number.

- *Multiline* fields let guests type multiple lines of text. You need this kind of field when you let visitors type in long notes, such as those in response to a "Let us know what you think!" or "Nature of problem:" field.

NOTE Dreamweaver includes a separate button for adding a multiline text field, called a *textarea* in HTML (see Figure 12-2).

- *Password* fields hide the characters a guest types from the prying eyes of passing spies. Whatever your web visitor types appears on-screen as a set of asterisks (*** in Windows) or bullets (••• on a Mac). (Be aware, however, that the information in the password field isn't completely secret: It's still transmitted as plain text, just like any other form field. The masking action takes place only in your visitor's browser. See the Frequently Asked Question on page 576.)

- **Max Chars/Num Lines**. Max Chars (maximum characters) lets you limit the number of characters a field accepts. It's a good way to ensure that guests type in the right information in the right place. For instance, if you use a field to collect a visitor's age, odds are you don't need to allot more than three characters; very few 1,000-year-olds surf the Web these days (and those who do don't like to reveal their ages).

When you specify a multiline text field, the Max Chars box morphs into the Num Lines box. In this case, you can't limit the amount of text someone types. (You can, however, use the Spry Text Area widget to limit the number of characters a multiline text field accepts, as described on page 603.) Instead, you specify the height of the text field in number of lines.

NOTE The limit you specify here affects only how tall the field is *on-screen*. Your visitors can type as many lines of information as they want (a scroll bar appears if the number of lines exceeds the size of the box).

- **Init val**. Here, you can specify the initial value of a field—starter text that automatically appears in the field so it isn't empty when a visitor begins the form. You can use this feature to include explanatory text inside the field itself, such as "Type your name in this box" or "Example: (212) 555-1212." Another common use is when you create an *update form*—a form for editing previously entered information. For example, to update your Facebook profile, you go to a page that has all your current information in it already. You change whatever information you want and then submit the form to update your profile. An update form requires a database and some server-side programming—in other words, you don't manually fill out the field's initial value property; that's done by programming on the server.

- **Disabled and Read-only**. You probably won't ever have any reason to use these two options—both make the text field uneditable. The Disabled option grays out the text field and prevents visitors from clicking into it, or even selecting any text that's already there (from the "Init val" property discussed above). In addition, when you disable a field, a browser doesn't submit that field's data when it submits the form itself.

The Read-only option lets a visitor select and copy anything in the text field, but doesn't let him change it.

Since forms are meant to collect information from visitors, don't taunt them with uneditable fields. Leave both options alone. So why do they exist? People usually use them in conjunction with JavaScript programming—for example, to disable a text field until a visitor selects another option. Why does Dreamweaver offer these options? Your guess is as good as ours.

Using the Password Field for Credit Card Numbers

Can I use the Password field for credit card numbers and other sensitive information?

Yes, but it doesn't give the information any extra security.

The Password field does one thing: It hides what people type into it. Someone looking over your visitor's shoulder can't read what he's typing—it looks like a bunch of dots—but once a browser submits that information over the Internet, it's unprotected.

To provide real security for form information, you need an encrypted connection between your web server and the visitor's computer. Most website creators use SSL (Secure Socket Layer) technology for this purpose. You can identify a site using SSL by its URL; it begins with *https://*. The "s" stands for secure and browsers usually indicate a secure connection by displaying a lock at the top or bottom of the browser window.

Web browsers understand SSL, but your web server must be specially configured to work in this mode. Contact your web host to see if their servers support SSL (the answer is usually yes). If so, they can tell you where to put your files and how to access them from a web browser. You don't have to make any special changes to your web pages, and once the server is set up, you put your web pages on it as you would for a non-secure website (Chapter 16 covers moving your files onto the Web).

Checkboxes and Checkbox Groups

Checkboxes (see Figure 12-4) are simple and to the point; a guest either checks them or not. A single checkbox is often used when you register with a web site— "By checking this box you agree to our terms and conditions." But you can also see checkboxes grouped together for questions that can have more than one answer. For example, suppose you offer visitors their choice of three email newsletters. In your form, you might include some text—"Check the boxes for the newsletters you want to receive"—and three corresponding checkboxes with labels that indicate the name of each newsletter.

Once you add a checkbox to a form, you can set up its options in the Property Inspector (see Figure 12-7):

- **Checked value**. Here's where you specify the information a browser sends to your form-processing program when a visitor selects the checkbox. Since visitors never actually see this information, it doesn't have to match the checkbox's label; it could transmit a coded response.

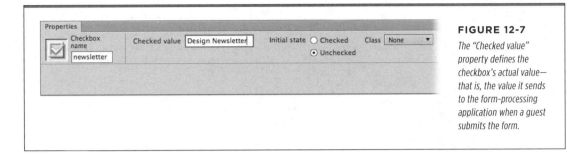

FIGURE 12-7

The "Checked value" property defines the checkbox's actual value— that is, the value it sends to the form-processing application when a guest submits the form.

- **Initial state**. If you like, you can have a checkbox already filled in when your web page first loads. You've probably seen this if you've ever signed up for something on a commercial site. There's usually a checkbox—already checked—near the bottom of the form with fine print like this: "Check here if you want to get daily, unsolicited email from our marketing department."

After you set these options, if you don't use Dreamweaver's accessibility options (discussed on page 256), return to the document window to add a text label next to the field. You want to let people know what the checkbox is for: "Yes, sign me up!", for example.

Checkboxes don't have to come in groups, but they often do. Dreamweaver includes a tool to make inserting multiple checkboxes easier, as discussed next.

■ CHECKBOX GROUPS

Checkboxes frequently travel in groups— "What activities do you like? Check all that apply." Here's how you set them up.

1. **On the Insert panel, click the Checkbox Group button.**

   The Checkbox Group window opens (see Figure 12-8).

2. **In the Name field, type a name.**

   This name applies to all the checkboxes in the group, saving you the trouble of typing in the name for each checkbox. The name you type is the name the browser submits to your web server, so follow the formatting rules for naming form fields: letters and numbers only, no spaces or funny characters, except an underscore or hyphen. (To see how Dreamweaver differentiates checkboxes that all have the same name, see the box on page 579.) Although each checkbox shares the same name, if someone selects multiple checkboxes, the browser sends the data from *all* the checked boxes to the server.

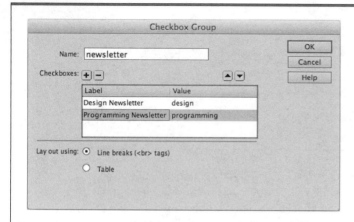

FIGURE 12-8

The Checkbox Group dialog box lets you quickly add multiple checkboxes to a page.

3. **In the Label column, click Checkbox and type in a label for the first box.**

For example, if you add a set of checkboxes so visitors can sign up for one or more newsletters, you might type the name of the newsletter here—"Design Newsletter," for example. This label will appear next to the checkbox.

> **NOTE** If you use the Checkbox Group tool, Dreamweaver skips the Accessibility Attributes window. You don't have any control over how Dreamweaver inserts the <label> tag; it just wraps the tag around the checkbox—the same as if you'd selected the "Wrap with label tag" option described in step 4 on page 572. Because the "Attach label tag using 'for' attribute (step 4 on page 572) is considered the better approach, you may wish to skip the Checkbox Group tool and just insert checkboxes one at a time.

4. **Hit the Tab key to jump to the Value column for that checkbox, and then type in a value.**

This is the value the browser passes to the web server when somebody selects the checkbox and submits the form—for example, "design" for the "Design Newsletter" option.

5. **Repeat steps 3–4 for the second checkbox in the group.**

You can create additional checkboxes by clicking the + button. Follow steps 3 and 4 for each checkbox you add.

6. **Select a layout for the group.**

Dreamweaver puts each checkbox on its own line. Choose whether you want Dreamweaver to do so using a line break (<br>) or by creating a table with one checkbox per row. Don't care for either option? Pick the "Line breaks" option—it's easier to modify—and read the Note below.

NOTE If you want a group of checkboxes to appear side by side instead of stacked one on top of the other, choose the "Line breaks" option in the Checkbox Group dialog box. Then, with Dreamweaver set to display the invisible line break character (see page 93), click the line break's gold shield in Design view, and hit Backspace or Delete to move the checkbox on the line below onto the same line as the current checkbox.

7. **Click OK to add the group of checkboxes to your page.**

   The checkboxes and their labels are essentially text (or buttons) on the screen. You can move the checkboxes around, change their labels, and, in the Property Inspector, alter each checkbox's properties.

UP TO SPEED

How Dreamweaver Uniquely IDs Checkboxes

When you insert checkboxes using the Checkbox Group tool, Dreamweaver inserts all the checkboxes with the same name, but gives each a unique ID. For example, if you insert two checkboxes with this tool, you might end up with HTML that looks like this:

```
<label><input   type="checkbox"
name="newsletter"
value="design" id="newsletter_0" />
Design newsletter</label>
<br />
<label><input type="checkbox"
name="newsletter" value="programming"
id="newsletter_1" />Programming newsletter
</label>
```

Notice that the two boxes have the same name—newsletter—but, since you need unique ID names to differentiate the checkboxes, Dreamweaver creates them by tacking _0, _1, and so on onto the end of each ID.

It's perfectly valid to use the same name for multiple checkboxes, but keep in mind (and tell your programmer) that the data is submitted as an *array*—a data format common to programming languages that lets you store multiple items under a single name. So the values of every checked box are sent in one group using the name you supplied in step 2, but using the unique ID that Dreamweaver added.

Radio Buttons and Radio Groups

Radio buttons, like checkboxes, are simple page elements (see Figure 12-4); they appear either selected (represented by a solid circle) or not (an empty circle).

Unlike checkboxes, radio buttons require your visitor to make a single choice from a group, just like the radio buttons on a car or the buttons on a blender. Radio buttons are ideal for multiple-choice questions that require a single answer, like, "What is your income: A. $10,000–35,000, B. $35,001–70,000, C. $70,001–100,000, D. None of your business."

In the Property Inspector, set the following options for a radio button (Figure 12-9):

- **Name**. Dreamweaver supplies the generic name *radio* (or radio2, radio3, and so on) when you insert a radio button. Make sure you change it to something more descriptive, and, when you insert a group of related radio buttons, give them all the *same name*. Your visitors should be able to select only one button in the group. To make sure that's the case, every button in the group needs to share the same name (although they should have different "checked values;" see the next bullet point).

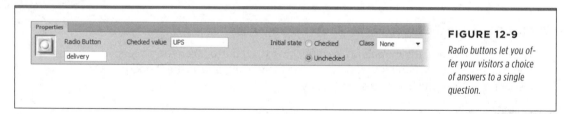

FIGURE 12-9

Radio buttons let you offer your visitors a choice of answers to a single question.

If, when you test your page, you notice that you can select more than one radio button at a time, you must have given them different names. (Consider using Dreamweaver's Radio Group object, described in the next section. It acts like a wizard, simplifying the process of creating group radio buttons.)

- **Checked value**. This is the information your form submits to the server if your visitor selects this button. Once again, the info doesn't have to match the button's on-screen label. If you filled out the Accessibility window's ID box, Dreamweaver uses the ID you supplied as the checked value. If you don't like it, change it here.

- **Initial state**. When you create a radio-button form, you can set a button as pre-checked when the page loads. To do your visitors this timesaving courtesy, turn on Checked for the button that holds the default value—the one they'll choose most often.

  Of course, if making a choice here is optional, leave all the buttons unselected by setting their initial state to Unchecked. However, once somebody *does* select a radio button, only the Reset button (if you add one) can unselect them *all* again (see page 585 to learn how to create a Reset button).

  Finally, you should add a text description for the entire group. For example, if you use radio buttons to let visitors choose a method of payment, your introductory text might say, "How would you like to pay for your item(s)?" There isn't any special HTML for creating a label for an entire group of buttons, so you just type the descriptive text next to the group of radio buttons.

■ RADIO GROUP

Although you can easily create a group of radio buttons using the Radio Button object, Dreamweaver makes it even simpler with the Radio *Group* object, a single dialog box that creates a group of radio buttons and their labels in one fell swoop. It works the same way as the Checkbox Group tool discussed on page 577, except that Dreamweaver inserts radio buttons instead of checkboxes.

Pull-Down Menus and Lists

While checkboxes and radio buttons let you ask multiple-choice questions, use them when your questions offer relatively few answer choices. Otherwise, your form can quickly become overcrowded with buttons and boxes. And therein lies the beauty of lists and pull-down menus (usually called *pop-up menus* on the Mac)—they offer many answer choices without taking up a lot of screen space (Figure 12-10 shows an example).

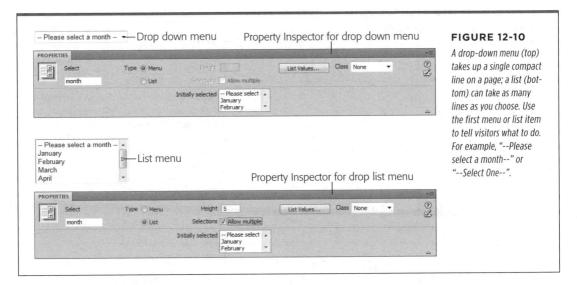

FIGURE 12-10

A drop-down menu (top) takes up a single compact line on a page; a list (bottom) can take as many lines as you choose. Use the first menu or list item to tell visitors what to do. For example, "--Please select a month--" or "--Select One--".

Once you insert a menu or list object into your document, adjust its settings in the Property Inspector.

- **Type**. Menus and lists differ in both appearance and function. A menu takes up just a single line on a page, and visitors click on that line to trigger a drop-down menu full of choices. A list displays all those choices on the page at once. Click the form element you want (Menu or List).

- **Height**. In the Height box—available only for lists—type in the number of lines you want the list to take up on the page. That can vary from a single line (in which case you might as well use a menu) to many lines (displaying a number of choices at once). If you specify a height that's smaller than the number of items in the list, Dreamweaver adds a vertical scroll bar.

- **Allow multiple**. Here's a key difference between menus and lists: If you turn on the "Allow multiple" option, a visitor can simultaneously select more than one item from a list, just by pressing the Ctrl (⌘) key while clicking items. (If you choose this option, be sure your instructions tell visitors they can select multiple items.)

- **List Values**. This button opens a dialog box where you type in the items that make up your menu or list. You specify two pieces of information for each item: a *label* (the text that appears in the menu or list on the web page) and a *value* (the information your form submits to the web server, which isn't necessarily the same thing as the label).

  To use this dialog box, type in an item label. Press Tab (or click in the Value column), and then type a value, if you like (see Figure 12-11 for details).

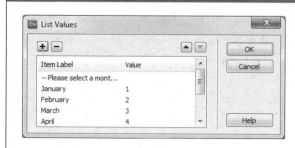

FIGURE 12-11

Using the + button, you can add an item to the end of a list; when you click inside the list's last item's Value column, pressing Tab creates a new list item. To delete an item, select it, and then click the minus-sign button. You can move an item higher or lower in the list by selecting the item and then clicking the up- or down-arrow buttons. Like radio buttons, pop-up menu items and list items always flock together—nobody ever creates just one.

NOTE A menu item's label isn't the same as the HTML <label> tag discussed on page 587. It's just the text that identifies an item in the menu.

Values are optional; if you don't specify one, the form submits the item's label *as* the value. Still, you'll often find a separate value useful. Imagine you design a pull-down menu on an e-commerce site so your visitors can select their credit cards' expiration month. Figure 12-11 shows what the items for such a pull-down menu might look like. It displays the names of the months, but the form actually transmits the *number* of the month to your form-processing program. When a visitor selects "April," the form submits 4.

Computer programs often work more easily with numbers than with names, while humans do the opposite. So when you offer visitors a pop-up menu of products, the label might use the human-friendly name of the product ("Blue Wool Cap"), while the value reflects a model number that your form-processing program readily understands (XSD1278, say).

Click OK when you finish building your menu or list. You can always return to this screen to edit the options: in the document window, click the menu or list and then, in the Property Inspector, click the List Values button. You return to the List Values dialog box.

As with other form elements, you can, and probably should, add some explanatory text alongside the menu or list in the document window. One easy method: You can automatically add a label to a menu or list using Dreamweaver's accessibility features, as described on page 256.

Giving Order to Your Forms

If you're not careful, creating forms can quickly lead to visual chaos. The different shapes and sizes of text boxes, radio buttons, and other form objects don't naturally align well with text. One solution: Use tables to control your forms' appearance.

If you simply place form labels and fields line after line, you end up with an ungainly zigzag pattern created by the differing lengths of label text and the form fields. The result is not only ugly, but hard to read.

To better organize a form, you can insert the form tag, then insert an HTML table made of two columns and as many rows as you have form fields; one column holds the label, the other the text box (or other form field). Align the text in the first column to the right, and you'll create a clean edge that effectively mirrors the edge created by the form fields.

To make this table-based solution work most effectively, set each text field to the same width, using the *Char Width* property (page 574) or Cascading Style Sheets and the CSS Width property (page 448).

You can also use CSS to lay out a form. You'll see this technique in action in the tutorial starting on page 612.

File Field

Receiving responses to checkboxes, radio buttons, and pull-down menus is all well and good, but what if you want your visitors to submit something a little meatier—like an entire file? Imagine a bulletin board system that lets guests post JPEG images of themselves, or upload word processing documents to share with others. Dreamweaver's File Field form object (see Figure 12-4) can help (but not without a little magic from your web server).

Before you get carried away with the possibilities the file field offers, you need to do a little research to see whether you can use it on your website. Although Dreamweaver lets you easily *add* a field so guests can upload images, text files, and other documents, you need to check with your web host to see if they permit anonymous file uploads (some don't for fear of receiving viruses or performance–choking large files). Then, of course, you have to ensure that the program that processes the form actually *does* something with the incoming file—stores it on the server, for instance. Dreamweaver doesn't have any built-in functions that help with this back-end work, but you can enlist some third-party solutions as described, in the box on page 585.

When you click the File Field button on the Insert panel's Forms category (or choose Insert→Form Objects→File Field), Dreamweaver inserts a text field *and* a Browse button; together, they constitute a single file field. When you click either one, you highlight both.

NOTE Browsers display file fields in different ways. For example, in Firefox and Internet Explorer, a file field looks like a text field with a button next to it. In Chrome and Safari, the field is simply a button with the text "Choose File" on it and, to the right of the button, either the text "No file chosen" (when the page first loads) or the name of the file (after a visitor selects a file from their computer).

The Browse button opens the standard Windows or Macintosh Open File dialog box, letting your visitor navigate to and select the file she wants to upload.

The Property Inspector offers only two settings (other than specifying a more creative name):

- **Char width**. Dreamweaver measures the width of text fields in characters; type *20* in the character width box and Dreamweaver creates a field 20 characters wide.

- **Max chars**. Leave this blank, as explained in Figure 12-12.

You haven't finished the file field until you add instructions or a label in the document window, something like "Click the Browse button to select a file to upload" (again, Dreamweaver simplifies this task with the Label option in the form's Accessibility window described on page 571).

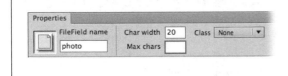

FIGURE 12-12

Avoid the "Max chars" field. Dreamweaver offers it to limit the number of characters a field accepts, but it doesn't have any effect on the file field, which automatically selects the full path to the file regardless of how long it is.

Hidden Field

Most form elements are designed to accept input from your guests: the value of a selected radio button, the text from a text field, or the choice from a menu of choices, for example. But visitors don't even know about, and don't ever see, one kind of form field: the *hidden* field.

NOTE Hidden fields aren't exactly hidden—it's true that visitors don't see them in a browser, but they (and their data) are visible if a visitor checks the page's HTML (using the browser's View→View Source or View Page Source command). In other words, despite their name, don't put anything into a hidden field that you wouldn't want someone to see.

Why, you're probably asking, would you need to submit a value you already know? Because hidden fields supply information to the programs that process forms—information that the program has no other way of knowing. Many web hosting services, for example, offer a generic form-processing program that collects information submitted with a form and emails it to the site's administrator. But how does the program know where to email the data? After all, it's a *generic* program that hundreds of other people use. The solution: A hidden field that stores the information required for the program to properly process the form—like *email=me@mydomain.com*.

To insert a hidden field, click the Insert panel's Hidden Field button (under the Forms category), or choose Insert→Form→Hidden Field. A gold shield icon appears on the page (this is Dreamweaver's symbol for HTML that you can't see in web browsers). Use the Property Inspector to give the field a name and a *value*—that is, the value you want the browser to submit to your form-processing program (in the example above, that value would be your email address).

NOTE   Gold shields indicating hidden fields appear only if, in the Preferences window's Invisible Elements category, you turn on the Hidden Form Fields checkbox (see the note on page 94), and, in the View menu, you turn on Invisible Elements (View→Visual Aids→Invisible Elements).

WORKAROUND WORKSHOP

Adding File-Upload Ability to Your Site

Imagine adding a "Job Application" page to your site, where applicants can upload their resumes for review. Or a web-based way for your clients to submit graphics files and word processing documents they want included in the pages you're building.

Dreamweaver lets you add a File Field to a form, but doesn't provide the tools you need to make this useful feature function on your site. To compensate for that glaring omission, you can turn to extensions that add this power to Dreamweaver. But before you shell out any hard-earned cash for the extensions listed next, make sure your web hosting company allows anonymous file uploads from a web form—some don't.

DMXZone (*www.dmxzone.com/index?3/1019*) offers three fee-based extensions for ASP, ASP.NET, and PHP. The Pure Upload extension offers many different settings to manage the process of uploading files to a site, including the ability to rename duplicate files and to add file information to databases.

WebAssist (one of the big players in the Dreamweaver extensions market) offers a commercial product, Universal Email, for uploading *and* downloading files from a server (*http://tinyurl.com/68dj2lt*). As its name indicates, this extension also handles sending the contents of a form as an email message. This extension works for PHP.

Buttons

No form is complete without a Submit button so your visitors can register their choices (see Figure 12-4). Only when guests click this button do their responses set out on their way to your form-processing application. People sometimes add a Reset button, which visitors can click if they make an error; it clears all their form entries, and resets all the form fields to their original values.

To add either type of button, use the Insert panel's Forms category or choose Insert→Form→Button. If the Accessibility window appears (see page 571), you don't need to add a label, since the button itself has "Submit," "Reset," or whatever text you wish emblazoned across its face, so just click the Cancel button.

The Property Inspector controls (Figure 12-13) for a freshly inserted button are:

- **Button name**. The button's name provides the first half of the "name/value" pair that the browser sends to your server (see page 563).

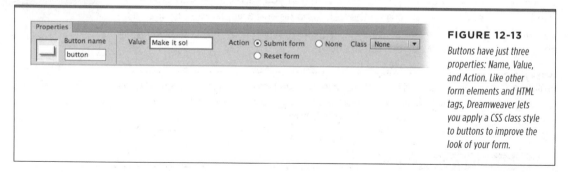

FIGURE 12-13

*Buttons have just three
properties: Name, Value,
and Action. Like other
form elements and HTML
tags, Dreamweaver lets
you apply a CSS class style
to buttons to improve the
look of your form.*

- **Value**. The value is the label that appears on a button. Dreamweaver proposes *Submit*, but you're free to substitute *Buy Now, Make It So*, or *Send my data on its merry way*.

What your visitors see printed on the button—"Click Me," for example—is the value transmitted along with the button's name when guests submit the form. This characteristic opens up some interesting possibilities. You could, for example, include *several* Submit buttons, each with a different label. If you create a form that works with a database application, for example, one button might say Delete, while another says Edit. Depending on which button your visitor clicks, the program processing the form either deletes the record from the database or modifies it.

- **Action**. The three Action options govern what happens when somebody clicks your button. The "Submit form" button transmits the form data to your form-processing program. The "Reset form" button resets all the fields to their original values. (The fields, checkboxes, or menu items aren't left blank or unselected, they return to their *initial* state, which you specified when you created the control. If you set the Initial State property of a checkbox to Checked and your visitor unchecked the box and then clicked the Reset button, the box becomes checked once again.)

The Reset button used to appear on nearly every form on the Web; these days it's much less frequent, mainly because it's unlikely that anyone would want to *completely* erase *everything* she's typed into a form. In addition, its presence offers the unfortunate possibility that a visitor, after painstakingly filling out a form, will mistake the Reset button for the Submit button, and click it—erasing everything she's typed. So if you include a Reset button, it's probably best not to put it right next to the Submit button.

NOTE While reset buttons aren't common on forms used to collect new information—"Sign up for our newsletter"—they do come in handy on a page intended to *update* information. An update form contains previously recorded information (like the shipping address for your *Amazon.com* account). In this case, a Reset button lets you erase any mistakes you make when you update your account information. Click the Reset button and the form goes back to displaying the original information, like your original shipping address.

Setting the button's action to None means that clicking the button has no effect on the *form*. "Gee *that's* useful," you're probably thinking. But while the button doesn't trigger an action related to the form, you *can* use it to trigger one of Dreamweaver's built-in behaviors (see Chapter 13). The only way to do that is to make the button available for programming by choosing None. This way, you get a common user interface element—the 3-D look of a beveled form button—that can trigger any of many different actions, like opening a new browser window or popping up a message on the screen. If you're a JavaScript programmer, you can also use this button to activate your own programs.

NOTE You can use a graphic as a Submit button, too, thus freeing you to be more creative with the look of the button. That's thanks to something called an Image Field. On the Insert panel, click the Image Field button or choose Insert→Form→Image Field to select the graphic you want to use. When a visitor clicks the image, it submits the form and all its data. (Image Fields do only one thing: submit form data. You can't use them as a Reset button, for example.)

The <label> Tag

As discussed on page 571, the <label> tag lets you associate a label with a particular form element, like a checkbox or text field. Of course, you can always place plain text next to a form element on a page. But because a <label> tag is "attached" to a particular form element, it's more helpful in explaining the function and layout of your form to people who use assistive technologies, like screen-reading software for the blind.

NOTE Labels also make forms more usable: by adding a <label> tag to a checkbox, for example, a visitor can click on the label text to check the box, extending the "clickable" region. Likewise, clicking a label on a text field places the cursor inside the text box so a visitor can start typing.

On the Insert panel's Forms category, the Label Tag button doesn't behave like other form elements. If you're in Design view when you add a label this way, Dreamweaver switches to Split view (Code and Design), drops a <label> tag into the HTML and places the cursor inside it. You're much better off inserting labels with Dreamweaver's form Accessibility option, as described on page 571. However, there are some cases when you don't want to put the label directly next to the form field; for example, when you use tables to lay out a form, you usually put the label in one table cell, and the form element in another. In such a case, you need to jump into Code view to add a label anyway, and this button can save you a little typing.

The <fieldset> Tag

The <fieldset> tag is a form-organization tool that lets you group related form fields. For example, if you create an online order form, you can organize all the "ship to" information—address, city, state, Zip code, and so on—into a single set. Again, this arrangement can help those using assistive technology to understand the organization and intent of a form.

The <fieldset> tag also has a visual benefit: Browsers display a border around fieldsets. In addition, the Legend tag (which Dreamweaver automatically adds whenever you insert a fieldset) lets you add a description of the fields grouped inside a fieldset. The legend appears at the top of the fieldset.

To use this tag, select the related form fields. You have to position the form fields next to each other on-screen, and you can organize them within other HTML elements, like a table. Then, on the Insert panel's Forms category, click the Fieldset button. In the Label window that appears, type a label (called, somewhat dramatically, a legend) for the fieldset, and then click OK.

In addition to displaying the label you type, Dreamweaver creates a simple border around the group of fields you select. Because different browsers display this border differently, make sure you preview the page (F12, or Option-F12 on a Mac) in a recent version of Internet Explorer, Firefox, Chrome, Safari, and Opera, or use Adobe's BrowserLab tool (page 760), to see how the label and the surrounding border look in different browsers.

■ Validating Forms

You might get frustrated when you review feedback submitted via a form on your web page, only to notice that your visitor failed to provide a name, email address, or some other critical piece of information. That's why, depending on the type of form you create, you might want to make certain information *mandatory*.

For instance, a form that signs up guests for an email newsletter isn't much use if the would-be reader doesn't type in an email address. Likewise, if you need a shipping address to deliver a product, you want to be sure that your visitor includes his address on the form.

Luckily, Dreamweaver includes a set of validation options that do exactly that. They're called Spry validation "widgets." (The term *widget* refers to any of the Spry-based, interactive web page elements that Dreamweaver helps you create, such as the Spry Menu Bar, Spry Validation Text Field, and Spry Tabbed Panels.) With a Spry validation widget, you can display a friendly "Hey, please fill out this box" message when someone tries to submit a form that's missing information. You can specify that visitors can't leave a particular field blank, or that a field must contain information in a specific format, such as a phone number, email address, or credit card number. If someone tries to submit the form without the correct information, your message appears. And instead of an annoying and amateurish JavaScript error window popping up, Spry form validation widgets display error messages right on the web page, and right next to the faulty form field. You can even change the field's look to highlight a problem (add a red background to the field, for example).

Emailing Form Results

I don't want to store form submissions in a database or anything fancy like that. I just want to get an email message that includes the information a guest submits. How do I do that?

This common function—available on countless websites—may seem like an easy task, but Dreamweaver doesn't supply a tool to automate the process. Basically, you need a program to collect the data and send it off in an email message. Most web hosting companies provide just such a program. They generally work like this: You build a form, set the form's Action property (see "Creating a Form") to point to the URL of the server's form-emailing program, and then add one or more hidden fields. The hidden fields contain information that the program uses—your email address, for example, and the URL of the page the browser should load after it submits the form. Since this form-emailing program varies from server to server, you need to contact your hosting company for details.

Many commercial Dreamweaver extensions can help you, too. For basic form mailing, the Mail Form extension for ASP and PHP is available from Felix One for $38 (*http://tinyurl.com/6cty3lq*). Two other extensions offer much more advanced emailing features, including the ability to mass-mail newsletters to email addresses stored in a database: WA Universal Email ($99) from WebAssist (*http://tinyurl.com/5uhm4g4*) works for PHP pages and also supports file uploads, and DMXZone sells both an ASP (*www.dmxzone.com/go?5578*) and a PHP (*www.dmxzone.com/go?5628*) version of its Smart Mailer extension ($49).

For all these extensions, however, your server has to support the appropriate programming language (ASP or PHP)—Part Six of this book has more on server-side programming.

Spry Validation Basics

Spry validation widgets let you verify input in a text field, a text area, a pull-down menu, a checkbox, or a group of radio buttons. You can make sure guests fill out a field, turn on a checkbox, select from a list, or click a radio button. You can limit input to a specific type of information, such as a date or phone number, and even limit the number of letters someone types into a text box.

The basic process for all form validation widgets is the same:

1. **Insert the Spry widget.**

   Buttons for inserting the seven types of Spry validation form fields appear in four places: on the Insert panel's Forms menu, in the dedicated Spry menu, from the Insert→Form submenu, and from the Insert→Spry submenu. The first few steps are the same as those for inserting any form field. The Input Tag Accessibility window appears, and you follow steps 3–5 on pages 571–573.

   If you already inserted a text field, multiline text box, checkbox, or pull-down menu on a page, you can add Spry validation to it by selecting the form element and then, on the Insert panel, clicking the appropriate Spry form button.

If you want to validate a text field, for instance, select the text field, and then click the Spry Validation Text Field button. You can't add validation to a group of already-placed radio buttons, however. To do that, you have to create them as part of the Spry Validation Radio Group widget (see page 611).

When you insert a widget, Dreamweaver adds more than just the HTML needed to validate the form field; it also inserts a <span> tag surrounding the field, a label, and the HTML necessary to display one or more error messages. In addition, the widget adds JavaScript programming to verify the validity of the information in the field, and CSS to style the appearance of the field and the error messages.

> **NOTE** When you save a web page after inserting a Spry widget, Dreamweaver pops up a window letting you know that it's added JavaScript and CSS files to the SpryAssets folder in the site's root folder (see the Tip on page 215).

2. **Rename the widget (optional).**

Once you insert a widget, you can rename it using the Property Inspector (see Figure 12-14). Dreamweaver assigns every Spry widget a generic ID like *sprytextfield1*, *sprytextfield2*, and so on. You can change this to something more descriptive, but for clarity's sake leave "spry" in the ID name. If you insert a Spry text field to collect a person's email address, for example, you might name the widget *spryEmail*.

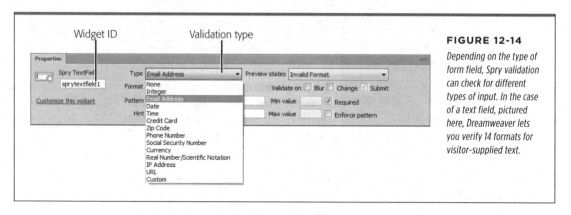

FIGURE 12-14

Depending on the type of form field, Spry validation can check for different types of input. In the case of a text field, pictured here, Dreamweaver lets you verify 14 formats for visitor-supplied text.

Dreamweaver applies the ID to a <span> tag that wraps around the actual form field, form label, and error messages that Spry creates. Don't get this ID confused with the ID you assigned to the form field—that's a different tag with its own ID. That's why it's a good idea to include "spry" in the ID you assign to the widget. If this all sounds confusing, do yourself a favor and don't bother renaming the widget. Dreamweaver can track the IDs just fine, and since the generic name Dreamweaver assigns is never visible on the form, no one visiting your site knows the difference.

3. **Assign a validation requirement.**

Use the Property Inspector to specify the type of validation you want to apply. The most basic type simply ensures that your guests type *something* into a form field, make a selection from a pull-down menu, turn on a checkbox, or select a radio button. But each type of form field has additional validation options. For example, you can make sure a visitor fills out a text field with numbers in the correct format for a credit card. The options for each field are discussed below.

NOTE Properties for a Spry widget appear in the Property Inspector only when you select the widget (as opposed to selecting the form field itself). To do that, mouse anywhere over the form field until a blue Spry tab appears (see Figure 12-15), and then click the tab to select the widget.

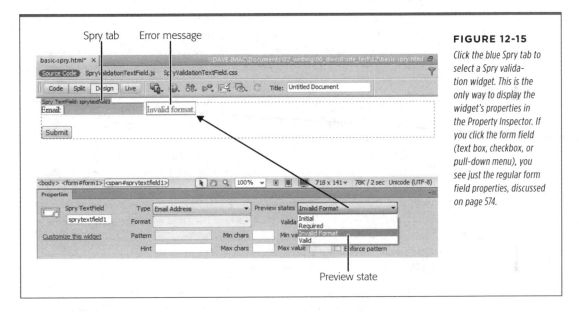

FIGURE 12-15

Click the blue Spry tab to select a Spry valida-tion widget. This is the only way to display the widget's properties in the Property Inspector. If you click the form field (text box, checkbox, or pull-down menu), you see just the regular form field properties, discussed on page 574.

4. **Select when the validation occurs.**

A browser validates form fields as soon as a visitor submits the form. So, when someone clicks the Submit button, the JavaScript in the web page checks to make sure your guest filled out everything correctly. If not, the form does not pass Go and one or more error messages appear, letting the visitor know what went wrong. In fact, Spry tools always validate information when a browser submits a form, and you can't turn this behavior off (that's why, in the Property Inspector, the Submit checkbox is checked and grayed out [see Figure 12-14]).

However, to provide more responsive feedback, you can also check to make sure the form has the right kind of info immediately after your visitor enters it. Say you add a text field to collect a visitor's email address, and some wisenheimer types in "I'm not telling" instead of his email address. You could present an error message—like "This is not a valid email address"—when he tries to submit the form. Or you could display an error message the moment he moves onto the next field. This kind of instant feedback can make it easier for your site visitors: They immediately see and can fix their mistakes instead of waiting until they submit the form.

You dictate *when* a field is valid by turning on one or both of the Property Inspector's "Validate on" checkboxes (circled in Figure 12-14). Dreamweaver lets you validate a form field when the field is "blurred," "changed," or both. "Blurred" doesn't mean the field suddenly gets fuzzy; it refers to the moment when a visitor clicks on another field or another part of the page. Also, if you type something into a text box and then press the Tab key to jump to another field (or click anywhere outside that field), the browser considers the text box "blurred." This blurred state is a great time to validate a text field, because you know the visitor is done with that field.

You can also validate a field when the field "changes." In this case, "change" means anything entered into the field. When a guest types into a text field, for example, each letter the person types represents a "change" to the field, so the browser validates the field following each keystroke. This can be a bit annoying, since an error message might appear the moment your visitor starts typing. For example, if you validate email addresses, the JavaScript looks for text in the form of *bob@somewhere.com*. So say Bob clicks in the field and starts to type. The moment he hits the 'b' key, he changes the field and JavaScript validates its contents. But since 'b' isn't a proper email address, Bob gets an "Invalid format" message. That's a bit rude. In a case like this, the blur option is better, since it waits until your visitor finishes filling out the field.

On the other hand, validating a pull-down menu field when it changes can be quite useful. Say you add a pull-down field to a form, and the first option is "Please make a selection." Obviously, you want people filling out the form to select something other than "Please make a selection." Imagine that someone starts to fill out the form and she scrolls down to an item in the menu. Then, for whatever reason, she changes her selection to "Please make a selection." This option isn't valid, and the browser should notify her immediately. If you have Dreamweaver validate the form when it changes, that's what will happen. But if you validate the page when the menu is "blurred," the browser notifies your guest only after she clicks somewhere else on the page—a few moments later, rather than immediately.

In general, "blur" works best for text fields and text areas, while "change" is better for checkboxes, radio buttons, and pull-down menus.

5. **Set other options for the widget.**

Some widgets have other settings that come in handy. For instance, with a text validation widget, you can limit the number of letters someone can type into a text area, and you can add "hints," like "Type your name in this box," to a text field widget. These options are discussed below.

6. **Modify error messages.**

Preventing incomplete fields solves only part of the valid-information problem. When a visitor leaves a required field blank, or types incorrect information into a field, you need to let him know what went wrong so he can fix it. Every form validation widget includes one or more error messages. An error message appears next to an invalid form field entry, for example, and different error messages appear under different circumstances. A Spry Validation Text Field left blank displays the message "A value is required," for example. A field filled with the wrong type of response—a word instead of a year in answer to "What year were you born?", for instance—triggers the error message "Invalid format."

You can customize each of these messages from the Property Inspector by first selecting the proper "preview state," which shows you where Dreamweaver will display the message and what the message will say. In Figure 12-15, for example, selecting Invalid Format displays the error message "Invalid format" if a guest leaves the field blank.

To change the error message, select the text in Design view and type in a new message. It's generally a good idea to come up with a friendly and descriptive notice. If you programmed a text field to accept a date in a particular format, for instance, you might change the "Invalid format" error message to something like "Please enter a date in the format 02/27/2013."

> **NOTE** Be careful when you select a Spry error message; you can inadvertently delete both it and the <span> tag that the Spry widget relies on. Without that <span> tag, the validation won't work. A good precaution is to select everything up to (but not including) the final period in the error message and then type in the new message.

Most validation widgets have more than one error message, so make sure you preview each of the "states." Some states have no error message, so you're just previewing the page in the selected state. For example, no error message appears when a form first loads, so the "Initial" option in the preview state menu just shows you what the form field will look like when a browser loads the page. Every other widget (except the checkbox widget) also includes a "Valid" preview state. This is how the form field looks when it receives input. There's no error message in this instance, but the form field's background changes to green. You create this green formatting with CSS, which you'll learn to do next.

TIP You can change the placement of a Spry form field error message by going into Code view and then moving the <span> tags containing the error message—it'll look something like *<span class="textfieldInvalid FormatMsg">Invalid format</span>*. Because each form field can have multiple error messages (for Required and Invalid formats, and so on), there may be more than one <span> element. However, keep in mind that each Spry form widget has *another* <span> tag that surrounds the label, the field, and the error messages—it looks something like *<span id="sprytextfield1">*. You can only move the error messages' <span> tags to another location *within* the surrounding widget's <span> tag. If you move them outside that span, the error messages no longer work.

Formatting Spry Error Messages and Fields

Spry error messages appear in red with a red outline. Fortunately, you're not stuck with this factory setting. CSS controls the display of the Spry widgets, and a single style controls the "invalid" error message format. When you insert a Spry validation widget, Dreamweaver adds its style sheet to the SpryAssets folder in your site's root folder (see page 215). Each Spry validation widget (text boxes, text areas, menus, and checkboxes) has its own external style sheet. Dreamweaver names the style sheet after the type of widget. For example, the style sheet for a Spry validation text field is *SpryValidationTextField.css*. If you add several types of Spry validation fields, you have to edit several style sheets to change the look of the error messages.

Fortunately, you don't have to hunt and peck through the .css file to modify an error message style. By using Dreamweaver's CSS Styles panel's Current view, you can easily identify the proper style, and then edit it. Here's how:

1. **Open the CSS Styles panel (see Figure 12-16) if it's not already open.**

   Choose Window→CSS Styles in either Windows or on a Mac, or Shift+F11 on Windows.

2. **At the top of the panel, click the Current button.**

   The Current view shows the styles and properties that Dreamweaver applies to the selection in the document window.

3. **Make sure you select the Cascade button (circled in Figure 12-16).**

   The Cascade button activates the Rules pane in the middle of the CSS Styles panel. It displays all the CSS styles that Dreamweaver applies to the selection in the order of their specificity—least specific on top, most specific at the bottom (see page 391 for a refresher on specificity). The style that most directly applies to the given selection is listed last.

4. **Select the Spry validation widget.**

   Mouse anywhere over the form field in Design view until a blue Spry tab appears, and then click the tab to select the widget.

5. **From the Property Inspector's "Preview states" menu, select the preview state you want to format.**

   Dreamweaver displays the error message that appears for the selected state—"A value is required" for the "required" state, for example. In addition, it displays

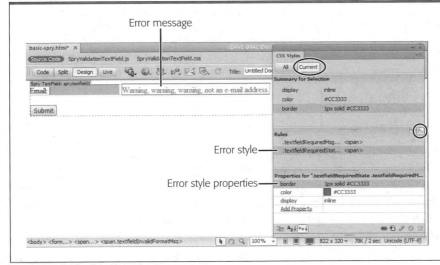

any formatting it applies to the form field in that state; for example, a text field in its "Valid" state has a green background. You can adjust the format of the form field as well.

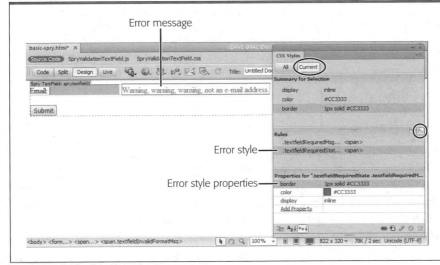

Error message

FIGURE 12-16

You can easily adjust the formatting of a Spry validation error message by clicking inside the message, selecting the Current button in the CSS Styles panel, identifying the style in the Rules pane, and then, in the Properties pane, editing the style properties. Or just double-click the style name to open the friendly CSS Rule Definition window.

Error style

Error style properties

6. **In the document window, click anywhere in the text of the error message or the form field you wish to format.**

The Styles panel displays the style in the Rules pane (see Figure 12-16). Its name is a rather long-winded group selector (beginning with something like *.textfieldRequiredState, .textfieldRequiredMsg*) made up of classes and descendent selectors (see page 381 for details on group styles). You don't really need to pay attention to the name, however, since you already selected the style you want to edit.

NOTE When you format an error message, just click inside the text. Don't try to select the entire message by triple-clicking it—if you do, you'll select more than the error message, and the CSS Styles panel won't display the message's style.

7. **Edit the style's properties.**

You can do this most easily by double-clicking the style's name in the Rules pane. That opens the CSS Rule Definition window, where you can edit CSS properties just as you would any other style, as described on page 139. You can also use the Properties pane for a more rapid edit, to quickly change the text color, for instance (see page 382 for more on how to use the Properties pane to edit and set CSS properties). Using the Properties pane also give you access to some CSS properties (like the box-shadow property discussed on page 421) that aren't listed in the Rule Definition window.

TIP Dreamweaver puts Spry error messages inside <span> tags and displays them inline (meaning on the same line as the form field). If you want to put the error message on its own line, change the *display* property (listed under the Block category in the CSS Rule Definition window) from *inline* to *block*.

In addition, you can move the <span> tags containing the error messages, and even change them from a <span> tag to a <div> or <p> tag. The exact tag type doesn't matter—but if you change the tag type (from <span> to <p>, for instance), make sure the class name remains the same. Spry depends on the proper class name to identify the error message. In addition, if you change the error message tag to a block-level element like a <p> or <div> tag, you should change the widget's outer <span> tag—<span id="sprytextfield2"> for instance—to a <div> tag; otherwise you'll have a block-level element (the error <div>) inside an inline element (the widget's <span>) which is invalid HTML. If you move the error message, it must remain inside the outer <span> tag that forms the Spry validation widget.

A few other styles affect the appearance of Spry form fields. For example, when you click in a Spry-enabled text field, its background color changes to yellow; when you click a Spry menu, its background also changes to yellow. Dreamweaver applies these colors to what's called the field's "focus state"—the moment when a visitor interacts with the field—but you can't preview or adjust the colors in the Rules or Property panes as described above. Instead, you have to edit the relevant CSS files themselves. The styles that control these focus states are:

- **Text field focus style**: *.textfieldFocusState input, input.textfieldFocusState*. You'll find it in the *SpryValidationTextField.css* file.

- **Text area focus style**: *.textareaFocusState textarea, textarea.textareaFocusState*. Located in the *SpryValidationTextarea.css* file.

- **Menu focus style**: *.selectFocusState select, select.selectFocusState*. Found in the *SpryValidationSelect.css* file.

In addition to these styles, another special style formats text fields and text area boxes when a visitor presses an invalid key on the keyboard (see the Tip on page 601).

TIP Dreamweaver's Live View can also help you style CSS elements controlled by JavaScript (like the Spry validation widgets). Page 494 has more information.

Spry Text Fields

Spry text fields have the most options of any Spry validation widget. Dreamweaver lets you choose from 14 validation types, and lets you control several other settings, such as limiting the minimum and maximum number of characters allowed.

First, decide whether you want to *require* your visitor to enter information in a field; if so, turn on the Required box in the Property Inspector (circled in Figure 12-17). A form almost always requires *some* information (an email address to sign up for a newsletter, for instance). But sometimes you want to make a response optional, such as when you ask for a phone number. In a case like that, you don't want to turn on the Required box, but you do want your guest to format the information accurately. That's where validation types come in.

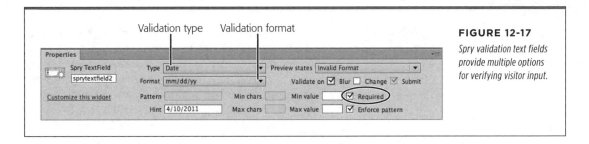

FIGURE 12-17

*Spry validation text fields
provide multiple options
for verifying visitor input.*

■ VALIDATION TYPES

To make sure your visitors supply answers in the appropriate format on your forms, validate the contents of a field. Use the Type menu in the Property Inspector to assign one of 14 validation options:

- **None**. This is the default setting. The JavaScript code Dreamweaver creates doesn't inspect the contents of the field to make sure it matches a particular format. Use this setting in combination with the Required checkbox when you don't care what someone types in, so long as they enter something. You might use this setting to capture the reason a customer wants to return a product, for example.

NOTE When you assign any validation option other than None, Dreamweaver adds an "Invalid format" error message to the page. You can change this message as described in step 6 on page 595.

- **Integer**. Use this option to verify that your guest enters a whole number, like one asking for their age or year of birth. If someone types in 1.25, JavaScript won't submit the form; it displays an "Invalid format" error message. (If you *do* want to allow decimal values, use the Real Number option discussed below.)

  If you specify integer validation, you can also assign minimum and maximum allowed values, as discussed on page 602.

- **Email**. This option looks for a validly formatted email address (like *missing@ sawmac.com*). It can't verify that the address is real, so someone could enter a fake address (like *nobody@nowhere.com*), but this option at least makes sure an honest visitor doesn't enter a typo.

- **Date**. When you require visitors to enter a specific date, use this option. If you create a form that schedules the use of a meeting room, for example, you could add a "Date needed" field. Dates comprise a month, day of the month, and year, which visitors can enter in many ways: 12-02-2013, 12/02/13, 02.12.13, and so on. To specify the format you want, use the Property Inspector's Format menu (see Figure 12-17).

NOTE With date validation, the option *yyyy* means visitors have to enter the full year (2022) to pass validation. However, *mm* and *dd* both allow single-digit values, like 1 for January, or 2 for the second day of the month—guests don't need to enter an initial zero (01 or 02, for example).

You specify the format for a month by *mm*, a day by *dd*, and the year by either *yy* (for just the last two digits of the year, like 13 for 2013) or *yyyy* (for a complete year, like 2013). You should also indicate the kind of separator you want between the month, day, and year, like a backslash (/) or a hyphen (-). So, for example, the option *mm/dd/yyyy* means that 1/2/2013 and 12/15/2013 are both valid entries, but 1-2-2013 or 12/15/13 are not.

TIP If you'll eventually store the responses from a date form field in a MySQL Date field, choose yyyy-mm-dd as the format since it matches the format MySQL uses.

- **Time**. This option validates time entries in one of several formats, such as 12:15 PM or 23:15. You can use it along with the date field to, say, capture the exact time of an event, so a guest could specify a beginning and an ending time on a meeting room scheduling form, for example. As with the Date format, you have to specify a Time format using the Property Inspector's Format menu. *HH* indicates the hour using 24-hour time—13 for 1 p.m., in other words; *hh* is the hour using nonmilitary time, *mm* represents minutes, *ss* indicates seconds, *tt* means before noon and after noon in AM or PM format, and *t* indicates the same thing using just a single letter, A or P.

  So the HH:MM option validates 13:35, but not 1:35 PM (guests must enter a zero for single-digit hours, minutes, and seconds). The hh:mm:ss tt option requires visitors to format time like this: 01:35:48 PM.

NOTE Whenever you require a visitor to type information in a specific format—12:45 PM, for instance—be sure to include clear instructions and perhaps an example. Something like, "Please enter the time you'd like to reserve using this format: 12:45 PM." You can also take advantage of a Spry text field's Hint setting, as described on page 602. You can prevent visitors from entering invalid letters, numbers, or symbols using the Enforce Pattern option described on page 601.

- **Credit Card**. An e-commerce site isn't much good if you don't give people a way to pay for their purchases. To make sure visitors enter a validly formatted credit card number, choose this option. If you accept only one type of card—like a Visa or MasterCard—you can specify it using the Property Inspector's Format menu. As with email addresses, the validation checks only that someone has correctly formatted the number—it doesn't actually check to see if this is a real (and not stolen!) credit card.

NOTE Be careful if you accept credit card numbers online. An awful lot of responsibility goes along with taking someone's credit card number, including potential liability if the card is stolen, or someone manages to steal the credit card numbers you collect. For an introduction to online payment processing, check out *http://tinyurl.com/5vbvkvy*.

- **Zip Code**. To mail a brochure, t-shirt, book, or any other product, you need a Zip code. Use the Zip Code validation format to make sure guests type it in correctly. The Format menu lets you specify a Zip code type and country. For example, US-5 means you want to see a five-digit US Zip code, like 97213, whereas US-9 is the nine-digit US Zip code format, composed of five digits, a hyphen, and four more numbers: 97213-1234. Dreamweaver also offers Canadian and UK Zip code formats, and you can create your own by specifying a custom pattern (see the next section).

- **Phone Number**. The US/Canada phone number format looks like this: (555) 555-1234, with the parentheses, space, and hyphen required. If you'd like a different format (555-555-1234, for example), you can define a custom pattern in the Pattern field, as described in the next section. For an alternative style, see page 601.

- **Social Security Number**. This option requires three numbers, a hyphen, two numbers, a hyphen, and three more numbers, like this: 555-12-4888. You should avoid requesting Social Security numbers. Many people are reluctant to disclose them for reasons of privacy and fear of identity theft, and by law, they don't have to.

- **Currency**. If you require someone to specify a monetary amount in a field— "How much money would you like to contribute to the home for wayward web designers?"—select the currency option to validate their responses. You can choose US or European formatting. US format appears like 1,000.00, while the same value in European format is expressed as 1.000,00. The comma (period for the European value) that indicates "thousands" (1,000) is optional; Java-Script considers both 1000.00 and 1,000.00 valid. However, it doesn't accept an opening dollar sign; if a visitor enters $1,000.00 into a currency field, she gets an "Invalid format" error message.

- **Real Number/Scientific Notation**. To allow decimal points in a field intended to capture numeric values, use this option. For a serious, scientific audience, this format even allows scientific notation, like 1.231e10.

- **IP Address**. Since we all like having people type the unique set of numbers that identify a computer on the Internet, you can make sure a form accepts only properly formatted IP addresses (like 192.168.1.1). The Format menu lets you choose between the current IPv4 and the newer, not yet fully implemented IPv6, or both—oh, please, does anyone really go around asking for people's IP addresses?

- **URL**. Make sure visitors enter properly formatted web addresses using this option. The address has to include the protocol (http://). So *http://www.sawmac.com* is valid, but *www.sawmac.com* isn't.

- **Custom**. If you're unhappy with the validation options Dreamweaver offers, you can create your own. That's described next.

■ CUSTOM VALIDATION

If you need information entered into a field in a very precise way and none of Dreamweaver's validation types fit the bill, you can create your own. Say your company has an internal ID system for employees. Each employee is assigned an ID composed of three numbers, a hyphen, and the first three letters (in uppercase) of the person's last name, like 348-MCF. To enforce this format, you can create your own validation "pattern." If a visitor's input matches the pattern, JavaScript considers the information valid and submits the form. If the input doesn't match, it displays an error message.

A pattern is just a series of symbols that indicate acceptable input; each letter in the pattern has a special meaning that defines the valid character type. AAA means "Accept three uppercase letters in a row as valid."

To create a custom validation, select a Spry text field widget and, from the Property Inspector's Type menu, choose Custom. Then, in the Pattern field, type the pattern you want (see Figure 12-18).

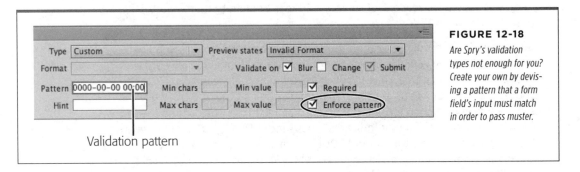

FIGURE 12-18

Are Spry's validation types not enough for you? Create your own by devising a pattern that a form field's input must match in order to pass muster.

Validation pattern

Here's a key to the symbols you use to create a pattern:

- **0 means a whole number between 0 and 9**. If you want to make sure that someone enters five digits, type *00000* in the Property Inspector's Pattern field. This pattern is the same as the one for a five-digit Zip code.

- **Type *A* to indicate a single uppercase alphabetic character**. The pattern A0A, for instance, is good for an uppercase letter, followed by a number, followed by another uppercase letter, like U5U.

- **A lowercase *a* identifies a lowercase alphabetic character**. The pattern *aaa*, then, matches *abc*, but not *ABC*.

- **To accept either an uppercase *or* a lowercase letter, use *B*.** The pattern *BBB* matches both *abc* and *ABC*.

- **To include numbers along with uppercase letters, use *X;*** the letter *x* matches both numbers and lowercase alphabetical characters. **Use *Y* for a case-insensitive match for numbers and letters**. *XXX* matches *B2B, BBB* and *123*, but not *b2b* or *bbb*. To match b2B or bb1, use YYY as the pattern.

- **Finally, use *?* as a kind of wild card**. It stands in for any character whatsoever, and you should use it when a character other than a letter or number (like a period, !, or $ symbol) is also valid.

You can include any required symbol, like a period, comma, or hyphen, as part of the pattern. In the employee ID example discussed above, the pattern to match that format is 000-AAA. In other words, three numbers, a hyphen, and then three uppercase letters. To match a phone number like 503-555-1234, use the pattern 000-000-0000. To match the MySQL DATETIME format, use 0000-00-00 00:00:00.

■ ENFORCING A PATTERN

You can make sure visitors can't even type in incorrect characters by turning on the "Enforce pattern" checkbox in the Property Inspector (circled in Figure 12-18). When you select this option, JavaScript prevents guests from entering invalid characters in the form field. It's a very useful way to prevent visitors from entering incorrect information in the first place.

For example, suppose you add a Spry text field and set its validation type to Zip code, using the US-Zip5 format. That box can accept only digits, and only five digits at that. If you turn on the "Enforce pattern" option for this field, a visitor can type only five numbers into the field. If a visitor types the letter A, the field remains blank. If the visitor types five numbers and then any other character (like another number or even a letter), that sixth character never appears.

For some validation formats, the "Enforce pattern" feature is even more useful. For example, if you choose a US/Canada phone number format, the Spry validation expects a number that looks like this: (503) 555-1212. Because the only part of the number that will vary from visitor to visitor is the actual numbers—not (,), -, or spaces—the Spry programming automatically adds those so visitors only need to type in the numbers, not any of the required punctuation.

You can choose the "Enforce pattern" option for any validation type except *None*. It even works with custom patterns.

TIP When someone types invalid characters into a form field that has the "Enforce pattern" option set, any text inside the box flashes bright red to indicate a problem. If you want to change that color, you can edit the styles responsible. For text fields, in the *SpryValidateTextField.css* file, the style is a group selector named *.textfieldFlashText input, input.textfieldFlashText*. In the *SpryValidationTextarea.css* file, a similar style named *.textareaFlashState textarea, textarea.textareaFlashState* applies to text fields.

SUPPLYING A HINT

When you require a very specific format for a field, you should provide clear instructions to visitors. You can have these instructions appear next to the label or below the form field.

Dreamweaver also lets you add a short "hint" inside a Spry text field. This hint appears when the form first loads, but the moment a visitor clicks into the field, it disappears; visitors are then free to type in a response.

To add a hint, select the Spry widget, and then, in the Property Inspector's Hint field, enter what you want to appear (see Figure 12-17).

Since text fields are relatively short, you don't have much room for instructions. A better use of the hint is an example of the format the field requires. If you want to collect an email address, for example, make the hint something like *your_email@ your_site.com*. If you're looking for a phone number, add a sample phone number, like (555) 555-1234. This lets visitors know that they should include the parentheses and hyphen.

LIMITING CHARACTERS AND ENFORCING A RANGE OF VALUES

At times, you may want to control the amount of text someone types into a field. If you create a member profile form as part of a "members-only" website, you might want to collect a person's age—so you want an integer that's at least two numbers long (no babies allowed!), but no more than three numbers long (no immortals either!). As you've read, HTML's "Max chars" property (see page 575) lets you control a text field's maximum number of characters, but HTML gives you no way to require *a minimum* number of characters. In addition, setting the "Max chars" property doesn't alert a visitor when she's typed the maximum number of characters allowed.

With Spry text fields, you can set both limits, using the Property Inspector's "Min chars" and "Max chars" fields (see Figure 12-19). Select the Spry widget by clicking the blue tab that appears when you mouse over the Spry text field, and then set the minimum and maximum number of characters. You can fill in either field, both fields, or neither. In the age example above, you'd type *2* in the "Min chars" box and *3* in the "Max chars" box.

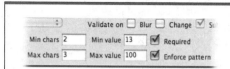

FIGURE 12-19

Go ahead, indulge your inner dictator. The Spry text field validation widget lets you control how many characters someone can type into a field.

Each setting has its own error message. You can view and edit the messages by choosing the appropriate state from the "Preview states" menu (see step 6 on page 593). For example, while the error message for the minimum number of characters reads "Minimum number of characters not met," you can change that to something more descriptive, like "You're too young to join our club."

Some validation fields let you enforce a *range* of values. If you select the Integer validation type (see page 597), the "Min value" and "Max value" boxes become active in the Property Inspector. Say you include a question on a form that reads, "Please rate the quality of our service from 1 to 10," and supply a text box for a response. In this case, set the "Min value" to *1* and the "Max value" to *10*; that way, JavaScript won't allow answers like 100, or –10.

You can set Min and Max values for other numeric validation types, too, like currency and real numbers. These two settings even work with the date and time validation types. Say you offer rebates to anyone who buys your product before a certain date—08/05/2013, for instance; the online rebate form includes a "Date purchased" field. In this instance, you can choose the Date validation type from the Format menu, select mm/dd/yyyy, and then, in the "Max value" field, type *08/05/2013*. If someone who buys the product on September 15, 2013, tries to claim the rebate, he gets an error message when he fills out the form.

NOTE Setting a minimum and maximum value for a text field that uses Time validation works reliably only if you use 24-hour time (like 18:00 for 6:00 PM). If you use one of the formats that requires the AM or PM notation, you can end up with inaccurate results. Spry treats 12:00 PM (noon) as later than 5:00 PM, and 8:00 AM as earlier than 12:00 AM (midnight).

Spry Text Area

A Spry text area has far fewer validation options than a normal text field. You can't select a type of validation or enforce a pattern on the text box's contents, for example. However, the Property Inspector does let you specify whether content is required, dictate the minimum and maximum number of characters allowed, and supply a hint that appears inside the text box when the form page loads (see Figure 12-20). These options works just like those for a standard text field, described on page 596.

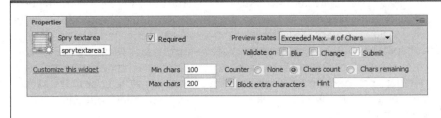

FIGURE 12-20

If you turn on the "Block extra characters" checkbox after you set a value in the "Max chars" field, anything someone types beyond that maximum character limit doesn't appear. HTML gives you no way to limit the amount someone can type into a multiline text box, so this Spry feature offers a nice workaround.

In addition, you can include a counter alongside the text area that tells your guest either how many characters they've entered (turn on the "Chars count" radio button you see in Figure 12-20), or how many more they *can* enter before they hit the limit ("Chars remaining"). That's helpful if you limit the amount of feedback a visitor can type in; you can include a message like "Please limit your feedback to under 300 letters" and either tally up the number of characters your guest enters or count down the number to zero (Figure 12-21).

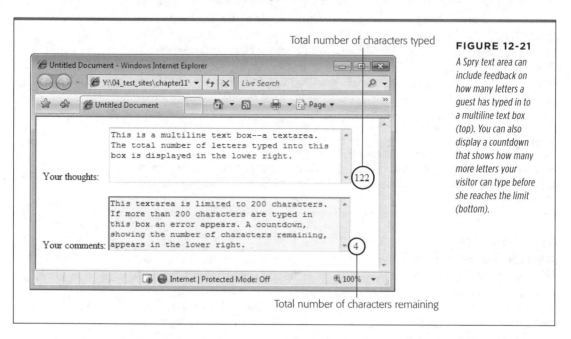

Total number of characters typed

FIGURE 12-21

A Spry text area can include feedback on how many letters a guest has typed in to a multiline text box (top). You can also display a countdown that shows how many more letters your visitor can type before she reaches the limit (bottom).

Total number of characters remaining

Both of these counters are helpful, but neither gives your guest a context for the number: 300? 300 what? Letters remaining, or letters already typed into the box? To add a clarifying message next to the number, you have to go into Code view. The best way to add the message is to select the text area field in Design view, click the Code or Split view button, and then find a <span> tag that looks something like *<span id="countsprytextarea2"> </span>*. In this example, "sprytextarea2" is the Spry widget's name. You must add your message either before or after the <span> tag, but not *inside* it. For a text area with the "Chars remaining" option turned on, you could change the code above to:

```
<span id="countsprytextarea2"> </span> characters remaining
```

This way, a visitor sees something like "300 characters remaining," as he types his message in the text box.

Spry Checkbox

The Spry checkbox validation lets you make sure that a visitor turns on a checkbox, an especially handy tool for those ubiquitous "I agree to your rules and conditions" disclaimers. In addition, you can add several checkboxes as a group, and require that your visitor select a minimum number of options ("Please make at least two choices") or a maximum number ("Please choose no more than two").

To add a single Spry checkbox, choose Insert→Form→Spry Validation Checkbox, or, in the Insert panel's Forms category, click the Spry Validation Checkbox button (Figure 12-22). The Spry checkbox that appears on the page already has the Required option selected in the Property Inspector. If you want just a single checkbox, you're done. But beyond the kind of "You must turn on this checkbox to free us from all legal responsibility" scenario, a single, required checkbox isn't so useful. After all, checkboxes more commonly come in groups as part of a multiple-choice question.

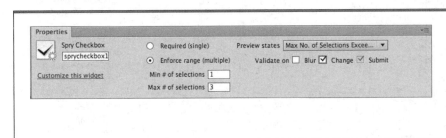

FIGURE 12-22

Use the Spry Validation Checkbox widget to make sure your site visitors turn on a checkbox (in cases where you want that to happen, of course).

Unfortunately, Dreamweaver doesn't include a simple "Add a group of Spry checkboxes" tool. If you insert several Spry checkboxes in a row, Dreamweaver creates a Spry widget for each one and JavaScript validates each box separately, rather than as a group. Nor can you insert a bunch of regular checkboxes, select them all, and then apply the Spry Validation Checkbox to them.

To create a group of related Spry checkboxes, you need to either go into Code view or execute a delicate keyboard dance to get all the code just right. If you want to stay in Design view, here's a way to insert a group of checkboxes that JavaScript validates simultaneously:

1. **Insert a Spry checkbox.**

    Use either the Insert→Form menu or the Insert toolbar. Dreamweaver inserts a checkbox with the familiar blue Spry tab. Add a label in the text field to the right of the checkbox (you can use the Input Tag Accessibility Attributes window described on page 571). Now, say you want to add another checkbox to the right of the one you just inserted.

2. **Click anywhere in the label text and then click <label> in the tag selector at the bottom of the document window (see top image in Figure 12-23).**

    In Code view or Split view, Dreamweaver highlights the current label. Your goal is to make sure your cursor is *outside* the <label> tag for the current checkbox. If you simply click to the right of the label and insert the next checkbox, one of two (bad) things can happen: You insert another checkbox inside the first checkbox's <label> tag—when this happens, Dreamweaver gets really confused and omits a <label> tag for the new checkbox. Or you insert the checkbox outside the Spry widget, meaning the new checkbox won't be validated along with the first checkbox.

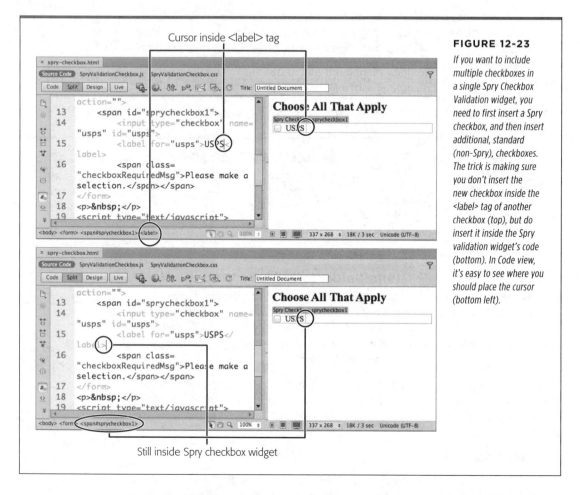

FIGURE 12-23

If you want to include multiple checkboxes in a single Spry Checkbox Validation widget, you need to first insert a Spry checkbox, and then insert additional, standard (non-Spry), checkboxes. The trick is making sure you don't insert the new checkbox inside the <label> tag of another checkbox (top), but do insert it inside the Spry validation widget's code (bottom). In Code view, it's easy to see where you should place the cursor (bottom left).

3. **Press the right arrow key until the <label> tag disappears from the tag selector at the bottom of the document window, but you still see something like <span#sprycheckbox1> (Figure 12-23, bottom).**

   When you no longer see <label> in the tag selector, your cursor is outside the label and you can insert another checkbox. The <span#sprycheckbox1> tag identifies the tag responsible for the Spry checkbox widget. As long as you see that in the tag selector, the next checkbox you insert receives Spry validation.

4. **Insert a *regular* (non-Spry) checkbox as described on page 576.**

   The cursor is already inside a Spry checkbox widget, so you don't want to insert another Spry checkbox.

5. **Repeat steps 2–4 to insert as many checkboxes as you need.**

    As long as you insert the checkboxes inside the Spry widget, they'll be part of the validation process.

TIP If you want to put each checkbox in its own paragraph, change the <span> tag that the Spry checkbox validation widget uses to a <div> tag. According to the rules of HTML, you can't wrap a <span> tag around block-level elements like a paragraph. Go into Code view, locate the opening span tag (it should look something like *<span id="sprycheckbox1">*), and change *span* to *div*. Then locate the closing tag, </span>, and change it to </div>.

---

6. **Click the blue Spry tab to select the widget; in the Property Inspector, select the "Enforce range" button, and then, in the "Min # of selections" and the "Max # of selections" fields, type *numbers* (see Figure 12-22).**

    You don't have to fill out both the Min and Max fields. If you have a question like "What type of food do you like (select as many as apply)," you might choose 1 for "Min # of selections" but leave the Max field blank. That way, you require at least one choice, but your visitor can choose as many other options as she wants.

    Or, you might have a question like "Select your four favorite foods." In this case, you'd type *4* in the Max field if you don't want more than four answers. (You could also type *4* in the Min field if you want to make sure you get exactly four choices.)

Spry Select

The Spry Validation Select widget validates the choices in pull-down menus, and has two options to determine whether or not a menu selection is valid (see Figure 12-24). Remember that a pull-down menu (which Dreamweaver creates using the <select> tag) consists of a label and a value (see page 581). The label is what someone sees when he makes a selection from the menu, and the value is what the browser sends over the Internet when it submits the form.

With a Spry menu, if a guest makes no selection, or if she makes an invalid selection, you can prevent JavaScript from submitting the form and have it display an error message instead. Say you have a menu listing all the months of the year. The label is the month's name and its value is a number (see Figure 12-11). Suppose you added "Please select a month" as the first item in the menu. This common technique lets visitors know that the menu's a list of months they should select from. Of course, when the browser submits the form, you want it to send the value for a month and *not* "Please select a month."

NOTE Although Dreamweaver inserts a pull-down menu when you add a Spry Validation Select widget, you can convert the menu to a list menu, as described on page 581. The same validation options apply.

To make sure this is the case, leave the value for "Please select a month" blank and, in the "Do not allow" section of the Property Inspector, turn on "Blank value" (see Figure 12-24).

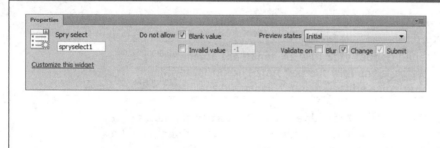

FIGURE 12-24

Clicking the "Customize this widget" link that appears when you select a Spry widget launches a web browser and accesses documentation on help .adobe.com that tells you which CSS styles affect the appearance of the widget. You can use this information to edit the supplied widget styles so that they match the look of your site.

Sometimes a label and a value are the same. For example, on a menu with a list of years ("In what year were you born?"), the label ("1967") is the same as the value ("1967"). In cases like this, it would be frustrating to have to set both the label and value for each menu item. Fortunately, you don't have to. As you read on page 582, a label doesn't require a value, and if you don't specify a value, the web browser submits the label *as* the value.

If you have a list without values, the "Blank value" validation option won't work. After all, even valid selections (the selected label) won't have a value explicitly set. In cases like this, use the "Invalid value" option in the Property Inspector to ensure that the form gets submitted. Here's how you set this option up: First, identify the invalid selection(s). There's just one in the example above, the label at the top of the menu ("Please select a month"). Assign an arbitrary value to the illegitimate selection(s). In this case, assign a value of -1 to "Please select a month." Then select the Spry widget and, in the Property Inspector, turn on the checkbox for "Invalid value" and enter -1 in the field next to it (see Figure 12-24). Should a guest select "Please select a month" from the list, JavaScript recognizes its value as invalid and prevents the form from winging its way to your server. (If this sounds confusing, you'll find a hands-on example in the tutorial on page 618.)

NOTE If your form menu has a long list of options, you might add a separator (like a row of hyphens, ---------) as a label, to demarcate groups of options. You could either forego assigning a value to that separator and use the "Blank value" validation option, or assign it an invalid value (like −1) and use the "Invalid value" setting. Now, if someone accidentally selects the separator, she can't submit the form.

Spry Password

A password like "sesame," "password," or "bob" isn't very secure. Any hacker with a dictionary (or access to an infinite number of monkeys) can easily infiltrate a password-protected web page or gain access to someone's personal information. If you ever add a signup form that requires someone to come up with a password, use Dreamweaver's Spry Password widget. This helpful tool lets you enforce a set of rules for password names so that visitors don't create easily hacked credentials. For example, you can say that a password must be at least eight characters long, have at least three numbers, and contain a minimum of two uppercase letters. This kind of password-naming strategy means visitors have to come up with hard-to-crack passwords like AB3859kirl.

NOTE Use the Spry Password widget only for forms where a visitor creates a password. Don't use it for a form where a visitor logs in with an already created password. After all, there's no point in telling a visitor that she needs a certain number of letters or numbers in her password if she already has a valid password.

To add a Spry password field, click the area in the form where you want to add the field, and then, on the Insert panel's Forms category, select the Spry Validation Password button or choose Insert→Form→Spry Validation Password. Then, just as with any form field you insert, the Input Tag Accessibility window opens; follow steps 3–5 on page 571–573 to insert the field.

NOTE If you want to turn an already existing text field in a form into a Spry password field, you first need to make sure the password option is turned on for that field (see page 575). Then select the field and click the Spry Validation Password button in the Insert Panel or choose Insert→Form→Spry Validation Password.

Once inserted, the password field has a blue Spry Password tab, and the Property Inspector shows the options for validating the field (see Figure 12-25). Since one of the goals of a good password is to make it hard to figure out, the validation options for the password widget try to enforce a pattern that's essentially a random collection of numbers, letter, and characters. The Min and Max characters options let you specify the length of a password. You can set either or both of these options, but at the very least, you should specify a minimum number of characters—8 is a solid amount—so that no one creates an easily hacked password like 1, A, or A1.

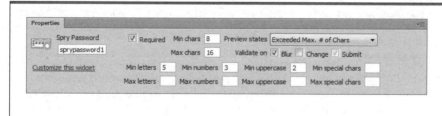

FIGURE 12-25

Use Dreamweaver's Spry Password Validation widget to make sure that new visitors create a suitably random and difficult-to-crack password for your site.

In addition, you can specify the *types* of characters visitors must include in their password. For example, you might decide that passwords should have at least four letters, two numbers, and one special character (like an exclamation point). That rule would make a password like ABCDE38! valid, but wouldn't let someone create a password like ABCDEFGH or 12345678. You can even dictate that passwords have a certain number of uppercase letters as well, just to mix things up. For example, say you type *6* in the "Min letters" box; if you do that, a valid password must have at least six letters in it. But to make sure there's a good mix of upper- and lowercase letters, you could set the "Min uppercase" value to 2, and the "Max uppercase" value to 4. That way, a visitor has to include at least a few uppercase and lowercase letters in his password.

Depending on which validation options you select for the password widget, you can customize up to four error messages: the "Required" message, which your page displays when a visitor leaves the password field blank and tries to submit the form; the "Min # of characters" message that appears when you specify a value in the "Min chars" box and your guest uses fewer characters; the "Max # of characters" message that appears when your visitor exceeds the specified number; and, finally, the "Invalid strength" message that appears if a guest types in a password that doesn't match the options you set ("Min letters" or "Min numbers," for example).

The "Invalid strength" error message that Dreamweaver supplies—"The password doesn't meet the specified strength"—doesn't really tell your visitor what he did wrong. So either change this message to something like "Please type a password that's at least 8 characters long and that contains letters, numbers, and at least one special character, like a period, question mark, or exclamation point" or, even better, provide those instructions on the form to begin with. That way, a visitor won't waste his time trying to decode the runes of your password requirements. (See step 6 on page 593 for instructions on editing Spry form validation error messages.)

Spry Confirm

The Spry Confirm validation widget comes in handy when you want to make sure someone correctly enters important information. For example, if you create a form for people to sign up for your email newsletter, you want to make sure they give you the correct email address. One way to do that is to have a visitor enter the same information twice, by adding a second field that asks her to type in her address again.

NOTE You can also use this double-checking maneuver with a "Create a password" field. A password field displays what the visitor types as dots or asterisks, so it's easy to make a mistake without ever realizing it. Adding a second, confirmation field can help make sure the visitor gets it right.

The Spry Confirm widget works only with text fields, and displays an error message if the value in one text field doesn't match the value in another text field. To use this widget, first add a text field—either a Spry text field, a Spry password field, or just a regular text field. That field is the original "Type your email" or "Create a password" box. Next, from the Insert panel's Forms category, add the Spry Confirm widget or choose Insert→Form→Spry Validation Confirm. (It's best to put this field directly after the original field, and use a label like "Please confirm your password.")

The options for a Spry Confirm widget are simple (see Figure 12-26). From the "Validate against" menu, simply select the name of the field you're comparing. For example, say you add a Spry Password validation widget, and you name that field *password1*. When you insert the Spry Confirm field, select *password1* in the Property Inspector's "Validate against" menu. Then, when someone fills out the form, she must type a password in the *password1* field. That password becomes *password1*'s value. Then, in the confirmation field, she types the same password. The Spry Confirm widget compares the two values. If they're different, the widget displays an error message, letting the visitor know she made a typo.

FIGURE 12-26

If the field you're comparing against is required, make sure you turn on the Required box for the confirmation field as well. Since the information is so important that you need a second field to confirm it, odds are that it's required anyway, so you almost always leave the Required box checked.

Spry Radio Group

Sometimes you want to make sure a visitor selects a radio button before she submits a form. For example, say you have an e-commerce site and you collect shipping information from a customer. For the shipping method, you want the customer to select either USPS, FedEx, or UPS. Since visitors have to choose a delivery method in order for you to ship a package, it's a good idea to make sure they click one of the radio buttons before submitting the form. This is where the Spry Radio Group comes in handy. Essentially, it's just like the radio group described on page 580, except that it displays an error message if a guest tries to submit the form without selecting a button.

To add a Spry Radio Group, use the Insert panel's Forms category or choose Insert→Form→Spry Validation Radio Group. The process is the same as inserting a regular radio group or a checkbox group. Once you add the group of buttons to a page, use the Property Inspector to set the validation options (see Figure 12-27). Dreamweaver gives you several ways to validate a radio group, but only one is really useful: The Required checkbox simply means that a radio button must be selected (and it doesn't matter which one).

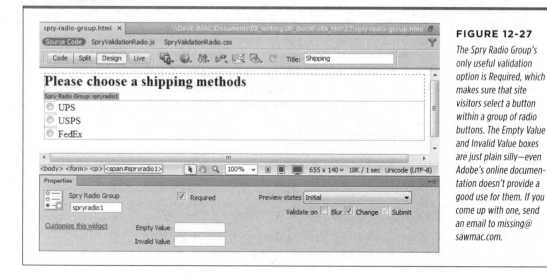

FIGURE 12-27

The Spry Radio Group's only useful validation option is Required, which makes sure that site visitors select a button within a group of radio buttons. The Empty Value and Invalid Value boxes are just plain silly—even Adobe's online documentation doesn't provide a good use for them. If you come up with one, send an email to missing@ sawmac.com.

The other two options—Empty Value and Invalid Value—produce error messages should a visitor select a radio button that you specify. In either of the boxes beside these options, enter the same value you used when you created the buttons. If a guest selects a button with the specified value, he sees one of two error messages when he tries to submit the form. In the case of Empty Value, the error message tells the visitor that he *hasn't* made a selection (huh?); and for the Invalid Value, the error message announces that the choice he made was invalid. Neither of these options seem like they would ever be useful. After all, do you really want to display an error message when someone clicks a radio button that says, in effect, "Ha, ha, you fool, you just released the hounds!"

■ Forms Tutorial

In this tutorial, you'll build a simple reservation form for Cafe Soylent Green's website (skip ahead to Figure 12-38 if you want to see the final result). To make sure the folks at the Cafe get all the information they need to book a reservation, you'll use Spry form validation tools.

NOTE To complete this tutorial, you need to download the practice files from *www.sawmac.com*. See the Note on page 54 for more details.

Once you download the tutorial files, open Dreamweaver and define a new site as described on page 40. Name the site *Forms*, and then select the Chapter12 folder (inside the MM_DWCS6 folder). (In a nutshell: Choose Site→New Site. In the Site

Definition window, type *Forms* into the Site Name field, click the folder icon next to the Local Site Folder field, navigate to and select the Chapter12 folder, and then click Choose or Select. Finally, click OK.)

Insert a Form and Add a Form Field

The first step in building a form is inserting a <form> tag. This tag will enclose all the fields within a form, and indicates where the form begins and ends. As noted earlier in this chapter, you can insert other HTML elements into the form, too, like text elements and <div> tags.

1. **Choose File→Open.** Double-click the file *reservation.html* in the Chapter12 folder to open it.

    If you have the Files panel open (Window→Files), just double-click *reservation.html*. The page is partly designed, with a banner, sidebar, and footer.

2. **Click the empty white space directly below the headline "Make a Reservation."** On the Insert panel, select the Forms category (see Figure 12-2).

    Alternatively, if you're using Dreamweaver's Classic view, described on page 38, or have docked the Insert panel to the top of the workspace (as pictured in Figure 12-28), click the Forms category to view form object buttons.

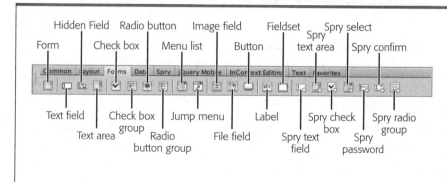

FIGURE 12-28

Normally, the Insert panel appears on the right of the screen, along with Dreamweaver's other panels (Files, CSS Styles, and so on). But if you choose the Classic workspace layout as described on page 38, the Insert panel becomes this Insert bar and sits across the top of the screen. Click the Forms tab to see all the form objects. If your monitor is wide enough (most are), the Classic view is usually the better way to go—it frees up space on the right side of your monitor for the CSS and Files panels.

3. **Click the Form button in the Insert panel's Forms category, or choose Insert→Form→Form.**

   A red, dashed rectangle appears in the document window, indicating the boundaries of the form.

4. **In the Property Inspector's Form ID field, type *reservation* (see Figure 12-29).**

   You just added an ID to your form.

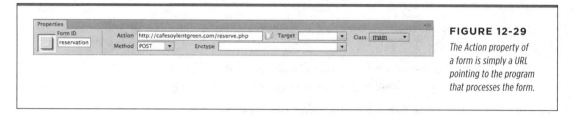

FIGURE 12-29

The Action property of a form is simply a URL pointing to the program that processes the form.

5. **In the Action field, type *http://cafesoylentgreen.com/reserve.php*.**

   Leave off the period after the URL in the sentence above (we added it to make our copy editors happy).

   A form's Action property identifies the Internet address of the program that processes the form. In this case, you've been spared the effort of writing (or hiring a programmer to write) the required form-processing software. That program already exists on the website whose address you just typed in, and it's waiting to process the form you're about to design.

6. **In the Method field, make sure you see POST selected.** Leave the Target and Enctype fields blank.

   The Method specifies how a form sends information to a form-processing program, and the POST option is the most common (see page 568).

   Now you're ready to insert a text field.

7. **In the document window, click inside the form—anywhere within the red dashed lines.** On the Insert panel, click the Text Field button or choose Insert→Form→Text Field.

   Dreamweaver displays the Input Tag Accessibility window (see Figure 12-30). If you don't see it, choose Edit→Undo to remove the text field you just inserted, use Dreamweaver's Preferences window to turn on the accessibility options for form objects as described in Figure 12-5, and then repeat this step.

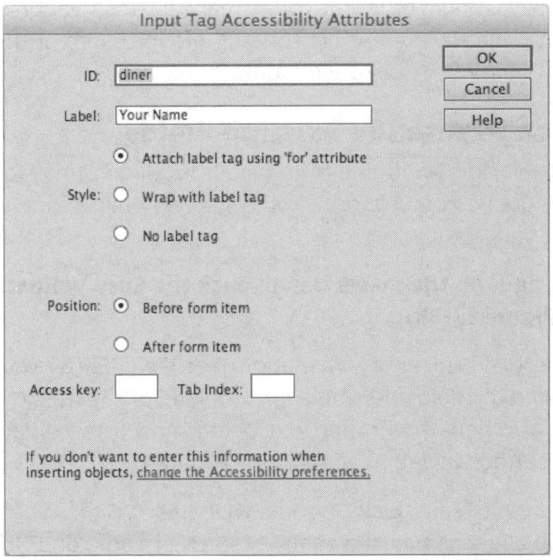

FIGURE 12-30

If you don't see the Input Tag Accessibility Attribute window when you insert a new form field, you (or someone using your computer) may have turned this feature off. To turn it back on, choose Edit→Preferences (Dreamweaver→Preferences on Macs); select the Accessibility category in the Preferences window, and make sure the "Form objects" box is checked.

8. **In the ID box, type *diner*.**

   Dreamweaver adds the name you type ("diner" here) to both the *name* and *ID* properties of the field's HTML. The form-processing program uses the *name* property to connect an ID with the value a visitor types in, in this case his name. When a guest types his name into the text field, the form-processing program receives information in what's called a name/value pair (*diner=Bob*, for instance; see page 563 for details).

   The ID uniquely identifies the form element. If you want, you can create an ID style to format this particular form field—for example, to assign a width or background color to this one field. Next, you'll add a label for the name field.

9. **In the Label box, type *Your name* and select "Attach label tag using 'for' attribute."** Then select the "Before form item" button.

   The window should now look like the one in Figure 12-30.

10. **Click OK to insert the text field.**

    The label and text field appear side-by-side on the page. The label's text resides inside the HTML <label> tag (page 587). Now you'll add another text field.

11. **Click to the right of the rectangular text box you just added and hit Enter (Return) to create a new line.** Repeat steps 7–10 to insert a new text field. Use the ID "email" and "Your email address" for the label.

Now you have two text boxes. But in order for you to make the reservation and confirm it with your patron, he *must* enter his contact info into both of these boxes—a perfect application for the Spry validation widgets.

Adding Spry Validation to Already Existing Fields

Fortunately, you don't have to decide whether a form field is required or has to be submitted in a certain way before you build a form. You can freely build a form and then later decide you need to validate it.

1. **Click the first text field and, on the Insert panel, click the Spry Validation Text Field button (see Figure 12-28).**

Alternatively, choose Insert→Form→Spry Validation Text Field. Either way, a blue outline appears around the field and a blue tab labeled Spry TextField appears above the field. In addition, the Property Inspector now lists validation settings for this newly inserted validation widget (see Figure 12-31).

The people at the café aren't really picky about what their visitor types in here—for example, they'll allow names like Jenny Stadler, or Omicron 9 from *@^$(&!(%^. However, they do require at least *some* name for the day of the reservation—"Omicron 9, your table is ready!" So you don't need a validation type or format for this field, but you will make one change.

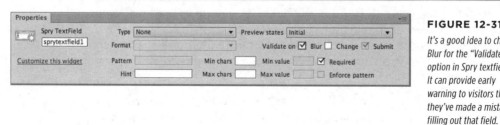

FIGURE 12-31

It's a good idea to choose Blur for the "Validate on" option in Spry textfields. It can provide early warning to visitors that they've made a mistake filling out that field.

2. **On the right side of the Property Inspector, check the "Blur" option for the "Validate on" setting.**

As mentioned on page 591, by setting "Validate on" to Blur for text boxes, the Spry JavaScript programming checks to make sure your guest has entered something into the box the moment they go anywhere else on the page. In other words, if a visitor clicks into the field and then immediately clicks outside of it without typing anything, they'll see an error message saying that they need to enter a "value." Next, you'll customize this error message.

3. **In the Property Inspector, choose Required from the "Preview states" menu (circled in Figure 12-32) to display the error message.** Select the text "A value is required," but don't delete it (see the Note below). Instead, type "Please type your name" in place of the selected text.

   The page should now look like Figure 12-32, right.

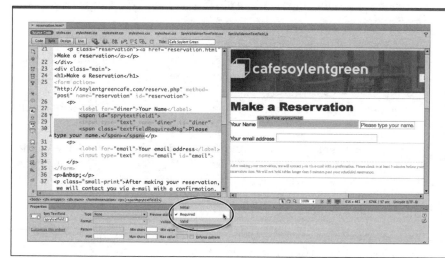

FIGURE 12-32

A Spry validation widget's "Preview states" option lets you see the error messages that appear if a visitor incorrectly fills out a form. With the error message visible in Design view, you can select and edit it.

> **NOTE**   When you replace the error message in step 3, don't delete the "A value is required" message before you type in the new one. If you do, you might accidentally delete the <span> tag responsible for making the error message work. As an added precaution, select all the text except for the period after the words "A value is required and then type in the new message." It's not common, but occasionally, if you select all the text, Dreamweaver actually deletes the <span> tag as well, breaking the validation widget.

4. **Choose File→Save.**

   Dreamweaver opens the Copy Dependent Files dialog box, letting you know the page now requires both a style sheet file and a JavaScript file for the new Spry Validation field.

5. **Click OK to close the Copy Dependent Files window.**

   If you look at the Files panel, you'll see a folder named SpryAssets (you may need to hit the refresh button in the Files panel), which Dreamweaver created and where it just saved the two new files (you can tell Dreamweaver to save those files in a different folder, as described in the Tip on page 215).

6. **Repeat steps 1 and 2 to add Spry validation to the email field.**

   Now, a visitor will also have to fill out this field before submitting the form. However, to make sure the visitor's entry looks like a real email address, you'll specify a validation type.

7. **With the Spry validation widget still selected, choose Email Address from the Property Inspector's Type menu.**

   You'll notice that an error message—"Invalid format"—appears on the page. This is the message that will appear when a visitor enters something incorrectly formatted ("blah" instead of jordan@yahoo.com, for example).

8. **In Design view, select the text "Invalid format" and type *Please type a valid email address*.**

   Spry validation widgets can, and often do, have more than one error message. For example, every required field includes an "A value is required" error message. But specifying a validation format, like an email address, adds another error message—"Invalid format." Multiple error messages let you craft messages specific to each type of error. You'll change the required error message for the email address now.

9. **Mouse over the email address form field and click the blue Spry Validation Textfield label to select the widget.** In the Property Inspector, choose Required from the "Preview states" menu (circled in Figure 12-32) to display another error message. Select the text "A value is required," and type *Please* type your email address.

   There are other types of form fields besides text boxes. In the next section you'll add a menu, radio buttons, and a Submit button.

Adding a Spry Validation Widget

You don't have to insert a regular form field and then convert it into a Spry validation field. If you haven't yet created a form, it's a lot easier to simply add a form field with Spry validation in one step.

1. **Click to the right of the error message for the email address field, and press Enter (Return) to create a new empty paragraph.** In the Forms panel click the Spry validation select button.

   The Input Tag Accessibility Attributes window appears.

2. **Type *diners* in the ID field, and *Number in party* for the label field.** Click OK to insert the field.

   Dreamweaver inserts a drop-down menu. The blue tab, which reads "Spry select: spryselect1," tells you that this form field is a Spry validation widget.

3. **Choose File→Save.**

   The Copy Dependent Files window appears again. Since this is a new type of validation widget, there are separate CSS and JavaScript files to control its look and behavior.

4. **Click OK to close the Copy Dependent Files window.** Click the Spry drop-down menu widget to select it.

   Remember that the form field and the Spry widget are separate items, and have separate controls in the Property Inspector. To control the validation, you select the widget (click the blue tab), but to alter the field—to add items to the drop down menu, for example—you must select the form field itself.

5. **Click the List Values button in the Property Inspector.**

   The List Values window appears (Figure 12-33). Here you'll add items to the menu.

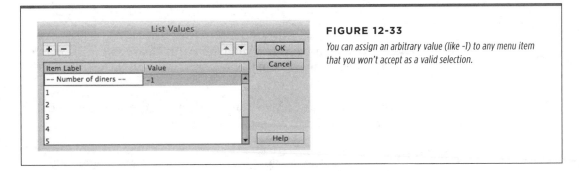

FIGURE 12-33

You can assign an arbitrary value (like -1) to any menu item that you won't accept as a valid selection.

6. **Click inside the field under Item Label and type** *-- Number of diners --*, **press the Tab key, and then type** *-1* **in the Value field.**

   The text ("--Number of diners --") will appear at the top of the drop-down menu. It's an instruction telling your visitor what to do. Of course, you want your guest to choose an option *other* than this text. If he does select it, the -1 serves as a kind of secret message that flags the Spry validation program that this option isn't valid. Before you get to that, though, add the valid selections to this form.

7. **Press the Tab key, and then type** *1*; **press the Tab key twice to create another list option, and then type** *2*. Continue adding options until you get to *7*, then add one last entry, *8+* (or until you've got the hang of adding menu items).

   The List Values window should look like Figure 12-33.

8. **Click OK to insert the menu.** Move your mouse over the menu, and then click the blue Spry tab to select it.

   You need to specify invalid menu selections.

9. **In the Property Inspector, turn off the "Blank value" box, turn on the "In-valid value" box, and then make sure** *-1* **appears in the field.** Then turn on the Change checkbox.

   The Property Inspector should look like Figure 12-34. Time to change the error message.

10. From the Property Inspector's "Preview states" menu, select Invalid.

In the document window, to the right of the form menu, you should see this red error message: "Please select a valid item."

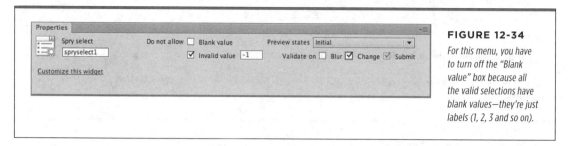

FIGURE 12-34

For this menu, you have to turn off the "Blank value" box because all the valid selections have blank values—they're just labels (1, 2, 3 and so on).

11. Replace the text *Please select a valid item* with *Please select the number in your party*. Click to the right of that error message and hit Enter (Return) to create a new paragraph.

Now you'll add two more Spry validation widgets to collect the date and time the visitor wishes to dine at the café.

> **NOTE** When you add a new paragraph after a Spry validation widget, make sure you're outside of that widget when you hit the Enter (Return) key. If you have the insertion point inside the error message and you press Enter (Return), Dreamweaver just inserts a line break (
 tag) within the error message. Anything you type at this point will simply be part of that error message. In Design view, just click to the right of the error message before hitting Enter (Return).

12. From the Insert panel's Spry category, click the Spry Validation Text Field button.

The Input Tag Accessibility Attributes window appears again.

13. Type *date* for the ID, and *Date* for the label. Click OK.

Dreamweaver inserts a new text field with Spry validation. Now you'll customize the validation settings to accept only a date.

14. From the Type menu in the Property Inspector, choose Date.

The date format requires a visitor to fill out the form with a properly formatted date. But which format is proper? You specify that with the format menu.

15. From the Format menu, select mm/dd/yyyy.

As discussed on page 597, you can format dates many ways. In this case, the café is looking for dates formatted like 1/29/2022.

16. Check the Blur and "Enforce pattern" boxes in the Property Inspector.

You checked Blur for the other text fields on the page so that the Spry widget checked to make sure your visitor typed something into the field as soon as she tabs away from it or clicks outside of the field. The "Enforce pattern" box limits the characters she can type in. For example, if you want dates formatted like 1/29/2022, you don't want anyone typing in "today" or "January 29th of the year 2022." In such a case, the "Enforce pattern" box limits what your visitor can type to numbers. In fact, the Spry widget is smart enough to automatically add the date format's forward slashes for the visitor.

Because a visitor won't know exactly what date format you're after, it's a good idea to add a hint.

17. **In the Hint box, type *1/29/2022*.**

    The Property Inspector should now look like Figure 12-35.

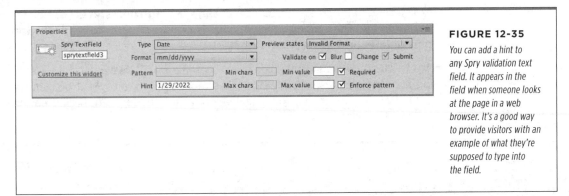

FIGURE 12-35

You can add a hint to any Spry validation text field. It appears in the field when someone looks at the page in a web browser. It's a good way to provide visitors with an example of what they're supposed to type into the field.

18. **Using the "Preview states" menu, select Invalid Format, and, in the document window, change the error message from "Invalid format" to "Please type a date like 1/29/2022."** Click the blue Spry widget tab, select Required from the "Preview states" menu, and edit the error message to say "Please type a date for your reservation."

    If you're still not sure how to edit error messages, turn to page 593 for a refresher. Now you'll add one last text field.

19. **Click to the right of the error message for the text field you just added.** Hit Enter (Return) to create a new paragraph.

    Follow steps 12–13 on page 620 to create another Spry validation text field. This time, use time for the ID, and "Time of reservation" for the label. Now you'll set some options for the widget in the Property Inspector.

20. **Follow steps 14–17 on page 620–621: choose Time from the Type menu, "hh:mm tt" from the Format menu, and type 12:30 PM in the Hint box.**

    The Property Inspector should look like Figure 12-36. The last thing to do is change the error messages.

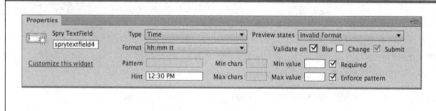

FIGURE 12-36

Dreamweaver lets you use many time formats, like 24-hour time (18:00). Whichever you choose, add a hint so your visitor knows how to type in the information.

21. **Repeat step 18 on page 621: change the "Invalid format" message to "Please type a time like 1:30 PM"; likewise, change the "Preview states" option to Required and then change the "A value is required" error to read "Please type a time for your reservation."**

At this point, the page should look like Figure 12-37. You're almost done building the form; you just need to add some radio buttons, a big text box, and a Submit button. After that, you'll tackle formatting the form so that it's easier to read and fill out.

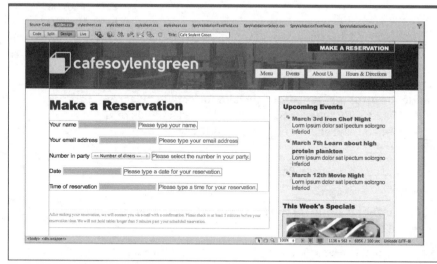

FIGURE 12-37

There's a lot of room for improving the look of this form. The fields are staggered, creating a hard-to-read form, and the error messages are a little intense. Don't worry, with a little CSS magic, you can redesign the form to be beautiful and more functional.

Adding a Group of Radio Buttons

When you want a visitor to select one option among many, as with a multiple-choice question, a group of radio buttons is the perfect solution.

1. **Click to the right of the error message for the last field in the form (the reservation time), and press Enter (Return) to create a new paragraph.** Type *Location preference*: in that paragraph.

   You'll be adding three radio buttons. Each will have its own label, but it's a good idea to add some text that identifies what the buttons are for. In this case, your visitor will choose a preferred location in the café (for example, at the bar or at a romantic corner table).

2. **In the Insert panel's Forms category, click the Radio Button icon (Figure 12-38).**

   The familiar Input Tag Accessibility Attributes window appears.

   Make sure you select the regular Radio Button here, not the Spry Validation Radio Group.

3. **Type *anywhere* in the ID field, "Anywhere is fine" in the label, and click the OK button.**

   Dreamweaver inserts a radio button on the page. You'll set a couple of preferences for the button next.

4. **Click the radio button to select it and in the Property Inspector type *location* in the Radio button name field, and check the Checked button (see Figure 12-38).**

   While Dreamwaver names all other form fields using the ID you supply in the Input Tag Accessibility Attributes window, it treats radio buttons differently. Usually, radio buttons travel in groups so a visitor can select one option among several. For a browser to treat related radio buttons as a single group, you must give each button in the group the same name. Here, you named the button *location*. You'll insert two more buttons and give them the same name.

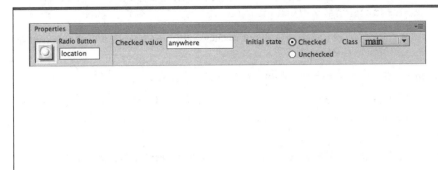

FIGURE 12-38

Selecting the Checked option for a radio button ensures that the button is pre-selected. In other words, if you want one button in a group of buttons to be the default, set its initial state to Checked. The same strategy works for checkboxes.

5. **Click to the right of the "Anywhere is fine" label, and repeat steps 2 and 3 above: type *bar* for the ID, and "At the bar" for the label.**

    Because this radio button is in a group with the "Anywhere is fine" button, it needs to share the same name.

6. **Select the radio button you just inserted and, in the Property Inspector, change its name from "radio" to "location."**

    You need to add one last button to complete the set.

7. **Add another radio button to the right of the "At the bar" label: use *corner* for the ID and "Corner table" for the label.**

    Make sure you name this button *location* so that it gets grouped with the other two buttons.

Adding a Multiline Text Box

To retrieve more than a single line of text—to receive a lengthy comment, complaint, recommendation, or movie review, for example—you should turn to a multiline text field (also called a Textarea in HTML).

1. **Click to the right of the "Corner table" label for the last radio button.** Hit Enter (Return) to create a new paragraph, and then click the Spry Validation Textarea button on the Insert panel (see Figure 12-28).

    The Input Tag Accessibility Attributes window appears.

2. **Type *comments* for the ID, and "Any comments or requests?"** for the label. Click OK to insert the Spry widget. Choose File→Save.

    The Copy Dependent Files window appears again. Since this textarea differs from a text field or a radio button, you need to add new CSS and JavaScript files.

3. **Click OK to close the Copy Dependent Files window, and click the blue Spry tab for the widget you just inserted.**

    As with all Spry widgets, you have to click the blue tab to select it and change its settings in the Property Inspector.

4. **In the Property Inspector, uncheck the Required box.**

    A visitor requesting a reservation isn't required to supply a comment or request, so you'll make this box optional. However, there are a few other useful options available to a Spry Validation Textarea.

5. **Type *300* in the Property Inspector's "Max chars" box, select the "Chars remaining" button, and then type *Please type no more than 300 characters* in the hint box.**

    The Property Inspector should look like Figure 12-39. These settings limit the amount of text a visitor can type into the text box. There's no way to do that with regular HTML, but you can use the JavaScript power of this Spry widget.

The hint box works just like the text hints you supplied for the date and time fields—it prints a message in the textarea box. Finally, the "Chars remaining" option provides a helpful counter to inform someone filling out the form how many more characters they can type in until they reach the limit you set. Unfortunately, Dreamweaver displays only a number, like 300, without any context for it; you'll remedy that next.

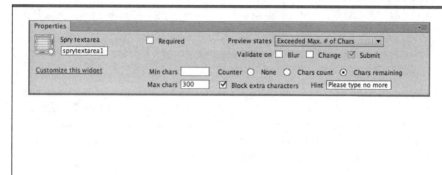

FIGURE 12-39

Selecting the Checked option for a radio button (and checkbox also) makes sure that button is pre-selected. In other words, in a group of radio buttons, if you want one button to be the default option, then set its "Initial state" to "Checked."

6. **If you're not already viewing the document in Split (Code and Design) view, click Split in the Document toolbar.**

   Alternatively, you can choose Window→Code and Design. In either case, you'll see the page's code and design side by side, as in Figure 12-40.

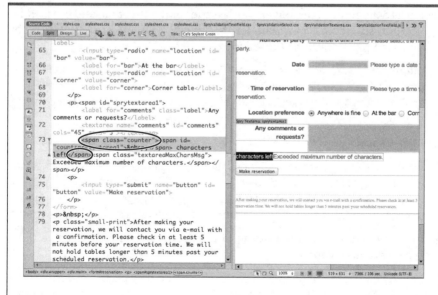

FIGURE 12-40

The <span id= "countsprytextarea1"> </span> code indicates the spot where the JavaScript programming will write the number of characters left. You don't want to put your message there, because JavaScript essentially deletes what's inside that span each time a visitor types in the box. Placing the "characters remaining" text just outside that <span> assures that the text will appear right next to the updating number of characters.

7. **In Design view, click the blue Spry tab for the textarea.**

You'll see the corresponding HTML selected in Code view. First, you'll move the character counter down below the text box.

8. **In the highlighted section in Code view, find and select** *<span id="countsp rytextarea1"> </span>* **and then press Ctrl+T (⌘-T) to open the quick tag editor (page 361).** Type *<span class="counter">* and hit Enter (Return). This wraps the selected <span> tag in a new <span> tag (circled in Figure 12-40).

Why wrap this in another <span>? So that a browser treats the counter and the text you're about to add as a single unit that you can style with CSS (which you'll do later in this tutorial)

The goal now is to add the words "characters left" so that visitors will see a message like "300 characters left" next to the text box. As a guest types, that message changes—"299 characters left," and so on—to reflect how many more characters he can type until he reaches the limit for the text box. The trick is figuring out where to place that text.

9. **Position your cursor between the two closing </span> tags in <span class="counter"><span id="countsprytextarea1"> </span></span>.** Type a space character followed by *characters left*.

See Figure 12-40 to see what your code should now look like. Finally, you'll see that Dreamweaver includes an error message when you set the "Max chars" option for a Spry textarea. You're almost done; you just need to add a Submit button.

10. **Click to the right of the red error message for the text area and press Enter (Return) to create a new paragraph.** Choose Insert→Form→Button or, on the Insert panel, click the Button icon (see Figure 12-28).

Alternatively, you can choose Insert→Form→Button. Either way, your old friend the Input Tag Accessibility window appears. This time, however, you don't need an ID or label. Buttons (like Submit) already have a message printed on them, so you don't need to add a label.

11. **Click Cancel.**

In the Input Tag Accessibility window, clicking Cancel doesn't actually cancel the process of inserting a form field—it just skips the steps for providing an ID and label for the field. A Submit button appears on the page. You can change the generic "Submit" message to something more reflective of the form's purpose.

12. **In Design view, click the button; in the Property Inspector's Value field, type *Make reservation*.**

You're done building the form. Save the page and preview it in a web browser (for example, choose File→"Preview in Browser" and select a browser, or press the F12 key [Option-F12] to launch your preferred browser). The form should look like Figure 12-41.

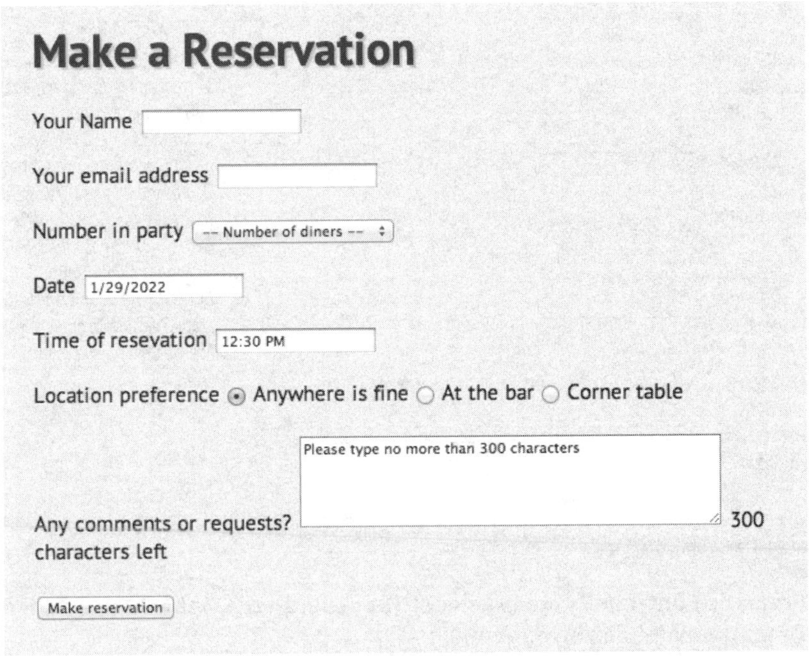

Make a Reservation

Your Name

Your email address

Number in party -- Number of diners -- ⬦

Date 1/29/2022

Time of resevation 12:30 PM

Location preference ⦿ Anywhere is fine ◯ At the bar ◯ Corner table

Please type no more than 300 characters

Any comments or requests? 300
characters left

Make reservation

FIGURE 12-41

This figure doesn't show the entire web page, just the form section (so the banner, sidebar and footer are missing). You can try submitting the form by clicking the "Make reservation" button, but you'll see a bunch of error messages since you didn't fill out the form. Victory!

Styling the Labels

At this point, you have a functioning form, but it doesn't look very good. The error messages are ugly, and the form fields create a jagged line that's neither easy to read nor attractive. The first step in improving this form is to position the fields so their left edges align (see Figure 12-42). To do this, you'll actually create and apply a style to the labels—in essence, you'll float (page 448) the labels to the left and give them a set width. That makes them behave much like the columns you created in the chapter on page layout (Chapter 11).

1. **In the CSS Styles panel, click the New Rule button.** In the New CSS Rule window, select Class from the Selector Type menu, type *.label* in the Selector Name box, and choose styles.css from the Rule Definition menu. Click OK to start building the style.

   The CSS Rule Definition window appears. (If you're still fuzzy on this whole CSS styles thing, turn back to page 125 for a refresher.) First, you'll style the text.

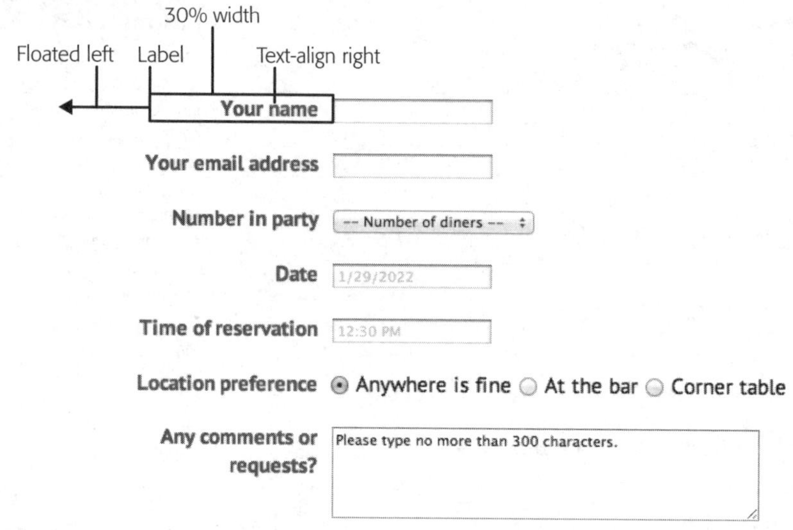

30% width

Floated left   Label   Text-align right

Your name

Your email address

Number in party   -- Number of diners --

Date   1/29/2022

Time of reservation   12:30 PM

Location preference ● Anywhere is fine ○ At the bar ○ Corner table

Any comments or   Please type no more than 300 characters.
requests?

FIGURE 12-42

One way to lay out a form is to create an HTML table (page 291) and put the form fields in one column and the labels in another. Another way, one that uses a lot less HTML, is to use the CSS Float property (page 448) to make the labels sit in one column, which forces the fields to wrap around each label and visually create a second column.

2. **From the Font-family menu select PTSansBold—the webfont you added to Dreamweaver back on page 169.**

   If you didn't complete the tutorial in Chapter 3 (or you're working on a different computer than you used for that tutorial), you won't see PTSansBold listed in the Font-family menu. Either turn back to page 169, and add the font, or simply choose a different font.

3. **In the Color box, type #205B0A (or use the color box to select a dark green color).**

   As mentioned on page 160, you can also specify colors in RGB format; here, that'd be rgb(32,91,10). Next you'll set up the properties that will position the label using the Float property.

4. **Click the Box category.** Set the Width to 30%, choose "left" from the Float menu, choose "left" from the Clear menu, uncheck the "Same for all" box under Padding, and then type *10px* in the Right padding box.

   The CSS Rule Definition window should now look like Figure 12-43. In a nutshell, these settings will float the labels to the left of the page, making the text fields wrap around their right side. The Clear setting makes sure that the labels don't attempt to wrap around the right side of any floated elements. Now you'll change the labels' alignment so they line up on the right side, against the form fields.

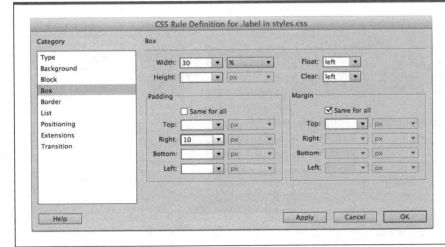

FIGURE 12-43

When floating a form label to the left, it's a good idea to also set the Clear property (page 449) to "left." This prevents the label from wrapping around the right side of another label. By setting the Clear property to left, you're telling the labels to always appear below other floated labels.

5. **Select the Block category, and choose "right" from the Text-align menu.**
   Click OK to complete the style.

   Setting the text-align property to "right" forces text to align its right edge with the right edge of its box—in other words, moving the label text to the right, as pictured in Figure 12-42.

6. **In the document window, click anywhere inside the label "Your name."** In the tag selector, click <label> (circled in Figure 12-44) to select the label tag. In the Property Inspector, make sure you select the HTML button and then, from the Class menu, choose "label."

   Make sure you select the <label> tag before applying the class. If you just click inside the text and choose "label" from the Class menu, Dreamweaver applies the class to the surrounding paragraph (the <p> tag), which won't provide the layout you're after.

NOTE After step 6, you might wonder why you didn't just create a tag style for the <label> tag instead of a class style you had to manually apply. Good question. In some cases you can, but if you add checkboxes or radio buttons to a form, you can't always go that route. That's because you usually add text before a group of boxes or buttons to introduce the group. In the form you're working on, the text "Location preference" works this way: It isn't in a <label> tag since it's not associated with any single form field. However, you do want to format it like the other labels ("Your name," "Your email address," and so on) on the page. So creating a class style—*.label*—lets you apply the same CSS style—and therefore the same format—to different types of tags.

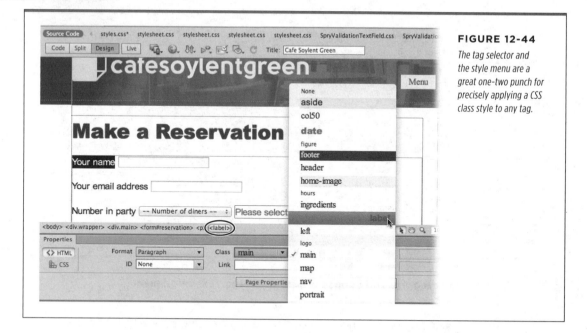

FIGURE 12-44

The tag selector and the style menu are a great one-two punch for precisely applying a CSS class style to any tag.

7. **Repeat step 6 for the other labels on the page.** When you get to the "Location preference" text (which isn't in a <label> tag), just select that text and choose "label" from the Class menu.

   Because "Location preference" isn't in its own tag, Dreamweaver wraps that text with a <span> tag and adds the class attribute to it, like this: <span class="label">Location preference</span>. If you preview the page now, you'll see that the Submit button and the " characters remaining" text sit on the left; they'd both look better indented with the form fields.

8. **In the CSS Styles panel, click the New Rule button.** In the New CSS Rule window, select Class from the Selector Type menu, type *.counter* in the Selector Name box, and choose styles.css from the Rule Definition menu. Click OK to start building the style.

   The class *.counter* comes from the <span> tag you added in step 8 on page 626. That span provides a way to format both the counter and the text "characters remaining."

9. **From the Font-family menu, select PTSansItalic, the webfont you added to Dreamweaver on page 169.** Type *.8* and select "em" for the Font-size, and choose a gray color for the Color property.

If you didn't complete the tutorial in Chapter 3 (or you're working on a different computer than you used for that tutorial), you probably won't see PTSansItalic in the Font-family menu. Just select the same font you selected in step 2 on page 628.

Currently, the counter sits uncomfortably to the right of the text area. It would look better directly underneath it.

10. **In the CSS Rule Definition window, click the Block category and choose "block" from the Display menu.** Select the Box category, uncheck the "Same for all" box under Margin, type *-5px* for the top margin, and *32%* for the left margin.

    As you learned on page 166, setting the CSS display property to "block" turns an element into a block-level element. Since a <span> tag normally sits on the same line as other content (like a form field), setting its display to block forces the element to drop down onto its own line. A small negative top margin moves the <span> up closer to the text box, while the left margin indents the text so that it sits underneath the textarea field.

11. **Click OK to complete the style.**

    Wow! You're really getting some practice in the finer details of obsessive-compulsive web design. No time to wash hands, we need to move on to our next task: indenting the Submit button.

12. **In the CSS styles panel, click the New CSS Rule button.** In the New CSS Rule window, select "class" from the Selector Type menu, type *.submit* in the Selector Name box, and choose styles.css from the Rule Definition menu. Click OK to start building the style.

    You're creating a special class that you can then apply to the paragraph containing the Submit button.

13. **In the CSS Rule Definition window, select the Box category.** Uncheck the Margin's "Same for all" box, and type *32%* in the left margin box. Click OK to complete the style.

    Nothing happens yet; because you created a class style, you need to apply it to the paragraph containing the button.

14. **In Design view, click the line containing the Submit button (either to the left or right of the button) and choose "submit" from the Property Inspector's Class menu.**

    The button indents to line up with the form fields. You're almost done styling the form. Your last task is to set the font and width for the form's text fields. As you read on page 574, you can use the "Char width" property to set the width for a text field. However, this requires setting that property on every text field. If you want all your text fields to be the same width, it's a lot easier to use CSS.

15. **In the CSS styles panel, click the New CSS Rule button.** In the New CSS Rule window, select "Compound (based on your selection)" from the Selector Type menu, type "textarea, input[type="text"]" in the Selector Name box, and choose styles.css from the Rule Definition menu. Click OK to start building the style.

What the heck is "textarea, input[type="text"]", you're probably asking. Well, first, it's a group selector (like the ones you read about on page 381), composed of two other, different selectors. The first selector, textarea, is just a tag selector that targets the HTML textarea element (in other words, the Comment box on this form). The second selector, input[type="text"], is an attribute selector (they target only input tags that have a "type" of "text"). This is useful since most form fields (buttons, checkboxes, and radio buttons, for example) use the <input> tag. If you tried to set a width (say 200 pixels) using a simple input tag style, you'd end up with 200-pixel-wide checkboxes! However, since you create text fields by setting the input tag's "type" attribute to "text"—<input type="text">—this very specific selector lets you style just text fields! (This little trick works in all current browsers, even Internet Explorer 7 and later.)

16. **In the CSS Rule Definition window, from the Font-family menu, select PT-SansReg, the webfont you added to Dreamweaver back on page 169.** Type *1.2em* for in the Font-size box.

If you didn't complete the tutorial in Chapter 3 (or you're working on a different computer than you used for that tutorial), you won't see PTSansReg in the Font-family menu. That's OK, just pick another font.

17. **In the CSS Rule Definition window, select the Box category.** Type *50%* for the width; uncheck the Margin's "Same for all" box, and type *-3px* in the Top box. Click OK to complete the style.

Setting the width property to 50% makes all the text boxes 50% the size of the <div> tag that holds the form. The negative top margin scoots those boxes up a few pixels so they align better with their labels on the left side of the form.

Styling Spry Error Messages

Your final task is to change the look of the Spry error messages. The border around the errors looks amateurish, and the messages would look better underneath the form fields instead of

1. **Click inside the error message for the first form field ("Please type your name").**

If you don't see an error message, mouse over that form field and select the blue "Spry Textfield" tab when it appears. In the Property Inspector, choose Required from the "Preview states" menu. The error message "Please type your name" appears.

2. **Make sure you have the CSS Styles panel open (Window→CSS Styles).** At the top of the panel, select the Current button, and then make sure you have the Cascade button (circled in Figure 12-45) selected.

A long-winded group selector (page 381), made up of a bunch of descendent selectors (page 377), controls the error message's style. The one you want is the last one listed in the Styles panel's Rules pane; it begins with *.textfieldRe-quiredState .textfieldRequiredMsg* (the middle pane in Figure 12-45).

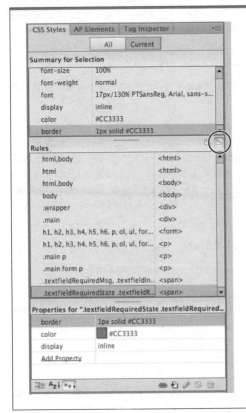

FIGURE 12-45

To format Spry widgets most easily, use the CSS Styles panel's Current view. If you have the Cascade button (circled) selected, then you merely need to click the element whose style you want to change. In this case, selecting the error message for a Spry validation text field highlights the appropriate style's name. Double-click the name to open the CSS Rule Definition window, and style away!

3. **In the Rules pane, double-click the style beginning with *.textfieldRequired-State .textfield-RequiredMsg* to open the CSS Rule Definition window.**

You'll change the font, font-size, and a few other properties of these error messages.

4. **In the Rule Definition window, from the Font-family menu, select PTSansI-talic (or pick any font you'd like).** In the Font-size box, type *.8em*.

Next you'll remove the border and make sure that the error messages appear underneath the form fields.

5. **Select the Block category, and choose "block" from the Display menu.** Select the Border category and delete the values from the Style, Width, and Color boxes. Select the Box category, uncheck the Margin's "Same for all" box, and type *32%* in the Left box. Click OK to complete the style.

   You may see all the error messages for the text boxes change to reflect the style changes you just made. However, the error message for the menu didn't change. Each type of Spry Validation widget (text field, menu, checkbox, text area) has its own CSS style to format error messages. So, unfortunately, if you use more than one type of validation in a form, you have to repeat the same formatting steps to get error messages that match. In the case of a pull-down menu error message, the style name begins with *.selectRequiredState .selectRequiredMsg*, and it's in an external style sheet named *SpryValidationSelect.css*.

6. **Repeat steps 2–5 above for the error message next to the menu, and the textarea.**

   Now all the error messages look the same. But if you preview the page, you'll notice that the hints inside the Date and "Time of reservation" fields really stand out. And because they're in large, bold, black type, it looks like someone has already filled them out. To make it clear that the text is merely a hint, you can use a visual cue, making the hint text a lighter color so it fades into the background. Fortunately, the style sheets for these Spry widgets already include a style for hints.

7. **In the CSS Styles menu, click the All button.**

   There are a lot of styles and style sheets attached to this page now.

8. **Scroll down the list of styles until you see *SpryValidationTextfield.css* (you may need to click the + [flippy triangle on Macs] to see all the styles in the style sheet).** Double-click the group style named *.textfieldHintState input, input.textfieldHintState* (top circled item in Figure 12-46).

   The CSS Rule Definition window appears.

9. **Choose a light-gray color from the Color box.** Click OK to complete the style.

   A different style in another style sheet controls the hint in the text area box. You'll need to edit that one, too.

10. **In the CSS styles panel, locate *SpryValidationTextarea.css* and double-click the group style *.textarea.textareaHintState, .textareaHintState textarea* (bottom circled item in Figure 12-46).** Change its color value to match the gray you selected in the previous step and click OK to complete the style.

    That was a lot of work, but you've finished the form!

11. **Choose File→Save All, and then press the F12 key (Option-F12).**

A web browser opens with the new form displayed.

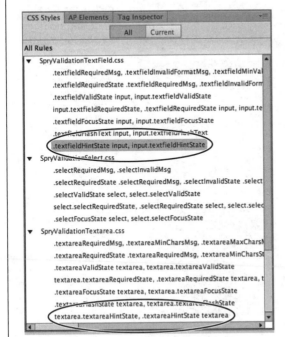

FIGURE 12-46

It won't be easy to find some styles using the Current view of the CSS Styles panel. On the other hand, the All view shows you all the styles and style sheets for the current web page.

12. **Click the "Make reservation" button.**

The form doesn't submit (see Figure 12-47). Instead, several error messages appear. Fill out the form correctly, and try to submit it again.

NOTE If, after you submit the form, you notice that some of the information you entered doesn't show up on the form-processing page ("Reservation submitted"), you may not have typed the name of the field exactly as specified in the tutorial. Form-processing programs are very particular—if you don't provide the exact name it's expecting, it won't correctly capture the form data. You can change the names of form elements by selecting them and using the Property Inspector.

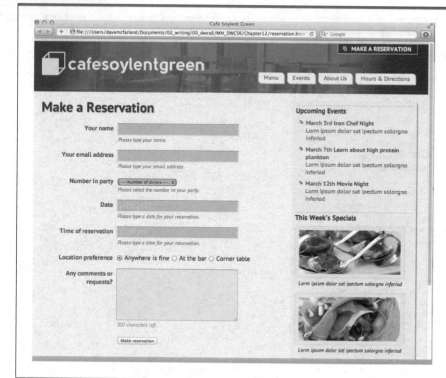

FIGURE 12-47

Dreamweaver's Spry Validation Form widgets can help ensure that your forms collect the information you want. Professional-looking error messages, placed next to the offending responses, give visitors clear feedback

Adding Interactivity with JavaScript

As a web designer, you can count on one thing: The Web will always be changing. Yesterday's technology is yesterday's news—remember Java applets, frames, and messages that scroll in your browser's status bar? (If you don't, you're lucky!) You can see the most recent web design innovations on sites like Google Maps, Flickr, and Facebook, all of which offer a high degree of interactivity without resorting to multimedia plug-ins like Flash. Google Maps, for example, lets you zoom in, zoom out, and scroll across a map of the world without loading a new web page for each view. Many of the most cutting-edge websites look and act like the kinds of complex programs you use right on your desktop computer.

JavaScript has grown from the simple language behind pop-up windows and image rollovers to a full-blown programming tool that can change the content of a web page as you look at it. It's the key to today's website interactivity. It can even update a page with new data that it downloads behind the scenes (that's why you can scroll to new sections of that Google map without loading new pages). Dreamweaver, which has always tried to provide tools to meet web designers' current needs, includes a set of JavaScript tools that let you add interactive page elements like drop-down navigation menus, tabbed panels, pop-up tooltips, and data-driven, sortable tables. That's what this chapter is all about.

■ Introducing Adobe's Spry Framework

You've already seen Spry in action in Chapters 4 and 12, where you learned about the Spry Menu Bar and Spry Validation widgets. But what exactly is Spry? It isn't just a Dreamweaver tool; it's a technology developed by Adobe, distributed freely and independently on the Adobe Labs website (*http://tinyurl.com/22da4k*).

It's officially called the "Spry Framework for Ajax," and it's a collection of JavaScript programs that let you, the web designer, offer your visitors sophisticated control of a web page through *widgets*, *effects*, and *data sets*. A widget includes web page elements like menu bars, form validation messages, or sets of tabbed panels that makes a site easier to use. For example, the Spry Menu Bar widget adds links to a compact navigation bar, so visitors can easily find their way around your site.

A Spry effect is a visual treat that doesn't necessarily improve how a web page works but adds cool eye candy. You can use a Spry effect to fade page elements in and out of view, for example.

Finally, a Spry data set is a presentation format that's more interactive than a standard HTML table. Imagine you have a table listing products your company sells. The table displays one product per row, with columns for the product's name, price, and availability. A visitor can sort a Spry data table by any of these columns, simply by clicking the name of the column. And that all happens without the browser ever having to reload the web page. Dreamweaver does this by letting you put data into a common HTML table and using that as the basis for an interactive table.

WORD OF WARNING

Spry's Days May Be Numbered

Adobe first introduced the Spry Framework back in Dreamweaver CS3 (circa 2007). At the time, Spry represented cutting-edge JavaScript programming and offered a sophisticated set of tools to let ordinary web designers supercharge their web pages with dynamic effects.

Unfortunately, Adobe stopped developing the Spry Framework several years ago, and there's been no update since 2008. In fact, the current version is still called a "pre-release." Adobe has also backed a competing framework, called jQuery (*http://jquery.com*). jQuery is the most popular JavaScript framework; millions of websites use it, and an active community of programmers (some from Adobe) maintain, update, and improve jQuery on an almost daily basis.

All of the Spry widgets discussed in this book still work in current (and older) browsers, so you can use them without worrying that your site's visitors won't be able to use them... for now. One day, the programming in the Spry Framework may not work in future browsers; and, at the very least, without any new work going into maintaining Spry, the Spry widgets you add won't take advantage of the latest and greatest JavaScript power offered by newer generations of web browsers.

In other words, you may wish to skip Spry if you're worried about adopting the latest trends in JavaScript on your site. There are many alternatives to the widgets discussed in this chapter, such as jQuery UI (*http://jqueryui.com*), which is a user-interface library that works with jQuery so you can easily added tabbed panels, accordions, dialog boxes, visual effects, and more.

■ Tabbed Panels

Some website visitors are loath to scroll; if they don't see what they want when a page first loads, they move on. Because of this, some web designers divide long passages of information into multiple pages so that each page presents small, easy-to-digest chunks. Of course, that means building several pages instead of just one, and it forces visitors to click through (and wait for) a series of pages. The Spry Tabbed Panels widget provide an alternative (see Figure 13-1). Instead of creating one long page, or several smaller pages, you organize information into blocks, and drop them into separate tabbed panels. That way, your content is always front and center, and your guests can easily visit different sections of your site by clicking a tab.

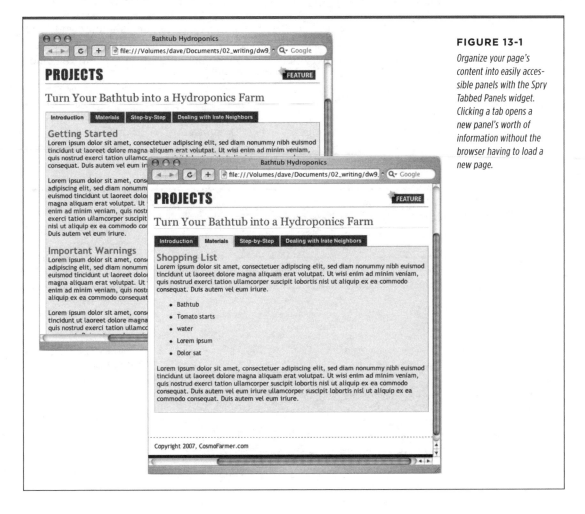

FIGURE 13-1

Organize your page's content into easily accessible panels with the Spry Tabbed Panels widget. Clicking a tab opens a new panel's worth of information without the browser having to load a new page.

Adding a Tabbed Panel

You can place Spry tabbed panels anywhere on a web page. But since the tabs form a single horizontal row, you need enough space to accommodate all the tabs. Unless you have only a couple of tabs with one-word text labels, you should place the tabbed panels in a fairly wide space, such as the main column of a web page or across the entire width of the page. To do so, follow these steps:

1. **In the document window, click where you wish to insert the panels.**

   For example, inside a <div> tag.

2. **Choose Insert→Spry→Spry Tabbed Panels, or, on the Insert panel's Spry category, click the Spry Tabbed Panels buttons.**

   You can find all the Spry goodies in the Insert panel's Spry category; you'll also find several Spry widgets (including Tabbed Panels) listed under the Layout category, and other Spry buttons grouped under other tabs (form validation Spry widgets appear under the Forms tab, for example).

   After you insert a tabbed panel, you see two tabs and two panels on the page (Figure 13-2); in addition, a blue tab appears above the panels indicating a Spry widget. The blue tab appears only in Dreamweaver's Design view, not in your guest's web browser. It gives you an easy way to select the widget and access its properties in the Property Inspector.

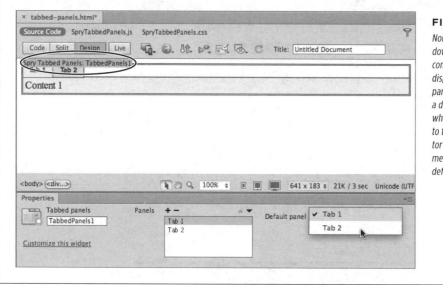

FIGURE 13-2

Normally, when a browser downloads a page containing Spry panels, it displays the first tab and panel. If you'd rather have a different panel visible when the page loads, go to the Property Inspector's "Default panel" menu and specify the default tab.

NOTE   When you save a page after inserting a Spry tabbed panel, Dreamweaver notifies you that it has added two files to your site: a CSS file (*SpryTabbedPanels.css*) that formats the panel group and a JavaScript file (*SpryTabbedPanels.js*) that makes the panels appear and disappear when visitors click the tabs. Dreamweaver saves both files in the SpryAssets folder in your site's root folder (see the Tip on page 215). Make sure you upload this folder when you move your site to your web server.

3. **In the Property Inspector, name the panel group.**

   This step is optional. Dreamweaver provides a generic name (*TabbedPanels1*, for example), so you don't really have to come up with a name; it never appears in a browser window. But if you ever take the plunge into manually modifying your Spry widgets in Code view, you may want to change the name to something more descriptive. If your tabbed panels house information about a product, for example, you might name the panel group *productPanels*. That'll help you identify code related to the panel group if you ever want to enhance or change the panels in Code view.

4. **Add additional panels and reorder the tabs.**

   If two panels aren't enough for your needs, use the Property Inspector to add more. Above the list of tab names, click the + button. To remove a panel, in the same list, click the name of a tab, and then click the minus-sign (-) button.

   You reorder panels by selecting a tab from the list, and then clicking the up or down arrow keys. The up arrow moves a panel to the left, while the down arrow moves it to the right.

NOTE   A Spry widget's properties appear in the Property Inspector only when you select the widget. To do so, click the blue tab above the elements inside the widget (circled in Figure 13-2).

Adding and Editing Panel Content

Each tabbed panel has two parts: a labeled tab and a panel containing content associated with the tab. In Figure 13-1, "Introduction," "Materials," "Step-by-Step," and "Dealing with Irate Neighbors" are each tabs, while the area of the page beginning with the "Shopping List" headline is the panel for the "Materials" tab.

To change the label on a tab, select and replace the tab's text in Design view. The label is normal HTML text, so you can just triple-click to select it, as you would any block of text.

Dreamweaver stores the text for the panel itself inside a <div> tag, so you can select it by clicking anywhere inside the panel and then choosing Edit→Select All (or Ctrl+A [⌘-A]). You can place any combination of HTML inside a panel: headlines, paragraphs, bulleted lists, forms, images, and Flash movies (you can even insert *another* tabbed panel if you like that kind of circus-sideshow-hall-of-mirrors effect).

To edit a panel's contents, you first need to make the panel visible. Since the entire point of the tabbed panels is to present a lot of information in overlapping panels, you see only one panel at a time. Fortunately, Dreamweaver offers a simple way to close the current panel and open another one so you can edit it: move your mouse over a hidden panel's tab, and an eye icon appears at the tab's right edge (see Figure 13-3). Click the eye to open the tab's panel for editing.

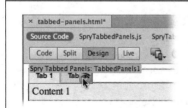

FIGURE 13-3

Dreamweaver displays an eye icon for all Spry widgets that have tabs and panels. Clicking the eye makes a currently hidden panel visible and ready to edit.

Formatting Tabbed Panels

The tabbed panels and the content inside them are just basic HTML, made to look good with a generous dose of CSS. The tab buttons are a simple bulleted list, while each panel is a separate div; Dreamweaver wraps all the panels together in another div. An external style sheet in the root folder's SpryAssets folder, *SpryTabbedPanels .css*, controls all the fancy formatting—tab buttons sitting side by side, borders, and background colors.

> **TIP** Dreamweaver stores Spry support files (the external CSS and JavaScript files that make Spry so spry) in a folder named SpryAssets in your site's root folder. If you don't like the name of that folder or you want to store those files elsewhere on your site, see page 215.

Dreamweaver supplies CSS styles to format the panels, the currently selected tab, and the tabs whose panels aren't currently visible. The general process of modifying the look of any element in a panel group is simple: Identify the element you want to modify (like a panel or tab), locate the style that controls that element, and then edit that style. If you want to change the text color of the currently selected tab, for example, open the *.TabbedPanelsTabSelected* class style in the *SpryTabbedPanels .css* file. The basic steps are as follows:

1. **Open the CSS Styles panel (Window→CSS Styles).**

   At the top of the panel, make sure you have the All button selected.

2. **Expand the list of styles for the *SpryTabbedPanels.css* style sheet.**

   Just click the + symbol (flippy triangle on Macs) next to the file's name to reveal all the styles for tabbed panels.

3. **In the Styles panel, double-click the style's name.**

The Style Definition window opens.

4. **Make your changes, and then, in the Style Definition window, click OK to finish editing the style.**

You can use the CSS Properties pane to edit the styles as well. (For a recap on editing CSS styles, see page 139.)

To help guide you in the process of modifying Spry panels, here's a list of panel elements and the styles that control them:

- **Spry tabbed panels group**: .TabbedPanels

Normally, the width of a collection of panels and tabs stretches to fit the available space. So if you place a panel group on an empty page, it stretches to fit the entire width of the browser window. Placed inside a div with a set width, the group of panels stretches to match the div's width. If you want to make the group of panels thinner, change the width property of the .TabbedPanels style. Normally it's set to 100%, but you could change this to 50% or a set pixel amount. The .TabbedPanels style floats the entire group of panels and tabs to the left, so any content that appears after the panel group wraps around the right side of the panels (see page 448 for more on floats). (To adjust the height of a group of panels, see the "Panels" bullet point, below.)

- **All tabs**: .TabbedPanelsTab

The Spry Tabbed Panels widget uses two types of tabs: one for the currently displayed panel, and one for tabs that aren't active. The .TabbedPanelsTab style controls both tabs. If you want to change the font on all of them, edit the .TabbedPanelsTab style, and then choose a new font family. To change the borders around the tabs, edit this style's Border property. To adjust the amount of space between the edge of the tab and the text label inside it, edit the style's Padding property (page 449). To change the space between tabs, edit the style's Margin property (page 449).

- **Not selected tab**: .TabbedPanelsTab and .TabbedPanelsTabHover

The .TabbedPanelsTab also dictates the basic look of an unselected tab, like its background color. In addition, a non-selected tab has a hover style—.TabbedPanelsTabHover—so that when a guest mouses over it, the tab highlights to indicate that you can click it. The basic style sheet supplied with Dreamweaver merely changes the tab's background color when a mouse moves over it, but you're free to change other settings, such as the font color.

NOTE Dreamweaver's Live view lets you instantly preview style changes without leaving the program. For example, with the CSS Styles panel open and your web page in Live view, you can edit the .TabbedPanelsTabHover style (change the background color, for instance) and immediately test that change by moving your mouse over the tab in Design view.

- **Currently selected tab**: *.TabbedPanelsTabSelected*

The *.TabbedPanelsTabSelected* style applies to the tab for a currently displayed panel. This style essentially overwrites the style properties inherited from the *.TabbedPanelsTab* style, which all the tabs share. The background color and text color differ from the other tab styles, but, again, you're free to modify the style (by picking a new font, for instance).

Be aware of a couple of things with this style. First, it has a set bottom border. You shouldn't eliminate it, unless you eliminate bottom borders on the *.Tabbed-PanelsTab* as well. Otherwise, you see a noticeable line separating the tab from its panel. In addition, if you change the background color of the tab and the panel (they're usually set to the same color to make it appear that they form a unified element), set the color of the bottom border to match. If you don't, you end up with a line separating the tab from the panel.

> **NOTE** If you make the text size for one type of tab larger or smaller than another, you end up with different heights for the different tabs. What's worse, the shorter tab no longer touches the top of the panel group. To fix this, add a *line-height* property (see page 161) to the *.TabbedPanelsTab* style that's large enough to force the two tabs to occupy the same height—use a pixel value so you can guarantee that the tabs will be the same height. You'll probably need to conduct some trial-and-error testing to get this right.

- **Panels**: *.TabbedPanelsContentGroup* or *.TabbedPanelsContent*

Two styles affect the panels. Dreamweaver applies the first, *.TabbedPanelsContentGroup*, to a <div> tag that wraps around the HTML of *all* the panels. The second wraps the content of each panel in a <div> tag with the *.TabbedPanelsContent* class applied to it. You can edit either style to adjust basic properties like font color, size, and so on. However, the *.TabbedPanelsContentGroup* controls the borders and background color for the panels; edit that style to change the panels' borders or backgrounds. Out of the box, Dreamweaver sets just the Padding property in the *.TabbedPanelsContent* style sheet—it adds space inside each panel so its contents don't butt right up against the borders of the panel.

Each panel is only as tall as the content inside it. If one panel has a lot of information and another just a little, the panels grow or shrink wildly as you switch among them. If you're a stickler for consistency, you can set a uniform height for all the panels by adding a height property to the *.TabbedPanelsContent* style. Be careful with height, however; before building a web page, it's difficult to judge how much content a panel will have (and thus how tall it needs to be). If the content inside a panel grows taller than the panel's height setting, you get some weird display problems, as explained on page 448.

TIP Safari, Firefox, and Chrome highlight the tab of a Spry panel when you click it. In Firefox, you'll see a fuzzy, dotted outline around the tab, and in Safari and Chrome you get a glowing blue outline. That's because the browser applies a "focus" state to the tab (see page 209). To remove it, you need to create a compound style named *.TabbedPanelsTab:focus*. Then you need to set the CSS *outline* property to *none*.

Unfortunately, you can't do this in Dreamweaver's Rule Definition window. To add this property, you first have to create the *.TabbedPanelsTab:focus* style (make sure to save this new style in the *SpryTabbedPanels.css* style sheet). When the CSS Rule Definition window opens, just click OK. This creates a style with no properties. Next, in the CSS Styles panel, find the style and select it. Then, in the Properties pane (see page 382), click the Add Property link, type *outline*, hit Tab, and then type *none*. You're done.

- **Content inside the panel**. Dreamweaver doesn't start you off with any styles that control the tags inside a panel of content. Although headlines and paragraphs inherit (see page 390) any text properties you add to the panel styles (*.TabbedPanelsContentGroup and.TabbedPanelsContent*), you might want to define a different look for headlines, paragraphs, lists, and other tags inside the panel. This is a perfect situation for descendent selectors. A descendent selector, as you read on page 377, lets you specify the look of a tag when it's inside another tag; using descendant selectors, you can customize the look of page elements based on where they appear on a page.

  In the case of a panel's style, say you want the paragraphs inside a panel to look different from other paragraphs on the page. Create a descendent selector style named *.TabbedPanelsContent p*, and then add any CSS properties you like. Or, to format the look of Heading 2 tags inside a panel, create a style named *.TabbedPanelsContent h2*. In other words, to control the look of any tag inside a panel, create an advanced style, and then name it *.TabbedPanelsContent* followed by a space and then the name of the tag you want to style.

◼ Accordions

The Spry Accordion widget is another space-saving widget that lets you stuff lots of content into a multi-paneled display (Figure 13-4). Like Spry tabbed panels, a Spry accordion contains panels of information, each with a labeled tab. But in this case, a browser stacks the tabs on top of each other instead of side by side. When you click the tab of a panel that's not currently visible, that panel rises with a smooth animated effect and exposes the content "underneath." In addition, you must set each panel's height, so if the content is taller than the panel itself, the browser adds a scroll bar to the panel's right edge. It's kind of like having a browser window inside a browser window. Dreamweaver's stock style sheet sets the height of each panel to 200 pixels, but you can change that (see the bullet point "Panels" on page 650).

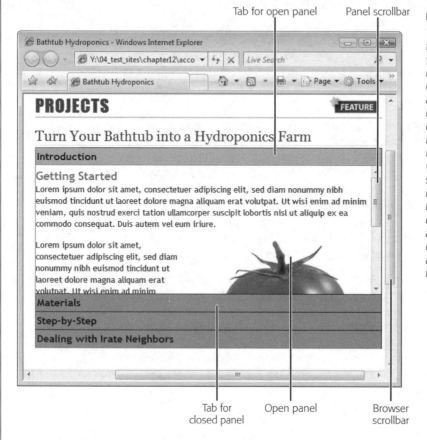

Tab for open panel   Panel scrollbar

Tab for   Open panel   Browser
closed panel   scrollbar

FIGURE 13-4

You have to specify a height for Accordion panels, so you always know how much room they take up on a page. A web browser automatically adds scroll bars to panels that have lots of content. The content in this image doesn't fit within the height of the panel, so a visitor has to use the small scroll bar to read all the information. Depending on how you look at it, the additional scroll bar provides a great way to present a lot of content in a little space or an annoying inconvenience that forces visitors to scroll.

Adding an Accordion

You can place a Spry accordion anywhere on a web page—on an empty page, inside a <div> tag, and so on.

1. **In the document window, click the area where you wish to insert the accordion.**

   For example, inside a <div> tag.

2. **Choose Insert→Spry→Spry Accordion, or, on the Insert panel, click the Spry Accordion button.**

After inserting an accordion, you see a tab (named "Label 1"), an open panel (with "Content 1" inside it), and another tab ("Label 2") at the bottom (see Figure 13-5); in addition, a blue Spry tab appears above the top tab, and the Property Inspector displays the accordion's properties.

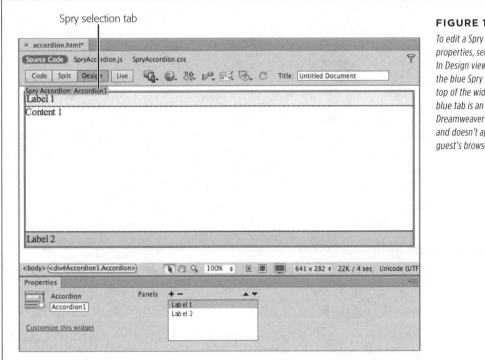

Spry selection tab

FIGURE 13-5

To edit a Spry widget's properties, select it. In Design view, click the blue Spry tab on top of the widget. The blue tab is an internal Dreamweaver control, and doesn't appear in a guest's browser.

TIP You can insert any Spry widget by dragging its icon from the Insert panel to anywhere on a web page.

3. **In the Property Inspector, name the accordion.**

   As with Spry tabbed panels, this step is optional.

4. **Add additional tabs and panels to the accordion.**

   If two panels aren't enough for your needs, use the Property Inspector to add more. Click the + button above the list of tab names. To remove a panel, click the name of the tab in the panels list, and then click the minus (–) button. (You can also reorder the panels by selecting a tab from the list, and then, in the Property Inspector, clicking the up or down arrow button.)

Adding and Editing Accordion Content

Dreamweaver divides accordions into sections, composed of a labeled tab and a content panel associated with that tab. It embeds each tab in its own <div> tag, and the content for each tab's panel inside another <div> tag. Dreamweaver then encloses each tab/panel pair in yet another div (and wraps the entire accordion [all of the tab/panel groups] in one final div).

To edit a tab's label, select its text in Design view, and then type in a new label. (Since Dreamweaver enclosed the label in a <div> tag, you can also just click the tab, and then press Ctrl+A [⌘-A] to select all the label's text.) Since accordion tabs span the width of the accordion, you can put a lot more words on an accordion tab than you can on the tabbed panel tabs described above.

As with those Spry tabbed panels, you have to make a panel visible to edit it: Mouse over the tab of a hidden panel, and then, at the right edge of the tab, click the eye icon. To select all the text inside a panel, click the panel, and then choose Edit→Select All (or Ctrl+A [⌘-A]). You can place any combination of HTML inside a panel: headlines, paragraphs, bulleted lists, forms, images, and Flash movies.

You'll run into one big problem if you add more content than fits inside an accordion panel's height: you can't see all the content in Dreamweaver! Remember, accordion panels occupy a fixed height. When you view the accordion in a browser, you can scroll inside the panel to see any content that doesn't fit that height (see Figure 13-4). But you don't get any scroll bars in Dreamweaver's Design view, so when you add more content than fits in the panel, you can't edit it. You work around this in two ways:

- Double-click the panel.

- Right-click (Control-click) the panel, and then, from the pop-up menu, choose Element View→Full.

Either way, the panel fully expands so you can see and edit all the content. In fact, all the panels in the accordion expand when you take either action. This "full" view is only visible in Dreamweaver in order to make it easier to edit content in the accordion panels. When someone views the page in a web browser, he sees only the top panel, and must click another tab to view another panel's content.

Formatting a Spry Accordion

When you add a Spry accordion to a web page, Dreamweaver links an external style sheet named *SpryAccordion.css* to the page. This CSS file contains all the styles that control the look of the accordion's tabs and panels. The process of modifying the appearance of those tabs follows the same general sequence as that for Spry tabbed panels (see page 642): Identify the element you want to format, and then open and edit that element's style to match your page's overall design.

To help you modify Spry accordions, here's a list of accordion elements and the styles that control them:

- **The accordion** (all tabs and panels): *.Accordion*

  The *.Accordion* class style controls the overall settings for the accordion. Dreamweaver applies the class to the <div> tag that surrounds the tabs and panels. If you add basic font formatting to this style, such as font color, size, and font family, the other tabs and panels inherit these same settings (for more on inheritance, see page 390).

  In addition, you set the left, right, and bottom borders that appear around the accordion using this style.

- **All tabs**: *.AccordionPanelTab*

  A web browser displays tabs inside a Spry accordion four possible ways (some design-inspired Adobe engineer got a little wild). As with a Spry tabbed panel, you see both a selected tab (the tab for the currently displayed panel) and a non-selected tab (the tab eagerly awaiting your click to reveal its hidden contents).

  In addition, both the selected and nonselected tabs have "focus" states that kick into action to format *all* the tabs when you click any *one* tab (*.Accordion-Focused .AccordionPanelTab* and *.AccordionFocused .AccordionPanelOpen .AccordionPanelTab*). In other words, click a single tab, and all the tabs change their appearance—"Yes sir, my tabs-in-arms and I are ready for your command!" Overall, the focus tabs are visually distracting (especially since the background colors are shimmering blue and electric purple). They aim to aid someone using a keyboard instead of a mouse to navigate the accordion panels (you can actually tab to the accordion, and then use the up and down arrow keys to hide and reveal panels).

  To alter the basic appearance of all tabs, edit the *.AccordionPanelTab* style. If you define a font family for this style, all the tabs will display that font. In addition, you define the padding inside each tab, and the borders that appear around each tab, in this style.

- **Not selected tab**: *.AccordionPanelTab*, *.AccordionPanelTabHover,* and *.AccordionFocused .AccordionPanelTab*

  The *.AccordionPanelTab* style also dictates the background color for unselected tabs. In addition, a non-selected tab has a hover style—*.AccordionPanelTab-Hover*—so that when a visitor mouses over the tab, the tab highlights to indicate that she can click it. The basic style sheet Dreamweaver supplies merely changes the tab's text color when as a mouse moves over it, but you're free to change other settings as well.

When guests click any tab, all unselected tags also change appearance, thanks to the *.AccordionFocused .AccordionPanelTab* style. Tabs also use this style when a visitor presses his keyboard's Tab key to access the accordion panels. The stock style sheet changes the background color to a bright blue. You can delete the style if you don't want the tabs changing color. (At the very least, for the sake of all who care about beauty in this world, change the electric blue to something less obnoxious.)

> **TIP** You'll see the same blurry blue outline with accordions that you saw when you clicked a tab in a tabbed panel (see the Tip on page 645). But in this case, Safari, Firefox, and Chrome place a fuzzy line around the entire accordion. To remove the outline, create an advanced style called *.Accordion:focus*, and then set that style's *outline* property to *none*.

- **Currently selected tab**: *.AccordionPanelOpen .AccordionPanelTab*, *.AccordionPanelOpen .AccordionPanelTabHover*, and *.AccordionFocused .AccordionPanelTab*

  The *.AccordionPanelOpen .AccordionPanelTab* style applies to the tab associated with the currently open panel. This style essentially overwrites style properties inherited from the *.AccordionPanelTab* style that all tabs share. In the stock style sheet, only the background color differs from the unselected tab styles, but, again, you're free to modify this. In addition, the text on a selected tab changes color when a visitor mouses over it, thanks to the *.AccordionPanelOpen .AccordionPanelTabHover* style. This subtle "you can click me" cue is useful for unselected tabs (since clicking one of *them* actually does something). But since clicking an already open tab doesn't do anything, this hover style is a needless distraction.

  A selected tab also changes color when you click its tab, or press the keyboard's Tab key to access the accordion (again, you see that hideous electric blue). The *.AccordionFocused .AccordionPanelTab* style is the culprit.

- **Panels**: *.AccordionPanelContent*

  Dreamweaver adds the *.AccordionPanelContent* class to the <div> tag that surrounds the HTML in an accordion panel. You can adjust the font settings for this style to affect only the text inside the panel. In addition, this style defines each panel's height. Dreamweaver sets the CSS *height* property to 200 pixels at first, but you can make this value larger to display a bigger panel, or smaller for a shorter one. If you remove the height property from the style, the content inside the first panel dictates the height of all the other panels. For example, if you have three lines of text in the first panel, each of the other panels will also be three text lines tall. If you do go this route, it's best to put the most content in the first panel; that way, the other panels will be tall enough to display all of their content without scroll bars. Unfortunately, you can't make the panels automatically adjust to fit whatever content is inside them.

- **Content inside the panel**. Dreamweaver supplies no styles to control the HTML tags in an accordion panel. You can follow the process described for Spry tabbed panels (under the bullet point "Content inside the panel" on page 645) to create descendent selectors that affect only tags inside the panels. Just use *.Accordion* as the first part of the selector. For example, *.Accordion p* formats paragraphs inside an accordion panel.

  Also note that content inside an accordion panel butts up against the panel's left and right edges. If you apply padding directly to the panel (in the *.AccordionPanelContent* style), the opening and closing panel animation isn't very smooth. It's a bit more work, but it's better to add padding to the tags that appear inside the panel. For example, if you want all Heading 2 tags to indent 5 pixels from both the left and right sides of the panel, create a descendent selector like *.Accordion h2*, and then set the left and right Margin properties to 5 pixels.

NOTE When you create descendent selectors, always keep the *cascade* in mind (page 391). This CSS concept provides a set of rules for handling styles that conflict. You can easily create conflicts as you add multiple descendent selectors to a page.

For example, say you create the main content region of a page using a div with an ID named *#mainContent*. If you want to create a descendent selector to format the paragraphs *inside* that main content region, you might name it *#mainContent p*. Now, say you insert a Spry accordion, and you want to create a unique look for the paragraphs inside it. You could then create a style named *.Accordion p*. Unfortunately, since the *#mainContent p* style is more specific (has greater influence) than the *.Accordion p* style, the styles in *#mainContent p* win. In other words, it would be impossible to change the size of paragraphs inside the accordion...unless you create a more specific style for the accordion, something like *#mainContent .Accordion p*.

■ Collapsible Panels

The Spry Collapsible Panel widget is like an accordion panel, except that it consists of just a single tab-and-panel pair (see Figure 13-6). The tab toggles the panel's display on and off; each click of the tab either opens or closes the panel. You decide whether the panel is opened or closed when the web page first loads. A closed collapsible panel is great for keeping information out of a visitor's face until she wants it—like a form for signing up for an email newsletter, or driving directions to your business. Use an already open panel on your page when you want to make an important announcement that, once read, can be quickly hidden with a click of the mouse.

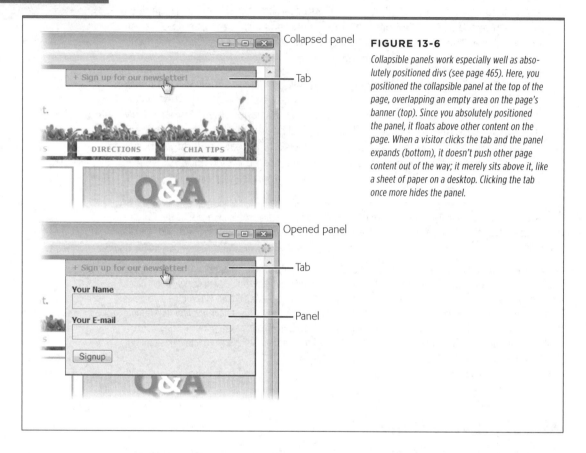

Tab

Opened panel

Tab

Panel

FIGURE 13-6

Collapsible panels work especially well as absolutely positioned divs (see page 465). Here, you positioned the collapsible panel at the top of the page, overlapping an empty area on the page's banner (top). Since you absolutely positioned the panel, it floats above other content on the page. When a visitor clicks the tab and the panel expands (bottom), it doesn't push other page content out of the way; it merely sits above it, like a sheet of paper on a desktop. Clicking the tab once more hides the panel.

Adding a Collapsible Panel

You can place a Spry collapsible panel anywhere on a web page—on an empty page, inside a <div> tag, and so on.

1. **In the document window, click where you want to insert the collapsible panel.**

   For example, inside a <div> tag.

2. **Choose Insert→Spry→Spry Collapsible Panel, or, on the Insert panel, click the Spry Collapsible Panel button.**

   After you insert a panel, you see a tab in the document window labeled "Tab," and an open panel labeled "Content." In addition, a blue Spry tab appears above the top tab, and the Property Inspector displays the properties for the panel (Figure 13-7).

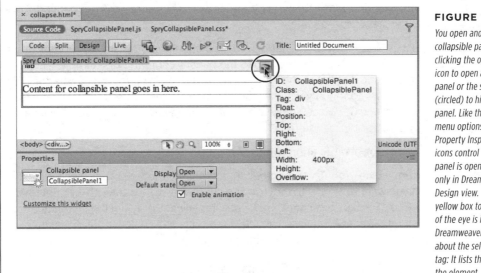

FIGURE 13-7
You open and close a collapsible panel by clicking the open-eye icon to open a closed panel or the shut-eye icon (circled) to hide an open panel. Like the Display menu options in the Property Inspector, the icons control whether the panel is open or closed only in Dreamweaver's Design view. The large yellow box to the right of the eye is information Dreamweaver supplies about the selected <div> tag: It lists the width of the element, as well as any other positioning information defined in the CSS.

3. **In the Property Inspector, name the collapsible panel.**

   As with Spry tabbed panels, this step is optional.

   Unlike tabbed panels and accordions, a collapsible panel is just a single tab/panel pair. You can't add additional tabs or panels. You can, however, place multiple collapsible panels on a page, stacked one on top of the next. This has two distinct advantages over an accordion: First, you don't have to have a panel open when the page loads—you can have three collapsible panels on a page with all three closed. A visitor clicks the tab of one panel and it opens, leaving the other panels unaffected.

   In addition, because each collapsible panel works independently of the others, a visitor can have all the panels open at once.

4. **From the Property Inspector's Display menu, choose either Open or Closed.**

   The Display menu controls whether the panel is opened or closed *in Design view only*. In other words, this setting is just to help you while you work within Dreamweaver; it doesn't affect how the panel appears when a visitor gets to the page.

5. **From the Property Inspector's "Default state" menu, choose either Open or Closed.**

This menu controls how the panel appears—open or closed—when a web browser first loads the page. In other words, a visitor sees the panel this way when he visits the page.

If you start with the panel closed, you should somehow inform visitors that they need to click the tab to see the panel's content. For example, you could simply add a + sign to the tab text, like this: "+ Sign up for our newsletter." Web designers commonly use the + sign to indicate that there's more information a click away. Or you could use text to let visitors know what to do: "Click here to sign up for our newsletter."

6. **Enable or disable animation.**

Turn on the Property Inspector's "Enable animation" checkbox (see Figure 13-7) if you want the panel to move in and out of view with a smooth "window-blind" effect. Turn off this checkbox if you simply want the panel to instantly appear and disappear from view with each tab click. The choice is purely aesthetic, so choose according to your design preference.

Adding Content to a Collapsible Panel

A collapsible panel consists of a simple combination of <div> tags: one marks the beginning and end of the widget, and it wraps around two other <div> tags, one for the tab, followed by another for the panel.

To edit a tab's label, select its text in Design view, and then type in a new label. Since Dreamweaver encloses the label in a <div> tag, you can also just click inside the tab, and then press Ctrl+A (⌘-A) to select all the label's text.

To edit the panel's content, you have to make the panel visible, and you control that either through the Property Inspector's Display menu (Figure 13-7) or by clicking the eye icon on the panel's tab (circled in Figure 13-7). To select all the text inside a panel, click anywhere inside it, and then choose Edit→Select All (or Ctrl+A [⌘-A]). You can place any combination of HTML inside a panel: headlines, paragraphs, bulleted lists, forms, and images.

Formatting a Collapsible Panel

When you add a Spry collapsible panel to a web page, Dreamweaver links the page to an external style sheet named *SpryCollapsiblePanel.css*, which contains all the styles that control the look of the tab and panel. You edit the styles the same way you edit Spry tabbed panels: namely, identify the element you wish to format, and then open and edit that element's style to match your page's design.

To help guide you in the process of modifying Spry collapsible panel styles, here's a list of panel elements and the styles that control them:

- **The collapsible panel**: .CollapsiblePanel

  This style controls the border that appears around a collapsible panel. You can alter its color or style, or remove it completely.

- **All tabs**: .CollapsiblePanelTab

  Four styles control how browsers display a collapsible panel's tab. Each style applies to the tab under different circumstances: when the panel is open, when it's closed, when a mouse moves over the tab, and when a guest clicks the tab (this last action gives the tab "focus").

  To alter the basic appearance of all the tabs, edit the .CollapsiblePanelTab style. For example, define a font family for this style and all tabs adopt that font. In addition, this style dictates the padding inside each tab, and the border that separates the tab and the panel beneath it.

- **Tab when panel is closed**: .CollapsiblePanelTab

  The .CollapsiblePanelTab style also dictates the properties, such as the background color, for the tab when the panel is closed.

TIP The same fuzzy outline you see in focused tabs for tabbed panels and accordions appears in the Spry collapsible panel, too. To remove the outline, create an advanced style called .CollapsiblePanel: focus, and then set that style's outline property to none.

- **Tab when moused over**: .CollapsiblePanelTabHover, .CollapsiblePanelOpen .CollapsiblePanelTabHover

  This long group selector applies to the hover state for tabs—both when the panel is open and when it's closed. If you want to define a different hover style for a tab when the panel is open, create two styles: .CollapsiblePanelTabHover for a tab when the panel is closed, and .CollapsiblePanelOpen .CollapsiblePanel TabHover for a tab when the panel is open. (If you go this route, you should either delete the supplied group selector style—.CollapsiblePanelTabHover, .CollapsiblePanelOpen .CollapsiblePanelTabHover—or change its name as described on page 141 so that it applies to only one of the tab states.)

- **Tab when panel is opened**: .CollapsiblePanelOpen .CollapsiblePanelTab, .CollapsiblePanelFocused .CollapsiblePanelTab

  The .CollapsiblePanelOpen .CollapsiblePanelTab descendent selector style applies to a tab when the panel is open. This style overwrites style properties inherited from the .CollapsiblePanelTab style. In Dreamweaver's stock style sheet, only the background color differs from the other tab style, but, again, you're free to change that.

  A tab also changes color when a visitor clicks it, or presses the Tab key to access it. The .CollapsiblePanelFocused .CollapsiblePanelTab style is the culprit here, so you want to edit it if you don't want this color change to take place.

- **Panel**: *.CollapsiblePanelContent*

  Dreamweaver applies the *.CollapsiblePanelContent* class to the <div> tag that surrounds the HTML in an accordion panel. You can adjust font settings for this style to affect only the text inside the panel, or add a background color to make the panel stand out from other page content.

- **Content inside the panel**. As with Spry tabbed panels and Spry accordions, Dreamweaver doesn't start you out with any styles that control specific tags inside a collapsible panel. You can use the same process described for Spry tabbed panels (under the bullet point "Content inside the panels" on page 645) to create descendent selectors that affect only tags inside a collapsible panel. Just use *.CollapsiblePanel*, followed by a space as the first part of the selector and then the tag name. For example, the style *.CollapsiblePanel p* formats paragraphs inside a collapsible panel.

  Also note that content inside a collapsible panel butts up against the panel's left and right edges. Avoid adding padding directly to the panel (the *.Collapsible-PanelContent* style), since it disrupts the panel's smooth opening and closing animation. In addition, the second time you open the panel, it's actually taller than it was the first time. Instead, add padding or margins to the tags inside the panel. For example, if you want all Heading 2 tags indented 5 pixels from both the left and right sides of the panel, create a descendent selector (like *.CollapsiblePanelContent h2*), and then set the left and right Margin properties to 5 pixels.

■ Spry Tooltips

Pop-up tooltips are a great way to give visitors supplementary information without visually overloading your web page. A tooltip waits in hiding until a visitor mouses over a word, sentence, or image, and then...bam! The tooltip appears. You can use tooltips to define web page features, display pictures and text, or even point to a web page with additional information. Netflix, for example, uses a simple presentation for the DVDs they rent—the listing includes just pictures, ratings, and a way to quickly add the DVD to your "To rent" list. However, when you mouse over a DVD in the main catalog, a tooltip appears, featuring a detailed summary of the movie. Dreamweaver includes a Spry tool for creating these kinds of useful pop-up boxes.

Adding a Spry Tooltip

A Spry Tooltip widget consists of a *trigger*—text or an image that your visitor mouses over—and the *tooltip* itself—the pop-up box. To add a tooltip:

1. **Select a word, sentence, image, or block-level element.**

   You can turn any block-level element into a trigger: a word, sentence, or paragraph; a headline; an image; or an entire <div> tag. Which way you go depends on the tooltip's purpose. For example, if you want to define important words in a document, select a single word to trigger the tooltip.

2. **Choose Insert→Spry→Spry Tooltip or, on the Insert panel, click the Spry Tooltip icon.**

When you insert a tooltip, Dreamweaver first adds an ID to the trigger—if you select an entire paragraph as a trigger, for example, Dreamweaver adds the ID name to the <p> tag like this: *<p id="spryTrigger1">*. If you select just a single word, Dreamweaver wraps the word in a <span> tag with the proper ID name:

```
<span id="spryTrigger1">word</span>
```

The exact name Dreamweaver assigns depends on whether you already added tooltips to the page, so you might have various IDs on the same page—spry-Trigger1, spryTrigger2, and so on.

TIP You don't have to select anything on a page to insert a tooltip. You can place the cursor anywhere on your page and complete step 2 above. Dreamweaver inserts a <span> tag into the document at the location of your cursor, along with the text "Tooltip trigger goes here." You can change the text to something more appropriate— "Move your mouse here for a pop-up list of directions," and even move the span to another location on the page (just cut and paste the tag). You can also delete the <span> tag, which lets you assign the tooltip to another tag, as described in step 4 below.

Dreamweaver also inserts a new <div> tag containing some placeholder text—"Tooltip content goes here." This is the tooltip itself and, depending on how big your web page is, you may not actually see it at first. That's because Dreamweaver adds tooltips to the very end of a web page, after all the other content. So if you have many paragraphs of text, images, and so on, you may need to scroll down to the bottom of the page to see and edit your tooltip. By default, the tooltip has a light yellow background, but you can change that as described on page 606.

NOTE Dreamweaver always makes tooltips visible so you can edit their content. However, when you view the page in a browser (or click the Live button [page 72]), the tooltips remain hidden until you hover over its trigger.

---

3. **In the Property Inspector, name the tooltip.**

As with the other Spry widgets, this step is optional. Changing the name alters the ID Dreamweaver applied to the tooltip <div> tag.

4. **If you want to change the ID name Dreamweaver applies to the tooltip trigger, click anywhere inside the trigger text.** In the Property Inspector, type a new name in the ID box.

In most cases, you'll skip this step. When you insert a tooltip, Dreamweaver correctly prepares all the HTML you need. But if you don't like the generic name Dreamweaver supplies (*sprytrigger1*, for example), you can change it.

5. **If you changed the trigger's ID in the previous step, then click the tooltip's blue Spry tab to select it, and then, from the Property Inspector's Trigger menu, select the ID name you typed in step 2.**

This step is optional as well, so you'll probably skip it. However, you might want to select the ID name of an existing page element. For example, say you have an image on your page and you gave it the ID name "logo." You can use this element as a trigger. First, insert a tooltip (without selecting any text, as described in the Tip on page 657) and then, from the Property Inspector's Trigger menu, select the ID of the element—for example #*logo*. (Don't forget to delete the original trigger <span> that Dreamweaver inserted.)

6. **In the Property Inspector, set one or more of the display options (Figure 13-8).**

Just where your tooltip pops up on a web page depends on where your visitor's mouse is when he moves over the tooltip's trigger. That is, if the trigger is an entire paragraph of text and a visitor moves his mouse over the top line of the paragraph, the tooltip appears near the top of the paragraph; if he mouses deep into the paragraph, the tooltip appears near the bottom of the paragraph. You can fine-tune these settings in the Property Inspector's tooltip options.

Here's how those options work:

- **Follow mouse**. When you select this option, the tooltip follows your guest's mouse as she moves her cursor around the trigger element. For example, say a visitor triggers a tooltip when she mouses over a large picture of the Eiffel Tower. If the visitor moves the mouse around the picture, the tooltip follows along. Since this can induce sea-sickness, you might want to leave this checkbox turned off, in which case, once the tooltip appears, it doesn't move.

- **Hide on mouse out**. This confusingly named option lets you keep a tooltip open as long as the mouse is over *either* the trigger element or the tooltip box itself. Normally, a tooltip disappears when you mouse off the trigger element. This is often a good idea, since you want the tooltip to disappear when a visitor moves his mouse off of a trigger and toward another area of your page. However, if the tooltip has content that a visitor might click—such as a set of links—turn this option on. If you don't, as soon as someone moves his mouse toward one of the links in the tooltips—at the same time moving the mouse off the trigger element—the tooltip disappears, and the visitor can never click the link! Turn on this option, and the tooltip remains visible while the mouse hovers over the trigger element or the tooltip; it disappears only when the mouse is no longer over either.

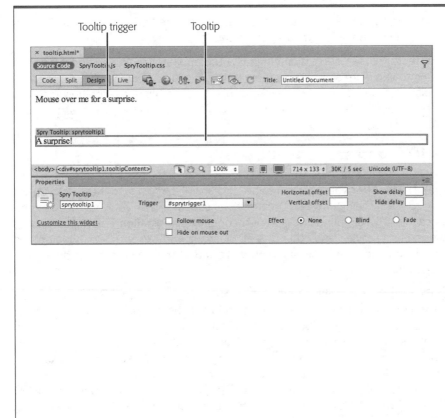

Tooltip trigger   Tooltip

- **Horizontal offset/Vertical offset**. Dreamweaver normally places tooltips 20 pixels to the right and 20 pixels down from the trigger element. If you want the tooltip to appear in a different location, type either a pixel or percentage value in the "Horizontal offset" box (to control its placement left and right of the cursor) or the "Vertical offset" box (to control the placement above or below the cursor). You can even use a negative value for either orientation. For example, -60% in the "Vertical offset" box positions a little more than half of the tooltip above the mouse's position. If you use a negative value for both offsets, you can make the tooltip appear directly over the trigger element.

- **Delay**. If you don't want a tooltip to appear right after it's triggered, type a number in the "Show delay" box. Browsers register the value in milliseconds, so if you type *1000*, the tooltip appears 1 second after a visitor mouses over the trigger. This feature may not seem very useful—after all, by the time one second passes a visitor has probably moved his mouse off the trigger, and the tooltip never appears. However, a smaller value, like 100, serves a good purpose:

It prevents a tooltip from appearing if the mouse momentarily travels over a trigger. This keeps your tooltips from suddenly flashing on- and off-screen as someone mouses over the trigger on his way to somewhere else.

The "Hide delay" option determines how long the tooltip hangs around *after* your guest moves her mouse off the trigger.

- **Effect**. You can add visual effects to the appearance and disappearance of the tooltip. Turn on the None radio button if you want the tooltip to appear or disappear in a blink. For a fancier display, choose Blind (the tooltip wipes into and out of existence like a window shade) or Fade (the tooltip fades in and out like a ghost).

Adding Content to a Tooltip

The HTML for a tooltip is very basic, just a single <div> tag placed at the end of your page's HTML. After you insert a tooltip, click inside the div, and then press Ctrl+A (⌘-A) to select the dummy text Dreamweaver supplies. Then add your own content. You can insert a simple paragraph or a complex combination of HTML, including images, Flash movies, and other divs. If you want, you can even turn a tooltip into a mini-web page—just make sure you don't add so much content that the tooltip doesn't fit in the browser window.

You can also edit the tooltip's trigger element—the text, paragraph, div, or image you selected before adding the tooltip. As mentioned above, Dreamweaver adds an ID to the trigger's HTML (or, if you selected just a word or two, wraps the selection in a <span> tag, and then adds an ID to that span). Unfortunately, you have no immediate way to identify a particular tooltip's trigger—it doesn't highlight, for example, when you select the tooltip. You need to either remember where the trigger is, or select the tooltip and then, in the Property Inspector, look for the ID name applied to it (see Figure 13-8). Once you know the ID, execute a search for that name using Dreamweaver's excellent Find and Replace tool, as described in Chapter 20.

Formatting a Tooltip

When you add a Spry tooltip to a web page, Dreamweaver links the page to an external style sheet named *SpryTooltip.css*, which contains only two styles. Leave the first one—*.iframeTooltip*—alone. It overcomes some browser display bugs related to the tooltip. The second style—*.toolTipContent*—defines the look of the pop-up. Out of the box, the style has just a single property—a light yellow background. However, you'll probably want to change the background color, add some padding to move the content away from the edges of the tooltip, and so on.

In addition, you may want to create styles that apply just to tags inside the tooltip— for example, to provide a unique look for paragraphs or a heading. Here, again, descendent selectors come to the rescue (see page 377). Since all tooltip content goes inside a <div> tag with the class *.tooltipContent* applied to it, you can create special styles that apply only to the content. For example, the descendent selector *.tooltipContent p* affects only paragraphs inside a tooltip.

You might also want to create a style to format the tooltip trigger. Dreamweaver doesn't help you out with this—the program doesn't supply a style to make the trigger stand out. In fact, unless you do something to alter the look of a trigger element, it's difficult for anyone to figure out that any particular element has a tooltip attached to it! For example, say you select a single word on a page, and then add a tooltip to it—perhaps the tooltip defines the word. When viewed in a web browser, that word doesn't look any different from any other word, so a visitor has no way of knowing that she should mouse over it.

One way to solve this problem is to create a class style—.*trigger*, for example—and apply it to the HTML tag for the trigger (see page 132 for instructions on applying a class to a tag). If you add tooltips to single words (as in the definition example), you might want to add a light background to highlight the word. You could also change the cursor style used for that class. For example, if you set the *cursor* property to "Help," the cursor changes to a question mark when a visitor mouses over the trigger.

Of course, if the trigger is obvious—for example, if it has the text "Mouse over me to see..."—you might not want or need any special style for the trigger.

■ Spry Data Sets

Dreamweaver lets you display data more dynamically than a plain-vanilla HTML table can. Spry data sets provide several ways to present data from a variety of sources, including basic HTML tables or XML files. With a Spry data set, you can create an interactive table that visitors can sort just by clicking the header of a table column.

Say a page has a table that lists all the employees in a company. The table includes each employee's name, the region of the country where he or she works, his or her phone number, and other important information. Sometimes you might want to see the list alphabetized by last name; other times you may want to sort the list by the regions in which they work (northeast, southeast, and so on). Normally, you'd have to create two web pages: one with a table of employees listed by last name, and another with employees listed by region.

With a Spry data set, you need only one page and one table, no matter how many columns you have. That's because a Spry table is interactive, just like a regular old Excel spreadsheet. Want to see employees organized by last name? Click the "Name" column. To group employees by region, click the "Region" column. A Spry table is interactive, instantaneous, and doesn't require loading another web page.

In addition, Spry data sets let you display detailed data on a single item in the table. Suppose you have a simple table that lists just employees' names and the regions in which they work. With Spry, you can add an "Up Close and Personal" section to the page, so that when you click an employee name in a table row, detailed information, such as the employee's phone number, photo, and email address, appear in another part of the page. Once again, this little trick doesn't require the browser to download a different web page. All this information appears on the same page and with a simple mouse click.

If you often add data tables to your site, or you simply have large amounts of related data that you want to display in interactive format, the Spry data set is perfect for you. You can store the data you want to make interactive in a plain HTML table, like those you read about in Chapter 6. The JavaScript programming included in the Spry data set reads the data from that HTML table and reformats it for presentation. If you have an HTML table, you can either create a separate page that displays the table, or include the table directly inside the page with the Spry data set. Keep in mind that Adobe wrote Spry data sets primarily to display repeating rows of information. Although an HTML file can hold any type of information, you should use a Spry data set for tables that contain lists of information, like product catalogs, employee records, and so on.

Storing Data in an HTML File

To get started with Spry data sets, you need a file containing data in basic HTML format. Dreamweaver provides two ways to create a Spry data set from an HTML table. The first is to create a separate file that contains a basic HTML table with all your data in it. You can then tell the Spry Data Set tool to load that file and its data, and then display it on your site. This means you have a simple HTML file that's easy to update, and another, fully designed page that displays the data using Dreamweaver's Spry data set tools.

The second method is to add the HTML table to the same page as the Spry data set. In other words, insert a basic HTML table on a page in your site, and then use the Spry data set tools to massage that data and turn it into an interactive super-table. When it does this, the Spry programming hides the original (HTML) table of data if that table is on the same page as the Spry data set, and displays only the Spry-formatted table on the page.

This second approach might sound a bit weird. After all, why add a table to a page, and then add some fancy JavaScript just to display data from the same table? If all you want to do is display a table of data, this approach is overkill—rather, create a nice-looking HTML table on your web page, and you're done. But if you want to tap the interactive capabilities of a Spry data set—to create a sortable table like the one discussed on page 671, for example, or the interactive master/detail display discussed on page 675 — this approach has a couple of advantages.

First, Spry uses JavaScript to load data into a data set. If the HTML table is in a separate file and a visitor has JavaScript turned off, then that separate HTML file never loads, and the visitor never sees the data—just an empty space where the data should be. In addition, search engines don't use JavaScript either, so any data that JavaScript loads is lost to a search engine. By putting the HTML table on the same page, search engines and visitors without JavaScript can still access the data (although they lose all the interactivity JavaScript provides).

Which method to use? If you want search engines to index the data you display, or you want to make sure the data's visible even for people who have JavaScript turned off, use the second approach: Add the HTML table to the same page that displays the data. The first approach is good if your data comes from a source other than the page that displays it—if, for example, another program exports the data as an HTML table—or if you want someone who's not Dreamweaver-savvy to have a simple way to update the data in the table.

In either case, you start by adding a basic HTML table containing all your data. The table doesn't have to be fancy—your site's visitors don't actually see this table. They just see the data pulled from the table and either placed onto *another* web page or completely reformatted and displayed on the same page, enhanced with interactive Spry effects. In fact, the table should be as simple as possible (see Figure 13-9). You don't need to worry about the table's width, cell padding and spacing, or any other formatting choices you make when you design regular HTML tables. Also, do yourself a favor and avoid merged cells and row spans (see page 308), which produce inconsistent results in your data. Finally, don't apply any styles to the rows, columns, or the table itself. This table, if it hasn't sunk in by now, is just for the data—you format the data's appearance when you add it to a web page using a Spry data set.

Make sure the top row of the table is a header row (see page 301) that identifies each column's data. In Figure 13-9, for example, the top row of cells contains table headers. Column 1 has the header "thumb," column 2's has "large," and so on. With descriptive header names, it's easier for you, later on, to identify and select the data you want to use in a Spry data set.

> **NOTE** You can also put images in table cells; use the same procedure you would for inserting an image into a web page (page 242). However, for those images to show up correctly on a page that uses the Spry data tools, you need to make sure that, if you create a separate file for the HTML table, you store that file (with its document-relative image links) in the same folder as the web page using the data. Otherwise, the paths to the images won't work, and the images won't show up on the final web page.
>
> Alternatively, you can use site root-relative links for your images (see page 187) and keep your HTML file anywhere in your site—any page on the site can display those images correctly.

Finally, you need to give the table an ID. The Spry programming requires this, and if you don't provide an ID, you can't extract the data from the table. To add an ID, select the table (click the table border, for example, or use one of the other methods mentioned on page 294), and then, in the Property Inspector's ID box (circled in Figure 13-9), type a name—a simple ID name, like *data*, works just fine.

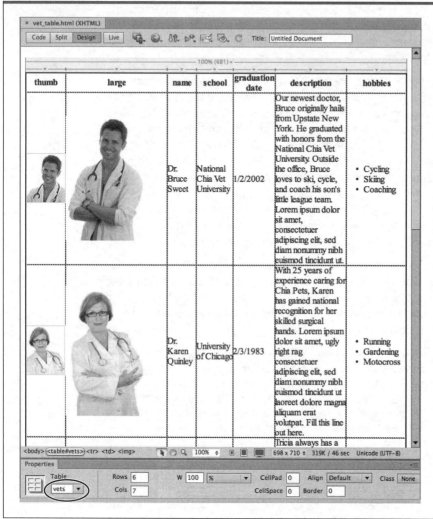

FIGURE 13-9

The Spry data set tool lets you extract data from a basic HTML table and manipulate it in fun, interesting, and interactive ways. You can even suck data from an existing table on your site (a nice way to reuse content that's already there). The only condition is that any table you use for Spry data must have an ID assigned to it (circled). See page 137 for details.

Dreamweaver also lets you store data in tags other than HTML tables. For example, you could create a series of <div> tags that store the data you wish to display. If you go this route, you need to have one <div> tag that surrounds all your data—and you have to apply an ID to it. You also need separate divs for each row and each column within a row, and you must apply a class to each of the row divs and another class to each of the column divs. For example, the basic HTML for a data file using divs might look like this:

```
<div id="data">

  <div class="row">

    <div class="column">Godzilla Chia</div>

    <div class="column">1955</div>

  </div>

  <div class="row">

    <div class="column">Bambi Chia</div>

    <div class="column">1960</div>

  </div>

</div>
```

You need the class names—.row and .column in this example—to let Dreamweaver know which divs hold one row of information, and how many columns are in each row. Unless you already have data set up in the format described in this paragraph, stick to HTML tables for storing data—they're a lot easier to create and maintain.

NOTE Because the Spry programming actually downloads the entire data file (the HTML file) and stores it in a browser's memory, Spry data sets work best with relatively few rows of data. If you build an HTML table with 1,000 rows of information, you're better off using a database instead. Otherwise you'll find that your Spry-driven data sets run slowly in web browsers.

Inserting a Spry Data Set

Dreamweaver provides an easy-to-follow wizard that lets you create both a complete Spry data set *and* all the HTML needed to display the data using one of four canned layouts. (You can create your own data set layouts, too, as described in the box on page 679.)

To begin using a Spry data set:

1. **Open a web page where you want to display Spry data, and then click in the area of the page where you want the Spry table to appear.**

    This could be an empty line inside the page's main <div>, for example. Just make sure there's enough room for the table to fit.

2. **Next, insert the Spry data set object by clicking the Spry Data Set button from the Insert panel's Data category or by choosing Insert→Spry→Spry Data Set.**

    The new Spry Data Set wizard opens (see Figure 13-10). From this point, there are just 3 more steps.

Selected data table   Select file   Preview file

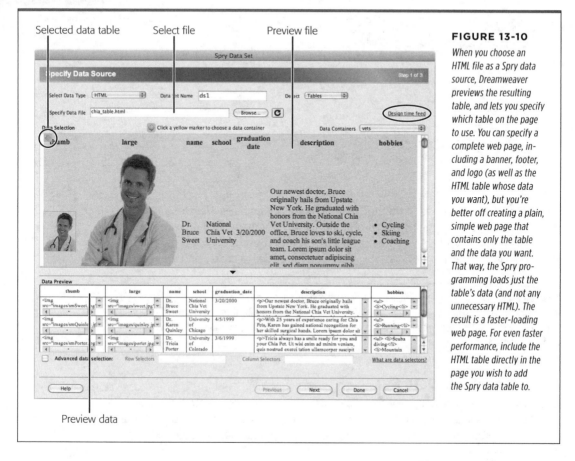

FIGURE 13-10

*When you choose an
HTML file as a Spry data
source, Dreamweaver
previews the resulting
table, and lets you specify
which table on the page
to use. You can specify a
complete web page, in-
cluding a banner, footer,
and logo (as well as the
HTML table whose data
you want), but you're
better off creating a plain,
simple web page that
contains only the table
and the data you want.
That way, the Spry pro-
gramming loads just the
table's data (and not any
unnecessary HTML). The
result is a faster-loading
web page. For even faster
performance, include the
HTML table directly in the
page you wish to add
the Spry data table to.*

Preview data

3. **Choose a data source.**

   The data source is an HTML file (see page 662 for details). You can specify a file
   on your computer, or even use an absolute URL to point to a file on your web
   server. (Due to security limitations of web browsers, you have to have the data
   file and the web page that displays the Spry data on the same server.)

   This window's many choices can make it a little intimidating, but setting the options
   correctly is a pretty simple process:

   1. **From the Select Data Type menu, choose HTML.**

NOTE You can also use an XML file as a data source. In step 1, choose XML instead of HTML, and select the XML file from your computer in step 4.

2. **In the Data Set Name field, type a name.**

   Dreamweaver supplies a generic name—like *ds1*—but change it to something more descriptive. If you add multiple data sets to a page, distinguishing among *ds1, ds2, and ds3* isn't as easy as among, say, *dsEvents, dsEmployees,* and *dsProducts.*

   Keep the *ds* prefix, however. If you ever go into Code view, this small step makes it easy for you to identify a reference to a Spry data set.

3. **From the Detect menu, select Tables.**

   You can actually select Divs, List, or Custom from this menu, too. As mentioned earlier, you can store data inside any nested group of HTML tags, such as a group of <div> tags or even a nested unordered list (the Detect menu lets you specify the HTML tag you used in the data file). However, HTML tables really are the most straightforward way to store data, so you're better off sticking with the Tables option.

4. **Click the Browse button, and locate and select an HTML file.**

   You can choose a separate file that has a table, or the same file you're working on if it has the data table you want to "Spry-ify." You can also type in an absolute URL that points to an HTML file—like http://www.chia-vet.com/vets/table.php. This is handy if you're not pulling data from an actual HTML file, but from a program that generates the HTML (for example, from a database on your web server). In that case, use the URL of the server-side program that generates the data.

   Keep in mind a couple of caveats when you work with absolute URLs. First, for the Spry data set to work, the data file and the web page that displays the data have to be on the same site. In other words, if you add a Spry data set to a web page residing at www.cosmofarmer.com and it specifies an XML file on www.chia-vet.com, the Spry data set won't work. In fact, a browser trying to view that Spry-enabled page displays a nasty error message.

   That error is part of a browser's built-in security. When a page on one site tries to use JavaScript to access and display data from another site, the browser smells something fishy—"Is this web page trying to pretend it's on another site?"—and spits out an error message.

5. **Identify the data container.**

The Spry data set tools let you specify any HTML page, including the page to which you're adding the Spry data (as long as it has a data table); you can also specify another fully designed HTML page on your site that just happens to have a table in it. The page might even have a couple of tables, so you need to tell Dreamweaver which one to use. As mentioned earlier, when you build an HTML data table for use with Spry, you must give it an ID. If you don't, Dreamweaver tells you that the file has no valid data containers, and you can't pick a table.

You can identify a data container two ways. The middle part of the Spry Data Set wizard window previews the HTML file containing the table. A yellow arrow indicates a valid table (that is, any HTML table with an ID). Click the yellow arrow, and it turns green indicating that Dreamweaver will use the information from that table for the Spry data set (circled on the left side of Figure 13-10). If you know the name of the ID you applied to the HTML table, then, in the top-right of the window, you can select it from the Data Containers menu.

After you select a table, in the bottom portion of the window, Dreamweaver previews the table's data. If the table has a row of table headers at the top, then the text in that row's cells appears as the name atop each column. For example, in Figure 13-10, the text "thumb" appears in the Data Preview pane at the top of the first column, because that text is inside a table header cell in the actual HTML file. (See the HTML preview in the middle of Figure 13-10.)

6. **Optionally specify advanced data selection rules.**

If you use HTML tables for data, then, at the bottom of the Specify Data Source window, you probably never need to turn on the "Advanced data selection" checkbox. However, if you're using nested <div> or <ul> tags to store data, then you *have to* choose this option, and then specify which tags are rows and which are columns. For instance, in the earlier nested div example, each <div> tag that acts as a single row has the class name *.row* applied to it; likewise, divs that act as single "cells" of information have the class name *.column*. So, to use the nested div example, you would need to turn on the "Advanced data selection" checkbox and, in the Row Selectors box, type *.row*, and in the Column Selectors box, type *.column*. (Dreamweaver uses the same syntax as CSS to specify a class selector.)

Or, even better, just use HTML tables and skip this entire step!

7. **Click the Next button.**

The Set Data Options window appears (see Figure 13-11), previewing the data and providing tools for setting various options for displaying the data.

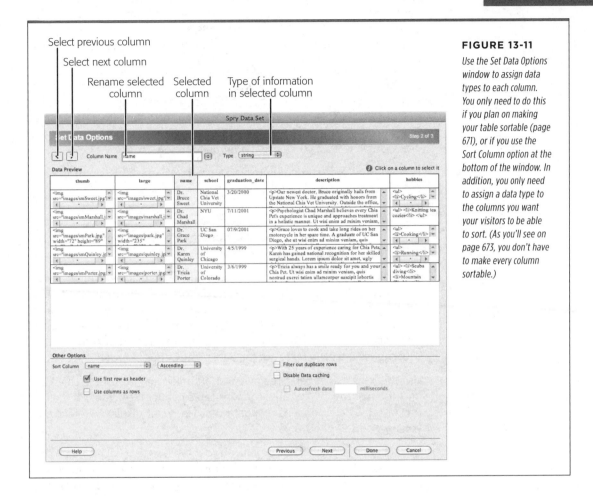

FIGURE 13-11

Use the Set Data Options window to assign data types to each column. You only need to do this if you plan on making your table sortable (page 671), or if you use the Sort Column option at the bottom of the window. In addition, you only need to assign a data type to the columns you want your visitors to be able to sort. (As you'll see on page 673, you don't have to make every column sortable.)

Select previous column

Select next column

Rename selected column

Selected column

Type of information in selected column

8. **Set column data types.**

Click each column, and then, from the Type menu, choose an option. This is necessary only if you want to sort the table before a browser displays the data (see the next step) or if you want to give your visitors the ability to sort the table by column. You can choose one of four types of data:

- String. Choose *string* for text. For example, if the column contains people's names, choose this option.

- **Number.** Choose *number* if a column contains, uh, numbers, of course. For example, if the column displays how many units of a particular product you have in stock, then, from the Type menu, choose *number*. For a sortable table (like the kind described on page 671), a visitor can then click the Units column and view product listings in the order of how many units are in stock.

- **Date.** Use this option if the column holds dates in the form of 3/29/2012—in other words, the month, followed by a forward slash, the day, another forward slash, and the year. You can specify the month and day with either one or two digits—03 and 3 both work—and the year with either two or four digits—12 and 2012 both work. However, if the column includes just years (such as 1977), then use the *number* option.

- **HTML.** Finally, if the column contains HTML markup (such as <img src="photo.jpg">), choose this option.

9. **Set additional options.**

   The Set Data Options window's bottom portion offers several ways to control how Spry displays the data from the HTML file:

   - **Sort column.** If you want to sort the data before it's displayed on the page, choose a column from this menu. For example, if you have an HTML table listing employee names and information, you could choose the employee name column to list staffers in alphabetical order. From the menu to the right, choose Ascending if you want the data sorted from A to Z or 1 to 100; choose Descending to put the data in the opposite order: Z–A or 100–1

   - **Use first row as header.** Dreamweaver automatically turns this checkbox on if the first row of the table contains table header (<th> tags). If the first row of table cells contains real data that you want displayed, make sure you turn off this checkbox.

   - **Use columns as rows.** If you organized your table so that each column contains data on a single record, turn on this checkbox. This configuration is common on pages that compare products. To give guests an easy-to-read, side-by-side comparison, each table row holds data for *different* records (for example, a row might display the prices of four different cellphones). If you set up your table like this, turn on this checkbox to make sure the data for each record remains grouped together.

   - **Filter out duplicate rows.** Turn on this checkbox only if your table has the same record with the identical data listed twice.

   - **Disable Data caching.** Sometimes, data needs to be as fresh as bread from a bakery. Stock prices, sports scores, and other time-sensitive info needs to be up-to-date. Since web browsers tend to download and store files in a cache (see the box on page 783), when you load a Spry data set page, you may be looking at data downloaded a week earlier. Turn on this checkbox to force the Spry programming to download the HTML data file every time it downloads the web page. This is especially true if the data comes from a frequently updated database.

However, if you modify the HTML data table only every now and again, keep this checkbox turned off. The web page loads more quickly if the browser doesn't have to constantly download the HTML data file.

- **Autorefresh data.** This option is available only if you turned on the "Disable Data caching" checkbox. Put a check in this box if your data changes *really* frequently—as in every few seconds or so. With this option set, a browser downloads the data file according to the schedule you specify in the milliseconds box. For example, if you type *1000* there (see Figure 13-11), the browser downloads the HTML data file every second. Normally, you use this option only when the HTML data comes from a server program that receives constantly updated information.

10. **Click Next, and then select a method for inserting the Spry data.**

The Choose Insert Options screen gives you the same option for HTML and XML data files.

Choosing a Data Layout

The last step for the Spry Data Set wizard is selecting how you want to insert the data into your web page. To make the process easier, Dreamweaver includes four ready-to-use layouts that insert the necessary HTML tags, add the data, attach an external CSS file with some basic formatting in it, and essentially perform all the heavy lifting so that you just need to massage the CSS to match the look of your site. You'll read about each of these options in the following sections.

Alternatively, you can just add the data set programming as described in the previous sections, and then add the data to your page by hand, using a panel built just for this purpose; see the box on page 679.

Note that once you finish with the Spry Data Set wizard and select one of the four layouts, you can't return to the wizard and change the layout, or alter any of the layout options you selected when you first inserted the layout into the page. You can, however, delete any of the Spry layouts on the page (for example, the Spry table the wizard inserted). You can then reinsert a different layout (or choose different layout options) by editing the Spry data set by double-clicking the data set's name in the Bindings panel (Window→Bindings).

■ SPRY TABLE

The first choice in the Choose Insert Options window, "Insert table," is the easiest way to present rows of information from an XML file in a quick and orderly fashion (see Figure 13-12). While the information might look like a regular HTML table, it's actually interactive, letting visitors click column headers to sort the data and mouse over rows to highlight them.

Row of data   Column header   Hover class applied

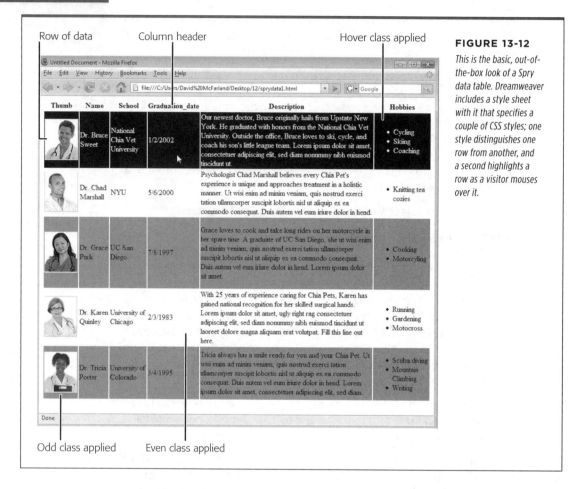

FIGURE 13-12

This is the basic, out-of-the-box look of a Spry data table. Dreamweaver includes a style sheet with it that specifies a couple of CSS styles; one style distinguishes one row from another, and a second highlights a row as a visitor mouses over it.

Odd class applied   Even class applied

To add this kind of Spry table, turn on the "Insert table" radio button in the Choose Insert Options window and then:

1. **Click the Set Up button.**

   The Insert Table window opens (see Figure 13-13).

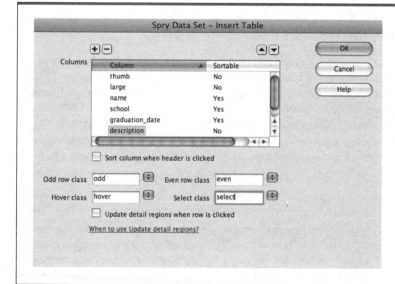

FIGURE 13-13

It doesn't always make sense to make a column sortable. For example, it's not useful to sort a column full of descriptive paragraphs (who wants to see a list of items based on whether their description begins with "A," "The," or "This"?), nor would you want to sort a column based on the name of thumbnail images.

2. **Remove and rearrange your table's columns.**

   Dreamweaver lists all the columns in the data set. Each column name appears inside a single table cell. If you don't want one of the columns and its data to appear in the table, click the column name and then press the minus (-) button to remove it. (If you want to bring back a column you deleted, press the + button, and then select the column name in the window that appears.)

   Removing a column from the Column list means only that Dreamweaver won't add that data to the table it's about to create. And, if you find you're *missing* data from a table after you create it, you can use the Bindings panel (discussed in the box on page 679) to drag those missing elements into the table.

   You can also rearrange the order of the columns. The name at the top of the list is the table's left-most column; the name at the bottom is the column on the far right. To reposition a column, click its name, and then press the up-arrow button to move the column to the left in the final table, or click the down-arrow button to move the column to the right.

3. **Assign sortable columns.**

   One of a Spry table's coolest features is its ability to instantly re-sort data simply by clicking a column's header. If someone visiting your web page wants to sort a Spry table differently from the way you presented it, he just needs to click a different header.

Columns aren't normally sortable—the Insert Spry Table window defaults to listing all the columns as non-sortable. To make a column sortable, select its name in the Column list, and then turn on the "Sort column when header is clicked" checkbox (see Figure 13-13).

4. **Assign CSS classes to table rows.**

A Spry table provides helpful visual feedback that makes it easy for you to read and interact with the data. You can more easily scan all the columns in a single, wide row of data if every other row has a distinct background (see the Spry table in Figure 13-12). Dreamweaver lets you assign a class style to a table's odd rows and another class style to its even rows. For a simple approach, create two classes, *.odd* and *.even*, each with different background colors. Then, in the Insert Spry Table window, select the appropriate class from the "Odd row class" menu and the "Even row class" menu.

Similarly, you can assign classes to rows based on how someone interacts with them. For example, you can make a row change color when someone mouses over any column in the row. Or you can change a row's color when someone clicks it (a kind of "this row is now selected" indicator). The *.hover* class controls the look of a row when a mouse passes over it, while the Spry programming applies the *.select* class when someone clicks a row. Both are useful if you use a master/detail layout for your table (described below), but since Dreamweaver has a simple tool for creating these types of layouts, you'll probably skip these options (unless you like the eye candy).

If you haven't yet created any class styles for these rows, just type in a class name (without the period). Even if you're not sure you want to change the look of the table's rows, assign classes to all four options (*.odd*, *.even*, *.hover*, and *.select*) anyway. Dreamweaver provides no way to return to the Insert Spry Table window, so if you later decide to add styles to the rows, you have to go into Code view and add them by hand using specific Spry syntax (visit the online Spry Developer's Guide to learn how: *http://tinyurl.com/ygy7xd6*). Save yourself this hardship by assigning the classes while you've got an easy-to-use dialog box.

5. **If you plan to include a detail region with your table (discussed next), turn on the "Update detail regions when row is clicked" checkbox.**

This option makes sure that the Spry programming changes a detail region when a visitor clicks a row in the table.

6. **Click OK, and then, in the Spry Data Set window, click Done.**

Dreamweaver inserts the table into the page. It's just an HTML table with a little extra Spry code. You can resize it and then adjust it just as you would a regular HTML table (see Chapter 7). The top row contains a series of table headers (<th> tags) with each column's name. The names are regular text, and you can change them to a more understandable label if you like.

The second row of cells represents the data. Dreamweaver displays just a single row, but when you preview the page in a browser, a table row appears for each row of data in the HTML or XML file. Even better, the Live view (page 72) lets you quickly preview a Spry table without leaving Dreamweaver. In Design view, each cell in this row has a Spry data placeholder (the element's name on a blue background). You can select a format for the placeholder as if it were regular HTML (for example, apply a CSS style to it or make it bold).

■ MASTER/DETAIL LAYOUT

One of the most exciting uses for Spry data is the so-called master/detail layout. When you select this option from the Choose Insert Options window, you create a page that lists all the rows in a data set (the *master* list), accompanied by a region of the page that displays details from a single, selected row (detailed information on the selected item, in other words). For example, in Figure 13-14, clicking Dr. Chad Marshall's box on the left fills the area on the right with detailed information about the good doctor.

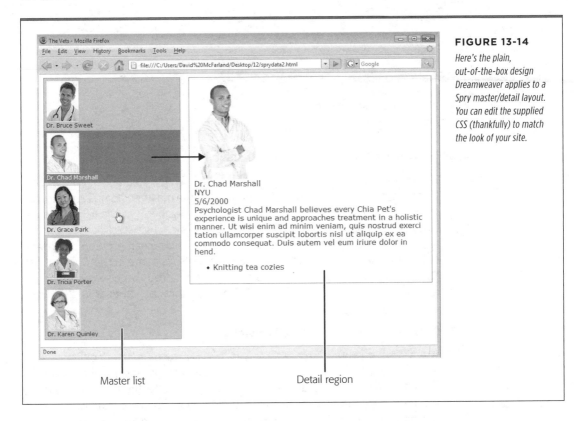

FIGURE 13-14

Here's the plain, out-of-the-box design Dreamweaver applies to a Spry master/detail layout. You can edit the supplied CSS (thankfully) to match the look of your site.

Master list

Detail region

To create a master/detail layout, click the "Insert master/detail layout" button in the Choose Insert Options screen and then:

1. **Click the Set Up button.**

The Insert Master/Detail Layout window opens (see Figure 13-15).

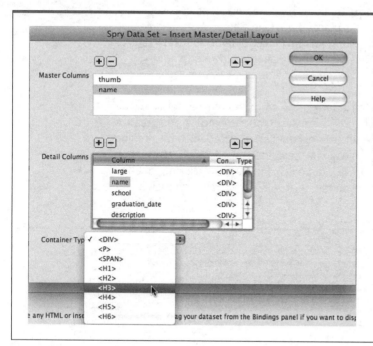

2. **Remove and rearrange the master columns.**

The top portion of the window lets you specify which columns of data appear in the master list. For example, in Figure 13-14, the master columns are the ones with the thumbnail image and the name of each doctor in the list on the left side of the page. To add a column of data to the master list, click the + button, and then, in the window that appears, select a column name. If you don't want one of the elements to appear in the table, click its name in the Columns list, and then press the minus (-) button to remove it. You can also rearrange the columns by using the up and down arrows, so that they appear in a different order in the list.

3. **Remove and rearrange detail columns.**

The procedure you use to add, remove, and rearrange master columns works for detail columns as well. However, in addition to choosing which columns should appear in the detail region, you can also specify the HTML tag that Spry applies to the data. For example, you might want to use a heading (an <h2> tag, for example) to list the title of an article, or a <p> tag for a long description.

4. **Click OK, and then, in the Spry Data Set window, click Done.**

Dreamweaver inserts all the HTML and Spry programming necessary to create the master/detail layout. In addition, it attaches an external style sheet—*Spry-MasterDetail.css*—that provides basic formatting for the elements on the page.

Basically, Dreamweaver creates the master list with a series of <div> tags stacked one on top of the other. The program puts each item in the master list in a div and applies the class *.MasterColumn* to it. If you want to change the look of each of those boxes (for example, add a top border line to separate each item in the list), edit the descendent selector style *.MasterDetail .MasterColumn*.

Likewise, Dreamweaver creates the detail region using a single div with the class *.DetailContainer*, while it applies a different HTML tag to each piece of data in the detail region (see step 3), and then applies the class *.DetailColumn* to each of them.

■ STACKED CONTAINERS

The third option in the Choose Insert Options window lets you create a series of stacked <div> tags with information from a Spry data set. This layout really isn't that useful. It doesn't offer any of the interactivity of a standard Spry table or the master/detail layout. You could just as easily build this table yourself without imposing all the download overhead—in the form of the data and Spry files required—on your visitors. However, you may want to use this layout if you can't get the data any other way—for example, if a database spits out the data from a web server, and it gets updated frequently.

To create a stacked layout, select the "Insert stacked containers" button in the Choose Insert Options screen, and then:

1. **Click the Set Up button.**

The Insert Stacked Containers window opens.

2. **Remove and rearrange columns.**

As with the Spry table and master/detail layouts, specify which columns you want to appear on the page. Also, as with step 3 in the master/detail layout instructions, you can specify the HTML tag where Dreamweaver puts the data. For example, you might want to use a heading (an <h2> tag, for example) to list the title of an article, or a <p> tag for a long description.

3. Click OK, and then, in the Spry Data Set window, click Done.

Dreamweaver inserts all the HTML and Spry programming necessary to create the layout. In addition, it attaches an external style sheet—*SpryStackedContainers.css*—that provides basic formatting for the elements on the page. The style sheet comes with just three styles, and they control the formatting for the overall div container (a class style named *.StackedContainers*), the div containing one row's worth of data (a descendent selector style named *.StackedContainers .RowContainer*) and a class style applied to the tag wrapped around each column of information (a descendent selector style named *.StackedContainers .RowColumn*).

■ STACKED CONTAINERS WITH SPOTLIGHT AREA

Since variety is the spice of life, Dreamweaver includes yet a fourth way to lay out your Spry data. The lovingly named Stacked Container with Spotlight Area layout looks much like the stacked container layout, except that it includes an area to left of the main data (the "spotlight") that's perfect for an employee photograph, a product shot, and the like.

As with the stacked container option, you could just as easily build this layout without Spry, but, since you asked, here's how you create one of these babies: First, click the "Insert stacked containers with spotlight area" button in the Choose Insert Options screen, and then:

1. Click the Set Up button.

The Insert Spotlight Area window opens. This window has two sections, one that lets you specify which column(s) should appear in the spotlight (on the left) and which should appear in the stacked column of data (on the right).

2. Remove, rearrange, and assign HTML tags to columns.

As with the basic Spry table and master/detail layouts, specify which columns you want to appear on the page. Since the spotlight area is small and tall, a column that contains paths to image files is a good bet here, and you want only one or two columns of data. You should display the longer, more detailed data on the right, in the stacked column region. Also, as with step 3 on page 676 (in the master/detail layout section), you can specify the HTML tag that the Spry programming wraps around the data. For example, you might want to use a heading (an <h2> tag, for example) to list the title of an article, or a <p> tag for a long description.

3. Click OK, and then, in the Spry Data Set window, click Done.

Dreamweaver inserts all the HTML and Spry programming necessary to create the layout. In addition, it attaches an external style sheet—*SprySpotlightColumn.css*—that provides basic formatting for the different elements on the page.

Build Your Own Spry Data Region

While Dreamweaver supplies four table layouts for displaying HTML and XML data, you can build your own layout using Dreamweaver's Spry Region tool. Basically a Spry region is a <div> or <span> tag in which you insert data from an HTML table or XML file. First, you have to specify a Spry data set, as described on page 665. Then you need to insert a Spry region using either the Spry Region button on the Insert panel or by choosing Insert→Spry→Spry Region.

You can then use the Bindings panel (Window→Bindings) to view all the data from the Spry data set, and drag it into the Spry region you created. There's basically little reason to use this tool, since you can just as easily build a complex layout using the CSS techniques described in Chapter 9 without resorting to JavaScript. However, if you're interested in learning more about this visit *http://tinyurl.com/c4oytyf*. (But keep in mind that Spry may be a short-lived technology not worth investing too much time in—see the box on page 638.)

Dreamweaver Behaviors

Dreamweaver behaviors are prepackaged JavaScript programs that let you add interactivity to your pages, even if you don't know the first thing about JavaScript. While Dreamweaver's behaviors were once revolutionary—JavaScript programming without any programming!—Adobe hasn't updated them in years. Many of the behaviors aren't very useful these days—you can get some of the same results with CSS, for example, Spry widgets have supplanted other behaviors, and some of the behaviors just don't work as advertised. That said, a few are still worth discussing.

Behavior Basics

To use a behavior, you need three elements: an HTML tag, an action, and an event:

- First, you select an HTML tag to apply the behavior to.

- Next, pick an action. The action is whatever the behavior is supposed to *do*—such as open a new browser window or hide an element on the page.

- Finally, you assign an event to the behavior. The event *triggers* the action, which usually involves a visitor interacting with your site, like clicking a Submit button on a form, moving a mouse over a link, or even simply loading the web page into the browser.

For instance, say that, when a visitor clicks a link, instead of just sending him to another page, you want a new browser window to pop up and load that linked page. In this case, the HTML tag is the link itself—an <a> tag; the *action* is opening another browser window and loading a web page in it; and the *event* takes place when your visitor clicks the link—his browser opens a new window and loads the new page. Voilà—interactivity!

■ Applying Dreamweaver Behaviors

Dreamweaver makes adding behaviors as easy as selecting a tag and choosing an action from a drop-down menu in the Behaviors panel.

The Behaviors Panel

The Behaviors panel is the control center for Dreamweaver's behaviors (Figure 13-16). On it, you can see the behaviors applied to a tag, add more behaviors, and edit the behaviors you already applied.

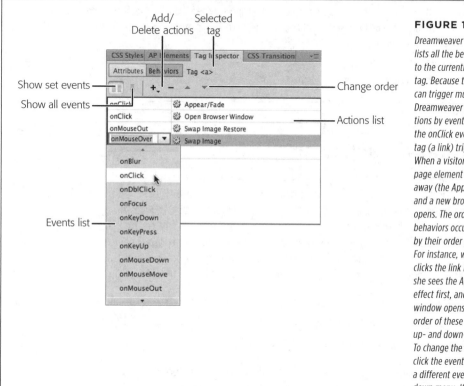

FIGURE 13-16

Dreamweaver's Behaviors panel lists all the behaviors applied to the currently selected HTML tag. Because the same event can trigger multiple actions, Dreamweaver groups the actions by event. In this example, the onClick event for an <a> tag (a link) triggers one action. When a visitor clicks this link, a page element appears or fades away (the Appear/Fade effect) and a new browser window opens. The order in which the behaviors occur is determined by their order in this panel. For instance, when a visitor clicks the link in this example, she sees the Appear/Fade effect first, and then a browser window opens. To change the order of these events, use the up- and down-pointing arrows. To change the type of event, click the event name and select a different event from the drop-down menu. If a unique event triggers each action, the order in which the events appear in the panel is irrelevant.

You open the Behaviors panel three ways:

- Choose Window→Behaviors.

- Press Shift+F4 to open the Tag Inspector, and then click the Behaviors button.

- If you have the Tag Inspector open, click the Behaviors button.

Dreamweaver shows you the currently selected tag at the top of the panel; a list of the behaviors applied to that tag, if any, appears below that. The panel breaks down each behavior into two parts: events and actions.

You can choose from two views in the Behaviors panel; switch between them using the buttons at the upper-left corner:

- "Show set events" gets down to the specifics: which behaviors you applied to a tag and which events trigger them. When you work on a web page, this view moves extraneous information out of your way.

- "Show all events" lists all the events *available* to a particular tag. This view isn't that useful, since you see a complete list of events for that tag when you select the tag and add an action.

Applying Behaviors, Step by Step

Open the Behaviors panel and proceed as follows:

1. **Select the object or tag to which you want to assign a behavior.**

   You have to attach a behavior to an HTML tag, such as a link (an <a> tag) or the page's body (the <body> tag). Take care, however; it's easy to accidentally apply a behavior to the wrong tag. Form elements, like checkboxes and text fields, are easy to target—just click one to select it. For other kinds of tags, consider using the Tag Selector, as described on page 26, for more precision.

2. **In the Behaviors panel, add an action.**

   Click the + button in the Behaviors panel and, from this "Add behavior" menu, select the action you wish to add (see Figure 13-17). You'll find a list of these behaviors and what they do beginning on page 684.

   Some actions are dimmed in the menu because your web page doesn't include an element that the action can affect. If your page lacks a form, for instance, you won't be able to select the Validate Form behavior. Other behaviors are grayed out because you have to apply them to a particular page element. For example, Jump Menu is off-limits until you add a list/menu field to the page and select it.

3. **In the dialog box that opens, set options for that action.**

   Each action has properties specific to it, and you set them in the dialog box. For instance, when you choose the Go To URL action, Dreamweaver asks what web page you want to load. (You'll find these actions described below, beginning on page 684.)

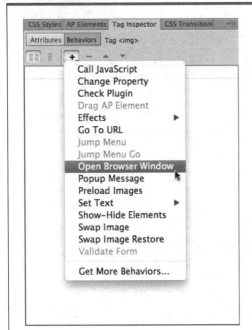

FIGURE 13-17

Dreamweaver grays out behaviors you can't apply to a currently selected tag. The reason? Your page is either missing a necessary object, or you selected an object that can't exhibit that behavior. For example, you can't apply the Show-Hide Elements behavior if your page doesn't have at least one tag with an ID applied to it.

4. **Click OK to apply the action.**

   At this point, Dreamweaver adds the HTML and JavaScript required to invoke the behavior to your page's underlying code. The behavior's action appears in the Behaviors panel.

   Unlike HTML objects, behaviors usually add JavaScript code in two places in a document: to the head of the document itself *and* to the HTML tag of the target behavior in the body of the page.

5. **Change the event, if desired.**

   When your newly created action shows up in the Behaviors panel, Dreamweaver displays, in the Events column, a default event (a trigger) for the selected tag and action. For example, if you add an Open Browser Window behavior to a link, Dreamweaver suggests the *onClick* event.

   However, this default event may not be the only one available. Links, for instance, can handle many events. An action could begin when your visitor's cursor moves *over* the link (the *onMouseOver* event), *clicks* the link (the *onClick* event), and so on.

To change the event for a particular behavior, click the event's name, and the Events drop-down menu appears (see Figure 13-16). Select a trigger from the list of available events for that tag.

When you're done, you can leave the Behaviors panel open to add more behaviors to the current tag, or to add behaviors to other tags. For the latter, select another tag using the document window or the Tag Selector, and repeat steps 2–5.

NOTE Dreamweaver sometimes displays a yellow warning bar above a document after you insert a behavior. It does so when it believes there's a mistake in a JavaScript program, and it tells you that the code was written incorrectly. In fact, this yellow bar often appears even if there is no JavaScript error. Close and re-open the page and the error bar goes away.

Editing Behaviors

Once you apply a behavior, you can edit it any time. Double-click the behavior in the Behaviors panel to reopen the Settings dialog box as described in step 3 of the previous instructions. Make any changes you like, and then click OK.

To remove a behavior from your web page, select it in the Behaviors panel, and then click the minus (-) button or press Delete. (If you *accidentally* delete a behavior, choose Edit→Undo Remove Behavior.)

A Quick Example

The brief example below shows you the behavior-creation process. In it, you'll use a behavior that makes an important message appear when a web page opens.

1. **Choose File→New to create a new, untitled document.**

   You'll start with a new page.

2. **Choose File→Save and save the file to your computer.**

   It doesn't matter where you save the page since you won't include any graphics or link to other pages.

   You start the process of adding a behavior by selecting a specific tag—in this case, the page's <body> tag.

3. **In the Tag Selector in the lower-left corner of the document window, click "<body>."**

   Once you select a tag, you can apply one or more behaviors to it. But first, make sure you have the Behaviors panel open. If you don't see it, choose Window→Tag Inspector or press Shift+F4, and then click the Behaviors button.

4. **Click the + button on the Behaviors panel.** From the "Add behavior" menu, choose Popup Message (see Figure 13-16).

   The Popup Message dialog box appears.

5. **In the message box, type "Visit our store for great gifts!",** and then click OK.

Dreamweaver adds the required JavaScript code to the page. Notice that the Behaviors panel lists the *action* called Popup Message next to the *event* called *onLoad*. The *onLoad* event triggers an action *after* a page and everything on it—graphics and so on—has loaded.

To see the page in action, preview it in a web browser by pressing F12 (Option-F12). (You can also use Dreamweaver's Live view, described on page 72, to see this behavior without leaving the program.)

> **NOTE** Dreamweaver behaviors rely on little JavaScript programs that run inside web browsers. For security reasons, Internet Explorer doesn't always like running JavaScript programs from your own computer. If the JavaScript you add to a page doesn't work when you preview it in IE, look for a narrow yellow bar just above the page. Click it and follow the instructions to allow the JavaScript on the page to run. This is only the case when you view a page that's sitting on your computer; once you move the page to the Web, Internet Explorer eases its security precautions and runs JavaScript programs without the warning.

■ Events

Events are at the heart of interactive web pages. They trigger behaviors based on your visitors' actions, like clicking a link, mousing over an image, or simply loading a page. But not all events work with all tags. For example, the *onLoad* event works only with web pages and images, not paragraphs, divs, or any other page element. The Event menu in the Behaviors panel can help; it lists only those events available for the tag you're targeting.

Current browsers—Internet Explorer 9, Safari, Firefox, and Chrome—support events for many HTML tags. Many events work with other tags as well, such as headline, paragraph, and div tags. But don't go crazy. Making an alert message appear when someone double-clicks a paragraph is more likely to win your site the Hard-To-Use Website of the Month award than a loyal group of visitors.

■ (Some of) the Actions, One by One

While events get the ball rolling, actions are, yes, where the action is. Whether it's opening a 200 x 200-pixel browser window or slowly fading in a photograph, you'll find an action for almost every type of interactivity you need.

In some cases, alas, the actions aren't very good. Dreamweaver CS6 is still saddled with behaviors that Adobe created for (and hasn't updated since) Dreamweaver CS4. Although Spry effects—part of the much-newer Spry Framework discussed in the last chapter—offer a fresh set of behaviors to play with, Adobe has only weeded out a few behaviors that aren't very useful or that don't work well. To be honest, you should skip most of these actions, but a few still worth trying are discussed below.

After you complete the steps required to set up an action as described on page 68, the new action appears in the Behaviors panel, and your web page is ready to test. At this point, you can click the event's name in the panel, where you can use the drop-down menu to change the event that triggers the action, as shown in Figure 13-16.

Spry Effects

Spry effects are a relatively new addition to Dreamweaver's arsenal of behaviors. They first appeared in Dreamweaver CS3 and are sophisticated visual effects that can do things like highlight elements on a page, make a photo fade in, or shake an entire sidebar of information as though it were in an earthquake. They're mostly eye candy and work well when you want to draw attention to an element, or create a dramatic introduction. It's easy to abuse these fun effects, however: If every part of your page blinks, shrinks, shakes, and flashes, most visitors will quickly grow tired of the nonstop action.

Spry effects are part of Adobe's Spry Framework, which you read about earlier in this chapter. To use an effect, you first have to apply an ID to the "target" element—the part of the page you want to affect. Every effect, except Slide, can target any element. (The Slide effect can target only <div> tags.)

You usually think of IDs as a way to format a unique element on a page using Cascading Style Sheets. But IDs are also handy when you want to add interactivity to a page. In fact, you can add an ID to HTML without ever creating a CSS style for it.

Recall that the HTML ID attribute marks a tag with a unique name. Because that name targets a specific area of your page, you can control that area using JavaScript. How you apply an ID to a tag depends on the tag, but here are the most common techniques:

- **Div tags**. Assign an ID to a div using the Property Inspector. Just select the <div> tag and then use the ID field to give it a unique name. In addition, you can wrap any collection of HTML tags (or even a single element, like an image) inside a <div> tag and apply an ID at the same time, using the Insert Div Tag tool (see page 440).

- **Images**. When you select an image in the document window, you can type an ID for that image in the Property Inspector's ID box.

- **Forms**. Select the form and type an ID in the ID field on the left edge of the Property Inspector.

- **Form fields**. When you insert a form field, you can set the field's ID in the Input Tag Accessibility Options window. You can later set or change a field's ID by selecting it and then using the ID field on the left edge of the Property Inspector.

- **Other elements**. To add an ID to paragraphs, headlines, bulleted lists, and other tags, select the tag in the Property Inspector and then type a name in the ID field.

After you apply an ID to the target, you add a Spry effect to the tag that triggers the effect (and that's usually a tag other than the target). For example, say you want the site's banner image to emerge on the page after the page loads. The target is the banner image, but you apply the effect to the <body> tag using the *onLoad* event.

■ APPEAR/FADE

To make an element fade in or out, use the Appear/Fade effect. To add a dramatic introduction to your site, you can fade in a large photograph on your home page after the page loads. Or you can have an "Important Announcement" box disappear when a visitor clicks it.

To use this effect:

1. **Select the tag that you want to trigger the fade in or out.**

   For example, a link could trigger the effect, such as an image inside a <div> tag that you want to fade out, or you could use the <body> tag coupled with the *onLoad* event.

2. **From the Actions list on the Behaviors panel, choose Effects→Appear/Fade.**

   The Appear/Fade window appears (see Figure 13-18).

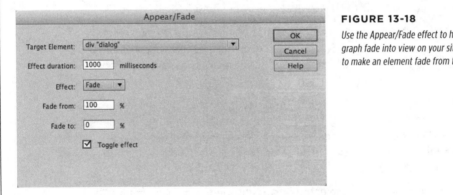

FIGURE 13-18

Use the Appear/Fade effect to have, say, a photo-graph fade into view on your site's home page, or to make an element fade from the page.

3. **Select a target element from the first menu.**

   Here's where you specify which page element should appear or fade away. The menu lists every tag on the page that has an ID applied to it. In addition, you may see <Current Selection> listed, which refers to the tag you selected in step 1. Choose this option if you want to apply the behavior to any <div> tag that contains some kind of message—like "We'll be closed February 2nd to celebrate Groundhog Day!" When a visitor clicks this <div> tag, the message fades away.

4. **Type an amount in the "Effect duration" field.**

This setting controls how long the fade in or out lasts. You set the duration in milliseconds, so typing *1000* gets you 1 second. If you want the target element to appear or disappear immediately, enter *0*.

5. **Choose the type of effect—Appear or Fade—from the Effects menu.**

If you want the target element to fade into view, you have to hide it to begin with. Otherwise the fade-in effect looks really weird: first you see the photo, then you don't, and *then* it fades in. To make the element invisible, add (or edit) a style for the target element, and then set the CSS *display* property (page 166) to *none*. Of course, if you go this route, you can't use the hidden element you selected in step 1 as the trigger; after all, you can't click or mouse over an element that's invisible.

6. **Type a percentage amount in the "from" and "to" fields.**

Depending on which type of effect (Appear or Fade) you select, you'll see either "Appear from" or "Fade from" and "Appear to" or "Fade to" in the Appear/Fade window. These two fields let you define the opacity of the target element. You'll commonly type *100* in the "Fade from" field and *0* in the "Fade to" field. Doing so makes the image fade completely out of view. However, if you like ghostly apparitions, you can fade from 100% to 25%, which makes a solid element transparent.

7. **Optionally, turn on the "Toggle effect" checkbox.**

This option turns the trigger tag into a kind of light switch that lets you fade the element in and out. Say you add an absolutely positioned div to a page that contains helpful hints on getting the most out of your website. You could then add a link that says "Show/hide hints." Add the Appear/Fade effect, target the AP div, and turn on the "Toggle effect" checkbox. Now, when a visitor clicks that link, the div fades into view if it were hidden, or it fades out of view if it were visible.

8. **Click OK to apply the behavior.**

Once you add the effect to a tag, you can edit or delete it just as you can any other behavior; see page 683 for details.

■ BLIND

Don't worry: The Blind effect won't hurt your eyes. It's actually just a way of simulating a window blind—either being drawn closed over an element to hide it or opened to reveal it. The basic concept and functionality is the same as the Appear/Fade effect: it lets you hide or reveal an element on a page. Follow the basic steps described in the previous section for Appear/Fade.

Once you select Blind from the Effects menu in the Behaviors panel, you can control all the basic elements of the effect from the Blind dialog box (Figure 13-19).

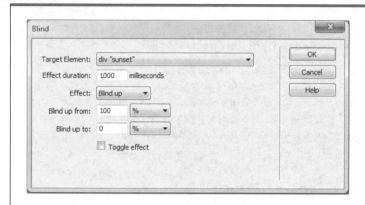

FIGURE 13-19

The "from" and "to" fields can hide or reveal just a portion of a div. If you set "Blind down from" to 0% and "Blind down to" to 50%, the effect reveals the contents of the div starting at the top and then it stops at the halfway mark—in other words, the bottom half of the div will still be invisible.

In the dialog box, use the Effect pull-down menu to choose in which direction the blind moves. If you want to display a hidden element on the page, choose "Blind down." To make an element disappear, choose "Blind up." This behavior is totally counterintuitive—you'd think raising a blind upward would actually reveal something. Fortunately, you can choose either direction for both revealing or hiding an element; the key is entering the correct percentage values in the "from" and "to" fields. If you wish to hide an already visible element, type *100* in the "from" field and *0* in the "to" field.

To make an element appear, you first need to set its *display* property (page 166) to *none* by creating a CSS style for the target element. Next, apply the Blind effect to a tag (for example, to a link or the <body> tag), and then select the direction for the blind (up or down) from the Effect menu. Finally, type *0* in the "from" field and *100* in the "to" field. The "Toggle effect" checkbox reverses the effect when a guest triggers the event again. For example, a link clicked for the first time might reveal a photo on the page; when clicked again, the photo disappears.

◼ GROW/SHRINK

The Grow/Shrink effect is another "now you see it, now you don't" effect. With it, you can make a photo, a paragraph, or a div full of content grow from a tiny speck on the screen to its full size, or you can make an element disappear altogether by shrinking it into nothingness. The basic setup is the same as with the Appear/Fade effect described in "Appear/Fade" on page 686. The Grow/Shrink window (Figure 13-20) lets you target any element that has an ID, set a duration for the effect, and then select whether to make the element appear (grow) or disappear (shrink). You can also have an element grow or shrink to a percentage of its full size. However, unless you target an image, displaying an element at less than its full size is usually unattractive and unreadable.

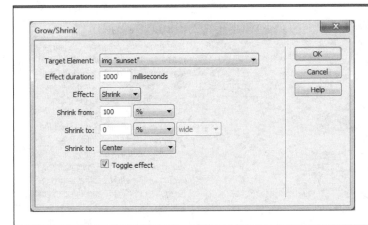

FIGURE 13-20

The "Grow from" menu ("Shrink from" if you selected the Shrink effect) determines the point on the page from which the element begins its growth on its way to achieving full size. You can make the element grow from either its center or from its top-left corner. The "center" option makes the element appear to come straight at you (or recede straight from you when you select Shrink).

HIGHLIGHT

Adding a background color to a paragraph, headline, or div is one way to create visual contrast and make an important piece of information stand out. A red box with white type will draw the eye quicker than a sea of black type on a white page. But if you really want to draw someone's attention, use the Highlight effect. Highlighting an element lets you add a flash of bright background color to it. For instance, on a form, you may have an important instruction for a particular form field ("Your password must be 10 characters long and not have !, #, or $ in it"). You could add the Highlight effect to the form field so that when a visitor clicks in the field, the instruction's background color quickly flashes, ensuring that the visitor sees the important information.

As with other Spry effects, you use the Behaviors panel to apply the Highlight effect to some triggering element (like a form field you click in, or a link you mouse over). Then set options in the Highlight window (see Figure 13-21): the target element (any tag with an ID), the duration of the effect, and background colors.

Colors work like this: The Start Color is the background color of the target element when the effect begins. The background subsequently fades from the Start Color to the End Color (time the duration of the fade using the "Effect duration" setting). Finally, the End Color abruptly disappears and the Color After Effect replaces it. The general settings suggested by Dreamweaver when you apply the effect aren't so good: white, red, white. Assuming the background color of your page is white, you don't get a flash effect so much as you get a "fade-to-a-color-that-immediately-disappears" effect. The effect looks a lot better if you set the Start Color to some bright, attention-grabbing highlight color, and the End Color to match the background of the target element. Then the effect looks like a bright flash that gradually fades away.

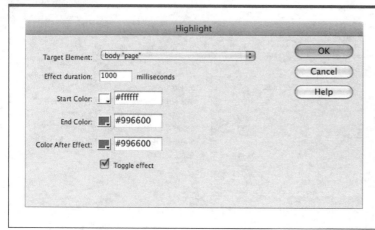

FIGURE 13-21

The "Toggle effect" checkbox lets you fade in a background color with a single action (for example, the click of a link) and then fade out the background when the same event occurs again (when a guest clicks the link a second time, for instance). But, for it to look good, make sure you set the Color After Effect to the same value as the End Color. Otherwise, the second time your visitor triggers the highlight (when she toggles the effect, in other words) the background won't fade smoothly back to its starting color.

However, instead of a flash, you may want an element's background to slowly fade to a different color and stay that color. In that case, set the Start Color to match the target element's current background, and use the same color for both the End Color and Color After Effect options.

■ SHAKE

The Shake effect is like adding an earthquake to a web page. The target element shakes violently left to right for a second or so. And that's all there is to it. When you apply this behavior, you have just one option: which element on the page to shake. You can shake any element with an ID—a div or even just a paragraph. It's kind of a fun effect...once...and maybe just for kids.

■ SLIDE

The Slide effect is just like the Blind effect, but instead of a "window blind" moving over an element to hide it (or moving off an element to reveal it), the element itself moves. Say you have a <div> tag that contains a gallery of photos. If you target that div with a "slide up" effect, the images all move upwards and disappear at the top edge of the div. Think of the <div> as a kind of window looking out onto the photos. When the photos move up past the "window," you can't see them any longer.

NOTE You can only use the slide effect on div tags that have IDs. You can't use it on, for example, an image, paragraph, or headline, and the div tag must have an ID applied to it.

You can make an element slide up or down using the Effect menu in the Slide window (Figure 13-22). And, as with the Blind effect, to make an element disappear, type *100* in the "from" field and *0* in the "to" field. To make an element slide either up or down and *appear* on the page, first create a style for the element's ID, and then apply the Slide behavior to some other element (a link or the body tag, for instance). Finally, type *0* in the "from" field and *100* in the "to" field.

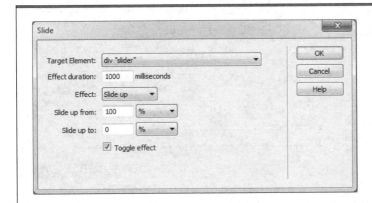

FIGURE 13-22

The Slide effect works just like the Blind effect described on page 687; the only difference is that the element itself moves and disappears (as opposed to a "blind" being drawn over the element).

SQUISH

The Squish effect offers no options other than selecting a target element. The effect hides an element by shrinking it down until it disappears. It behaves exactly like the Grow/Shrink effect (page 688) with the Shrink effect selected (see Figure 13-20). Since it doesn't provide any timing controls, you're better off sticking with the more versatile Grow/Shrink effect.

Open Browser Window

Sometimes, when a visitor action opens a new browser window, you want to dictate the size of that window. If you have a link to a "Sign up for our newsletter form," for example, you may want to open the sign-up page in a window that matches the exact width and height of the form. Or, when a visitor clicks on a thumbnail image, you may want to open a new window whose dimensions match that of the full-size photo—and prevent that window from displaying all the distracting browser "chrome," like the location bar, status bar, toolbar, and so on.

Enter Dreamweaver's Open Browser Window action (Figure 13-23). Use this behavior to tell your visitor's browser to open a new window to a height and width *you* desire. In fact, you can even dictate what elements the browser window includes. Don't want the toolbar, location bar, or status bar? No problem; this action lets you include or exclude the frills.

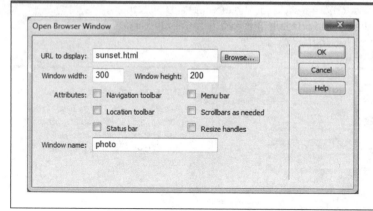

FIGURE 13-23

Here, you can define the properties of the new window, including what web page loads into it, its dimensions, and so on. If you leave the "Window width" and "Window height" properties blank, you'll get different results in different browsers. In Firefox, Chrome, and Opera, you won't get a new window—the page opens up a new tab. In Internet Explorer and Safari, you get a new window, but it's the same size as the window that spawned it.

To open a new browser window, you start, as always, by selecting the tag to which you want to attach the behavior. You can attach it to any HTML tag, but you usually want to add it to a link with an *onClick* event, or to the <body> tag with the *onLoad* event.

NOTE Most browsers have pop-up blockers. This nifty feature prevents a browser from opening a new browser window unless the visitor initiates the request. In other words, you probably won't be able to open a new browser window when a page loads in the current window, but you can open a new browser window based on a visitor's action—like clicking a link.

Once you select this action from the + menu in the Behaviors panel, you see the dialog box shown in Figure 13-23.

Specify the following options:

- **URL to display**. In this box, type in the URL or path to the page you want to load, or click Browse and find the page on your computer (the latter is a near-foolproof way to ensure functional links). If you want to load a web page that's on somebody else's site, don't forget to type in an *absolute* URL, one beginning with *http://*.

- **Window width, Window height**. Next, define the width and height of the new window. Specify these values in pixels; most browsers require a minimum window size of 100 x 100 pixels. Also, if the width and height you specify are larger than the available space on your visitor's monitor, the window fills the monitor (but won't ever generate a wider or taller window).

- **Attributes**. Turn on the checkboxes for the elements you want the new window to include. Figure 13-24 shows the different pieces of a standard browser window. Note that in most browsers, you can't really get rid of the resize handle, so even if you leave that option turned off it still appears and a visitor will still be able to resize the window.

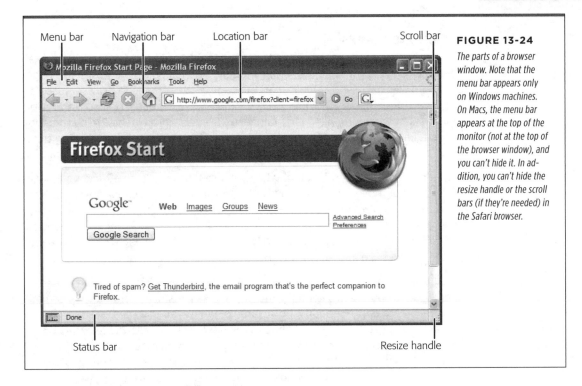

FIGURE 13-24

The parts of a browser window. Note that the menu bar appears only on Windows machines. On Macs, the menu bar appears at the top of the monitor (not at the top of the browser window), and you can't hide it. In addition, you can't hide the resize handle or the scroll bars (if they're needed) in the Safari browser.

- **Window name**. Give the new window a name (using letters and numbers only). If you include spaces or other symbols, Dreamweaver displays an error message and lets you correct the mistake. The name won't actually appear on your web page, but it's useful for targeting links or actions from the original window.

Once you set up the Open Browser Window action, you can load web pages into the new window from the original page; simply use the name of the new window as the link's target. For example, you could add the Open Browser Window behavior to a link labeled "Open photo gallery" that, when clicked, opens a small new window showcasing a photo. You could include additional links on the main page that load additional photos into that small window.

If you use more than one Open Browser Window behavior on a single page, make sure you give each new window a unique name. If you use the same name, your page might retain the first new window's settings and you might not get the width, height, or other settings you want in the new window.

When you click OK, your newly created behavior appears in the Actions list in the Behaviors panel.

Image Actions

Images make web pages stand out, but using Dreamweaver behaviors with images can make them come to life.

■ PRELOAD IMAGES

It takes time for images to load over the Internet. A 64 KB image, for instance, takes about 1 second to download over a DSL modem. Add 10 images of this size to a page, and it can take a while to actually load the page. However, once a browser loads an image, it stores that image in its *cache*, as described on page 783, so if the page requires that same graphic again, it loads extremely quickly. The Preload Images action takes advantage of this concept by downloading images and storing them in the browser's cache *before* the page actually needs them.

Preloading is especially important when you use mouse rollover effects on a page. When a visitor moves her mouse over a button, it may, for example, appear to light up. If the rollover image weren't preloaded, the light-up graphic wouldn't appear when your visitor rolled over the button; in fact, it wouldn't even begin to download until she rolled her cursor over the button. The resulting delay would make your button feel less like a rollover and more like a layover.

If you use the Insert Rollover Image command (see page 276), you don't need to apply the Preload Images action by hand because Dreamweaver adds it automatically. But there are exceptions. For example, when you use the CSS *background* property (page 262) to add an image to the hover state of a link (see page 206), a new background image appears when a visitor mouses over the link. But the browser loads that image only when a visitor triggers the hover state, not before. In a case like this, you want to add the Preload Images action to the event.

To do so, select the <body> tag. You can apply the Preload Images behavior to any tag, but it really only makes sense to attach it to the <body> tag using an *onLoad* event, so that when the first web page loads, the browser begins downloading the images.

If you add rollover images to your page, this behavior may already be applied to the <body> tag. If that's the case, just select the tag (click <body> in the Tag Selector) and then double-click the Preload Images action that should already be listed in the Behaviors panel. If it isn't, choose Preload Images from the + menu in the Behaviors panel. Either way, Dreamweaver displays the Preload Images dialog box.

Click the Browse button and navigate to the graphics file you want to preload, or type in the path and (if the graphic is on the Web) the absolute URL. Dreamweaver adds the image to the Preload Images list. To preload another image, click the + button and repeat the process. Continue until you add all the images you want to preload.

You can remove an image from the preload list by selecting it and then clicking the minus (-) button. (Be careful not to delete any images required for a rollover effect you already created—the Undo command doesn't work here.)

When you click OK, you return to your document and your new action appears in the Behaviors panel. You can edit it, if you like, by changing the event that triggers it. But unless you're trying to achieve some special effect, you usually use the *onLoad* event on the <body> tag. That's all there is to it. When your page loads in a browser, the browser continues to load and store the graphics you specified quietly in the background. They'll appear almost instantly when they're called by a rollover action or even by a shift to another page that incorporates the graphics.

■ SWAP IMAGE

The Swap Image action exchanges one image on your page for another (see Figure 13-25). (See the end of this section for detail on Swap Image's sibling behavior, Swap Image Restore.)

Simple as that process may sound, swapping images is one of the most visually exciting things you can do on a web page. It works something like rollover images, except that you don't have to trigger the swap with a mouse click or mouse pass. You can use *any* tag-and-event combination. For instance, you can create a mini slideshow by listing the names of pictures down the left side of a web page and inserting an image in the middle of the page. Add a Swap Image action to each slide name, and the appropriate picture replaces the center image when a visitor clicks on a new name.

To make this behavior work, your page has to include a *starter image*, and the images you want to swap in have to match the width and height of that starter graphic. If they don't, the browser resizes and distorts the swapped pictures to fit the "frame" dictated by the original image.

To add the Swap Image behavior, first identify the starter image (choose Insert→Image, or use any of the other techniques described in Chapter 5). Give your image an ID in the Property Inspector so JavaScript knows which image to swap out. (JavaScript doesn't really care about the original graphic itself, but rather about the space that it occupies on the page.)

TIP You can swap more than one image at a time with a single Swap Image behavior. Using this trick, not only can a button change to another graphic when you mouse over it, but any number of other graphics on the page can change at the same time. An asterisk (*) next to the name of an image in the Swap Image dialog box (Figure 13-26) indicates that the behavior will swap in a new image for that particular graphic. In the example in Figure 13-25, you can see that two images—*horoscope* and *ad*, both marked by asterisks—swap as a result of a single action.

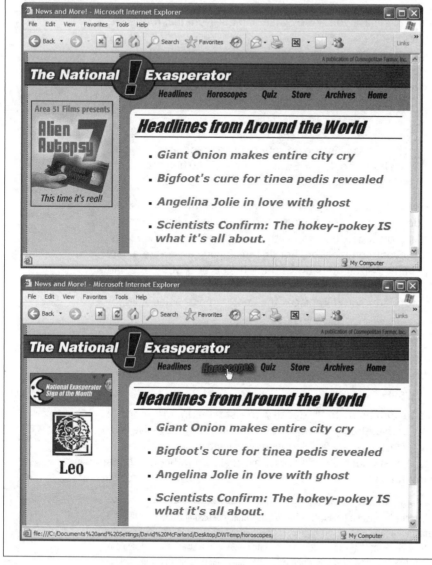

FIGURE 13-25

You can use the Swap Image behavior to simultaneously change multiple graphics with a single mouseover. A humble web page (top) comes to life when a visitor moves her mouse over the Horoscopes button (bottom). Not only does the graphic for the button change, so does the ad in the left sidebar; it's replaced with a tantalizing look at the "Sign of the Month." The Swap Image action lets you easily get this type of effect, sometimes called a disjoint rollover.

Now select the tag you want to associate with the Swap Image behavior—you can choose a link, a paragraph, another image, or even the starter image itself. When you choose this action's name from the Behaviors panel, the Swap Image dialog box appears, as shown in Figure 13-26.

- **Images**. From the list, click the name of the starter image.

- **Set source to**. Here's where you specify the *image* file you want to swap in. If it's a graphics file in your site folder, click Browse to find and open it. You can also specify a path or an absolute URL to another website, as described on page 196).

- **Preload images**. Preloading ensures that image downloads don't slow down the swap-in.

- **Restore images onMouseOut**. You get this option only when you apply the Swap Image behavior to a link. When you turn on this checkbox, the previous image reappears when a visitor moves *off* the link.

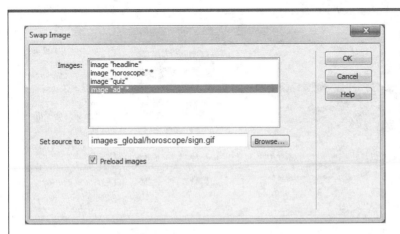

FIGURE 13-26

Some actions, like Swap Image, can automatically add behaviors to a web page. In this case, the "Preload images" and "Restore images onMouseOut" options actually add a Swap Image Restore action to the onMouseOut event of the currently selected tag and a Preload Images action to the onLoad event of the <body> tag.

■ SWAP IMAGE RESTORE

The Swap Image Restore action returns the last set of swapped images to its original state. Most designers use it in conjunction with a rollover button so that the button returns to its original appearance when the visitor moves his cursor off the button.

You'll probably never find a need to add this behavior yourself; Dreamweaver automatically adds it when you insert a rollover image and choose the "Restore images onMouseOut" option when you set up a regular Swap Image behavior. (The Swap Image Restore dialog box offers no options to set.)

Popup Message

Use the Popup Message behavior to send important messages to your visitors, as shown in Figure 13-27. Your visitor must click OK to close the dialog box. But because a pop-up message demands immediate attention, reserve this behavior for important announcements.

FIGURE 13-27

Here, a pop-up message indicates a sale going on at Chia-Vet.com. While the Popup Message behavior is easy to use, you can't customize the look of the dialog box. The browser controls that, and it looks different from browser to browser. For a better-looking pop-up, you could create an absolutely positioned div (see page 465) containing a nicely styled message, and then add one of the Spry effects (like Fade, Blind, or Shrink) to a Close button inside the div, so that when a visitor clicks the button, the div disappears.

To create a pop-up message, select the tag that you want to trigger the behavior. For example, adding this action to the <body> tag with an *onLoad* event makes the message appear when a visitor first loads the page; adding the same behavior to a link with an *onClick* event makes the message appear when your visitor clicks the link.

From the Add Action menu (+ button) in the Behaviors panel, choose Popup Message. In the Popup Message dialog box, type the message that you want to appear. Then click OK.

TIP JavaScript programmers, your message can also include any valid JavaScript expression. To embed JavaScript code in a message, place it inside braces ({ }). If you want to include the current time and date in a message, for example, add this: {*new Date()*}. If you just want to display a brace in the message, add a backslash, like this: \{. The backslash lets Dreamweaver know that you *really* do want a { character—and not just a bunch of JavaScript—to appear in the dialog box.

■ The Widget Browser

Dreamweaver includes another way to add interactivity to your web pages with easy-to-use, preprogrammed JavaScript: the Widget Browser. You already encountered the term "widget" in the discussions above of Spry form validation, the Spry menu bar, and the other Spry mini-programs. The widgets available from the Widget Browser are similar in that they use a collection of preprogrammed JavaScript, HTML, and CSS to add useful interactivity to a page. For example, you can use widgets to add slideshows, Google Maps, HTML5 video, Twitter updates, and more to your pages.

However, these widgets aren't built into Dreamweaver, nor do most of them use Adobe's Spry (JavaScript) Framework. In fact, most of the widgets you find in the Browser aren't programmed by Adobe engineers, they're created by other programmers and placed on the Adobe Exchange website (discussed on page 917). Because of this, the widgets don't necessarily provide the same ease-of-use as Dreamweaver's built-in Spry tools or behaviors. In addition, since third parties provide the widgets for free, their quality varies.

To find widgets, you use the Widget Browser, a standalone program. And for that, you need an Adobe account:

1. **Visit *https://www.adobe.com/cfusion/membership* and click the "Create an Adobe Account" button.**

   The "Join Adobe" page appears with a long form for you to fill out.

2. **Fill out the form, and then press Continue.**

   Fortunately, much of the form is optional, so you can leave most of it blank if you wish. You just need to supply your name, email address, city, state, zip code, and a password. Once you complete the sign-up, you can use the email address and password you used to log into Adobe.com to take part in members-only areas of the site, like forums, the Exchange discussed on page 917, and Adobe's BrowserLab tool for previewing your web pages in different browsers and operating systems (see page 760). You use this same login info to sign into Adobe through the Widget Browser so you can browse and download Dreamweaver widgets.

Once you have an Adobe ID, you can launch the Widget Browser and begin to view, select, and install widgets. You open the Browser from the Application bar, then click the Extend Dreamweaver button (circled in Figure 13-28) and select Widget Browser from the drop-down menu.

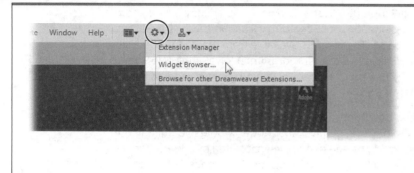

FIGURE 13-28

You open the Widget Browser from Dreamweaver's Application bar. However, since the Browser's a standalone program, you'll also find it in either C:\Program Files\Adobe\Adobe Widget Browser folder (Windows) or the Applications→Adobe folder (Macs). Just double-click the Widget Browser icon to launch it.

The first time you start the Browser, you have to click through a couple of those corporate "Yes, I agree to whatever you say" dialog boxes, but eventually you'll see the Widget Browser window (see Figure 13-29). Before you can add a widget to a Dreamweaver page, you must first find one you like and add it to your widget library.

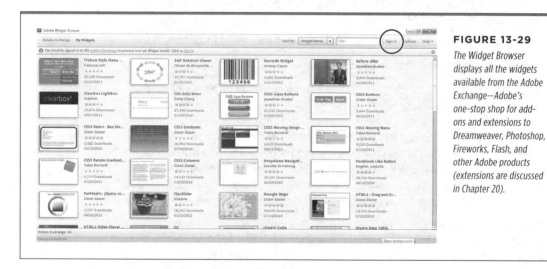

FIGURE 13-29

The Widget Browser displays all the widgets available from the Adobe Exchange—Adobe's one-stop shop for add-ons and extensions to Dreamweaver, Photoshop, Fireworks, Flash, and other Adobe products (extensions are discussed in Chapter 20).

Find and Install Widgets

The Widget Browser lets you view all the widgets the Adobe Exchange offers. It also lets you install and configure widgets for use in Dreamweaver. To find a widget and add it to your library:

1. **Launch the Widget Browser from the Application bar.**

2. **Click the Sign In link (circled in Figure 13-29), and log in using the Adobe account you created earlier.**

   If you haven't yet created an Adobe account, click the Create Account button: you'll go to the Adobe sign-up page described above.

   The Browser displays all the widgets available from Adobe.com. You can use the "Sort by" menu to display widgets by name, author, date posted, rating, or number of downloads. You can also type a search term in the box to the right of the "Sort by" menu to search for particular widgets. For example, type "video" and the Browser displays widgets related to adding video to a web page.

3. **Select a widget from the list.**

   A details page for that widget appears (top image in Figure 13-30), explaining what it does, who created it, what browsers it works with, and more. Some important details to keep in mind are the widget's rating, how many times it's been downloaded, and when it was added to the Exchange. If the widget has a low rating, you probably should skip it. Likewise if it was uploaded two years ago (meaning there's been no recent update); the widget's author might not maintain it any longer, and you run the risk of adding a widget that might not work in newer browsers.

4. **Click the Preview button to preview the widget in action (bottom image in Figure 13-30).**

   The Preview pane shows how the widget should behave—it's basically a mini-browser that displays the widget's HTML and CSS and runs its JavaScript programming. The preview is a good way to see whether you like the widget before you add it.

5. **If you like the widget, click the "Add to My Widgets" button in the bottom-right of the window.**

   A window appears displaying the widget's "License."

6. **Click the Accept button in the License window.**

   The Widget Added window appears. At this point, you can click the "Go to My Widgets" button to see all the widgets you've installed. To return to the list of available widgets from Adobe, click the "Adobe Exchange" link in the top left of the Widget Browser.

Once you add a widget to your collection, you can add it to a web page in Dreamweaver as described on page 706. However, you'll probably want to customize its look and functionality to match your site, a process described next.

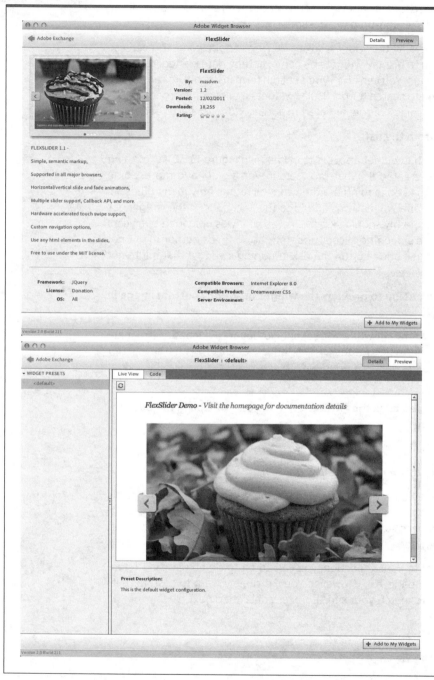

FIGURE 13-30

Viewing a widget in the Adobe Exchange lets you review its details (top image), including when it was uploaded to Adobe.com, how many times it's been downloaded, its user rating, and the author's description of the widget. The widget preview screen (bottom) displays what the widget will look like and how it will work in a browser. You see the FlexSlider widget in the bottom image here. The small area with the photo of a cupcake is actually a mini-browser window into which you can click and mouse around to see how the widget performs.

Configuring Widgets

Every widget has at least one standard configuration, or "preset." This is how the widget looks and works if you simply add it to a web page in Dreamweaver. Some widgets even have several designs, which you choose among when you insert the widget into a web page. However, you'll probably want to tweak those presets to better fit your site's design. Fortunately, most widgets let you customize them, from making simple modifications such as changing the colors used, to more elaborate alterations that affect how the widget works. For example, the Google Maps widget lets you display a map centered over a longitude and latitude you specify, dictate the type of map (for example, "road," "satellite," "terrain"), and even add custom markers to highlight a specific location (such as your business).

Since each widget is different, the configuration options vary from widget to widget; in addition, the widget authors are responsible for adding those options, so one widget might offer just a few settings, while another offers dozens. Regardless of the widget, however, the basic process of customizing it is the same:

1. **In Dreamweaver, launch the Widget Browser from the Application bar (see Figure 13-28).**

   Alternatively, open the application from the C:\Program Files\Adobe\Adobe Widget Browser folder (Windows) or Applications→Adobe folder (Macs).

2. **Click the My Widgets link in the top-left of the Browser (see Figure 13-29).**

   You can only configure a widget you've added to your list of widgets, so follow the steps above to find and add a widget to your "My Widgets" collection.

3. **Select the widget you want to customize, and then click the Preview button in the top-right of the Browser (see Figure 13-31).**

   The Widget Browser displays a preview of the widget in action on the right, and a list of presets on the left. A preset represents one set of options for the widget. Some widgets have just a single preset (called <default>), and others have many. For example, the Google Maps widget in Figure 13-31 has one <default> preset and eight additional developer presets. You customize the widget by adding your own presets, which appear under the "My Presets" category. If you click on a preset, you'll see a preview of the widget using that preset's options on the right.

   The real fun lies in creating your own presets.

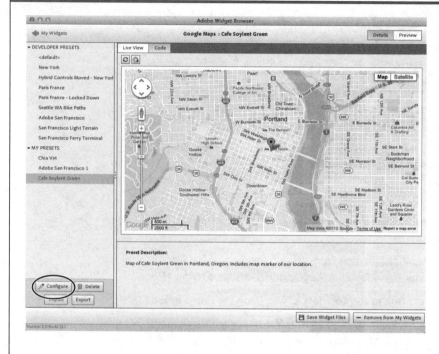

FIGURE 13-31

Once you add a widget to your "My Widgets" list, you can preview it in the Widget Browser. Clicking one of the presets changes the preview. For example, in this image you can see a custom preset created by the web designer at Cafe Soylent Green. It's a Google Map that includes a small marker in the center, indicating the location of the cafe. You can delete one of these custom presets, but not any of the preinstalled developer presets. However, you can export or import either type of preset. To export a preset (to share with another designer or to add your customized preset to Dreamweaver on a different machine), first select the preset and then click the Export button. This creates an XML file, which you can then import by clicking the Import button (you have to have the original widget installed in the Widget Browser to import a preset for that widget, though).

4. **Click the "Configure" button (circled in Figure 13-31).**

   The Configure window appears (Figure 13-32). Its left-hand column lists categories of options (for example, General, Controls, and Marker for the Google Maps widget). Each widget has its own categories and sets of options. Some widgets, like the Spry Content Slideshow, have just a few options, while others, like the Lightbox Gallery widget, sport dozens of options divided into multiple categories.

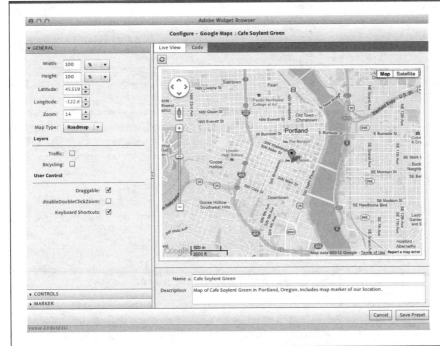

FIGURE 13-32

Every widget is different—they do different things and have different settings, so the list of categories and options in the left-hand column of the Configure window will vary from widget to widget. In the case of this Google Maps widget, there are three categories of options. The first lets you set the size of the map, the latitude and longitude of the center of the map, and how much the map should initially be zoomed in, as well as a few other options.

5. **Choose your configuration options.**

   This step is pretty open-ended; since each widget has its own options, there aren't any specific recommendations here. Your best bet is to look at all the options and all the categories: Most are pretty self-explanatory (for example, the Map Type menu lets you pick a type of Google map, like a road map or satellite view). Change one option and then click in the preview window to see the effect of that change.

6. **Once you're satisfied with your changes, type a name and description in the bottom of the Configure window, and then click the Save Preset button.**

   A new preset with the name you supplied appears in the "My Presets" category in the widget preview.

NOTE To edit a preset you already created, select it from the My Presets list, and then click Configure. Make any changes you want, but don't change the preset's name in the Configure window; just click the Save Preset button and the Widget Browser updates that preset. You can't, however, change the settings of the Developer Presets—the Widget Browser always saves a copy when you configure a developer preset and saves it in the My Presets list.

At this point, you're ready to use the widget. You'll turn to Dreamweaver to do that.

TIP If you do use the Google Maps widget, you need a way to determine the latitude and longitude you want to display for that map. For example, if you want to add a Google Map with your business' location so potential customers can find you, you'll need the latitude and longitude of your location. If you don't have a GPS, you can use the free Geocoder.us (*http://geocoder.us/*) online service. Just visit the site, type in your address, and hit the Search button.

Adding a Widget to a Web Page

Once you find a widget, download it, and customize it, you're ready to add it to a web page. You don't need the Widget Browser at this point, so you can close it and return to Dreamweaver.

1. **Open the page where you want to add a widget.**

2. **Click on the page where you want the widget placed.**

   You need to make sure that there's enough room for the widget to fit. For example, the Spry Slideshow widget is 700 pixels wide, so if you try to place it in a <div> that's only 500 pixels wide, you'll end up with some weird results. Not all widgets let you set a size, nor do they tell you the dimensions in their details page, so you have to experiment.

3. **Choose Insert→Widget.**

   Alternatively, you can click the Widget button (a gear icon) on the Common category of the Insert panel. The Widget window appears (Figure 13-33).

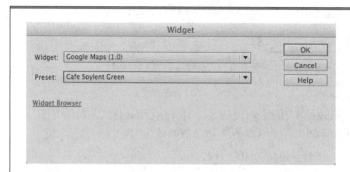

FIGURE 13-33

Dreamweaver's Widget window includes a list of all the widgets you installed using the Widget Browser. In addition, the Preset menu lists all the developer presets as well as any custom presets you created for the widget. Click the Widget Browser link to launch the Browser.

4. **Select the widget you want to insert from the Widget menu, select the preset you wish to use from the Preset menu, and then click OK to insert the widget.**

Dreamweaver deposits all the necessary HTML, CSS, and JavaScript into the page and, in Design view, surrounds the widget with a blue box with a blue tab at the top. In addition, widgets usually include additional files, such as external style sheets, JavaScript files, and sample images. When you save the file, Dreamweaver lets you know what files it added to your site.

5. **If necessary, customize the widget's HTML.**

Some widgets don't require any edits after you add them to a web page. For example, once you set up the Google Maps widget's settings in the Widget Browser, you're done. Just insert the widget into a page in Dreamweaver and, voila, you have a Google map right on the page.

Other widgets require further modification of the HTML. For example, the Lightbox widget comes with a simple set of thumbnail images. You need to replace them with your own thumbnails (see page 242 for information on working with images). In addition, each thumbnail links to a larger version of the image, so you have to update the link applied to each thumbnail (see page 191 for information on editing links).

Likewise, the Spry Slideshow widget adds a bunch of images to your site and includes <div> tags filled with information about each one. Not only do you need to replace the supplied images with your own, you have to edit the text in each div to match the details of your photos. Unfortunately, you're on your own with this step. Unlike Spry widgets, which include helpful windows or customizable options displayed in the Property Inspector, any changes you make to a widget must be done in the HTML. Some widgets include instructions.

Once you insert a widget, the only way to update its settings is to get into the code and edit it. Changes you make in the Widget Browser won't have any effect at this point. If you do want to replace a widget you already inserted with one that uses different presets, you have to delete the widget from your page and then reinsert it with the new presets. To delete a widget, click it's blue tab, and then press Delete.

NOTE Unfortunately, deleting a widget from a page by selecting its blue tab and hitting Delete doesn't always remove all the code the widget inserted. For example, the Lightbox widget leaves behind two lines of code even after you deleted the widget from the page:

```
<script src="../Scripts/jquery.js" type="text/javascript"></script>
```

```
<script src="../Scripts/lightbox.js" type="text/javascript"></script>
```

You can remove those lines by hand in Code view.

If you want to make changes to the appearance of a widget and the Widget Browser doesn't offer any settings to do that, you have to turn to the widget's CSS. A great way to analyze and update the CSS of a widget is to click the Live button, and then click the Inspect button. Inspect mode lets you mouse around a page, click on an element, and see all the CSS styles that affect that element's appearance. You can read more about Inspect mode on page 494.

Add Flash and Other Multimedia

As you learned in previous chapters, you can bring your website to life with interactive and animated pages using Cascading Style Sheets (Chapter 3), Spry widgets, Dreamweaver effects and behaviors (Chapter 13), and images (Chapter 5). But as you've probably seen by now, today's web pages go even further—they blink, sing, and dance with sound, video, and advanced animation.

You can create these effects too, but you'll need some outside help. Programs like Flash (see Figure 14-1) let you create and display complex multimedia presentations, such as slick animations, interactive games, and video tutorials.

In this chapter, you'll learn to embed these media files in your pages, and you'll see why Flash, a versatile program that lets you both develop and play back multimedia, provides amazingly fast and smooth web animations and complex visual interaction.

NOTE Flash isn't as popular as it once was, and HTML5, CSS, and JavaScript let you do many of the things that were once only possible with Flash—but for the full story, see the box on page 711.

■ Flash: An Introduction

A few years ago, if you wanted to add smooth animation, slideshows, or any other high-quality interactive effects to a web page, Flash was the only game in town. Thanks to the Flash plug-in (available in almost all web browsers), web developers could use the Flash authoring program to make "movies" that played inside a browser and add programming logic so those movies respond to visitor feedback—mouse movement, clicks, and keyboard input. However, the JavaScript programming language and the speedy JavaScript engines in today's browsers provide an alternative to many simple forms of animation and interactivity. Dreamweaver's Spry widgets, like Spry tabbed panels and the Spry accordion, are good examples of the interactive effects JavaScript offers.

FIGURE 14-1

Some websites, like the Get the Glass game, are created entirely with Flash. Its ability to handle interactivity, animation, and video playback makes it a great technology for online games and entertainment websites. But you still need an HTML file to display the Flash movie. (Unfortunately, this remarkable web site is no longer online.)

But for really high-quality animation, games, and interactivity, there's still no replacement for Flash. For example, the fantastic "Get the Glass" game (*www.gettheglass .com*) merges game play, video, and animation into an engaging game (as well as a powerful marketing tool for the California Milk Processor Board). This kind of presentation is simply outside the ability of JavaScript (at this point). That's why many entertainment company websites (especially those for movie companies) and consumer-oriented product sites, still turn to Flash to create an immersive, interactive experience (see *http://marvel.com/avengers_movie/,* for example).

Flash provides other benefits as well. It not only plays Flash-created animations, but it also plays third-party audio and video files. And its advanced programming features let you add a level of sound, video, and interactivity that can make plain HTML pages look dull by comparison.

In addition, Flash movies look and work exactly the same way in every browser, whether you use a Windows, Mac, or even Linux PC. That kind of cross-platform compatibility is rare. And finally, the ubiquity of Flash on the web means that nearly every desktop browser—in fact, 90 percent of them—have a Flash player installed.

However, that 90 percent figure covers desktop computers only. Two of the most popular devices for surfing the Web, the iPhone and the iPad, don't support Flash at all. So if you think you'll have visitors using their iPhones or iPads to search for your business's hours of operation, street address, and phone number, make sure you at least provide your most crucial information in HTML format. Said another way: Don't make your site's home page one big Flash movie (as some sites do). Otherwise iPhone/iPad guests will be staring at a blank page.

Of course, all this power comes at a price. You need Adobe Flash or a similar program, like Swish (*www.swishzone.com*), Toon Boom (*www.toonboom.com*), or Anime Studio (*http://anime.smithmicro.com*) to produce full-fledged movies. And although these programs aren't necessarily difficult to get started with, they represent one more expense and one more technology you have to learn.

NOTE Creating external movies, animations, and applications is an art (and a book or two) unto itself. This chapter is a guide to *inserting* these goodies into your web page and assumes that a cheerful programmer near you has already *created* them. For the full scoop on creating Flash files, pick up a copy of *Flash CS6: The Missing Manual*.

FREQUENTLY ASKED QUESTION

Is Flash Still Important?

I hear that Flash is dead. Is that true?

When Apple famously announced that it wouldn't ever support Flash on the iPhone or iPad, many people believed that was the beginning of the end for Flash. In many ways, it was. While Adobe still promotes Flash, they've begun developing new tools for HTML5, CSS, and JavaScript—the languages of the web—and have stopped working on the mobile version of Flash.

Many of the latest browsers provide tools that let you build modules similar to those previously possible only with Flash. For example, Flash used to be the only way you could embed cross-platform movies in a web page. Now, HTML5's <video> tag lets you add videos to a site without requiring a browser plug-in. Likewise, faster computers and browsers now make it possible to create slick animations using JavaScript only. Sites like Google's HTML5 Rocks (*www.html5rocks.com*) demonstrate the kinds of highly interactive experiences available in the latest crop of browsers.

However, while a Flash-less future may be here one day, right now Flash is still useful in some cases. HTML5's <video> and <audio> tags are exciting, but Microsoft's still-popular Internet Explorer 8 browser doesn't understand them, and thus can't play video or audio files embedded that way. In addition, different browsers support different video formats, so while you can use the high-quality H.264 movie format in Safari, Chrome, and Internet Explorer 9 and above, you need to use a different format for Firefox and Opera. In other words, using the <video> tags means you need to create three versions of your video for it to work in common browsers.

Likewise, while JavaScript is powerful, it can't create the kind of complex, smooth-running animations that sites like Get the Glass (see Figure 14-1) can. Flash is still used extensively in many projects, like museum exhibits, that require smooth and consistent animation and interactivity.

In a nutshell, it may not be the best time to take on a career as a Flash programmer. In addition, if you need to build sites that are accessible on mobile devices (including the popular iPhone and iPad), you probably want to stay away from Flash. However, in some cases, including video, Flash still has a role to play...for now.

Insert a Flash Movie

To add a Flash movie to a page, position your cursor where you want the movie to appear and then choose Insert→Media→SWF (.swf is the file extension for Flash movies) or, in the Common category of the Insert panel, choose SWF from the Media menu (circled in Figure 14-2). Either way, you'll see the Select File dialog box. Navigate to the Flash file you want to embed (look for the .swf extension) and double-click it. Dreamweaver automatically recognizes the width and height of the movie and generates the appropriate HTML so you can embed it in your page. You'll see a gray rectangular placeholder with the Flash logo in the center; you can adjust the movie's settings as described in the next section.

> **TIP** You can also drag a Flash movie from the Files panel into the document window. Dreamweaver automatically adds the correct code.

> **NOTE** When you insert a Flash movie, an Object Tag Accessibility Options window appears. This window lets you set options intended to make accessing Flash content easier, but they don't really work in most browsers. If you don't want to set these options, just click Cancel, and Dreamweaver still inserts the Flash movie. To permanently turn off this window, open the Preferences window (Edit→Preferences [Dreamweaver→Preferences]), click the Accessibility category, and then turn off the Media checkbox.

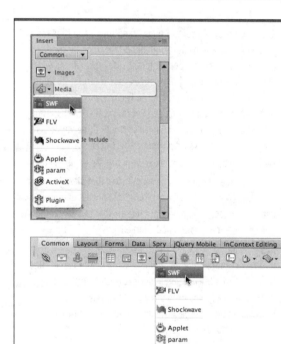

FIGURE 14-2

The Media menu in the Insert panel's Common category (top) is where old web technologies go to die. Only Flash and Flash Video are commonly used on websites these days. If you use the Classic Workspace (see page 38), you can find the Media menu at the top of the screen (bottom).

NOTE When you save a web page after inserting a Flash movie, Dreamweaver pops up a dialog box informing you that it needs to save two files on your site—*expressInstall.swf* and *swfobject_modified.js*. These files make it possible to notify Flash-less visitors (and those with older versions of the program) that they need to download the current Flash plug-in (see page 718 for details).

Change Movie Properties

You'll rarely have to change the default properties Dreamweaver assigns Flash movies. But if you do—say you resize a movie and want to change it back to its original size, or you want to swap in a different movie altogether—the Property Inspector is the place to go.

The Two Lives of the <object> Tag

If you choose View→Code after you insert a Flash movie, you may be surprised by the amount of HTML Dreamweaver deposits in your page. You may also encounter some HTML tags you've never heard of, including <object> and <param>. These tags provide browsers with the information they need to launch the Flash player and play a Flash movie.

Due to differences between Internet Explorer and all other browsers, Dreamweaver has to insert the <object> tag twice: once for IE (with all the proper settings for that browser) and once for other browsers. To do this, Dreamweaver uses IE conditional statements—HTML comments that only Internet Explorer understands—to send special instructions to just IE (and even to specific versions of IE). You can learn more about conditional comments at *http://tinyurl.com/9osegt*.

Dreamweaver started using the <object> tag like this in Dreamweaver CS4. It replaces the old way of embedding Flash movies, which involved inserting two tags, the <object> and the <embed> tags. This new method is standards-compliant, which means that most pages where you use Dreamweaver CS6 to add a movie will pass W3C validation (the same validator used with Dreamweaver CS6's W3C Validation tool described on page 773). That wasn't true in versions of Dreamweaver prior to CS4, which produced invalid HTML that failed the W3C validator.

Ironically, if you insert a Flash movie into an HTML5 document (page 10), the code Dreamweaver inserts actually produces invalid HTML5! One step forward, two steps back.

■ RENAME YOUR MOVIE

Just as you learned that JavaScript can control images and buttons, so it can control Flash movies. Dreamweaver assigns a generic name to each movie you embed—*FlashID, FlashID2, FlashID3*, and so on. This act of naming your movie is important—the auto-install option discussed on page 718 requires a name—but the exact name isn't. If you want, you can change the name in the Name field, the box directly below "SWF" at the top-left of the Property Inspector panel (see Figure 14-3). However, there's no real need to since no one visiting the page will ever see it.

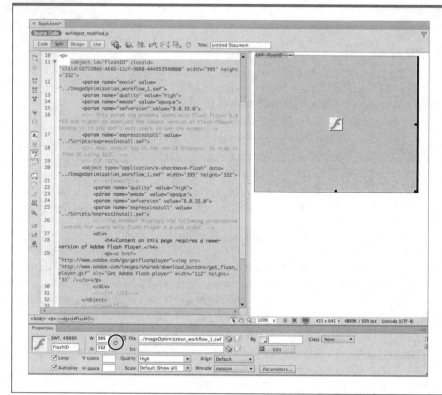

FIGURE 14-3

Use the Property Inspector to set the display and playback controls for a Flash movie. Avoid the V space, H space, and Align settings. CSS handles those same formatting options.

REPLACE YOUR MOVIE

The File box specifies your movie's location on your hard drive. To swap out the current movie, type a new path into the File field or click the nearby folder icon and browse to the new movie.

> **NOTE** In previous versions of Dreamweaver, you could preview a Flash movie by clicking a Play button in the Property Inspector. Adobe removed that button in Dreamweaver CS6. If you want to see a Flash movie play now, you either have to use Live View (page 72) or preview the page in a browser (page 73).

SET THE SRC PROPERTY

The Src field indicates the location of your original Flash file (the one with the .fla extension). When you first insert a Flash movie, the Src box is blank. If you think you'll want to edit the original Flash file, tell Dreamweaver where to find it.

To do that, click the Edit button in the Property Inspector. Dreamweaver asks you to locate the original file, the one with the .fla extension. Double-click it and Dreamweaver launches the Flash program and opens the file for editing. Make any changes you wish (or not) and, in Flash, click Done. Flash exports the updated .swf file to your site, replacing the previous version of the movie. In addition, the Src property box now points to your original .fla file. That way, if you need to work on the movie in the future, you just press the Edit button. Dreamweaver launches Flash, and it opens your original movie for editing.

■ CHANGE YOUR MOVIE'S SIZE

Although enlarging GIF or JPEG images by dragging their edges usually results in a pixellated mess, you can often resize Flash movies without a problem. If you use Flash's vector-based tools to create your movie, you can scale them nicely. However, if the Flash movie contains bitmap images, such as GIFs, PNGs, JPEGs, or embedded video, leave the movie at its original size. If you resize a movie that has bitmaps, the images distort and pixellate.

To resize a movie, do one of the following:

- Select the movie in the document window and drag one of the three resizing handles at its edges. To maintain the movie's proportions, press Shift as you drag the lower-right corner handle.

- Select the movie in the document window and type new width and height values into the Property Inspector's W and H boxes. You can also use percentage values, in which case your movie scales to fit the browser window.

If you make a complete mess of your page by resizing your movie beyond recognition, just click the Reset Size button in the Property Inspector (circled in Figure 14-3).

> **NOTE** If you want to insert a Flash movie that fills 100% of a browser window, you first need to set the movie's height and width to 100%. Then you need to create a few CSS styles. First, create a tag style for the <body> tag with the *padding* (page 449) and *margin* (page 449) values set to 0, and the *height* and *width* (page 448) values set to 100%. Next, create a style for the <html> tag with the same settings as the <body> tag (a group selector—discussed on page 381—makes the process of creating the styles more efficient). If the Flash movie is nested within other tags, like a <div> or a <p> tag, you need to remove the padding and margin for those tags and set their heights and widths to 100% as well. Finally, choose an appropriate Scaling setting for the movie, as discussed on the next page.

■ SET PLAYBACK OPTIONS

The Loop and Autoplay checkboxes control movie playback. When you turn on Loop, the movie plays over and over endlessly, an approach advertisers often use in animated banner ads. The Autoplay option starts playback as soon as the page loads into a browser.

Neither of these options overrides any programming instructions you embed in the Flash movie, however. So if you added a Stop command to the final frame of your movie, the movie stops at that frame regardless of the Loop setting.

■ LEAVE MARGINS UNSPECIFIED

Skip the V space and H settings in the Property Inspector. They're intended to add space to the top and bottom (V) and the left and right (H) edges of your movie, but they produce invalid code for the HTML 4.01 strict and HTML5 document types (see page 7 for more on doctypes). In addition, you can't control each of the four margins individually.

Instead, use Cascading Style Sheets and the CSS *margin* property (discussed on page 449) to add space around your movie. You can create an ID style (page 124) using the movie's name. For example, you might create an ID style named *#FlashID*.

■ SELECT A QUALITY SETTING

If your Flash movie requires a lot of processing muscle—if it's heavy on animation and action, for example—it may overwhelm older computers, making playback slow and choppy. Not every computer has a 3-gigahertz processor and 16 gigabytes of memory (not yet, anyway). Until that day, you may need to adjust the quality settings of your Flash movie so it looks good on all computers.

By default, Dreamweaver sets the movie quality to High, but you can choose any of the following four settings from the Quality menu in the Property Inspector:

- **High** provides the best quality, but the movie may run slower on older computers.

- **Low** looks terrible. This setting sacrifices quality by eliminating all *antialiasing* (edge-smoothing) in a movie, leaving harsh, jaggy lines on the edges of every image. Movies set to low quality look bad on *all* computers, so pass it by.

- **Auto Low** forces the movie to start in low-quality mode, but switches automatically to high-quality playback if the visitor's computer is fast enough.

- **Auto High** makes the movie switch to low-quality mode only if the visitor's computer requires it. This way, you can deliver a high-quality image to most visitors, while still letting those with slow computers view the movie. This mode is the best choice if you want to provide a high-quality image but still make your movie play back at reasonable speed for those with older computers.

■ ADJUST YOUR MOVIE'S SCALE

Scaling only becomes an issue when you specify *relative* dimensions for your movie, setting its size to, say, 90% of the width of a browser window. That's because the movie grows or shrinks as your visitor's browser grows or shrinks, and you have no control over what your visitors does with her browser—one person may prefer a small horizontal browser at the bottom of her screen, while another may use a tall, narrow window.

Enter Dreamweaver's Scale property. It lets you determine *how* Flash scales your movie. For example, in Figure 14-4, the top movie's original size is 334 pixels high by 113 pixels wide. If you resize the movie using the W and H attributes so that it's *350* pixels high and 113 pixels wide, one of three things will happen, depending on your Scale setting:

- **Show All**. This setting, the default, maintains the original aspect ratio (proportions) of your movie (second from top in Figure 14-4). In other words, although the overall *size* of the movie may change as a visitor fusses with his browser, its width-to-height ratio won't. Show All keeps your movie from distorting (but it may also cause white borders on the top, bottom, or either side of your movie; to hide the borders, make the movie's background color the same color as your web page).

- **No Border**. This setting resizes a movie according to your specifications *and* maintains its aspect ratio, but it may also crop the sides of the movie. Notice how the top and bottom of the Chia Vet logo are chopped off in Figure 14-4 (third image from top).

- **Exact Fit**. This option may stretch your movie's picture either horizontally or vertically. In Figure 14-4 (bottom), "Chia Vet" is stretched wider than normal.

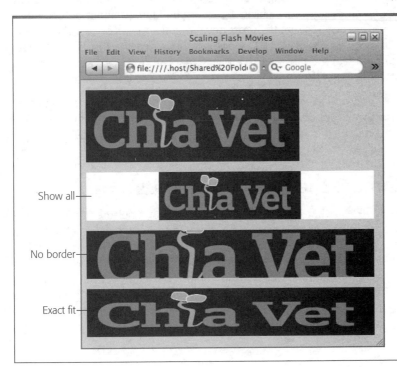

FIGURE 14-4

This browser window shows the results of choosing different settings in the Property Inspector's Scale menu. A Flash movie's Scale property specifies how a movie scales when you set its width and height properties to something different from that of the original movie. If you resize a movie, press F12 (Option-F12) to see how it looks in a web browser, and then, if necessary, choose a different setting from the Scale drop-down menu in the Property Inspector.

■ ALIGN YOUR MOVIE

You can align Flash movies relative to the paragraphs around them just as you can align images relative to the surrounding text. In fact, the Property Inspector's movie alignment options work exactly the same way as its text alignment properties. For example, when you choose Right from the Align menu, Dreamweaver positions the movie at the right edge of the screen and wraps text around its left side. (If the movie is inside a cell, Align→Right moves the movie to the right edge of the cell.) However, for strict document types and HTML5, the Align property is invalid. As with the margin settings discussed above, you're better off using CSS properties, such as the *float* property described on page 448.

■ BACKGROUND COLOR

To set a background color for a Flash movie, use the "Bg Color" box in the Property Inspector. This color overrides any background color set in the movie itself and becomes the movie's placeholder color when a page has loaded but the movie hasn't.

■ WMODE

Wmode stands for "Window mode" and it controls how your movie interacts with other HTML elements on the page. The standard setting, *opaque*, is useful when you include HTML that needs to appear on top of a movie—the classic example is a drop-down menu like the Spry Navigation Bar you learned about on page 210. The opaque setting ensures that the drop-down menu appears on top of the Flash movie. The *transparent* option lets HTML appear above a movie, too, but it also lets any HTML *underneath* the movie—like a page's background color—show through any transparent areas of the movie.

Finally, the *window* option is the exact opposite of the opaque option: It makes sure a Flash movie always appears above any HTML element on a page—even above a drop-down navigation menu that would normally appear over the movie.

■ Automate the Flash Download

Even though the Flash plug-in is nearly universal, you can't be sure that every visitor's browser has it. In addition, you may have created a Flash movie that runs only in the latest version of the plug-in, so a visitor might have the Flash plug-in, but not the correct *version* of it. The result? A movie that either doesn't play back at all or doesn't play back as it should. Guests who fall into this category have to choose from three equally unpalatable options: go to a different website to download the plug-in, skip the multimedia show (if you've built a second, plug-in-free version of your site), or skip your website entirely.

The Land of Obsolete Web Technology

Dreamweaver CS6 includes several other options in the Media menu of the Insert panel (see Figure 14-2). Some have been around since Dreamweaver was in training pants, and most of them don't see much use on today's Web; they either don't work for many users, or creating the content to work with these technologies is so hard that few web designers bother. In addition, some of the technologies look like they're being phased out by their creators.

Shockwave is a web technology that's been around a long time. It's the Internet-ready form of movies created with Adobe Director. Historically, Director was a program for creating CD-ROMs. But when the Web exploded onto the scene, Director quickly morphed into a web authoring tool, and its movie-creation tool was called Shockwave. As a result of its CD background, Shockwave offers complex programming possibilities, which makes it ideal for detailed, interactive presentations, and game-makers still use it.

However, most people won't find a use for it. Flash provides much of the same functionality for websites using simpler programming and, consequently, it's the much more common choice for web designers. In addition, the Shockwave plug-in isn't installed with web browsers, so visitors have to download it, the full version of which weighs in at a hefty 11.7MB for Windows PCs and 11.1 MB for Macs.

But if you just can't do without Shockwave, you can insert a Shockwave movie into a web page just as you would any other multimedia file. Choose where you want to insert the movie, and then choose Insert→Media→Shockwave, or choose Shockwave from the Media menu on the Common category of the Insert panel. Either way, a Select File dialog box appears. Find and double-click the Shockwave movie file (look for the .dcr extension).

Dreamweaver also includes tools for inserting other multimedia and plug-in files. In fact, these tools have been around since much earlier incarnations of Dreamweaver, when there really *were* other media types like Java applets, ActiveX controls, and other plug-in technology. However, Java applets never really took off (their performance never quite lived up to the hype), and ActiveX controls are limited to Internet Explorer for Windows.

Fortunately, Dreamweaver provides a built-in solution for both scenarios. When you embed a movie in a web page, Dreamweaver includes code that detects your visitor's browser plug-ins. If a visitor either doesn't have the Flash plug-in or doesn't have the right version of it, the page displays a message alerting the visitor (see Figure 14-5) and offering a button (labeled "Get Adobe Flash Player") that takes guests to the plug-in download. If your visitor has at least version 6 of the plug-in, she can take advantage of its "express install" feature, which lets her upgrade to the latest version with just a mouse click.

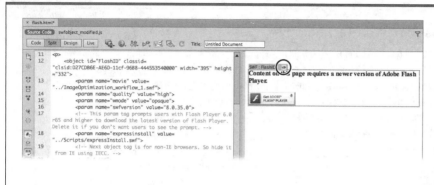

FIGURE 14-5

Here's the message a web browser displays if a visitor doesn't have the Flash player installed, has an old version of the player, or is viewing the page on a device that doesn't support Flash (like an iPhone or iPad). You can customize this message, but it's a good idea to leave the Flash player icon in place—it includes a link to a page on Adobe .com where your visitor can download the player.

You won't see the "missing Flash file" message in Design view; Dreamweaver keeps it hidden. But you can see and edit it by clicking the eye icon (circled in Figure 14-5).

WARNING Make sure you edit the message that appears when the Adobe plug-in isn't available (see Figure 14-5). It assumes that you can download and install the Flash player. Mobile devices that don't support Flash (like the iPhone and iPad) will display this same message—and telling visitors to download software that won't run on their device is just rude. Instead, change the message to something like "Your browser either doesn't support the Flash plug-in or you need to download a newer version of it to see this content."

To make all this happen, Dreamweaver adds two files to your website, both of them inside a folder named Scripts: *expressInstall.swf* and *swfobject_modified.js*. When you move your finished web pages and Flash movies to your web server (see Chapter 16), be sure to move the Scripts folder as well.

◼ Add Flash Videos

In addition to playing back animations and hosting games, the Flash player plays back videos, too. In fact, *Flash Video*, as this feature is called, is likely the most common way to play video on the Web. If you've visited a little site called YouTube, you've seen Flash Video in action. High among this format's advantages—compared to competing standards like QuickTime or Windows Media Video—is that you can reasonably count on every visitor having the new Flash program to view your videos.

Dreamweaver makes it a snap to embed videos. Unfortunately, Flash can't play back videos in just any old format, like MPEG or AVI, without a little help. And Dreamweaver can't transform videos in these formats to the Flash Video format (which has the extension .flv). Instead, you need one of several Adobe products to create Flash video files. If you bought the Adobe Creative Suite, you're in business; it includes the Flash Video encoder. Otherwise, you need Flash CS6, CS5, or CS4 Pro.

ADD FLASH VIDEOS

NOTE For a quick intro to creating Flash videos, visit *http://tinyurl.com/63lkad9*. Adobe also dedicates an entire section of their site to Flash video: *www.adobe.com/devnet/video*.

Fortunately, creating the .flv file is the hard part. Dreamweaver makes the rest easy. Follow these few simple steps to inserts a Flash video into your page, complete with DVD-like playback controls.

1. **Click the place on the page where you want to insert the video.**

   Like other Flash movies, you'll want an open area of your page.

2. **Choose Insert→Media→FLV.**

   Or, from the Common category of the Insert panel, select FLV from the Media menu, and the Insert FLV window appears (see Figure 14-6). You can also just drag the .flv file from the Files panel and drop it onto the document window.

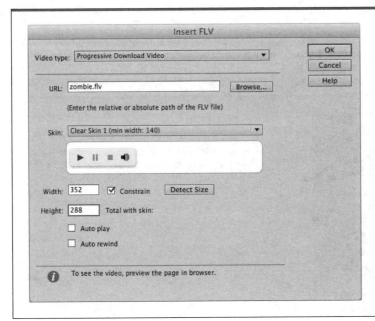

FIGURE 14-6

The Insert FLV window is probably the easiest way to add video to your website. To play the video, all your visitors need is the Flash player, which in many cases comes preinstalled with their browser.

CHAPTER 14: **ADD FLASH AND OTHER MULTIMEDIA**   721

3. **Select Progressive Download Video from the "Video type" menu.**

Dreamweaver provides two download options, Progressive Download Video and Streaming Video. The latter requires you to have some expensive software (a Flash server) or a Flash video-streaming service, which can run you anywhere from $10 a month to a couple of hundred dollars a month. Streaming video is usually reserved for live events or to handle very large numbers of viewers. That's why websites for TV networks like ABC.com use streaming servers—it's an efficient way to distribute video when thousands of people watch the same video at the same time.

If you choose Progressive Download, your video doesn't have to download completely before it begins playing back, so viewers don't have to wait, say, 30 minutes while your 40 MB movie downloads. Instead, the video starts as soon as the first section of the file arrives on their machine, and plays back as the rest of the movie downloads. That's how YouTube videos work.

4. **Click the Browse button and select the Flash video file (.flv) you want to add to the page.**

Due to differences in how operating systems work, you're best off putting your Flash video file in the same folder as your web page. If you want to put it elsewhere (in a dedicated Flash video folder, for instance, or even on a different web server), use absolute links (see page 186).

5. **Select a skin.**

A *skin* is a set of playback controls for your video; it includes buttons that start, pause, and stop the video; a progress bar; and various volume-adjustment controls (see Figure 14-7).

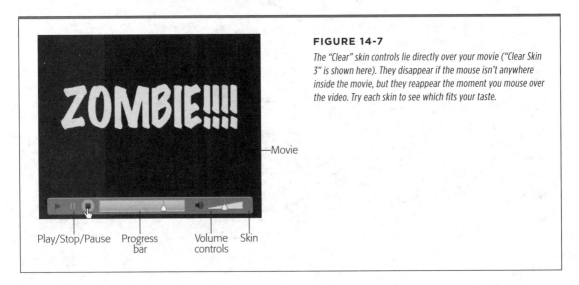

FIGURE 14-7

The "Clear" skin controls lie directly over your movie ("Clear Skin 3" is shown here). They disappear if the mouse isn't anywhere inside the movie, but they reappear the moment you mouse over the video. Try each skin to see which fits your taste.

—Movie

Play/Stop/Pause   Progress   Volume   Skin
bar   controls

Dreamweaver adds the controls to your video, and offers nine styles—actually, three types of controllers, each with three different graphical styles.

6. **Click the Detect Size button.**

   Flash videos contain *metadata*—information embedded inside the video file that describes its features, like its dimensions, file size, and so on. The Flash video encoder adds this metadata when you create a movie. Clicking the Detect Size button extracts the movie's width and height measurements, adds the width and height of the playback controls, and then automatically fills in the width and height boxes in the Insert FLV window (see Figure 14-7).

   If, for whatever reason, your file doesn't include metadata, you have to enter the width and height values yourself—these settings specify how much space the video occupies on your page. Note that entering these dimensions won't actually distort your video—making it really, really thin or really, really wide, for example. No matter what size you enter, Dreamweaver preserves the original aspect ratio of your movie, and adds extra, empty space to fill any area not occupied by it. For example, say your movie is 352 pixels wide and 288 pixels tall. If you enter a dimension of 100 x 288, respectively, the movie won't stretch like you're watching it in a fun-house mirror. Instead, the movie appears 100 pixels wide and 82 pixels tall, with 53 pixels of blank space above and below it.

7. **If you want, turn on the Autoplay checkbox.**

   Doing so makes the movie play as soon as enough video data's been downloaded from the Web. Otherwise, a visitor has to press the play button to begin the movie.

8. **If you want, turn on the "Auto rewind" checkbox.**

   After playback, your movie automatically "rewinds" to the first frame if you turn on this checkbox. But you may not always want to abide by the old video-store credo "Be Kind, Rewind." If your movie ends with a dramatic message—"Stay tuned for the next exciting installment of Blind Mole Rats from Mars!"—you might prefer to leave the movie on its last frame when it's complete.

9. **Click OK to add the Flash video to your page.**

   This step installs the necessary code not only for the video, but for detecting the Flash plug-in as well (described on page 718). You can check out the newly inserted video by pressing F12 (Option-F12) to preview the page in a browser.

NOTE When you upload your web page and Flash video to your site (see Chapter 16), you need to upload four additional files that Dreamweaver secretly adds: the two files (and the *Scripts* folder) discussed on page 718, the file *FLVPlayer_progressive.swf*, and the .swf (Flash movie) file for the skin you selected. That last file is named after the skin you chose—for example, *Clear_Skin_1.swf*. Save yourself some work: When uploading your Flash-filled web page (uploading details are on page 798), choose to include "dependent files;" that way, Dreamweaver grabs these three files for you.

■ Other Video Options

Flash video is great. It looks good and plays back smoothly...in those devices that have the Flash plug-in. Unfortunately, two common devices—the iPhone and iPad—don't support Flash or Flash Video. When a visitor with an iPhone goes to a page with a Flash video embedded in it, she won't be able to watch it. If you want to make sure visitors with Apple's iOS (that's the operating system in iPhones and iPads) can view your movies, you have a couple of choices.

First, you can use YouTube. While YouTube originally used only Flash Video, it now supports a wider range of video options. When you upload a video to YouTube, it converts the movie to Flash Video as well as to other common video formats. For example, when someone with Internet Explorer visits a YouTube page, he gets a Flash video; but if the visitor is using an iPad, YouTube sends an MPEG4 file instead. In other words, YouTube does all the hard work for you. Best of all, you can even embed your YouTube-hosted videos on your own web pages, too.

Another option is HTML5. HTML5 introduced the <video> tag, which lets you embed video straight into a web page, without the need for a plug-in like the Flash player or QuickTime. Excitement from Google and other companies about the <video> tag has given way to frustration among web developers, however. The original idea behind the tag—to provide a simple way to add video to a web page—has turned into a lot more work than expected. As it turns out, browser makers have settled on 3 different formats—H.264, Ogg Theora, and WebM—and, of course, the various browsers out there play different formats. Even worse, Internet Explorer 8 and earlier don't understand the <video> tag at all! For the average web developer, this means taking a video and "encoding" it into several formats, including Flash Video, and putting in the proper HTML to make sure everybody (including IE 8 and earlier owners) can view it. That's a lot of work. If you're game for that, you can find in-depth explanations of adding HTML video to a web page at *www.netmagazine.com/tutorials/add-html5-video-your-site* and *http://webdesign.about.com/od/video/ss/html5-video.htm*.

If you're happy with YouTube, which many businesses use routinely, here's how to put video on YouTube.com and include it in a web page on your site:

1. **Get a video.** Obviously you'll need to make a video, have one already made, or get one from your client or boss. YouTube accepts QuickTime .mov, Windows .avi, .mpg files, and even Flash Video (.flv) or the new Google-owned format WebM. You can even record directly from a webcam. You can upload both standard-definition (640 x 480 pixels) and high-definition videos (1280 x 720 pixels). Your movies should be no longer than 15 minutes.

> **NOTE** In some cases, you can upload really long videos—up to 12 hours long. If you really want to upload your "My sleeping habits in real time" video to YouTube, visit *http://support.google.com/youtube/bin/answer .py?hl=en&answer=71673* to find out how.

2. **Get an account at *www.youtube.com*.** If you don't already have an account, you need to go to YouTube and sign up. It's free and easy.

3. **Upload a video.** Once you have an account and log in, click Upload at the top of YouTube's home page. Then click "Upload video," select a video file from your computer, and then click OK. The video begins to upload, and you'll see a page that lets you set its properties, such as its title and description.

4. **Select and copy the "embed" code.** Once you finish uploading the file, you'll see an "Embed" button. Click it and copy the HTML code there. The embed code is a snippet of HTML that lets you put the video on any page of your site. (You can also find the embed code listed on the movie's page on YouTube—in fact, on any movie page on YouTube, so if you want to embed a movie you didn't create but that you found while surfing YouTube, you can: just click the Share button on the movie page, then the Embed button to select the HTML snippet.)

   Return to Dreamweaver and add the code to your page. Since you copied a snippet of raw HTML code, you need to add the code in Code view. The easiest way to do that is to click where you want to add the video in Design view, and then click the Code view button; Dreamweaver has put the cursor in the right place and you simply choose Edit→Paste to add the code.

While YouTube was once considered just a place to stash your home videos, blooper reels, and illegally copied TV shows, it's more and more a place where businesses put product demos, instructional videos, and other videos promoting their companies. In addition to showcasing the video on your site, you make it possible for a few of the billions of eyeballs that visit YouTube each month to stumble across your video and learn about your product or business—free marketing can't be beat.

There are a few other reasons why YouTube is a good video-hosting option. Video takes a lot of bandwidth and server processing power. Putting video on your own server can easily slow down your site and cost you extra money once you hit your web host's monthly bandwidth allotment. In addition, YouTube does all the hard work of making your video ready for pretty much any browser or device—Internet Explorer 6, Firefox, iPad, iPhone, Android—and not just browsers that have the Flash player installed.

Adding Sound to Web Pages

Hey man, I'm a rock star-in-training, and I want to surprise the world with my cool tunes. How do I put my music on my website?

Lots of technologies let you add music and sound to your site. Most require plug-ins, which limit your audience because few people are going to rush off to another website to download and install more software just to enjoy your site—unless you're U2 or Miley Cyrus.

As a result, the ubiquitous Flash provides the best and fastest way to add sound to your site. Flash supports several audio formats, such as MP3, WAV (Windows), and AIFF (Mac), and if you have QuickTime installed, it handles even more formats. You'll have to dip into the Flash Help files to learn how to import audio, but it's not too hard. If you just want ambient background music on a page, you can even create a very small (like a 1 pixel x 1 pixel) Flash movie that simply plays back

music. Follow the steps on page 712 for inserting the Flash movie into your page.

There are also a few Dreamweaver extensions that let you add sound and music to your site. Speaker from HotDreamweaver (*www.hotdreamweaver.com/speaker*, $20) lets you insert MP3 files that play back when you click a small icon. Trio Solutions (*http://components.developers4web.com*) sells more than a dozen MP3 player extensions; each lets you insert CD-player-like controls (Play, Pause, Stop, Fast-Forward) to control playback and some let you create a playlist of multiple songs.

HTML5 also added an <audio> tag, but it has some of the same problems as the <video> tag discussed above—different browsers support different audio formats and there's no support in Internet Explorer 8 and earlier. You can read about the <audio> tag at *http://tinyurl.com/mo39ha*.

Managing a Website

PART

4

Introducing Site Management

As the dull-sounding name *site management* implies, organizing and tracking your website's files is one of the least glamorous, most time-consuming, error-prone aspects of being a web designer. On the Web, your site may look beautiful, run smoothly, and appear as a gloriously unified whole, but behind the scenes, it's nothing more than a collection of various files—HTML pages, images, Cascading Style Sheets, JavaScript code, Flash movies, and so on—that must all work together. The more files you have to keep track of, the more apt you are to misplace one. And a single broken link or missing graphic can interfere with the operation of your entire site, causing personal—even professional—embarrassment.

Fortunately, computers excel at tedious organizational tasks. Dreamweaver's site management features take care of the complexities of dealing with a website's many files, freeing you to concentrate on the creative aspects of the site. In fact, even if you're a hand-coding HTML junkie and you turn your nose up at all visual web page editors, you may find Dreamweaver worth its weight in gold just for the features described in this and the next two chapters.

The first three parts of this book described how to create, lay out, and embellish your site. This part offers a bird's-eye view of the production process as you see your site through to completion and, ultimately, put it up on the Internet.

To get the most out of Dreamweaver's site management features, you need to be familiar with some basic principles for organizing web files.

■ The Structure of a Website

When you build a website, you probably spend hours adding carefully planned links, helpful labels, and clear, informative navigation tools. You want your *site architecture*—the structure of your site—to make it easy for visitors to understand where they are, where they can go, and how to return to where they just came from (see Figure 15-1). Behind the scenes, it's equally important to organize your site files with just as much clarity and care, so you can find *your* way around when you update or modify the site. And, just as on your computer, a website's main organizational tool is the humble *folder*.

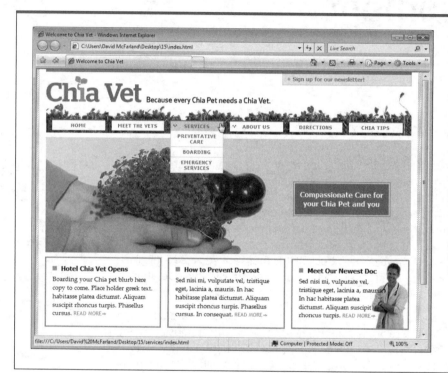

FIGURE 15-1

A good site (even a made-up one) has an easy-to-understand structure. It divides content into logical sections, and includes a prominent navigation bar—the row of buttons below the Chia-Vet logo in this image—to give visitors quick access to that content. When you build a site, its "architecture" provides a useful model for creating and naming the behind-the-scenes folders that hold the site's files.

You probably organize files on your computer every day, creating, say, a folder called Personal, within which are folders called Financial Planning and Vacation Pictures. Inside the Vacation Pictures folder, you might have separate folders for memories of Maui, Yosemite, and the Mall of America.

The same principle applies to the folders that make up a website: All websites have one primary folder—the *root folder*—and that folder usually contains additional folders where you further subdivide and organize your site's files. Collectively, the root folder and its subfolders hold all of a site's web pages, graphics, and other files.

A sensible site structure (see Figure 15-2) makes it easy to maintain your site because it's logically organized—it gives you quick access to whatever graphic, style sheet, or movie you're looking for. But don't fall into the trap of becoming so obsessed with bins that you put every graphic or web page in its own folder; adding structure to your site should make your job easier, not harder.

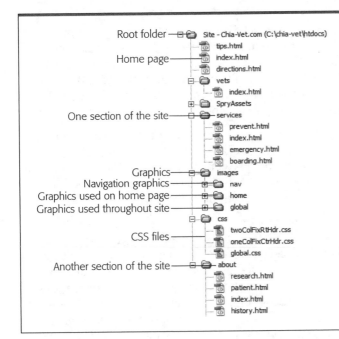

Root folder — Site - Chia-Vet.com (C:\chia-vet\htdocs)
tips.html
Home page — index.html
directions.html
vets
index.html
SpryAssets
One section of the site — services
prevent.html
index.html
emergency.html
boarding.html
Graphics — images
Navigation graphics — nav
Graphics used on home page — home
Graphics used throughout site — global
css
twoColFixRtHdr.css
CSS files — oneColFixCtrHdr.css
global.css
Another section of the site — about
research.html
patient.html
index.html
history.html

FIGURE 15-2

Here's a sample structure for a website. The root (main) folder, htdocs, ultimately holds all the site's pages. The home page, index.html, is in the root folder, while other pages reside within subfolders—one folder for each section of the site. The home page uses lots of graphics that don't appear anywhere else on the site; a folder named "home" inside the "images" folder helps keep those in order. In addition, since many pages share the same logo and other graphics, the site includes a folder called "global." Finally, to keep all the graphics used for navigational buttons and links orderly, the site includes a folder called "nav." Also notice that the "services" folder (like the folder for each section of the site) has its own default page, here called index.html, which can contain additional subfolders (see the box on page 735).

NOTE If you already have a website that suffers from lack of organization, it's not too late. Dreamweaver can help you reorganize your files quickly and accurately. Take the following rules to heart and then turn to "Managing Files and Folders" on page 49.

Here, then, are some guidelines for effective site organization:

- **Plan for future growth**. Like ever-spreading grapevines, websites grow. Today you may have only enough words and pictures for 10 web pages, but tomorrow you'll put the finishing touches on your new 1,000-page online catalog. It may seem like overkill to create a lot of folders for a small site, but better to start with a solid structure today than find yourself knee-deep in files tomorrow.

  For instance, it's useful to create separate folders for graphics that appear within each section of the site. If a section of your site is dedicated to promoting your company's products, for example, create a folder called *products* for your product web pages. Create an additional subfolder called *images* to store the pictures of those products. Then, when you add more products or images, you know right where to put them.

NOTE While you can start with no organizational plan and later use Dreamweaver to bring your site into shape (see page 49), you may run into unforeseen problems if your site has been up and running for a while. That's because search engines may have already indexed your site, and other websites may have linked to your pages. If you suddenly rearrange your site, people who try to access your site from a search engine may be foiled, and those cherished links from the outside world may no longer work. If that's the case, you're better off leaving the site as it is, and begin the organization process with new files only.

- **Follow the site's architecture**. Take advantage of the work you've already done in organizing your site's content. For instance, the Chia Vet site content is divided into five sections: Meet the Vets, Services, About Us, Directions, and Chia Tips, as shown in Figure 15-1. Following this structure, it makes sense to create folders—*vets, services, about*, and so on—in the site's root folder for each section's respective web pages. If one section is particularly large, add subfolders.

- **Organize files by type**. After you create folders for each section of your site, you'll probably need to add folders to store other types of files, like graphics, Cascading Style Sheets, external JavaScript files, and PDF files. Most sites, for instance, make extensive use of graphics, with several images per page. If that's the case for you, file those images neatly and efficiently.

  One way to organize your graphics is to create a folder for images that appear on your home page and another for images that appear elsewhere on the site. Often, the home page is visually distinct from other site pages and contains graphics that are not only unique to it, but which might change frequently. You can create a folder—such as *images_home*—in the root folder for images that appear only on your home page. Create another folder—*images_global*, for example—to store graphics that appear on all or most of the other pages, like the company logo, navigation buttons, and other frequently used icons. When you add these images to other pages on your site, you'll know to look for them in this folder. Alternatively, you could create an *images* folder in the root of your site and add subfolders such as *home, global*, and *nav* (see Figure 15-2). The choice of an organizational system is yours; just make sure you have one.

- **Use understandable names**. While file names like *1a.gif, zDS.html*, and *f.css* are compact, they aren't very obvious. Make sure your file names mean something. Clear, descriptive names like *site_logo.gif* or *directions.html* make it a lot easier to locate files and update pages.

  This principle is especially important if you work as part of a team. If you're constantly explaining to coworkers that *345g.gif* is the banner for the home page, changing the file name to *home_banner.gif* could save you some aggravation. There's a tradeoff here, however, as long file names can waste precious bytes, bloating your pages and slowing down load time. For instance, a site full of file names like *this_is_the_image_that_goes_in_the_upper_right_corner_of_the_home_page.gif* is probably not a good idea.

NOTE Dreamweaver employs the industry-standard .html extension for web pages—as in *index.html*. Another common extension is .htm (a holdover from the days when Windows could handle only three-letter extensions). It doesn't really matter which you use, and if you're used to .htm, you can easily change the extension Dreamweaver uses. Just choose Edit→Preferences (Dreamweaver→Preferences) to open the Preferences window, select the New Document category, and then type *.htm* in the default extension box.

It's also helpful to add a prefix to related files. For example, use *nav_* at the beginning of a graphic name to indicate that it's a navigation button. This way, you can quickly identify *nav_projects.png*, *nav_quiz.png*, and *nav_horoscopes.png* as graphics used in a page's navigation bar, or *bg_body.png* and *bg_column.png* as graphics used as backgrounds. As a bonus, when you view the files on your computer or in Dreamweaver's Files panel (see Figure 15-3), they appear neatly sorted by name; in other words, all the *nav_* files cluster together in the file list. Likewise, if you have rollover versions of your navigation graphics, give them names like *nav_projects_hover.gif* or *nav_ horoscopes_h.gif* to indicate that they're the highlighted (or rollover) state of the navigation button. (If you use Fireworks, its button-creation tools automatically use names like *nav_projects_f1.gif* and *nav_projects_f2.gif* to indicate two different versions of the same button.)

And, as mentioned in "Naming Your Files and Folders" on page 49, to make sure your files work on any web server, stick to letters, numbers, hyphens (-), and the underscore (_) character in file and folder names.

- **Be consistent**. Once you come up with an organization that works for you, follow it. Always. If you name one folder *images*, for instance, don't name another *graphics* and a third *pretty_pictures*. And certainly don't put web pages in a folder named *images* or JavaScript files in a folder named *style_sheets*.

In fact, if you work on more than one website, you may want to use a single naming convention and folder structure for all your sites, so that switching from one project to another goes more smoothly. If you name all your graphics folders *images*, then no matter what site you're working on, you know where to look for GIFs, PNGs and JPEGs.

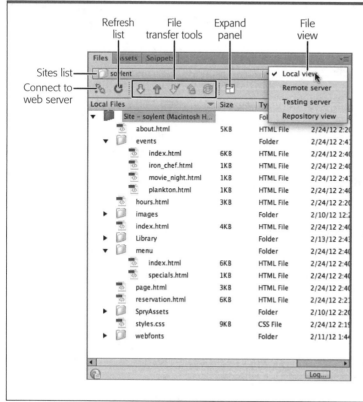

Refresh list
File transfer tools
Expand panel
File view

Sites list
Connect to web server

FIGURE 15-3

Dreamweaver's Files panel, logically enough, lists files in the currently active website. A list of all the websites you defined in Dreamweaver appears on the Sites drop-down menu. To work on a different site, select its name from the list (but be aware that you could inadvertently select files on your local drive, potentially tripping up Dreamweaver's site management tools—see the box on page 54 for details). You can use the Files panel to connect to a web server and transfer files back and forth between your local and remote sites, as described on page 798. You can tell whether you're looking at the files on your computer, the web server, the testing server, or a Subversion repository (page 810) by looking at the name that appears at the top of the file column. In this figure, for example, you're looking at files on your computer, since "Local Files" appears at the top of the Files column.

NOTE It's usually best to put only files that make up your website in the root folder and its subfolders. Keep your source files—the original Photoshop, Fireworks, Flash, or Word documents—stored elsewhere on your computer. That way, you're much less likely to accidentally transfer a 14.5 MB Photoshop file to your web server (a move that would *not* gain you friends in the IT department). That said, if you do like keeping all your files together, check out Dreamweaver's *cloaking* feature (described on page 804). Using it, you can prevent Dreamweaver from transferring certain file types to your web server when you use the program's FTP feature.

FREQUENTLY ASKED QUESTION

All Those Index Pages

Why are so many web pages named index.html *(or* index.htm*)?*

If you type a URL like *www.missingmanuals.com* into a web browser, the Missing Manuals home page opens on your screen. But how did the web server know which of the site's pages to send to your browser? After all, you didn't ask for a particular page, like *www.missingmanuals.com/index.html*.

When a web server gets a request that doesn't specify a page, it looks for a default web page—often named *index.html* or *index.htm*. It does the same thing even when the URL you type specifies (with a slash) a folder inside the site root, like this: *www.missingmanuals.com/cds/*. In this case, the server looks for a file called *index.html* inside the "cds" folder, and, if it finds the file, sends it to your browser.

If the server doesn't find an *index.html* file, two things can happen, both undesirable: The browser can display either an ugly error message or a listing of all the files inside the folder. Neither result helps to your visitors.

While your site still functions if you don't give the main page inside each folder a default page name, it's good form to name that file *index.html*. This avoids the "404 File Not Found error" when someone requests just a folder name and not a specific file inside that folder.

Web servers can use different names for these default pages—*default.html*, for example—although *index.html* works on most web servers. In fact, you can specify any page as a default, so long as you set up your web server to look for that default page. When working with a server-side programming language, like PHP, ASP, or .NET, the index page will end with a file extension appropriate to that language: for example, *index.php*. *index .asp*, or *index.aspx*. Most web servers already predefine multiple default page names, so if it doesn't find a file named *index.html*, it may automatically look for one called *index.php*.

■ Setting Up a Site (in Depth)

Organizing and maintaining a website—creating new folders and web pages; moving, renaming, and deleting files and folders; and transferring pages to a web server—can require going back and forth between a couple of programs. With Dreamweaver's site management features, however, you can perform all those tasks from within one program. But to take advantage of this simplicity, you must first make Dreamweaver aware of your site; in other words, you need to give Dreamweaver some basic information about it.

Setting up a site in Dreamweaver involves showing the program which folder contains your website files (the *root folder*) and setting a few other options. You already know the very basics of setting up a site using Dreamweaver's Site Setup window (page 40). Here, you'll get a detailed explanation of the options available in Site Setup.

Start by choosing Site→New Site. That opens the Site Setup window (see Figure 15-4). It includes four categories of options where you specify the details of your site—Dreamweaver labels the categories Site, Servers, Version Control, and Advanced Settings.

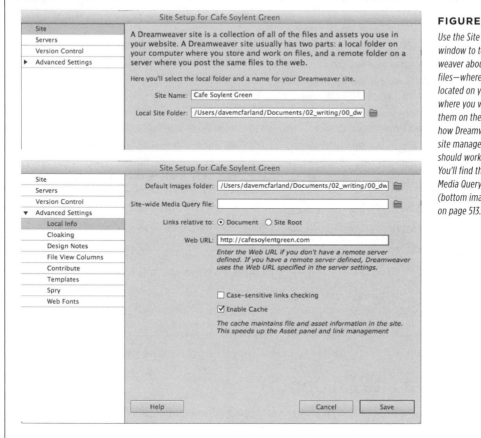

FIGURE 15-4

Use the Site Setup window to tell Dreamweaver about your site files—where they're located on your computer, where you want to put them on the Web, and how Dreamweaver's site management tools should work with them. You'll find the "Site-wide Media Query file" option (bottom image) discussed on page 513.

You've encountered the Site category several times already (page 40, for example): It's where you tell Dreamweaver where on your computer it can find your website files. The Servers and Version Control settings help Dreamweaver work with your remote server; you'll learn about these settings in Chapter 17 (see page 787).

You'll find the Advanced Settings options (Figure 15-4, bottom) useful for different situations, described below. You'll learn about the "Local info" options next, the Cloaking options on page 804, the Design Notes category on page 817, the Templates option in Chapter 19, the Spry option on page 215, and the Web Fonts option on page 146. The settings are called "Advanced" for a reason and you may not ever feel the need to visit or change them.

The most important category in the Site Setup window is the first: Site (top image in Figure 15-4). Filling out the following two options are all you need to get started using Dreamweaver effectively.

■ SITE NAME

In the "Site name" field, type a name that briefly identifies the site for you—and Dreamweaver. This is the name that appears in, among other places, the File panel's Site drop-down menu (see Figure 15-3 for a glimpse of that), so you can tell what site you're working on. It's just for identifying your site while you work in Dreamweaver—it doesn't appear on your actual site pages.

■ LOCAL SITE FOLDER

Identify your site's local folder—the folder on your hard drive that contains all the site's files. (This is also known as a local root folder.) Click the folder icon to the right of "Local site folder" to browse for the folder. See the box on page 46 for more information on local site folders.

> **NOTE** If you're confused about which folder is your local site folder, ask yourself this question: "Which folder on my computer will contain (or contains) my site's home page?" That's your local site folder. All your site's other files and folders should go inside this one.

The Dreamweaver tools that manage your sites' files rely on the local site folder. Once you set up a site, you see all its files listed in the Files panel. In the Advanced Settings area, the "Local info" tab tells Dreamweaver how to work with the files on your computer.

The "Local info" category under the Advanced Settings menu (bottom image in Figure 15-4) has some other useful settings that can help Dreamweaver work with your site's files, as described below.

■ DEFAULT IMAGES FOLDER

When you want to display a graphic on a web page, you tell the page where to find the image by pointing to its file location. That location has to be inside the local root folder or one of its subfolders. In other words, if you link to a graphic that's sitting *outside* of the root folder on your hard drive, a web browser will never find it.

Dreamweaver offers a feature that puts images in the right place even if you forget to. When you add a stray graphics file to a page on your site, Dreamweaver automatically copies the file into your default images folder. In fact, even if you drag a graphic from your desktop onto a web page-in-progress, Dreamweaver copies the file to the default images folder without missing a beat.

You identify the default images folder the same way you select the local site folder. Click the folder icon and locate the folder on your local drive. If you haven't set up the folder yet, click the "New Folder" button to create it on the spot. (For example, you might add a folder to your local root folder and name it *images*.)

■ SITE-WIDE MEDIA QUERY FILE

Media Query files are discussed in depth on page 510, but in a nutshell they determine the width of your guest's screen and load a CSS file that applies different style sheets based on that width. In other words, you can style your pages to look different depending on whether your visitor has a mobile phone, a tablet, or a monitor. A site-wide Media Query file is just a file that makes it faster for you to use media queries on your pages. You don't *have* to use media queries on your site, so you can leave this option empty if you want. Chapter 11 discusses Media Queries in-depth and how to use Dreamweaver to work with different screens on mobile, tablet, and desktop browsers.

■ LINKS RELATIVE TO

As discussed on page 185, you can set up links in your web pages in a variety of ways. When you link from one page to another on your site, Dreamweaver lets you create either a *document-relative* link or a *root-relative* link. As explained on page 186, document-relative links are often the easiest way to go, but Dreamweaver gives you the flexibility to choose. Click either the Document or Site Root radio button. Then, whenever you embed a link in your pages, Dreamweaver creates the link using that setting.

> **NOTE** You can override this setting and use whichever type of link you wish—document-relative or site root-relative—when you create the link, as described in step 4 on page 194.

FREQUENTLY ASKED QUESTION

Bringing Your Own Website

I already have a website. Will Dreamweaver work with it?

Yes. In fact, Dreamweaver's site management features are an invaluable aid in organizing the files of an existing site. As you can read in "Managing Files and Folders" on page 49, you can use Dreamweaver to rearrange, rename, and reorganize files—tasks that are extremely difficult and time-consuming to do by hand.

Furthermore, Dreamweaver lets you clean up and reorganize a site without breaking links. So Dreamweaver is just as useful for working with a completed site as it is for creating one from scratch.

To work on an existing site, make sure it has its own root folder—in other words, that its home page, graphics, CSS files, other web pages, and any subfolders, all reside in one main site folder. Then set up a new site in Dreamweaver as described above, and choose this folder as the local site folder.

■ WEB URL

This option serves two functions: First, if you use absolute URLs to link to pages within your site (see page 186), you must fill out the Web URL field for Dreamweaver's link-management features to work. Type in your site's full URL, beginning with *http://*. Dreamweaver uses this address to check for broken links within your site and correctly rewrite links if you move pages around. For example, say your webmaster told you to link a form to http://www.yourdomain.com/cgi/formscript .php instead of using a document-relative link. In this case, you'd type http://www .yourdomain.com/ in the Web URL box. Now, if you move or rename the *formscript .php* page from within Dreamweaver, the program is smart enough to update the absolute link in the form.

This setting is also incredibly valuable in one particular situation: if you use site root-relative links, but the site you're working on isn't actually located in the site root on the web server. For example, say you run the marketing department at International ToolCo. You manage just the web pages for the marketing department, and they're located in a folder called *marketing* on the web server. In essence, you manage a sub-site, which acts as an independent site within the larger International ToolCo site. Maybe your webmaster demands that you use site root-relative links—man, is that guy bossy.

NOTE If you set up Dreamweaver to upload and download files from your web server as described on page 785, you've already told Dreamweaver your website's URL (see step 10 on page 791). If that's the case, the Web URL option in the "Local info" box will be grayed out.

This is a potentially tricky situation. Here's why: Site root-relative links always begin with a forward slash (/), indicating the root folder on the web server (for a refresher on this concept, see page 187). Normally, if you add a root-relative link to, say, the main page in a folder named *personnel* located inside the local root folder, Dreamweaver would write the link like this: */personnel/index.html.* But in this case, that wouldn't work. The *personnel* folder is actually located inside the *marketing* folder on the web server. So the link should be */marketing/personnel/index.html.* In other words, Dreamweaver normally thinks that your local root folder maps exactly to the web server's root folder.

You can solve this dilemma by adding a URL that points to the "sub-site" in the Site Definition window's Web URL box. In this example, you'd type http://www .intltoolco.com/marketing/ in the box. Then, whenever you add a root–relative link, Dreamweaver begins it with */marketing/* and then adds the rest of the path to the URL. In summary, *if* you use site root-relative links *and* you're working solely on pages located inside a subdirectory on the actual server, *then* fill out the absolute URL to that subdirectory. Finally, add this whole rigmarole to the list of reasons why document-relative links are easier to manage in Dreamweaver.

NOTE Strangely, the first use of the Web URL box mentioned above—that is, managing absolute URLs pointing to files in your site—doesn't work with the second option—sub-sites. For example, if you specify a subdirectory like http://www.intltoolco.com/marketing/ in the Web URL box, Dreamweaver isn't able to keep track of absolute links within this site. So if you had to use the URL www.intltoolco.com/marketing/cgi/form.php to point to a form page within your site, and then you move that form page, Dreamweaver won't update the page that uses that absolute link.

■ CASE-SENSITIVE LINKS

Some web servers (namely, those that use the Unix and Linux operating systems) are sensitive to the case you use in file names. For example, both consider *INDEX .html* and *index.html* different files. If your server uses either OS, turn on the "Use case-sensitive link checking" checkbox to make sure Dreamweaver doesn't mistake one file for another when it checks links. Say you link to a file named *INDEX.html*, but change the name of another file named *index.html* to *contact.html*. Without this option turned on, Dreamweaver may mistakenly update links to *INDEX.html* because it considers that file the same as *index.html*.

In real-world use, you probably won't need this option. First, it's not possible to have two files with the same name but different combinations of upper- and lowercase letters in the same folder on a Windows or Mac machine. So if your local root folder is on a Windows or Mac computer, you'll never be able to get into this situation. In addition, it's confusing (and just plain weird) to use the same name but different cases for your files.

■ CACHE

The cache is a small database of information about the files in your site. It helps Dreamweaver's site management features work more efficiently. In almost all cases, you want to keep this checkbox turned on. However, if you have a really large site, composed of tens of thousands of web pages, Dreamweaver might act pretty sluggishly when you perform basic tasks like moving files around within the site or checking for broken links.

Once you provide the local information for your site, click Save to close the Site Definition window and begin working.

■ Managing Dreamweaver Sites

When you work with Dreamweaver, always keep in mind that you'll have a set of files on your computer for each site you work on as well as a "site" that you've set up in Dreamweaver. The files on your computer will always be there (until you or your mischievous cat delete them): They exist even without Dreamweaver. However, when you use Dreamweaver, you'll also have a list of all the sites you've set up within the program using the process described in Setting Up a Site (in Depth) on page 735. These Dreamweaver "sites" are nothing more than the information Dreamweaver needs to locate and work with your web files and to connect to your web server. You can edit and delete a Dreamweaver "site" without doing any harm to the actual site files on your computer.

Editing or Removing Sites

Sometimes you need to edit the information associated with a site. Perhaps you want to rename the site, or you reorganized your hard drive and moved the local root folder, so you want to let Dreamweaver know the new location.

To edit a site, open the Manage Sites dialog box (choose Site→Manage Sites or, in the Files panel, choose Manage Sites from the bottom of the Site drop-down menu) and double-click the name of the site you want to edit. The Site Setup window opens (top image in Figure 15-4). Now you can type a new name in the Site Name box, choose a new local root folder, or make any other changes you want. Click OK to close the dialog box when you're done.

TIP If you want to edit the current site's information, there's a shortcut. In the Files panel (Figure 15-3), double-click the name of the site in the Sites menu. (Mac owners need to click once to select the name in the menu, and then click again to open the Site Definition window.)

Once you finish designing a site, you may want to remove it from Dreamweaver's list of sites. Open the Manage Sites dialog box (see Figure 15-5) as described above, click to select the site you wish to delete, and then click the button that looks like a minus sign (that's the Delete Site button).

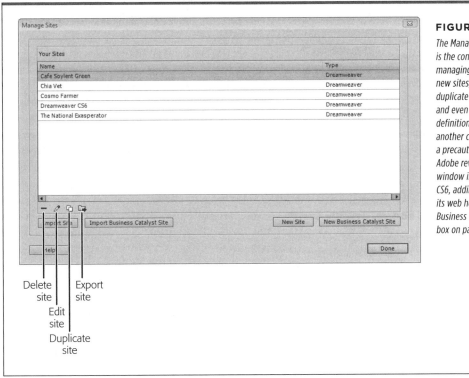

FIGURE 15-5

The Manage Sites window is the control center for managing your sites. Add new sites, edit old ones, duplicate a site definition, and even export site definitions for use on another computer, or as a precautionary backup. Adobe revamped this window in Dreamweaver CS6, adding support for its web hosting service, Business Catalyst (see the box on page 744).

Delete site

Edit site

Duplicate site

Export site

A warning appears telling you that you can't undo this action. Don't worry; deleting the site here doesn't actually *delete* the site's web pages, images, or other files from your computer. It merely removes the site from Dreamweaver's list of sites. (You can always go back and set up the site again by following the steps on page 735.) Click Done to close the Manage Sites window.

NOTE If you do, in fact, want to delete the actual web pages, graphics, and other site components, you can either switch to the desktop (Windows Explorer or the Finder, for example) and delete them manually, or delete them from within Dreamweaver's Files panel, as described on page 52.

UP TO SPEED

Local vs. Live Site Folders

A site folder (also called a *root* folder) is a site's main, hold-everything bin. It contains every component that makes up your website: all web page documents, graphics, CSS style sheets, JavaScript files, and so on.

The word "site" in the name "site folder" implies that this folder holds your entire site. It's the master, outer, main folder, in other words, the folder in which you may have plenty of subfolders. Remember that, in most cases, your website exists in two locations: on your computer as you work on it and on the Internet where people can enjoy the fruits of your labor. In fact, most websites in the universe live in two places at once—one copy on the Internet and the original on some web designer's hard drive. (In some cases, you'll also have what's called a "testing server," often used so you can test dynamic, database-driven websites before publishing them to the Internet—you'll learn about testing servers in Chapter 21.)

The copy on your own computer is called the *local site*. Think of it as a sort of development area, where you build your site,

test it, and modify it. (With database-driven sites, you do your testing on a testing server, and use the local site to store the files as you work on them. As you'll read on page 929, it's common for the files on your local site and testing server to be one and the same.)

Because the local site isn't on a web server, the public can't see it, and you can freely edit and add to it without affecting the pages your visitors see. The folder for the version of the site you keep on your computer, therefore, is called the *local site folder*.

After you add or update a file, you move it from the local site to the *remote server*. The site on the remote server mirrors the local site. Because you create a remote site by uploading your local site to a server, it has the same folder structure as your local site and contains the same polished, fully functional web pages. The local site also includes all the half-finished, typo-ridden drafts you're working on. Chapter 17 explains how to use Dreamweaver's FTP features to upload only your ready-for-prime-time local site and how to work with a remote server.

Exporting and Importing Sites

When you set up a site, Dreamweaver stores that site's information in its own private files. If you want to work on your site using a different computer, therefore, you must re-set up the site for *that* copy of Dreamweaver. In a design firm where several people work on many different sites, that's a lot of extra setup. In fact, even if there's just one of you working on two computers, duplicating your efforts takes extra work.

Dreamweaver lets you import and export site setups so you can put your time to better use. For example, you can back up your site set-up files in case you have to reinstall Dreamweaver, and you can export a site setup for others to use.

NOTE Exporting a site in Dreamweaver doesn't actually export your site files—all of the web pages, folders, and so on—it just exports the setup options you used when you set up the site. In other words, you just export and import the information that lets Dreamweaver work with your site's files.

To export a site setup:

1. **Choose Site→Manage Sites.**

   The Manage Sites window appears, listing all the sites you defined (Figure 15-5).

2. **Select a site from the list, and then click Export Site button (the folder with the arrow on it).**

   If you haven't told Dreamweaver about your remote server, skip to step 4.

3. **Select either "Back up my settings" or "Share settings with other users" and click OK.**

   If the site setup includes remote server information (so Dreamweaver can connect to your web server and move files onto it as described on page 785), you'll see a dialog box called "Exporting site" (Figure 15-6). If you simply want to make a backup of your site definition because you need to reinstall Dreamweaver, select the "Back up my settings" radio button.

   The other option, "Share settings," isn't all that useful. It's intended to let you share your site settings with a person working on another copy of the same site on their own computer. When you elect to share settings, Dreamweaver doesn't include the username and password you use to connect to the remote (web) server, a good thing. But it also excludes the site-file paths you defined because, presumably, the person you're sharing the settings with has her site files in a different location on her computer from your paths. For that reason, it's just as easy for that person to simply create her own site setup following the instructions on page 735.

   The Export Site panel appears.

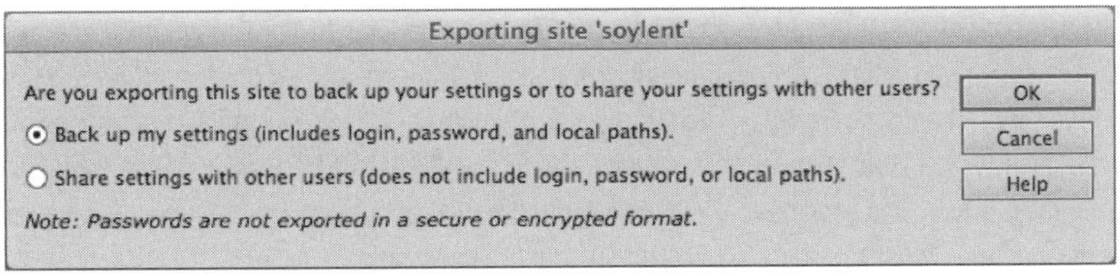

FIGURE 15-6

This dialog box lets you back up your site settings or share them (minus your login information) with other people.

4. **In the Export Site panel, specify where you want to save the file and give it a name.**

   If you're making a backup, save the file outside the local root folder (for example, with the Photoshop, Fireworks, and Word source files for your site). Because the export file can potentially contain the username and password you use to move files to your remote site, you don't want to keep the file anywhere in your local root folder—you might mistakenly upload it to the web server, where someone might find it and wreak havoc with your site.

Dreamweaver uses the extension *.ste* for site definition files.

TIP You can export multiple sites in a single step. Select all the sites you want to export (Ctrl-click [c-click] the names of the sites), and then click the Export button. You won't however, be able to name each export file in this step—just the first one. In addition, Dreamweaver saves all the site definitions you export this way in the same folder. You can, of course, move and rename them on your computer. Just make sure to keep the .ste file extension at the end of each file name.

Once you create a site setup file, you can import it into Dreamweaver as follows:

1. **Choose Site→Manage Sites.**

    The Manage Sites panel appears.

2. **Click the Import Site button (see Figure 15-5).**

    The Import Site panel appears. Navigate to the set-up file—look for a file ending in .ste. Select it, and then click OK.

If you import the site setup options to a computer other than the one you used to export it, you may need to perform a few more steps. If Dreamweaver can't find the location of the local site folder in the site setup file, it asks you to select a local site folder on the new computer, as well as a new default Images folder.

UP TO SPEED

Business Catalyst

Dreamweaver CS6 includes the ability to create or import Business Catalyst websites. Business Catalyst is Adobe's commercial web hosting company. However, it's more than just a place to park your web files: It offers many tools to supercharge your (or your client's) online presence. It includes a CMS (or content management system) so you can edit pages using a web browser and without any knowledge of HTML or CSS, as well as web analytics so you can track how many visitors come to your site, where they come from, what they click on, and how long they stay. And that's just for the basic $9-per-month package.

For a higher fee (prices ranges from $9 to $79 per month), you can add complete e-commerce functionality (including credit-card processing), a blog, email marketing, a "customer relationship management" system for collecting and analyzing customer information, and even database-based web applications.

However, creating a Business Catalyst site isn't like building the types of web pages you've been reading about in this book. Business Catalyst is a "system" that has a lot of functionality right out of the box. In other words you don't start by creating regular web pages: you start by creating a Business Catalyst site, and downloading all the specially created Business Catalyst web files to your computer. You can then add various modules to the site—photo galleries, product catalogs, web forms, and so on, from the Business Catalyst panel (Windows→Business Catalyst). And you can customize the CSS and HTML of Business Catalyst template files (similar to Dreamweaver templates discussed in Chapter 19) from within Dreamweaver.

To learn more about Business Catalyst visit *http://www .businesscatalyst.com*. The site also includes training videos to learn how Business Catalyst works (*www.businesscatalyst .com/training*) and specific information on using Dreamweaver with Business Catalyst (*http://www.businesscatalyst.com/ support/dw*). For even more information on Business Catalyst visit Adobe TV's "Learn Business Catalyst" show at *http:// tv.adobe.com/show/learn-business-catalyst/*.

Viewing Files in the Files Panel

Once you set up your local site, you can use Dreamweaver's Files panel as your command center for organizing your files, creating folders, and adding new web pages. To open the Files panel, choose Window→Files, or press F8 (Shift-F).

In its most basic incarnation, the Files panel lists the files in the current site's local root folder. This list looks and acts very much like Windows Explorer or the Mac's Finder; you see names, file sizes, and folders. You can view the files inside a folder by clicking the + symbol (flippy triangle on Macs) next to the folder (or simply by double-clicking the folder name). Double-click a web page to open it in Dreamweaver. You can also see the size of a file, the type of file it is, and the last time you modified it. That's a lot of information to fit in that space, so if you find this new view a little too crammed with information, you can hide any columns you don't like—see page 820.

> **NOTE** You can open certain types of files in an outside program of your choice by defining an external editor for that file type. For example, you can tell Dreamweaver to open GIF files in Fireworks, Photoshop, or another image editor. See page 268 for more.

You can view your site's files four ways, using the View drop-down menu (shown in Figure 15-3):

- **Local view** lists the files in your local root folder. Dreamweaver displays folders in this view as green.

- **Remote server** displays the files in your remote site folder, in other words, the files on your web server (see the box on page 46). Of course, before you post your site to the Web, this list is empty. Dreamweaver adds files to this folder only after you set up a connection to a remote server and upload files to it. Dreamweaver displays folders in this view as yellow on Windows PCs and blue on Macs.

- **Testing server view** is useful when you create the dynamic, database-driven sites discussed in Chapter 22. No files appear in this view until you set up a testing server (see page 929) and connect Dreamweaver to it. When you do, Dreamweaver displays folders in this view in red.

- **Repository view** gives you a peek inside a file-versioning system called Subversion. You'll learn about this advanced file-management tool on page 810.

You can view any combination of these two views side by side—for example, you can see a list of your local files next to a list of the files on your web server—by clicking the Expand Panel button (see Figure 15-3). This undocks the Files panel from the side of the screen, turning it into a floating window (see Figure 15-7). You'll find this most useful when you want to compare files on your local computer with those on your web server or testing server.

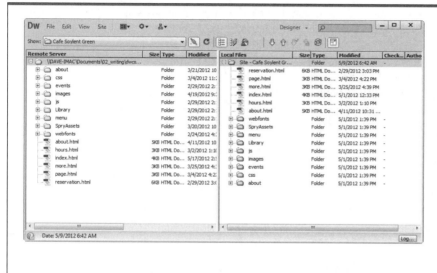

FIGURE 15-7

Click the Expand/Collapse button shown in Figure 15-3 to maximize the Files panel and display two views simultaneously. This way, you can view both your remote server and local site at the same time. Local files normally appear on the right, but might be on the left, depending on the preference you set under the Site category of the Preferences window. (If you want to change this, press Ctrl+U [⌘-U] to open Preferences and then click the Site category.) The view that appears opposite the local files view—Remote Server, Testing, or Repository—depends on which view you selected before clicking the Expand button. To change views, click a different view button.

Modifying the Files Panel View

Dreamweaver stocks the Files panel with loads of information: the file name, the size of the file, the type of file (web page, graphic, and so on), and the date you last modified it. This is all useful to know, but if you have a relatively small monitor, you may not be able display everything without having to scroll left and right. What's worse, the file names themselves often get clipped by other columns of information.

There are a couple of ways to fix this. First, you can resize the width of each column by dragging one of the dividers that separates the column names (for example, the vertical line between the "Local Files" and "Size" columns in Figure 15-3). Using this technique, you can at least display the full name of each file.

If you don't like the number of columns Dreamweaver displays, you can hide any or all of them. After all, how useful is listing the type of each file? The folder icon clearly indicates when you're looking at a folder and each file's extension—for example, .html for a web page or .jpg for a JPEG graphic—clearly indicates the file's type. For most folks, that's enough.

Unfortunately, there's no program-wide setting to control which columns appear. You have to define the visible columns on a site-by-site basis:

1. **Choose Site→Manage Sites and double-click the name of the site whose Files panel you want to modify.**

   The Site Setup window opens.

2. **Click the Advanced Settings category to display the list of options, and select File View Columns (see top image in Figure 15-8).**

   Dreamweaver lists all the columns the Files panel can display and indicates which it currently displays ("Show") or hides ("Hide"). Under the Type heading, all the files initially say "Built In" to indicate columns that Dreamweaver displays by default. As you'll read on page 821, you can add your own customized columns to this list.

3. **Double-click the column you want to change.**

   For example, double-clicking the Type column displays the options you see in Figure 15-8, bottom: Column Name, "Associate with Design Notes," and "Share with all users of this site." Most of the options are dimmed out because they only apply to custom columns, described on page 821.

4. **Change the alignment of the column (Left, Right, or Center) from the Align menu, and turn on or off the Show checkbox to show or hide a column.**

   For example, to hide a column, turn off the Show checkbox.

5. **Click the Save button to close that column's settings.**

   Repeat steps 3–5 for any other columns you wish to edit, and when you're done, click the Save button on the Site Setup window.

You can change the order of the columns, too—perhaps a file's Modified date is more important to you than its size. Select a column and click the up or down arrow. The up arrow moves the column to the left in the Files panel, while the down arrow scoots a column over to the right.

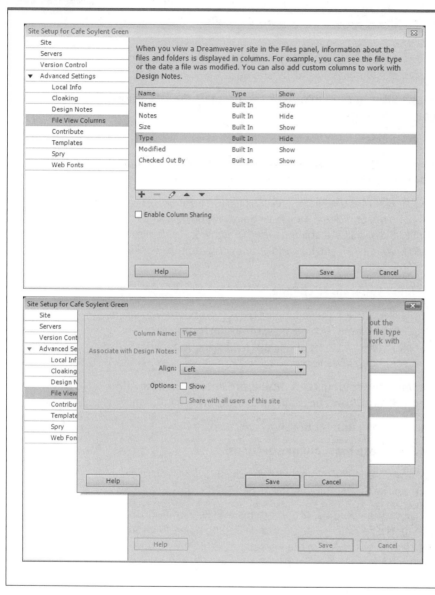

FIGURE 15-8

Use the File View Columns category to show or hide columns in the Files panel. You can rearrange the columns by selecting one and clicking the up or down arrow (top image). The up arrow moves the column to the left in the Files panel, while the down arrow moves it to the right. You can also use the File View Columns category to work with Dreamweaver's collaborative note-sharing feature called Design Notes. Instructions on using Design Notes start on page 817.

Changing the New Page Default

Whenever you create a new web page—by choosing File→New or by right-clicking (Control-clicking) an existing file in the Files panel—Dreamweaver gives you a blank document window. But what if you always want your pages to have special HTML comments indicating that your company created the page, or you always want to include a link to the same external style sheet?

Every new web page you create is actually an untitled copy of a default template document called *Default.html*. You can find this file in Dreamweaver's configuration folder. On Windows it's in *C:\Program Files\Adobe\Adobe Dreamweaver CS6\configuration\DocumentTypes\NewDocuments*. On a Mac, you can find it in the *Applications→Adobe Dreamweaver CS6 →Configuration→DocumentTypes→New-Documents* folder.

Save a copy of this folder so you can always return to the original, Dreamweaver-supplied file. In Windows XP, use the folder name *C:\Documents and Settings\[your user name]\Application Data\ Adobe\Dreamweaver CS6\en_US\Configuration*. In Windows Vista, use *C:\Users\[your user name]\AppData\Roaming\Adobe\ Dreamweaver CS6\en_US\Configuration*. On a Mac, try *Volume Name→Users→[your user name]→Library→Application Support→Adobe→Dreamweaver CS6→en_US→Configuration*.

You can then open a file from the NewDocument folder in your personal configuration folder and edit it however you like: change or add HTML comments, meta tags, pre-canned links to a style sheet, or whatever, so that all subsequent new pages inherit these settings. Also, make sure you don't touch an HTML fragment that probably appears to you to be incorrect: namely, the *charset*=" snippet, which appears at the end of the <meta> tag. This fragment of HTML is indeed incomplete, but when you create a new page, Dreamweaver correctly completes the code according to the alphabet (a.k.a. character set) your page uses—Chinese, Korean, Western European, or UTF-8, for example.

You'll notice lots of other files in this folder. Since Dreamweaver can create lots of different file types—Cascading Style Sheets, Active Server Pages, and so on—you'll find a default blank file for each. You can edit any of these—but don't, unless you know what you're doing. You can easily damage some of the more complex file types, especially those that involve dynamic websites.

Site Assets

Web pages integrate lots of different elements: PNGs, GIFs, JPEGs, links, colors, JavaScript files, and Flash movies, to name just a few. On a large site with lots of files, it's a challenge to locate a particular image or remember an exact color.

To simplify the process, Dreamweaver provides the Assets panel. For want of a better generic term, Dreamweaver defines the term *asset* to mean any element you use on a web page, such as a JPEG, a link, or even an individual color.

Viewing the Assets Panel

Dreamweaver lists your site's assets on the nine category "pages" of the Assets panel (Figure 15-9). To open the panel, choose Window→Assets.

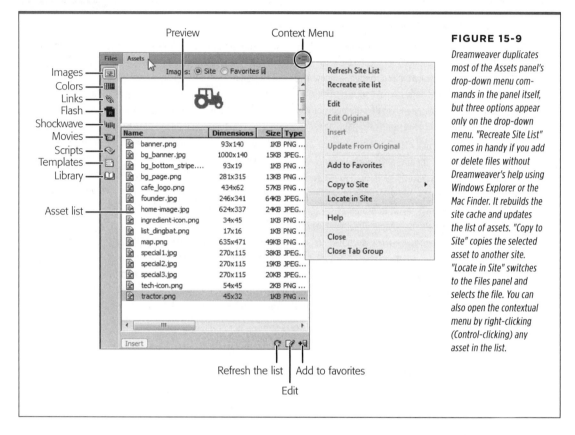

Preview   Context Menu

Images
Colors
Links
Flash
Shockwave
Movies
Scripts
Templates
Library

Asset list

Refresh the list | Add to favorites

Edit

FIGURE 15-9

Dreamweaver duplicates most of the Assets panel's drop-down menu commands in the panel itself, but three options appear only on the drop-down menu. "Recreate Site List" comes in handy if you add or delete files without Dreamweaver's help using Windows Explorer or the Mac Finder. It rebuilds the site cache and updates the list of assets. "Copy to Site" copies the selected asset to another site. "Locate in Site" switches to the Files panel and selects the file. You can also open the contextual menu by right-clicking (Control-clicking) any asset in the list.

Select an asset by clicking its name; Dreamweaver previews the asset above the Assets list. To preview a movie, click the green arrow that appears in the preview window.

Dreamweaver divides your site's assets into nine categories, represented by icons on the left of the Assets panel. To view the assets in a particular category, click its icon:

- **The Images category lists all the GIF, JPEG, and PNG files in your site**. Dreamweaver lists the dimensions of each image next to its name so you can quickly identify whether *logo1.gif* or *logo2.gif* is your 728 x 90 pixel banner logo. You can also see the images' sizes, types, and locations (you may need to scroll to the right to see all this).

- **The Colors category shows you all the colors specified in your site's pages and style sheets**. These include link colors, background colors, and text colors.

- **The Links category lists all external links**—and not just standard *http://* links, but also email links, FTP addresses, and JavaScript links.

- **The three multimedia categories—SWF (meaning Flash movies), Shockwave, and Movies (meaning Flash video or QuickTime movies)—are roughly equivalent**. They each display movie files with their corresponding extensions: .swf (Flash), .dcr (Shockwave), .flv (Flash video), and .mov or .mpg (QuickTime and MPEG). Unfortunately, the Movies category hasn't kept up with the times: Thanks to HTML5 video (see page 724), there are other movie formats to think about, such as MPEG4 (.mp4), Ogg Vorbis (.ogv), and WebM (.webm). The Movies category doesn't list any movies with those extensions.

- **The Scripts category lists JavaScript files**. It includes only external script files your web pages link to, such as those Dreamweaver's Spry Framework uses (Chapter 13). Dreamweaver doesn't include scripts embedded *in* a web page—like those that Dreamweaver behaviors create—here.

- **The last two categories—Templates and Library—are advanced assets that streamline website production**. They're discussed in Chapters 18 and 19.

You can switch between two views for each asset category—Site and Favorites—by clicking the radio buttons near the top of the Assets panel. The Site option lists all the assets in your site for the chosen category. Favorites lets you create a select list of your most important and frequently used assets (see page 753).

If you add additional assets as you work on a site—for example, if you create a GIF image in Fireworks and import it into your site—you need to update the Assets panel. To do so, click the Refresh Site List button (see Figure 15-9).

Inserting Assets

The Assets panel's prime mission is to make it easy for you to add assets to your site by dragging the asset from the panel into your document window. For example, you can add graphics, colors, and links to your pages with a simple drag-and-drop operation. Note that most of the categories on the panel refer to external files you commonly find on web pages: images, Flash and Shockwave files, movies, and scripts.

You can drop an asset anywhere on a page you'd normally insert an object—in a table cell, a <div> tag, at the beginning or end of a page, or within a paragraph. You can also add script assets to the head of a page (see Figure 15-10). (If you're billing by the hour, you may prefer the long way: click in the document window to plant the insertion point, click the asset's name, and then click Insert at the bottom of the Assets panel.)

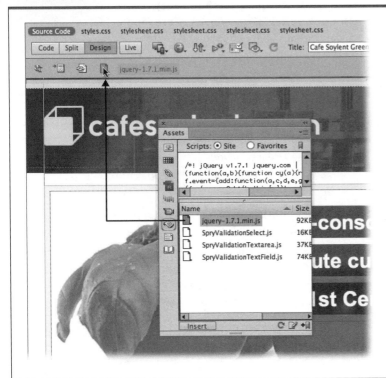

FIGURE 15-10

Although you'll insert most assets into the body of a web page, you can (and usually should) place script files at the head of the page. To do this, choose View→Show Head Content. Then drag the script from the Assets panel into the head pane, as shown here. (Adding a script asset doesn't copy the JavaScript code into the web page. Instead, just as with external style sheets, Dreamweaver links to the script file so that when a browser loads the page, it looks for and then loads the JavaScript file from the website.)

■ ADDING COLOR AND LINK ASSETS

Color and link assets work a bit differently from other asset files. Instead of standing on their own, they *add* color or a link to text or images you select in the document window. (You can add colors to any text selection, or add links to images and text.) This makes it easy to quickly add a frequently used link—the URL to download the Adobe Reader, for example.

To do so, start by highlighting the text (to change its color or turn it into a link) or image (to turn it into a link). In the Assets panel, click the appropriate category button—Colors or Links. Click the color or link you want, and then click Apply. Alternatively, you can drag the color or link asset from the panel to the selected text or image.

In the case of a link, Dreamweaver simply adds an <a> tag to the selection, with the proper external link. For color, Dreamweaver pops up the New CSS Rule window and asks you to create a new CSS style—you then need to go through the whole rigmarole described on page 125. Unfortunately, Dreamweaver's not smart enough to update the text color of any style already applied to the selected text. In other words, applying colors with the Assets panel is more trouble than it's worth.

However, there is one way to use the color assets effectively, sort of. As you'll recall (or not) from page 157, the Dreamweaver color-picker lets you sample a color off the screen. So if you want to use a color from the Assets panel, make sure you have the Assets panel open and the color assets visible; then, when you want to select a color (for example, to add a color to text in the CSS Rule Definition window), click the color box (the cursor changes to an eye dropper), and then click a color in the Assets panel.

Favorite Assets

On a large site, you may have thousands of images, movies, colors, and external links. Because scrolling through long lists of assets is a chore, Dreamweaver lets you create a compact list of your favorite, frequently used assets.

For example, you might come up with five main colors that define your site's color scheme, which you'll use much more often than the miscellaneous colors on the Assets list. Add them to your list of favorite colors. Likewise, adding graphics you use over and over—logos, for example—to a list of favorites makes it easy to locate and insert those files into your pages. (You can also use Dreamweaver's Library and template features for this function. They're similar but more powerful tools to keep frequently used items at the ready. Turn to Chapters 18 and 19 for the details.)

■ IDENTIFYING YOUR FAVORITES

If the color, graphic, or other element you want to add to your Favorites list already appears on your Assets panel, highlight it in the list and then click the "Add to Favorites" button (see Figure 15-9).

Even quicker, you can add favorites as you go, snagging them right from your web page. If you're working on your site's home page, for example, and you insert a company logo, that's a perfect time to make the logo a favorite. Simply right-click (Control-click) the image. From the shortcut menu, choose "Add Image to Favorites." Dreamweaver instantly adds the graphic to your list of favorites *within that asset category*—meaning that you'll see the file when you're in the Favorites view *and* you have the Image category selected. You can use the same shortcut for colors, links, and script, Flash, Shockwave, or QuickTime files.

When it comes to colors and links, you can turn them into favorites another way: In the Assets panel, select the Color or URLs category, click the Favorites radio button, and then click the New Asset button (see Figure 15-11).

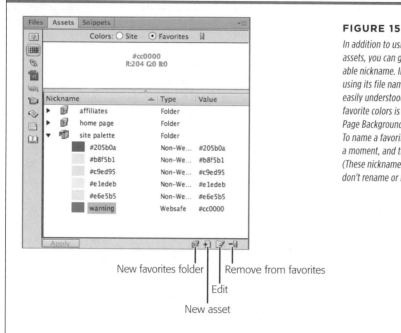

FIGURE 15-11

In addition to using folders to organize your Favorite assets, you can give favorite assets an easily identifi- able nickname. Instead of listing a favorite image using its file name—148593.gif, for instance—use an easily understood name like New Product. Naming favorite colors is particularly helpful; a nickname like Page Background is more descriptive than #FF6633. To name a favorite asset, click to select it, pause a moment, and then click again to edit its name. (These nicknames only apply in the Assets panel; you don't rename or retitle your files.)

New favorites folder

Remove from favorites

Edit

New asset

Then:

- If you're adding a favorite color, the Dreamweaver color box appears. Select a color using the eyedropper (see page 157).

- If you're adding a favorite link, the Add URL window opens. Type either an absolute URL (a web address starting with *http://*) in the first field or an email address (for instance, mailto:*info@cafesoylentgreen.com*). Next, type a name for the link—such as *Acrobat Download* or *Info Email*—in the Nickname field and then click OK.

Your new color or link appears in your Favorites list.

■ USING YOUR FAVORITES

You insert assets from your Favorites list into web pages just as you would any other asset; see page 751.

■ REMOVING FAVORITES

Removing an asset from your Favorites list is just as straightforward as adding one: select it in the Favorites list and then press Delete. The "Remove from Favorites" button (see Figure 15-11) on the Assets panel does the same thing. Yet another ap- proach is to use the contextual menu (Figure 15-10).

Don't worry; removing an asset from your Favorites list *doesn't* delete that asset from the Assets panel (or your site). You can still find it by clicking the Site radio button.

■ ORGANIZING FAVORITE ASSETS

On a large site with lots of important assets, even a Favorites list can get unwieldy. That's why you can set up folders within the asset categories of the Favorites panel to organize your assets. For example, if you use lots of ads on a site, create a folder in the Image assets category of your Favorites list called Ads or, for even greater precision, create multiple folders for different types of ads: Banner Ads, Half Banner Ads, and so on.

You can then drag assets into the appropriate folders and expand or contract the folder to show or hide the assets inside. These folders simply help you organize your Assets panel; they don't actually appear anywhere within the structure of your site. Moving a Favorite asset into a folder doesn't change the location of files within your site.

To create a Favorites folder, click the appropriate asset category button on the left edge of the Assets panel (any except the bottom two, since, alas, you can't create folders for templates and Library items). Click Favorites at the top of the Assets panel (you can't create folders in Site view). Finally, click the New Favorites Folder button (see Figure 15-11) at the bottom of the Assets panel. When Dreamweaver displays the new folder with its naming rectangle highlighted, type a new name for the folder and then press Enter (but don't use the same name for more than one folder).

To put an asset into a folder, just drag it there from the list. And if you're really obsessive, you can even create subfolders by dragging one folder onto another.

GEM IN THE ROUGH

Nothing Could Be Kuler

Adobe's Kuler web tool (*http://kuler.adobe.com*) is an online gallery of color palettes. It lets you build your own sets of colors and offers tools based on the science of color theory to create harmonious color combinations for your site. Even better, you can see thousands of palettes created by *other* web designers, showcasing everything from cool and subtle schemes to loud and vibrant color mixes. It's a great site if you're eager for a little color inspiration.

To make it even easier for you to use this site, the extension developer WebAssist has a free Dreamweaver extension named PalettePicker. This simple add-on is essentially a floating palette within Dreamweaver that lets you browse or search Kuler's large collection of color palettes. When you find colors you like, you can use Dreamweaver's color box and eyedropper tool to sample a color from the PalettePicker palette just as you'd sample a color from a picture on a web page. You can find the extension at *http://tinyurl.com/3vg8pjc*. To learn how to use and install extensions, turn to page 916.

Testing Your Site

As you no doubt realize by now, building a website involves quite a few steps. At any point in the process, you can easily introduce errors that affect the performance of your pages. Mistakes both small (like typos) and site-shattering (think broken links) occur frequently in the web development cycle.

Unfortunately, web designers often neglect to develop a set of best practices for testing their sites. This chapter offers helpful techniques for testing your site, and shows you how Dreamweaver's wide array of site-testing tools can help.

Site Launch Checklist

Don't wait until you finish your site before you develop a thorough strategy for regular testing. If you do, serious design errors may have so completely infested your pages that you have to start over, or at least spend many hours fixing problems you could have prevented early on. These guidelines help you avoid that predicament:

- **Preview early and often**. The single best way to make sure a page looks and functions the way you want it to is to preview it in as many browsers as possible. For a quick test, click the Live View button in Dreamweaver's Document toolbar (page 72). This is a great way to quickly check JavaScript components and view the way a browser displays pages with complex CSS. However, since Dreamweaver's built-in browser is WebKit (basically what you find in Google's Chrome, Apple's Safari browser, and the web browser in many mobile phones), Live view doesn't necessarily show you how your page will look in other popular browsers, like Internet Explorer, Firefox, or Opera.

To see how your layouts, CSS, and JavaScript features hold up elsewhere, use Dreamweaver's Preview command (File→Preview in Browser) to test your pages in every browser you can get your hands on (Dreamweaver lists your installed browsers when you click Preview, and you select one from the list). Make sure the graphics look right, your layout remains intact, and Cascading Style Sheets and Dreamweaver behaviors work as you intend.

For a thorough evaluation, however, you should preview your pages using every combination of browser *and* operating system you think your site's visitors may use. At the very least, try to test your pages using Internet Explorer 6, 7, 8, and 9 on Windows; Chrome on Window PCs and Macs; Firefox on Windows and Macs; and Safari on the Mac. According to the Market Share website (*http://bit.ly/q7UEdA*), Internet Explorer 8 for Windows is still the most popular web browser, followed by Internet Explorer 9, Chrome, and Firefox. Including all versions, Internet Explorer claims over 53 percent of the worldwide market for browsers (as of January 2012).

TIP If you already have a site up and running, you can find useful browser information in your site's *log files*. They track information about visits to your site, including which browsers and platforms your visitors use.

NOTE Most web hosting companies provide access to these files and the software that analyzes the confusing code inside them. You can use this information to see, for example, whether *anyone* who visits your site still uses Internet Explorer 6. If no one does, that's one less browser you have to design for. And if you don't have access to your log files, you can use Google Analytics (*www.google.com/analytics/*), a free service that tracks guests who visit your website. You just need to sign up for a Google Analytics account and add a little snippet of JavaScript to each page of your site.

Unfortunately, you'll discover that what works in one browser/operating system combination may not work in another. That's why you should preview your designs *early* in the process of constructing your site. If you design a page that doesn't work well in Internet Explorer 8 on Windows, for example, it's better to catch and fix that problem immediately than to discover it after you build 100 pages based on that design. In other words, once you create a page design you like, don't plow ahead and continue building your site! Check that page in multiple browser/operating system combos, fix any problems, and then, Grasshopper, begin to build.

To test your pages, enroll your friends and family so you can check your pages on as many setups as possible. You can also use Dreamweaver's built-in support for Adobe's BrowserLab to get screenshots of your designs.

NOTE Internet Explorer 6 is often where most web pages fall apart. This old and crotchety browser is full of bugs that often cause hair-pulling bouts of hysteria among web designers. Most of the problems relate to the CSS that lays out your page (see Chapter 9). Professional web designers recommend previewing your page in Firefox, Safari, or Internet Explorer 9 first. Get the page working right in those browsers, and then preview it in IE 6 to fix bugs.

If you design with just IE 6 in mind, you'll find that your site might not work in Firefox, Safari, and, in many cases, the ever-growing population of IE 9 browsers. Fortunately, in the United States, Internet Explorer 6 is all but dead—most statistics report that less than 1 percent of the US population uses it. Many US web designers don't even test for IE 6 any longer. However, it still has a strong presence in China and other nations around the world, so if you're designing for a global audience, you may still need to test your designs in IE 6.

- **Validate your pages**. HTML and CSS errors can easily slip into your code if you edit your files with a text editor or work on pages someone else created. These errors, called validation errors, are often the source of cross-browser display problems, messed-up layouts, and incorrect formatting.

   Previous versions of Dreamweaver included a tool that let you compare your web pages against agreed-upon standards for HTML and other web languages. It wasn't completely reliable, so Adobe removed that feature from Dreamweaver CS5.

   However, in Dreamweaver CS5.5, Adobe resurrected the validator! But this time, instead of relying on its own engineers to create the perfect validator, Dreamweaver CS5.5 and, now, CS6 use the industry-standard W3C validator. The W3C, or World Wide Web Consortium, develops most of the technologies web designers rely on, like HTML and CSS, and they've always provided a very good validator. The validator resides online, but Dreamweaver CS6 makes the testing process simple by incorporating it directly into Dreamweaver. You'll learn how to use it on page 773.

While you do the bulk of your checking during page development, you should do some troubleshooting at the end of the process, too, just before you move a page (or an entire site) to your web server:

- **Check the spelling on your pages**. Amazingly, people often overlook this simple step. As a result, you can easily find otherwise professional-looking pages undermined by sloppy spelling. To learn how to use Dreamweaver's built-in spell-checker, see page 116.

- **Check your links**. A website can be a complex and twisted collection of interconnected files. Web pages, graphics, videos, and other types of files all have to work together. Unfortunately, if you move or delete one file, problems can ripple through your entire site. Use Dreamweaver's Check Links command to identify and fix broken links (see page 765).

- **Run site reports**. It's always the little things. When you build a website, small errors inevitably creep into your pages. While not necessarily life-threatening, forgetting to title a page or add an Alt property to an image does diminish the quality and professionalism of a site. Use Dreamweaver's site-reporting feature to quickly identify these problems (see page 779).

Previewing Web Pages in BrowserLab

Adobe's free BrowserLab service is like having a legion of Windows and Macintosh PCs with various browsers and browser versions at your beck and call. Basically, BrowserLab provides screenshots of your web pages so you can see how your designs hold up in different browsers. If you're on Windows and don't have access to a Mac, or vice versa, BrowserLab is a simple way to cross-test your pages. You can even test interactive page elements, like Spry drop-down menus.

BrowserLab Setup

Dreamweaver lets you tap into BrowserLab as if you were previewing your page in a local web browser, by choosing File→Preview In Browser→BrowserLab. However, you need to do a little setup before you can get it to work:

1. **Get an Adobe Account at** *https://www.adobe.com/cfusion/membership/index.cfm.*

   It's free and you only need to supply a few pieces of information, like your name, email address, city, country, and Zip code.

2. **Visit** *https://browserlab.adobe.com* **and click the Sign In button at the top-right of the page.**

   A form appears asking for your Adobe ID (that's your email address) and the password you supplied when you signed up for your Adobe account.

3. **Type in your email address and password, and then click the Sign In button.**

   The first time you sign in, you have to accept the Terms of Use agreement. You know these things: lots of legal mumbo-jumbo that nobody reads.

   Once you sign in, you go to the main Adobe BrowserLab screen. There's not much to it, but this is where you'll preview your web pages. But before you do that, you should set up a *browser set*.

4. **Click the Browser Sets button (see Figure 16-1) and check off the browsers in which you want to test your pages.**

   That becomes your browser set. As of this writing, BrowserLab supports 11 browsers, and they refine the list as new browsers and browser versions come out. The more browsers you choose, the slower the service runs, since it must take a separate screenshot for each browser, so here's one strategy to streamline the testing process: First, choose only a handful of browsers as your Default Browser Set. Pick the popular browsers that you don't have easy access to. For example, if you're on Windows, you may have Internet Explorer 9, Firefox, and Chrome installed, but not IE 6, 7, or 8, or any of the Mac browsers. In that case, select IE 6 and 7, and Safari for Macs. If you're on a Mac, choose all the Internet Explorer versions, but since Chrome and Firefox are pretty much the same on Window PCs as they are on Macs, just test your page on your own computer using Chrome and Firefox for Mac. You should use this basic browser set for your routine testing as you build your pages.

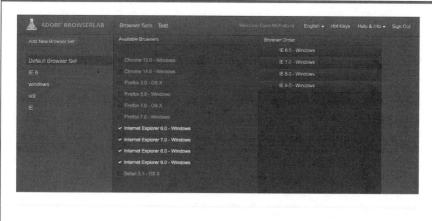

FIGURE 16-1

Adobe's BrowserLab service creates screenshots of your web pages in a variety of browsers, browser versions, and operating systems. Click the Browser Sets button at the top of the screen to define which browsers you want to preview in, and create different browser sets. Once you tell BrowserLab which browser set to use, click the Test button at the top of the screen to return to the page that displays your test results.

Then, create a second browser set (click the Add New Browser Set button). Name it something like "Complete Set," and check all the browsers you don't have access to. Most likely, this will include quite a few browsers, and it'll take some time to test this set, so use it after you finish testing with your Default Browser Set. In other words, get your pages to look good in the Default Browser Set, and then, as one last check, use the complete browser set to check your pages.

Testing Pages in BrowserLab

Once you set up an account and create your browser sets, you're ready to start testing your pages. BrowserLab lets you test directly from Dreamweaver, or you can test pages directly within BrowserLab, so long as BrowserLab can grab those pages from the Web.

To view a page from within Dreamweaver, open the page you want to check, and then choose File→Preview In Browser→BrowserLab. Dreamweaver opens a small, floating Adobe BrowserLab panel (see Figure 16-2). If you don't have a web browser open, Dreamweaver launches one and goes to the BrowserLab website. If you're not logged in, you have to do so using your Adobe membership credentials as described in step 3 on the opposite page.

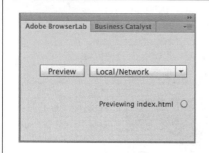

FIGURE 16-2

The Adobe BrowserLab panel opens when you preview a page using the service. You can also access the panel by choosing Window→Extensions→Adobe BrowserLab. Clicking the Preview button is the same as choosing File→Preview In Browser→BrowserLab. The file location menu (the one labeled Local/Network here) is described in the Note below.

NOTE BrowserLab can be a bit finicky. If you have trouble connecting to the service, launch a web browser, visit *http://browserlab.adobe.com*, and sign in using the Adobe account you created earlier (page 760). Then return to Dreamweaver, open the web page you want to test, and choose File→Preview In Browser→BrowserLab. You'll have to switch back to your web browser when the green light appears in the BrowserLab panel to see the results.

The BrowserLab site displays a message asking you to wait, letting you know it's busy creating screenshots of the tested page. This can take a while (30 seconds or more), so be patient. Once BrowserLab's done, it displays a screenshot of your page (see Figure 16-3).

If you have a browser open and you already logged into BrowserLab, Dreamweaver won't switch you to your browser so you can see BrowserLab's results; you'll just sit there staring at Dreamweaver. Look for a green light to appear next to "Connected to BrowserLab" in the BrowserLab panel (Figure 16-2), and then switch over to your browser to see the updated screenshots.

NOTE The Adobe BrowserLab panel lets you choose whether to preview a "Local/Network" page (meaning the page you're currently working on in Dreamweaver) or a page from your server. Usually, the Local/Network option is the way to go. You only want to use the server option for database-driven pages (like those discussed in Chapter 21) and other pages that depend on information on your web server. And even if you create those kinds of sites, you can still use the Local option if you set up a testing server on your own system (see page 929 to learn how). However, to test local dynamic pages in BrowserLab, you must first click the Live View button in Dreamweaver (page 72).

FIGURE 16-3

Use the View menu to select different views of your tested pages. Pictured here is the 2-up View, meaning you see two screenshots from two different browsers side-by-side. Use the Browser Version menu to display the screenshot from another one of the browsers in a browser set. In the page location field, you can type in an absolute URL pointing to a page that already exists on the Web, and have BrowserLab test that page.

Browser version · Choose browsers to test · View screenshots · Page location · Preview delay · Reload page · View menu · Zoom

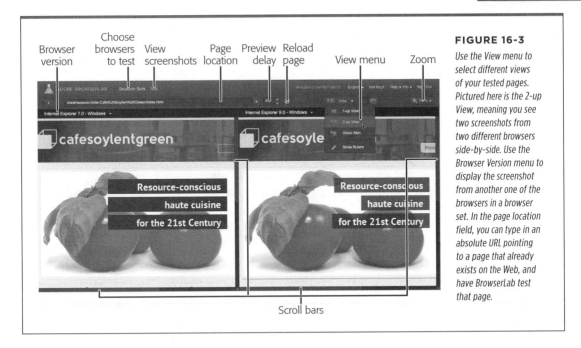

Scroll bars

You can use BrowserLab's Browser Version menu to see screenshots from different browsers or use the Browser Sets menu to choose a collection of browsers to test (after which BrowserLab creates screenshots for all the browsers listed in the new browser set).

Use BrowserLab's View menu to see two screenshots side-by-side (select "2-up View") or use the Onion Skin view to see the screenshots superimposed on top of each other. The latter can help you identify page elements that appear at different widths in different browsers and can highlight differences in how different browsers interpret margin and padding settings.

NOTE BrowserLab includes a "Preview delay" setting (see Figure 16-3) that forestalls the screen capture for a specified number of seconds. This is useful if a page has to download a lot of files, like the web fonts discussed on page 146, or if you have JavaScript that runs when a page loads and alters the look of the page. Without a delay, BrowserLab could take a screenshot before it's downloaded all the page elements it needs—this is a big problem with web fonts since BrowserLab will take a screenshot with standard computer fonts, instead of the beautiful and fancy fonts you assigned. If your previews don't look right, try changing the setting to 5 seconds and previewing again.

Unfortunately, BrowserLab can't tell you *why* your page looks different in different browsers. For that, you have to brush up on your CSS.

▰ CAPTURING JAVASCRIPT INTERACTIVITY

Some screenshot services can only take a picture of a page when it first loads. Because these services give you static screenshots of a page's HTML, they can't capture page effects your visitors might trigger, like a menu that drops down when your guest mouses over a navigation element. BrowserLab, with the aid of Dreamweaver's Live view, can capture screenshots of most kinds of JavaScript interactivity, such as the drop-down menu in the Spry Menu Bar (page 210) or the look of a validation error in a Spry validation field (page 588).

To do this kind of testing, you need to use Dreamweaver's Live view (discussed on page 72), which lets you preview a page, complete with interactivity, directly in Dreamweaver. Just click the Live view button in the Document window (see Figure 16-4), which displays your page using the WebKit browser (the same one behind Chrome and Safari). You can move your mouse over a JavaScript-powered Spry Menu Bar and see a drop-down menu, or click on a Spry collapsible panel to display a normally hidden panel (page 651).

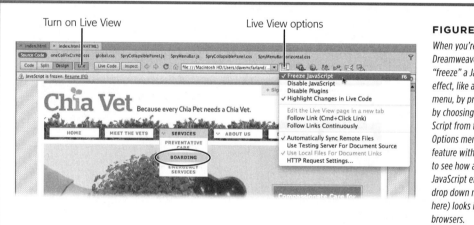

Turn on Live View

Live View options

FIGURE 16-4

When you're in Live view, Dreamweaver lets you "freeze" a JavaScript effect, like a drop-down menu, by pressing F6 or by choosing Freeze Java-Script from the Live view Options menu. Use this feature with BrowserLab to see how a dynamic JavaScript effect (like the drop down menu circled here) looks in different browsers.

If you want to see what a JavaScript effect looks like in other browsers, you need to "freeze" the page once you trigger the effect and then preview it in Browser-Lab. To freeze JavaScript in Live View, hit the F6 key or choose Freeze JavaScript from the View→Live View Options menu (see Figure 16-4). Once you do, choose File→Preview in Browser→BrowserLab. BrowserLab captures screenshots of the page in the chosen browsers.

Find and Fix Broken Links

Broken links are inevitable. If you delete a file from your site, move a page or a graphic outside Dreamweaver, or simply type an incorrect path name to a file, you may end up with broken links and missing graphics. In the B.D. era (Before Dreamweaver), you could fix such problems only by methodically examining every link on every page in your site. Fortunately, Dreamweaver's link-checking features automate the process.

NOTE In this context, a link doesn't mean just a hyperlink connecting one page to another. Dreamweaver checks links to external files, such as PNGs, GIFs, and JPEGs that reside in different folders, external CSS style sheets, and JavaScript files. For example, if a graphic is missing or isn't in the place your page specifies, Dreamweaver reports a broken link.

Finding Broken Links

Dreamweaver's Check Links Sitewide command scans an entire site's worth of files, and reports all the links and paths that don't lead to a file. (It's one of Dreamweaver's site management features, meaning that you have to set up a local site before you can use this command; see page 735 for instructions.) Note that Dreamweaver checks only links and paths *within* the local site folder; it doesn't check links that lead to other people's sites (see the Note on page 766 for a tool that can help with *that* annoying chore).

TIP If your local site contains a lot of pages, you may not want to check links in one or more folders whose pages *you know* have no broken links. You can exclude files from the Check Links Sitewide operation using the Cloaking feature described on page 804. Doing so also makes the link-checking operation go faster.

■ CHECKING JUST ONE PAGE

To check links on an open page, save it in your local site folder and choose File→Check Page→Links (or press Shift+F8). Dreamweaver scans the page and opens the Link Checker window, which lists any broken links (see Figure 16-5). If Dreamweaver doesn't find any—you HTML god, you—the window comes up empty.

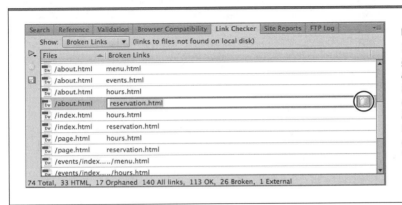

FIGURE 16-5

The Check Links Sitewide command generates a list of all external links and orphan files (files with no links to them). If you wish, click the Save (floppy disk) button to save all this information into a tab-delimited text file. You can also fix a broken link directly inside this panel using the "Browse for File" button (circled).

Testing Your Sites in Multiple Browsers

How can I test my website if I have only a couple of the most common browsers on my computer?

If you don't have every browser ever created on your Windows, Mac, and Linux machines (you *do* have all three, don't you?), you can use Adobe's BrowserLab service as discussed on page 760 (at least to tackle the Windows and Mac sides).

But there are alternatives as well, such as CrossBrowserTesting.com (*http://CrossBrowserTesting.com*), which costs $30 a month (ouch) for 150 minutes of use and offers an added benefit: interactive testing. You see your page running remotely on a PC under your control so you can test features that a screenshot can't capture, like Flash movie playback, animation, and JavaScript interactions.

Another service, BrowserStack (*www.browserstack.com*) also lets you test interactively via your web browser. For $19 a month, it's like renting multiple Windows and Mac machines with multiple versions of IE, Chrome, Firefox, and Safari installed.

Browsershots (*www.browsershots.org*) is a free alternative, which provides screenshots for a wide range of browsers on Windows and Linux systems.

Windows users can try out a program named IETester (*www.my-debugbar.com/wiki/IETester/HomePage*). It lets you see

how your pages look in multiple versions of IE, including 6, 7, 8, 9, and 10. Microsoft also offers an IE preview program named SuperPreview: http://www.microsoft.com/expression/products/SuperPreview_Overview.aspx

You can also see what a page looks like in Internet Explorer 6, 7, 8, 9 (and even 5.5) for free with NetRenderer (*http://ipinfo.info/netrenderer*), though your pages need to be on a publicly accessible website. Visit *http://ipinfo.info/netrenderer*, type in the URL of the page, and in a few moments you'll see a screenshot. Unfortunately, it doesn't take a picture of a complete web page—just the top part that you'd normally see on-screen—but it is free.

If you're a Mac person with an Intel chip at the heart of your system, you can install Windows on your machine using Apple's Bootcamp technology (*www.apple.com/support*) or use third-party "virtualization" software that runs Windows and Mac OS X simultaneously on the same computer (and believe it or not, the universe does *not* implode). VMWare Fusion for Macs (*www.vmware.com/products/fusion*) and Parallels Desktop (*www.parallels.com/products/desktop*), for example, let you run multiple versions of Windows (XP, Vista, and Windows 7) as well as Mac OS X.

NOTE Although Dreamweaver can't check links to the outside world, a free tool from the W3C can. You can find its link checker at *http://validator.w3.org/checklink*. This tool checks both internal links (to pages on the same site) and external links (to pages on other sites). The only possible downside: The pages you check must already be on the Web. Likewise, the link checker from Webmaster Toolkit provides a free online link-checking service at http://bit.ly/hcik3. Another free online link-checker, from 1-hit.com, also checks internal and external links: *http://bit.ly/4v8wwi*.

■ CHECKING SPECIFIC PAGES

You can check links on specific pages of your site from the Link Checker panel:

1. **Choose Window→Results→Link Checker.**

   The Link Checker panel opens.

2. **Use the Files panel to select the site you want to check.**

   If you're already working on the site, skip this step.

3. **In the Files panel, select the files you want to check.**

   For techniques on selecting files and folders in the Files panel, see the box below.

NOTE   Selecting a folder in the Files panel makes Dreamweaver scan all the files in that folder.

---

4. **In the Link Checker panel, click the tiny grayed-out arrow on the left; it turns green when you mouse over it.** From the menu that opens, choose "Check Links for Selected Files/Folders in Site."

   Alternatively, you can right-click (Control-click) the selected files, and then, from the shortcut menu, choose Check Links→Selected Files.

   Either way, Dreamweaver scans the pages and displays any broken links in the Link Checker panel (Figure 16-5).

UP TO SPEED

Selection Shortcuts for the Files Panel

You'll often want to use the link-checking tools in Dreamweaver's Results panel on more than one page in your website. Fortunately, the link checker can work on multiple pages in the Files panel.

To select several consecutively listed files at once, click the first file name, scroll if necessary, and then Shift-click the last one. Dreamweaver highlights all the files between your first and final clicks.

To select nonconsecutive files, click each one while pressing the Ctrl (⌘) key.

Once you select one or more files, you can deselect any single one by Ctrl-clicking (⌘-clicking) it once again.

Dreamweaver also includes a snazzy command for selecting recently modified files in the Files panel. Suppose you want

to select all the files you created or changed today (to see if the links work or to upload them to your web server). To do so, click the panel's contextual-menu button in the upper-right corner of the Files panel. From the menu that appears, select Edit→Select Recently Modified.

The Select Recently Modified window appears. You can either specify a range of dates (for example, files you created or changed between July 1, 2012, and July 7, 2012) or a number of days (to specify all the files you modified in, say, the last 30 days). (The last option—Modified By—works only with Adobe's Contribute program.) Set the options, click OK, and Dreamweaver selects the appropriate files in the Files panel.

■ **CHECKING AN ENTIRE WEBSITE**

You can check all the links on all the pages in your site in any of three ways. For all three techniques, you have to have your website selected in the Files panel (press F8 [Shift-⌘-F] to open the Files panel, and then use the panel's menu to select your site).

- Choose Site→Check Links Sitewide or use the keyboard shortcut Ctrl+F8 (⌘-F8).

- Open the Files panel and then right-click (Control-click) any file. From the shortcut menu, choose Check Links→Entire Local Site.

- Open the Link Checker panel (Window→Results→Link Checker, click the arrow on the left of the panel, and then, from its menu, choose "Check Links for Entire Current Local Site."

Once again, Dreamweaver scans your site and lists files containing broken links in the Link Checker panel.

Fixing Broken Links

Of course, simply finding broken links is only half the battle. You also need to *fix* them. The Link Checker panel provides a quick and easy way to do that:

1. **In the Link Checker panel, click a path in the Broken Links column.**

    Dreamweaver highlights the path, and displays a tiny folder icon to the right (circled in Figure 16-5).

> **TIP** The Link Checker panel shows you which pages *contain* broken links, but doesn't show you the text or images of the broken links themselves, which can make it difficult to figure out how to fix them ("Was that a button that links to the home page?"). In cases like that, *double-click* the file name in the Link Checker panel's left column. Dreamweaver opens the Web page and, even better, highlights the link on the page.

> **NOTE** Once you determine where the link should lead ("Oh yeah. That's the button to the haggis buffet menu."), you can fix the link right on the page or go back to the Link Checker panel and make the change as described in the next step.

2. **Click the tiny folder icon.**

    The Select File dialog box opens. From here, you can navigate to and (in the next step) select the correct page—the one that the link *should* have opened.

    If you prefer, you can type the correct path directly in the Link Checker panel. But that's usually not a good idea, since it's difficult to understand the path from one page to another just by looking at the Link Checker panel. Searching for the proper page using the Select File dialog box is a much more accurate and trouble-free method.

3. **In the Select File dialog box, double-click the name of the correct web page.**

    The dialog box disappears, and Dreamweaver fixes the link.

    If your site contains other links that point to the same missing file, Dreamweaver asks if you'd like to fix those links, too—an amazing timesaver that can quickly repair broken links on dozens of pages.

NOTE Dreamweaver's behavior is a bit odd when it comes to fixing the same broken link, however. Once you fix one link, it remains selected in the Link Checker panel. You must click another broken link, or one of the buttons in the window, before Dreamweaver asks if you'd like to fix that same broken link on other pages.

4. **Continue to fix broken links, following steps 1–3.**

   Once you repair all the broken links, you can close the Results panel by double-clicking anywhere along the top row of tabs (for example, double-click the Link Checker tab). Double-clicking any tab reopens the Results panel.

Listing External Links

Although Dreamweaver doesn't verify links to external websites on your pages, it can list those links after you run the link checker. To see this list, choose External Links from the Link Checker panel's Show menu (see Figure 16-6). The list includes absolute URLs leading to other sites (like *http://www.yahoo.com*) as well as email links (like *mailto:reservations@cafesoylentgreen.com*).

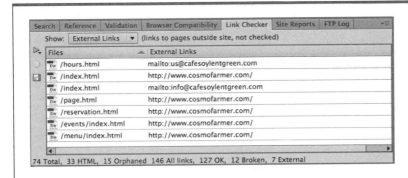

FIGURE 16-6

Although Dreamweaver can't check external links, you can use this window to change the URL of one.

This window is especially useful if you include a link to a certain external website several times throughout your site and decide to change it. For example, if you discover through testing (or through the W3C Link Checker mentioned in the Note on page 766) that an external link you peppered throughout your site no longer works, then:

1. **Choose Site→Check Links Sitewide (or press Ctrl+F8 [⌘-F8]).**

   Dreamweaver scans your site, and then opens the Link Checker panel.

2. **From the Show drop-down menu, choose External Links.**

   The window lists links you created to sites outside your own.

3. **Click the external link you want to change.**

   Dreamweaver highlights the link, indicating that you can now edit it.

4. **Type in the new URL, and then press Enter (Return).**

   If other pages contain the old URL, Dreamweaver asks if you want to fix them as well. If so, click Yes; the deed is done.

Orphaned Files

The Link Checker panel also provides a list of files that aren't used by *any* of your site's pages—*orphaned files*, as they're called. You wind up with an orphaned file when, for example, you save a GIF to your site folder but then never use it on a web page. Or suppose you eliminate the only link to an old page that you don't need anymore, making it an orphaned file. Unless you think you may link to it in the future, you can delete it to clean up unnecessary clutter.

In fact, that's the primary purpose of the Orphaned Files list: to identify old and unused files so you can delete them. Here's how it works:

1. **Choose Site→Check Links Sitewide, or press Ctrl+F8 (⌘-F8).**

   Dreamweaver opens the Link Checker panel.

2. **From the Show menu, choose Orphaned Files.**

   The list of orphaned files appears (see Figure 16-7).

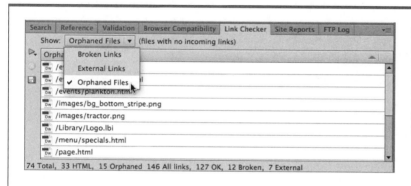

FIGURE 16-7

Identify (and delete) unused files with Dreamweaver's Orphaned Files option in the Link Checker panel. This panel can also list external links and broken links; use the Show menu to choose a type of link.

3. **Select the files you want to delete.**

   Ctrl-click (⌘-clicking) files to select them.

4. **Press Delete.**

   Dreamweaver asks if you really want to delete the files. Click OK if you do or Cancel if you suddenly get cold feet.

Before you get spring-cleaning fever and delete all orphaned files in your site, however, keep a few pointers in mind:

- Just because your site doesn't *currently* use a file doesn't mean you won't need it again later. For example, say you have an employee-of-the-month page. In March, you included a photo of Robin Albert, your best salesperson. In April, someone else got the award, so you removed Robin's photo from the page. The photos still resides on your computer; it's just that no web page currently uses it, making it an orphan. But next month you may need the photo again, when Robin develops a spurt of motivation. So make sure a file really is useless before deleting it.

- More important, Dreamweaver may flag files your site actually *needs* as orphaned. For example, some sites include what's called a *splash page*: an introductory page that first appears when someone comes to the site. It can be a page with a bold graphic and the text "Click here to enter the site." Or it may be a fancy Flash movie intended to make a big impact on your visitors. Usually, this page is nothing more than a welcome mat that leads to the *real* home page. Since it's simply an introductory page, no other page in the site links to it. Unfortunately, that's precisely what Dreamweaver considers an orphaned file.

- If you write your own JavaScript, you may reference graphic files and web pages. Dreamweaver doesn't keep track of references in your JavaScript code, and identifies those files as orphans (unless you insert or link to them elsewhere in the page or site).

    On the other hand, Dreamweaver is somewhat smarter when it comes to Spry widgets and Dreamweaver behaviors. It can track files referenced as part of its own JavaScript programs—for example, graphics files you use in a rollover effect—and doesn't list them as orphaned.

The bottom line is that while this report can be useful, use it cautiously when you delete files.

Changing a Link Throughout a Site

Suppose you create a page to teach your visitors the basics of HTML. You think this page would be really, really helpful, so you create links to it from every page on your site. After a while, you realize that you just don't have the time to keep the page up-to-date, but you still want to help your visitors get this information. Why not change the link so it points to a more current and informative source? Using Dreamweaver's Change Link Sitewide command, you can do just that. The process differs depending on whether you want to change a link that points to the outside world or a link that points to another page on your site.

1. **Choose Site→Change Link Sitewide.**

    The Change Link Sitewide dialog box opens (see Figure 16-8).

    This dialog box offers two fields: "Change all links to" and "Into links to." Understanding what you're supposed to do at this point is easier if you imagine that the first label actually says "Change all links that *currently* point to." In other words, you first indicate where those links point to now, and then you indicate where they should point. To change links that point outside your site, go to step 2; to change links that lead within your site, see step 3.

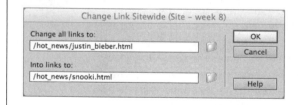

FIGURE 16-8

Dreamweaver uses a root-relative link to specify the page whose URL you want to change, as indicated by the slash (/). Don't worry, this doesn't mean that Dreamweaver makes the link root-relative. It's just how Dreamweaver identifies the location of the page in the site. See page 187 for more on root-relative links.

2. **For links to a page outside your site, type the old web address in the "Change all links to" field.** For example, if your aim is to round up every link that now points to Yahoo and redirect it to Google, type *http://www.yahoo.com* here.

   Then, in the "Into links to" field, type the URL of the new web address. In this example, type in *http://www.google.com*. The links on your site that used to lead to Yahoo will now to point to Google. Skip to step 4.

   > **TIP** As a shortcut to following steps 1, 2, and 3, you can select a file in the Files panel and *then* choose Site→Change Link Sitewide. Dreamweaver automatically adds the selected file's path to the "Change all links to" field.

3. **To change links to a page *within* your site, click the folder icon to the right of the "Change all links to" field.** This brings up the "Select Link to Change" dialog box. Browse to the old link, the one you want to change throughout your site, and then click OK (Windows) or Open (Macs).

   Next, you need to specify the file that the link should point to *now*. Click the folder icon beside "Into links to" to open the "Select Link to Change" dialog box again. Select a file in the local site folder, and then click OK (Windows) or Open (Macs).

   Your new link can point to graphics, Cascading Style Sheets, or any other file you can include in a web page. You'll get unpredictable results, however, if you change a link that points to a graphic file into, say, a link that points to a web page, or vice versa. Make sure the "before" and "after" links share the same file type, whether that's a web page, style sheet, or graphic.

   > **TIP** For another way to change one external link into another, see Figure 16-6.

4. **Click OK in the Change Link Sitewide box to make the change.**

   The same Update Files dialog box you encountered in the last chapter appears, listing every page that the change will affect.

5. **Click Update to update the pages.**

   Dreamweaver scans your site and updates the pages.

Validating Web Pages

The Web is a far-flung collection of technologies, programming languages, and people, all working together. When you think about it, it's pretty amazing that an 11-year-old in Fargo, North Dakota, can create a website millions of people around the world can view, and that dozens of different browsers, from Internet Explorer to cellphones, can browse the same site. This kind of global communication owes its success in large part to the World Wide Web Consortium (the W3C), an organization composed of representatives from universities, research institutions, corporations, and government agencies dedicated to creating standards for different Internet-related technologies.

The W3C developed standards for HTML5, CSS, XML, and other Web languages, and continues to create new standards as technologies evolve. Thanks to these standards, companies have a guide to follow when they create new websites or new web browsers.

It sure would be great if all companies followed the standards when building web browsers, and all web designers followed the standards when building web pages. Then anyone with any web browser could view any web page. What a wonderful world *that* would be—you'd never have to test your pages in different browsers.

Of course, this kind of utopian thinking hasn't always been applied by the major browser makers. As a result, web developers have been forced to come up with techniques to deal with the way different browsers display HTML. Dreamweaver CS4 and earlier included a built-in web page validator, but it wasn't always accurate and frequently came up with results that were different from the definitive online validator offered by the W3C (*http://validator.w3.org*). Because of that, Dreamweaver CS5 dropped the validator. However, because validation is important, CS5.5 added the validator back in—but this time, rather than using its own tool, Adobe decided to use the online validator offered by the W3C.

> **NOTE** Because Dreamweaver CS6 uses the W3C's online validator, you have to have an Internet connection to use this feature.

Steps for Validating Web Pages

Dreamweaver's validation tool works on only one page at a time, and only with a page you've opened in the document window. To validate an open page:

1. **Choose File→Validate→Validate Current Document (W3C).**

Dreamweaver opens a W3C Validator Notification window, letting you know that Dreamweaver is going to send the page to the W3C online validator—uh yeah, that's what you just asked Dreamweaver to do, so turn on the "Don't show this dialog again" box and then click OK.

If it's not already open, the W3C Validation tab opens in the results panel at the bottom of screen.

NOTE There's another choice under the File→Validate menu: Validate Live Document (W3C). You can select this option when you use Dreamweaver's Live View (page 72). For a plain HTML file, the Validate Live Document option isn't any different from the Validate Current Document, but it's handy when working with some types of server-side pages, like the PHP pages discussed in Chapter 21, or a page created by a content management system like WordPress, Joomla, or Drupal.

In content management systems, what looks like a single web page from a visitor's perspective is usually many different files pieced together using information from a database to create a single HTML file. This means you can't just open a file in a WordPress site in Dreamweaver and validate it—instead, you need to view a WordPress page in Live View to see the finished HTML page and then choose File→Validate→Validate Live Document (W3C).

---

2. **Review the results.**

Dreamweaver displays the results in the Validation panel (Figure 16-9) and divides each message into four columns: the first includes an icon that indicates the severity of the error, the second lists the file name, the third lists the line of code the message applies to, and the fourth describes the validation error or message.

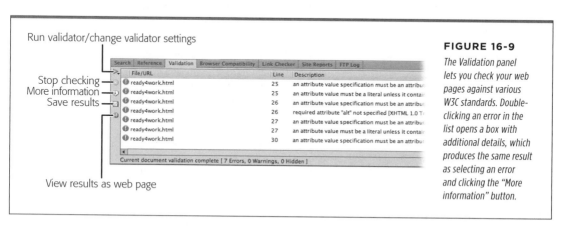

Run validator/change validator settings

Stop checking
More information
Save results

View results as web page

FIGURE 16-9

The Validation panel lets you check your web pages against various W3C standards. Double-clicking an error in the list opens a box with additional details, which produces the same result as selecting an error and clicking the "More information" button.

The icon at the beginning of the message helps you determine which errors are important. A red stop sign identifies a violation of the standards for the page's doctype (HTML 4.01 Transitional, XHTML 1.0 Transitional, HTML5, and so on).

In some cases, this warning can indicate that a mandatory tag (like the <body> tag) is missing—a serious problem.

Other stop-sign errors aren't necessarily fatal. For example, when Dreamweaver inserts a Spry Collapsible Panel (page 651), it adds a *tabindex* property to a <div> tag that represents the panel's tab. In HTML5, you can add a tabindex to any tag, but in HTML 4.01 or XHTML, the tabindex attribute is reserved for links and form elements, so adding a Spry Collapsible panel to a non-HTML5 page results in invalid HTML. Dreamweaver's JavaScript programming relies on this property to control how the panel works when a user tabs through the links on a page. But even though this is technically invalid code, it won't cause any problems for your site's visitors.

Less serious problems are flagged with little message balloons. These may inform you that the page has *no* problems, or point out optional fixes.

> **NOTE** Dreamweaver's validation feature doesn't help with CSS files. To make sure your CSS files are valid, you can use the W3C's CSS Validator (*http://jigsaw.w3.org/css-validator*), which lets you either point to a file out on the web, upload a CSS file (or an HTML file with an internal CSS style sheet), or simply paste a CSS style sheet into an online form. The CSS Validator then checks your style sheet to make sure you didn't make any mistakes in writing your CSS.

3. **Fix the errors.**

Alas, Dreamweaver can't fix all these validation errors. For errors related to improperly written code, you can let Dreamweaver automatically fix them as described on page 332.

For other errors, it's up to you and your knowledge of HTML to go into the code and fix problems. For assistance, check out the HTML reference (see page 370).

To get started, double-click an error in the Validation results panel. If you started in Design view, the web page switches to Split view, with the cursor place next to the invalid HTML. You can then delete or modify the offending code. Keep in mind, though, that the code Dreamweaver produces is the result of many thousands of hours of engineering and testing. Unless you're sure you know how to fix a problem, you may just want to trust the code Dreamweaver produces.

> **TIP** You may find that you constantly get a particular validation error, like the "there is no attribute tabindex" error that pops up when you use a Spry Collapsible Panel in an XHTML or HTML 4.01 page. Because that extra attribute is required by the Spry Collapsible panel but doesn't actually cause any problem, you might want to ignore it.

NOTE   To hide particular types of errors, right click (Control-click) the error message in the W3C Validation tab of the results panel and then choose Hide Error. From then on, when you validate any page that has this error (even pages on other sites), you won't see an error message in the Results panel. (To make Dreamweaver display an error you previously hid, click the triangle icon in the top left of the results panel and choose "settings." The W3C Validator Preferences menu opens; click Manage to open the hidden errors window, select the error that you want to make visible, and then click Remove.)

■ Cleaning Up HTML (and XHTML)

You've been reading about what great HTML Dreamweaver writes, and how, no matter what doctype you pick (XHTML 1, HTML 4.01, or HTML5, for example), Dreamweaver adds the correct tags in the correct order. But there are exceptions to every rule. In the process of formatting text, deleting elements, and—in general—building a web page, it's quite possible to end up with less-than-optimal HTML. While Dreamweaver usually catches potentially sloppy code, you may nonetheless run across instances of empty tags, redundant tags, and nested tags in your Dreamweaver pages.

For example, in the normal course of adding, editing, and deleting content on a page (either by hand or even in Dreamweaver's Design view), you can occasionally end up with code like this:

```
<div> </div>
```

This empty tag doesn't serve any purpose, and only adds unnecessary HTML to your page. Remember, the less code your page uses, the faster it loads. Eliminating redundant tags can improve your site's download speed.

Another possible source of errors is you. When you type HTML in Code view or open pages created by another program, you may introduce errors that you need to clean up later.

Aware of its own limitations (and yours), Dreamweaver provides a command designed to streamline the code in your pages: Clean Up HTML (if you're using Dreamweaver's XHTML mode, the command is called Clean Up XHTML). This command not only improves the HTML in your page, it can strip out other nonessential code, such as comments and special Dreamweaver markup code, and it can eliminate a specific tag or tags.

NOTE   The Clean Up HTML command doesn't fix really bad errors, like missing closing tags or improperly nested tags. You can have Dreamweaver automatically fix these types of problems when opening a file (see page 332).

To use this command:

1. **Open a web page you want to clean up.**

Unfortunately, this great feature works on only one page at a time—no cleaning up a site's worth of pages in one fell swoop! Accordingly, it's best to first use the Site Reports feature (see page 779) to identify problem pages, and then open them in Dreamweaver and run this command.

2. **Choose Commands→Clean Up HTML (or Clean Up XHTML).**

The Clean Up HTML/XHTML window appears (see Figure 16-10).

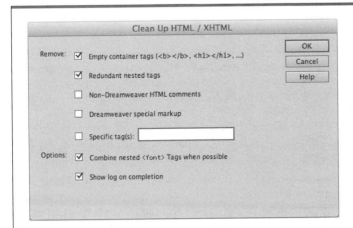

FIGURE 16-10

The Clean Up HTML/XHTML command lets you strip out redundant and useless code. You can even use it to strip out unnecessary tags by specifying the tag in the "Specific tag(s)" field (although the "Find and Replace" command provides a much more powerful way to identify and remove HTML tags; see Chapter 20).

TIP The Clean Up HTML command is extremely useful. Once you try it a few times, you'll probably want to use it on all your pages. Unfortunately, it doesn't come with a keyboard shortcut. This is a classic example of where Dreamweaver's keyboard-shortcut editor is just the white knight you need; using it, you can add a keystroke combination to trigger this command from the keyboard. See page 911 for details.

3. **Turn on the checkboxes for the options you want.**

Here's a rundown:

- "Empty container tags" deletes tags that don't actually contain anything. For example, you may have deleted text you set in boldface, leaving behind opening and closing bold tags without any text in between: <strong> </strong>. Or you may have deleted an image within a link, leaving behind a useless pair of <a> tags. It's always a good idea to turn on this option.

- "Redundant nested tags" deletes tags that appear within other tags of the same type, like this: <strong>You can't get any <strong>bolder</strong> than bold</strong>. The inner set of bold tags does no good, so choosing this option would produce this HTML: <strong> You can't get any bolder than bold</strong>. This option is extremely useful.

- "Non-Dreamweaver HTML comments" deletes any comments *not* inserted by Dreamweaver as part of its site management tools. For example, the Dreamweaver Template tool (Chapter 19) inserts HTML comments to help you identify different parts of the template. But web designers also place notes within code as instructions or to explain parts of the code. (These comments are invisible in a browser, by the way. They appear only in Code view, or in Dreamweaver's document window as a gold comment icon.) However, if the page is finished and you doubt you'll need the information the comments contain, you can decrease the file size of a page a little bit by using this option.

> **NOTE** Dreamweaver's Clean Up HTML command doesn't strip out CSS comments. If you use Dreamweaver's CSS Layouts or Spry widgets, you'll find the style sheets loaded with CSS comments. For a quick way to remove those types of comments, visit *http://tinyurl.com/6kcmq4g*. There, you can download a "stored query" (a reusable search) to use with Dreamweaver's "Find and Replace" tool.

- "Dreamweaver special markup" deletes any special code that Dreamweaver inserts. Dreamweaver relies on certain code in some of its features, including tracing images, libraries (Chapter 18), and templates (Chapter 19). Choosing this option eliminates the special code that makes those features work, so use this option with care. (Since the template feature can add a fair amount of this specialized code, Dreamweaver includes a Template Export command that lets you export an entire site with all the template code removed; see page 882.)

- "Specific tag(s)" deletes HTML tags you specify. Type the name of the tag (without brackets) in the field like this: *font*. To remove multiple tags at once, separate each tag name by a comma, like this: *font, blink*.

  Be careful with this option. Since it lets you remove *any* tag from a page, you could easily delete an important and necessary tag (like the <body> tag) from your page by accident. Furthermore, Dreamweaver's "Find and Replace" command provides a much more powerful tool for doing this kind of surgery (see Chapter 20).

- "Combine nested <font> tags when possible" combines multiple *font* properties into a single tag. Hopefully, you've moved to CSS for all your text formatting needs, so you don't use the <font> tag in your HTML, nor do you need this option.

- If you want to see a report of all the changes Dreamweaver makes to a page, turn on "Show log on completion."

4. **Click OK to clean up the page.**

   If you selected "Show Log on Completion," a dialog box appears, listing the types and number of changes that Dreamweaver made to the page.

NOTE When running this command on an XHTML page, Dreamweaver also checks to make sure the syntax of the page matches the requirements of an XHTML document. Among other concerns, all tags in XHTML must be lowercase, and you have to correctly terminate any empty tags—
 for the line break tag, for example. Dreamweaver fixes such problems.

As long as you keep the page open, you can undo the changes Dreamweaver makes. Suppose you asked Dreamweaver to remove comments, and then you suddenly realized you really did need them. Ctrl+Z (⌘-Z) does the trick.

TIP While Dreamweaver generally does a good job of avoiding extra, and unnecessary, HTML tags, you'll still find pages that have empty paragraphs with just a single nonbreaking space (page 95) in them, like this:

```
<p>  </p>
```

Dreamweaver inserts these paragraphs whenever you're in Design view and hit the Enter (Return) key. Dreamweaver fills that <p> tag with whatever you type, but if you don't type anything it leaves this empty <p> tag: well, it's not quite empty since it holds a nonbreaking space, so the "Clean up HTML" command's "Empty container tags" option won't clean up this useless tag. Instead, turn to Dreamweaver's "Find and Replace" tool (Chapter 20), and perform a "Source Code" search for <p> </p>; leave the "Replace" value as empty, and Dreamweaver will strip these almost-empty <p> tags from your page (or site).

Site Reporting

The Clean Up HTML command is a great way to make sure your code is well-written. But what if you forget about it until after you build all 500 pages of your site? Do you have to open each page and run the command—whether there's a problem or not?

Fortunately, no. Dreamweaver's Site Reports feature makes identifying problems throughout a site a snap. Dreamweaver not only locates the problems that the Clean Up HTML command can fix, it checks your pages for other problems, such as missing titles, empty Alt properties for images, and other issues that can make your site less accessible to disabled web surfers.

TIP To save time when running a report, you can exclude selected folders from a Site Report using the cloaking feature described on page 779.

After you run a report, Dreamweaver displays a list of pages with problems. Unfortunately, the Site Reports feature only *finds* problems, it doesn't fix them. You have to open and fix each page individually.

To run a report on one or more web pages, proceed like this:

1. **Choose Site→Reports.**

   The Reports window opens (see Figure 16-11).

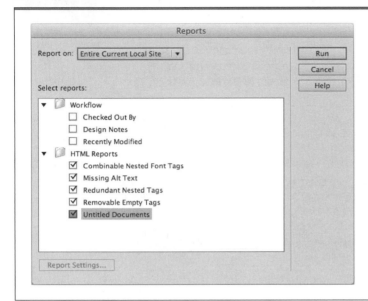

FIGURE 16-11

Dreamweaver's Site Reports feature makes quick work of finding common page errors. You won't use all these options, but at the very least, make sure you check for missing Alt text (page 254) and any untitled documents before you put a new website up on the Internet.

2. **From the "Report on" menu, select the files you want to analyze.**

   Dreamweaver can report on a single web page, on multiple pages, or even on an entire site. Choose Current Document to check the web page you have open at the moment. Select Entire Current Local Site to check every web page in the local site folder, including folders within the site folder. This option is great when you want to check your entire site prior to uploading it to a web server and making it "live" (more on that in the next chapter).

   Choosing "Selected Files in Site" checks only the files you choose in the Files panel. You need to open the Files panel and then select files in the local file list for this option to work. (See the box "Selection Shortcuts for the Files Panel" on page 767 for ways to select files.) Choose this option when you modify pages on or add pages to a site and you're ready to move them to your server.

   The Folder option checks all web pages in a selected folder. After you choose it, an empty field and a folder icon appear. Click the folder icon; a dialog box gives you the opportunity to locate and select the folder you want to check, including any folders inside it. You can also use this option to check pages that aren't actually part of the current site.

3. Select the types of reports you want Dreamweaver to generate.

Dreamweaver displays two kinds of reports in the Reports window. The first set, Workflow Reports, deals mostly with features that facilitate working with others as part of a production team (see the following chapter). The last option in this group—Recently Modified—generates a list of files that you either created or modified within a certain number of days or within a range of dates (February 1 of last year to the present, say). When you run this type of report, Dreamweaver lists the files in the Site Reports panel *and* opens a web page listing those files in your browser.

NOTE The Recently Modified site report looks for files created or changed in the last seven days, but you can adjust that timeframe. In the Reports window, select Recently Modified, and then click Report Settings (Figure 16-11). A window appears where you can change the range of dates to check.

In fact, you'll find the technique described on page 767 more useful. It not only identifies recently modified files, it also selects them in the Files panel, giving you many more options for acting on this information. For example, with those files selected, you can upload them to your server, run find-and-replace operations on just those files, or apply many other tools.

The second type of report, HTML Reports, is useful for locating common errors, such as forgetting to title a web page or forgetting to add an Alt property to an image.

Three of the HTML Report options—Combinable Nested Font Tags, Redundant Nested Tags, and Removable Empty Tags—search for pages with common code mistakes. These problems are the same ones fixed by the Clean Up HTML command (see page 776).

Turn on Missing Alt Text to search for pages with images that lack a text description (see page 254).

Finally, turn on Untitled Documents to identify pages that are either missing a title or still have Dreamweaver's default title.

NOTE The Site Report command doesn't identify XHTML syntax errors like those fixed by the Clean Up XHTML command (see page 776).

4. Click Run.

Dreamweaver analyzes the pages you specified and produces a report listing pages that match your settings (see Figure 16-12). Each line in the Results window displays the name of the file, the line number where the error occurs, and a description of the error.

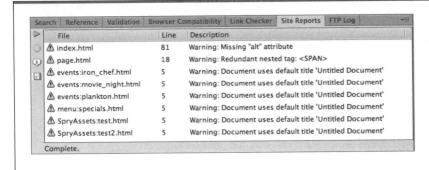

FIGURE 16-12

If you decide that it's taking too long for Dreamweaver to generate the report, you can always stop it. In the Results panel's left-hand toolbar, click the icon that looks like a stop sign with an X through it (the stop sign icon is normally grayed out, but it's bright red when Dreamweaver is busily generating a site report for you).

5. **In the Results panel, double-click the file to open it.**

   Dreamweaver opens the file and highlights the offending code.

6. **Fix the problem according to its type.**

   For a page containing Combinable Nested Font Tags, Redundant Nested Tags, or Removable Empty Tags errors, use the Clean Up HTML command as described on page 776.

   For pages missing a title, add one by opening the page and typing a title in the document window's Title box as described on page 25.

   You can add missing Alt properties using the Property Inspector, as described on page 254, but, if the same image is missing its Alt property on several pages, you may find it faster to use Dreamweaver's powerful "Find and Replace" command (see Chapter 20).

7. **Continue opening files from the Results window and fixing them until you correct each mistake.**

   Unfortunately, Dreamweaver doesn't provide a quick, one-step method to fix any of these problems. Except when using the "Find and Replace" command for adding missing Alt text, you must open and fix each page individually.

   If you want to save the results of your report, click the Save Report button. Dreamweaver opens a Save As dialog box, and lets you save the report as an XML file (so you can file it in the "Files I don't really need" folder on your desktop).

■ Download Statistics

Remember the old joke that WWW really stands for "World Wide Wait"? Even as more and more people upgrade to speedy cable and DSL modems, file size is a web designer's constant foe. What takes only a moment to load from your computer's hard drive could take minutes to travel across the Internet. The more information you put into a web page, the more time it takes to load.

You can judge how big your page is, and therefore how long it'll take to load, by looking at the status bar at the bottom of the document window. You'll see download stats that look something like this: *9k/2 sec*. This tells you the file size of the page (9k in this instance) and how long it'll take a visitor to download the page (2 seconds) using a 56 Kbps modem.

The file size and download time takes into account linked files like images, external CSS style sheets, and JavaScript files. This information provides a realistic picture of download speed, since not only does a browser have to download these files, it also has to fetch any files that a page uses (like a photo) from across the Internet.

The file size and download time can be misleading, however. That's because, if you use the same external files on *other* pages in your site (for example, if you use a common external style sheet or a logo that appears on each page), your visitors may have already "cached" those files and their browsers don't need to download the files again (see the box on the next page).

UP TO SPEED

Caching In

Behind the scenes, web browsers store the graphics they download in a part of your computer's hard drive called a *cache*. This is a speed trick. If you click your Back button to return to a web page whose graphics files the browser has already downloaded, the browser simply pulls them out of the cache—off of your hard drive, in other words—instead of re-downloading them. This makes the page load more quickly, since retrieving information from a hard drive is generally much faster than getting it through a modem.

As a web designer, you can capitalize on this standard browser feature by reusing the same graphics files on more than one page of your site. For instance, you can create a navigation bar composed of small graphic buttons (Home, Contact Us, Products, and so on). If you reuse those buttons on other pages of the site, those pages appear to download more quickly.

This same trick works for external CSS style sheets. A browser needs to download a complete style sheet with hundreds of formatting commands only once, and any page on your site can reuse it.

NOTE People hate to wait. You may think that the graphic design of your site is so compelling that people will stick around even if it takes a full minute to download that graphics-heavy home page. Think again. Research shows that 10 seconds is the maximum amount of time someone stays focused on a task while waiting. That means that if you're designing a website for people to view over DSL, you should keep your pages below a few hundred kilobytes (KB)—and that's if you want it to take 10 seconds for your page to appear. Most site owners want their site to load a lot faster than that.

Now that millions of people use their phones to browse the Web, designers are back to where they started in 1995—worrying about shaving every last KB of size from their web pages.

A Firefox plug-in called YSlow is a great tool for testing your download times. It can analyze bottlenecks and help you determine why a page downloads slowly. You can get the plug-in at *http://developer.yahoo.com/yslow*. It even has a tool that compresses graphics more than tools like Photoshop or Fireworks do.

Moving Your Site to the Internet

B uilding web pages on your computer is a big accomplishment, but it's not the whole job. Your beautifully designed and informative site will languish in obscurity unless you move it from your hard drive to a web server.

Fortunately, once your site is ready for prime time, you can put it on a server without ever leaving the comfort of Dreamweaver. The program includes simple commands for transferring files back and forth between the server and your desktop. All you need to do is provide Dreamweaver with the information it needs to connect to your server.

NOTE Dreamweaver CS6 includes many enhancements to its file transfer abilities. It's now a lot faster, allowing multiple, simultaneous connections to a server. In other words, the old Dreamweaver transferred files one at a time, but now the program can send multiple files at once.

■ Adding a Remote Server

As you work on your website on your computer—whether you build the site from scratch or add and modify existing pages—you keep your files in a *local root folder* (see page 46), often called a *local site* for short. You can think of the local site as a work-in-progress; you'll routinely have partially finished documents sitting on your computer.

After you perfect and test your pages using the techniques described in Chapter 16, you're ready to transfer those pages to a server that's connected to the Internet; this web server stores copies of your site files so it can dispense them to visitors.

Dreamweaver calls this server the *remote server*, and you can transfer your local site files to it several ways:

- **FTP**. By far, the most common method is *FTP*, or File Transfer Protocol. Just as HTTP is the process by which web pages are transferred from servers to web browsers, so FTP is the traditional way to transfer files from one drive to another over the Internet. If your site resides at a web hosting company or your Internet Service Provider (ISP), you'll use this option or, even better, the SFTP option discussed next. One downside of FTP is that none of the information you transfer using it—including your user name and password—is encrypted. It's possible, therefore (though very unlikely), for someone monitoring the flow of data over the Internet to spot your user name and password and log into your web server and wreak havoc on your site.

- **SFTP** stands for Secure FTP. This transfer method encrypts *all* your data, including your user name and password, so information you transfer this way is unintelligible to Internet snoops. It's the ideal way to connect to a web server, and in many cases, it's also faster. Unfortunately, not all web hosting companies offer this advanced option, so you may be stuck with regular FTP. If you're not sure if you can use SFTP, try it—Dreamweaver will tell you if it's unable to transfer files that way. Should that be the case, just switch to FTP.

- **FTP over SSL/TSL**, also called FTPS, provides security that regular FTP lacks. It encrypts your login information, and, optionally, all the data—web pages, images, and so on—that you transfer as well. Because your user name and password are secure, SFTP is a better choice for file transfers, but if your server runs Windows, SFTP isn't available. If that's the case, you can try a couple of other options. FTP over SSL/TSL comes in two flavors, implicit (an older and less-well-supported method) and explicit (the newer, now-standard form of FTPS). If you know your web server runs Windows, try connecting using this order: FTP over SSL/TSL (explicit encryption); if that doesn't work, try implicit encryption, and, finally, if that fails, use plain old FTP.

- **Local/network**. If you work on an intranet, or if your company's web server is connected to the company network, you may also be able to transfer files just as you would any other files on your office network (using the Network Neighborhood, My Network Places, or "Connect to Server" command, depending on your operating system).

- The last two options—**WebDAV and RDS**—are file-management systems used for collaborative web development. They're not very common, so you're unlikely to ever use them, but you'll learn about them on pages 795 and 796.

Beyond Dreamweaver

Do I have to use Dreamweaver to move my files to the Web?

No. If you use another program to FTP files, like FileZilla (Windows, Mac, and Linux), Cyberduck (Windows and Mac), CuteFTP (Windows), or RBrowser (Mac), you can continue to use it and ignore Dreamweaver's Remote Site feature.

However, if you've never used Dreamweaver to move files, you may want to at least try it because it simplifies much of the process. For example, to move a file from your computer

to a web server using a regular FTP program, you must first browse for the file on your local machine and then navigate to the proper folder on your server. Dreamweaver saves you both steps; when you select the file in the Files panel and click the Put button (see page 798), Dreamweaver automatically locates the file on your computer and transfers it to the correct folder on your server.

Setting Up a Remote Server with FTP or SFTP

You can set up a remote server only if you first set up a *local* site on your computer, as described on page 40. If you built your site in Dreamweaver, you should already have a local site set up. Once you do, you need to tell Dreamweaver how to connect to the remote server so it can transfer your local site files to your server:

1. **Choose Site→Manage Sites.**

   The Manage Sites dialog box opens, listing all the sites you've defined so far. You're about to tell Dreamweaver how to connect to a web server so you can create a living, Internet-based *copy* of one of these hard drive-based local sites.

NOTE Even if all you want to do is copy a live website from the Internet to your computer, you need a local site on your computer, and you want to point Dreamweaver to a folder within that local site—even if it's just an empty folder—so it has a place to store the files you download.

2. **Click the name of the site you want to put on the Internet, and then click the "Edit the currently selected site" button, also known as the pencil icon in the lower-left corner of the Manage Sites window.**

   Alternatively, just double-click the site name in the list. The Site Setup window appears for the selected site, as shown in Figure 17-1.

NOTE You can set up your local site and remote server simultaneously, when you first begin creating your site, as described on page 40. Even then, however, Dreamweaver requires that you first give the site a name and choose a local site folder. At that point, you can rejoin the steps described here.

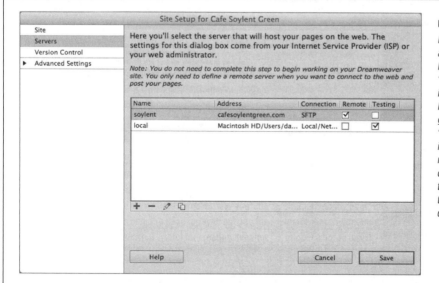

FIGURE 17-1

In addition to setting up a local site, Dreamweaver lets you set up both "remote" servers (meaning the web server on the Internet where people go to see your site) and "testing" servers (meaning a server—frequently running on your own computer—usually used to test dynamic sites, like the PHP-driven pages described in Chapter 21).

3. Click the Servers option.

The Servers category of the Site Setup window is where Dreamweaver lists your "remote" and "testing" servers. The remote server contains the site the world can see, while the testing server acts as a test area, usually for dynamic, database-driven sites. If you're building a website without using PHP, ASP, ColdFusion, or some other server-side programming language, you won't need to set up a testing server.

Initially, the Servers category is empty: You need to add a remote server.

> **NOTE** Dreamweaver lets you define as many remote and testing servers as you want, but you probably won't ever have a need for "infinity" servers. However, you may need to upload the same site to two different servers—perhaps you have a high-traffic website and put the site on several servers to balance the load. In that case, you can define a second, third, and even a fourth server. Note, though, that you can only "turn on" one remote server at a time. In other words, you can only upload and download to and from the server that has the Remote checkbox selected.

4. Click the + button.

A new pane pops up (see Figure 17-2). Here, you supply the information necessary for Dreamweaver to connect to the server.

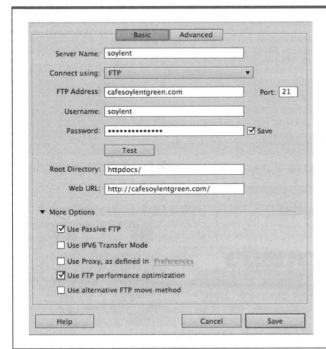

FIGURE 17-2

To connect to a server, you need to know its address, the FTP user name and password, and the name of the folder where the server stores your files. You get all this information when you sign up with a web hosting company. You usually don't need to change the "More Options" settings when you transfer files using FTP, though they can help if you're having connectivity problems (see the box on page 792). (If you use SFTP, the "More Options" menu doesn't appear.)

5. **Type a name in the Server Name field.**

   Dreamweaver only uses this name internally; it's not something anyone else will see, so name it anything you like, such as "My Server" or "Hosting Company."

6. **From the "Connect using" drop-down menu, choose either FTP or SFTP.**

   Ideally, you'll use SFTP—it's more secure and usually faster—but your web hosting company may not offer it, in which case you'll have to choose FTP.

NOTE If you're not sure whether your server supports SFTP, try it out. Follow these set-up instructions using SFTP as the "Connect using" option, and then click the Test button. If Dreamweaver can't connect, try FTPS (discussed next). If you still can't tap the server, try regular FTP. And if Dreamweaver *still* can't connect, you probably typed the wrong user name, password, or FTP address.

7. **Fill in the "FTP address" field.**

This is the address of your web server. It's usually something like www.cafe soylentgreen.com. It never includes directories, folders, or slashes (like www. cafesoylentgreen.com/menu); never includes codes for the FTP protocol (ftp:// ftp.cafesoylentgreen.com) or HTTP protocol (http://www.cafesoylentgreen .com); and it may simply be a domain name, such as cafesoylentgreen.com. It can also be an IP address, like *64.226.43.116*. In most cases, it's the address you type in a web browser's address window (minus the *http://*) to get to your site's home page.

If you don't know the host name, there's only one way to find out: call or email your web hosting company or ISP, or check its website.

8. **In the Username field, type your user name, and then type your password in the Password field.**

Dreamweaver uses bullets (••••) to display your password so that office evil-doers can't see what you type. If you want Dreamweaver to remember your password each time you use the program, turn on the Save checkbox. This way, you won't have to type your password each time you connect to the server.

WARNING For security reasons, don't turn on the Save box if you access the Web using computers at, say, your local library, community college, or anywhere else where people you don't trust can use the machine. Otherwise, you might awaken one morning to find the following splattered across your home page: "Hi there! Welcome to Jack's house of illegally acquired and unlawfully distributed music, featuring Justin Bieber's greatest hits."

---

9. **In the Root Directory box, type the path to your server's root directory.**

Here you specify the path to the *folder* on the web server that contains your web-page files. This folder is known as the root folder, and it's the counterpart to the folder on your hard drive that holds the files you work on with Dreamweaver. Common names for this folder include *docs, www, htdocs, public_html, httpdocs*, and *virtual_html*.

When you connect to your server using FTP, you rarely connect to that root folder itself, however. You often connect *outside* that folder, sometimes to an administrative folder for your web account, which the web host fills with folders for log reports of your site's traffic and other housekeeping files.

The path you type in the Root Directory box depends on where on the server Dreamweaver's FTP tool connects—and that all depends on how your web host set up the web server, so the only way to know what to type into this box is to contact your web host.

In many cases, you only have to type the name of the root folder followed by a slash, like this: *htdocs/.* You're specifying the path from the folder that Dreamweaver initially connects to via FTP—the web hosting company's administrative folder—to your site's root folder. In this example, Dreamweaver connects to a folder that contains the root folder, so you simply say, "Hey Dreamweaver, you're in the wrong place. Go inside the htdocs folder to find my site."

However, sometimes you need to use a much longer path, one that includes lots of folders, like this:

/var/www/mysite.com/htdocs/.

This type of path includes the entire path from the top level of the server's hard drive through several folders and, finally, to your root folder (htdocs) on the server. Again, there's no real way to tell, so ask your web hosting company.

10. **Type your site's web address in the Web URL box.**

   This is simply what you'd type in your web browser's address line to get to your site: www. cafesoylentgreen.com/, for example. Sometimes, though, you might work on files in a subdirectory of the site's root folder. For example, if you work in corporate web design, you might oversee a self-contained site for the marketing department, which means the URL to reach the files you work on might be www.mycompany.com/marketing. If that's the case, then also include the subdirectory's name: www.cafesoylentgreen.com/marketing.

NOTE What you type into the Web URL box when you set up a remote server can affect how Dreamweaver checks and updates links. See "Web URL" on page 738 for details.

---

11. **Click the Test button.**

   Dreamweaver attempts to connect to your server. If it succeeds, you'll see a box that says, "Dreamweaver connected to your Web server successfully." If it didn't succeed, you'll get an error message. See the box on page 792 for the most common problems and solutions.

NOTE When Dreamweaver can't connect to a server, one of the first things you should try (after double-checking your user name and password) is turning on the "Use passive FTP" checkbox. See the box on page 792 for more.

---

12. **Click Save to save these settings.**

   Dreamweaver returns to the Servers category of the Site Setup window (Figure 17-1).

13. **Click Save once again to return to the Manage Sites window, and then click Done.**

   At this point, you're ready to connect to your web server and transfer files. If you're the only person working on the site, Dreamweaver's Get and Put commands will do the trick (page 798). If, however, you're part of a development team, you can use Dreamweaver's Check In/Check Out feature, described on page 807, to make sure a co-worker doesn't accidentally erase your hard work.

More Remote Server Options for FTP

The steps discussed above will be probably be all you ever need to FTP your files, but Dreamweaver offers a few more options, as well as some advanced settings that apply to all types of connections (see "Advanced Remote Server Settings" on page 797).

> **NOTE** The options listed below aren't available (or necessary) when you connect using SFTP.

To see the additional options for FTP connections, click the More Options arrow (see Figure 17-2). Most of these checkboxes should remain turned off, but here's what they do:

- **Use Passive FTP**. Select this if you're unable to make an FTP connection and you know that you correctly typed your FTP address, user name, password, and root directory name (see steps 7–9 on page 790). This option can overcome firewall problems: hardware- or software-based gateways that control incoming and outgoing traffic through a network. Firewalls protect your company's network or your personal computer from hackers, but they also limit how computers inside the network—behind the firewall—connect to the outside world.

FREQUENTLY ASKED QUESTION

When Your Remote Site Is Too Remote

Help! I can't connect to my web server. What should I do?

Things don't always go smoothly when you try to connect to the outside world. That's doubly true when you try to connect to a web server, since you depend on a variety of things—your Internet connection, the networks connecting you to the server, the server itself, and the FTP software that runs the show—working together in harmony. Dreamweaver presents an error message if you can't successfully establish an FTP connection with your server. The error box frequently contains useful information that can help you diagnose the problem. Here are some of the most common:

- **"Remote host cannot be found"** usually means that you typed in an incorrect FTP host address (step 7 on page 790).

- **"Cannot open server folder"** usually means you mistyped the name of the root directory, or you've got the wrong name for it (see step 9 on page 790).

Unfortunately, there are lots of reasons why Dreamweaver may not be able to connect to a server, so sometimes the error message isn't particularly helpful—you'll often get a really large dialog box listing all those reasons. Even if you simply got your login or password incorrect, Dreamweaver spits out a long list of possible problems.

The first thing to do is double- (and triple-) check your user name and password. Here are a few other suggestions: Make sure you're connected to the Internet (open a web browser and see if you can visit a site); return to the Site Setup window for the site, open the Servers pane, and turn on the "Use passive FTP" option under More Options (sometimes this just makes things work); in the same window, turn off the "Use FTP performance optimization" checkbox; and if you have another FTP program, like FileZilla or Cyberduck, see if you can connect to your server using the same settings you gave Dreamweaver. If all these steps fail, visit this page on the Adobe website for additional troubleshooting tips: *http://tinyurl.com/2crmqey*.

- **Use IPV6 Transfer Mode**. You probably won't need to turn on this checkbox, but the day has finally arrived that the normal IP addresses we've used for years—like 192.16.16.62—have all been used up. The new standard—called IPV6—contains many, many, many more possible addresses (340,282,366,920,938,463,463,374, 607,431,768,211,456 to be precise), so we shouldn't be running out any time soon. If your web server uses an IPV6 address (which looks something like 1A23:120B :0000:0000:0000:7634:AD01:004D), your web hosting company will tell you.

- **Use Proxy**. If you can't connect to the remote server and your company's system administrator confirms that you have a firewall, check the Use Proxy box (also in Site Setup→Servers→More Options), and click the Preferences link to open the Site category of the Preferences window. Here you'll need to enter the name of the firewall host computer and its port number. Your firewall configuration may also require passive FTP. Check with your administrator to see if this is the case, and, if so, head back to the More Options section and turn on the checkbox next to "Use passive FTP."

- **Use FTP performance optimization**. Dreamweaver normally turns on this box because it helps speed up file transfers between your computer and your web server. However, it can also be a source of connection problems. If you can't connect to your server, try turning off this box.

- **Use alternative FTP move method**. If everything's okay when you connect to your server but you're getting errors when you move files there, turn on this option. This transfer method is slower than FTP, but more reliable. It's also handy if you use Adobe's Contribute program and take advantage of its "rollback" feature (to learn more about Contribute, visit *www.adobe.com/contribute/*).

NOTE When you set up a remote server, you'll see an "Advanced" button, which lets you set some additional options that you can usually skip, but turn to page 797 if you want to see what they do.

Setting Up a Remote Server Using FTP over SSL/TLS

As mentioned earlier, FTP isn't the safest way to transfer files: Your user name and password are transmitted "in the clear" over the Internet, and some nefarious hacker could grab that information and use it to log into your web server, wreck your site, and ruin your reputation. That's pretty unlikely, but still possible. SFTP is a much better option, but it's not available on Windows servers, so if your site is hosted on a server running Windows (as opposed to Linux/Unix, the more common web server operating system), try to use "FTP over SSL/TLS."

FTP over SSL/TLS (also known as FTPS or FTPSE) comes in two flavors, implicit encryption and explicit encryption. You should use explicit encryption since it's newer, has more features, and is an agreed-upon standard. Implicit encryption is only offered to support older servers, which don't offer explicit encryption.

Most of the settings for FTP over SSL/TLS are the same as those for regular FTP, so you can follow steps 1–10 on page 787, but instead of choosing FTP from the "Connect using" menu, choose "FTP over SSL/TLS." The main difference between regular FTP and FTP over SSL/TLS is the use of a "server certificate" to "authenticate" the web server. This just means that the web server has a special file on it (kind of like an identification card) that "proves" it is what it says it is, so you know that you're really connecting to your web server and not some evil server pretending to be your server (jeez, these web guys are paranoid).

Basically, if your server is set up for FTPS, you choose either None or Trusted Server from the Authentication menu (see Figure 17-3). You'll need to contact whoever is in charge of your server (your web host or your company's IT department) to determine which option you need. Once you make a selection, click Test to see if Dreamweaver can connect to your server. If not, see the troubleshooting advice in the box on page 792.

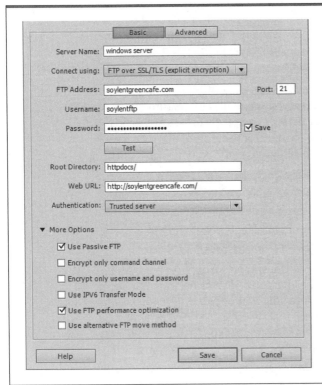

FIGURE 17-3

If you use "FTP over SSL/TLS" to connect to your web server, you have a few additional choices listed under "More Options." "Encrypt only command channel" only obscures your login and the commands you send to the server. The actual data, like web pages and images, goes out uncloaked. This translates to faster uploads and downloads. The "Encrypt only username and password" just hides your login information and is a fine choice unless you're uploading particularly sensitive information that you don't want the rest of the world to see.

Setting Up a Remote Server over a Local Network

If you work on an intranet, or if your company's web server is connected to the company network, you may be able to transfer site files just as you'd move any files from machine to machine. Dreamweaver provides the same file-transfer functions as with FTP, but the setup is simpler.

Follow steps 1–5 from the previous instructions (page 787), but in step 6, choose Local/Network from the "Connect using" menu. This brings up menus and fields for collecting your connection information in the Site Setup box (see Figure 17-4).

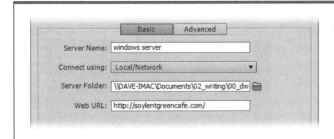

FIGURE 17-4

If your company keeps its web server in your office, the "remote site" might not be that remote. In such a case, choose a folder on your local network as the "remote" folder.

Click the folder icon next to "Remote folder." In the resulting dialog box, navigate to and select your site's remote site folder. On a local network, this folder isn't *truly* remote, because your company's web server is still within the walls of your building, but you get the idea.

Wrap up with steps 10, 12, and 13 of the previous instructions. At this point, you're ready to connect to the "remote" server and transfer files as described on page 798.

Setting Up a Remote Server with WebDAV

Dreamweaver also allows access to a remote site using *WebDAV*, short for Web-based Distributed Authoring and Versioning. Like FTP, it's a standard, or *protocol*, for transferring files. Like SFTP, it uses a secure connection (called SSL, or Secure Socket Layer) that encrypts all your data as it passes back and forth between your computer and your web server. But unlike both of those technologies, WebDAV addresses the kinds of problems you encounter when you collaborate on website development with other people.

For instance, all kinds of havoc can result if two people edit a page simultaneously; whoever uploads the page to the server *second* winds up wiping out the changes made by the first person. WebDAV supports a check-in and check-out system that works similarly to Dreamweaver's Check In and Check Out tools (see page 807) to make sure only one person works on a file at a time and no one tramples on anyone else's files. In fact, Dreamweaver's Check In/Check Out feature works seamlessly with WebDAV.

Both Microsoft Internet Information Server (IIS) and Apache Web Server work with WebDAV. Colleges and universities commonly use WebDAV, but that's not the case with web hosting companies, so it's pretty unlikely that you'll find commercial web hosts that offer it. To find out if your server can handle WebDAV (and to find out the necessary connection information), consult your web server's administrator (for example, call or email your web hosting company).

Setting up WebDAV access to a remote site is similar to setting up FTP access. Follow steps 1–5 on page 787, and then:

1. **Choose WebDAV from the "Connect using" menu.**

   The Site Definition window displays the WebDAV settings, which require just four pieces of information.

2. **In the URL box, type in the address of the WebDAV server.**

   In most cases, this is the URL of your website, so it begins with either *http://* or *https://*. The "s" in *https* means you'll connect securely to the server using SSL. The normal *http://* method doesn't use encryption, which means that, just as with regular FTP, your computer sends your user name, password, and data "in the open" as it travels across the Internet. Note that just adding an "s" won't suddenly make your file transfers secure; the receiving server needs to be set up to accept *https* connections (a technically challenging task).

3. **In the Username and Password fields, type in your credentials.**

   Turn on the Save checkbox so you don't have to type in your password each time you move files to your server (but heed the Warning on page 790).

4. **Click the Test button to see if your connection works.**

   If Dreamweaver succeeds, it proudly tells you. Unfortunately, if it fails, you'll get an error message that isn't exactly helpful. WebDAV isn't nearly as finicky as FTP, so if there's an error, you most likely just typed the URL, password, or login info incorrectly, or WebDAV just isn't available for the server.

NOTE Due to the different possible server configurations for WebDAV, Dreamweaver may not be able to connect even if your server has WebDAV turned on. If that's the case, you'll need to use FTP or another method to connect to your server.

The rest of the process is identical to the FTP setup process, so follow steps 10, 12, and 13 starting on page 791. At that point, you're ready to connect to your server and transfer files, as described on page 798.

Setting Up a Remote Server with RDS

RDS (Remote Development Services) is a feature of Adobe's ColdFusion Server. It lets designers work on web files and databases in conjunction with a ColdFusion application server. If you're using something other than a ColdFusion server, you don't need to worry about this option.

To create a remote site in Dreamweaver that works with RDS, follow steps 1–5 on page 787. In step 6, choose RDS from the "Connect using" drop-down menu.

The Site Definition window displays a version number, a short description, and a Settings button. Click Settings to open the Configure RDS Server window. Fill in the dialog box as directed by your server administrator or help desk.

Advanced Remote Server Settings

No matter which connection method you use (FTP, Local/Network, and so on), each remote server has a set of advanced options that you access by clicking the Advanced tab when you add a server (see Figure 17-5):

- **If you don't want to synchronize files, turn off the "Maintain synchronization information" box**. Dreamweaver's synchronization feature is useful to keep all the files in your site up to date. It helps you maintain the most recent versions of your files on the remote server by keeping track of when you change a file on your computer.

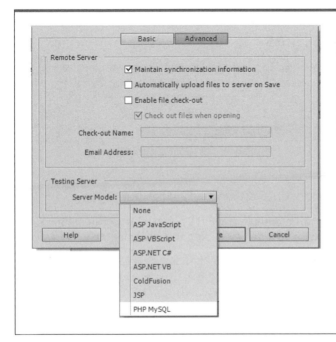

FIGURE 17-5

If you use Dreamweaver's Check In/Check Out feature and you work on your site in several locations (for example, from home and your office), use a different check-out name for each location (BobAtHome and BobAtWork, for example). That way, you know which files you checked out to your home computer and which to your computer at work.

When you synchronize a site, Dreamweaver moves the most recent files onto your server (you'll learn about this feature in detail on page 813). If you don't want Dreamweaver to synchronize your files, definitely turn off this checkbox. When it's on, Dreamweaver inserts little files named *dwsync.xml* throughout your site in folders named *_notes*. These files hold synchronization information about each site file, but don't clutter up your site with them if you don't synchronize. In addition, Dreamweaver spends time determining the synch status of each file, so your file transfers go more quickly with this turned off.

- **Leave "Automatically upload files to server on Save" turned off**. Not only will this slow things down—Dreamweaver has to connect and move the saved file to the server every time you press Ctrl+S (⌘-S)—it also means you may save half-finished pages on your remote server.

- **If you work with a team of developers, you may want to use Dreamweaver's Check In/Check Out tools discussed on page 807.** If you do, turn on "Enable file check in and check out." Then fill in the corresponding options as explained in Figure 17-5. If you do wind up using the Check Out feature (see page 808), you can save yourself some clicks by turning on "Check out files when opening." (Fill in your name and email address, too.) Now you can check out a file from the remote server just by double-clicking its name in the Site Files list. If you work on your own, *do not* turn on this setting, since it slows down the process of moving files to and from the server and adds unnecessary files (used to determine who has what file checked out) to both your server and your own computer.

■ Transferring Files

Once you tell Dreamweaver *how* to send off your web pages to your server, you can set about actually *doing* so. Thanks to Dreamweaver's Files panel, the whole process takes only a few steps.

Moving Files to Your Web Server

To transfer files to your server:

1. **Open the Files panel.**

   Choose Window→Files (keyboard shortcut: F8 [Shift-⌘-F]).

2. **From the drop-down Site menu in the Files panel, choose the name of the site whose files you wish to move (if it isn't already selected).**

   The Files panel displays files for the selected site. You can use the File View drop-down menu to see either a list of the files on your local site or a list of the files on your remote server (see Figure 17-6). You can see local and remote server files side by side if you first choose "Remote server" from the File View menu and then click the Expand button on the Files panel.

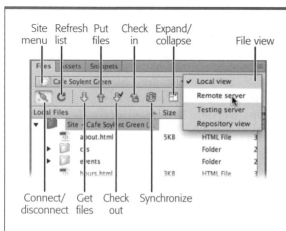

FIGURE 17-6

The Files panel offers toolbar buttons for uploading and downloading your web files to and from the web server that actually dishes them out to your site's adoring public. (See Chapter 15 for much more on this important window.)

NOTE The color of the folders in the Files panel lets you know which view you're currently in: Green folders mean Local view (your computer), beige (blue on the Mac) mean Remote view, and red folders indicate the Testing view (if you have a testing server, as described on page 929).

3. **From the file list in the Files panel, select the files you want to upload to the server.**

   To move a folder and every file inside it, just select the folder. (In other words, you can transfer your *entire* website to the server by simply selecting the local site folder—the folder listed at the very top of the Local Files list.) If you change only a few files on your site, you can selectively upload those files (or folders of changed files) using any of the techniques described on page 798.

NOTE If you don't see the files you want to upload in the Files list, you may have selected "Remote server." Select "Local view" to see only those files on your computer, and then click the Refresh button on the Files panel (Figure 17-6).

When you use do-it-yourself FTP programs like FileZilla or Cyberduck, you have to specify a folder location for every file you transfer to the web server. Here's one of the great advantages of letting Dreamweaver do your file shuffling; it already *knows* where your files should go on the remote server. The local and remote sites are, after all, mirror images, so Dreamweaver simply puts your local files in the corresponding folders on the remote server.

For example, suppose you select the file *mayo.html*, which is in a folder called condiments, which itself is in the local root folder. When you transfer *mayo .html*, Dreamweaver automatically puts it in the condiments folder in the root folder on the remote server. In fact, if the condiments folder doesn't exist on the remote server, Dreamweaver creates it for you and *then* puts the file into it. Now that's service!

You're now ready to go live with your web page.

4. **Click the "Put files" button—the up-arrow icon in the Files panel.**

   Alternatively, you can use the keyboard shortcut Ctrl+Shift+U (⌘-Shift-U).

   Several things happen when you do this. First, if you're using an FTP connection, Dreamweaver attempts to connect to your server. As you can see in the status window that opens, it may take a moment or so to establish the connection; once it does, the Connect button (see Figure 17-6) displays a bright green light.

   Next, if any of the files you're transferring are currently open and have unsaved changes, Dreamweaver asks if you want to save the files before it transfers them. Click Yes to save the file; if you have multiple unsaved files, click Yes To All. Dreamweaver then begins the transfer.

In addition, as Dreamweaver transfers your pages, it asks if you want to transfer any *dependent files* (see Figure 17-7). That includes graphics, external CSS files, or movies that a browser needs to display your pages properly.

The dependent files feature can save you considerable time and hassle because you don't have to hunt for and upload each graphic file or external style sheet yourself. On the other hand, if all the dependent files are *already* on the server, having Dreamweaver transfer the same files again is a waste of time. Fortunately, Dreamweaver prevents this wasted effort as described in the next step.

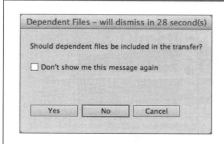

FIGURE 17-7

The File Transfer command's Dependent Files feature makes sure that Dreamweaver copies to the server all the files a browser needs to display your web pages correctly—graphics, external style sheets, movies, and so on. The feature also includes a time limit—you'll see a "will dismiss in xx seconds" message. If you don't click a button within 30 seconds, Dreamweaver assumes you mean "No" and uploads just the files you selected.

NOTE If you turn on the "Don't show me this message again" box in the Dependent Files dialog box and then click Yes, from that moment forward, Dreamweaver copies dependent files without asking you. On the other hand, if you turn on the "Don't show me this message again" box and click No, Dreamweaver *never* copies dependent files.

If you turn off the Dependent Files dialog box and change your mind later, hold down the Alt (Option) key when you transfer a file (using any method except a keyboard shortcut). Or choose Edit→Preferences→Site Category (Dreamweaver→Preferences→Site Category) to turn this feature on or off.

5. **Click Yes to transfer dependent files, or No to transfer only the files you selected.**

   Dreamweaver copies the files to the server. If you copy a file that's inside a folder that doesn't exist on the remote server, Dreamweaver creates an eponymous server-side folder in the same step. In fact, Dreamweaver creates as many subfolders as necessary to make sure it transfers every local file to a mirror folder on the remote site. (Try doing *that* with a regular FTP program.)

   If you choose to transfer dependent files as well, Dreamweaver may or may not put the dependent file on the server, depending on your settings. If you didn't turn off the "Maintain Synchronization Information" checkbox when you defined your remote site (see page 797), Dreamweaver determines whether the dependent file already exists on the server and, if it does, whether your local copy is a newer version. If the dependent file doesn't exist on the server or your local copy is newer (meaning you made changes to it locally but haven't yet moved it to the Web), Dreamweaver sends it when you tell it to transfer dependent files.

However, if Dreamweaver thinks that it's the same file, or that the copy of the file on the server is newer, it won't make the transfer. This behavior is a huge time-saver, since you won't have to repeatedly upload the same 50 navigation buttons each time you say "Yes" to transferring dependent files. But best of all, Dreamweaver still transfers dependent files that really *are* new.

NOTE Dreamweaver's ability to correctly determine whether a dependent file on your computer is the same as a file on the server depends on its Site Synchronization feature, described on page 813.

Dreamweaver's accuracy with this tool is good, but it has been known to get it wrong. If Dreamweaver isn't moving a dependent file, you can select that file and upload it manually (for example, select it in the Files panel and then click the Put button). Dreamweaver always obeys a direct order to move a selected file.

6. **Continue using the Put button to transfer all the files in your website to the remote site.**

    Depending on the number of files you transfer, this operation can take some time. Transferring files over the Internet using FTP isn't nearly as fast as copying files from one hard drive to another (see Figure 17-8 on next page).

■ OTHER WAYS TO MOVE FILES TO YOUR WEB SERVER

To copy a current document to your server without using the Files panel at all, you can go directly to the Put command. Say you finish building or modifying a page and want to immediately move it to the Web. Just choose Site→Put, or press Ctrl+Shift+U (⌘-Shift-U), or use the toolbar shortcut shown in Figure 17-8; Dreamweaver automatically copies the fresh page to the proper folder online.

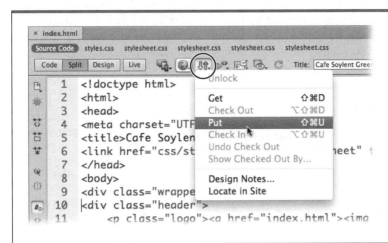

FIGURE 17-8

Click the File Status button (circled) and choose Put to quickly move a file to your server. You can also use this menu to retrieve a copy of a file from the server (Get), use Check In and Check Out tools (page 807), or review Design Notes (page 817) for the page. Note that Check In and Check Out are only available when you've turned on the Check In/Check Out tool as described on page 798. To highlight this file in the Files panel, choose "Locate in Site."

A Little More Background on File Transfers

Dreamweaver lets you keep working as it dutifully moves files in the background. You can edit a web page, create a new style sheet, and so on. However, there are some things you *can't* do while Dreamweaver transfers files. For example, you can't edit the site definition (since this could affect how you connect to the remote server). Dreamweaver lets you know if you try to take a forbidden action while it's working with the server.

If you find Dreamweaver's background activity window a nuisance, click the Hide button and it temporarily disappears. In addition, if you accidentally start uploading a 10,000-page website, you probably don't want to wait until Dreamweaver's done; click the Cancel button to stop the transfer.

When Dreamweaver finishes moving files around, you can see a record of its actions by clicking the Log button in the bottom-right corner of the Files panel. This log differs from the raw FTP log discussed in the box on page 804. This plain-language report lets you know what Dreamweaver did—"Put successful," "Get successful," and so on. If you see a "Not transferred" message, Dreamweaver tried to Get or Put a file, but both the local and remote server copies were identical, so it didn't do anything. See the previous Note for more.

Getting Files from Your Web Server

So far, this chapter has described getting your hard drive-based pages *to* the Internet. Sometimes, however, you want to download one or more files *from* your server. Perhaps you made a horrible (and irreversible) mistake on the local copy of a file and you want to retrieve the unblemished version from the Web, effectively using the remote server as a last-ditch backup system. Maybe you've taken over a design job for a client, and the only files they have are on the server, so you need to copy the entire site to your desktop computer. Or perhaps someone uploaded files to the site and you want to download a copy to your own computer (although the Synchronize feature described on page 813 would also work).

To get files from your remote site to your local drive, open the Files panel (press F8 [Shift-⌘-F]) and proceed as follows:

1. **From the Site pull-down menu, choose the site whose files you wish to retrieve.**

   As with all of Dreamweaver's site management features, downloading files from a web server depends on first defining a site.

2. **From the Files panel's View menu, choose "Remote server."**

   Dreamweaver tells you that it's attempting to connect to the web server. Once it makes the connection, it lists the files and folders on the server, and turns the Connect button a bright green. (Dreamweaver automatically disconnects after 30 minutes of inactivity, at which point the green dot turns black.)

NOTE To change the disconnect time limit, press Ctrl+U (⌘-U) to open the Preferences window. Click the Site category and change the number listed in the Minutes Idle box. Be aware, however, that some web servers have their own settings and may disconnect you sooner than you specify.

3. **From the Remote Server file list, select the files you want to download.**

   For techniques on selecting files in the Files panel, see page 767. To download a folder and every file inside it, just click the folder. This technique also lets you get your *entire* website from the server; just select the remote server's root folder, which appears at the very top of the Remote Server file list.

TROUBLESHOOTING MOMENT

Don't Replace the Wrong File

One strange feature of the Files panel's Get and Put commands may get you in trouble. Suppose, having just added new information to your home page (*index.html*), you want to transfer that page to your server. You select it in the Local Folder list—but then you accidentally click Get instead of Put.

Not knowing your true intention, Dreamweaver dutifully prepares to retrieve the file from the server, which, of course, will replace (wipe out) the newly updated home page on your computer.

Fortunately, before causing such damage, Dreamweaver also displays a warning message asking if you really want to overwrite the local file. Click No or Cancel to save your hard work.

There may be times when you *do* want to wipe out your local copy—if, for example, your cat walks across your keyboard, types illegible code, presses Ctrl+S to save the ruined page,

and Ctrl+Q to quit Dreamweaver (keeping you from using Undo to fix the mistakes). In this common situation, you'll want to replace your local copy with the remote server copy. To do so, press Yes when Dreamweaver warns you and you'll rectify your cat's errors. Oh yeah, this is also a useful trick if *you* ever make a mistake on a page you can't fix and want to return to the working copy on your server.

Dreamweaver also includes a useful Compare button to help you sort out the differences between a local and a remote file. Clicking this button compares the two so you can identify which changes you made. This way, you can salvage changes you made to the local copy and discard errors you (or your cat) may have introduced to the page. You can learn more about this feature on page 363.

4. **Click the "Get files" button (the down arrow).**

   Alternatively, click Ctrl+Shift+D (⌘-Shift-D).

   If, as you retrieve a file from your server, you have the *local* version of that file open with unsaved changes in it, Dreamweaver warns you that you'll lose those changes. (No surprise there; copying a file from the remote server automatically replaces the same file on the local site, whether it's open or not.) Dreamweaver also warns you if you're about to replace a local file that's *newer* than the remote one. And finally, Dreamweaver offers to transfer any dependent files, as described in Figure 17-7.

5. **Click Yes to transfer dependent files, or No to transfer only the files you selected.**

   Dreamweaver copies the files to your local site folder, creating any folders necessary to replicate the structure of the remote site.

Troubleshoot Using the FTP Log

If you have problems moving files using Dreamweaver's FTP command, you may be able to find some clues to the problem in the records Dreamweaver keeps when it transfers files. If you've used other FTP programs, you may have seen little messages that the web server and FTP program send back and forth, like this:

```
< 200 PORT command successful
>LIST< 150 Opening ASCII mode data connec-
tion for file list
```

Dreamweaver sends and receives this information, too, but it keeps it hidden. To see the FTP log, choose Window→Results,

and then click the FTP Log tab. Any errors Dreamweaver encounters appear here.

For example, if you come across a "cannot put file" error, it may mean that you're out of space on your web server. Contact your ISP or your server administrator for help. WebDAV connections also produce a log of file-transfer activity, but it's not very easy to decipher.

And Secure FTP (SFTP) produces no log in Dreamweaver—hush, hush, it's a secret.

Cloaking Files

You may not want *all* your files transferred to and from your remote site. For example, as part of its Library and Template tools, Dreamweaver creates folders inside your local root folder. These folders don't do you any good on the web server; their sole purpose is to help you build your site locally. Likewise, you may have Photoshop (.psd), Flash (.fla), Illustrator (.ai), or Fireworks CS6 (.fw.png) files in your local site folder. They're inaccessible from a web browser and can take up a lot of disk space, so you shouldn't transfer them to your server when you move your site online.

> **NOTE** If you work on a website with other people, you probably *will* want to have the Library and Templates folders on the server. That way, your colleagues can get at those files as well.

To meet such challenges, Dreamweaver includes a feature called *cloaking*. It lets you hide folders and specific file types from many file-transfer operations, including Get/Put, the Check In/Check Out feature (page 807), and site synchronization (page 813). In fact, you can even hide files from many sitewide Dreamweaver actions, including site reports (see page 779), search-and-replace functions (Chapter 20), the ability to check and change links sitewide (page 771), and the Assets panel (page 749). There's one exception: files linked to library items (see Chapter 18) or templates (Chapter 19) can still "see" items even if they're in cloaked Library and Templates folders.

Dreamweaver lets you cloak folders and file types (those that end with a specific extension, such as .fla or .psd). It even lets you cloak a single file anywhere on your site. Implementing each type of cloak requires a different technique.

To hide specific types of files:

1. **Choose Site→Manage Sites.**

   The Manage Sites window opens, listing all the sites you defined in Dreamweaver.

2. **Double-click the site of interest to open it for editing.**

   Alternatively, select the site, and then click the Edit button (the pencil icon) in the lower-right corner of the Manage Sites window. Either way, that site's Site Setup window opens.

3. **Click the arrow next to Advanced Settings to expand that list of options.** Click the Cloaking category.

   The cloaking settings appear (see Figure 17-9). The factory setting is On for every site you define. (If you want to turn cloaking off, turn off the "Enable cloaking" box.)

TIP You can quickly turn cloaking on and off by right-clicking (Control-clicking) any file or folder in the Files panel and then selecting Cloaking→Enable Cloaking from the shortcut menu. A checkmark next to Enable Cloaking means that cloaking is turned on.

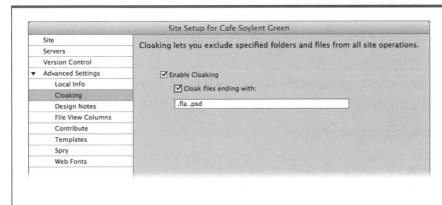

FIGURE 17-9

The Cloaking category of the Site Definition window lets you turn cloaking on and off—a feature that lets you hide folders, specific file types, and individual files from sitewide operations, like transferring files to the web server or searching and replacing text. In this window, you can specify which types of files to hide by listing their extensions (.psd for Photoshop files, for example).

4. **Turn on the "Cloak files ending with" checkbox.**

Dreamweaver identifies file types by their extensions—.fla for Flash files, for example. If you use Fireworks, which uses the extension .png, don't add the .png extension to this box. If you're using Fireworks CS6, then add .fw.png to the list (the latest version of Fireworks adds .fw to its older .png file extension so as not to confuse the byte-heavy Fireworks file with the lean, compress PNG file format).

NOTE Mac programs don't always add these file name suffixes, but without them, Dreamweaver can't cloak, so if you use a Mac, make sure you add an extension when you save a file. Some programs have a "Hide File Extension" checkbox that appears when you save a file—make sure you have this *turned off*.

---

5. **In the text box, type the extensions of the files you want to cloak.**

Each extension should start with a period followed by three or four letters. Fireworks CS6 is an exception: For those files, type .fw.png. To specify multiple extensions, separate them with a space.

6. **Click Save and then Done to close this and the Manage Sites window.**

In the Files panel, cloaked files will have a red slash through them.

You can also cloak a single folder or file using the Files panel, like this:

7. **Open the Files panel by pressing F8 (Shift-⌘-F).**

Alternatively, choose Window→Files.

8. **Right-click (Control-click) any folder or file in the Local Files view.**

A shortcut menu appears with many site-related options.

9. **Select Cloaking→Cloak.**

Dreamweaver adds a red slash through the file or folder's icon in the Files panel. When you cloak a folder, Dreamweaver hides all the files and folders *within it* as well, as indicated by the red slashes through their icons.

Once you cloak a folder, it and any folders inside it disappear from Dreamweaver's file-transfer functions. Dreamweaver also hides individual files you cloak and any files with an extension you specified in the Preferences window.

As with everything in life, there are exceptions, however. You can override the cloaking, for example, by selecting a cloaked file or folder and then using the Get or Put buttons as described on page 798. Dreamweaver assumes that since you specifically selected that file or folder, you want to override the cloaking feature.

Dreamweaver also ignores cloaking if you answer Yes in the Dependent Files message box when you Put or Get files. In that case, Dreamweaver transfers all dependent files, even if you cloaked them (this applies when you try to Put or Get library and template files as well).

■ Check In and Check Out

If you're the sole developer for a website, the Files panel's Put and Get buttons are fine for transferring files. But if you're on a team of developers, those simple tools can get you in trouble.

Suppose your boss emails you an important announcement that she wants posted on your site's home page immediately. So you download the home page from the web server and start to edit it. At the same time, your co-worker Bob notices a typo on the page. He downloads it, too.

You're a much faster worker than Bob, so you add the critical news to the home page and move it back to the server. But then Bob transfers *his* corrected home page, *overwriting* your edits and eliminating that urgent notice you just added. (An hour later, your phone rings. It's the boss.)

Without some kind of system to monitor who has what file and to prevent people from overwriting each other's work, collaborative web development is a chaotic mess. Fortunately, Dreamweaver's Check In and Check Out system provides a civilized answer to the problem, specifically designed for group web development. It works like your local public library: When you check out a file, no one else can have it. When you're finished, you check the file back in, releasing control of it, and allowing someone else on the team to check it out and work on it.

To use the Check In/Check Out feature effectively, you first need to turn it on. You'll find that setting under the Advanced options when you set up your remote server (as described in "Advanced Remote Server Settings" on page 797 and pictured in Figure 17-5). In addition, you must keep a few things in mind:

- When you develop a website solo, your local site usually contains the most recent versions of your files. You make any modifications or additions to the pages on your computer and *then* transfer the edited pages to your web server.

  But in a collaborative environment, where many people work on the site at once, the files on your hard drive may not be the latest ones. After all, your co-workers, like you, have been updating pages and transferring them to the server. The home page sitting in your local site folder may be several days older than the file on the remote site, which is why checking out a file from the *remote server*, rather than editing the copy on your computer, is so important. It guarantees that you have the latest version of the file. (Dreamweaver can automatically check out a file whenever you open it from the list of local files. See page 808 for details.)

- In a collaborative environment, nobody should post files to the server using any method except Dreamweaver's Check In/Check Out system.

  The reason is technical, but worth slogging through: When Dreamweaver checks out a file, it doesn't actually *lock* the file. Instead, it places a small, invisible text file (with the three-letter suffix .lck) on both the remote server and in your local site folder. This file indicates who has checked out the website file. When

Dreamweaver connects to the remote server, it uses these text files to determine which web files are in use by others.

And that's why your site-development team needs to use Dreamweaver exclusively to transfer files: only Dreamweaver understands the .lck files. Other FTP programs, like WS_FTP (Windows) and Fetch (Mac), gladly ignore them and can easily overwrite checked-out files. This risk also applies when you simply copy files back and forth over the office network.

NOTE Adobe's word-processor-like web-page editing program, Contribute, also takes advantage of the Check In/Check Out feature, so you can use the two programs on the same site.

- All Dreamweaver-using team members must configure their remote site to use Check In and Check Out. If just one person doesn't do it, you risk overwritten files.

NOTE WebDAV people are free of these last two constraints. As long as everyone working on the site uses programs that support the WebDAV protocol, they can work seamlessly with people using Dreamweaver, and vice versa.

Checking Out Files

When you work collaboratively and want to work on a file, you check it out from the web server. Doing so makes sure that *you* have the latest version of the file, and that nobody else can make changes to it.

WARNING Dreamweaver's Check In/Check Out feature only works if everyone on the team uses it. Everyone needs to have Dreamweaver and everyone needs to turn on this feature, as described on page 798. If even a single person doesn't use Dreamweaver and this system, you'll probably run into problems.

If you're used to creating sites by yourself, this Check In/Check Out business may feel a little strange; after all, when it's just you working on a site, the local site (the files on your computer) contains the latest version of all your site files. But when you work with a group, you need to consider the *remote server*—the drive that everyone can access, edit, and add new pages to—the master repository of your site's files.

NOTE There's nothing to check out when you create a new page. Since the only version of that file in the universe lies on your computer, have no fear that someone else may work on it at the same time as you. In this case, you only need to check the file *into* the site when you're done.

You check out a file using the Files panel; if it's not open, press F8 (Shift-⌘-F) or choose Window→Files. Then select the site you want to work on from the Site dropdown menu (shown at the top of Figure 17-10).

Checked out   Check out   Check in

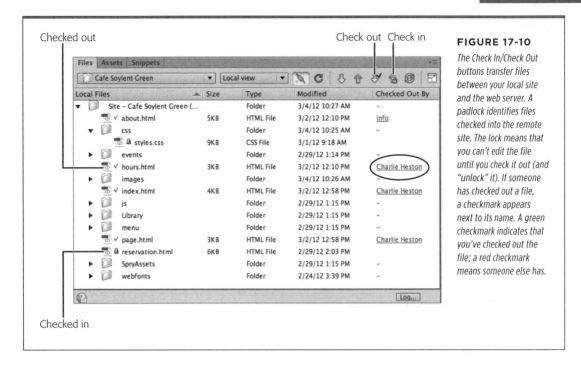

Checked in

FIGURE 17-10

The Check In/Check Out buttons transfer files between your local site and the web server. A padlock identifies files checked into the remote site. The lock means that you can't edit the file until you check it out (and "unlock" it). If someone has checked out a file, a checkmark appears next to its name. A green checkmark indicates that you've checked out the file; a red checkmark means someone else has.

Now you're ready to begin. From the Local Files list in the Files panel, select the files you want to check out from the server—or, to check out an entire folder and every file inside it, select the folder.

In some instances, you may want to select a file from the "Remote server" list as well. For example, you might need to modify a page you didn't create and which you've never checked out before. In such a case, the file isn't *in* your local site, so you have to get it from the remote server. Select "Remote server" from the Files panel (see Figure 17-6); Dreamweaver connects to and then displays the remote server files. Select the ones you want to check out.

TIP If, when you set up your remote server (see page 798), you select the "Check Out File when Opening" option, you can also check out (and open) a file by double-clicking it in the Files panel. This is a quick way to open a page you want to edit while still using Dreamweaver's Check Out feature.

In any case, now just click the Check Out button in the Files panel (see Figure 17-10), or use the keyboard shortcut Ctrl+Alt+Shift+D (⌘-Option-Shift-D). (Not enough fingers? See page 911 to learn how to change Dreamweaver's shortcuts.)

Subversion in Dreamweaver

Dreamweaver includes support for one popular version control system called *Subversion*. Well, at least it's popular among coders. Subversion is a free program that developers usually use to manage files as part of a large programming project. It has powerful features to make sure that multiple users don't overwrite each others' changes, and to make it easy to "roll back" to previous versions of a file if something goes wrong.

To take advantage of Dreamweaver's Subversion support, you first need to set up a *Subversion server*—a separate piece of software running on either your own computer, on a server on your network, or even on a server somewhere on the Internet. You can download the software at *http://subversion.apache .org/packages.html*. You can also find companies that offer free or cheap Subversion hosting (in other words, they take care of the mess of setting up a Subversion server for you). Next, you need to create what's called a Subversion *repository*—a way of identifying a set of files that belong to a particular project. For example, each web project would probably be its own repository. You can learn more about how to set up Subversion at *http://svnbook.red-bean.com*.

For Dreamweaver users, it's important to keep in mind that a Subversion repository is independent of the website running on your web server. In other words, you'll have a Subversion repository, local files on your computer, and another set of files out on the Web (that is, on your remote server).

You can set up Subversion support for a site in Dreamweaver by choosing Site→Manage Sites and then choosing a site to edit. In the Site Definition window, select the Version Control category and choose Subversion from the Access menu. Then fill out the other settings, such as the server address, repository path, your user name, and password.

Once you do this, you'll connect to the repository when you choose Repository View from the File View menu (see Figure 17-6). In addition, when you use the Check In and Check Out buttons on the Files panel, you'll check files in and out from the Subversion repository. Dreamweaver CS6 includes the ability to copy, move, delete, and revert (go back to a previous version of) files in the repository.

Unfortunately, if you want to perform sitewide changes, like updating templates or changing the footer information throughout your site, you need to check out the *entire* website from the repository.

If you develop websites on your own, Subversion is definitely overkill. Even if you toil in a small workgroup, unless you have someone with the system administrator know-how to set up a Subversion server and repository, you're probably better off with something simpler, like Dreamweaver's Check In/Check Out system or even WebDAV. Probably the most important feature of Subversion is the ability to go back to a previous version of a file that has somehow been wrecked.

If you're not going to use Subversion, it's definitely worth investing in some basic backup software like Retrospect Remote or Apple's Time Machine. Even most simple backup software lets you keep hourly, daily, weekly, or monthly file backups, and lets you go back in time to retrieve older versions of files. Or, take the low-tech approach: Just back up your site every day and store the copied files in a folder named something like *June_10_2012*. That way, you'll have a daily backup you can turn to if you need to recover a lost file.

However, if your company or organization does use Subversion, you can get in-depth information on using Dreamweaver with it at *http://tinyurl.com/3kxo5wu*.

Dreamweaver asks if you want to check out dependent files, too. Click Yes if you think the page you're checking out uses files you haven't downloaded. Dreamweaver then copies the dependent files to your computer, so the page you check out displays its current images, CSS style sheets, and any other linked files. It doesn't *check out* a dependent file, however, so if you do want to *edit* the dependent file—if, for example, you need to edit the styles in a linked external style sheet—you must also check out that dependent file, by selecting it from the Files list and clicking the check out button.

> **NOTE** When you edit a web page you check out, you may run into a weird problem if you edit the CSS that page uses. If the page has an external style sheet and you didn't check out the style sheet, you won't be able to edit any styles on the page. Instead, you'll get a message saying that the styles file is locked and Dreamweaver will ask if you want to check it out. Click the Check Out button and Dreamweaver tries to check it out. If Dreamweaver informs you that someone else has checked it out, click Cancel and wait until the other person checks the style sheet back in. Then check it out and make your changes. Bottom line: Check out your site's external style sheets if you want to edit the CSS in your pages.

When you check out files, Dreamweaver copies them to your computer and marks them as checked out so others can't change them. Like uploading and downloading files, checking out files can take time, depending on the speed of your Internet connection.

After you check out a file, Dreamweaver displays a green "checked-out" checkmark in the Files panel next to its name (see Figure 17-10). You can now open and edit the file, and, when you're done, check the file back in.

If you attempt to check out a file that someone has already checked out, Dreamweaver tells you as much. It also gives you the option to override the person's checkout—but unless you're the boss, resist the temptation, for two reasons. First, your colleague may have made some important changes to the page, which you'll wipe out with your shenanigans. Second, because you so rudely stole the file, they may stop bringing you donuts in the morning.

A better way to work with someone who's checked out a file that you need is to use Dreamweaver's email feature. You can see who checked out the file by consulting Dreamweaver's Checked Out By column (see the circled entry in Figure 17-10). Even better, if you click the name, Dreamweaver opens your email program and addresses a message to that person, so you can say: "Hey Bob, you've had the home page checked out for two days! I need to work on it, so check it back in!"

The name and email address Dreamweaver uses depends on the information your co-workers provided when they configured their computers for remote site use (you provided this same information when you configured your computer). See the Advanced options on page 798 for more.

Checking In Files

When you're ready to move a page you've been editing back onto the server, you check it in. (You also check in *new* files you create.)

To check in files, open the Files panel (press F8 [Shift-⌘-F]), choose the relevant site from the Site drop-down menu, and, using the Local Folder file list in the Files panel, select the files you want to check in to your server. As always, you can click a folder to check *it* in, too, along with every file inside it.

The files you check in should be files you checked out, or brand-new files that have never been on the server. If you attempt to check in a file that someone else has checked out, Dreamweaver warns you with a message box. Click Cancel to stop the check-in so you don't overwrite the checked-out file. Dreamweaver also warns you if you try to check in a file that's older than the copy on the server. Again, unless you're sure this is what you want to do, click Cancel.

Manual Check Out Override

Occasionally, you may want to erase the checked-out status of a file. Suppose, for example, someone who's checked out a lot of files suddenly catches the plague and can't continue working on the site. To free those files so others can work on them, you have to undo his check-out (and quarantine his cubicle).

To do the former, make sure you have the Files panel in Remote Server view (this trick won't work with the local files displayed). Then, right-click (Control-click) the checked-out file and select Undo Checkout from the menu that appears.

Dreamweaver warns you that whoever checked out the file won't be able to check it back in. (This is, in fact, false. That person can still check in the file, overwriting whatever's on the web server. So you can see why you should override the check-out only when the person who checked it out is very unlikely to check it back in—stranded on a deserted island, perhaps.)

When the operation's complete, a padlock icon appears next to the file.

You can also use this technique on a file *you've* checked out. For example, if, after checking out a file, you make a horrible mistake on the page and wish to revert to the copy on the server.

NOTE If you want to check in the page you're currently working on, use the toolbar in the document window (see Figure 17-8).

You can check in the selected files in any of the usual ways:

- Click the Check In button on the Files panel (see Figure 17-6).
- Use the keyboard shortcut Ctrl+Alt+Shift+U (⌘-Option-Shift-U). (See page 911 to learn how to change any Dreamweaver shortcut to something less cumbersome.)

Dreamweaver asks if you want to check in any dependent files at the same time. You should transfer dependent files only if you first checked them out, or if the dependent files are new and have never been uploaded to the server. If you attempt to check in a dependent file that someone else has checked out, Dreamweaver warns you with a message box—click the No button in this box so you don't overwrite someone's checked-out file.

After you click through all the message boxes, Dreamweaver copies the files to your remote server. Once you check in a file, Dreamweaver locks your local copy—you'll see a padlock icon next to its name in the Local Files list of the Files panel (see Figure 17-10)—that's so you don't accidentally change the local version of the file. If you wish to modify the file in some way, check it out from the server.

NOTE Dreamweaver's Site Report feature (page 779) lets you see which files are checked out and by whom. Skip it. On a large site, the report can take a long time to run, it isn't always accurate, and you can't do the things you're most likely to do with checked-out files (like checking them back in).

FREQUENTLY ASKED QUESTION

Get and Put, In and Out

I'm using Dreamweaver's Check In and Check Out buttons to transfer my files. What do the Get and Put buttons do if I use the Check In/Check Out feature?

If you use Check In and Check Out, the Get and Put commands function slightly differently than described on page 798. *Get*, in this case, copies the selected file or files to your local site. However, Dreamweaver adds a small lock icon next to each of the "gotten" files in your "Local files" list. The files are locked, and you shouldn't edit them. Remember, checking out a file is the only way to prevent others from working on it simultaneously. If you edit a locked file on your computer, nothing stops someone else from checking out the page, editing it, and checking it back in.

But you may still find the Get command useful in such a situation. For example, suppose someone just updated the site's external style sheet. The pages you're editing use this style sheet, so you want to get the latest version. You don't want to edit the style sheet itself, so you don't need to check it out. If

you use Get instead of checking out the pages, you can keep a reference copy on your computer without locking anyone else out of the file and without having to check it back in.

Put, on the other hand, simply—and blindly—transfers the file on your local site to the remote site. If you use the Check In/Check Out feature and you haven't also checked out the file, using Put is a bad idea. The remote site should be your reference copy; several rounds of revisions may have been made to a file since you last checked it out. Your local copy will be hopelessly out of date, and moving it to the server destroys the most recent version of the file.

However, if you *do* have the file checked out, you can use Put to transfer your local copy to the server so your site's visitors see it. For example, say you're updating the home page with 20 new news items. To keep your site up-to-the-minute fresh, you can Put the home page after you add each news item. Then the whole world will see each item as soon as possible. When you completely finish editing the home page, check it in.

■ Synchronizing Site Files

As you may suspect, when you keep two sets of files—on your local site and remote server—it's easy to lose track of which files are the most recent. For example, say you finish working on your website and move all the files to the server. The next day, you notice mistakes on a bunch of pages, so you make corrections on the copies in your local site. But in your rush to fix the pages, you didn't keep track of which ones you corrected. So although you're ready to move the corrected pages to the server, you're not sure *which* ones you need to transfer.

When you use the Check In/Check Out feature, you avoid this problem altogether. Using this system, the version on the server is *always* considered the latest and most definitive copy—*unless* you or someone else has checked out that file. In that case, whoever checked out the file has the most recent version.

But if you're operating solo and don't use the Check In/Check Out feature, you may get good mileage from Dreamweaver's Synchronize command, which lets you compare the remote and local sites and transfer only the newer files in either direction. (In fact, since the Synchronize command uses the Get and Put methods of transferring files, you may not get the results you expect if you synchronize your site while also using Check In and Check Out, as described in the box on page 813.)

To synchronize your sites:

1. **Make sure you turn on the "Maintain synchronization information" checkbox when you set the server options (see the Advanced options mentioned on page 797).**

   Dreamweaver automatically turns this option on when you set up a server (see Figure 17-5).

2. **Choose Site→Synchronize Sitewide.**

   Alternatively, you can right-click anywhere inside the Files panel. From the shortcut menu that appears, select Synchronize. In either case, the Synchronize Files dialog box appears (see Figure 17-11).

FIGURE 17-11

Using the Synchronization command, you can copy newer files from your computer to the web server or get newer files from the remote site.

3. **Using the Synchronize drop-down menu, specify the files you want to update.**

   You can either synchronize all the files in the current site, or just the files you select from the "Local site" list. This last option is good when you have a really big site and want to limit this operation to just a single section of the site—one folder, for example.

4. **Using the Direction drop-down menu, choose the destination for newer files.**

   You have three choices. *Put newer files to remote* updates the web server with any newer files in your local site folder. It also copies any *new* files on the local site to the remote server. Use this option when you've done heavy editing to the local site and want to move all the new or modified pages to your server.

   Get newer files from remote does the reverse: It updates your local site folder with any newer (or new) files from the remote site. Here's one instance where the synchronize feature comes in handy in team-design situations. If you've been out of the office for a while, click this option to download copies of the latest site files. (Note that this doesn't check out any files; it merely makes sure you have copies of the latest files on your computer. This is one example where synchronization works well with Check In/Check Out, since it refreshes your local copy of the site with the latest files, including graphics and external CSS style sheets, that any pages you do check out may depend on.)

Get and put newer files is a two-way synchronization. Dreamweaver transfers any new files on the local site to the remote site and vice versa. For example, if you update a page on your computer, Dreamweaver moves that file to the web server; if someone has made changes to a file on the server that is more recent than the copy on your computer, Dreamweaver downloads that file to your hard drive. The result is that both "sides" contain the latest files.

5. **Turn on the Delete checkbox, if desired.**

The way Dreamweaver words this option reflects the option you selected in the previous step. If you move newer files to the remote site, it says, "Delete remote files not on local drive." It's a useful option when, for example, you spent the afternoon cleaning up the local copy of your site, deleting old, orphaned graphics files and web pages, and you want Dreamweaver to update the web server to match.

If you chose to transfer newer files *from* the remote site, Dreamweaver lets you "Delete local files not on remote server." Use this feature when your local site is hopelessly out of date with the remote site. Perhaps you work on the site with a team, but you've been on vacation for two months (this is, of course, a hypothetical example). The site may have changed so significantly that you want to get your local copy in line with the website.

WARNING Of course, you should proceed with caution when using *any* command that automatically deletes files. There's no Undo for these delete operations, and you don't want to accidentally delete the only copy of a particular page, graphic, or external Cascading Style Sheet.

If you chose the "Get and put newer files" option in step 4, Dreamweaver dims and makes unavailable the Delete checkbox. This option truly synchronizes the two; Dreamweaver copies newer files on the remote site (including files that exist on the server but not on your computer) to your local site, and vice versa.

6. **Click Preview to begin the synchronization process.**

Dreamweaver connects to the remote site and compares the two sets of files—if your site is large, this comparison takes a long time. When it finishes, the Synchronize preview window appears (Figure 17-12), listing which files Dreamweaver will delete and which it will transfer, and providing an additional set of options for working with the listed files.

NOTE Synchronization is a slow process. Dreamweaver needs to connect to the remote server, and then compare the remote server files with your local files. On a site with even a dozen or so pages and lots of graphics, synchronizing files can take minutes. This is one reason why, if you only need to synchronize files in one folder, you should first select that folder in the Files panel, and then, in step 3 above, choose "Selected files only." Also make sure to take advantage of the cloaking feature described on page 804, so Dreamweaver doesn't waste time trying to synchronize files that you don't want on the web server to begin with.

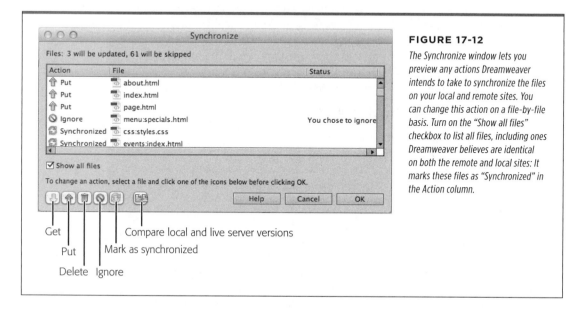

FIGURE 17-12

The Synchronize window lets you preview any actions Dreamweaver intends to take to synchronize the files on your local and remote sites. You can change this action on a file-by-file basis. Turn on the "Show all files" checkbox to list all files, including ones Dreamweaver believes are identical on both the remote and local sites: It marks these files as "Synchronized" in the Action column.

7. **Change the action Dreamweaver takes on the listed files.**

   The preview box tells you what Dreamweaver plans to do with a file—Get it, Put it, or delete it. You can override these actions by selecting a file from the list and clicking one of the action buttons at the bottom of the window. For example, if you realize that Dreamweaver is going to delete a file that you *know* you need, select the file in the list and click the "Ignore file" button (the red circle with a line through it).

   Most of these options are useful only if you know Dreamweaver made a mistake—for example, when the program says you should Get a file, but you know your local copy is identical to the server's copy. In that case, you could select the file and click the "Mark as synchronized" button to tell Dreamweaver that they're identical. However, if you knew exactly which files were identical and which ones needed updating, you wouldn't need to use the Synchronize feature in the first place, right?

One option can come in quite handy. The "Compare local and remote versions" button lets you compare the code in the local file to the code in the remote file so you can identify exactly what differs between the two. You can use this feature to, for example, see exactly what changes were made to the remote copy of the file. You'll learn about this feature in detail in "Comparing Versions of a Web Page" on page 363.

8. **Click OK to proceed, or Cancel to stop the synchronization.**

   If you click OK, Dreamweaver commences copying and deleting the chosen files. If you want to stop the process, click the Cancel button in the Background File Activity window.

9. **Click Close.**

TIP If you just want to *identify* newer files on the local site without synchronizing them (to run a report on them, for example), click the contextual menu in the top-right corner of the Files panel and choose Edit→Select Newer Local. Dreamweaver connects to the remote server and compares the files, and then, in the Files panel's "Local view" list, highlights files on the local site that are newer than their remote counterparts.

You can also identify newer files on the remote server: Choose Edit→"Select Newer on Remote server" from the Files panel's contextual menu.

Finally, you can identify files on your computer you either created or modified within a given date range, using the Select Recently Modified command described in the box on page 767.

■ Communicating with Design Notes

Lots of questions arise when a team works on a website: Has this page been proof-read? Who is the author of the page? Where did this graphic come from? Usually, you must rely on a flurry of emails to ferret out the answers.

But Dreamweaver's Design Notes dialog box (Figure 17-13) eliminates much of that hassle by letting you attach information, such as a web page's status or author, to a file.

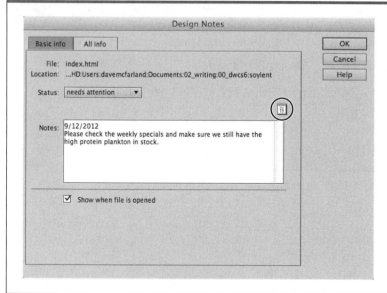

FIGURE 17-13

If you want the Design Notes window to open whenever someone opens a page, turn on the "Show when file is opened" checkbox. This option makes sure that no one misses an important note attached to a page, because Dreamweaver automatically opens the note when it opens the page. (This option has no effect when you add notes to GIFs, JPEGs, PNGs, or anything other than a file that Dreamweaver can open and edit, such as a web page or an external style sheet.)

You can open these notes (from the Files panel, from a currently open document, or automatically), edit them, and even share them with others. That way, it's easy to leave notes for other people, such as, "Hey Bob, can you make sure that this is the most recent photo of Brad and Angelina?" You can even add notes to files other than web pages, including folders, images, and external Cascading Style Sheets—anything, in fact, that appears in the Files panel.

Setting Up Design Notes

You can't use Design Notes unless you turn the feature on. To find out if it's on, open the Site Setup dialog box by double-clicking the site's name in the Manage Sites dialog box (choose Manage Sites from the Site menu or the drop-down menu in the Files panel). In the Advanced Setting window, click Design Notes. As you can see in Figure 17-14, two checkboxes pertain to the notes feature:

- **Maintain Design Notes**. This checkbox lets you create and read notes using Dreamweaver's File→Design Notes command (see "Viewing Design Notes" on page 820).

- **Enable Upload Design Notes for sharing**. If you use Design Notes as part of a team, turn on this checkbox, which makes Dreamweaver upload design notes to the remote site, so that your fellow team members can read them.

NOTE Design Notes are especially useful for keeping track of pages built and maintained by a team of web developers. But if you're a solo operator and still want to use them—maybe you're the type with a hundred Post-it notes taped to the edges of your monitor—then turn off "Upload Design Notes for sharing." You'll save time and server space by preventing Dreamweaver from transferring the note files to the server.

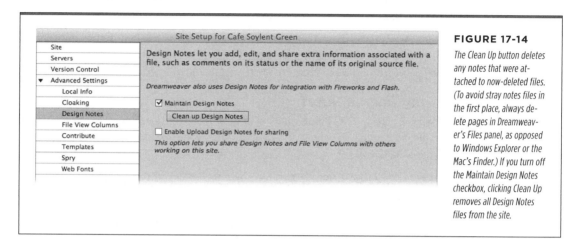

FIGURE 17-14

The Clean Up button deletes any notes that were attached to now-deleted files. (To avoid stray notes files in the first place, always delete pages in Dreamweaver's Files panel, as opposed to Windows Explorer or the Mac's Finder.) If you turn off the Maintain Design Notes checkbox, clicking Clean Up removes all Design Notes files from the site.

Click OK to close the Site Definition dialog box. You can double-click another site in the Manage Sites dialog box to turn on its Design Notes feature, or click Done.

To add a Design Note to a document you're working on, choose your favorite method:

- Choose File→Design Notes.

- From the File Status menu in the Document toolbar (see Figure 17-8), choose Design Notes.

- Right-click (Control-click) a file in the Files panel (or an external object, such as a graphic or movie, in the document window), and choose Design Notes from the shortcut menu.

In any case, the Design Notes window opens (Figure 17-13). If you like, you can use the Status drop-down menu to let your team members know where the file stands. For example, is it ready to move to the server? Is it just a draft version? Or is there something wrong with it that requires attention? Dreamweaver provides eight options: "draft," "revision1," "revision2," "revision3," "alpha," "beta," "final," and "needs attention."

The note itself, which you type into the Note box, could be a simple question for the page's author ("Are you sure 'Coldplay: Defining a New Musical Language for the Modern Age' is an appropriate title for this article?") or it could offer more information about the status of the page ("Still need studio shot for high-energy plankton milk shake").

TIP Click the calendar icon (circled in Figure 17-13) to pop the date into your note—a great way to keep a running tally of notes and the dates they were written.

When you click OK, Dreamweaver creates a file with all the note information in it. This file ends with the extension .mno and begins with the name of the file; for the file *index.html*, for example, Dreamweaver would name the note *index.html.mno*.

Dreamweaver stores notes in a folder called *_notes* that it keeps in the same folder as the relevant page or file. For example, if you add notes to the home page, Dreamweaver stores the *_notes* folder inside the root folder.

Viewing Design Notes

You can view Design Notes in a number of ways. If the note's author turned on "Show when file is opened," of course, the Design Notes window opens automatically when you open that page.

Otherwise, to look at a note, you have any number of options:

- Choose File→Design Notes.

- Choose Design Notes from the File Status drop-down menu in the document window's toolbar.

- Double-click the small yellow balloon icon in the Notes column of the Files panel. (You'll only see this column if you turned on this option in the Site Definition window, as described below.)

- Right-click (Control-click) an embedded object, like a graphic or Flash movie, right in the document window, and choose Design Notes from the shortcut menu.

- Right-click (Control-click) a file in the Files panel and choose Design Notes from the shortcut menu.

Organizing the Columns in the Files Panel

Columns in the Files panel identify a file's name, size, modification date, type, and so on.

This may be more information than you're interested in—or it may not be enough. So remember that Dreamweaver lets you show or hide columns, change their order, or even create new ones with information it retrieves from a file's Design Notes.

NOTE You can adjust the relative width of these columns by dragging the dividing line between the column names. You can also sort all the pages listed in this window by clicking the relevant column's name. Click "Modified," for example, to sort the files so the newest ones appear first. Click a second time to reverse the sort, placing oldest files first.

When you set up a website in the Site Definition window, you can view the column setup by clicking the File View Columns category (Figure 17-15).

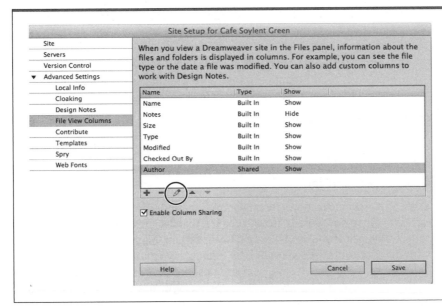

FIGURE 17-15

Dreamweaver's Files panel has a handful of set columns: Name, Notes, Size, Type, Modified, and Checked Out By. You can't delete these columns, but you can hide them as described below after clicking the Edit button (circled). You can also create custom columns to display information that matches your work requirements (for example, a column listing the author of each web article).

Once you see the screen shown in Figure 17-15, you can perform any of these stunts:

- **Reorder columns**. Click a column name in the Site Definition window to select it. Then click the up and down arrow buttons to move the column one spot to the left or right, respectively, in the Files panel.

- **Deleting columns**. Click the column name, and then click the minus-sign (-) button to delete the column. (Dreamweaver doesn't let you delete the built-in columns Name, Notes, Type, Modified, and so on.)

- **Adding Columns**. You can add columns of your own, as described next.

To hide a column (or show a hidden column), select the column in the File View Options category of the Site Setup window, and then click the Edit button (circled in Figure 17-15). In the window that opens, hide the column by turning off the Show checkbox. (You display a hidden column by turning on this checkbox.) You can also change how Dreamweaver aligns the text in the column (left, right, or center) using the Align menu. It's a good idea to hide columns you don't need, since they take up space in the Files panel, often hiding parts of file names.

Creating Custom Columns

Your Files panel offers columns for all the usual information bits: Name, Checked Out, and so on. But you may someday wish there were a column that showed each page's status, so that your Files panel could show you which files need proofreading, who wrote each article, or which pages are being held until a certain blackout date.

You can add columns of your own design, although the process isn't streamlined by any means. It involves two broad efforts: First, using an offshoot of the Design Notes feature described earlier, you set up the new columns you want to display. Then, using the column-manipulation dialog box shown in Figure 17-15, you make the new columns visible in the Files panel.

■ PHASE 1: DEFINING THE NEW INFORMATION TYPES

You create new kinds of informational flags—primarily for use as new columns in the Files panel—using the Design Notes dialog box. Here's the rundown:

1. **Choose File→Design Notes.**

   The Design Notes window appears. (You can summon it in various other ways, as described on page 820.)

2. **Click the "All info" tab.**

   This peculiar window shows the programmery underbelly of the Dreamweaver Notes feature (see Figure 17-16). It turns out that it stores every kind of note as a name/value pair. If you used the main Notes screen (Figure 17-12) to choose Beta from the Status drop-down menu, for example, you'll see a notation that says "status=beta". *Status* is the info nugget's description; *beta* is its value. If you turn on the option called "Show when file is opened," you'll see "showOnOpen=true". And if you typed *Badly needs updating* as the note itself, you'll see "notes=Badly needs updating" on this screen.

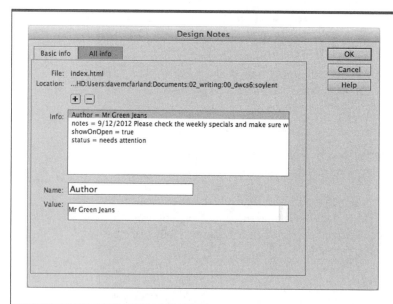

FIGURE 17-16

Dreamweaver lets you create your own types of notes in the "All info" tab of the Design Notes window. This lets you add more information to a page, such as its author or designer. Deleting a note you added is a simple matter of clicking on the note in the Info box and then clicking the minus (-) button.

But those are just the built-in info types; you're free to create your own.

3. **Click the + button.**

   You may wonder why you'd do this; after all, you can type a lot of information in the Notes box under the Basic Info tab. The primary benefit is that you can display this information in the Files panel.

4. **Type the name of the new note in the Name field.**

   It may be *Author*, for example, so that you can note who wrote the text of each page. Or it could be *Artist*, if you wish to add a note to each image specifying who created it. Maybe you need a column called *Hold Until*, which reminds you when certain information is OK to publish online.

5. **Press Tab to jump to the Value field, and then type the contents of the note.**

   You can enter the actual name of the author or artist—Jennifer Jones, for example—or the actual "Hold Until" date.

   Repeat steps 3–5 to add more notes.

NOTE Keep the value short—one or two words. Otherwise, the narrow Files panel column chops off the latter part of it. If you've got enough screen real estate, you can resize the columns by dragging the divider bars between column names.

---

6. **Click OK.**

   The dialog box closes.

■ PHASE 2: ADDING THE COLUMN

Just creating a new note type gets you halfway home; now you have to tell Dreamweaver to display that information in the Files panel.

To add a column to the Files panel:

1. **Open the Site Setup window for the particular site and select the File View Columns category under the Advanced Setting options.**

   To edit a site, choose Site→Manage Sites, and then double-click the name of the site from the Manage Sites window. Expand the Advanced Settings category on the left side of the window and the File View Columns options appear.

2. **Click the + button.**

   A pane appears (Figure 17-17) for adding the information for the new column.

3. **In the Column Name box, type the column heading you want to appear in the Files panel.**

   Make it short and descriptive. If possible, it should match the note type (*Author*, *Artist*, *Hold Until*, or whatever).

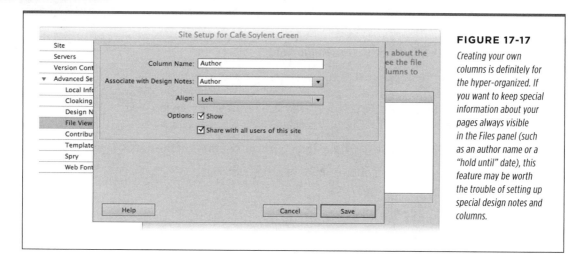

FIGURE 17-17

Creating your own columns is definitely for the hyper-organized. If you want to keep special information about your pages always visible in the Files panel (such as an author name or a "hold until" date), this feature may be worth the trouble of setting up special design notes and columns.

4. **Press Tab.** Type the name of the Design Note you wish to use for this column.

   This is the name part of the name/value pair described in step 4 of the previous instructions. For example, if you add a note named Author to a file, you would type *Author* here. Capitalization matters; so if you named the Design Note *Author*, type it with a capital A.

   There's a drop-down menu here, too, but it always lists the same four options: Status, Assigned, Due, and Priority. If you choose Status, you'll get a column that reflects your choice from the Status drop-down menu in the Design Notes window (see step 2 on page 822). The other three options do nothing *unless* you create a matching note type in step 4 of the previous instructions. (It would be nice if this drop-down menu listed *all* the note names you created, so you didn't have to remember them.)

   Before you wrap up the column-adding procedure, you can, if you wish, choose an alignment option for the text in the column (left, right, or center). Check to make sure that the Show checkbox is turned on (otherwise, your new column won't appear, and you've just defeated the purpose of this whole exercise). Finally, turn on "Share with all users of this site" if you like.

The Share feature works like this: The next time you connect to your remote server, Dreamweaver uploads a file containing your newly defined column information. The next time another member of the team connects to the remote site, *his* copy of Dreamweaver downloads this file, so that his Files panel shows the same columns yours does.

NOTE The column-sharing feature can be very handy; it lets everyone working on a site share the same information. But it works properly only if everyone on the team has the "Enable column sharing" checkbox turned on (see Figure 17-15).

5. **Click OK.**

You should now see the new column in your Files panel. (You may need to widen the panel to see all the columns. You can also click the Expand Files Panel button [Figure 17-8] to expand the Panel.)

Dreamweaver CS6 Power

Snippets and Libraries

O K, so you finished the design for your company's new website. It looks great and your boss is ecstatic. But you've really only just begun. You have to build hundreds of pages before you launch the site. And once the site's online, you need to make endless updates to keep it fresh and inviting.

This is where Dreamweaver's Snippets and Library features come in, streamlining the sometimes tedious work of building and updating site pages.

As you create more and more web pages (and more and more websites), you may find yourself crafting the same page elements over and over again. Many of your pages may share common elements that always stay the same: a copyright notice, a navigation bar, or a logo, for example. And you may find yourself frequently using complex components, such as a pull-down menu that lists all the countries you ship products to or a particular design for photos and their captions.

Recreating the same components time after time is tiresome and—thanks to Dreamweaver—unnecessary. Dreamweaver provides two subtly different tools for reusing common page elements: *Snippets* and *Library items*.

■ Snippets Basics

Snippets aren't fancy or complex, but they sure save time. A snippet is simply a chunk of code you store away and then plunk into your web pages as necessary. They can be as simple as boilerplate legal text, or as complex as HTML, CSS, or JavaScript code (or code from any other programming language you encounter). For example, say you always use the same table design to list product specifications in your company's catalog. Each time you want to create a similar table, you could go through all the same steps to build it—or you could turn that table into a snippet, and then, with a simple double-click, add it to page after page of your site. Or say you use the popular jQuery JavaScript library on each site you build, and have to include the code to link to jQuery's JavaScript file—rather than type that code each time, just have Dreamweaver drop the pre-typed code into the page for you.

You keep these code chunks in the Snippets panel (see Figure 18-1), and summon them in a couple of ways:

- Choose Window→Snippets.

- Windows people can press Shift-F9. (There's no Mac keyboard shortcut for the Snippets panel, but you can create your own, as described on page 911.)

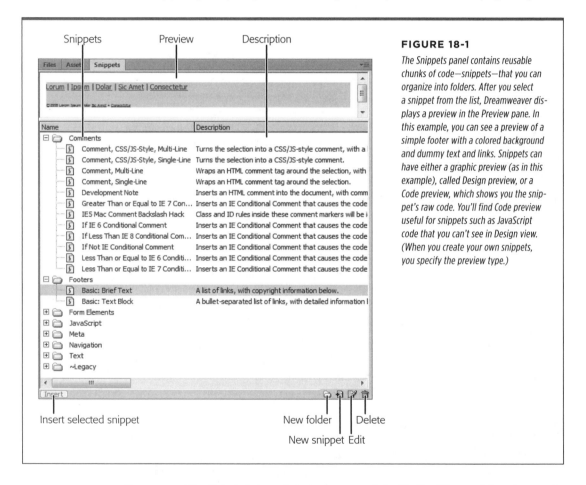

Snippets   Preview   Description

FIGURE 18-1

The Snippets panel contains reusable chunks of code—snippets—that you can organize into folders. After you select a snippet from the list, Dreamweaver displays a preview in the Preview pane. In this example, you can see a preview of a simple footer with a colored background and dummy text and links. Snippets can have either a graphic preview (as in this example), called Design preview, or a Code preview, which shows you the snippet's raw code. You'll find Code preview useful for snippets such as JavaScript code that you can't see in Design view. (When you create your own snippets, you specify the preview type.)

Insert selected snippet   New folder   Delete
                                 New snippet Edit

Once open, the Snippets panel appears, grouped with the Files and Assets panels. You'll see a set of stock Dreamweaver snippets, but above and beyond those, you can quickly build your own collection.

■ Using Snippets

Snippets come in two varieties: those that are simple blocks of code, and those that wrap around a currently selected element in a document. For example, in the Snippets panel's Text folder, you'll find a snippet called Service Mark. Adding this snippet to a page instantly inserts the code *^{sm}*, creating a superscript service mark (^{sm}) symbol.

But on occasion, you'll want to wrap code around something you've already typed. You may, for example, want to add an HTML comment to your page (a message that won't appear in web browsers, but that helps you or other web designers decipher the page). The "Comment, multi-line" snippet (in the Comments folder of the Snippets panel) helps you quickly add such a note. It wraps whatever you select with opening (<!--) and closing HTML comment markers (-->). Adding an HTML comment is as easy as typing the comment in your page, selecting it, and then double-clicking this snippet. This may sound a lot like the Apply Comment button in the Coding toolbar described in Figure 7-7, but the cool thing about this snippet is that it works in Design view, too, not just in Code view.

> **NOTE** Unfortunately, unless the snippet's description (which you find in the Snippet Panel's Description column) specifies that the snippet wraps, you can't tell whether it will or not. You either have to try out the snippet or open it in Editing mode to see. (And while you have the snippet open, you can add a note to its description indicating its ability, or inability, to wrap.)

To add a snippet to a web page, click in the document where you want the item to go, or select the object you wish to wrap with a snippet. Then do one of the following:

- On the Snippets panel, double-click the name of the snippet.

- On the Snippets panel, select the snippet, and then click the panel's Insert button.

- Drag the snippet from the panel into the document window. (If the snippet is supposed to wrap a selection, drag the snippet *onto* the selected object.)

While you can use snippets in either Design or Code view, some make sense only in Code view. For example, you typically have to insert the JavaScript snippets that come with Dreamweaver in the <head> section of a page, inside <script> tags. To use these snippets, you have to switch to Code view, insert the <script> tags, and then put the snippets inside.

> **TIP** To quickly insert a snippet you recently used, select the snippet's name from Insert→Recent Snippets. Better yet, create a keyboard shortcut for your favorite snippets, and then insert them with a keystroke, as described on page 911.

Snippets simply dump their contents into a document—essentially copying the snippet code and pasting it into your web page; Dreamweaver doesn't step in to make sure that you're adding the code correctly. Unless you're careful—and have some knowledge of HTML—you may end up adding snippets that make your web page impossible to view. (For advice on how to avoid such pitfalls, see the box on page 836.)

Creating Snippets

Dreamweaver comes with a lot of snippets, and you may find many of them irrelevant to what you want to do. No problem—you can easily create your own. Here's how:

1. **Create and select the content you wish to turn into a snippet.**

   You could, for instance, select a table in Design view, or select the opening and closing <table> tags (as well as all the code between them) in Code view. Or, if you want to save a form select menu (see page 581) that took you half an hour to build, then, in Design view, just click the form menu.

   If you want to make a snippet out of code that isn't visible in Design view, such as a JavaScript program or content that appears in the <head> section of a page, you need to switch to Code view first.

2. **In the Snippets panel, click the New Snippet button.**

   The Snippet window appears (Figure 18-2), displaying the code you selected in the Insert field.

NOTE If you skip step 1 and just click the New Snippet button, you can either type the code or, in the Insert box, paste a previously copied selection (see step 6).

---

3. **Title the snippet.**

   The name you type in the Name field appears in the Snippets panel. Make sure to give your snippet a name that clearly describes what it does.

4. **In the Description field, type identifying details.**

   This step is optional, but useful. Use this field to describe when and how to use the snippet, and whether or not the snippet wraps a selection.

5. **Select a snippet type.**

   "Wrap selection" makes the code wrap around a selection when you use the snippet. The "Insert block" option is for a snippet that's a single block of code you want to insert into a document, like a copyright notice or a form menu.

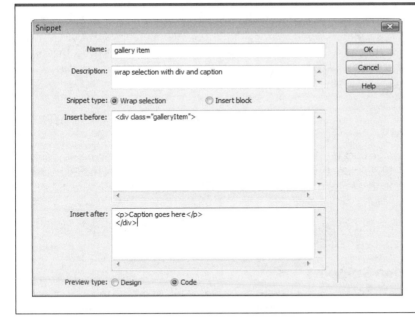

FIGURE 18-2

The Snippet window lets you create reusable chunks of HTML called snippets. For snippets that wrap around a currently selected object—for example, a snippet that adds a link to any selected text or graphic—you put code in the two Insert boxes. The code that appears before the selected object goes in the top box, and the code that goes after the object appears in the bottom box. In this example, the snippet wraps the current selection in a <div> tag with a predefined class applied to it.

6. **If necessary, add the code for the snippet.**

   If you initially selected code in the document window, it automatically appears in the "Insert before" field for a snippet that wraps around other code. For snippets that are just a single block of code, the code appears in the "Insert code" box.

   If you create a wrapping snippet, you need to add some code in the "before" field and some in the "after" field. For example, say you create a lot of photo galleries, and you want to wrap each photo in its own <div> tag with some room for a caption. Instead of adding that HTML manually over and over again, you can create a snippet that wraps the image with the appropriate HTML. For example, the code that goes before the image might include an opening <div> tag with a class applied to it, and the code that goes after the image can include the HTML for the caption and the closing </div> tag. In this case, in the "Insert before" field, you might type <div class="galleryItem">, and in the "Insert after" field, type the HTML that goes after the image, maybe something like <p>Caption goes here</p></div>.

7. **Select a "Preview type."**

The preview type determines how the snippet appears in the Snippets panel's Preview pane. *Design* means the snippet looks as it would in Design view—a table snippet appears as a table, for instance. *Code* means the code itself appears in the Preview pane, so a snippet for a horizontal rule would preview like this: <hr>. Use Code preview for snippets, like JavaScript code, that aren't visible in Design view.

8. **Click OK.**

Dreamweaver adds the snippet to the Snippets panel; you can then drop it in your web pages using any of the techniques described on page 831.

If you need to go back and edit a snippet—change the code, snippet type, description, or name—in the Snippets panel, select the snippet, and then click the Edit Snippet button + ✎. You can also right-click (Control-click) the snippet name, and then, from the shortcut menu, select Edit.

Whichever method you choose, the Snippet window in Figure 18-2 opens. Make your changes, and then click OK.

Organizing Snippets

To keep your snippets organized, you can create folders and store them by category. To add a folder to the Snippets panel, click ▣ (see Figure 18-1). An untitled folder appears; type in a name for it. If you select a folder before clicking ▣, Dreamweaver creates the new folder *inside* that folder. You can move folders around by dragging them into and out of other folders. However, folders are always listed in alphabetical order, so you can't re-order folders by dragging them in the Snippets panel.

TIP To drag a folder or snippet outside a folder to the top level of the Snippets list, you have to drag it all the way to the *bottom* of the Snippets panel, below any other folders. If you try to drag it to the top, Dreamweaver puts the folder or snippet inside the list's top folder.

To move a snippet into or out of its folder, simply drag it. If you drag a snippet over a closed folder without releasing the mouse, that folder expands to reveal the folders and snippets inside, if any.

To delete a snippet, select it in the Snippets panel, and then click the Delete Snippet button (the trash can; see Figure 18-1). Quicker yet, press Delete.

NOTE Storing lots of snippets slows down the Snippets panel. You'll probably never use many of the snippets that come with Dreamweaver, so it's best to remove the ones you don't use. An excellent candidate is the Legacy folder listed at the bottom of the panel. This folder, which really should be called the Old Garbage folder, is full of out-of-date, you-really-shouldn't-use-them snippets that Adobe added to much earlier versions of Dreamweaver. If you don't want to permanently delete these snippets, you can move them out of the Snippets folder in the main Adobe Dreamweaver CS6 Configuration folder and store them in a separate folder on your hard drive. (For more on the Configuration folder and how to find it, see the box on page 923.)

Built-In Snippets

Most of Dreamweaver's stock snippets offer solutions to problems you may never encounter, like a page footer with two lists of links and a copyright notice in it. In addition, many Dreamweaver snippets use older design techniques (like tables to lay out content) that are best avoided. However, most web developers find at least a few built-in snippets worth using. Here are some highlights:

- **Close Window Button**. When you create a pop-up window (page 691), this snippet lets you add a Close button to let people dismiss the window. The Close Window Button snippet (in the Form Elements folder) places a form button with the words "Close Window" on it, complete with the JavaScript necessary to close the window when your visitor clicks the button.

- **Dropdown Menus**. If you create a lot of forms for your sites (see Chapter 12), you'll find some other useful snippets in the Form Elements folder, especially in the Dropdown Menus subfolder. For example, the "Numbers 1-12" snippet inserts a menu with the numbers 1 to 12 already coded into it—great for capturing credit card expiration dates on an e-commerce site. (To create an even more useful drop-down snippet, see the tutorial at the end of this chapter.)

- **HTML Comments**. You can use the Comment Multi-Line snippet (in the Comments folder) to "comment-out," or hide, HTML. And this works in Design view, so just select the element you want to hide and apply this comment. This is a good way to temporarily hide some HTML—for example, to test what a page looks like with and without different chunks of HTML. To make the HTML visible again, go into Code view, because the Coding toolbar has a handy tool for quickly un-commenting HTML (see Figure 7-6).

- **IE Conditional Comments**. Sometimes older versions of Internet Explorer just don't get things right. This is frequently the case with CSS. To overcome browser differences, you sometimes need to provide IE with CSS code (or HTML or JavaScript code) that differs from the code you send to other browsers. You can insert special code (in the form of so-called conditional comments) that only IE understands. Dreamweaver provides a handful of code snippets (the last five listed in the Snippets panel's Comments folder) that create the necessary code for adding IE-oriented conditional comments. (For more information on why and how to use IE Conditional Comments, visit *http://bit.ly/H9m6UT*.)

Library Basics

Imagine this situation: You manage a relatively large website consisting of thousands of pages. At the bottom of each one sits a simple copyright notice: "Copyright My-BigCompany. We reserve all rights—national, international, commercial, noncommercial, and mineral—to the content contained on these pages."

Each time you add another page to your site, you *could* retype the copyright message, but that invites both typographic errors and carpal tunnel syndrome. And if you must *format* this text, too, you're in for even more work.

A Snippet of Caution

Snippets aren't as smart as other features in Dreamweaver. While the program usually warns you before you make a mistake, it doesn't make a peep if you incorrectly add a snippet.

For instance, when you use one of Dreamweaver's Form snippets to add, say, a text field to a page, it doesn't check to see if you're really putting the snippet into a form. Therefore, it doesn't let you know if you're missing the required <form> tag, and it certainly doesn't add the tag itself. Furthermore, if you're working in Code view, Dreamweaver lets you add snippets to the <head> section of a page (or even outside the <html> tags altogether), which is useful for creating dynamic web pages that include server-side programming, but creates messy and invalid HTML in normal web pages.

Furthermore, snippets don't take advantage of Dreamweaver's site management features to keep track of links or paths to images. Suppose you create a snippet that includes an image. If you insert that snippet into another page, the image may not show up correctly. If you create a snippet that includes a document-relative link (page 186) from one page to another page on your site, that link may not work when you add the snippet to yet another page.

So it's best to create snippets that don't involve images or links—but there are workarounds. For instance, you can create snippets with fake links—use nothing but the # symbol for the link, for example—and update the link after you insert the snippet into the page. For images, you can use Dreamweaver's Image Placeholder object (page 245) to simulate a graphic in a snippet (choose Insert→Image Objects→Image Placeholder). After you add the snippet to the page, update the placeholder with the details (location, size, and so on) for the real image file.

If you want to create reusable content that can keep track of links and images, see "Creating and Using Library Items" on page 838.

Fortunately, Dreamweaver's Library feature can turn anything you select in the document window (a paragraph, an image, a table) into a reusable chunk of HTML that you can easily drop into any Dreamweaver document. The Library, in other words, is a great place to store copyright notices, navigation bars, announcements, or any other chunks of frequently used HTML.

So far, this description sounds pretty much like the snippets described in the previous section. But Library items have added power: When you add HTML to a web page using a Library item, that code remains linked to the original Library item, the one Dreamweaver created and stored in your site. Thanks to this link, whenever you update the *original* Library item, you get a chance to update every page that uses that item, too.

Suppose your company is bought, and the legal department orders you to change the copyright notice to "Copyright MyBigCompany, a subsidiary of MuchBigger-Company" on each of the website's *10,000 pages*. If you had cleverly inserted the original copyright notice as a Library item, you could take care of this task in the blink of an eye. Just open the item in the Library, make the required changes, save it, and let Dreamweaver update all the pages for you (see Figure 18-3).

NOTE   You can achieve a similar effect to Dreamweaver Library items using Server-side Includes. This option, discussed on page 937, is a bit more technical but provides even faster site updates than Library items.

Compared to snippets, Library items are much smarter. They possess the unique ability to update the same material on an entire site's worth of files in seconds, and can successfully deal with links and images. Unlike snippets, however, Dreamweaver's Library feature is site-specific: Each site you set up in Dreamweaver has its own Library, and Dreamweaver stores that Library's files along with all the site's other files. You can't use a Library item from one site when you're working on a page from another site.

FIGURE 18-3

Library items are great for small chunks of HTML that you use frequently on a site. Here, on an old version of The Museum of Modern Art's home page, many of the navigation options on the page (circled) are Library items. If the Museum needed to add or remove a navigation link, they could update the Library item to change every page on the site in one simple step. In fact, since a Library item is a chunk of HTML, you could replace the left-hand navigation bar with plain-text links (instead of graphics), or any other valid HTML code.

■ Creating and Using Library Items

To create a Library item, start by opening the Library window. Click the Assets tab (to the right of the Files tab) or choose Window→Assets, and then click the Library items button (it looks like an open book, circled in Figure 18-4) to reveal the Library category.

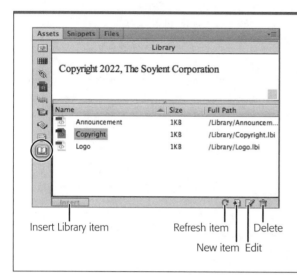

FIGURE 18-4

The Assets panel's Library category lists the name, file size, and location of each Library item in the currently open site. When you select an item from the list, you see a small preview. In this example, the Library item "Copyright" is, shockingly, a copyright notice.

Insert Library item   Refresh item   Delete

New item   Edit

NOTE Keep in mind that Library items can contain only page elements that appear in the document window—in other words, only HTML from the <body> section of a web page. You can't include anything that appears in the <head> of a page, like Cascading Style Sheets, Spry widgets (Chapter 13), or meta tags. This means you can't store Dreamweaver behaviors or Spry widgets in your Library (but you *can* include them with a Dreamweaver template, discussed in the next chapter). Furthermore, Library items must include a complete set of HTML tags—both an opening and a closing tag—as well as all the tags necessary to complete the original object. For example, Dreamweaver doesn't let you turn just a single cell, row, or column of a table into a Library item. If you try, Dreamweaver will add the *entire* table to the Library.

Now select the part of your document you want to save as a Library item: a blob of text, a graphic, or whatever. This might be just a few words, or an entire paragraph or headline. You can even select a <div> tag (page 438) containing other tags.

TIP Use the Tag Selector (see page 26) to make sure you choose the precise tag you want. Sometimes, though, you want the content *inside* a tag. To select the contents inside a table cell, for example, click at the beginning of the content, and then drag until you select everything in the cell, or, click in the cell and choose Edit→Select All.

Next, add the selection to the Library. As you may expect, Dreamweaver provides several ways to do this:

- Drag the highlighted selection into the list of Library items.

- Click the New Item button (Figure 18-4).

- Choose Modify→Library→Add Object to Library.

The new item appears in the Assets panel, bearing the jaunty name "Untitled." Type in a more useful name, such as *Copyright notice* or *Logo*. Your new Library element is now ready to use.

NOTE Even though you can't turn a CSS style into a Library item, you *can* turn HTML that you've styled with CSS into a Library item. For example, you can add to the Library a paragraph that has a CSS class style applied to it. When you attempt to add this paragraph to the Library, Dreamweaver warns you that the item may not look the same when you place it in other documents—because the style sheet information doesn't come along for the ride. To make sure the Library item appears correctly, make sure you attach the same style sheet to any page where you use that item. External style sheets (see page 123) make this easy.

Adding Library Items to a Page

To add a Library item to a web page, drag it out of the Assets panel's Library items list onto your page. (The long way: Click to plant your insertion point on the page, click the Library item you want in the Assets panel, and then, in the Assets panel, click the Insert button, shown in Figure 18-4.)

NOTE Library Items (.lbi files) also appear in the Files panel in a site's Library folder. Dragging a Library item from the Files panel to a page, however, *doesn't* insert it into the page. It adds the name of the Library item file (not its contents) with a link to the .lbi file—not something you want to do.

When you insert a Library item into a page (or turn a selected item *into* a Library item), it, sprouts a light yellow background. The highlighting indicates that Dreamweaver intends to treat the item as a single object, even though it may include many different HTML elements. You can select it or drag it around, but you can't edit it. (Unfortunately, if you turn a nontransparent graphic into a Library item—like a logo, for example—Dreamweaver doesn't give you the helpful yellow background.)

Remember, too, that the placed Library item links to the original item in the Library. The copy in your document automatically changes to reflect any changes you make to the copy in the Library, using the technique described next.

TIP At some point, you may want to sever the connection between the Library and a Library item you placed on a page—to modify a copyright notice on just a single page, for example. Select the item on the page, and then, in the Property Inspector, click "Detach from original" (Figure 18-5). Dreamweaver removes the comment tags (see the box on page 843), thus breaking the link to the Library.

You can also insert the HTML of a Library item *without* maintaining a link to the Library by pressing the Ctrl (Option) key as you add the item to your document. This treats the HTML more like a snippet, since Dreamweaver doesn't update the HTML on this page if you change the original Library file.

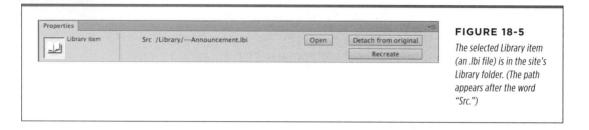

FIGURE 18-5

The selected Library item (an .lbi file) is in the site's Library folder. (The path appears after the word "Src.")

■ Editing Library Items

You'll appreciate the real power of Library items when it's time to make a change. When you update the original file in the Library, all the pages graced with that linked item update, too.

Start by opening the Library, as described on page 838. Then:

1. **Open the Library item you want to edit.**

   You can do this by double-clicking the Assets panel's Library item, by highlighting it and then clicking the Edit button (Figure 18-4), or by highlighting a Library item on a web page and then, in the Property Inspector, clicking the Open button (Figure 18-5). (You can also open the Library item file—an .lbi file—in the Library folder of your site's root by double-clicking it in the Files panel.)

   Dreamweaver opens what looks like a normal web page, but it contains only the text, graphics, or other elements of the Library file.

2. **Edit away.**

   A Library item is only a selection of HTML, it's not a complete web page. That means you must not add *page* properties, like a title or background color, or one of the behaviors discussed in Chapter 13. (Dreamweaver actually lets you do this, but that adds invalid HTML to the Library item as well as to every page that uses that Library item.) Also, you can insert Library items only in the body of a web page, so stick with objects that would normally appear in the document window, such as links, images, tables, and text. Don't add any code that appears in the head of a web page, such as Cascading Style Sheets, meta tags, behaviors, or Spry widgets.

   Since Library items can't contain style sheets, if the HTML in your Library item relies on a style, you'll have trouble previewing it correctly. Dreamweaver's Design-Time Style Sheet tool comes in handy here. It lets you temporarily "add" a style sheet while you design a page, without actually adding the CSS code to the page. For more on this useful feature, turn to page 405.

NOTE Don't turn any of Dreamweaver's Spry widgets into Library items. For example, if you use the Spry Menu Bar (page 210), you might be tempted to turn the menu into a Library item so you can reuse it. Problem is, all Spry features combine HTML, JavaScript, and CSS code placed in different parts of a page's code. When you select the Spry widget on the page and then turn it into a Library item, only the HTML goes along for the ride—the CSS, which makes the widget look good, and the JavaScript, which makes the widget work, aren't included. The solution? Use Dreamweaver templates instead (see the next chapter).

3. **Choose File→Save.**

   Dreamweaver checks to see if any pages use the Library item and, if they do, it opens the Update Library Items window. A list of the pages that use that item appears.

4. **Click Update.**

   Dreamweaver opens the Update Pages window, updates the HTML in all the pages that use the Library item, and then lists all the files that it changed.

   On the other hand, you don't necessarily have to click Update. Perhaps you have a lot of changes to make to the Library item, and you just want to save the work you've done so far. You're not done editing it yet, so you don't want to waste time updating pages you'll just have to update again later. You can always update them another time (see the box on page 865); to do that, click Don't Update. (Once you finish making changes and save the file for the final time, *then* you can update the site.)

5. **Click Done.**

   As you can see, the Library is an incredible timesaver that greatly simplifies the process of changing common page elements.

Renaming Library Elements

To rename something in your Library, click its name in the Assets panel. Pause briefly, click again, and Dreamweaver highlights the name, ready for your edit. Type the new name, and then press Enter (Return).

If you already added the item to your web pages, Dreamweaver prompts you to update those pages. Click Update. Otherwise, the link between those pages and the Library breaks.

NOTE If you accidentally click Don't Update, don't panic. Simply change the Library item back to its original name, and then *re*-rename it. And don't forget to click Update this time!

Deleting Library Elements

You can delete unnecessary elements from your Library any time, but use caution. When you delete something from the Library, Dreamweaver leaves behind every copy of it you placed on your pages—complete with links to the now-deleted Library item.

In other words, you can't edit the copies embedded in your web pages until you break those links. If you do indeed want to edit them, you have to break the links manually on each page where the Library item appears by selecting the item and then clicking the "Detach from original" button (see Figure 18-5).

Now that you've been warned, here are the instructions to get rid of a Library item. In the Assets panel, click the item, and then do one of the following:

- Click 🗑.

- Press Delete.

- Right-click (Control-click) the item's name, and then, from the shortcut menu, choose Delete.

TIP If you ever accidentally delete an item from the Library, you can re-create it, provided you used it on one of the web pages in your site.

NOTE Open the page containing the Library item, and then click the item to select it. In the Property Inspector, click Recreate (Figure 18-5) to make the item anew. A new item appears in the Library, using the name and HTML from the item you selected.

■ Snippets and Library Tutorial

In this tutorial, you'll do two things: First, create some useful snippets for common form elements. Second, you'll turn an announcement on the Café Soylent Green site into a reusable Library item, and then add it to several pages on the site.

NOTE You need to download the tutorial files from *www.sawmac.com* to complete this tutorial. See the Note on page 54.

Once you download the tutorial files and open Dreamweaver, set up a new site as described on page 40: Name the site *Snippets and Library*, and then select the Chapter18 folder (it's inside the MM_DWCS6 folder). In a nutshell: choose Site→New Site. In the Site Setup window, type *Snippets and Library* into the Site Name field, click the folder icon next to the Local Site Folder field, navigate to and select the Chapter18 folder, and then click Select or Choose. Finally, click Save.

Under the Hood of Library Items

Behind the scenes, Dreamweaver stores the HTML for Library items in basic text files. Those files' names end with the extension .lbi, and they stay in the Library folder inside your local site folder.

When you insert a Library item into a web page, Dreamweaver inserts the item's HTML, and adds a set of comment tags. These tags refer to the original Library file, and help Dreamweaver remember where the Library item begins and ends. For instance, if you turn the text "Copyright 2011" into a Library item called *copyright*, and insert it into a web page, Dreamweaver adds the following HTML to the page:

```
<!-- #BeginLibraryItem "/Library/
copyright.lbi" -->Copyright 2011<!--
#EndLibraryItem-->
```

Avoid using hyphens in Library item names. Why? Since HTML comments use hyphens, <!-- -->, some versions of Firefox get tripped up by additional hyphens, and respond by hiding the contents of the item or displaying raw HTML code instead.

In addition, although you can't edit a Library item on a page in Design view, you can muck around with the code in Code view. In the example above, you could change 2011 to 2012 in Code view. Don't do it! Dreamweaver obliterates your changes the minute you try to save the web page. If you want to make a change to a Library item, edit the *original* Library item, or detach the item from the Library (as described in the Tip on page 839) and then edit it.

Creating a Snippet

1. **With your site freshly defined, make sure you have the Files panel open.**

   If it isn't, press the F8 key (Shift-⌘-F) or choose Window→Files.

2. **In the Files panel, double-click the file *snippet.html*.**

   A page with several form pull-down menus opens. The page includes menus for the months of the year, the names of US states, and the numbers 1 to 31. You can use menus like these on your web pages for a variety of jobs: for example, to let readers specify task to-do dates, to select a destination state for a product shipment, or simply select a month for their astrological sign. Dreamweaver's own snippets don't include these useful menus, but, fortunately, you can add them yourself.

3. **In Design view, click the first form menu at the top of the page, the one to the right of the words "Months of year."**

   You've selected the menu and its underlying HTML code. To add this as a snippet, you need to open the Snippets panel.

4. **Choose Window→Snippets.**

   The Snippets panel is your control center for adding, editing, and deleting snippets.

5. **At the bottom of the panel, click the New Snippet button (Figure 18-1).**

   The Snippet window opens. Dreamweaver automatically copies the code for the menu into the "Insert before" window. You just need to name the snippet, and add a few more details.

6. **In the Name box, type *Month Menu*, and in the description box, type *A list of month names, with numeric values* as pictured in Figure 18-6.**

   The snippet's name and description will appear in the Snippets panel once you finish creating the snippet. In this case, the description you wrote identifies what appears in the menu (a list of month names) and what value the snippet applies when a visitor selects a month from the list—a "numeric value." In other words, your description identifies the name/value pair for this form field. (See Chapter 12 for more information on how forms work.)

7. **Select "Insert block."**

   Clicking this button identifies the snippet as a chunk of standalone HTML, and Dreamweaver changes the code's label from "Insert before" to "Insert code." You can simply plop down standalone code like this anywhere on a page.

   If you want a snippet to wrap around a selected graphic or text, like a link or table cell. Select the "Wrap selection" button and include the closing code in the "Insert after" box.

8. **At the bottom of the window, select the Design button.**

   You just told Dreamweaver to display the snippet visually when you select it in the Snippets panel. In other words, when you select this snippet in the panel, Dreamweaver previews the form menu in your page-in-progress, it doesn't display just a bunch of code.

9. **The window should now look like Figure 18-6.** Click OK to create your new snippet.

   The snippet should now appear in the Snippets panel, ready for you to insert it into a page.

NOTE If you select a folder (or a file inside a folder) in the Snippets panel when you create a snippet, Dreamweaver stores the new snippet in that folder. To move it out of the folder and up to the top-level list of the Snippets panel, drag the snippet—Month Menu here—to the very bottom of the panel. Or, to move the snippet to another folder in the Snippets panel, just drag the snippet to that folder—in this case, the Form Elements folder would be appropriate.

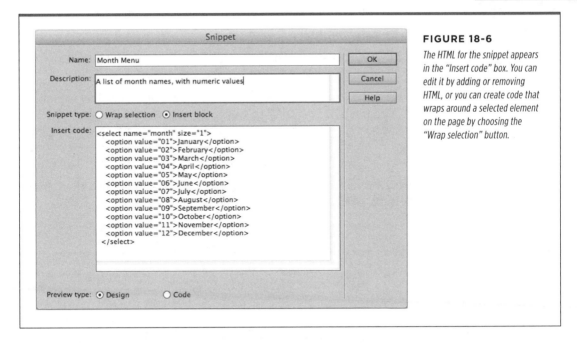

FIGURE 18-6

The HTML for the snippet appears in the "Insert code" box. You can edit it by adding or removing HTML, or you can create code that wraps around a selected element on the page by choosing the "Wrap selection" button.

10. **Select the Files panel by clicking the Files tab or by pressing the F8 key (Shift-⌘-F), and then double-click the file *reservation.html*.**

This step opens Café Soylent Green's reservation form. You'll insert your new snippet as part of this form.

11. **Return to the Snippet panel once again by clicking the Snippets tab or by choosing Window→Snippets.**

Now for the moment of truth.

12. **Drag your new snippet—Month Menu—from the Snippets panel to the right of the label "Month" (below "number of diners" drop-down menu).**

Ta-da! Dreamweaver adds the new menu. Now, whenever you need to add a menu that lists the months of the year, don't bother creating it from scratch, just use the snippet!

13. **At the top of the document window, click the *snippet.html* tab.** Click the third menu (the one with days of the month), and then repeat steps 5–12.

Name this new snippet *Days of month* and, as a description for the snippet, type *numerical days of the month*. Insert this new snippet to the right of the label "Day" (below the menu you just added to the form) on the reservation.html page. You can close the file *snippet.html* when you're done.

Creating a Library Item

Now you'll see one way in which Dreamweaver's powerful site management tools can help you create and update your websites more effectively:

1. **Open the file about.html.**

   For example, double-click its name in the Files panel, or choose File→Open and select the *about.html* file in the site's root folder.

   In the main column, near the middle of the page is a green box that says, "Café Soylent Green is now open 7 days a week!" This box is a simple <span> element with some text in it. The cafe uses this box for important announcements, and it appears on various pages of the site. Since you need to keep these announcements up to date, creating an easily updated Library item is an efficient choice.

2. **Click anywhere inside the box (in the text, for example), and then, in the Tag Selector, click <span.announcement> (Figure 18-7).**

   You can use this selected <span> as the basis for a new Library item.

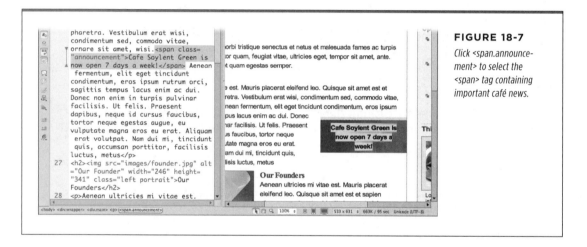

FIGURE 18-7

Click <span.announcement> to select the <span> tag containing important café news.

3. **Choose Window→Assets, and then click the Library button.**

   The Assets panel opens, and displays the Library category.

4. **On the Assets panel, click the New Library Item button (Figure 18-4).**

   A warning message appears, saying that the Library item may not look the same in other pages. Dreamweaver's telling you that Library items can contain only HTML from the body of a web page—they can't include Cascading Style Sheets. (You can still include HTML that has a style applied to it, just as this <div> tag does, so long as you make sure that any *pages* to which you add the Library item have the appropriate style sheets attached.)

The text in this example *is* formatted using a style sheet, so, sure enough, it won't look the same in pages that don't have the same style sheet applied to them. In this exercise, however, this isn't a problem, since all the pages on the site share the same linked external style sheet.

Click OK to dismiss the warning (and feel free to turn on the "Don't warn me again" checkbox while you're at it). The announcement item appears in the Library list, with the "Untitled" name highlighted for editing.

5. **Type *news* to name the new item on the Assets panel, and then press Enter (Return).**

   You just checked this standard blob of text into your Library. It's ready to use anywhere else on your site. Notice that the span's background has changed to yellow in the document window—that's Dreamweaver's way of letting you know that this is a Library item.

6. **In the Files panel, double-click the file *hours.html*.**

   You'll frequently jump between the Files panel and the Assets panel, so the keyboard shortcut to open the Files panel comes in handy: click the F8 key (Shift-⌘-F). The Assets panel doesn't have a keyboard shortcut, but you can create one as described on page 911.

   The Hours & Directions page doesn't have an announcement box, so you'll add one.

7. **Switch back to the Assets panel and drag the "news" Library item to the left of the letter "H" in the second headline—"Hours"— as pictured in Figure 18-8.**

   If you accidentally drop the Library somewhere else on the page, just choose Edit→Undo and try again. You can recognize the newly inserted Library item by its yellow background. Click the text in the item, and notice that you can't edit it; Dreamweaver treats the item as a single object.

8. **Add the "news" Library item to two other pages on the site: *ingredients .html*, and *philosophy.html*.**

   Open the page (by double-clicking its name in the Files window), and then repeat step 7. You can actually insert this Library item anywhere you want on the page.

   (You can close and save the pages as you go, or leave them open. Leave at least one open at the end and go on to step 9.)

9. **Save the pages you added the Library item to by selecting File→Save All.**

10. **This just in!**

    New things are happening at the Café all the time, so it's time to update this announcement. Fortunately, you used a Library item, so it's easy to make the change.

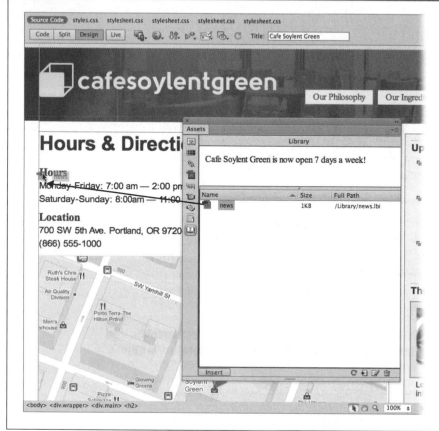

FIGURE 18-8

In addition to dragging a Library item into the document window, you can insert the item by finding the insertion point in the document window, and then, in the Assets panel, clicking the Insert button.

11. **In the Library in the Assets panel, double-click the "news" item.**

    The Library item opens up, ready for editing. Notice that it doesn't have any of the formatting you saw on the web page—that's because there's no CSS file attached to the item, so you see only the plain HTML version of the announcement box.

12. **Select the text and type *"Cafe temporarily (we hope) closed due to health inspection. We are sorry for the inconvenience."*** Choose File→Save.

    The Update Library Items dialog box appears (Figure 18-9), listing the four pages in the site that use this announcement box.

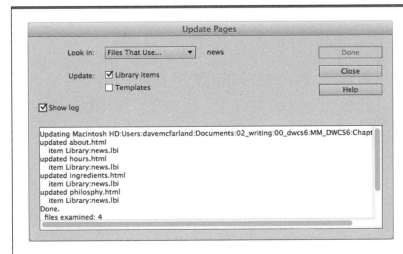

FIGURE 18-9

The Update Pages dialog box appears whenever you update a Library item. If you turn on the "Show log" checkbox, Dreamweaver displays all the changes it made, including the names of the pages it updated and the total number of pages changed. This window also appears when you update Template files, as discussed in the next chapter.

13. **Click Update.**

    Dreamweaver opens the Update Pages dialog box, and then updates all the pages that use the "news" item.

14. **Click Close to close the Update Pages dialog box.**

    And now if you open *about.html, hours.html,* philosophy.html and *ingredients .html,* you'll see that Dreamweaver updated the announcement box on all four pages.

    Now imagine that you just used this auto-update feature on a 10,000-page site. Sit back and smile.

TIP If you use a particular Library item on some pages of your site but not all, you'll want to know which pages you changed so you can move just those pages up to your server. You won't want to upload your entire website when you change just a handful of pages. Dreamweaver's Select Recently Modified command can help (see the box on page 767). You can also use Dreamweaver's synchronization feature to make sure you get the most recent pages from your computer to your server (see page 813).

Templates

Some web designers handcraft their sites with loving care, changing layouts, colors, fonts, banners, and navigation page by page. But that approach isn't always practical—or desirable.

Consistency from page to page is a good thing. Web pages that look and act similarly reassure visitors; they can concentrate on each page's unique content when the navigation bar and left sidebar stay the same. But even more important, a handcrafted approach to web design is often unrealistic when you need to crank out content on a deadline.

That's where *templates* come in. Frequently, the underlying design of many website pages is identical. An employee directory at a company site, for instance, may consist of individual pages dedicated to each employee. Each page has the same navigation bar, banner, footer, and layout. Only a few particulars change from page to page, like the employee's name, photograph, and contact information. This is a perfect case for templates.

This chapter shows you how templates can make quick work of building pages where most, if not all, of the pages use repetitive elements.

■ Template Basics

Templates let you build pages that share a similar structure and graphic identity, quickly and without having to worry about accidentally deleting or changing elements. Templates come in handy when you design a site where other, less Dreamweaver-savvy, individuals will build individual pages. By using a template, you, the godlike Dreamweaver guru, can limit the areas that these underlings can modify in each page.

A new page based on a template—also called a *template instance*, or a *child page*—looks just like the template, except that page authors can edit only designated areas of the page, called, logically enough, *editable regions*. In Figure 19-1, you can see that the question-and-answer text is an editable region; the rest of the page remains consistent (and is, in fact, locked).

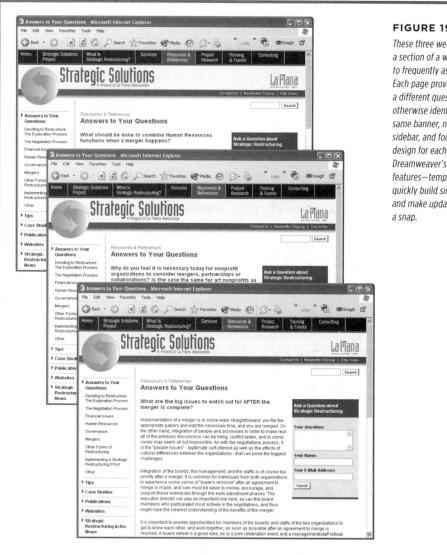

FIGURE 19-1

These three web pages are part of a section of a website dedicated to frequently asked questions. Each page provides the answer to a different question, but they're otherwise identical, sharing the same banner, navigation buttons, sidebar, and footer. Why rebuild the design for each one? Enter one of Dreamweaver's great timesaving features—templates—which help you quickly build similar-looking pages, and make updating page designs a snap.

A Dreamweaver template can be very basic, consisting of nothing more than one or more areas that a page author can change (the editable regions) along with other areas that he can't edit (the *locked regions*). At the same time, you can build templates that give page authors an impressive amount of flexibility. Here's an overview of the features you can tap when you create and use templates:

- **Editable regions**. These are the basic building blocks of a template. An editable region is that part of a page—a paragraph, the contents of a <div> tag, or a headline, for example—that page authors can change as they build template-based pages. Templates can include multiple editable regions—a sidebar and the main content section of a page, for example.

- **Editable tag attributes**. There may be times when you want to make a particular tag *property* editable. For example, say you have a banner ad at the top of a page—the banner ad is just a basic image file, and each page should have a different ad. You want to make sure that no one can delete the image (after all, those ads are paying for your site), but you do want someone to be able to swap in a new image. In other words, no one should mess with the <img> tag; they should only be able to assign a new file by changing the <img> tag's *src* attribute. To keep someone from deleting the image but still allow them to change pictures, you'd make just the *src* property editable. (You could also make the image's *alt* property editable, and if the *width* and *height* properties vary from image to image, you can make those editable as well.)

  Or you might want a unique headline design for each section of your site. To get that, when you build the site template, assign a class to the <body> tag and make the class name editable. Then, when you create pages for different sections of the site, you add a class name specific to each section. For example, for a site's About Us page, you could set the body's class to *.about*. Once you do, you can use a descendent selector (like *.about h1*) to create a custom style for all the headlines on just that page. On template-based pages showcasing your company's products, change the class to *.products*, and then add a descendent selector style *.products h1* to your style sheet and you'll have a unique look for all the <h1> tags on product pages.

- **Repeating regions and repeating tables**. Some web pages, like those that showcase the products a company sells, include *lists* of items. For pages like these, Dreamweaver lets you define *repeatable regions* in your template. For example, your design for a page of product listings might include each product's picture, name, and price, organized in a table with multiple rows (Chapter 6). As the template builder, you may not know in advance how many products the page will eventually list, so you can't fully design the page. You can, however, use Dreamweaver to define a row—or any selection of HTML—as a repeating region, so that page authors can add new rows of product information as needed.

- **Optional regions and editable optional regions**. *Optional regions* make templates even more flexible. They let you show or hide content—from a single paragraph to an entire <div> tag full of other tags—on a page-by-page basis.

Suppose you create a template that showcases your company's products. Some products go on sale while others remain full price, so you add an *optional region* to the product descriptions that displays a big "On Sale!" logo. When you create a new product page, you could *show* the optional region for products that are on sale and keep it *hidden* for the others.

Editable optional regions are similar, but have the added benefit of being editable. Maybe you're creating a template for an employee directory, giving each employee his or her own page with contact information. Some employees want their picture displayed on the page, while others don't (you know the type). Solution: Add an editable optional region that includes space for a photo. You add a different photo for each page, except for the shyer types; for them, you simply hide the photo area.

Facilitating page creation is only one of the benefits of templates. You'll also find that templates greatly simplify the process of updating a website's design. Like Library items (Chapter 18), pages based on templates retain a reference to the original template file. Dreamweaver passes any changes you make to that template to all the pages you created from it, which can save you hours of time and trouble when it comes time to update your site's look or structure. Imagine how much time you'll save when your boss asks you to add "just one more" button to a site's navigation bar. Instead of updating thousands of pages by hand, you need to update only a single template file.

■ Creating a Template

The first step in creating a template is to build a basic web page and tell Dreamweaver that you'd like to use it as a template. You do that two ways: build a regular, plain old web page and turn it into a template, or create a blank, empty template file and add sections for text, graphics, tables, and other content.

Turning a Web Page into a Template

The easiest way to create a template is to base it on a web page in your current site folder. Although you can create templates based on web pages that *aren't* part of your current local site, you may run into problems with links and paths to images, as described in a moment.

Once you open the page, choose File→ Save As Template or, in the Common category of the Insert panel (see Figure 19-2), click the Templates button and then select Make Template from the drop-down menu. The Save As Template window (Figure 19-3) includes the name of the current local site in the Site drop-down menu; meanwhile, all templates for that site show up in the Existing Templates box.

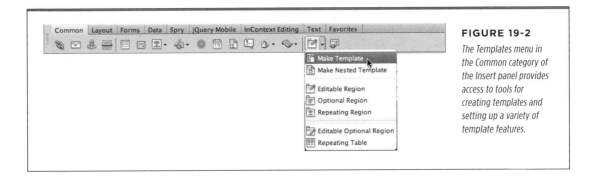

FIGURE 19-2

*The Templates menu in
the Common category of
the Insert panel provides
access to tools for
creating templates and
setting up a variety of
template features.*

NOTE At this point, you could theoretically use the Site drop-down menu to save a template in any local site folder you set up (see Chapter 15 for a discussion of local sites), but be careful with this option. If your page contains images, external style sheets, and links and you save it as a template for another local site, Dreamweaver doesn't copy the images or style sheets from the first site folder to the second one. As a result, the paths to the image files and links don't work correctly, and the page won't show any styling.

If you must use a page from one site as a template for another, copy the web page, graphics, and style sheets into the new site's root folder, open the page from there, and create the template as described here.

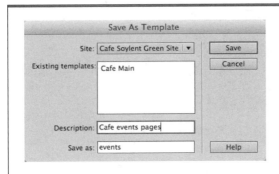

FIGURE 19-3

The Save As Template dialog box lets you save your template in any of the local site folders you defined. Stick to your current local site to avoid broken links, missing images, disappearing style sheets, and similar problems.

Dreamweaver includes a Description field where you can add a brief note characterizing the template. The description appears when you select a template as the basis for new pages. It's useful when *other* people build a site using your templates and aren't sure whether *templateA1, templateA2,* or *templateA3* is the correct choice; a simple note that says "Use this template for all FAQ pages" makes it clear.

Finally, in the "Save as" box, type a name for the new template, and then click Save. Choose Yes when Dreamweaver asks if you want to update links on the page. If you choose No, all page-relative links break, styles from external style sheets won't work, and all the images on the page appear as broken-image icons.

Dreamweaver saves the page in the Templates folder of your local site root folder. It adds the extension .dwt to indicate that it's a Dreamweaver template. (For dynamic web pages, Dreamweaver adds the .dwt *before* the file's extension. For example, a PHP template may have a name like *maintemplate.dwt.php*.)

NOTE Don't get carried away building too many templates for a site. It doesn't make any sense to create 20 templates for a 20-page site. You should only need a handful of templates to cover the different types of pages you have on a site. In fact, you might just need a single template to dictate the look of all your site's pages.

Building a Template from Scratch

It's easiest to create a web page first and then save it as a template, but you can also build a template from scratch. Open the Asset panel's Templates category by choosing Window→Assets and then clicking 🔲 (see Figure 19-4). Then click the New Template button at the bottom of the Assets panel. Once Dreamweaver adds a new, untitled template to the list, give it a new name. Something descriptive like "Press release" or "Employee page" helps you keep track of your templates.

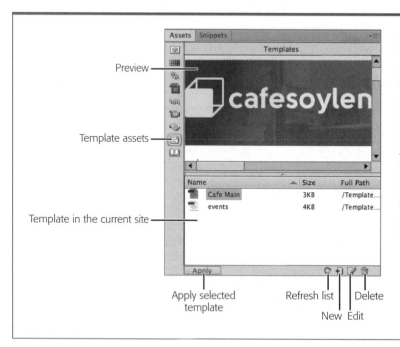

FIGURE 19-4

The Templates category of the Assets panel lists the name, file size, and location of each template in the current local site. The Apply button applies a template to the current open web page. The Refresh Site List button updates the list of templates—if you just created a template and don't see it listed, click this button. The New Template button creates a new, blank template in the Templates folder. Select a template from the list and click the Edit Template button to open and edit the template.

After you create a blank template, open it by double-clicking its name in the Assets panel (or by selecting its name and then clicking the Edit button at the bottom of the Assets panel). It opens just like any web page so you can get busy designing it with the unchanging elements of your site—logo, navigation bar, and so on. You'll learn how to add editable regions next.

Defining Editable Regions

Your next task is to specify which parts of your template you want locked and which you want editable. By default, *everything* on a page is locked. After all, the main reason to use a template is to maintain a consistent, unchanging design and structure among pages. To make a template usable, you have to define the area or areas that page authors *can* change.

To add an editable region to a template, start by selecting the part of the page you want to make changeable. You can designate as editable anything in the document window (that is, any HTML between the <body> tags).

NOTE You can always add Cascading Style Sheets, JavaScript code, and meta tags to the <head> of a template-based page. Any <head> content in the original template files stays put in the page you create from it, however. For example, you can't remove an external style sheet applied to a template from a page based on that template.

For templates you create from scratch, place your cursor at the point where you want to insert an editable region. For templates you build from an existing page, drag across your page to select the elements you wish to make editable, or, for greater precision, use the Tag Selector (see page 26) to make sure you select the exact HTML you want.

Now tell Dreamweaver that you want to make the selected elements editable. You can use any of these techniques:

- In the Common category of the Insert panel (Figure 19-2), select Editable Region from the Template menu.

- Choose Insert→Template Objects→Editable Region.

- Press Ctrl+Alt+V (⌘-Option-V).

- Right-click (Control-click) the selection and then, from the shortcut menu, choose Templates→New Editable Region.

When the New Editable Region dialog box appears, type a name for the region (you can't use the same name twice) and then click OK. You return to your template, where the name you gave the region appears in a small blue tab above the editable region, outlined in blue.

> **NOTE** When you use CSS to lay out a page, you usually create separate <div> tags (see page 438) for the different areas of a page. For example, you might wrap the main content area in one div, the banner in another, and the footer in yet another. For divs you use to structure the layout of a page, you want to make them editable by selecting just the *contents* of the <div> tag, not the tag itself. Here's one instance where you want to *avoid* the Tag Selector (page 26), which selects the entire div element, tags and all. If you turned the <div> tag into an editable region, someone modifying the page could delete the tag entirely, which could wreak untold havoc on your CSS-based layout.
>
> Fortunately, Dreamweaver has a handy shortcut for selecting just the contents of a <div> tag. Click anywhere inside the <div> tag and then press Ctrl+A (⌘-A) or choose Edit→Select All. Then turn this selection into an editable region, and the <div> tags will remain *outside* that region, so no one can inadvertently delete them.

You may find that a single editable region is all you need—for example, when you put text for a product review in just a single area of a page (a section of a page enclosed by a <div> tag, for example). However, if you need to be able to edit *multiple* areas of a page, just add more editable regions to the template. For instance, when you create a template for an employee page, you can create editable regions for the employee's name, telephone number, and photo. If you change your mind and want to lock a region, select the editable region and then choose Modify→Templates→Remove Template Markup. Dreamweaver removes the code that makes the region editable.

> **WARNING** You can rename an editable region by clicking the blue tab on the template page and typing a new name in the Property Inspector. However, if you already built pages based on the template, that's not a good idea. Because template-based pages identify regions by their name, Dreamweaver can lose track of where content should go when you rename a region. Skip ahead to Figure 19-18 for a workaround.

Once you add at least one editable region to a template, you're ready to start adding pages to your site and filling them up with content. (Of course, you may need some of the more advanced template features—you'll learn how to add them to a template starting on page 866.)

FREQUENTLY ASKED QUESTION

When Save Won't Behave

I keep getting an error message when I save my template. What's going on?

If you add an editable region *inside* certain block-level elements, like a paragraph or a heading, Dreamweaver pops up a warning message when you save the template, explaining that you can't create additional paragraphs or headings inside this region on any pages you build from this template. This just means that you selected the *contents* of a paragraph or heading (not the actual paragraph or heading tag itself) when you made the region editable. Dreamweaver considers anything outside the editable region locked, so you can't change those tags. Since it's improper HTML to have a paragraph, heading, or other block-level elements inside *another* paragraph or heading, Dreamweaver won't let you add a paragraph, heading, bulleted list, or any other block-level element inside the editable contents of the locked paragraph or heading.

This characteristic may not be such a bad thing, however. Imagine you created a template for other people to use as they build a website. You have a Heading 1 with a style applied to it, and you want to make sure it looks the same on every page.

You wouldn't want anyone changing the heading tag, and possibly erasing the style. In addition, you don't want them to change the Heading 1 to a Heading 2 or a Heading 3; nor do you want them to completely erase the <h1> tag and type paragraph after paragraph of their random thoughts. You just want them to type in new text for the page title. Selecting just the text inside the heading (as opposed to the <h1> tag *and* the text) and turning it into an editable region does just that. Viva micro-management!

If this is in fact what you want to do, you can save yourself the bother of having to constantly see the "You placed an editable region inside a block tag" warning box each time you save the template by simply turning on the "Don't show me this message again" checkbox. However, if you made a mistake and *do* want to allow people to change the heading or add more headings and paragraphs in this region, you need to do two things: First, unlock the editable region you created (see above), and then select the text *and* the tag (the Tag Selector [page 26] is the best way to make sure you select a tag), and turn that selection into an editable region.

Building Pages Based on a Template

Building a template is only a prelude to the actual work of building your site. Once you finish your template, it's time to produce pages.

To create a new document based on a template, choose File→New to open the New Document window (see Figure 19-5). Click the "Page from Template" button, and then, from the Site list, select the site you're working on. All the templates for that site appear in the right-hand column. Select the template you wish to use, and then click Create.

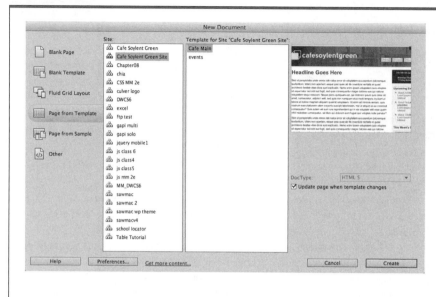

FIGURE 19-5

The Page From Template category of the New Document window lets you build new pages based on a template. Be careful of the middle "Site" column. It lets you pick any site that you've set up in Dreamweaver and open a new page based on a template from that site. It's a bad idea to pick a site other than the one you're working on. In fact, if you do, Dreamweaver doesn't bring along any of the assets of that template (for example, style sheets, images, linked-to pages, and so on) so you'll end up with a broken template-based page. Why, Adobe, why?

NOTE If you don't want your new web page linked to a template (so that future changes to the template won't affect this page), turn off the "Update page when template changes" checkbox. The result is a new page that looks just like the template, but has no locked regions; you can edit the entire page. This is a useful technique when you want to create a new template starting with the general design and structure of an existing one. (Be aware that Dreamweaver remembers this choice the next time you create a new template-based page. In other words, future pages you create from a template will *also* be unlinked—unless you remember to turn the "Update page" checkbox back on.)

A new web page document opens, based on the template, bearing a tab in the upper-right corner that identifies the underlying template name. Dreamweaver outlines any editable regions in blue; a small blue tab displays each region's name (Figure 19-6).

Dreamweaver makes it obvious which areas of a page are off-limits; your cursor changes to a "forbidden" symbol (a circle with a line through it) when you venture into a locked area.

Editable head content   Tabs of editable regions   Template name

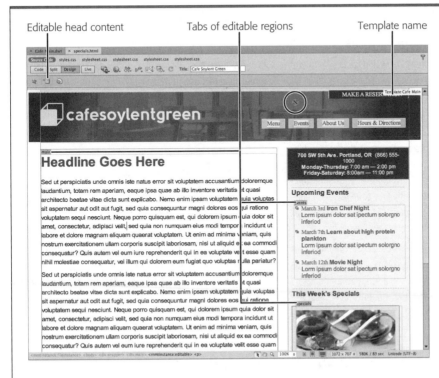

FIGURE 19-6

This page is based on a template called "Cafe main," as you can tell from the little tab in the document window's upper-right corner. You can modify this page's editable regions, which Dreamweaver labels with small tabs. In this example, one editable region, called "main," fills the main section of the page, while two additional editable regions (named "events" and "specials") appear within the right sidebar. You can edit the title of any page created from a template. All other parts of the page are locked (circled); you can make changes to these parts only in the original template file.

To add content to an editable region, click anywhere inside the region. You can type inside it, add graphics, or add any other object or HTML you can normally add to a document. You can also change the document's title and add a Spry menu bar (Chapter 4), Spry widget (Chapter 13), Cascading Style Sheet (see Chapter 3), and meta tags (items that go in the <head> of an HTML document).

Once you finish adding content, save the file and close it. You can create additional pages based on the same template by following the steps as above (choose File→New to open the New Document window, click the "Page from Template" button, select the template, and so on). If you need to make a site-wide change to the template-based pages (add a navigation button, for example), you edit the template as described on page 864. You might also find that the basic editable region doesn't provide the control you need. Fortunately, Dreamweaver's advanced template regions—described on page 866—might help.

Under the Hood of Templates

Dreamweaver saves templates as HTML files in the Templates folder inside your current local site folder (see Chapter 15 for information on local sites). Each template bears the file extension .dwt to distinguish template pages from regular web pages.

Dreamweaver treats files in the Templates folder differently from normal web pages, so don't save anything but .dwt files there. In addition, since Dreamweaver expects to find the Templates folder in the local root folder of your site, don't move it or change its name in any way (don't even change the capital "T" in "Templates," even if you're a low-key type of person). If you do, your templates won't work.

As with Library items, Dreamweaver uses HTML comment tags to indicate the name of a template. If you inspect the HTML code of a template-based document, you'll see that, immediately following the opening <html> tag, Dreamweaver inserts a comment tag with the text "InstanceBegin" followed by the

location and name of the template. Additional comment tags indicate areas of the page you can modify, plus special template features like template parameters used for optional regions. For instance, the title of a page based on a template is always editable; its comment tag might look like this:

```
<!-- InstanceBeginEditable
name="doctitle" -->
<title>My New Page</title>
<!-- InstanceEndEditable -->
```

The first comment indicates the editable region's beginning and also includes the editable region's name. When you edit pages based on the template, you can change only the HTML between these comment tags. Everything else on the page is locked, even when you work in Code view.

Applying Templates to Existing Pages

What happens if you create a web page, and *then* decide you want it to share the look of a template? No problem. Dreamweaver lets you apply a template to any web page in your site. You can even swap one template for another.

To apply a template to a page you already created:

1. **Choose File→Open to open the page you want to alter.**

   The page opens.

2. **Choose Window→Assets.** Click the Assets panel's Templates button (see Figure 19-4).

   The Assets panel appears and reveals a list of your site's templates.

   NOTE You can also apply a template to a page by choosing Modify→Templates→Apply Template to Page. Select the name of the template from the window that appears and then skip to step 5.

3. **Click a template in the list in the Assets panel, and then click Apply.**

   The Inconsistent Region Names dialog box opens (Figure 19-7).

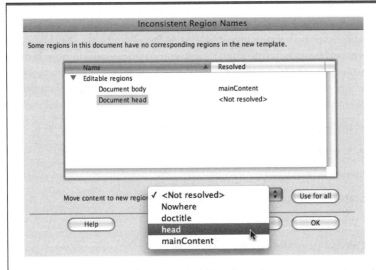

FIGURE 19-7

When you apply a template to an existing page, you must tell Dreamweaver what to do with the material already on the page by selecting one of the template's editable regions from a pop-up menu, which takes charge of all editable regions in the page you're converting.

4. **In the list under "Editable regions," choose "Document body."**

   To the right, in the Resolved column, you see "<Not resolved>." This is Dreamweaver's way of saying it doesn't know what to do with the contents of the current page. You need to pick one of the template's editable regions.

5. **From the "Move content to new region" menu, select an editable region.**

   If you want to keep the material, select the name of an editable region from the list—that'll copy the content there. Otherwise, choose Nowhere, which, in effect, creates a new blank page based on the template.

   Unfortunately, you can only select a single editable region. If the original page has several content regions, Dreamweaver pushes them all into that single editable region.

6. **If "Document head" also appears in the window, select it and choose "head" from the "Move content to new region" menu.**

   This step preserves any special information you added to the head of your page, like Cascading Style Sheets, meta tags, and custom JavaScript programs. Unfortunately, Dreamweaver always replaces the title of your original page with the default title of the template. You have to re-enter the title (see Figure 1-16) after you apply the template.

7. **Click OK.**

   Your new page appears.

■ Updating a Template

Templates aren't useful just for rapidly building pages; they also make quick work of site updates. Template-based pages maintain a link to their original template; Dreamweaver automatically passes changes you make to the original template along to every page built from it. If you used templates to build your site, you probably won't cry on your keyboard when the boss asks you to add an additional button and a link to the navigation bar. Instead of editing every page, you can simply open the template file, update the navigation bar, and let Dreamweaver apply the update to all your pages.

You update a template (and all the pages based on it) like this:

1. **Choose Window→Assets.**

   The Assets panel appears.

2. **Click the Templates button.**

   A list of the site's templates appears.

3. **Double-click the template's name to open it.**

   Alternatively, you can select the template in the Assets panel, and then click the Edit button to open the original template (.dwt) file. The template opens.

> **TIP** You can also open a template by double-clicking the appropriate template file name (.dwt) in the Templates folder in the Files panel.

4. **Edit the template as you would any web page.**

   Since this is the original template file, you can edit any of the HTML in the document, including Cascading Style Sheets, meta tags, and layers. You can also add or remove editable regions.

   Take care, however, to edit *only* the areas that you did *not* mark as editable regions. The reason: When you update your pages, any region marked as editable in a template file isn't passed on to pages based on that template. After all, the template dictates only the design of those pages' *non*-editable regions. In other words, if you make a change to an editable region in a template, Dreamweaver won't pass that change on to any existing template-based pages.

> **NOTE** Be careful when you remove editable regions from a template. If you already built some pages based on the template, Dreamweaver warns you when you save the newly configured template. As described below, you can either *delete* the content you added to that region in each of the pages you created, or you can move it to another editable region on the page.

5. **Choose File→Save.**

   If you already created pages based on this template, Dreamweaver opens the Update Template Files dialog box. It lists all the files that use the template.

6. **Click Update to update all the files based on the template.**

   Dreamweaver automatically applies the changes you made to the pages based on the template. Then it opens the Update Pages dialog box. If you want to see a list of all the files Dreamweaver changed, turn on the "Show log" checkbox.

   On a large site, this automatic update feature can be an incredible time-saver, but you may *not* want to click Update, at least not right now. Perhaps you're just saving some of your hard work on the template but aren't quite finished perfecting it—why waste time updating all those pages more than once? In such a scenario, click the Don't Update button. Remember, you can always update the pages later (see the box below).

7. **Click Close.**

   The Update Pages dialog box closes.

Remember that you need to update all your files, even if you make a simple change to the template, like changing its name.

POWER USERS' CLINIC

Wait to Update

Whenever you modify and save a template, Dreamweaver gives you the option of updating any pages in the site descended from that template. The same holds true for Library items; if you change a Library item, Dreamweaver asks if you want to pass that change on to all the pages with that item. Very often, you'll say yes.

But there are times when you want to wait to update your site. If you're making a lot of changes to templates or multiple Library items, you may wish to wait until you finish all your edits before you let the changes ripple through your pages. After all, it can take some time to update large sites.

Dreamweaver lets you update pages that use templates and Library items any time. Just choose Modify→Templates→Update Pages or Modify→Library→Update Pages.

Both menu options open the same window, the Update Pages dialog box.

At this point, you can update pages that use a specific template or Library item by going to the "Look in" menu, choosing "Files that Use," and then selecting the appropriate name from the drop-down menu. If you want to update all the pages in a site, choose Entire Site, and then, from the drop-down menu, select the name of the local site. Turn on both the Templates and "Library items" checkboxes to update all pages.

To see the results of Dreamweaver's work, turn on the "Show log" checkbox, which displays all the files Dreamweaver updated.

Unlinking a Page from a Template

If you're confident that you won't make any further changes to a page's template and you want to edit a page's locked regions, you can break the link between the page and its template by choosing Modify→Templates→Detach from Template.

You can now edit all the HTML in the page, just as you can on a regular web page—which is, in fact, what you have now. You removed all references to the original template, so any changes to the template no longer affect this page.

NOTE If you unlink a nested template from its master template, Dreamweaver removes only the code provided by the original master template. Any editable regions you added to the nested template remain.

■ Using Repeating Regions

The humble editable region is the heart of all templates—after all, the whole point of a template is to provide an easy way to create new pages with new content. You may find that templates with editable regions are all you ever need for your site. However, Dreamweaver provides several other template features that might come in handy.

Some web pages have types of content that repeat over and over on a page. For example, a catalog page may display row after row of the same product information—picture, name, price, and description. An index of Frequently Asked Questions may list questions and the dates visitors posted them. Dreamweaver provides a couple of ways to turn content like this into an editable region in a template.

You could, of course, make the entire area where the repeating content appears editable. For example, you could use one of Dreamweaver's CSS layouts (see Chapter 9) to build a template for a FAQ page. The list of questions and answers go inside the page's main <div> tag. You can turn this div into an editable region. The downside to this approach is that you won't have any ability to enforce (or easily update) the HTML used to lay out the questions and answers, since another designer could edit or delete everything in the div.

Fortunately, Dreamweaver provides a pair of template tools to address the problem: *repeating regions* and *repeating tables*. Both let you create areas of a page that include editable (and uneditable) regions that you can repeat any number of times (see Figure 19-8).

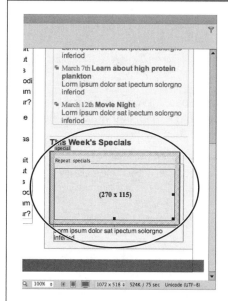

FIGURE 19-8

A repeating region lets page authors add multiple instances of repeating information. Left: In this template, you see a repeating region labeled "specials" (circled). Right: A complete page based on this template includes two repeating editable regions (circled). If another page requires more cafe specials, you can easily add one to each list by clicking the + button at the top of the repeating region in the template-based page (right). Even with the ability to dictate how many repeating regions appear on a page, the master template still controls the page's basic design. That means page authors can't change the box that surrounds the specials or the headline "This Week's Specials."

Adding a Repeating Region

You add a repeating region the same way you add an editable region. Select the area of the template where you want to repeat information; it usually contains at least one element that you have made editable. It could be a single list item (the <li> tag), a table row (<tr> tag), or even an entire <div> tag.

> **NOTE** You can make a repeating region that *doesn't* include an editable region. For example, a template for a movie review web page could include a repeating region that's simply a graphic of a star. A page author adding a new movie review could repeat the star graphic to match the movie's rating—four stars, for example. (There's just one caveat—see the Tip on page 871.)

Next, tell Dreamweaver that the elements you selected represent a repeating region. You can use any of these techniques:

- On the Common category of the Insert panel, select the Repeating Region option from the Templates menu.

- Choose Insert→Template Objects→Repeating Region.

- Right-click (Control-click) the selection and choose Templates→New Repeating Region from the shortcut menu.

When the New Repeating Region dialog box appears, type a name for the region and then click OK. You return to your template, where the name you gave the region appears in a small blue tab above it (see Figure 19-8).

WARNING Dreamweaver lets you name a repeating region even if that name is already in use by an editable region. But don't repeat names—multiple template areas with the same name make Dreamweaver act unpredictably.

FREQUENTLY ASKED QUESTION

Hindered by Highlighting

I'm distracted by the tabs and background colors that Dreamweaver uses to indicate templates and Library items. How do I get rid of them?

When you use templates or Library items, you see blue tabs and yellow backgrounds, respectively, to indicate editable regions and Library items. Although these visual cues don't appear in a web browser, they can get in your way and even alter a page's layout while you work in Dreamweaver. Fortunately, you can change the background color of these items and even turn highlighting off altogether.

Choose Edit→Preferences or press Ctrl+U (⌘-U). In the Preferences Category list, click Highlighting. To change the background color of editable regions, locked regions, and Library

items, use the color box (see page 157) or type in a hexadecimal color value (see page 160). To remove the highlighting, turn off the Show checkbox next to the appropriate item.

Often, it's useful to keep highlighting on to help you keep track of editable regions and Library items. If you want to turn off highlighting temporarily, simply choose View→Visual Aids→Invisible Elements, or use the keyboard shortcut Ctrl+Shift+I (⌘-Shift-I) to toggle these visual cues off and on. This technique has the added benefit of hiding table borders, layer borders, image maps, and other invisible elements.

Adding a Repeating Table

Dreamweaver's *repeating table* tool is essentially a shortcut to creating a table with repeating rows. If you had time on your hands, you could achieve the same effect by adding a table to the page, selecting one or more rows, and applying a repeating region to the selection.

To use the repeating table tool:

1. **In the template page, click where you want to insert the table.**

   You can't insert a repeating table into an editable, repeating, or optional region, as you'll see in "Making an Attribute Editable", coming up on page 872. You must be in an empty, locked area of the template.

2. **On the Common category of the Insert panel, select the Repeating Table option from the Templates menu.**

   Alternatively, you can choose Insert→Template Objects→Repeating Table. Either way, the Insert Repeating Table window appears (Figure 19-9).

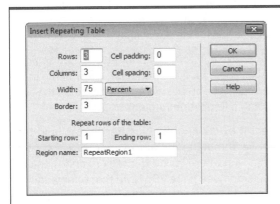

FIGURE 19-9

The Insert Repeating Table dialog box lets you kill three birds with one stone: It adds a table to a page, turns one or more rows into a repeating region, and adds editable regions in each table cell inside the repeating region.

3. **Fill out the basic properties of the table.**

   The top part of the window lets you set up the basic structure of the table: rows, columns, cell padding, cell spacing, width, and border. Basically, it's the same information you provide when you create any table, as described on page 291. You usually start a repeating table with two rows—one for a heading, another to contain the information you want to repeat.

4. **In the "Starting row" box, type the number of the row where the repeating region should begin.**

   Often you'll have just one repeating row: a row of product information, for example. You may want to use the top row for labels indicating the information contained in the rows below. If that's the case, enter *2* at this step, leaving the first row as an uneditable part of the template.

   It's conceivable, however, that you may want each entry to take up *two* rows. The first would list Product Name and Description; the second would contain a cell for a photo and a cell for the price. You set up this effect in this step and the next.

5. **In the "Ending row" box, type the number of the last repeating row.**

If you want to repeat only a single row, enter the same number you provided in step 4. If you want to create a double repeating row, add 1 to the number you provided in step 4. For example, if you need three rows for each repeating entry, add 2 to the number you entered in step 4.

6. **Type a name for this repeating region.**

Don't use the same name as another template region. You'll run the risk of unpredictable results on template-based pages.

7. **Click OK.**

Dreamweaver inserts a table into the page. A blue tab with the name of the repeating region appears, as do blue tabs in each cell of each repeated row. These tabs indicate new editable regions—one per cell.

Since these new editable regions have uninformative names like *EditRegion4*, you may want to rename them. Click the blue tab and type a new name in the Property Inspector. (But do so *before* you create any pages based on the template—see the warning on "Adding a Repeating Region".)

To remove a repeating region, select it by clicking the blue Repeat tab, and then choose Modify→Templates→Remove Template Markup. A more accurate way to select a repeating region is to click anywhere inside the region, and then click <mmtemplate: repeat> in the Tag Selector (see page 26). Note that removing a repeating region doesn't remove any editable regions you added inside the repeating region. If you want to rename a repeating region, heed the warning on page 686.

Working with Repeating Regions

Repeating regions work a bit differently from editable regions. In most cases, a repeating region includes one or more editable regions (which you can edit using the instructions above). However, Dreamweaver provides special controls to let you add, remove, and rearrange repeating entries (see Figure 19-10).

These regions let page editors add repeating page elements—like rows of product information in a list of products. To add a repeating entry, click the + button to the right of the Repeat region's blue tab. You can then edit any editable regions within the entry. Click inside an editable region inside a repeating entry and click + again to add a new entry *after* it.

Deleting a repeating entry is just as easy; click inside an editable region within the entry you want to delete, and then click the - button.

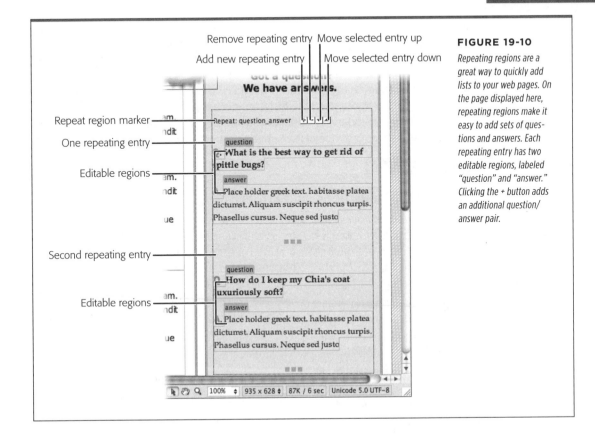

FIGURE 19-10

Repeating regions are a great way to quickly add lists to your web pages. On the page displayed here, repeating regions make it easy to add sets of questions and answers. Each repeating entry has two editable regions, labeled "question" and "answer." Clicking the + button adds an additional question/answer pair.

TIP You can create repeating regions that don't have any editable regions—for example, you can create a repeating region with a star in it, and repeat the region several times to indicate the rating for a product. Although you can use the + button to repeat such regions, you can't delete those regions using the - button (-). In other words, you're stuck with any extra stars you add. The only workaround is to add an editable region to the repeating region—then Dreamweaver lets you remove the repeating regions.

To rearrange entries in a repeated-region list, click inside an entry's editable region. Click the up or down arrows to move the entry up or down in the list (to alphabetize it, for example).

■ Using Editable Tag Attributes

An editable region lets you—or, more likely, page-author jockeys—change areas of HTML, like a paragraph, image, or an entire table, on new pages they create from your template. However, when you create a template for others to use, you may want to limit the page authors' editing abilities. For example, you may want to allow budding web designers to change the source of the image used in a banner ad without letting them change the width, height, and class applied to the image. Or you might want to use templates but still let others assign a class to the <body> tag—a move normally forbidden on template-based pages. You can use Dreamweaver's Editable Tag Attribute to specify which tag properties your successors can change.

FREQUENTLY ASKED QUESTION

Editable Regions, Repeating Regions, and Errors

When I try to insert an editable region inside a repeating region, I get the following error: "The selection is already in an editable, repeating, or optional region." What's that about?

This error message essentially means you're trying to add a template region where it doesn't belong. It appears most often when you attempt to put a repeating or optional region inside an editable region. That kind of nesting is a no-no; page authors can change anything inside an editable region on template-based pages, and as such, Dreamweaver can't touch it.

However, you may get this error message seemingly by mistake. For instance, it's perfectly OK to add an editable region inside a repeating region, and it's even OK to add a repeating region inside an optional region, and vice versa.

But say one day you select text inside a repeating region and try to turn it into an editable region, and boom—error message. What probably happened was, when you selected the text, Dreamweaver actually selected part of the hidden code used to define a template region (see the box on page 862) and thought you were trying to put an editable region inside it. To avoid confusion, use the Tag Selector to select the page element you want to turn into an editable region. In the Tag Selector, you can click <p> to select the paragraph inside the repeating region. Alternatively, go into Code view (see page 335), and then select whatever part of the code inside the repeating region you wish to make editable.

NOTE Before you make a tag attribute editable, first set that property to a default value in the template: for example, add a class to the <body> tag if you want to make the class editable. Doing so inserts a default value and makes the attribute appear in the Editable Tag Attribute window (see steps 3 and 7 in the following instructions).

Making an Attribute Editable

To make a tag attribute editable:

1. **Select the tag whose property you want to make editable.**

   Using the Tag Selector (see page 26) is the most accurate way.

2. **Choose Modify→Templates→Make Attribute Editable.**

   The Editable Tag Attributes window opens (Figure 19-11).

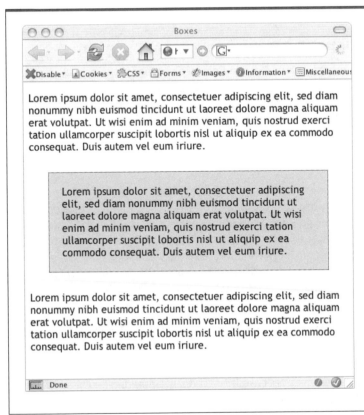

FIGURE 19-11

Dreamweaver gives you detailed control over template pages. To make just a single property of a single tag editable on pages based on your template, turn on the "Make attribute editable" checkbox. In this case, the ID attribute of the body tag is editable, allowing page designers the freedom to apply different CSS styles to the body of each template-based page. They could change the ID name from page to page, and use descendent selectors to target styles that apply only to elements within pages that have that specific ID.

3. **Select an attribute from the menu or add a new attribute with the Add button.**

   The Attribute menu displays only those properties you already set for the selected tag. In other words, if you select an image, you probably see the *src*, *width*, and *height* properties listed. But unless you set the image's alternative text, the *alt* property won't appear.

   To add a property, click the Add button. In the window that appears, type in the appropriate property name. For example, to make the *alt* (alternate text) attribute of a graphic editable, you'd type *alt* in here.

   NOTE If you want page editors to be able to change a CSS class or ID applied to the <body> tag on template-based pages—to apply different fonts, background colors, or any of the many CSS formatting options to each template-based page—you *have* to make the Class or ID attribute editable. (See page 124 for more on CSS classes and IDs.)

4. **Make sure you turn on the "Make attribute editable" checkbox.**

If you decide at some point that you no longer want people to be able to edit this property, you can return to this dialog box and turn off editing, as described in a moment.

5. **Type a name in the Label field.**

What you type here should be a simple description of the editable tag and property, which helps page authors correctly identify editable properties. For example, you could use *Product Image* if you make a particular image's *src* property editable.

6. **Choose a value type from the menu.**

Your choices are:

- **Text.** Use this option when a property's value is a word. For example, you can change the image tag's *Align* property to *top, middle, baseline,* and so on. Or, when using Cascading Style Sheets, you could make a tag's *Class* property editable to allow page authors to apply a particular custom style to the tag—*content, footer,* and *URL*. Use this last option to let page authors edit the path to a file, like an image's *src* property or a link's *href* property. Using its site management tools, Dreamweaver keeps track of these paths and updates them when you move pages around your site.

- **Color.** If the property requires a web color, like a background hue, select this option. It makes Dreamweaver's color box available to people who build pages from the template.

- **True/False.** You shouldn't use this option. It's intended for Dreamweaver's Optional Regions feature (discussed below), and doesn't apply to *HTML* properties.

- **Number.** Use this choice for properties that require a numeric value, like an image's *Height* and *Width* properties.

7. **Type a default value into the Default field.**

This step is optional. The default value defines the initial value for this property, when people first create a page based on the template. They can then modify this value for that particular page. If you already set this property in the template, its value automatically appears in this box.

8. **Click OK to close the window.**

Dreamweaver adds code to the template page that allows page authors control of the attribute. To set this attribute on pages created from the template, see the instructions on the next page.

If you later decide that you *don't* want a particular tag property to be editable, Dreamweaver can help. Open the template file, select the tag with the editable attribute, and choose Modify→Templates→Make Attribute Editable. In the window that appears, turn off the "Make attribute editable" checkbox (Figure 19-11). Unfortunately, doing so doesn't remove *all* of the template code Dreamweaver added. Even after you turn off editing for an attribute, Dreamweaver leaves behind the parameter used to control the tag's property. To eliminate *this* extra code, see the box on page 881.

Changing Properties of Editable Tag Attributes

Unlike editable or repeating regions, you can't readily see an editable tag attribute on template-based pages. There's no blue tab that identifies them, as there are for editable regions; in fact, nothing appears in Design view to indicate that there are *any* editable *tag* properties on the page. The only way to find out is to choose Modify→Template Properties to open the Template Properties dialog box (see Figure 19-12).

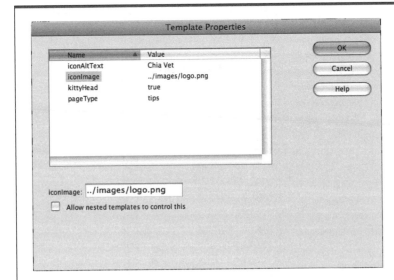

FIGURE 19-12

The Template Properties window lets you control editable tag attributes and other parameters for optional regions. Depending on which parameter you select, the options at the bottom of the window change. In this case, the src property of an image tag has been made editable. To change the image tag's src property, click Dreamweaver's familiar "Browse for File" button and select a new graphic.

Dreamweaver displays all the editable tag attributes for this page in this window. In addition, it displays all the parameters defined for this page, including optional regions, as discussed in the box on page 881.

To change the value of a template property—in other words, to edit the property of an editable tag—select its name from the list and fill out the option that appears at the bottom of the window. For example, in the case of color properties, use the color box to pick a color. If the property is a path (like a link or an image's *src* property), click the folder icon to browse to the file.

Once you finish setting the editable properties for the page, click OK to close the window.

FREQUENTLY ASKED QUESTION

The Broken-Link Blues

Why aren't the links in my templates working?

When you created the link in the template file, you probably typed a path into the Property Inspector's Link field—a recipe for heartbreak. Instead, always select the target web page for a link by clicking the folder icon in the Property Inspector, or by pressing Ctrl+L (⌘-L). In other words, when you add links to a template, always link to pages within the site by browsing to the desired file.

Dreamweaver saves templates in the Templates folder inside the local root folder; all document-relative links need to be relative to this location. (Absolute links, like those to other websites, aren't a problem; neither are root-relative links; see page 185 to learn the difference.) The reason you should browse to, rather than type in, your links is so that Dreamweaver can create a proper relative link.

Imagine this situation: You create a template for all the classified ads that appear on your site. You store all the ads for April 2001 inside a series of folders like this: classifieds→2001→april, as shown in the site diagram here.

A link from a page in the *april* folder to the home page would follow the path marked 1 here. So when you create a link in your template, you can create a link to the home page by typing the path ../../../index.html.

That choice is logical if you're thinking about the page (in the *april* folder) you'll create from the template—but it won't work.

Dreamweaver stores templates in the Templates folder, so the correct path would be path 2, or ../*index.html*. When you create a new page based on the template and save it in the *april* folder, Dreamweaver, in its wisdom, automatically rewrites all the paths in the page so that the links work correctly.

The beauty of Dreamweaver is that you don't have to understand how all this works. Just remember to use document-relative links in your templates and create them by clicking the folder icon in the Property Inspector.

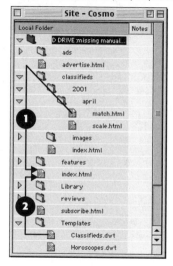

■ Using Optional Regions

Templates provide consistent design. While consistency is generally a good thing, it can also get boring. Furthermore, there may be times when you want the flexibility to include information on some template-based pages but not on others.

Dreamweaver provides a template tool aimed at letting you vary a page's design while still maintaining page-to-page consistency: *optional regions*. An optional region is simply part of a template you can hide or display on each template-based page (see Figure 19-13). When a page author creates a new page based on the template, she can turn the region on or off.

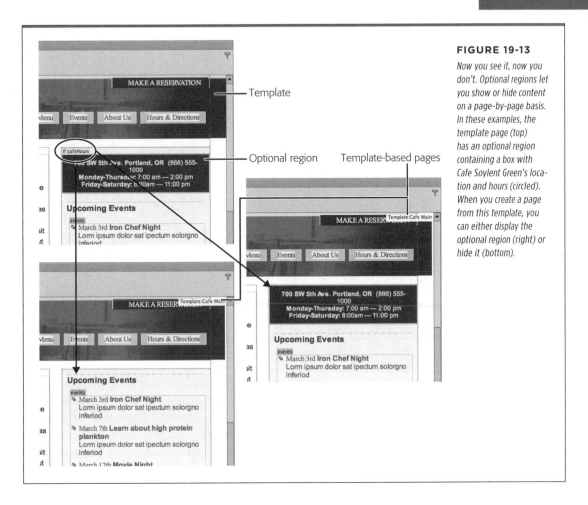

FIGURE 19-13

Now you see it, now you don't. Optional regions let you show or hide content on a page-by-page basis. In these examples, the template page (top) has an optional region containing a box with Cafe Soylent Green's location and hours (circled). When you create a page from this template, you can either display the optional region (right) or hide it (bottom).

Adding an Optional Region

Creating an optional region is a snap. Just select the HTML code you want to make optional and do one of the following:

- On the Common category of the Insert panel, select the Optional Region option from the Templates menu.

- Choose Insert→Template Objects→Optional Region.

- Right-click (Control-click) the selection and choose Templates→New Optional Region from the shortcut menu.

In the New Optional Region window, type a name (see Figure 19-14). Make sure not to use the same name as any other region on the page, and—although Dreamweaver lets you—don't use spaces or other punctuation marks. (Following the rules for nam-ing files as described in page 48 ensures that the optional region works properly.) Click OK to close the window and create the new optional region. Dreamweaver adds a light blue tab with the word "If," followed by the name you gave the region (Figure 19-13).

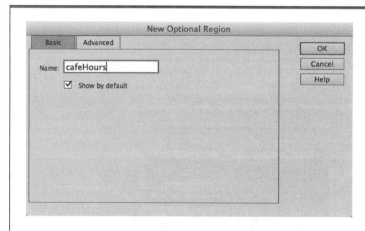

FIGURE 19-14

The Optional Regions feature lets you show or hide specific content on template-based pages. Turning on the "Show by default" checkbox tells Dreamweaver to display the region when you first create a template-based page. That's a good idea if you want most of your pages to display the content—you'll save yourself the effort of turning on the optional region each time you create a template-based page.

A FEATURE TO AVOID

Nested Templates

Dreamweaver includes yet another template feature called "nested templates." Nested templates let you create a template with a very basic design so you can create new templates based on that original one, refining the design as you do so. This way, you can have a single template that dictates your core layout, and then create specialized templates for particular types of pages or sections on your site.

This might sound like a great way to provide templates that both maintain your site's basic layout via a master template and let you create pages designed for different purposes. However, in execution, nested templates are confusing, don't

always work, and aren't that necessary. With the flexibility that the optional regions discussed in this chapter give you, you can customize individual template-based pages while using only a single template file.

When it comes to nested templates, our advice is stay away.

Locking Optional Regions

An optional region can include editable regions, repeating regions, *and* locked regions. For example, if you want to allow a page editor to turn on or off a graphic ("This item on sale!!!!"), insert the graphic outside an editable region on the page, and then make it an optional region as described above. Since anything not inside an editable region is locked, a page editor can't change the graphic or ruin its for-matting—he can only make it visible or hidden.

Repeating Optional Regions

An optional region can also include repeating regions. For example, suppose you create a repeating region (see page 866) that lets a page editor add row after row of links to a list of related articles. You could then turn this repeating region into an optional region, as described above, so that if a particular page had no related articles, the page editor could simply hide the entire "related articles" section of the page.

Optional Editable Regions

Dreamweaver's Optional Editable Region command inserts an optional region with an editable region *inside* of it. To use it, click on the spot in the template where you'd like to add it, and then choose Insert→Template Objects→Optional Editable Region (alternatively, you can choose this option from the Templates menu in the Common category of the Insert panel). The New Optional Region window appears; give it a name, and then follow the steps above for adding an optional region (see page 877).

This technique doesn't offer a lot of control; it's hard to insert HTML *outside* the editable region, for example. So if you want an image or table that's optional but *not* editable, it's usually better to just create the editable region as described on page 857 and turn it (and any other HTML you wish to include) into an optional region.

> **NOTE** The Optional Editable Region command doesn't let you name the editable region; it automatically assigns a generic name like *EditRegion7*. You can select the editable region and change its name in the Property Inspector, but do so *before* you build any pages based on this template (see the warning on page 858).

Advanced Optional Regions

A basic optional region is a rather simple affair: It either appears or it doesn't. But Dreamweaver offers more complex logic for controlling them. For example, you may want several different areas of a page to be either hidden or visible at the same time—perhaps an "On Sale Now!" icon at the top of a page *and* a "Call 1-800-SHIZZLE to order" message at the bottom of the page. When one appears, so does the other.

Because these objects sit in different areas of the page, you have to create two separate optional regions. Fortunately, using Dreamweaver's advanced settings for optional regions, you can easily have a *single* region control the display of one or more additional areas of a page. Here's how:

1. **Create the first optional region using the steps in "Adding Optional Regions" on page 876.**

   Give the region a name using the Basic tab of the New Optional Region window (Figure 19-15).

2. **Select the part of the page—an image, paragraph, or table—you want to turn into a second optional region.**

   In this case, you want to make the display of this region dependent on the optional region added in step 1. If the first region is visible on the page, this second region also shows.

3. **On the Common category of the Insert panel, choose the Optional Region item from the Templates menu.**

The New Optional Region window appears.

4. **Click the Advanced tab.**

The optional region's advanced options appear (see Figure 19-15). Here, you want the first optional region you created to control the display of this new region. So instead of giving this region a name, you simply select the name of the first optional region in the next step.

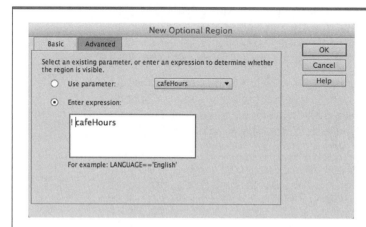

FIGURE 19-15

The Advanced section of the New Optional Region dialog box lets you more precisely control the display of optional content. You can make the region appear only when another region is visible, or use Dreamweaver's template expression language to create a more complex behavior. In this case, the selected region appears only when another region— named "kittyHead"—is not visible (the ! is the programming equivalent of "is not").

5. **Click the "Use parameter" button and select the name of the first optional region from the menu.**

This step is what makes the first optional region control this second region. If a page displays the first region, it also displays the second region.

6. **Click OK to close the window and create the new optional region.**

You can continue adding optional regions this way, using the Advanced tab and selecting the name of the first optional region from the menu. As a result, the first optional region controls the display of many other areas of the page.

Editing and Removing Optional Regions

After you insert an optional region, you can always return to the New Optional Region dialog box to change the region's name, alter its default settings, or use advanced options. To edit an optional region, first select it using one of these techniques:

- Click the region's blue tab in the document window.

- Click anywhere inside the optional region in the document window and then click the <mmtemplate:if> tag in the Tag Selector (see page 26 for details on the Tag Selector).

When you select an optional region, Dreamweaver displays an Edit button in the Property Inspector. Click it to reopen the New Optional Region window. You can then change the region's properties.

To remove an optional region, select it by using one of the techniques listed previously and then choose Modify→Templates→Remove Template Markup. Dreamweaver removes most of the code associated with the optional region (but see the box below).

POWER USERS' CLINIC

Understanding Template Parameters

When you insert an optional region, Dreamweaver adds special code to the head of the web page. Called a *template parameter*, this code is responsible for showing or hiding an optional region.

In fact, Dreamweaver uses parameters when you make a tag attribute editable, too. A typical parameter for an optional region might look like this:

```
<!-- TemplateParam name="SaleBug"
type="boolean" value="true" -->
```

The <!-- and --> are HTML comment markers that hide this code from web browsers. TemplateParam tells Dreamweaver that the comment is actually part of the program's Template features—specifically, a template parameter.

A parameter has three parts: name, type, and value. The name is the name you give the editable region. The type—"Boolean" above—indicates that the value of this parameter can be only one of two options: true or false. In this example, the value is "true," which simply means that the optional region called SaleBug is visible. (Don't worry; you don't have to actually edit this code by hand to turn optional regions on and off, as you'll see below.)

In programming jargon, a template parameter is known as a *variable*. In simpler terms, it's just a way to store information that can change. Dreamweaver reacts differently depending on the parameter's value: show the region if the parameter's true, hide it if the parameter's false.

Editable tag attributes also use parameters to store the values you enter for tag attributes. For example:

```
<!-- TemplateParam name="PageColor"
type="color" value="#FFFFFF" -->
```

On template-based pages, you can change the value of an editable tag's parameter using the Modify→Template Parameters menu (see "Changing Properties of Editable Tag Attributes").

Unfortunately, when you delete an optional region from a template, or remove the ability to edit a tag attribute, Dreamweaver always leaves these parameter tags hanging around in the head of the template document. Keeping in mind that Dreamweaver adds these parameter tags directly before the closing </head> tag, you can find and remove them in Code view.

Hiding and Showing Optional Regions

When working with template-based pages, you can hide or show the optional region. As with Editable Tag Attributes, you use the Template Properties window to control the display of optional regions. On template-based pages, you can show or hide an optional region by choosing Modify→Template Properties to open the Template Properties dialog box (see Figure 19-16). Next, select the name of the optional region. To make all the page elements in the region visible, turn on the "Show" checkbox at the bottom of the window. To hide all the optional regions, turn off the checkbox.

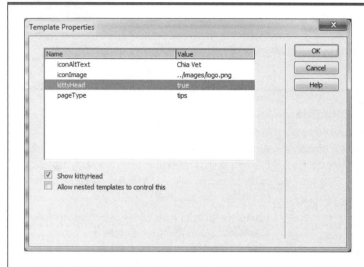

FIGURE 19-16

The Template Properties window displays optional regions as well as editable tag attributes. Template properties for optional regions—in this example, "kittyHead"—have a value of either true or false. "True" lets people see the contents of the region, while "false" hides the region. (You use the "Allow nested templates to control this" option with nested templates—see the box on page 878.)

Exporting a Template-Based Site

The good news about Dreamweaver's sophisticated templating features is that it lets you build complex web pages that are easy to create and update. The not-so-good news is that you need some behind-the-scenes code to achieve this ease of use. Dreamweaver's template features rely on HTML comment tags to identify editable, optional, and repeating page regions, as well as nested templates and editable tag attributes (see the box titled "Under the Hood of Templates").

Although this code is only for Dreamweaver's use and has no effect on how a web browser displays the page, it does increase, by a small amount, the size of your pages. That's probably why Dreamweaver includes a feature that lets you export an entire site into a new folder on your computer *without* any template markup code—to give you the leanest HTML possible. The following steps show you how to do that.

> **NOTE** While it's certainly possible to perform this file-slimming procedure, truth be told, it's not really necessary—the code Dreamweaver adds is minimal, so it won't have much effect on the download speed of your site.

1. **Choose Modify→Templates→Export Without Markup.**

   Dreamweaver uses the currently active site, so make sure you select the site you want to export in the Files panel. The Export Site Without Template Markup window appears, which offers just three options.

2. **Click the Browse button, and then select a destination folder for the exported site.**

    Select a folder *other* than the current local site folder. You always want to keep the original files in the local folder, since they're the ones that retain the template markup, making future updates possible.

3. **Turn on the export options you want.**

    The Export window includes two options. The first, "Keep template data files," creates an XML file for each template-based page. In other words, when you export the site, there's one HTML page (without any template code) and an XML file (which includes all the template code as well as the page contents).

    Theoretically, you could then go back and choose the File→Import→XML into Template to recreate the page, complete with the original template information. However, in practice, you probably won't. For one thing, this process creates lots of additional files that you wouldn't want to move to a website. In addition, when you want to work on the site to edit and update it, you should use the original files in the site's local folder, since they have the useful template code in them.

    The "Extract only changed files" option speeds up the process of exporting a large template-based site. This option forces Dreamweaver to export only pages you changed since the last export. Unfortunately, it doesn't tell you *which* files it exports until after the fact. So, to make sure you get those newly exported files to your server, you need to keep track of the files you change by hand.

4. **Click OK to export the site.**

    Dreamweaver goes through each page of the site, stripping out template code and exporting it to the folder you specified.

    You can use Dreamweaver's FTP feature to upload the files to your server (see page 798), but you need to create a new site and define the folder with the *exported* files as a local root folder. Whenever you need to add or update template-based pages, use the original site files, and then export the changed files. You can then switch to the site containing the exported files and transfer the new or updated files to your server. If that sounds like a lot of work, it is. Every change you make means exporting the site again. You're better off just leaving the template code in your pages, or use this command only if you're absolutely sure that you're done using templates for your site.

■ Template Tutorial

In this tutorial, you'll create a template for the Cafe Soylent Green website. Then you'll build a page based on that template and enjoy an easy site-wide update courtesy of Dreamweaver's templates feature.

Once you download the tutorial files and open Dreamweaver, set up a new site as described in "Setting Up a Site" on page 40; when you do, name the site *Templates*, and then select the Chapter19 folder (inside the MM_DWCS6 folder). (Here's how you set up a site in a nutshell: Choose Site→New Site. In the Site Setup window, type *Templates* into the Site Name field, click the folder icon next to the Local Site Folder field, navigate to and select the Chapter19 folder, and then click Choose or Select. Finally, click OK.)

Creating a Template

1. **Open the Files panel by pressing the F8 key (Shift-⌘-F).**

   Of course, if it was already open, you just closed it. Press F8 (Shift-⌘-F) again.

2. **In the Files panel, find and double-click the page *design.html*.**

   It's usually easier to create a template from an existing web page rather than from scratch, which you then save as a template. For the purpose of getting to bed before midnight tonight, pretend that you just designed this beautiful page.

3. **Choose File→Save As Template.**

   The Save As Template dialog box opens (see Figure 19-17).

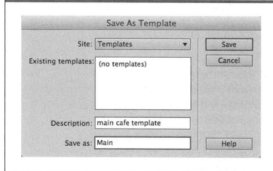

FIGURE 19-17

The first step in creating a template from a regular web page is to choose File→Save As Template. You only need to provide a name for the new template, but a brief description can help when you have lots of templates in a site; the description appears in the New Document window when you create a new template-based page.

4. **In the description field, type "main cafe template."**

   This description appears in the New Template window when you create a page based on this template.

5. **In the "Save as" box, name the template *Main*, and then click Save.** In the Update Links window, click Yes.

   Behind the scenes, Dreamweaver creates a new folder—Templates—in the site's root folder, and saves the file as *Main.dwt* inside it. A new template is born. You can see it in the newly created Templates folder in the Files panel and in the Templates page of the Assets panel (see the Note below).

The template is a model for other pages. And although those other pages will be *based* on this template's design, they won't be identical. The next step is to identify those areas of the design you want to change from page to page—the editable regions, in other words.

NOTE Templates don't always immediately show up in the Templates category of the Assets panel. Sometimes you need to click the Refresh Site List button (the circular arrow in the bottom-right of the Assets panel) to see a newly added template.

---

6. **Click inside the green "Headline" text and choose Edit→Select All.**

   The headline and paragraph of text below it live inside a <div> tag on this page. Choosing Select All when the cursor is inside a div selects everything inside the div, but not the <div> tag itself. In this case, you want to put content inside this div when you create new pages based on this template, so you'll turn the current selection into an editable region.

7. **Choose Insert→Template Objects→Editable Region.**

   Here, as in the following steps, you can also, from the Insert panel's Common category, go to the Templates menu and choose the Editable Region option, or just press Ctrl+Alt+V (⌘-Option-V).

   The New Editable Region dialog box appears.

8. **Type *Content*, and then click OK.**

   A small blue tab, labeled *Content*, appears above the headline (see Figure 19-18). You just added one editable region—the most basic type of template region. You'll add other types of template regions later, but lets build a few template-based pages first.

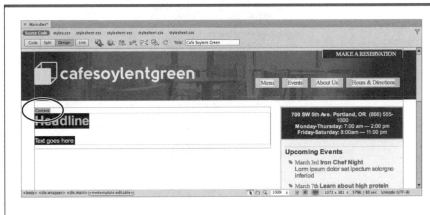

FIGURE 19-18

A template file with an editable region. If you don't see the blue box representing the region (circled), you may have turned off the display of invisible elements. To turn them on, choose View→Visual Aids, and then click Invisible Elements.

9. **Choose File→Save, and then File→Close.**

Congratulations! You just created your first template.

Creating a Page Based on a Template

Now it's time to get down to business and build some web pages:

1. **Choose File→New.**

The New Document window opens.

2. **On the window's far left side, click the "Page from Template" button.**

A list of all the defined sites appears in the Site list.

3. **Make sure you have the site you set up for this tutorial (Templates) selected in the Site column.** From the templates list, select Main, and make sure you have the "Update page when template changes" checkbox (in the right of the window) turned on.

If you don't turn on the "Update page" checkbox, the new page doesn't link to the original template, and therefore doesn't update when you make changes to that template.

4. **Click Create.**

Lo, a new web page appears—one that looks (almost) exactly like the template (Figure 19-19).

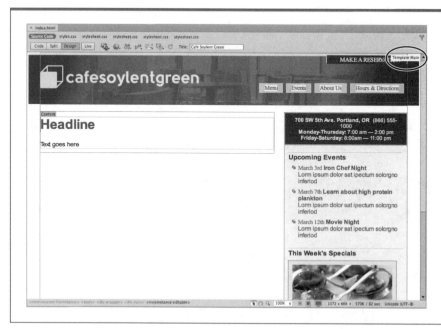

FIGURE 19-19

In template-based pages, blue tabs identify editable areas, and the yellow tab at the top-right lists the template's name (circled).

5. **Choose File→Save.** Click the Site Root button and save the file as *index.html* in the root folder. In the Document toolbar's Title field (at the top of the document window), type *Welcome to Cafe Soylent Green.*

   To indicate that it's your template's offspring, the document window has a yellow tab in the upper-right corner that reads "Template:Main." Dreamweaver indicates your editable region with a blue tab. Now it's time to add some content.

6. **Choose File→Open.** In the Open file window, click the Site Root button, and then double-click the file *text-index.html*.

   You can also open this file by double-clicking its name in the Files panel. The *text-index.html* page contains the content for the site's home page. It's just a matter of copying and pasting the text from one page to the other.

7. **Click the <body> tag in the Tag Selector (bottom-left of the document window) to select all the page contents, and then choose Edit→Copy.**

   Clicking the <body> tag in the Tag Selector is the best way to select an entire page's worth of content. As you read on step 6 on page 885 above, just clicking into a page and choosing Edit→Select All doesn't necessarily select everything on a page; if the cursor is inside a <div> tag, then only the contents inside that div are selected.

8. **At the top of the document window, click the *index.html* tab to switch to the template-based page.** Click the blue tab labeled "Content" (just above the headline.

   Remember that you can add content only to an editable region. If you move your mouse over the banner, navigation, or footer areas of the page, you see a black "forbidden" symbol. You can't insert the cursor anywhere but inside editable regions. Clicking the blue tab selects everything inside that region. Since it's just placeholder text anyway, you'll replace it with the content you just copied.

9. **Choose Edit→Paste.**

   Dreamweaver replaces the dummy text with the new content. Thanks to the power of CSS, the plain-look HTML you just copied and pasted is instantly formatted (if only web design were so simple!). Of course, on your own site, you'd probably copy and paste text from an email message or Word document. Then you'd use Dreamweaver's tools to create headlines, paragraphs, links, and bulleted lists, and then create your own CSS to style the page.

   You're done with this page!

10. **Save and close the file.**

    Time to create another page...well actually four more pages! You could repeat steps 1–9 above to create the new pages, but if you're starting off with a simple HTML page that you'd like to apply a template to, there's a better way.

11. **Open the file *about.html*.** Choose Modify→Templates→Apply Template to Page.

The Select Template window appears. Since there's only a single template for this site, the choice isn't hard.

12. **Select Main and then press Select.**

The Inconsistent Region Names window appears (see Figure 19-20). Since you're starting with an HTML file, you need to tell Dreamweaver where in the template-based page it's supposed to move this already-existing content. In general, you simply tell Dreamweaver to place the body of the page into an editable region, and the head of the page (which includes any already existing title) into the head of the template-based page.

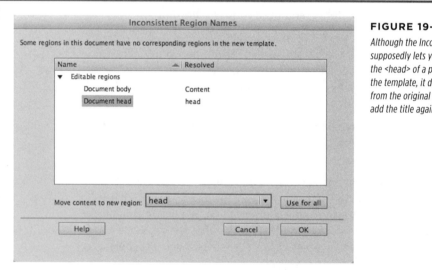

FIGURE 19-20

Although the Inconsistent Region Names supposedly lets you move content from the <head> of a page into the <head> of the template, it doesn't preserve the title from the original HTML file—you have to add the title again.

13. **Select "Document body" and then choose "Content" from the "Move content to new region" menu.**

This will place the page's content into the editable "Content" region from the template.

14. **Select "Document head" and choose "head" from the "Move content to new region" menu.** Click OK.

The Inconsistent Region Names window disappears and a new template-based page appears. Unfortunately, applying a template to an existing page wipes out that page's title (even when you choose to move the document head to the head of the new template-based page).

15. **Type *"About Cafe Soylent Green"* for the title.**

    Now, you just need to repeat these steps for four more pages.

16. **Repeat steps 11–14 for the *events.html, menu.html, hours.html,* and *reserva-tion.html* files.** Add appropriate titles to each page. Choose File→Save All to save all the new pages, and then choose File→Close All to close all the open files.

    Now you'll turn to an advanced template feature: optional regions.

Creating and Using Optional Regions

You may have noticed that two of the pages you just created—*hours.html* and *events.html*—have the same content in the right sidebar. While it's useful to display the hours and location on other pages, it's a bit weird to duplicate that information on the *hours.html* page. The same is true for the *events.html* page and the events listing in the sidebar. Fortunately, using optional regions, you can hide or show that information on a page-by-page basis.

1. **Return to Dreamweaver.** In the Assets panel, click the Templates button (see Figure 19-4), and then double-click the Main template to open it.

   The original template, the *Main.dwt* file, opens. You can also open the .dwt file by double-clicking its name inside the Templates folder in the Files panel.

   You'll first turn the box with the location and hours in it into an optional region.

2. **Click inside the dark-green box in the sidebar on the right.** In the Tag Selector in the bottom-left of the document window, and then click <div.hours> to select the entire <div> tag.

   Alternatively, you could click inside that div and choose Edit→Select All twice; the first time selects the contents of the div, while the second time selects the <div> tag itself.

3. **Choose Insert→Template Objects→Optional Region.**

   You can also use the Template menu in the Insert panel. Either way, the New Optional Region window opens.

4. **Type Hours in the Name field and then click OK.**

   You'll turn the events listing into an optional region as well.

5. **Click at the beginning of the "Upcoming Events" headline and then drag down the sidebar until you select the headline and all three bulleted items.**

   The events listings aren't contained in their own <div> tag, they're just made up of a headline followed by a bulleted list.

6. **Choose Insert→Template Objects→Optional Region.** In the New Optional Region window, type *Events* in the Name field, and then click OK.

   The Template file should look like Figure 19-21.

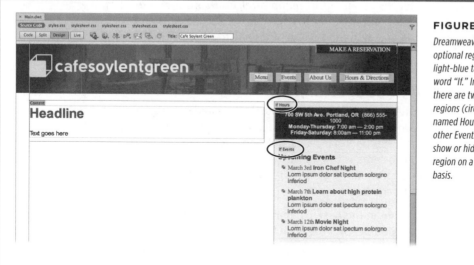

FIGURE 19-21

Dreamweaver identifies optional regions with a light-blue tab and the word "If." In this case, there are two optional regions (circled), one named Hours and the other Events. You can show or hide either region on a page-by-page basis.

7. **Choose File→Save.**

   The Update Template Files window appears. Whenever you update a template, Dreamweaver updates any template-based pages built using that template.

8. **Click the Update button, and when Dreamweaver completes the update, click Done.**

   Now you'll hide the hours box on the *hours.html* page.

9. **Open the file *hours.html*.** Choose Modify→Template Properties.

   The Template Properties window appears (Figure 19-22).

10. **Select Hours and then turn off the Show Hours checkbox at the bottom of the window.** Click OK.

    The Template Properties window closes and the hours and location box in the sidebar disappears. You could bring back that box by opening the Template Properties window again, selecting Hours, and then turning on the "Show Hours" checkbox.

11. **Open the file *events.html*.** Choose Modify→Template Properties. Select Events and then turn off the Show Events checkbox at the bottom of the window. Click OK.

    The Template Properties window closes and the events listing in the sidebar disappears.

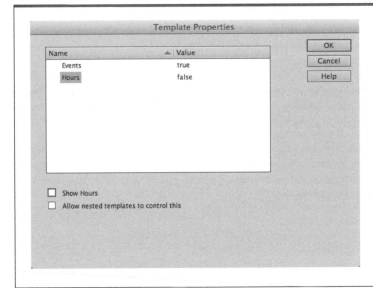

FIGURE 19-22

The Template Properties window does double duty. It lets you hide or show optional regions, and it lets you set values for editable tag attributes. The "Allow nested templates to control this box" option applies only to nested templates, which, as mentioned in the box on page 878, you should avoid.

12. **Choose File→Save All to save all the new pages, and then choose File→Close All to close all open files.**

    Next you'll see the real power of Dreamweaver templates.

Updating a Template

Now the fun begins. Remember, the pages you just created maintain a reference to the original template. In this final phase of the tutorial, you're going to make a few changes to the template.

1. **Return to Dreamweaver.** In the Assets panel, click the Templates button, and then double-click the Main template to open it.

   The original template, *Main.dwt*, opens. You can also open the file by double-clicking its name inside the Templates folder in the Files panel.

   There are a couple of things you need to change. First, you need to update the copyright notice.

2. **In the footer, locate "Copyright 2022" and change it to the current year.**

   Change the year to 2012 or whatever the current year happens to be. You'll also add a link here.

3. **On the same line in the footer, select the text "Cosmopolitan Farmer."** In the Property Inspector's link field, type *http://www.cosmofarmer.com*.

   There's a new food special that needs to appear in the right sidebar.

4. **In the right sidebar, click at the end of the last paragraph and press Enter (Return).**

   You just need to add an image and some text.

5. **Choose Insert→Image.** In the Select Image Source window, navigate to the *images* folder and double-click *special3.jpg* to insert the image.

   The Image Tab Accessibility window appears.

6. **Type Grilled Mozzarella in the "Alternate text" box and then click OK.** Press the right arrow key to deselect the image and move the cursor to the right; type Yummy grilled mozzarella.

   You could add more specials, update the events listing, change the banner and navigation bar. In short, Dreamweaver will pass on any changes you make to the non-editable areas of the template to the pages you built based on that template. Time to see the magic happen.

7. **Choose File→Save.**

   Dreamweaver displays the Update Template Files window. This is the moment of truth.

8. **Click Update.**

   Dreamweaver opens the Update Pages dialog box and updates the appropriate web pages, adding the copyright year, the link, and the new cafe special. In this case, you based only two pages on the template, so Dreamweaver updates only two pages, as indicated by the list of changes Dreamweaver displays when it's finished.

   NOTE   If, after you update pages based on a template, you don't see the number of updated pages listed in the Update Pages window, turn on the Show Log checkbox.
   ---

9. **Click "Close" to close the Update Pages dialog box.** Finally, open any of the template-based files: *index.html, about.html, and so on.*

   Notice that Dreamweaver updated the copyright and sidebar in all of those pages (see Figure 19-23). This series of events happened because you changed the template to which the page was genetically linked. Ah, the power!

FIGURE 19-23

Here's the finished tutorial page, complete with a useful Chia tip, a box with a link to a related web page, and a helpful question and answer.

Find and Replace

You've probably encountered find-and-replace tools in word processing programs and even some graphics software. As its name implies, the command finds a piece of text (*webmaster*, for example) and *replaces* it with another piece of text (*webmistress*). Like Microsoft Word, Dreamweaver can search and replace text in the body of your web pages. But it also offers variations on this feature that enhance your ability to work within the tag-based world of HTML.

What's more, Dreamweaver lets you find and replace text on *every* page of your site simultaneously, not just the current, open document. In addition, you can *remove* every appearance of a particular HTML tag, or search and replace text that matches very specific criteria. For example, you can find every instance of the word "Aardvark" that appears within a paragraph styled with the class name *animal*. These advanced find-and-replace maneuvers are some of the most powerful—and underappreciated—tools in Dreamweaver. If you learn how to use them, you can make changes to your pages in a fraction of the time it would take using other methods.

TIP You can use Find and Replace feature to search an entire site's worth of files. This is powerful, but it can also be slow, especially if some folders hold files you don't want to search—old archives, for example. You can use Dreamweaver's cloaking feature to hide files from find-and-replace operations. See page 804 for details.

Find and Replace Basics

To start a search, press Ctrl+F (⌘-F), or choose Edit→Find and Replace. The Find and Replace window opens (see Figure 20-1). Now all you have to do is fill in the blanks and set up the search.

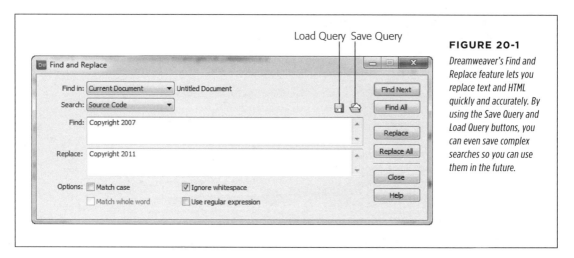

Load Query Save Query

FIGURE 20-1

Dreamweaver's Find and Replace feature lets you replace text and HTML quickly and accurately. By using the Save Query and Load Query buttons, you can even save complex searches so you can use them in the future.

Whether you perform a simple text search or a complex, tag-based search-and-replace, the procedure for using the Find and Replace feature is basically the same. First, you need to tell Dreamweaver *where* to search (within highlighted text on a page, in a file, a folder, or on your entire website). Next, tell it *what* to search for (text, HTML, or a particular tag with a specific attribute). Finally, you dictate what the replacement item is. This last step is optional; you can use the Find and Replace window as a way to locate an item on a page or on your site, without changing it to anything.

> **TIP** After you enter the Find and Replace criteria, click the Save Query button (see Figure 20-1). A Save dialog box appears; you can type in a name for your query, which Dreamweaver saves as a .dwr ("Dreamweaver replace query") file. You can save this file anywhere on your computer. If it's a query you'll use for a particular site, you might want to save it with that site's files. To reuse a query, click the Load Query button in the Find and Replace window and locate the .dwr file. After the search-and-replace criteria load, you can click any of the four action buttons—Find Next, Find All, Replace, or Replace All.

Basic Text and HTML Searches

Dreamweaver can search all the source code in a page or focus on text that appears in the document window.

- Source code searches let you find and replace any code on a page, including words, letters, and symbols. This means *anything* you see in Code view, such as HTML, CSS, or server-side programming code used to create the dynamic database-driven sites described in Part Six of this book. Code searches are the only type of search Dreamweaver allows on non-web page files, such as external JavaScript files or external CSS files.

- Text searches are more refined. They only look for text that appears within the <body> element of a page. That is, Dreamweaver ignores HTML tags, properties, and comments when it executes a text search—in short, it ignores anything that doesn't appear as actual words in the document window. By using a text search when you want to change the word "table" to "elegant wood table," for example, you won't accidentally change the very useful HTML <table> tag into a browser-choking <elegant wood table> tag.

If you've used the Find and Replace feature in other programs, the following routine will be familiar.

Phase 1: Determine the Scope of Your Search

Using the "Find in" pull-down menu (see Figure 20-2), choose any of these options:

- **Selected Text**. Searches only the highlighted section of the page you're working on. This can be useful if you're working in Code view and you want to search the code in just a certain section of the page, such as the head of the document. But it also comes in handy if you have a large HTML table full of data, and you want to search and replace just the content inside that table—just select the table (for example, click <table> in Tag selector [see page 26] or use any of the techniques described on page 294), and then choose the Selected Text option when executing a Find and Replace command.

- **Current Document**. Searches the web page you're working on.

- **Open Documents**. Searches all currently open Dreamweaver documents. This option is handy if you're working on a bunch of pages at once and you realize you made the same typo on each.

- **Folder**. Search all web pages in a particular folder. Dreamweaver also searches web pages in all folders *within* the selected folder. You can use this option to search pages that aren't part of the current site.

- **Selected Files in Site**. To use this option, open the Files panel and select the files you want to search in the local file list (see page 767 for details).

- **Entire Current Local Site**. Searches every web page in the current site folder, including pages in folders *inside* the site folder. This option is invaluable when you need to change a basic piece of information throughout your site. For instance, if your company hires a new boss, you can replace every instance of "Mark Jones" with "Joe Smith."

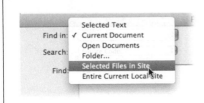

FIGURE 20-2

The effect of the Find and Replace command isn't limited to the current document. You can also search multiple web pages, or even an entire site.

NOTE Using the Find and Replace command is one of the best ways to quickly make changes to an entire site, but it's also one of the easiest ways to wreck a site's worth of web pages. Dreamweaver *can't* undo Find and Replace changes to files that aren't open when you execute the command. So be careful. If you plan on making extensive changes, make a backup copy of your files first!

Phase 2: Specify What to Search For

For your next trick, you'll tell Dreamweaver what you want to search for. Use the Search pop-up menu to choose one of these two options:

- **Text**. This makes Dreamweaver search for a certain word or phrase that appears in the *body* of the documents you specify. Type the text you want to find into the Search field. If you're searching for a pattern in your text, enter a *regular expression* here and turn on the "Use regular expression" checkbox. (See the box on page 905 for more on searching using regular expressions.)

- **Source Code**. Basic text searches are useful, but they're limited to text that appears in the body of a page (what you see in the document window). If you want to search and replace *code*, you need the Source Code option.

  Source-code searches work identically to text searches, except that Dreamweaver searches *everything* within a file—text, HTML, JavaScript, CSS, and so on—and replaces any part of the file. Using this option, you could search for any instance of the tag <img src="mark_jones_photo.jpg">, for example, and then replace it with <img src="joe_smith_photo.jpg">.

  (If you're in Code view, Dreamweaver automatically selects the Source Code option.)

  As you fill in the Search field, be aware that some plain-English words are also special words in HTML, JavaScript, or CSS. If you replace *table* with *desk* using a source-code Find and Replace command by mistake, you'll completely destroy any <table> tags on the page.

  You can also enter a regular expression to search for patterns in your HTML source code (see the box on page 905).

Phase 3: Provide the Replacement Text

If you want to change the text that Dreamweaver finds, type the replacement text into the Replace box. It may be the word or words you want to swap in (for a text search), or actual HTML code (for a source-code search).

TIP Dreamweaver won't let you create a new line in the Search or Replace boxes—for example, if you want to replace some source code with two lines of HTML. At least it won't let you do it the normal way. If you hit the Enter key, Dreamweaver begins the search rather than inserting a new line. To add another line, use Shift-Enter (Shift-Return).

If you just want to find text without replacing it, skip this step.

NOTE If you want to find the specified text and replace it with *nothing* (that is, deleting every occurrence of the text), leave the Replace field blank and perform a replace operation, described in Phase 5.

Phase 4: Choose the Search Settings

Dreamweaver gives you three options to govern its search and replace; some are quite complex:

- The **Match Case** option limits the Find command to text that exactly matches the case (capitalization and lowercase) of the text in the Search field. If you search for the text *The End* with the Match Case box turned on, Dreamweaver finds a match in "The End is near," but not in "You're almost at the end." Use this trick to find every instance of *Web* and replace it with *web*.

- **Match Whole Word** searches for an entire word—not a portion of a larger word. For example, if you turn this option on, a search for *Rob* matches only "Rob," and not any parts of "Robert," "robbery," or "problem." If you don't select this option, Dreamweaver stops on "rob" in all four instances, and could cause serious problems if you also *replace* "Rob" with something like "Bob" (unless, of course, you've come up with a new word for thefts committed by people named Bob: Bobbery). (Note that if you selected the Match Case option, Dreamweaver matches *Rob* in "Rob" and "Robert," but *not* in "robbery" and "problem," since they don't include a capital R.)

- The **Ignore Whitespace** option treats multiple spaces, tabs, non-breaking spaces, and carriage returns as single spaces during a search. For instance, if you search for *the dog* and turn on this option, Dreamweaver matches "the dog" as well as "the   dog"—even if the multiple spaces are actually the HTML non-breaking space character * * (see page 95).

NOTE To Mac users: Unfortunately, in the Mac version of Dreamweaver, the Find and Replace function doesn't treat non-breaking space characters as spaces, so if you have *the dog* in your HTML and search for *the dog*, even with the Ignore Whitespace box checked, the search will find nothing.

Unless you have a good reason, always leave this option turned on. The HTML of a page can contain lots of extra spaces, line breaks, and tabs that don't appear in a web browser or in Dreamweaver's document window. For example, in the HTML of a document, it's possible to have two lines of code that look like this:

```
<p>This sentence will appear on one

line in a Web browser</p>
```

Even though this text would appear on a single line in the document window, a search for "one line" *without* the Ignore Whitespace box turned on would find no match; the carriage return after "one" is not an exact match for the space character in "one line."

> **NOTE** You can't turn on the Ignore Whitespace option when you have the Use Regular Expression checkbox turned on.

- The **Use Regular Expression** option matches patterns in text. For a discussion of this advanced technique, see the box on page 905.

Phase 5: Take Action

Finally, you're ready to set the search in motion by clicking one of the four action buttons in the Find and Replace window (see Figure 20-1):

- **Find Next** locates the next instance of your search term. If you're searching the current document, Dreamweaver highlights the matching text. If you're searching an entire website or a folder of pages, Dreamweaver opens the file *and* highlights the match. You can cycle through each instance of the search term by clicking this button repeatedly.

> **TIP** As in other programs (notably Microsoft Word), you can press Enter to repeat the Find Next function (Windows only). If you click in the document window—or even closed the Find window—you can press F3 (⌘-G) to repeat the Find Next function.

- **Find All** locates every instance of the search term, all at once, and shows them to you in a list in the Search tab of the Results panel (Figure 20-3). The name and location of each file (if you searched multiple files) appear to the left, and the matched text appears to the right. Dreamweaver displays part of the sentence in which the matched word or words appear. It underlines the exact match with a squiggly red line, so you can see the search in context and identify text you may *not* want to replace.

    Unlike the Find Next action, Find All doesn't automatically open any of the web pages containing matches. To open a matched page, double-click its name in the results list. Only then does Dreamweaver open the page and highlight the match.

- **Replace** locates the next instance of the search term *and* replaces it with the text in the Replace field, leaving the replaced text highlighted for your inspection.

  You can use this button in combination with Find Next to selectively replace text. First, click Find Next. Dreamweaver locates and highlights the next match. To replace the text, click Replace. Otherwise, click Find Next to search for the next match, and repeat the cycle. This cautious approach lets you supervise the replacement process and avoid making changes you didn't intend.

- **Replace All** is the ultimate power tool. It finds every instance of the search term and replaces it with the text in the Replace field. Coupled with the Find in Entire Local Site option, you can quickly make site-wide changes (and mistakes—so back up all your files before you Replace All!).

  When you click this button, Dreamweaver warns that you can't undo this operation on any closed files. You can erase mistakes you make with Find and Replace in *open* documents by choosing Edit→Undo in each document, but Dreamweaver *permanently* alters closed files that you search and replace. So be careful! (On the other hand, changes to open documents aren't permanent until you close those files.)

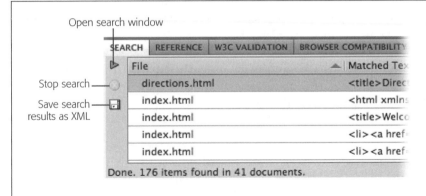

FIGURE 20-3

The green-arrow button reopens the Find and Replace window. Click the red Stop button to abort the current search (for example, when you inadvertently begin a search for "the" in a 10,000-page website). You can also save a rather useless XML file that provides a report of the results of the search (remember the old adage: Just because you can doesn't mean you should).

TIP Before you take the plunge and click the Replace All button, it's a good precautionary step to click Find All first and then preview the results in the Results panel (Figure 20-3). This way, you can be sure that you're going to change exactly what you *want* to change.

If you use the Find All or Replace All commands, the Find and Replace window closes, and the results of the search appear in the Search tab (see Figure 20-3). You can reopen the window (with all your previous search criteria still in place) by clicking the green arrow on the Search tab (called the Find and Replace button), but only if you haven't selected anything else—like text on a page—first.

■ Advanced Text Searches

If you want greater control over a text search, use the Find and Replace command's *advanced* text search option, which lets you confine a search to text either inside or outside a specific tag.

For example, when Dreamweaver creates a new blank document, it sets the page's *Title* property to *Untitled Document*. Unfortunately, if you forget to change it, a site can quickly fill up with untitled web pages. A basic text search doesn't identify this problem, because it searches only the body of a page; titles appear in the head. And a source-code search for *Untitled Document* would turn up the words "untitled document" *wherever* they appeared in the page, not just inside the <title> tag.

In cases like this, an advanced text search is your best choice. Simply set the Find and Replace command to search for *Untitled Document* whenever it appears within the <title> tag. To use advanced text search, follow the same general routine as described on the previous pages. But before using one of the action buttons, you make a few additional setup changes to the dialog box.

Limiting the Search by Tag

Choose Text (Advanced) from the Search pop-up menu to make the expanded controls appear (see Figure 20-4). Now, from the menu next to the + and – buttons, choose either Inside Tag or Not Inside Tag. For example, consider this line of code: "Stupid is as <strong>stupid</strong> does." The first instance of "stupid" isn't inside the <strong> tag, but the second one is.

> **NOTE** A more descriptive name for the first option would be "*Enclosed* By Tag"; Dreamweaver actually searches for text that's between *opening and closing* tags. In fact, an advanced text search using this option doesn't identify text that's literally inside a tag. For example, searching for "Aliens" inside an <img> tag—<img src="ufo.jpg" alt="Aliens live among us.">—won't work, but a search for "Aliens" between opening and closing <strong> tags—<strong>Aliens live among us.</strong>—would work. In the first example, *Aliens* appears as part of the <img> tag, while in the second, *Aliens* is enclosed by the opening and closing <strong> tags.

Once you specify whether you're looking for text inside or outside tags, you can choose a specific HTML tag from the Tag menu identified in Figure 20-4. The menu lists all HTML tags—not just those with both an opening and closing tag. So the image tag (<img>) still appears, even though Dreamweaver won't search for text inside of it.

> **TIP** A great way to search for text in both the title and body of a web page is to choose the Inside Tag option and then select *html* from the Tag menu. That way, you can search for any text that appears within the opening html tag,<html>, and the closing tag, </html>, of the page—which, since those tags start and end any web document, is *all* the text on a page. This trick is handy when you want to change text that might appear in the body *and* the title of a page (for example, a company name).

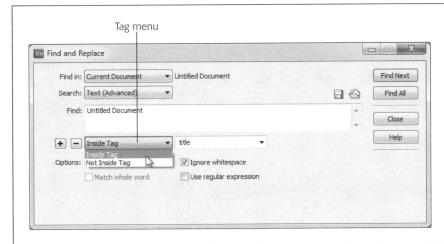

Tag menu

FIGURE 20-4

Use an advanced text search to limit your search to text that appears within a particular HTML tag. Conversely, you can use it to search for text that doesn't appear within a tag.

Limiting a Search by Attribute

To limit the search further, click the + button (see Figure 20-5); yet another set of fields appears. Using the Tag Modifier menu—next to the + and – buttons—you can choose from any of six options that break down into three groups:

- **With Attribute/Without Attribute**. To limit the search, you can specify that a tag must either have (With Attribute) or not have (Without Attribute) a specific property.

For example, say the following lines of code appear throughout a website:

```
<p>For assistance, please email

<a href="mailto:mail@chia-vet.com">

Chia Vet.</a></p>
```

Now, for the sake of argument, say you need to change that line to read "For assistance, please email Customer Service." A basic text find-and-replace would incorrectly change the words "Chia Vet" to "Customer Service" *everywhere* on the site.

However, an advanced text search using the With Attribute option lets you specifically target the text "Chia Vet" wherever it appears inside an <a> tag whose *href* attribute is set to *mailto:mail@chia-vet.com*. You could then just change that text to "Customer Service" while leaving all other instances of "Chia Vet" alone. (To learn about the different HTML tags and attributes, use Dreamweaver's built-in code reference; see page 370.)

After you choose With Attribute, use the menu on the right to select *which* of the tag's properties you want to find. (Dreamweaver automatically lists properties appropriate for the tag you specify.) For example, if you search inside a <table> tag, the menu lists properties such as *align*, *background*, *bgcolor*, and so on.

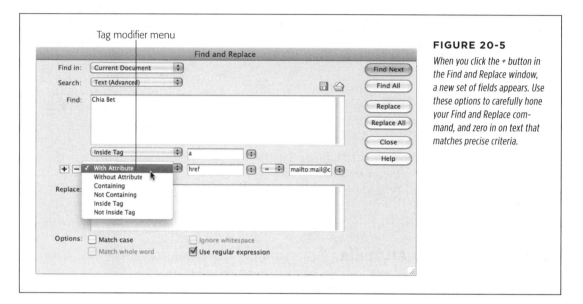

FIGURE 20-5

When you click the + button in the Find and Replace window, a new set of fields appears. Use these options to carefully hone your Find and Replace command, and zero in on text that matches precise criteria.

Advance to the next pop-up menu to choose a type of comparison: = (equal to), != (not equal to), > (greater than), or < (less than). You'll only use the less than or greater than options when a property's value is a number, such as the *width* property of a table cell. For example, you could use the comparison option to locate all table cells wider than 100 pixels (width > 100). (This setting has no effect on values that are words, such as *center* in this example: <td align="center">.)

Finally, type the value of the property in the last field. If you were searching for a black-colored background, the value would be *#000000* (the hex value for black).

You can also click the menu and choose "[any value]"—a useful option when you want to find tags that have a certain property, but you're not interested in the property's value. For example, if you want to find all <table> tags with a background color (no matter whether the color's #336699, #000000, or #FFFFFF), choose the *bgcolor* attribute and "[any value]."

- **Containing/Not Containing**. These options let you specify whether a tag contains (or doesn't contain) specific text or a particular secondary tag.

When you choose this option, a different set of fields appears. Choose either Text or Specific Tag from the menu to the right, and then either enter some text or select a tag in the last field in the row. For example, another (less error-proof) solution to the problem above would be to search for the text "Chia

Vet" wherever it appears inside a <p> (paragraph) tag that *also contains* the text "please email."

- **Inside Tag/Not Inside Tag**. These last two choices are identical to those described in "Limiting the search by tag" above. They let you specify whether the tag is inside—or not inside—a specific tag. Use these to limit a search, for example, to text that appears only within a <span> tag that itself is *inside* an <h1> tag.

If you like, you can add even more restrictions to your search, adding new rules by clicking the + button and repeating the setup just described. When you're really on a roll, it's even possible to add so many modifiers that the Find and Replace window actually grows past the bottom of your monitor. To remove a modifier, click the minus sign (–) button.

POWER USERS' CLINIC

Turbocharge Your Searches

If you want to find the phone number 555-123-5473 on your site, no problem; just type *555-123-5473* into the search field. But what if you want to find *every* phone number—555-987-0938, 555-102-8870, and so on—on a web page or across a site?

In such a case, you need to use *regular expressions*, the geeky name for a delightfully flexible search language carried over from early UNIX days, which consists of wildcard characters that let you search for *patterns* of text instead of actual letters or numbers. Each phone number above follows a simple pattern: three numbers, a dash, three more numbers, another dash, and four more numbers.

To search for a pattern, you use a variety of symbols combined with regular text characters to tell Dreamweaver what to find. For example, in the world of regular expressions, "\d" stands for "any number." To find three numbers in a row, you could search for \d\d\d, which would find 555, 747, 007, and so on. There's even shorthand for this: \d{3}. The number between the braces ({}) indicates how many times in a row the preceding character must appear to match. To finish up the example of the phone numbers, you could use a regular expression like this: \d{3}-\d{3}-\d{4}. The \d{3} finds three numbers, while the hyphen (-) following it is just the hyphen in the phone number, and \d{4} finds four numbers.

Here are some of the other symbols you'll encounter when using regular expressions:

- . (period) stands for any character, letter, number, space, and so on.

- \w stands for any letter or number (but not spaces, tabs, , or line breaks).

- * (asterisk) represents the preceding character, zero or more times (and is always used after another character). This is best explained with an example: The regular expression colou*r, for instance, matches both "colour" and "color"—the * following the u indicates that the u is optional (it can appear zero times). This would also match "colouuuuur" (handy for those times when you've fallen asleep on the keyboard).

To see a complete list of regular-expression characters Dreamweaver understands, as well as a short tutorial on regular expressions, visit *http://tinyurl.com/3zw4oj6*. A full-length discussion of regular expressions could—and does—fill a book of its own; check out *Mastering Regular Expressions*, Third Edition (O'Reilly, 2006) by Jeffrey E. F. Friedl *(http://oreilly.com/catalog/9780596528126)* or, for made-to-order regular expressions, visit the Regular Expression Library at *http://regexlib.com*.

For an example of using regular expressions in Dreamweaver, see "A Powerful Example: Adding Alt Text Fast" on page 908.

■ Advanced Tag Searches

If you find the number of options an advanced text search offers overwhelming, you haven't seen anything yet. Dreamweaver's tag search adds even more choices to help you quickly search for, and modify, HTML tags. You can use a tag search to strip out unwanted HTML tags (for example, if you're migrating a very old site to CSS, you could remove the <font> tag), transform one tag into another (you could turn old-style *bold* [<b>] into the more widely accepted *strong* [<strong>] tag), and perform a host of other powerful actions.

In its basic outline, a tag search is much like the regular text search described on page 896. But this time, from the Search menu, you should choose Specific Tag. Now a Tag menu appears next to the Search menu, and the dialog box expands to display a new set of fields (see Figure 20-6). Some of them are the same as the controls you see when you do an advanced text search (page 902), such as the Tag Modifier menu and the + button that lets you add additional restrictions to the search.

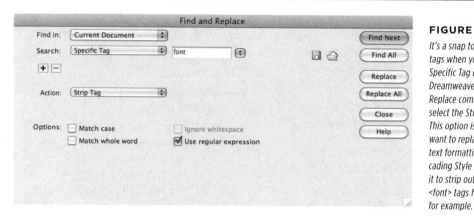

FIGURE 20-6

It's a snap to remove tags when you use the Specific Tag option with Dreamweaver's Find and Replace command—just select the Strip Tag action. This option is handy if you want to replace old-style text formatting with Cascading Style Sheets. Use it to strip out unwanted <font> tags from old sites, for example.

But a key difference here is the Action menu (Figure 20-7), which lets you specify the action Dreamweaver performs on tags that match the search criteria when you click Replace or Replace All (if you intend to search, but not replace, then these options don't apply):

- **Replace Tag & Contents**. Replaces the tag, and anything enclosed by the tag (including other tags), with whatever you put into the With box to the right of this menu. You can either type or paste text or HTML here.

- **Replace Contents**. Only replaces everything enclosed by the tag with text or HTML that you specify. The tag itself remains untouched.

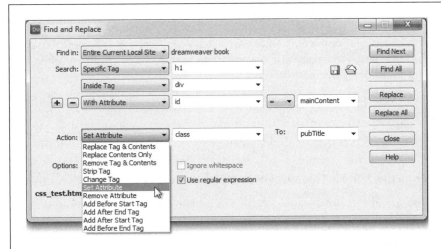

FIGURE 20-7

Once Dreamweaver finds a specific tag, it can perform any of 11 different actions on the tag or its contents.

NOTE Depending on which tag you're searching for, you might not see all the actions listed here. For example, the <img> tag doesn't have both an opening and a closing tag like the <p> tag does, so you won't see any of the options, such as Replace Contents Only, that affect the content between an opening and closing tag.

- **Remove Tag & Contents**. Deletes the tag and *everything* inside.

- **Strip Tag**. Deletes the tag from the page, but leaves anything enclosed by the tag untouched. The outmoded <font> tag is a perfect candidate for this action.

- **Set Attribute**. Adds an attribute to the tag. For example, you could set the *alt* property of an image this way (see the example in the next section).

- **Remove Attribute**. Removes an attribute from a tag. You could remove the not-at-all-useful *lowsrc* attribute from all image tags on your pages, for example.

- **Add Before (After) Start (End) Tag**. The last four actions in the menu simply offer variations on the same theme. Each lets you place content in a web page just before or after the tag for which you're searching.

To understand how this works, remember that most HTML tags come in pairs. The paragraph tag, for example, has an opening tag (<p>) and a closing tag (</p>). Say you searched for a paragraph tag; you could add text or HTML *before* or *after* the start tag (<p>), or *before* or *after* the end tag (</p>). (For an example of when you might use this feature, see the box on page 910.)

■ A Powerful Example: Adding Alt Text Fast

You've just put the finishing touches on the last page of your brand-new, 1,000-page site. You sit back and smile—and then snap bolt upright when you notice you forgot to add an Alt description for the site's banner graphic (see page 254). This graphic, called *site_banner.gif*, appears on every single one of those 1,000 pages. With rising dread, you realize you have to open each page, select the graphic, and add the *alt* property by hand.

And then you remember Dreamweaver's advanced tag-based Find and Replace feature.

Here's what you do. Press Ctrl+F (⌘-F) to open the Find and Replace window. Set up the dialog box like this:

1. **From the "Find in" menu, choose Entire Current Local Site.**

   You want to fix *every* page on your site (remember to make a backup first!).

2. **From the Search pop-up menu, choose Specific Tag; from the pop-up menu to its right, choose "img."**

   You'll start by identifying every image (the <img> tag).

3. **In the next row, use the three pop-up menus to choose With Attribute, "src," and the equals sign (=).**

   This tells Dreamweaver to look for specific images—in this case, images with a *src* attribute (the path that tells a browser where on the web server to find the image file) with a specific value.

4. **Type .*site_banner\.gif in the box next to the = sign.**

   For this exercise, assume you stored the graphics file in a folder called *images* located in the root folder of the site. The name *site_banner.gif* is the name of the image file. The .* is the magic, and you'll learn its purpose in a moment (ditto the backslash hanging out before the second period).

5. **Click the + button.**

   Another row of Tag Modifier menus appears.

6. **From this new row of menus, choose Without Attribute and "alt."**

   You've further limited Dreamweaver's search to only those images that don't already have the *alt* attribute. (After all, why bother setting the *alt* property on an image that already has it?)

7. **From the Action menu, choose Set Attribute; from the Tag menu, choose "alt."**

   You've just told Dreamweaver what to do when you click the Replace or Replace All button. When Dreamweaver finds an <img> tag that matches the search criteria, it will then *add* an *alt* property to that tag.

In this example, you might type *Chia Vet* in the To field; you've just specified the *alt* text for Dreamweaver to add to the image.

8. **Turn on "Use regular expressions."**

Regular expressions, described on page 905, let you search for specific patterns of characters and, in this case, help you accurately identify the banner graphic file everywhere it appears.

You know you're looking for the file *site_banner.gif* wherever it appears on the site. Unfortunately, if you just type *site_banner.gif* as the value of the *src* property in step 3, Dreamweaver can't succeed in its task. That's because the *src* attribute—the part of the <img> tag that includes the name of the file—varies from page to page. Depending on where a page is relative to the graphic, the src might be *site_banner.gif*, *images/site_banner.gif*, or even *../../../images/site_banner.gif*. What you need is a way to match every *src* attribute that ends in *site_banner.gif*.

A simple regular expression, *.*site_banner\.gif*, does the trick. The period stands for *any* character (6, g, or even %, for example), while the * (asterisk) means "zero or more times." When you add these codes to the graphic name, *site_banner.gif*, you instruct Dreamweaver to find every *src* value that ends in *site_banner.gif*.

In other words .* will match *images/*, *../../images/*, and so on. It will even match nothing at all in the case where the web page is actually inside the *images* folder and the *src* property is then just *site_banner.gif*.

Note the backslash before the last period: \.gif. In the world of regular expressions, a period means "any character," so simply using *site_banner.gif* would not only match *site_banner.gif*, but also *site_banner1gif*, *site_bannerZgif*, and so on—in other words, any character that sits between *site_banner* and *gif*. The backslash tells Dreamweaver to treat the next character literally; it's just a period with no special regular-expression power.

The dialog box should look like the one in Figure 20-8.

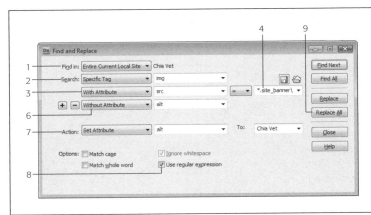

FIGURE 20-8

The numbers shown here correspond to the steps in this example, in which you want to add an <alt> tag to every occurrence of the banner logo for the benefit of people who can't, or don't want to, see graphics in their browsers.

9. **Click the Replace All button and sit back.**

In a matter of moments, Dreamweaver updates all 1,000 pages.

To test this out first, you might try a more cautious approach: Click the Find Next button to locate the first instance of the missing *alt* property; verify that it's correct by looking in the Search box (see Figure 20-8), and then click the Replace button to add the proper *alt* value. Double-check the newly updated page to make sure everything worked as planned. You can continue updating pages one at a time this way, or, once you're sure it works correctly, press Replace All.

FREQUENTLY ASKED QUESTION

Convenient Copyright Notices

I want to add a copyright notice to the bottom of each page in my website. Is there a way to automate this process so I don't have to edit every page by hand?

You bet. Use Dreamweaver's Find and Replace command to add text or HTML to the bottom of any web page. The trick is knowing how to use the command's Specific Tag option.

First, choose Edit→Find and Replace to open the Find and Replace window. Next, choose Entire Current Local Site from the "Find in" menu, and choose Specific Tag from the Search menu. Choose "body" from the Tag menu. Remember, the <body> tag in HTML encloses everything that appears inside a browser window; it's equivalent to what you see in the document window.

From the Action menu, choose Add Before End Tag. The end tag in this case is </body>. Since </body> marks the end of any content in a web page, whatever appears directly before this closing tag will appear at the bottom of the page (you can probably see where this is going).

Now, in the text field next to the Action menu, type (or paste) the copyright notice you want on each page. You may want to first design the copyright message using Dreamweaver, and then copy and paste the HTML into this field.

Click Replace All. Dreamweaver handles the rest.

You may not want to put the copyright notice at the *very end* of the page's HTML, as in this example. You might want it to go inside a particular <div> tag that's already on the page. Let's say that that div has an ID of *footer*. In that case, you would search for a <div> tag from the Tag menu and then select "With attribute" ID equal to "footer." Then you could use either the Add Before End Tag or Add After Start Tag options to place the copyright notice either at the end or the beginning of that div.

TIP To get a full description of every Dreamweaver menu, see Appendix B, "Dreamweaver CS6, Menu by Menu."

Customizing
Dreamweaver

Whether you're a hard-core HTML jockey who prefers to be knee-deep in Code view, or a visually oriented, drag-and-drop type who never strays from Design view, Dreamweaver lets you work the way you want.

By now, you're probably already using the Favorites tab on the Insert panel to store your most frequently used objects, as discussed on page 31. But don't stop there. Dreamweaver gives you the power to add, change, and share keyboard shortcuts, too—it's a simple way to tailor the program to your needs. And if that's not a big enough efficiency boost, you can add features that even Adobe's engineers never imagined, from simple productivity add-ons like QuickLink (see page 200) to advanced server behaviors that help power complete e-commerce sites. Dreamweaver's design lets amateur and professional programmers alike write new features and functions using HTML, JavaScript, and XML (Extensible Markup Language). You'll find hundreds of these extras, called *extensions*, to explore. And best of all, you can try many of them for free.

Keyboard Shortcuts

As you use Dreamweaver, you'll hit the same keyboard shortcuts and travel to the same palettes and menus time and again; perhaps you use a lot of graphics and Flash movies on your site, for example, and you're constantly using keyboard shortcuts to insert them. You may find that, after the thousandth time, Ctrl+Alt+F (⌘-Option-F) hurts your pinkie and uses too many keys to be truly efficient. On the other hand, the things you do all the time—like inserting text fields into forms or adding rollover images—may not have shortcuts at all, so you have no choice but to go to a menu.

To speed up your work and save your tendons, you can define or redefine shortcuts for most Dreamweaver commands using the program's keyboard-shortcut editor.

Dreamweaver stores its keyboard shortcuts in sets. It's easy to switch between them—a useful feature when you share your computer with someone who likes different keystrokes. Four sets of shortcuts come with the program, but you'll most likely never need to switch from the standard set:

- **Dreamweaver Standard**. When you first fire up Dreamweaver, the program turns on this set of keyboard shortcuts. It's the same one available since Dreamweaver 8.

- **Dreamweaver MX 2004**. Some shortcuts have changed since Dreamweaver MX 2004—for example, Shift+F5 now opens the Tag Editor window, whereas Ctrl+F5 did so in MX 2004. But the changes are so minor that it's not really necessary to use this set.

- **BBEdit**. If you're a Mac user with a code-editing past, you may have spent a lot of time learning the shortcuts for Bare Bones Software's popular BBEdit. If so, you can choose this set.

- **HomeSite**. Likewise, if you're adept at the Windows HTML text editor HomeSite, you may want to use its keyboard shortcuts. Don't remember HomeSite? That's because it hasn't been available for years, so you probably won't ever need this.

You access Dreamweaver's shortcut sets from the Keyboard Shortcuts dialog box. Choose Edit→Keyboard Shortcuts (Dreamweaver→Keyboard Shortcuts on Macs). Be patient—the sets can take some time to load. Once the dialog box appears (see Figure 21-1), you can switch sets by choosing a new one from the Current Set menu.

Make Your Own Shortcut Set

What if you want a set that *combines* BBEdit shortcuts with the ones you use most from Dreamweaver? Or you're a radical individualist who wants to remap *every* command to keys of your liking? No problem. You can't alter any of Dreamweaver's four standard shortcut sets, so you first want to make a copy of one of them.

Choose Edit→Keyboard Shortcuts (Dreamweaver→Keyboard Shortcuts). In the Keyboard Shortcuts window, use the Current Set pop-up menu to choose the set you wish to copy, and then click the Duplicate Set button, 🔳. Dreamweaver asks you to name the new set; once you do, click OK.

You can delete or rename any set you create—once you figure out that 🔘 is the Rename Set button. The 🗑 button, of course, lets you delete a set.

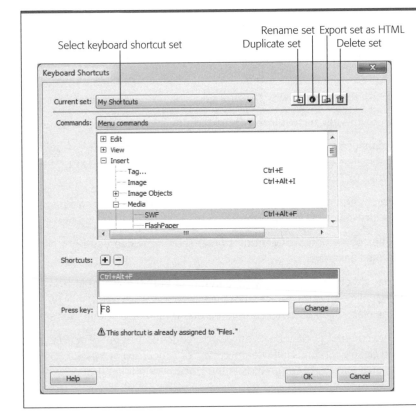

FIGURE 21-1

The Keyboard Shortcuts window lets you select or duplicate a shortcut set, as well as add or remove your own keyboard shortcuts, for every menu item in Dreamweaver. You can also create keyboard shortcuts for snippets (see Chapter 17). When you attempt to create a shortcut that another command already uses, Dreamweaver warns you. If you wish, you can ignore the warning and reassign the keys to the new command.

NOTE Dreamweaver lets you delete the four main keyboard shortcut sets. If you want one of them back, don't worry. The actual file isn't gone. You just need to edit a file called *mm_deleted_files.xml* in your Dreamweaver Configuration folder. Remove the line that lists the shortcut set you want to get back and save the file. Then quit and restart Dreamweaver. (Note that each account holder on Windows and Mac OS X has their own Configuration folder. See the box on page 923 for more details.)

Changing Keyboard Shortcuts

Once you duplicate a set of shortcuts, you can select any command and alter its shortcut. Start by choosing Edit→Keyboard Shortcuts (Dreamweaver→Keyboard Shortcuts) to open the Shortcuts window, if it's not already open. Then:

1. **From the Commands pop-up menu, choose the command type.**

   Dreamweaver organizes shortcuts into seven (Windows) or four (Macintosh) primary categories. They don't always make sense: For example, the Copy and Paste commands appear in the Code editing category, even though you use them at least as frequently when you edit a document in Design view. In addition, quite a few commands appear in multiple categories (though you only need to change a keyboard shortcut once to change it across all categories).

   Browse to see which commands have (or could have) keyboard shortcuts:

   - Menu commands, such as Insert→Image, appear in Dreamweaver's menus.

   - You might use the Code editing commands when you edit HTML. However, you could just as easily use them in Design view—they include Cut, Paste, and Move to Top of Page, to name a few.

   - Document editing commands let you select text and objects on a page, as well as preview a page in a browser.

   - The Files panel options (Windows only) show up when you right-click a file in the Files panel.

   - Site panel commands (Windows only) include those available from the contextual menu at the top-right of the Files panel, such as Site→New Site. (On the Mac, many of these commands are in the Menu commands set.)

   - The Site commands (Windows only) are an odd assortment of actions that let you close a window, quit Dreamweaver, or cancel an FTP session. On the Mac, you'll find these commands in the Document editing group.

   - Snippets are pieces of reusable code you select from the Snippets panel, as discussed in Chapter 17.

2. **In the list below the Commands menu, click the command whose keyboard shortcut you want to change.**

   You'll find menu commands grouped by menu name: Commands you see in the File drop-down menu, like Open and Save, fall under File. Click the + (Windows) or flippy triangle (Mac) next to the menu name to display its commands. For example, in Figure 21-1, the Insert menu is expanded as is its submenu, Media.

   If the command already has a keyboard shortcut, it appears in the right-hand column. If it doesn't, you see an empty space.

3. **Click inside the "Press key" field, and then press the new keystroke.**

   Unless you assign the shortcut to an F-key or the Esc key, you must begin your shortcut with the Ctrl key (⌘-key). For example, you can assign a shortcut to the F8 key, but not to the letter R; you'd have to press Ctrl+R (⌘-R) instead.

NOTE Your operating system may use some of its own keyboard shortcuts, and you can't assign any of those OS shortcuts to Dreamweaver. For example, in Windows, Ctrl+Esc opens Windows' Start Menu, while on Macs, the Dashboard uses the F12 key. If you try to assign an operating system shortcuts to Dreamweaver, your computer won't let you.

Of course, many commands already have shortcuts. If you choose an already assigned key combination, Dreamweaver tells you which command has dibs. You can pick a different key combination, or click the Change button to reassign the shortcut to your command. The original command now has no shortcut.

4. **Click the Change button.**

Dreamweaver saves the new shortcut in your custom set.

Repeat the steps above to assign other keystrokes. When you finish, click OK to close the dialog box.

FREQUENTLY ASKED QUESTION

Sharing Shortcuts

How do I share my keyboard set with other people?

Dreamweaver stores your keyboard shortcuts as XML files, but finding them can be tricky. They're in different locations depending on your operating system. Each keyboard set lives in an XML file; the file's name ends with the extension .xml. For example, if you create a new set of keyboard shortcuts named My Shortcuts, the XML file would be *My Shortcuts.xml*.

In Windows XP, you'll find the custom keyboard set on your main hard drive in *Documents and Settings→[Your Name] →Application Data→Adobe Dreamweaver CS6→en_US→ Configuration→Menus→Custom Sets.* In Windows Vista and Windows 7, they're in *C:\Users\[Your user name]\AppData\ Roaming\Adobe\Dreamweaver CS6\en_US\Configuration\ Menus\Custom Sets.* (Note that Windows normally hides these files from you; see the Note on page 916 to get around this little problem.)

Mac OS X squirrels these files away in your *[User name]→ Library→Application Support→Adobe→Dreamweaver CS6→ en_US→Configuration→Menus→Custom Sets.* (Mac OS X Lion [version 10.7] normally hides your Library folder from view, but see the note on page 917 to flush it out.)

Depending on the language you use, you might see something other than "en_US" (which stands for English), such as "de_DE" for German, or "ja_JP" for Japanese.

You can copy these files and place them in the Custom Sets folder on other computers. Once you do, Dreamweaver users on those machines can use the Keyboard Shortcuts window (Edit→Keyboard Shortcuts or, on the Mac, Dreamweaver→Keyboard Shortcuts) to select the new set, just as though you created it in that copy of Dreamweaver.

What if a command you use often doesn't have a shortcut at all? No problem, you can create one. As a matter of fact, Dreamweaver lets you assign *two* keyboard shortcuts to every command—one for you, and one for your left-handed spouse, for example.

To give a command a first or additional shortcut:

1. **Choose the command.**

Follow the first two steps of the preceding instructions.

2. **Click the + button next to the word "Shortcuts."**

The cursor automatically pops into the "Press key" field.

3. **Press the keys for the shortcut, and then click Change again.**

Repeat these steps to assign another set of keystrokes; when you finish, click OK.

Deleting shortcuts is just as easy. Simply click the command in the list, and then click the minus sign (–) next to "Shortcuts."

Create a Shortcut Cheat Sheet

Unless your brain is equipped with a 400-gig hard drive, you'll probably find it hard to remember all of Dreamweaver's keyboard shortcuts.

Fortunately, Dreamweaver offers a printable cheat sheet. At the top of the Shortcuts window, there's a handy "Export Set as HTML" button (labeled with the odd icon ; see Figure 21-1). Click this button to name and save a simple HTML page that lists all the commands and keyboard shortcuts for the currently selected command set. Once you save the file, print it out or use it as an online reference—it's a great way to keep a record of your shortcuts for yourself or a team of designers.

> **NOTE** Windows owners: Windows normally hides certain files, such as important system files, from sight. This includes the Configuration folder discussed in the box on page 923 and the Menus folder discussed in the box on page 915. To access these folders, you need to make hidden files visible. XP users should follow the steps at *http://tinyurl.com/259yhu5*, and Windows Vista and 7 users should do so at *http://tinyurl.com/6hxlo4o*.

■ Dreamweaver Extensions

While keyboard shortcuts give you an easy way to access frequently used commands, they're not much help if the command you want doesn't exist. Suppose, for example, you use Dreamweaver's Open Browser Window behavior (page 691) to load a new web page into a window that measures exactly 200 x 300 pixels. What if you want to center the window in the middle of your visitor's monitor? Dreamweaver's behavior doesn't do that. What's a web designer to do? You could go to the Adobe site and request the new feature (*http://tinyurl.com/jbmlm*) in hopes that the bustling team of programmers will add it to the next version of the program. But you'd have to wait—and there's no guarantee that Adobe would add it.

Instead, legions of hard-core Dreamweaver fans have taken this wish-list feature into their own hands. As it turns out, amateur (and pro) programmers can enhance Dreamweaver relatively easily by writing new feature modules using the basic languages of the Web: HTML, JavaScript, and XML. (In fact, HTML forms, JavaScript programs, and XML documents constitute much of Dreamweaver's code. The objects in the Insert panel, for example, are actually HTML pages stored within Dreamweaver's Configuration folder, and Adobe wrote all of Dreamweaver's menus as an XML file.)

Because of this "open architecture," you can add new functions and commands—called *extensions*—to Dreamweaver by downloading the work of one of those programmers and installing it in your own copy of the program. A Dreamweaver extension can take many forms, and they change how the program works in a variety of ways. You can add an icon to the Insert panel, a behavior to the Behaviors panel, or a command in the Commands menu. It might even be an entirely new floating window, like the Property Inspector, that you use to alter some aspect of your page.

Best of all, while you might need some programming ability to *create* extensions, you don't need any to *use* them. You can download and install hundreds of extensions from the Web, many of them for free. In addition, you can find many sophisticated extensions, like those for creating e-commerce sites, commercially available.

NOTE   Mac OS X Lion owners: While previous versions of Mac OS X let you view application preferences, plug-ins, and data in your Library folder, OS X Lion [version 10.7] now hides the Library folder from sight. Here's how you uncover it: In the Finder, click Go to see a list of destinations (Documents, Desktop, and so on). Hold down the Option key and the Library folder pops up in the list of destinations. Click Library→Application Support→Adobe→Dreamweaver CS6—en_US→Configuration.

Browse the Exchange

The largest collection of add-ons awaits you at the Adobe Exchange website (*www.adobe.com/exchange*), where you'll find hundreds of free and commercial extensions. Although some come from Adobe itself, an army of talented Dreamweaver users write the vast majority of them.

NOTE   You've been introduced to the Exchange in Chapter 13; you just might not have known it—the Widget Browser mentioned in Chapter 13 is another way to browse offerings on the exchange. However, the Widget Browser is limited to just the widgets described in Chapter 13. The Exchange has both widgets *and* Dreamweaver extensions.

Using the Exchange is straightforward:

1. **In your browser, go to *www.adobe.com/exchange* and then click the Dreamweaver link under "Exchanges by Product."**

   You can also get to the Exchange from within Dreamweaver by choosing Commands→Get More Commands.

2. **Sign in.**

   You can *browse* the site without signing in, but to *download* any of the extensions, you need to get a free Adobe ID and sign in, using the Exchange Sign In form—click the *Your account* link in the top-left corner of the web page.

3. Browse the extensions.

Once you log into the site, the home page highlights new and popular extensions. A list of extension categories—Accessibility, DHTML/Layers, Navigation, and so on—appears on the right. Click any of them to see a list of extensions in that category. Click one of the sorting tabs (circled in Figure 21-2) to view staff picks or the newest, most popular, or highest-rated extensions.

Use the menu to the right of "License type" to view extensions that match a particular license—for example, if you want free stuff, select Open Source or Freeware and then click the Filter button.

If you're looking for a *particular* extension, the Search command is your best bet. Type the extension's name or a few descriptive words into the Search Dreamweaver field, and then click Search.

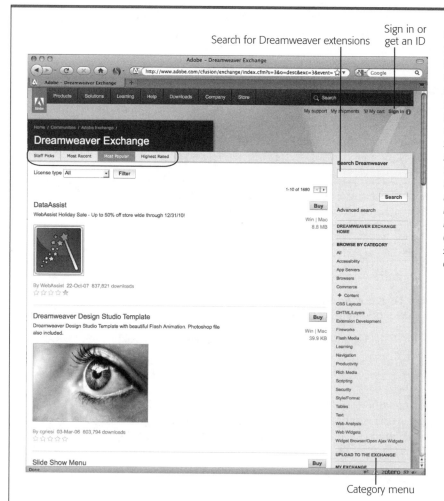

Search for Dreamweaver extensions

Sign in or get an ID

Category menu

FIGURE 21-2

The Dreamweaver Exchange lets you check out its offerings freely, and even buy commercial third-party extensions. But if you want to download a free extension, you have to get an Adobe ID and log into the site. Unfortunately, the marketing machine must be appeased, so you need to provide personal information and face a (fortunately optional) survey of your web development habits.

NOTE Extensions have been around for many versions of Dreamweaver. Unfortunately, each version added a few kinks for extension developers, so not all extensions work with Dreamweaver CS6. (Many that were compatible with Dreamweaver CS4, however, *do* work with Dreamweaver CS6.) Most extension developers list the Dreamweaver versions their extensions work with; you can also check for version compatibility on the Dreamweaver Exchange site (*http://tinyurl.com/yvbfxf*); see Figure 21-2.

4. **Click an extension's name to go to its web page.**

   You'll find lots of information there, including a description of how the extension works, a button to either purchase or download it, information about which version of Dreamweaver and which operating system (Windows or Mac) it works with, and buttons to add the extension to Favorites and Alerts lists. The Favorites option lets you create a personal list of the extensions you like best; sign up on the Alerts list and the author sends you an email whenever she updates the extension.

   When you click the Download button for an extension, your browser either starts downloading the extension or shuttles you off to the author's website. A Buy button, on the other hand, always sends you to the site where you buy the extension directly from its creator.

Find a Good Extension

How do you figure out which extensions are worth checking out? First, you can find recommendations scattered throughout this book in special boxes labeled "Extension Alert" (see page 200 for an example).

The Exchange also provides information to help you separate the wheat from the chaff. Adobe tests many of the extensions. Those that pass a basic set of tests—meaning that it installs OK, it works, and it doesn't blow up your computer—get a Basic approval rating. Some extensions pass a more rigorous test that determines if the extension works in a way that's "Dreamweaver-like." In other words, these extensions look, feel, and act like other aspects of the program, so you won't need to learn a new interface. Adobe gives them an Adobe Approved rating, indicated by the word "Adobe" in the approval section of an extension's details page.

NOTE Adobe used to test all the extensions, but that appears to have been too much work. An extension with an approval rating of None means that Adobe hasn't tested it.

Of course, these approval ratings only let you know if an extension works; they don't tell you whether it's *useful*. As an extra aid, Dreamweaver aficionados (including you) can rate each extension on a scale of 1 (worst) to 5 stars (best) and even add a detailed review of the extension. An extension's average rating gives you a good indication of how handy it is. When you browse the Exchange, look for the star rating at the bottom of each extension (see Figure 21-2). You can also click the Highest Rated link to sort the list of extensions from most to least number of stars.

Other Extension Sources

Unfortunately, the glory days of free extensions are mostly over. While you can still find plenty of extensions for free, many developers realized they couldn't survive by giving away their work. The upside is that there are now more excellent, polished, well-documented commercial extensions than ever—and many even offer customer support. Here are a few highlights:

- **WebAssist** (*www.webassist.com*) is one of the largest and most professional extension-development companies. It offers a wide variety of high-quality extensions, including a few for free.

- **Felix One** (*http://tinyurl.com/65oesd6*) offers an impressive collection of extensions if PHP or ASP is your bag. You need to register at the site, but it's free.

- **Project Seven** (*www.projectseven.com*) offers free extensions and several excellent commercial extensions that let you create animated HTML and CSS menus, scrolling areas of text, CSS-based page layouts, photo galleries, and more.

- **Trent Pastrana** (*www.fourlevel.com*) sells extensions that build photo galleries, whiz-bang effects (like menus that slide onto a page), and scrollers that move text up and down (or left and right) across a page. He also provides several free extensions.

- **Trio Solutions** (*http://tinyurl.com/6k8q2zg*) sells lots of inexpensive extensions that let you add CSS-style calendars, insert Flash music players into a page, and much more.

- **Hot Dreamweaver** (*www.hotdreamweaver.com*) sells extensions for server-side needs, like sending form submissions as emails, adding Captcha (those little hard-to-read pictures of letters and numbers that you have to type into a form to prove you're a human), and uploading files to a web server.

- **DMXZone** (*www.dmxzone.com/index?3*) offers a range of extensions, including those that let you build a Facebook fan page for your business, embed an MP3 player on a page so visitors can listen to audio, and extensions for PHP and ASP server-side programming that let you add forms so guests can upload files to your server. They even have a bunch of free extensions, like YouTubizer, that make it easy to embed YouTube videos on a page.

Download and Install Extensions

Once you find a great extension, download it to your computer. You can save the downloaded file anywhere on your machine, but you may want to create a special folder for it. That way, if you ever need to reinstall Dreamweaver, you can quickly find and add your collection of extensions.

Extension file names end with .mxp, which stands for Macromedia Exchange Package (from the days before Adobe bought Macromedia), or the newer .zxp file type (essentially the same file, just zipped). Those special file formats work with Adobe's Extension Manager—the program that actually installs the extension in Dreamweaver.

Extension Manager

To add or remove a Dreamweaver extension, use the Extension Manager, a standalone program integrated into Dreamweaver. The Extension Manager handles add-ons for many Adobe programs, not just Dreamweaver. It lets you install extensions, turn them on and off, and remove them. It's handy if you also use Adobe's Photoshop, Illustrator, Flash, or Fireworks programs—you get a single place to manage all your extensions.

You can launch the Extension Manager from within Dreamweaver by choosing Help→Manage Extensions (Commands→Manage Extensions); see Figure 21-3.

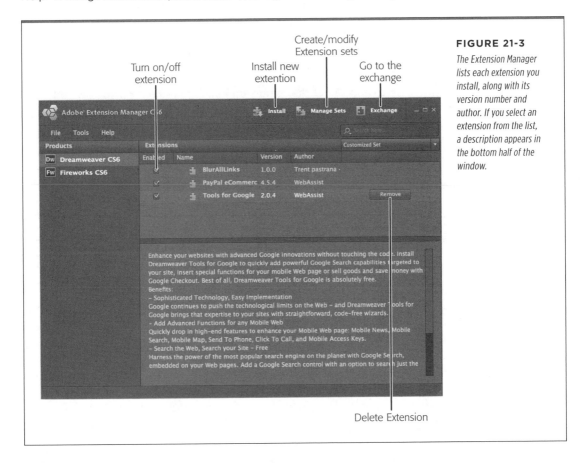

FIGURE 21-3

The Extension Manager lists each extension you install, along with its version number and author. If you select an extension from the list, a description appears in the bottom half of the window.

Turn on/off extension

Install new extention

Create/modify Extension sets

Go to the exchange

Delete Extension

To add an extension:

1. **Download an extension package (a .mxp, or .zxp file) from the Exchange or another website.**

   See instructions above.

2. **In Dreamweaver, choose Help→Manage Extensions (Commands→Manage Extensions).**

   You can also select Extension Manager from the Extension menu in the Application Bar (see Figure 1-7). Either way, Dreamweaver launches the Extension Manager, which lists all the extensions you've installed.

3. **Choose Dreamweaver CS6 from the left-hand list of Adobe products.**

   Since the Extension Manager handles extensions for several programs, you need to specify which program you're using. If you don't have any other Adobe products installed on your machine, Dreamweaver CS6 is your only option.

4. **Choose File→Install Extension.**

   You can also click the Install Extension button. The Select Extension window appears, listing the folders on your hard drive.

5. **Navigate to and select the extension package (.mxp or .zxp file) you want to add.**

   A disclaimer appears with a lot of legal text. In brief, it frees Adobe from liability if your computer melts down as a result of installing the extension.

6. **Click Accept in the Disclaimer window.**

   A message may appear that asks you to quit and restart Dreamweaver. If so, follow the directions.

TIP A faster way to install an extension is to simply double-click the .mxp, or .zxp file after you download it. This launches the Extension Manager and installs the extension.

To remove an extension, select it from the list and choose File→Remove Extension, or click the Remove button.

If you install a lot of extensions, Dreamweaver may take longer than usual to load; it needs to process every extension file as it starts up. If you want to temporarily turn off an extension (as opposed to deleting it), open the Extension Manager and turn off the Enable box next to the extension's name. To turn it back on, simply turn on the checkbox again. You may need to restart Dreamweaver to make the extension available again.

Another option is to use the Extension Manager's Manage Sets feature (see Figure 21-3.) Clicking this option opens a Manage Extension Sets window where you can create different collections or sets of extensions that you can toggle on and off. This is really only useful if you have a lot of extensions installed and you use some extensions on some sites and others on another site. For example, if you're building a PHP-driven website, you might create a collection of extensions that add features for PHP-based pages. You could turn on that set of extensions when you're working on PHP pages, and pick a different set when you work on regular HTML sites.

Make Your Own Extensions

The Exchange is a great resource for finding useful extensions, but what if you can't find the extension you need? Create your own.

Writing extensions requires in-depth knowledge of HTML and JavaScript and is beyond the scope of this book. But when you create a command that lets you complete a weekly task in a fraction of the time it previously took, the effort may just be worth it. For more information, visit the Dreamweaver Support Center at *http:// help.adobe.com/en_US/dreamweaver/cs/extend/*.

POWER USERS' CLINIC

The Secret Life of Extensions

Where do extensions go? The basic answer is inside Dreamweaver's Configuration folder. But Dreamweaver actually supplies you with multiple configuration folders: a main folder located with the program file itself and account-specific folders for each user account on a computer. Windows and Macs let multiple users each have an account on a single computer—one for you, one for your spouse, and one for your pet ferret, say. Of course, you may be the only one using your computer, so there'd be only one configuration folder for your account and one in the main application folder.

On a Windows machine, you find the main configuration folder in *C:\Program Files\Adobe\Adobe Dreamweaver CS6 \ configuration* (assuming that C is your main drive and you're on an x86 [32-bit Windows] system—if you're using a 64-bit version of Windows then you'll find the configuration folder in *C:\Program Files (x86)\Adobe\Adobe Dreamweaver CS6 \ configuration*). On a Mac, you find it in *Applications→Adobe Dreamweaver CS6→Configuration*. The individual account configuration folders are located in folders dedicated to each user. In Windows XP, they're at *C:\Documents and Settings\ [Your user name]\Application Data\Adobe\Dreamweaver CS6\en_US\Configuration*. In Windows Vista and Windows 7, look for *C:\Users\[Your user name]\AppData\Roaming\Adobe\ Dreamweaver CS5.5\en_US\ Configuration*. (Normally the AppData folder is hidden, so you may need to make it visible as described in the note on page 916.)

On a Mac, try *Volume Name→Users→[Your user name]→ Library→Application Support→Adobe→Dreamweaver CS5.5→en_US→Configuration*. (Mac OS X 10.7 [Lion] owners won't usually see their Library folder—see the note on page 917, to learn how to access it.)

As mentioned in the box on page 915, "en_US" means English. If you installed Dreamweaver using a different language, this folder will be named something else, such as "de_DE" for German.

Dreamweaver records some changes you make in your personal configuration folder, such as when you add an extension, delete a keyboard shortcut set (see page 911), or save a workspace layout (see page 37).

The main Configuration folder holds many of the files that control Dreamweaver's look and operation. For instance, Dreamweaver describes its entire menu structure, including menu items and submenus, in a file called *menus.xml*. When Dreamweaver starts, it reads this file and uses the information inside it to draw the menus on the screen.

The Configuration folder holds many subfolders, each with a special purpose. For example, the Objects subfolder contains files that tell Dreamweaver which icon buttons appear on the Insert bar and how each one works.

Depending on the type of extension you downloaded—command, object, behavior, or whatever—the Extension Manager stores the file (or files) it requires in one or more folders inside the Configuration folder. Because all the files in the Configuration folder are crucial to the way Dreamweaver works, don't delete the folder or any of the files inside it. In fact, because the Extension Manager automatically makes any required changes to the Configuration folder, there's no reason for you to even look inside it. (The only exception is when you want to copy your keyboard shortcut set to another computer [see page 915].)

Working with Server-Side Programming

So far in this book, you've learned to build and maintain websites using Dream-weaver's powerful design, coding, and site management tools. The pages you've created use straightforward HTML, and you can immediately preview them in a web browser. The web cognoscenti often call these kinds of pages *static*, because they don't change once you finish building them (unless you edit them, of course). For many websites, especially those where you carefully handcraft the design and content on a page-by-page basis, static web pages are the way to go.

But imagine landing a contract to build an online catalog of 10,000 products. After the initial excitement disappears (along with your plans for that trip to Hawaii), you realize that even using Dreamweaver's Template tool (Chapter 19), building 10,000 pages is a lot of work!

For jobs like that, most developers use a database to store information about the many products the company sells, along with a kind of page template that's programmed to serve up just-in-time product-info pages. These dynamically created pages work their magic using a server-side programming language like PHP, ASP, ColdFusion, Java, or Ruby. When a visitor clicks a link to learn more about a product, he's actually requesting this template file, which talks to the database, retrieves information for a product, and then returns a fully-formed web page—one that looks just like a page you'd create by hand.

All major e-commerce sites work this way. Visit *www.amazon.com*, for example, and you'll find more books than you could read in a lifetime. In fact, you'll find more products—DVDs, CDs, even outdoor lawn furniture—than could fit inside a Wal-Mart. In just an hour, you could browse through hundreds of products, each with its own web page. Do you really think Amazon hired an army of web developers to create a web page for each product it sells? Not a chance.

Instead, when you search for a book on Amazon.com, your search triggers a computer program, running on what's called an *application server*, that searches Amazon's large database of products. When the program finds products that match your search criteria, it merges information about that product with HTML page elements (a banner, navigation buttons, a copyright notice, and so on) to stitch together a web page on the fly and send it to your browser. You see a page that's been created, perhaps for the first time ever (Figure 22-1).

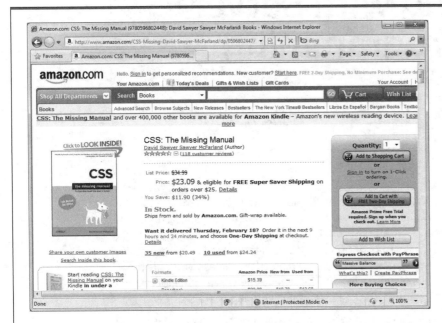

FIGURE 22-1

An infinite number of monkeys couldn't create a web page for each product Amazon.com sells. The solution? A dynamic website, which follows programmed instructions to create pages made up of content chunks pulled from a database. That's the way to go if you've got a site with loads of pages, all of which present similar information.

NOTE Luckily, you're not limited to *either* "static" *or* "dynamic" web pages. Websites frequently use both—static pages for custom designs and handcrafted content and dynamic pages for mass-produced catalog pages, for example.

Dynamic websites are generally the realm of professional programmers. If you're reading this chapter, you're either already programming these types of pages using PHP, ColdFusion, Ruby on Rails, C#, or some other programming language...or you're interested in learning how to do so.

NOTE This chapter won't teach you how to program; its sole purpose is to show you how to set up Dreamweaver to work with dynamic websites. If you're interested in getting started with server-side programming, PHP is a very popular first step. Facebook and the popular blogging system WordPress use PHP. A good place to start learning the language is with *PHP Solutions: Dynamic Web Design Made Easy* (friendsofED) by David Powers or *Head First PHP & MySQL* (O'Reilly Media) by Lynn Beighley and Michael Morrison.

What About Dreamweaver's Server-Side Tools?

I own a previous version of this book, which included tutorials for building database-driven websites with Dreamweaver. Where did they go?

It's true that Dreamweaver includes tools for connecting to a database, adding and retrieving information from that database, password-protecting pages, and a lot more. Unfortunately, those tools, called "server behaviors," have been left stagnant for several versions of the program. Adobe apparently doesn't have any interest in updating them and the code the program produces is just plain unprofessional—it's old and outdated. It's a mystery why Adobe doesn't just remove these tools.

Regardless, you probably want to steer clear of Dreamweaver's server behaviors and either learn how to program yourself, or use a pre-programmed content management system like WordPress, Joomla, or Drupal to handle your database needs. Alternatively, you can jump to a third-party solution like *WebAssist.com*, which sells its own set of PHP server behaviors.

But if you really want to try Dreamweaver's built-in tools, you can find the chapters dealing with Dreamweaver's server-side programming tools from the last edition of this book in an online appendix; visit *http://sawmac.com/dwcs6/* to get the chapters and tutorial files.

■ Pieces of the Puzzle

Dynamic websites are more complex than simple static sites. Static sites require only the computer you use to build your pages and a web server to dish them out. In fact, as you can see by previewing your site with a web browser on your own computer, you don't even need a web server to effectively view a static website.

Dynamic web pages, by contrast, require more horsepower and a mix of technologies (see Figure 22-2). Not only is there a web server that handles requests for web pages, but you need two other types of servers, an *application server* and a *database server.*

You'll still use a lot of HTML (and CSS) in building a dynamic site—for example, to provide the page layout, add banner graphics, and display navigation bars. But you'll augment that mix with some form of programming code. The application server processes that code, often retrieving information from the database server, and then it sends a completed HTML page to the web server, which, in turn, sends that page to your site's visitor.

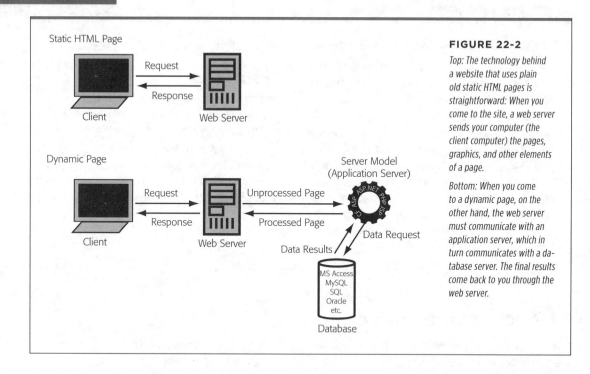

FIGURE 22-2

Top: The technology behind a website that uses plain old static HTML pages is straightforward: When you come to the site, a web server sends your computer (the client computer) the pages, graphics, and other elements of a page.

Bottom: When you come to a dynamic page, on the other hand, the web server must communicate with an application server, which in turn communicates with a database server. The final results come back to you through the web server.

NOTE When you talk about websites, a *server* refers to the software that dishes out particular types of information—web pages, database results, or a program's output. It doesn't necessarily mean a separate computer; web hosting firms can (and frequently do) have web, database, and application servers all running happily together on a single machine.

Because dynamic websites always coordinate the work of these servers, you can't just open dynamic site pages in your browser as you build them, as you can with a regular web page. You have to view dynamic pages through a web server that has an appropriate application server running. You also have to set up a database, and connect that database to your application server.

Although this arrangement can be quite complex, it's not difficult to set up a basic web server, application server, and database on your own computer, so you can build and test database-driven web pages. It's also easy to connect to remote computers that are already configured to serve up dynamic, database-driven web pages.

NOTE The term *web application* refers to web pages that work together to complete a task. All the various pages that make up an online shopping site—pages that let you search a database of products, view individual product pages, and add products to a shopping cart, for example—are collectively considered a web application.

■ Dynamic Websites: The Setup

Now that your head is spinning and you're considering some noble career alternative like farmer, firefighter, or carpenter, it's time to set up Dreamweaver to work with an application server and database.

You can configure your setup several ways. One involves using what Dreamweaver calls a *testing server*. Remember how you can create a website on your own computer (the *local site*) before posting it online for all to see (the *remote site*)? Here, the concept is similar. When you build web applications, it's a good idea to keep all your work-in-progress pages on your own computer, just as you did when you created static pages. After all, you don't want to fill up an online database with test data, or put half-finished product pages on the Internet. But because dynamic websites require an application server and database to work, you need to set up a *testing server* to store and preview your dynamic pages—a real web server, an application server, and a database, in other words—all running on the same machine, your own computer.

Then, when you finish building your site, you transfer these pages to your remote site using Dreamweaver's built-in FTP feature (see Chapter 17). If you work in a group setting with other web developers, you can set up the testing server on a machine that's part of your group's local network. Each developer can then connect to the testing server and retrieve files to work on. (Dreamweaver's Check In/Check Out feature, described on page 807, is ideal for this type of environment.)

> **NOTE** You can always use your remote site as a testing server. If you go this route, you should have a fast Internet connection. Otherwise, testing your dynamic pages may just test your patience, as you constantly upload pages to the server for testing.

Finally, whenever you work on dynamic files directly on a remote server, be aware that mistakes you make along the way may affect a database that *other* dynamic pages use. If, while hurriedly trying to complete your website, you accidentally create a page that deletes records from your database, important information may no longer be available on your site. So whenever possible, keep your testing server separate from the server that stores your finished and perfected site.

Setting Up a Testing Server

If you want to set up your own local testing server and are new to server-side programming, start out with AMP, which stands for Apache, MySQL, and PHP. This is the most common trio of web server, database server, and application server; you'll find AMP at almost all hosting companies, and it's a great foundation for server-side programming. Even better, it's easy to set up on both Windows and Mac PCs.

■ WINDOWS

For Windows, WAMP is a good choice. It's a simple installer for putting Apache, MySQL, and PHP on your computer. It's free and works with Windows 7 and 8, Windows Vista, and Windows XP. You can find the software at *www.wampserver .com/en*. Because the software changes somewhat frequently, you'll find instructions that match changes to the WAMP installer at *www.uptospeedguides.com/wamp*.

■ MACS

For the Mac, MAMP provides a simple way to get Apache, MySQL, and PHP up and running. MAMP is free and available from *www.mamp.info*. The MAMP software changes (as does its website) frequently, so make sure you get the most up-to-date directions at *www.uptospeedguides.com/mamp*.

If you plan to follow along with the tutorials in this section of the book, it's a good idea to download and install WAMP or MAMP now.

Localhost and the Local Site Root Folder

If you followed the previous instructions and installed a testing server on your computer, you've already visited a web page at either http://localhost/ or http://localhost/MAMP (the home pages for WAMP and MAMP, respectively). You may be wondering, what's this *localhost* thing? For a computer, "localhost" is just another way of saying "me." When you instruct a browser to go to http://localhost, you're merely telling it to look for a web server running on the same computer as the browser is. Normally, when you visit a website, you type a web address like *http://www.google.com*. That sends your browser out over the Internet looking for a web page located on some computer identified as *www.google.com*. When you set up a web server on your own computer and want to view the web pages you create there, your browser need look no further than your own system and *its* web server, a.k.a. that testing server you created earlier.

But once the browser asks your local testing server to give it a web page, where does the server find that page on your computer? When you work with static web pages (like the ones you built earlier in this book), you can keep your website files pretty much anywhere you want: on your desktop, in your Documents folder, on an external hard drive, and so on. Dynamic pages, on the other hand, work only with the help of a web server (and its companions, the application and database servers). The web server expects files for a website to reside in a particular location on your computer.

That folder is called the *site root* folder (you may also hear it referred to as the *document root*). The exact name and location of the site root folder varies from system to system. For example, different web hosting companies have different setups, and might name the folder *htdocs, webdocs*, or *public_html*. WAMP uses a folder named *www* as the site root (*C:\WAMP\www*, for example), while MAMP uses a folder called *htdocs*; head over to Applications→MAMP→htdocs.

In the case of WAMP, if you type http://localhost/my_page.html into your browser, the browser requests a file named *my_page.html* from the web server running on your computer. The server then looks inside *C:\Program Files\WAMP\www* for a file named *my_page.html*; if it finds it, the server sends the file back to the browser. On a Mac running MAMP, the web server looks in Applications→MAMP→htdocs for the file *my_page.html*.

> **NOTE** If you don't specify a particular file—for example, if you just surf to http://localhost/—the web server looks for a "default file" (usually named *index.html* or *index.php*).

Remember, when you work on a dynamic, database-driven site, you need to keep your website files inside the site root folder of your testing server.

> **NOTE** You can also put your site files in a folder *inside* the site root folder. If you placed a folder named *store* in the *www (WAMP) or htdocs (MAMP)* folder, you could visit a web page named *products.php* inside that folder by browsing to http://localhost/store/products.php.

In addition, as you start to build more and more dynamic sites, you might want to have separate folder names for each site. For example, you could put the site files for clientX in a folder named *clientX* inside the *www* or *htdocs* folder. Then you could test that client's web pages by typing http://localhost/clientX/ into a browser. However, it's more elegant to have separate local sites for each client; that way, you can type something like http://clientX/ into a web browser and your local web server would find the files just for that one client. To do this, you create what are called *virtualhosts* for each site. You can learn how to do that by following the instructions at *www.uptospeedguides.com/wamp/virtualhosts* or *www.uptospeedguide.com/mamp/virtualhosts*. MAMP users can also buy MAMP Pro ($59 and worth every penny), which provides a simple program for creating and managing separate websites on the same server.

Setting Up Dreamweaver

After you set up a testing server on your computer, the next step (as with any web site you work on in Dreamweaver) is setting up a website. The process of setting up a dynamic site, however, is slightly different from that for a static site:

1. **Start Dreamweaver, and then choose Site→New Site.**

   The Site Setup window opens (see Figure 22-3). You need to give this new site a name and tell Dreamweaver where to find the site files.

2. **Name the site in the first box.**

   You can use any name you like; it only shows up in Dreamweaver's Files panel. (This is the same step as described on page 40.)

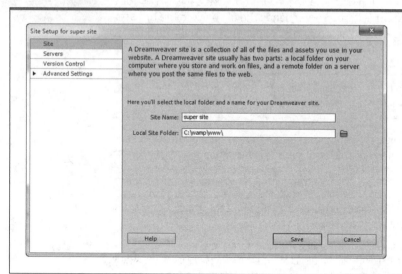

FIGURE 22-3

Setting up a dynamic site starts the same way as setting up a regular, plain old HTML site: name the site and tell Dreamweaver where to find its files.

3. **In the next box, click the folder icon on the far right, and then navigate to and select the folder where you'll store your local files.**

   Again, this is the same step you used to set up a static website; however, if you've set up a local testing environment using a program like MAMP or WAMP, this folder should match the local root folder for the testing server. In the case of WAMP, you'll find that root folder at C:\WAMP\www; MAMP puts it in Applications→MAMP→htdocs. (If you installed Apache yourself, or used a program other than WAMP or MAMP, your local root folder will be elsewhere on your system; for non-AMP programs, refer to the program's website to see where it creates local root folders.)

   You just told Dreamweaver the name you want to use for the new site and selected the local site's folder.

4. **Click Servers in the left-hand list of categories (see Figure 22-4).**

   You use this screen to set up both the remote and the testing servers for your dynamic site. In other words, you use this screen to add FTP information so you can upload your site files to your live web server (as described on page 785), *and* you use this screen to tell Dreamweaver where your local testing server resides.

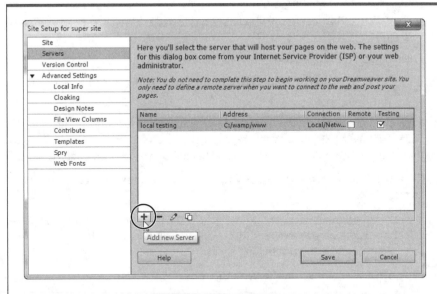

FIGURE 22-4

*Dreamweaver lets you
add more than one server
to a site, crucial if you're
building a dynamic site.
Dynamic sites, just like
static websites, need a
regular old web server
on the Internet, and you
have to tell Dreamweaver
how to connect to it via
FTP (this is discussed in
Chapter 17). In addition to
that, dynamic sites need
a testing server, and you
have to give Dreamweaver
the connection details for
that as well.*

5. **Click the Add New Server button (circled in Figure 22-4).**

    The Basic server settings window appears (see Figure 22-5). Here, you tell
    Dreamweaver how to connect to your testing server and where it can find the
    files for your site.

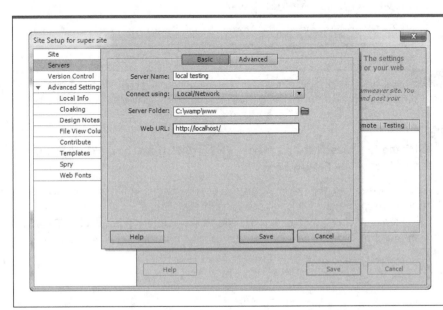

FIGURE 22-5

*You want to test your
dynamic site locally (on
your own computer)
before you upload your
files to a live server on
the Web. To do that, you
need to tell Dreamweaver
where to find the local
testing server. Your setup
window should look like
this when you're done.*

6. **In the Server Name box, type local testing.**

It doesn't really matter what you type here—the name just helps you identify your server in the Servers window (Figure 22-4). In this case, use *local testing* since that denotes both a testing server and the fact that it's "local" (on your own computer).

The next step tells Dreamweaver how to connect to that server.

7. **Choose Local/Network from the "Connect using" drop-down menu.**

This is the same window you used to set up connections to both local and remote servers, so even though you're setting up a local site, you'll see options like FTP, SFTP, FTP over SSL/TLS, WebDAV and RDS here (see page 785 for more on these). Because you're setting up a local testing server, choose Local/Network.

8. **Click the folder icon and select your local site folder (basically the same as step 2).**

If you're using WAMP, the *root* folder is at *C:\WAMP\www*; if you use MAMP, select Applications→MAMP→htdocs. Next, you need to provide a web address so you can connect to your testing server.

9. **Type http://localhost/ in the Web URL box.**

Although Dreamweaver asks for a "Web" URL, don't type in the address for your site out on the Web. Dynamic pages only work when you have a web server, and you just set one up, called a testing server, on your own computer. Therefore, you have to tell Dreamweaver to direct a web browser to your own, local, testing server. That way, when you use Dreamweaver's File→Preview in Browser command, Dreamweaver opens a browser and tells it to find the page on the web server at http://localhost/.

The Site Setup window should now look like Figure 22-5. Lastly, you'll tell Dreamweaver that you want to create PHP pages.

> **NOTE** If you run MAMP and can't change the port Apache uses as described in the MAMP setup instructions at *www.uptospeedguides.com/mamp/*, you need to add the port number 8888 to the URL, like this: http://localhost:8888/.

10. **Click the Advanced tab and choose PHP MySQL from the drop-down Server Model menu (see Figure 22-6).**

This lets Dreamweaver know the type of web pages you'll create. (This step doesn't do too much else, but it does ensure that Dreamweaver adds the proper file extension when you create a new file. For example, if you select PHP MySQL from this list, Dreamweaver appends ".php" to file names when you create a new page. If you're using a language that Dreamweaver doesn't list, like Ruby on Rails, you can still use Dreamweaver to edit those files; Live view still displays the site, and you can still preview it using a web browser to launch the page from your local testing server.

11. **Click the Save button.** In the Site Setup window, turn off the "Remote" checkbox and turn on the "Testing" checkbox (see Figure 22-4).

This last step identifies this server as the testing server and, when Dreamweaver previews your pages in a browser, it loads the pages from this server. You're just about done.

NOTE If you forget to turn on the "Testing" checkbox as described in step 11, Dreamweaver pops up an error message when you try to use the Preview in Browser command with a PHP page. Dreamweaver tells you that you need to set up a testing server to preview the page and gives you the option to go to the Site Setup window to add one. If this happens, click Yes, and just turn on the Testing checkbox for the appropriate server.

12. **Click Save to save the new site.**

Whew! That took a few steps, but you've successfully set up a local site so you can build and view dynamic pages. You're now ready to start *creating* those pages.

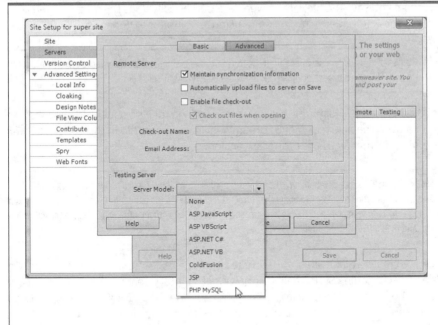

FIGURE 22-6

The Advanced server settings in the Site Setup window let you choose options related to your live web server on the Internet (they're listed under "Remote server"), and pick the server model you'll use when you build your pages. The list includes ASP JavaScript, ASP VBScript, ASP.NET C#, ASP.NET VB, ColdFusion, JSP, and PHP MySQL. The only effect these options have is when you build a new, blank web page—Dreamweaver creates a file with the correct file extension (.aspx or .jsp, for example), but that's about it.

■ Creating a Dynamic Page

Once you set up an application server and a database server, you're ready to connect to a database, retrieve information, and display it on a web page.

You already know how to handle the first step: Design an HTML page to display the database information. Dynamic pages differ from regular HTML pages in a couple ways. For starters, the name of a dynamic file doesn't end with .html. Depending on which server model you use, dynamic pages end in .php (for PHP pages), .asp (ASP), .aspx (.NET), or .cfm or cfml (ColdFusion). The file extension you use is important: A web server uses it to identify the type of page requested. If a server gets a request for an .html file, it simply finds it and sends it to the web browser. But if it gets a request for a page that ends in, say, .php, it sends the page to the application server to sort out all the messy programming.

The good news is that the basic process of creating a new, blank, dynamic page is the same as creating a regular HTML page:

- Choose File→New to open the New Document window. Select the Blank Page category; from the Page Type list, choose a dynamic page type (PHP, for example). From the Layout list, choose a layout (or none if you wish to start with a fresh, blank page), and then click the Create button.

    When you save the file, Dreamweaver automatically adds the proper extension: .asp for ASP pages, .cfm for ColdFusion, or .php for PHP pages.

> **NOTE** When you create a new page from the New Document window, Dreamweaver lets you select many different types of dynamic pages, including JSP, ASP.NET, and ASP JavaScript.

- Or, more simply, just right-click (Control-click) in the Site panel and choose New File from the shortcut menu. Dreamweaver creates a file in the correct server model format, with the proper extension.

> **NOTE** For ASP pages, just renaming a file in the Sites panel (from *about.html* to *about.asp*, for example) does *not* give the file the code necessary to apply the correct server model to the page. However, PHP and ColdFusion pages don't start life with any special code in them, so you could start with an .html page, change the extension to .php, and then add PHP programming.

Once you create a blank page, you can use any of the page-building tools described in this book—Cascading Style Sheets, Spry widgets, Library items, and so on—to design it. Even though the file is officially a PHP page (or an ASP or ColdFusion page), it still contains lots of HTML. Unlike a plain-vanilla HTML page, though, this one can also contain server-side programming that lets the page communicate with a database.

Finally, you can edit your newly created page in Design view, Split view, or Code view, but to add server-side programming, you need to switch to Code view.

■ Using Server-Side Includes

Even if you don't want to dive into the weird (but wonderful) world of server-side programming, you can still take advantage of one timesaving featured that dynamic web pages offer: server-side includes (SSIs). SSIs are like the Dreamweaver Library items discussed in Chapter 18; they're individual files with code that you can reuse on pages throughout a site. They're great for banners, footers, copyright notices, sidebars, and other chunks of HTML you use throughout a site. For example, you might use the same banner (logo, navigation bar, search box, and so on) at the top of each page. Instead of replicating that HTML over and over again, you can store it in a single file and "include" that file on your site's pages.

The advantage to this approach is that if you need to change anything on the banner, you open its file, make the change, save it, upload it to your web server, and voilà, your site is updated. Server-side includes actually make site updates easier than Library items. As you can read on page 840, when you make a change to a Library item, Dreamweaver has to update all the relevant pages on your site: granted, that process is fast and automated, but it still requires that you upload all the changed files to your web server—and if the Library item appears on 10,000 pages, you have to update and upload 10,000 pages! That takes time.

Web servers incorporate server-side includes into a web page on the fly, when a visitor requests the page. That means that you can update your site by changing and uploading only the Include file: now that's fast and efficient!

With SSIs, the web server acts like an automated copy-and-paste machine. Say your home page includes an SSI that holds the HTML for the page's banner. When someone requests that page, the web server opens the file (*index.php*, for example), sees the SSI for the banner, opens the banner file (*banner.php*, for example), copies its code, pastes it into the home page, and then sends the just-constructed page to your visitor. If the guest goes to another page on the site, the server again copies the banner code and pastes it into the newly requested page. While all this repeated copying and pasting might sound inefficient, servers are fast—so fast that the use of server-side includes are extremely common on the Web.

Creating a Server-Side Include

SSIs are simply text files that contain programming code, HTML, or both. They can be as simple as a paragraph of text with a copyright notice, or as complex as the programming required to retrieve information from a database with no HTML at all. Generally, SSI file names end in the extension of the programming language you're using (.php for example). In addition, since the SSI gets added to a web page, it shouldn't include the elements of a complete HTML file. In other words, just like a Dreamweaver Library item, the SSI should contain no doctype, <head> tag, or style sheets: it's just a text file that's empty save for the content you wish to appear on another page.

Here's a simple way to create an SSI:

1. **Choose File→New.**

   Dreamweaver opens the New Document window.

2. **Click Blank Page in the left-hand list of categories, choose a page type that matches your programming language (PHP, for example), and then click Create.**

   Dreamweaver creates a new blank page. However, it's full of the usual scaffolding required by web pages, including a doctype and <html>, <head>, and <body> tags. You don't need (or want) any of that for the small snippet of HTML you'll add to the Include.

3. **Click the Code or Split button in the Document toolbar, position your cursor in Code view, and then select and delete all the text.**

   For example choose Edit→Select All, and then Edit→Cut. Now that you have a truly empty page, you can save it.

4. **Choose File→Save, and use the extension that matches your programming language.**

   For example, save the file as *banner.php*.

   TIP One common practice among web developers is to include both .inc and the file extension used by the programming language in the file name: for example, banner.inc.php. The .inc in the middle makes it clear that the file is an include.

5. **Add content to the Server-Side Include.**

   You can switch to Design view for this and use the tools you're already familiar with, such as the Insert bar, to add HTML. Note, however, that you can't add styles to the Include file—the SSI is just a *part* of a complete web page, so you need to add any styles you want to the page itself. However, if you use Dream-weaver's Design Time Style Sheet feature (page 405), you can overcome this limitation; it "tricks" Dreamweaver into thinking that the SSI actually does have a style sheet attached to it, and you can edit the styles.

   NOTE When you add links or images to an SSI, always use root-relative paths (see page 187). An SSI is simply copied and pasted by the server into other files on your site. If the server pastes the SSI into a file that's within a folder or subfolder of your site, a document-relative path probably won't work when the SSI gets pasted into the page.

Adding a Server-Side Include to a Web Page

Once you create an SSI, you can add it to any dynamic page on your site, that is, any page that ends in .php or another server-side programming extension.

1. **Open the page you wish to add the SSI to.**

   This page must end in .php (or .asp or .cfm). They have to be dynamic pages, because you're about to add some code to them.

2. **Click the spot in the page where you want to insert the SSI.**

   While you can do this in Design view, it's usually less error-prone to do it in Code view. For example, it's easy in Design view to add an SSI within a page's <p> tag, and if the SSI includes divs, headers, or other block-level HTML, you'll generate invalid HTML.

   Say you create an SSI banner for your site. To add it to a page, you'd go into Code view and place the cursor just after the opening <body> tag. Alternatively, if you want to insert a footer SSI (like a copyright notice and contact information), you can click just before the closing </body> tag.

3. **Choose Insert→Server-Side Include.**

   Dreamweaver opens a Select File dialog box.

4. **Navigate to and select the SSI you created.** Click OK (Open on Macs).

   Dreamweaver adds the necessary code to attach the SSI. For example, in PHP it will look something like this:

   ```
   <?php require_once('banner.php'); ?>
   ```

   If the SSI contains any HTML, Dreamweaver displays the HTML in Design view so you can see your full-fledged page. (You won't however, see the results produced by any server-side programming, such as request for database information.)

You can continue to use the SSI on additional pages on the site; you can even use it in Dreamweaver templates (Chapter 19), so that you can combine these two time-saving features.

NOTE When you add a Server-Side Include to a page, make sure you use a document-relative path (see page 186.)

■ Working with Related PHP Files

As discussed on page 353, Dreamweaver provides a special toolbar for identifying files associated with a web page, such as an external style sheet or a JavaScript file. This "related files" toolbar not only shows you which files have been added to a page, but, with just a click of the mouse, it lets you jump directly to the code for that file. Dreamweaver considers server-side includes "related files" too, so you can easily edit an SSI by clicking its name in the toolbar.

In fact, server-side programming often involves adding lots of files to a page: files for connecting to a database server, for running a database query, for sending email, and more. For example, the popular blogging system WordPress uses a single file, *index.php*, to control an entire blog—this one file manages every one of the blog's pages, from the home page to a category page to a single blog post. To do this, the *index.php* file includes tons (really, a *lot*) of other PHP files. If you're using a program other than Dreamweaver, the only way to edit a WordPress site is to open each file individually. Dreamweaver, however, can "discover" related PHP files and display them in the Related Files toolbar for easy access. To do this, you need to follow a few steps:

1. **Open a PHP file.**

   If you use the Insert Server-Side Include command discussed previously, Dreamweaver automatically sees these PHP files and displays them in the Related Files toolbar with no further effort on your part. But you might also include PHP files within *other* Include files. In cases like that, you need to tell Dreamweaver to "discover" them.

2. **Click the Discover link in the information toolbar in the document window (see Figure 22-7, top).**

   Dreamweaver finds all the PHP files the currently open dynamic page uses. That may be just a few files or, in the case of a complex PHP application like WordPress, quite a few. For example, in the bottom image in Figure 22-7, you can see that the Related Files toolbar is chock-full of file names.

3. **Select a related file to work on.**

   Once Dreamweaver discovers all related PHP files, you can use the Related Files toolbar as you normally would to open a file. If there are a lot of files, as is the case with WordPress, navigate through the list by clicking the left and right arrow buttons, or click the Show More button to see a drop-down menu of all the related files. Select a name from that list to open the file in Code view.

4. **Filter the list if necessary.**

   You may not want to see or work on some of the files that Dreamweaver discovers. For example, in the case of WordPress, you'll see many PHP files listed, most of which you never want to touch since they're part of the core WordPress program and editing them might break your blog.

   Fortunately, you can filter the list of related files to see just the ones you want. The Filter button in the top-right corner of the Related Files toolbar lets you do two things: First, clicking it pops up a menu that lets you filter by file type— meaning that you can show or hide JavaScript, CSS, or PHP files, along with any other file type that your web page references. By default, Dreamweaver selects all the file types, so to hide one, click the Filter button, and then click the relevant extension (.css, .php, .js, and so on). To show those file types later, select them again from the Filter menu.

You can also create a custom filter. Click the Filter button, choose Custom Filter, and a dialog box pops up. Type in the file names and/or file types you want to see. For example, with WordPress, you're interested in editing the PHP theme files—the ones WordPress uses to create your blog's look. To show the relevant files, enter their names separated by a semicolon, like this: *index.php*; *footer.php*; *header.php*, and so on. You can also filter by file type. To show all JavaScript files plus *index.php*, *footer.php*, and *header.php*, type this in the Related Files toolbar: *index.php*; *footer.php*; *header.php*;.js.

When you're done, click OK to close the Custom Filter window. Now, in the Related Files toolbar, Dreamweaver displays only the files you specified.

NOTE Custom filters are useful but, unfortunately, Dreamweaver doesn't remember a custom filter, so once you close a file, that filter is lost and you have to recreate it the next time you want to use it. In addition, you can't filter by folder—all PHP files within a particular folder only—although that would be really helpful when you work with certain CMS systems, like WordPress, which keep files related to the design of the site in one particular folder. Maybe next time.

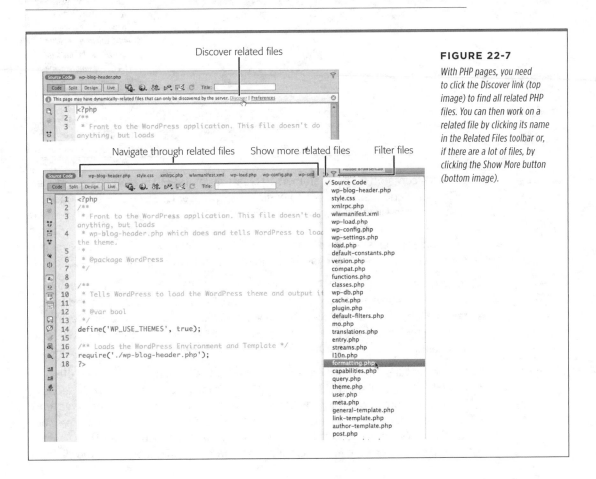

Discover related files

Navigate through related files   Show more related files   Filter files

FIGURE 22-7

With PHP pages, you need to click the Discover link (top image) to find all related PHP files. You can then work on a related file by clicking its name in the Related Files toolbar or, if there are a lot of files, by clicking the Show More button (bottom image).

PHP Code Hints

Dreamweaver includes advanced code-hinting for the server-side programming language PHP (but not for other server-side technologies, like .NET, ColdFusion, Java Server Pages, and Ruby on Rails). Not only does Dreamweaver support code-hinting for built-in PHP functions, it also makes note of variables, functions, and classes that you create (see Figure 22-8).

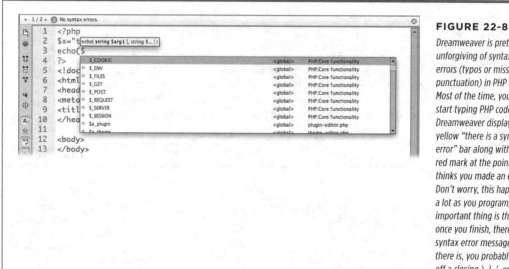

FIGURE 22-8

Dreamweaver is pretty unforgiving of syntax errors (typos or missing punctuation) in PHP code. Most of the time, you start typing PHP code and Dreamweaver displays a yellow "there is a syntax error" bar along with a red mark at the point it thinks you made an error. Don't worry, this happens a lot as you program; the important thing is that, once you finish, there's no syntax error message. If there is, you probably left off a closing), }, ', or ".

Since it's common for programmers to create multiple PHP files and then add them all to (or include them all in) a master file, Dreamweaver CS6 searches through all the files referenced in the current working file and analyzes them. Then, as you type more PHP code, Dreamweaver displays code hints based on the names of the variables, functions, and classes you defined in those files. In other words, Dreamweaver personalizes its code hints for your site and for the PHP programming you added to it.

In addition, since many PHP frameworks, like CakePHP and Zend, and many PHP-based content management systems (CMSes), like WordPress, Joomla and Drupal, rely on many separate PHP files, Dreamweaver includes something called site-specific code hints. This is only available for PHP-based websites and it's intended to let you identify which folders Dreamweaver scans to create its code hints for your site.

Dreamweaver's site-specific code hints have a few benefits. First, if you often include PHP files outside the root folder (for example, the Zend framework keeps its include files outside the web-accessible root folder), you can tell Dreamweaver to scan the folder above the current local root folder. Second, many CMS systems and PHP frameworks use tons of files with tons of variables, functions, and class names. Sites like these use the files internally, in the programming that drives the systems.

You, as a programmer, don't ever need to see most of them, and you certainly don't want their elements cluttering up your code-hint window.

You can turn site-specific code hints on by choosing Site→Site-Specific Code Hints. This opens a new window (see Figure 22-9). If you're using either WordPress, Joomla, or Drupal, you can select your environment from the top Structure menu, and Dreamweaver automatically identifies the proper folders, files, and paths. Click OK and you're done.

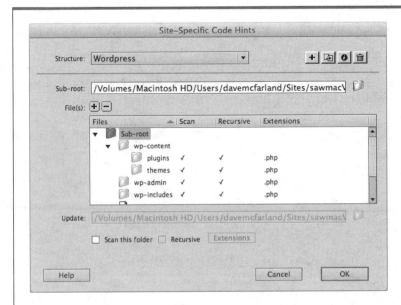

FIGURE 22-9

To add the function names, class names, and variable names you use in your site's PHP code to Dreamweaver's Code Hint feature, you need to choose Site→Site-Specific Code Hints and tell Dreamweaver which files and folders to scan.

If, however, you're using a PHP framework or some other PHP CMS, you need to tell Dreamweaver which folders to analyze by following these steps:

1. **Identify the folder containing your site and all the PHP files you want Dreamweaver to scan by clicking the folder icon and selecting a folder.**

   If you don't have any PHP files outside your local root folder, you can skip this step because Dreamweaver automatically selects the local root folder. However, you may have PHP files one level up from the local folder. In this case, click the folder icon and select the folder one level up that contains both the PHP files and your local site root.

2. **Click the + button.**

   The Add File/Folder window appears. You can click another icon to select either one particular PHP file, or to select a folder's worth of PHP files. If you pick a folder, turn on the checkbox labeled Recursive if you want Dreamweaver to scan the files in subfolders within this main folder. You can ensure that Dreamweaver searches only .php files by clicking the + button to the right of the Extensions label and typing in *.php*. Dreamweaver won't look through any other files and, as a result, it displays code hints faster. However, if you do use other extensions for your PHP files, such as .inc, make sure to add those as well.

You can prevent Dreamweaver from scanning a folder you added from the main Site-Specific Code Hints window, too. Select the folder from the Files list and turn off the "Scan this folder" checkbox. You can also turn off recursive scanning and change the file extensions from this window.

3. **Click OK to finish.**

   Dreamweaver scans the selected files and creates a list of code hints for your site.

NOTE You may find that Dreamweaver doesn't always automatically pop up a box for site-specific code hints as it does for regular PHP functions. You may need to coax Dreamweaver into displaying them by using the keyboard shortcut Ctrl+space bar.

Getting Help

Hard as it may be to believe, even a book as voluminous and detailed as this one may not answer all your questions about Dreamweaver. Fortunately, a range of other resources awaits you when a feature's giving you trouble.

Getting Help from Dreamweaver

There's plenty of assistance built right into Dreamweaver itself, from beginner tutorials to Dreamweaver's online documentation and online support center. You'll find details below.

Detailed Assistance

Adobe provides online documentation for Dreamweaver, accessible by choosing Help→Dreamweaver Help (or by pressing the F1 key). This launches your web browser and loads the documentation for Dreamweaver CS6. The opening page lists categories like "Creating Pages with CSS" and "Previewing pages," where you can get detailed information on various aspects of the program.

NOTE If you prefer your documentation printed, you can download a PDF of the entire Dreamweaver manual. Choose Help→Dreamweaver Help (or press the F1 key) to access the online help documents. You'll find a link in the top-right corner of the screen labeled "View Help PDF" that downloads a hefty Adobe Acrobat file.

Adobe also offers a more interactive version of their online help system called Community Help. It's like a Google for Dreamweaver (and other Adobe products). When you search for a Dreamweaver-related topic—"templates," for example—you get a list of pages that have something to do with Dreamweaver templates. However, rather than search the entire Web, including Joe's "I just learned Dreamweaver 2 seconds ago and now I'm an expert" blog, Community Help searches only websites Adobe has determined have good and accurate information. That includes Adobe's own website, but other useful sites as well, such as CreativePro (*www.creativepro.com*) and CommunityMX (*www.communitymx.com*).

You can even search for help (on the Web and from Adobe's Community Help system) from within Dreamweaver. Its Application bar includes a simple search box (see Figure A-1). Type a term in the box and click the magnifying glass icon to launch a browser and retrieve a list of results that match your search term. Of course, as with all things free on the Internet, you may or may not find an exact answer to your question.

FIGURE A-1.

Dreamweaver's Application bar provides a quick way to search the Web for Dreamweaver tips, tricks, and information.

Dreamweaver's Help menu provides other useful jumping-off points for exploring topics like the Spry Framework and a few commercial Adobe services ("Hi, Dreamweaver engineers. This is marketing, do you mind if we add a couple of links to your Help menu?").

If you're interested in refreshing your knowledge of HTML, Dreamweaver's Reference window (select Help→Reference or press Shift-F1) provides in-depth information on HTML; unfortunately, this content hasn't been updated for HTML5, so if you need to keep up with the latest changes in HTML you're better off with the official W3C documentation (*http://dev.w3.org/html5/html-author/*) or the Mozilla Developer Network (*https://developer.mozilla.org/en/HTML/HTML5*). However, skip the CSS, JavaScript, JSP, and other guides in the Reference—they're outdated. In addition, you might be tempted to select the CSS Advisor option—after all, CSS is tricky and who wouldn't want their own advisor to help out? Avoid the CSS Advisor! While it started off as a way of collecting answers to common cross-browser CSS bugs, it's now a place where confused designers go to ask questions about Dreamweaver, and those questions usually go unanswered. If you do have a Dreamweaver question, you're better off visiting the Dreamweaver forums (discussed next), where you'll find many experts willing to help.

■ Getting Help from Adobe

You can also get up-to-date and personalized support from Adobe, ranging from technical notes available on Adobe's site to pay-as-you-ask support plans.

Adobe's Dreamweaver Website

The Dreamweaver support page (*www.adobe.com/support/dreamweaver,* also available at Help→Dreamweaver Support Center) is command central for finding help from Adobe. Here you can search the vast database of technical notes (short articles on specific problems) that just may hold the answer you seek, find basic tutorials on getting started with Dreamweaver, see a list of top Dreamweaver issues (and their answers), and review a list of the most recent Dreamweaver technical notes.

You can also click the Contact Support link (in the right-hand navigation bar) to go to a page listing common setup problems and their solutions, as well as phone numbers you can call for product help, installation help, and software activation help.

Paid Support

If you have deep pockets, you can tap into three levels of personalized, fee-based support from Adobe, ranging from $175 for five "incidents" to the whole-hog luxury of the Gold Support program (for pricing on this option, Adobe tells you to "contact your Adobe reseller"—watch out!). For more information on these programs, go to *www.adobe.com/support/programs/creativesuite*. Each program has its own phone number, so determine the type of support (from Bronze to Gold) you need.

Adobe used to let you buy a single "incident" to answer one nagging problem, but now they only sell the five-incident pack, so if you have just a single nagging question, first try to one of the free resources listed here. After that, customers in the U.S. and Canada should call 1-866-MYADOBE for the five-incident service.

The Forums

Adobe provides online forums that offer free advice from many helpful souls. To get to the forums, choose Help→Adobe Online Forums, which launches a web browser that takes you to the forums page.

The forums are a terrific source of information, offering almost real-time answers on Dreamweaver and related web-design techniques. Adobe sponsors several forums and newsgroups. Of most interest to average Dreamweaver users are the FAQ forum (answers to the most frequently asked questions), the General Discussion forum (answers to basic questions), and the Application Development forum, where people discuss Dreamweaver's dynamic web page features. If you're struggling with Dreamweaver's Spry tools, the Spry forum is a good place to seek help. In addition, you'll find forums for BrowserLab (discussed on page 760), Dreamweaver extensions, and the Dreamweaver widget browser. Odds are one of the many knowledgeable experts who always seem to be hanging around will come back with an answer, sometimes within minutes.

You can find Dreamweaver's forums at *http://forums.adobe.com/community/ dreamweaver.*

Dreamweaver CS6, Menu by Menu

Dreamweaver CS6: The Missing Manual is quite complete; in its pages, you'll find descriptions of every major Dreamweaver function (and most minor ones). In the interest of completeness, however, here's a quick reference to every command in every menu—and the answer to the occasional "What does that mean?" mystery.

■ File Menu

The commands in Dreamweaver's File menu include basic functions like saving and closing files, and controlling an open Dreamweaver document:

- **New**. Opens the New Document window, which lets you create a new, blank Dreamweaver document using any of several types of web page, from basic HTML pages to dynamic pages like PHP or ASP files. If you create Dreamweaver page templates, they show up here, too.

- **New Fluid Grid Layout**. This option, new in Dreamweaver CS6, provides a basic framework for creating a site that works in mobile, tablet, and desktop browsers. Using some pre-packaged CSS and JavaScript as well as a fancy user interface, you can basically "draw" three layouts—one for smartphones, one for tablets, one for desktop computers—that use the same HTML content.

- **Open**. Opens the standard Open File dialog box so you can navigate to and open an existing Dreamweaver document. You can set the Enable drop-down menu to display only specific types of documents—only HTML pages or style sheets, for example.

- **Browse in Bridge**. Bridge is Adobe's own file manager. It's like Windows Explorer or the Mac's Finder function. It lets you browse, find, and open documents. But since Dreamweaver sports the very useful Files panel (page 49), you already have a way to manage your site files. In addition, Bridge is part of Adobe's graphics heritage, so it works best with image files—in other words, Photoshop and Illustrator files, *not* Dreamweaver documents. Note that this option won't do anything if you bought only the standalone version of Dreamweaver. Adobe Bridge is only available as part of the entire Adobe Creative Suite.

- **Open Recent**. Displays a submenu that lists the 10 most recently opened documents. Selecting a document from the list opens it. The last option in this menu, "Reopen Documents on Startup," is kind of cool. If you quit Dreamweaver with documents still open and have this option checked, Dreamweaver automatically reopens those documents the next time you launch the program.

- **Open in Frame**. Opens an existing HTML page within one frame of a frameset. To make this command available, you must have a frameset open and have clicked inside one of its frames to select the frame—you can't open an HTML page just by loading a Frameset document. The Select HTML file dialog box opens and lets you navigate to the file you want to insert into the frame. You can also choose to make the file's URL relative to the document or the root folder, as described in Chapter 5. (Frames are an old technology, and professional designers no longer use them.)

- **Close**. Closes the currently open Dreamweaver document. If you have unsaved changes, Dreamweaver gives you the opportunity to save them. This action also closes the files in the "related files" toolbar (see page 353).

- **Close All**. Closes *all* the currently open documents. If you have unsaved changes in any of them, Dreamweaver gives you the opportunity to save them.

- **Save** (Save Frameset/Save Frame). Saves any changes you made to your document. Dreamweaver dims the Save command if you haven't made any changes to the document since the last time you saved it.

- **Save As** (Save Frameset As/Save Frame As). This command works slightly differently than in other programs. Like most other programs, it saves a copy of the current document under a new name, but it also leaves the *original* document and reverts that file to its *last* saved state. In other words, only the Save As copy has the most recent changes you made to the original file...weird.

- **Save All**. Saves changes to all your open documents, including other web pages, external CSS and JavaScript files, and any files listed in the Related Files bar (see "Related Files" on page 353). This is a great command to make sure you save all your changes to every document you edited since opening Dreamweaver.

- **Save All Related Files**. Saves changes to the document you're currently editing, as well as files that the current document uses, such as external CSS and Java-Script files, and server-side programs such as PHP Includes. This is a good way to make sure you save every edit that affects the current file, whether you made the change in a CSS file, the HTML source code, or an external JavaScript file.

- **Save as Template**. Saves the current document as a Dreamweaver template with the suffix .dwt. The "Save as Template" dialog box appears so you can specify the template's file name, and indicate which site it belongs to. Dreamweaver automatically saves all template documents in a Templates subfolder in the selected site's folder. You'll find templates discussed in Chapter 19.

- **Revert**. Undoes any changes you made to a document since the last time you saved it. Edit→Undo is often a better choice; it takes a few more steps to undo all the changes you made, but it can actually undo changes *past* your last save. So if you're one of those gotta-save-it-every-5-seconds types, the Undo command is for you.

- **Print Code**. Prints what you see in Code view of the current document.

- **Import**. Lets you import data from other sources into your Dreamweaver document. For example, you can import XML data into a template or tabular data from a CSV (comma separated value) file into an HTML file. Windows users can also choose to import text from a Microsoft Word document or tabular data from an Excel spreadsheet.

- **Export**. Extracts tabular data or template data in XML format from your Dreamweaver document, for use in other applications.

- **Convert**. Converts older HTML pages into a variety of more modern formats, like HTML 4.01 Strict, two forms of XHTML, or HTML5. Unfortunately, it's kind of hit-or-miss: This feature can't always update older files to modern standards.

- **Preview in Browser**. Opens the current document in your web browser. By selecting Edit Browser List, you can add new browsers to, or delete browsers from, your browser list, or specify a preferred browser. Dreamweaver CS6 also lets you preview pages in "Adobe BrowserLab"—this option, described on page 760, uses an online Adobe service to take screenshots of the current page in different browsers.

- **Multiscreen Preview**. Opens a window that displays the current web page in three different "viewports." It's intended to help you work with Media Queries (Chapter 11) to preview how a page looks on different devices, like smartphones, tablets, and desktop browsers.

- **Check Page**. Checks the current page for a variety of problems, such as broken links and misspellings. You can also access the link-checker from the Results panel to check an entire site's worth of files—choose Window→Results, and then click the Link Checker tab to check links. The Browser Compatibility option is particularly useless, so skip it.

- **Validate**. Lets you check XML files to make sure they conform to XML standards and document type definitions. In other words, it checks to make sure your XML is correct. In addition, you can check an HTML file using the W3C's online validator—from right within Dreamweaver. Select the "Validate current document" option and Dreamweaver connects to the Web, contacts the W3C validator, and checks your page's HTML. If it finds errors, it lists them in the W3C validation pane below the Property Inspector. If you're working on a server-side page (like a WordPress page), then choose the Validate Live Document option: this first processes a page through a web server and then contacts the W3C site. That way, you're actually checking the finished HTML (after the server has completed all its server-side antics and produced a real HTML file).

- **Compare with Remote/Compare with Testing**. Lets you use a third-party code-comparison tool to see how the local copy of a page differs from either the remote copy (the one on your web server) or the copy on your testing server. It identifies all code differences. You can learn more about this feature on page 363.

- **Design Notes**. Opens the Design Notes window (Chapter 17), where you can add additional information about an open document, set its status, and choose to have the Design Note appear whenever you open the document.

NOTE To use Design Notes, make sure you select the Maintain Design Notes option in the Site Definition window's "Design notes" section; see page 817.

- **Exit (Windows only)**. Exits Dreamweaver. If any of your open Dreamweaver documents have unsaved changes, the program prompts you to save them before quitting. (Mac users will find a "Quit Dreamweaver" option under the Dreamweaver menu.)

■ Edit Menu

The Edit menu lets you make common changes to your documents, like copying and pasting text:

- **Undo**. Undoes the most recent change you made to your document. Choose this command repeatedly to step progressively backwards through your changes, even *after* you save the document. You can take 50 steps back in time, unless you change Dreamweaver's default in Preferences→General.

- **Redo** (Repeat). Restores whatever changes you just made using the Undo command. Selecting Redo multiple times moves you progressively forward through the changes you made. If you just used a command other than Undo, Repeat appears instead of Redo. This property lets you repeat the last action. For example, if you just pressed Delete, the Repeat command presses it again.

- **Cut**. Deletes the selected text or objects from a document, and copies them to the invisible Windows or Macintosh Clipboard so you can paste them elsewhere. (The Clipboard holds only one selection at a time.)

- **Copy**. Copies the selected text or object to the Clipboard so you can paste it elsewhere—without disturbing the original.

- **Paste**. Places the most recent selection from the Clipboard into your document at the insertion point.

- **Paste Special**. Opens the Paste Special window, which lets you choose how to paste a Clipboard item into your document. Options range from Text Only for just plain text to increasingly more elaborate options, which force Dreamweaver to attempt to preserve various kinds of formatting, such as styles, bold text, italic text, bulleted lists, and so on. See page 87.

- **Clear**. Deletes the selected text or object from a document without placing it in the Clipboard.

- **Select All**. Selects everything in a document so you can make document-wide changes in one fell swoop. If you have the cursor inside a table cell or <div> tag, however, Select All selects just the contents of that cell or div.

- **Select Parent Tag**. Broadens the current selection to include everything within its *parent tag*, including the content. For example, if you have a table cell selected, this command increases the selection to include the entire table *row*. Choose the command a second time and you increase the selection to include the entire table. In short, this command ensures that any changes you make apply to the entire tag.

- **Select Child**. Narrows the current selection to include everything within the *child tag*, including its contents. If you select a table row, choosing this command decreases that selection to include only the first table *cell* and its contents.

- **Find and Replace**. Lets you search a document—or an entire site—for a specific word, tag, or piece of source code, and replace it with something different (see Chapter 20). This command lets you make these changes either en masse or one instance at a time.

- **Find Selection**. This command lets you find another instance of the current selection. Say you select the word "mothball" on a page. This command searches the page for another example of "mothball."

- **Find Again**. Uses the most recent search setting from the "Find and Replace" window to search the current document, highlighting the next instance of the search item.

- **Go to Line**. Opens the Go To Line dialog box. Type in a number, and Dreamweaver positions the cursor at the beginning of the specified line of code (available only in Code view).

- **Show Code Hints**. Immediately displays any code hints (overriding the delay set in the Preferences window) available for the current tag. Code Hints, described in Chapter 7, provide a drop-down menu of tag properties appropriate to the current tag (available only in Code view, and only when you use the Insert Tag command [⌘-T]).

- **Refresh Code Hints**. Doesn't seem to do much of anything.

- **Code Hint Tools**. When you work in Code view, this command lets you access Dreamweaver's color picker, its "Browse for File" button, and its list of fonts so you don't have to type in things like *#FF6633, ../../images/dog.gif*, or *Arial, Helvetica, sans-serif* every time you use a color, link to a file, or want to use a font. In addition, you can display a pop-up menu of all the ID, class, and element names on a page, which you'll find useful for JavaScript programming.

- **Indent Code**. Adds one indent before the selected line of code (available only in Code view).

- **Outdent Code**. Removes one indent from the selected line of code (available only in Code view).

- **Balance Braces**. When you edit a script in Code view, this command helps you check for unbalanced braces (that is, an introductory "{" without a closing "}") by highlighting the matching tags enclosing the selected code. It doesn't do anything for plain HTML, but if you're writing a JavaScript program or using a dynamic programming language like PHP or ASP, it helps identify missing braces—a common source of programming errors. Works with opening and closing parentheses, and brackets ([and]) as well.

- **Repeating Entries**. Lets you cut, copy, paste, and delete repeating regions in templates. You can learn about repeating regions in Chapter 19.

- **Code Collapse**. Hides a selection of code in Code view so you see only the code you want to work on. You'll find this feature discussed on page 348, and since the same options are available more directly from the coding toolbar, you can skip this command.

- **Edit with External Editor** (Windows). If you haven't already specified an external HTML code editor, such as BBEdit or Notepad, this command opens the Preferences window and selects the File Types/Editors category so you can find and select a text editor on your hard drive. Once you specify an editor, this command opens the current document in that editor. You can change the editor setting from the Edit→Preferences (Dreamweaver→Preferences) window.

- **Tag Libraries**. Lets you modify the way Dreamweaver writes code for various types of tags, such as those for HTML, PHP, ASP, ColdFusion, and so on. You can create new tag libraries for other types of tag-based languages, or modify the ones that ship with Dreamweaver.

- **Keyboard Shortcuts** (Windows). Opens the Keyboard Shortcuts window, and shows you all of Dreamweaver's current keyboard shortcuts. You can create a new set of shortcuts for specific sites or programs, or export the settings to HTML so you can share your settings with others. (You must duplicate the factory settings before you add or delete your own shortcuts, however.) You'll find details on page 911. (On the Mac, this option appears under the Dreamweaver menu.)

- **Preferences** (Windows). Opens the Preference window, which is full of options that customize the way Dreamweaver works. You can choose from 19 categories of preferences, including those that let you edit the color and format of HTML tags, create shorthand versions of CSS styles, and change the order in which Dreamweaver's info panels appear on-screen. (On the Mac, this option appears under the Dreamweaver menu.)

■ View Menu

The View menu controls the document window's appearance. A checkmark in the menu lets you know which view you're in:

- **Code**. Displays the file's source code.

- **Split Code**. Displays the file's source code in split view, side by side. You can use this feature to edit both the HTML near the top of the page (on one side of the document window), and HTML elsewhere on the page (on the other side of the Document window.) But it's most useful when you use it in conjunction with Dreamweaver's Related Files feature (page 353). In Split Code view, you can view the HTML of the page in one pane, and the CSS of an external style sheet in the other.

- **Design**. Displays the file's visual design.

- **Code and Design**. Splits the document window into two panes: source code on the left (or top), visual design on the right (or bottom). You can adjust where the split panes appear, and adjust how much of each pane you see by dragging the center divider left or right or up or down.

- **Split Vertically**. When you're in Code and Design view, you see the page's code and its design side by side...great for really wide monitors. Unselecting this option displays the Code and Design views one on top of the other—unless you have an unusually tall monitor, this option doesn't let you see much of either.

- **Design View on Left/Top**. When you're in Code and Design view, this option dictates where Dreamweaver puts the Design view pane relative to the Code view pane. If you select Split Vertically, you can display the Design view either to the right or the left of the Code view; when you stack Code and Design views on top of each other, you can place the Design view either above or below the Code view.

- **Switch Views**. Switches your cursor position between Code and Design views... of course, so does just clicking into the code in Code view, or clicking into the design in Design view!

- **Refresh Design View**. Updates the Design view to reflect changes you make directly to the source code in either Code view or Split view.

- **Refresh Styles**. Who knows? You can only select it when viewing a page in Live View, and even then it doesn't seem to do anything.

- **Live View**. Displays a web page as it would appear in a web browser (actually, as it would appear in Apple's Safari or Google's Chrome browser). You can preview JavaScript, Flash movies, and other interactive page features in this view.

- **Live View Options**. Lets you control the display of Live View. You can pause JavaScript—a useful way to see the HTML that JavaScript creates on the fly—disable JavaScript, turn off plug-ins, and control settings that affect how Dreamweaver displays the page in Live View.

- **Live View Browser**. Dreamweaver CS6 includes the ability to navigate while you're in Live View. Click a link on a page in Live View and it takes you to another page (but only if you turned on that feature in the Live View Options menu). The Live View Browser lets you control the navigation just as you would in a web browser (page backward or forward, for example), view recent pages, and open the currently visited page in a new tab so you can edit it.

- **Live Code**. In Live View, choose this option to display the HTML as it appears to a web browser—useful for pages that include JavaScript that can dynamically change the HTML of a page by adding classes to tags and even inserting or removing entire chunks of HTML. This feature is a good way to make sure the JavaScript code you write does what you want it to do to the HTML of a page. This feature is also good for server-side pages composed of multiple server-side includes (page 937): for example, to view what the HTML looks like for a site using the WordPress content management system (see page 358).

- **Inspect**. This option lets you inspect the CSS of page elements in Live View. Discussed on page 494, this feature is a great way to inspect page styles in dynamically generated server-side pages (such as PHP pages), which you often can't see in Design view.

- **Head Content**. Opens a new menu bar in the main document window that contains shortcuts to the head section of an HTML page. You can use these menu items to highlight your document's title tags, meta tags, and scripts, and then, in the Property Inspector, to edit their content.

- **Noscript Content**. When you insert JavaScript code into the document window, you can include what're called <noscript> tags—information that appears in browsers that don't understand JavaScript (of which there are few), or which have their JavaScript turned off. After selecting this option, all the information inside <noscript> tags appears in the document window. To hide this information, select this menu option again.

- **Table Mode**. Lets you switch between the standard Table view and Expanded Tables view. Expanded Tables view simply adds borders and a bit of padding to table cells to make it easier to select and edit cells in a table in which you've removed all padding, borders, and cell spacing. It doesn't have any effect on your final table, it just alters the way it looks within Dreamweaver.

- **Visual Aids**. Lets you summon on-screen symbols that represent typically invisible page elements, like image maps, anchors, the borders of a <div> tag, and the grid used in the new Fluid Grid layouts.

- **Style Rendering**. Lets you hide or show the effects of all style sheets on a page, or selectively display the formatting changes a style sheet applies to a particular type of media—screens only, for example, or printers only.

- **Code View Options**. Lets you adjust the way your HTML appears in Code view. You can turn on (or off) options that wrap lines of text to fit in the document window, add line numbers, highlight invalid HTML, turn on syntax coloring, and indent lines of code.

- **Window Size**. Lets you change the size of the page that Dreamweaver displays in the document window. Best used in conjunction with Media Queries (Chapter 11) to see how a page looks on different-size screens, such as the 320- x 480-pixel screen of an iPhone.

- **Magnification**. Lets you zoom in, zoom out, and generally magnify your view of the document window. It has no effect on the HTML or how a page displays in a web browser, it merely zooms in to get a close-up view of the page or zooms out to get a bird's eye view.

- **Rulers**. When you choose Show, Dreamweaver displays rulers along the top and left sides of the document window. Using the options you find here, you can choose your ruler units: pixels, inches, or centimeters. You can also reset the orientation of the two rulers so that both start from zero in the screen's upper-left corner.

- **Grid**. Places a grid of vertical and horizontal lines over the document window that you use as a guide as you build your layouts. Selecting Edit Grid opens the Grid Setting dialog box, where you can adjust the grid's colors, spacing, behaviors, and line appearance.

- **Guides**. Shows, hides, locks, and erases guidelines you drag from a ruler onto the current page. Also controls options for guides, and displays guidelines that mark the visible area of a browser window for monitors of different resolutions.

- **Tracing Image**. Adjusts the document's background tracing image. You can load a new tracing image, make a current one visible, or adjust its position.

- **Display External Files**. You can insert images and other files into a page from your own or other websites on the Internet. When you insert an image from another site, you can type in or paste an absolute URL. Dreamweaver even displays the image in Design view, but only if you check this option. Because this feature requires an Internet connection to display the image, pages with links to external files may take longer to display in Dreamweaver (since it has to get the images and files from the Web). If you have lots of external images and files and your pages open sluggishly in Dreamweaver, uncheck this option.

- **Color Icons**. Dreamweaver's interface underwent an overhaul in version CS4— the once-bright icons were made hip, dull, and gray, and they're still hip, dull, and gray in CS6. If you'd rather have the colorful icons from Dreamweaver CS3, turn this option on.

- **Hide Panels** (Show Panels). Hides all open panels. If you've already hidden the panels, the command says Show Panels instead; it restores the panels to their original positions.

- **Toolbars**. Displays toolbars for use with Dreamweaver. Select Document from the submenu to display the Document toolbar at the top of the document window. It displays the current page's title and offers common commands, like display options, file-management options, code-navigation options, and browser previews. The Standard toolbar displays buttons for common commands, such as opening files, closing files, and cutting, copying, and pasting content. The Style Rendering toolbar lets you toggle style sheets off and on, like the Style Rendering menu described earlier in this section. The Coding toolbar appears along the left edge of Code view and provides options for working with HTML, JavaScript, CSS, and PHP code, such as wrapping the code in comments, indenting the code, and so on.

- **Related Files**. Lists all external CSS, JavaScript, and server-side programming files the current page uses. Select one and you'll see the code for that file. Better yet, just use the Related Files toolbar that appears in the document window—it's much faster.

- **Related Files Options**. Lets you filter the files displayed in the Related Files toolbar (page 353). For example, you can hide all server-side includes, display just external CSS files, or create a custom filter to show files that match a certain pattern (like all PHP files that include *DB* in the file name). You'll find filters most useful for really complicated server-side programs (like WordPress, Joomla, or Drupal) that often overwhelm the Related Files toolbar with dozens of included PHP files.

- **Code Navigator**. Pops open the Code Navigator window so you can scan all CSS rules that apply to the current HTML element (see "Using the Code Navigator").

- **Show Spry Tooltips**. Shows or hides Spry tooltips when you work on a web page in Design view (see page 656 for more on Spry tooltips).

■ Insert Menu

The Insert menu adds selected page elements to a document at the cursor's current position. The commands listed here correspond to the buttons on the Objects panel:

- **Tag**. Opens the Tag Chooser window, which provides access to all tags Dreamweaver understands (no HTML5, for example). That includes HTML 4 tags, as well as any tag in Dreamweaver's Tag Library (see the Tag Libraries entry under Edit Menu above). You can insert any tag and set any of its properties from this window. However, Dreamweaver doesn't make sure you insert the tag correctly, so you should understand HTML (or the tag language you're using) before trying this option.

- **Image**. Inserts an image file, such as a JPG, PNG, or GIF, into the current document. The Select Image Source window appears so you can navigate to the file on your hard drive. You can choose to make the URL for the file relative to either the document or to the site root folder.

- **Image Objects**. Lets you insert placeholder graphics, rollover images, or HTML from Fireworks.

- **Media**. Inserts media files including Flash, Flash Video, Shockwave, Java applets, plug-ins, and Active X files into a document. In most cases, the standard Select File window appears, which you can use to navigate to the desired file.

- **Media Queries**. Opens the Media Queries window and lets you assign different style sheets to a page based on the width of a browser's screen. Useful for building sites whose design adapts to a smaller screen, like the one on smartphones. See page 510 for more on Media Queries.

- **Table**. Inserts a new table into a document. The Insert Table dialog box appears and lets you format the table by specifying the number of rows and columns; the table width; measurements for cell padding, cell spacing, and the table border; and whether or not and where to include table headers.

- **Table Objects**. Provides a way to insert tabular data (see the Import entry under File Menu above) and add other table-related tags such as the table header tag—<th>—into a page. The tag options in this menu assume you understand HTML and let you just insert tags without making sure you're doing it correctly.

- **Layout Objects**. Lets you insert absolutely positioned divs, regular divs, and divs used by the fluid grid layout tool discussed on page 521. This menu also includes Dreamweaver's new Spry widgets, like the Spry Navigation Bar discussed in Chapter 5, and the Spry panel widgets discussed in Chapter 14.

- **Form**. Inserts Form Objects—the <form> tag, text fields, buttons, checkboxes, or lists—into a document. (If you don't insert the <form> tag when you insert a form object, Dreamweaver prompts you to do so.)

- **Hyperlink**. Inserts a link. The Insert Hyperlink dialog box lets you specify the label for the link, the link's address, as well as many other link options, such as the target window and tab index.

- **Email Link**. Creates a new email link at the insertion point. The Insert Email Link dialog box appears; you specify both the email address and the link's label (such as "Click to email me").

- **Named Anchor**. Inserts a named anchor so you can add links to specific positions *within* a page. See page 202.

- **Date**. Inserts the current date into a document. The Insert Date dialog box lets you format the appearance of the day of the week, the date, and the time. You can also automatically update the date each time you save the document.

- **Server-Side Include**. Opens a Find File window, from which you select a file that dynamically adds content to your page. Learn more about server-side includes on page 937.

- **Comment**. Inserts an HTML comment into your page. Web browsers don't display comments, but Dreamweaver represents them as little gold shields in Design view. Use comments to leave notes for yourself and colleagues about the page. For example, you might add a comment indicating where a member of you web design team should put an ad.

- **HTML**. This menu includes lots of specific HTML tags, such as those for a horizontal rule, frames, text objects (many of which are also available under the Text menu), script objects for JavaScript, and head tags that go in the *head* portion of a web page—including meta tags, such as keywords and content descriptions that some search engines use.

- **Template Objects**. When you work on template files, this menu lets you insert many of Dreamweaver's template features, such as Optional, Editable, and Repeating Regions.

- **Recent Snippets**. Lists the most recently inserted snippets. Select a snippet from the list and Dreamweaver inserts it into the document. You'll see snippets discussed in Chapter 18.

- **Widget**. Like the Spry widgets discussed in this book, a widget is a JavaScript-powered add-on for a page. However, these widgets usually aren't as nicely integrated into Dreamweaver as the Spry widgets are, and while some widgets come from Adobe, third-party programmers write most of them. You download widgets from Adobe.com using Dreamweaver's Widget Browser, available from the Application bar (see Figure 13-28). Once you download and install a widget, you can use this menu to add it to a page (see page 706).

- **Spry**. Inserts any Dreamweaver Spry object, including the Spry Navigation Bar (Chapter 4), Spry Form Validation widgets (Chapter 12), and Spry Data and Layout widgets (Chapter 13).

- **jQuery Mobile**. Lets you insert code needed to build mobile applications using the jQuery Mobile JavaScript library. For example, you can insert a page or specialized user interface elements like a toggle switch. See page 537.

- **InContext Editing**. Lets you insert tags related to Adobe's Business Catalyst web hosting service. This online commercial service (as in "you gotta pay") lets non-web-savvy individuals update specially created web pages.

- **Data Objects**. Inserts server behaviors associated with Dreamweaver's dynamic database-driven website tools. As discussed on page 6, these archaic tools haven't been updated for years, and are best avoided.

- **XSLT Objects** (visible only when you work on an XSL file). Inserts various objects to convert XML data into a browser-readable format. (You could also use these with Dreamweaver's antiquated server behaviors.)

- **Customize Favorites**. Lets you add your favorite objects from the Insert panel into a special "favorites" toolbar so your most common objects, images, divs, roll-overs, tables, and so on are just a click away. See page 31 for more.

- **Get More Objects**. Opens the Adobe Exchange website in your desktop browser (outside of Dreamweaver, in other words). You can search for and download extensions and objects to add new features to Dreamweaver. Go to Commands→Manage Extensions to integrate downloaded extensions into Dreamweaver.

■ Modify Menu

Commands in the Modify menu adjust the properties of common document objects, like links, tables, and layers:

- **Page Properties**. Opens the Page Properties window, where you can specify document-wide attributes—such as a page's title, background and link colors, margins, and background image—or select a *tracing image* to use as a reference for designing the page.

- **Template Properties**. Opens the Template Properties window, where you can modify settings for template features, like the visibility of optional regions, the properties of editable attributes, and the values of any template expressions you create. Available only when you work on template-based pages, as described in Chapter 19.

- **Selection Properties**. When you select this item (as indicated by a checkmark in the menu), Dreamweaver displays the Property Inspector on-screen, which you use to edit the current settings of selected page elements. This command is the same as choosing Window→Properties.

- **CSS Styles**. Controls the display of the CSS Styles panel. A checkmark tells you that the panel is open. This item has the same effect as choosing CSS Styles from the Window menu.

- **Media Queries**. Opens the Media Queries window (see the Media Queries entry under Insert Menu above).

- **Font Families**. Opens the Edit Font List window so you can create your own sets of fonts for use with CSS.

- **Web Fonts**. Opens the Web Fonts Manager window. This feature, new in Dreamweaver CS6, lets you select your own "web fonts," freeing you from the limited set of standard fonts normally available for web pages (see page 146).

- **Edit Tag**. Opens a dialog box with detailed options for the HTML tag highlighted in the current document. This advanced feature is for the true HTML geek—it gives you access to *tons* of properties for a specific tag (not just the ones Dreamweaver displays in the Property Inspector). Unfortunately, some of the properties only apply to specific browsers, and it doesn't list newer properties (like those for HTML5) at all. Skip this option: The Tag Inspector, which provides a less-intrusive panel with a more comprehensive list of options, is a better option. Choose Window→Tag Inspector to open it.

- **Quick Tag Editor**. Lets you edit an HTML tag without leaving Design view. If you don't have anything selected on a page, the Quick Tag editor prompts you to enter a new HTML tag at the insertion point (by choosing from an alphabetical menu). If you have text or an object already selected when you open the Quick Tag Editor, the window displays the selection's HTML tags so you can edit them.

- **Make Link**. Turns a highlighted page element (graphic or text) into a link. The standard Select File dialog box appears; choose the document you want a browser to open when someone clicks the link.

- **Remove Link**. This command is available only when you select a link or have the cursor positioned inside a link in Design view. Remove Link deletes hyperlinks by removing the <a> tag from the selected text or image.

- **Open Linked Page**. Opens the linked page in a new document window. This command is available only when you have a link selected or have the cursor positioned inside a link in Design view. (You can also hold down the Ctrl key [⌘] and double-click a link to open the linked page.)

- **Link Target**. Sets a link's target window, defining whether a browser opens the linked page in the same window or a new one. You can choose from _blank, _parent, _self, or _top targets, or manually define the target in the Set Target dialog box. This command is available only when you have a link selected or have the cursor inside a link. (See Chapter 4 for details on links.)

- **Table**. Opens a list of options to modify a selected table. You can adjust the number of rows and columns, add row or column spans, or completely clear cells' defined heights and widths (see Chapter 6).

- **Image**. Opens a list of options to modify a selected image, including optimizing it in Fireworks or editing it with one of Dreamweaver's new built-in image-editing features, such as the Crop, Resample, and Sharpen tools. See page 253 for more.

- **Frameset**. Offers options to split the current page into *frames*. Alternatively, you can choose the Edit No Frames Content command, which creates alternative web page content that older browsers, those without frame support, can read. You won't find frames used on the Web very much any more, and professional web designers stay away from them—they're an outdated and clunky way to format pages.

- **Arrange**. Lets you change the Z-index (the front-to-back order) of overlapping positioned elements. You can send one absolutely positioned element in front of another, send it to the back, and so on. You can also tell Dreamweaver to disallow overlapping elements altogether. If you select two or more absolutely positioned elements, you can choose from one of this menu's alignment options to align the components, like the tops of the two elements. See Chapter 9 for more on absolutely positioned elements.

- **Convert**. Don't use this menu! Adobe created it to take a table-based layout and turn it into a layout using CSS absolute positioning. It doesn't work well at all. Better to recreate your design using the CSS layout techniques described in Chapter 9. The reverse option listed here—converting absolutely positioned elements to table layout—produces awful HTML and no benefit (unless you're building a "Retro Web Design Circa 1998" website).

- **Library**. Lets you add selected document objects to a site's Library folder (Chapter 18). You can also update the current document, or multiple documents, to reflect any changes you make to a Library object.

- **Templates**. These commands work with Dreamweaver's—or your own—templates (see Chapter 19). Using these commands, you can apply a preexisting template to the current page, separate the page from its template, or update the page to reflect changes you made to its template. If you have a template file open, you can create or delete editable regions (remove the template markup, in other words) and update all site files based on that template. You can also add repeating template regions and editable tag attributes.

◼ Format Menu

The commands in this menu let you format and modify a document's text:

- **Indent**. In the case of bulleted or numbered lists, this option indents the selected list items to create a nested (indented) list (see page 111). For other HTML tags, this option wraps the element in a <blockquote> tag (an HTML tag used to represent a quotation). In cases where it's against the rules of HTML to wrap the selected tag in a <blockquote>—an HTML table, for example—this option simply inserts an empty <blockquote> tag (really, though, a better approach to indenting text is to use the CSS Margin property, as described on page 449).

- **Outdent**. Turns selected bulleted or numbered list items into paragraph tags; for nested list items, it removes the indent. If your cursor's within a <blockquote> tag, this option removes the blockquote.

- **Paragraph Format**. Applies a paragraph format, such as Heading 1, Heading 2, or preformatted text, to all the text in the current block-level element. You can also go to this menu's submenu and choose "None" to remove the paragraph formatting.

- **Align**. Aligns text in the selected paragraph to the left margin, center, or right margin of a document. If the paragraph sits inside a table cell or layer, Dreamweaver aligns it with the left, center, or right of that cell or layer (the CSS text-align property [page 156] is a better option).

- **List**. Turns the selected paragraph into an ordered, unordered, or definition list. You can edit the list's format by selecting the submenu's Properties option.

- **Style**. Applies predefined text styles—such as bold, italic, or strikethrough—to the selected text.

- **CSS Styles**. Lets you create new CSS styles, and then apply them to selected text (Chapter 3). You can also choose to attach an existing style sheet to the current document, or export the document's own style sheet so you can use it in other sites.

- **Color**. Opens the standard Windows or Mac color-picker dialog box so you can apply color to the selected text. In general, the color box, which appears in the CSS Property panel, the Property Inspector, and the CSS Rule Definition window, is a better way to assign web colors to text.

■ Commands Menu

Use the Commands menu to apply advanced features to your Dreamweaver document. Some menu items, such as the Record commands, eliminate repetitive tasks; others, such as the Clean Up HTML command, fix common problems in a single sweep:

- **Start/Stop Recording**. Records a series of actions that you can apply to other parts of a document with a click of your mouse. When you select the Start Recording command, Dreamweaver records each of your actions until you choose Stop Recording. Note that Dreamweaver retains only one recorded command at a time.

- **Play Recorded Command**. Reapplies the most recently recorded command.

- **Edit Command List**. Opens a list of all saved commands. You can rename the commands, or delete them permanently.

- **Get More Commands**. Opens the Adobe Exchange for Dreamweaver website in a new browser window so you can search for and download new Dreamweaver extensions and commands. Dreamweaver downloads extensions to your Extension Manager (see page 916).

- **Get AIR Extension**. Takes you to Adobe's website, where you can download a Dreamweaver extension that lets you use Dreamweaver to create Adobe AIR applications—desktop-based programs that work (without a web browser) using common Web technologies like HTML, JavaScript, and Flash.

- **Manage Extensions**. Opens the Extension Manager, a program that lets you manage extensions you download from the Adobe Exchange website (page 917). The Extension Manager helps you install, delete, and selectively disable extensions.

- **Check Spelling**. Checks the current document for spelling errors (see page 116).

- **Apply Source Formatting**. Lets you apply Dreamweaver's formatting preferences to existing HTML and CSS documents. (Normally, changes you make to Dreamweaver's HTML source formatting, defined in the Preferences window and the *SourceFormat.txt* file, apply only to newly created documents.)

- **Apply Source Formatting to Selection**. Same as the previous command, Apply Source Formatting, but applies only to selected content. This command lets you selectively apply source formatting so you can, for example, make sure that Dreamweaver nicely formats a <table> element but leaves the rest of your finely crafted HTML alone. Works with CSS as well.

- **Clean Up HTML/XHTML**. Opens a list of options to correct common HTML problems, such as empty tags or redundant nested tags. Once you select what you want to fix, Dreamweaver applies those changes to the current document, and, if requested, provides a log of the number and type of changes it made (see Chapter 16).

- **Clean Up Word HTML**. If you import HTML generated by Microsoft Word, you often end up with unnecessary or cluttered HTML tags that can affect your site's performance. This command opens a list of options that corrects common formatting problems in Word's HTML. Dreamweaver applies the selected changes to the document and, if requested, displays a log of the number and type of changes it made.

- **Externalize JavaScript**. Lets you take all the JavaScript code in a web page and dump it into an external JavaScript file. This can make web pages download more quickly and lets you reuse common JavaScript programs throughout your site. See the note on page 371.

- **Remove FLV Detection**. If you used Dreamweaver CS3 to add a Flash Movie, and you then delete that Flash movie, this command removes the JavaScript code left behind. Again, this only applies if you have old Flash video pages you created way back when, with Dreamweaver CS3.

- **Optimize Image**. Opens the selected image in the Image Preview window so you can experiment with different compression settings to find the best balance between file size and image quality. See "Inserting an Image from Photoshop" on page 247.

- **Sort Table**. Sorts the information in a selected table alphabetically or numerically, in ascending or descending order. You can't apply this command to tables that include *rowspans* or *colspans*.

Site Menu

As its name suggests, the commands in this menu apply to your entire website rather than single documents. These commands help keep your site organized, and promote collaboration between large workgroups:

- **New Site**. Opens the New Site window, where you can set up a site to start working in Dreamweaver.

- **New Business Catalyst Site**. This command lets you set up a site to work with Adobe's Business Catalyst service. Business Catalyst is Adobe's web hosting company for businesses; it lets you build websites that incorporate e-commerce, blogs, a customer management system, email newsletters, and so on.

- **Manage Sites**. Opens the Manage Sites panel where you can create, delete, or edit site definitions. See Chapter 15.

> **NOTE** The next five menu commands let you transfer files between your computer (the *local* site) and a web server (the *remote* site). These commands, in other words, don't work unless you first define a local and remote site in the Site Definition window. In addition, you have to download the files you want to work on by *selecting* them in the Site window (see below).

- **Get**. Copies files (those you select in the Site window) from the remote server to your local site folder so you can edit them. Note that if you have Dreamweaver's file Check In and Check Out feature active (see Check In and Check Out below), you can't edit the downloaded files if someone downloaded a copy before you did.

- **Check Out**. Copies files (those you select in the Site window) from the remote server to your local site, and marks them on the remote server as *checked out*. No one else can make changes to the document until you upload it back onto the remote server.

- **Put**. Uploads files (those you select in the Site window) from your local site to the remote site. The uploaded files replace the previous version of the document.

- **Check In**. Uploads files you've checked out and copied to your local site back up to your remote site, and makes them available for others to edit. Once you check a file in, the version on your local site becomes read-only (you can open it, but you can't edit it).

- **Undo Check Out**. Removes the checked-out status of selected files. Dreamweaver doesn't upload the file back to the remote server, so any changes you made to the file locally aren't transmitted to the server. In addition, your local copy of the file becomes read-only.

- **Show Checked Out By**. Lets you see who's checked out a file.

- **Locate in Site**. When you select this option while working on a document, it opens the Site window and highlights that document in the site's local folder.

> **NOTE** See Chapter 17 for the full scoop on local sites, remote sites, and checking files in and out.

- **Reports**. Opens the Reports window, and lists options for generating new reports (see Chapter 17). Reports can monitor pages (such as design notes in them and their check-out status) and highlight common HTML problems (such as missing Alt text, empty tags, untitled documents, and redundant nested tags). You can generate a report on an open document, multiple documents, or your entire site.

- **Site-Specific Code Hints**. This option, available only for PHP websites, lets you specify how code hints (the tooltips that pop up as you type programming code) work. This advanced feature is for serious PHP programmers.

- **Synchronize Sitewide**. Opens the Synchronization window, which lets you compare all your local files with the files on your web server. Use it to make sure you transfer all the files you update locally to your web server, or that you transfer all the site files on the server to your local site.

- **Check Links Sitewide**. Analyzes the current site for broken links, external links, and orphaned pages, and then generates a report of all the problems it found. You can fix problematic links directly in the Report window—or click the file name to open the errant file in a new document window, with the link highlighted and ready to repair.

- **Change Link Sitewide**. Replaces a broken link throughout your site in one step. In the Change Link dialog box, you specify the incorrect link; below it, you enter the correct link. Dreamweaver searches your site, replacing every instance of the old link.

- **Advanced**. Provides access to advanced site options, such as the FTP Log—a record of all FTP file transfer activity; "Recreate Site Cache," which forces Dreamweaver to rescan the site's files and update its cache to reflect any changes to the files or links in the site; "Remove Connection Scripts" to remove the script files Dreamweaver creates to work with dynamic, database-driven websites; and "Deploy Supporting Files" to move necessary programming files to your server when you use Dreamweaver's ASP.NET server model to build dynamic pages. (Since Dreamweaver no longer provides the tools to easily build .NET pages, this last menu option is, uh, useless.)

- **PhoneGap Build Service**. PhoneGap is a free tool that makes creating mobile apps using HTML, CSS, and JavaScript easier. PhoneGap is an online service that can build apps for iOS, Android, WebOS, Blackberry, and other mobile devices (see the box on page 560 for more information on this new feature in Dreamweaver CS6).

Window Menu

This menu controls which panels and windows Dreamweaver displays or hides at the moment. A checkmark in the menu denotes open panels:

- **Insert**. Opens the Insert panel, from which you can insert various types of objects (such as images, layers, or forms) into your document. The Insert panel also contains options to switch between Layout and Standard table views, and to add dynamic elements (such as Spry widgets) to your pages.

- **Properties**. Opens the Property Inspector, where you can edit the properties for a selected object. The options in the Property Inspector depend on the selected page element.

- **CSS Styles**. Opens the CSS (Cascading Style Sheet) Styles panel, from which you can define and edit CSS styles, or apply existing ones to selected text.

- **jQuery Mobile Swatches.** Opens the jQuery Mobile Swatches window, which lets you apply different design "themes" to jQuery Mobile page elements. This option works only with the jQuery mobile pages discussed on page 537.

- **AP Elements**. Opens the AP Elements panel, which lists all the elements on a page you positioned using CSS positioning properties. See Chapter 9 for details.

- **Multiscreen Preview**. Opens the Multiscreen preview window so you can compare a live version of a web page at three different sizes—for smartphones, tables, and desktop browsers. See page 507.

- **Business Catalyst**. Opens the Business Catalyst panel. You need to sign up for Adobe's business web hosting service (*www.businesscatalyst.com*) for this panel to work. It lets you add code so you can work with sites that this commercial ($$$) web-hosting company manages.

- **Databases**. Opens the Databases panel so you can work on dynamic websites. This panel lets you connect your site to a database, view the structure of the database, and even preview data currently stored in the database. As mentioned on page 6, Dreamweaver's built-in database and server-side programming features are old and obsolete, so this menu option (and the next three) are best avoided.

- **Bindings**. Opens the Bindings panel, which lets you create database queries for dynamic sites. In addition, the panel displays and lets you add dynamic data to a web page.

- **Server Behaviors**. Opens the Server Behaviors panel, the control panel for viewing, editing, and adding advanced features to dynamic web pages.

- **Components**. Opens the Components panel, for use with ColdFusion sites. This advanced feature lets ColdFusion developers take advantage of prewritten, self-contained programs, which makes building complex dynamic sites easier.

- **Files**. Opens the Files panel. From this window, you can open any file, and transfer files between your computer and your remote server.

- **Assets**. Opens the Assets panel, which conveniently groups and lists all the assets (such as colors, links, scripts, graphics, library items, and templates) you use in your site.

- **Snippets**. Opens the Snippets panel, which contains snippets of HTML, JavaScript, and other types of code. You can create your own snippets to save your fingers from retyping code you use often on a site.

- **CSS Transitions**. Opens the CSS Transitions window, which lets you add, edit, and remove animated transitions between two different CSS styles. You can read about this window—new in Dreamweaver CS6—on page 405.

- **Tag Inspector**. Opens the Tag Inspector panel, which lists *all* the properties available for the currently selected HTML tag. This uber-geek option is like the Property Inspector on steroids.

- **Behaviors**. Opens the Behaviors panel, which lets you associate *behaviors* (such as swapping images on a mouse rollover or checking for necessary plug-ins) to selected page elements (see Chapter 13).

- **History**. Displays the History panel, a record of all the actions you took in working on the current document.

- **Frames**. Displays the Frames panel so you can select the frames and framesets you want to edit. Frames are an old and finicky web-page building technique and are best avoided.

- **Code Inspector**. Opens a pop-up window that displays the HTML for the current document. It's different than plain Code view, since the code sits in a pop-up window. While you can edit the code directly in this window, it's often easier just to use Dreamweaver's Code view or "Code and Design" view (View→Code and Design).

- **Results**. Lets you open Dreamweaver's many site-wide tools, such as the Find and Replace, Link Checker, and Reports commands. Pick the operation of choice from the submenu.

- **Extensions**. This menu lets you tap into Adobe's web page testing service, BrowserLab (page 760). (In previous version of Dreamweaver, the menu used to list other services, which have since been discontinued. It's a mystery why they didn't just make this menu option read "BrowserLab.")

- **Workspace Layout**. Lets you choose pre-set layouts of panels and windows. You can also use this menu to save the position and size of Dreamweaver's current panels and windows setup. This is great for customizing your Dreamweaver work environment.

- **Hide Panels**. Closes all currently open panels. Choosing Show Panels reopens only those panels displayed before you selected Hide Panels.

- **Application Frame (Macs only)**. New in Dreamweaver CS6 for Mac, the Application Frame treats all of Dreamweaver's panels and windows as one big window (or frame.) Grabbing the bottom right corner of the frame (usually the bottom-right corner of the Files panel) lets you resize the frame. Some people like this unified feel, some don't. If you don't like it, uncheck this option. When you do, all the windows and panels act as individual units you can resize independently of each other.

- **Application Bar.** Opens and closes the Application bar at the top of the screen. Generally the Application bar isn't that useful, as it takes up vertical space and offers shortcuts, like switching between Code view and Design view or setting up a new site, that are just as easy to do with other commands in the program. On Macs, you can only turn off the Application bar if you also turn off the Application Frame (discussed above).

- **Cascade**. By default, when you have multiple documents open, you switch from page to page by clicking tabs that appear at the top of the document window. If you prefer to have all open documents floating and resizable within the document area, this and the next two options let you "undock" the current documents. The cascade option resizes each open document and places them one on top of the other. Windows folks can re-dock pages by clicking the Maximize button on any currently open document. Mac people can select the Combine As Tabs option.

- **Tile Horizontally** (Windows only). Places all open documents one on top of the other. The documents don't float on top of each other; rather, they fill the available document area as row upon row of thin, horizontal windows. With more than a few documents open, you see so little of each page that it's difficult to work on any one.

- **Tile Vertically** (Windows only). Just like the previous command, except that Dreamweaver positions the documents vertically, like stripes going down the screen.

- **Tile** (Mac Only). This has the same effect as Tile Vertically above.

- **Combine As Tabs** (Mac only). Returns either tiled or cascaded documents (see those options above) to the single, unified tab interface.

- **Next Document, Previous Document** (Mac only). This pair of commands let you step through all your open documents, bringing each one front-and-center in turn so you can edit it.

- **List of Currently Open Documents**. Lists all the documents currently open at the bottom of this menu. Selecting one brings it to the front so you can edit it. But with the document tabs atop the document window, why bother?

■ Help Menu

The Help menu offers useful links and reference documents that give you more information about using, troubleshooting, and extending Dreamweaver:

- **Dreamweaver Help**. Launches Adobe Community Help in your desktop browser, with the Adobe Dreamweaver CS6 reference already selected. Nice. From here, you can even search the Web for more information on using Dreamweaver. Really nice.

- **Business Catalyst Help**. Opens a web browser and takes you to the Dreamweaver support section of the Business Catalyst website. You can learn how to use Dreamweaver to build and manage sites built for this Adobe-owned web hosting service.

- **Spry Framework Help**. An online reference to working with and programming Spry widgets, like those discussed in Chapter 13. It doesn't have any information on how to use the Spry tools built into Dreamweaver; instead, it gives programming-oriented web designers who want to jump into Code view more in-depth information on Spry coding itself, and expands on Dreamweaver's Spry features.

- **Get started with Business Catalyst InContext Editing**. As of this writing, this link takes you to a page on Adobe.com that says Adobe is discontinuing the InContext Editing service. D'oh! Presumably, this option will eventually (perhaps even as you read this) take you to a page describing Adobe's business web-hosting service, Business Catalyst (*www.businesscatalyst.com*).

- **Reference**. Opens the Reference panel, a searchable guide to HTML tags, Cascading Style Sheets, and JavaScript commands. Almost all the guides are woefully out of date, so it's best to avoid them. The HTML reference, however, still provides information on the HTML 4.01 tags you'll use while building web pages in Dreamweaver; however it has no information on any of the new tags offered in HTML5 (unfortunately, Dreamweaver doesn't offer any tools, aside from handcoding, to add HTML5 tags to your web pages).

- **Dreamweaver Support Center**. Opens the Community Help section of Adobe's online Dreamweaver Help and Support site, which provides access to tutorials, videos, and troubleshooting tips.

- **Dreamweaver Exchange**. Launches your desktop browser and loads the home page for Adobe Marketplace & Exchange on Adobe.com. You'll have to take the extra step of clicking the "Dreamweaver" link on the page to find extensions that add new features to Dreamweaver (see Chapter 20 for details).

- **Manage Extensions**. Same as the Manage Extensions option listed under Commands Menu above.

- **CSS Advisor**. Takes you to Adobe's ill-fated, out-dated, and pretty near useless CSS Advisor website. While the site had good intentions—to chronicle browser bugs and offer workarounds—it's ended up being a place where confused souls post questions about Dreamweaver (people with questions should instead visit the online forums, discussed next).

- **Adobe Online Forums**. Opens an index of available online forums on Adobe's website. You can interact with other Adobe customers, post questions, share techniques, or answer questions posted by others. Requires Internet access and a newsgroup reader.

- **Complete/Update Adobe ID Profile**. Dreamweaver CS6 is the first version of Dreamweaver to require owners to create an Adobe ID for the Adobe website. This menu option lets you update your profile (if you want to change your email address or password, for example).

- **Activate**. As part of Adobe's attempt to stop piracy of their software, Dreamweaver's Software Activation module contacts Adobe and makes sure that your copy of Dreamweaver isn't activated on anyone else's computer. Adobe lets you install Dreamweaver on one desktop and one laptop of the same operating system. If you don't activate your software, the program stops working after 30 days. (If you've already activated the software, this option doesn't appear in the Help menu.)

- **Deactivate**. If you get a new computer, *do not forget* to deactivate the software on your old one. Use this menu option to do so. Deactivating the software lets you install it on another computer. (You won't see this option unless you've already activated your software.)

- **Updates**. Launches the Adobe updater. It finds updates for Dreamweaver (and every other Adobe product on your computer).

- **Adobe Product Improvement Program**. Opens a window that lets you participate in this Adobe project, which collects information about your use of Dreamweaver. According to Adobe, all the information is anonymous.

- **About Dreamweaver** (Windows only). Opens an About Dreamweaver window, showing your software's version number. (On the Macintosh, you'll find this command in the Dreamweaver menu.)

Index